# Architectural Woodw
## 2nd Edition

A Specification of Qualities, Methods, and Workmanship
Requisite to the Production and Installation of Architectural Millwork

Adopted and Published Jointly, Effective October 1, 2014,
As the Successor, Replacement, and Latest Edition of the
Architectural Woodwork Standards
By the Following Sponsor Associations:

**Architectural Woodwork Institute (AWI)**
46179 Westlake Drive, Suite 120, Potomac Falls, VA 20165
Phone: 571-323-3636 / Fax: 571-323-3630
www.awinet.org

**Architectural Woodwork Manufacturers Association of Canada (AWMAC)**
Unit 02A, 4803 Centre Street NW, Calgary, Alberta T2E 2Z6, Canada
Phone: 403-981-7300
www.awmac.com

**Woodwork Institute (WI)**
P. O. Box 980247, West Sacramento, CA 95798-0247
Phone: 916-372-9943 / Fax: 916-372-9950
www.woodworkinstitute.com

Joint Standards Committee Members:
Myron Jonzon - Chair • Mike Bell - Vice Chair • Clare Smith - Secretary

| AWI | WI | AWMAC |
|---|---|---|
| Michael Bell - Florida | Bill Fenstermacher - California | Kerry DePape - Saskatchewan |
| Randy Jensen - Alabama | Mike Hansen - California | Myron Jonzon - Alberta |
| William Munyan - North Carolina | Bruce Humphrey - California | Jim Taylor - British Columbia |
| Shows Leary - New York | Dennis Milsten - Washington | Martin Boutet - Quebec |

Executive Editor:
**Stanley R. (Rob) Gustafson, CAE, CSI**
CEO - Woodwork Institute

© 2014 jointly by the Architectural Woodwork Institute (AWI), Architectural Woodwork Manufacturers Association of Canada (AWMAC), and Woodwork Institute (WI). All rights reserved under Pan American and International Copyright Conventions.

Price: $125.00 USD

# INTRODUCTION

## INTRODUCTORY STATEMENT

Like all architectural components of the construction process, woodwork design and configuration possibilities are limited only by the creativity of the design professional. We have included architectural wood products which through evolution have become fixtures of our daily lives and have developed a measurable guideline to ensure these products meet these standards.

While these Architectural Woodwork Standards (AWS) are to be applied to the production and installation of all architectural wood products, the performance of wood products once installed outside of a climate controlled (interior) environment (as identified in Section 2 of these standards) cannot be measured by these standards. Wood products installed in non-climate controlled environments will have varying degrees of performance and should be governed by contractual agreements between the manufacturers and the buyers.

It is the intent of these standards to assist the design professional to specify a variety of millwork products which meet the functional and esthetic requirements of their clients. Encompassing all products in these standards is not possible; but by understanding and applying these standards and implementing the services provided by the signatory Sponsor Associations, the design professional will best serve their client needs and can be confident their quality criteria will be achieved.

When design professionals reference the AWS for their projects, they also assume the obligation that the quality standards are met.

## DISCLAIMERS

The Sponsor Associations shall not be responsible to anyone for the use of or reliance upon these standards. The Sponsor Associations shall not incur any obligation nor liability for damages, including consequential damages, arising out of or in connection with the use, interpretation of, or reliance upon these standards.

These *Architectural Woodwork Standards* (AWS) provide the minimum criteria for the concept, design, fabrication, finishing, and installation of architectural woodwork. Provisions for mechanical and electrical safety have not been included. References to life-safety requirements are included for information only. Governmental agencies or other national standards-setting organizations provide the standards for life-safety requirements.

While the AWS does establish Assembly and Installation standards for all wood products, the joint flushness and gap tolerance performance for wood products once installed outside of climate controlled (interior) environments (as identified in Section 2 of these standards) cannot be governed by these Standards.

Illustrations are intended to assist in understanding the standards and may not include all requirements for a specific product or unit, nor do they show the only method of fabrication. Such partial drawings shall not be used to justify improper or incomplete design and/or construction.

The appendix is provided as an additional resource to the manufacturer, design professional, educator, user, or certifying organization. The Appendix is only part of the standards when referenced.

This AWS includes citations and quotes from other industry Standards that are neither developed nor published by the Sponsor Associations. The reference to and usage of is not a validation of these citations and quotations outside the context of the AWS. Only when these citations and partial quotations are applied in concert with all other related provisions of this AWS are these citations and partial quotations recognized for application to architectural woodwork.

If a conflict is found in these standards, it shall be brought to the attention of the Joint Standards Committee (JSC) by way of the AWS Improvement Suggestion Form (found at end of Users Guide and the Inside Back Cover) and until specifically addressed, the least restrictive requirement shall prevail.

# SPONSOR ASSOCIATIONS

# Architectural Woodwork Institute (AWI)

The Architectural Woodwork Institute is a nonprofit international trade association of architectural woodwork manufacturers, industry suppliers, and design professionals. AWI was established in 1953 as an expansion of the Millwork Cost Bureau and is dedicated to goals that include:

- Updating, maintaining and promoting the Architectural Woodwork Standards;
- Providing networking, industry specific education, and learning opportunities for both members and the design community.
- Researching innovative materials and methods of compliance, engineering, fabrication, finishing, and installation.
- And through AWI's network of over twenty-five chartered AWI chapters, operating regionally on principles of sharing knowledge, education, and networking.

**AWI's education and networking events include:**

- Face-to-face and online based seminars and workshops for AWI members, the construction industry, and design professionals (including AIA Continuing Education System (CES) credits).
- Best Practices Groups for owners and top management of manufacturing member companies.
- Fall Annual Meeting and Convention.
- Spring Meeting & Leadership Conference.

**AWI's Publications and web content, include:**

- Design Solutions – AWI's quarterly journal with circulation of over 20,000 architects and designers.
- AWI eCost Book - a web-based manufacturing labor hour calculation system.
- LEED® Resources – Simplifies the key points to assist woodworkers with LEED® point reporting process.
- Numerous member-centered education, resources and networking activities.
- AWI's Safety Solutions – a web-based resource for safety and OSHA compliance information.
- AWI's annual Cost of Doing Business Report – provides manufacturing members with financial performance benchmarks, wage and compensation data and business trends.

- For more information about AWI, please visit the AWI website www.awinet.org or call the AWI National Office at 571-323-3636.

**The AWI Quality Certification Program**

In 1995, AWI's Board of Directors established the Quality Certification Program (QCP) to give measurable confirmation that the architectural woodwork, specified as a QCP Certified Project meets the quality grade required and established in the Architectural Woodwork Standards.

Since 2007, the AWI Quality Certification Corporation (AWI QCC), an independent, international credentialing body, has been the sole administrator of the AWI Quality Certification Program. To fulfill its mission to inspect, report, enforce and assist in architectural woodwork standards compliance, the QCP annually performs more than 500 inspections of firms and projects throughout North America, Asia, Africa, and Europe.

The design professional's reputation depends on others when they specify architectural woodwork. The Quality Certification Program (QCP) provides the means to measure, confirm and report that the quality specified is the quality provided.

QCP provides design professionals and owners a means of verifying the skills and competence of the architectural woodwork manufacturers on a project-specific basis. Inspections, reports and documentation give the design professional and owner clear justification to reject any woodwork that does not meet contract documents. A major benefit of QCP is that it provides the means to prevent noncompliant woodwork from being installed on the job site.

Design professionals are encouraged to include QCP's suggested specification language in their contract documents:

Quality Standard: Unless otherwise indicated, comply with "Architectural Woodwork Standards" for grades of interior architectural woodwork, construction, finishes, and other requirements.

Quality Assurance: Provide AWI Quality Certification Program (QCP) [labels] [certificates] indicating that woodwork [including installation] complies with requirements of grades specified. This project has been registered as AWI/QCP Number _____.

OR, the contractor, upon award of the work, shall register the work under this Section with the AWI Quality Certification Program at www.awiqcp.org or by calling QCC toll free 1-855-345-0991.

In fulfilling its mission to inspect, report, enforce and assist in architectural woodwork standards compliance, the AWI Quality Certification Program retains a team of experienced compliance inspectors, each of whom have at least fifteen years of experience in the architectural woodwork industry. Each inspector has passed the initial qualification testing, receives ongoing training by the QCC and has agreed to adhere to the QCC conflict of interest policy.

The QCP licenses eligible woodworking firms to certify that a project's work complies with the project contract documents and the Architectural Woodwork Standards (AWS). QCP verifies compliance with the contract documents and the standards through the inspection process.

Compliance inspections are performed for each new QCP Licensee's first two registered certified projects, or any registered project where request has been made to QCP administration for a compliance inspection by the project's design professional, the general contractor or project owner. Each year QCP performs compliance inspections on dozens of randomly chosen registered QCP projects throughout North America.

Woodworking firms earn their licensee certification credentials by successfully completing comprehensive testing, rigorous inspections, and by submitting no less than ten trade references. Moreover, QCP Licensees must demonstrate the ability to fabricate, finish, and/or install work in accordance with the quality grade criteria set forth in the Architectural Woodwork Standards (AWS).

The AWI Quality Certification Program is endorsed by leading construction organizations that values quality, including the U.S. General Services Administration (GSA) and the American Subcontractors Association (ASA). For more information about the AWI QCP, please visit the QCP website www.awiqcp.org or call the QCP National Office toll free at (855) 345-0991.

Consult the awiqcp.org website for additional inspection services.

# SPONSOR ASSOCIATIONS

## Architectural Woodwork Manufacturers Association of Canada (AWMAC)

The Architectural Woodwork Manufacturers Association of Canada (AWMAC)/Association des Manufacturiers de la Menuiserie Architecturale du Canada has its roots in the 1920s millwork industry in Vancouver, Canada. Evolving from regional associations, it has become a nonprofit national registered association. AWMAC's strength is the linkage between the national association, the regional AWMAC Chapters, and the manufacturer, supplier, educational, associate, and design professional members. Today, AWMAC is the national voice of the Canadian architectural woodwork industry and is committed to:

- Partnering with other associations to define and improve architectural woodwork standards.
- Collaborating with educational institutions to enhance the apprentice and technical programs and to ensure a quality human resource for the architectural woodwork industry.
- Communicating the traditional, new, and innovative architectural woodwork assembly methods and materials to governments, industry, design professionals, and their associations
- Publishing The Sounding Board, a newsletter, and the Salary/Business Conditions Survey.
- In conjunction with AWMAC, AWMAC Chapters provide:
  - Seminars from raw "green" products to installed architectural woodwork for architects, designers, and members.
  - Annual Awards that celebrate the best in quality, service, and design for manufacturers, associates, and design professionals.
  - Administration of the Guarantee and Inspection Service (GIS); initiated in 1990, the GIS Program (when specified by the design professional) monitors and guarantees projects that specify AWMAC standards.

### GUARANTEE AND INSPECTION SERVICE (GIS)
AWMAC regional chapters manage the GIS monitoring program, initiated in 1990. AWMAC GIS Certified Inspectors review, inspect and report on pre-tender specifications if requested, sample units when specified and shop drawings. Inspectors also perform a comprehensive final inspection of the architectural woodwork for the project owner. The AWMAC GIS program offers, through its members in good standing, a two year AWMAC Guarantee Certificate on projects which have the recommended GIS wording specified in the tender documents.

### GIS MANDATE
In order to ensure that the quality of materials and workmanship of the architectural woodwork specified are in compliance with the current AWMAC Architectural Woodwork Standards (AWS), the AWMAC Guarantee and Inspection Service program (GIS) must be specified and be considered an integral component of the scope of work.

### GIS OBJECTIVE
The objectives of the Guarantee and Inspection Service are:
1. To assist the design authority in achieving "good architectural woodwork."
2. To offer the owner, customer, design authority, and woodwork contractor an assurance that strict monitoring of the architectural woodwork requirements on a given project will meet the specified AWMAC standards.

### GIS WORDING FOR SPECIFICATIONS
Architectural woodwork shall be manufactured and/or installed to the current AWMAC Architectural Woodwork Standards and shall be subject to an inspection at the factory and/or site by an appointed AWMAC Certified Inspector. Inspection costs shall be included in the tender price for this project. (Contact your local AWMAC Chapter for details of inspection costs). Shop drawings shall be submitted to the AWMAC Chapter office for review before work commences. Work that does not meet the AWMAC Architectural Woodwork Standards, as specified, shall be replaced, reworked and/or refinished by the architectural woodwork contractor, to the approval of AWMAC, at no additional cost to the owner.

If the woodwork contractor is an AWMAC Manufacturer member in good standing, a two (2) year AWMAC Guarantee Certificate will be issued. The AWMAC Guarantee shall cover replacing, reworking and/or refinishing deficient architectural woodwork due to faulty workmanship or defective materials supplied and/or installed by the woodwork contractor, which may appear during a two (2) year period following the date of issuance.

If the woodwork contractor is not an AWMAC Manufacturer member they shall provide the owner with a two (2) year maintenance bond, in lieu of the AWMAC Guarantee Certificate, to the full value of the architectural woodwork contract.

### CONTACT
For more information about AWMAC and the GIS Program visit our website at www.awmac.com and contact your local AWMAC Chapter office.

# SPONSOR ASSOCIATIONS

 Woodwork Institute (WI)

Established in 1951 as a not-for-profit trade organization dedicated to the preservation of the use of wood as a building material, Woodwork Institute (WI) has grown to a national organization whose primary purpose is to assure excellence and craftsmanship in woodwork.

As the Institute has grown, so too has its Quality Control Options. As a means of establishing quality control, WI along with AWI and AWMAC has collaborated on the Architectural Woodwork Standards (AWS). This book is the essence of building and installing quality products.

Unique to WI are its certification programs which include the Certified Compliance Program (CCP), the Monitored Compliance Program (MCP) and the Certified Seismic Installation Program (CSIP).

As well, WI provides Independent Inspection Services (IIS) for projects and Expert Witness Services (EWS), when requested by a party to the contract.

### DIRECTORS OF ARCHITECTURAL SERVICE (DAS)

Our Director's of Architectural Services provide a wealth of knowledge to the architectural community and the construction industry. Their primary focus is compliance verification (inspection services) through CCP, MCP and CSIP.

Concentrating on the design community, the DAS are available to review specifications, answer millwork related Requests for Information, consult on design issues and present seminars for continuing education units as required by the Architectural Institute of America (AIA). As well, the DAS are available to assist a design professional should they need an impartial opinion about millwork fabricated or installed on a project.

Focusing on fabricators and installers the DAS are available for free and unbiased consultation regarding specification interpretation, compliance issues, shop-drawing protocol, standards interpretation and other matters.

### CERTIFIED COMPLIANCE PROGRAM (CCP)

The Certified Compliance Program is a discipline of quality control used in conjunction with the AWS which provides an unbiased means of ensuring conformance to a project's plans and specifications. CCP, together with the use of the desired Grade(s) in the specifications, informs all parties of the design professional's expectations, without bidder discrimination.

By specifying CCP for both shop drawings and fabrication/installation of millwork products the design professional is assured that all items conform to the contract documents and the requirements of the AWS.

CCP does not restrict bidding or bidders. Anyone may use the CCP inspection service without the requirement of being a member or licensee.

Evidence of certification is provided by issuance of a Certified Compliance Certificate, listing the items certified, the applicable AWS Grade, and whether installation is included. Additionally, if so specified, shop drawings and each elevation of casework and/or countertops are labeled with an individually serial-numbered "Certified Compliance Label."

### MONITORED COMPLIANCE PROGRAM (MCP)

The Monitored Compliance Program is a discipline of quality affirmation used in conjunction with the AWS which provides ongoing reviews/inspections of a project from its beginning through completion.

The design professional, in specifying MCP, is ensuring that strict conformance to his/her design intent is adhered to throughout the millwork fabrication and installation process.

Shop drawings, millwork products, finishing and installation (of all involved parties) will be progressively inspected for compliance to the contract documents and the specified AWS Grade(s). Reports will be issued to all involved parties at each review/inspection.

Evidence of compliance is provided by issuance of a Monitored Compliance Certificate, listing the items certified, the applicable AWS Grade(s) and whether installation is included. Additionally, if so specified, shop drawings and each elevation of casework and/or countertops are labeled with an individually serial-numbered "Compliance Label".

### CERTIFIED SEISMIC INSTALLATION PROGRAM (CSIP)

Certified Seismic Installation Program is WI's most recent certification program. It is a standalone Quality Control and Seismic Compliance Option, but can be specified in conjunction with CCP or MCP. CSIP offers design professionals and property owners specified use of WI's seismic casework pre-approvals from the Office of Statewide Health Planning and Development (OSHPD) without additional engineering costs and/or requirements. It further assures:

- Proper backing has been installed in the walls when and where required.
- Certified acknowledgement that the project's seismic casework installation requirements meet OSHPD and/or the Division of State Architect (DSA) compliance requirements.

### INDEPENDENT INSPECTION SERVICE (IIS)

The Independent Inspection Service is available on a fee basis with respect to issues pertaining to the architectural woodwork industry as defined within or covered by the AWS.

### EXPERT WITNESS SERVICE (EWS)

Expert Witness Service is available on a fee basis with respect to issues pertaining to the architectural woodwork industry as defined within or covered by the AWS.

For more information please visit WI's website at www.woodworkinstitute.com or call the administrative office at (916) 372-9943.

# CONTRIBUTING ASSOCIATIONS

## The Following Associations Are Gratefully Acknowledged:

American Institute of Architects (AIA)

American National Standards Institute (ANSI)

American Society of Interior Designers (ASID)

American Society for Testing and Materials (ASTM)

Builders Hardware Manufacturers Association (BHMA)

Composite Panel Association (CPA)

Construction Specifications Canada (CSC)

Construction Specifications Institute (CSI)

The Engineered Wood Association (APA)

Hardwood Plywood & Veneer Association (HPVA)

Interior Design of Canada (IDC)

International Solid Surface Fabricators Association (ISSFA)

International Wood Products Association (IWPA)

Laminating Materials Association (LMA)

National Electrical Manufacturers Association (NEMA)

National Fire Protection Association (NFPA)

National Hardwood Lumber Association (NHLA)

Royal Architectural Institute of Canada (RAIC)

Scientific Equipment & Furniture Association (SEFA)

Stair Manufacturer Association (SMA)

Western Wood Products Association (WWPA)

Window and Door Manufacturers Association (WDMA)

Wood Moulding and Millwork Producers Association (WMMPA)

# Architectural Woodwork Standards

# USER'S GUIDE

# USER'S GUIDE

Sponsored by the Architectural Woodwork Institute, the Architectural Woodwork Manufacturers Association of Canada, and the Woodwork Institute (hereinafter called the Sponsor Associations), these joint standards represent the best of what all three organizations have to offer in defining the minimum requirements of material and workmanship for the fabrication and installation of architectural woodwork in a climate controlled interior environment. The joint standards are based on three definitive levels of materials and workmanship: Economy, Custom, and Premium Grade.

These standards are both a voluntary and a definitive document, intended to spell out the requirements for satisfactory performance when referenced as part of contract documents. Sections in the document are interrelated and are intended to be used together, not in part. For example, if a project specification requires compliance with Section 10, then compliance with Sections 1-5 along with the Appendix and the Glossary are also required, as applicable.

The **INSIDE FRONT COVER** provides an important **PRODUCT ADVISORY** regarding dimensional change problems in architectural woodwork and its review and consideration is recommended by the Sponsor Associations.

The **INSIDE BACK COVER** provides reference for access to an **AWS IMPROVEMENT SUGGESTION FORM** which can be filled out and submitted online through any of the Sponsor Associations web sites.

Each **SECTION** is organized into two distinct elements, that of:

- **Introductory Information** - Consisting of educational materials and resources relevant to the Section that are not standards or compliance requirements, and:
  - Specific specification requirements.
  - General recommendations.
- **Compliance Requirements** - Consisting of the standards requirements (rules) which are further organized into:
  - **Basic Considerations,** including grades, general subject matter and industry practices applicable to the scope of work.

- **Product**, covering minimum manufacturing (material, machining, and assembly) requirements.
- **Installation**, minimum installation requirements (not applicable to Sections 1-5).
- **Test** - covers the ways of verifying compliance with the standards (not applicable to Sections 1-4).

### THE FOLLOWING ARE NOT PART OF THE AWS FOR COMPLIANCE PURPOSES:

- Introduction
- Table of Contents
- Introductory Information Portion of Each Material or Product/Installation Section
- Design Ideas
- Index

### THE AWS IS SUBDIVIDED AS FOLLOWS:

- **Introduction** - Provides an Introductory Statement, Disclaimers and a brief description about the Sponsor Associations.
- **User's Guide** - Provides a tool to enhance your understanding of the philosophy behind the layout of these standards.
- **Table of Contents**
- **Preface** - Provides information in areas of importance that should be reviewed in advance of using the standards.
- **Section 1 - Submittals** - Addresses minimum submittal requirements, including shop drawings, samples, etc., and is further subdivided as follows:
  - Table of Contents
  - Introductory Information
    - Specify Requirements For
    - Recommendations
  - Compliance Requirements
    - **GENERAL**
      - Basic Considerations
        - Grades
        - Industry Practices
    - **PRODUCT**
      - Scope
      - Default Stipulation
      - Rules
        - Basic Rules
        - Section 6-12 Rules

- **Section 2 - Care & Storage** - Addresses minimum care and storage (environmental condition) requirements to be maintained before, during, and after the delivery, storage, and installation of product and is further subdivided as follows:
  - Table of Contents
  - Introductory Information
    - Specify Requirements For
    - Recommendations
  - Compliance Requirements
    - **GENERAL**
      - Basic Considerations
        - Grades
        - Industry Practices
    - **PRODUCT**
      - Scope
      - Default Stipulation
      - Rules
        - Basic Rules

- **Section 3 - Lumber** - Addresses the minimum acceptable performance and appearance characteristics of lumber to be used within the standards' product Sections 6-12. This section does not attempt to establish raw material grades. It defines the minimum characteristics for lumber when used in a product governed by Sections 6-12 based on the specified Grade of work (Economy, Custom, or Premium) and is further subdivided as follows:
  - Table of Contents
  - Introductory Information
    - Specify Requirements For
    - Recommendations
  - Compliance Requirements
    - **GENERAL**
      - Basic Considerations
        - Grades
        - Industry Practices
    - **PRODUCT**
      - Scope
      - Default Stipulation
      - Rules
        - Basic Rules
        - Hardwood Material Rules
        - Softwood Material Rules

# USER'S GUIDE

- **Section 4 - Sheet Products** - Addresses the minimum acceptable performance and appearance characteristics of panel materials to be used within the standards' product Sections 6-12. This section does not attempt to establish raw material grades. It defines the minimum characteristics for panels when used in a product governed by Sections 6-12 based on the specified Grade of work (Economy, Custom, or Premium) and is further subdivided as follows:
  - Table of Contents
  - Introductory Information
    - Specify Requirements For
    - Recommendations
  - Compliance Requirements
    - **GENERAL**
      - Basic Considerations
        - Grades
        - Industry Practices
    - **PRODUCT**
      - Scope
      - Default Stipulation
      - Rules
        - Basic Rules
      - Hardwood Veneer Material Rules
      - Softwood Veneer Material Rules
      - HPDL Material Rules
      - LPDL Material Rules
      - Vinyl Film Material Rules
      - MDO Material Rules
      - HDO Material Rules
      - Hardboard Material Rules
      - Balance Sheet Material Rules
      - Backer Material Rules
      - Epoxy Material Rules
      - Natural Stone Material Rules
      - Engineered Stone Material Rules
      - Solid Surface Material Rules
      - Solid Phenolic Material Rules

- **Section 5 - Finishing** - Addresses the minimum acceptable performance and appearance characteristics for factory and field finishing used within the standards' product Sections 6-12 and is further subdivided as follows:
  - Table of Contents
  - Introductory Information
    - Specify Requirements For
    - Recommendations
  - Compliance Requirements
    - **GENERAL**
      - Basic Considerations
        - Grades
        - Industry Practices
    - **PRODUCT**
      - Scope
      - Default Stipulation
      - Rules
        - Basic Rules
        - Application Rules
    - **TESTS**
      - Basic Considerations

- **Section 6 - Millwork** - Addresses the minimum acceptable millwork fabrication and installation requirements for standing and running trim, door frames, window frames, sashes, blinds and shutters, screens, ornamental and miscellaneous millwork based on the specified Grade of work (Economy, Custom, or Premium) and is further subdivided as follows:
  - Table of Contents
  - Introductory Information
    - Specify Requirements For
    - Recommendations
  - Compliance Requirements
    - **GENERAL**
      - Basic Considerations
        - Grades
        - Industry Practices
    - **PRODUCT**
      - Scope
      - Default Stipulation
      - Rules
        - Basic Rules
        - Material Rules
        - Machining Rules
        - Assembly Rules
    - **INSTALLATION**
      - Preparation and Qualification Requirements
      - Rules
        - Basic Rules
        - Product Specific Rules
    - **TESTS**
      - Basic Considerations

- **Section 7 - Stairwork & Rails** - Addresses the minimum acceptable millwork fabrication and installation requirements for wood stairs, integral trim, handrails and guardrails based on the specified Grade of work (Economy, Custom, or Premium) and is further subdivided as follows:
  - Table of Contents
  - Introductory Information
    - Specify Requirements For
    - Recommendations
  - Compliance Requirements
    - **GENERAL**
      - Basic Considerations
        - Grades
        - Industry Practices
    - **PRODUCT**
      - Scope
      - Default Stipulation
      - Rules
        - Basic Rules
        - Material Rules
        - Machining Rules
        - Assembly Rules
    - **INSTALLATION**
      - Preparation and Qualification Requirements
      - Rules
        - Basic Rules
    - **TESTS**
      - Basic Considerations

- **Section 8 - Wall/Ceiling Surfacing & Partitions** - Addresses the minimum acceptable millwork fabrication and installation requirements for wood veneer, solid wood, stile and rail wood, decorative laminate, solid surface and solid phenolic wall/ceiling and partition surfacing, based on the specified Grade of work (Economy, Custom, or Premium) and is further subdivided as follows:
  - Table of Contents
  - Introductory Information
    - Specify Requirements For
    - Recommendations

# USER'S GUIDE

## THE AWS IS SUBDIVIDED (continued)

- **Section 8 - Wall/Ceiling Surfacing & Partitions** (continued)
  - Compliance Requirements
    - **GENERAL**
      - Basic Considerations
        - Grades
        - Industry Practices
    - **PRODUCT**
      - Scope
      - Default Stipulation
      - Rules
        - Basic Rules
        - Material Rules
        - Machining Rules
        - Assembly Rules
    - **INSTALLATION**
      - Preparation and Qualification Requirements
      - Rules
        - Basic Rules
    - **TESTS**
      - Basic Considerations

- **Section 9 - Doors -** Addresses the minimum acceptable millwork fabrication and installation requirements for passage doors of flush and stile & rail construction with wood and HPDL faces, based on the specified Grade of work (Economy, Custom, or Premium). This section is further subdivided as follows:
  - Table of Contents
  - Introductory Information
    - Specify Requirements For
    - Recommendations
  - Compliance Requirements
    - **GENERAL**
      - Basic Considerations
        - Grades
        - Industry Practices
    - **PRODUCT**
      - Scope
      - Default Stipulation
      - Rules
        - Basic Rules
        - Material Rues
        - Machine/Assembly Rules
    - **INSTALLATION**
      - Preparation and Qualification Requirements
      - Rules
        - Basic Rules
    - **TESTS**
      - Basic Considerations

- **Section 10 - Casework -** Addresses the minimum acceptable millwork fabrication and installation requirements for wood, decorative laminate and solid phenolic faced casework, based on the specified Grade of work (Economy, Custom, or Premium). This section is further subdivided as follows:
  - Table of Contents
  - Introductory Information
    - Specify Requirements For
    - Recommendations
  - Compliance Requirements
    - **GENERAL**
      - Basic Considerations
        - Grades
        - Industry Practices
    - **PRODUCT**
      - Scope
      - Default Stipulation
      - Rules
        - Basic Rules
        - Material Rules
        - Machining Rules
        - Assembly Rules
    - **INSTALLATION**
      - Preparation and Qualification Requirements
      - Rules
        - Basic Rules
    - **TESTS**
      - Basic Considerations

- **Section 11 - Countertops -** Addresses the minimum acceptable millwork fabrication and installation requirements for tops, wall caps, splashes and sills of high pressure decorative laminate, wood, solid surface, solid phenolic, epoxy resin and natural/engineered stone, based on the specified Grade of work (Economy, Custom, or Premium). This section is further subdivided as follows:
  - Table of Contents
  - Introductory Information
    - Specify Requirements For
    - Recommendations
  - Compliance Requirements
    - **GENERAL**
      - Basic Considerations
        - Grades
        - Industry Practices
    - **PRODUCT**
      - Scope
      - Default Stipulation
      - Rules
        - Basic Rules
        - Material Rules
        - Machining Rules
        - Assembly Rules
    - **INSTALLATION**
      - Preparation and Qualification Requirements
      - Rules
        - Basic Rules
    - **TESTS**
      - Basic Considerations

- **Section 12 - Historic Restoration Work -** Addresses the minimum acceptable millwork fabrication and installation requirements for historic restoration work, including stripping, repairs and finishing. This section is further subdivided as follows:
  - Table of Contents
  - Introductory Information
    - Specify Requirements For
    - Recommendations
  - Compliance Requirements
    - **GENERAL**
      - Basic Considerations
        - Grades
        - Industry Practices

# USER'S GUIDE

## THE AWS IS SUBDIVIDED   (continued)

- **Historic Restoration Work**   (continued)
  - **PRODUCT**
    - Scope
    - Default Stipulation
    - Rules
      - Basic Rules
      - Material Rules
      - Machining Rules
      - Assembly Rules
      - Repair Rules
      - Stripping Rules
      - Finishing Rules
  - **INSTALLATION**
    - Preparation and Qualification Requirements
    - Rules
      - Basic Rules

- **Appendix -** Provides additional resources to the manufacturer, design professional, educator, user, or certifying organization and is only part of these standards when referenced. For your convenience where the **APPENDIX** is referenced it is flagged by the following icon:

- **Design Ideas -** Provides additional resources to the design professional, educator, or user. For your convenience where **DESIGN IDEAS** is referenced it is flagged by the following icon:

- **Glossary -** Provides definitions of terms used throughout these standards.

- **Index**

## FORMAT WITHIN EACH SECTION:

The **Introductory Information** portion is in triple column, text book format with a non-shaded header including Section number, title, and Introductory Information statement recognizing that the included text is non-compliant in nature. There is also a black edge tab with Section number for ease of navigation.

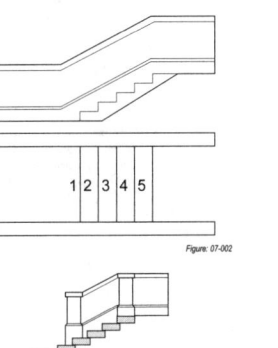

Each page also includes a footer stating the page number, document name, edition, and effective publication date.

However in the Compliance Requirements portion the footer also includes an Errata statement advising "As may be updated by errata at awinet.org, awmac.com or aws-errata.com."

# USER'S GUIDE

**FORMAT WITHIN EACH SECTION** (continued)

The **Compliance Requirement Sections** have a grey shaded header with Section number, title, and compliance requirements statement recognizing that the included text is part of the standards for compliance purposes. There is also a grey shaded edge tab with Section number for your ease of navigation.

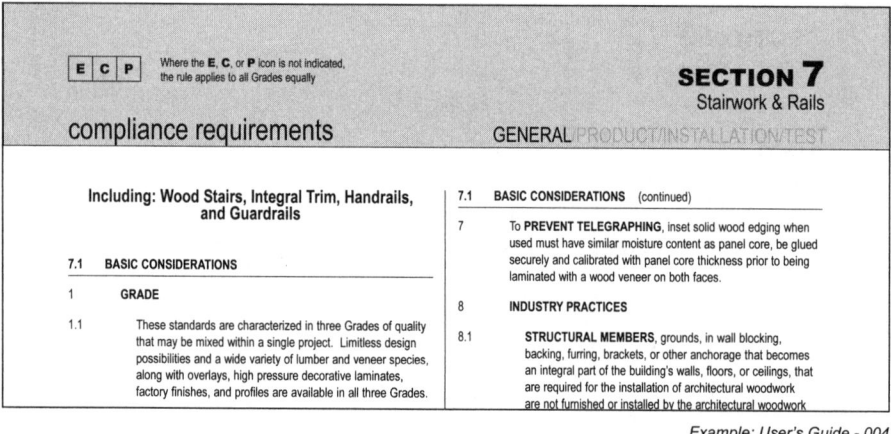

All text is laid out in two column or table numerical, outline format, wherein each statement, issue, or rule becomes a specific, uniquely referenced item. Additional discussion or qualifications to an item are indented to the right, immediately below, or listed subsequently.

The following is an example of the **"General"** portion:

*Example: User's Guide - 004*

The **Product** and **Installation** portions add an additional table format to express particular requirements that are applicable only to a particular Grade or Grades of work.

- The **Product** portion is divided into Basic, Material, Machining, and Assembly sub-sections. They are intended to be read with the understanding that the more general rules are listed first in the Basic sub-section with the more specific or detailed rules following in other sub-sections.

- The concept of "Unless Specified Otherwise" is a significant aspect of these standards. When referenced in contract documents, these standards shall establish the minimum contractual compliance requirements for materials, fabrication, installation, and workmanship - in the absence of any specific contractual requirement to the contrary. If there is a conflict between the contract documents and these standards, the contract documents shall prevail.

- As a rule of thumb, unless otherwise noted, the statements or rules contained within the **General**, **Product**, **Installation** and **Test** portions of each section are equally applicable to all Grades of work.

- Otherwise, within the **Product** or **Installation** portions, when a rule applies specifically to a particular Grade or Grades of work, it is shown by a bold E, C, and/or P in the corresponding right-hand columns to indicate Economy, Custom, or Premium Grade, respectively. If there are no columns or letters, it applies to all grades.

- Headers or footers are used on a column-by-column and page to page basis to indicate where there is additional coverage of a topic on a previous or a subsequent page.

| 7.4.5 Material Rules | | | | | | |
|---|---|---|---|---|---|---|
| ▲ From previous column | | | | | | |
| 10 | | For OPAQUE FINISH: | | | | |
| 10 | 1 | Medium density fiberboard (MDF) is permitted. | | | | |
| 10 | 2 | Veneer is permitted; however: | | | | |
| 10 | 2 | 1 | SPECIES shall be of manufacturer's choice, closed grain hardwood conforming to HPVA definitions and characteristics for: | | | |
| 10 | 2 | 1 | 1 | Grade - D. | E | C | P |
| 10 | 2 | 1 | 2 | Grade - C. | | C | P |
| 10 | 2 | 1 | 3 | Grade - B. | | | P |
| 11 | | For TRANSPARENT FINISH, VENEER: | | | | |
| 11 | 1 | | SPECIES of manufacturer's choice, hardwood conforming to HPVA definitions and characteristics for: | | | |
| 11 | 1 | 1 | Grade - B. | E | | P |
| 11 | 1 | 2 | Grade - A. | | C | P |
| 11 | 1 | 3 | Grade - AA. | | | P |
| 11 | 2 | SLICING of: | | | | |
| 11 | 2 | 1 | Manufacturer's choice. | E | | |
| 11 | 2 | 2 | Plain sliced. | | C | P |
| 11 | 3 | MATCHING ADJACENT LEAVES be: | | | | |
| 11 | 3 | 1 | Manufacturer's choice. | E | | |
| 11 | 3 | 2 | Book matched. | | C | P |
| 11 | 4 | MATCHING WITHIN PANEL FACE be: | | | | |
| 11 | 4 | 1 | Running. | E | | |
| 11 | 4 | 2 | Balance. | | C | P |
| 11 | 5 | MATCHING BETWEEN ADJACENT PANELS be: | | | | |
| 11 | 5 | 1 | Manufacturer's choice. | E | | |
| 11 | 5 | 2 | Compatible for color and grain. | | C | |
| 11 | 5 | 3 | Well matched for color and grain, and: | | | P |
| 11 | 5 | 4 | END, SEQUENCE, and BLUEPRINT MATCHING shall be specified. | | | |
| Continues next column ▼ | | | | | | |

*Example: User's Guide - 005*

- Unique to Sections 10 and 11, additional specific material, fabrication, and installation requirements have been provided for casework and/or countertops to be used in a laboratory-type setting. These requirements are only applicable if a project's contract documents specifically require compliance to such.

For further clarification or explanation, call your local Sponsor Association.

Architectural
Woodwork Standards

# TABLE
# OF
# CONTENTS

# TABLE OF CONTENTS

## INTRODUCTION
Introductory Statement & Disclaimers ............................................. 2
Sponsor Associations ........................................................................ 3
Contributing Association Acknowledgements ................................ 6

## USER'S GUIDE
Product Advisory ..................................................... Inside Front Cover
AWS Improvement Suggestion Access ................... Inside Back Cover
Section Organization ........................................................................ 8
Non-Compliance Portions ................................................................ 8
AWS Subdivision ............................................................................... 8
Format Within Each Section ........................................................... 11

## PREFACE
Architectural Woodwork Standards ............................................... 18
Variations in Natural Wood Products ............................................. 19
Moisture and Architectural Woodwork .......................................... 20
Architectural Woodwork Specifications ........................................ 20
Architectural Woodwork Drawings ................................................ 21
Systems of Measurement ............................................................... 22
Forest Management Certification .................................................. 22
Casework Refinishing/Refacing/Refurbishing .............................. 22
Warranty/Guarantee Language ..................................................... 22

## SECTION 1 - Submittals
Table of Contents ............................................................................ 24
Introductory Information ................................................................ 25
Compliance Requirements ............................................................. 27
    General ........................................................................................ 27
    Product ........................................................................................ 28

## SECTION 2 - Care & Storage
Table of Contents ............................................................................ 36
Introductory Information ................................................................ 37
Compliance Requirements ............................................................. 41
    General ........................................................................................ 41
    Product ........................................................................................ 41

## SECTION 3 - Lumber
Table of Contents ............................................................................ 44
Introductory Information ................................................................ 46
Compliance Requirements ............................................................. 58
    General ........................................................................................ 58
    Product ........................................................................................ 60

## SECTION 4 - Sheet Products
Table of Contents ............................................................................ 70
Introductory Information ................................................................ 73
Compliance Requirements ............................................................. 89
    General ........................................................................................ 89
    Product ........................................................................................ 90

## SECTION 5 - Finishing
Table of Contents .......................................................................... 108
Introductory Information .............................................................. 110
    AWS Finishing Systems .......................................................... 112
Compliance Requirements ........................................................... 117
    General ...................................................................................... 117
    Product ...................................................................................... 118
    Tests .......................................................................................... 125

## SECTION 6 - Millwork
Table of Contents .......................................................................... 128
Guide Specifications ..................................................................... 131
Introductory Information .............................................................. 132
Compliance Requirements ........................................................... 145
    General ...................................................................................... 145
    Product ...................................................................................... 147
    Installation ................................................................................ 160
    Tests .......................................................................................... 164

# TABLE OF CONTENTS

## SECTION 7 - Stairwork & Rails
- Table of Contents .................................................. 168
- Guide Specifications ............................................. 171
- Introductory Information ..................................... 172
- Compliance Requirements ................................... 175
  - General .............................................................. 175
  - Product .............................................................. 176
  - Installation ........................................................ 183
  - Tests .................................................................. 187

## SECTION 8 - Wall/Ceiling Surfacing and Partitions
- Table of Contents .................................................. 190
- Guide Specifications ............................................. 194
- Introductory Information ..................................... 195
- Compliance Requirements ................................... 212
  - General .............................................................. 212
  - Product .............................................................. 214
  - Installation ........................................................ 225
  - Tests .................................................................. 231

## SECTION 9 - Doors
- Table of Contents .................................................. 234
- Guide Specifications ............................................. 238
- Introductory Information ..................................... 239
- Compliance Requirements ................................... 251
  - General .............................................................. 251
  - Product .............................................................. 254
  - Installation ........................................................ 270
  - Tests .................................................................. 274

## SECTION 10 - Casework
- Table of Contents .................................................. 278
- Guide Specifications ............................................. 284
- Introductory Information ..................................... 285
- Compliance Requirements ................................... 295
  - General .............................................................. 295
  - Product .............................................................. 301
  - Installation ........................................................ 327
  - Tests .................................................................. 333

## SECTION 11 - Countertops
- Table of Contents .................................................. 336
- Guide Specifications ............................................. 341
- Introductory Information ..................................... 342
- Compliance Requirements ................................... 350
  - General .............................................................. 350
  - Product .............................................................. 352
  - Installation ........................................................ 364
  - Tests .................................................................. 370

## SECTION 12 - Historic Restoration Work
- Table of Contents .................................................. 374
- Guide Specifications ............................................. 376
- Introductory Information ..................................... 377
- Compliance Requirements ................................... 379
  - General .............................................................. 379
  - Product .............................................................. 380
  - Installation ........................................................ 382

## APPENDIX
- Table of Contents .................................................. 386
- Reference Source Directory ................................. 387
- Reference Source Listings .................................... 388
- Preservative & Water-Repellent Treatments ....... 390
- Fire-Retardant Coatings ....................................... 390
- Fire Codes ............................................................. 390
- ADA Requirements ............................................... 390
- Rated Fire Door Assemblies ................................. 390
- Building Code Requirements ............................... 390
- Seismic Fabrication and Installation Requirements ........ 390
- Adhesive Guidelines ............................................. 391
- Specific Gravity & Weight of Hardwoods ........... 392
- Joinery Details ...................................................... 394
- SEFA Chemical and Stain Resistance .................. 396
- Casework Integrity ............................................... 398
- Casework Refinishing/Refacing/Refurbishing Guidelines ........ 403
- Fractional/Decimal/Millimeter Conversion Table ........ 404
- Miscellaneous Conversion Factors ....................... 405

# TABLE OF CONTENTS

**DESIGN IDEAS**

| | |
|---|---|
| Table of Contents | 408 |
| Introduction | 408 |
| Base and Base Cap Patterns | 409 |
| Picture Mold Patterns | 412 |
| Casing Patterns | 413 |
| Panel Mold Patterns | 416 |
| Crown Mold Patterns | 417 |
| Bed Mold Patterns | 419 |
| Handrail Patterns | 420 |
| Chair Rail Patterns | 421 |
| Architectural Ornamentation | 423 |
| Stile & Rail Door Design Examples | 436 |
| Casework Design Examples | 440 |
| Cabinet Design Series (CDS) | 469 |

**GLOSSARY** .................................................. 490

**INDEX** ........................................................ 512

**SECTIONS 1 - 12**, the **APPENDIX**, and **DESIGN IDEAS**
have further detailed Tables of Content..

# Architectural Woodwork Standards

# PREFACE

# PREFACE

## ARCHITECTURAL WOODWORK STANDARDS

### PURPOSE
Provide design professionals with logical and simple means to comprehensively specify elements of architectural woodwork for use in climate controlled environments.

Provide compliance criteria to ensure that manufacturers/installers bidding on a project compete on an equal basis and are obligated to perform work of equal quality.

Provide industry information, terminology, and test criteria to properly determine compliance.

### OVERVIEW
These standards are based on three Grades of quality that may be mixed within a single project. Limitless design possibilities and a wide variety of lumber and veneer species, along with overlays, high-pressure decorative laminates, factory finishes, and profiles are available in all three Grades.

- **ECONOMY GRADE** defines the minimum quality requirements for a project's workmanship, materials, or installation and is typically reserved for woodwork that is not in public view, such as in mechanical rooms and utility areas.

- **CUSTOM GRADE** is typically specified for and adequately covers most high-quality architectural woodwork, providing a well-defined degree of control over a project's quality of materials, workmanship, or installation.

- **PREMIUM GRADE** is selectively used in the most visible and high-profile areas of a project, such as reception counters, boardrooms, and executive areas, providing the highest level of quality in materials, workmanship, or installation.

These standards cannot address every contingency; however, this document is the most comprehensive architectural woodworking standard available.

When these standards are referenced, the client is protected, and the manufacturer/installer has a clear direction for what is required.

These standards are not restrictive; they merely establish the minimum rules by which all parties shall conform. Issues not clearly defined in the contract documents or in these standards will be resolved by selection, fabrication, finishing, and/or installation at the option of the manufacturer or installer.

### FIRST-CLASS WORKMANSHIP
It is intended that architectural woodwork specified to meet these standards will conform to "First-Class Workmanship" as defined within these standards and the glossary.

### DEFAULT STIPULATION
When these standards are referenced as a part of the contract documents and no Grade is specified, Custom Grade will be the default stipulation. In the absence of material specifications, it will be the manufacturer's option to select materials suitable for opaque finish.

### EXCEPTION
These standards are a guide from which the design professional is free to deviate.

When the design professional, as part of the contract documents, deviates from these standards, the contract document takes precedence over the Standards. Such deviations cannot be adjudicated using the Standards as a basis.

These standards are intended for typical commercial, institutional and/or residential applications and environments and might not perform as expected in abusive or other environments where special design considerations should be taken.

### DISCLAIMERS
The sponsors of these standards shall not be responsible to anyone for the use of or reliance upon these standards.

The sponsors of these standards shall not incur any obligation nor liability for damages, including consequential damages, arising out of or in connection with the use, interpretation of, or reliance upon these standards.

These standards provide the minimum criteria for the concept, design, fabrication, finishing, and installation of architectural woodwork. Provisions for mechanical and electrical safety have not been included. References to life-safety requirements are included for information only.

Governmental agencies or other national standards-setting organizations provide the standards for life-safety requirements.

Illustrations are intended to assist in understanding these standards and might not include all requirements for a specific product or unit, nor do they show the only method of fabrication. Such partial drawings shall not be used to justify improper or incomplete design and/or construction.

### APPENDIX
Is provided as additional resources to the manufacturer, design professional, educator, user, or certifying organization and is only part of these standards when referenced. For your convenience where referenced it is flagged by the following icon:

### DESIGN IDEAS
Are provided as additional resources to the design professional, educator, or user. For your convenience where referenced it is flagged by the following icon:

### CITATIONS and QUOTES
Other industry standards, neither developed nor published by the Sponsor Associations, are used within the Architectural Woodwork Standards. The reference to and usage of is not a validation of these citations and quotations outside the context of the AWS. Only when these citations and partial quotations are applied in concert with all other related provisions of this Architectural Woodwork Standard are these citations and partial quotations recognized for application to architectural woodwork.

### CONFLICT
If found in these standards, it shall be brought to the attention of the Joint Standards Committee (JSC) by way of the AWS Improvement Suggestion Form (for which access is referenced on the inside back cover) and until specifically addressed, the least restrictive requirement shall prevail.

# PREFACE

## IMPROVEMENT

The Sponsor Associations encourage your suggestions for changes, revisions, and/or improvements to these standards. Access reference to the AWS Improvement Suggestion Form can be found on the inside back cover or on each of the Sponsor Associations' websites (www.awinet.org, www.awmac.com, or www.woodworkinstitute.com). Simply follow the form's instructions.

## TOLERANCES

The tolerances found within the AWS fall into two categories in Sections 6 – 11:

- Factory fabricated joinery, assembly and construction - found in the Product portion
- Field installation joinery and assembly - found in the Installation portion

Specific locations where the tolerances apply are found in the Tests portion of each Section.

Most fabrication and installation assemblies include solid wood to solid wood joints, solid wood to wood veneer joints, solid wood to wood based products (HPDL, LPDL, Solid Phenolic and panel products), solid wood to non-wood based products (which can be drywall, glass, metal, stone, acrylics, and other surfaces), and non-wood to non-wood joints.

Tolerances found in the AWS include:

- Flatness of wood based panel products
- Solid wood to solid wood joints and assemblies
- Solid wood to wood veneer joints and assemblies
- Wood veneer to wood veneer joints and assemblies
- Solid wood to wood based product joints and assemblies
- Solid surface to solid surface joints and assemblies

Because of the differences of expansion and contraction of non-wood products compared to solid wood and wood based products, the AWS does not apply tolerances regarding flatness or joinery to these non-wood based products.

## IMPORTANT PRODUCT ADVISORY REGARDING DIMENSIONAL CHANGE PROBLEMS IN ARCHITECTURAL MILLWORK

This advisory concerns prevention of dimensional problems in architectural woodwork products as the result of uncontrolled relative humidity. It is further intended as a reminder of the natural dimensional properties of wood and wood-based products such as plywood, particleboard, and high pressure decorative laminate (HPDL) and of the routine and necessary care and responsibilities which must be assumed by those involved.

For centuries, wood has served as a successful material for architectural woodwork, and as history has shown wood products perform with complete satisfaction when correctly designed and used. Problems directly or indirectly attributed to dimensional change of the wood are usually, in fact, the result of faulty design, or improper humidity conditions during site storage, installation, or use.

Wood is a hygroscopic material, and under normal use and conditions all wood products contain some moisture. Wood readily exchanges this molecular moisture with the water vapor in the surrounding atmosphere according to the existing relative humidity. In high humidity, wood picks up moisture and swells. In low humidity, wood releases moisture and shrinks. As normal minor fluctuations in humidity occur, the resulting dimensional response in properly designed construction will be insignificant. To reduce humidity related problems, the appropriate recommendations from Section 2 of the AWS should be considered. Uncontrolled extremes can likely cause problems.

Oxidation is a reaction of acids in wood (e.g., tannic acid), with iron, oxygen, and moisture, whether this be relative humidity or direct moisture. Control of moisture is a simple way to protect wood products from stains as a result of oxidation.

Together with proper design, fabrication, and installation, humidity control is obviously the important factor in preventing dimensional change problems.

Architectural woodwork products should be manufactured as designed from wood that has been dried to an appropriate average moisture content and maintained at this condition up to the time of delivery. Subsequent dimensional change in wood is and always has been an inherent natural property of wood. These changes cannot be the responsibility of the manufacturer or products made from it. Specifically:

- Responsibility for dimensional change problems in wood products resulting from design rests with the designer/architect/specifier.
- Responsibility for dimensional change problems in wood products resulting from improper relative humidity exposure during site storage and installation rests with the general contractor.
- Responsibility for dimensional change problems in wood products resulting from humidity extremes after occupancy rests with engineering and maintenance.

## VARIATIONS IN NATURAL WOOD PRODUCTS

Wood is a natural material with variations in color, texture, and figure. These variations are influenced by the natural growing process and are uncontrollable by the manufacturer.

The color of wood within a tree varies between the "sapwood" (the outer layers of the tree that continue to transport sap), which is usually lighter in color, and the "heartwood" (the inner layers in which the cells have become filled with natural deposits).

Various species, veneer cuts, and/or lumber milling options produce different grain patterns (figures) which influence the selection process. There will be variations of grain patterns within any selected species.

The manufacturer cannot select solid lumber cuttings within a species by grain and color in the same manner in which veneers might be selected.

Color, texture, and grain variations may occur in architectural woodworking.

# PREFACE

## MOISTURE AND ARCHITECTURAL WOODWORK

The moisture content of wood is crucial. If wood is not properly dried and/or seasoned, the best of workmanship cannot prevent moisture-related defects such as surface checks, cracking, bowing, twisting, and glue-line failure that might occur during production and afterward. In severe cases, a product can even be destroyed; unfortunately, most moisture defects are irreversible.

Wood is a hygroscopic material, expanding when it takes on moisture, shrinking when it loses moisture. How much moisture will be absorbed or how fast lumber will dry depends upon the present moisture content of the wood, the wood species, the relative humidity, and the temperature of the surrounding air. The drying process of lumber has to be slow enough to avoid stress between the surface and the core because too much stress results in surface checks, cracks, split ends, and other drying effects.

If wet and dry pieces of wood are placed in an area, they will absorb or lose moisture until all pieces have the same final moisture content (Equilibrium Moisture Content or EMC). For instance, if you make furniture, cabinets, picture frames, or clocks for inside a home, an office, or other heated live-in area, all wooden parts will eventually dry to approximately 6-12% wood moisture (extreme climate zones might have slightly higher or lower values).

For lasting quality and beauty, use only wood with a moisture content between 6-12%. Moisture-related defects might occur if only one piece has a higher or lower moisture content than 6-12%. Without control of the moisture content, occurrences of moisture related defects increases dramatically.

Many manufacturers reduce the occurrences of moisture problems by buying only kiln-dried wood. Kiln-dried wood should have a moisture content between 6-12%. Even though the wood might be dried properly when it leaves the dry kiln, it can change in moisture content during manufacturing, transportation, or storage. Manufacturers might inadvertently further complicate the problem by assembling a project with materials that have dissimilar moisture contents.

To reduce the risk of moisture damage, the U.S. Department of Agriculture, Forest Service, Forest Products Laboratory recommends in their General Technical Report 113 that:

- Large assemblies, such as ornamental beams, cornices, newel posts, stair stringers, and handrails, should be built up from comparatively small pieces.

- Wide door and window casing and base molding should be hollow-backed.

- Backband trim, if mitered at the corners, should be glued and splined before erection.

- Large solid pieces, such as wood stile and rail paneling, should be designed and installed so that the panels are free to move across the grain. Narrow widths are preferable.

## ARCHITECTURAL WOODWORK SPECIFICATION GUIDELINES

Specifications, along with the architectural drawings, are the road map for a project's success. Use of these standards will greatly reduce the text of your specifications and their development time. They eliminate the need to worry about every fabrication and material detail.

- **Budget constraints** should be communicated up front so that all parties can work together toward a successful resolution.

- **Requirements for each GRADE** are specifically defined within these standards; however, **special requirements** or **unusual applications** will need to be noted.

- **Compliance programs**, which all Sponsor Associations offer, are cost-effective and help enforce your contract documents. They ensure the performance and compliance of your architectural woodwork project's contract documents. With some, written status reports are issued during the project's progression, affording you timely notification of noncompliant findings.

- **Avoid conflict** in your specifications that might allow for interpretation other than what was envisioned. Use of certain words can make a big difference:

- Requiring compliance to Example A **AND** Example B means that the end result will be in full compliance with both.

- Requiring compliance to Example A **OR** Example B means that compliance to either is acceptable.

- **Enforce** your contract documents and their intent; however, be open-minded to proposed changes and cost savings. Materials and their availability are in constant flux; therefore, listen and be open to change when it does not affect your design intent.

- **Pre-qualify** your bidders to ensure their performance ability. Seek out and take advantage of our industry's knowledge and experience.

- **Guide specifications** for some and/or all of the AWS Product Sections are offered by the Sponsor Associations on an individual association basis:

  - The **ARCHITECTURAL WOODWORK INSTITUTE** (AWI) offers an online specification writing guide tool – AWI Build-a Spec to provide design professionals and specification writers with the ability to author architectural woodwork specifications that are complete and accurate in reference to the Architectural Woodwork Standards. Building a specification that reflects the exact project has never been easier and empowers the author to leverage their specification with the full power of the AWS. This allows upfront clarification of design intent while generating enforceable Architectural Woodwork specifications. This is not meant to compete with other specification writing tools, but rather supplement them with an enhanced application of detailed fine woodworking standards.

    This specification writing guide tool can be found at www.awinet.org

# PREFACE

- The **ARCHITECTURAL WOODWORK MANUFACTURERS ASSOCIATION OF CANADA** (AWMAC) offers Construction Specifications Canada (CSC) / Devis de Construction Canada (DCC) Master Formatted, guide specifications in digital, interactive, Word file formats .doc (Word 2003) and .docx (Word 2007).

  Included in the guide specifications is wording for AWMAC's national quality control program, the Guarantee and Inspection Service (GIS) which is administered locally in Canada by AWMAC's chapters.

  The Master Format sections covered by the guide specifications are:
  - 064100 Architectural Wood Casework
  - 064200 Wood Paneling
  - 064600 Wood Trim
  - 081400 Wood Doors
  - 123553 Laboratory Casework

  Downloads are available at: http://www.awmac.com/aws-guide-specifications

- The **WOODWORK INSTITUTE** (WI) offers CSI (Construction Specifications Institute) Master Formatted, guide specifications in digital, interactive, Word and plain text formats. Word file formats include .rtf (rich text format), .doc (Word 2003) and .docx (Word 2007). Specifically, WI offers guide specifications, including CCP, MCP and CSIP quality control options, for:
  - Wood Standing and Running Trim
  - Wall Paneling
  - Wood Passage Doors
  - Casework, including Green and Laboratory
  - Countertops

  Downloads are available at: http://www.woodworkinstitute.com/publications/aws_guide_specs.asp

## ARCHITECTURAL WOODWORK DRAWINGS - GUIDELINES

For design professionals, the proper use of these standards will greatly reduce drafting time. It is not necessary to produce standard joinery details on your drawings. Requirements for each **GRADE** are defined throughout these standards; however, **SPECIAL REQUIREMENTS or UNUSUAL APPLICATIONS** need to be noted and detailed.

### CASEWORK AND COUNTERTOPS:
Indicate the **CONSTRUCTION TYPE** desired:

- **FRAMELESS** construction.
- **FACE FRAME** construction (not recommended for decorative laminate faced or solid phenolic casework, and standards are not provided for such).

These standards define the following basic casework **CONSTRUCTION TYPES**:

- Wood Faced - **FRAMELESS**
- Wood Faced - **FACE FRAME**
- Decorative Laminate Faced - **FRAMELESS**
- Solid Phenolic Constructed - **FRAMELESS**

Casework elevations are not necessary if the **CASEWORK DESIGN SERIES (CDS)** numbers, which can be found in **DESIGN IDEA**s are utilized; however, a floor plan indicating each design number selection and relative dimensions is required.

When casework elevations are shown, they should indicate:

- The basic overall dimensions.
- Dimensions of items required to be of predetermined or controlled size.
- Dimensions required for installation of items of equipment.
- Whether sliding or hinged doors are desired, including swing if hinged.
- Thickness of cabinet doors if other than nominal 3/4" (19 mm) is required.
- If and where locks are required.
- Required details not shown in these standards or those that involve installation of unusual equipment.
- Shelf location and whether fixed or adjustable.
- Material and load capacity required.
- Type of countertop.

### STANDING AND RUNNING TRIM
Elevations should indicate the placement of standing and running trim, including cross section details along with overall dimensions should be shown for all trim types. If a finish schedule is used in lieu of elevations, it should be comprehensive enough to clearly indicate all of the above.

### ARCHITECTURAL WALL AND CEILING SURFACING
Elevations should indicate the placement of architectural wall surfacing, including each panel size, along with edge, corner, reveal, ceiling, and base treatments.

Door and/or other woodwork matching should be so indicated. Reveals, dimensions and locations should be as specified; however, a minimum of 1/4" (6.4 mm) wide reveal is recommended. If a finish schedule is used in lieu of elevations, it should clearly indicate all of the above.

### DOORS
Include a comprehensive door and hardware schedule indicating the location, type, size, and handling of each door, along with applicable requirements for:

- Pair and/or transom matching
- Room and/or panel matching
- Transom panel or Dutch door edge and/or shelf treatment
- Special core blocking
- Glass and louver cutouts
- Undercut tolerances
- Flame spread, acoustical, x-ray, and/or other ratings/requirements
- Hardware

Include elevations of typical door types to indicate glass and louver cutout sizes and locations.

# PREFACE

## SYSTEMS OF MEASUREMENT

These standards are written with the U.S. Customary System of Measurement followed by the metric system in brackets.

The system of measurement used in the original design of a project's architectural drawings will dictate which system of measurement within these standards is used for verification of compliance.

The metric number is typically a "soft" conversion of the U.S. Customary System of measurement. In order to make the metric number more conceptually coherent and consistent, most conversions for less than 3" (76 mm) in dimension are "soft" converted to the nearest 0.1 mm; for measurements above 3" (76 mm), the "soft" value is converted to the nearest 1 mm.

Exceptions to this convention will occur as, for example, 1220 mm is commonly used for 48", as opposed to 1219 mm.

## FOREST MANAGEMENT CERTIFICATION:

The Sponsor Associations acknowledge and have adopted the International Wood Products Association's (IWPA) Statement on Certification as modified below.

- We acknowledge the interest in certified timber products and verification of good forest management.
- A number of certification and verification systems are in operation or in development today, and we make no judgment against or endorsement of any single plan.
- Certification can serve as an audit of work already being done toward improved forest management. An absence of certification, however, does not mean there is a lack of quality forest management.
- We wish to recognize the efforts that many countries and companies are making with regard to improved forest management practices. Further, we strongly endorse the right of individual countries and companies that become involved with certification or the verification of forest management to pursue the development of their own internal auditing system or the selection of one that is already established.
- Global consensus has not been reached regarding the scope and viability for any single system of certification to be appropriate for all locations and conditions. Efforts are being made to develop an international framework of mutual recognition between credible and market-oriented sustainable forest management standards and certification systems.

The development of a mutual recognition process should ensure that these various certification or verification systems:

- Do not discriminate against different forest types.
- Should be regularly reviewed and updated.
- Should be transparent.
- Should be cost-effective.

We strongly endorse the development of a mutual recognition system and support any and all efforts that will further enhance management of the world's forests and the growth of global and sustainable trade in wood products.

## CASEWORK REFINISHING/REFACING/REFURBISHING

Is typically required to be done in the field and is not covered by these standards; however, guidelines can be found in the **APPENDIX**.

## WARRANTY/GUARANTEE LANGUAGE

There have been repeated requests for "industry standard" warranty or guarantee language, both on the part of design professionals and woodwork manufacturers. It is not the purpose or intent of this publication to give legal advice with regard to warranties. Such language varies from governing body to governing body.

**CAUTION**: You might use the following language as a starting point; however, the sponsors of these standards assume no liability whatsoever from its use. It is advised that warranty language be reviewed by competent counsel for the state or province in which it is intended.

Architectural woodwork is guaranteed to be of good material and workmanship and free from defects that render it unserviceable for the use for which it is intended. Natural variations in the color or texture of the wood are not to be considered defects. The quality of architectural woodwork is safeguarded while it is in the manufacturer's possession. To be protected by this guarantee, products must not be stored in damp warehouses or placed in moist or freshly plastered buildings. The woodwork must not be subjected to abnormal heat or dryness. Permanent-type heat and air conditioning must be in operation a sufficient length of time to "cure" the building before any woodwork or doors are delivered to the site. (Temporary-type heat sources might either add excessive moisture or create excessive dryness, depending upon the type of fuel. Thus, temporary heating can be a source of woodwork problems and should be avoided).

Adhere to the requirements in Section 2 for range and maintenance of relative humidity. Acclimatize delivered woodwork to the job site for a minimum of 72 hours before installation.

Woodwork must be inspected upon arrival, and all claims or complaints must be filed before painters' finish is applied. Doors must be properly sealed on all surfaces, including top and bottom edges, to prevent absorption of moisture. The manufacturer will not be responsible for defects resulting from neglect of these precautions.

The manufacturer agrees, within a period of __(insert year)__ year(s) after delivery date, to repair or replace (in the white, unfinished, if so furnished originally) without charge any woodwork that is defective within the meaning of this guarantee. The manufacturer does not agree to be responsible for any work that was not originally performed by them. The manufacturer _ __(insert does or does not)__ agree to pay charges for finishing or installing replaced woodwork. This guarantee is not effective if goods are repaired or replaced without first obtaining the manufacturer's written consent.

# Architectural Woodwork Standards

# SUBMITTALS

## SECTION 1

# SECTION 1
Submittals

## table of contents

### INTRODUCTORY INFORMATION

Introduction ..................................................................... 25
What to Expect .............................................................. 25
Purpose ........................................................................... 25
Level of Detail ................................................................ 25
Approvals ........................................................................ 25
Scheduling ..................................................................... 25
The Process .................................................................... 25
Specify Requirements For ......................................... 26
Recommendations ....................................................... 26

### COMPLIANCE REQUIREMENTS

#### GENERAL

Basic Considerations .................................................. 27
    Grades ........................................................................ 27
    Range of Color ........................................................ 27
    Industry Practices .................................................. 27
        Submittals ........................................................ 27
        Compliance ...................................................... 27

#### PRODUCT

Scope ............................................................................... 28
Default Stipulation ...................................................... 28
Rules ................................................................................ 28
    Errata .......................................................................... 28
    Basic Rules ............................................................... 28
        Submittals ............................................................ 28
        Rules ..................................................................... 28
        Drawing Sheets .................................................. 28
        Cover or Title Sheet ......................................... 28
        Material List ........................................................ 29
        Drawings ............................................................. 29
        Samples ............................................................... 29
        Mock-ups ............................................................ 29
        First Class Workmanship ................................ 29

Section Rules ................................................................. 30
    Section 6 .................................................................. 30
        Listing ................................................................... 30
        Drawings ............................................................. 30
    Section 7 .................................................................. 30
        Listing ................................................................... 30
        Drawings ............................................................. 30
    Section 8 .................................................................. 31
        Listing ................................................................... 31
        Drawings ............................................................. 31
    Section 9 .................................................................. 31
        Listing ................................................................... 31
        Drawings ............................................................. 31
    Section 10 ............................................................... 32
        Listing ................................................................... 32
        Drawings ............................................................. 32
    Section 11 ............................................................... 32
        Listing ................................................................... 32
        Drawings ............................................................. 32
    Section 12 ............................................................... 33
        Listing ................................................................... 33
        Drawings ............................................................. 33
    Samples and Mock-ups ...................................... 33

# SECTION 1
## Submittals

## introductory information

### INTRODUCTION

Section 1 begins the Architectural Woodwork Standards. At the beginning of every woodwork project is the submittal stage. This section deals with the various items that are the foundation of every project – Shop Drawings, Approvals, Samples and Scheduling. Each of the Product Sections (6 through 12) have criteria pertaining to their specific products.

Quality assurance can be achieved by adherence to the AWS and will provide the owner a quality product at competitive pricing. Use of a qualified Sponsor Member firm to provide your woodwork will help ensure the manufacturer's understanding of the quality level required. Illustrations in this Section are not intended to be all inclusive, other engineered solutions may be acceptable. In the absence of specifications; methods of fabrication are the manufacturer's choice. The design professional, by specifying compliance to the AWS increases the probability of receiving the product quality expected.

### WHAT TO EXPECT

The key to achieving a detailed and useful set of shop drawings is concise and continual communication between design professional and manufacturer.

The manufacturer shall submit samples, product data and shop drawings of sufficient detail and scale to demonstrate compliance with the AWS Grade specified.

### PURPOSE

Shop drawings are the means by which the design concept is turned into reality, serving as the primary instructions for woodwork engineering and fabrication, and as a guide for other trades. As the primary communication among manufacturer, general contractor and design professional, shop drawings serve a valuable coordinating function. Shop drawings should indicate methods of construction, exact material selections, finishes, method of attachment and joinery, exact dimensions and should include the manufacturer's technical suggestions.

### LEVEL OF DETAIL

The level of detail required on shop drawings is established by the complexity of the project. The specifier is at liberty to specify any level of detail as a requirement of the project and of the contract documents. It should be noted that requirements for local codes and utilization of fire retardant wood products is to be researched and directed by the design professional and are not the responsibility of the manufacturer.

What constitutes the minimum expectation for a set of shop drawings is not simple, since there are many variables as to the complexity, quality and type of work being specified.

### APPROVALS

For the design professional, the approval stage provides an opportunity, prior to fabrication, to review the manufacturer's proposed shop drawings. Shop drawings, however, are not an extension of the design development process; therefore, changes by either party of intent or concept made during shop drawing review may result in a change of cost and/or time.

During the review process the design professional should consider the following:

- Unless noted otherwise, two copies are necessary for checking purposes. After being reviewed, one marked copy should be returned to the contractor or manufacturer.

- Those charged with review of shop drawings should be familiar with woodwork fabrication, and have an understanding or working knowledge of the referenced standards as well as design concept.

- Deviations from the contract documents are often recommendations for improvement, and not necessarily a criticism of design. It is as wrong for a reviewer to arbitrarily stamp "Revise and Resubmit" on a shop drawing that proposes a change, as it is wrong to automatically accept shop drawings because they contain duplicates of the original plans.

For the manufacturer, shop drawings are drawings, diagrams, schedules and other data specifically prepared to illustrate their portion of the work. Their purpose is to demonstrate the way by which the manufacturer proposes to conform to the information given and the design concept expressed in the Contract Documents.

The four common levels of approval are:

- Approved
- Approved As Noted
- Revise and Resubmit
- Rejected

Approvals are generally indicated by a stamp on the cover sheet of the shop drawings. When selecting "Approved As Noted" rather than "Revise and Resubmit," the design professional can often save weeks of production time provided the concept and all changes are clearly marked on the drawings.

### SCHEDULING

Most projects are encumbered by a tight production schedule, especially for the finish trades such as woodworking, painting, carpeting and wall coverings. Prompt review of shop drawings and accurate coordination of multiple trades can save weeks of time and eliminate problems before construction begins.

The design professional should work with the manufacturer through the contractor to determine the maximum "approval-to-fabrication" timeline needed to keep the job on schedule (e.g., "Shop drawings must be returned approved to fabricate seven (7) days after submittal").

**Schedules vs Drawings** - In some cases shop drawings are not required to communicate the necessary quality, type, quantity and details of an item. Tabular schedules are used instead, generally for such items as doors, frames, stock factory cabinets, closet shelves, and furniture items.

### THE PROCESS

It is the responsibility of the contractor to coordinate the manufacturer's shop drawings with work of all other trades and to ensure that hold-to/guaranteed dimensions are actually enforced.

It is the responsibility of the design professional or contractor, depending on contract relationships, to communicate design and field changes to all parties so that if dimensions are changed, each subcontractor can be held responsible for their work.

# SECTION 1
## Submittals

*introductory information*

### SPECIFY REQUIREMENTS FOR

- **MOCK-UPS**
- **HARDWARE SAMPLES**
- **MOLDING SAMPLES**
  - Unless a catalog item, samples are typically not furnished until full-size details (in the shop drawings) have been approved.
- **FINISH SAMPLES**
  - Design professionaL shall provide a sample (suggested minimum of 5" x 8" {122 mm x 196 mm}) indicating the desired color, sheen and/or transparency as applicable.

### RECOMMENDATIONS

- That only **TWO SETS** of shop drawings are required to be submitted for initial design professional review.
  - If the review is Approved or Approved as Noted, the design professional keeps one copy, and a marked set is returned to the manufacturer with a request for the required number of final copies.
  - If the review is not Approved or Approved as Noted, the design professional returns one set requesting correction and resubmittal. The other set is kept by the design professional to check against the resubmittal.

# SECTION 1
## Submittals
### GENERAL/PRODUCT

## compliance requirements

**Includes: Shop Drawings, Profile and Veneer Flitch Samples, Finish Samples, Hardware Samples**

### 1.1 BASIC CONSIDERATIONS

**1 GRADES**

1.1 None; shop drawing requirements are the same for all architectural woodwork projects regardless of Grade specified.

2 **RANGE OF COLOR** shall be expected on finished wood products due to variance in wood color within the same species and even within the same log.

**3 INDUSTRY PRACTICES**

3.1 **SUBMITTALS** are submitted to the contractor, design professional, and/or owner for review prior to fabrication, and:

3.1.1 Are the property of the manufacturer, and the manufacturer is not responsible for errors caused by their unauthorized use by others.

3.1.2 The manufacturer is encouraged to make technical suggestions and raise questions based upon working experience; however:

3.1.2.1 Changes incorporated within shop drawings, in themselves, are not a request for approval.

3.1.2.2 Changes to material or design must be specifically identified in separate written documentation within the submittal package, requesting approval of the suggested changes.

3.1.2.2.1 Means and methods such as joinery details are not considered material changes.

3.2 **RESPONSIBILITY OF:**

3.2.1 **CODE/REGULATION** research, and compliance direction is that of the design professional, not of the manufacturer and/or installer.

3.2.2 **COORDINATION** of manufacturer's shop drawing with work of all other trades and assurance that hold-to/guaranteed dimensions are actually enforced is that of the general contractor, not of the manufacturer and/or installer.

3.2.3 **COMMUNICATION** of design and field changes to all parties so that if dimensions are changed, each subcontractor can be held responsible for their work, is that of the design professional or contractor, depending on contract relationships.

# SECTION 1
## Submittals

**GENERAL/PRODUCT** — compliance requirements

### 1.2 SCOPE

1. All materials and products covered under the scope of these standards.

### 1.3 DEFAULT STIPULATION

1. Not used or applicable for this section.

### 1.4 RULES

1. The following rules shall govern unless a project's contract documents require otherwise.
2. These rules are intended to provide a well-defined degree of control over a project's quality of submittals.
3. **ERRATA**, published on the Sponsor Associations' websites at www.awinet.org, www.awmac.com, or www.aws-errata.com, **shall take precedence over these rules**, subject to their date of posting and a project's bid date.

#### 1.4.4 Basic Rules

| | | | | |
|---|---|---|---|---|
| 1 | | | | **SUBMITTALS** shall: |
| 1 | 1 | | | Be submitted to the contractor, design professional, and/or owner for review prior to fabrication, and: |
| 1 | 2 | | | If applicable, note project phasing on shop drawings. |
| 1 | 3 | | | Be specifically created illustrating the project requirements. |
| 1 | 4 | | | Allow reuse of a portion of the Contract Documents in the creation of shop drawings if permitted by the design professional prior to the original shop drawing submittal, and: |
| 1 | 4 | 1 | | Copies with notations are not acceptable. |
| 1 | 4 | 2 | | Be in compliance with the following rules. |
| 2 | | | | **RULES** shall apply to all Grades equally. |
| 3 | | | | **DRAWING SHEETS** shall: |
| 3 | 1 | | | Be of size required to convey design concept. |
| 3 | 2 | | | A minimum of 11" x 17" (279 x 432 mm), except: |
| 3 | 2 | 1 | | Door submittals may be a minimum 8.5" x 11" (216 x 279 mm). |
| 3 | 3 | | | Numbered. |
| 3 | 4 | | | Dated. |
| 3 | 5 | | | Be electronic submittals if requested and/or approved by the design professional, and: |
| 3 | 5 | 1 | | Are in Portable Document Format (PDF) only. |

*Continues next column*

#### 1.4.4 Basic Rules

*From previous column*

| | | | | |
|---|---|---|---|---|
| 4 | | | | **COVER** or **TITLE SHEET** is required and shall include as applicable: |
| 4 | 1 | | | Project name and address. |
| 4 | 2 | | | Design professional firm and contact information, including phone, fax and email. |
| 4 | 3 | | | Contractor firm and contact information, including phone, fax and email. |
| 4 | 4 | | | Manufacturer firm and contact information, including phone, fax and email. |
| 4 | 5 | | | Installer firm and contact information, including phone, fax and email. |
| 4 | 6 | | | Finisher firm and contact information, including phone, fax and email. |
| 4 | 7 | | | AWS Grade requirement if same throughout, or: |
| 4 | 7 | 1 | | If multiple grades apply Cover or Title Sheet shall indicate the applicable Grades and scope, and the drawings shall individually indicate which Grade. |
| 4 | 8 | | | A Table of Contents listing all items in the woodworker's submittal package including: |
| 4 | 8 | 1 | | Number and title of each shop drawing page. |
| 4 | 8 | 2 | | Names of material, hardware, etc. lists. |
| 4 | 8 | 3 | | Description of finish samples supplied. |
| 4 | 8 | 4 | | Description of substitution and/or change requests, which shall be itemized separately from the shop drawings, and shall: |
| 4 | 8 | 4 | 1 | Be submitted as soon as possible, and no later than the time of shop drawing submittal. |
| 4 | 8 | 4 | 2 | Include the reason for the request. |
| 4 | 8 | 4 | 3 | Include a comparison of the requested product or design to that specified or shown, including technical data from the product manufacturers and/or detailed drawings as applicable. |
| 4 | 8 | 4 | 4 | Include a statement of the cost impact and possible impact to other trades. |
| 4 | 8 | 4 | 5 | Include a statement of possible schedule impact. |
| 4 | 8 | 5 | | When contract documents are in variance to these standards, a listing of all variant items with reference to the contract document and the AWS citation. |

*Continues next column*

# SECTION 1
## Submittals
### compliance requirements — GENERAL/PRODUCT

## 1.4.4 Basic Rules

▲ From previous column

| | | | |
|---|---|---|---|
| 5 | | | **MATERIAL LIST** shall include as applicable: |
| 5 | 1 | | Items to be used for exposed, semi-exposed, and/or concealed surfaces, including: |
| 5 | 1 | 1 | Lumber species and cut for transparent finish; however: |
| 5 | 1 | 1 | Cut is not relevant for items exposed on several sides such as turnings, railings, and some moldings. |
| 5 | 1 | 2 | Veneer species, cut, leaf match/balance, panel match, and room match for transparent finish, and: |
| 5 | 1 | 2 | If specified, flitch number and supplier. |
| 5 | 1 | 3 | Lumber and veneer species only for opaque finish. |
| 5 | 1 | 4 | Panel core type and thickness with any special compliance requirements, such as: |
| 5 | 1 | 4 | Moisture resistant. |
| 5 | 1 | 4 | Fire retardant. |
| 5 | 1 | 4 | NAUF (No Added Urea Formaldehyde) or ULEF (Ultra Low Emitting Formaldehyde). |
| 5 | 1 | 4 | CARB (California Air Resources Board). |
| 5 | 1 | 5 | Laminates, including applicable NEMA grade and thickness. |
| 5 | 1 | 6 | Solid phenolic core. |
| 5 | 1 | 7 | Solid surface. |
| 5 | 1 | 8 | Speciality work, such as metal, glass, fabric, etc. |
| 5 | 1 | 9 | All adhesive types being used, including: |
| 5 | 1 | 9 | Where they are being used and indication of the adhesive type used at detail drawings. |
| 5 | 1 | 10 | Hardware (except fasteners) with manufacturer's specification sheet. |
| 5 | 1 | 11 | Finishing requirements, including AWS System number, sheen and required application steps. |
| 6 | | | **DRAWINGS** shall show: |
| 6 | 1 | | Each item of woodwork in plan, elevation and section as needed to clearly indicate what is provided, its location, and its method(s) of construction and attachment, and: |
| 6 | 1 | 1 | Provide a reference plan drawn in minimum 1/4" = 1'-0" (1:50) scale showing location(s) of all work to be provided. |
| 6 | 1 | 2 | Plan and elevation views shall be drawn in minimum 3/8" = 1'-0" (1:20) scale. |
| 6 | 1 | 3 | Detailed section views shall be drawn in minimum 1-1/2" = 1'-0" (1:10) scale as required within each product section below. |
| 6 | 1 | 4 | Be sufficient in detail scale, minimum 3" = 1'-0" (1:5) scale, to clearly indicate unique features in construction. |

Continues next column ▼

## 1.4.4 Basic Rules

▲ From previous column

| | | | |
|---|---|---|---|
| 6 | | | **DRAWINGS** (continued) |
| 6 | 2 | | Internal blocking, where required, for woodwork installation, showing center line height or horizontal location and materials, for: |
| 6 | 2 | 1 | Side or back wall runs of all countertops not otherwise supported by casework or support brackets. |
| 6 | 2 | 2 | Wall or ceiling applied surfacing and/or standing and running trim. |
| 6 | 2 | 3 | Wall mounted shelf standards. |
| 6 | 2 | 4 | Door and window frames. |
| 6 | 2 | 5 | Wood or wood product blocking is required where nails are allowed for woodwork attachment. |
| 6 | 2 | 6 | Casework by a standard convention such as: |

| | | | |
|---|---|---|---|
| 7 | | | **SAMPLES**, if required, for: |
| 7 | 1 | | **HARDWARE** shall include one sample of each decorative and functional hardware item. |
| 7 | 2 | | **FINISHING** shall: |
| 7 | 2 | 1 | Be a minimum of 12" x 12" (304 mm x 304 mm) for panel products. |
| 7 | 2 | 2 | Be as wide as practical if on lumber by a minimum of 12" (304 mm) in length. |
| 7 | 2 | 3 | Be on material representative of that to be used for the project. |
| 7 | 2 | 4 | Bear a label identifying the date, job name, the design professional, the contractor, the manufacturer, the finisher and the finish system name and number and steps used. |
| 7 | 2 | 5 | At Transparent finish, require a minimum of three (3) sets, bound together, of three (3) samples each, indicating the range of color and grain to be expected for each finish selection. |
| 7 | 2 | 6 | At Opaque finish, require a minimum of three (3) samples for each color selection. |
| 8 | | | **MOCK-UPS** shall be provided as required by contract documents. |
| 9 | | | **FIRST-CLASS WORKMANSHIP** is required in compliance with these standards. |

# SECTION 1
## Submittals

GENERAL/PRODUCT compliance requirements

### 1.4.5 Section 6 - 12 Rules

| | | | | |
|---|---|---|---|---|
| 1 | | | | **SECTION 6 - MILLWORK:** |
| 1 | 1 | | | **LISTING** requirements shall additionally include: |
| 1 | 1 | 1 | | Related material requirements and specifications, and if applicable: |
| 1 | 1 | 1 | 1 | Wood treatments. |
| 1 | 1 | 1 | 2 | Adhesive. |
| 1 | 1 | 2 | | Trim schedule for each room or area, including as applicable: |
| 1 | 1 | 2 | 1 | Detail section reference. |
| 1 | 1 | 2 | 2 | Blocking requirements. |
| 1 | 1 | 3 | | Column, pilaster, cornice, finial, and/or pediment for each location, including: |
| 1 | 1 | 3 | 1 | Opening number. |
| 1 | 1 | 3 | 2 | Location. |
| 1 | 1 | 3 | 3 | Elevation reference. |
| 1 | 1 | 3 | 4 | Section reference. |
| 1 | 1 | 4 | | Frame, sash, screen, blind, and/or shutter schedule for each room or area, including as applicable: |
| 1 | 1 | 4 | 1 | Opening number and location. |
| 1 | 1 | 4 | 2 | Elevation and/or section references. |
| 1 | 1 | 4 | 3 | Opening size. |
| 1 | 1 | 4 | 4 | Handing and premachining requirements. |
| 1 | 1 | 4 | 5 | Hardware types and locations. |
| 1 | 1 | 4 | 6 | Screen specifications. |
| 1 | 2 | | | **DRAWINGS** requirements shall additionally include as applicable: |
| 1 | 2 | 1 | | Frame, sash, screen, blind, and/or shutter members, drawn in full (1:1) scale profile, except: |
| 1 | 2 | 1 | 1 | Members too large to fit on a single sheet may be drawn in segments, or at half scale, 1:2 ratio. |
| 1 | 2 | 2 | | Frame, sash, screen, blind, and/or shutter construction details drawn to a minimum 3" = 1'-0" (1:5) scale. |
| 1 | 2 | 3 | | Frames in section detail with elevations as necessary for coordination with other trades. |
| 1 | 2 | 4 | | Sash, screen, blind, and/or shutter in elevation. |
| 1 | 2 | 5 | | Column, pilaster, cornice, finial, and/or pediment construction details minimum 1-1/2" = 1'-0" (1:10 mm) scale, except: |
| 1 | 2 | 5 | 1 | Be sufficient in detail scale, minimum 3" = 1'-0" (1:5) scale, to clearly indicate unique features in construction. |

▼ Continues next column

### 1.4.5 Section 6 - 12 Rules

▲ From previous column

| | | | | |
|---|---|---|---|---|
| 1 | | | | **SECTION 6** (continued) |
| 1 | 2 | | | **DRAWINGS** (continued) |
| 1 | 2 | 6 | | **DETAILED SECTIONS**, minimum 1-1/2" = 1'-0" (1:10) scale, of: |
| 1 | 2 | 6 | 1 | Corners, inside and outside. |
| 1 | 2 | 6 | 2 | Joints within the woodwork item. |
| 1 | 2 | 6 | 3 | Joints between the woodwork item and other trim. |
| 1 | 2 | 6 | 4 | Woodwork item meeting features provided by other trades. |
| 1 | 2 | 6 | 5 | Attachment. |
| 1 | 2 | 6 | 6 | Relationships to adjacent trim members or features. |
| 2 | | | | **SECTION 7 - STAIRWORK & RAILS:** |
| 2 | 1 | | | **LISTING** requirements shall additionally include related material requirements and specifications. |
| 2 | 2 | | | **DRAWINGS** requirements shall additionally include as applicable: |
| 2 | 2 | 1 | | Professional Engineer seals if required of the manufacturer in the contract documents. |
| 2 | 2 | 2 | | Rails and trim members, shown in full-size profile. |
| 2 | 2 | 3 | | Plan and elevation views drawn to a minimum 3/4" = 1'-0" (1:20) scale for each: |
| 2 | 2 | 3 | 1 | Rise and run of stair. |
| 2 | 2 | 3 | 2 | Section of balustrade. |
| 2 | 2 | 4 | | **DETAILED SECTIONS**, minimum 1-1/2" = 1'-0" (1:10) scale, of: |
| 2 | 2 | 4 | 1 | Joinery. |
| 2 | 2 | 4 | 2 | Attachment. |
| 2 | 2 | 4 | 3 | Relationships to adjacent features. |
| 2 | 2 | 4 | 4 | Handrail brackets and other hardware. |
| 2 | 2 | 5 | | Location of field joints at all multi length pieces of stringers, riser and treads if such pieces cannot be made out of one piece of material in length. |

▼ Continues next column

# compliance requirements

## SECTION 1 — Submittals
### GENERAL/PRODUCT

### 1.4.5 Section 6 - 12 Rules
▲ From previous column

| | | | | | |
|---|---|---|---|---|---|
| 3 | | | | | **SECTION 8 - WALL/CEILING SURFACING & PARTITIONS:** |
| 3 | 1 | | | | **LISTING** requirements shall additionally include: |
| 3 | 1 | 1 | | | Cut, match, and balance of veneer leaves within the panel. |
| 3 | 1 | 2 | | | Match and balance of panels to adjacent panels. |
| 3 | 1 | 3 | | | Match and balance of panels within an elevation. |
| 3 | 1 | 4 | | | Match and balance of panels within a room. |
| 3 | 1 | 5 | | | Match and balance of panels to adjacent doors or casework. |
| 3 | 1 | 6 | | | Panel core type and thickness. |
| 3 | 1 | 7 | | | Backing or balance sheet, including thickness and material description. |
| 3 | 1 | 8 | | | Edgebanding, including thickness and material description. |
| 3 | 1 | 9 | | | Related material specifications, such as: |
| 3 | 1 | 9 | 1 | | Reveals. |
| 3 | 1 | 9 | 2 | | Metal panels or accents. |
| 3 | 1 | 9 | 3 | | Plastic resin materials. |
| 3 | 1 | 9 | 4 | | Adhesive types. |
| 3 | 1 | 10 | | | Orientation of veneer grain and/or directional pattern. |
| 3 | 2 | | | | **DRAWINGS** requirements shall additionally include as applicable: |
| 3 | 2 | 1 | | | Trim members, shown in full-size profile. |
| 3 | 2 | 2 | | | Plan and elevation views for each panel location. |
| 3 | 2 | 3 | | | **DETAILED SECTIONS**, including: |
| 3 | 2 | 3 | 1 | | Vertical and horizontal sections. |
| 3 | 2 | 3 | 2 | | Corner joints, both inside and outside. |
| 3 | 2 | 3 | 3 | | Panel to panel joints. |
| 3 | 2 | 3 | 4 | | Panel to base or floor joint. |
| 3 | 2 | 3 | 5 | | Panel to crown or ceiling joint. |
| 3 | 2 | 3 | 6 | | Attachment. |
| 3 | 2 | 3 | 7 | | Hardware. |

Continues next column ▼

### 1.4.5 Section 6 - 12 Rules
▲ From previous column

| | | | | | |
|---|---|---|---|---|---|
| 4 | | | | | **SECTION 9 - DOORS:** |
| 4 | 1 | | | | **LISTING** requirements shall additionally include: |
| 4 | 1 | 1 | | | Panel core type and thickness for slab door. |
| 4 | 1 | 2 | | | Solid or veneer edgebanding, including: |
| 4 | 1 | 2 | 1 | | Adhesive type. |
| 4 | 1 | 2 | 2 | | Any fire rated components. |
| 4 | 1 | 3 | | | Match and/or balance of door veneer leaves, including: |
| 4 | 1 | 3 | 1 | | Within door face. |
| 4 | 1 | 3 | 2 | | To adjacent paneling. |
| 4 | 1 | 4 | | | Stile and rail construction, including: |
| 4 | 1 | 4 | 1 | | Solid or veneered core. |
| 4 | 1 | 4 | 2 | | Core type and thickness. |
| 4 | 1 | 5 | | | Frame schedule, including as applicable: |
| 4 | 1 | 5 | 1 | | Opening number and location. |
| 4 | 1 | 5 | 2 | | Elevation and/or section references. |
| 4 | 1 | 5 | 3 | | Handing and premachining requirements. |
| 4 | 1 | 5 | 4 | | Hardware types and locations. |
| 4 | 1 | 5 | 5 | | Glass lite openings with size, type and location. |
| 4 | 1 | 5 | 6 | | Louver openings with size, type and location. |
| 3 | 1 | 6 | | | Orientation of veneer grain and/or directional pattern. |
| 4 | 2 | | | | **DRAWINGS** requirements shall additionally include as applicable: |
| 4 | 2 | 1 | | | Trim members, shown in full-size profile. |
| 4 | 2 | 2 | | | Manufacturer's specifications or cut sheet showing construction. |
| 4 | 2 | 3 | | | **DETAILED SECTIONS**, minimum 1-1/2" = 1'-0" (1:10) scale, of: |
| 4 | 2 | 3 | 1 | | Construction Type, 3, 5, or 7-ply for slab doors; solid or veneered for stile and rail. |
| 4 | 2 | 3 | 2 | | Panel core type and thickness. |
| 4 | 2 | 3 | 3 | | Diagram of hardware blocking locations at slab doors. |
| 4 | 2 | 3 | 4 | | Stile and rail construction, including that of stiles, rails, raised panels, and moldings. |
| 4 | 2 | 3 | 5 | | Stile and rail joints. |
| 4 | 2 | 3 | 6 | | Louvers and/or lites. |
| 4 | 2 | 3 | 7 | | Flame spread rating. |

Continues next column ▼

# SECTION 1
## Submittals

GENERAL/PRODUCT — compliance requirements

### 1.4.5 Section 6 - 12 Rules

▲ From previous column

| | | | | |
|---|---|---|---|---|
| 5 | | | | **SECTION 10 - CASEWORK:** |
| 5 | 1 | | | **LISTING** requirements shall additionally include: |
| 5 | 1 | 1 | | Exposed surface materials and if HPDL, its thickness. |
| 5 | 1 | 2 | | Semi-exposed surface materials and if HPDL, its thickness. |
| 5 | 1 | 3 | | Concealed surface materials. |
| 5 | 1 | 4 | | Inside face of cabinet door material and if HPDL, its thickness. |
| 5 | 1 | 5 | | Panel core type and thickness. |
| 5 | 1 | 6 | | Edgebanding material and thickness. |
| 5 | 1 | 7 | | Drawer box material and construction. |
| 5 | 1 | 8 | | Drawer slides or guides. |
| 5 | 1 | 9 | | Hinges including finish. |
| 5 | 1 | 10 | | Adjustable shelf pins, brackets, and/or standards including finish. |
| 5 | 1 | 11 | | Miscellaneous finish hardware, including finish. |
| 5 | 1 | 12 | | Glass type(s) and thickness. |
| 5 | 1 | 13 | | Special metal work and/or specialty items. |
| 5 | 1 | 14 | | Adhesive type(s). |
| 5 | 1 | 15 | | Other materials such as plastic resin or acrylic. |
| 3 | 1 | 16 | | Orientation of veneer grain and/or directional pattern. |
| 5 | 2 | | | **DRAWINGS** requirements shall include additionally, as applicable: |
| 5 | 2 | 1 | | Reference plan, so work areas can be located in building. |
| 5 | 2 | 2 | | Trim and/or scribe shown in full-size profile. |
| 5 | 2 | 3 | | Casework, shown in plan, elevation, and section view, minimum ½" = 1'-0" (1:30) scale, including: |
| 5 | 2 | 3 | 1 | Countertops, per the specific requirements for countertops listed below. |
| 5 | 2 | 3 | 2 | Details need not be drawn if properly referenced to a supplementary provided document. |
| 5 | 2 | 3 | 3 | Dimensions necessary to construct cabinets. |
| 5 | 2 | 3 | 4 | Dimensions and attachment method of face-frame members. |
| 5 | 2 | 3 | 5 | Type and thickness of drawer members, including heights and depths. |
| 5 | 2 | 3 | 6 | Type and thickness of cabinet doors. |
| 5 | 2 | 3 | 7 | Section of each cabinet type or configuration. |
| 5 | 2 | 3 | 8 | Details of all joinery and connections. |
| 5 | 2 | 3 | 9 | Specification and location of special metal work and/or specialty items. |
| 5 | 2 | 3 | 10 | Provision for field dimensions. |
| 5 | 2 | 3 | 11 | Section details showing method of cabinet attachment to walls, floors, and ceilings. |

Continues next column ▼

### 1.4.5 Section 6 - 12 Rules

▲ From previous column

| | | | | |
|---|---|---|---|---|
| 5 | | | | **SECTION 10** (continued) |
| 5 | 2 | | | **DRAWINGS** (continued) |
| 5 | 2 | 3 | | Casework (continued) |
| 5 | 2 | 3 | 12 | Blocking or strapping requirements and their locations (blocking to be furnished by others) shown on cabinet elevations with dimensions off finished floor. |
| 6 | | | | **SECTION 11 - COUNTERTOPS:** |
| 6 | 1 | | | **LISTING** requirements shall include, as applicable: |
| 6 | 1 | 1 | | Panel core type and thickness. |
| 6 | 1 | 2 | | Exposed material(s) description and thickness. |
| 6 | 1 | 3 | | Backing sheet material(s) and thickness at countertop and/or splash. |
| 6 | 1 | 4 | | Adhesive type. |
| 6 | 1 | 5 | | Sealing compound type used at sink cutouts and/or splashes. |
| 6 | 1 | 6 | | Orientation of veneer grain and/or directional pattern. |
| 6 | 2 | | | **DRAWINGS** shall include, as applicable: |
| 6 | 2 | 1 | | Each countertop, including indication of field joints, if applicable, and: |
| 6 | 2 | 1 | 1 | Type, quantity and layout of joint fasteners. |
| 6 | 2 | 2 | | Sink size, type, mounting and location if provided to manufacturer prior to shop drawing submittal. |
| 6 | 2 | 3 | | Support brackets with notation, if furnished by others. |
| 6 | 2 | 4 | | In elevation view; and: |
| 6 | 2 | 4 | 1 | Interface to casework and support brackets. |
| 6 | 2 | 5 | | In section detail, minimum 3" = 1'-0" (1:5) scale, showing: |
| 6 | 2 | 5 | 1 | Front and/or end overhang. |
| 6 | 2 | 5 | 2 | Front and/or end edge types. |
| 6 | 2 | 5 | 3 | Splash type and height. |
| 6 | 2 | 5 | 4 | Drip groove. |
| 6 | 2 | 5 | 5 | End splash return. |
| 6 | 2 | 6 | | Attachment of casework, including fastener type, quantity and layout. |

Continues next column ▼

## 1.4.5 Section 6 - 12 Rules

▲ From previous column

| 7 | SECTION 12 - HISTORIC RESTORATION WORK: | | | |
|---|---|---|---|---|
| 7 | 1 | | | The above AWS basic and specific section shop drawing requirements shall prevail for specific product types. |
| 7 | 2 | | | A written Restoration and Conservation Program shall be developed with a qualified wood conservator and submitted for each phase of the restoration process, outlining: |
| 7 | 2 | 1 | | Where existing wood materials will need to be removed, repaired, and retained, including. |
| 7 | 2 | 2 | | The means and methods to catalog the wood members, remove, crate and protect, store, and reinstall. |
| 7 | 2 | 3 | | A plan for protection of surrounding materials, including interface with other trades. |
| 7 | 2 | 4 | | A plan to retain toxic and/or offensive off-gassing and provide adequate ventilation. |
| 7 | 2 | 5 | | A plan to date-stamp all new work in letters minimum 1/4" (6.4 mm) high noting the month, year, and the installer's or manufacturer's name in an area not exposed to view as a record of when the work was installed. |
| 7 | 3 | | | **LISTING** requirements shall include, as applicable: |
| 7 | 3 | 1 | | Items to be repaired, including description, location, original material, and material to be used in repair. |
| 7 | 3 | 2 | | Items to be replaced, including description, location, material to be used, and basis for design. |
| 7 | 3 | 3 | | Specific restoration requirements for: |
| 7 | 3 | 3 | 1 | Removal. |
| 7 | 3 | 3 | 2 | Storage. |
| 7 | 3 | 3 | 3 | Repair or patching. |
| 7 | 3 | 3 | 4 | Replacement criteria. |
| 7 | 3 | 3 | 5 | Stripping. |
| 7 | 3 | 3 | 6 | Refinishing. |
| 7 | 3 | 3 | 7 | Installation. |
| 7 | 3 | 3 | 8 | Adhesive type(s). |
| 7 | 3 | 4 | | Material requirements, see: |
| 7 | 3 | 4 | 1 | Applicable AWS Sections above, if not otherwise specified. |
| 7 | 4 | | | **DRAWINGS** shall include plan, elevation, and section views, as applicable, of: |
| 7 | 4 | 1 | | See applicable AWS Section(s) above. |
| 7 | 4 | 2 | | Reference plan showing location of each item to be repaired or replaced. |
| 7 | 4 | 3 | | Relationship of items to be repaired or replaced to building and architectural features. |

Continues next column ▼

## 1.4.5 Section 6 - 12 Rules

▲ From previous column

| 7 | SECTION 12 (continued) | | | |
|---|---|---|---|---|
| 7 | 4 | | | **DRAWINGS** (continued) |
| 7 | 4 | 4 | | Section details in minimum 1-1/2" = 1'-0" (1:10) scale, of: |
| 7 | 4 | 4 | 1 | Trim members in full scale. |
| 7 | 4 | 4 | 2 | Fabrication. |
| 7 | 4 | 4 | 3 | Joinery. |
| 7 | 4 | 4 | 4 | Attachment. |
| 7 | 5 | | | **SAMPLES** and **MOCK-UPS** shall include: |
| 7 | 5 | 1 | | Design professional's written acceptance of all representative visual qualities before proceeding with work, including: |
| 7 | 5 | 1 | 1 | Any altered or modified methods and techniques used, as required, to achieve intended results. |
| 7 | 5 | 2 | | Acceptable samples, suitably marked, during the restoration process as a standard for work to be performed. |
| 7 | 5 | 3 | | For new work, prepare and have approved samples representative of all: |
| 7 | 5 | 3 | 1 | New molding and/or decorative profiles. |
| 7 | 5 | 3 | 2 | Panel, frame, stile and rail door, railing, and/or otherwise unique millwork assemblies. |
| 7 | 5 | 3 | 3 | Typical trim joinery and casework construction. |
| 7 | 5 | 3 | 4 | Fasteners. |
| 7 | 5 | 4 | | For restoration work, perform sample restoration work of the following general processes on existing materials in an area directed by the design professional, of sufficient scope to demonstrate the effectiveness of proposed materials and techniques of each process: |
| 7 | 5 | 4 | 1 | To remove existing finishes. |
| 7 | 5 | 4 | 2 | Of patching, plugging, and/or cut-ins. |
| 7 | 5 | 4 | 3 | Of refinishing. |

# SECTION 1
Submittals

notes

# Architectural Woodwork Standards

# CARE & STORAGE

## SECTION 2

# SECTION 2
Care & Storage

## table of contents

### INTRODUCTORY INFORMATION

| | |
|---|---|
| Introduction | 37 |
| Important Product Advisory regarding Dimensional Change | 37 |
| Care | 37 |
| Relative Humidity and Moisture Content (Table: 2-001) | 38 |
| Equilibrium Moisture Content Values (Table: 2-002) | 39 |
|     Recommendations | 40 |
|         Climate Control Maintenance | 40 |
|         Cleaning | 40 |
|         Avoid | 40 |
|         Use | 40 |

### COMPLIANCE REQUIREMENTS

#### GENERAL

| | |
|---|---|
| Basic Considerations | 41 |
|     Grades | 41 |
|     Dimensional Change Responsibility | 41 |
|     Industry Practices | 41 |
|         Off Gas Reduction | 41 |

#### PRODUCT

| | |
|---|---|
| Scope | 41 |
| Default Stipulation | 41 |
| Rules | 41 |
|     Errata | 41 |
|     Basic Rules | 41 |
|         Delivery | 41 |
|         Handling | 41 |
|         Storage | 41 |
|         Installation | 42 |
|         After Install and Acceptance | 42 |
|         Severe Damage | 42 |

# SECTION 2
## Care & Storage

## introductory information

### INTRODUCTION

Section 2 handles one of the most important aspects of preserving a good woodworking installation. Storage, jobsite conditions and relative humidity requirements before, during and after installation are covered here.

Quality assurance can be achieved by adherence to the AWS and will provide the owner a quality product at competitive pricing. Use of a qualified Sponsor Member firm to provide your woodwork will help ensure the manufacturer's understanding of the quality level required. Illustrations in this Section are not intended to be all inclusive, other engineered solutions may be acceptable. In the absence of specifications; methods of fabrication are the manufacturer's choice. The design professional, by specifying compliance to the AWS increases the probability of receiving the product quality expected.

### IMPORTANT PRODUCT ADVISORY REGARDING DIMENSIONAL CHANGE PROBLEMS IN ARCHITECTURAL MILLWORK

This advisory concerns prevention of dimensional problems in architectural woodwork products as the result of uncontrolled relative humidity. It is further intended as a reminder of the natural dimensional properties of wood and wood-based products such as plywood, particleboard, and high pressure decorative laminate (HPDL) and of the routine and necessary care and responsibilities which must be assumed by those involved.

For centuries, wood has served as a successful material for architectural woodwork, and as history has shown wood products perform with complete satisfaction when correctly designed and used. Problems directly or indirectly attributed to dimensional change of the wood are usually, in fact, the result of faulty design, or improper humidity conditions during site storage, installation, or use.

Wood is a hygroscopic material, and under normal use and conditions all wood products contain some moisture. Wood readily exchanges this molecular moisture with the water vapor in the surrounding atmosphere according to the existing relative humidity. In high humidity, wood picks up moisture and swells. In low humidity, wood releases moisture and shrinks.

As normal minor fluctuations in humidity occur, the resulting dimensional response in properly designed construction will be insignificant. To reduce humidity related problems, the appropriate recommendations from Section 2 of the AWS should be considered. Uncontrolled extremes can likely cause problems.

Together with proper design, fabrication, and installation, humidity control is obviously the important factor in preventing dimensional change problems.

Architectural woodwork products are manufactured as designed from wood that has been kiln dried to an appropriate average moisture content. Subsequent dimensional change in wood is and always has been an inherent natural property of wood. These changes cannot be the responsibility of the manufacturer or products made from it. Specifically, responsibility for dimensional change problems in wood products resulting from:

- Design rests with the designer/architect/specifier.

- Improper relative humidity exposure during site storage and installation rests with the general contractor.

- Humidity extremes after occupancy rests with engineering and maintenance.

### CARE

All construction related products, regardless of material, have particular care and storage requirements. Woodwork is not unique in this respect.

Architectural woodwork should be treated like fine furniture, particularly that which is constructed of wood finished with a transparent finish system. Modern commercial finishes are durable and resistant to moisture.

- **Finish Maintenance** - With the exception of true oil-rubbed surfaces, modern finishes do not need to be polished, oiled, or waxed. In fact, applying some polishing oils, cleaning waxes, or products containing silicone may impede the effectiveness of touch-up or refinishing procedures in the future.

No abrasives, chemical or ammonia cleaners should be used to clean woodwork surfaces. Routine cleaning is best accomplished with a soft, lint-free cloth lightly dampened with water or an inert household dust attractant. Allowing airborne dust, which is somewhat abrasive, to build up will tend to dull a finish over time.

Remove oil or grease deposits with a mild flax soap, following the directions for dilution on the container.

- **Impact** - Avoid excessive or repetitive impact, however lightly applied. The cellular structure of the wood will compact under pressure. Many modern finishes are flexible, and will show evidence of impact and pressure applied to them.

- **Heat** - Avoid localized high heat, such as a hot pan or plate, or a hot light source, close to or in contact with the finished surface. Exposure to direct sunlight will alter the appearance of woodwork over time.

- **Humidity** - Maintain the relative humidity around the woodwork in accordance with the guidelines published in these standards, every hour of every day, to minimize wood movement.

- **Moisture** - Architectural woodwork, when properly finished, is relatively durable and resistant to moisture. Prevent direct contact with moisture, and wipe it dry immediately should any occur. Allowing moisture to accumulate on, or stay in contact with, any wood surface, no matter how well finished, will cause damage.

- **Oxidation** - Is a reaction of acids in wood (e.g., tannic acid), with iron, oxygen, and moisture, whether this be relative humidity or direct moisture. Control of moisture is a simple way to protect wood products from stains as a result of oxidation.

- **Abuse** - Use the trims, cabinets and fixtures, paneling, shelving, ornamental work, stairs, frames, windows, and doors as they were intended. Abuse of cabinet doors and drawers, for example, may result in damage to them as well as to the cabinet parts to which they are joined.

- **Refinishing** - Contact a local Sponsor Association member, to explore the options for repair or refinishing. It is often cost effective to replace damaged woodwork elements rather than attempting large scale, on site refinishing.

# SECTION 2
## Care & Storage

## introductory information

### RELATIVE HUMIDITY AND MOISTURE CONTENT

The space in which architectural woodwork is to be installed should be engineered with appropriate humidity controls to maintain its optimum relative humidity. Wood for architectural woodwork manufacturing use needs a moisture content within an optimum range.

A major cause for failure in architectural woodwork is the lack of controls for maintaining a consistent, year round, appropriate relative humidity in a building or building space. Wood is susceptible to movement, shrinkage, expansion and warpage when exposed to air that has not been humidified. Without considerations made to properly regulate the relative humidity in any space containing architectural woodwork, some degree of failure of the woodwork can be expected.

The range of relative humidity change should not exceed 30 percentage points. Relative humidity outside the range shown on Table 2-001 below for the respective region is particularly harmful to wood and wood products.

The table and map that follow (adapted from USDA's The Wood Handbook (latest edition), published by their Forest Products Laboratory) shows the Optimum Moisture Content and the Indoor Relative Humidity required to hold such MC within the general areas of the United States and Canada.

Some of these areas have additional micro-climates not shown or referenced.

TABLE: 2-001 - RELATIVE HUMIDITY and OPTIMUM MOISTURE CONTENT

| Geographical Location | Optimum Moisture Content | | Optimum Climate Controlled Relative Humidity |
|---|---|---|---|
| | Non-Climate Controlled Interior or Exterior Environment | Climate Controlled Environment | |
| Most of U.S. and Canada | 9-15% | 5-10% | 25-55% |
| Damp Southern Coastal areas of the U.S. and Canadian Eastern Coastal Provinces | 10-15% | 8-13% | 43-70% |
| Dry Southwestern U.S. | 7-12% | 4-9% | 20-50% |
| Alberta, Saskatchewan, and Manitoba in Canada | 10-15% | 4-9% | 20-50% |

# SECTION 2
## Care & Storage

# introductory information

*TABLE: 2-002* - **EQUILIBRIUM MOISTURE CONTENT VALUES AT VARIOUS TEMPERATURES AND HUMIDITIES**

The following table indicates relative humidity must average between 25% and 55% to maintain wood moisture content between 5-10%. This range is best suited for most of the U.S. and Canada. While temperature has an impact on relative humidity, temperature alone has little effect on wood products if the relative humidity is maintained within recommended ranges.

Wet bulb lowering in degrees Fahrenheit (columns); Dry bulb temperature in degrees Fahrenheit (rows). Each cell: upper figure = relative humidity (%), lower figure = equilibrium moisture content (%).

| Dry Bulb °F | 2 | 3 | 4 | 5 | 6 | 7 | 8 | 9 | 10 | 11 | 12 | 13 | 14 | 15 | 16 | 17 | 18 | 19 | 20 | 21 | 22 | 23 | 24 | 25 | 26 | 27 | 28 | 29 |
|---|---|---|---|---|---|---|---|---|---|---|---|---|---|---|---|---|---|---|---|---|---|---|---|---|---|---|---|---|
| 40 | 83/17.6 | 75/14.8 | 68/12.9 | 60/11.2 | 52/9.9 | 45/8.6 | 37/7.4 | 29/6.2 | 22/5.0 | 15/3.5 | 8/1.9 | | | | | | | | | | | | | | | | | |
| 45 | 85/18.3 | 78/15.6 | 72/13.7 | 64/12.0 | 58/10.7 | 51/9.5 | 44/8.5 | 37/7.5 | 31/6.5 | 25/5.3 | 19/4.2 | 12/2.9 | 6/1.5 | | | | | | | | | | | | | | | |
| 50 | 86/19.0 | 80/16.3 | 74/14.4 | 68/12.7 | 62/11.5 | 56/10.3 | 50/9.4 | 44/8.5 | 38/7.6 | 32/6.7 | 27/5.7 | 21/4.8 | 16/3.9 | 10/2.8 | 5/1.5 | | | | | | | | | | | | | |
| 55 | 88/19.5 | 82/16.9 | 76/15.1 | 70/13.4 | 65/12.2 | 60/11.0 | 54/10.1 | 49/9.3 | 44/8.4 | 39/7.6 | 34/6.8 | 28/6.0 | 24/5.3 | 19/4.5 | 14/3.6 | 9/2.5 | 5/1.3 | | | | | | | | | | | |
| 60 | 89/19.9 | 83/17.4 | 78/15.6 | 73/13.9 | 68/12.7 | 63/11.6 | 58/10.7 | 53/9.9 | 48/9.1 | 43/8.3 | 39/7.6 | 34/6.9 | 30/6.3 | 26/5.6 | 21/4.9 | 17/4.1 | 13/3.2 | 9/2.3 | 5/1.3 | 1/0.2 | | | | | | | | |
| 65 | 90/20.3 | 84/17.8 | 80/16.1 | 75/14.4 | 70/13.3 | 66/12.1 | 61/11.2 | 56/10.4 | 52/9.7 | 48/8.9 | 44/8.3 | 39/7.7 | 36/7.1 | 32/6.5 | 27/5.8 | 24/5.2 | 20/4.5 | 16/3.8 | 13/3.0 | 8/2.3 | 6/1.4 | 2/0.4 | | | | | | |
| 70 | 91/20.9 | 86/18.2 | 81/16.5 | 77/14.9 | 72/13.7 | 68/12.5 | 64/11.6 | 59/10.9 | 55/10.1 | 51/9.4 | 48/8.8 | 44/8.3 | 40/7.7 | 36/7.2 | 33/6.6 | 29/6.0 | 25/5.5 | 22/5.0 | 19/4.3 | 15/3.7 | 12/2.9 | 9/2.3 | 6/1.5 | 3/0.7 | | | | |
| 75 | 91/21.0 | 86/18.5 | 82/16.8 | 78/15.2 | 74/14.0 | 70/12.9 | 66/12.0 | 62/11.2 | 58/10.5 | 54/9.8 | 51/9.3 | 47/8.7 | 44/8.2 | 41/7.7 | 37/7.2 | 34/6.7 | 31/6.2 | 28/5.6 | 24/5.1 | 21/4.7 | 18/4.1 | 15/3.5 | 12/2.9 | 10/2.3 | 7/1.7 | 4/0.9 | 1/0.2 | |
| 80 | 92/21.2 | 87/18.7 | 83/17.0 | 79/15.5 | 75/14.3 | 72/13.2 | 68/12.3 | 64/11.5 | 61/10.9 | 57/10.1 | 54/9.7 | 50/9.1 | 47/8.6 | 44/8.1 | 41/7.7 | 38/7.2 | 35/6.8 | 32/6.3 | 29/5.8 | 26/5.4 | 23/5.0 | 20/4.5 | 18/4.0 | 15/3.5 | 12/3.0 | 10/2.4 | 7/1.8 | 5/1.1 |
| 85 | 92/21.3 | 88/18.8 | 84/17.2 | 80/15.7 | 76/14.5 | 73/13.5 | 70/12.5 | 66/11.8 | 63/11.2 | 59/10.5 | 56/10.0 | 53/9.5 | 50/9.0 | 47/8.5 | 44/8.1 | 41/7.6 | 38/7.2 | 36/6.7 | 33/6.3 | 30/6.0 | 28/5.6 | 25/5.2 | 23/4.8 | 20/4.3 | 18/3.9 | 15/3.4 | 13/3.0 | 11/2.4 |
| 90 | 92/21.3 | 89/18.9 | 85/17.3 | 81/15.9 | 78/14.7 | 74/13.7 | 71/12.8 | 68/12.0 | 65/11.4 | 61/10.7 | 58/10.2 | 55/9.7 | 52/9.3 | 49/8.8 | 47/8.4 | 44/8.0 | 41/7.6 | 39/7.2 | 36/6.8 | 34/6.5 | 31/6.1 | 29/5.7 | 26/5.3 | 24/4.9 | 22/4.6 | 19/4.2 | 17/3.8 | 15/3.3 |
| 95 | 92/21.3 | 89/19.0 | 85/17.4 | 82/16.1 | 79/14.9 | 75/13.9 | 72/12.9 | 69/12.2 | 66/11.6 | 63/11.0 | 60/10.5 | 57/10.1 | 55/9.5 | 52/9.1 | 49/8.7 | 46/8.2 | 44/7.9 | 42/7.5 | 39/7.1 | 37/6.8 | 34/6.4 | 32/6.1 | 30/5.7 | 28/5.3 | 26/5.1 | 23/4.8 | 22/4.4 | 20/4.0 |
| 100 | 93/21.3 | 89/19.0 | 86/17.5 | 83/16.1 | 80/15.0 | 77/13.9 | 73/13.1 | 70/12.4 | 68/11.8 | 65/11.2 | 62/10.6 | 59/10.1 | 56/9.6 | 54/9.2 | 51/8.9 | 49/8.5 | 46/8.1 | 44/7.8 | 41/7.4 | 39/7.0 | 37/6.7 | 35/6.4 | 33/6.1 | 30/5.7 | 28/5.4 | 26/5.2 | 24/4.9 | 22/4.6 |
| 110 | 93/21.4 | 90/19.0 | 87/17.5 | 84/16.2 | 81/15.1 | 78/14.1 | 75/13.3 | 73/12.6 | 70/12.0 | 67/11.4 | 65/10.8 | 62/10.4 | 60/9.9 | 57/9.5 | 55/9.2 | 52/8.8 | 50/8.4 | 48/8.1 | 46/7.7 | 44/7.5 | 42/7.2 | 40/6.8 | 38/6.6 | 36/6.3 | 34/6.0 | 32/5.7 | 30/5.4 | 28/5.2 |
| 120 | 94/21.3 | 91/19.0 | 88/17.4 | 85/16.2 | 82/15.1 | 80/14.1 | 77/13.4 | 74/12.7 | 72/12.1 | 69/11.5 | 67/11.0 | 65/10.5 | 62/10.1 | 60/9.7 | 58/9.4 | 55/9.0 | 53/8.7 | 51/8.3 | 49/7.9 | 47/7.7 | 45/7.4 | 43/7.2 | 41/6.8 | 40/6.6 | 38/6.3 | 36/6.1 | 34/5.8 | 33/5.6 |

Diagonal reference curves on the chart indicate 13% moisture, 10% moisture, and 5% moisture lines.

### EXAMPLES OF MOISTURE EQUILIBRIUM TABLE USE

The above may be used as a guide in determining whether or not the conditions in a construction area are suitable for receiving woodwork. For example: if woodwork with an 8% average moisture content is to be installed and the average temperature in the building will be maintained at 70°F, it can be determined by following the 70°F column horizontally to the right until the lower moisture content figures of 8.3% and 7.7% are reached.

Here the upper figures in the same squares show that ideally a relative humidity of between 44% and 40% should be maintained in order to achieve dimensional equilibrium. After the woodwork is painted or finished, moisture changes in the wood are retarded so that maintenance of relative humidity between the practical limits shown on the curve (between 5%-10% m.c.) of the humidity table, i.e., 25%-55% relative humidity, is usually satisfactory.

### TO USE TABLE

Obtain wet and dry bulb readings. Subtract wet bulb reading from dry bulb reading. Find dry bulb on left margin of table and follow across to the column where the value at the top corresponds with the difference between wet and dry readings. At point of intersection, the upper figure in the square gives relative humidity in percent and the lower figure gives equilibrium moisture content of the woodwork.

# SECTION 2
## Care & Storage

## introductory information

### RECOMMENDATIONS

- **CLIMATE CONTROL MAINTENANCE** of relative humidity every hour of every day, within the ranges shown previously in this section is important. Uncontrolled extremes such as those listed below will likely cause problems:
  - Relative humidity, above or below the ranges shown previously in this section.
  - Sudden changes in the allowable relative humidity, especially when it is repetitive.

- **CLEANING** should be routine and accomplished with a soft, lint-free cloth lightly dampened with water or an inert household dust attractant. Allowing airborne dust, which is somewhat abrasive, to build up will tend to dull a finish over time.
  - Remove oil or grease deposits with a mild flax soap, following its directions for dilution.
  - Do not use abrasives, chemical or ammonia cleaners on fine architectural woodwork surfaces.

- **AVOID**:
  - Excessive or repetitive impact, however lightly applied. The cellular structure of the wood will compact under pressure. Many modern finishes are flexible and will show evidence of impact and pressure applied to them.
  - Localized high heat, such as a hot pan or plate, or a hot light source, close to or in contact with the finished surface. Exposure to direct sunlight will alter the appearance of fine woodwork over time.

- **USE** trims, cabinets and fixtures, paneling, shelving, ornamental work, stairs, frames, windows, and doors as they were intended.
  - Abuse of cabinet doors and drawers, for example, may result in damage to them as well as to the cabinet parts to which they are joined.

# SECTION 2
## Care & Storage

**compliance requirements** — GENERAL/PRODUCT

**Including: Care and Moisture Considerations Before, During, and After Installation**

## 2.1 BASIC CONSIDERATIONS

**1   GRADES** - None

1.1   Care and storage requirements are the same for all architectural woodwork projects, regardless of Grade specified or required.

**2.1   DIMENSIONAL CHANGE RESPONSIBILITY** in wood products resulting from:

2.1.1   Improper design rests with the design professional.

2.1.2   Improper relative humidity exposure during site storage and installation rests with the contractor.

2.1.3   Humidity extremes after occupancy rests with the owner.

**3   INDUSTRY PRACTICES**

3.1   **OFF GAS REDUCTION** by raising the temperature in a building for a sustained period is unacceptable and will negatively affect the appearance and performance of architectural millwork.

3.1.1   Open joints, warped paneling/doors, and other defects caused by such are not to be considered a defect.

# SECTION 2
## Care & Storage

**GENERAL/PRODUCT** — compliance requirements

### 2.2 SCOPE

1. All materials and products covered under the scope of these standards.

### 2.3 DEFAULT STIPULATION

1. Not used or applicable for this section.

### 2.4 RULES

1. The following rules shall govern unless a project's contract documents require otherwise.

2. These rules are intended to provide a well-defined degree of control over a project's quality of finishing.

3. **ERRATA**, published on the Sponsor Associations' websites at www.awinet.org, www.awmac.com, or www.aws-errata.com, **shall take precedence over these rules**, subject to their date of posting and a project's bid date.

### 2.4.4. Basic Rules

| | | | | |
|---|---|---|---|---|
| 1 | **DELIVERY** shall be: | | | |
| | 1 | Made in accordance with a progress schedule furnished by the contractor, and: | | |
| | 1 | 1 | For climate controlled applications, in an area in which: | |
| | 1 | 1 | 1 | Wet work is dry. |
| | 1 | 1 | 2 | Overhead work is complete. |
| | 1 | 1 | 3 | Area is room clean. |
| | 1 | 2 | For non-climate controlled interior or exterior applications, in an area which is: | |
| | 1 | 2 | 1 | Clean. |
| | 1 | 2 | 2 | Protected from direct moisture. |
| | 1 | 2 | 3 | Protected from direct sunlight. |
| 2 | **HANDLING** shall: | | | |
| | 1 | Be with clean hands or gloves. | | |
| | 2 | Include protection from marks or damage. | | |
| 3 | **STORAGE** shall be: | | | |
| | 1 | Flat on a level surface. | | |
| | 2 | Clean. | | |
| | 3 | At least 4" (101.6 mm) off the floor or ground. | | |
| | 4 | Protected from: | | |
| | 4 | 1 | Sunlight, wide swings in relative humidity, and/or abnormal heat or cold. | |
| | 4 | 2 | Moisture. | |

*Continues next column*

### 2.4.4. Basic Rules

▲ From previous column

| | | | | |
|---|---|---|---|---|
| 3 | **STORAGE** (continued) | | | |
| | 5 | For climate controlled applications: | | |
| | 5 | 1 | In a clean, closed building or area with operational HVAC system, and: | |
| | 5 | 1 | 1 | Relative humidity between 25-55% inclusive. |
| | 5 | 1 | 2 | Maintained Optimum Moisture Content between 5 - 10% inclusive, except in: |
| | 5 | 1 | 2 | 1 | The damp Southern Coastal areas of the U.S. and Canadian Eastern Coastal Provinces shall be between 8 - 13% inclusive. |
| | 5 | 1 | 2 | 2 | The dry Southwestern U.S., and Alberta, Saskatchewan, and Manitoba in Canada shall be between 4 - 9% inclusive. |
| 4 | **INSTALLATION** shall only occur after materials have been acclimatized for a minimum of 72 hours, and: | | | |
| | 1 | For climate controlled applications, that: | | |
| | 1 | 1 | Is between 60 - 90 degrees Fahrenheit (15.5 - 32 degrees Celsius) inclusive. | |
| | 1 | 2 | Has a maintained Relative Humidity between 25 - 55% inclusive, except in: | |
| | 1 | 2 | 1 | The damp Southern Coastal areas of the U.S. and Canadian Eastern Coastal Provinces shall be between 43 - 70% inclusive. |
| | 1 | 2 | 2 | The dry Southwestern U.S., and Alberta, Saskatchewan, and Manitoba in Canada shall be between 20 - 50% inclusive. |
| 5 | **AFTER INSTALL** and **ACCEPTANCE:** | | | |
| | 1 | At climate controlled applications: | | |
| | 1 | 1 | Woodwork shall be maintained in the same environmental conditions as during its storage and/or installation. | |
| | 1 | 2 | Temperature in a building or area of a building shall not be raised or lowered for a sustained period (more than 24 hours) for any reason as it may negatively affect the appearance and performance of architectural woodwork. | |
| | 2 | At non-climatic controlled interior or exterior applications woodwork shall: | | |
| | 2 | 1 | Have its finish maintained, refinishing as necessary (especially oiled finishes). | |
| | 2 | 2 | Be protected from excessive moisture and standing water. | |
| 6 | **SEVERE DAMAGE** can result from not adhering to the above rules: | | | |
| | 1 | Fabricator/Installer shall not be held responsible for the damage caused by not adhering to the above. | | |

# Architectural Woodwork Standards

# LUMBER

## SECTION 3

# SECTION 3
Lumber

## table of contents

### INTRODUCTORY INFORMATION

| | |
|---|---|
| Introduction | 46 |
| Lumber | 46 |
| Architectural Woodwork Standards | 46 |
| Wood as a Plant | 46 |
| Annual Rings | 46 |
| Softwoods and Hardwoods | 46 |
| Heartwood | 46 |
| Sapwood | 47 |
| Medullary Rays | 47 |
| Photodegradation | 47 |
| Oxidation | 47 |
| Comparative Table of Wood Species | 47 |
| Specie Descriptions | |
|     Alder, Red | 49 |
|     Anigre | 49 |
|     Ash, White | 49 |
|     Basswood | 49 |
|     Beech, American | 49 |
|     Beech, European | 49 |
|     Birch, Yellow | 49 |
|     Cedar, Western Red | 49 |
|     Cherry, American Black | 50 |
|     Cypress, Yellow | 50 |
|     Fir, Douglas | 50 |
|     Hickory, Pecan Group | 50 |
|     Hickory, True Group | 50 |
|     Mahogany, African | 50 |
|     Mahogany, American | 50 |
|     Makore | 50 |
|     Maple, Soft Group | 50 |
|     Maple, Hard Group | 50 |
|     Oak, English Brown | 51 |
|     Oak, Red | 51 |
|     Oak, White | 51 |
|     Pecan | 51 |
|     Pine, Ponderosa | 51 |
|     Pine, Eastern White | 51 |
|     Pine, Southern Yellow | 51 |
|     Pine, Sugar | 51 |
|     Poplar, Yellow | 51 |
|     Redwood | 52 |
|     Teak | 52 |
|     Walnut, American Black | 52 |
| Other Species | 52 |
| Endangered Species | 52 |
| Use of Reclaimed Timber | 52 |
| Engineered Products | 53 |
| Aesthetic Characteristics | 53 |
|     Color | 53 |
|     Sapwood and Heartwood | 53 |
|     Grain | 53 |
|     Open Grain and Closed Grain | 53 |
|     Figure | 53 |
|     Finishing Characteristics | 53 |
| Methods of Sawing | 53 |
|     Plain Sawn | 53 |
|     Quarter Sawn | 54 |
|     Rift Sawn | 54 |
| Availability and Size Limitations | 54 |
| Veneered Construction | 54 |
| Dimension Stability, Relative Humidity and Moisture Content | 54 |
| Adaptability for Exterior Use | 55 |
| Preservative Treatments | 55 |
| Flame Spread Classification | 55 |
| Fire Retardant Wood | 56 |
| Specify Requirements For | 57 |

# table of contents

# SECTION 3
## Lumber

## COMPLIANCE REQUIREMENTS

### GENERAL
- Basic Considerations ..... 58
  - Grades ..... 58
  - Lumber Association Grades ..... 58
  - Lumber Rules ..... 58
  - Contract Documents ..... 58
  - Transparent Finishes ..... 58
  - Engineered Wood ..... 58
  - Reconstituted Wood ..... 58
  - Special and Unusual Characteristics ..... 58
  - Mahogany, American ..... 58
  - Lauan, Tanguile ..... 58
  - Cherry, Walnut ..... 58
- Industry Practices ..... 59
  - Gluing ..... 59
  - Specification ..... 59
  - Species ..... 59

### PRODUCT
- Scope ..... 60
- Default Stipulation ..... 60
- Rules ..... 60
  - Errata ..... 60
  - Basic Rules ..... 60
    - Aesthetic ..... 60
    - Visible Surfaces ..... 60
    - Board ..... 60
    - Member ..... 60
    - Lumber ..... 60
    - Moisture Content ..... 60
    - Exterior ..... 60
    - Gluing ..... 60
    - Adhesive ..... 60
    - Philippine Mahogany ..... 60
    - Species Not Specifically Covered ..... 60
  - Basic Material Rules ..... 60
    - Finished Thickness ..... 61
    - Finished Width ..... 61
    - Machine Sanded ..... 61
  - Hardwood Material Rules ..... 61
    - Applying To ..... 61
    - Gluing for Thickness ..... 61
    - Gluing for Width ..... 61
    - Oak, Rift Grain ..... 62
    - Natural Ash, Birch and Maple ..... 62
    - Maximum Length ..... 62
    - Opaque Finish ..... 63
      - Not Matching for Color ..... 63
      - Filling ..... 63
      - Quantity, Spacing and Distribution of Natural Characteristics ..... 63
      - Natural Characteristics (permitted) ..... 63
    - Transparent Finish ..... 64
      - Matching ..... 64
      - Filling ..... 64
      - Quantity, Spacing and Distribution of Natural Characteristics ..... 64
      - Natural Characteristics (permitted) ..... 64
  - Softwood Material Rules ..... 66
    - Applying To ..... 66
    - Gluing for Width ..... 66
    - Gluing for Thickness ..... 66
    - Maximum Length ..... 66
    - Opaque Finish ..... 66
      - Filling ..... 66
      - Quantity, Spacing and Distribution of Natural Characteristics ..... 66
      - Natural Characteristics (permitted) ..... 66
    - Transparent Finish ..... 67
      - Filling ..... 67
      - Natural Characteristics (permitted) ..... 67
      - Natural Characteristics (size) ..... 67

# SECTION 3
## Lumber

### introductory information

### INTRODUCTION

Section 3 is the first of two "material" sections and covers hardwood and softwood lumber. Included is a basic primer identifying wood characteristics and considerations. Basic rules pertaining to all solid wood as well as specific Hardwood Rules and Softwood Rules make up most of this section.

Quality assurance can be achieved by adherence to the AWS and will provide the owner a quality product at competitive pricing. Use of a qualified Sponsor Member firm to provide your woodwork will help ensure the manufacturer's understanding of the quality level required. Illustrations in this Section are not intended to be all inclusive, other engineered solutions may be acceptable. In the absence of specifications; methods of fabrication are the manufacturer's choice. The design professional, by specifying compliance to the AWS increases the probability of receiving the product quality expected.

### LUMBER

Lumber used in architectural woodwork is divided into two groups:

- **Hardwoods**: Lumber obtained from angiosperms, usually deciduous trees (broad leaf trees). There are more angiosperms on Earth than any other plant group, over 200,000 species. About 900 of those species are commonly available for lumber or veneer throughout the world.
- **Softwoods**: Lumber obtained from gymnosperms, about 600 of which are coniferous trees such as pine, spruce and fir. The gymnosperms are among the largest and oldest living plants.

The above groups have no relationship to the density or "hardness" within or between various species. Some softwoods are harder than some hardwoods, and hardness varies greatly between species within each group.

### ARCHITECTURAL WOODWORK STANDARDS (AWS)

The selection of the proper wood species for an architectural design can be the end result of a number of contributing factors and conditions. Intended use, costs, hardness, and relative stability are among many important considerations.

Lumber grades should always be referenced when specifying architectural woodwork. Selection of an AWS Grade (Economy, Custom, or Premium) for the finished product will define both materials and workmanship for that product. Lumber grades defined by the lumber manufacturers' associations allow some defects which the manufacturer must remove (cut out), or otherwise work around (by gluing, etc.).

The architect and designer may make his selection from a large variety of foreign and domestic species, now commercially available. The unique quality that wood imparts to design is that each species has its own distinguishing characteristics. Once the species is chosen, its effectiveness may vary according to the manner in which it is sawn, sliced as veneer, treated, and finished. This Section is designed to advise the architect and designer in the comparisons, considerations, and species which should be evaluated before decisions are made and specifications are written. This Section will help you correlate and tabulate the information needed. An informed choice will reward the owner with the best possible performance by a natural building material.

### WOOD AS A PLANT

The trunk and its branches: The cross section of a tree shows the following well-defined features in succession from the outside to the center: (1) bark and cambium layer, (2) wood, which in most species is clearly differentiated into sapwood and heartwood, and (3) pith, the small central core. The pith and bark, of course, are excluded from finished lumber.

Most branches originate at the pith, and their bases are inter-grown with the wood of the trunk as long as they are alive. These living branch bases constitute inter-grown or tight knots. After the branches die, their bases continue to be surrounded by the wood of the growing trunk and therefore loose or encased knots are formed. After the dead branches fall off, the stubs become overgrown, and subsequently clear wood is formed.

Growth in thickness takes place in the cambium layer by cell division. No growth in either diameter or length takes place in wood already formed; new growth is purely the addition of new cells, not the further development of existing cells.

### ANNUAL RINGS

Most species grown in temperate climates produce well-defined annual growth rings, which are formed by the difference in density and color between wood formed early and late in the growing season. The inner part of the growth ring formed first is called "spring wood," and the outer part formed later in the growing season is called "summer wood."

Spring wood is characterized by cells having relatively large cavities and thin walls. Summer wood cells have smaller cavities and thicker walls, and consequently are more dense than spring wood. The growth rings, when exposed by conventional methods of sawing, provide the grain or characteristic pattern of the wood. The distinguishing features of the various species are thereby enhanced by the differences in growth ring formation.

Some tropical species, on the other hand, experience year long even growth which may result in less obvious growth rings.

### SOFTWOODS and HARDWOODS

Native species of trees and the wood produced by these trees are divided into two botanical classes: hardwoods, which have broad leaves; and softwoods, which have needle-like or scale-like leaves. This botanical classification is sometimes confusing, because there is no direct correlation between calling a species a hardwood or softwood and the hardness or softness of the wood itself. Generally, hardwoods are more dense than softwoods, but some hardwoods are softer than many softwoods. If hardness is a desired characteristic, refer to the Comparative Table of Wood Species later in this section.

### HEARTWOOD

Heartwood consists of inactive cells formed by changes in the living cells of the inner sapwood rings, presumably after their use for sap conduction and other life processes of the tree have largely ceased. The cell cavities of heartwood may also contain deposits of various materials that frequently provide a much darker color. Not all heartwood, however, is darker.

# SECTION 3
## Lumber

## introductory information

The infiltrations of material deposited in the cells of heartwood usually make lumber cut from there more durable when exposed to weather. All wood, with the possible exception of the heartwood of Redwood and Western Red Cedar, should be preservative-treated when used for exterior applications.

### SAPWOOD

Sapwood contains living cells and performs an active role in the life processes of the tree. It is located next to the cambium and functions in sap conduction and storage of food. Sapwood commonly ranges from 1" to 2" (25-50 mm) in thickness. The Maples, Hickories, Ashes, and some of the Southern Yellow Pines and Ponderosa Pine may have sapwood 3" to 6" (76-152 mm) in thickness, especially in second growth trees.

### MEDULLARY RAYS

Medullary rays extend radially from the pith of the log toward the circumference. The rays serve primarily to store food and transport it horizontally. They vary in height from a few cells in some species to four or more inches in the Oaks, and produce the fleck (sometimes called flake) effect common to the quarter-sawn lumber in these species.

### PHOTODEGRADATION

Photodegradation is the effect on the appearance of exposed wood faces caused by exposure to both sun and artificial light sources. If an entire face is exposed to a light source, it will photodegrade somewhat uniformly and hardly be noticeable, whereas partially exposed surfaces or surfaces with shadow lines might show nonuniform photodegradation. Some woods, such as American Cherry, Fir and Walnut, are more susceptible than others, and extra care should be taken to protect against the effects of nonuniform photodegradation.

### OXIDATION

Oxidation is the effect on the appearance of exposed wood faces caused by exposure to atmosphere. This is analogous to browning reactions in freshly cut fruit; for instance, apples. Hardwoods can develop deep yellow to reddish brown discolorations on the surface of the wood when exposed to air immediately after sawing or peeling.

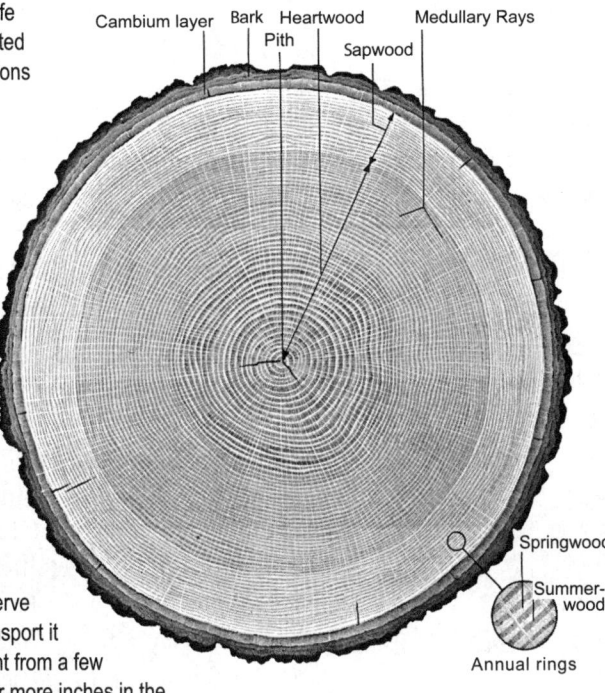

Figure: 3-001

These discolorations are especially noticeable on Cherry, Birch, Red Alder, Sycamore, Oak, Maple, and Sweet Gum. Some species, such as Alder, Oak, Birch, and Maple, develop these discolorations during air-seasoning. A related gray stain on several varieties of Southern Oaks also appears to be oxidative in nature. Proper selection, sanding, and finishing can minimize the effects of oxidation. Care should be taken when using filler, as it might not change the same as the wood.

### COMPARATIVE TABLE OF WOOD SPECIES

In order to simplify species selection, the following Comparative Table of Wood Species has been prepared showing pertinent characteristics of some species of domestic and foreign woods used by the architectural woodwork industry. The table can aid a design professional in proper species selection after studying the characteristics.

Careful analysis of the table will make it possible for an architect, designer or specification writers (who may have only a limited knowledge of architectural wood species) to make an informed selection. It is our intent that this tool will enhance understanding between the manufacturer of the woodwork you have designed and your profession, thereby enabling the building industry to better service the client.

- **Cost** has been broken into Low, Moderate, High, and Very High (V. High). The cost of lumber, as with other commodities, is influenced by supply and demand, both of which are constantly changing.

- **Hardness** is broken into Soft, Medium, Hard and Very Hard and takes into consideration the ability of the lumber species to sustain stress; resist indentation, abuse and wear; and to carry its anticipated load in applications such as shelving and structural members.

- **Dimensional stability** is helpful in selecting woods for use where humidity conditions may vary widely and where design or fabrication of a wood product does not allow free movement or the use of sheet products. The column figures indicate extreme conditions and show the maximum amount of movement possible in a 12" (305 mm) wide piece of unfinished wood where its moisture content increases or decreases from 10% to 5%. The possible change in dimension demonstrates that unfinished interior woodwork must be carefully protected prior to finishing by keeping it in rooms where relative humidity is between 25% and 55%. The column also shows the variation between species, and between flat grain and edge grain where such cuts are available commercially.

# SECTION 3
Lumber

## introductory information

*Table: 3-002* - **COMPARATIVE WOOD SPECIE VALUES**

| Species | Costs [1] | Practical Size Limits [2] | | | Hardness | Dimensional Stability [3] |
| --- | --- | --- | --- | --- | --- | --- |
| | | **Thickness** | **Width** | **Length** | | |
| Alder, Red | Low | 1-1/2" | 5-1/2" | 10' | Soft | 10/64" |
| Anigre | High | 1-1/2" | 5-1/2" | 12' | Very Hard | No data |
| Ash, White | Moderate | 2-1/2" | 5-1/2" | 12' | Hard | 10/64" |
| Basswood | Low | 2-1/2" | 5-1/2" | 10' | Soft | 10/64" |
| Beech, American | Low | 1-1/2" | 5-1/2" | 12' | Hard | 14/64" |
| Beech, European | Moderate | 2-1/2" | 7-1/2" | '16' | Hard | No data |
| Birch, Yellow - natural | Moderate | 1-1/2" | 5-1/2" | 12 | Hard | 12/64" |
| Birch, Yellow - select red | Moderate | 1-1/2" | 4-1/2" | 11 | Hard | 12/64" |
| Birch, Yellow - select white | Moderate | 1-1/2" | 4" | 11' | Hard | 12/64" |
| Cedar, Western Red | High | 3-1/4" | 11" | 16' | Soft | 10/64" |
| Cherry, American Black | High | 2-1/2" | 4" | 7' | Hard | 9/64" |
| Fir, Douglas - flat grain | High | 3-1/4" | 11" | 16' | Medium | 10/64" |
| Fir, Douglas - vertical grain | High | 1-1/2" | 11" | 16' | Medium | 6/64" |
| Hickory, True Group | Low | 1-1/2" | 4-1/2" | 12' | Very Hard | 11/64" |
| Mahogany, African - plain sawn | High | 2-1/2" | 9" | 15' | Medium | 7/64" |
| Mahogany, African - quarter sawn | V. High | 2-1/2" | 5-1/2" | 15' | Medium | 5/64" |
| Mahogany, American | High | 2-1/2" | 11" | 15' | Medium | 6/64" |
| Makore | High | 1-1/2" | 5-1/2" | 12' | Very Hard | No data |
| Maple, Hard - natural | Moderate | 3-1/2" | 7-1/2" | 12' | Very Hard | 12/64" |
| Maple, Hard - select white | Moderate | 2-1/2" | 5-1/2" | 12' | Very Hard | 12/64" |
| Maple, Soft - natural | Moderate | 3-1/2" | 7-1/2" | 12' | Medium | 9/64" |
| Oak, English Brown | V. High | 1-1/2" | 4-1/2" | 8' | Hard | No data |
| Oak, Red - plain sawn | Moderate | 2-1/2" | 7-1/4" | 12' | Hard | 11/64" |
| Oak, Red - rift sawn | High | 1-1/16" | 3-1/2" | 8' | Hard | 7/64" |
| Oak, Red - quarter sawn | High | 1-1/16" | 5-1/2" | 8' | Hard | 7/64" |
| Oak, White - plain sawn | Low | 1-1/2" | 5-1/2" | 10' | Hard | 11/64" |
| Oak, White - rift sawn | High | 3/4" | 3" | 8' | Hard | 7/64" |
| Oak, White - quarter sawn | High | 3/4" | 4" | 8' | Hard | 7/64" |
| Pecan Group, Hickory | Low | 1-1/2" | 4-1/2" | 12' | Hard | 11/64" |
| Pine, Eastern or Northern White | Moderate | 1-1/2" | 9-1/2" | 14' | Soft | 8/64" |
| Pine, Ponderosa | Moderate | 1-1/2" | 9-1/2" | 16' | Soft | 8/64" |
| Pine, Southern Yellow | Low | 1-1/2" | 7-1/2" | 16' | Medium | 10/64" |
| Pine, Sugar | Moderate | 3-1/4" | 11" | 16' | Soft | 7/64" |
| Poplar, Yellow | Low | 2-1/2" | 7-1/2" | 12' | Medium | 9/64" |
| Redwood, flat grain heartwood | Moderate | 2-1/2" | 11" | 16' | Soft | 6/64" |
| Redwood, vert. grain heartwood | Moderate | 2-1/2" | 11" | 16' | Soft | 3/64" |
| Teak | V. High | 1-1/2" | 5-1/2" | 8' | Hard | 6/64" |
| Walnut, American Black | Moderate | 2-1/2" | 4" | 6' | Hard | 10/64" |

(1) Market conditions will cause these relationships to vary. These are raw costs without consideration of labor.
(2) Maximum practical sizes without lamination/gluing. Only 10% of any order is required to be at maximum sizes.
(3) These figures represent possible width change in a 12" (304.8 mm) board when moisture content is reduced from 10% to 5%. Figures taken are for plain sawn unless indicated otherwise in the species column.

# SECTION 3
## Lumber

## introductory information

### ALDER, RED (Alnus rubra)

Red Alder (also know as Oregon, Pacific Coast and Western Alder) has become an important utility lumber. Stable, economical and plentiful, it is used as a core for veneer and in the solid for mass produced furniture. The inner bark turns a reddish orange when exposed to the air, hence the name. Sourced predominately from the states of Oregon and Washington. Varies in color from almost white to pale pinkish brown and there is no visible boundary between heartwood and sapwood. Moderately light in weight and intermediate in most strength properties with relatively low shrinkage.

### ANIGRE (Aningeria poteria)

Anigre grows in Africa and is most common in the tropical areas of east Africa. The color varies from light yellowish brown with a pinkish tinge in the heartwood to golden brown. The grain is straight with uniform texture but can be wavy producing a mottled figure. Overall working characteristics are fair. Good nailing, screwing, gluing and staining properties. Used for cabinetwork and furniture.

### ASH, WHITE (Fraxinus americana)

While White Ash has always enjoyed widespread use for industrial products where hardness, shock resistance, stability and strength were important, its acceptance for architectural woodwork is increasing. It is open grained and has a strong and pronounced grain pattern. The heartwood is light tan or brown and its sapwood creamy white. Color contrast between the two is minor and its blonde effect makes it particularly appealing when a light or near natural finish is desired. Finished with darker tones it presents a bold effect. Its cost is moderate and it is readily available in lumber form. In veneered form some size limitation may be experienced but it can be easily produced on special order.

### BASSWOOD (Tilia americana)

Basswood is well suited to woodcarving and pattern making. Its critical quality is there being no contrast between early wood and late wood. This is unusual in wood, as normally the late wood would tear as you attempt to work against its natural bias. Otherwise basswood is almost featureless. Creamy white to light tan in color with a pink hue; yellows when a finish is applied. Has a straight grain with fine and even texture. Shrinkage in width and thickness during drying is high; however, seldom warps in use.

### BEECH, AMERICAN (Fagus grandfolia)

Beech grows in Eastern U.S. and adjacent Canadian Provinces. Color varies from nearly white sapwood to reddish brown heartwood; however, sometimes there is no clear demarcation between them. Heavy in weight with hard and strong properties that are highly suitable for steam bending. Machines smoothly, wears well, is well suited for turning and is easily treated with preservatives. Used for flooring, furniture, veneer, woodenware and when treated, for railroad ties.

### BEECH, EUROPEAN (Fagus sylvatica)

European Beech grows from the southern parts of Scandinavia to Sicily and from the French Atlantic coast to Poland. The color varies from pale pink brown heartwood to reddish brown tone when steamed and may have some dark veining. The grain is straight and fine with an even texture. The steam bending properties are exceptionally good. Stains well and is permeable for preservation treatment. Used for cabinetwork, furniture, flooring, heavy construction and marine piling (when pressure treated).

### BIRCH, YELLOW - natural, select red, select white (Betula alleghaniensis)

Yellow Birch has been and continues to be one of the prominent wood species used for architectural woodwork. This is due not only to its attractive appearance but also to its general availability both as lumber and as veneered products, its adaptability to either paint or transparent finish, and its abrasion resistance. The heartwood of the tree varies in color from medium to dark brown or reddish brown while its sapwood, which comprises a better than average portion of the tree, is near white. Despite its wide usage some confusion exists as to the common terms used to describe Birch lumber and/or veneer. Virtually all commercially used Birch is cut from the Yellow Birch tree, not from the White Birch tree, which botanically is a distinct species. The term "Natural" or "Unselected" Birch means that the lumber or veneer may contain both the sapwood, or white portion, as well as the heartwood, or dark portion, of the tree in unrestricted amounts. The term "Select Red" Birch describes the lumber or veneer produced from the heartwood portion of the tree, and the term "Select White" Birch describes the lumber or veneer produced from the sapwood portion of the tree. To obtain "Red" or "White" Birch exclusively requires selective cutting with corresponding cost premium as well as considerable restriction on the width and length availability in lumber form. Birch, in veneer form, is readily available in all "selections" and is usually rotary cut. While some sliced veneer is produced which simulates the same grain effect as lumber, its availability and cost reflect the same cutting restrictions that are incurred in producing the "select" forms of Birch lumber.

### CEDAR, WESTERN RED (Thuja plicata)

Found in the Pacific Northwest and along the Pacific Coast to Alaska. With nearly white sapwood which is typically narrow, its heartwood runs reddish or pinkish brown to dull brown. It is generally straight grained with uniform coarse grain. With very low shrinkage, its lightweight, moderately soft, low in strength; however, very resistant to decay. Principally used for shingles, exterior siding, decks, standing and running trim, sash and doors.

# SECTION 3
## Lumber

### introductory information

**CHERRY, AMERICAN BLACK** (Prunus serotina)

Wild Black American Cherry is a fine and especially stable close grained cabinet and veneer wood. Its heartwood color ranges from light to medium reddish brown. Its sapwood, which is a light creamy color, is usually selectively eliminated from the veneer and lumber. In some respects it resembles Red Birch, but has a more uniform grain and is further characterized by the presence of small dark gum spots which, when sound, are not considered as defects but add to its interest. Cherry is available in moderate supply as lumber and architectural paneling and is usually plain sawn or sliced. Exceptionally rich appearance is achieved with transparent finishes which, together with its machining characteristics, justifies its identity with Early American cabinetry and furniture manufacturing, thus adding to its prestige as one of our most desirable native woods.

**FIR, DOUGLAS** - (Pseudotsuga taxifolla)

Douglas Fir is a large, fast growing species and is native to the northwest. It accounts for much of the lumber produced in North America. While the preponderance of its production is developed for structural and construction type products, some of its upper grades are used for stock millwork and specialized woodwork. Its heartwood is reddish tan while its sapwood is creamy yellow. Since its growth rings are conspicuous, a rather bold grain pattern develops when either plain sawn for lumber or rotary cut as is common in plywood. Some lumber and veneer is cut edge or vertical grain, producing a superior form of the product since the tendency to "grain-raise" is greatly reduced.

**HICKORY, PECAN GROUP** (Carya cordiformis, illinoensis, aquatica and myristiciformis)

Harvested typically in the Eastern half of the U.S. Sapwood is white to nearly white and relatively wide with somewhat darker heartwood. Predominately used for implement handles, furniture and decorative paneling.

**HICKORY, TRUE GROUP** (Carya ovata, glabra, and lacinosa)

Harvested typically in the Middle to Southern Atlantic and Central U.S. The sapwood is white and usually quite wide with reddish heartwood. It is extremely tough, heavy, hard, strong and experiences considerable shrinkage in drying. Typically used for implement handles, ladder rungs, furniture and flooring.

**MAHOGANY, AFRICAN** - (Khaya ivorensis)

This, one of the true Mahoganies, is perhaps the most widely used of the several Mahogany species. This is due to its excellent cutting and working characteristics and versatility. While its use has been largely for interior purposes, its innate stability and moderate decay resistance justifies its consideration for selected and demanding exterior applications. It has a very pleasing open grain, with its heartwood ranging in color from light to medium dark reddish brown. In lumber form it is more readily available as plain sawn and selectively so as quartersawn. In veneer form the quarter or "ribbon striped" cut predominates, but plain sliced, as well as many of the exotic "figure" cuts, can be produced on special order.

**MAHOGANY, AMERICAN** (Swietenia macrophylla - CITES listed)

This Mahogany species is commonly known as "Honduras Mahogany," but actually encompasses all of this species that grow throughout Mexico, Brazil, Peru, and Central America. Its traditional identity with casework and furniture justifies its position as one of the finest woods for this purpose. Its stability, workability, warm appearance, and firm grain make it a favorite of all woodworking craftsmen. It is a semi open grain wood, with its heartwood color ranging from light tan to a rich golden brown depending to some extent on the country of its origin. Its outstanding stability and decay resistance expands its potential to include exterior applications for "monumental" projects. It is most generally available as plain sawn lumber and plain sliced veneer with different veneer cuts available on special order.

**MAKORE** (Tieghemella heckelii, Tieghemella africana)

Makore grows in Western and Middle Africa. The color varies from pink to reddish brown. The grain has a fine texture with closed pores and can be straight, interlocked or wavy. Generally easy to work, although sections with interlocked grain can cause tear out during planing. Suitable for turning and is easy to glue and finish. Used for cabinetwork, furniture, flooring, boat building and turned objects.

**MAPLE, SOFT GROUP** (Acer saccharinum, rubrum, negundo and macrophyllum)

Typically found in Eastern U.S. with some in the Oregon Pacific Coast. Similar in appearance to hard Maple, heartwood is somewhat lighter in color than sapwood and wider. Soft Maple is not as heavy, heard or strong as Hard Maple. Typically used for railroad ties, furniture, veneer and wooden ware.

**MAPLE, HARD GROUP** - natural or select white (Acer saccharum and nigrum)

Hard Maple is very similar in general characteristics to Yellow Birch. It is heavy, hard, strong, and resistant to shock and abrasion. The heartwood of the tree is reddish brown and its sapwood is near white with a slight reddish brown tinge. Another natural characteristic is the prevalence of dark mineral streaks (predominantly in the heartwood), which can be minimized in the sapwood by selective cutting. Like Birch, common usage of descriptive terms does occasion some confusion. The term "Natural" or "Unselected" Maple indicates that the lumber or veneer may contain both the white sapwood and the darker heartwood. The term "White" Maple means that the lumber or veneer is selected and separated from the pieces containing the dark heartwood. Unlike Birch, the heartwood is so low in content that no comparable selection is available. Maple's close identity with furniture and specialized industrial use overshadows its potential for architectural woodwork. Its modest cost, and pleasing, mild grain pattern warrants its consideration, especially on items subject to hard usage.

# SECTION 3
## Lumber

## introductory information

### OAK, ENGLISH BROWN (Quercus robur)

The English Brown Oak, or Pollard Oak is a tree which varies in height from 60'-130' (18-40 m) depending on soil conditions. It varies in color from a light tan to a deep brown with occasional black spots. It produces burls and swirls which are very brittle and fragile, but beautiful work can be obtained with their use. English Brown Oak is considered one of the finest woods in use today. English Brown Oak is obtained from trees which have had their tops cut out before reaching maturity. This pruning leads to the production of a number of new branches around the cut, and if these are subsequently lopped off, more new branches are formed. This wood is difficult to season and to work, tending to warp and twist in drying and to tear in working. The best figure is obtained from trees which have been cut out regularly every few years, the branches never being left sufficiently long for the production of large knots. The constant exposure of freshly cut surfaces promotes attack from parasites, the result being that a considerable portion of these trees become decayed sooner or later. This has made the timber relatively scarce and costly.

### OAK, RED - (Quercus rubra)

Red Oak is one of the most abundant of our domestic hardwoods. Its moderate cost, strength, wearability, and appealing grain characteristics make its use widespread. It is open grained and in its plain sawn or sliced form expresses a very strong "cathedral" type grain pattern. The heartwood is reddish tan to brown and very uniform in color. Its sapwood is lighter in color and minimal in volume, making its elimination by selective cutting very easy. Red Oak is also available in rift sawn or sliced form, which produces a very uniform straight grained effect. Less frequently it is quarter sawn or sliced, still producing a straight grain but with the fleck (sometimes called flake) of the medullary ray accented. Some sacrifice in width and length availability occurs when producing either rift or quarter sawn lumber.

### OAK, WHITE (Quercus alba)

White Oak, like Red Oak, is perhaps one of the best known hardwoods in the world, and its use for architectural woodwork is widespread. It is hard and strong. Its heartwood has good weathering characteristics, making its use for selected exterior applications appropriate. It is open grained and in its plain sawn form is highly figured. The heartwood varies considerably in color from light grayish tan to brown, making the maintenance of color consistency difficult. Its sapwood is much lighter in color, is fairly prevalent, and its elimination is accomplished by selective ripping. White Oak is often rift sawn or sliced, producing a very straight grained effect or frequently quarter sawn or sliced, producing straight grain, but with the fleck (sometimes called flake) of the medullary ray greatly pronounced. The special cuts mentioned are more readily attained in veneer form since the solid lumber cutting techniques greatly restrict its width and length potential.

### PECAN - (see Hickory, Pecan Group)

### PINE, PONDEROSA (Pinus ponderosa)

Ponderosa Pine is said to be the softwood species most commonly used for exterior and interior woodwork components. Its heartwood is tannish pink, while its sapwood is a lighter creamy pink. Its supply is extensive; found in commercial quantities in every state west of the Great Plains. Ponderosa Pine grows in pure stands and is abundant in mixed stands. Also, like most Pines, the proportion of sapwood is high and its heartwood has only a moderate natural decay resistance. Fortunately, its receptivity to preservative treatment is high, and since all Pines should be so treated when used on the exterior, it can be used interchangeably with them.

### PINE, EASTERN WHITE (Pinus strobus)

Found from Maine to Northern Georgia and the Great Lake States, it is typically called White Pine. Heartwood light brown, often with a reddish tinge and turns darker when exposed to air. Has relatively uniform texture, straight grain, low shrinkage and high stability. It's light weight, moderately low in strength and stiffness. Extensively used in patterns, sash, doors, furniture, interior woodwork, knotty paneling and caskets.

### PINE, SOUTHERN YELLOW - short leaf (Pinus echinata)

Southern Yellow Pine, commonly called Short Leaf Pine, is commercially important in Arkansas, Virginia, Missouri, Louisiana, Mississippi, Texas, and South and North Carolina, and is found in varying abundance from New York and south central Pennsylvania, south and westerly to eastern Texas and Oklahoma. The yellowish wood is noticeably grained, moderately hard, strong, and stiff. A cubic foot of air dried Southern Yellow Pine weighs 36 to 39 pounds. It is used extensively in house building, including framing, ceiling, weather boarding, panels, window and door frames, casing, and carved work. The grain shows well in natural finish or when stained. Frames of overstuffed furniture, chairs, desks, agricultural machinery, wood pulp, mine props, barrels, and crates are also made of this Pine.

### PINE, SUGAR (Pinus lambertiana)

The world's largest species of pine typically found in California and South Western Oregon. It's heartwood is buff to light brown and sometimes tinged with red. It's straight grained with fairly uniform texture, low shrinkage and dimensionally stable, lightweight, soft, and moderately low in strength and stiffness. Used almost exclusively for boxes, sashes, doors, frames, general millwork and foundry patterns.

### POPLAR, YELLOW (Liriodendron tulipfera)

Yellow Poplar, sometimes incorrectly called "Whitewood," is an extremely versatile and moderately priced hardwood that is well adapted to general interior woodwork usage. It is even textured, close grained, stable, of medium hardness, and has an inconspicuous grain pattern. The heartwood is pale greenish yellow while the sapwood is white. Occasional dark purple streaks also occur. The tight, close grain results in outstanding paintability, while its modest figure and even texture permits staining to simulate more expensive hardwood. Due to its indistinct grain figure, Poplar is seldom used for decorative veneered products. Its white sapwood is not appropriate for use in exterior applications.

# SECTION 3
## Lumber

## introductory information

### REDWOOD - heartwood (Sequoia sempervirens)

Redwood is the product of one of nature's most impressive accomplishments. The enormous size and unique inherent characteristics of this tree produce a material ideally suited for exterior applications. Its heartwood color is a fairly uniform brownish red, while its very limited sapwood is lemon colored. In its plain sawn form medium "cathedral" type figure develops, while in the vertical grain a longitudinal striped figure results. Its availability in "all heartwood" form with its outstanding natural resistance to decay accounts for its wide usage for exterior purposes. It is considered a very stable wood and its paint retention qualities are excellent. Redwood's principal identity with painted exterior application should not preclude its consideration for either exterior or interior use with transparent finish. Its pleasing and uniform color lends to a variety of such finishes suggesting the warmth and honesty of wood in its natural state. The size of the trees yields lumber of unusually character free widths and lengths.

### TEAK (Tectona grandis)

Teak is one of the most versatile and valuable woods and has attained great prestige value. The figure variations are extensive and it is available in both lumber and veneered products. Adding to its appeal is its distinctive tawny yellow to green to dark brown color, often with light and dark accent streaks. It is perhaps most appealing in plain sawn or sliced cuts. While it has unique stability and weathering properties, making it ideal for exterior applications, its high cost usually limits its use to decorative interior woodwork, most often in veneer form. Its great beauty and interest dictate it being finished in its near "natural state."

### WALNUT, AMERICAN BLACK (Juglans nigra)

American Black Walnut is perhaps our most highly prized domestic wood species. Its grain pattern variations are extensive and in veneered form produces, in addition to its normal plain sliced cut, quartered or "pencil striped" as well as specialty cuts such as crotches, swirls, burls, and others. Its heartwood color varies from gray brown to dark purplish brown. The sapwood, which is very prevalent in solid lumber, is cream colored and its complete elimination by selective cutting is very costly. Fortunately, if this natural effect is felt to be undesirable, its appearance can be neutralized by sap staining in the finishing process. The growth conditions of Walnut result in significant width and length limitations in its lumber form. Its potential is best expressed in veneered products.

### OTHER SPECIES

There are many other species, both domestic and imported, used in woodworking. Nearly all are ecologically sound and appropriate for use. Using hardwoods for architecture gives value to the species, encouraging improved forest management techniques and the continuation of the species.

### ENDANGERED SPECIES

For a current list of endangered species see the Convention on International Trade in Endangered Species (CITES) Appendix I restricted table at www.cites.org.

### USE OF RECLAIMED TIMBER AND LUMBER

Interest in timber reclaimed from old logs cut from old growth forests and lumber salvaged from old structures has increased recently.

Sources and types of reclaimed materials coming from underwater salvage as well as demolished buildings and structures vary greatly in their type, quality, availability. aesthetics and cost. A sample of the material used for selection may not match actual available material in species, color, texture, surface quality or structural composition when it comes time to make a purchase. Design professionals and specifiers should be aware of the limitations of availability of species, cut, quantity, lead time, waste factor and cost of material. These materials are normally sold "as is" and are not returnable.

Design professionals need to be aware that there is no NHLA Grade for reclaimed materials, therefore there are no measurable characteristics and defects established by which to reject unsuitable materials once they are delivered. It is advisable that the design professional and woodworker see the material at the supplier to determine the availability and suitability for the intended use.

Logs harvested over 100 years ago and transported by water often sank en route to mills. The resulting "lost underwater forest" lay on the bottoms of rivers and lakes until recently as proper environmental and mechanical procedures for retrieving them have been developed.

Reclaimed submerged materials are utilized in all aspects of construction of furniture, architectural woodwork and musical instruments. Submerged lumber is generally processed in both solid lumber, plain sliced and rotary veneer.

The uniqueness of the harvesting procedures, the high quality of the material and unusual aesthetic qualities are a few of desirable traits associated with this special material.

# SECTION 3
## Lumber

## introductory information

### ENGINEERED PRODUCTS

Structural Composite Lumber (SCL) — A man made composite that utilizes grain oriented wood strands from a variety of tree species, providing an alternative to dimension lumber. The material is engineered for strength and stability. While SCL is not really "lumber," it is marketed as a lumber substitute. SCL can be specified as core, stile backers, and core for stiles and rails, so long as all other criteria of the AWS are met in relation to its use.

### AESTHETIC CHARACTERISTICS

One of the qualities which contributes to the widespread use of wood is the option offered for aesthetic selection. It varies between species, between two logs of the same species, and between two boards from the same log. Aesthetic considerations in specifying wood are influenced by the following characteristics:

- **Color** - The basic hue of the species, which may be further enhanced by the finishing process employed.
- **Sapwood** and **heartwood** - The color of wood within a tree varies between the "sapwood" (the outer layers of the tree that continue to transport sap), which is usually lighter in color than the "heartwood" (the inner layers in which the cells have become filled with natural deposits). If desired, sapwood may be stained in the finishing process to blend with the heartwood. This difference in color is so pronounced in certain species that the sapwood is marketed under a different nomenclature from the heartwood.

  Some examples are:

  - Select White Birch - sapwood of Yellow or Paper Birch
  - Select Red Birch - heartwood of Yellow Birch
  - Natural Birch - both sapwood and heartwood of any Birch
  - Select White Ash - sapwood of White or Green Ash
  - Select Brown Ash - heartwood of Black Ash
  - Natural Ash - both sapwood and heartwood of any Ash
  - Select White Maple - sapwood of the Sugar Maple

- **Grain** - The appearance produced by the arrangement of wood fibers and pores of the species. Lumber grain may not match veneer grain.

- **Open Grain** and **Closed Grain** - Open grain woods are said to be ring porous and usually show a distinct grain pattern. Close grain woods are said to be diffuse-porous with even grain. The size and distribution of the cellular structure of the wood influences the appearance and uniformity. Open grain hardwoods, such as Elm, Oak, Ash, and Chestnut are ring-porous species. These species have distinct figure and grain patterns. Close grain hardwoods, such as Cherry, Maple, Birch, and Yellow Poplar, are diffuse-porous species. Most North American diffuse-porous woods have small, dense pores resulting in less distinct figure and grain. Some tropical diffuse-porous species (e.g., Mahogany) have rather large pores.

- **Figure** - Various species produce different grain patterns (figures), which influence the selection process. There will be variations of grain patterns within any selected species. The manufacturer cannot select solid lumber cuttings within a species by grain and color in the same manner in which veneers may be selected.

- **Finishing Characteristics** - The many species of wood vary considerably in their receptivity to the multitude of finishing processes on the market. Some woods, because of their open pores, will accept fillers while tighter grained woods will not. Some will show greater contrast between the "early wood" and the "late wood" when stained than others. Design professionals should take into consideration the finish that will be applied when selecting a particular species. Consult with a Sponsor Association member about finishing prior to selection or specification. Providing large samples of the desired finish to manufacturers during the design phase and bidding process will assure the designer of obtaining an acceptable final product, while enabling the manufacturer to be aware of exactly what is required. Lumber might not accept transparent finishes in the same manner as veneer and special finishing techniques may be required.

### METHODS OF SAWING

Lumber is typically furnished plain sawn unless otherwise specified. Sawing methods, and the selection of boards after sawing the log, as shown below, produce the following types of lumber:

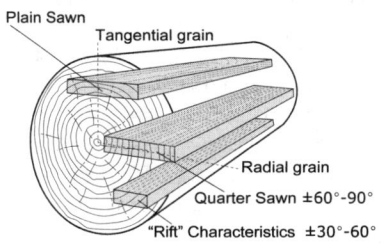

Figure: 3-003

- **Plain Sawn** - Plain sawing, the most common type of lumber sawing, yields broad grain, the widest boards and least waste. The annular rings are typically 30 degrees or less to the face of the board.

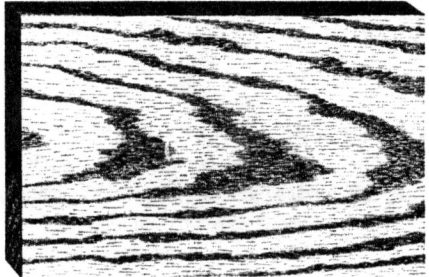

Figure: 3-004

# SECTION 3
Lumber

## introductory information

### METHODS OF SAWING   (continued)

- **Quarter Sawn** - Most often cut as Rift and Quartered, and then sorted for appearance, quarter sawn lumber is available in certain species, yields a straight grain, narrow boards, and fleck (sometimes called flake) or figure which runs across the grain in some species (notably the Oaks). Dimensional stability across the grain is the best. The annular rings run approximately 60 to 90 degrees to the face of the board, with the optimum being 90 degrees. Quartered lumber is generally narrower and more expensive than plain sawn of the same species.

Figure: 3-005

- **Rift Sawn** - Rift sawing produces small flecks caused by cutting through the wood rays. Only certain species produce these flecks, primarily Red and White Oak. Rift cutting reduces yield and increases cost. The annular rings run about 30 to 60 degrees to the face of the board, with the optimum being 45 degrees.

Figure: 3-006

### AVAILABILITY and SIZE LIMITATIONS

The supply of lumber is in constant flux throughout the world. It is affected by many factors such as current demand, export regulations of the country of origin, natural forces of weather, fire, disease, political situations, etc. Certain trees (species) naturally grow larger, thus producing longer and wider lumber. Other trees are smaller and produce narrow and shorter boards. The manufacturer must work with the available lumber, which must be considered when selecting any species. Consult a Sponsor Association member before specifying an uncommon species, or thickness, and/or long lengths which may not typically be available. If available, the cost may be substantially higher. Economies can be realized by detailing and specifying thicknesses and widths within the finish sizes of these standards.

### VENEERED CONSTRUCTION

Lumber can be used to secure wide and thick members in species with limited cutting potential. An acceptable technique is to apply thin lumber or veneer to the faces and edges of a compatible density lumber, structural composite lumber (SCL), or a medium density fiberboard core.

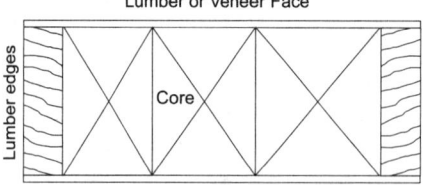

Figure: 3-007

### DIMENSIONAL STABILITY, RELATIVE HUMIDITY, and MOISTURE CONTENT

All woods are affected significantly by moisture and to a lesser degree by heat. Lumber swells and shrinks primarily in two directions: thickness and width. There is insignificant change in length. The changes in dimension due to moisture vary with different species, thus influencing the selection of lumber to use and the design elements.

Prevention of dimensional problems in architectural woodwork products as a result of uncontrolled relative humidity is possible. Wood products perform, as they have for centuries, with complete satisfaction when correctly designed and used. Problems directly or indirectly attributed to dimensional change of the wood are usually, in fact, the result of faulty design or improper humidity conditions during site storage, installation, or use.

Wood is a hygroscopic material, and under normal conditions all wood products contain some moisture. Wood readily exchanges this moisture with the water vapor in the surrounding atmosphere according to the relative humidity. In high humidity, wood picks up moisture and swells. In low humidity, wood releases moisture and shrinks. As normal minor changes in humidity occur, the resulting dimensional response in properly designed construction will be insignificant. To avoid problems, it is recommended that the appropriate recommendations from Section 2 of the AWS be maintained. Uncontrolled extremes are likely to cause problems. Together with proper design, fabrication, and installation, humidity control is the important factor in preventing dimensional change problems. The book *Understanding Wood* by Bruce Hoadley contains excellent data of wood and moisture.

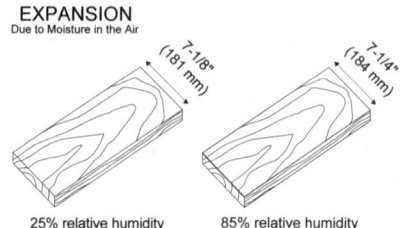

Figure: 3-008

# SECTION 3
## Lumber

## introductory information

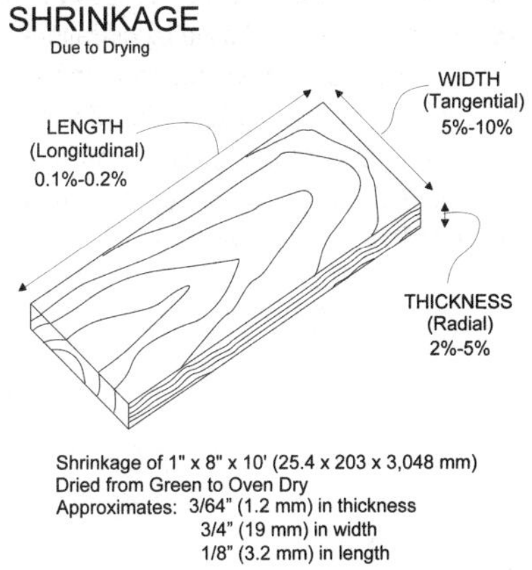

### SHRINKAGE
Due to Drying

Shrinkage of 1" x 8" x 10' (25.4 x 203 x 3,048 mm)
Dried from Green to Oven Dry
Approximates: 3/64" (1.2 mm) in thickness
3/4" (19 mm) in width
1/8" (3.2 mm) in length

*Figure: 3-009*

Wood is anisotropic in its shrinkage characteristics. It shrinks most in the direction of the annual rings when it loses moisture from the cell walls. This illustration from USDA's The Wood Handbook (latest edition), published by their Forest Products Laboratory, shows the typical distortion of cuts from various parts of a log.

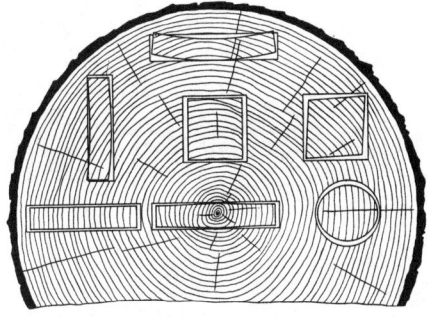

*Figure: 3-010*

Moisture can also cause iron stain (oxidation) in wood, also referred to as blue/black stain. Iron stain is a natural reaction of acids with iron, oxygen, and moisture (either high relative humidity or direct moisture) in wood. Control of moisture is a simple way to protect wood products from iron stain.

### ADAPTABILITY FOR EXTERIOR USE

Years of performance have shown certain species to be more durable for exterior applications. Heartwood shall be furnished when these species are designated for external use, excluding the sapwood. The following is a list of species generally considered acceptable for exterior use, from USDA's The Wood Handbook (latest edition), published by their Forest Products Laboratory:

- Cherry, Black
- Chestnut
- Douglas, Fir
- Eastern and Western Red Cedar
- Locust, Black
- Mahogany, American
- Oak, White
- Redwood, heartwood
- Spanish Cedar
- Teak, old growth

Baldcypress (Taxodium distichum) has a long tradition as a species resistant to decay, but beware! There are at least nine other species of four different genus which are marketed under the common name cypress. Only the heartwood of Baldcypress, often marketed as Tidewater or Red Cypress, is decay resistant. Sinker Cypress, that is old trees which have been brought up from below water in which they have been submerged for some time and properly cured and dried, is also resistant. None of this Cypress will come from new cutting, but as salvaged wood.

### PRESERVATIVE TREATMENTS

Modern technology has developed methods of treating certain species to extend their life when exposed to the elements. Some lumber species used for exterior architectural woodwork may be treated with an industry tested and accepted formulation. One such formulation is a liquid containing 3-iodo-2-propynyl butyl carbamate (IPBC) as its active ingredient, which must be used according to manufacturer's directions.

The Window & Door Manufacturers Association (WDMA), through the treatments and coatings committee, has reviewed information from third party testing laboratories which indicates that the number of formulations at the stated in use concentration meet the requirements of WDMA I.S.4 (latest edition). The formulations are acceptable for use under the WDMA Hallmark Water Repellent Non Pressure Preservative Treatment Certification Program and are adopted to meet all requirements.

### FLAME SPREAD CLASSIFICATIONS

This is the generally accepted measurement for fire rating of materials. It compares the rate of flame spread on a particular species with the rate of flame spread on untreated Oak. Most authorities accept the following classes for flame spread:

- Class I or A.        0-25
- Class II or B.       26-75
- Class III or C.      76-200

# SECTION 3
## Lumber

## introductory information

*Table: 3-011* - **FLAME SPREAD and SMOKE DEVELOPED INDEXES**

Common woods species, adapted from USDA's The Wood Handbook (latest edition), published by their Forest Products Laboratory, and based on 3/4" (19 mm) thick solid lumber:

| Species | Flame Spread Index | Smoke Developed Index |
|---|---|---|
| **SOFTWOODS** | | |
| Yellow Cedar | 78 | 90 |
| Baldcypress | 145 - 150 | --- |
| Cedar, Western Red | 70 | 213 |
| Fir, Douglas | 70 - 100 | --- |
| Fir, Pacific Silver | 69 | 58 |
| Hemlock, Western | 60 - 75 | --- |
| Pine, Eastern White | 85 - 215 | --- |
| Pine, Ponderosa | 105 - 230 | --- |
| Pine, Red | 142 | 229 |
| Pine, Southern | 130 - 195 | --- |
| Pine, Western White | 75 | --- |
| Redwood | 70 | --- |
| Spruce, Eastern | 65 | --- |
| Spruce, Sitka | 74 - 100 | --- |

| Species | Flame Spread Index | Smoke Developed Index |
|---|---|---|
| **HARDWOODS** | | |
| Birch, Yellow | 105 - 110 | --- |
| Cottonwood | 115 | --- |
| Maple | 104 | --- |
| Poplar, Yellow | 170-185 | --- |
| Oak, Red / White | 100 | 100 |
| Sweetgum | 140-155 | --- |
| Walnut | 130 - 140 | --- |

## FIRE RETARDANT WOOD

The natural fire retardant qualities and acceptability of treatments vary among the species. Where items of architectural woodwork are required to have a flame spread classification to meet applicable building and safety codes, the choice of lumber species must be a consideration. Most treated species are structural softwoods.

Following are some references to assist in making these choices. Additional data on various species may be available from USDA's The Wood Handbook (latest edition), published by their Forest Products Laboratory.

- **Built-up construction** to Improve Fire Rating: In lieu of solid lumber, it is often advisable, where a fire rating is required, to build up members by using treated cores clad with untreated veneers not thicker than 1/28" (1 mm). Some existing building codes, except where locally amended, provide that facing materials 1/28" (1 mm) or thinner finished dimension are not considered in determining the flame spread rating of the woodwork.

  In localities where basic model building codes have been amended, it is the responsibility of the specifier to determine whether the application of the facing material specified will meet the code.

- **Fire retardant treatments** (FRT): Some species may be treated with chemicals to reduce flammability and retard the spread of flame over the surface. This usually involves impregnating the wood, under pressure, with salts suspended in a liquid. The treated wood must be re-dried prior to fabrication. FRT wood may exude chemicals in relative humidity above 85%, damaging finishes and corroding metals in contact with the FRT surface. Consult with a manufacturer about the resulting appearance and availability of treated woods prior to specification.

  Hardwoods currently being treated (Flame spread less than 25) include 4/4 Red Oak, and 4/4 to 8/4 Poplar. These woods can be machined after treatment, although machining may void the label classification. Fire retardant treatment does affect the color and finishing characteristics of the wood.

According to the traditional model codes in the USA and subject to local code modifications, untreated wood and wood products can usually be used in up to 10% of the combined surface area of the walls and ceiling. Casework, furniture, and fixtures are rarely fire rated, and can be built of combustible materials.

# SECTION 3
## Lumber

## introductory information

**SPECIFY REQUIREMENTS FOR**

- **UNIFORM COLOR**; special finishing techniques might be required (see Section 5).

- **SPECIAL CHARACTERISTICS**, such as sapwood, heartwood, ribbon stripe, quarter sawn, rift sawn, or vertical grain are only required if so specified.

  - **Natural** as a type selection of a species allows an unlimited amount of heartwood or sapwood within a face and is the default selection.

  - **Select Red** or **White** means all heartwood or sapwood, respectively for Birch and Maple.

  - **Select Brown** means all heartwood for Ash.

- **EXTERIOR APPLICATIONS**, where species selection should take decay resistance into consideration. The following species, when selected for **heartwood only**, exhibit the listed decay resistance adapted from USDA's *The Wood Handbook* (latest edition) published by their Forest Products Laboratory:

  - **DECAY RESISTANT WOODS:**

    **VERY RESISTANT:**
    *Domestic*:
    - Locust, Black
    - Yew, Pacific

    *Import*:
    - Goncalo Alves
    - Lignumvitae
    - Ipe (Iapacho)
    - Purpleheart
    - Jarrah
    - Teak (Old Growth)

    **RESISTANT:**
    *Domestic*:
    - Baldcypress (Old Growth)
    - Juniper
    - Cedar
    - Oak, White
    - Cherry, Black
    - Redwood (Old Growth)
    - Chestnut
    - Walnut, Black
    - Cypress, Arizona

    *Import*:
    - Mahogany, American
    - Spanish Cedar

    **MODERATELY RESISTANT:**
    *Domestic*:
    - Baldcypress (Young Growth)
    - Redwood (Young Growth)
    - Fir, Douglas
    - Tamarack
    - Larch, Western

    *Import*:
    - Avodire
    - Mahogany, African
    - Benge
    - Meranti, Dark Red
    - Bubinga
    - Sapele
    - Keruing
    - Teak (Young Growth)

- If none of the above species is specified, these standards require exterior woodwork to be treated with an industry-tested and accepted preservative formulation listed by **WDMA**.

# SECTION 3
## Lumber
### GENERAL/PRODUCT

## compliance requirements

### Including: Hardwood and Softwood

## 3.1  BASIC CONSIDERATIONS

1. **GRADES**

    1.1  **GRADE CLASSIFICATIONS ECONOMY, CUSTOM,** and **PREMIUM** are used within these standards only in reference to the acceptable quality of workmanship, material, or installation in a completed architectural woodwork product covered in sections 6 - 12.

    1.1.1  In this section, the use of these classifications is only for the purpose of identifying lumber that can be used in finished products meeting those Grades.

    1.1.2  These classifications are not intended to be used as Grades of raw material or to judge a stand alone board or member.

2. **LUMBER ASSOCIATION RULES** shall not be used, since even their highest Grades permit defects unacceptable in architectural woodwork and are not based upon the use of the whole piece, but rather on a percentage of the piece.

    2.1  The appearance of a piece in the end product is of importance, not whether it is cut from a larger board that contained defects that can be eliminated.

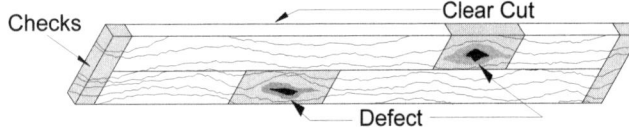

*Figure: 3-012*

3. **LUMBER RULES**

    3.1  Apply only to surfaces visible after manufacture and installation.

    3.2  Establish criteria as to which, if any, natural or seasoning characteristics are acceptable.

    3.3  Limit the extent of characteristics that will be permitted based on an exposed area's size and proximity of characteristics to one another.

    3.4  Do not apply to special varieties of species that display unusual characteristics desirable for aesthetic and design reasons.

## 3.1  BASIC CONSIDERATIONS   (continued)

4. **CONTRACT DOCUMENTS** shall govern if in conflict with these standards.

5. **TRANSPARENT FINISHES** in lumber may not be accepted in the same manner as plywood; special finishing techniques might be required (see Section 5).

6. **RECONSTITUTED LUMBER** is typically manufactured from sliced wood veneer, which in some cases are dyed, then glued up and sawn in such a manner as to imitate dimensional lumber species. Use of these engineered products are allowed only if specified and/or approved by the owner and/or design professional.

7. **SPECIAL** and **UNUSUAL CHARACTERISTICS**, for example **HICKORY, PECAN, BUTTERNUT, KNOTTY PINE, WORMY CHESTNUT, PECKY CYPRESS,** and **WATTLED WALNUT** are not covered by these standards, and:

    7.1  If their use is contemplated, individual ranges of characteristics and availability should be investigated and specified accordingly.

8. **MAHOGANY, AMERICAN** varies in color from a light pink to a light red, reddish brown to a golden brown or yellowish tan, and:

    8.1  Figure or grain includes plain sliced, plain to broken stripe, mottled, fiddleback, swirl and crotches.

    8.2  It can turn darker or lighter in color after machining.

9. **LAUAN, TANGUILE,** and other species are native to the Philippine Islands and are sometimes referred to as Philippine Mahogany; however, they are not a true Mahogany.

    9.1  **MAHOGANY** is a generic term and should not be specified without further definition, such as American or African Mahogany.

10. **CHERRY, WALNUT,** and certain other hardwood species are required to be specified by origin, such as American Cherry, American Walnut, or English Brown Oak, because they can be significantly different in color and texture.

## 3.1 BASIC CONSIDERATIONS (continued)

### 11 INDUSTRY PRACTICES

11.1 Lumber is furnished plain sawn unless otherwise specified.

11.2 Hardwood is typically not recommended for exterior use.

11.2.1 Exceptions include Apitong, American Mahogany, White Oak, Teak, and Tanguile.

11.3 Lumber is dimensioned in the following conventional order: thickness, followed by width (across the grain direction), followed by length (with the grain direction); see drawing:

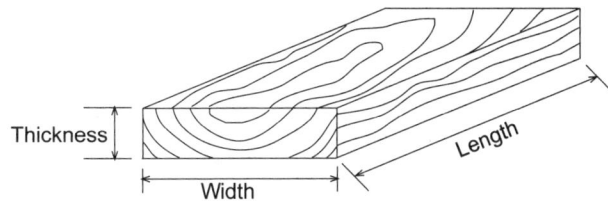

*Figure 3-013*

11.4 **GLUING** for thickness and/or width is permitted as governed by these standards; see drawing:

*Figure 3-014*

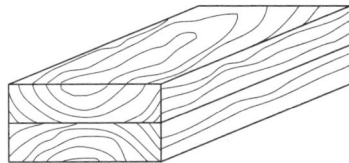

*Figure 3-015*

11.5 **SPECIFICATION:**

11.5.1 Of **PHILIPPINE MAHOGANY** permits the use of Lauan, Tanguile, and other natural Philippine species.

11.5.2 By the generic term **MAHOGANY** means genuine Mahogany, such as American or African.

11.6 **SPECIES** not specifically covered by these standards shall be as agreed to between owner/design professional and manufacturer/installer as to length requirements and size/exposed area of permitted natural characteristics.

# SECTION 3
## Lumber
### GENERAL/PRODUCT — compliance requirements

Where the **E**, **C**, or **P** icon is not indicated, the rule applies to all Grades equally | E | C | P |

## 3.2 SCOPE

1. All materials and products covered under the scope of these standards.

## 3.3 DEFAULT STIPULATION

1. Not used or applicable for this section

## 3.4 RULES

1. The following rules shall govern unless a project's contract documents require otherwise.

2. These rules are intended to provide a well-defined degree of control over a project's quality of materials and workmanship.

3. **ERRATA**, published on the Associations' websites at www.awinet.org, www.awmac.com, or www.aws-errata.com, shall **TAKE PRECEDENCE OVER THESE RULES**, subject to their date of posting and a project's bid date.

### 3.4.4 Basic Rules

1. **AESTHETIC** Grade rules apply only to exposed and semi-exposed surfaces visible after installation.

2. **VISIBLE SURFACES** shall be sound lumber, free of decay, shake, pith, wane and warp.

3. **"BOARD"** refers to a piece of lumber before gluing for width or thickness.

4. **"MEMBER"** refers to a piece of lumber after gluing for width or thickness.

5. **LUMBER** shall be plain sawn.

6. Lumber is **DIMENSIONED** by thickness, followed by width (across the grain direction), followed by length (with the grain direction).

7. **SPECIAL CHARACTERISTICS**, such as sapwood, heartwood, ribbon stripe, quarter sawn, rift sawn, and vertical grain are not required unless specified.

8. **MOISTURE CONTENT** of lumber shall be in compliance with Section 2.

9. **EXTERIOR** use of lumber for architectural millwork requires the lumber to be preservative treated in accordance with WDMA I.S. 4 (latest edition), unless the lumber is classified as "Resistant or Very Resistant" in accordance with USDA's The Wood Handbook (latest edition), published by the Forest Products Laboratory.

10. **GLUING** for thickness and/or width is permitted as governed by this Section.

11. **ADHESIVE** used to glue for thickness, width, or lay-up of veneered construction shall be for the intended purpose, applied in accordance with the manufacturer's instructions, and be:

    11.1 Type I when intended for non-climate controlled interior or exterior use.

    11.2 Type II when intended for climate controlled use.

12. **PHILIPPINE MAHOGANY** shall permit the use of Lauan, Tanguille, and other natural Philippine species.

13. **SPECIES NOT** specifically **COVERED** by these standards shall be as agreed to between design professional and manufacturer/installer as to length requirements and size/exposed area of permitted natural characteristics.

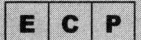

Where the **E**, **C**, or **P** icon is not indicated, the rule applies to all Grades equally

# SECTION 3
## Lumber

### compliance requirements

**GENERAL/PRODUCT**

## 3.4.5 Basic Material Rules

| | | | |
|---|---|---|---|
| 1 | | Minimum **FINISHED THICKNESS** of S4S and profiled members: | |
| 1 | 1 | Nominal 4/4 or 1" (25 mm) = | 11/16" (18 mm) |
| 1 | 2 | Nominal 5/4 or 1-1/4" (32 mm) = | 15/16" (24 mm) |
| 1 | 3 | Nominal 6/4 or 1-1/2" (38 mm) = | 1-3/16" (30 mm) |
| 1 | 4 | Nominal 8/4 or 2" (51 mm) = | 1-1/2" (38 mm) |
| 1 | 5 | Nominal 10/4 or 2-1/2" (64 mm) = | 2" (51 mm) |
| 1 | 6 | Nominal 12/4 or 3" (76 mm)) = | 2-1/2" (64 mm) |
| 1 | 7 | Nominal 16/4 or 4" (102 mm) = | 3-1/2" (89 mm) |
| 1 | 8 | *[Illustration showing Nominal Thickness and Finished Thickness]* | |
| 2 | | Minimum **FINISHED WIDTH** of S4S and profiled members: | |
| 2 | 1 | Nominal 1" (25 mm) = | 11/16" (18 mm) |
| 2 | 2 | Nominal 2" (51 mm) = | 1-1/2" (38 mm) |
| 2 | 3 | Nominal 3" (76 mm) = | 2-1/2" (64 mm) |
| 2 | 4 | Nominal 4" (102 mm) = | 3-1/2" (89 mm) |
| 2 | 5 | Nominal 5" (127 mm) = | 4-1/4" (108 mm) |
| 2 | 6 | Nominal 6" (152 mm) = | 5-1/4" (133 mm) |
| 2 | 7 | Nominal 8" (203 mm) = | 7" (178 mm) |
| 2 | 8 | Nominal 10" (254 mm) = | 9" (229 mm) |
| 2 | 9 | Nominal 12" (305 mm) = | 11" (279 mm) |
| 2 | 10 | Nominal 12+" (305+ mm) = | 1" (25 mm) less than nominal size |
| 2 | 11 | *[Illustration showing Nominal Width and Finished Width]* | |
| 3 | | When **MACHINE SANDED**, a reduction of 1/32" (1 mm) off the above thicknesses or widths is permitted. | |

## 3.4.6 Hardwood Material Rules

| | | |
|---|---|---|
| 1 | | **APPLYING** to only the following species: |
| | | ALDER — MAPLE, HARD & SOFT |
| | | ASH — OAK, RED |
| | | BIRCH — OAK, WHITE |
| | | CHERRY, AMERICAN — POPLAR |
| | | LAUAN — TEAK |
| | | MAHOGANY, AFRICAN — WALNUT, AMERICAN |
| | | MAHOGANY, AMERICAN |
| 1 | 1 | For **SPECIES NOT LISTED**, length requirements and size/exposed area of permitted natural characteristics shall be as agreed to between owner/design professional and manufacturer/installer. |
| 2 | | **GLUING** for **THICKNESS** is permitted when finished dimensions exceed 1-1/16" (27 mm). |
| 3 | | **GLUING** for **WIDTH** is permitted when: |
| 3 | 1 | Finished dimensions exceed 6" (152 mm), or: |
| 3 | 1 | 1 — 4-1/4" (108 mm) at Rift sawn White/Red Oak; quarter sawn White/Red Oak, Maple, and Walnut; and select White/Red Birch, White Ash, Alder and Cherry. |
| 3 | 2 | Direction of the end grain of boards glued for width shall be alternated, see example: |
| 3 | 2 | 1 — *[Illustration of boards glued for width with alternating end grain]* |
| 4 | | Lumber of the **SAME SPECIES** but of **DIFFERENT ORIGINS** shall not be mixed on a project (example: American and European Cherry). |
| 5 | | If only the generic term **MAHOGANY** is specified, it shall mean African or American Mahogany. |
| 6 | | Specifications calling for **PHILIPPINE MAHOGANY** shall permit the use of Lauan, Tanguile, and other natural Philippine species of wood. |
| 7 | | **OAK, RIFT GRAIN**, shall permit twenty-five percent (25%) of the exposed surface area of each board to contain medullary ray flake. |
| 8 | | **NATURAL ASH, BIRCH**, and **MAPLE** shall permit both sapwood and heartwood in any board. |

Continues next column ▼

Architectural Woodwork Standards

# SECTION 3
## Lumber

**GENERAL PRODUCT** — compliance requirements

Where the **E**, **C**, or **P** icon is not indicated, the rule applies to all Grades equally | E | C | P |

### 3.4.6 Hardwood Material Rules

▲ From previous column

**9 MAXIMUM LENGTH** required for thickness up to 1-1/2" (38 mm):

- 9.1 Boards required to be longer than those listed may be glued and joined for length or furnished in multiple pieces.
- 9.2 **ALDER:**
  - 1  2" (51 mm) in width = 9'-10" (2997 mm).
  - 2  3" (76 mm) in width = 8'-10" (2692 mm).
  - 3  4" (102 mm) in width = 7'-6" (2286 mm).
  - 4  5" (127 mm) in width = 6'-10" (2083 mm).
  - 5  6" (152 mm) or wider is not usually available.
- 9.3 **ASH, NATURAL:**
  - 1  2" to 3" (51 mm to 76 mm) in width = 15'-6" (4724 mm).
  - 2  4" (102 mm) in width = 14'-6" (4420 mm).
  - 3  5" (127 mm) in width = 13'-6" (4115 mm).
  - 4  6" (152 mm) in width = 12'-6" (3810 mm).
  - 5  7" to 8" (178 mm to 203 mm) in width = 10'-6" (3200 mm).
  - 6  9" (229 mm) in width = 8'-10" (2692 mm).
- 9.4 **ASH, SELECT BROWN** or **WHITE:**
  - 1  2" to 4" (51 mm to 102 mm) in width = 11'-6" (3505 mm).
  - 2  5" to 6" (127 mm to 152 mm) in width = 10'-6" (3200 mm).
  - 3  7" (178 mm) in width = 8'-6" (2591 mm).
  - 4  8" to 9" (203 to 229 mm) in width = 7'-10" (2388 mm).
- 9.5 **BIRCH, NATURAL:**
  - 1  2" to 4" (51 mm to 102 mm) in width = 10'-6" (3200 mm).
  - 2  5" to 6" (127 mm to 152 mm) in width = 9'-6" (2896 mm).
  - 3  7" (178 mm) in width = 8'-6" (2591 mm).
  - 4  8" to 9" (203 mm to 229 mm) in width = 7'-6" (2286 mm).
- 9.6 **BIRCH, SELECT RED** or **WHITE:**
  - 1  2" to 4" (51 mm to 102 mm) in width = 9'-6" (2896 mm).
  - 2  5" to 6" (127 mm to 152 mm) in width = 8'-6" (2591 mm).
  - 3  6" (152 mm) or wider is not usually available.
- 9.7 **CHERRY, AMERICAN:**
  - 1  2" to 4" (51 mm to 102 mm) in width = 9'-10" (2997 mm).
  - 2  5" to 6" (127 mm to 152 mm) in width = 8'-10" (2692 mm).
  - 3  7" (178 mm) in width = 7'-10" (2388 mm).
  - 4  8" (203 mm) or wider is not usually available.
- 9.8 **LAUAN; MAHOGANY, AMERICAN** and **AFRICAN:**
  - 1  2" to 9" (51 mm to 229 mm) in width = 15'-10" (4826 mm).

Continues next column ▼

### 3.4.6 Hardwood Material Rules

▲ From previous column

**9 MAXIMUM LENGTH** (continued)

- 9.9 **MAPLE, NATURAL:**
  - 1  2" to 3" (51 mm to 76 mm) in width = 14'-10" (4521 mm).
  - 2  4" (102 mm) in width = 13'-10" (4216 mm).
  - 3  5" (127 mm) in width = 12'-10" (3912 mm).
  - 4  6" to 7" (152 mm to 178 mm) in width = 10'-10" (3302 mm).
  - 5  8" to 9" (203 mm to 229 mm) in width = 8'-10" (2692 mm).
- 9.10 **MAPLE, WHITE:**
  - 1  2" (51 mm) in width = 14'-10" (4521 mm).
  - 2  3" to 4" (76 mm to 102 mm) in width = 11'-10" (3607 mm).
  - 3  5" (127 mm) in width = 10'-10" (3302 mm).
  - 4  6" to 7" (152 mm to 178 mm) in width = 8'-10" (2692 mm).
  - 5  8" (203 mm) or wider is not usually available.
- 9.11 **OAK, RED** or **WHITE** (except Rift or Quarter Sawn):
  - 1  2" (51 mm) in width = 14'-10" (4521 mm).
  - 2  3" to 4" (76 mm to 102 mm) in width = 13'-10" (4216 mm).
  - 3  5" to 6" (127 mm to 152 mm) in width = 11'-10" (3607 mm).
  - 4  7" (178 mm) in width = 9'-10" (2997 mm).
  - 5  8" to 9" (203 mm to 229 mm) in width = 8'-10" (2692 mm).
- 9.12 **OAK, RED** or **WHITE, RIFT** or **QUARTER SAWN:**
  - 1  2" to 3" (51 mm to 76 mm) in width = 13'-10" (4216 mm).
  - 2  4" (102 mm) in width = 11'-10" (3607 mm).
  - 3  5" to 6" (127 mm to 152 mm) in width = 9'-10" (2997 mm).
  - 4  7" (178 mm) in width = 7'-10" (2388 mm).
  - 5  8" (203 mm) or wider is not usually available.
- 9.13 **POPLAR:**
  - 1  2" to 6" (51 mm to 152 mm) in width = 15'-10" 4826 mm).
  - 2  7" (178 mm) in width = 13'-10" (4216 mm).
  - 3  8" to 9" (203 mm to 229 mm) in width = 12'-10" (3912 mm).
- 9.14 **TEAK:**
  - 1  2" (51 mm) in width = 9'-6" (2896 mm).
  - 2  3" to 4" (76 mm to 102 mm) in width = 8'-6" (2591 mm).
  - 3  5" to 7" (127 mm to 178 mm) in width = 7'-6" (2286 mm).
  - 4  8" (203 mm) or wider is not usually available.

Continues next column ▼

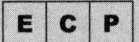

Where the **E**, **C**, or **P** icon is not indicated, the rule applies to all Grades equally

# SECTION 3
## Lumber

**compliance requirements**  GENERAL PRODUCT

### 3.4.6 Hardwood Material Rules

▲ From previous column

| 9 | | | MAXIMUM LENGTH (continued) | | | |
|---|---|---|---|---|---|---|
| 9 | 15 | | WALNUT, AMERICAN: | | | |
| 9 | 15 | 1 | 2" (51 mm) in width = 9'-6" (2896 mm). | | | |
| 9 | 15 | 2 | 3" to 4" (76 mm to 102 mm) in width = 8'-6" (2591 mm). | | | |
| 9 | 15 | 3 | 5" (127 mm) in width = 7'-6" (2286 mm). | | | |
| 9 | 15 | 4 | 6" (152 mm) in width = 5'-6" (1676 mm). | | | |
| 9 | 15 | 5 | 7" (178 mm) or wider is not usually available. | | | |
| 10 | | | OPAQUE FINISH allows: | | | |
| 10 | 1 | | NOT MATCHING for COLOR when glued for thickness or width. | | | |
| 10 | 2 | | NATURAL CHARACTERISTICS if they are inconspicuous after two coats of finish. | | | |
| 10 | 3 | | FILLING of checks, splits, or other open characteristics which is the responsibility of the millwork manufacturer. | | | |
| 10 | 4 | | QUANTITY, SPACING and DISTRIBUTION of NATURAL CHARACTERISTIC in any one board's exposed face of: | | | |
| 10 | 4 | 1 | NONE in any face smaller than 200 square inches (129,032 square mm), with: | E | C | P |
| 10 | 4 | 1 | 1 ONE permitted for each additional 100 square inches (64,516 square mm). | E | C | P |
| 10 | 4 | 1 | 2 A maximum of FIVE in any board. | E | C | P |
| 10 | 4 | 1 | 3 NO knots, pitch streaks, or pitch pockets within 18" (457 mm) of one another. | E | C | P |
| 10 | 4 | 2 | NONE in any face smaller than 300 square inches (193,548 square mm), with: | E | C | P |
| 10 | 4 | 2 | 1 ONE permitted for each additional 150 square inches (96,774 square mm). | E | C | P |
| 10 | 4 | 2 | 2 A maximum of FOUR in any board. | E | C | P |
| 10 | 4 | 2 | 3 NO knots, pitch streaks, or pitch pockets within 24" (610 mm) of one another. | E | C | P |
| 10 | 4 | 3 | NONE in any face smaller than 400 square inches | E | C | P |
| 10 | 4 | 3 | 1 ONE permitted for each additional 200 square inches (129,032 square mm). | E | C | P |
| 10 | 4 | 3 | 2 A maximum of THREE in any board. | E | C | P |
| 10 | 4 | 3 | 3 NO knots, pitch streaks, or pitch pockets within 36" (9(414 mm) of one another. | E | C | P |
| 10 | 5 | | The following NATURAL CHARACTERISTICS: | | | |
| 10 | 5 | 1 | BARK POCKET - None. | | | |
| 10 | 5 | 2 | BIRDSEYE, Sound - Unlimited. | | | |
| 10 | 5 | 3 | BIRDSEYE, Checked and Filled - Unlimited. | | | |

Continues next column ▼

### 3.4.6 Hardwood Material Rules

▲ From previous column

| 10 | | | OPAQUE FINISH (continued) | | | |
|---|---|---|---|---|---|---|
| 10 | 5 | | The following NATURAL CHARACTERISTICS (continued) | | | |
| 10 | 5 | 4 | BURL, Sound: | | | |
| 10 | 5 | 4 | 1 < 1" (25 mm) in diameter. | E | C | P |
| 10 | 5 | 4 | 2 < 3/4" (19 mm) in diameter. | E | C | P |
| 10 | 5 | 5 | CHECK, Filled: | | | |
| 10 | 5 | 5 | 1 < 3/32" (2 mm) wide x 9" (229 mm) long. | E | C | P |
| 10 | 5 | 5 | 2 < 1/16" (2 mm) wide x 6" (152 mm) long. | E | C | P |
| 10 | 5 | 5 | 3 < 1/32" (1 mm) wide x 4" (102 mm) long. | E | C | P |
| 10 | 5 | 6 | HONEYCOMB - None: | | | |
| 10 | 5 | 7 | KNOT, Sound and Tight: | | | |
| 10 | 5 | 7 | 1 < 1" (25 mm) in diameter. | E | C | P |
| 10 | 5 | 7 | 2 < 5/8" (16 mm) in diameter. | E | C | P |
| 10 | 5 | 7 | 3 < 3/8" (10 mm) in diameter. | E | C | P |
| 10 | 5 | 8 | KNOT, Checked and Filled: | | | |
| 10 | 5 | 8 | 1 < 3/4" (19 mm) in diameter. | E | C | P |
| 10 | 5 | 8 | 2 < 1/2" (13 mm) in diameter. | E | C | P |
| 10 | 5 | 8 | 3 < 1/4" (6 mm) in diameter. | E | C | P |
| 10 | 5 | 9 | KNOT, Open and Filled: | | | |
| 10 | 5 | 9 | 1 < 1/2" (13 mm) in diameter. | E | C | P |
| 10 | 5 | 9 | 2 < 1/4" (6 mm) in diameter. | E | C | P |
| 10 | 5 | 9 | 3 < 1/8" (3 mm) in diameter. | E | C | P |
| 10 | 5 | 10 | MINERAL STAIN - Unlimited | | | |
| 10 | 5 | 11 | PATCH ≤ 1-1/2" (38 mm) wide x 3-1/2" (89 mm) long. | | | |
| 10 | 5 | 12 | PITCH POCKET or STREAK, Filled: | | | |
| 10 | 5 | 12 | 1 < 1/16" (2 mm) wide x 6" (152 mm) long or 1/8" (3 mm) wide x 4" (102 mm) long. | E | C | P |
| 10 | 5 | 12 | 2 < 1/16" (2 mm) wide x 3" (76 mm) long or 1/8" (3 mm) wide x 2" (51 mm) long. | E | C | P |
| 10 | 5 | 13 | SAPWOOD - Unlimited. | | | |
| 10 | 5 | 14 | SHAKE, Filled: | | | |
| 10 | 5 | 14 | 1 ≤ 1/4" (6 mm) wide x 3" (76 mm) long. | E | C | P |
| 10 | 5 | 14 | 2 ≤ 1/8" (3 mm) wide x 3" (76 mm) long. | E | C | P |
| 10 | 5 | 14 | 3 ≤ 1/16" (2 mm) wide x 2" (51 mm) long. | E | C | P |
| 10 | 5 | 15 | SPLIT, Filled: | | | |
| 10 | 5 | 15 | 1 ≤ 3/32" (2 mm) wide x 8" (203 mm) long. | E | C | P |
| 10 | 5 | 15 | 2 ≤ 1/16" (2 mm) wide x 6" (152 mm) long. | E | C | P |
| 10 | 5 | 15 | 3 ≤ 1/32" (1 mm) wide x 4" (102 mm) long. | E | C | P |
| 10 | 5 | 16 | STICKER BOARD DISCOLORATION - Unlimited. | | | |

Continues next column ▼

# SECTION 3
## Lumber

GENERAL/PRODUCT — compliance requirements

Where the **E**, **C**, or **P** icon is not indicated, the rule applies to all Grades equally | E | C | P |

### 3.4.6 Hardwood Material Rules

▲ From previous column

| | | | | | E | C | P |
|---|---|---|---|---|---|---|---|
| 10 | | | **OPAQUE FINISH** (continued) | | | | |
| 10 | 5 | | The following **NATURAL CHARACTERISTICS** (continued) | | | | |
| 10 | 5 | 17 | **WORM HOLE**, Filled: | | | | |
| 10 | 5 | 17 | 1 | ≤ 1/8" (3 mm) in diameter. | E | C | P |
| 10 | 5 | 17 | 2 | ≤ 1/16" (2 mm) in diameter. | E | **C** | P |
| 10 | 5 | 17 | 3 | No worm holes allowed. | E | C | **P** |
| 11 | | | **TRANSPARENT FINISH** allows: | | | | |
| 11 | 1 | | **MATCHING**, when glued for thickness or width or when veneered construction is utilized, shall be: | | | | |
| 11 | 1 | 1 | Not required. | | E | C | P |
| 11 | 1 | 2 | Compatible for color and grain. | | E | **C** | P |
| 11 | 1 | 3 | Well matched for color and grain. | | E | C | **P** |
| 11 | 2 | | **FILLING** of checks, splits, or other open characteristics is the responsibility of the finisher. | | | | |
| 11 | 3 | | **QUANTITY, SPACING** and **DISTRIBUTION** of **NATURAL CHARACTERISTIC** in any one board's exposed face of: | | | | |
| 11 | 3 | 1 | **FOUR** with: | | E | C | P |
| 11 | 3 | 1 | 1 | NO knots, pitch streaks, or pitch pockets within 24" (610 mm) of one another. | **E** | C | P |
| 11 | 3 | 2 | **THREE** with: | | E | **C** | P |
| 11 | 3 | 2 | 1 | NO knots, pitch streaks, or pitch pockets within 36" (914 mm) of one another. | E | **C** | P |
| 11 | 3 | 3 | **TWO** with: | | E | C | **P** |
| 11 | 3 | 3 | 1 | NO knots, pitch streaks, or pitch pockets within 48" (1219 mm) of one another. | E | C | **P** |
| 11 | 3 | 4 | For: **ALDER**, **MAHOGANY**, African, **ASH**, Natural, **MAPLE**, Hard or Soft, Natural, **BIRCH**, Natural, **POPLAR**, **LAUAN**, **RED & WHITE OAK**, **MAHOGANY**, American, **TEAK** | | | | |
| 11 | 3 | 4 | 1 | NONE in any face smaller than 300 square inches (193,548 square mm), with: | **E** | C | P |
| 11 | 3 | 4 | 1 | 1 | ONE permitted for each additional 100 square inches (64,516 square mm). | **E** | C | P |
| 11 | 3 | 4 | 2 | NONE in any face smaller than 400 square inches (258,064 square mm), with: | E | **C** | P |
| 11 | 3 | 4 | 2 | 1 | ONE permitted for each additional 150 square inches (96,774 square mm). | E | **C** | P |

Continues next column ▼

▲ From previous column

| | | | | | E | C | P |
|---|---|---|---|---|---|---|---|
| 11 | | | **TRANSPARENT FINISH** (continued) | | | | |
| 11 | 3 | | **QUANTITY, SPACING** and **DISTRIBUTION** of **NATURAL CHARACTERISTIC** (continued) | | | | |
| 11 | 3 | 4 | For: **ALDER** | | | | |
| 11 | 3 | 4 | 3 | NONE in any face smaller than 600 square inches (387,096 square mm), with: | E | C | **P** |
| 11 | 3 | 4 | 3 | 1 | ONE permitted for each additional 200 square inches (129,032 square mm). | E | C | **P** |
| 11 | 3 | 5 | For: **ASH**, Select Brown, **BIRCH**, Select Red & White, **MAPLE**, Select White | | | | |
| 11 | 3 | 5 | 1 | NONE in any face smaller than 200 square inches (129,032 square mm), with: | **E** | C | P |
| 11 | 3 | 5 | 1 | 1 | ONE permitted for each additional 100 square inches (64,516 square mm). | **E** | C | P |
| 11 | 3 | 5 | 2 | NONE in any face smaller than 350 square inches (225,806 square mm), with: | E | **C** | P |
| 11 | 3 | 5 | 2 | 1 | ONE permitted for each additional 150 square inches (96,774 square mm). | E | **C** | P |
| 11 | 3 | 5 | 3 | NONE in any face smaller than 500 square inches (322,580 square mm), with: | E | C | **P** |
| 11 | 3 | 5 | 3 | 1 | ONE permitted for each additional 200 square inches (129,032 square mm). | E | C | **P** |
| 11 | 3 | 6 | For: **CHERRY**, American, **RED & WHITE OAK**, Rift/Quarter Sawn, **WALNUT**, American | | | | |
| 11 | 3 | 6 | 1 | NONE in any face smaller than 150 square inches (96,744 square mm), with: | **E** | C | P |
| 11 | 3 | 6 | 1 | 1 | ONE permitted for each additional 75 square inches (48,387 square mm). | **E** | C | P |
| 11 | 3 | 6 | 2 | NONE in any face smaller than 200 square inches (129,032 square mm), with: | E | **C** | P |
| 11 | 3 | 6 | 2 | 1 | ONE permitted for each additional 100 square inches (64,516 square mm). | E | **C** | P |
| 11 | 3 | 6 | 3 | NONE in any face smaller than 300 square inches (193,548 square mm), with: | E | C | **P** |
| 11 | 3 | 6 | 3 | 1 | ONE permitted for each additional 150 square inches (96,774 square mm). | E | C | **P** |
| 11 | 4 | | The following **NATURAL CHARACTERISTICS**: | | | | |
| 11 | 4 | 1 | **BARK POCKET** - None. | | | | |
| 11 | 4 | 2 | **BIRDSEYE**, Sound - Unlimited. | | | | |

Continues next column ▼

 Where the E, C, or P icon is not indicated, the rule applies to all Grades equally

# compliance requirements

## SECTION 3
### Lumber
### GENERAL / PRODUCT

### 3.4.6 Hardwood Material Rules
▲ From previous column

| | | | | | | | |
|---|---|---|---|---|---|---|---|
| 11 | | | **TRANSPARENT FINISH** (continued) | | | | |
| 11 | 4 | | The following **NATURAL CHARACTERISTICS**: | | | | |
| 11 | 4 | 3 | **BIRDSEYE**, Checked: | | | | |
| 11 | 4 | 3 | 1 | Unlimited. | E | C | P |
| 11 | 4 | 3 | 2 | ≤ 10% of face. | E | C | P |
| 11 | 4 | 3 | 3 | None. | E | C | P |
| 11 | 4 | 4 | **BURL**, Sound: | | | | |
| 11 | 4 | 4 | 1 | Unlimited. | E | C | P |
| 11 | 4 | 4 | 2 | ≤ 1" (25 mm) in diameter. | E | C | P |
| 11 | 4 | 4 | 3 | ≤ 1/2" (13 mm) in diameter. | E | C | P |
| 11 | 4 | 5 | **CHECK**: | | | | |
| 11 | 4 | 5 | 1 | ≤ 3/32" (2 mm) wide x 8" (203 mm) long. | E | C | P |
| 11 | 4 | 5 | 2 | ≤ 1/16" (2 mm) wide x 6" (152 mm) long. | E | C | P |
| 11 | 4 | 5 | 3 | ≤ 1/32" (1 mm) wide x 4" (102 mm) long. | E | C | P |
| 11 | 4 | 6 | **HEARTWOOD**, in Select White Ash, Birch, and Maple - None. | | | | |
| 11 | 4 | 7 | **HONEYCOMB** - None. | | | | |
| 11 | 4 | 8 | **KNOT**, Sound and Tight: | | | | |
| 11 | 4 | 8 | 1 | ≤ 3/8" (10 mm) in diameter. | E | C | P |
| 11 | 4 | 8 | 2 | ≤ 1/4" (6 mm) in diameter. | E | C | P |
| 11 | 4 | 8 | 3 | ≤ 1/8" (3 mm) in diameter. | E | C | P |
| 11 | 4 | 9 | **KNOT**, Checked: | | | | |
| 11 | 4 | 9 | 1 | ≤ 1/2" (13 mm) in diameter. | E | C | P |
| 11 | 4 | 9 | 2 | ≤ 1/4" (6 mm) in diameter. | E | C | P |
| 11 | 4 | 9 | 3 | None. | E | C | P |
| 11 | 4 | 10 | **KNOT**, Open - None. | | | | |
| 11 | 4 | 11 | **MINERAL STAIN**: | | | | |
| 11 | 4 | 11 | 1 | Unlimited. | E | C | P |
| 11 | 4 | 11 | 2 | ≤ 10% of face. | E | C | P |
| 11 | 4 | 11 | 3 | None. | E | C | P |
| 11 | 4 | 12 | **PATCH**: | | | | |
| 11 | 4 | 12 | 1 | ≤ 1-1/2" (38 mm) wide x 3-1/2" (89 mm) long, and inconspicuous from 60". | E | C | P |
| 11 | 4 | 12 | 2 | ≤ 1-1/2" (38 mm) wide x 3-1/2" (89 mm) long, and inconspicuous from 36". | E | C | P |
| 11 | 4 | 12 | 3 | None. | E | C | P |
| 11 | 4 | 13 | **PITCH POCKET** or **STREAK**: | | | | |
| 11 | 4 | 13 | 1 | ≤ 1/16" (2 mm) wide x 6" (152 mm) long or 1/8" (3 mm) wide x 4" (102 mm) long. | E | C | P |
| 11 | 4 | 13 | 2 | None. | E | C | P |

Continues next column ▼

### 3.4.6 Hardwood Material Rules
▲ From previous column

| | | | | | | | |
|---|---|---|---|---|---|---|---|
| 11 | | | **TRANSPARENT FINISH** (continued) | | | | |
| 11 | 4 | | The following **NATURAL CHARACTERISTICS**: | | | | |
| 11 | 4 | 14 | **SAPWOOD**, in unselected species - Unlimited. | | | | |
| 11 | 4 | 15 | **SAPWOOD**, in select Red Birch and Brown Ash - None. | | | | |
| 11 | 4 | 16 | **SAPWOOD** in Cherry, and Walnut: | | | | |
| 11 | 4 | 16 | 1 | Unlimited. | E | C | P |
| 11 | 4 | 16 | 2 | ≤ 10% of face. | E | C | P |
| 11 | 4 | 16 | 3 | ≤ 5% of face. | E | C | P |
| 11 | 4 | 17 | **SHAKE**: | | | | |
| 11 | 4 | 17 | 1 | ≤ 1/8" (3 mm) wide x 3" (76 mm) long. | E | C | P |
| 11 | 4 | 17 | 2 | None. | E | C | P |
| 11 | 4 | 18 | **SPLIT**: | | | | |
| 11 | 4 | 18 | 1 | ≤ 3/32" (2 mm) wide x 8" (203 mm) long. | E | C | P |
| 11 | 4 | 18 | 2 | ≤ 1/16" (2 mm) wide x 6" (152 mm) long. | E | C | P |
| 11 | 4 | 18 | 3 | ≤ 1/32" (1 mm) wide x 4" (102 mm) long. | E | C | P |
| 11 | 4 | 19 | **STICKER BOARD DISCOLORATION**: | | | | |
| 11 | 4 | 19 | 1 | ≤ 10% of face. | E | C | P |
| 11 | 4 | 19 | 2 | None. | E | C | P |
| 11 | 4 | 20 | **WORM HOLE**, Filled: | | | | |
| 11 | 4 | 20 | 1 | ≤ 1/8" (3 mm) in diameter. | E | C | P |
| 11 | 4 | 20 | 2 | ≤ 1/16" (2 mm) in diameter. | E | C | P |
| 11 | 4 | 20 | 3 | No worm holes allowed. | E | C | P |

©2014 AWI | AWMAC | WI 2nd Edition, October 1, 2014
As may be updated by errata at awinet.org, awmac.com, or aws-errata.com

# SECTION 3
## Lumber

GENERAL **PRODUCT**

**compliance requirements**

Where the **E**, **C**, or **P** icon is not indicated, the rule applies to all Grades equally | E | C | P |

## 3.4.7 Softwood Material Rules

| 1 | | **APPLYING** only to the following species:<br>CEDAR, WESTERN RED     HEMLOCK<br>PINE, SUGAR     FIR, DOUGLAS<br>PINE, PONDEROSA     REDWOOD | | | |
|---|---|---|---|---|---|
| 1 | 1 | For **SPECIES NOT LISTED**, length requirements and size/exposed area of permitted natural characteristics shall be as agreed to between owner/design professional and manufacturer/installer. | | | |
| 2 | | **GLUING** for **WIDTH** is permitted when finished dimensions exceed 7" (178 mm). | | | |
| 2 | 1 | Direction of the end grain of boards glued for width shall be alternated. | | | |
| 2 | 2 | | | | |
| 3 | | **GLUING** for **THICKNESS** is permitted when finished dimensions exceed 1-1/2" (38 mm). | | | |
| 4 | | **VERTICAL GRAIN** shall have a minimum average of 5 growth rings per inch at exposed surfaces. | | | |
| 5 | | **MAXIMUM LENGTH** required for thickness up to 1-1/2" (38.1 mm): | | | |
| 5 | 1 | **DOUGLAS FIR, HEMLOCK, & WESTERN RED CEDAR:** | | | |
| 5 | 1 | 1 | 4" to 8" (102 mm to 203 mm) in width = 15'-8" (4,775 mm). |
| 5 | 1 | 2 | 10" (254 mm) in width = 13'-8" (4,166 mm). |
| 5 | 1 | 3 | 12" (305 mm) is not usually available. |
| 5 | 2 | **PONDEROSA** or **SUGAR PINE**: | | | |
| 5 | 2 | 1 | 4" to 12" (102 mm to 305 mm) in width = 15'-8" (4,775 mm). |
| 5 | 3 | **REDWOOD**: | | | |
| 5 | 3 | 1 | 4" to 12" (102 mm to 305 mm) in width = 19'-8" (5,994 mm). |
| 5 | 4 | **BOARDS** required to be **WIDER** than those listed above may be glued for width. | | | |
| 5 | 5 | **BOARDS** required to be **LONGER** than those listed as available above may be glued and joined or furnished in two pieces for length at the option of the manufacturer. | | | |
| 6 | | **OPAQUE FINISH** allows: | | | |
| 6 | 1 | **NATURAL CHARACTERISTICS** only if they are inconspicuous after two coats of finish are applied. | | | |
| 6 | 2 | **FILLING** of checks, splits, or other open characteristics which is the responsibility of the millwork manufacturer. | | | |

Continues next column ▼

## 3.4.7 Softwood Material Rules

▲ From previous column

| 6 | | | | **OPAQUE FINISH** (continued) | | | |
|---|---|---|---|---|---|---|---|
| 6 | 3 | | | **QUANTITY, SPACING** and **DISTRIBUTION** of **NATURAL CHARACTERISTIC** in any one board's exposed face of: | | | |
| 6 | 3 | 1 | | **NONE** in any face smaller than 200 square inches (129,032 square mm), with: | E | C | P |
| 6 | 3 | 1 | 1 | **ONE** permitted for each additional 100 square inches (64,516 square mm). | E | C | P |
| 6 | 3 | 1 | 2 | **FIVE** in any board. | E | C | P |
| 6 | 3 | 1 | 3 | **NO** knots, pitch streaks, or pitch pockets within 18" (457 mm) of one another. | E | C | P |
| 6 | 3 | 2 | | **NONE** in any face smaller than 400 square inches (258,064 square mm), with: | E | C | P |
| 6 | 3 | 2 | 1 | **ONE** permitted for each additional 150 square inches (96,774 square mm). | E | C | P |
| 6 | 3 | 2 | 2 | **FOUR** in any board. | E | C | P |
| 6 | 3 | 2 | 3 | **NO** knots, pitch streaks, or pitch pockets within 24" (610 mm) of one another. | E | C | P |
| 6 | 3 | 3 | | **NONE** in any face smaller than 600 square inches (387,096 square mm), with: | E | C | P |
| 6 | 3 | 3 | 1 | **ONE** permitted for each additional 200 square inches (129,032 square mm). | E | C | P |
| 6 | 3 | 3 | 2 | **THREE** in any board. | E | C | P |
| 6 | 3 | 3 | 3 | **NO** knots, pitch streaks, or pitch pockets within 36" (914 mm) of one another. | E | C | P |
| 6 | 4 | | | The following **NATURAL CHARACTERISTIC**: | | | |
| 6 | 4 | 1 | | **BARK POCKET** - None. | | | |
| 6 | 4 | 2 | | **BIRDSEYE**, Sound - Unlimited. | | | |
| 6 | 4 | 3 | | **BIRDSEYE**, Checked and Filled - Unlimited. | | | |
| 6 | 4 | 4 | | **BURL**, Sound: | | | |
| 6 | 4 | 4 | 1 | $\leq 1"$ (25 mm) in diameter. | E | C | P |
| 6 | 4 | 4 | 2 | $\leq 3/4"$ (19 mm) in diameter. | E | C | P |
| 6 | 4 | 5 | | **CHECK**, Filled: | | | |
| 6 | 4 | 5 | 1 | $\leq 3/32"$ (2 mm) wide x 9" (229 mm) long. | E | C | P |
| 6 | 4 | 5 | 2 | $\leq 1/16"$ (2 mm) wide x 6" (152 mm) long. | E | C | P |
| 6 | 4 | 5 | 3 | $\leq 1/32"$ (1 mm) wide x 4" (102 mm) long. | E | C | P |
| 6 | 4 | 6 | | **HONEYCOMB** - None. | | | |

Continues next column ▼

| E | C | P | Where the E, C, or P icon is not indicated, the rule applies to all Grades equally |

**SECTION 3**
Lumber

## compliance requirements

GENERAL/PRODUCT

### 3.4.7 Softwood Material Rules

▲ From previous column

| | | | | | | | |
|---|---|---|---|---|---|---|---|
| 6 | | | OPAQUE FINISH (continued) | | | | |
| 6 | 4 | | The following **NATURAL CHARACTERISTICS** (continued) | | | | |
| 6 | 4 | 7 | **KNOT**, Sound and Tight: | | | | |
| 6 | 4 | 7 | 1 | ≤ 1" (25 mm) in diameter. | E | C | P |
| 6 | 4 | 7 | 2 | ≤ 5/8" (16 mm) in diameter. | E | **C** | P |
| 6 | 4 | 7 | 3 | ≤ 3/8" (10 mm) in diameter. | E | C | **P** |
| 6 | 4 | 8 | **KNOT**, Checked and Filled: | | | | |
| 6 | 4 | 8 | 1 | ≤ 3/4" (19 mm) in diameter. | E | C | P |
| 6 | 4 | 8 | 2 | ≤ 1/2" (13 mm) in diameter. | E | **C** | P |
| 6 | 4 | 8 | 3 | ≤ 1/4" (6 mm) in diameter. | E | C | **P** |
| 6 | 4 | 9 | **KNOT**, Open and Filled: | | | | |
| 6 | 4 | 9 | 1 | ≤ 1/2" (13 mm) in diameter. | E | C | P |
| 6 | 4 | 9 | 2 | ≤ 1/4" (6 mm) in diameter. | E | **C** | P |
| 6 | 4 | 9 | 3 | ≤ 1/8" (3 mm) in diameter. | E | C | **P** |
| 6 | 4 | 10 | **MINERAL STAIN** - Unlimited. | | | | |
| 6 | 4 | 11 | **PATCH** ≤ 1-1/2" (38 mm) wide x 3-1/2" (89 mm) long. | | | | |
| 6 | 4 | 12 | **PITCH POCKET** or **STREAK**: | | | | |
| 6 | 4 | 12 | 1 | < 1/16" (2 mm) wide x 6" (152 mm) long or 1/8" (3 mm) wide x 4" (102 mm) long. | E | C | P |
| 6 | 4 | 12 | 2 | < 1/16" (2 mm) wide x 3" (76 mm) long or 1/8" (3 mm) wide x 2" (51 mm) long. | E | C | **P** |
| 6 | 4 | 13 | **SAPWOOD** - Unlimited. | | | | |
| 6 | 4 | 14 | **SHAKE**, Filled: | | | | |
| 6 | 4 | 14 | 1 | ≤ 1/4" (6 mm) wide x 3" (76 mm) long. | E | C | P |
| 6 | 4 | 14 | 2 | ≤ 1/8" (3 mm) wide x 3" (76 mm) long. | E | **C** | P |
| 6 | 4 | 14 | 3 | ≤ 1/16" (2 mm) wide x 2" (51 mm) long. | E | C | **P** |
| 6 | 4 | 15 | **SPLIT**, Filled: | | | | |
| 6 | 4 | 15 | 1 | ≤ 3/32" (2 mm) wide x 8" (203 mm) long. | E | C | P |
| 6 | 4 | 15 | 2 | ≤ 1/16" (2 mm) wide x 6" (152 mm) long. | E | **C** | P |
| 6 | 4 | 15 | 3 | ≤ 1/32" (1 mm) wide x 4" (102 mm) long. | E | C | **P** |
| 6 | 4 | 16 | **STICKER BOARD DISCOLORATION** - Unlimited. | | | | |
| 6 | 4 | 17 | **WORM HOLES**, Filled: | | | | |
| 6 | 4 | 17 | 1 | ≤ 1/8" (3 mm) in diameter. | E | C | P |
| 6 | 4 | 17 | 2 | ≤ 1/16" (2 mm) in diameter. | E | **C** | P |
| 6 | 4 | 17 | 3 | No worm holes allowed. | E | C | **P** |

Continues next column ▼

### 3.4.7 Softwood Material Rules

▲ From previous column

| | | | | | | | |
|---|---|---|---|---|---|---|---|
| 7 | | | **TRANSPARENT FINISH** allows: | | | | |
| 7 | 1 | | **MATCHING**, when glued for thickness or width or when veneered construction is utilized, shall be: | | | | |
| 7 | 1 | 1 | Not required. | E | C | P |
| 7 | 1 | 2 | Compatible for color and grain. | E | **C** | P |
| 7 | 1 | 3 | Well matched for color and grain. | E | C | **P** |
| 7 | 2 | | **FILLING** of checks, splits, or other open characteristics which is the responsibility of the finisher. | | | | |
| 7 | 3 | | **QUANTITY, SPACING** and **DISTRIBUTION** of **NATURAL CHARACTERISTIC** in any one board's exposed face of: | | | | |
| 7 | 3 | 1 | **NONE** in any face smaller than 400 sq. in. (258,064 sq. mm), with: | E | C | P |
| 7 | 3 | 1 | 1 | **ONE** permitted for each additional 200 sq. in. (129,032 sq. mm). | **E** | C | P |
| 7 | 3 | 2 | **FOUR**, with: | E | C | P |
| 7 | 3 | 2 | 1 | **NO** knots, pitch streaks, or pitch pockets within 24" (610 mm) of one another. | **E** | C | P |
| 7 | 3 | 3 | **NONE** in any face smaller than 600 sq. in. (387,096 sq. mm), with: | E | **C** | P |
| 7 | 3 | 3 | 1 | **ONE** permitted for each additional 300 sq. in. (193,548 sq. mm). | E | **C** | P |
| 7 | 3 | 4 | **THREE**, with: | E | **C** | P |
| 7 | 3 | 4 | 1 | **NO** knots, pitch streaks, or pitch pockets within 36" (914 mm) of one another. | E | **C** | P |
| 7 | 3 | 5 | **NONE** in any face smaller than 900 sq. in. (580,644 sq. mm), with: | E | C | **P** |
| 7 | 3 | 5 | 1 | **ONE** permitted for each additional 400 sq. in. (258,064 sq. mm). | E | C | **P** |
| 7 | 3 | 6 | **TWO**, with: | E | C | **P** |
| 7 | 3 | 6 | 1 | **NO** knots, pitch streaks, or pitch pockets within 48" (1219 mm) of one another. | E | C | **P** |
| 7 | 4 | | The following **NATURAL CHARACTERISTICS**: | | | | |
| 7 | 4 | 1 | **BARK POCKET** - None. | | | | |
| 7 | 4 | 2 | **BIRDSEYE**, Sound - Unlimited. | | | | |
| 7 | 4 | 3 | **BIRDSEYE**, Checked: | | | | |
| 7 | 4 | 3 | 1 | Unlimited. | E | C | P |
| 7 | 4 | 3 | 2 | ≤ 10% of face. | E | **C** | P |
| 7 | 4 | 3 | 3 | None. | E | C | **P** |

Continues next column ▼

# SECTION 3
## Lumber

**GENERAL PRODUCT** — compliance requirements

Where the **E**, **C**, or **P** icon is not indicated, the rule applies to all Grades equally | **E** | **C** | **P** |

### 3.4.7 Softwood Material Rules

▲ From previous column

| | | | | | E | C | P |
|---|---|---|---|---|---|---|---|
| 7 | | **TRANSPARENT FINISH** (continued) | | | | | |
| 7 | 4 | The following **NATURAL CHARACTERISTICS** (continued) | | | | | |
| 7 | 4 | 4 | **BURL**, Sound: | | | | |
| 7 | 4 | 4 | 1 | ≤ 3/4" (19 mm) in diameter. | E | C | P |
| 7 | 4 | 4 | 2 | ≤ 5/8" (16 mm) in diameter. | E | **C** | P |
| 7 | 4 | 4 | 3 | ≤ 1/2" (13 mm) in diameter. | E | C | **P** |
| 7 | 4 | 5 | **CHECK:** | | | | |
| 7 | 4 | 5 | 1 | ≤ 3/32" (2 mm) wide x 8" (203 mm) long. | **E** | C | P |
| 7 | 4 | 5 | 2 | ≤ 1/16" (2 mm) wide x 6" (152 mm) long. | E | **C** | P |
| 7 | 4 | 5 | 3 | ≤ 1/32" (1 mm) wide x 4" (102 mm) long. | E | C | **P** |
| 7 | 4 | 6 | **HONEYCOMB** - None. | | | | |
| 7 | 4 | 7 | **KNOT**, Sound and Tight: | | | | |
| 7 | 4 | 7 | 1 | ≤ 3/4" (19 mm) in diameter. | **E** | C | P |
| 7 | 4 | 7 | 2 | ≤ 1/2" (13 mm) in diameter. | E | **C** | P |
| 7 | 4 | 7 | 3 | ≤ 1/4" (6 mm) in diameter. | E | C | **P** |
| 7 | 4 | 8 | **KNOT**, Checked: | | | | |
| 7 | 4 | 8 | 1 | ≤ 1/2" (13 mm) in diameter. | **E** | C | P |
| 7 | 4 | 8 | 2 | ≤ 1/4" (6 mm) in diameter. | E | **C** | P |
| 7 | 4 | 8 | 3 | None. | E | C | **P** |
| 7 | 4 | 9 | **KNOT**, Open - None. | | | | |
| 7 | 4 | 10 | **MINERAL STAIN:** | | | | |
| 7 | 4 | 10 | 1 | Unlimited. | **E** | C | P |
| 7 | 4 | 10 | 2 | ≤ 10% of face. | E | **C** | P |
| 7 | 4 | 10 | 3 | None. | E | C | **P** |
| 7 | 4 | 11 | **PATCH:** | | | | |
| 7 | 4 | 11 | 1 | ≤ 1-1/2" (38 mm) wide x 3-1/2" (89 mm) long, and inconspicuous from 60". | **E** | C | P |
| 7 | 4 | 11 | 2 | ≤ 1-1/2" (38 mm) wide x 3-1/2" (89 mm) long, and inconspicuous from 36". | E | **C** | P |
| 7 | 4 | 11 | 3 | None. | E | C | **P** |
| 7 | 4 | 12 | **PITCH POCKET** or **STREAK:** | | | | |
| 7 | 4 | 12 | 1 | ≤ 1/16" (2 mm) wide x 6" (152 mm) long or 1/8" (3 mm) wide x 4" (102 mm) long. | **E** | C | P |
| 7 | 4 | 12 | 2 | ≤ 1/16" (2 mm) wide x 3" (76 mm) long or 1/8" (3 mm) wide x 2" (51 mm) long. | E | **C** | P |
| 7 | 4 | 12 | 3 | None. | E | C | **P** |
| 7 | 4 | 13 | **SAPWOOD**, in unselected species - Unlimited. | | | | |
| 7 | 4 | 14 | **SAPWOOD**, in All Heart Redwood - None. | | | | |

Continues next column ▼

### 3.4.7 Softwood Material Rules

▲ From previous column

| | | | | | E | C | P |
|---|---|---|---|---|---|---|---|
| 7 | | **TRANSPARENT FINISH** (continued) | | | | | |
| 7 | 4 | The following **NATURAL CHARACTERISTICS** (continued) | | | | | |
| 7 | 4 | 15 | **SHAKE:** | | | | |
| 7 | 4 | 15 | 1 | ≤ 1/8" (3 mm) wide x 3" (76 mm) long. | **E** | C | P |
| 7 | 4 | 15 | 2 | ≤ 1/16" (2 mm) wide x 2" (51 mm) long. | E | **C** | P |
| 7 | 4 | 15 | 3 | None. | E | C | **P** |
| 7 | 4 | 16 | **SPLIT:** | | | | |
| 7 | 4 | 16 | 1 | ≤ 1/16" (2 mm) wide x 6" (152 mm) long. | **E** | C | P |
| 7 | 4 | 16 | 2 | ≤ 1/32" (1 mm) wide x 4" (102 mm) long. | E | **C** | P |
| 7 | 4 | 16 | 3 | None. | E | C | **P** |
| 7 | 4 | 17 | **STICKER BOARD DISCOLORATION:** | | | | |
| 7 | 4 | 17 | 1 | ≤ 10% of the face. | **E** | C | P |
| 7 | 4 | 17 | 2 | None. | E | **C** | P |
| 7 | 4 | 17 | 3 | None. | E | C | **P** |
| 7 | 4 | 18 | **WORM HOLES:** | | | | |
| 7 | 4 | 18 | 1 | ≤ 1/8" (3 mm) in diameter. | **E** | C | P |
| 7 | 4 | 18 | 2 | ≤ 1/16" (2 mm) in diameter. | E | **C** | P |
| 7 | 4 | 18 | 3 | None. | E | C | **P** |

**Applicable TESTS, may be found in Sections 6 - 11; however, these tests are only applicable to the exposed and semi-exposed portions of installed millwork products.**

# Architectural Woodwork Standards

# SHEET PRODUCTS

### SECTION

4

# SECTION 4
## Sheet Products

## table of contents

### INTRODUCTORY INFORMATION

- Introduction ............................................................. 73
- Plywood .................................................................. 73
- Types of Panel ........................................................ 73
    - Industrial Grade Particleboard ........................... 73
    - Moisture Resistant Particleboard ....................... 73
    - Fire Retardant Particleboard .............................. 73
    - Medium Density Fiberboard (MDF) ..................... 73
    - Moisture Resistant MDF ..................................... 73
    - Veneer Core ........................................................ 73
    - Hardboard ........................................................... 74
    - Lumber Core ....................................................... 74
        - Staved ........................................................... 74
        - Full Length .................................................... 74
        - Banded .......................................................... 74
    - Agrifiber / Agrofiber ........................................... 74
    - Combination ...................................................... 74
    - Forming .............................................................. 74
    - Solid Phenolic .................................................... 74
    - Other Panel Material .......................................... 74
        - Engineered Wood/Panels .............................. 74
        - Bamboo ......................................................... 75
- Characteristics of Core Performance Table ............ 75
- Decorative Face Material and Construction Balance ........................... 75
- Types of Plywood Panels ........................................ 76
    - Particleboard Core ............................................. 76
    - Medium Density Fiberboard (MDF) Core ........... 76
    - Veneer Core ....................................................... 76
    - Lumber Core ....................................................... 76
    - Combination Core .............................................. 76
- Wood Veneers ........................................................ 76
    - Hardwood ........................................................... 76
    - Softwood ............................................................ 76
    - Veneer Grain ...................................................... 76
    - Figure ................................................................. 76
    - Special Characteristics ...................................... 76
    - Natural ................................................................ 76
    - Select Red or White ........................................... 76
- Species .................................................................. 76
    - Reconstituted Veneers ....................................... 76
- Speciality Sheet Products ...................................... 77
- Panel Adhesive ....................................................... 77
- Fire Retardance ...................................................... 77
- Photodegradation ................................................... 77
- Oxidation ................................................................. 77
- Types of Veneer Cuts ............................................. 77
    - Plain Slicing ........................................................ 77
    - Quarter Slicing .................................................... 77
    - Rift Slicing .......................................................... 78
    - Rotary Slicing ..................................................... 78
- Common Hardwood Veneer Species and Cuts Table ........................... 78
- Wood Veneer Species Table .................................. 79
- Product Advisory .................................................... 80
- Matching Adjacent Wood Veneer Leaves .............. 81
    - Book Matching .................................................... 81
    - Slip Matching ...................................................... 81
    - Random Matching .............................................. 81
    - End or Butt Matching ......................................... 81
- Matching Within Individual Panel Faces ................. 82
    - Running Match ................................................... 82
    - Balance Match .................................................... 82
    - Balance and Center Match ................................. 82
    - Slip, Center, Book Match ................................... 82
- Speciality or Sketch Matches of Wood Veneers ..... 83
    - Sunburst Match .................................................. 83
    - Box Match ........................................................... 83
    - Reverse or End Grain Box Match ....................... 83
    - Herringbone or V Book Match ............................ 83
    - Diamond Match ................................................... 83
    - Reverse Diamond Match .................................... 84
    - Parquet Match .................................................... 84
    - Swing Match ....................................................... 84
    - Book and Butt Match .......................................... 84
- Matches Between Panels ....................................... 84
    - Not Matched ....................................................... 84
    - Sequence Matched ............................................ 84

# SECTION 4
## Sheet Products

## table of contents

### INTRODUCTORY INFORMATION (continued)

- Sequence Matched & Custom Width .................. 84
- Blueprint Matched .................. 84
- Decorative Laminate Overlays and Prefinished Panel Products .......... 85
  - Medium Density Overlay (MDO) .................. 85
  - High Density Overlay (HDO) .................. 85
  - Thermoplastic Sheet .................. 85
  - Vinyl Films .................. 85
  - High Pressure Decorative Laminate (HPDL) .................. 85
  - Low Pressure Decorative Laminate (LPDL) .................. 85
    - Melamine .................. 85
    - Polyester .................. 85
- Common HPDL Types .................. 85
  - General Purpose .................. 85
  - Vertical .................. 85
  - Postforming .................. 85
  - Cabinet Liner .................. 85
  - Backing Sheet .................. 85
  - Flame Retardant .................. 86
- Color Through Laminates .................. 86
- Solid Phenolic Core (SPC) .................. 86
- Static Dissipative Laminates .................. 86
- Chemical Resistant Decorative Laminates .................. 87
- Metal Faced Laminates .................. 87
- Flame Spread Rating of Laminates .................. 87
- Natural Wood Laminates .................. 87
- Specialty Sheet Products .................. 87
- Solid Surfaces .................. 88
- Other Core Products .................. 88
- Specify Requirements For .................. 88
- Recommendations .................. 88

### COMPLIANCE REQUIREMENTS

#### GENERAL
- Basic Considerations .................. 89
  - Grades .................. 89
  - Classifications .................. 89
  - Panel Association Grades .................. 89
  - Sheet Product Requirements .................. 89
  - Contract Documents .................. 89
  - Low Density Fiberboard .................. 89
  - Continuous Pressure Laminates .................. 89
  - Industry Practices .................. 89
    - Panel Grain Direction .................. 89

#### PRODUCT
- Scope .................. 90
- Default Stipulation .................. 90
- Rules .................. 90
  - Errata .................. 90
  - Basic Rules .................. 90
    - Aesthetic .................. 90
    - Grain Direction .................. 90
    - Species .................. 90
    - Reference Standards .................. 90
    - Panel Layup .................. 90
    - Thickness Tolerance .................. 91
    - Squareness Tolerance .................. 91
    - Straightness Tolerance .................. 91
    - Cathedral .................. 91
  - Hardwood Veneer Material Rules .................. 91
    - Applies To .................. 91
    - Core .................. 91
    - Veneer .................. 91
    - Edges .................. 91
    - Backing Species .................. 91
    - Figure .................. 91
    - Natural .................. 91
    - Grain .................. 91
    - Rift Grain Oak .................. 91

# SECTION 4
## Sheet Products

## table of contents

**COMPLIANCE REQUIREMENTS** (continued)

**PRODUCT** (continued)

Rules (continued)

Hardwood Veneer Material Rules (continued)
- Veneer Face Grade Requirements ................................... 91
- Veneer Face Grade Descriptions ..................................... 92
- Terminology Definitions .................................................. 93
- Allowable Face Grade Characteristics Tables .................. 94
  - Ash, Beech, Birch, Maple, and Poplar ....................... 95
  - Mahogany (African or American), Anigre, Makore, and Sapele ............................................. 96
  - Red and White Oak ................................................. 97
  - Pecan and Hickory .................................................. 98
  - Walnut and Cherry .................................................. 99

Softwood Veneer Material Rules ........................................... 100
- Applies To ....................................................................... 100
- Type I Adhesive .............................................................. 100
- Core ................................................................................ 100
- Vertical Grain ................................................................. 100
- Transparent Finish ......................................................... 100
- Face Grade Descriptions ................................................ 100
- Allowable Face Grade Characteristics Tables ................ 100
  - Western Red Cedar, White Pine, Vertical Grain Douglas Fir/Redwood ............................................ 101
  - Rotary Cut Douglas Fir ............................................ 102

HPDL Material Rules ............................................................. 103
LPDL Material Rules ............................................................. 104
Vinyl Film Material Rules ...................................................... 104
MDO Material Rules ............................................................. 104
HDO Material Rules ............................................................. 104
Hardboard Material Rules .................................................... 104
Particleboard Material Rules ................................................ 105
Medium Density Fiberboard (MDF) Material Rules ............. 105
Balance Sheet Material Rules .............................................. 105
Backer Material Rules .......................................................... 105
Epoxy Resin Material Rules ................................................. 105
Natural Stone Material Rules ............................................... 105

Engineered Material Rules ................................................... 105
Solid Surface Material Rules ................................................ 106
Solid Phenolic Material Rules .............................................. 106

# SECTION 4
## Sheet Products

## introductory information

### INTRODUCTION

Section 4 is the second "material" section. This section includes a wide range of sheet goods, Hardwood and Softwood Veneers, High Pressure Decorative Laminate, Overlays, Backers, Solid Surface, Solid Phenolic, Epoxy Resin, and Natural and Manufactured Stone. This section identifies common panel cores and panel surfaces referred to in subsequent product sections. It contains material rules specific to all of the sheet products the section covers.

Quality assurance can be achieved by adherence to the AWS and will provide the owner a quality product at competitive pricing. Use of a qualified Sponsor Member firm to provide your woodwork will help ensure the manufacturer's understanding of the quality level required. Illustrations in this Section are not intended to be all inclusive, other engineered solutions may be acceptable. In the absence of specifications; methods of fabrication are the manufacturer's choice. The design professional, by specifying compliance to the AWS increases the probability of receiving the product quality expected.

### PLYWOOD

The term "plywood" is defined as a panel manufactured of three or more layers (plies) of wood or wood products (veneers or overlays and/or core materials), generally laminated into a single sheet (panel).

### TYPES OF PANELS

There are a wide range of panel materials available for the fabrication of architectural woodwork.

Property and performance characteristics are influenced by the panel grade, panel thickness, and materials used for the core:

- Surface uniformity has a direct relationship to the performance of the face veneers.
- Dimensional stability relates to the effect of exposure to wide swings in temperature and relative humidity.
- Screw holding and bending strength are influenced by and should be considered in design engineering.

Architectural panels with applied decorative surface materials are made up of a variety of core types including: Particleboard, Medium Density Fiberboard (MDF), Veneer, Hardboard, Lumber, Combination and Agrifiber/Agrofiber.

### PRIMARY CORE MATERIALS

- **Industrial Grade Particleboard** - Sometimes referenced as composite core, is made of wood particles of various sizes that are bonded together with a synthetic resin or binder under heat and pressure.

Medium Density Industrial Particleboard is used in the broadest applications of architectural woodwork. It is especially well suited as a core for veneers and decorative laminates.

When used as panels without surface plies, the product is referred to as particleboard. When used as an inner core with outer wood veneers, the panel is referred to as particle core plywood.

Industrial particleboard is commercially classified by "density," which is measured by the weight per cubic foot of the panel product.

- Medium Density (M series) = generally between 40-50 pounds per ft$^3$ (640-800 kg per m$^3$).
- High Density (H series) = generally above 50 pounds per ft$^3$ (800 kg per m$^3$).

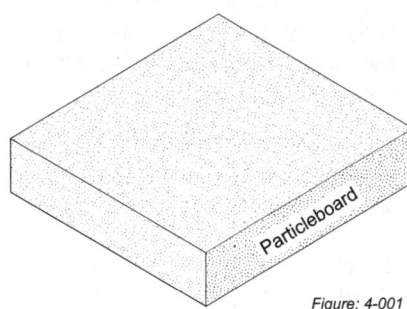

*Figure: 4-001*

- **Moisture resistant particleboard** - Some Medium Density Industrial Particleboard is bonded with resins more resistant to swelling when exposed to moisture. The most common grades are ANSI A-208.1 (latest edition) Type M-2-Exterior Glue and M-3-Exterior Glue.

- **Fire Retardant Particleboard** - Some Medium Density Industrial Particleboard has been treated during manufacture to carry a UL stamp for Class I flame spread rating (Flame spread 20, Smoke developed 450). Fire retardant Medium Density Fiberboard is also available.

- **Medium Density Fiberboard (MDF)** - Sometimes referenced as composite core, is made of wood particles reduced to fibers in a moderate pressure steam vessel, combined with a resin, and bonded together under heat and pressure.

- Due to the finer texture of the fibers used in manufacturing Medium Density Fiberboard (MDF) it is smoother than Medium Density Particleboard. The uniform texture and density of the fibers create a homogenous panel that is very useful as a core for paint, thin overlay materials, veneers and decorative laminates. MDF is among the most stable of the mat formed panel products. When used as an inner core with outer wood veneers, the panel is referred to as MDF core plywood.

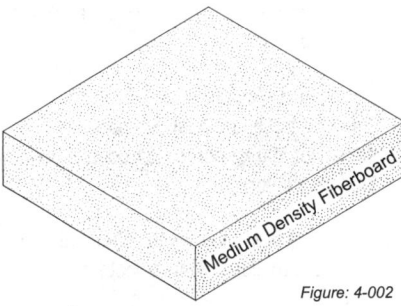

*Figure: 4-002*

- **Moisture Resistant Mdf** - Can be manufactured to meet the ANSI A-208.2 (latest edition) reduced thickness swell criteria.

- **Veneer** - Is separated into two groups according to materials and manufacturing:
  - **Hardwood Veneer** - Panels manufactured of hardwood veneers.
  - **Softwood Veneer** - Panels manufactured of softwood veneers.

Hardwood or Softwood Veneers used as a core is not recommended in many areas of the AWS due to poor stability, but do have many other structural characteristics. It is recommended that veneer core panels be used only when they can be housed or in areas where warping in not a significant issue.

# SECTION 4
## Sheet Products

### introductory information

**PRIMARY CORE MATERIALS** (continued)

- **Veneer** (continued)

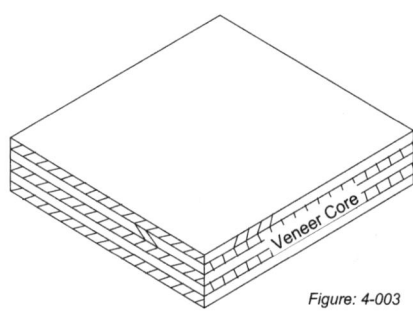

*Figure: 4-003*

What many think of as traditional "plywood", is a panel core made up of an odd number of plies, 3 or more (except when the center is constructed of two unidirectional plies), alternating layers of veneers, all less than 1/4" (6.4 mm) thick, pressed and glued into a single sheet. The two outside veneer layers are the Face and Back. The interior veneer bands are cross bands and parallel bands. The latter is sometimes referenced as centers. Veneer bands are layered at right angles to the adjoining veneer layer.

- **Hardboard** - Is defined as inter felted fibers consolidated under heat and pressure to a density of 500 kg per m³ (31 pounds per cubic foot) or greater.

Hardboard is available with either one side (S1S) or two sides (S2S) smooth.

There are typically two types of hardboard core used by architectural manufacturers:

- Standard (untempered).

- Tempered, which is standard hardboard subjected to a curing treatment increasing its stiffness, hardness, and weight.

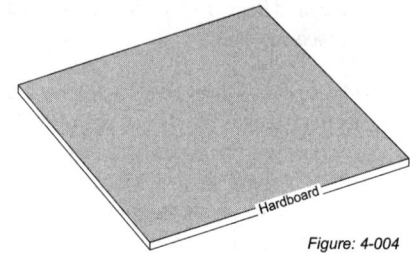

*Figure: 4-004*

- **Lumber** - Is where the center ply, called the "core" is composed of strips of lumber edge glued into a solid slab. This type is usually 5-ply, 3/4" (19 mm) thick, but other thickness from 1/2" (12.7 mm) to 1-1/8" (28.6 mm) are manufactured for special uses. There are three main types:

  - Staved - is where the core strips are random length and butt joined.

  - Full Length - is where the core strips are one piece in length.

  - Banded - is where the outside strips run full length and the others are random length. Banding may be the same species of lumber as the rest of the core, but it is usually matched to the face and might include all four edges. Banded plywood is typically produced for special uses, such as furniture, desk tops, and cabinet doors.

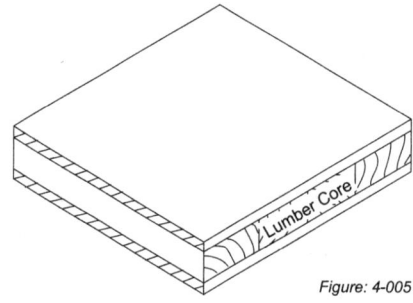

*Figure: 4-005*

- **Agrifiber/Agrofiber** - Panel products made from straw and similar fiber are appearing in the marketplace. Panels shall meet the performance characteristics of ANSI A208.1 or ANSI A208.2 standards.

The characteristics of agrifiber/agrofiber core material performance vary by manufacturer, and are not included in the following table.

- **Combination** - A balanced hybrid blend of veneer and composition core materials offering some of the properties of both. Typically these cores have internal layers which are constructed of three or five plies of veneer or a center layer of wafer board (randomly oriented wafers) or other wood fiber which are sandwiched between thin laminations of a composite product like MDF, particleboard, hardboard, etc.

Typically these products result in stronger, lighter weight, dimensionally stable panels with increased screw holding ability, and superior surface flatness. Combination panels shall meet the standards of particleboard or MDF as stated in this manual, density excepted.

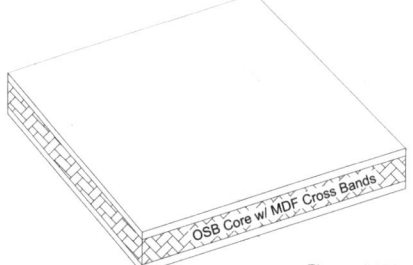

*Figure: 4-006*

- **Forming (Bendable)** - Assembled and/or machined cores made of hardboard, veneer, particleboard and/or MDF for radius work are manufactured under various trade names. When used for freestanding work these Forming Cores must be a balanced panel but if bound (restrained) the panel is not required to be balanced.

- **Solid Phenolic (SP)** - A composite of solid phenolic resins molded with a homogeneous core of organic fiber reinforced phenolic and one or more integrally cured surfaces of compatible thermoset nonabsorbent resins. SP has seen some use in recent years as wall surfacing, casework parts, and countertops.

- **Other Panel Material** - Shall meet the minimum performance characteristics of ANSI A208.1, ANSI A208.2 or ANSI/HPVA HP-1 (latest edition) standards.

  - Engineered Wood/Panel - Is a general term used to describe any wood or plant fiber composite panel. Such products as Particleboard, MDF, SCL and LVL are described as an engineered wood or plant fiber. Typically they are made from wood or plant fiber or wood pieces and have specific esthetic and physical attributes.

# SECTION 4
## Sheet Products

## introductory information

**PRIMARY CORE MATERIALS** (continued)

- **Other Panel Material** (continued)

  - **Bamboo** is a building material attracting much attention due to its quick replenishing and growing cycles as a green product. It is a grass product and not a true wood product. Due to its relatively new emergence in use as a building material, the performance evaluation as a stable and viable building material has not been established. The Architectural Woodwork Standards does not cover or endorse the use of bamboo and encourages the design professional to consult with Bamboo manufacturers and distributors as to its characteristics and viability as an architectural millwork product.

*Table: 4-007* - **CHARACTERISTICS OF CORE PERFORMANCE**

It is important for the reader to understand the difference between "flatness" and "dimensional stability" characteristics. Particleboard and MDF are the recommended cores for high pressure decorative laminate and wood veneer work because of their excellent flatness. Fair dimensional stability (expansion/contraction in panel size) is acceptable unless the product is exposed to wide swings in relative humidity, generally below 25% or above 55% with swings of more than 30 points.

| Core Type | Flatness (Warp Resistance) | Visual Edge Quality | Surface Uniformity | Dimensional Stability | Screw Holding Face | Bending Strength |
|---|---|---|---|---|---|---|
| Particleboard, Medium Density | Excellent | Good | Excellent | Fair | Fair | Good |
| Particleboard, Moisture Resistant | Excellent | Good | Good | Fair | Fair | Good |
| Particleboard, Fire Retardant | Excellent | Fair | Good | Fair | Fair | Good |
| Medium Density Fiberboard (MDF) | Excellent | Excellent | Excellent | Fair | Good | Good |
| MDF, Moisture Resistant | Excellent | Excellent | Excellent | Fair | Good | Good |
| MDF, Fire Retardant | Excellent | Excellent | Excellent | Fair | Good | Good |
| Veneer | Fair | Good | Fair | Excellent | Excellent | Excellent |
| Lumber | Good | Good | Good | Good | Excellent | Excellent |
| Combination | Good | Fair | Excellent | Good | Excellent | Excellent |

Various characteristics above are influenced by the grade and thickness of the core and specific gravity of the core species. Visual Edge Quality is rated before treatment with edgebands or fillers and Visual Edge Quality of lumber core assumes the use of "clear edge" grade. Surface Uniformity has a direct relationship to the performance of veneers placed over the surface. Dimensional Stability is usually related to exposure to wide swings in relative humidity. Screw Holding and Bending Strength are influenced by proper design and engineering.

### DECORATIVE FACE MATERIAL AND CONSTRUCTION BALANCE

All panels may be used as cores for the application of decorative faces (e.g. veneer, plastic laminate) to the face and back. The whole is referred to as a panel. The parts being a core covered by a face and a balancing back. To achieve balanced construction, panels must be an odd number of layers (plies) symmetrical from the center line; e.g., inner plies, except the innermost middle ply, should occur in pairs, using materials and adhesives on both sides that contract and expand, or are moisture permeable, at the same rate.

A ply may consist of a single veneer, particleboard, medium density fiberboard, or hardboard. Each pair of inner plies should be of the same thickness and direction of grain at 90 degrees. Each ply of each pair is placed on opposite sides of the innermost ply or layer, alternating grain directions from the center out. (Particleboard and MDF do not have a specific grain orientation).

The thinner the facing material, the less force it can generate to cause warping. The thicker the core, the more it can resist a warping movement or force.

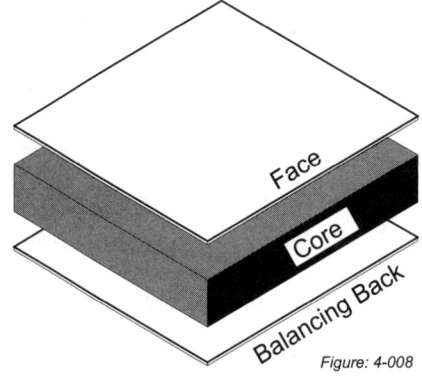

*Figure: 4-008*

# SECTION 4
## Sheet Products

## introductory information

### TYPES OF PLYWOOD PANELS:

- **Particleboard Core**

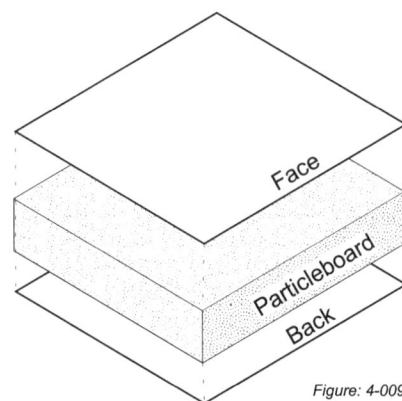

*Figure: 4-009*

- **Medium Density Fiberboard (MDF) Core**

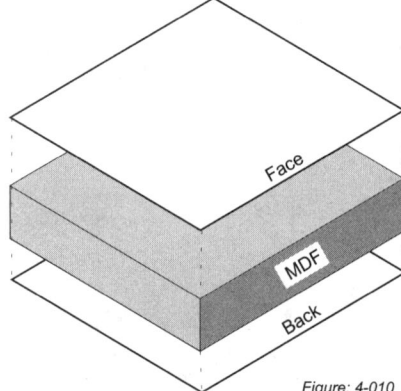

*Figure: 4-010*

- **Veneer Core**

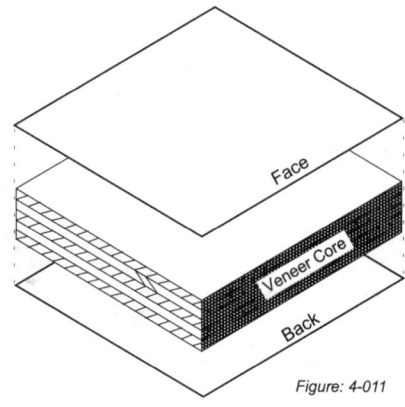

*Figure: 4-011*

- **Lumber Core**

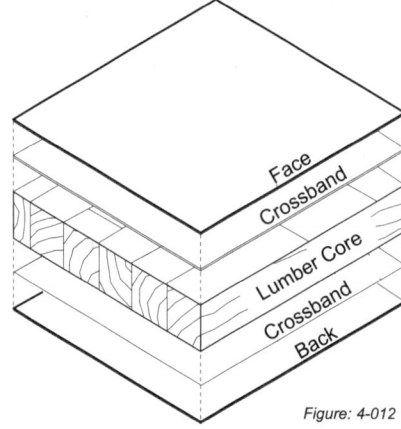

*Figure: 4-012*

- **Combination Core**

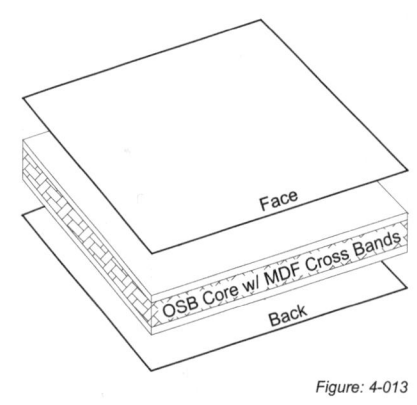

*Figure: 4-013*

### WOOD VENEERS

Wood veneer is produced by veneer manufacturers in a variety of "industry standard" thicknesses. The slicing process is controlled by a number of variables. The thickness of the raw veneer has little bearing on the ultimate quality of the end product so long as show-through and sand-through is avoided.

- **Hardwood Veneer - Species**: Available in many domestic and imported wood species. Normally cut as plain sliced. Rift sliced and quarter sliced available in certain species at additional cost.

- **Softwood Veneer - Species**: Most common is Douglas Fir; Pines are available; other softwoods in limited supply. Most softwood veneer is Rotary cut. Plain sliced softwood veneer and "vertical grain" (quarter sliced) softwood veneer are limited in availability with long lead times and higher prices associated with special orders.

  Rotary-cut softwood sheets are typically manufactured in various grades referring to the appearance of the face, back, and interior plies of the sheet and are intended for exterior (with a fully waterproof glue line) or interior (with a moisture resistant, but not waterproof, glue line). Clear faces, free of patches, are not typically available.

- **Veneer Grain** might not match the grain of solid stock, and it might not accept transparent finishes in the same manner; additional finishing steps might achieve similar aesthetic value.

- **Figure** is not a function of a species grade, and special desires must be so specified.

- **Special Characteristics**, such as sapwood, heartwood, ribbon stripe, birdseye and comb grain, must be so specified.

- **Natural,** as a type of wood species selection, allows an unlimited amount of heartwood and/or sapwood within a face and is the default selection, unless specified otherwise.

- **Select Red or White** simply means all heartwood or all sapwood, respectively, and must be so specified.

- **Species**, such as Hickory, Pecan, Butternut, or Maple, may exhibit special character or figure and users are advised to thoroughly investigate the expected grain and color of these species.

- **Reconstituted Veneers** are logs that are first sliced into veneer leaves, the leaves may be dyed, then glued under pressure in a mold to produce a large laminated block. The laminated block is then sliced across the glue line to create a faux grain with a designed appearance that is highly repeatable. Not all pre-dyed veneers are colorfast, consult with manufacturer.

# SECTION 4
## Sheet Products

## introductory information

### SPECIALTY SHEET PRODUCTS

Plywood with textured faces, prefinished plywood, overlaid plywood, composition sheets, flame spread rated plywood, moisture resistant plywood, lead lined sheets, projectile resistant armor (bullet proofing), reconstituted veneers, bamboo sheets, acrylic sheets, or PVC sheets are the products of the individual manufacturer, and are covered by their manufacturer's specification - not by these standards.

### PANEL ADHESIVES

Are defined as:
- **Type I** Waterproof bond for limited exterior use (2 Cycle Boil Test plus Shear Test).
- **Type II** Water resistant bond for interior use (3 Cycle Soak Test).

### FIRE RETARDANCE

Sheets are available with various types of fire retardant treated core, such as veneer, lumber, particleboard, and mineral core.

Flame-spread rating will vary for different species of untreated face veneers on treated cores, directly with the density of the untreated face veneers; the higher the density, the higher the flame spread rating.

Refer to the latest edition of the Underwriters' Laboratories listings for various flame-spread ratings available bearing U.L. Labels.

### PHOTODEGRADATION

The effect on the appearance of exposed wood faces caused by exposure to both sun and artificial light sources is called photodegration. If an entire face is exposed to a light source, it will photodegrade somewhat uniformly and hardly be noticeable, whereas partially exposed surfaces or surfaces with shadow lines might show nonuniform photodegradation. Some woods, such as American Cherry and Walnut, are more susceptible than others, and extra care should be taken to protect against the effects of nonuniform photodegradation.

### OXIDATION

The effect on the appearance of exposed wood faces caused by exposure to atmosphere is called oxidation. This is analogous to browning reactions in freshly cut fruit; for instance, apples. Hardwoods can develop deep yellow to reddish brown discolorations on the surface of the wood when exposed to air immediately after sawing or peeling. These discolorations are especially noticeable on Cherry, Birch, Red Alder, Sycamore, Oak, Maple, and Sweet Gum. Some species, such as Alder, Oak, Birch, and Maple, develop these discolorations during air-seasoning. A related gray stain on several varieties of Southern Oaks also appears to be oxidative in nature. Proper selection, sanding, and finishing can minimize the effects of oxidation.

### VENEER CUTTING

The manner in which a log segment is cut with relation to the annual rings will determine the appearance of the veneer. When sliced, the individual pieces of veneer, referred to as leaves, are kept in the order in which they are sliced, thus permitting a natural grain progression when assembled as veneer faces. The group of leaves from one slicing is called a flitch and is usually identified by a flitch number and the number of gross square feet of veneer it contains. The faces of the leaves with relation to their position in the log are identified as the tight face (toward the outside of the log) and the loose face (toward the inside or heart of the log). During slicing the leaf is stressed on the loose face and compressed on the tight face. When this stress is combined with the natural variation in light refraction caused by the pores of the wood, the result is a difference in the human perception of color and tone between tight and loose faces.

### FOUR COMMON VENEER CUTS

- **Plain Slicing** (or Flat Slicing) - This is the slicing method most often used to produce veneers for architectural woodwork. Slicing is done parallel to a line through the center of the log. A combination of cathedral and straight grain patterns results, with a natural progression of pattern from leaf to leaf.

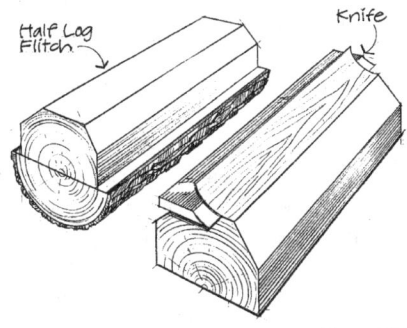

Figure: 4-014

- **Quarter Slicing** (or Quarter Cut) - Quarter slicing simulates the quarter sawing process of solid lumber, roughly parallel to a radius line through the log segment. In many species the individual leaves are narrow as a result. A series of stripes is produced, varying in density and thickness from species to species. "Fleck" (sometimes called flake) is a characteristic of this slicing method in Red and White Oak.

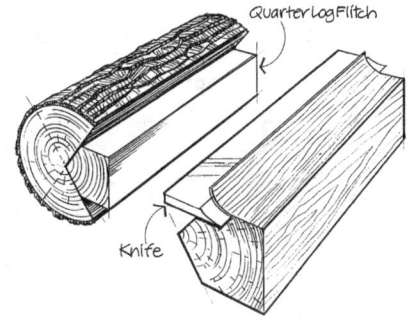

Figure: 4-015

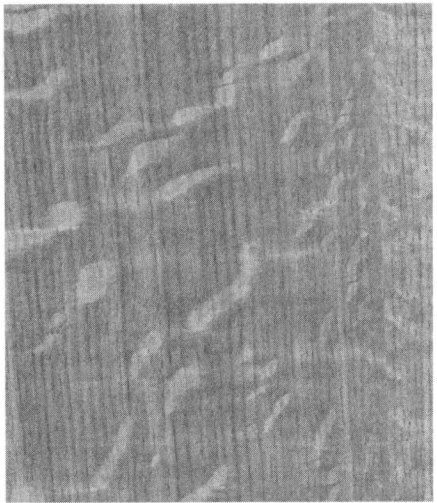

Figure: 4-016

# SECTION 4
## Sheet Products

## introductory information

- **Rift Slicing** (or Rift Cut) - Rift veneers are produced most often in Red and White Oak. Note that rift veneers and rift sawn solid lumber are produced so differently that a "match" between rift veneers and rift sawn solid lumber is highly unlikely. In both cases the cutting is done slightly off the radius lines minimizing the "fleck" (sometimes called flake) associated with quarter slicing.

- **Rotary Slicing** - The log is center mounted on a lathe and "peeled" along the general path of the growth rings like unwinding a roll of paper, providing a generally bold random appearance.

When transparent finish is specified; rotary sliced hardwood veneers are sometimes specified for:

- Wall Surfacing: Institutional panel faces.
- Doors: Institutional flush door faces.
- Cabinets: Semi-exposed (interior) surfaces and used in a limited way for exposed surfaces.

Some species may possess a special figure, for example birds eye, which is achieved by rotary slicing.

Careful consideration, specification, and communication are recommended when rotary cut is contemplated.

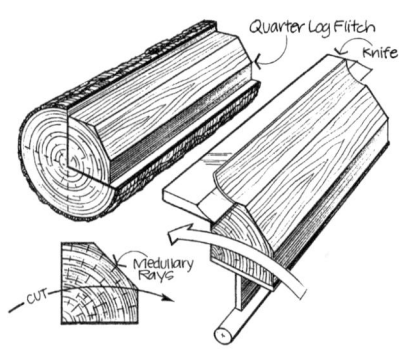

*Figure: 4-017*

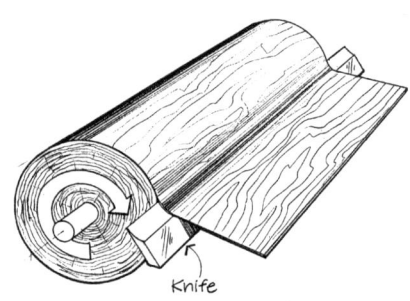

*Figure: 4-018*

*Table: 4-019* - **COMMON HARDWOOD VENEER SPECIES and CUTS**

| SPECIES | ROTARY | PLAIN SLICED | QUARTER SLICED | RIFT |
|---|:---:|:---:|:---:|:---:|
| Anigre |  | ● | ● |  |
| Ash |  | ● | ● |  |
| Beech |  | ● | ● |  |
| Birch | ● | ● |  |  |
| Cherry |  | ● | ● |  |
| Hickory |  | ● |  |  |
| Lauan | ● |  | ● |  |
| Mahogany, African |  | ● | ● |  |
| Mahogany, American |  | ● | ● |  |
| Makore |  | ● | ● |  |
| Maple | ● | ● | ● |  |
| Oak, Red | ● | ● | ● | ● |
| Oak, White |  | ● | ● | ● |
| Pecan |  | ● |  |  |
| Poplar | ● | ● |  |  |
| Sapele |  | ● | ● |  |
| Walnut |  | ● | ● |  |

# SECTION 4
## Sheet Products

## introductory information

*Table: 4-020 -* **WOOD VENEER SPECIES** - General characteristics of selected species:

| WOOD VENEER SPECIES - General characteristics of selected species: | | | | | | |
|---|---|---|---|---|---|---|
| **SPECIES** | **CUT (1)** | **WIDTH TO** | **LENGTH** | **FLITCH SIZE** | **COST (2)** | **AVAILABILITY** |
| Alder | Plain Sliced | 12" (305 mm) | 10' (3048 mm) | Medium | Moderate | Moderate |
| Anigre | Plain Sliced | 12" (305 mm) | 10' (3048 mm) | Large | Moderate | Good |
| Anigre | Quarter Sliced | 8" (203 mm) | 12' (3658 mm) | Medium | High | Good |
| Anigre, Figured | Quarter Sliced | 8" (203 mm) | 12' (3658 mm) | Medium | Very High | Limited |
| Ash, American | Plain Sliced | 12" (305 mm) | 10' (3048 mm) | Large | Moderate | Moderate |
| Ash, American | Quarter Sliced | 6" (153 mm) | 10' (3048 mm) | Medium | High | Moderate |
| Ash, European | Plain Sliced | 10" (254 mm) | 10' (3048 mm) | Medium | Moderate | Limited |
| Ash, European | Quarter Sliced | 6" (153 mm) | 10' (3048 mm) | Small | Moderate | Moderate |
| Beech, European | Plain Sliced | 10" (254 mm) | 10' (3048 mm) | Large | Moderate | Good |
| Beech, European | Quarter Sliced | 6" (153 mm) | 10' (3048 mm) | Medium | High | Good |
| Birch, Natural | Rotary | 36" (914 mm) | 10' (3048 mm) | Large | Low | Good |
| Birch, Natural | Plain Sliced | 8" (203 mm) | 10' (3048 mm) | Small | Medium | Limited |
| Birch, Select Red and White | Rotary | 36" (914 mm) | 10' (3048 mm) | Large | Moderate | Good |
| Birch, Select Red and White | Plain Sliced | 8" (203 mm) | 10' (3048 mm) | Small | High | Limited |
| Cedar, Western Red | Plain Sliced | 18" (457 mm) | 10' (3048 mm) | Medium | Moderate | Limited |
| Cedar, Western Red | Quarter Sliced | 8" (203 mm) | 10' (3048 mm) | Medium | Moderate | Limited |
| Cherry, American (3) | Plain Sliced | 12" (305 mm) | 12' (3658 mm) | Medium | Moderate | Good |
| Cherry, American (3) | Quarter Sliced | 6" (153 mm) | 10' (3048 mm) | Small | High | Moderate |
| Ebony | Plain Sliced | 6" (153 mm) | 10' (3048 mm) | Very Small | Extreme | Very Limited |
| Fir, Douglas (Vertical Grain) | Quarter Sliced | 18" (457 mm) | 12' (3658 mm) | Large | Moderate | Good |
| Hickory | Plain Sliced | 12" (305 mm) | 12' (3658 mm) | Medium | Moderate | Good |
| Hickory | Quarter Sliced | 6" (153 mm) | 10' (3048 mm) | Small | Moderate | Moderate |
| Jatoba | Plain Sliced | 12" (305 mm) | 12' (3658 mm) | Medium | Moderate | Good |
| Lacewood | Quarter Sliced | 6" (153 mm) | 10' (3048 mm) | Small | High | Very Limited |
| Lauan (4) | Plain Sliced | 15" (381 mm) | 12' (3658 mm) | Medium | Moderate | Good |
| Lauan (4) | Quarter Sliced | 8" (203 mm) | 10' (3048 mm) | Small | Moderate | Moderate |
| Mahogany, African (5) | Plain Sliced | 18" (457 mm) | 12' (3658 mm) | Large | Moderate | Good |
| Mahogany, African (5) | Quarter Sliced | 10" (254 mm) | 12' (3658 mm) | Medium | High | Moderate |
| Mahogany, American (5) (Swietenia macrophylla CITES listed (6)) | Plain Sliced | 18" (457 mm) | 12' (3658 mm) | Large | Moderate | Very Limited |
| Mahogany, American (5) (Swietenia macrophylla CITES listed (6)) | Quarter Sliced | 10" (254 mm) | 12' (3658 mm) | Medium | High | Very Limited |
| Makore | Plain Sliced | 15" (381 mm) | 12' (3658 mm) | Large | Moderate | Moderate |
| Makore | Quarter Sliced | 8" (203 mm) | 12' (3658 mm) | Medium | High | Limited |
| Maple, American | Rotary | 36" (914 mm) | 10' (3048 mm) | Large | Low | Good |
| Maple, American | Plain Sliced | 12" (305 mm) | 12' (3658 mm) | Medium | Moderate | Good (2) |
| Maple, American | Quarter Sliced | 6" (153 mm) | 10' (3048 mm) | Small | High | Limited |
| Maple, Birds Eye | Rotary | 24" (610 mm) | 10' (3048 mm) | Medium | Very High | Limited |
| Meranti | Plain Sliced | 18" (457 mm) | 12' (3658 mm) | Large | Moderate | Good |
| Meranti | Quarter Sliced | 10" (254 mm) | 12' (3658 mm) | Medium | High | Moderate |

# SECTION 4
## Sheet Products

## introductory information

*Table: 4-020 - WOOD VENEER SPECIES* (continued)

| SPECIES | CUT (1) | WIDTH TO | LENGTH | FLITCH SIZE | COST (2) | AVAILABILITY |
|---|---|---|---|---|---|---|
| Oak, English Brown | Plain Sliced | 12" (305 mm) | 10' (3048 mm) | Medium | High | Limited |
| | Quarter Sliced | 8" (203 mm) | 10' (3048 mm) | Small | Very High | Limited |
| Oak, Red | Rotary | 36" (914 mm) | 10' (3048 mm) | Large | Low | Good |
| | Plain Sliced | 18" (457 mm) | 12' (3658 mm) | Large | Low | Good |
| | Quarter Sliced | 8" (203 mm) | 10' (3048 mm) | Medium | Moderate | Good |
| | Rift | 8" (203 mm) | 10' (3048 mm) | Medium | Moderate | Good |
| Oak, White | Plain Sliced | 12" (305 mm) | 12' (3658 mm) | Medium | Low | Good |
| | Quarter Sliced | 8" (203 mm) | 10' (3048 mm) | Small | Moderate | Good |
| | Rift | 8" (203 mm) | 10' (3048 mm) | Small | Moderate | Good |
| Poplar | Plain Sliced | 15" (381 mm) | 10' (3048 mm) | Medium | Low | Good |
| Rosewood, American | Plain Sliced | 10" (254 mm) | 10' (3048 mm) | Small | Very High | Very Limited |
| Sapele | Plain Sliced | 15" (381 mm) | 10' (3048 mm) | Large | Moderate | Good |
| | Quarter Sliced | 8" (203 mm) | 10' (3048 mm) | Medium | Moderate | Moderate |
| Sycamore | Plain Sliced | 15" (381 mm) | 12' (3658 mm) | Medium | High | Moderate |
| | Quarter Sliced | 8" (203 mm) | 10' (3048 mm) | Small | High | Limited |
| Teak | Plain Sliced | 12" (305 mm) | 12' (3658 mm) | Medium | High | Moderate |
| | Quarter Sliced | 5" (127 mm) | 10' (3048 mm) | Small | High | Limited |
| Walnut (3) | Plain Sliced | 15" (381 mm) | 12' (3658 mm) | Large | Moderate | Good |
| | Quarter Sliced | 6" (152 mm) | 10' (3048 mm) | Small | High | Moderate |
| Wenge | Plain Sliced | 10" (254 mm) | 10' (3048 mm) | Small | High | Limited |

(1) When only Plain Sliced is listed, the width dimension for quartered Cut is narrower.
(2) Seasonal factors may affect availability.
(3) Cherry, Walnut and certain other hardwood species are required to be specified by origin, such as American Cherry, American Walnut, or English Brown Oak, because they can be significantly different in color and figure.
(4) Lauan (White and Red), Tanguile, and other species are native to the Philippine Islands and are sometimes referred to as Philippine Mahogany; however, they are not a true Mahogany The generic term Mahogany should not be specified without further definition.
(5) Mahogany, American and African vary in color from a light pink to a light red, reddish brown to a golden brown or yellowish tan. Some Mahogany turns darker or lighter in color after machining. The figure or grain runs from plain sliced, plain stripe to broken stripe, mottled, fiddleback, swirl, and crotches.
(6) CITES, Convention on International Trade in Endangered Species or Wild Fauna and Flora.

**PRODUCT ADVISORY:**

Due to adverse reaction of some veneers laminated to fire rated (FR), ultra low emitting formaldehyde (ULEF or NAUF), medium density fiberboard (mdf) causing discoloration of the wood veneer even months after installation, major core manufacturers have issued disclaimers in the use of FR cores. They strongly suggest that use of FR ULEF mdf and particleboard cores should be done after testing compatibility of adhesives, wood veneer and cores. Any resulting discoloration with the use of these cores may be exempt in their warranties. Use of FR ULEF cores should only be considered after consultation with the board supplier.

# SECTION 4
## Sheet Products

# introductory information

**MATCHING ADJACENT WOOD VENEER LEAVES**

It is possible to achieve certain visual effects by the manner in which the leaves are arranged. Matching of adjacent wood veneer leaves, as with the effect of different veneer cuts, can alter the appearance of a given panel or an entire installation. To create a particular appearance, the veneer leaves of a flitch are edge glued together in patterns.

Individual leaves of veneer in a sliced flitch increase or decrease in width as the slicing progresses. Thus, if a number of panels are manufactured from a particular flitch, the number of veneer leaves per panel face will change as the flitch is utilized. The manner in which these leaves are "laid up" within the panel requires specification.

Rotary cut veneers are difficult to match; therefore most matching is done with sliced veneers. The matching of adjacent veneer leaves must be specified. Special arrangements of leaves such as "diamond" and "box" matching are available. Consult your manufacturer for choices.

- **Book Matching** - A common match used in the industry. Every other piece of veneer is turned over so adjacent pieces (leaves) are opened like the pages of a book.

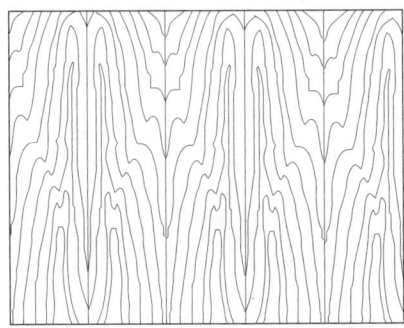

Figure: 4-021

Visual Effect - Veneer joints match, creating a symmetrical pattern. Yields maximum continuity of grain. When sequenced panels are specified, prominent characteristics will ascend or descend across the match as the leaves progress from panel to panel.

Barber Pole Effect in Book Match - Because the tight side and loose side of the veneer leaf faces alternate in adjacent pieces of veneer, they may accept stain differently, and this may result in a noticeable color variation. Book matching also accentuates cell polarization, causing the perception of different colors. These natural characteristics are often called barber pole, and are not a manufacturing defect.

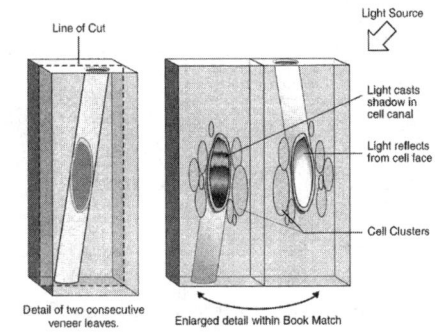

Figure: 4-022

- **Slip Matching** - Often used with quarter sliced and rift sliced veneers. Adjoining leaves are placed (slipped out) in sequence without turning, resulting in the same face sides being exposed.

Visual Effect - Grain figure repeats; but joints do not show visual grain match.

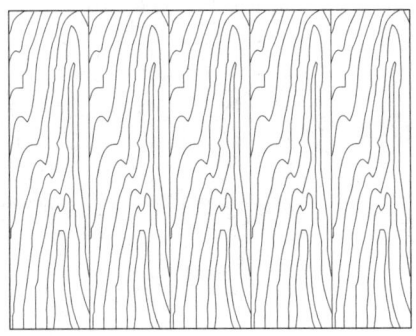

Figure: 4-023

The lack of grain match at the joints can be desirable. The relatively straight grain patterns of quartered and rift veneers generally produce pleasing results and a uniformity of color because all faces have the same light refraction.

- **Random Matching** - Veneer leaves are placed next to each other in a random order and orientation, producing a "board by board" effect in many species.

Visual Effect - Casual or rustic appearance, as though individual boards from a random pile were applied to the product. Conscious effort is made to mismatch grain at joints.

Degrees of contrast and variation may change from panel to panel. This match is more difficult to obtain than book or slip match, and should be clearly specified and detailed.

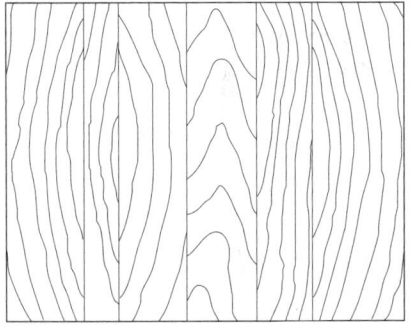

Figure: 4-024

- **End** or **Butt Matching** - Often used to extend the apparent length of available veneers for high wall panels and long conference tables.

Leaves are individually book (or slip) matched, first end to end and then side to side, alternating end and side.

Visual Effect - Yields best continuous grain patterns for length as well as width. Minimizes misalignment of grain pattern.

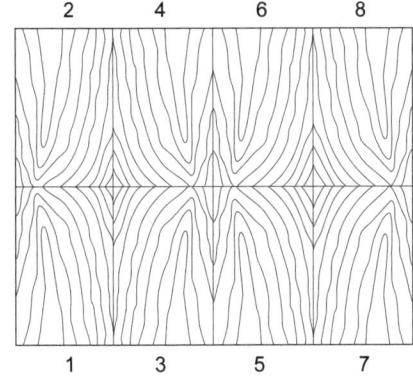

Figure: 4-025

Architectural Woodwork Standards

# SECTION 4
## Sheet Products

### introductory information

#### MATCHING WITHIN INDIVIDUAL PANEL FACES

The individual leaves of veneer in a sliced flitch increase or decrease in width as the slicing progresses. Thus, if a number of panels are manufactured from a particular flitch, the number of veneer leaves per panel face will change as the flitch is utilized. The manner in which these leaves are "laid up" within the panel requires specification, and is classified as follows:

- **Running Match** - The panel face is made from components running through the flitch consecutively. Any portion of a component left over from a face is used as the beginning component or leaf in starting the next panel. **This method is the default for Custom Grade.**

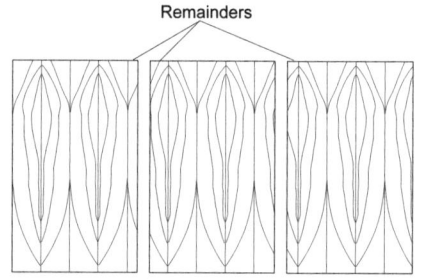

*Figure: 4-026*

- **Balance Match** - Each panel face is assembled from veneer leaves of uniform width before edge trimming. Panels may contain an even or odd number of leaves, and distribution may change from panel to panel within a sequenced set. While **this method is the default for Premium Grade,** it must be specified for other Grades, and it is the most common assembly method at moderate cost.

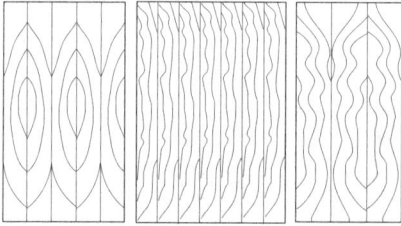

*Figure: 4-027*

- **Balance and Center Match** - Each panel face is assembled of an even number from veneer leaves of uniform width before edge trimming. Thus, there is a veneer joint in the center of the panel, producing horizontal symmetry. A small amount of figure is lost in the process. Considered by some to be the most pleasing assembly at a modest increase in cost over Balance Match.

*Figure: 4-028*

- **Slip, Center, Book Match** - Each panel face is assembled of an even (four or more) number of veneer leaves. The veneer leaves are laid out as a slip matched panel face; then at the center, one half of the leaves are booked to the other half. Quarter and rift sliced veneers are generally used for this match, which allows for a pleasing balance of sweep and character marks.

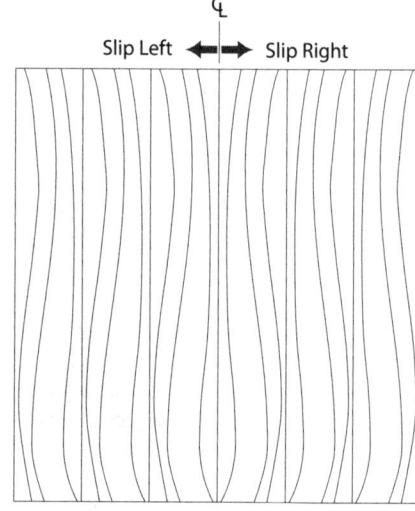

*Figure: 4-029*

# SECTION 4
## Sheet Products

## introductory information

### SPECIALTY OR SKETCH MATCHES OF WOOD VENEERS

There are regional variations in the "names" of the following veneer leaf matching techniques, drawn as squares for simplicity. It is strongly recommended that the design professional use both names and drawings to define the desired effect, using a rectangle, polygon, circle, ellipse, or other shape. Rift sliced, quarter sliced, and highly figured veneers are generally used for these speciality matches. The different matches of veneer cause the reflection of light to vary from adjoining leaves, bringing "life" to the panel. Due to the inherent nature of the layup process, alignment at corners might vary.

- **Sunburst Match** - is made of six or more veneer leaves cut at the appropriate angle with the grain radiating from the center. These veneer leaves are then book matched, assembled, and trimmed for final size.

*Figure: 4-030*

- **Box Match** - is made of four leaves with the grain running parallel to the perimeter of the panel. The leaves are cut at the appropriate angle and end matched.

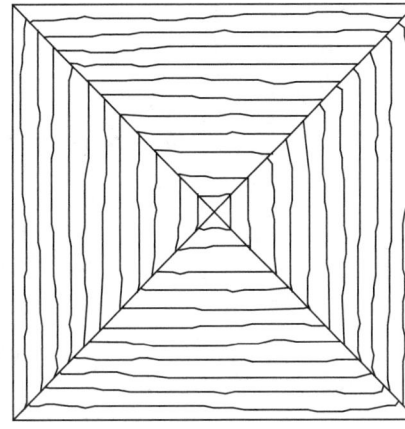

*Figure: 4-031*

- **Reverse or End Grain Box Match** - is made of four leaves with the grain running at right angles to the perimeter of the panel. The leaves are cut at the appropriate angle and book matched.

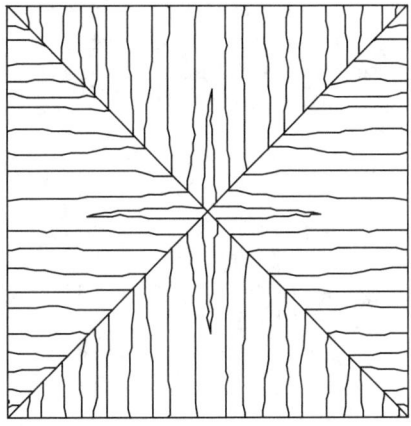

*Figure: 4-032*

- **Herringbone or V Book Match** - is one or more pairs of assembled slipped or booked leaves. Each assembled set of leaves is cut at generally 45 degrees to one edge of the panel. The assembled set of leaves is then end matched to the adjoining assembled set of leaves.

*Figure: 4-033*

- **Diamond Match** - is made of four leaves with the grain running 45 degrees to the perimeter of the panel and surrounding the center. The leaves are cut at the appropriate angle and end matched.

*Figure: 4-034*

# SECTION 4
## Sheet Products

### introductory information

- **Reverse Diamond Match** - is made of four leaves with the grain running 45 degrees to the perimeter of the panel and radiating from the center. The leaves are cut at the appropriate angle and book matched.

*Figure: 4-035*

- **Parquet Match** - is made by dividing the panel into multiple equal sized pieces and cutting the veneer to the same size. Each veneer leaf is joined at right angles to the adjoining piece of veneer.

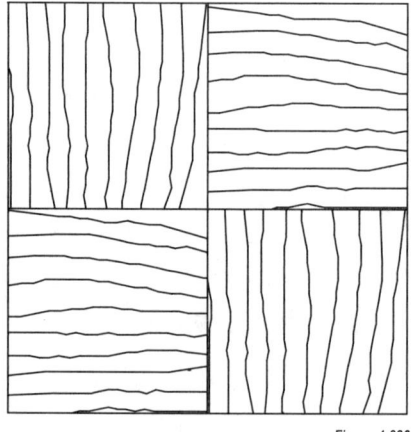

*Figure: 4-036*

- **Swing Match** - is made by dividing the panel into multiple paired sets. For each paired set, two leaves of veneer are cut at half the width of the set. One of these two veneer leaves is rotated 180 degrees and joined to the other. This pair is then adjoined to the other pairs assembled in the same way.

*Figure: 4-037*

- **Book** and **Butt Match** - is made by book matching highly figured veneer leaves (such as burl) 1, 3, 5, and 7 (set A) of the 8 leaf sequence. The remaining leaves 2, 4, 6, and 8 (set B) are also book matched. Set B is then flipped up and over the top end of set A, resulting in an end match.

*Figure: 4-038*

### MATCHES BETWEEN PANELS

- **Not Matched** - Veneered panels are generally manufactured without matching and may or may not be similar in grain and color.

- **Sequence Matched** - Veneered panels may be sourced and/or manufactured in sequence. These panels will be well matched for grain and color.

- **Sequence Matched & Custom Width** Generally veneered panels are manufactured in 4'x 8' and occasionally in 4'x 10' panels. The design professional may specify veneered sequence panels in custom width for the specific project and/or elevation. These panels will be well matched for grain and color.

- **Blueprint Matched** - The design professional may specify blueprint matched panels which will be custom sized height and width as well as sequencing for the specific project and/or elevation. These panels will be matched for grain and color.

# SECTION 4
## Sheet Products

## introductory information

### DECORATIVE LAMINATES, OVERLAYS, and PREFINISHED PANEL PRODUCTS

Decorative surfacing materials are often applied to wood product cores such as industrial particleboard, fiberboard, hardboard, etc. Terminology and definitions of these overlay products follow, broadly grouped as:

- **Medium Density Overlay (MDO)** - Pressed resin impregnated paper overlays, highly resistant to moisture, applied to suitable cores for both interior and exterior uses. The seamless panel face and uniform density furnishes a sound base for opaque finishes and paint.

- **High Density Overlay (HDO)** - Is a thermosetting phenolic resin impregnated, cellulose fiber overlay that provides a hard, smooth, uniformly textured surface of such character that further finishing is not necessary. Some evidence of underlying grain may appear.

- **Thermoplastic Sheet** - Semi rigid sheet or roll stock extruded from a nonporous acrylic/polyvinyl chloride (PVC) alloy solid color throughout. Withstands high impact. Minor scratches and gouges are less conspicuous due to the solid color.

- **Vinyl Films** - Polyvinyl chloride (PVC) film, either clear or solid color, used extensively for decorative vertical surfaces in mobile homes, recreational vehicles, commercial panels and movable walls. Some films are available with scuff resistant top coatings.

- **High Pressure Decorative Laminate (HPDL)** - Is a stand alone product that can be laminated onto a core as the face of a sheet product or directly onto a structure as a covering. Decorative laminate is produced in a one step process by fusing together, under heat and pressure, multiple layers of kraft paper saturated with phenolic resin, together with a layer of melamine saturated decorative paper.

The assembly offers resistance to wear and many common stains and chemicals. Common uses include casework exteriors, countertops, and wall paneling.

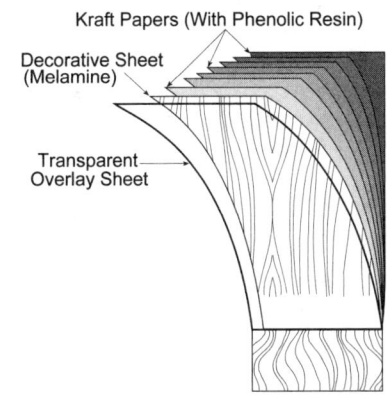

*Figure: 4-039*

Some decorative laminates utilize a white background paper to achieve the high fidelity, contrast, and depth of color in their printed patterns, which leaves a white line at the exposed edges of the laminate and can be extremely noticeable in darker colors.

- **Low Pressure Decorative Laminate (LPDL)** - Decorative thermally fused panels flat pressed from a thermoset polyester or melamine resin impregnated web. Most products are prelaminated to Industrial Particleboard or Medium Density Fiberboard cores when they arrive at the woodwork fabricator. Performance characteristics are similar to High Pressure decorative laminate except for the impact test.

Thermally fused papers and foils are similar to that used in the manufacture of decorative laminate. Saturated with reactive resins and partially cured during manufacture to allow for storage and handling, the papers achieve final curing when they are hot press laminated to a core, providing a hard, permanent thermoset bond between the paper and the core.

- Melamine - Impregnated papers, the most common, are noted for their hardness, scratch resistance, and color stability.

- Polyester - Impregnated papers are noted for their chemical, stain, water, and impact resistance; color clarity; and machinability.

### COMMON HPDL TYPES

The basic types form the majority of applications of high pressure decorative laminate in North America are:

- **General Purpose (HGS and HGL)** Used for most horizontal applications, such as desk tops and self-edged kitchen countertops, "HG" laminates offer durability, resistance to stains, and resistance to heat.

- **Vertical (VGS and VGL)** A slightly thinner material, "VG" laminates are produced for areas which will receive less wear and impact than typical horizontal materials. They are an excellent choice for cabinet doors, the sides of casework, primarily decorative display shelves and vertical panels.

- **Post-forming (HGP and VGP)** Specifically for applications where a radiused surface is desirable, "P" laminates offer strong performance in both horizontal and vertical applications.

A major advantage of formed surfaces on the exposed corners of casework and service counters is the edge's resistance to chipping damage. Most chip damage occurs at sharp 90° corners. Surfaces are thermoformed under controlled temperature and pressure.

- **Cabinet Liner (CLS)** A thin vertical sheet, this type is designed for areas where the surface, which is not considered decorative, generally white or off white in color, but will need to withstand less wear, such as the inside surfaces of cabinets and closets.

- **Backing Sheet (BKL)** Backing materials are essential in the fabrication of decorative laminate clad surfaces to prevent warping and to protect against dimensional instability of both laminate and core in conditions of changing temperature and humidity. Backing sheets are non decorative, and both economical and effective in the creation of a successful application. Produced without a decorative face and available as standard (slightly thinner than decorative) or regrind (reclaimed decorative laminate with decorative sheet sanded off).

# SECTION 4
## Sheet Products

## introductory information

### COMMON HPDL TYPES (continued)

- **Flame Retardant (HGF)** Some of these laminates are capable of providing flame retardant characteristics as determined by test methods required by the authority having jurisdiction. HGF is the most common type used.

In summary, these common decorative laminate types have the limitations of high pressure decorative laminate:

- They are for interior use only, and will not be successfully used outdoors or under heavy exposure to the ultraviolet rays of the sun.
- They should not be used as cutting surfaces, because knives and other sharp tools will readily deface the surface and lower its other performance capabilities.
- They should not be exposed to caustic chemicals, such as drain and toilet bowl cleaners, which can permanently etch the surface.
- While they offer outstanding heat resistance, exposure to constant heat from a curling iron, an electric skillet or coffee pot, for example can harm the surface and may cause it to delaminate, discolor or blister.

### COLOR THROUGH DECORATIVE LAMINATES

The interest in specifying solid color decorative laminates and the resurgence of interest in very pale pastels and neutral shades have caused increasing concern with the brown line visible at glued decorative laminate edges.

Color through decorative laminates were formulated specifically to provide light colors without this brown line.

Color through decorative laminate may be applied to cores in three basic ways:

- As sheets, to form a decorative face with a true monolithic look;
- As edge trims, to match a face of conventional decorative laminate or to accent a natural material such as wood or leather;
- As decorative inlays.

Color through decorative laminate is produced with multiple layers of decorative papers, rather than the decorative plus kraft composition of conventional laminate. As a result, this material is slightly stiffer and slightly more brittle when flexed.

Selection of adhesive should take into consideration that a visible glue line may detract. Adhesive should be untinted.

### SOLID PHENOLIC LAMINATES (SP).

High pressure decorative laminates are produced by several manufacturers in thicknesses adequate to preclude the use of a core (minimum 1/8" (3.2 mm).

Unlike conventional sheets, they may be drilled and tapped, and offer significant screw holding capacity.

Depending on thickness, these laminates may be used for many flat applications, such as toilet and dressing room partitions, workbenches, shelving, and table tops.

Panels are heavy for their size—an asset in sturdiness of the end application, but a factor which must be considered when planning for time and cost of labor and transportation as well as for support structures.

### STATIC-DISSIPATIVE LAMINATES

High pressure decorative laminate is a good electrical insulator—in fact, it was for the specific purpose of electrical insulation that the product was originally developed.

HPDL does not store static electricity, and it is therefore a suitable material for use in hospital areas, i.e.: operating rooms, X-ray rooms, and computer room controlled environments where the accumulation and retention of static electricity must be avoided.

However, the growing need for work surfaces in areas such as electronic clean rooms, where electrostatic charges must be actively, continuously channeled away, has triggered the development of specifically conductive (static-dissipative) laminates such as: Anti Static, Static Dissipative and Conductive.

These HPDL sheets have a conductive layer enclosed in, or backing, the sheet. Connected to suitable grounding, they create a decorative, sturdy, practical work surface. Applications include electronic workbench tops and work areas around instrument monitoring devices, in lab testing environments, around photo equipment and on computer desktops.

Antistatic laminates are produced in a number of compositions, thicknesses, colors and patterns. Consult manufacturers' literature for details.

# SECTION 4
## Sheet Products

## introductory information

### CHEMICAL-RESISTANT DECORATIVE LAMINATES

Chemical resistant HPDL offers the familiar advantages of HPDL: resistance to wear, conductive and radiant heat, and impact; as well as ease in cleaning, color fastness, and relatively light weight. Although this product may resist some chemicals, depending on the testing methods of the individual manufacture's, it is the design professional's responsibility to select the appropriate material for the chemical resistance required.

These laminates may be applied on vertical as well as horizontal surfaces, to extend protection to cabinet doors and sides. And they may be post-formed for seamless edges.

Adhesives should be specified carefully. Edges which may be exposed to chemical attack should be glued with chemical-resistant adhesives. Formulation of chemical-resistant decorative laminate differs from producer to producer. Consult product literature to make sure the material you specify meets the needs of your projects.

They are available in varying thicknesses and a number of color and patterns depending on manufacturer.

### METAL-FACED LAMINATES

High pressure decorative laminates are produced with metal veneers and a backer of kraft paper and phenolic resin.

The material used for much of the metal laminates is interior-type anodized aluminum. Other materials, including copper and nickel alloys may be specified in various formats; however, some metals, such as stainless steel or plated metal, are not conducive to machining with woodworking equipment.

### FLAME SPREAD RATING of DECORATIVE LAMINATES

Safer materials for interiors are a primary concern for commercial and institutional design professionals across North America. The threat of fire and its concomitant hazard of smoke has created a critical need for interior materials that address this concern without aesthetic sacrifice.

Manufacturers of decorative laminate materials offer fire and smoke retardant grades for interior application. The addition of fire retardant does not affect the performance characteristics of decorative laminate; wear and stain resistance, ease of maintenance, and color stability remain very strong.

Rated high pressure decorative laminates are evaluated and certified according to ASTM-E-84 test procedures (cataloged as ASTM-E-84 Tunnel Test; and as Test No. 723 by Underwriters Laboratories, Inc. Similar Canadian testing is cataloged as CAN4-512-79).

With appropriate choices of core and adhesive, panels clad with fire-rated decorative laminate may be produced to comply with Class 1, I, or A, fire codes. Finished panels, already certified, may also be specified from some decorative laminate manufacturers.

Major applications of rated decorative laminate include door, wall, and wainscot cladding in corridors, stairwells, entries, and elevators; as well as surfacing on fixtures and casework. These materials are supplied in both horizontal and vertical types, in a wide range of colors and patterns.

They may not be post-formed; the special formulation that produces fire retardant is not compatible with heat forming.

Adhesive choice for fire-rated decorative laminate is important. As with many types of fire retardant particleboard, some PVA adhesives are incompatible with the fire-retardant chemical composition of the decorative laminate material. Resorcinol adhesives are best for both chemical compatibility and flame spread rating of the end product. Contact adhesives do surprisingly well in some cases. Verify test ratings with your decorative laminate manufacturer.

### NATURAL WOOD LAMINATES

An excellent example of the ongoing evolution of the high pressure decorative laminate process. Presently, natural wood laminates may be specified in two formats; both feature thin veneers of woods bonded under high pressure and heat to a core of kraft papers and phenolic resins. One process leaves the face of the wood untreated, and ready to finish. The other adds a protective face of melamine resin.

Performance characteristics vary with the presence or absence of the melamine resin. In both cases, the ease of cutting and bonding, as well as the wear resistance, improve in comparison to raw wood veneer. With the melamine face, the natural wood assumes much of the easy care and long wear properties of conventional high pressure decorative laminate.

Sequence matching of natural wood laminate panels is extremely limited; consult the laminate manufacturer.

### SPECIAL SHEET PRODUCTS

Included in this classification are special panel products such as lead lined panels for X-ray areas, bullet resistant panels, honeycomb core panels when light weight is a consideration, etc.

- **Lead Lined Panels** - Usually a sheet of lead of a specified thickness, to meet X-ray shield requirements, is laminated between 2 layers of core material. A decorative overlay and balancing sheet can then be applied as required.

- **Bullet Resistant Panels** - Available as steel plate, glass, polycarbonate, acrylic or fiberglass reinforced material which can offer protection against many available small arms fire, depending upon the thickness specified. These panels are usually built into the interior of the structure of the counter, teller's lines, judge's benches, etc.

# SECTION 4
## Sheet Products

## introductory information

### SOLID SURFACE

Is a manufactured, filled cast polymeric resin panel. The fillers enhance both its performance properties and aesthetics. With a homogeneous composition throughout its thickness, solid surface requires no finish coat and is capable of being fabricated with inconspicuous seams and repaired to its original finish. Products (and manufacturer's warranties) vary and should be fabricated according to manufacturer's recommendations, including the use of unique fasteners and adhesives. Many decorative inlays are available. Consult your manufacturer about performance issues, materials, colors, and patterns. To ensure color and pattern match it is suggested to use same batch material at adjacent sheets.

### OTHER PANEL PRODUCTS

Many new panel products are available, from recycled glass and epoxy impregnated metal shavings to plastic or acrylic panels created from a variety of natural and recycled materials. The options are wide spread and the sheer volume of products make it difficult to quantify. The AWS acknowledges these products and encourages design professionals to verify with individual product manufacturers that their products meet required performance standards. The AWS does not at present address these products.

### SPECIFY REQUIREMENTS FOR

- **UNIFORM COLOR**, certain finishing techniques might be required to achieve uniformity (see Section 5).

- **CHARACTERISTICS**, such as sapwood, heartwood, ribbon stripe, quarter sawn, rift sawn, or vertical grain.

  - Natural, Sapwood and Heartwood are color and cut subsets of Ash, Beech, Birch, Maple, and Poplar. (see HPVA table).
  
  - Natural as a type of wood species selection, allows an unlimited amount of heartwood and/or sapwood within a face.
  
  - Sapwood is all sapwood and is generally referred to for example as Select White for Maple and Birch.
  
  - Heartwood is all heartwood and is generally referred to for example as Select Red for Birch.

- **SPECIAL FIGURE** characteristics.

- **TYPE I WATERPROOF BOND** for limited non climate controlled interior or exterior use (compliant with 2 Cycle Boil and Shear Tests).

- **FLAME SPREAD** and/or smoke development ratings.

- **SPECIALITY SHEET PRODUCTS**, such as plywood with textured faces, prefinished plywood, overlaid plywood, composition sheets, flame spread rated plywood, moisture resistant plywood, lead lined sheets, projectile resistant armor (bullet resistant), reconstituted veneers, bamboo sheets, acrylic sheets, or PVC sheets which are the products of an individual manufacturer, are covered by their manufacturer's specification - not by these standards.

### RECOMMENDATIONS

- **VENEER CORE PANELS** should not be used for cabinet doors because they are likely to warp, and:

  - Rotary cut softwood sheets with clear faces, free of patches, are not typically available.
  
  - Formaldehyde emission regulations should be carefully researched before shipping product into an unfamiliar area.

- **CHECKING or WARPAGE** of wood veneered sheets can be avoided by proper environmental maintenance, such as being:

  - Protected from extremes in relative humidity and temperature.
  
  - Finished on both surfaces to retard moisture movement in and out of the panel.
  
  - Placed in locations that avoid directly facing air vents and/or radiant heat sources.

- **LAMINATION OVER EXISTING OVERLAYS**

  - The application of any thickness of HPDL over the top of existing HPDL is not permitted. Experience shows that the adhesion of the new laminate to the existing surface is very low, often resulting in delamination and failure of the glue line.
  
  - Likewise, the application of HPDL over existing thermoset decorative overlay (melamine) is strongly discouraged. Some fabricators report success by aggressively sanding the melamine surface, followed by applying sufficient contact adhesive and adequate pressure. Delamination is a defect. The risk of delamination is high. Specify or use this procedure with care.

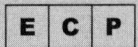 Where the **E**, **C**, or **P** icon is not indicated, the rule applies to all Grades equally

# SECTION 4
## Sheet Products

## compliance requirements

### GENERAL/PRODUCT/TEST

Including: Hardwood and Softwood Veneer, High Pressure Decorative Laminate, Thermally Fused Overlays, Vinyl Film, Medium and High Density Overlays, Hardboard, Backers, Solid Surface, Solid Phenolic, Epoxy Resin, and Natural/Manufactured Stone

### 4.1 BASIC CONSIDERATIONS

1. **GRADE CLASSIFICATIONS ECONOMY, CUSTOM**, and **PREMIUM** are used within these standards only in reference to the acceptable quality of workmanship, material, or installation in a completed architectural woodwork product.

1.2 This material section deals with sheet products, which are a component of finished products covered in Sections 6 - 12.

1.2.1 In this section, the use of Grade classifications is only for the purpose of identifying sheet products that can be used in finished products meeting those Grades.

1.2.2 These Grade classifications are not intended to be used as Grades of raw material or to judge a stand alone sheet.

2. **PANEL ASSOCIATION GRADES**, by themselves, should not be used for architectural woodwork, because even their highest grades might permit unacceptable defects, and:

2.1 The appearance of a piece in the end product is of primary importance, not whether it is cut from a larger sheet that contained characteristics which can be eliminated.

3. **SHEET PRODUCT REQUIREMENTS**

3.1 Apply only to surfaces visible after manufacture and installation.

3.2 Establish criteria as to which, if any, natural characteristics are acceptable.

3.3 Limit the extent of characteristics that will be permitted based on an exposed area's size and the proximity of characteristics to one another.

3.4 Do not apply to special varieties of species that display unusual characteristics desirable for aesthetic and design reasons.

4. **CONTRACT DOCUMENTS** shall govern if in conflict with these standards.

### 4.1 BASIC CONSIDERATIONS (continued)

5. **LOW DENSITY FIBERBOARD (LDF)** sheets have distinct weight advantages; however, they typically offer substantially less in performance characteristics. LDF is permitted in general paneling products and/or woodwork fabrication, with the exception of casework.

5.1 LDF may be used for casework construction, provided its performance characteristics meet or exceed those required of particleboard.

6. **CONTINUOUS PRESSURE LAMINATES** (melamine or polyester based) are an alternative to and may be used in lieu of HPDL, provided they conform to the same standards as HPDL.

7. **INDUSTRY PRACTICES**

7.1 **PANEL GRAIN DIRECTION** is indicated by its size listing; for example, 48" x 96" (1219 mm x 2438 mm) means the grain direction runs with the 96" (2438 mm) direction, whereas a 96" x 48" (2438 mm x 1219 mm) panel's grain direction runs with the 48" (1219 mm) dimension.

# SECTION 4
## Sheet Products

**compliance requirements**

### 4.2 SCOPE

1. All sheet products used for the fabrication or production of the architectural woodwork covered by these standards.

### 4.3 DEFAULT STIPULATION

1. If not otherwise specified or indicated in the contract documents, sheet products shall match the default stipulation of the applicable product portion of these standards.

### 4.4 RULES

1. The following rules shall govern unless a project's contract documents require otherwise.

2. These rules are intended to provide a well defined degree of control over a project's quality of materials and workmanship.

3. **ERRATA**, published on the Sponsor Associations' websites at www.awinet.org, www.awmac.com, or www.aws-errata.com, shall **take precedence over these rules**, subject to their date of posting and a project's bid date.

### 4.4.4 Basic Rules

| | | |
|---|---|---|
| 1 | | **AESTHETIC** grade rules apply only to exposed and semi-exposed surfaces visible after installation. |
| 2 | | **GRAIN DIRECTION** is indicated by a panel's size listing. |
| 3 | | **SPECIES** not covered by these standards shall be as agreed to between owner/design professional and manufacturer/installer as to length requirements and size/exposed area of permitted natural characteristics. |
| 4 | | **REFERENCE STANDARDS**, adopted for the performance, fabrication, and appearance of face veneers, laminates, overlays, backers, and cores are as follows: |
| 4 | 1 | Hardwood Plywood - ANSI/HPVA HP-1 (latest edition). |
| 4 | 2 | Softwood Plywood - US Plywood Standard APA PS-1 (latest edition). |
| 4 | 3 | Medium-Density Overlay (MDO) - US Plywood Standard APA PS-1 (latest edition). |
| 4 | 4 | High-Density Overlay (HDO) - US Plywood Standard APA PS-1 (latest edition). |
| 4 | 5 | Thermally Fused Overlay (Melamine or Polyester) - NEMA - LD-3 (latest edition) for face characteristic only. |
| 4 | 6 | High-Pressure Laminate (HPDL) - NEMA - LD-3 (latest edition). |
| 4 | 7 | Hardboard - ANSI A135.4 (latest edition). |
| 4 | 8 | Particleboard - ANSI A208.1 (latest edition) - Grade M2 or better. |
| 4 | 9 | Medium-Density Fiberboard (MDF) - ANSI A208.2 (latest edition). |
| 4 | 10 | Oriented Strand Board (OSB) - APA PS-2 (latest edition). |
| 4 | 11 | Agrifiber – shall meet or exceed the performance properties of particleboard or MDF as stated in this manual. |
| 4 | 12 | Combination Core – shall meet or exceed the performance characteristics of ANSI A208.1 or ANSI A208.2 standards. |
| 5 | | Additional **REQUIREMENTS,** if so specified: |
| 5 | 1 | **FIRE RETARDANT CORE** shall be color tinted or otherwise documented. |
| 5 | 2 | **MOISTURE RESISTANT CORE** shall be color tinted or otherwise documented. |
| 5 | 3 | **WATERPROOF ADHESIVE.** |
| 6 | | **PANEL LAY-UP:** |
| 6 | 1 | Shall be for interior use, unless specified otherwise. |
| 6 | 2 | Shall be constructed with an odd number of plies. |
| 6 | 3 | Requires **BALANCED CONSTRUCTION** of faces, thickness, and moisture content to produce a warp-free panel suitable for its intended use. |

Continues next column ▼

Where the **E**, **C**, or **P** icon is not indicated, the rule applies to all Grades equally

## compliance requirements

# SECTION 4
Sheet Products

GENERAL/**PRODUCT**/TEST

### 4.4.4 Basic Rules

| | | |
|---|---|---|
| | ▲ | From previous column |
| 6 | | **PANEL LAYUP** (continued) |
| 6 | 4 | Shall have a rigid glue line, and: |
| 6 | 4 | 1 | **DELAMINATION** or **SEPARATION** is not allowed. |
| 6 | 5 | Shall **NOT USE CONTACT ADHESIVE** unless otherwise indicated in these standards. |
| 6 | 6 | Requires **CORES** of veneer, lumber, particleboard, MDF, or a combination thereof, and: |
| 6 | 6 | 1 | Veneer core shall not be used for cabinet door or drawer front components. |
| 6 | 7 | **SURFACE** distortions or defects, such as bubbling, blistering, cracking, crazing or ridges in the exposed face veneer, shall not occur. |
| 6 | 8 | Except as indicated in Section 9 for wood doors only, **TELEGRAPHING** shall not exceed 0.004" (0.10 mm) in any 3" (76.2 mm) span. |
| 6 | 9 | When **VENEER WITH BACKER SHEET** is specified, it shall be pressed using hard setting glues that develop a rigid glue line (not a contact adhesive) on appropriate core material, and if required, panel to be balanced with appropriate balance material. |
| 6 | 10 | **LAMINATION OVER EXISTING HPDL** is not permitted. |
| 7 | | **THICKNESS TOLERANCE** shall be as established by ANSI/HPVA HP-1 and equal to: |
| 7 | 1 | +0/-1/32" (0 / 0.8 mm) for nominal thickness less than 1/4" (6 mm). |
| 7 | 2 | +0/-3/64" (0 / 1.2 mm) for nominal thickness of 1/4" (6 mm) or greater. |
| 8 | | **SQUARENESS TOLERANCE** shall be as established by ANSI/HPVA HP-1 and equal to: |
| 8 | 1 | 3/32" (2.4 mm) for panels 48" x 48" (1220 mm x 1220 mm) or greater. |
| 8 | 2 | 1/16" (1.6 mm) for panels smaller than 48" x 48" (1220 mm x 1220 mm). |
| 9 | | **STRAIGHTNESS TOLERANCE** shall be as established by ANSI/HPVA HP-1 and equal to: |
| 9 | 1 | 1/16" (1.6 mm) for edges less than 96" (2440 mm) in length. |
| 9 | 2 | 3/32" (2.4 mm) for edges 96" (2440 mm) or greater. |
| 10 | | **CATHEDRAL** type figure shall be achieved by: |
| 10 | 1 | A single component in "AA" Face Grade. |
| 10 | 2 | The split heart method in Face Grades "A - D", and: |
| 10 | 2 | 1 | Each half of a split heart shall be subject to the minimum component width requirements for Face Grade "B." |

### 4.4.5 Hardwood Veneer Material Rules

| | | |
|---|---|---|
| 1 | **APPLIES** to the following common species: ANIGRE, ASH, BEECH, BIRCH, CHERRY, HICKORY, LAUAN, MAHOGANY American, MAKORE, MAPLE, OAK Red & White, PECAN, POPLAR, SAPELE, WALNUT |
| 2 | **CORE** shall be manufacturer's choice. |
| 3 | **VENEER** shall be of sufficient thickness so as not to permit show through of cross banding after sanding or finishing. |
| 4 | **EDGES** of multi leaf faces shall appear parallel. |
| 5 | **BACKING SPECIES** shall be manufacturer's choice. |
| 6 | **FIGURE** is not a function of a species grade, and special requirements shall have been so specified. |
| 7 | **NATURAL** allows unlimited heartwood and/or sapwood within a face. |
| 8 | **GRAIN** direction shall be manufacturer's choice unless otherwise specified in the contract documents or required within Sections 6 - 12. |
| 9 | **RIFT GRAIN OAK** shall allow up to twenty-five percent (25%) of the exposed surface area to contain medullary ray flake. |
| 10 | **VENEER FACE GRADE REQUIREMENTS** (based on the following ANSI/HPVA HP-1 definitions and characteristics) shall be for: |

| | | | | | | |
|---|---|---|---|---|---|---|
| 10 | 1 | | **OPAQUE FINISH:** | | | |
| 10 | 1 | 1 | Grade - D. | E | | |
| 10 | 1 | 2 | Grade - C. | E | C | |
| 10 | 1 | 3 | Grade - B. | E | C | P |
| 10 | 2 | | **TRANSPARENT FINISH:** | | | |
| 10 | 2 | 1 | Grade - B. | E | | |
| 10 | 2 | 2 | Grade - A. | E | C | |
| 10 | 2 | 3 | Grade - AA. | E | C | P |

Continues next column ▼

# SECTION 4
## Sheet Products

GENERAL / **PRODUCT** / TEST

## compliance requirements

Where the **E**, **C**, or **P** icon is not indicated, the rule applies to all Grades equally | E | C | P |

### 4.4.5 Hardwood Veneer Material Rules
▲ From previous column

**10 VENEER FACE GRADE REQUIREMENTS** (continued)

| 10 | 3 | | For **PRESELECTED FLITCHES,** the following characteristics are applicable only when: |
|---|---|---|---|
| 10 | 3 | 1 | Design professional has determined, in advance of bid, which characteristics and/or defects are acceptable or are to be eliminated for the total face appearance. |
| 10 | 3 | 1 | 1 | Yield and leaf width/length are directly related to this determination and therefore there may be waste/yield implications. |

**11 VENEER FACE GRADE DESCRIPTIONS** - Range from AA through D, primarily based on appearance features with fewer natural characteristics allowed in higher grades.

| 11 | 1 | **GRADE - AA -** Veneer shall be smooth, tight cut, and full length. When the face consists of more than one veneer component or piece, the edges shall appear parallel and be edge matched. All components of a book or slip matched face shall be from the same flitch. Rotary cut faces may be whole piece or multi piece with edge joints tight and no sharp color contrast at the joints. Species specified for natural color will allow color contrasts but shall be book matched or conform to the type of matching as specified. The components of plain sliced (flat cut) and multi piece rotary faces will be book matched unless otherwise specified with a running, balanced, or center matched arrangement. Unless otherwise specified, components in plain sliced faces will have a matching arrangement selected by the manufacturer. Plain sliced faces will consist of two or more components with no component less than 6" (152 mm) wide except for outside components, which may be less than 6" (152 mm) to allow for certain types of matching or panel edge loss. No plain sliced components will have a split heart. No full quartered cut is allowed in plain sliced faces. The width of any single component in quarter cut, rift cut faces shall not be less than 3" (76 mm) except for outside components, which may be less than 3" (76 mm) to allow for certain types of matching or panel edge trim loss. |

Continues next column ▼

### 4.4.5 Hardwood Veneer Material Rules
▲ From previous column

**11 VENEER FACE GRADE DESCRIPTIONS** (continued)

| 11 | 2 | **GRADE - A -** Veneer shall be smooth, tight cut, and full length. When the face consists of more than one veneer component or piece, the edges shall appear parallel and be edge matched. All components of a book or slip matched face shall be from the same flitch. Rotary cut faces may be whole piece or multi piece with edge joints tight; however, no sharp color contrasts are permitted at the joints, and the face will provide a good general appearance. Species specified for natural color will allow color contrasts, but shall be book matched or conform to the type of matching as specified. The components of plain sliced (flat cut) and multi piece rotary faces will be book matched, unless otherwise specified with a running, balanced, or center matched arrangement. Unless otherwise specified, components in plain sliced faces will have a matching arrangement selected by the manufacturer. Plain sliced faces will consist of two or more components with no component less than 5" (127 mm) wide except for outside components, which may be less than 5" (127 mm) to allow for certain types of matching or panel edge trim loss. Split heart is permitted if manufactured cathedral is achieved. No full quarter cut is allowed in plain sliced faces. The width of any single component in quarter cut, rift cut, or comb grain faces shall not be less than 3" (76 mm) except for outside components, which may be less than 3" (76 mm) to allow for certain types of matching or panel edge trim loss. In some species, sapwood is permitted; however, in other species, it may be permitted by agreement between buyer and seller. |
| 11 | 3 | **GRADE - B -** Veneer shall be smooth, tight cut, and full length as described for the various species. All components of a book or slip matched face shall be from the same flitch. Slip or book matched veneers are available if specified by the buyer. If not specified, multi piece faces will be pleasingly matched. Sharp color contrasts at the joints are not permitted. Species specified for natural color will allow color contrasts, but shall be book matched or conform to the type of matching as specified. Plain sliced faces will consist of two or more components with no component less than 4" (102 mm) wide to allow for certain types of matching or panel edge trim loss. Some full quarter cut is permitted in plain sliced faces. For some species, unlimited sapwood is allowed, and in other species, a percentage of sapwood is allowed. |

Continues next column ▼

 Where the **E**, **C**, or **P** icon is not indicated, the rule applies to all Grades equally

# SECTION 4
## Sheet Products

## compliance requirements

GENERAL / **PRODUCT** / TEST

### 4.4.5 Hardwood Veneer Material Rules

▲ From previous column

| 11 | | VENEER FACE GRADE DESCRIPTIONS (continued) |
|---|---|---|
| 11 | 4 | **GRADE - C -** Permits unlimited color streaks and spots and color variation. An unlimited number of small burls and pin knots are allowed with no restrictions on the size of the dark pin knot centers, as long as the diameter of pin knots does not exceed 1/4" (6.4 mm) in diameter. The size of sound and repaired knotholes and similar shaped openings cannot exceed 1/2" (9.5 mm) in diameter, with a specified number allowed based on individual species. Faces shall provide a sound face, free of open defects, with only minimal areas of rough grain. |
| 11 | 5 | **GRADE - D -** Permits unlimited color streaks and spots and color variation. An unlimited number of small burls and pin knots are permitted with no restrictions on the size of dark pin knot centers, as long as the diameter of pin knots does not exceed 1/4" (6.4 mm) in diameter. The size of repaired and sound knotholes and similar shaped openings cannot exceed 3/4" (19 mm) (repaired) and 1" (25.4 mm) (sound) diameters, with a specified number based on individual species. Faces shall provide a sound face, free of open defects. The size or percentage of rough grain on the panel surface depends on the species. |
| 11 | 6 | **OTHER SPECIES -** May be covered by these standards, provided the buyer and seller agree to a species grouping as a basis for the evaluation and grade of the unlisted species. It is obviously not workable to try to develop and include the individual grade requirements for every known species. |
| 11 | 7 | **SPECIALTY GRADES -** Applicable to veneer in which the features of greatest significance are unusual characteristics that are not covered within grades AA-D. Characteristics shall be as agreed upon between buyer and seller. Species such as Wormy Chestnut, Birds Eye Maple, and English Brown Oak, which have unusual decorative features, are considered a Speciality Grade. |
| 11 | 8 | **NOTE -** Variance from these standards might invalidate certain criteria and tests. |
| 11 | 8 | 1 | Example - Strong color contrasts will occur when rotary natural Birch leaves are slip matched. |

Continues next column ▼

### 4.4.5 Hardwood Veneer Material Rules

▲ From previous column

| 12 | | **TERMINOLOGY DEFINITIONS** for use with following ANSI/HPVA HP-1 (latest edition) Characteristic charts: |
|---|---|---|
| 12 | 1 | **BARK POCKET:** Bark around which normal wood has grown. |
| 12 | 2 | **BRASHNESS:** Condition of wood characterized by low resistance to shock and by abrupt failure across the grain without splintering. |
| 12 | 3 | **BURL, BLENDING:** A swirl, twist, or distortion in the grain of the wood which usually occurs near a knot or crotch but does not contain a knot and does not contain abrupt color variation. A blending burl is detectable at 1.8 m to 2.4 m (6 feet to 8 feet) as a swirl or roundel. |
| 12 | 4 | **BURL, CONSPICUOUS:** A swirl, twist, or distortion in the grain of the wood which usually occurs near a knot or crotch. A conspicuous burl is associated with abrupt color variation and/or a cluster of small dark piths caused by a cluster of adventitious buds. |
| 12 | 5 | **COMB GRAIN:** A quality of rift cut veneer with exceptionally straight grain and closely spaced growth increments resembling the appearance of long strands of combed hair. |
| 12 | 6 | **CROSS BAR:** Irregularity of grain resembling a dip in the grain running at right angles, or nearly so, to the length of the veneer. |
| 12 | 7 | **FLAKE:** See Fleck, Ray. |
| 12 | 8 | **FLECK, RAY:** Portion of a ray as it appears on the quartered or rift cut surface. Fleck is often a dominant appearance feature in Oak. |
| 12 | 9 | **GUM POCKETS:** Well defined openings between rings of annual growth, containing gum or evidence of prior gum accumulations. |
| 12 | 10 | **GUM SPOTS AND STREAKS:** Gum or resinous material or color spots and streaks caused by prior resin accumulations sometimes found on panel surfaces. |
| 12 | 11 | **HAIRLINE:** A thin, perceptible line showing at the joint of two pieces of wood. |
| 12 | 12 | **HEARTWOOD:** The non active or dormant center of a tree, generally distinguishable from the outer portion (sapwood) by its darker color, sometime referred to as heart. |

Continues next column ▼

# SECTION 4
## Sheet Products

**compliance requirements**

---

### 4.4.5 Hardwood Veneer Material Rules

▲ From previous column

**12 TERMINOLOGY DEFINITIONS** (continued)

| | | |
|---|---|---|
| 12 13 | | **KNOT:** Cross section of tree branch or limb with grain usually running at right angles to that of the piece of wood in which it occurs, further defined as: |
| 12 13 | 1 | **CONSPICUOUS PIN:** Sound knots 6.4 mm (1/4 inch) or less in diameter containing dark centers. |
| 12 13 | 2 | **HOLES:** Openings produced when knots drop from the wood in which they were embedded. |
| 12 13 | 3 | **OPEN:** Opening produced when a portion of the wood substance of a knot has dropped out or where cross checks have occurred to produce an opening. |
| 12 13 | 4 | **SOUND TIGHT:** Knots that are solid across their face and fixed by growth to retain their place. |
| 12 13 | 5 | **SPIKE:** Knots cut from 0° to 45° to the long axis of limbs. |
| 12 14 | | **REPAIRS:** A patch, shim, or filler material inserted and/or glued into veneer or a panel to achieve a sound surface. |
| 12 15 | | **RIFT CUT:** A straight grain appearance achieved through the process of cutting at a slight angle to the radial on the half round stay log or through the use of veneer cut in any fashion that produces a straight grain with minimal ray fleck. |
| 12 16 | | **ROUGH CUT:** Irregular shaped areas of generally uneven corrugation on the surface of veneer, differing from the surrounding smooth veneer and occurring as the veneer is cut by the lathe or slicer. |
| 12 17 | | **RUPTURED GRAIN:** A break or breaks in the grain or between springwood and summerwood caused or aggravated by excessive pressure on the wood by seasoning, manufacturing, or natural processes. Ruptured grain appears as a single or series of distinct separations in the wood such as when springwood is crushed leaving the summerwood to separate in one or more growth increments. |
| 12 18 | | **SAPWOOD:** The living wood of lighter color occurring in the outer portion of a tree, sometimes referred to as sap. |
| 12 19 | | **SLIGHT:** Visible on observation, but does not interfere with the overall aesthetic appearance with consideration of the applicable grade of the panel. |
| 12 20 | | **SPLITS:** Separations of wood fiber running parallel to the grain. |
| 12 21 | | **STREAKS, MINERAL:** Sharply contrasting elongated discolorations of the wood substance. |
| 12 22 | | **VINE MARK:** Bands of irregular grain running across or diagonally to the grain which are caused by the growth of climbing vines around the tree. |

Continues next column ▼

---

### 4.4.5 Hardwood Veneer Material Rules

▲ From previous column

**12 TERMINOLOGY DEFINITIONS** (continued)

| | | |
|---|---|---|
| 12 23 | | **WORMHOLES:** Holes resulting from infestation of worms. |
| 12 24 | | **WORM TRACKS:** Marks caused by various types of wood attacking larvae. Often appear as sound discolorations running with or across the grain in straight to wavy streaks. Sometimes referred to as "pith flecks" in certain species of Maple, Birch and other hardwoods because of a resemblance to the color of pith. |
| 13 | | **SUMMARY TABLES of ALLOWABLE WOOD VENEER FACE GRADE CHARACTERISTICS**, printed with permission from the Hardwood Plywood and Veneer Association and their ANSI/HPVA HP1 (latest edition), are as follows: |
| 13 | 1 | Tables for **STAND ALONE DOOR FACES** are in Section 9. |
| 13 | 2 | Table: 4-040 - **ASH, BEECH, BIRCH, MAPLE,** and **POPLAR.** |
| 13 | 3 | Table: 4-041 - **MAHOGANY** (African or American), **ANIGRE, MAKORE,** and **SAPELE.** |
| 13 | 4 | Table: 4-042 - **RED** and **WHITE OAK.** |
| 13 | 5 | Table: 4-043 - **PECAN** and **HICKORY.** |
| 13 | 6 | Table: 4-044 - **WALNUT** and **CHERRY.** |
| 13 | 7 | The following tables are not intended to create a face grade, they are **INTENDED ONLY TO ESTABLISH THE ACCEPTABLE REQUIREMENTS AND/OR CHARACTERISTICS AFTER THE WOODWORK IS COMPLETED OR INSTALLED.** |

 Where the **E**, **C**, or **P** icon is not indicated, the rule applies to all Grades equally

# SECTION 4
## Sheet Products

## compliance requirements

**GENERAL/PRODUCT/TEST**

*Table: 4-040* - **ASH, BEECH**[a], **BIRCH, MAPLE,** and **POPLAR** (ANSI/HPVA HP-1 (latest edition))

| Cut | Plain Sliced (Flat Cut), Quarter Cut, Rotary Cut | | | | | | | | | |
|---|---|---|---|---|---|---|---|---|---|---|
| Grade Description | AA | | | A | | | B | | C | D |
| Color and Matching | Sap | Heart | Nat. | Sap | Heart | Nat. | Sap | Heart | Nat. | | |
| Sapwood | Yes | No | Yes | Yes | No | Yes | Yes | No | Yes | Yes | Yes |
| Heartwood | No | Yes | Yes | No | Yes | Yes | No | Yes | Yes | Yes | Yes |
| Color Streaks or Spots | Slight | | | Slight | | Yes | Yes | | | Yes | Yes |
| Color Variation | Slight | Yes | | Slight | | Yes | Yes | | | Yes | Yes |
| Sharp Color Contrast at Joints | Yes if Slip, Plank, or Random matched | | | Yes if Slip, Plank, or Random matched | | | Yes if Slip, Plank, or Random matched | | | Yes | Yes |
| Type of Matching, | | | | | | | | | | | |
|   Book Matched | Yes | | | Yes | | | Specify | | | -- | -- |
|   Slip Matched | Specify | | | Specify | | | Specify | | | -- | -- |
|   Pleasing Matched | -- | | | -- | | | Yes | | | -- | -- |
| Nominal Minimum Width of Face Components[b]   Plain Sliced   Quarter   Rotary | 6" (152 mm) 3" (76 mm) 6" (152 m) | | | 5" (127 mm) 3" (76 mm) 5" (127 mm) | | | 3" (76 mm) 3" (76 mm) 4" (102 mm) | | | No Limit | No Limit |
| Natural Characteristics | | | | | | | | | | | |
| Small Conspicuous Burls & Pin Knots   Combined Average Number | 1 per 5 sq ft (2 per 1 m²) 6 per 32 sq ft | | | 1 per 3 sq ft (4 per 1 m²) 10 per 32 sq ft | | | 1 per 2 sq ft (6 per 1 m²) 16 per 32 sq ft | | | No Limit | No Limit |
| Conspicuous Burls, Maximum Size | 1/4" (6.4 mm) | | | 3/8" (9.5 mm) | | | 1/2" (12.7 mm) | | | No Limit | No Limit |
| Conspicuous Pin Knots,   Average Number   Maximum Size, Dark Part   Total | No | | | 1 per 8 sq ft (4 per 3 m²) 4 per 32 sq ft 1/8" (3.2 mm) 1/4" (6.4 mm) | | | 1 per 4 sq ft (3 per 1 m²) 8 per 32 sq ft 1/8" (3.2 mm) 1/4" (6.4 mm) | | | No Limit | No Limit |
| Scattered, Sound and Repaired Knots,   Combined Average Number   Maximum Size - Sound   Maximum Size - Repaired   Average Number - Repaired | No | | | No | | | 1 per 8 sq ft (4 per 3 m²) 4 per 32 sq ft 3/8" (9.5 mm) 1/8" (3.2 mm) 1 per 8 sq ft (4 per 3 m²) | | | 1 per 4 sq ft (3 per 1 m²) 8 per 32 sq ft 1/2" (12.7 mm) 1/2" (12.7 mm) 1 per 8 sq ft (4 per 3 m²) | 1 per 3 sq ft (4 per 1 m²) 10 per 32 sq ft 1" (25.4 mm) 3/4" (19 mm) 1 per 6 sq ft (2 per 1 m²) |
| Mineral Streaks | No; Maple, Slight | | | Slight | | | Slight | | | Yes | Yes |
| Bark Pockets | No | | | No | | | Few to 1/8" x 1" (3.2 mm x 25.4 mm) | | | Few to 1/4" x 2" (6.4 mm x 50.8 mm) | 1/4" x 2" (6.4 mm x 50.8 mm) |
| Worm Tracks | Slight | | | Slight | | | Slight; Ash, Yes | | | Yes | Yes |
| Vine Marks | Slight | | | Slight | | | Slight | | | Yes | Yes |
| Cross Bars | Slight | | | Slight | | | Yes | | | Yes | Yes |
| Manufacturing Characteristics | | | | | | | | | | | |
| Rough Cut/Ruptured Grain | No | | | No | | | Slight | | | Two 8" (203 mm) dia. areas or equivalent | 5% of panel |
| Blended Repaired Tapering Hairline Splits | Two 1/32" x 3" (0.8 mm x 76 mm) on panel ends only | | | Two 1/16" x 6" (1.6 mm x 152 mm) | | | Four 1/8" x 8" (3.2 mm x 203 mm) | | | Four 3/16" x 8" (4.8 mm x 203 mm) | Six 1/4" x 10" (6.4 mm x 203 mm) |
| Repairs | Very small blending | | | Small blending | | | Blending | | | Yes | Yes |
| Special Characteristics | | | | | | | | | | | |
| Quartered | 1" in 12" (25.4 mm in 305 mm) maximum grain slope; 2-1/2" in 12" (63.5 mm in 305 mm) maximum grain sweep | | | | | | | | | | |

Open splits, open joints, open bark pockets, or doze not allowed in above grades.
[a] American or European
[b] Outside components will be different size to allow for edge trim loss and certain types of matching.

# SECTION 4
## Sheet Products

GENERAL / **PRODUCT** / TEST

## compliance requirements

Where the **E**, **C**, or **P** icon is not indicated, the rule applies to all Grades equally | **E** | **C** | **P** |

*Table: 4-041* - **MAHOGANY** (African or American), **ANIGRE**, **MAKORE**, and **SAPELE** (ANSI/HPVA HP-1 (latest edition))

| Cut | \multicolumn{5}{c}{Plain Sliced (Flat Cut), Quarter Cut, Rotary Cut} |||||
|---|---|---|---|---|---|
| Grade Description | AA | A | B | C | D |
| **Color and Matching** | | | | | |
| Sapwood | No | No | No | Yes | Yes |
| Heartwood | Yes | Yes | Yes | Yes | Yes |
| Color Streaks or Spots | Slight | Slight | Occasional | Yes | Yes |
| Color Variation | Slight | Slight | Moderate | Yes | Yes |
| Sharp Color Contrast at Joints | Yes if Slip, Plank, or Random matched | Yes if Slip, Plank, or Random matched | Yes if Slip, Plank, or Random matched | Yes | Yes |
| Type of Matching<br>   Book Matched<br>   Slip Matched<br>   Pleasing Matched | <br>Yes<br>Specify<br>-- | <br>Yes<br>Specify<br>-- | <br>Specify<br>Specify<br>Yes | <br>--<br>--<br>-- | <br>--<br>--<br>-- |
| Nominal Minimum Width of Face Components [a]<br>   Plain Sliced<br>   Quarter<br>   Rotary | <br>6" (152 mm)<br>3" (76 mm)<br>6" (152 m) | <br>5" (127 mm)<br>3" (76 mm)<br>5" (127 mm) | <br>3" (76 mm)<br>3" (76 mm)<br>4" (102 mm) | No Limit | No Limit |
| **Natural Characteristics** | | | | | |
| Small Conspicuous Burls & Pin Knots, Combined Average Number | 1 per 5 sq ft<br>(2 per 1 m²)<br>6 per 32 sq ft | 1 per 3 sq ft<br>(4 per 1 m²)<br>10 per 32 sq ft | 1 per 2 sq ft<br>(6 per 1 m²)<br>16 per 32 sq ft | No Limit | No Limit |
| Conspicuous Burls, Maximum Size | 1/4" (6.4 mm) | 3/8" (9.5 mm) | 1/2" (12.7 mm) | No Limit | No Limit |
| Conspicuous Pin Knots,<br>   Average Number<br>   Maximum Size, Dark Part<br>   Total | No | 1 per 8 sq ft<br>(4 per 3 m²)<br>4 per 32 sq ft<br>1/8" (3.2 mm)<br>1/4" (6.4 mm) | 1 per 4 sq ft<br>(3 per 1 m²)<br>8 per 32 sq ft<br>1/8" (3.2 mm)<br>1/4" (6.4 mm) | No Limit | No Limit |
| Scattered Sound and Repaired Knots,<br>   Combined Average Number<br>   Maximum Size - Sound<br>   Maximum Size - Repaired<br>   Average Number - Repaired | No | No | 1 per 8 sq ft<br>(4 per 3 m²)<br>4 per 32 sq ft<br>3/8" (9.5 mm)<br>1/8" (3.2 mm)<br>1 per 8 sq ft<br>(4 per 3 m²) | 1 per 4 sq ft<br>(3 per 1 m²)<br>8 per 32 sq ft<br>1/2" (12.7 mm)<br>1/2" (12.7 mm)<br>1 per 8 sq ft<br>(4 per 3 m²) | 1 per 3 sq ft<br>(4 per 1 m²)<br>10 per 32 sq ft<br>1" (25.4 mm)<br>3/4" (19 mm)<br>1 per 6 sq ft<br>(2 per 1 m²) |
| Mineral Streaks | No | Slight | Occasional | Yes | Yes |
| Bark Pockets | No | No | Few to 1/8" x 1"<br>(3.2 mm x 25.4 mm) | Few to 1/4" x 2"<br>(6.4 mm x 50.8 mm) | 1/4" x 2"<br>(6.4 mm x 50.8 mm) |
| Worm Tracks | No | No | Slight | Few | Yes |
| Vine Marks | Slight | Slight | Yes | Yes | Yes |
| Cross Bars | Occasional | Occasional | Yes | Yes | Yes |
| **Manufacturing Characteristics** | | | | | |
| Rough Cut/Ruptured Grain | No | No | Slight | Slight | Two 8" dia. areas or equivalent |
| Blended Repaired Tapering Hairline Splits | Two 1/32" x 3" on (0.8 mm x 76 mm) panel ends only | Two 1/16" x 6"<br>(1.6 mm x 152 mm) | Four 1/8" x 8"<br>(3.2 mm x 203 mm) | Four 3/16" x 8"<br>(4.8 mm x 203 mm) | Six 1/4" x 10"<br>(6.4 mm x 254 mm) |
| Repairs | Very Small Blending | Small Blending | Blending | Yes | Yes |
| **Special Characteristics** | | | | | |
| Unfilled Worm Holes | No | No | No | 1/16" (1.6 mm) max. dia. | 1/16" (1.6 mm) max. dia. |
| Quartered | \multicolumn{5}{l}{1" in 12" (25.4 mm in 305 mm) maximum grain slope; 2-1/2" in 12" (63.5 mm in 305 mm) maximum grain sweep} |||||

Open splits, open joints, open bark pockets, or doze not allowed in above grades.
[a] Outside components will be different size to allow for edge trim loss and certain types of matching.

Where the **E**, **C**, or **P** icon is not indicated, the rule applies to all Grades equally

# SECTION 4
## Sheet Products

## compliance requirements

GENERAL/**PRODUCT**/TEST

*Table: 4-042 - **RED** and **WHITE** OAK*   (ANSI/HPVA HP- 1 (latest edition) as modified by notes 'd' and 'e')

| Cut | Plain Sliced (Flat Cut), Quarter Cut, Rotary Cut ||||||||
|---|---|---|---|---|---|---|---|---|
| Grade Description | AA || A || B || C | D |
| | Red | White | Red | White | Red | White | | |
| **Color and Matching** ||||||||||
| Sapwood | No | No | 5% [a] | Yes [a] | 10-20% [b] | Yes | Yes | Yes |
| Heartwood | Yes | Yes | Yes | Yes | Yes | Yes | Yes | Yes |
| Color Streaks or Spots | Yes | Yes | Yes | Yes | Yes | Yes | Yes | Yes |
| Color Variation | Slight | Slight | Slight | Slight | Yes | Yes | Yes | Yes |
| Sharp Color Contrast at Joints | Yes if Slip, Plank, or Random matched || Yes if Slip, Plank, or Random matched || Yes if Slip, Plank, or Random matched || Yes | Yes |
| Type of Matching<br>    Book Matched<br>    Slip Matched<br>    Pleasing Matched | Yes<br>Specify<br>-- || Yes<br>Specify<br>-- || Specify<br>Specify<br>Yes || --<br>--<br>-- | --<br>--<br>-- |
| Nominal Minimum Width of Face Components [c]  Plain-Sliced<br>Quarter<br>Rotary | 6" (152 mm)<br>3" (76 mm)<br>6" (152 mm) || 5" (127 mm)<br>3" (76 mm)<br>5" (127 mm) || 3" (76 mm)<br>3" (76 mm)<br>4" (102 mm) || No Limit | No Limit |
| **Natural Characteristics** ||||||||||
| Small Conspicuous Burls & Pin Knots, Combined Average Number | 1 per 4 sq ft<br>(3 per 1 m²)<br>6 per 32 sq ft || 1 per 2-2/3 sq ft<br>(4 per 1 m²)<br>12 per 32 sq ft || 1 per 1-1/3 sq ft<br>(8 per 1 m²)<br>24 per 32 sq ft || No Limit | No Limit |
| Conspicuous Burls, Maximum Size | 1/4" (6.4 mm) || 3/8" (9.5 mm) || 1/2" 12.7 mm) || No Limit | No Limit |
| Conspicuous Pin Knots,<br>  Average Number<br>  Maximum Size, Dark Part<br>  Total | No || 1 per 3 sq ft<br>(4 per 1 m²)<br>10 per 32 sq ft<br>1/8" (3.2 mm)<br>1/4" (6.4 mm) || 1 per 2 sq ft<br>(6 per 1 m²)<br>16 per 32 sq ft<br>1/8" (3.2 mm)<br>1/4" (6.4 mm) || No Limit | No Limit |
| Scattered Sound and Repaired Knots,<br>  Combined Average Number<br>  Maximum Size - Sound<br>  Maximum Size - Repaired<br>  Average Number - Repaired | No || No || 1 per 8 sq ft<br>(4 per 3 m²)<br>4 per 32 sq ft<br>3/8" (9.5 mm)<br>1/8" (3.2 mm)<br>1 per 8 sq ft<br>(4 per 3 m²) || 1 per 4 sq ft<br>(3 per 1 m²)<br>8 per 32 sq ft<br>1/2" (12.7 mm)<br>1/2" (12.7 mm)<br>1 per 8 sq ft<br>(4 per 3 m²) | 1 per 3 sq ft<br>(4 per 1 m²)<br>10 per 32 sq ft<br>1" (25.4 mm)<br>3/4" (19 mm)<br>1 per 6 sq ft<br>(2 per 1 m²) |
| Mineral Streaks | No || Slight, Blending || Few to 12"<br>(305 mm) || Yes | Yes |
| Bark Pockets | No || No || Few to 1/8" x 1"<br>(3.2 mm x 25.4 mm) || Few to 1/4" x 2"<br>(6.4 mm x 50.8 mm) | 1/4" x 2"<br>(6.4 mm x 50.8 mm) |
| Worm Tracks | No || No || Slight || Few | Yes |
| Vine Marks | No || Slight || Yes || Yes | Yes |
| Cross Bars | Slight || Slight || Yes || Yes | Yes |
| **Manufacturing Characteristics** ||||||||||
| Rough Cut/Ruptured Grain | No || No || Slight || Slight | Two 8" (203 mm) dia. areas or equivalent |
| Blended Repaired Tapering Hairline Splits | Two 1/32" x 3" on<br>(0.8 mm x 76 mm)<br>panel ends only || Two 1/16" x 6"<br>(1.6 mm x 152 mm) || Four 1/8" x 8"<br>(3.2 mm x 203 mm) || Four 3/16" x 8"<br>(4.8 mm x 203 mm) | Six 1/4" x 10"<br>(6.4 mm x 254 mm) |
| Repairs | Very Small Blending || Small Blending || Blending || Yes | Yes |
| **Special Characteristics** ||||||||||
| Ray Fleck [d] | Slight, Blending || Slight, Blending || Slight, Blending || Yes | Yes |
| Rift and Comb Grain | <u>Rift</u> permits 1" in 12" (25.4 mm in 305 mm) max. grain slope, 2-1/2" in 12" 63.5 mm in 305 mm) max. grain sweep, fleck not to exceed 3/8" (9.5 mm) in width.<br><u>Comb</u> permits 1/2" in 12" (1`2.7 mm in 305 mm) max. grain slope, 1/2" in 12" (1`2.7 mm in 305 mm) max. grain sweep, fleck not to exceed 3/32" (2.4 mm) in width. ||||||||

Unfilled worm holes, open splits, open joints, open bark pockets, or doze not allowed in above grades.
[a] Sap allowed in rotary only unless otherwise specified.  [b] 10% sap allowed in rift, comb, and plain-sliced; 20% sap allowed in rotary.
[c] Outside components will be different size to allow for edge trim loss and certain types of matching.
[d] Unless otherwise specified, quartered permits unlimited fleck.

©2014 AWI | AWMAC | WI  2nd Edition, October 1, 2014
As may be updated by errata at **awinet.org**, **awmac.com**, or **aws-errata.com**

Architectural Woodwork Standards  97

# SECTION 4
## Sheet Products

GENERAL / **PRODUCT** / TEST

## compliance requirements

Where the **E**, **C**, or **P** icon is not indicated, the rule applies to all Grades equally | **E** | **C** | **P** |

*Table: 4-043* - **PECAN** and **HICKORY**  (ANSI/HPVA HP-1 (latest edition))

| Cut | Plain-Sliced (Flat Cut), Quarter-Cut, Rotary Cut | | | | |
|---|---|---|---|---|---|
| Grade Description | AA | A | B | C | D |
| **Color and Matching** | | | | | |
| Sapwood | Yes | Yes | Yes | Yes | Yes |
| Heartwood | Yes | Yes | Yes | Yes | Yes |
| Color Streaks or Spots | Yes | Yes | Yes | Yes | Yes |
| Color Variation | Yes | Yes | Yes | Yes | Yes |
| Sharp Color Contrast at Joints | Yes if Slip, Plank, or Random matched | Yes if Slip, Plank, or Random matched | Yes if Slip, Plank, or Random matched | Yes | Yes |
| Type of Matching<br>  Book-Matched<br>  Slip-Matched<br>  Pleasing-Matched | <br>Yes<br>Specify<br>-- | <br>Yes<br>Specify<br>-- | <br>Specify<br>Specify<br>Yes | <br>--<br>--<br>-- | <br>--<br>--<br>-- |
| Nominal Minimum  Plain-S.<br>Width of<br>Face Components [a]  Quarter<br>  Rotary | 6" (152 mm)<br>3" (76 mm)<br>6" (152 mm) | 5" (127 mm)<br>3" (76 mm)<br>5" (127 mm) | 3" (76 mm)<br>3" (76 mm)<br>4" (102 mm) | No Limit | No Limit |
| **Natural Characteristics** | | | | | |
| Small Conspicuous Burls & Pin Knots-<br><br>Combined Avg. Number | 1 per 1 sq ft<br>(11 per 1 m²)<br>32 per 32 sq ft | 2 per 1 sq ft<br>(22 per 1 m²)<br>64 per 32 sq ft | No Limit | No Limit | No Limit |
| Conspicuous Burls - Max. Size | 1/4" (6.4 mm) | 3/8" (9.5 mm) | 1/2" (12.7 mm) | No Limit | No Limit |
| Conspicuous Pin Knots [b]<br>Avg. Number<br><br>Max. Size: Dark Part<br>           Total | 1 per 2 sq ft<br>(6 per 1 m²)<br>16 per 32 sq ft<br>1/8" (3.2 mm)<br>1/4" (6.4 mm) | 2 per 1 sq ft<br>(22 per 1 m²)<br>64 per 32 sq ft<br>1/8" (3.2 mm)<br>1/4" (6.4 mm)" | No Limit<br><br><br>1/8" (3.2 mm)<br>1/4" (6.4 mm)" | No Limit | No Limit |
| Scattered Sound and Repaired Knots-Combined Avg. Number<br><br>  Max. Size - Sound<br>  Max. Size - Repaired<br>  Avg. No. - Repaired | No | No | 1 per 8 sq ft<br>(4 per 3 m²)<br>4 per 32 sq ft<br>3/8" (9.5 mm)<br>1/8" (3.2 mm)<br>1 per 8 sq ft<br>(4 per 3 m²) | 1 per 3 sq ft<br>(4 per 1 m²)<br>10 per 32 sq ft<br>1/2" (12.7 mm)<br>1/2" (12.7 mm)<br>1 per 8 sq ft<br>(2 per 1 m²) | 1 per 3 sq ft<br>(6 per 1 m²)<br>10 per 32 sq ft<br>1" (25.4 mm)<br>3/4" (19 mm)<br>1 per 6 sq ft<br>(3 per 1 m²) |
| Mineral Streaks | Slight | Slight | Yes | Yes | Yes |
| Bark Pockets | No | Small, Occasional | Few to 1/4" x 2"<br>(6.4 mm x 50.8 mm) | Few to 3/8" x 4"<br>(9.5 mm x 102 mm) | To 1/2" wide<br>(12.7 mm) |
| Worm Tracks | No | Slight | Few | Yes | Yes |
| Vine Marks | Slight | Occasional | Yes | Yes | Yes |
| Cross Bars | Slight | Occasional | Yes | Yes | Yes |
| **Manufacturing Characteristics** | | | | | |
| Rough Cut/Ruptured Grain | No | No | Slight | Two 8" (203 mm) dia. areas or equivalent | 5% of panel |
| Blended Repaired<br>  Tapering Hairline Splits | Two 1/32" x 3" on<br>(0.8 mm x 76 mm)<br>panel ends only | Two 1/16" x 6"<br>(1.6 mm x 152 mm) | Four 1/8" x 8"<br>(3.2 mm x 203 mm) | Four 3/16" x 8"<br>(4.8 mm x 203 mm) | Six 1/4" x 10"<br>(6.4 mm x 254 mm) |
| Repairs | Very Small Blending | Small Blending | Blending | Yes | Yes |
| **Special Characteristics** | | | | | |
| Bird Peck [c] | No | Slight | Yes | Yes | Yes |
| Knife Marks | Knife marks might occur in these dense species. | | | | |
| Quartered | 1" in 12" (25.4 mm in 305 mm) maximum grain slope; 2-1/2" in 12" (63.5 mm in 305 mm) maximum grain sweep | | | | |

Unfilled worm holes, open splits, open joints, open bark pockets, or doze are not allowed in above grades.

[a] Outside components will be a different size to allow for edge trim loss and certain types of matching.

[b] For Pecan and Hickory, conspicuous pin knots mean sound knots 1/4" (6.4 mm) or less in diameter with dark centers larger than 1/16" (1.6 mm). Blending pin knots are sound knots 1/4" (6.4 mm) or less in diameter with dark centers 1/16" (1.6 mm) or less and are allowed in all Grades.

[c] To achieve a more rustic appearance, bird peck shall be specified.

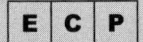 Where the **E**, **C**, or **P** icon is not indicated, the rule applies to all Grades equally

# SECTION 4
## Sheet Products

## compliance requirements

GENERAL/**PRODUCT**/TEST

*Table: 4-044 -* **WALNUT** and **CHERRY** (ANSI/HPVA HP-1 (latest edition))

| Cut | Plain-Sliced (Flat Cut), Quarter-Cut, Rotary Cut | | | | |
|---|---|---|---|---|---|
| Grade Description | AA | A | B | C | D |
| **Color and Matching** | | | | | |
| Sapwood [a] | No | No [a] | No [a] | Yes | Yes |
| Heartwood | Yes | Yes | Yes | Yes | Yes |
| Color Streaks or Spots | Slight | Slight | Yes | Yes | Yes |
| Color Variation | Slight | Slight | Yes | Yes | Yes |
| Sharp Color Contrast at Joints | Yes if Slip, Plank, or Random Match | Yes if Slip, Plank, or Random Match | Yes if Slip, Plank, or Random Match | Yes | Yes |
| Type of Matching:<br>  Book-Matched<br>  Slip-Matched<br>  Pleasing-Matched | Yes<br>Specify<br>-- | Yes<br>Specify<br>-- | Specify<br>Specify<br>Yes | --<br>--<br>-- | --<br>--<br>-- |
| Nominal Minimum Width of Face Components: [b]<br>  Plain Sliced<br>  Quarter<br>  Rotary | 6" (152 mm)<br>3" (76 mm)<br>6" (152 mm) | 5" (127 mm)<br>3" (76 mm)<br>5" (127 mm) | 3" (76 mm)<br>3" (76 mm)<br>4" (102 mm) | No Limit | No Limit |
| **Natural Characteristics** | | | | | |
| Small Conspicuous Burls & Pin Knots, Combined Average Number | 1 per 4 sq ft (3 per 1 m²)<br>8 per 32 sq ft | 1 per 1-1/3 sq ft (8 per 1 m²)<br>24 per 32 sq ft | 2 per 1 sq ft (22 per 1 m²)<br>64 per 32 sq ft | No Limit | No Limit |
| Conspicuous Burls, Maximum Size | 1/4" (6.4 mm) | 3/8" (9.5 mm) | 1/2" (12.7 mm) | No Limit | No Limit |
| Conspicuous Pin Knots, [c]<br>  Average Number<br>  Maximum Size, Dark Part<br>  Total | 1 per 5 sq ft (3 per 1 m²)<br>6 per 32 sq ft<br>1/8" (3.2 mm)<br>1/4" (6.4 mm) | 1 per 2 sq ft (6 per 1 m²)<br>16 per 32 sq ft<br>1/8" (3.2 mm)<br>1/4" (6.4 mm) | 1 per 1 sq ft (11 per 1 m²)<br>32 per 32 sq ft<br>1/8" (3.2 mm)<br>1/4" (6.4 mm) | No Limit | No Limit |
| Scattered Sound and Repaired Knots, Combined Average Number<br>  Maximum Size - Sound<br>  Maximum Size - Repaired<br>  Average Number - Repaired | No | No | 1 per 8 sq ft (4 per 3 m²)<br>4 per 32 sq ft<br>3/8" (9.5 mm)<br>1/8" (3.2 mm)<br>1 per 8 sq ft (4 per 3 m²) | 1 per 4 sq ft (3 per 1 m²)<br>8 per 32 sq ft<br>1/2" (12.7 mm)<br>1/2" (12.7 mm)<br>1 per 8 sq ft (4 per 3 m²) | 1 per 3 sq ft (4 per 1 m²)<br>10 per 32 sq ft<br>1" (25.4 mm)<br>3/4" (19 mm)<br>1 per 6 sq ft (2 per 1 m²) |
| Mineral Streaks | Slight | Slight | Yes | Yes | Yes |
| Bark Pockets | No | No | Few to 1/8" x 1" (3.2 mm x 25.4 mm) | Few to 1/4" x 2" (6.4 mm x 50.8 mm) | 1/4" x 2" (6.4 mm x 50.8 mm) |
| Worm Tracks | No | No | Slight | Few | Yes |
| Vine Marks | Slight | Occasional | Yes | Yes | Yes |
| Cross Bars | Slight | Occasional | Yes | Yes | Yes |
| **Manufacturing Characteristics** | | | | | |
| Rough Cut/Ruptured Grain | No | No | Slight | Slight | Two 8" (203 mm) dia. areas or equivalent |
| Blended Repaired Tapering Hairline Splits | Two 1/32" x 3" (0.8 mm x 76 mm) on panel ends only | Two 1/16" x 6" (1.6 mm x 152 mm) | Four 1/8" x 8" (3.2 mm x 203 mm) | Four 3/16" x 8" (4.8 mm x 203 mm) | Six 1/4" x 10" (6.4 mm x 254 mm) |
| Repairs | Very Small Blending | Small Blending | Blending | Yes | Yes |
| **Special Characteristics** | | | | | |
| Gum Spots and Streaks, Cherry only | Occasional Spots | | Gum Spots and Streaks in Cherry | | |
| Quartered | 1" in 12" (25.4 mm in 305 mm) maximum grain slope; 2-1/2" in 12" (63.5 mm in 305 mm) maximum grain sweep | | | | |

Unfilled worm holes, open splits, open joints, open bark pockets, or doze are not allowed in above grades.
[a] Sapwood is allowed in Grades A and B; however, the percentage shall be agreed upon between buyer and seller.
[b] Outside components will be a different size to allow for edge trim loss and certain types of matching.
[c] For Walnut and Cherry, conspicuous pin knots mean sound knots 1/4" (6.4 mm) or less in diameter with dark centers larger than 1/16" (1.6 mm). Blending pin knots are sound knots 1/4" (6.4 mm) or less in diameter with dark centers 1/16" (1.6 mm) or less and are allowed in all Grades.

©2014 AWI | AWMAC | WI 2nd Edition, October 1, 2014
As may be updated by errata at **awinet.org**, **awmac.com**, or **aws-errata.com**

Architectural Woodwork Standards

# SECTION 4
## Sheet Products

GENERAL / **PRODUCT** / TEST

**compliance requirements**

Where the **E**, **C**, or **P** icon is not indicated, the rule applies to all Grades equally | E | C | P |

### 4.4.6 Softwood Veneer Material Rules

| | | | | | | | |
|---|---|---|---|---|---|---|---|
| 1 | Applies only to the following species: **DOUGLAS FIR, REDWOOD, WESTERN RED CEDAR,** and **WHITE PINE**. | | | | | | |
| 2 | **TYPE I ADHESIVE** is required at non climatic controlled interior or exterior applications. | | | | | | |
| 3 | **CORE** shall be manufacturer's choice, within the provisions of these standards. | | | | | | |
| 4 | **VERTICAL GRAIN** shall have over 90% of the visible face, a minimum average of: | | | | | | |
| 4 | 1 | 5 annual growth rings per 1" (24.4 mm) in width. | | | E | C | P |
| 4 | 2 | 10 annual growth rings per 1" (24.4 mm) in width. | | | E | **C** | P |
| 4 | 3 | 15 annual growth rings per 1" (24.4 mm) in width. | | | E | C | **P** |
| 5 | For **TRANSPARENT FINISH**, boat, router, and/or sled patches shall be limited to 12 in any 4' x 8' (1239 mm x 2438 mm) panel and proportionately reduced for smaller size panels. | | | | E | **C** | **P** |
| 6 | **FACE GRADE REQUIREMENTS** (based on the following Voluntary Product Standard - PS1 (latest edition) and ANSI/HPVA HP-1 (latest edition) definitions and characteristics as indicated) for: | | | | | | |
| 6 | 1 | **WESTERN RED CEDAR** and **WHITE PINE**, rotary, and knotty sliced (ANSI/HPVA HP-1 (latest edition)) are as follows: | | | | | |
| 6 | 1 | 1 | Grade - **B**. | | E | C | P |
| 6 | 1 | 2 | Grade - **A**. | | E | **C** | **P** |
| 6 | 2 | **DOUGLAS FIR** and **REDWOOD**, vertical grain sliced (ANSI/HPVA HP-1 (latest edition)) are as follows: | | | | | |
| 6 | 2 | 1 | Grade - **A**. | | | | |
| 6 | 3 | **DOUGLAS FIR**, rotary sliced (Voluntary Product Standard - PS1 (latest edition)) for: | | | | | |
| 6 | 3 | 1 | **OPAQUE FINISH** are: | | | | |
| 6 | 3 | 1 | 1 | Grade - **B**. | E | C | P |
| 6 | 3 | 1 | 2 | Grade - **A**. | E | **C** | **P** |
| 6 | 3 | 2 | **TRANSPARENT FINISH** are: | | | | |
| 6 | 3 | 2 | 1 | Grade - **A**. | | | |
| | Continues next column | | | | | | |

### 4.4.6 Softwood Veneer Material Rules

| | | | |
|---|---|---|---|
| ▲ From previous column | | | |
| 7 | **SUMMARY TABLES of ALLOWABLE WOOD VENEER FACE GRADE CHARACTERISTICS** are as follows: | | |
| 7 | 1 | *Table: 4-045* - **WESTERN RED CEDAR, WHITE PINE,** and **VERTICAL GRAIN DOUGLAS FIR/REDWOOD**, was: | |
| 7 | 1 | 1 | Reprinted with permission from the Hardwood Plywood Veneer Association and their ANSI/HPVA HP-1 (latest edition). |
| 7 | 2 | *Table: 4-046* - **DOUGLAS FIR**, was: | |
| 7 | 2 | 1 | Reprinted with permission from the US Plywood Standard APA PS-1 (latest edition). |
| | Continues next column ▼ | | |

Where the **E**, **C**, or **P** icon is not indicated, the rule applies to all Grades equally

# SECTION 4
## Sheet Products

## compliance requirements

GENERAL/PRODUCT/TEST

*Table: 4-045* - **WESTERN RED CEDAR, WHITE PINE**, and **VERTICAL GRAIN DOUGLAS FIR/REDWOOD** (ANSI/HPVA HP-1 (latest edition))

| Species | Western Red Cedar | | White Pine | | Douglas Fir | Redwood |
|---|---|---|---|---|---|---|
| Cut | Plain Sliced (Flat Cut), Quarter Cut, Rotary Cut | | | | Sliced Vertical Grain | |
| Grade Description | A | B | A | B | A | A |
| **Color and Matching** | | | | | | |
| Sapwood | Yes | | | | Limited - No Bright Sapwood | Yes |
| Heartwood [a] | Yes | | | | Yes [a] | |
| Color Streaks or Spots | Slight | Yes | Slight | Yes | No | No |
| Color Variation | No | Slight | No | Yes | Slight | Slight |
| Stain, Blue or Brown | No | Slight | No | Slight | No | No |
| **Type of Matching** | | | | | | |
| Book Match | Not Applicable | | | | Yes - Matched for color and grain at the joints | |
| Random Match | Yes, for pleasing appearance | | | | Not Applicable | |
| Slip Match | Not Applicable | | | | Yes, for color | |
| End Match | Specify - Not readily available | | | | Specify - Not readily available | |
| **Natural Characteristics** | | | | | | |
| Burls | Yes | | | | Small | |
| Pin Knots | Yes | | | | No | Yes |
| Sound Knots, maximum size | 2" (50.8 mm) | | 3-1/2" (89 mm) | | No | |
| Spike Knots, maximum size | 2" (50.8 mm) | 3-1/2" (89 mm) | 2" (50.8 mm) | 3-1/2" (89 mm) | No | |
| Repaired Knot Holes, maximum size | 3/4" (19 mm) | 1-1/2" (38 mm) | 3/4" (19 mm) | 1-1/2" (38 mm) | No | |
| Pitch Streaks | Small | | | | Small | No |
| Pitch Pockets | Few to 1/8" x 1" (3.2 mm x 25.4 mm) | Few to 1/8" x 2" (3.2 mm x 50.8 mm) | Few to 1/8" x 1" (3.2 mm x 25.4 mm) | Few to 1/8" x 2" (3.2 mm x 50.8 mm) | No | |
| Crow's Foot | Slight | Occasional | Slight | Yes | No | |
| **Manufacturing Characteristics** | | | | | | |
| Rough Cut | No | Slight | No | Slight | No | |
| Blended, Repaired, Tapering, Hairline Splits | Yes | | | | Yes | |
| Repairs | Blending | | | | Blending | |
| **Special Characteristics** | | | | | | |
| Cross Bar | Not Applicable | | | | No | |

Unfilled worm holes, open splits, open joints, or doze are not allowed in above Grades.
[a] Heartwood must have 6 or more annual rings per 1" (25.4 mm).

# SECTION 4
## Sheet Products

GENERAL/**PRODUCT**/TEST

## compliance requirements

Where the **E**, **C**, or **P** icon is not indicated, the rule applies to all Grades equally | **E** | **C** | **P** |

*Table: 4-046* - **ROTARY CUT DOUGLAS FIR**   (US Plywood Standard APA PS-1 (latest edition))

| Species | Douglas Fir | | |
|---|---|---|---|
| Cut | Rotary Cut | | |
| Grade Description | N | A | B |
| **Color and Matching** | | | |
| Sapwood | Yes - 100% | Yes | Yes |
| Heartwood | Yes - 100% | Yes | Yes |
| Color Streaks or Spots | No | Yes | Yes |
| Color Variation | Well Matched | Yes | Yes |
| Stain | No | Yes | Yes |
| **Type of Matching** | | | |
| Rotary Sliced | Yes | | |
| **Natural Characteristics** | | | |
| Chipped or Depressed Areas | Less than 1/8" x 1/4" (3.2 mm x 6.4 mm) | Less than 1/2" x 2" (12.7 mm x 50.8 mm) | Less than 1/2" x 2" (12.7 mm x 50.8 mm) |
| Cracks or Checks | Less than 1/32" (0.8 mm) wide | Less than 3/16" (4.8 mm) wide | Less than 3/16" (4.8 mm) wide |
| Knots, tight | No | No | Yes, maximum 1" (25.4 mm) dia. |
| Pitch Streaks | Average 3/8" (9.5 mm) wide and blended in color with wood | Average 3/8" (9.5 mm) wide and blended in color with wood | Average 1" (25.4 mm) wide and blended in color with wood |
| Pitch Pockets | No | No | No |
| Splits | Repaired - less than 1/16" x 2" (1.6 mm x 50.8 mm) | Repaired - less than 1-1/4" (31.8 mm) x unlimited | Open - less than 1/32" (0.8 mm) |
| Worm or borer holes | No | No | Yes |
| **Manufacturing Characteristics** | | | |
| Rough Cut | No | No | Yes, maximum 5% of face |
| Repairs | Maximum 6, well matched | Maximum 18, excluding shims | Unlimited |
| Patches | Maximum 3 "Router Patches" 1" x 3-1/2" (25.4 mm x 88.9 mm) | Boat, Router, or Sled, maximum 2-1/4" x 4-1/2" (57.2 mm x 114 mm) | Maximum 4" (102 mm) wide |
| Shims | Maximum 3/16" x 12" (4.8 mm x 305 mm) | Yes | Yes |

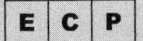

Where the **E**, **C**, or **P** icon is not indicated, the rule applies to all Grades equally

# SECTION 4
## Sheet Products

## compliance requirements

GENERAL / **PRODUCT** / TEST

### 4.4.7 HPDL Material Rules

**8** — **SHALL BE CONSTRUCTED** (in conformance with NEMA LD3 (latest edition)) of multiple layers of phenolic resin saturated kraft paper in combination with a layer of decorative melamine saturated paper, fused together under heat and pressure with the following minimum performance properties, and:

**8.1** — Laminate types are abbreviated as "HGS/L" and "VGS/L" for horizontal and vertical general purpose; "HGP" and "VGP" for post-forming; "HGF" for fire rated, "CLS" for cabinet liner; and "BKL" for backer in accordance with latest NEMA usage. See Table below:

*Continues next column* ▼

### 4.4.7 HPDL Material Rules

▲ From previous column

**9** — **CORE** shall be manufacturer's choice, within the provisions of these standards.

**10** — If **FLAME SPREAD** required, it shall:

**10.1** — Be **CLASS 1**.

**10.2** — Have minimum 0.028" (0.71 mm) thick **BACKING SHEET**.

**10.3** — Be **BONDED** with a Class 1, rigid set adhesive.

**11** — Shall be within the **THICKNESS** range indicated below in *Table 4-047*:

*Table: 4-047* - **HPDL TYPES** and **MINIMUM PERFORMANCE REQUIREMENTS**

|  | HGS | HGL | VGS | VGL | HGP | VGP | HGF | CLS | BKL |
|---|---|---|---|---|---|---|---|---|---|
| Nominal thickness inch / (mm) | 0.048" (1.2) | 0.039" (1.0) | 0.028" (0.7) | 0.020" (0.5) | 0.039" (1.0) | 0.028" (0.7) | 0.048" (1.2) | 0.020" (0.5) | 0.020" (0.5) |
| Thickness tolerance ± inch / (mm) | 0.005" (0.12) | 0.005" (0.12) | 0.004" (0.10) | 0.004" (0.10) | 0.005" (0.12) | 0.004" (0.10) | 0.005" (0.12) | 0.004" (0.10) | 0.004" (0.10) |
| Wear (cycles, min.) | 400 | 400 | 400 | 400 | 400 | 400 | 400 | 400 | n/a |
| % Dim change (cross-direction) | 0.9 | 1.0 | 1.2 | 1.3 | 1.4 | 1.4 | 0.9 | 2.0 | n/a |
| Stain (variety of agents) | No effect 1-10 Moderate effect 11-15 | | | | | | | Moderate effect 1-15 | n/a |
| Cleanability (cycles, maximum) | 20 | | | | | | | | n/a |
| Light | Slight effect | | | | | | | Moderate effect | n/a |
| High temperature | Slight effect | | | | | | | Moderate effect | n/a |
| Radiant heat (seconds, minimum) | 125 | 100 | 80 | 60 | 100 | 80 | 75 | n/a | n/a |
| Boiling water | No effect | | | | Slight effect | | No effect | Moderate effect | n/a |
| Impact (inches, min.) | 50 | 35 | 20 | 15 | 30 | 20 | 45 | 10 | n/a |

Test procedures and minimum requirements shall comply with NEMA-LD3 (latest edition) for HPDL.

**DIMENSIONAL BEHAVIOR** - is similar to that of wood; when humidity varies, the width of a laminate (cross-direction) undergoes greater dimensional changes than the length by a ratio of nearly two to one.

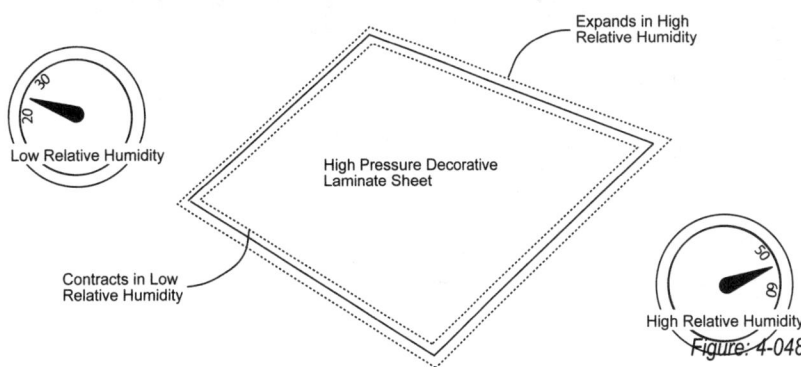

*Figure: 4-048*

# SECTION 4
## Sheet Products

GENERAL/**PRODUCT**/TEST

**compliance requirements**

Where the **E**, **C**, or **P** icon is not indicated, the rule applies to all Grades equally | E | C | P |

### 4.4.8 LPDL Material Rules

1. Shall be melamine, polyester, or foil resin impregnated paper thermally fused under pressure to an approved core, conforming to the following minimum performance properties taken in part from NEMA LD3 (latest edition):

| PROPERTY | MINIMUM PERFORMANCE |
|---|---|
| Wear | Solid Color, 400 Cycles |
| | Wood Grain, 125 Cycles |
| Scuff | No Effect |
| Stain | No Effect on Agents 1-23 |
| | Moderate on Agents 24-29 |
| Cleanability | No Effect (Cleaned in 20 or Fewer Strokes) |
| Light | Slight |
| High Temperature | Slight |
| Radiant Heat | No Effect (After 60 Seconds) |
| Boiling Water | No Effect |
| Impact | 15" (380 mm) Without Fracture |

2. **CORE** shall be manufacturer's choice, within the provisions of these standards.

3. Shall have **BALANCE SHEET**.

### 4.4.9 Vinyl Film Material Rules

1. Shall be a minimum of 2 mils in **THICKNESS**.

2. **CORE** shall be manufacturer's choice, within the provisions of these standards.

3. Shall be opaque or reverse printed.

4. Shall conform to the following average property requirements:

| PROPERTY | VALUE | TEST PROCEDURE |
|---|---|---|
| Mil Thickness | 2 Minimum | Caliper Gauge |
| Light Stability | 300 hrs with no change | ASTM-E-42-64 |
| Flame Retardance | Self Extinguishing (free film) | ASTM E-82-67 |
| Gloss Level | 10-45 | Gardner Glossmeter |
| Abrasion Resistance | Opaque 25-60 | MG loss - 1000 Cyc., CS 10 |
| | Reverse Prints 30-45 | |
| | Reverse Prints 6000-11000 | Cycles to Print Failure, CS 17 |

5. Shall not have **SURFACE APPEARANCE** affected when exposed to the following agents:

| | | |
|---|---|---|
| Water | Coffee | Olive Oil |
| Beet Juice | Vinegar | Alcohol |
| Mustard | Shoe Polish | Mercurochrome |
| Washable Inks | Crayon | Tea |
| Household Detergents and Soaps | | |

### 4.4.10 MDO Material Rules

1. Shall be (in conformance with APA PS1 (latest edition)) a thermosetting phenolic resin impregnated cellulose fiber sheet or sheets containing not less than 34% phenolic resin after pressing.

2. **CORE** shall be manufacturer's choice, within the provisions of these standards.

3. Shall have **BALANCE SHEET**.

### 4.4.11 HDO Material Rules

1. Shall be (in conformance with APA PS1 (latest edition)) a thermosetting phenolic resin impregnated cellulose fiber sheet or sheets, not less than 0.012" (0.30 mm) in thickness after pressing.

2. Shall be allowed in lieu of paint grade wood veneer for opaque finish.

3. **CORE** shall be manufacturer's choice, within the provisions of these standards.

4. Shall have Balance sheet.

### 4.4.12 Hardboard Material Rules

1. Shall be (in conformance with CAP/ANSI A135.4 (latest edition)) a panel manufactured of interfelted lignocellulosic fibers, consolidated under heat and pressure to a density of 31 lb/ft$^3$ or greater with the following minimum performance properties based on 1/4" (6.4 mm) thickness, as follows for:

   1. **STANDARD GRADE:**

   | PROPERTY | PERFORMANCE | | | |
   |---|---|---|---|---|
   | Water Absorption | 25% Maximum | | | |
   | Thickness Swelling | 20% Maximum | E | C | P |
   | Modulus of Rupture | 4500 psi | | | |
   | Tensile Strength - Parallel | 2200 psi | | | |
   | Tensile Strength - Perpendicular | 90 psi | | | |

   2. **TEMPERED GRADE:**

   | PROPERTY | PERFORMANCE | | | |
   |---|---|---|---|---|
   | Water Absorption | 20% Maximum | | | |
   | Thickness Swelling | 15% Maximum | E | C | P |
   | Modulus of Rupture | 6000 psi | | | |
   | Tensile Strength - Parallel | 3000 psi | | | |
   | Tensile Strength - Perpendicular | 130 psi | | | |

# SECTION 4
## Sheet Products

**compliance requirements** — GENERAL/PRODUCT/TEST

> Where the **E**, **C**, or **P** icon is not indicated, the rule applies to all Grades equally

### 4.4.13 Particleboard Material Rules

1. Shall be (in conformance with ANSI A208.1 (latest edition)) a generic term for a composite panel primarily composed of cellulosic materials (usually wood), generally in the form of discrete pieces or particles, as distinguished from fibers, bonded together with a bonding system, and which may contain additives to a density between 40-50 lb/ft³ (640-800 kg/m³), requiring:
   1. **GRADE M2** or better with the following minimum properties:
      
      | PROPERTY | VALUE |
      |---|---|
      | Thickness Swelling | 5.5% Maximum |
      | Modulus of Rupture (M-2) | 1885 psi |
      | Modulus of Rupture (M-3) | 2393 psi |

### 4.4.14 Medium Density Fiberboard (MDF) Material Rules

1. Shall be (in conformance with ANSI A208.2 (latest edition)) a panel composed of cellulosic fibers and a bonding system cured under heat and pressure. MDF density is typically between 31 lbs/ft³ (500 kg/m³) and 62 lbs/ft³ (1000 kg/m³). For formaldehyde emission limits, thin MDF is defined as MDF with a thickness less than or equal to 0.315 inches (8 mm), requiring:
   1. **GRADE 130** or better with the following minimum properties:
      
      | PROPERTY | VALUE |
      |---|---|
      | Thickness Swelling | 11% Maximum |
      | Modulus of Rupture (Grade 130) | 3130 psi |
      | Modulus of Rupture (Grade 155) | 4050 psi |

### 4.4.15 Balance Sheet Material Rules

1. Where required within the Product Sections, shall include:
   1. **WOOD VENEER** of the same thickness and compatible species.
   2. **HPDL** of the same material and thickness.
   3. **OVERLAY** of the same material and thickness.

### 4.4.16 Backer Material Rules

1. Where required within the Product Sections, shall include:

### 4.4.16 Backer Material Rules

| | | | E | C | P |
|---|---|---|---|---|---|
| 1 | 1 | Brown colored, minimum 0.002" (0.05 mm) thick, factory applied, hot-melt coating of blended wax petroleum, copolymer resins, and anti oxidants with swipe controlling agents. | E | C | P |
| 1 | 2 | Polyester or melamine overlay. | E | C | P |
| 1 | 3 | Man made wood fiber veneers, impregnated with acrylic melamine, fortified, high load resin system, a minimum of 0.020" (0.51 mm). | E | C | P |
| 1 | 4 | Synthetic polymer treated backing sheet 0.017" (0.43 mm) - 0.019" (0.48 mm) nominal thickness, designed for use with HPDL. | E | C | P |
| 1 | 5 | Dark brown colored, 0.015" (0.38 mm) nominal thickness, phenolic resin impregnated kraft paper. | E | C | P |
| 1 | 6 | Thermoset resin treated wood fiber, brown colored, 3-ply construction, a minimum of 0.020" (051 mm) in thickness. | E | C | **P** |
| 1 | 7 | Minimum 0.020" (0.51 mm) thick laminate, conforming to NEMA LD3 (latest edition). | E | C | **P** |

### 4.4.17 Epoxy Resin Material Rules

1. Shall be a panel produced from a composite of epoxy resin, silica, inert fillers, and organic hardeners, cast and cured in ovens at elevated temperatures, homogenous throughout, and nonabsorbent, with the following minimum performance properties:

   | PROPERTY | VALUE | TEST PROCEDURE[1] |
   |---|---|---|
   | Compressive Strength | 30,000 psi minimum | ASTM-D-695 |
   | Density | 120 lbs./ft³ | ASTM-D-792 |
   | Flexural Strength | 11,000 psi minimum | ASTM-D-790 |
   | Hardness (Rockwell M) | 100(Min.) | ASTM-D-785 |
   | Water Absorption | 0.05% minimum | ASTM-D-570 |

   [1] Latest edition

### 4.4.18 Natural Stone Material Rules

1. Shall not be subject to minimum performance properties established by these standards, because it is a natural product.

### 4.4.19 Engineered Stone Material Rules

1. Shall be as specified and subject to the manufacturer's instructions and these standards.

# SECTION 4
## Sheet Products

GENERAL / **PRODUCT** / TEST

Where the **E**, **C**, or **P** icon is not indicated, the rule applies to all Grades equally | E | C | P |

# compliance requirements

### 4.4.20 Solid Surface Material Rules

1. Shall be a manufactured, filled cast polymeric resin panel. Fillers may be used to enhance both its performance properties and aesthetics. With a homogeneous composition throughout its thickness, solid surface requires no finish coat and is capable of being fabricated with inconspicuous seams and the following minimum performance properties:

| PROPERTY | VALUE | TEST PROCEDURE [1] |
|---|---|---|
| Abrasion Resistance | Pass | ANSI-Z124.7 |
| Bacterial Resistance | Pass | ASTM-G-22 |
| Boiling Water Surface Resistance | No visible effect | NEMA LD3-3.05 |
| Color Stability (200 Hrs.) | No visible effect | NEMA LD-3 |
| Fungal Resistance | Pass | ASTM-G-22, or ISO.846 |
| Gloss (60° Gardner) | 5-20 minimum | NEMA LD-3 |
| Hardness (Rockwell M) | 90 minimum | ASTM-D-785 |
| | 50 minimum | Barcol |
| High Temp. Resistance | No visible effect | NEMA LD-3-3.06 |
| Impact Resistance | No failure | NEMA LD-3-3.08 |
| Izod Impact | 0.25 ft.-lbs./in. of notch | ASTM-D-256 |
| Radiant Heat Resistance | No visible effect | NEMA LD-3-3.010 |
| Specific Gravity [2] | 1.5 gram/cm$^3$ minimum | |
| Stain Resistance | Pass | ANSI-Z-124 |
| Surface Flammability | Meet or exceed applicable code and regulations | |
| Tensile Strength | 4,000 psi minimum | ASTM-D-638 |
| Tensile Modulus | 500,000 psi minimum, or 25,000 psi minimum at 1/8" nominal material | ASTM-D-638 |
| Tensile Elongation | 1% maximum, or 10% maximum at 1/8" nominal material | ASTM-D-638 |
| Thermal Expansion | 2.3 x 10$^{-5}$ in./in./F° max. | ASTM-D696 |
| Water Absorption | 1% maximum, 24 hr | ASTM-D-570 |

[1] Latest edition
[2] Approximate weight per 12" x 12" (305 x 305 mm):
   1/8" (3 mm) 1.02 lbs. (0.544 kg),
   1/4" (6 mm) 2.10 lbs. (0.953 kg),
   1/2" (13 mm) 4.20 lbs. (1.905 kg),
   3/4" (19 mm) 6.20 lbs. (2.812 kg).

2. Shall be **COLOR** and **PATTERN MATCHED**, use of same batch materials is required for adjacent sheets.

3. **REPAIRS**, while fully functional might be visible.

### 4.4.21 Solid Phenolic Material Rules

1. Shall be a panel composed of melamine impregnated decorative surface papers superimposed over a varying number of kraft phenolic core sheets to achieve a desired thickness, with the following minimum performance properties:

| PROPERTY | VALUE | TEST PROCEDURE [1] |
|---|---|---|
| Compressive Strength | 24,000 psi minimum | ASTM-D-695 |
| Density | 90 lbs./ft$^3$ | ASTM-D-792 |
| Flame Test | Self-Extinguishing | ASTM-D-635 |
| Flexural Strength | 15,000 psi minimum | ASTM-D-790 |
| High Temp. Resistance | No Visible Effect | NEMA LD-3-3.06 |
| Impact Resistance (1/2 lb. Ball at 120") | No Effect | NEMA LD-3-3.08 |
| Modulus of Elasticity | 1,400,000 psi minimum | ASTM-D-790 |
| Screw Pull Out [2] | 340 lbs. (154 kg) minimum at 3/8" (9.5 mm) penetration 680 lbs. (308 kg) minimum at 3/4" (19 mm) penetration | |
| Shear Strength | 2,000 psi minimum | |
| Tensile Strength | 15,000 psi minimum | ASTM-D-638 |
| Thickness Tolerance | ± 1/32" (0.8 mm) minimum | |
| Water Absorption | 3% maximum | ASTM-D-570 |

[1] Latest edition
[2] Resistance based on 1/4" (6.4 mm) machine screw

**Applicable TESTS, may be found in Sections 6 - 11; however, these tests are only applicable to the exposed and semi-exposed portions of installed millwork products.**

# Architectural Woodwork Standards

# FINISHING

## SECTION 5

# SECTION 5
## Finishing

## table of contents

### INTRODUCTORY INFORMATION

| | |
|---|---|
| Introduction | 110 |
| Purpose | 110 |
| Factory / Field Finishing | 110 |
| Important Considerations | 110 |
|     Specifications | 110 |
|     Varying Costs | 110 |
|     Intermixing Systems | 110 |
|     Application | 110 |
|     Curing | 110 |
|     Prefinished Wood Panels | 110 |
|     Panel Products | 111 |
|     Barber Pole | 111 |
|     Grain | 111 |
|         Open | 111 |
|         Closed | 111 |
|     Color and Grain Enhancement | 111 |
|     Color Match and Consistency | 111 |
|     Sheen | 111 |
|     Transparent | 111 |
|     Blotchy Appearance | 111 |
| Techniques to Consider | 111 |
|     Sanding | 111 |
|     Wash Coat | 112 |
| Blue Stain | 112 |
| Fire Retardant Treated Wood and Coatings | 112 |
| AWS Finishing Systems | 112 |
| General Performance Characteristics Table | 113 |
| Specific Performance Characteristics Table | 114 |
| Usage and Performance Score Comparison Table | 115 |
| Specify Requirements For | 116 |
| Recommendations | 116 |

### COMPLIANCE REQUIREMENTS

#### GENERAL

| | |
|---|---|
| Basic Considerations | 117 |
|     Grade | 117 |
|         Classifications | 117 |
|     Compliance Requirements | 117 |
|     Contract Documents | 117 |
|     Aesthetic Compliance | 117 |
|     Listing | 117 |
|     Factory or Field | 117 |
|     Industry Practices | 117 |
|         Door Manufacturer | 117 |
|         Finisher of Wood Components | 117 |
|         Finishing Systems | 117 |

#### PRODUCT

| | |
|---|---|
| Scope | 118 |
|     Typical Inclusions | 118 |
|     Typical Exclusions | 118 |
| Default Stipulation | 118 |
| Rules | 118 |
|     Errata | 118 |
|     Basic Rules | 118 |
|         Finisher | 118 |
|         Samples | 118 |
|     Aesthetic Rules | 119 |
|         Overall Appearance | 119 |
|         Application Techniques | 119 |
|         Incompatibility | 119 |
|         Paneling | 119 |
|         Trim and Frames | 119 |
|         Doors | 119 |
|         Casework | 119 |
|         Defects and Workmanship | 119 |
|         First Class Workmanship | 120 |

# SECTION 5
## Finishing

## table of contents

**COMPLIANCE REQUIREMENTS** (continued)

**PRODUCT** (continued)
- Material Rules .................................................. 120
  - Priming and Sealing ..................................... 120
  - Flow Properties ........................................... 120
  - Chemical Resistance ................................... 120
- Application Rules ............................................ 121
  - Sanding ....................................................... 121
  - Factory Priming .......................................... 121
  - Ventilation ................................................... 121
  - Over spray .................................................. 121
  - Removal ..................................................... 121
  - Cleaning ..................................................... 121
  - Scratches ................................................... 121
  - Consistency ................................................ 121
  - Film Thickness ........................................... 121
  - Filler ........................................................... 121
  - Thoroughly Dry ........................................... 121
  - Sapwood .................................................... 121
  - Staining ...................................................... 121
  - Generic Coating Schedule .......................... 121
  - System Coating Schedule .......................... 122
    - System 1 ............................................... 122
    - System 2 ............................................... 122
    - System 3 ............................................... 122
    - System 4 ............................................... 122
    - System 5 ............................................... 122
    - System 6 ............................................... 123
    - System 7 ............................................... 123
    - System 8 ............................................... 123
    - System 9 ............................................... 123
    - System 10 ............................................. 123
    - System 11 ............................................. 124
    - System 12 ............................................. 124
    - System 13 ............................................. 124
  - After Finishing ............................................ 124
  - Touch up .................................................... 124

**TESTS**
- Basic Considerations ...................................... 125
  - Visual Testing ............................................. 125
  - Testing for Consistency .............................. 125
  - Sheen Testing ............................................ 125

# SECTION 5
## Finishing

## introductory information

### INTRODUCTION

Section 5 pertains to shop and field finishing of architectural woodwork. Thirteen finishing systems are outlined with application rules and methods of testing.

Quality assurance can be achieved by adherence to the AWS and will provide the owner a quality product at competitive pricing. Use of a qualified Sponsor Member firm to provide your woodwork will help ensure the manufacturer's understanding of the quality level required. Illustrations in this Section are not intended to be all inclusive, other engineered solutions may be acceptable. In the absence of specifications; methods of fabrication are the manufacturer's choice. The design professional, by specifying compliance to the AWS increases the probability of receiving the product quality expected.

### PURPOSE

The purpose of finishing woodworking is twofold. First, the finish is used traditionally as a means to enhance or alter the natural beauty of the wood. Second, the finish shall offer protection to the wood from damage by moisture, contaminants, and handling. It is important to understand that a quality finish must offer acceptable performance and also meet the aesthetic requirements of the project.

The AWS illustrates a number of finishing systems. The finishing system provides a protective surface for the product. Some of these systems are in general use; others are intended for special conditions and can only be applied under a strictly controlled environment. The cost of the systems vary, the higher performing finishes usually being more costly than the lower performing finishes. Unnecessary cost could be added to a project through over specification.

When specifying, use the system name as set forth in the AWS. Involve your woodwork manufacturer early in the design process to evaluate the systems in relation to your project requirements. Choose performance characteristics which meet, but do not exceed, the needs of your project in the interest of value engineering.

The listing of a finish system in the AWS does not imply an endorsement of the materials and/or methods or compliance with federal and/or local Environmental Protection Agency or other requirements.

### FACTORY or FIELD FINISHING

Both are permitted, provided there is no violation of applicable codes or regulations.

- **Factory finishing** is usually specified for high quality work where superior appearance and performance of the finish is desired. Benefits of factory finishing include consistency, control of film thickness, environmental compliance, and curing/drying of the finish in a controlled atmosphere. Its use assumes a maximum degree of manufacturer prefabrication so that site installation can be performed with a minimum amount of cutting, fitting, and adjustment to facilitate project completion.

- **Field finishing** is typically specified when there is not a demand or specific need for a superior appearance and is not necessarily part of the woodwork contract. This would normally be specified in the painting specification section. The finisher/painter is responsible for examining and accepting the woodwork as supplied prior to the commencement of finishing. The finisher/painter is responsible for meeting or exceeding the control sample for surface performance characteristics (such as color, texture, and sheen), including proper surface preparation, shading, and blending of color, and other requirements as defined in this standard when so referenced.

- **Wood parts on decorative laminate cabinets**: finish is required on all wood pulls, trims, applied molding, edge bands, drawer boxes, and interior wood parts of decorative laminate casework.

### IMPORTANT CONSIDERATIONS:

- **Specifications** too often, call for finishes based on samples or guide language from a specialty manufacturer.

Select the performance criteria which best meets the needs of your client from the finish tables. Finish chemistry, performance, value to performance ratio, and your finisher's abilities should be considered.

- **Varying costs** of finish systems typically relate directly to their performing characteristics.

- **Intermixing systems** will likely cause quality and/or performance problems; they are usually not compatible with each other.

Examples include the over specification of polyurethane or polyester topcoats when they are neither necessary or available from a custom fabricator.

- **Application** of finish material in excess of manufacturer's film thickness recommendations can cause the finish to fail.

Brush applied finishes are not recommended for factory finished architectural woodwork, and are not covered by the AWS.
Application techniques and other variances make the execution of the finish system difficult to determine. These standards provide the minimum requirements. The desired end result is to provide a finish that is both durable and achieves the desired appearance.

- **CURING** of finish systems have a wide range of variance. Shortest cure time is UV cured coatings, and longest being water based air dry coatings. Heat and air movement will speed the recoat and cure time.

For the most part the method should not concern the design professional or specification writer. It is the performance of the topcoat which is important.

UV (ultraviolet light) is typically used for high volume, repetitive applications, and requires special reactors to cure. A number of prefinished panel products are coated with materials designed specifically for UV curing. A wide range of UV cured roll coat flat line panel finishes are available. Just as there are in the conventional spray/air cured coatings. Consult with the fabricator for performance tests and details

- **Prefinished Wood Panels** and decorative overlays have aesthetic and performance characteristics which meet or exceed the AWS, and should be evaluated, approved and specified by the design professional when desired.

# SECTION 5
## Finishing

## introductory information

- **Panel products** and/or wood doors require balanced coats of finishing materials for stability and to remain free of warp.

- **Barber pole** effect is most evident when veneer leaves are book matched. Because book matched veneer panels or door faces are made up by turning every other piece (leaf) of veneer over, like the pages of a book, the face of one leaf and the back of the next leaf is exposed. This exposes the "tight" and "loose" face of the leaves. One of the most striking examples of Barber Pole effect can be seen in book matched rift and quarter cut Oak. Check with your manufacturer when you are considering specifying rift or quartered veneers.

- **Grain** can significantly impact a finish's visual appearance and smoothness. If a filled finish is required it must be so specified. As a rule, close grain woods do not require filler. See Table.

  For finishing purposes, the following woods are classified as:

  **Open Grain**

  | | |
  |---|---|
  | Ash | Mahogany, Philippine |
  | Butternut | Oak, Red |
  | Chestnut | Oak, White |
  | Mahogany, African | Walnut |
  | Mahogany, American | |

  **Close Grain**

  | | |
  |---|---|
  | Alder, Red | Gum |
  | Beech | Maple |
  | Birch | Pine |
  | Cherry | Poplar |
  | Fir | |

- **Color** and **grain enhancement** of a system, from the addition of a single stain, to a multiple step build of one color on another with wash coats in between for enhanced appearance is not included in the basic systems and needs to be specified.

  Aesthetically, systems may vary from no stain, to a single stain, to a multiple step application. Some samples will require multiple color and finish steps in order to meet the architect's requirements. The system specified may not include all steps necessary to match the architect's example or requirements.

Color and grain enhancement of some finishes require the build of one color step on another. This will sometimes require an additional protective wash coat between color steps. Generally, this procedure adds to the depth and beauty of the finish. Each added step increases costs and shall be specified.

- **Color match** and **consistency** is often misleading. The best case achievable using a natural product like wood in a wide variety of lighting conditions is a good "blend" of color and tone throughout the project area. The natural color of the wood product is altered by the application of even a clear topcoat. Further alteration is achieved through the use of stains, glazes, bleaches, etc. Wood changes color; especially Cherry, Fir, American and African Mahogany, Walnut, Teak, and others. Filled nail holes will not change with wood. The apparent consistency of the color is a combination of light reflectance, cellular structure, natural characteristics, applied colors, and sheen.

  Color and "matching" of a sample are often highly subjective. Individual perception, ambient lighting, and reflectivity influence judgement. Design professionals are encouraged to consult directly with a manufacturer during the design and selection phase of each project.

- **Sheen** is the result of many factors, including finishing techniques, processes, stains, topcoats and the wood itself. Coating manufacturers use a variety of names for different sheens. An untrained eye can see a 10 point or greater difference in sheen.

  The following sheen ranges were developed by measuring the reflectance of a direct light source at a 60 degree angle with a gloss meter:

  - Flat = 8 - 14
  - Satin = 15 - 25
  - Satin Gloss = 26 - 49
  - Semi gloss = 50 - 70
  - Gloss = 71 - 90

- **Transparent** finishes are applied in varying operations, typically consisting of some combination of hand sanding to remove job handling marks, staining, filling, sealing, sanding, and surface coating. Some exotic species have a high natural oil content and do not accept finishes similar to other hardwoods; because of this, the most common finish used is penetrating oil without any filling or sealing dyes or pigments in a stain.

- **Blotchy appearance** occurs because some wood species exhibit an uneven distribution of large and small pores in their structure. The occurrence of this is readily apparent in such hardwood species as Maple and Birch and, to a lesser degree, in Cherry. This irregular distribution of pores usually causes an uneven absorption of stain, hence, an apparent blotchy appearance in the finish. Reduction of the blotching condition can sometimes be achieved by proper sanding, wash coating (prior to staining) or by choosing non penetrating pigments, such as dyes, alcohol stains or glaze. When these steps are required or desired, they shall be specified in addition to finish system selection.

### TECHNIQUES TO CONSIDER

While a blotchy appearance and the "barber pole effect" may occur in any species, due to the natural characteristics of wood, there are steps that can be taken to reduce these effects. The following are two of the techniques that are of particular importance.

- **Sanding** - While the selection of species, cut and match are major factors in the final appearance of a project, the first step, in controlling the quality of finished appearance, is proper sanding.

  An important element of this standard is the statement "just prior to staining." Specifications that indicate "factory shall finish sand prior to shipment" do not provide a correct solution for proper surface preparation. Such a directive fails to take into account the length of time panels will be stored at the job site, potential damage from handling and the effects of changes in the relative humidity. Proper sanding can only be done, just prior to staining/finishing.

# SECTION 5
## Finishing

## introductory information

### TECHNIQUES TO CONSIDER (continued)

- **Sanding** (continued)

  The successful sanding of panels, or flush doors, is best accomplished with a hand block, powered pad sander, wide belt sander or stroke sander, exerting uniform pressure over the entire surface. Depending upon the condition of the surface it may be necessary to use successively finer grits of abrasive to properly prepare the surface, brushing off the surface between grits. The AWS sets forth the smoothness requirement for all Grades of work. Proper and complete surface preparation is the key factor in the successful finish procedure.

- **Wash Coat** - A wash coat is a thin coat of material, usually clear lacquer or vinyl sealer (6 to 10 parts thinner to one part sealer, topcoat). A wash coat can fulfill several purposes such as: to stiffen the small wood fibers that are raised by the staining operation, so they can be cut off easily with fine sandpaper (320 grit), to seal the stain, particularly if it is a bleeding type, to aid in the wiping and clean up of filler, and to minimize excessive penetration of stain or filler to minimize blotchiness. As with any finish process, samples should always be prepared to ensure that the desired finish is achieved.

### IRON STAIN

Iron stain occurs in some species of veneers when natural tannic acid in the wood comes in contact with iron and or moisture. Enough moisture may occur during heavy rains or high humidity in buildings not yet temperature controlled.

To prevent iron stain, never use steel wool on the bare wood. Fine particles of the wool will cling to the wood and cause trouble later. If you use shellac (a solvent for iron), it should not be stored in iron containers. To remove iron stain prior to finishing, we recommend a solution of oxalic acid crystals. The solution is made by dissolving 12 ounces of crystals in one gallon of lukewarm water. Use a plastic or rubber container. Wear rubber gloves while working with the solution. Apply it to the stained areas with a brush or sponge.

To remove the oxalic acid, use a sponge and a bucket filled with lukewarm water. Squeeze the sponge to remove excess water and wipe the entire surface of the Oak wood to remove the acid residue. Rinse the sponge frequently in clean lukewarm water as you wipe. Pour out the water and add 1 qt. of fresh lukewarm water to the bucket. Add 2 tbsp. baking soda to the water and stir with a spoon to dissolve. Insert a fresh sponge into the solution and squeeze out the excess water. Wipe the entire surface of the Oak to neutralize any remaining acid residue and stop the bleaching process. Allow the surface to dry and sand with 150 to 180 grit sandpaper. The entire surface should be treated to avoid spotting. Failure to rinse the treated area adequately may have a damaging effect on the finish subsequently applied, or may cause damage to nearby glass, porcelain or other surfaces in confined areas. Damage may not result immediately, but may result during storage or after installation.

### FIRE RETARDANT TREATED WOOD and COATINGS

Fire retardant treatments may affect the finishes intended to be used on the wood, particularly if transparent finishes are planned. The compatibility of finishes should be tested before they are applied.

"Fire retardant" coatings usually are of the intumescent type. They may be water based or solvent based, but both contain ingredients which, under the influence of heat, produce gases and char like products, resulting in the formation of a thick nonflammable crust that effectively insulates combustible cores from heat and flame. However, these ingredients are for the most part water sensitive and therefore reduce durability and range of usage of the coatings.

These coatings only delay the spread of fire and help contain it to its origin. To be of appreciable value, fire retardant coatings must be applied in strict conformance with the manufacturer's instructions. These finishes are not particularly durable and their use should be restricted to application over interior surfaces.

The need for, and effectiveness of, fire retardant and fire resistant finishes depends on the type of construction, nature of occupancy, and other technical features of the building. Because these finishes are considerably more expensive and have reduced durability, their use should be carefully limited to those areas where confining fire spread is the overwhelming consideration; for example, interior entrances, hallways, stairwells and ceilings.

### AWS FINISHING SYSTEMS

Apply to both transparent or opaque applications, unless otherwise indicated: Specification of a system requires listing both the system number and the name, along with any desired enhancements.

**SYSTEM - 1**, Lacquer, Nitrocellulose

**SYSTEM - 2**, Lacquer, Pre Catalyzed

**SYSTEM - 3**, Lacquer, Post Catalyzed

**SYSTEM - 4**, Latex Acrylic, Water Based

**SYSTEM - 5**, Varnish, Conversion

**SYSTEM - 6**, Oil, Synthetic Penetrating (available in transparent only)

**SYSTEM - 7**, Vinyl, Catalyzed

**SYSTEM - 8**, Acrylic Cross Linking, Water-Based

**SYSTEM - 9**, UV Curable, Acrylated Epoxy, Polyester or Urethane

**SYSTEM - 10**, UV Curable, Water Based

**SYSTEM - 11**, Polyurethane, Catalyzed

**SYSTEM - 12**, Polyurethane, Water Based

**SYSTEM - 13**, Polyester, Catalyzed

# SECTION 5
## Finishing

## introductory information

*Table: 5-001* - **GENERAL PERFORMANCE CHARACTERISTICS of AWS FINISHING SYSTEMS:**

| | Lacquer, Nitrocellulose | Lacquer, Pre Catalyzed | Lacquer, Post Catalyzed | Latex Acrylic, Water Based | Varnish, Conversion | Oil, Synthetic Penetrating (available in transparent only) | Vinyl, Catalyzed | Acrylic Cross Linking, Water-Based | UV Curable, Acrylated Epoxy, Polyester or Urethane | UV Curable, Water Based | Polyurethane, Catalyzed | Polyurethane, Water Based | Polyester, Catalyzed |
|---|---|---|---|---|---|---|---|---|---|---|---|---|---|
| | **1** | **2** | **3** | **4** | **5** | **6** | **7** | **8** | **9** | **10** | **11** | **12** | **13** |
| General Durability | 2 | 2 | 3 | 2 | 4 | 1 | 4 | 2 | 5 | 5 | 5 | 3 | 5 |
| Repairability | 5 | 4 | 3 | 3 | 3 | 5 | 4 | 4 | 1 | 3 | 2 | 4 | 1 |
| Abrasion Resistance | 2 | 4 | 4 | 3 | 4 | 1 | 4 | 4 | 5 | 4 | 5 | 4 | 5 |
| Finish Clarity | 5 | 4 | 5 | 2 | 3 | 5 | 3 | 4 | 5 | 5 | 3 | 4 | 4 |
| Yellowing in Time | 1 | 2 | 3 | 5 | 4 | 2 | 1 | 4 | 3 | 5 | 4 | 4 | 3 |
| Finish Flexibility | 1 | 2 | 3 | 3 | 4 | 5 | 4 | 3 | 2 | 3 | 4 | 4 | 1 |
| Moisture Resistance | 3 | 3 | 4 | 1 | 4 | 1 | 5 | 3 | 5 | 4 | 5 | 4 | 5 |
| Solvent Resistance | 1 | 2 | 4 | 1 | 5 | 1 | 5 | 3 | 5 | 5 | 5 | 4 | 5 |
| Stain Resistance | 2 | 4 | 5 | 3 | 5 | 1 | 5 | 4 | 5 | 5 | 5 | 4 | 5 |
| Heat Resistance | 1 | 2 | 5 | 1 | 5 | 1 | 5 | 3 | 5 | 5 | 5 | 4 | 5 |
| Household Chemical Resistance | 3 | 4 | 5 | 3 | 5 | 2 | 5 | 4 | 5 | 5 | 5 | 4 | 5 |
| Build/Solids | 2 | 3 | 3 | 3 | 4 | 1 | 4 | 3 | 5 | 4 | 4 | 3 | 4 |
| Drying Time | 5 | 5 | 5 | 2 | 4 | 2 | 5 | 4 | 5 | 5 | 3 | 5 | 2 |

5 = Excellent to 1 = Poor. The numerical ratings are subjective judgments based on the general performance of generic products. Special formulations and facilities will influence some of the performance characteristics.

**NOTES** for *Table: 5-002* on following page.

Testing was evaluated in an ISO 9000-certified laboratory using the following ASTM test criteria: Chemical Resistance Testing - ASTM D1308 (latest edition), Wear Index - Abrasion Resistance Testing - ASTM D4060 (latest edition), Cold Check Resistance - ASTM D1211 (latest edition), Cross Hatch Adhesion - ASTM D3359 (latest edition).
Baseline data for application prior to testing: A. 45-55% humidity at 70-80 degrees Fahrenheit; B. Water-borne coatings must be cured in a dehumidified atmosphere and can be assisted with infrared light and good air movement.
Performance indicator numbers are used, with the following definitions:

<u>For chemical resistance and wear index - abrasion resistance:</u>
    5 - No effect from the test.
    4 - Minimal effect or slight change and little repair required.
    3 - Some effect; noticeable change, and the coating will recover with minimal repairs.
    2 - Moderate effect, performance adversely affected and repairs required.
    1 - Poor performance and film failure is imminent and repairs difficult.

<u>For cross-hatch adhesion:</u>
    5 - Edges of the cuts are completely smooth; none of the squares of the lattice are detached.
    4 - Small flakes of the coating are detached at intersections; less than 5% of the area is affected.
    3 - Small flakes of the coating are detached along the edges and at the intersections of cuts; 5 to 15% of the area is affected.
    2 - Coating has flaked along the edges and on parts of the squares; 15 to 35% of the area is affected.
    1 - Coating has flaked along the edges of the cuts in large ribbons and whole squares have detached; 35 to 65% of the area is affected.

# SECTION 5
## Finishing

### introductory information

*Table: 5-002* - SPECIFIC PERFORMANCE CHARACTERISTICS for AWS FINISHING SYSTEMS for TRANSPARENT and OPAQUE TOPCOATS:

| | Lacquer, Nitrocellulose | Lacquer, Pre Catalyzed | Lacquer, Post Catalyzed | Latex Acrylic, Water Based | Varnish, Conversion | Oil, Synthetic Penetrating (available in transparent only) | Vinyl, Catalyzed | Acrylic Cross Linking, Water-Based | UV Curable, Acrylated Epoxy, Polyester or Urethane | UV Curable, Water Based | Polyurethane, Catalyzed | Polyurethane, Water Based | Polyester, Catalyzed |
|---|---|---|---|---|---|---|---|---|---|---|---|---|---|
| | 1 | 2 | 3 | 4 | 5 | 6 | 7 | 8 | 9 | 10 | 11 | 12 | 13 |
| Vinegar | 3 | 4 | 5 | 4 | 5 | 3 | 5 | 5 | 5 | 5 | 5 | 4 | 5 |
| Lemon Juice | 3 | 4 | 5 | 4 | 5 | 3 | 5 | 5 | 5 | 5 | 5 | 4 | 5 |
| Orange Juice | 3 | 4 | 5 | 4 | 5 | 3 | 5 | 5 | 5 | 5 | 5 | 4 | 5 |
| Catsup | 3 | 4 | 5 | 4 | 5 | 2 | 5 | 5 | 5 | 5 | 5 | 4 | 5 |
| Coffee | 3 | 4 | 5 | 4 | 5 | 2 | 5 | 5 | 5 | 5 | 5 | 4 | 5 |
| Olive Oil | 2 | 3 | 5 | 3 | 5 | 2 | 5 | 5 | 5 | 5 | 5 | 4 | 5 |
| Boiling Water | 3 | 4 | 5 | 4 | 5 | 3 | 5 | 5 | 5 | 5 | 5 | 4 | 5 |
| Cold Water | 5 | 5 | 5 | 5 | 5 | 3 | 5 | 5 | 5 | 5 | 5 | 4 | 5 |
| Nail Polish Remover | 1 | 2 | 3 | 2 | 4 | 1 | 2 | 2 | 5 | 5 | 4 | 3 | 4 |
| Household Ammonia | 3 | 4 | 5 | 4 | 5 | 2 | 4 | 2 | 5 | 5 | 5 | 4 | 5 |
| VM&P Naphtha | 3 | 4 | 5 | 4 | 5 | 1 | 4 | 5 | 5 | 5 | 5 | 4 | 5 |
| Isopropyl Alcohol | 1 | 2 | 3 | 1 | 5 | 2 | 4 | 3 | 5 | 5 | 5 | 4 | 5 |
| Wine | 3 | 4 | 5 | 4 | 5 | 2 | 4 | 5 | 5 | 5 | 5 | 5 | 5 |
| Windex™ | 3 | 3 | 4 | 3 | 5 | 2 | 3 | 4 | 5 | 4 | 5 | 4 | 5 |
| 409 Cleaner™ | 3 | 3 | 4 | 4 | 5 | 1 | 4 | 4 | 5 | 5 | 5 | 4 | 5 |
| Lysol™ | 3 | 5 | 5 | 4 | 5 | 2 | 4 | 3 | 5 | 5 | 5 | 4 | 5 |
| 33% Sulfuric Acid | 3 | 4 | 5 | 3 | 5 | 1 | 4 | 5 | 5 | 5 | 5 | 4 | 5 |
| 77% Sulfuric Acid | 1 | 2 | 3 | 1 | 1 | 1 | 2 | 1 | 4 | 3 | 4 | 3 | 4 |
| 28% Ammonium Hydroxide | 1 | 2 | 3 | 1 | 5 | 1 | 4 | 2 | 5 | 5 | 5 | 3 | 5 |
| Gasoline | 1 | 2 | 5 | 2 | 5 | 1 | 4 | 5 | 5 | 5 | 5 | 4 | 4 |
| Murphy's Oil Soap™ | 5 | 5 | 5 | 5 | 5 | 2 | 4 | 4 | 5 | 5 | 5 | 5 | 5 |
| Vodka 100 Proof | 3 | 4 | 5 | 4 | 5 | 2 | 4 | 3 | 5 | 5 | 5 | 4 | 5 |
| 1% Detergent | 3 | 4 | 5 | 4 | 5 | 3 | 4 | 5 | 5 | 5 | 5 | 5 | 5 |
| 10% TSP | 3 | 4 | 5 | 4 | 4 | 1 | 5 | 2 | 5 | 5 | 5 | 5 | 5 |
| **SUBTOTAL** | 65 | 86 | 110 | 82 | 114 | 46 | 100 | 95 | 119 | 117 | 118 | 97 | 117 |
| Wear | 2 | 3 | 4 | 2 | 5 | 1 | 4 | 4 | 5 | 5 | 5 | 5 | 4 |
| Cold Check | 5 | 5 | 5 | 5 | 5 | 5 | 5 | 5 | 5 | 5 | 5 | 5 | 5 |
| Adhesion | 5 | 5 | 5 | 5 | 5 | 5 | 5 | 5 | 5 | 5 | 5 | 5 | 5 |
| **TOTAL SCORE** | 77 | 99 | 124 | 94 | 129 | 57 | 114 | 109 | 134 | 132 | 133 | 112 | 131 |

**NOTES** are on previous page.

# SECTION 5
## Finishing

## introductory information

The following system overview tables are intended to give an overview of and help identify the correct standard or specialty finishing system to meet a project's needs; however, they are only relative to the topcoat, not any prior color or filler coats.

Differences between systems of 10 points or fewer are not generally considered significant enough to justify the typical added expense of a higher-rated system. This systems listing does not imply an endorsement of the materials or compliance with applicable codes and regulations. Due to changing environmental regulations and finish technologies, design professionals need to discuss finish options with a manufacturer located in the area of the project.

*Table: 5-003* - USAGE and PERFORMANCE SCORE COMPARISONS for AWS FINISHING SYSTEMS for TRANSPARENT and OPAQUE TOPCOATS:

| | TYPICAL USAGE | SCORE | WHY AND WHY NOT |
|---|---|---|---|
| 1 - Lacquer, Nitrocellulose | Use in climate controlled environment for trims, furniture, paneling, and ornamental work. | 77 | Why - Repairable; widely available; quick-drying<br>Why not - Lack of durability and resistance to most solvents and water; yellows over time. |
| 2 - Lacquer, PreCatalyzed | Use in climate controlled environment for furniture, casework, paneling, ornamental work, stair parts (except treads), frames, windows, blinds, shutters, and doors. | 99 | Why - Repairable; stain-, abrasion-, chemical-resistance.<br>Why not - Some yellowing; moderate build. |
| 3 - Lacquer, PostCatalyzed | Use in climate controlled environment for furniture, casework, paneling, ornamental work, stair parts (except treads), frames, windows, blinds, shutters, and doors. | 124 | Why - Repairable; finish clarity; stain-, heat-, abrasion-, chemical-resistance.<br>Why not - Some yellowing; moderate build. |
| 4 - Latex Acrylic, Water Based | Use in climate controlled environment for furniture, casework, paneling, ornamental work, stair parts (except treads), frames, windows, blinds, shutters, and doors. | 94 | Why - Low VOCs; finish clarity (some formulations); stain resistance; yellowing resistance.<br>Why not - Low durability; solvent- and heat-resistance; slow drying time. |
| 5 - Varnish, Conversion | Use in climate controlled environment for furniture, casework, paneling, ornamental work, stair parts, frames, windows, blinds, shutters, and doors. | 129 | Why - Durable; widely available; good build.<br>Why not - Occasional lack of finish clarity. |
| 6 - Oil, Synthetic Penetrating | Use in climate controlled environment on furniture or trims requiring a close-to-the-wood look or very low sheen. | 57 | Why - Close-to-wood, antique look; low sheen.<br>Why not - Labor-intensive to apply and maintain, refreshing finish required from time-to-time; low resistance properties to most substances. |
| 7 - Vinyl, Catalyzed | Use in climate controlled environment, often on kitchen, bath, office furniture, and laboratory casework. | 114 | Why - Durable; widely available; fast drying.<br>Why not - Occasional lack of finish clarity. |
| 8 - Acrylic Cross Linking, Water-Based | Use in climate controlled environment for furniture, casework, paneling, ornamental work, stair parts, frames, windows, blinds, shutters, and doors. | 109 | Why - Fine durability; excellent abrasion-, solvent-, stain-, and chemical-resistance; moderately fast-drying; resists moisture<br>Why not - Possibility of discoloration over time. |
| 9 - UV Curable, Acrylated Epoxy, Polyester or Urethane | Use in climate controlled environment, doors, paneling, flooring, stair parts, and casework, where applicable; consult your finisher before specifying. | 134 | Why - Low VOCs; durable; near 100% solids usage; quick-drying (cure), may qualify as Green Guard.<br>Why not - Difficult to repair with UV finish, as this requires a handheld UV lamp; availability varies; easy repair with lacquers or conversion varnish. |
| 10 - UV Curable, Water Based | Use in climate controlled environment, doors, paneling, flooring, stair parts, and casework where applicable; consult your finisher before specifying. | 132 | Why - Low VOCs; quick-drying (cure), maybe Green Guard.<br>Why not - Difficult to repair with UV finish, requires handheld UV lamp; availability varies; easy repair with lacquers or conversion varnish. |
| 11 - Polyurethane, Catalyzed | Use in climate controlled environment; some formulas available for exterior environments; floors, stairs, high-impact areas; some doors; generally not good for casework, paneling, windows, blinds, and shutters. | 133 | Why - Durable; good build.<br>Why not - Slow-drying; very difficult to repair; some formulations hazardous to spray-personnel without air make-up suits. |
| 12 - Polyurethane, Water Based | Use in climate controlled environment for furniture, casework, paneling, ornamental work, stair parts, frames, windows, blinds, shutters, and doors. | 112 | Why - Improved durability; excellent abrasion-, solvent-, stain-, and chemical-resistance; moderately fast-drying; resists moisture.<br>Why not - Tannins in some wood species may cause discoloration over time. |
| 13 - Polyester, Catalyzed | Use in climate controlled environment for furniture, casework, paneling, ornamental work, blinds, shutters, and some doors. | 131 | Why - Durable; good build; can be polished.<br>Why not - Not widely available; slow-curing; requires special facilities and skills; very difficult to repair; brittle finish flexibility. |

# SECTION 5
## Finishing

### introductory information

**SPECIFY REQUIREMENTS FOR**

- FIRE RESISTANCE
- CHEMICAL RESISTANCE
- Use of **FILLER**, **WASH COAT**, or **STAIN**
- FILLED FINISH
- **AWS** finishing system for transparent or opaque application:
  - **SYSTEM - 1**, Lacquer, Nitrocellulose
  - **SYSTEM - 2**, Lacquer, Pre Catalyzed
  - **SYSTEM - 3**, Lacquer, Post Catalyzed
  - **SYSTEM - 4**, Latex Acrylic, Water-Based
  - **SYSTEM - 5**, Varnish, Conversion
  - **SYSTEM - 6**, Oil, Synthetic Penetrating (available in transparent only)
  - **SYSTEM - 7**, Vinyl, Catalyzed
  - **SYSTEM - 8**, Acrylic Cross Linking, Water-Based
  - **SYSTEM - 9**, UV Curable, Acrylated Epoxy, Polyester or Urethane
  - **SYSTEM - 10**, UV Curable, Water-Based
  - **SYSTEM - 11**, Polyurethane, Catalyzed
  - **SYSTEM - 12**, Polyurethane, Water-Based
  - **SYSTEM - 13**, Polyester, Catalyzed

**RECOMMENDATIONS**

- If **FIELD FINISHED**, include in Division 09 of the specifications:
  - "Before finishing, all exposed portions of woodwork shall have handling marks or effects of exposure to moisture removed with a thorough, final sanding over all surfaces of the exposed portions, using appropriate grit sandpaper, and shall be cleaned before applying sealer or finish."
  - "Concealed surfaces of all architectural woodwork that might be exposed to moisture, such as those adjacent to exterior concrete walls, shall be primed."

- **REVIEW** the **GENERAL** portion of Sections 3 and 4 for an overview of the characteristics and the minimum acceptable requirements of lumber and/or sheet products that might be used herein.

- Avoid **BRUSH-APPLIED** finishes for architectural woodwork; they are not covered by these standards.

- Avoid **BLEACHED VENEERS** because of potential finishing problems.

- Avoid **JOBSITE FINISHING** because a factory-controlled finishing environment offers a superior finished product; however, jobsite finishing is permitted, provided there is no violation of applicable codes and regulations.

- Avoid **EXTERIOR WOOD DOORS** finished in a dark color that will absorb heat when exposed to direct sunlight or without adequate overhead soffit protection.

- For **CHEMICAL RESISTANCE**, these standards have adapted SEFA's (Scientific Equipment and Fixture Association) standard list of 49 chemicals/concentrations, their required methods of testing, and their minimum acceptable results as the minimum acceptable chemical-resistance requirement for finishes used at exposed and semi-exposed surfaces, when such is required by specification.

- **SEFA's** chemical listing, methods of testing, and minimum acceptable results can be found in **APPENDIX**.

- **FIRE-RETARDANT** or **RESISTANT FINISHES** are subject to applicable codes and regulations, the use of fire-rated cores in lieu of fire-retardant finishes is recommended.

- Some **PRE-FINISHED** wood panels or decorative overlays have aesthetic and performance characteristics that meet or exceed these standards without using a listed or recommended finish system.

  - Such products should be evaluated and/or specified by the design professional.

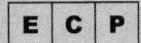 Where the **E**, **C**, or **P** icon is not indicated, the rule applies to all Grades equally

# SECTION 5
## Finishing

## compliance requirements

**GENERAL**/PRODUCT/TEST

### Including: Factory and Field Finishing

**5.1 BASIC CONSIDERATIONS**

**1 GRADE**

1.1 **CLASSIFICATIONS** of **ECONOMY**, **CUSTOM**, and **PREMIUM** are used within these standards only in reference to the acceptable quality of workmanship, material, or installation in a completed architectural woodwork product.

1.2 Section deals with finish application, which is a component of finished products covered in Sections 6 - 12.

1.2.1 Grade classifications are only for the purpose of identifying finish applications that can be used in finished products meeting those Grades.

1.2.2 They are not intended to be used as a Grade or to judge a particular finish system.

**2 COMPLIANCE REQUIREMENTS**

2.1 Apply only to surfaces visible after fabrication and installation.

2.2 Establish criteria as to which, if any, application characteristics are acceptable.

2.3 Address priming, when required.

3 **CONTRACT DOCUMENTS** shall govern if in conflict with these standards.

4 **AESTHETIC COMPLIANCE** requirements apply only to surfaces visible after manufacturing, installation and finishing.

5 **LISTING** of a finish system in these standards does not imply an endorsement of such or compliance with applicable codes and regulations.

**5.1 BASIC CONSIDERATIONS** (continued)

7 **FACTORY** or **FIELD** finishing are permitted, provided there is no violation of applicable codes or regulations.

7.1 **FACTORY** finishing is usually specified for high-quality work where superior appearance and performance of the finish is desired.

7.2 **FIELD** finishing is typically specified when there is not a demand or specific need for a superior appearance and is not necessarily part of the woodwork contract.

7.2.1 The finisher is responsible for examining and accepting the woodwork as supplied prior to the commencement of finishing.

7.2.2 The finisher is responsible for meeting or exceeding the control sample for surface performance characteristics (such as color, texture, and sheen), including proper surface preparation, shading, and blending of color, and other requirements as defined in this standard when so referenced.

**8 INDUSTRY PRACTICES**

8.1 **DOOR MANUFACTURERS** typically offer only their own standard finishes. If one or more acceptable door manufacturers are listed in a project's specifications, it indicates that each manufacturer's standard finish system is acceptable.

8.2 **FINISHING** of **WOOD COMPONENTS** on **DECORATIVE LAMINATE** casework (including pulls, trims, moldings, and edgebanding) is included in the manufacturer's scope of work.

8.3 **FINISHING SYSTEMS** are applied per the manufacturer's recommendations.

# SECTION 5
## Finishing

GENERAL / **PRODUCT** / TEST

**compliance requirements**

*Where the E, C, or P icon is not indicated, the rule applies to all Grades equally* | E | C | P |

### 5.2 SCOPE

1. All factory finishing of architectural woodwork.

2. **TYPICAL INCLUSIONS**

   2.1 The application of transparent or opaque finish on all architectural woodwork specified to be factory prefinished and/or jobsite finished within the architectural woodwork contract.

   2.2 The application of primer prior to delivery to the jobsite for final paint finish to be applied later by others.

   2.3 Raw wood parts on decorative laminate cabinets, except as specified in the contract documents, such as wood finger pulls or wood drawer bodies incorporated into the assembly.

   2.4 All preparatory work, labor, equipment, materials, and related supplies to produce the specified finish.

3. **TYPICAL EXCLUSIONS**

   3.1 All painting or priming of building surfaces not specified within the architectural woodwork contract.

   3.2 All finishing of architectural woodwork specified within the painting specifications.

   3.3 Jobsite touch up after delivery or installation.

   3.4 Brush applied topcoat finishes, except as called out under the scope of work for the custom woodwork manufacturer, such as faux finishes.

   3.5 Items to receive subsequent coats of finish materials by others.

   3.6 Exterior painting or priming.

### 5.3 DEFAULT STIPULATION

1. If not otherwise specified or indicated in the contract documents, all work under this section shall meet the same Grade as the item being finished, and/or the finishing system selected shall be the choice of the finishing contractor.

### 5.4 RULES

1. The following rules shall govern unless a project's contract documents require otherwise.

2. These rules are intended to provide a well defined degree of control over a project's quality of finishing.

3. **ERRATA**, published on the Sponsor Associations' websites at www.awinet.org, www.awmac.com, or www.aws-errata.com, **shall take precedence over these rules**, subject to their date of posting and a project's bid date.

#### 5.4.4 Basic Rules

| | | | | |
|---|---|---|---|---|
| 1 | | | | **FINISHER** shall: |
| | 1 | | | Determine and report in writing before the start of finishing, and: |
| | 1 | 1 | | Material or finish system requirements in violation of applicable codes or regulations, and: |
| | 1 | 1 | 1 | It shall **NOT** be the responsibility of the finisher to comply with a specification requirement or finishing system that is illegal or otherwise disallowed in a particular area by some regulatory agency. |
| | 1 | 2 | | Any condition that might affect proper finish application. |
| | 1 | 3 | | Moisture content of product and/or surrounding wall surfaces, such as drywall or plaster, above 12%. |
| | 1 | 4 | | **FILLED FINISH** is only required if so specified. |
| 2 | | | | **SAMPLES** shall |
| | 1 | | | Be submitted and approved before finishing of product, and: |
| | 1 | 1 | | Due to variance in wood color within the same species and even within the same log, a range of color shall be expected on finished wood products, and: |
| | 1 | 1 | 1 | To establish an acceptable sheen and color range, a minimum of three samples shall be submitted. |
| | 1 | 2 | | Shall be at least 12" x 12" (305 mm x 305 mm) if on a panel product, and: |
| | 1 | 2 | 1 | Protected from light. |
| | 1 | 2 | 2 | Be as wide as practical if on lumber by a minimum of 12" (305 mm) in length. |
| | 1 | 3 | | Shall be on material representative of that to be used for the project. |
| | 1 | 4 | | Shall each bear a label identifying the job name, the design professional, the contractor, and the finish system number. |

*Continues next column* ▼

Where the **E**, **C**, or **P** icon is not indicated, the rule applies to all Grades equally

# SECTION 5
## Finishing

**compliance requirements** — GENERAL/PRODUCT/TEST

### 5.4.4 Basic Rules
▲ From previous column

| | | | | | |
|---|---|---|---|---|---|
| 3 | | **AESTHETIC RULES** apply only to exposed and semi-exposed surfaces visible after installation. | | | |
| 4 | | **OVERALL APPEARANCE** shall be: | | | |
| 4 | 1 | Compatible in color and grain. | E | C | P |
| 4 | 2 | Well matched for color and grain. | E | C | P |
| 5 | | **APPLICATION TECHNIQUES** and other variances make the execution of the finish system difficult to determine. These standards provide the minimum requirements. The desired end result is to provide a finish that is both durable and achieves the desired appearance. | | | |
| 6 | | **INCOMPATIBILITY** of finish to wood shall be prevented, and: | | | |
| 6 | 1 | It is the responsibility of the finisher to: | | | |
| 6 | 1 | 1 — Conduct, as applicable, a test sample to check for species of wood that reacts unfavorably with certain finishes. | | | |
| 6 | 1 | 2 — Apply a sealer, if required, before finishing to nullify such a chemical reaction. | | | |
| 7 | | **PANELING** requires: | | | |
| 7 | 1 | Adjacent panels to be finished together to achieve maximum uniformity of color, and: | | | |
| 7 | 1 | 1 — If possible, entire elevations shall be finished together. | | | |
| 8 | | **TRIM** and **FRAMES** require only the exposed faces and edges to be topcoated. | | | |
| 9 | | **DOORS** require: | | | |
| 9 | 1 | Two faces and two vertical edges to be finished and: | | | |
| 9 | 1 | 1 — The top/bottom edges and hardware preparation areas at hinges and lock edges to be sealed. | | | |
| 9 | 2 | An equal number of coats of the same material applied to each side. | | | |
| 9 | 3 | Pairs of doors and openings with sidelights and transoms finished together to achieve maximum uniformity of color. | | | |
| 9 | 4 | **FINISHES**, other than those furnished by a door manufacturer, be specified to be applied by the woodwork finisher. | | | |
| 10 | | **CASEWORK** requires: | | | |
| 10 | 1 | All exposed exterior, exposed interior and semi-exposed surfaces be finished. | | | |
| 10 | 2 | All six faces of cabinet doors receive the same number of coats to prevent warping and/or twisting. | | | |

Continues next column ▼

### 5.4.4 Basic Rules
▲ From previous column

| | | | | | |
|---|---|---|---|---|---|
| 11 | | **DEFECTS and WORKMANSHIP:** | | | |
| 11 | 1 | Regardless of requirements otherwise stated in these standards, final sanding prior to the application of finishing materials is the responsibility of the finisher. | | | |
| 11 | 2 | **HANDLING, MACHINING,** or **TOOL MARKS** are not allowed. | | | |
| 11 | 3 | **INDENTATIONS** and **SCRAPES** shall be for: | | | |
| 11 | 3 | 1 — Opaque - Filled or patched. | E | C | P |
| 11 | 3 | 2 — Transparent - Filled or patched. | E | C | P |
| 11 | 3 | 3 — Transparent - Steamed out. | E | C | P |
| 11 | 4 | **MOISTURE EFFECTS**, such as raised grain or blue stain, shall be removed. | | | |
| 11 | 5 | **PARTICLES** and **DUST** shall be removed. | | | |
| 11 | 6 | At finish, **SANDING SCRATCHES** shall be: | | | |
| 11 | 6 | 1 — Inconspicuous beyond 72" (1830 mm). | E | C | P |
| 11 | 6 | 2 — Inconspicuous beyond 36" (915 mm). | E | C | P |
| 11 | 6 | 3 — Not permitted. | E | C | P |
| 11 | 7 | **ORANGE PEEL** (slight depressions in the surface similar to the skin of an orange) shall be: | | | |
| 11 | 7 | 1 — Inconspicuous beyond 72" (1830 mm). | E | C | P |
| 11 | 7 | 2 — Inconspicuous beyond 36" (915 mm). | E | C | P |
| 11 | 7 | 3 — Not permitted. | E | C | P |
| 11 | 8 | **RUNS** (running of wet finish film in rivulets) shall be: | | | |
| 11 | 8 | 1 — Inconspicuous beyond 36" (915 mm). | E | C | P |
| 11 | 8 | 2 — Not permitted. | E | C | P |
| 11 | 9 | **SAGS** (partial slipping of finish film creating a curtain effect) shall be: | | | |
| 11 | 9 | 1 — Inconspicuous beyond 72" (1830 mm). | E | C | P |
| 11 | 9 | 2 — Inconspicuous beyond 36" (915 mm). | E | C | P |
| 11 | 9 | 3 — Not permitted. | E | C | P |
| 11 | 10 | **BLISTERING** (small, swelled areas like water blisters on human skin) shall be: | | | |
| 11 | 10 | 1 — Inconspicuous beyond 36" (915 mm). | E | C | P |
| 11 | 10 | 2 — Not permitted. | E | C | P |
| 11 | 11 | **BLUSHING** (whitish haze, cloudy) shall be: | | | |
| 11 | 11 | 1 — Inconspicuous beyond 36" (915 mm). | E | C | P |
| 11 | 11 | 2 — Not permitted. | E | C | P |

Continues next column ▼

# SECTION 5
## Finishing

GENERAL / PRODUCT / TEST

compliance requirements

Where the **E**, **C**, or **P** icon is not indicated, the rule applies to all Grades equally — **E** **C** **P**

### 5.4.4 Basic Rules

▲ From previous column

| | | | | E | C | P |
|---|---|---|---|---|---|---|
| 11 | **DEFECTS and WORKMANSHIP** (continued) | | | | | |
| 11 | 12 | | **CHECKING** or **CRAZING** (crowfeet or irregular line separation) shall be: | | | |
| 11 | 12 | 1 | Inconspicuous beyond 36" (915 mm). | E | C | P |
| 11 | 12 | 2 | Not permitted. | | C | P |
| 11 | 13 | | **CRACKING** (formation like dried mud) shall be: | | | |
| 11 | 13 | 1 | Inconspicuous beyond 36" (915 mm). | E | C | P |
| 11 | 13 | 2 | Not permitted. | | C | P |
| 11 | 14 | | **PARTICLES** shall be: | | | |
| 11 | 14 | 1 | Inconspicuous beyond 36" (915 mm). | E | C | P |
| 11 | 14 | 2 | Not permitted. | | C | P |
| 11 | 15 | | **ADHESIVE SPOTS** shall be: | | | |
| 11 | 15 | 1 | Inconspicuous beyond 36" (915 mm). | E | C | P |
| 11 | 15 | 2 | Not permitted. | | C | P |
| 11 | 16 | | **FILLED NAIL HOLES** shall be: | | | |
| 11 | 16 | 1 | Inconspicuous beyond 108" (2745 mm). | E | C | P |
| 11 | 16 | 2 | Inconspicuous beyond 72" (1830 mm). | | C | P |
| 11 | 16 | 3 | Inconspicuous beyond 36" (915 mm). | | | P |
| 11 | 17 | | **FIELD REPAIRS** and **TOUCH UPS** shall be: | | | |
| 11 | 17 | 1 | Inconspicuous beyond 108" (2745 mm). | E | C | P |
| 11 | 17 | 2 | Inconspicuous beyond 72" (1830 mm). | | C | P |
| 11 | 17 | 3 | Inconspicuous beyond 36" (915 mm). | | | P |
| 12 | **FIRST CLASS WORKMANSHIP** is required in compliance with these standards. | | | | | |

### 5.4.5 Material Rules

| | | | | E | C | P |
|---|---|---|---|---|---|---|
| 1 | **PRIMING/SEALING**: | | | | | |
| 1 | 1 | | Is required when factory finishing is required, and: | | | |
| 1 | 1 | 1 | Shall be of a compatible material and conform to the following application requirements: | | | |
| 1 | 1 | 2 | **STANDING** and **RUNNING TRIM** shall be sealed at 1 mil dry. | | C | P |
| 1 | 1 | 3 | **BACKS** of wood wall and ceiling surfacing shall be sealed at 2 mil dry. | | C | P |
| 1 | 1 | 4 | **CASEWORK** shall be sealed at 1 mil dry. | | C | P |
| 1 | 1 | 5 | **DECORATIVE LAMINATE** faced woodwork shall be sealed at 1 mil dry. | | C | P |
| 2 | **FLOW PROPERTIES** requires capability of drying and/or curing free of streaks, sags, or mottle. | | | | | |
| 3 | **CHEMICAL RESISTANCE**, if so specified, at exposed horizontal surfaces shall pass a 24 hour exposure test, whereas exposed vertical surfaces and semi-exposed surfaces shall pass a 1 hour exposure test (ASTM 1308, latest edition). | | | | | |

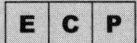

Where the **E**, **C**, or **P** icon is not indicated, the rule applies to all Grades equally

# SECTION 5
## Finishing

**compliance requirements** — GENERAL/**PRODUCT**/TEST

### 5.4.6 Application Rules

|  | | |  |
|---|---|---|------|
| 1 | | | Requires **SANDING** before and during all finishing procedures and: |
| 1 | 1 | | Exposed surfaces being block sanded parallel with the grain direction and the appropriate grit paper to prevent unacceptable blotchy and/or nonuniform appearance after staining or finishing. |
| 1 | 2 | | Removal of handling marks or effects of exposure to moisture. |
| 1 | 3 | | Steaming out of deep scratches. |
| 1 | 4 | | Easing of sharp edges with a light sanding. |
| 1 | 5 | | Removal of all raised grain, cross sanding, burnishing and machining marks, sanding inconsistencies, and/or defects. |
| 1 | 6 | | Light sanding between coats per manufacturer's recommendations. |
| 2 | | | **FACTORY PRIMING** with one coat of primer applied to appropriate surfaces is required, however: |
| 2 | 1 | | Factory sanding of the primed surfaces, after priming is not required. |
| 3 | | | **VENTILATION**, adequate and continuous, is required with sufficient heat to maintain temperatures above 65° F for 24 hours before, during, and 48 hours after application of finishes. |
| 4 | | | **OVER SPRAY** protection is required to prevent spray or droppings from fouling surfaces not being finished, as is: |
| 4 | 1 | | Repair of damage as a result of inadequate or unsuitable protection. |
| 5 | | | **REMOVAL** of electrical plates, surface hardware, fittings, and fastenings prior to finishing operation is required, and: |
| 5 | 1 | | Removed items are to be carefully stored, cleaned, and replaced on completion of work in each area, and: |
| 5 | 2 | | Use of solvent for cleaning that might remove permanent finish is not allowed. |
| 6 | | | **CLEANING** of surfaces with a dry brush or a tack cloth before applying sealer, stain, or primer is required. |
| 7 | | | **SCRATCHES**, dents, marks, screw and nail holes, and rough edges shall be properly repaired before finishing. |
| 8 | | | **CONSISTENCY** of each coat shall be as recommended by the manufacturer. |
| 9 | | | **FILM THICKNESS** shall conform to manufacturer's data or recommendation. |

*Continues next column*

### 5.4.6 Application Rules

*From previous column*

| # | | | Rule | E | C | P |
|---|---|---|------|---|---|---|
| 10 | | | **FILLER** (including paste types) when specified shall be applied before sealers or topcoats. | E | C | P |
| 11 | | | **THOROUGHLY DRY** each coat before sanding or applying additional coats. | | | |
| 12 | | | **SAPWOOD** treatment: | | | |
| 12 | 1 | | At **EXPOSED SURFACES**: | | | |
| 12 | 1 | 1 | Blending is not required. | E | C | P |
| 12 | 1 | 2 | Sapwood must be blended in the final finish appearance. | E | C | P |
| 12 | 2 | | At **SEMI-EXPOSED SURFACES**, blending is not required. | | | |
| 13 | | | **STAINING** at: | | | |
| 13 | 1 | | Dark stain finishes, the surface shall be wash coat sealed. | | | |
| 13 | 2 | | Oil stain shall be wipe applied in small areas at a time. | | | |
| 13 | 3 | | Non grain raising dye stains can be spray applied. | | | |
| 13 | 4 | | Open grain species shall be stained before applying sealer. | | | |
| 14 | | | **GENERIC COATING SCHEDULE**: | | | |
| 14 | 1 | | **CONCEALED CASEWORK SURFACES** that abut walls, floors, and ceilings, require a sanding sealer or self seal system. | E | C | P |
| 14 | 2 | | **SEMI-EXPOSED** surfaces, including wood drawer sides and cabinet interiors and [bracketed items if specified] requires: | | | |
| 14 | 2 | 1 | Wash coat (only at stained finish on close grain). | | | |
| 14 | 2 | 2 | [Stain]. | | | |
| 14 | 2 | 3 | Sanding sealer. | | | |
| 14 | 2 | 4 | Sand. | | | |
| 14 | 2 | 5 | First topcoat. | E | C | P |
| 14 | 2 | 6 | Second topcoat. | E | C | P |

*Continues next column*

©2014 AWI | AWMAC | WI  2nd Edition, October 1, 2014
As may be updated by errata at **awinet.org**, **awmac.com**, or **aws-errata.com**

# SECTION 5
## Finishing

### compliance requirements

**Where the E, C, or P icon is not indicated, the rule applies to all Grades equally** | E | C | P |

## 5.4.6 Application Rules

▲ From previous column

| 14 | | | GENERIC COATING SCHEDULE (continued) | | | |
|---|---|---|---|---|---|---|
| 14 | 3 | | EXPOSED surfaces with [bracketed items if specified] requires: | | | |
| 14 | 3 | 1 | Wash coat (only at stained finish on close grain). | | | |
| 14 | 3 | 2 | [Stain]. | | | |
| 14 | 3 | 3 | Sanding sealer. | | | |
| 14 | 3 | 4 | Sand. | | | |
| 14 | 3 | 5 | First topcoat. | | | |
| 14 | 3 | 6 | Second topcoat. | E | C | P |
| 14 | 3 | 7 | Third topcoat. | E | C | P |
| 14 | 3 | 8 | And INCLUDES wood components on decorative laminate casework. | | | |

| 15 | | | SYSTEM COATING SCHEDULE: | | | |
|---|---|---|---|---|---|---|
| 15 | 1 | | SYSTEM - 1, LACQUER, NITROCELLULOSE including [bracketed items if specified] requires at: | | | |
| 15 | 1 | 1 | CLOSE GRAIN woods: | | | |
| 15 | 1 | 1 | 1 Wash coat, nitrocellulose (only at stained finish). | E | C | |
| 15 | 1 | 1 | 2 Wash coat, vinyl (only at stained finish). | | C | P |
| 15 | 1 | 1 | 3 [Stain]. | | | |
| 15 | 1 | 1 | 4 Sealer, nitrocellulose. | E | C | |
| 15 | 1 | 1 | 5 Sealer, vinyl. | | C | P |
| 15 | 1 | 1 | 6 First topcoat. | | | |
| 15 | 1 | 1 | 7 Second topcoat. | E | C | P |
| 15 | 1 | 2 | OPEN GRAIN woods (including filled finish) requires: | | | |
| 15 | 1 | 2 | 1 Wash coat, nitrocellulose (only at filled finish). | | C | |
| 15 | 1 | 2 | 2 Wash coat, vinyl (only at filled finish). | | C | |
| 15 | 1 | 2 | 3 [Stain]. | | | |
| 15 | 1 | 2 | 4 Filler (only at filled finish). | | C | P |
| 15 | 1 | 2 | 5 Sealer, nitrocellulose. | E | C | |
| 15 | 1 | 2 | 6 Sealer, vinyl. | | C | P |
| 15 | 1 | 2 | 7 First topcoat. | | | |
| 15 | 1 | 2 | 8 Second topcoat (only at filled finish). | | C | |
| 15 | 1 | 2 | 9 Second topcoat. | | C | P |

Continues next column ▼

## 5.4.6 Application Rules

▲ From previous column

| 15 | | | SYSTEM COATING SCHEDULE (continued) | | | |
|---|---|---|---|---|---|---|
| 15 | 2 | | SYSTEMS - 2 and 3, LACQUER, PRE AND POST CATALYZED including [bracketed items if specified] requires at: | | | |
| 15 | 2 | 1 | CLOSE GRAIN woods: | | | |
| 15 | 2 | 1 | 1 Wash coat, vinyl (only at stained finish). | | | |
| 15 | 2 | 1 | 2 [Stain]. | | | |
| 15 | 2 | 1 | 3 Sealer, vinyl. | | | |
| 15 | 2 | 1 | 4 First topcoat. | | | |
| 15 | 2 | 1 | 5 Second topcoat. | E | C | P |
| 15 | 2 | 2 | OPEN GRAIN woods (including filled finish): | | | |
| 15 | 2 | 2 | 1 Washcoat, vinyl (only at filled finish). | E | C | P |
| 15 | 2 | 2 | 2 [Stain]. | | | |
| 15 | 2 | 2 | 3 Filler (only at filled finish). | E | C | P |
| 15 | 2 | 2 | 4 Sealer, vinyl. | | | |
| 15 | 2 | 2 | 5 First topcoat. | | | |
| 15 | 2 | 2 | 6 Second topcoat. | E | C | P |
| 15 | 3 | | SYSTEM - 4, LATEX ACRYLIC, WATER BASED including [bracketed items if specified] requires at: | | | |
| 15 | 3 | 1 | CLOSE and OPEN GRAIN woods; | | | |
| 15 | 3 | 1 | [Stain]. | | | |
| 15 | 3 | 2 | Sealer, water reduced. | | | |
| 15 | 3 | 3 | First topcoat, water reducible acrylic. | | | |
| 15 | 3 | 4 | Second topcoat, water reducible acrylic. | E | C | P |
| 15 | 4 | | SYSTEM - 5, VARNISH, CONVERSION including [bracketed items if specified] requires at: | | | |
| 15 | 4 | 1 | CLOSE GRAIN woods: | | | |
| 15 | 4 | 1 | 1 Wash coat, reduced conversion varnish (only at stained finish). | E | C | |
| 15 | 4 | 1 | 2 Wash coat, vinyl (only at stained finish). | | C | P |
| 15 | 4 | 1 | 3 [Stain]. | | | |
| 15 | 4 | 1 | 4 Sealer, reduced conversion varnish. | E | C | |
| 15 | 4 | 1 | 5 Sealer, vinyl. | | C | P |
| 15 | 4 | 1 | 6 First topcoat. | | | |
| 15 | 4 | 1 | 7 Second topcoat. | E | C | P |

Continues next column ▼

# SECTION 5
## Finishing

**compliance requirements** — GENERAL/PRODUCT/TEST

ECP: Where the **E**, **C**, or **P** icon is not indicated, the rule applies to all Grades equally

### 5.4.6 Application Rules

▲ From previous column

| | | | | | | E | C | P |
|---|---|---|---|---|---|---|---|---|
| 15 | | | | **SYSTEM COATING SCHEDULE** (continued) | | | | |
| 15 | 4 | | | **SYSTEM - 5, VARNISH, CONVERSION** (continued) | | | | |
| 15 | 4 | 2 | | **OPEN GRAIN** woods (including filled finish): | | | | |
| 15 | 4 | 2 | 1 | [Wash coat, reduced conversion varnish] (only at filled finish). | | E | C | P |
| 15 | 4 | 2 | 2 | [Wash coat, vinyl] (only at filled finish). | | E | C | **P** |
| 15 | 4 | 2 | 3 | [Stain]. | | | | |
| 15 | 4 | 2 | 4 | Filler (only at filled finish). | | E | **C** | **P** |
| 15 | 4 | 2 | 5 | Sealer, reduced conversion varnish. | | **E** | **C** | P |
| 15 | 4 | 2 | 6 | Sealer, vinyl. | | E | C | **P** |
| 15 | 4 | 2 | 7 | First topcoat. | | | | |
| 15 | 4 | 2 | 8 | Second topcoat. | | E | C | **P** |
| 15 | 5 | | | **SYSTEM - 6, OIL, PENETRATING** including [bracketed items if specified] requires at: | | | | |
| 15 | 5 | 1 | | **CLOSE** and **OPEN GRAIN** woods: | | | | |
| 15 | 5 | 1 | 1 | [Simulated oil finish]. | | **E** | C | P |
| 15 | 5 | 1 | 2 | First coat, penetrating oil. | | | | |
| 15 | 5 | 1 | 3 | Sealer, catalyzed vinyl. | | **E** | C | P |
| 15 | 5 | 1 | 4 | Scuff sand with appropriate grit. | | **E** | C | P |
| 15 | 5 | 1 | 5 | Brass wool rubdown. | | **E** | **C** | P |
| 15 | 5 | 1 | 6 | Second coat, penetrating oil. | | **E** | **C** | P |
| 15 | 5 | 1 | 7 | Wax coat. | | E | **C** | **P** |
| 15 | 6 | | | **SYSTEM - 7, VINYL, CATALYZED** including [bracketed items if specified] requires at: | | | | |
| 15 | 6 | 1 | | **CLOSE GRAIN** woods: | | | | |
| 15 | 6 | 1 | 1 | Wash coat, vinyl (only at stained finish). | | E | **C** | P |
| 15 | 6 | 1 | 2 | Wash coat, vinyl, catalyzed (only at stained finish). | | E | C | **P** |
| 15 | 6 | 1 | 3 | [Stain]. | | | | |
| 15 | 6 | 1 | 4 | Sealer, vinyl. | | **E** | **C** | P |
| 15 | 6 | 1 | 5 | Sealer, vinyl, catalyzed. | | E | C | **P** |
| 15 | 6 | 1 | 6 | First topcoat. | | | | |
| 15 | 6 | 1 | 7 | Second topcoat. | | E | **C** | **P** |

Continues next column ▼

### 5.4.6 Application Rules

▲ From previous column

| | | | | | | E | C | P |
|---|---|---|---|---|---|---|---|---|
| 15 | | | | **SYSTEM COATING SCHEDULE** (continued) | | | | |
| 15 | 6 | | | **SYSTEM - 7, VINYL, CATALYZED** (continued) | | | | |
| 15 | 6 | 2 | | **OPEN GRAIN** woods including filled finish: | | | | |
| 15 | 6 | 2 | 1 | [Wash coat, vinyl] (only at filled finish). | | E | **C** | P |
| 15 | 6 | 2 | 2 | [Wash coat, vinyl, catalyzed] (only at filled finish). | | E | C | **P** |
| 15 | 6 | 2 | 3 | [Stain]. | | | | |
| 15 | 6 | 2 | 4 | Sealer, vinyl. | | **E** | **C** | P |
| 15 | 6 | 2 | 5 | Filler (only at filled finish). | | E | C | **P** |
| 15 | 6 | 2 | 6 | Sealer, vinyl, catalyzed. | | E | C | **P** |
| 15 | 6 | 2 | 7 | First topcoat. | | | | |
| 15 | 6 | 2 | 8 | Second topcoat. | | E | **C** | **P** |
| 15 | 7 | | | **SYSTEM - 8, ACRYLIC CROSS LINKING, WATER BASED** including [bracketed items if specified] requires at: | | | | |
| 15 | 7 | 1 | | **CLOSE GRAIN** woods: | | | | |
| 15 | 7 | 1 | 1 | Wash coat, acrylic (only at stained finish). | | **E** | **C** | **P** |
| 15 | 7 | 1 | 2 | [Stain]. | | | | |
| 15 | 7 | 1 | 3 | Sealer, acrylic. | | | | |
| 15 | 7 | 1 | 4 | First topcoat. | | | | |
| 15 | 7 | 1 | 5 | Second topcoat. | | **E** | **C** | **P** |
| 15 | 7 | 2 | | **OPEN GRAIN** woods, including filled finish: | | | | |
| 15 | 7 | 2 | 1 | [Wash coat, acrylic] (only at filled finish). | | **E** | **C** | **P** |
| 15 | 7 | 2 | 2 | [Stain]. | | | | |
| 15 | 7 | 2 | 3 | Sealer, acrylic. | | | | |
| 15 | 7 | 2 | 4 | Filler (only at filled finish). | | **E** | **C** | **P** |
| 15 | 7 | 2 | 5 | First topcoat. | | | | |
| 15 | 7 | 2 | 6 | Second topcoat. | | **E** | **C** | **P** |
| 15 | 8 | | | **SYSTEM - 9 and 10, UV CURABLE, ACRYLATED EPOXY, POLYESTER, URETHANE**, applicable only to **PREMIUM GRADE** and including [bracketed items if specified] requires at: | | | | |
| 15 | 8 | 1 | | **CLOSE** and **OPEN GRAIN** woods: | | | | |
| 15 | 8 | 1 | 1 | [Stain]. | | | | **P** |
| 15 | 8 | 1 | 2 | Sealer with B-stage curing. | | | | **P** |
| 15 | 8 | 1 | 3 | Sealer with full cure. | | | | **P** |
| 15 | 8 | 1 | 4 | First topcoat with B-stage curing. | | | | **P** |
| 15 | 8 | 1 | 5 | Second topcoat with full cure. | | | | **P** |

Continues next column ▼

# SECTION 5
## Finishing

**compliance requirements**

## 5.4.6 Application Rules

▲ From previous column

| | | | | | | | |
|---|---|---|---|---|---|---|---|
| 15 | | | | **SYSTEM COATING SCHEDULE** (continued) | | | |
| 15 | 9 | | | **SYSTEM - 11 and 12, POLYURETHANE, CATALYZED, or WATER BASED** including [bracketed items if specified] requires at: | | | |
| 15 | 9 | 1 | | **CLOSE GRAIN** woods: | | | |
| 15 | 9 | 1 | 1 | Wash coat, reduced vinyl sealer (only at stained finish). | | | |
| 15 | 9 | 1 | 2 | [Stain]. | | | |
| 15 | 9 | 1 | 3 | Sealer, vinyl. | | | |
| 15 | 9 | 1 | 4 | First topcoat. | | | |
| 15 | 9 | 1 | 5 | Second topcoat. | E | C | P |
| 15 | 9 | 2 | | **OPEN GRAIN** woods (including filled finish): | | | |
| 15 | 9 | 2 | 1 | [Wash coat, reduced vinyl sealer] (only at filled finish). | E | C | P |
| 15 | 9 | 2 | 2 | [Stain]. | | | |
| 15 | 9 | 2 | 3 | Filler (only at filled finish). | E | C | P |
| 15 | 9 | 2 | 4 | Sealer, vinyl. | | | |
| 15 | 9 | 2 | 5 | First topcoat. | | | |
| 15 | 9 | 2 | 6 | Second topcoat. | E | C | P |
| 15 | 10 | | | **SYSTEM - 13, POLYESTER, CATALYZED**, applicable only to **PREMIUM GRADE** and including [bracketed items if specified] requires at: | | | |
| 15 | 10 | 1 | | **CLOSE** and **OPEN GRAIN** woods: | | | |
| 15 | 10 | 1 | 1 | [Stain]. | E | C | P |
| 15 | 10 | 1 | 2 | First sealer, polyester. | E | C | P |
| 15 | 10 | 1 | 3 | Second sealer, polyester. | E | C | P |
| 15 | 10 | 1 | 4 | Sand with appropriate grit. | E | C | P |
| 15 | 10 | 1 | 5 | Topcoat, polyester. | E | C | P |
| 15 | 10 | 1 | 6 | Rub and polish, mechanical. | E | C | P |
| 16 | | | | **AFTER FINISHING:** | | | |
| 16 | 1 | | | Remove all spilled, splashed, or spattered finish materials. | | | |
| 16 | 2 | | | Remove all fingerprints or other marks. | | | |
| 16 | 3 | | | Provide a final dusting of all exterior and interior surfaces, including drawers. | | | |
| 16 | 4 | | | Provide properly labeled touch up materials to allow for minor touch up. | | | |
| 17 | | | | **TOUCH UP** of: | | | |
| 17 | 1 | | | Factory finished materials are the responsibility of the installation contractor. | | | |
| 17 | 2 | | | Jobsite finished materials are the responsibility of the finishing contractor. | | | |

Where the **E**, **C**, or **P** icon is not indicated, the rule applies to all Grades equally

# SECTION 5
## Finishing

## compliance requirements
### GENERAL/PRODUCT/TEST

### 5.5 BASIC CONSIDERATIONS

1. The tolerances typically found within the Architectural Woodwork Standards fall into two categories:

   1.1 Factory fabricated joinery, assembly and construction - found in the **PRODUCT** portion.

   1.2 Field installation joinery and assembly - found in the **INSTALLATION** portion.

2. Most fabrication and installation assemblies include solid wood to solid wood joints, solid wood to wood veneer joints, solid wood to wood based products (HPDL, LPDL, Solid Phenolic and panel products), solid wood to non-wood based products (which can be drywall, glass, metal, stone, acrylics, and other surfaces), and non-wood to non-wood joints.

3. Tolerances found in the AWS include:

   3.1 Flatness of wood based panel products.

   3.2 Solid wood to solid wood joints and assemblies.

   3.3 Solid wood to wood veneer joints and assemblies.

   3.4 Wood veneer to wood veneer joints and assemblies.

   3.5 Solid wood to wood based product joints and assemblies.

   3.6 Solid surface to solid surface joints and assemblies.

4. Because of the differences of expansion and contraction of non-wood products compared to solid wood and wood based products, the AWS does not apply tolerances regarding flatness or joinery to these non-wood based products.

5. **VISUAL TESTING** is only applicable to exposed surfaces:

   5.1 View finished surfaces in the ambient conditions in which they will be installed and used.

   5.1.1 Perception of color varies with the light source and between individuals.

   5.2 Tests apply only to new work at the time of installation.

   5.2.1 They shall not be applied to refinishing conditions, except as agreed in advance between buyer and seller.

### 5.5 BASIC CONSIDERATIONS (continued)

6. **TESTING** for **CONSISTENCY** of **GRAIN** and **COLOR**:

   6.1 Compliance with standards for color and grain are highly subjective, and:

   6.1.1 Each person's perception of color is unique.

   6.1.2 The apparent color of a finished wood species is affected by many variables, such as:

   6.1.2.1 Ambient lighting.

   6.1.2.2 Cellular structure of the individual piece of wood.

   6.1.2.3 Cutting or slicing of the wood.

   6.1.2.4 Machining and sanding of the surface.

   6.1.2.5 Orientation of the surface to the viewer.

   6.2 Compliance shall be evaluated (by comparison to an approved panel, minimum 8" x 12" [203 x 305 mm], that has been signed and dated and protected from light) based on the following conditions:

   6.2.1 Viewing of the surfaces in the lighting and orientation in which they will be installed.

   6.2.2 Observing a color and tone blending that is not significantly lighter than the lightest of the range, nor darker than the darkest of the range.

   6.2.3 Because of natural variations in color and grain, it cannot be expected that all panels will match one particular sample exactly; however, shall match within the sample range submitted.

7. **SHEEN TEST**

   7.1 Compliance shall be evaluated by comparison to the approved range of sample panels, that has been signed and dated and protected from light based on the following conditions:

   7.1.1 Testing of the surfaces with a gloss meter, parallel to the grain, in identical lighting conditions:

   7.1.1.1 When comparisons of sheen tests between the approved sample panels and the installed work show sheen readings within 10 points of each other they shall be considered to be in compliance.

# SECTION 5
Finishing

notes

# Architectural Woodwork Standards

# MILLWORK

## SECTION 6

# SECTION 6
Millwork

## table of contents

### INTRODUCTORY INFORMATION

- Guide Specifications .................................................. 131
- Introduction ............................................................... 132
- Methods of Production ............................................. 132
  - Flat Surfaces ...................................................... 132
  - Molded Surfaces ................................................ 132
- Smoothness of Flat and Molded Surfaces ............... 132
- Design and Use of Resources .................................. 132
- Examples of Standing and Running Trim and Rail Parts ............ 133
- Examples of Standing and Running Trim ................ 134
- Examples of Standing and Running Trim and Rails .............. 135
- Radius Moldings ........................................................ 136
  - Solid Machined .................................................. 136
  - Core Veneered ................................................... 136
  - Laminated Plies ................................................. 136
  - Block Laminated ................................................ 136
  - Kerfed ................................................................. 136
  - Cross Grain ........................................................ 136
- Solid Lumber Paneling Patterns ............................... 137
- Built up Moldings for Larger Profiles ...................... 138
  - Ceilings .............................................................. 138
  - Chair Rails ......................................................... 138
  - Fireplaces .......................................................... 139
  - Doors and Windows .......................................... 139
  - Base ................................................................... 139
- Design Ideas ............................................................. 139
- Built up Cornice and Wall Trim Examples .............. 140
- Door Frame and Jamb Examples ............................ 141
- Frame Joinery Examples .......................................... 141
- Window Sash and Frame Examples ........................ 141
- Sash Joinery Examples ............................................ 141
- Glazing Examples .................................................... 141
- Thermal Integrity ..................................................... 141
- Blinds and Shutters .................................................. 142
- Screens ..................................................................... 142
- Ornamental Woodwork ............................................ 142
  - Typical Sources ................................................. 142
  - Fire Retardant Solid Lumber ........................... 143
  - Sources for Wood Ornamentation ................... 143
  - Working with an Artisan .................................. 143
- Design Ideas ............................................................. 144
- Specify Requirements For ....................................... 144
- Recommendations .................................................... 144

# SECTION 6
## Millwork

# table of contents

## COMPLIANCE REQUIREMENTS

### GENERAL
- Basic Considerations ..................................................... 145
  - Grades ................................................................. 145
    - Economy ........................................................... 145
    - Custom ............................................................. 145
    - Premium ........................................................... 145
  - Contract Documents ................................................. 145
  - Acceptable Compliance Requirements ........................ 145
  - Aesthetics Compliance Requirements .......................... 145
  - Exposed Surfaces ..................................................... 145
  - Semi-Exposed Surfaces ............................................. 145
  - Concealed Surfaces .................................................. 145
  - Prevent Telegraphing ................................................ 145
  - Industry Practices .................................................... 145
    - Flame Spread Rated Wood Door Frames ................ 145
    - Structural Members ............................................. 145
    - Wall, Ceiling and/or Opening Variations ................ 145
    - Priming .............................................................. 145
    - Radius Moldings .................................................. 146
      - Method of Fabrication ..................................... 146

### PRODUCT
- Scope ...................................................................... 147
  - Typical Inclusions .................................................... 147
  - Typical Exclusions ................................................... 147
- Default Stipulation ..................................................... 148
- Rules ...................................................................... 148
  - Errata .................................................................. 148
  - Basic Rules ........................................................... 148
    - Aesthetics .......................................................... 148
    - Woodwork .......................................................... 148
    - Lumber .............................................................. 148
    - Sheet Products ................................................... 148
    - Exposed Surfaces ............................................... 148
    - Semi-Exposed Surfaces ....................................... 148
    - Concealed Surfaces ............................................ 148
    - Standing and Running Trim .................................. 148

- Multiple Options ...................................................... 148
- Frame Spread Ratings .............................................. 149
- Specific Profile ........................................................ 149
- Special Ornamental Detail ........................................ 149
- Cathedral ............................................................... 149
- Exterior Application ................................................. 149
- Gluing and Laminating ............................................. 149
- Cutouts .................................................................. 149
- First Class Workmanship .......................................... 149
- Material Rules ......................................................... 149
  - Lumber, Veneered Profile and Sheet Products ........... 149
  - Natural and Manufactured Defects ........................... 149
  - Figure .................................................................. 149
  - Warp .................................................................... 149
  - Radius Woodwork .................................................. 149
  - Opaque Finish ....................................................... 150
  - Transparent Finish ................................................. 150
  - Exposed Surfaces .................................................. 150
    - For Transparent Finish ........................................ 150
  - Semi-Exposed Surfaces .......................................... 151
  - Concealed Surfaces ............................................... 151
  - Door and Window Frames ....................................... 151
  - Sash .................................................................... 151
  - Blinds and Shutters ................................................ 152
  - Screens ................................................................ 152
  - Closet and Utility Shelving ...................................... 152
  - Glass ................................................................... 153
  - Factory Finishing ................................................... 153
- Machining Rules ...................................................... 153
  - Exposed Surfaces .................................................. 153
    - Smoothness ....................................................... 153
    - HPDL, PVC, and Prefinished Wood ...................... 153
  - Trim ..................................................................... 154
  - Solid Machined and Block Laminated ...................... 154
  - Intersections ......................................................... 154
  - Dadoes ................................................................ 154
  - Standing and Running Trim .................................... 154

# SECTION 6
Millwork

## table of contents

**COMPLIANCE REQUIREMENTS** (continued)
  **PRODUCT** (continued)
    Rules (continued)
      Machining Rules (continued)
- Window Frames .................................................. 154
- Sash ..................................................................... 154
- Screens ............................................................... 154
- Blinds and Shutters ............................................. 155
- Ornamental Woodwork ........................................ 155

      Assembly Rules ........................................................ 155
- Joints at Assembled Woodwork .......................... 155
  - Flushness Test D ............................................ 155
  - Gap Test A ...................................................... 156
  - Gap Test B ...................................................... 156
  - Gap Test C ...................................................... 156
- Flatness or Warp Test E ..................................... 156
- Applied Moldings ................................................ 156
- Miter Joints and Caps ......................................... 156
- Stile and Rail Assemblies ................................... 156
- Sheet Products ................................................... 156
- Built up Items ...................................................... 156
- Standing and Running Trim ................................ 157
- Door Frames ....................................................... 157
- Window Frames .................................................. 157
- Sash ..................................................................... 158
- Blinds and Shutters ............................................. 158
- Screens ............................................................... 158
- Ornamental Millwork ........................................... 158
- Miscellaneous Millwork ....................................... 159

**INSTALLATION**
- Care, Storage and Building Conditions ................... 160
- Contractor is Responsible for ................................... 160
- Installer is Responsible for ....................................... 160
- Rules ......................................................................... 160
  - Errata .................................................................. 160
  - Basic Rules ........................................................ 161
    - Aesthetics ...................................................... 161
    - Transparent Finished .................................... 161
    - Repairs ........................................................... 161
    - Installer Modifications ................................... 161
    - Woodwork ....................................................... 161
    - These Standards ............................................ 161
    - Gaps Tests I ................................................... 161
    - Flushness Tests J .......................................... 162
    - Fastening and Fasteners ............................... 162
    - Glue ................................................................ 162
    - Equipment Cutouts ........................................ 163
    - Hardware ........................................................ 163
    - Areas of Installation ...................................... 163
    - First Class Workmanship .............................. 163
  - Product Specific Rules ...................................... 163
    - Standing and Running Trim .......................... 163
    - Closet Rods ................................................... 163
    - Door & Window Frames ................................ 163
    - Blinds and Shutters ...................................... 163
    - Screens .......................................................... 163
    - Ornamental Millwork ..................................... 163

**TESTS**
- Basic Considerations ............................................... 164
  - Fabricated and Installed ................................... 164
    - Smoothness ................................................... 164
    - KCPI ............................................................... 164
    - Sanding .......................................................... 164
  - Gaps, Flushness, Flatness and Alignment ....... 164
    - Illustrations ................................................... 165

## introductory information

**SECTION 6**
Millwork

# Guide Specifications

Are available through the Sponsor Associations in interactive digital format including unique and individual quality control options.
The Guide Specifications are located at:

## Architectural Woodwork Institute (AWI)
www.awinet.org

## Architectural Woodwork Manufacturers Association of Canada (AWMAC)
http://awmac.com/aws-guide-specifications

## Woodwork Institute (WI)
www.woodworkinstitute.com/publications/aws_guide_specs.asp

# SECTION 6
## Millwork

## introductory information

### INTRODUCTION

Section 6 includes information on standing & running trim, door frames, window frames, sashes, blinds & shutters, screens, ornamental & miscellaneous millwork composed of solid wood and/or sheet products and their related parts.

Quality assurance can be achieved by adherence to the AWS and will provide the owner a quality product at competitive pricing. Use of a qualified Sponsor Member firm to provide your woodwork will help ensure the manufacturer's understanding of the quality level required. Illustrations in this Section are not intended to be all inclusive. Other engineered solutions are acceptable. In the absence of specifications; methods of fabrication are the manufacturer's choice. The design professional, by specifying compliance to the AWS increases the probability of receiving the product quality expected.

### METHODS OF PRODUCTION
#### Flat Surfaces:
- Sawing - This produces relatively rough surfaces that are not utilized for architectural woodwork except where a "rough sawn" texture or finish is desired for design purposes.

To achieve the smooth surfaces generally required, the rough sawn boards are further surfaced by the following methods:

- Planing - Sawn lumber is passed through a planer or jointer, which has a revolving head with projecting knives, removing a thin layer of wood to produce a relatively smooth surface.

- Abrasive Planing - Sawn lumber is passed through a powerful belt sander with tough, coarse belts, which remove the rough top surface.

#### Molded Surfaces:
Sawn lumber is passed through a molder or shaper that has knives ground to a pattern which produces the molded profile desired.

### SMOOTHNESS OF FLAT AND MOLDED SURFACES

Planers and Molders: The smoothness of surfaces which have been machine planed or molded is determined by the closeness of the knife cuts. The closer the cuts to each other (i.e., the more knife cuts per inch [KCPI]) the closer the ridges, and therefore the smoother the resulting appearance.
Sanding and Abrasives: Surfaces can be further smoothed by sanding. Sandpapers come in grits from coarse to fine and are assigned ascending grit numbers. The coarser the grit, the faster the stock removal. The surface will show the striations caused by the grit. Sanding with progressively finer grit papers will produce smoother surfaces.

### DESIGN AND USE OF RESOURCES

Moldings should be cut from lumber approximately the same size as the finished piece to make the best use of our natural resources. Designing moldings with the size of typical boards in mind has several advantages.

The typical 1" x 4" (25.4 mm x 101.6 mm) will yield a very nice 3/4" (19 mm) thick molding, but will not be thick enough to develop a molding which is a full 1" (25.4 mm) thick in finish dimension. The typical 2" x 4" (50.8 mm x 101.6 mm) piece of lumber can be made into moldings about 1-3/4" (44.5 mm) thick in a similar manner.

Deep or large moldings are often best cut from more than one piece and built up to make the final profile. Just as in the manufacturing of single moldings, this process minimizes waste and reduces the tendency of the finished profiles to twist, warp, cup, or bow as a result of removing too much material from either side of the initial board.

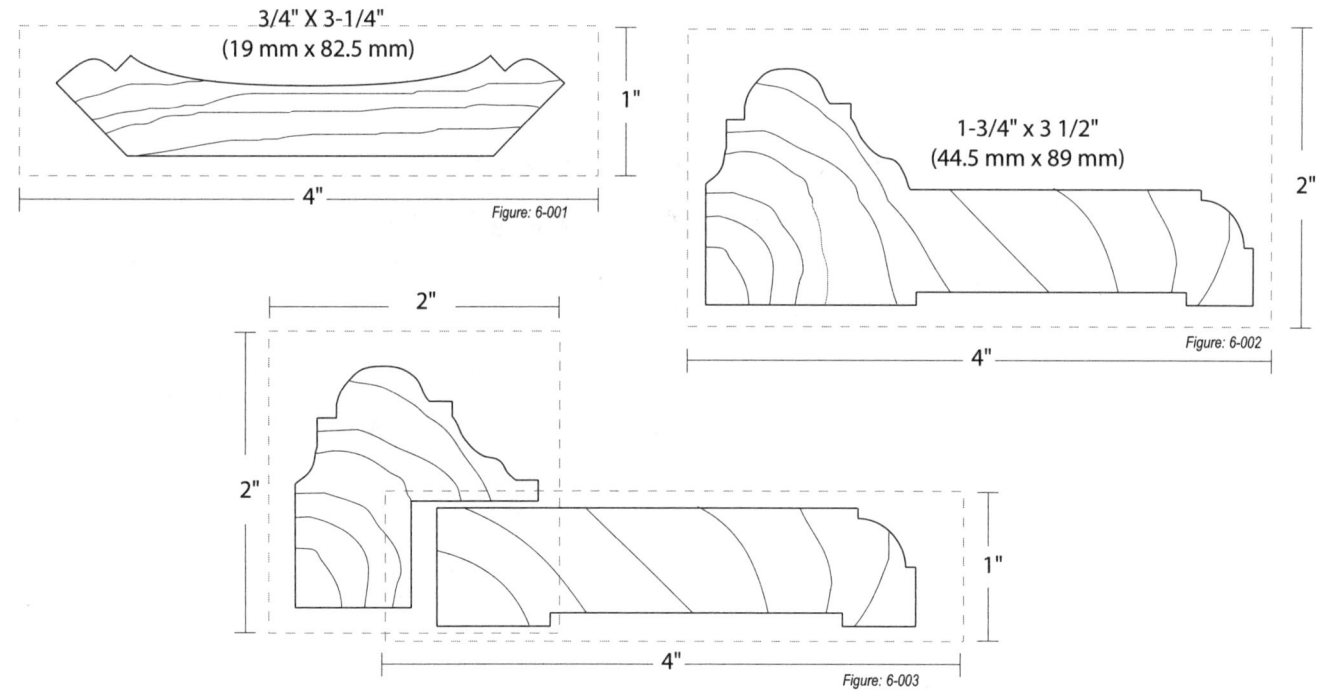

Figure: 6-001
Figure: 6-002
Figure: 6-003

# SECTION 6
## Millwork

## introductory information

**EXAMPLES OF STANDING and RUNNING TRIM and RAIL PARTS**

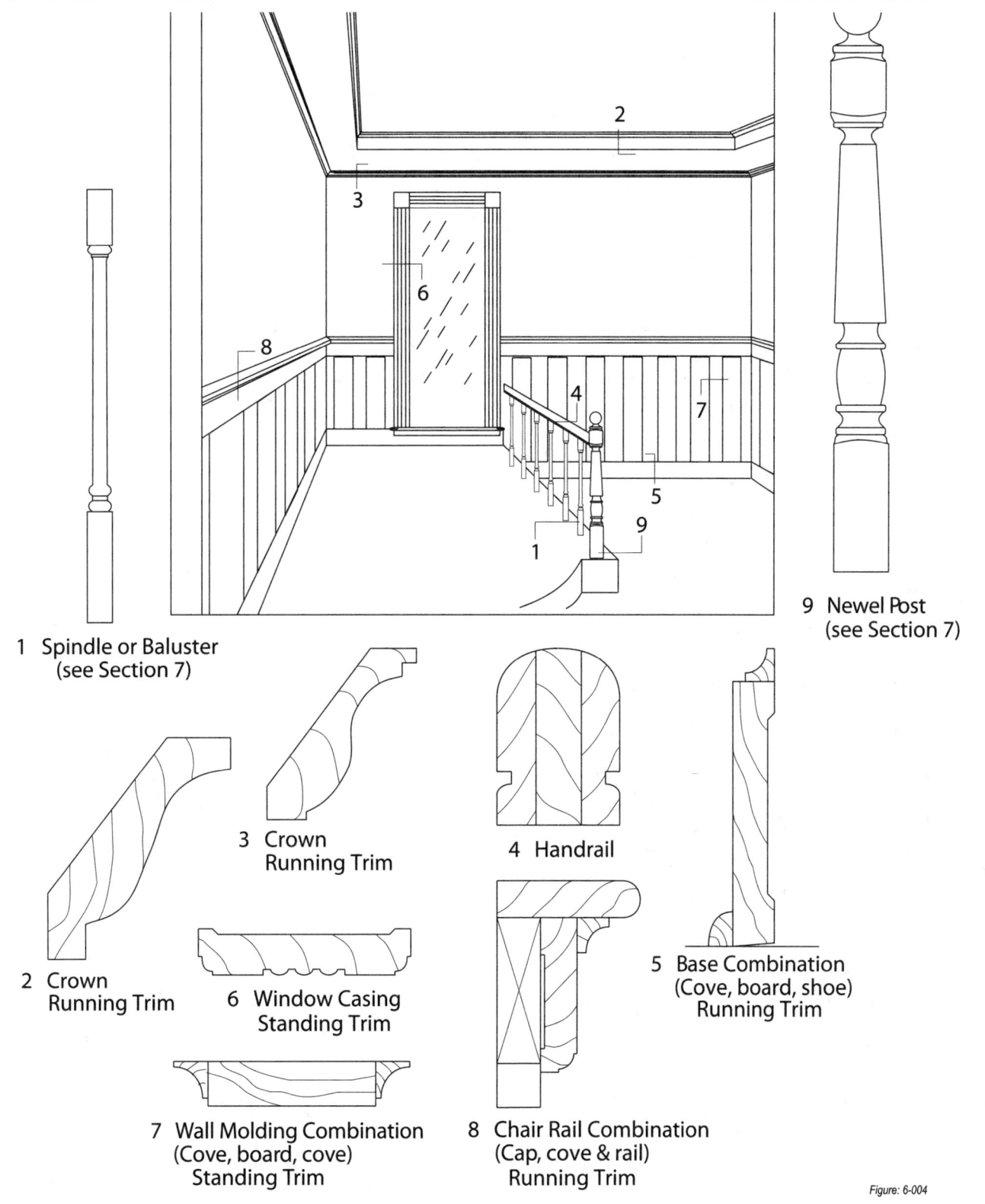

1. Spindle or Baluster (see Section 7)
2. Crown Running Trim
3. Crown Running Trim
4. Handrail
5. Base Combination (Cove, board, shoe) Running Trim
6. Window Casing Standing Trim
7. Wall Molding Combination (Cove, board, cove) Standing Trim
8. Chair Rail Combination (Cap, cove & rail) Running Trim
9. Newel Post (see Section 7)

Figure: 6-004

# SECTION 6
Millwork

## introductory information

**EXAMPLES OF STANDING and RUNNING TRIM**

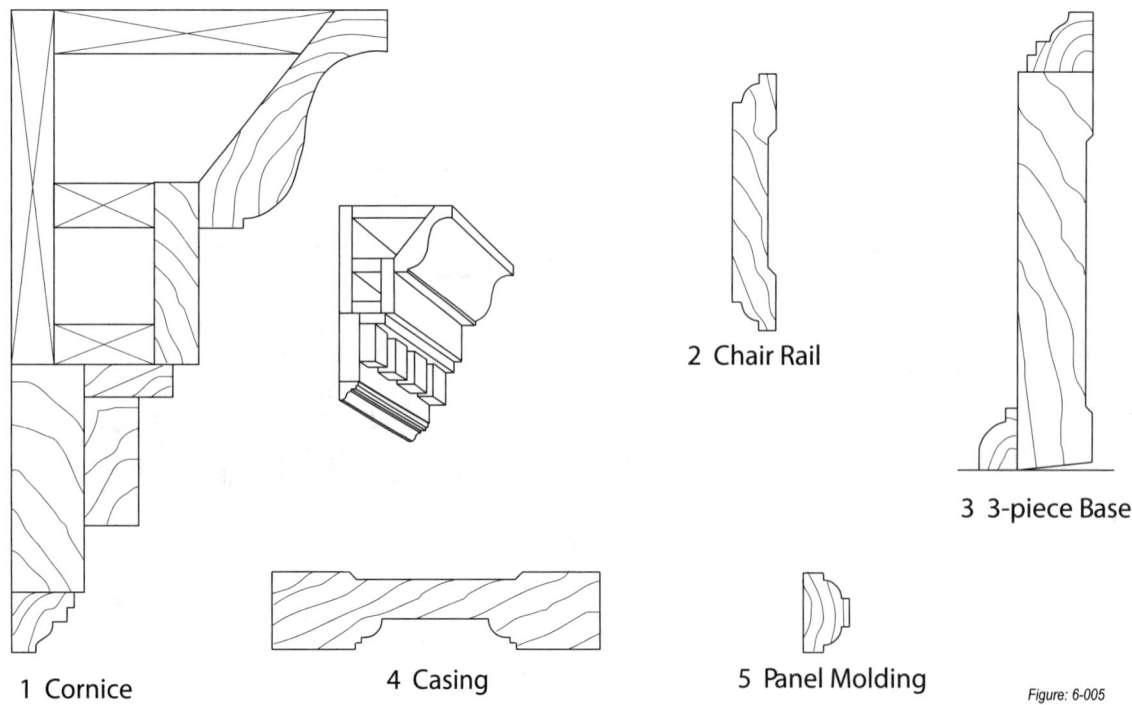

1 Cornice
2 Chair Rail
3 3-piece Base
4 Casing
5 Panel Molding

*Figure: 6-005*

# SECTION 6
## Millwork

# introductory information

**EXAMPLES OF STANDING** and **RUNNING TRIM** and **RAIL**

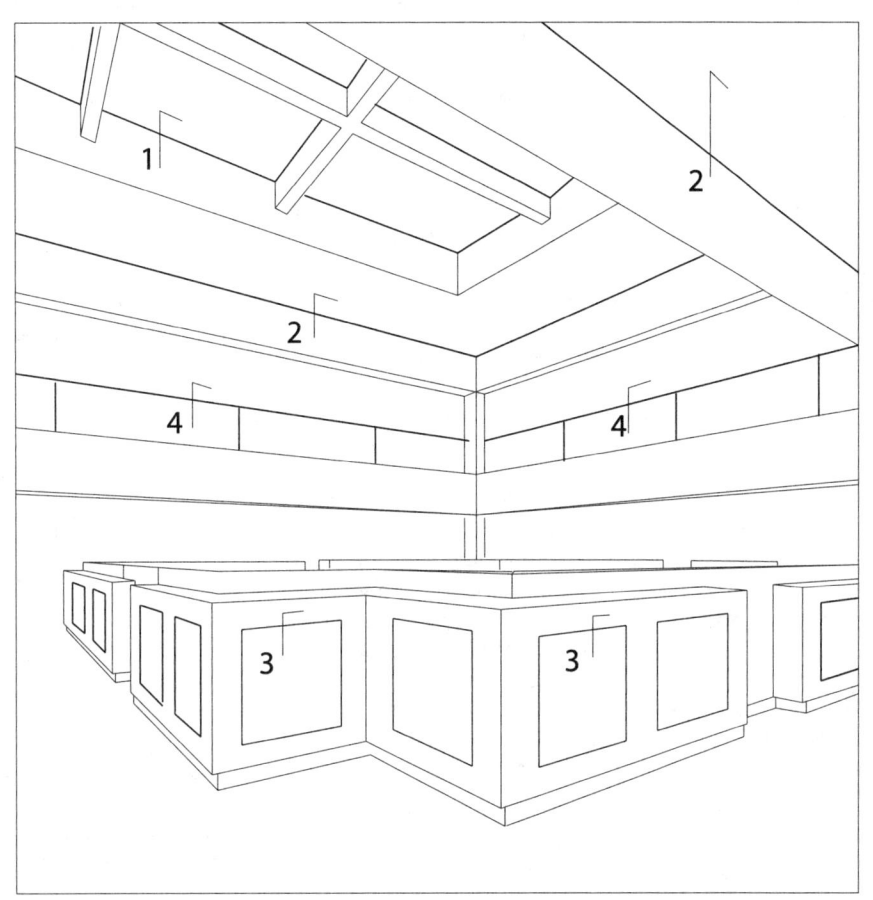

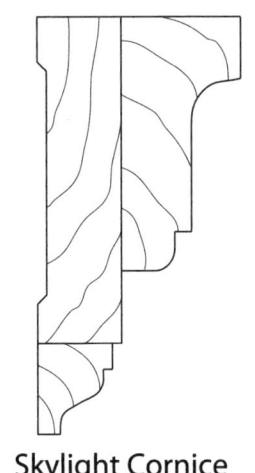

1 Skylight Cornice

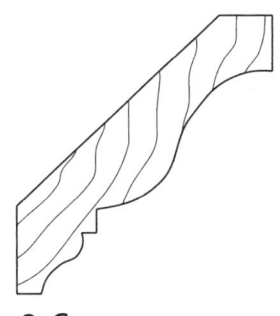

2 Crown

3 Panel Molding

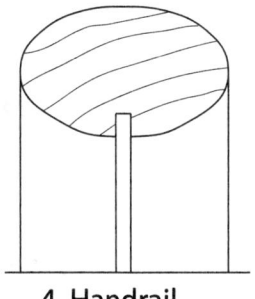

4 Handrail

*Figure: 6-006*

# SECTION 6
Millwork

## introductory information

### RADIUS MOLDINGS

Both traditional and nontraditional architectural styles often call for radius standing and running trim either in plan, elevation, or both. In situations where the size of the molding and the radius to which it is to be formed is such that a straight molding will not conform to the core, the architectural manufacturer can use several methods to fabricate radius moldings. Moldings applied to radii can be segmented, (typically only by direct specification) bent or steam bent, laminated and formed, preshaped, or machined to the radius. Manufacturers will fabricate the moldings in the longest practical lengths, with the purpose of minimizing the field joints.

- **Solid Machined** (Illustration A) woodwork typically starts with a large, often glued up piece of material, from which several nested pieces can be machined. Characteristically, this method limits the length of pieces that can be developed without a joint. It also yields a piece of material with the grain straight on the face, not following the curve. Profiles with a flat face can be machined from sheet products with an edgeband applied, yielding larger pieces with more consistent grain.

- **Core Veneered** (Illustration B) woodwork consists of core machined from lumber or panel product to which finish material is laminated as an exposed face. This technique is limited to certain profiles; however, it offers the ability to minimize glue joints and control grain directions.

- **Laminated Plies** (Illustration C) woodwork consists of thin, bendable plies of lumber in a form that will hold its shape without having to be secured to another surface. The curved piece can then be milled to the desired profile. The glue lines follow the edge grain and the curve, thus minimizing their visibility. The species of wood and the tightness of the radius determine the maximum thickness of each ply.

- **Block Laminated** (Illustration D) woodwork is made of solid machined pieces, glued up typically in a staggered fashion for width and length. When dealing with some cross sections, it can be advantageous to combine band sawing and laminating; however, it must be limited to certain profiles. It does, however, offer the ability to minimize glue joints, is used in radius jambs and often becomes the core for core veneered woodwork.

- **Kerfed** (Illustration E) woodwork consists of lumber with repeated saw cuts on the back face of the piece, perpendicular to the bend. The tightness of the radius determines the spacing and depth of the kerfs. Kerfing allows the piece to be bent to the required radius and then secured in place to hold the bend. Kerfing could result in "flats" on the face, which show in finishing. When dealing with a large radius, it is sometimes possible to stop the kerf prior to going through an exposed edge. In most cases, however, the kerf runs through, and the edge must be concealed.

**Cross Grain** in band sawn or laminated members and edges in veneer laminated members or where multiple layers are exposed by shaping may cause objectionable color variation when finished.

Unless specifically called out, the architectural manufacturer will have the option of which method to use for fabricating radius molding. Since the fabrication method determines the final appearance of the pieces, especially regarding the direction of grain and visibility of glue joints, the architect or designer may wish to specify the method. It is recommended that an architectural woodwork firm be consulted before making a selection. Mockups may be required to visualize the end product.

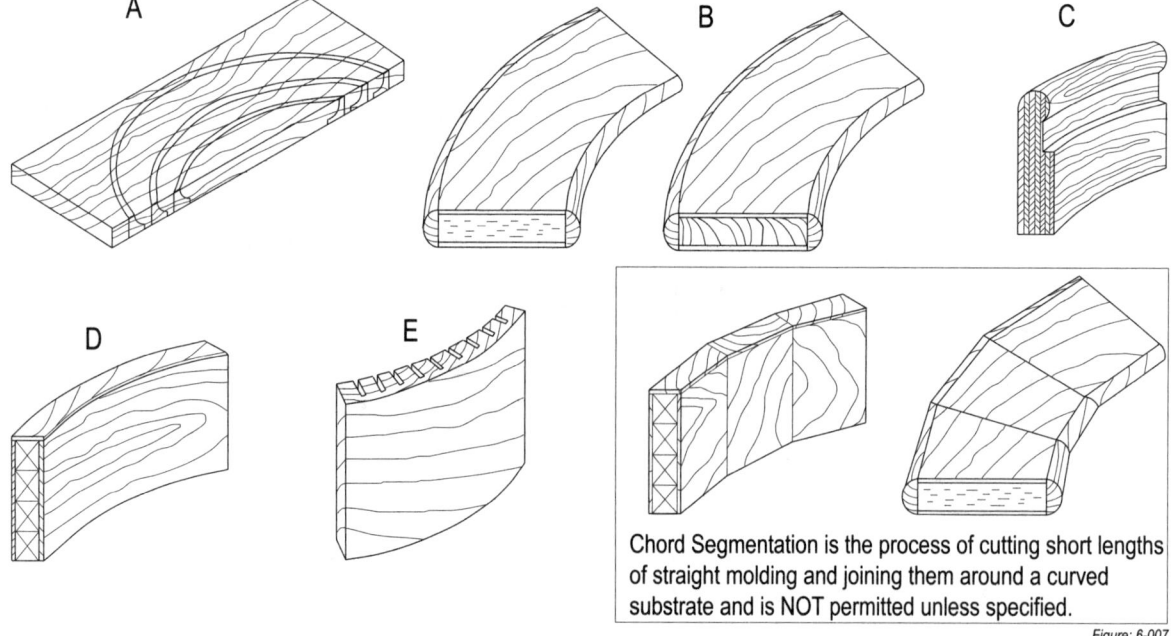

Chord Segmentation is the process of cutting short lengths of straight molding and joining them around a curved substrate and is NOT permitted unless specified.

*Figure: 6-007*

136 Architectural Woodwork Standards ©2014 AWI | AWMAC | WI 2nd Edition, October 1, 2014

# SECTION 6
## Millwork

## introductory information

**SOLID LUMBER PANELING PATTERNS**

The variety of solid lumber paneling is only limited by the imagination of the design professional. Virtually any machinable profile can be custom manufactured. The following profiles are some of the traditional patterns associated with solid board paneling. They are not dimensioned intentionally, allowing the design professional to determine the scale and proportions most appropriate for the project.

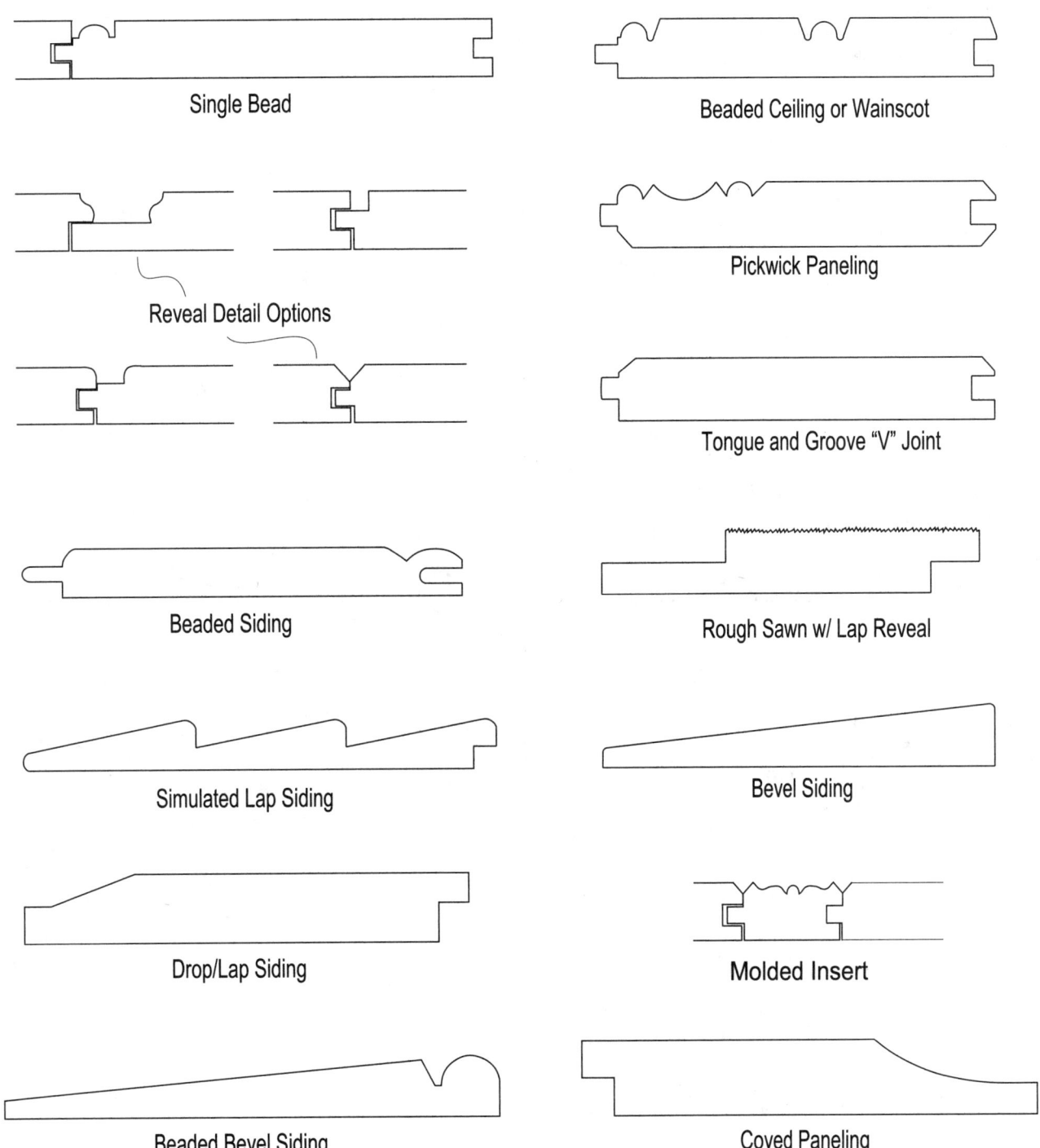

Figure: 6-008

# SECTION 6
## Millwork

# introductory information

**BUILT UP MOLDINGS FOR LARGER PROFILES**

Used with permission of the Wood Molding and Millwork Producers Association.

- **Ceilings** are the most obvious area for "built up" moldings. This is primarily true of rooms with high ceilings. In low ceiling rooms (8' [2438 mm]), single molding profiles usually work best.

A series of "built up" moldings would have a tendency to make a low ceiling appear even lower. But if your ceilings are high (10' [2540 mm] or higher), there is no limit to the rich three dimensional elegance you can add to the room's appearance with the creative application of moldings. Below are several suggested combinations. Let your imagination create your own combinations and designs.

- **Chair Rails** are a very traditional method of breaking up walls, adding both interest and protection. They prevent the wall from being bumped or scuffed by chairs and can also be used to separate two types of decorating material such as paneling, wallpaper, and paint. Following are some variations of "built up" chair rail combinations.

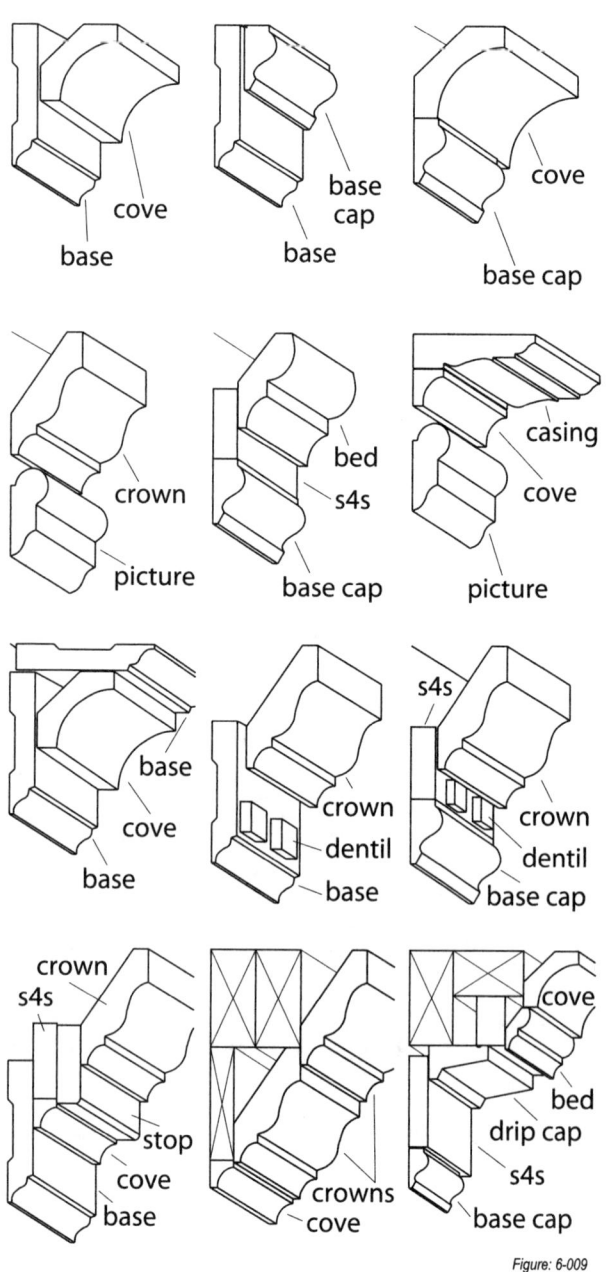

Figure: 6-009

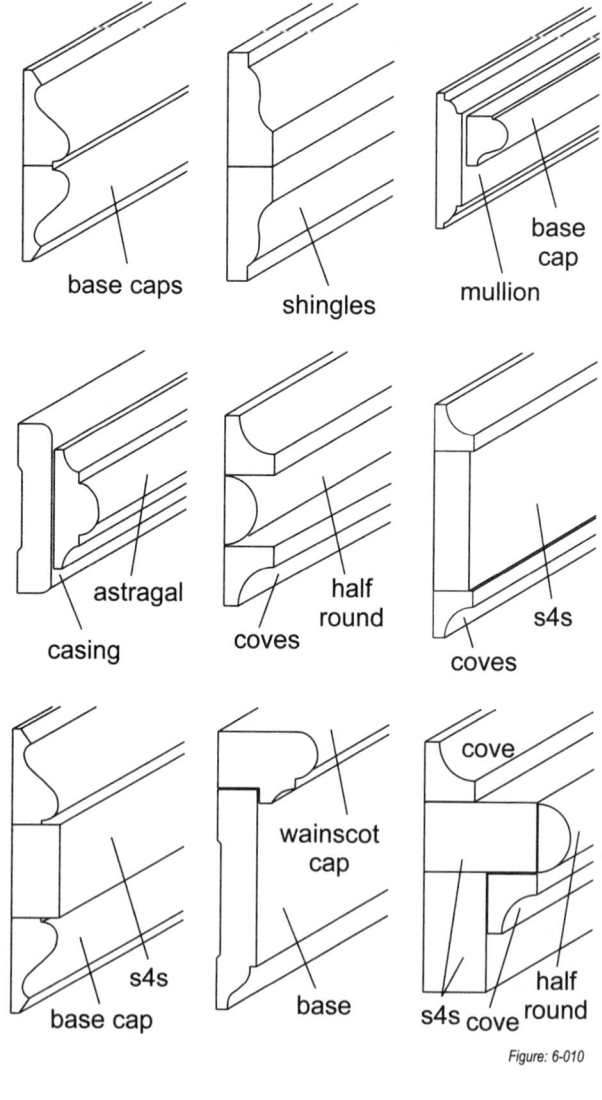

Figure: 6-010

138 Architectural Woodwork Standards ©2014 AWI | AWMAC | WI 2nd Edition, October 1, 2014

# SECTION 6
## Millwork

## introductory information

- **Fireplaces** highlighted or framed with "built up" moldings is an excellent way to add depth and richness. Below are a few creative but simple to install profile combinations.

*Figure: 6-011*

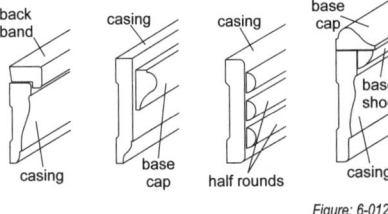
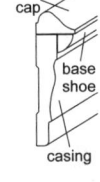

*Figure: 6-012*

- **Doors** and **Windows** are most commonly done with single molding profiles, but by adding other patterns, the basic trim can easily be transformed into a window or door casing of classical depth and beauty. Installing plinth blocks at the bottom of casing further enhances the traditional look.

*Figure: 6-013*

*Figure: 6-014*

- **Base** the elaborate look of elegance can even be carried through to base moldings where the wall meets the floor, as illustrated in the following variations.

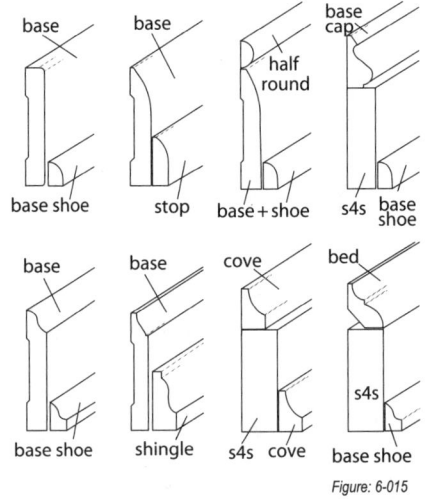

*Figure: 6-015*

### DESIGN IDEAS

Include molding illustrations such as:

- Base and base cap patterns
- Casing patterns
- Panel mold patterns
- Crown mold patterns
- Bed mold patterns
- Handrail patterns
- Chair rail patterns

# SECTION 6
Millwork

## introductory information

**BUILT-UP CORNICE** and **WALL TRIM EXAMPLES**

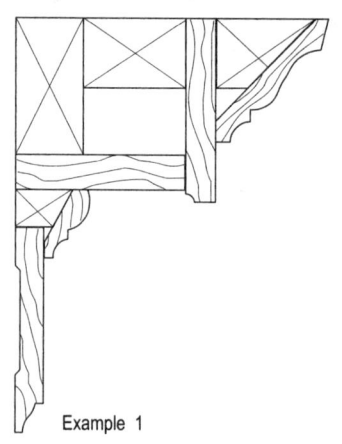
Example 1

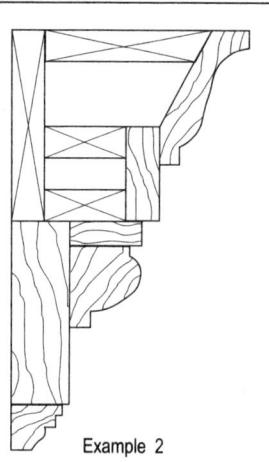
Example 2

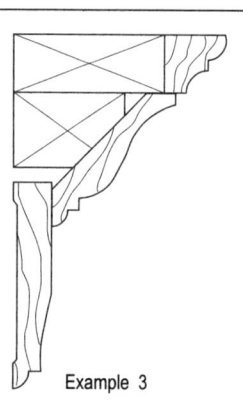
Example 3

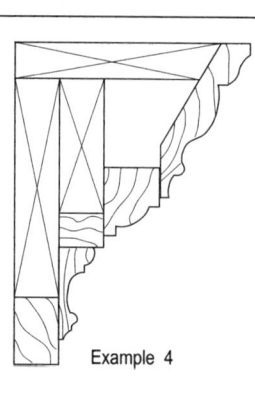
Example 4

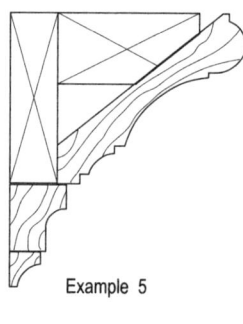
Example 5

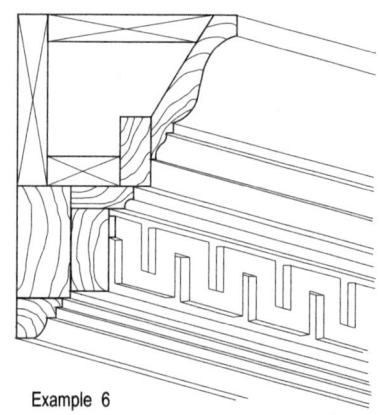
Example 6

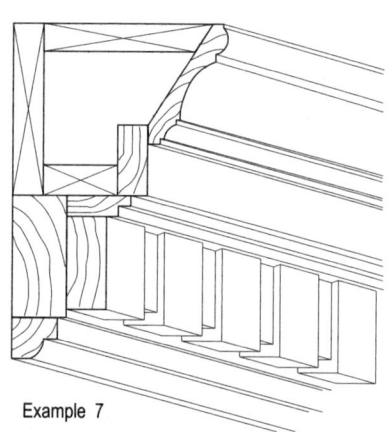
Example 7

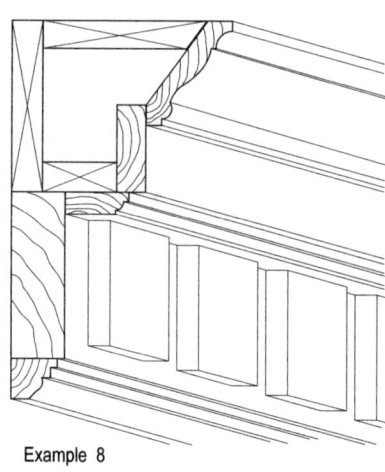
Example 8

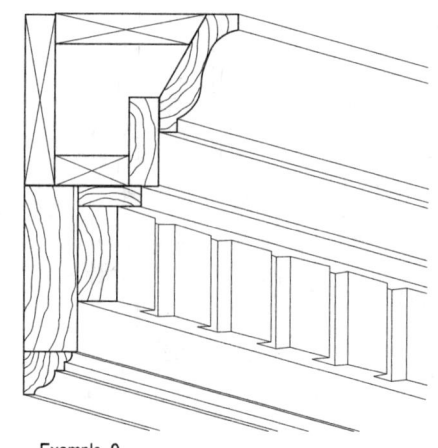
Example 9

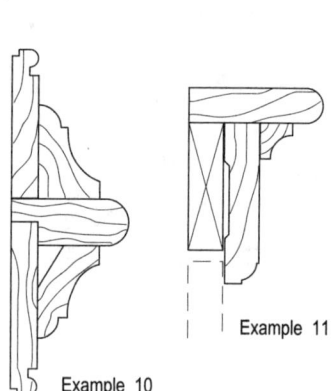
Example 10

Example 11

*Figure: 6-016*

# SECTION 6
## Millwork

## introductory information

### DOOR FRAME and JAMB EXAMPLES:

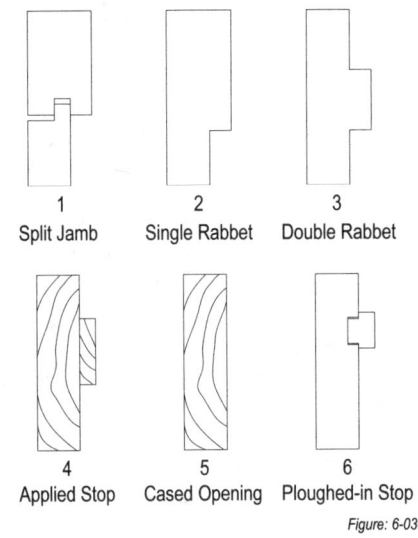

Figure: 6-030

### FRAME JOINERY EXAMPLES:

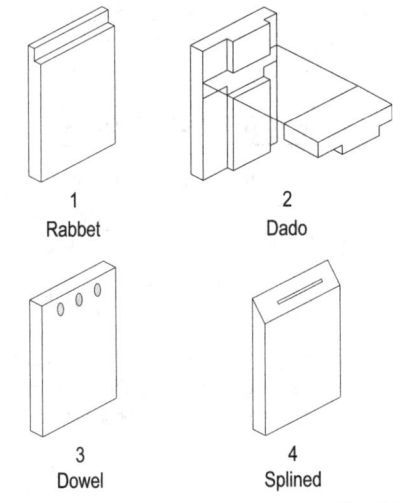

Figure: 6-031

**Labeled** (flame spread-rated) jamb assemblies are typically available in 20-, 45-, 60-, and 90-minute classifications of limited design/species; however, new designs/ratings are in ongoing development. Only firms recognized by applicable code officials are authorized to label a frame assembly. If a label will be required by the applicable code officials, it is the obligation of the design professional to so specify, and the obligation of the manufacturer to assure a properly licensed assembly. These standards do not cover labeled frames.

### WINDOW SASH and FRAME EXAMPLES:

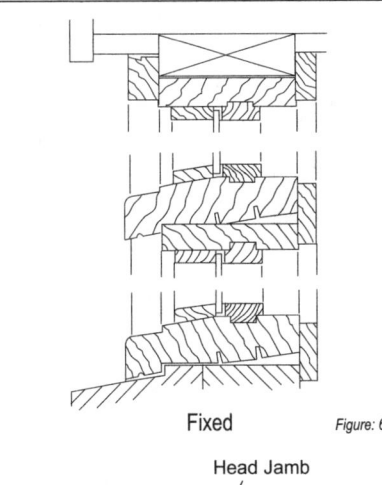

Figure: 6-032

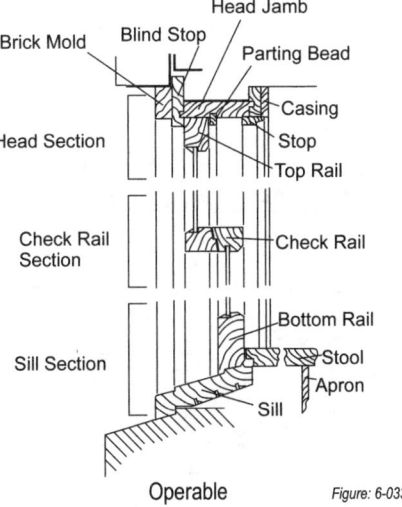

Figure: 6-033

### SASH JOINERY EXAMPLES:

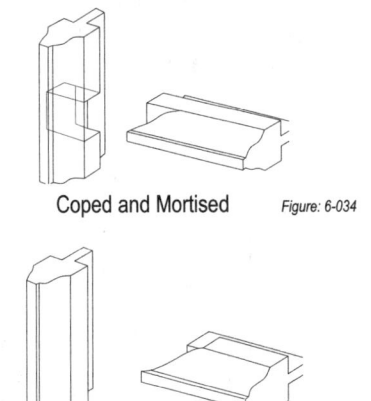

Figure: 6-034

Figure: 6-035

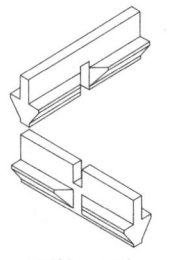

Half-Lapped     Figure: 6-036

### GLAZING EXAMPLES:

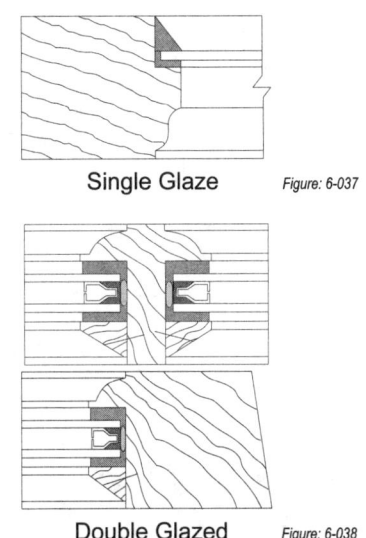

Single Glaze     Figure: 6-037

Double Glazed     Figure: 6-038

### THERMAL INTEGRITY:

Wood is a natural insulator that retains heat in winter without a thermal break, resists conductance of cold temperatures 2000 times better than aluminum, and is approximately 30% more thermally efficient than comparable aluminum windows. Wood's minimal conduction keeps the inside wood surface of windows warm in the winter and cool in the summer. Wood windows are available in single-, double-, and triple-glazing systems, increasing thermal efficiency.

**Performance Testing** is applicable only to complete exterior window units and, if required, must be specified and may include all or part of ASTM E 283, Air Infiltration; E 330, Loading; and/or E 547, Water Penetration. ASTM tests must be specified for the current ASTM Grade Level.

# SECTION 6
## Millwork

### introductory information

#### BLINDS and SHUTTERS

- **Hardware** must be specified, as it dictates the details of construction.

- **Manufacturer** does not typically supply, machine for, or install operating hardware, locking devices, pulls, lifts, etc.

Typical bead detail examples:

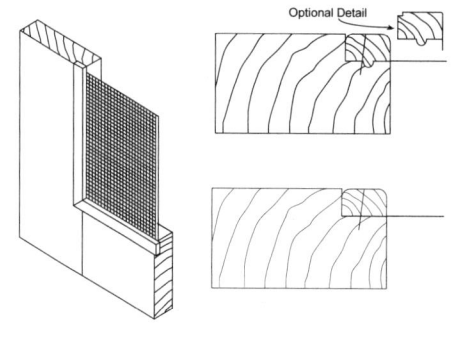

*Figure: 6-040*

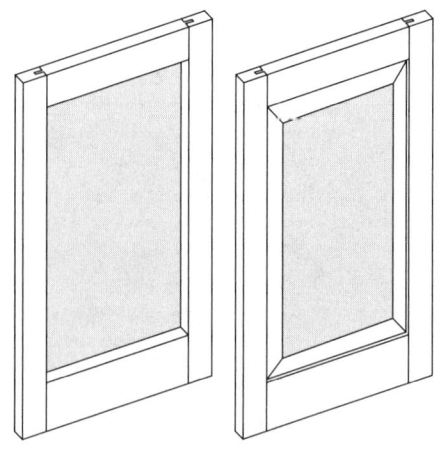

Flat Panel    Raised Panel

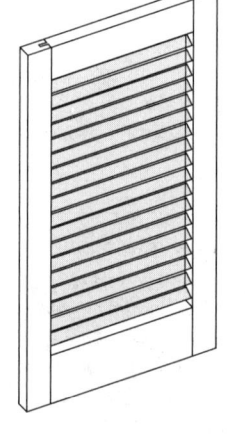

Louvered    *Figure: 6-039*

#### SCREENS:

- **Hardware** must be specified, as it dictates the details of construction.

- **Manufacturer** does not typically supply, machine for, or install operating hardware, locking devices, pulls, lifts, etc.

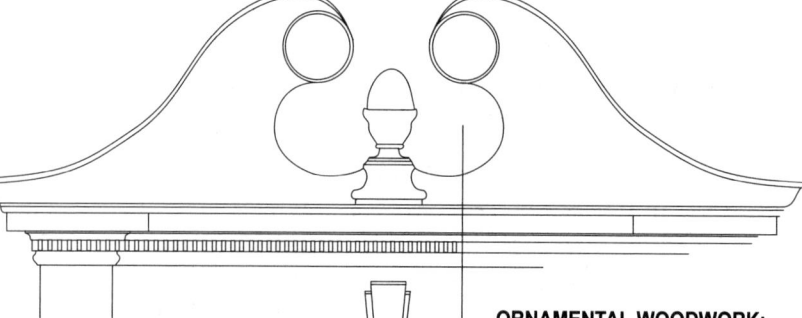

#### ORNAMENTAL WOODWORK:

**Typical Sources** of wood ornamentation are either mass-produced or custom carved and tooled.

- Mass-produced product is often limited in available species, sizes, and design, and is often a variety of historical styles, which might lack detail; however, can be appropriate for many applications.

- Custom carved or tooled work has a special appearance, with depth and clarity or crispness that machine tooling often cannot achieve. There will be slight irregularities because it is done by a skilled artisan; however, this is deemed desirable as it lends character and credence to the work, including tool-marked surface, which can be sanded smooth or left as a texture.

*Figure: 6-041*

## introductory information

**ORNAMENTAL WOODWORK**   (continued)

There are four methods of depicting a design in wood:

- **Incised**: Designs are simply made by shallow grooves in the surface of the material.

- **Relief**: Most architectural carving is carved in relief. The degree to which the design is lifted off the surface is described as low or high relief.

- **Pierced**: Some voids in the design are literally cut through the material and are termed pierced carvings.

- **Sculpture**: Carving in-the-round or sculptural works are incorporated into architectural surroundings.

Ornamental woodwork can be considered any addition to the purely functional and may partly rely on context for its aesthetic appeal. Among various definitions, the one pertinent here is: "Something that lends grace or beauty; a manner or quality that adorns." Ornamentation is defined as a decorative device or embellishment. A good example is the molding which can have functional uses such as covering joints, or with a profile, can be a design element. The profile can be further embellished or enriched by decorative carving.

Architectural carving combines the flat surfaces and clearly defined lines of geometry with the interpretive modeling of naturalistic forms.

Historic preservation, conservation and restoration disciplines are extensions of ornamental woodwork. Aspects of this work include, but are not limited to, stripping, repair, reconstruction, reuse of historic material, addition of new material, and special documentation for the work.

The United States Department of the Interior (www.doi.gov/), the National Park Service (www.nps.gov/), and the Historic Sites and Monuments Board of Canada (www.parkscanada.gc.ca/) publish documents related to work under their jurisdiction. The most recent publications from these entities will provide valuable information for the design professional and the woodwork fabrication, finishing, and installation.

There are a number of related arts which are incorporated into wood constructions, such as stained glass, ceramic tiles, mosaic, fabric, plaster or composition ornament, faux finishes, metal hardware and stone inlays.

Excludes standing and running trim except as incorporated as integral parts of elements.

Unless required by the details and/or woodwork specifications, the manufacturer shall not:

- Provide or prepare for electrical, telephone, mechanical, or plumbing equipment;

- Install woodwork or furnish common in wall blocking, furring or hanging devices for the support or attachment of the woodwork;

- Supply exposed materials other than wood or plastic laminate;

- Factory finish; or

- Supply "stock" or specialty products. If they are to be supplied, they must be specified by a brand name or manufacturer.

**Fire-Retardant Solid Lumber** may affect the finishes intended to be used on the wood, particularly if transparent finishes are planned. The compatibility of finishes should be tested before they are applied.

### Sources for Wood Ornamentation

There are two possible sources for wood ornamentation, machine-produced elements and the custom carver.

- The mass-produced product is often limited in available species, sizes and design, which is often a variety of historic styles which may lack detail, however can be appropriate for many applications. Often the detail lacks clarity because of the tooling, sanding or finish. However, the product is relatively inexpensive, consistent in appearance and appropriate for many applications.

- On the other hand, there are a number of reasons to contact a custom carver.

  - When the pieces required are impractical or impossible to shape on conventional factory machinery. Examples are tapering profiles as in keystones, acute (interior) corners such as in Gothic tracery and compound curves as in stair handrails.

  - When small quantities are specified which are impractical or too expensive to fabricate by computerized methods.

  - When there is a need to replicate missing (hand carved) elements for restoration or renovation.

  - When elements of specified dimensions are required and unavailable otherwise.

  - When a particular wood species is required.

  - When customized logos or lettering is desired.

  - When patterns are required for casting in another material such as plaster, metal, or glass.

  - When uniqueness is valued by the customer.

Hand tooled and carved work has a special appearance. It has a depth and clarity or crispness which machine tooling often cannot achieve. Because it is done by a skilled artisan there will be slight irregularities, but this is deemed desirable as it lends character and credence to the work. Whether the surface is sanded smooth or the texture of tool marks is left, is one of the points of discussion between the millwork company and carver.

### Working with an Artisan

The custom carver usually works by him- or herself in a studio situation, but this does not necessarily indicate limitations either in quality, production time or fabrication capability. Work is done on a commission basis, so it is common to expect reasonable lead times.

What the woodcarver will need to know (from millwork specifier or customer):

- Type of element - molding, capital, bracket, etc.

- Sizes - drawings showing elevations and Sections are absolutely necessary for accurate cost estimates, whether provided by the millwork company or drawn by the carver. Often the carver will redraw computer-generated designs or ones not full sized.

# SECTION 6
Millwork

## introductory information

### ORNAMENTAL WOODWORK (continued)

**Working with an Artisan** (continued)

- Species of wood and who will supply the "blanks". Finishes (paint grade, gilding, faux finish) should also be discussed.
- Context and/or installed location should be made clear in order to understand lighting and the degree of detail necessary.
- Intended schedule or completion date.
- Budget if available as the carver can propose subtle changes in order to oblige a tight budget.

The millwork company should make reasonable efforts to provide as much information as possible as to design, and material. If providing blanks, effort should be made to fabricate them as accurately as possible. Material should be straight grained and contain a minimum of glue lines and therefore, grain directional changes. Consultation concerning what should be provided (sizes, species, special fabrication such as turning) with the carver is essential.

What to expect from the carver:

- The carver provides skill and knowledge through experience. The majority of the cost may be in the labor. Carving is a unique product which adds immeasurably to the character and attractiveness of the overall project.
- The carving should closely resemble what is represented in drawings and verbal descriptions.
- The product should be cleanly carved without distracting irregularities and chips or fuzz in the recesses. The agreed upon surface treatment: sanded, tool textured, primed or gilded, etc. should be consistent throughout.
- Work should be done in a timely manner as agreed upon.
- Quality in artistic handwork is often a subjective matter, but proper communication and agreement among parties should reduce variance of interpretation.

### DESIGN IDEAS

Includes illustrations of base, picture, casing, panel, crown, bed, handrail and chair rail moldings; along with a large number of historic ornamental woodwork illustrations. These design ideas are not exhaustive and are for the reader to use as a starting guide.

### SPECIFY REQUIREMENTS FOR:

- Flame spread ratings or special code compliance.
- Window performance testing and/or labeling and hardware.
- Glass type and thickness.
- Wood species for exterior sash, shutters, or screens and frame parts, exposed, semi-exposed or concealed shall be of any species listed in Section 3, suitable for exterior use as being resistant, moderately resistant, or very resistant.
- Closet and utility shelving shelf size, thickness, and support system needed to meet the load-carrying requirements of the project; otherwise, the minimal requirements of the standards shall prevail. Shelf deflection information can be found in Section 10.
- ADA or barrier-free compliance design and requirements.

### RECOMMENDATIONS

- If **FIELD FINISHED,** include in Division 09 of the specifications:

  - **BEFORE FINISHING,** exposed portions of woodwork shall have handling marks or effects of exposure to moisture, removed with a thorough, final sanding over all surfaces of the exposed portion and shall be cleaned before applying sealer or finish.

  - At **CONCEALED SURFACES** - Architectural woodwork that may be exposed to moisture, such as those adjacent to exterior concrete walls, etc., shall be primed.

- **REVIEW** the **GENERAL** portion of Sections 3 and 4 for an overview of the characteristics and the minimum acceptable requirements of lumber and/or sheet products that might be used herein.

- **STRUCTURAL MEMBERS,** grounds, in wall blocking, backing, furring, brackets, or other anchorage which becomes an integral part of the building's walls, floors, or ceilings, required for the installation of architectural woodwork are not to be furnished or installed by the architectural woodwork manufacturer or installer.

- At **WOOD SASH** and **WINDOWS,** the finish coats will be flowed onto the glass area approximately 1/16" (1.6 mm) to properly seal against weather, wind, and rain. It is not recommended to use a razor blade to scrape the glass, as it might break the seal. A broad-blade putty knife is recommended to be used to protect the seal between the glass and the wood members.

- **FABRICATION METHODS** can affect the final appearance, especially regarding the direction of the grain and the visibility of the glue joints. As a design professional, you may wish to specify the method; however, it is recommended that an architectural woodwork firm be consulted before making a particular selection. Mock-ups may be required to visualize the end product.

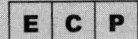
Where the **E**, **C**, or **P** icon is not indicated, the rule applies to all Grades equally

# SECTION 6
## Millwork

## compliance requirements

**GENERAL**/PRODUCT/INSTALLATION/TEST

Including: Standing & Running Trim, Door Frames, Window Frames, Sashes, Blinds & Shutters, Screens, Ornamental & Miscellaneous Millwork Composed of Solid Wood and/or Sheet Products

### 6.1 BASIC CONSIDERATIONS

1 **GRADE**

1.1 These standards are characterized in three Grades of quality that may be mixed within a single project. Limitless design possibilities and a wide variety of lumber and veneer species, along with overlays, high pressure decorative laminates, factory finishes, and profiles are available in all three Grades.

1.2 **ECONOMY GRADE** defines the minimum quality requirements for a project's workmanship, materials, or installation and is typically reserved for woodwork that is not in public view, such as in mechanical rooms and utility areas.

1.3 **CUSTOM GRADE** is typically specified for and adequately covers most high quality architectural woodwork, providing a well defined degree of control over a project's quality of materials, workmanship, or installation.

1.4 **PREMIUM GRADE** is typically specified for use in those areas of a project where the highest level of quality, materials, workmanship, and installation is required.

2 **CONTRACT DOCUMENTS** shall govern if in conflict with these standards.

3 **ACCEPTABLE REQUIREMENTS** of lumber and/or sheet products used within this woodwork product section are established by Sections 3 and 4, unless otherwise modified herein.

4 **AESTHETIC COMPLIANCE REQUIREMENTS** apply only to surfaces visible after fabrication and installation.

5 **EXPOSED SURFACES INCLUDE:**

5.1 Visible surfaces of standing/running trim, door/window frames, sashes, screens, blinds, shutters, and miscellaneous woodwork, excluding:

5.1.1 Top horizontal surfaces 80" (2032 mm) or more above the finished floor, unless visible from above.

5.1.2 Bottom horizontal surfaces 42" (1067 mm) or less above the finished floor.

### 6.1 BASIC CONSIDERATIONS (continued)

6 **SEMI-EXPOSED SURFACES INCLUDE:**

6.1 Top horizontal surfaces 80" (2032 mm) or more above the finished floor, unless visible from above.

6.2 Bottom horizontal surfaces 42" (1067 mm) or less above the finished floor.

7 **CONCEALED SURFACES INCLUDE:**

7.1 Non visible surfaces attached to and/or covered by another.

7.2 Non visible blocking, spacers, etc., used for attachment.

8 To **PREVENT TELEGRAPHING**, inset solid wood edging when used must have similar moisture content as panel core, be glued securely and calibrated with panel core thickness prior to being laminated with a wood veneer on both faces.

9 **INDUSTRY PRACTICES**

9.1 **FLAME SPREAD RATED WOOD DOOR FRAMES** shall be of the manufacturer's standard design and construction, conforming to the requirements of their applicable labeling service.

9.1.1 These standards do not cover labeled frames.

9.1.1.1 Only firms recognized by applicable code officials are authorized to label a frame assembly. If a label will be required by the applicable code officials, it is the obligation of the design professional to so specify, and the obligation of the manufacturer to assure a properly licensed assembly.

9.2 **STRUCTURAL MEMBERS**, grounds, in wall blocking, backing, furring, brackets, or other anchorage that becomes an integral part of the building's walls, floors, or ceilings, that are required for the installation of architectural woodwork are not furnished or installed by the architectural woodwork manufacturer or installer.

9.3 **WALL, CEILING,** and/or **OPENING VARIATIONS** in excess of 1/4" (6.4 mm) or **FLOORS** in excess of 1/2" (12.7 mm) in 144" (3658 mm) of being plumb, level, flat, straight, square, or of the correct size are not acceptable for the installation of architectural woodwork, nor is it the responsibility of the installer to scribe or fit to tolerances in excess of such.

9.4 **PRIMING** of architectural woodwork is not the responsibility of the manufacturer and/or installer, unless the material is being furnished prefinished.

## SECTION 6
Millwork

GENERAL/PRODUCT/INSTALLATION/TEST

compliance requirements

Where the **E**, **C**, or **P** icon is not indicated, the rule applies to all Grades equally

### 6.1 BASIC CONSIDERATIONS (continued)

**9 INDUSTRY PRACTICES** (continued)

9.5 **RADIUS MOLDINGS** are laminated and formed, preshaped, or machined to the radius and fabricated in the longest practical lengths to minimize installer joints.

9.5.1 The **METHOD of FABRICATION**, unless specified otherwise, is the manufacturer's choice.

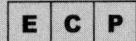 Where the E, C, or P icon is not indicated, the rule applies to all Grades equally

# SECTION 6
## Millwork

## compliance requirements

GENERAL / **PRODUCT** / INSTALLATION / TEST

### 6.2 SCOPE

1. All exposed interior and exterior standing and running wood trim members, door frames, window frames, sashes, blinds and shutters, screens, and ornamental and miscellaneous millwork that are not structural in nature.

2. **TYPICAL INCLUSIONS,** Interior or Exterior:

   2.1 Base; shoe, casing, picture, ceiling, apron, and stool molds.

   2.2 Wood thresholds, plinth, corner blocks, and other exposed wood trim.

   2.3 Wood wainscoting and caps, wall, ceiling, soffit, or decorative paneling.

   2.4 Decorative turned or boxed wood columns, pilasters, false beams, screens, or louvers, including brackets, corbels, pedestals, finials, drops, and lookouts.

   2.5 Band sawn, scrolled, turned, or carved ornamental woodwork.

   2.6 Solid, paneled, or veneered wood door jambs/frames with sidelights, louvers, transoms, and borrowed lights, including extensions, linings, stops, mullions, transom bars, sills, other components, and flame spread ratings.

   2.7 Mill built sliding door and sash pockets, including operating hardware.

   2.8 Cleat and standards/bracket supported shelves, including hook strips, cleats, rods, and required hardware.

   2.9 Cornice moldings, corner and edge boards, fascia and soffits, water tables, and casing.

   2.10 Metal sash surrounds.

   2.11 Wood belt and base courses, verge boards, and miscellaneous moldings.

   2.12 Decorative sun screens, trellises, louvers, blinds, and window/porch screens.

   2.13 Board and cleat, louvered, or paneled blinds or shutters, fixed or active.

   2.14 Seat and bench parts, duck boards, and similarly worked wood members.

   2.15 Sheet products applied in the form of multiple boards, including decorative laminate or other sheet products.

   2.16 Staff moldings, blind stops, and parting beads, attached flashing, sill pans, inside/back linings, and balances.

### 6.2 SCOPE (continued)

2. **TYPICAL INCLUSIONS** (continued)

   2.17 Wood caps, pediments, casing, stucco molds, or stops for exterior door frames.

   2.18 Columns, pilasters, brackets, corbels, paneling, and moldings integral to a frame's design.

   2.19 Elliptical, segment, or full circle head, arched, peaked, gothic, irregular, and divided entrance specialty units.

   2.20 Frames and sash for double hung, hopper, tilt/turn, casement, awning, sidelights, clerestory, and fixed windows.

   2.21 Glass and glazing unless specified otherwise; open sash may be included by agreement.

   2.22 Ornamental woodwork making use of molded, shaped, and carved elements to create a decorative appearance.

3. **TYPICAL EXCLUSIONS**

   3.1 Any structural wood framing, timbers or sheet products, sheathing, siding, decking, or planking and S4S boards or battens.

   3.2 Any composition or plaster wallboards or coverings, lath, shingles, or shakes.

   3.3 Any bucks, grounds, stripping, furring, in wall blocking, reglets, cant strips, or waste molding.

   3.4 Any wood members not exposed.

   3.5 Non wood, carved, or embossed moldings, including paper, vinyl, or foil wrapped.

   3.6 Commodity frames not governed by these standards.

   3.7 Machining of frames for hardware supplied by others.

   3.8 Any metal stops, frames, or wood cores for metal frames.

   3.9 Hardware, except as noted above.

   3.10 Priming or painting, glass and glazing, weather stripping, operating hardware, and/or sash balances.

   3.11 Flush or stile and rail doors.

   3.12 Premanufactured or stock window units.

   3.13 Fence posts or fence material where standard stock lumber yard material is indicated.

# SECTION 6
## Millwork

GENERAL/**PRODUCT**/INSTALLATION/TEST

**compliance requirements**

Where the **E**, **C**, or **P** icon is not indicated, the rule applies to all Grades equally | E | C | P |

## 6.2 SCOPE (continued)

### 3 TYPICAL EXCLUSIONS (continued)

- 3.14 Metal sash, skylights, screens, or weather stripping/milling for same.
- 3.15 Cabinet sash and hardware.
- 3.16 Roller screens and hardware.
- 3.17 Factory assembled shelving units.
- 3.18 In wall or ceiling blocking.
- 3.19 Premanufactured or stock screen units.
- 3.20 Providing or preparing for electrical, telephone, mechanical, or plumbing equipment.
- 3.21 Supplying exposed materials other than those covered herein or specified to be included.
- 3.22 Factory finish.

## 6.3 DEFAULT STIPULATION

1. If not otherwise specified or indicated in the contract documents, work shall be unfinished, Custom Grade, solid stock softwood intended for opaque finish.

## 6.4 RULES

1. The following rules shall govern unless a project's contract documents require otherwise.
2. These rules are intended to provide a well defined degree of control over a project's quality of materials and workmanship.
3. **ERRATA**, published on the Sponsor Associations' websites at www.awinet.org, www.awmac.com, or www.aws-errata.com, **shall take precedence over these rules**, subject to their date of posting and a project's bid date.

### 6.4.4 Basic Rules

| | | |
|---|---|---|
| 1 | | **AESTHETIC** grade rules apply only to exposed and semi-exposed surfaces visible after installation. |
| 2 | | **WOODWORK** not addressed herein shall be manufactured from solid stock, laminated stock, veneered stock, or a combination thereof. |
| 3 | | **LUMBER** shall conform to the requirements established in Section 3. |
| 4 | | **SHEET PRODUCTS** shall conform to the requirements established in Section 4. |
| 5 | | **EXPOSED SURFACES** include: |
| 5 | 1 | Visible surfaces of standing/running trim, door/window frames, sashes, screens, blinds, shutters, and miscellaneous woodwork, including: |
| 5 | 1 | 1 | Top horizontal surfaces less than 80" (2032 mm) above the finished floor, unless visible from above. |
| 5 | 1 | 2 | Bottom horizontal surfaces 42" (1067 mm) or more above the finished floor. |
| 6 | | **SEMI-EXPOSED SURFACES** include: |
| 6 | 1 | Top horizontal surfaces 80" (2032 mm) or more above the finished floor, unless visible from above. |
| 6 | 2 | Bottom horizontal surfaces less than 42" (1067 mm) above the finished floor. |
| 7 | | **CONCEALED SURFACES** include: |
| 7 | 1 | Non visible surfaces attached to and/or covered by another. |
| 7 | 2 | Non visible blocking, spacers, etc., used for attachment. |
| 8 | | **STANDING** and **RUNNING TRIM** shall be furnished as material only, not assembled. |

Continues next column ▼

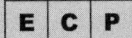

Where the **E**, **C**, or **P** icon is not indicated, the rule applies to all Grades equally

# SECTION 6
## Millwork

**compliance requirements** — GENERAL / PRODUCT / INSTALLATION / TEST

### 6.4.4 Basic Rules

▲ From previous column

| | | |
|---|---|---|
| 9 | | Where **MULTIPLE OPTIONS** are permitted, it shall be the manufacturer's choice unless specified otherwise. |
| 10 | | **FLAME SPREAD RATING**, if required, shall be so specified. |
| 11 | | **SPECIFIC PROFILE**, if required, shall be so specified or drawn. |
| 12 | | **SPECIAL ORNAMENTAL DETAIL** or joinery, if required, shall be so specified or drawn. |
| 13 | | **CATHEDRAL** type figure shall be achieved by: |
| 13 | 1 | A single component in "AA" Face Grade. |
| 13 | 2 | The split heart method in Face Grades "A - D", and: |
| 13 | 2 | 1 | Each half of a split heart shall be subject to the minimum component width requirements for Face Grade "B." |
| 14 | | **EXTERIOR APPLICATION** requires: |
| 14 | 1 | Type I, waterproof adhesive. |
| 14 | 2 | Sheet products be of exterior type. |
| 14 | 3 | Nails and screws be corrosion resistant. |
| 14 | 4 | Preservative treatment of exposed and concealed exterior frame members in accordance with Section 3. |
| 15 | | Where **GLUING** or **LAMINATION** occurs: |
| 15 | 1 | Delamination or separation shall not occur beyond that which is allowed in Sections 3 & 4. |
| 15 | 2 | Use of **CONTACT ADHESIVE** is not permitted unless otherwise indicated, and if used shall: |
| 15 | 2 | 1 | Comply with the Heat Resistance Test listed in the **APPENDIX**. [a] |
| 15 | 2 | 2 | Not be allowed at non phenolic backed wood veneer applications. |
| 16 | | **CUTOUTS** require: |
| 16 | 1 | At **SOLID SURFACE** or **HPDL** exposed surfaces have a minimum 1/4" (6.4 mm) radius at inside corners. |
| 17 | | **FIRST CLASS WORKMANSHIP** is required in compliance with these standards. |

### 6.4.5 Material Rules

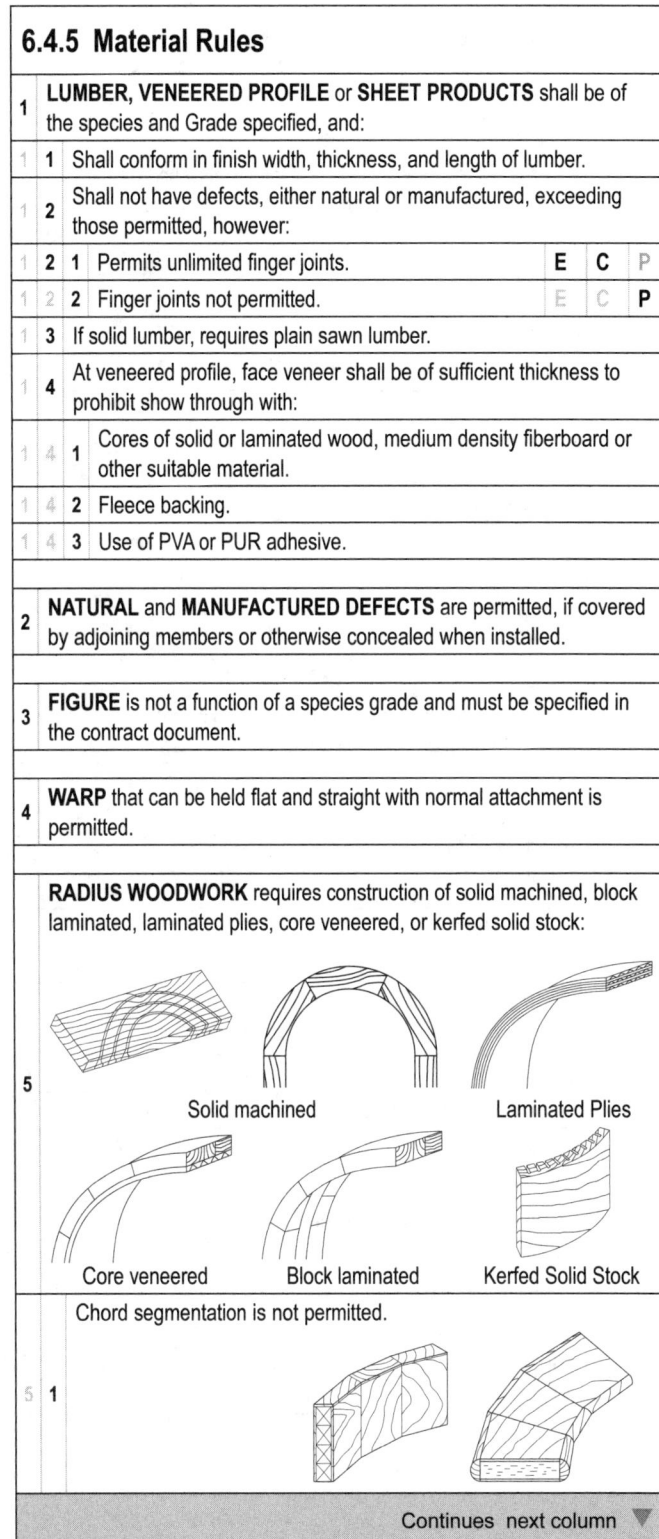

| | | | |
|---|---|---|---|
| 1 | | | **LUMBER, VENEERED PROFILE** or **SHEET PRODUCTS** shall be of the species and Grade specified, and: |
| 1 | 1 | | Shall conform in finish width, thickness, and length of lumber. |
| 1 | 2 | | Shall not have defects, either natural or manufactured, exceeding those permitted, however: |
| 1 | 2 | 1 | Permits unlimited finger joints. **E C P** |
| 1 | 2 | 2 | Finger joints not permitted. E C **P** |
| 1 | 3 | | If solid lumber, requires plain sawn lumber. |
| 1 | 4 | | At veneered profile, face veneer shall be of sufficient thickness to prohibit show through with: |
| 1 | 4 | 1 | Cores of solid or laminated wood, medium density fiberboard or other suitable material. |
| 1 | 4 | 2 | Fleece backing. |
| 1 | 4 | 3 | Use of PVA or PUR adhesive. |
| 2 | | | **NATURAL** and **MANUFACTURED DEFECTS** are permitted, if covered by adjoining members or otherwise concealed when installed. |
| 3 | | | **FIGURE** is not a function of a species grade and must be specified in the contract document. |
| 4 | | | **WARP** that can be held flat and straight with normal attachment is permitted. |
| 5 | | | **RADIUS WOODWORK** requires construction of solid machined, block laminated, laminated plies, core veneered, or kerfed solid stock: Solid machined, Laminated Plies, Core veneered, Block laminated, Kerfed Solid Stock. Chord segmentation is not permitted. |
| 5 | 1 | | |

Continues next column ▼

Architectural Woodwork Standards

# SECTION 6
## Millwork

GENERAL/**PRODUCT**/INSTALLATION/TEST

Where the **E**, **C**, or **P** icon is not indicated, the rule applies to all Grades equally | **E** | **C** | **P** |

**compliance requirements**

### 6.4.5 Material Rules

▲ From previous column

| | | | | | | |
|---|---|---|---|---|---|---|
| 5 | | **RADIUS WOODWORK** (continued) | | | | |
| 5 | 2 | Members of solid stock or block laminations shall be furnished in such sections as to avoid pronounced cross grain and reduce joints to a minimum, and: | | | | |
| 5 | 3 | Glue shall be selected for color to avoid a prominent glue line. | | | | |
| 6 | | For **OPAQUE FINISH**: | | | | |
| 6 | 1 | Medium density fiberboard (MDF) is permitted. | | | | |
| 6 | 2 | Veneer is permitted; however: | | | | |
| 6 | 2 | 1 | **SPECIES** of manufacturer's choice, closed grain hardwood conforming to ANSI/HPHA HP-1 (latest Edition) definitions and characteristics for: | | | |
| 6 | 2 | 1 | 1 | Grade - **D**. | E | C | P |
| 6 | 2 | 1 | 2 | Grade - **C**. | E | **C** | P |
| 6 | 2 | 1 | 3 | Grade - **B**. | E | C | **P** |
| 7 | | For **TRANSPARENT FINISH, VENEER**: | | | | |
| 7 | 1 | **SPECIES** of manufacturer's choice, hardwood conforming to ANSI/HPHA HP-1 (latest Edition) definitions and characteristics for: | | | | |
| 7 | 1 | 1 | Grade - **B**. | **E** | C | P |
| 7 | 1 | 2 | Grade - **A**. | E | **C** | P |
| 7 | 1 | 3 | Grade - **AA**. | E | C | **P** |
| 7 | 2 | **SLICING** of: | | | | |
| 7 | 2 | 1 | Manufacturer's choice. | **E** | C | P |
| 7 | 2 | 2 | Plain sliced. | E | **C** | **P** |
| 7 | 3 | **MATCHING ADJACENT LEAVES** be: | | | | |
| 7 | 3 | 1 | Manufacturer's choice. | **E** | C | P |
| 7 | 3 | 2 | Book matching. | E | **C** | **P** |
| 7 | 4 | **MATCHING WITHIN PANEL FACE** be: | | | | |
| 7 | 4 | 1 | Running. | **E** | **C** | P |
| 7 | 4 | 2 | Balance. | E | C | **P** |
| 7 | 5 | **MATCHING BETWEEN ADJACENT PANELS** be: | | | | |
| 7 | 5 | 1 | Manufacturer's choice. | **E** | **C** | P |
| 7 | 5 | 2 | Compatible for color and grain. | E | **C** | P |
| 7 | 5 | 3 | Well matched for color and grain. | E | C | **P** |
| 7 | 5 | 4 | **END, SEQUENCE**, and **BLUE PRINT MATCHING** shall be specified. | | | |

Continues next column ▼

### 6.4.5 Material Rules

▲ From previous column

| | | | | | | |
|---|---|---|---|---|---|---|
| 8 | | **EXPOSED SURFACES**: | | | | |
| 8 | 1 | Require end grain be kept to a minimum. | **E** | **C** | P |
| 8 | 2 | Require ends be self returned with no end grain showing. | E | **C** | **P** |
| 8 | 3 | Require sheet product edges to be edgebanded with the same species as the face: | **E** | C | **P** |
| 8 | 4 | For **TRANSPARENT FINISH**: | | | | |
| 8 | 4 | 1 | Permits hardwood or softwood. | **E** | C | P |
| 8 | 4 | 2 | Permits only one species for the entire project. | E | **C** | **P** |
| 8 | 4 | 3 | Prohibits finger joints. | **E** | **C** | **P** |
| 8 | 4 | 4 | Requires adhesive, used for laminating, to be selected for color to avoid a prominent glue line. | **E** | **C** | **P** |
| 8 | 4 | 5 | Requires lumber (including block segments or veneer of laminated material) and sheet products to be compatible in color and grain. | **E** | **C** | P |
| 8 | 4 | 6 | Requires lumber (including block segments or veneer of laminated material) to be well matched for color and grain; sheet products shall be compatible in color with solid stock, and adjacent sheet products shall be well matched for color and grain. | E | C | **P** |
| 8 | 4 | 7 | Requires radius frames to be constructed of laminated plies or core veneered. | E | **C** | **P** |
| 8 | 4 | 8 | Requires **INTERSECTIONS** of radius and straight members to be splined or half lapped, securely glued, and mechanically fastened. | **E** | **C** | **P** |
| 8 | 4 | 9 | At **BLOCK LAMINATION**: | | | |
| 8 | 4 | 9 | 1 | Requires segments to be cut from the same board, when practical. | E | **C** | **P** |
| 8 | 4 | 9 | 2 | Requires segment joints to be staggered. | **E** | **C** | **P** |
| 8 | 4 | 9 | 3 | Requires adjacent segment ends to have a similar grain angle. | **E** | **C** | **P** |

Continues next column ▼

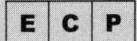

Where the **E**, **C**, or **P** icon is not indicated, the rule applies to all Grades equally

# SECTION 6
## Millwork

## compliance requirements
GENERAL/**PRODUCT**/INSTALLATION/TEST

### 6.4.5 Material Rules
▲ From previous column

| # | # | # | Description | E | C | P |
|---|---|---|---|---|---|---|
| 8 | | | **EXPOSED SURFACES** (continued) | | | |
| 8 | 4 | | For **TRANSPARENT FINISH** (continued) | | | |
| 8 | 4 | 10 | At **VENEER LAMINATIONS**: | | | |
| 8 | 4 | 10 | 1 | Requires exposed layers to be resawn from the same or matched boards. | E | C | P |
| 8 | 4 | 10 | 2 | Requires veneer layers to be reassembled in the same order and orientation as cut. | E | C | P |
| 8 | 4 | 11 | Have visible **EDGES**, **REVEALS**, and/or **SPLINES**, when appropriate, that are: | | | |
| 8 | 4 | 11 | 1 | Full length. | | | |
| 8 | 4 | 11 | 2 | Manufacturers' choice. | E | C | P |
| 8 | 4 | 11 | 3 | Match species of panel face. | E | C | P |
| 8 | 4 | 11 | 4 | Compatible for color and grain. | E | C | P |
| 8 | 4 | 11 | 5 | Well matched for color and grain. | E | C | P |
| 8 | 4 | 11 | 6 | A minimum of 0.020" (0.5 mm) nominal thickness that precludes show through of core. | E | C | P |
| 9 | | | **SEMI-EXPOSED SURFACES**: | | | |
| 9 | 1 | | **OPAQUE** finish, permits natural and manufacturing defects, provided the surface is filled solid. | | | |
| 10 | | | **CONCEALED SURFACES**: | | | |
| 10 | 1 | | Permits voids, wane, and unfilled knots. | | | |
| 10 | 2 | | Requires blocking or shims to be of a compatible material. | | | |
| 11 | | | **DOOR** and **WINDOW FRAMES**: | | | |
| 11 | 1 | | **FLAT STYLE** cased opening or with applied stop, shall be: | | | |
| 11 | 1 | 1 | Minimum of 11/16" (17 mm) in thickness. | E | C | P |
| 11 | 1 | 2 | Minimum of 3/4" (19 mm) in thickness. | E | C | P |
| 11 | 1 | 3 | Minimum of 1-1/16" (27 mm) in thickness at cased opening. | E | C | P |
| 11 | 1 | 4 | Stops shall be 3/8" (9 mm) in thickness. | E | C | P |
| 11 | 1 | 5 | Stops shall be 1/2" (13 mm) in thickness. | E | C | P |
| 11 | 2 | | **RABBETED STYLE** shall be: | | | |
| 11 | 2 | 1 | Minimum of 1-1/16" (27 mm) in thickness. | E | C | P |
| 11 | 2 | 2 | Minimum of 1-5/16" (33 mm) in thickness. | E | C | P |
| 11 | 2 | 3 | Minimum of 1-1/2" (38 mm) in thickness. | E | C | P |

Continues next column ▼

### 6.4.5 Material Rules
▲ From previous column

| # | # | # | Description | E | C | P |
|---|---|---|---|---|---|---|
| 11 | | | **DOOR** and **WINDOW FRAMES** (continued) | | | |
| 11 | 3 | | **PLOUGHED STYLE** with T-stop, shall be: | | | |
| 11 | 3 | 1 | Minimum of 3/4" (19 mm) in thickness. | E | C | P |
| 11 | 3 | 2 | Minimum of 1-1/16" (27 mm) in thickness. | E | C | P |
| 11 | 3 | 3 | Stops shall be minimum 3/4" (19 mm) in thickness set in 1/4" (6 mm) groove. | E | C | P |
| 11 | 4 | | **SPLIT STYLE** with T-stop, shall be: | | | |
| 11 | 4 | 1 | Minimum of 11/16" (17 mm) in thickness at thin member. | E | C | P |
| 11 | 4 | 2 | Minimum of 3/4" (19 mm) in thickness. | E | C | P |
| 11 | 5 | | **VENEERED CONSTRUCTION**: | | | |
| 11 | 5 | 1 | Shall be of the same species. | | | |
| 11 | 5 | 2 | Is permitted for use only in climate controlled environments, and face veneer shall: | | | |
| 11 | 5 | 2 | 1 | Be of sufficient thickness to prohibit show through. | | | |
| 11 | 5 | 2 | 2 | Extend over the edgebands when edgebands exceed 1/8" (3.2 mm) in thickness. | E | C | P |
| 11 | 6 | | **FLAME SPREAD RATING** shall be of the manufacturer's permitted design and construction in conforming with the requirements of their applicable labeling service. | | | |
| 12 | | | **SASH**: | | | |
| 12 | 1 | | **LUMBER SPECIES** shall be: | | | |
| 12 | 1 | 1 | Pine, Fir, Hemlock, or Larch. | E | C | P |
| 12 | 1 | 2 | Idaho White Pine, Northern White Pine, American or African Mahogany, or Douglas Fir. | E | C | P |
| 12 | 1 | 3 | Ponderosa and Sugar Pine, Teak (except at opaque finish), American Mahogany, White Oak, or Western Red Cedar. | E | C | P |
| 12 | 2 | | Shall be a minimum of 1-3/8" (35 mm) in thickness. | E | C | P |
| 12 | 3 | | Shall be a minimum of 1-3/4" (44 mm) in thickness. | E | C | P |
| 12 | 4 | | May require the minimum thickness to be different than this standard in consideration of the size of the window and the applicable codes. | | | |

Continues next column ▼

Architectural Woodwork Standards

# SECTION 6
## Millwork

GENERAL/**PRODUCT**/INSTALLATION/TEST

**compliance requirements**

Where the **E**, **C**, or **P** icon is not indicated, the rule applies to all Grades equally | **E** | **C** | **P** |

### 6.4.5 Material Rules

▲ From previous column

| 13 | | | | BLINDS and SHUTTERS: | | | |
|---|---|---|---|---|---|---|---|
| 13 | 1 | | | LUMBER SPECIES shall be: | | | |
| 13 | 1 | 1 | | Pine, Fir, Hemlock, or Larch. | E | C | P |
| 13 | 1 | 2 | | Idaho White Pine, Northern White Pine, American or African Mahogany, or Douglas Fir. | E | **C** | P |
| 13 | 1 | 3 | | Ponderosa and Sugar Pine, Teak (except at opaque finish), American Mahogany, White Oak, or Western Red Cedar. | E | C | **P** |
| 13 | 2 | | | STILES and RAILS shall be: | | | |
| 13 | 2 | 1 | | Solid stock. | | | |
| 13 | 2 | 2 | | Minimum of 3/4" (19 mm) in thickness. | | | |
| 13 | 3 | | | PANELS: | | | |
| 13 | 3 | 1 | | FLAT shall be: | | | |
| 13 | 3 | 1 | 1 | SOLID WOOD: | | | |
| 13 | 3 | 1 | 1 | Minimum 1/2" (12.7 mm) in thickness and maximum 23-3/4" (603 mm) across the grain in width. | **E** | C | P |
| 13 | 3 | 1 | 2 | Minimum 3/4" (19 mm) in thickness and maximum 13-3/4" (350 mm) across the grain in width. | E | **C** | P |
| 13 | 3 | 1 | 3 | Not permitted. | E | C | **P** |
| 13 | 3 | 1 | 2 | SHEET PRODUCT: | | | |
| 13 | 3 | 1 | 2 | 1 | Minimum 1/4" (6.4 mm) in thickness. | **E** | C | P |
| 13 | 3 | 1 | 2 | 2 | Minimum 1/2" (12.7 mm) in thickness. | E | **C** | P |
| 13 | 3 | 2 | | RAISED shall be: | | | |
| 13 | 3 | 2 | 1 | SOLID WOOD: | | | |
| 13 | 3 | 2 | 1 | 1 | Permitted in any dimension. | **E** | C | P |
| 13 | 3 | 2 | 1 | 2 | Minimum 3/4" (19 mm) in thickness and maximum in width 13-3/4" (350 mm) across the grain. | E | **C** | P |
| 13 | 3 | 2 | 1 | 3 | Not permitted. | E | C | **P** |
| 13 | 3 | 2 | 2 | VENEERED: | | | |
| 13 | 3 | 2 | 2 | 1 | Minimum 1/2" (12.7 mm) in thickness. | **E** | C | P |
| 13 | 3 | 2 | 2 | 2 | Minimum 3/4" (19 mm) in thickness. | E | **C** | **P** |

Continues next column ▼

### 6.4.5 Material Rules

▲ From previous column

| 14 | | | | SCREENS: | | | |
|---|---|---|---|---|---|---|---|
| 14 | 1 | | | Shall be solid lumber. | | | |
| 14 | 1 | | | LUMBER SPECIES shall be: | | | |
| 14 | 1 | 1 | | Pine, Fir, Hemlock, or Larch. | E | C | P |
| 14 | 1 | 2 | | Idaho White Pine, Northern White Pine, American or African Mahogany, or Douglas Fir. | E | **C** | P |
| 14 | 1 | 3 | | Ponderosa and Sugar Pine, Teak (except at opaque finish), American Mahogany, White Oak, or Western Red Cedar. | E | C | **P** |
| 14 | 2 | | | FRAME THICKNESS shall be: | | | |
| 14 | 2 | 1 | | Manufacturers' choice. | **E** | C | P |
| 14 | 2 | 2 | | Minimum of 3/4" (19 mm). | E | **C** | P |
| 14 | 2 | 3 | | Minimum of 1" (25 mm). | E | C | **P** |
| 14 | 3 | | | FRAME PARTS shall be coped: | | | |
| 14 | 3 | 1 | | Not required. | **E** | C | P |
| 14 | 3 | 2 | | With mortise and tenon, slot mortise and tenon, or doweled joinery. | E | **C** | P |
| 14 | 3 | 3 | | With haunched blind mortise and tenon or doweled joinery. | E | C | **P** |
| 14 | 3 | 4 | | With half lap joints permitted at intersecting muntins. | E | **C** | **P** |
| 14 | 4 | | | SCREEN MOLD shall be of sufficient thickness and width to cover wire edges. | | | |
| 14 | 5 | | | WIRE CLOTH shall be: | | | |
| 14 | 5 | 1 | | Nylon or fiberglass mesh. | **E** | C | P |
| 14 | 5 | 2 | | Aluminum or bronze wire (18 x 14 mesh). | E | **C** | P |
| 14 | 5 | 3 | | Bronze wire (18 x 14 mesh). | E | C | **P** |
| 14 | 5 | 4 | | Secured: | | | |
| 14 | 5 | 4 | 1 | At manufacturers' option. | **E** | C | P |
| 14 | 5 | 4 | 2 | At a maximum of 3" (76 mm) on center with staples. | E | **C** | P |
| 14 | 5 | 4 | 3 | By force into a kerf by use of a spline or a projecting bead. | E | C | **P** |
| 15 | | | | CLOSET and UTILITY SHELVING: | | | |
| 15 | 1 | | | Shall be one type of material for each project: | | | |
| 15 | 1 | 1 | | Medium Density Fiberboard (MDF), particleboard, or veneer core product. | **E** | C | P |
| 15 | 1 | 2 | | Medium Density Fiberboard (MDF), particleboard with UV filled coating, or veneer core product. | E | **C** | P |
| 15 | 1 | 3 | | Medium Density Fiberboard (MDF), thermoset overlay on particleboard, or veneer core product. | E | C | **P** |

Continues next column ▼

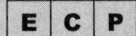 Where the **E**, **C**, or **P** icon is not indicated, the rule applies to all Grades equally

## compliance requirements

GENERAL/**PRODUCT**/INSTALLATION/TEST

# SECTION 6
Millwork

### 6.4.5 Material Rules

▲ From previous column

| | | | | | | |
|---|---|---|---|---|---|---|
| 15 | | | **CLOSET** and **UTILITY SHELVING** (continued) | | | |
| 15 | 2 | | Shelf thickness shall be a minimum of 3/4" (19 mm). | | | |
| 15 | 3 | | Wood shelf rods shall be a minimum of 1-3/8" (34.9 mm) in diameter. | | | |
| 15 | 4 | | Ends and back cleats shall be a minimum of 3/4" (19 mm) thick by: | | | |
| 15 | 4 | 1 | 3-1/2" (89 mm) wide when receiving a clothes rod or hooks. | | | |
| 15 | 4 | 2 | 1-1/2" (38 mm) wide when not receiving a clothes rod or hooks. | | | |
| 16 | | | **GLASS**: | | | |
| 16 | 1 | | Shall conform to applicable codes and regulations; these standards shall not supersede such regulations. | | | |
| 16 | 2 | | Safety type, shall conform to the Consumer Product Safety Commission's Safety Standard for Architectural Glazing Materials. | | | |
| 16 | 3 | | Putty shall conform to Federal Specification TT-P-791a. | | | |
| 16 | 4 | | Clear, single strength, shall be furnished within the appropriate size limitation; however: | | | |
| 16 | 4 | 1 | When required because of limitations, double strength shall be furnished. | | | |
| 16 | 5 | | Obscure type, shall be roll figured sheet glass, 1/8" (3.2 mm) in thickness, of standard pattern set with the smooth side facing the exterior or corridor, unless otherwise specified. | | | |
| 16 | 6 | | Wire type, whether polished or obscure, shall be 1/4" (6.4 mm) in thickness. | | | |
| 16 | 7 | | Float type, shall be 1/4" (6.4mm) in thickness. | | | |
| 16 | 8 | | Beveled type, at exterior openings, shall be set with the beveled face to the outside. | | | |
| 16 | 9 | | Leaded or zinc cane installation, shall have the individual light carefully fitted together with cane intersections neatly soldered and the whole assembly watertight. Reinforcing bars shall be provided where necessary. | | | |
| 16 | 10 | | Insulating units shall have the panes hermetically sealed and separated by a dehydrated air space. | | | |
| 17 | | | When **FACTORY FINISHING** is specified, concealed surfaces shall be factory sealed at 1 mil dry. | E | C | P |

### 6.4.6 Machining Rules

| | | | | | | |
|---|---|---|---|---|---|---|
| 1 | | | **EXPOSED SURFACES** shall comply with: | | | |
| 1 | 1 | | **SMOOTHNESS REQUIREMENTS** (see **SMOOTHNESS** in **TESTS**), and: | | | |
| 1 | 1 | 1 | Sharp edges shall be eased with a fine abrasive. | E | C | P |
| 1 | 1 | 2 | **TOP FLAT WOOD** surfaces, those that can be sanded with a drum or wide belt sander, with: | | | |
| 1 | 1 | 2 | 1 Minimum 15 KCPI or 100 grit sanding. | E | C | P |
| 1 | 1 | 2 | 2 120 grit sanding. | E | C | P |
| 1 | 1 | 2 | 3 150 grit sanding. | E | C | P |
| 1 | 1 | 3 | **PROFILED** and/or **SHAPED WOOD** surfaces require: | | | |
| 1 | 1 | 3 | 1 Minimum 15 KCPI or 100 grit sanding. | E | C | P |
| 1 | 1 | 3 | 2 Minimum 20 KCPI or 120 grit sanding. | E | C | P |
| 1 | 1 | 3 | 3 120 grit sanding. | E | C | P |
| 1 | 1 | 4 | **TURNED WOOD** surfaces require: | | | |
| 1 | 1 | 4 | 1 Minimum 15 KCPI or 100 grit sanding. | E | C | P |
| 1 | 1 | 4 | 2 120 grit sanding. | E | C | P |
| 1 | 1 | 4 | 3 180 grit sanding. | E | C | P |
| 1 | 1 | 5 | **CROSS SANDING**, excluding turned surfaces, require: | | | |
| 1 | 1 | 5 | 1 Is not a defect. | E | C | P |
| 1 | 1 | 5 | 2 Is not allowed. | E | C | P |
| 1 | 1 | 6 | **TEAR OUTS**, knife nicks, or hit or miss machining is not permitted. | | | |
| 1 | 1 | 7 | **KNIFE MARKS** are not permitted where sanding is required. | | | |
| 1 | 1 | 8 | **GLUE** or **FILLER**, if used, shall be inconspicuous and match the adjacent surface for smoothness. | | | |
| 1 | 2 | | **HPDL**, **PVC**, and **PREFINISHED WOOD** edges shall be machined flush and filed, sanded, or buffed to remove machine marks and sharp edges, and: | | | |
| 1 | 2 | 1 | **OVERLAP** (See Test F illustrations in **TESTS**) such as shall not exceed: | | | |
| 1 | 2 | 1 | 1 0.005" (0.13 mm) for a maximum length of 2" (50.8 mm) in any 12" (305 mm) run. | E | C | P |
| 1 | 2 | 1 | 2 0.005" (0.13 mm) for a maximum length of 1" (25.4 mm) in any 24" (610 mm) run. | E | C | P |
| 1 | 2 | 1 | 3 0.003" (0.08 mm) for a maximum length of 1" (25.4 mm) in any 48" (1220 mm) run. | E | C | P |

Continues next column ▼

# SECTION 6
Millwork

GENERAL/**PRODUCT**/INSTALLATION/TEST

Where the **E**, **C**, or **P** icon is not indicated, the rule applies to all Grades equally | **E** **C** **P**

## compliance requirements

### 6.4.6 Machining Rules

▲ From previous column

| | | | | | | | |
|---|---|---|---|---|---|---|---|
| 1 | | | **EXPOSED SURFACES** (continued) | | | | |
| 1 | 2 | | **HPDL**, **PVC**, and **PREFINISHED WOOD** edges (continued) | | | | |
| 1 | 2 | 2 | **CHIP OUT** (See Test G illustrations in TESTS) such as 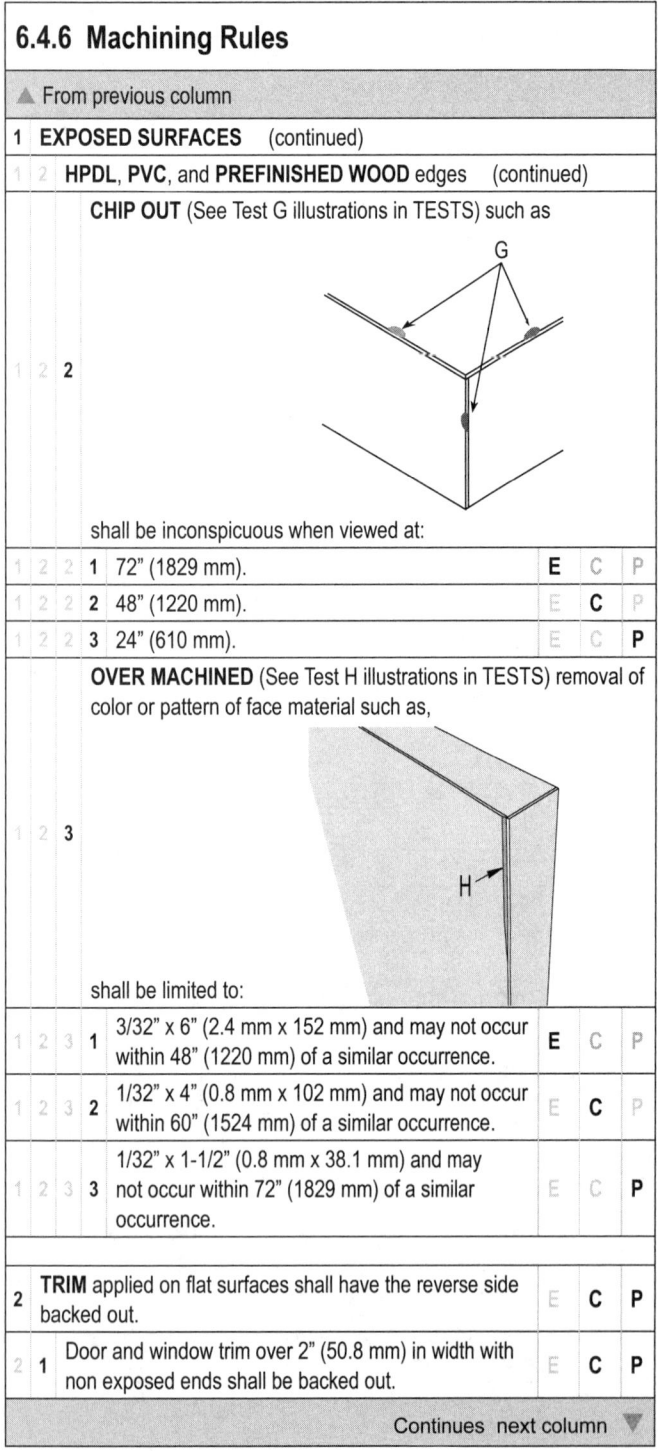 shall be inconspicuous when viewed at: | | | | |
| 1 | 2 | 2 | 1 | 72" (1829 mm). | E | C | P |
| 1 | 2 | 2 | 2 | 48" (1220 mm). | | C | P |
| 1 | 2 | 2 | 3 | 24" (610 mm). | | | P |
| 1 | 2 | 3 | **OVER MACHINED** (See Test H illustrations in TESTS) removal of color or pattern of face material such as, shall be limited to: | | | | |
| 1 | 2 | 3 | 1 | 3/32" x 6" (2.4 mm x 152 mm) and may not occur within 48" (1220 mm) of a similar occurrence. | E | C | P |
| 1 | 2 | 3 | 2 | 1/32" x 4" (0.8 mm x 102 mm) and may not occur within 60" (1524 mm) of a similar occurrence. | | C | P |
| 1 | 2 | 3 | 3 | 1/32" x 1-1/2" (0.8 mm x 38.1 mm) and may not occur within 72" (1829 mm) of a similar occurrence. | | | P |
| 2 | | | **TRIM** applied on flat surfaces shall have the reverse side backed out. | | | C | P |
| 2 | 1 | | Door and window trim over 2" (50.8 mm) in width with non exposed ends shall be backed out. | | E | C | P |

Continues next column ▼

### 6.4.6 Machining Rules

▲ From previous column

| | | | |
|---|---|---|---|
| 3 | **SOLID MACHINED** and **BLOCK LAMINATED** members shall be divided to minimize the exposure of cross grain in the face of the member, and: | | |
| 3 | 1 | Angle of grain at the face of the curved member shall not exceed 30 degrees, unless a small part size requires otherwise. 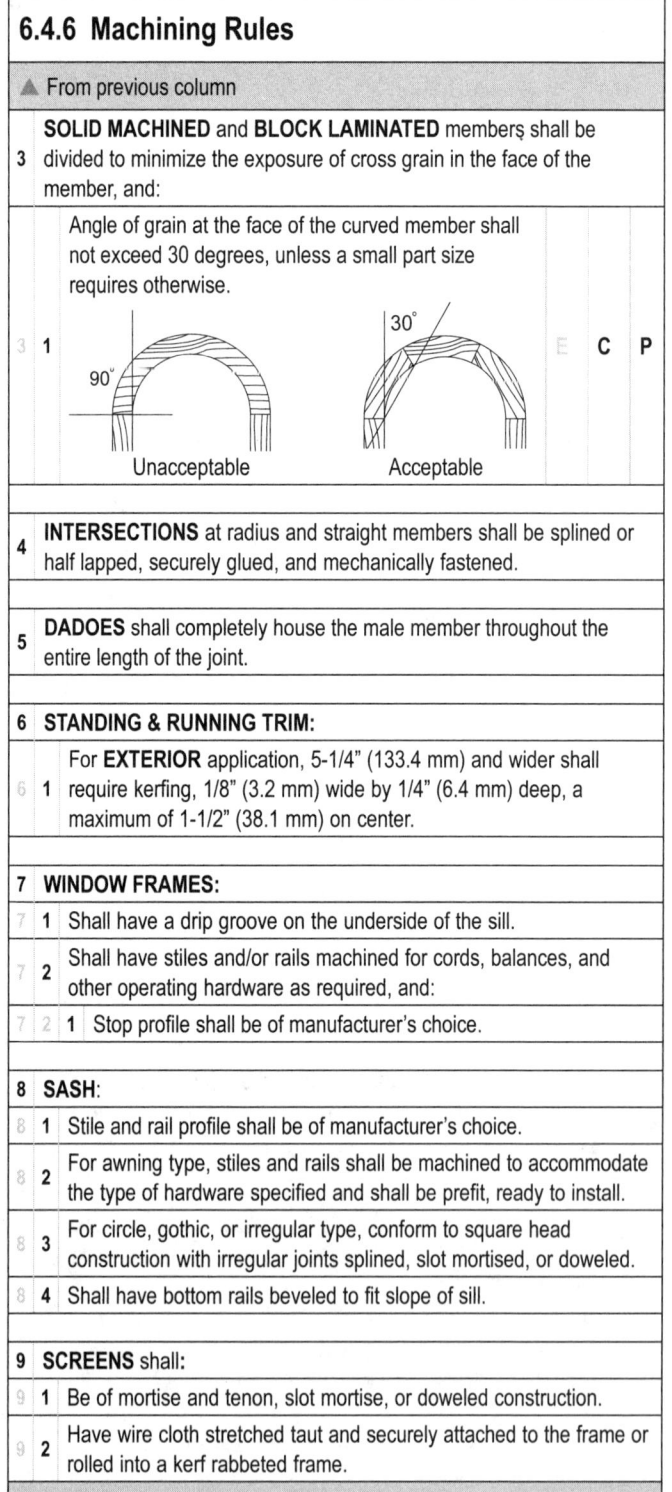 Unacceptable / Acceptable | C P |
| 4 | **INTERSECTIONS** at radius and straight members shall be splined or half lapped, securely glued, and mechanically fastened. | | |
| 5 | **DADOES** shall completely house the male member throughout the entire length of the joint. | | |
| 6 | **STANDING & RUNNING TRIM:** | | |
| 6 | 1 | For **EXTERIOR** application, 5-1/4" (133.4 mm) and wider shall require kerfing, 1/8" (3.2 mm) wide by 1/4" (6.4 mm) deep, a maximum of 1-1/2" (38.1 mm) on center. | |
| 7 | **WINDOW FRAMES:** | | |
| 7 | 1 | Shall have a drip groove on the underside of the sill. | |
| 7 | 2 | Shall have stiles and/or rails machined for cords, balances, and other operating hardware as required, and: | |
| 7 | 2 | 1 | Stop profile shall be of manufacturer's choice. |
| 8 | **SASH**: | | |
| 8 | 1 | Stile and rail profile shall be of manufacturer's choice. | |
| 8 | 2 | For awning type, stiles and rails shall be machined to accommodate the type of hardware specified and shall be prefit, ready to install. | |
| 8 | 3 | For circle, gothic, or irregular type, conform to square head construction with irregular joints splined, slot mortised, or doweled. | |
| 8 | 4 | Shall have bottom rails beveled to fit slope of sill. | |
| 9 | **SCREENS** shall: | | |
| 9 | 1 | Be of mortise and tenon, slot mortise, or doweled construction. | |
| 9 | 2 | Have wire cloth stretched taut and securely attached to the frame or rolled into a kerf rabbeted frame. | |

Continues next column ▼

# SECTION 6
## Millwork

**compliance requirements** — GENERAL/PRODUCT/INSTALLATION/TEST

Where the **E**, **C**, or **P** icon is not indicated, the rule applies to all Grades equally

### 6.4.6 Machining Rules

▲ From previous column

| 9 | | | **SCREENS** (continued) | | | |
|---|---|---|---|---|---|---|
| 9 | 3 | | Have molds neatly mitered and securely attached to the frame. | | | |
| 9 | 4 | | Be of manufacturer's choice frame width and profile. | | | |
| 10 | | | **BLINDS** and **SHUTTERS**: | | | |
| 10 | 1 | | Shall be of mortise and tenon, or doweled construction. | | | |
| 10 | 2 | | Slats shall overhang each other a minimum of 1/8" (3.2 mm), and: | | | |
| 10 | 2 | 1 | **STATIONARY SLATS** shall be mortised into stiles and set at an angle 45 to 60 degrees from horizontal, and: | | | |
| | | | Round edge slats shall be set in routed slot. | | | |
| 10 | 2 | 1 | 1 | | | |
| 10 | 2 | 1 | 2 | Flat edge slats shall be set in dado slot. | E | C | P |
| 10 | 2 | 1 | 3 | Flat edge slats shall be set in dado slot with molding applied to face rails to cover dado. | E | C | P |
| | | | **MOVABLE SLATS** shall pivot on a wood, metal, or nylon dowel, and: | | | |
| 10 | 2 | 2 | | | | |
| 10 | 2 | 2 | 1 | Pivot pins for damp coastal climates shall be nylon, stainless steel, or brass. | | | |
| 10 | 2 | 2 | 2 | Have a vertical control bar set to movable slats with curved staples to allow movement. | | | |
| 11 | | | **ORNAMENTAL MILLWORK:** | | | |
| 11 | 1 | | Permits cut sawn edges at scroll work. | | | |
| 11 | 2 | | Requires turnings to be clean, cut, sanded, and well matched for alignment. | | | |

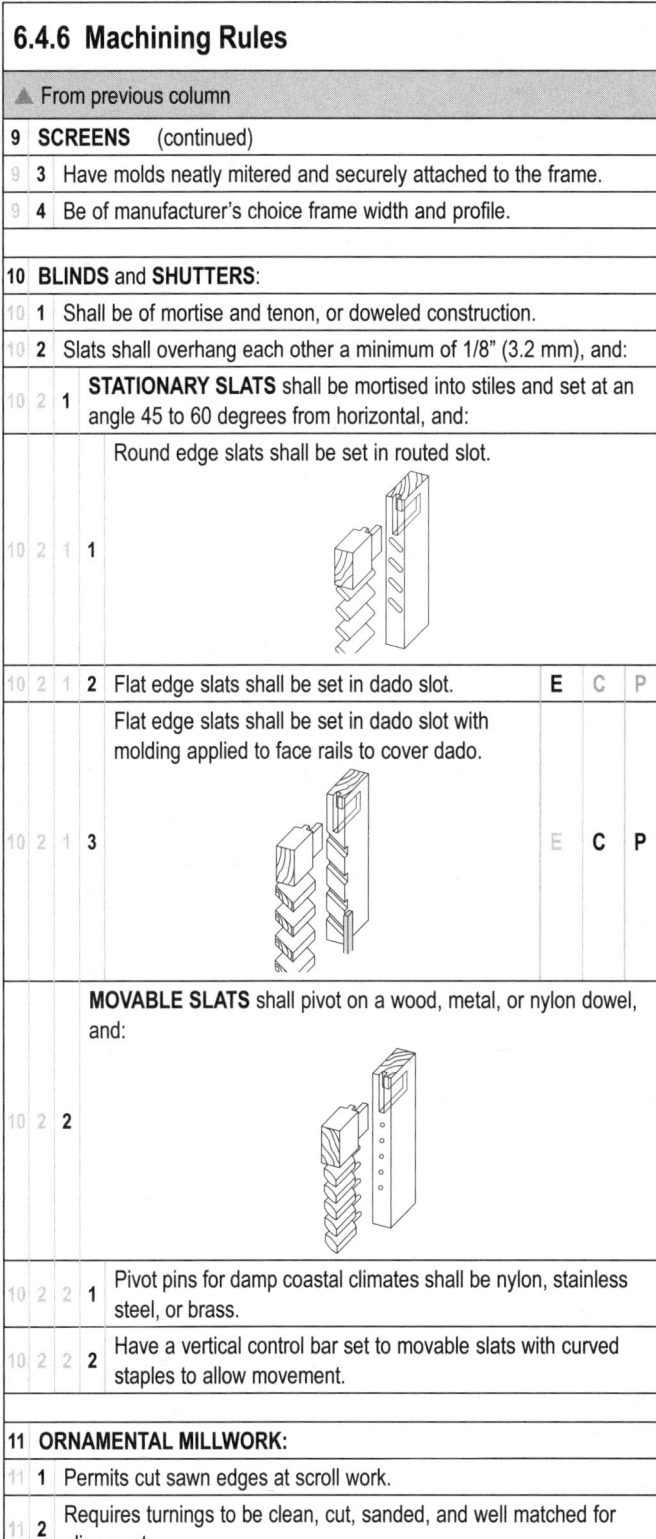

### 6.4.7 Assembly Rules

| 1 | | | These standards do not establish Grade rules for joint flushness and/or gap tolerances for woodwork products installed in a non climate controlled environment; however: | | | |
|---|---|---|---|---|---|---|
| 1 | 1 | | Prior to installation, the flushness and/or gap tolerances of woodwork products intended for non climate controlled environments shall meet the test requirements herein. | | | |
| 2 | | | **JOINTS** at **ASSEMBLED WOODWORK** shall: | | | |
| 2 | 1 | | Be neatly and accurately made. | | | |
| 2 | 2 | | Be securely glued, with: | | | |
| 2 | 2 | 1 | Adhesive residue removed from exposed and semi-exposed surfaces. | | | |
| 2 | 3 | | Be reinforced with glue blocks where essential. | | | |
| 2 | 4 | | Utilize clamp nail, biscuit spline, butterfly, scarf, or dowel joinery. | E | C | P |
| 2 | 5 | | Utilize biscuit spline, butterfly, scarf, or dowel joinery. | E | C | P |
| 2 | 6 | | Be **MECHANICALLY FASTENED** with nails or screws, where practical, with fasteners: | | | |
| 2 | 6 | 1 | Countersunk. | | | |
| 2 | 6 | 2 | Located in molding quirks or reliefs where possible. | E | C | P |
| 2 | 7 | | **NOT PERMIT** visible fasteners at exposed surfaces of sheet products. | | | |
| 2 | 8 | | Require **FLUSHNESS VARIATIONS** at exposed surfaces (See Test D illustrations in TESTS), when mitered or butted, such as not to exceed at: | | | |
| 2 | 8 | 1 | Wood to wood: | | | |
| 2 | 8 | 1 | 1 | 0.010" (0.25 mm). | E | C | P |
| 2 | 8 | 1 | 2 | 0.007" (0.18 mm). | E | C | P |
| 2 | 8 | 1 | 3 | 0.005" (0.13 mm). | E | C | P |
| 2 | 8 | 2 | Non wood to non wood: | | | |
| 2 | 8 | 2 | 1 | 0.025" (0.64 mm). | E | C | P |
| 2 | 8 | 2 | 2 | 0.015" (0.38 mm). | E | C | P |
| 2 | 8 | 2 | 3 | 0.010" (0.25 mm). | E | C | P |

Continues next column ▼

# SECTION 6
## Millwork

GENERAL / **PRODUCT** / INSTALLATION / TEST

**compliance requirements**

Where the **E**, **C**, or **P** icon is not indicated, the rule applies to all Grades equally — | E | C | P |

### 6.4.7 Assembly Rules

▲ From previous column

| 2 | JOINTS at ASSEMBLED WOODWORK (continued) | | | |
|---|---|---|---|---|
| | Allow **GAPS** at exposed surface (see Test A illustrations in TESTS), when mitered or butted, such as, | | | |
| 2 | 9 | not to exceed: | | | |
| 2 | 9 | 1 | 0.025" (0.64 mm) wide by 20% of the joint length. | E | C | P |
| 2 | 9 | 2 | 0.015" (0.38 mm) wide by 20% of the joint length. | E | C | |
| 2 | 9 | 3 | 0.010" (0.25 mm) wide by 20% of the joint length. | E | | P |
| | Allow **GAPS** at exposed surface joints of parallel members (See Test B illustrations in TESTS), such as | | | |
| 2 | 10 | not to exceed: | | | |
| 2 | 10 | 1 | 0.025" x 9" (0.64 mm x 229 mm) shall not occur within 48" (1219 mm) of a similar gap in the same joint. | E | C | P |
| 2 | 10 | 2 | 0.015" x 6" (0.38 mm x 152 mm) shall not occur within 60" (1524 mm) of a similar gap in the same joint. | E | C | |
| 2 | 10 | 3 | 0.010" x 4" (0.25 mm x 102 mm) shall not occur within 72" (1829 mm) of a similar gap in the same joint. | E | | P |
| | Allow **GAPS** at exposed surface joints (See Test C illustrations in TESTS) when mitered or butted, such as | | | |
| 2 | 11 | not to exceed at: | | | |
| 2 | 11 | 1 | 0.025" (0.64 mm). | E | C | P |
| 2 | 11 | 2 | 0.015" (0.38 mm). | E | C | |
| 2 | 11 | 3 | 0.010" (0.25 mm). | E | | P |

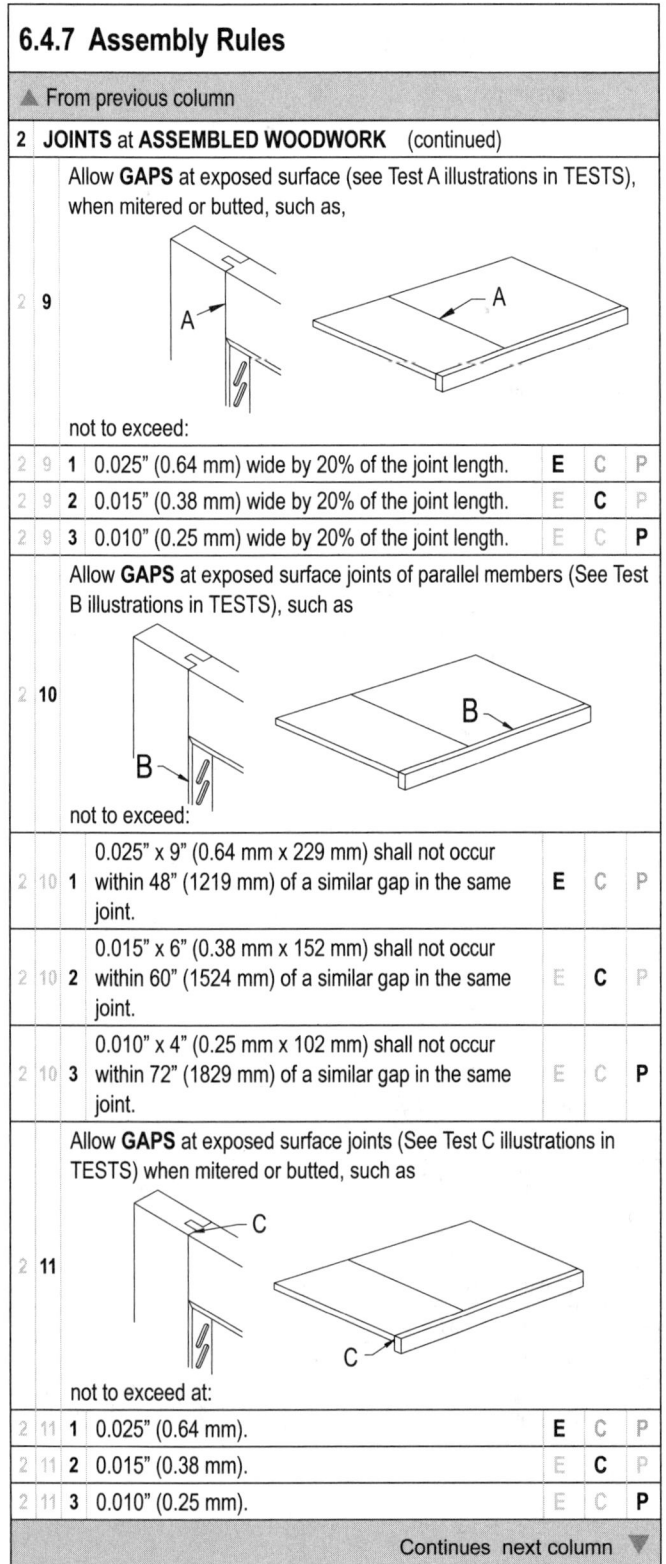

Continues next column ▼

### 6.4.7 Assembly Rules

▲ From previous column

| 2 | JOINTS at ASSEMBLED WOODWORK (continued) | | | |
|---|---|---|---|---|
| 2 | 12 | Allows use of **FILLER**: | | | |
| 2 | 12 | 1 | If inconspicuous when viewed at 36" (914 mm). | E | C | P |
| 2 | 12 | 2 | If inconspicuous when viewed at 24" (610 mm). | E | C | |
| 2 | 12 | 3 | NOT ALLOWED. | E | C | P |

| 3 | **FLATNESS** or **WARP** of installed and removable sheet products (see Test E illustrations in TESTS) such as shall not to exceed grade tolerance listed for 12" (303 mm) diagonal, width and/or length or as lineal ratio (not geometric ratio) thereof. Example, twice the grade tolerance listed for 24" (610 mm), three times the tolerance for 36" (914 mm): | | | |
|---|---|---|---|---|
| 3 | 1 | 0.045" (1.1 mm) per 12" (305 mm) or portion thereof. | E | C | P |
| 3 | 2 | 0.030" (0.8 mm) per 12" (305 mm) or portion thereof. | E | C | |
| 3 | 3 | 0.020" (0.5 mm) per 12" (305 mm) or portion thereof. | E | | P |

| 4 | **APPLIED MOLDINGS** shall be spot glued and mechanically fastened. | | | |
| 5 | **MITER JOINTS** and **CAPS** shall be well fitted and cleaned. | | | |
| 6 | **STILE** and **RAIL ASSEMBLIES** shall be built up in units as large as practical, and: | | | |
| 6 | 1 | Members shall be mortised and tenoned, doweled, or splined. | E | C | P |
| 7 | **SHEET** and **LAMINATED LUMBER PANELS** shall be allowed to move, float, expand or contract in reaction to ambient humidity changes. | | | |
| 8 | **BUILT UP ITEMS** shall be soundly fabricated with half lapped, mitered, shoulder mitered, tongued, or equivalent construction. | | | |

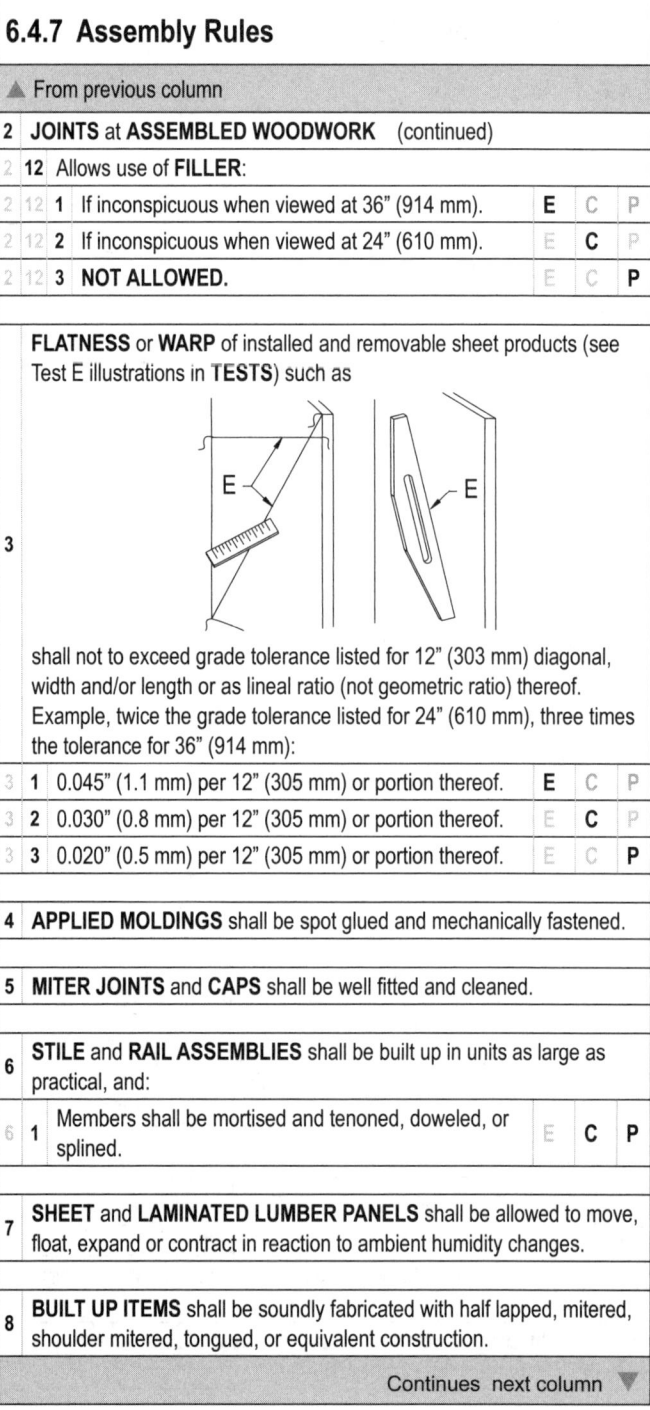

Continues next column ▼

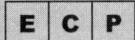

Where the **E**, **C**, or **P** icon is not indicated, the rule applies to all Grades equally

# SECTION 6
## Millwork

## compliance requirements

GENERAL / **PRODUCT** / INSTALLATION / TEST

### 6.4.7 Assembly Rules

▲ From previous column

| | | | E | C | P |
|---|---|---|---|---|---|
| 9 | | **STANDING & RUNNING TRIM** shall require: | | | |
| 9 | 1 | Radius moldings to be glued up for length in the longest practical lengths. | E | C | P |
| 9 | 2 | Exterior trim to be furnished as material only; items required to be assembled shall be so specified. | | | |
| 10 | | **DOOR FRAMES:** | | | |
| 10 | 1 | Flame spread rated shall be of the manufacturer's standard design and construction, conforming to the requirements of their applicable labeling service. | | | |
| 10 | 2 | With molded edges, other than square or with 1/16" (1.6 mm) or more in radius, shall have mitered joints. | E | C | P |
| 10 | 3 | With square heads shall have: | | | |
| 10 | 3 | 1 | Jambs furnished machined KD (knocked down). | | | |
| 10 | 3 | 2 | Stops cut to approximate length; however, not mitered or coped. | | | |
| 10 | 3 | 3 | Heads and sills dadoed to receive side jambs, or vice versa. | | | |
| 10 | 4 | With side jambs shall be dadoed into the sills and heads. | | | |
| 10 | 5 | With transom bars shall have them dadoed into side jambs. | | | |
| 10 | 6 | With mullions shall have them dadoed into sills and heads. | | | |
| 10 | 7 | For exterior opaque finished applications, shall have sill and jamb dadoes coated with mastic. | E | C | P |
| 10 | 8 | Shall be shipped: | | | |
| 10 | 8 | 1 | As oversize material for installer cutting and joinery. | E | C | P |
| 10 | 8 | 2 | As appropriately labeled pre-sized sets with premachined joinery. | E | C | P |
| 10 | 8 | 3 | As pre-sized, built up assemblies in as large as practical sections for safe transportation and installation, with: | E | C | P |
| 10 | 8 | 3 | 1 | Joints glued and fit tight, true, and secure. | E | C | P |
| 10 | 9 | At radius heads: | | | |
| 10 | 9 | 1 | Jambs shall be furnished assembled. | E | C | |
| 10 | 9 | 2 | Curved stops and casing shall be attached to frame. | E | C | |
| 10 | 9 | 3 | Joints at intersection of radius and straight members shall be splined or half lapped. | E | C | P |

Continues next column ▼

### 6.4.7 Assembly Rules

▲ From previous column

| | | | E | C | P |
|---|---|---|---|---|---|
| 11 | | **WINDOW FRAMES:** | | | |
| 11 | 1 | With molded edges, other than square or with 1/16" (1.6 mm) or more in radius, shall have mitered joints. | E | C | P |
| 11 | 2 | With transom bars shall have them dadoed into side jambs. | | | |
| 11 | 3 | With square edge members shall have the heads and sills dadoed to receive side jambs, or vice versa. | | | |
| 11 | 4 | With glazed openings shall be trimmed on both sides with wood stops; however, one side shall be removable and the removable stop shall be on exterior side of exterior frames, with: | | | |
| 11 | 4 | 1 | Stops shipped loose as material only. | E | C | P |
| 11 | 4 | 2 | Stops shipped in properly labeled sets, cut to size. | E | C | P |
| 11 | 4 | 3 | Stops tacked in place. | E | C | P |
| 11 | 5 | Shall include sills and applied exterior trim. | | | |
| 11 | 6 | Shall have stiles and/or rails machined for cords, balances, and other operating hardware as required. | | | |
| 11 | 7 | Shall have, at opaque finished exterior applications, the sill and jamb dadoes coated with mastic. | E | C | P |
| 11 | 8 | Shall include machining for: | | | |
| 11 | 8 | 1 | Operating hardware (if templates or a physical sample is provided prior to shop drawing preparation); however, it is not required to be furnished or installed. | | | |
| 11 | 8 | 2 | Weather stripping (provided templates or a physical sample is provided prior to shop drawing preparation); however, it is not required to be furnished or installed. | | | |
| 11 | 8 | 3 | Sash balances (provided templates or a physical sample is provided prior to shop drawing preparation); however, it is not required to be furnished or installed. | | | |
| 11 | 9 | Shall not include machining for non operating hardware, such as locking devices, pulls, lifts, etc., nor is it required to be furnished or installed. | | | |
| 11 | 10 | When glass is furnished and installed, it shall be bedded in a glazing compound prior to the installation of a face compound or wood bead, and: | | | |
| 11 | 10 | 1 | Glazing materials and the method of glazing are optional. | | | |
| 11 | 10 | 2 | Glass shall be cut slightly scant to prevent binding and set so as to prevent shifting. | | | |
| 11 | 10 | 3 | Glazier's points shall be spaced a maximum of 16" (406 mm) on center with a minimum of one on each edge of each light. | | | |
| 11 | 10 | 4 | Bedding of glass is required. | E | C | P |
| 11 | 10 | 5 | When putty (excluding primeless putty or glazing compound) is used, glass rabbets shall be primed with linseed oil before glazing. | | | |

Continues next column ▼

# SECTION 6
Millwork

GENERAL/**PRODUCT**/INSTALLATION/TEST

**compliance requirements**

Where the **E**, **C**, or **P** icon is not indicated, the rule applies to all Grades equally | **E** | **C** | **P** |

## 6.4.7 Assembly Rules

▲ From previous column

| | | | | | | | |
|---|---|---|---|---|---|---|---|
| 12 | **SASH** | | | | | | |
| 12 | 1 | Half lap joints are permitted at intersecting muntins, and: | | | | | |
| 12 | 1 | 1 | Bar and muntin alignment shall: | | | | |
| 12 | 1 | 1 | 1 | Be at right angles to each other and to the sash member. | | | |
| 12 | 1 | 1 | 2 | Align with each other vertically and horizontally. | | | |
| 12 | 1 | 1 | 3 | Align with similar members on the adjoining sash. | | | |
| 12 | 2 | Mullions shall be dadoed into heads and sills. | | | | | |
| 12 | 3 | At double glazed units requires one stop to be left loose for finishing. | | | | | |
| 12 | 4 | If glass is furnished and installed, it shall conform to the requirements set herein. | | | | | |
| 13 | **BLINDS** and **SHUTTERS**: | | | | | | |
| 13 | 1 | Require dadoed or equivalent joinery. | | | | | |
| 14 | **SCREENS** require: | | | | | | |
| 14 | 1 | They be assembled under pressure and pinned. | | | | | |
| 15 | **ORNAMENTAL MILLWORK:** | | | | | | |
| 15 | 1 | Woodwork shall be manufacturer sized except where installer adjustments are required. | | | | | |
| 15 | 2 | Column fabrication for opaque finish shall allow finger joints, with: | | | | | |
| 15 | 2 | 1 | Maximum of one per 96" (2400 mm) or portion thereof in any individual member. | | | | |
| 15 | 2 | 2 | Joints offset a minimum of 3" (76 mm) from adjacent joints. | | | | |
| 15 | 2 | 3 | Joints perpendicular to the face of the column resulting in the appearance of a single horizontal line with column upright. | | | | |
| 15 | 2 | 4 | Compliance Tests C and Flushness shall apply to such joints. | | | | |
| 15 | 3 | **SHEET PRODUCTS** | | | | | |
| 15 | 3 | 1 | Of **SOLID LUMBER** shall be: | | | | |
| 15 | 3 | 1 | 1 | Edge glued for width. | E | C | P |
| 15 | 3 | 1 | 2 | Maximum 10" (254 mm) in width. | E | C | P |
| 15 | 3 | 1 | 3 | Not permitted. | E | C | P |
| 15 | 3 | 2 | With **RAISED PANEL RIMS**: | | | | |
| 15 | 3 | 2 | 1 | Mitered and glued to sheet product body. | E | C | P |
| 15 | 3 | 2 | 2 | Mitered, splined, or doweled to sheet product body. | E | C | P |
| 15 | 3 | 3 | With **PANEL PRODUCT CENTERS** require: | | | | |
| 15 | 3 | 3 | 1 | No edge treatment. | E | C | P |
| 15 | 3 | 3 | 2 | Edge covered by veneer or concealed by molding. | E | C | P |

Continues next column ▼

## 6.4.7 Assembly Rules

▲ From previous column

| | | | | | | | |
|---|---|---|---|---|---|---|---|
| 15 | At **ORNAMENTAL MILLWORK** (continued) | | | | | | |
| 15 | 3 | **SHEET PRODUCTS** (continued) | | | | | |
| 15 | 3 | 4 | With **LOOSE JOINTS** between sections require: | | | | |
| 15 | 3 | 4 | 1 | No preparation. | E | C | P |
| 15 | 3 | 4 | 2 | Manufacturer preparation, utilizing mortise and tenon, dowel, or spline joinery. | E | C | P |
| 15 | 3 | 4 | 3 | Manufacturer assembly (if practical), utilizing mortise and tenon, dowel, or spline joinery. | E | C | P |
| 15 | 3 | 5 | With **OUTSIDE CORNERS** require: | | | | |
| 15 | 3 | 5 | 1 | No preparation. | E | C | P |
| 15 | 3 | 5 | 2 | Manufacturer prepared and shipped loose for installer fitting. | E | C | P |
| 15 | 3 | 5 | 3 | Manufacturer prepared, glued, and braced (if practical). | E | C | P |
| 15 | 3 | 6 | With **INSIDE CORNERS** require: | | | | |
| 15 | 3 | 6 | 1 | No preparation. | E | C | P |
| 15 | 3 | 6 | 2 | Shipped oversize for installer fitting. | E | C | P |
| 15 | 3 | 7 | With **APPLIED MOLDINGS**, contained wholly within an individual item or used as rim or panel retention members, require: | | | | |
| 15 | 3 | 7 | 1 | Mitered corners. | | | |
| 15 | 3 | 7 | 2 | No preparation. | E | C | P |
| 15 | 3 | 7 | 3 | Manufacturer application with spot glue and finish nails. | E | C | P |
| 15 | 3 | 7 | 4 | Manufacturer application with spot glue, finish nails, and: | E | C | P |
| 15 | 3 | 7 | 4 | 1 | Filled and sanded. | | |
| 15 | 3 | 8 | With **HISTORIC WORK** requires: | | | | |
| 15 | 3 | 8 | 1 | Repairs to be of the same machining, joinery, and assembly methods as original, reversible adhesives, etc. | | | |
| 15 | 3 | 8 | 2 | New work match existing, except when hand made non uniform profiles occur, a similar profile shall be selected by the design professional. | | | |

Continues next column ▼

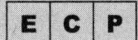

Where the **E**, **C**, or **P** icon is not indicated, the rule applies to all Grades equally

# SECTION 6
## Millwork

## compliance requirements

GENERAL/**PRODUCT**/INSTALLATION/TEST

### 6.4.7 Assembly Rules

▲ From previous column

| 16 | | | | At **MISCELLANEOUS MILLWORK** such as: | | | |
|---|---|---|---|---|---|---|---|
| 16 | 1 | | | **DECORATIVE SUN SCREENS** or **LOUVERS** shall be soundly constructed, with: | | | |
| 16 | 1 | 1 | | All members dadoed together and, where design permits, assembled in the mill. | | | |
| 16 | 2 | | | **BOXED BEAMS, COLUMNS, PILASTERS, SEATS, BENCHES**, and overhead **TRELLISES** shall be soundly constructed, with: | | | |
| 16 | 2 | 1 | | Tongued, shoulder mitered, mortised and tenoned, or doweled joints; securely glued, nailed, and reinforced with glue blocks or metal brackets, as appropriate. | | | |
| 16 | 3 | | | **STAVED COLUMNS** or **NEWELS** shall be of lock joint, tongue, or spline construction and securely glued with: | | | |
| 16 | 3 | 1 | | Caps and bases furnished loose. | | | |
| 16 | 4 | | | **HANDRAILS** and **CROOKS** shall be furnished mill cut and doweled unless jobsite conditions dictate otherwise. | | | |
| 16 | 5 | | | **CLOSET & UTILITY SHELVING,** shall have: | | | |
| 16 | 5 | 1 | | Shelves and dividers furnished: | | | |
| 16 | 5 | 1 | 1 | Unassembled. | | | |
| 16 | 5 | 1 | 2 | Cut to width in lengths suitable for installer fitting. | | | |
| 16 | 5 | 2 | | Cleats furnished as lineal footage. | | | |
| 16 | 5 | 3 | | Shelves with unsupported length exceeding 36" (914 mm) shall: | | | |
| 16 | 5 | 3 | 1 | Be a minimum of 1" (25.4 mm) in thickness, or: | | | |
| 16 | 5 | 3 | 1 | 1 | Have a minimum 3/4" x 2" (19 mm x 51 mm) applied frontdrop edge. 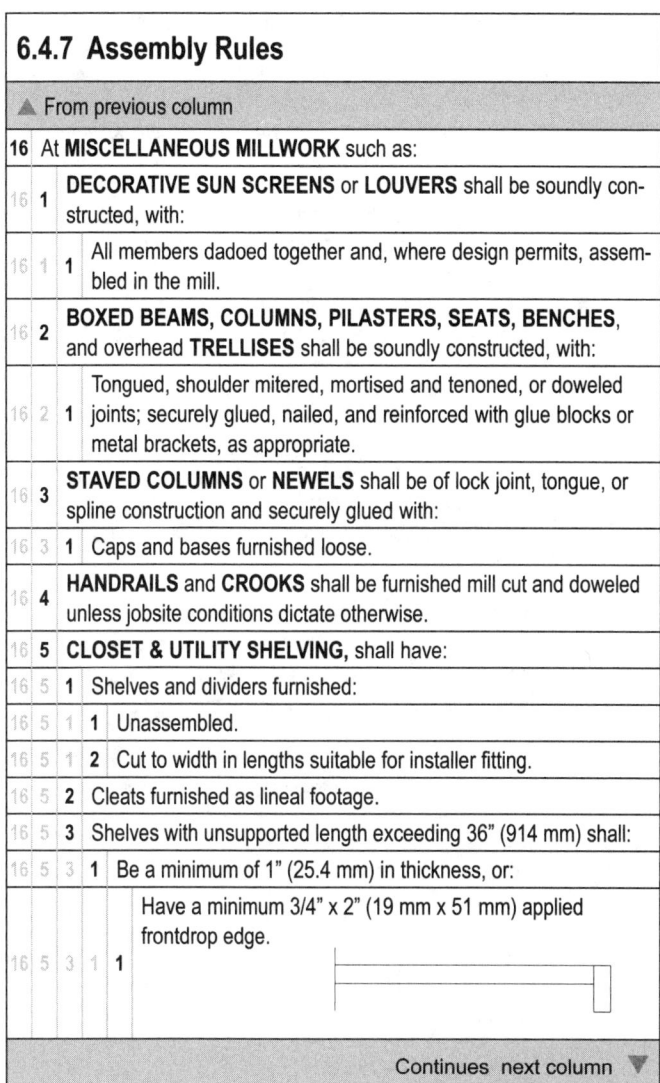 | | |

Continues next column ▼

### 6.4.7 Assembly Rules

▲ From previous column

| 16 | | | | At **MISCELLANEOUS MILLWORK** (continued) | | | |
|---|---|---|---|---|---|---|---|
| 16 | 5 | | | **CLOSET & UTILITY SHELVING** (continued) | | | |
| 16 | 5 | 4 | | Exposed edges of sheet good cleats and shelves are defined as visible in normal use position, and: | | | |
| 16 | 5 | 4 | 1 | Do not require edge work. | E | C | P |
| 16 | 5 | 4 | 2 | Shall be edgebanded to match face with edges eased, and: | E | C | P |
| 16 | 5 | 4 | 2 | 1 | Sequence of lamination is optional. | E | C | P |
| 16 | 5 | 4 | 3 | Adjoining adjustable shelves shall have ends edgebanded. | | | |
| 16 | 5 | 4 | 4 | When miter folded, shall have no open gaps, and: | | | |
| 16 | 5 | 4 | 4 | 1 | Shall be filed or sanded just enough to remove sharpness. | | | |
| 16 | 5 | 4 | 5 | Gaps between the end of the shelf and the wall up to 1/4" (6.4 mm) are allowed. 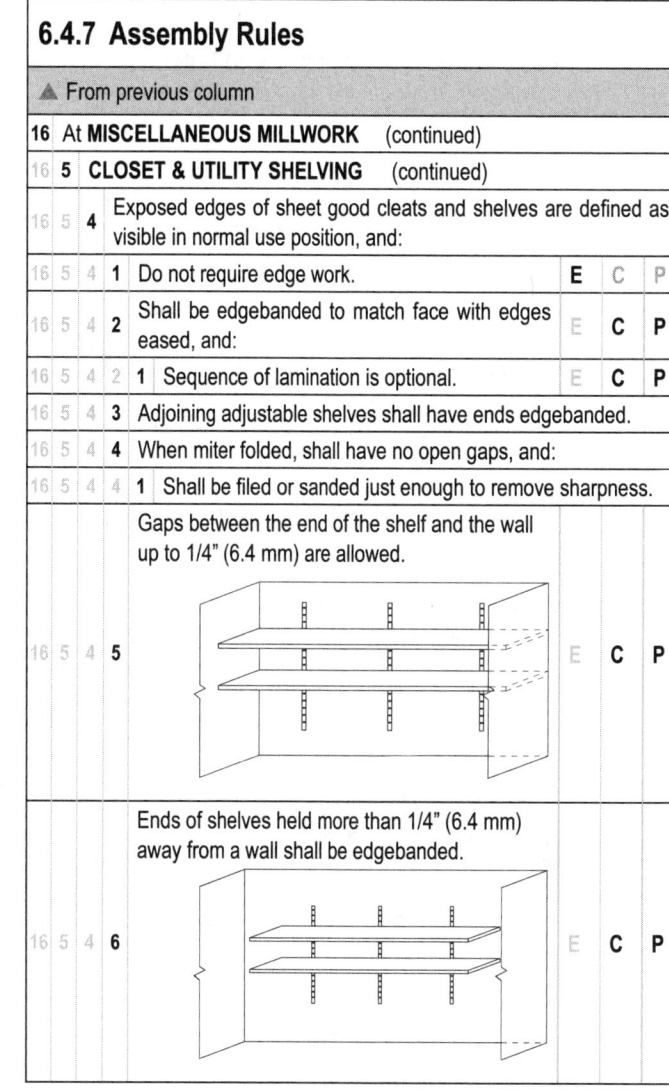 | E | C | P |
| 16 | 5 | 4 | 6 | Ends of shelves held more than 1/4" (6.4 mm) away from a wall shall be edgebanded. | E | C | P |

# SECTION 6
## Millwork

**GENERAL/PRODUCT/INSTALLATION/TEST**

**compliance requirements**

*Where the E, C, or P icon is not indicated, the rule applies to all Grades equally* — **E | C | P**

### 6.5 PREPARATION and QUALIFICATION REQUIREMENTS

**1 CARE, STORAGE,** and **BUILDING CONDITIONS** shall be in compliance with the requirements set forth in Section 2 of these standards.

1.1 Severe damage to the woodwork can result from noncompliance. The manufacturer and/or installer of the woodwork shall not be held responsible for damage that might develop by not adhering to the requirements.

**2 CONTRACTOR IS RESPONSIBLE FOR**

2.1 Furnishing and installing structural members, grounds, in wall blocking, backing, furring, brackets, or other anchorage required for architectural woodwork installation that becomes an integral part of walls, floors, or ceilings to which architectural woodwork, such as wall applied surfacing, standing and running trim, wall mounted shelf standards and door/window frames shall be installed.

2.1.1 In the absence of contract documents calling for the contractor to supply the necessary in wall blocking/backing in the wall or ceilings, either through inadvertence or otherwise, the architectural woodwork installer shall not proceed with the installation until such time as the in wall blocking/backing is installed by others.

2.1.2 Preparatory work done by others shall be subject to inspection by the architectural woodwork installer and may be accepted or rejected for cause prior to installation.

2.1.2.1 **WALL, CEILING,** and/or opening variations in excess of 1/4" (6.4 mm) or **FLOORS** in excess of 1/2" (12.7 mm) in 144" (3658 mm) of being plumb, level, flat, straight, square, or of the correct size are not acceptable for the installation of architectural woodwork, nor is it the responsibility of the installer to scribe or fit to tolerances in excess of such.

2.1.3 Installation site being properly ventilated, protected from direct sunlight, excessive heat and/or moisture, and that the HVAC system is functioning and maintaining the appropriate relative humidity and temperature.

2.2 Priming the architectural woodwork in accordance with the contract documents prior to its installation:

2.2.1 If the architectural woodwork is factory finished, priming by the factory finisher is required.

### 6.5 PREPARATION and QUALIFICATION (continued)

**3 INSTALLER IS RESPONSIBLE FOR**

3.1 Having adequate equipment and experienced craftsmen to complete the installation in a first class manner.

3.2 Checking architectural woodwork specified and studying the appropriate portions of the contract documents, including these standards and the reviewed shop drawings to familiarize themselves with the requirements of the Grade specified, understanding that:

3.2.1 Appearance requirements of Grades apply only to surfaces visible after installation.

3.2.2 For transparent finish, special attention needs to be given to the color and the grain of the various woodwork pieces to ensure they are installed in compliance with the Grade specified.

3.3 Verification that installation site is properly ventilated, protected from direct sunlight, excessive heat and/or moisture, and that the HVAC system is functioning and maintaining the appropriate relative humidity and temperature.

3.4 Verification that required priming of woodwork has been completed by others before woodwork is installed.

3.5 Verification that woodwork has been acclimated to the field conditions for a minimum of 72 hours before installation is commenced.

3.6 Woodwork specifically built or assembled in sequence for match of color and grain is installed to maintain that same sequence.

### 6.6 RULES

1 The following rules shall govern unless a project's contract documents require otherwise.

2 These rules are intended to provide a well defined degree of control over a project's quality of installation.

3 **ERRATA**, published on the Sponsor Associations' websites at www.awinet.org, www.awmac.com, or www.aws-errata.com, shall **TAKE PRECEDENCE OVER THESE RULES**, subject to their date of posting and a project's bid date.

 Where the **E**, **C**, or **P** icon is not indicated, the rule applies to all Grades equally

# SECTION 6
## Millwork

**compliance requirements** — GENERAL/PRODUCT/**INSTALLATION**/TEST

### 6.6.4 Basic Rules

| | | | | | E | C | P |
|---|---|---|---|---|---|---|---|
| 1 | | | AESTHETIC grade rules apply only to exposed and semi-exposed surfaces visible after installation. | | | | |
| 2 | | | TRANSPARENT FINISHED woodwork shall be: | | | | |
| 2 | 1 | | Installed with consideration for color and grain. | | E | C | P |
| 2 | 2 | | Compatible in color and grain. | | E | C | P |
| 2 | 3 | | Well matched for color and grain, and: | | E | C | P |
| 2 | 3 | 1 | Sheet products shall be compatible in color with solid stock. | | E | C | P |
| 2 | 3 | 2 | Adjacent sheet products shall be well matched for color and grain. | | E | C | P |
| 3 | | | REPAIRS are allowed, provided they are made neatly and are inconspicuous when viewed at: | | | | |
| 3 | 1 | | 72" (1830 mm). | | E | C | P |
| 3 | 2 | | 48" (1219 mm). | | E | C | P |
| 3 | 3 | | 24" (610 mm). | | E | C | P |
| 4 | | | INSTALLER MODIFICATIONS shall comply to the material, machining, and assembly rules within the PRODUCT portion of this section and, if applicable, the finishing rules in Section 5. | | | | |
| 5 | | | WOODWORK shall be: | | | | |
| 5 | 1 | | Securely fastened and tightly fitted with flush joints, and: | | | | |
| 5 | 1 | 1 | Joinery shall be consistent throughout the project. | | | | |
| 5 | 2 | | Of maximum available and/or practical lengths. | | E | C | P |
| 5 | 3 | | Trimmed equally from both sides when fitted for width. | | E | C | P |
| 5 | 4 | | Splined or doweled when miters are over 4" (100 mm) long. | | E | C | P |
| 5 | 5 | | Profiled or self mitered when trim ends are exposed. | | E | C | P |
| 5 | 6 | | Self mitered when trim ends are exposed. | | E | C | P |
| 5 | 7 | | Mitered at outside corners. | | | | |
| 5 | 8 | | Mitered or butted for S4S at inside corners. | | E | C | P |
| 5 | 9 | | Coped at inside corners, except S4S shall be mitered. | | E | C | P |
| 5 | 10 | | Installed plumb, level, square, and flat within 1/8" (3.2 mm) in 96" (2438 mm), and when required: | | | | |
| 5 | 10 | 1 | Grounds and hanging systems set plumb and true. | | E | C | P |

Continues next column ▼

### 6.6.4 Basic Rules

▲ From previous column

| | | | | | E | C | P |
|---|---|---|---|---|---|---|---|
| 5 | | | WOODWORK (continued) | | | | |
| 5 | 11 | | Installed free of: | | | | |
| 5 | 11 | 1 | Warp, twisting, cupping, and/or bowing that cannot be held true. | | | | |
| 5 | 11 | 2 | Open joints, visible machine marks, cross sanding, tear outs, nicks, chips, and/or scratches. | | | | |
| 5 | 11 | 3 | Natural defects exceeding the quantity and/or size limits defined in Sections 3 & 4. | | | | |
| 5 | 12 | | Smooth and sanded without cross scratches in conformance to the product portion of this section. | | | | |
| 5 | 13 | | Scribed at: | | | | |
| 5 | 13 | 1 | Flat surfaces. | | E | C | P |
| 5 | 13 | 2 | Shaped surfaces. | | E | C | P |
| 6 | | | THESE STANDARDS do not establish Grade rules for joint flushness and or gap tolerances for woodwork products installed in a non climate controlled environment, however: | | | | |
| 7 | | | GAPS at field joints (see Test I illustrations in TESTS) such as, 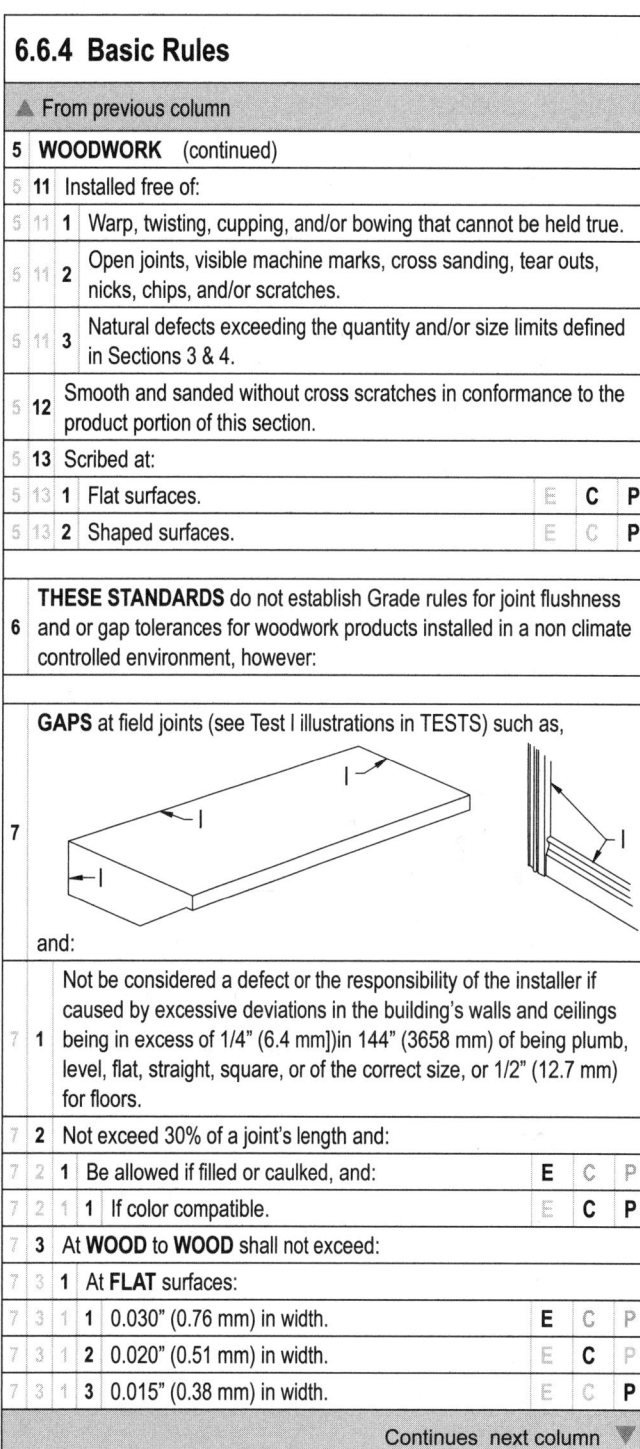 and: | | | | |
| 7 | 1 | | Not be considered a defect or the responsibility of the installer if caused by excessive deviations in the building's walls and ceilings being in excess of 1/4" (6.4 mm) in 144" (3658 mm) of being plumb, level, flat, straight, square, or of the correct size, or 1/2" (12.7 mm) for floors. | | | | |
| 7 | 2 | | Not exceed 30% of a joint's length and: | | | | |
| 7 | 2 | 1 | Be allowed if filled or caulked, and: | | E | C | P |
| 7 | 2 | 1 | 1 | If color compatible. | E | C | P |
| 7 | 3 | | At WOOD to WOOD shall not exceed: | | | | |
| 7 | 3 | 1 | At FLAT surfaces: | | | | |
| 7 | 3 | 1 | 1 | 0.030" (0.76 mm) in width. | E | C | P |
| 7 | 3 | 1 | 2 | 0.020" (0.51 mm) in width. | E | C | P |
| 7 | 3 | 1 | 3 | 0.015" (0.38 mm) in width. | E | C | P |

Continues next column ▼

# SECTION 6
## Millwork

**GENERAL/PRODUCT/INSTALLATION/TEST** — compliance requirements

### 6.6.4 Basic Rules (From previous column)

**7 GAPS** (see Test I illustrations in TESTS) (continued)

- 7.3 At **WOOD** to **WOOD** (continued)
  - 7.3.2 At **SHAPED** surfaces:
    - 7.3.2.1 0.040" (1.02 mm) in width. — **E**
    - 7.3.2.2 0.025" (0.64 mm) in width. — **C**
    - 7.3.2.3 0.015" (0.38 mm) in width. — **P**
- 7.4 At **WOOD** to **NON WOOD** shall not exceed:
  - 7.4.1 At **FLAT** and **SHAPED** surfaces:
    - 7.4.1.1 0.075" (1.91 mm) in width. — **E**
    - 7.4.1.2 0.050" (1.27 mm) in width. — **C**
    - 7.4.1.3 0.035" (0.89 mm) in width. — **P**
- 7.5 At **NON WOOD** to **NON WOOD** and/or **ALL ELEMENTS** shall not exceed:
  - 7.5.1 At **FLAT** surfaces:
    - 7.5.1.1 0.075" (1.91 mm) in width. — **E**
    - 7.5.1.2 0.050" (1.27 mm) in width. — **C**
    - 7.5.1.3 0.035" (0.89 mm) in width. — **P**
  - 7.5.2 At **SHAPED** surfaces:
    - 7.5.2.1 0.120" (3.05 mm) in width. — **E**
    - 7.5.2.2 0.075" (1.91 mm) in width. — **C**
    - 7.5.2.3 0.050" (1.27 mm) in width. — **P**

**8 FLUSHNESS** of field joinery (see Test J illustrations in TESTS) such as, [illustration labeled J, J] and:

- 8.1 Of **WOOD** to **WOOD** shall not exceed:
  - 8.1.1 At **FLAT** surfaces:
    - 8.1.1.1 0.025" (0.64 mm). — **E**
    - 8.1.1.2 0.015" (0.38 mm). — **C**
    - 8.1.1.3 0.010" (0.25 mm). — **P**
  - 8.1.2 At **SHAPED** surfaces:
    - 8.1.2.1 0.040" (0.97 mm). — **E**
    - 8.1.2.2 0.025" (0.65 mm). — **C**
    - 8.1.2.3 0.020" (0.51 mm). — **P**

*Continues next column*

### 6.6.4 Basic Rules (From previous column)

**8 FLUSHNESS** of joinery (continued)

- 8.2 Of **WOOD** to **NON WOOD** shall not exceed:
  - 8.2.1 At **FLAT** and **SHAPED** surfaces:
    - 8.2.1.1 0.075" (1.91 mm). — **E**
    - 8.2.1.2 0.050" (1.27 mm). — **C**
    - 8.2.1.3 0.035" (0.89 mm). — **P**
- 8.3 Of **NON WOOD** to **NON WOOD** and/or **ALL ELEMENTS** shall not exceed:
  - 8.3.1 At **FLAT** surfaces:
    - 8.3.1.1 0.075" (1.91 mm). — **E**
    - 8.3.1.2 0.050" (1.27 mm). — **C**
    - 8.3.1.3 0.035" (0.89 mm). — **P**
  - 8.3.2 At **SHAPED** surfaces:
    - 8.3.2.1 0.120" (3.05 mm). — **E**
    - 8.3.2.2 0.075" (1.91 mm). — **C**
    - 8.3.2.3 0.050" (1.27 mm). — **P**

**9 FASTENING** and **FASTENERS** shall:

- 9.1 Include the use of construction adhesive, finish nails, trim screws, pins and/or staples, except:
  - 9.1.1 Staples with a crown exceeding 3/16" (4.8 mm) are not permitted.
- 9.2 Not permit the use of drywall or bugle head screws.
- 9.3 Require exposed fasteners to be countersunk.
- 9.4 Require exposed fasteners to be set in quirks and reliefs where possible. — **C P**
- 9.5 Require exposed fasteners to be inconspicuous when viewed at 24" (610 mm). — **C P**
- 9.6 Allow use of construction adhesive for inconspicuous fastening.
- 9.7 Not permit exposed fastening through decorative laminate.
- 9.8 **REQUIRE** allowable fastener holes, when:
  - 9.8.1 Prefinished materials to be filled by the installer with matching filler furnished by the manufacturer.
  - 9.8.2 Unfinished materials to be filled by the paint contractor or others.

**10 GLUE** and filler residue is not permitted on exposed faces.

*Continues next column*

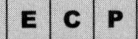

Where the **E**, **C**, or **P** icon is not indicated, the rule applies to all Grades equally

# SECTION 6
## Millwork

**compliance requirements** — GENERAL/PRODUCT/**INSTALLATION**/TEST

### 6.6.4 Basic Rules

▲ From previous column

| | | | | | |
|---|---|---|---|---|---|
| 11 | | **EQUIPMENT CUTOUTS**, including electrical and plumbing, shall be cut out by the installer, provided templates are furnished prior to installation, and: | | | |
| 11 | 1 | Shall be neatly cut and properly sized to be covered by standard cover plates or rosettes. | | | |
| 11 | 2 | Cutouts in HPDL shall have radiused inside corners. | | | |
| 12 | | **HARDWARE** shall be: | | | |
| 12 | 1 | Installed neatly without tear out of surrounding stock. | E | C | P |
| 12 | 2 | Installed per manufacturer's instructions. | | | |
| 12 | 3 | Installed using furnished fasteners and fasteners' provisions. When fastener provisions are countersunk, fasteners shall be countersunk. | | | |
| 12 | 4 | Adjusted for smooth operation, within limits of the specified hardware. | | | |
| 13 | | **AREAS OF INSTALLATION** shall be left broom clean. | | | |
| 13 | 1 | Debris shall be removed and dumped in containers provided by the contractor. | | | |
| 13 | 2 | Items installed shall be cleaned of pencil or ink marks. | | | |
| 14 | | **FIRST CLASS WORKMANSHIP** is required in compliance with these standards. | | | |

### 6.6.5 Product Specific Rules

| | | | | | |
|---|---|---|---|---|---|
| 1 | | **STANDING** and **RUNNING TRIM** shall require: | | | |
| 1 | 1 | Running joints be diagonal scarf or butted, if butted must use a dowel biscuit spline or spline. | E | C | P |
| 1 | 2 | Running joints on multimember trim be staggered from adjacent members. | E | C | P |
| 1 | 3 | Large, one piece or multimember moldings be installed with back blocking as needed. | | | |
| 1 | 4 | **MULTIPLE JOINTS** in running trim shall not be within: | | | |
| 1 4 | 1 | 24" (609 mm). | E | C | P |
| 1 4 | 2 | 36" (914 mm). | E | C | P |
| 1 4 | 3 | 48" (1220 mm). | E | C | P |
| 1 | 5 | Base be scribed to the floor, only if so specified: however: | | | |
| 1 5 | 1 | If not scribed it shall be caulked. | E | C | P |
| 1 | 6 | Miters over 4" (102 mm) long be joined with spline, dowel, or biscuit spline. | E | C | P |

Continues next column ▼

### 6.6.5 Product Specific Rules

▲ From previous column

| | | | | | |
|---|---|---|---|---|---|
| | 2 | **CLOSET RODS** shall be supported at a minimum of 48" (1219 mm) on center. | | | |
| 3 | | **DOOR & WINDOW FRAMES** shall: | | | |
| 3 | 1 | Have rough wood bucks secured at openings. | | | |
| 3 | 2 | Be set plumb. | | | |
| 3 | 3 | Be seated on the floor. | | | |
| 3 | 4 | Be securely fastened through shims into the framing. | | | |
| 3 | 5 | Have **LEGS** set square with header and parallel to each other within: | | | |
| 3 5 | 1 | 3/16" (4.8 mm). | E | C | P |
| 3 5 | 2 | 1/8" (3.2 mm). | E | C | P |
| 3 5 | 3 | 1/16" (1.6 mm). | E | C | P |
| 3 | 6 | Allow horns to be removed before installation. | | | |
| 3 | 7 | Require fire door frames to be installed per the manufacturers' basic instructions. | | | |
| 3 | 8 | Not permit prehung and pre-cased door/jamb assemblies that are fastened only through the casing. | E | C | P |
| 4 | | **BLINDS** and **SHUTTERS** | | | |
| 4 | 1 | If installed in a frame, screen, blind, or shutter, shall have a maximum clearance of 1/8" (3.2 mm) at all sides and be set uniformly within 1/8" (3.2 mm) of the frame face. | | | |
| 5 | | **SCREENS** | | | |
| 5 | 1 | If installed in a frame, screen, blind, or shutter, shall have a maximum clearance of 1/8" (3.2 mm) at all sides and be set uniformly within 1/8" (3.2 mm) of the frame face. | | | |
| 6 | | **ORNAMENTAL MILLWORK** | | | |
| 6 | 1 | Wood filler strip to cover a maximum of 1-1/2" (38 mm). | E | C | P |
| 6 | 2 | Scribe/fillers securely fastened with trim screws. | E | C | P |
| 6 | 3 | Scribe/fillers securely fastened with sheet goods adhesive, face nails, or pins. | E | C | P |
| 6 | 4 | Exposed surface scribed to the wall with a scribe strip, 1/32" (0.8 mm) maximum gap. | E | C | P |

# SECTION 6
## Millwork

GENERAL/PRODUCT/INSTALLATION/**TEST**

**compliance requirements**

Where the **E**, **C**, or **P** icon is not indicated, the rule applies to all Grades equally

### 6.7 BASIC CONSIDERATIONS

1. The tolerances typically found within the AWS fall into two categories:

   1.1 Factory fabricated joinery, assembly and construction - found in the **PRODUCT** portion.

   1.2 Field installation joinery and assembly - found in the **INSTALLATION** portion.

2. Most fabrication and installation assemblies include solid wood to solid wood joints, solid wood to wood veneer joints, solid wood to wood based products (HPDL, LPDL, Solid Phenolic and panel products), solid wood to non-wood based products (which can be drywall, glass, metal, stone, acrylics, and other surfaces), and non-wood to non-wood joints.

3. Tolerances found in the AWS include:

   3.1 Flatness of wood based panel products.

   3.2 Solid wood to solid wood joints and assemblies.

   3.3 Solid wood to wood veneer joints and assemblies.

   3.4 Wood veneer to wood veneer joints and assemblies.

   3.5 Solid wood to wood based product joints and assemblies.

   3.6 Solid surface to solid surface joints and assemblies.

4. Because of the differences of expansion and contraction of non-wood products compared to solid wood and wood based products, the AWS does not apply tolerances regarding flatness or joinery to these non-wood based products.

5. **FABRICATED** and **INSTALLED** woodwork shall be tested for compliance to these standards as follows:

   5.1 **SMOOTHNESS** of exposed surfaces:

### 6.7 BASIC CONSIDERATIONS (continued)

   5.1.1 **KCPI** (Knife Cuts Per Inch) is determined by holding the surfaced board at an angle to a strong light source and counting the visible ridges per inch, usually perpendicular to the profile.

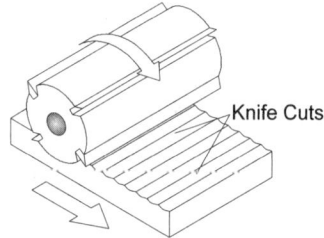

*Figure: 6-054*

   5.1.2 **SANDING** is checked for compliance by sanding a sample piece of the same species with the required grit of abrasive, and:

   5.1.2.1 Observation with a hand lens of the prepared sample and the material in question will offer a comparison of the scratch marks of the abrasive grit.

   5.1.2.2 Reasonable assessment of the performance of the finished product will be weighed against absolute compliance with the standard.

   5.1.2.3 A product is sanded sufficiently smooth when knife cuts are removed and remaining sanding marks are or will be concealed by applied finishing coats.

   5.1.2.4 Grain raise at unfinished wood, due to moisture or humidity in excess of the ranges set forth in this standard, shall not be considered a defect and must be sanded prior to finishing.

6. **GAPS, FLUSHNESS, FLATNESS**, and **ALIGNMENT** of product and installation require:

   6.1 Maximum gaps between exposed components shall be tested with a feeler gauge at points designed to join where members contact or touch.

   6.2 Joint length shall be measured with a ruler with minimum 1/16" (1 mm) divisions and calculations made accordingly.

   6.3 Reasonable assessment of the performance of the finished product will be weighed against absolute compliance with the standards.

# SECTION 6
## Millwork

### compliance requirements
GENERAL/PRODUCT/INSTALLATION/TEST

**6.7 BASIC CONSIDERATIONS** (continued)

6 **GAPS, FLUSHNESS, FLATNESS**, and (continued)

6.4 The following is intended to provide examples of how and where compliance testing is measured:

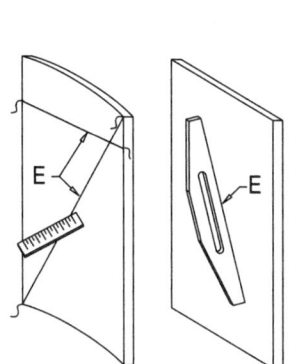
Measured on the concave face

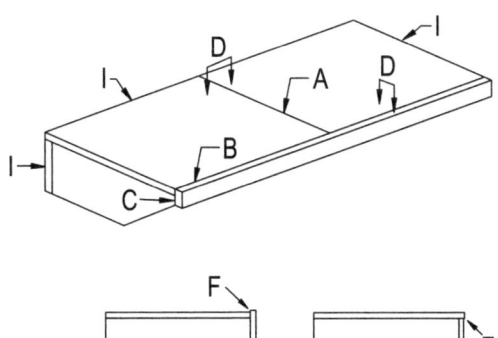

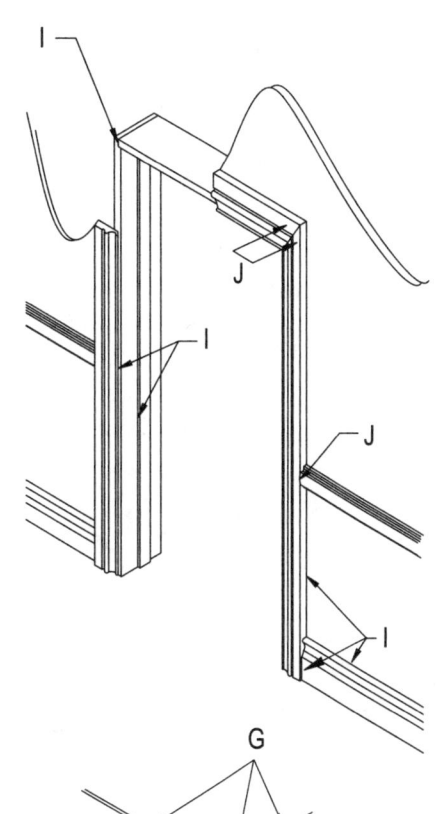

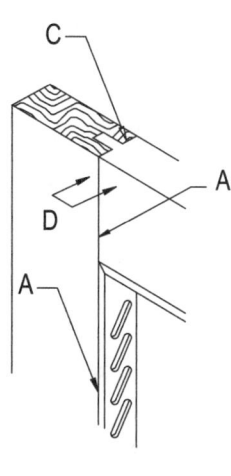

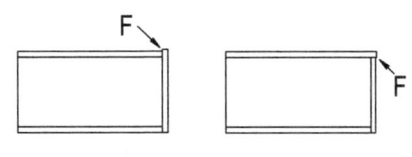

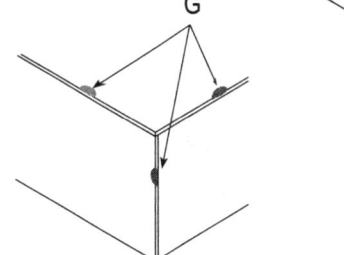

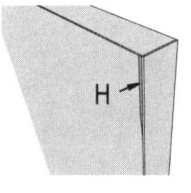

Figure: 6-055

A - Fabrication Gaps When Surfaces Are Mitered Or Butted
B - Fabrication Gaps When Parallel Pieces Are Joined
C - Fabrication Gaps When Edges Are Mitered Or Butted
D - Fabrication Flushness Between Two Surfaces
E - Flatness Of Panel Product
F - Overlap (Flushness Of Laminate)
G - Chip Out
H - Over Machining
I - Installation Gaps
J - Installation Flushness

# SECTION 6
Millwork

notes

# Architectural Woodwork Standards

# STAIRWORK & RAILS

## SECTION 7

# SECTION 7
## Stairwork & Rails

## table of contents

### INTRODUCTORY INFORMATION

- Guide Specifications ............ 171
- Introduction ............ 172
- Design Summary ............ 172
    - Critical Steps in Stair Designer ............ 172
    - Custom Designed Stairs ............ 172
        - Design Flexibility ............ 172
        - Cost Effective ............ 172
        - No Restrictions ............ 172
- Advisory ............ 172
    - Contract Documents ............ 172
    - Cross Grain ............ 172
    - Edges ............ 172
    - Curved Members ............ 172
    - Run and Riser Dimension Points ............ 172
- Typical Stair Runs ............ 172
    - Straight ............ 172
    - Turning ............ 172
    - Winding ............ 173
- Stair and Handrail/guardrail Nomenclature ............ 173
- Handrail/guardrail Component Nomenclature ............ 174
- Handrail/guardrail Fabrication ............ 174
- Handrail/guardrail Joinery ............ 174
- Specify Requirements For ............ 174
- Recommendations ............ 174

### COMPLIANCE REQUIREMENTS

**GENERAL**
- Basic Considerations ............ 175
    - Grades ............ 175
        - Economy ............ 175
        - Custom ............ 175
        - Premium ............ 175
    - Contract Documents ............ 175
    - Acceptable Requirements ............ 175
    - Aesthetic Compliance ............ 175
    - Exposed Surfaces ............ 175
    - Concealed Surfaces ............ 175
    - Solid Wood Edges ............ 175
    - Industry Practices ............ 175
        - Structural Members ............ 175
        - Wall, Ceiling and Floor ............ 175
        - Priming ............ 175
        - Radius Molding ............ 175

**PRODUCT** ............ 176
- Scope ............ 176
    - Typical Inclusions ............ 176
    - Typical Exclusions ............ 176
- Default Stipulation: ............ 176
- Rules ............ 176
    - Errata ............ 176
    - Basic Rules ............ 176
        - Aesthetic ............ 176
        - Lumber ............ 176
        - Sheet Products ............ 176
        - Woodwork ............ 176
        - Backing Sheet ............ 176
        - Exposed Surfaces ............ 176
        - Concealed Surfaces ............ 176
        - Standing and Running Trim ............ 176
        - Multiple Options ............ 176
        - Flame Spread Rating ............ 176
        - Specific Profile ............ 176
        - Special Ornamental Detail ............ 176

# SECTION 7
## Stairwork & Rails

## table of contents

### COMPLIANCE REQUIREMENTS (continued)

#### PRODUCT (continued)

##### Basic Considerations (continued)

###### Basic Rules (continued)

- Radius Moldings ........................................ 176
- Transparent Finish .................................... 176
- Cathedral ................................................... 177
- Stairwork ................................................... 177
- Gluing or Lamination ................................ 177
- Cut outs .................................................... 177
- Priming ..................................................... 177
- First Class Workmanship ......................... 177

###### Material Rules ............................................... 177

- Species ..................................................... 177
- Dimensions ............................................... 177
- Defects ...................................................... 177
- Treads ....................................................... 177
- Closed Stringers ....................................... 177
- Figure ........................................................ 177
- Warp .......................................................... 177
- Soffit and Spandrel Panels ...................... 177
- Opaque Surfaces ..................................... 178
- Transparent Finish ................................... 178
- Exposed Surfaces .................................... 178
- Concealed Surfaces ................................. 179
- Boxed or Curbed Stringers ...................... 179
- Stringer Turnouts ..................................... 179
- Glue up ..................................................... 179
- Risers ........................................................ 179
- Factory Finishing ..................................... 179

###### Machining Rules ........................................... 179

- Exposed Surfaces .................................... 179
  - Smoothness .......................................... 179
  - Edges .................................................... 179
    - Overlap, Test F ................................. 179
    - Chip out, Test G ............................... 180
    - Over Machined, Test H .................... 180
  - Band Sawn of Blocked Members ......... 180
- Intersections ............................................. 180
- Dadoes ...................................................... 180
- Profile ........................................................ 180
- Face Stringers .......................................... 180
- Shoe Rail .................................................. 180
- Scotia or Cove Mold ................................. 180
- Closed Stringers ....................................... 180
- Treads ....................................................... 180
- Risers ........................................................ 181
- Rails .......................................................... 181
- Newel Posts .............................................. 181

###### Assembly Rules ............................................ 181

- These Standards ..................................... 181
- Joints at Assembled Woodwork .............. 181
  - Handrail/Guardrail ................................ 181
  - Mechanically Fastened ........................ 181
  - Gap, Test A ........................................... 182
  - Gap, Test B ........................................... 182
  - Gap, Test C ........................................... 182
  - Filler ...................................................... 182
- Flatness or Warp, Test E ......................... 182
- Applied Moldings ..................................... 182
- Miter Joints ............................................... 182
- Built up Items ........................................... 182
- Stairwork ................................................... 182

### INSTALLATION

- Care, Storage and Building Conditions ......... 183
- Contractor is Responsible for ........................ 183
- Installer is Responsible for ............................ 183
- Rules ............................................................... 184
  - Errata ......................................................... 184
  - Basic Rules ............................................... 184
    - Aesthetics ............................................. 184
    - Transparent Finished .......................... 184
    - Installer Modifications ........................ 184
    - Repairs .................................................. 184
    - Woodwork ............................................. 184
    - These Standards .................................. 184

# SECTION 7
## Stairwork & Rails

## table of contents

**COMPLIANCE REQUIREMENTS** (continued)

  **INSTALLATION** (continued)

    Rules (continued)

      Basic Rules (continued)

        Gaps, Tests I .................................................. 185

        Flushness, Tests J ........................................... 185

        Fastening and Fasteners ................................. 186

        Glue .................................................................. 186

        Equipment Cutouts .......................................... 186

        Hardware ......................................................... 186

        Areas of Installation ......................................... 186

  **TESTS**

    Basic Considerations ............................................. 187

      Fabricated and Installed .................................. 187

      Smoothness ..................................................... 187

        KCPI ................................................................ 187

        Sanding .......................................................... 187

    Gaps, Flushness, Flatness and Alignment ........... 187

      Illustrations ...................................................... 188

## introductory information

**SECTION 7**
Stairwork & Rails

# Guide Specifications

Are available through the Sponsor Associations in interactive digital format including unique and individual quality control options. The Guide Specifications are located at:

## Architectural Woodwork Institute (AWI)
www.awinet.org

## Architectural Woodwork Manufacturers Association of Canada (AWMAC)
http://awmac.com/aws-guide-specifications

## Woodwork Institute (WI)
www.woodworkinstitute.com/publications/aws_guide_specs.asp

# SECTION 7
## Stairwork & Rails

# introductory information

## INTRODUCTION

Section 7 includes information on wood stairs, integral trim, handrails, and guardrails and their related parts.

Quality assurance can be achieved by adherence to the AWS and will provide the owner a quality product at competitive pricing. Use of a qualified Sponsor Member firm to provide your woodwork will help ensure the manufacturer's understanding of the quality level required. Illustrations in this Section are not intended to be all inclusive. Other engineered solutions are acceptable. In the absence of specifications; methods of fabrication shall be the option of the manufacturer. The design professional, by specifying compliance to the AWS increases the probability of receiving the product quality expected.

## DESIGN SUMMARY

This short summary is a collection of options and illustrations about the challenges of designing and building safe stairs. The *AWS* cannot and does not offer this data as advice on code compliance. Safe stairs and design and engineering to meet local codes remains the responsibility of the design professional.

**Critical steps in stair design:**

- Check local code.
- Consult with an experienced stair builder to double check your geometry.
- Pre clear your stair design with the local building officials.

Custom designed stairs offer:

- **Design flexibility:** The use of custom designed stairs in a building allows the design professional freedom of expression while meeting the functional needs of the client.

Since custom woodwork is normally produced by a specialty architectural woodwork firm, dimensions can easily be changed prior to actual fabrication, if required by job conditions. Special situations such as designing for the disabled can readily be accommodated by the custom architectural woodwork manufacturer.

- **Cost effective:** Custom woodwork competes favorably with mass produced millwork, and offers practically limitless variations of design and material. Most woodwork lasts the life of the building, quality counts.

- **No restrictions:** Custom architectural woodwork permits complete freedom of selection of the numerous hardwoods and softwoods available for transparent or opaque finish. Other unique materials available from woodwork manufacturers require no further finishing at all, such as plastic laminates and decorative overlays. These materials can be fashioned into a wide variety of profiles, sizes, and configurations. The design professional has the best of both worlds, high quality and freedom of choice.

## ADVISORY

**Contract documents**, furnished by the design professional, should clearly indicate or delineate material, fabrication, installation, and applicable building code/regulation requirements.

**Cross grain** in band sawn or laminated members might cause objectionable color variation when finished.

**Edges** in veneer laminated members or where multiple layers are exposed by shaping might cause objectionable color variation when finished.

**Curved members**, depending on the Grade, can be band sawn, block laminated, or veneer laminated at the option of the manufacturer.

**Run** and **Rise Dimension Points**

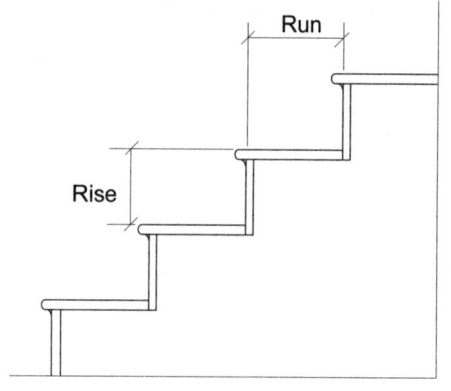

*Figure: 07-001*

**TYPICAL STAIR RUNS:**

- **STRAIGHT**

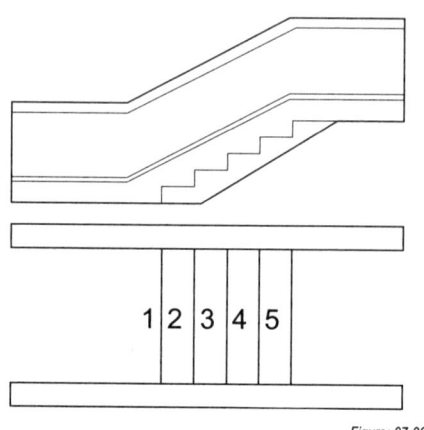

*Figure: 07-002*

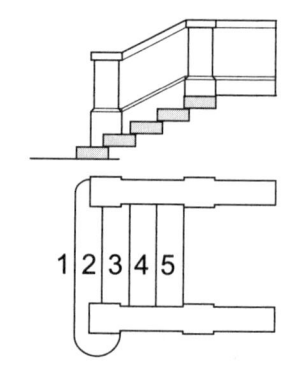

*Figure: 07-003*

- **TURNING**

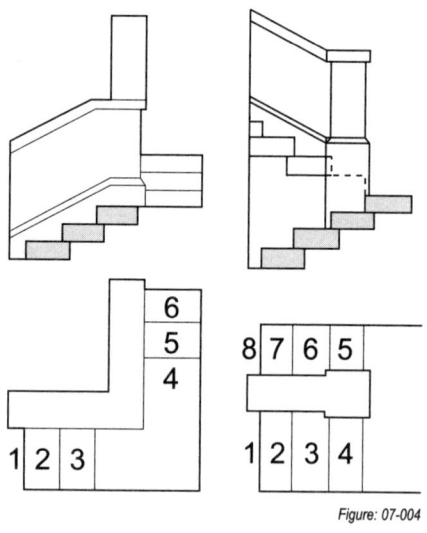

*Figure: 07-004*

# SECTION 7
## Stairwork & Rails

# introductory information

**TYPICAL STAIR RUNS** (continued)

- **WINDING**

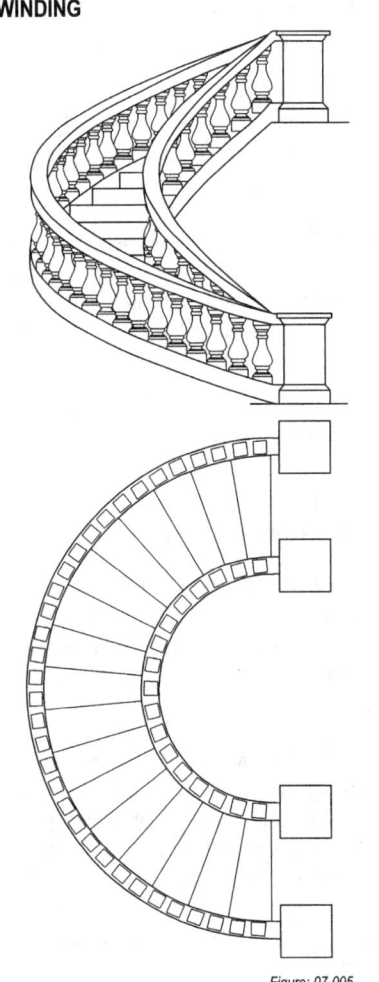

*Figure: 07-005*

**STAIR and HANDRAIL/GUARDRAIL NOMENCLATURE:**

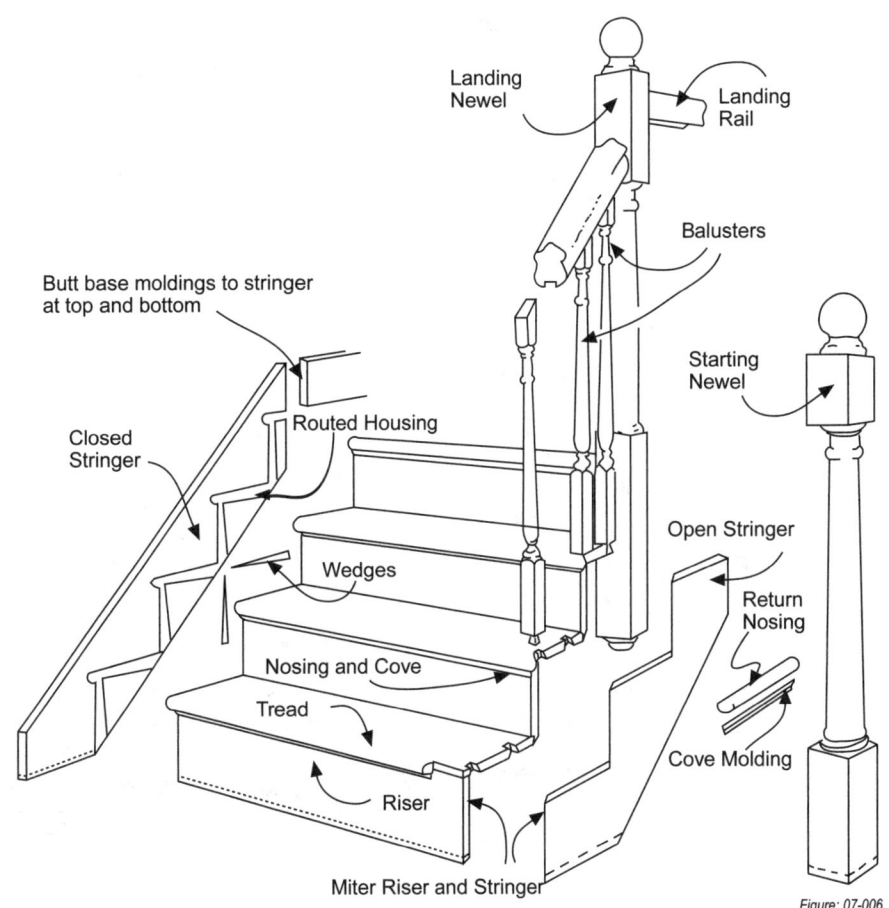

*Figure: 07-006*

# SECTION 7
## Stairwork & Rails

### introductory information

### HANDRAIL/GUARDRAIL COMPONENT NOMENCLATURE

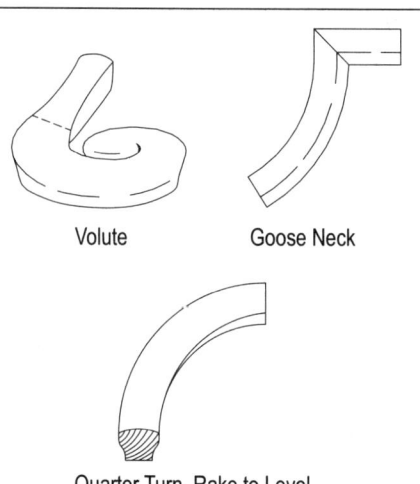

Volute

Goose Neck

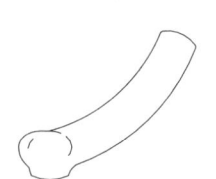

Quarter Turn, Rake to Level

*Figure: 07-007*

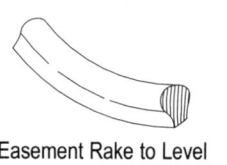

Half Turn      Starting Easement

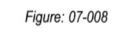

Easement Rake to Level

*Figure: 07-008*

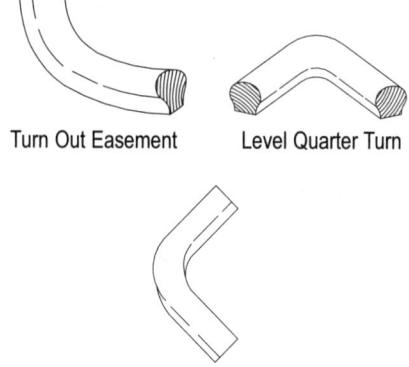

Turn Out Easement      Level Quarter Turn

Half Turn, Double Rake

*Figure: 07-009*

### HANDRAIL/GUARDRAIL FABRICATION

Large dimension rail fabrication techniques are typically the option of the manufacturer. Lamination on a radius depends on many factors:

Typical lamination orientations:

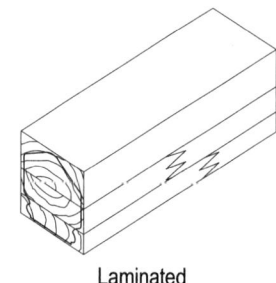

Laminated

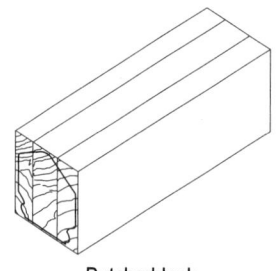

Butcherblock

*Figure: 07-010*

### HANDRAIL/GUARDRAIL JOINERY

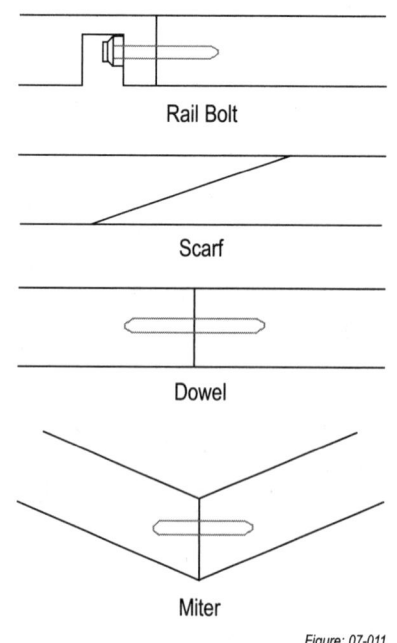

Rail Bolt

Scarf

Dowel

Miter

*Figure: 07-011*

Guard/Handrail illustrations may not be compliant with current or applicable codes.

### SPECIFY REQUIREMENTS FOR

- Flame Spread rating.
- Special code or regulation compliance.

### RECOMMENDATIONS

- If **FIELD FINISHED**, include in Division 09 of the specifications:
  - **BEFORE FINISHING**, exposed portions of woodwork shall have handling marks or effects of exposure to moisture, removed with a thorough, final sanding over all surfaces of the exposed portions, and shall be cleaned before applying sealer or finish.
  - At **CONCEALED SURFACES**, architectural woodwork that might be exposed to moisture, such as those adjacent to exterior concrete walls, shall be primed.

- **REVIEW** the GENERAL portion of Sections 3 and 4 for an overview of the characteristics and the minimum acceptable requirements of lumber and/or sheet products that might be used herein.

- **STRUCTURAL MEMBERS**, grounds, in wall blocking, backing, furring, brackets, or other anchorage which becomes an integral part of the building's walls, floors, or ceilings, required for the installation of architectural woodwork are not to be furnished or installed by the architectural woodwork manufacturer or installer.

- **DESIGN CONSIDERATIONS** - Stairs, rails, and handrail/guardrails are subject to building code requirements. Code restrictions apply to rise, run, handrail, and guardrail heights, structural strength and other issues. It is the responsibility of the design professional to comply with applicable building code(s) and regulations, and:

- **CONSULTATION** with an experienced stair builder is strongly recommended.

Where the **E**, **C**, or **P** icon is not indicated, the rule applies to all Grades equally

## compliance requirements

# SECTION 7
## Stairwork & Rails

**GENERAL**/PRODUCT/INSTALLATION/TEST

### Including: Wood Stairs, Integral Trim, Handrails, and Guardrails

### 7.1 BASIC CONSIDERATIONS

**1  GRADE**

1.1 These standards are characterized in three Grades of quality that may be mixed within a single project. Limitless design possibilities and a wide variety of lumber and veneer species, along with overlays, high pressure decorative laminates, factory finishes, and profiles are available in all three Grades.

1.2 **ECONOMY GRADE** defines the minimum quality requirements for a project's workmanship, materials, or installation and is typically reserved for woodwork that is not in public view, such as in mechanical spaces and utility areas.

1.3 **CUSTOM GRADE** is typically specified for and adequately covers most high quality architectural woodwork, providing a well defined degree of control over a project's quality of materials, workmanship, or installation.

1.4 **PREMIUM GRADE** is typically specified for use in those areas of a project where the highest level of quality, materials, workmanship, and installation is required.

2 **CONTRACT DOCUMENTS** shall govern if in conflict with these standards.

3 **ACCEPTABLE REQUIREMENTS** of lumber and/or sheet products used within this woodwork product section are established by Sections 3 and 4, unless otherwise modified herein.

4 **AESTHETIC COMPLIANCE** requirements apply only to surfaces visible after fabrication and installation.

5 **EXPOSED SURFACES INCLUDE:**

5.1 All visible surfaces of stringers, skirt boards, treads, risers, and balustrades.

6 **CONCEALED SURFACES INCLUDE:**

6.1 All non visible surfaces attached to and/or covered by another.

6.2 All non visible in wall blocking or spacers used for attachment.

### 7.1 BASIC CONSIDERATIONS (continued)

7 To **PREVENT TELEGRAPHING**, inset solid wood edging when used must have similar moisture content as panel core, be glued securely and calibrated with panel core thickness prior to being laminated with a wood veneer on both faces.

8 **INDUSTRY PRACTICES**

8.1 **STRUCTURAL MEMBERS**, grounds, in wall blocking, backing, furring, brackets, or other anchorage that becomes an integral part of the building's walls, floors, or ceilings, that are required for the installation of architectural woodwork are not furnished or installed by the architectural woodwork manufacturer or installer.

8.2 **WALL, CEILING**, and/or opening variations in excess of 1/4" (6.4 mm) or **FLOORS** in excess of 1/2" (12.7 mm) in 144" (3658 mm) of being plumb, level, flat, straight, square, or of the correct size are not acceptable for the installation of architectural woodwork, nor is it the responsibility of the installer to scribe or fit to tolerances in excess of such.

8.3 **PRIMING** of architectural woodwork is not the responsibility of the manufacturer and/or installer, unless the material is being furnished prefinished.

8.4 **RADIUS MOLDINGS** are laminated and formed, pre shaped, or machined to the radius and fabricated in the longest practical lengths to minimize installer joints.

# SECTION 7
## Stairwork & Rails

GENERAL / **PRODUCT** / INSTALLATION / TEST

**compliance requirements**

Where the **E**, **C**, or **P** icon is not indicated, the rule applies to all Grades equally — | E | C | P |

## 7.2 SCOPE

1    Wood stairs and allied wood stair material.

1.1    **TYPICAL INCLUSIONS:**

1.1.1    Wood stringers of skirt boards.

1.1.2    Treads, risers, nosing, and scotia.

1.1.3    Starting steps.

1.1.4    All wedges and glue blocks.

1.1.5    Newels, balusters, handrails, guardrails, and crooks.

1.1.6    Well hole trim.

1.1.7    Shoe rail, fillet, and spandrels.

1.1.8    All other wood parts of a stair.

1.1.9    Installation; if uninstalled, stair materials shall be furnished machined KD (knocked down).

1.2    **TYPICAL EXCLUSIONS:**

1.2.1    Any rough horses, structural wood framing, or timbers.

1.2.2    Any metal handrail/guardrail brackets or safety nosing.

1.2.3    Any flooring.

1.2.4    Priming and/or finishing of any kind.

## 7.3 DEFAULT STIPULATION

1    If not otherwise specified or indicated in the contract documents, all work shall be unfinished, Custom Grade, solid stock softwood intended for opaque finish.

## 7.4 RULES

1    The following rules shall govern unless a project's contract documents require otherwise.

2    These rules are intended to provide a well defined degree of control over a project's quality of materials and workmanship.

3    **ERRATA**, published on the Sponsor Associations' websites at www.awinet.org, www.awmac.com, or www.aws-errata.com, **shall take precedence over these rules**, subject to their date of posting and a project's bid date.

### 7.4.4 Basic Rules

1    **AESTHETIC** grade rules apply only to exposed and semi-exposed surfaces visible after installation.

2    **LUMBER** shall conform to the requirements established in Section 3.

3    **SHEET PRODUCTS** shall conform to the requirements established in Section 4.

4    **WOODWORK** not addressed herein shall be manufactured from solid stock, laminated stock, veneered stock, or a combination thereof.

5    **BACKING SHEET** shall conform to the requirements established in Section 4.

6    **EXPOSED SURFACES** include:

     6.1    All visible surfaces of stringers, skirt boards, treads, risers, and balustrades.

7    **CONCEALED SURFACES** include:

     7.1    All non visible surfaces attached to and/or covered by another.

     7.2    All non visible blocking or spacers used for attachment.

8    **STANDING** and **RUNNING TRIM** shall be furnished as material only, not assembled.

9    Where **MULTIPLE OPTIONS** are permitted, it shall be the manufacturer's choice unless specified otherwise.

10    **FLAME SPREAD RATING**, if required, shall be so specified.

11    **SPECIFIC PROFILE**, if required, shall be so specified or drawn.

12    **SPECIAL ORNAMENTAL DETAIL** or joinery, if required, shall be so specified or drawn.

13    **RADIUS MOLDINGS** are laminated and formed, pre shaped, or machined to the radius and fabricated in the longest practical lengths to minimize installer joints.

14    **TRANSPARENT FINISH**, if species is not specified, the use of either hardwood or softwood (plywood or solid stock) of one species for the entire job is permitted at the manufacturer's option.

*Continues next column* ▼

# SECTION 7
## Stairwork & Rails

**compliance requirements** — GENERAL/**PRODUCT**/INSTALLATION/TEST

Where the **E**, **C**, or **P** icon is not indicated, the rule applies to all Grades equally

### 7.4.4 Basic Rules

▲ From previous column

| 15 | | | **CATHEDRAL** type figure shall be achieved by: |
|---|---|---|---|
| 15 | 1 | | A single component in "AA" Face Grade. |
| 15 | 2 | | The split heart method in Face Grades "A - D", and: |
| 15 | 2 | 1 | Each half of a split heart shall be subject to the minimum component width requirements for Face Grade "B." |
| 16 | | | **STAIRWORK**, including handrail/guardrails, shall conform to applicable codes and requirements, and: |
| 16 | 1 | | Nothing in these standards shall overrule such. |
| 17 | | | Where **GLUING** or **LAMINATION** occurs: |
| 17 | 1 | | Delamination or separation shall not occur. |
| 17 | 2 | | Use of contact adhesive is not permitted, unless otherwise indicated, and: |
| 17 | 2 | 1 | Shall comply with the Heat Resistance Test listed in the **APPENDIX**.  |
| 18 | | | **CUT OUTS** require: |
| 18 | 1 | | That at **HPDL** exposed surfaces have a minimum 1/4" (6.4 mm) radius at inside corners. |
| 19 | | | **PRIMING** is not the responsibility of the manufacturer and/or installer, unless the material is furnished prefinished. |
| 20 | | | **FIRST CLASS WORKMANSHIP** is required in compliance with these standards. |

### 7.4.5 Material Rules

| 1 | | **SPECIES** and AWS Grade of lumber or sheet products shall be as specified, and: | | | |
|---|---|---|---|---|---|
| 1 | 1 | Plain sawn lumber is required. | | | |
| 2 | | **DIMENSIONS** of finished lumber shall conform to Section 3. | | | |
| 3 | | **DEFECTS**, natural or manufactured, shall not exceed those permitted, except: | | | |
| 3 | 1 | Unlimited finger joints are permitted. | E | C | P |
| 3 | 2 | Are permitted if covered by adjoining members or otherwise concealed when installed. | | | |
| 4 | | **TREADS** shall be a minimum of 1" (25.4 mm) in thickness. | | | |
| 5 | | **CLOSED STRINGERS** shall be a minimum of 3/4" (19 mm) in thickness. | | | |
| 6 | | **FIGURE** is not a function of a species grade and must be specified in the contract document. | | | |
| 7 | | **WARP**, which can be held flat and straight with normal attachment is permitted. | | | |
| 8 | | **RADIUS WOODWORK** shall be constructed of solid machined, block laminated, laminated plies, core veneered, or kerfed solid stock, 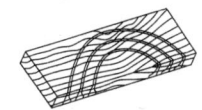    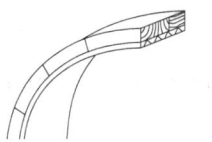 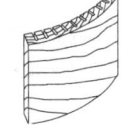  Solid machined   Block laminated   Laminated Plies   Core veneered   Kerfed Solid Stock   and: | | | |
| 8 | 1 | Solid stock or block lamination members shall be furnished in such sections as to avoid pronounced cross grain and reduce joints to a minimum. | | | |
| 8 | 2 | glue shall be selected for color to avoid a prominent glue line. | | | |
| 9 | | **SOFFIT** and **SPANDREL PANELS** shall conform to Section 8. | | | |

Continues next column ▼

# SECTION 7
## Stairwork & Rails

GENERAL / **PRODUCT** / INSTALLATION / TEST

## compliance requirements

Where the **E**, **C**, or **P** icon is not indicated, the rule applies to all Grades equally — **E** | **C** | **P**

### 7.4.5 Material Rules
▲ From previous column

| | | | | | | E | C | P |
|---|---|---|---|---|---|---|---|---|
| 10 | | | **For OPAQUE FINISH:** | | | | | |
| 10 | 1 | | Medium density fiberboard (MDF) is permitted. | | | | | |
| 10 | 2 | | Veneer is permitted; however: | | | | | |
| 10 | 2 | 1 | **SPECIES** shall be of manufacturer's choice, closed grain hardwood conforming to ANSI/HPHA HP-1 (latest Edition) definitions and characteristics for: | | | | | |
| 10 | 2 | 1 | 1 | Grade - **D**. | | E | | |
| 10 | 2 | 1 | 2 | Grade - **C**. | | | C | |
| 10 | 2 | 1 | 3 | Grade - **B**. | | | | P |
| 11 | | | **For TRANSPARENT FINISH, VENEER:** | | | | | |
| 11 | 1 | | **SPECIES** of manufacturer's choice, hardwood conforming to ANSI/HPHA HP-1 (latest Edition) definitions and characteristics for: | | | | | |
| 11 | 1 | 1 | 1 | Grade - **B**. | | E | | |
| 11 | 1 | 1 | 2 | Grade - **A**. | | | C | |
| 11 | 1 | 1 | 3 | Grade - **AA**. | | | | P |
| 11 | 1 | 2 | **SLICING** of: | | | | | |
| 11 | 1 | 2 | 1 | Manufacturer's choice. | | E | | |
| 11 | 1 | 2 | 2 | Plain sliced. | | | C | P |
| 11 | 1 | 3 | **MATCHING ADJACENT LEAVES** be: | | | | | |
| 11 | 1 | 3 | 1 | Manufacturer's choice. | | E | | |
| 11 | 1 | 3 | 2 | Book matched. | | | C | P |
| 11 | 1 | 4 | **MATCHING WITHIN PANEL FACE** be: | | | | | |
| 11 | 1 | 4 | 1 | Running. | | E | | |
| 11 | 1 | 4 | 2 | Balance. | | | C | P |
| 11 | 1 | 5 | **MATCHING BETWEEN ADJACENT PANELS** be: | | | | | |
| 11 | 1 | 5 | 1 | Manufacturer's choice. | | E | | |
| 11 | 1 | 5 | 2 | Compatible for color and grain. | | | C | |
| 11 | 1 | 5 | 3 | Well matched for color and grain, and: | | | | P |
| 11 | 1 | 5 | 4 | **END, SEQUENCE,** and **BLUEPRINT MATCHING** shall be specified. | | | | |

Continues next column ▼

### 7.4.5 Material Rules
▲ From previous column

| | | | | | E | C | P |
|---|---|---|---|---|---|---|---|
| 12 | | | **EXPOSED SURFACES:** | | | | |
| 12 | 1 | | End grain shall be kept to a minimum. | | E | C | P |
| 12 | 2 | | Ends to be self returned with no end grain showing. | | E | C | P |
| 12 | 3 | | Medium density fiberboard (MDF) is permitted for opaque finish. | | | | |
| 12 | 4 | | Sheet product edges shall be edgebanded with the same species as the face. | | | C | P |
| 12 | 5 | | Plain sliced veneer is required for transparent finish. | | | | |
| 12 | 6 | | Manufacturers' choice veneer is permitted for opaque finish. | | | | |
| 12 | 7 | | **TRANSPARENT FINISH:** | | | | |
| 12 | 7 | 1 | Hardwood or softwood is permitted. | | | | |
| 12 | 7 | 2 | Only one species is permitted for the entire project. | | | C | P |
| 12 | 7 | 3 | Finger joints are prohibited. | | | C | P |
| 12 | 7 | 4 | Adhesive used for laminating shall be selected for color to avoid a prominent glue line. | | | C | P |
| 12 | 7 | 5 | Lumber (including block segments or veneer of laminated material) and sheet products are to be compatible in color and grain. | | | C | P |
| 12 | 7 | 6 | Lumber (including block segments or veneer of laminated material) are to be well matched for color and grain; sheet products shall be compatible in color with solid stock, and adjacent sheet products shall be well matched for color and grain. | | | | P |
| 12 | 7 | 7 | Intersections of radius and straight members are to be splined or half lapped, securely glued, and mechanically fastened. | | | C | P |
| 12 | 7 | 8 | **BLOCK LAMINATION:** | | | | |
| 12 | 7 | 8 | 1 | Segments shall be cut from the same board. | | | C | P |
| 12 | 7 | 8 | 2 | Segment joints shall be staggered. | | | | |
| 12 | 7 | 8 | 3 | Adjacent segment ends shall have similar grain angle. | | | C | P |
| 12 | 7 | 9 | **VENEER LAMINATIONS:** | | | | |
| 12 | 7 | 9 | 1 | Exposed layers shall be sawn from the same or matched boards. | | | C | P |
| 12 | 7 | 9 | 2 | Veneer layers shall be reassembled in the same order and orientation as cut. | | | C | P |

Continues next column ▼

# SECTION 7
## Stairwork & Rails

**compliance requirements** — GENERAL/**PRODUCT**/INSTALLATION/TEST

Where the **E**, **C**, or **P** icon is not indicated, the rule applies to all Grades equally

### 7.4.5 Material Rules

▲ From previous column

| | | | | | | |
|---|---|---|---|---|---|---|
| 12 | | | **EXPOSED SURFACES** (continued) | | | |
| 12 | 7 | | **TRANSPARENT FINISH** (continued) | | | |
| 12 | 7 | 10 | Visible panel edges, reveals, and/or splines, when appropriate, shall be: | | | |
| 12 | 7 | 10 | 1 Full length. | | | |
| 12 | 7 | 10 | 2 Manufacturers' choice. | E | C | P |
| 12 | 7 | 10 | 3 Same species as panel face. | E | C | P |
| 12 | 7 | 10 | 4 Compatible for color and grain. | E | C | P |
| 12 | 7 | 10 | 5 Well matched for color and grain. | E | C | P |
| 12 | 7 | 10 | 6 A minimum of 0.020" (0.5 mm) nominal thickness that precludes show through of core. | E | C | P |
| 13 | | | **CONCEALED SURFACES:** | | | |
| 13 | 1 | | Allows defects such as voids, wane, or unfilled knots. | | | |
| 13 | 2 | | Required blocking or shims shall be of a compatible material. | | | |
| 14 | | | **BOXED** or **CURB STRINGERS**, shall be of two or more members. | | | |
| 15 | | | **STRINGER TURNOUTS**, including quarter turns, half turns, and the like, shall be of laminated or veneered face construction, and: | | | |
| 15 | 1 | | Such turns shall be a continuous part of the straight stringer, where feasible. | | | |
| 16 | | | **GLUE UP** is permitted of handrails, guardrails, newel posts, and balusters. | | | |
| 17 | | | **RISERS**, bull nosed or radius, shall be veneered construction with one piece face. | | | |
| 18 | | | **FACTORY FINISHING**, when specified, shall have concealed surfaces factory sealed at 1 mil dry. | E | C | P |

### 7.4.6 Machining Rules

| | | | | | | |
|---|---|---|---|---|---|---|
| 1 | | | **EXPOSED SURFACES** shall comply with: | | | |
| 1 | 1 | | **SMOOTHNESS REQUIREMENTS** (see **SMOOTHNESS** in **TESTS**) and: | | | |
| 1 | 1 | 1 | **SHARP EDGES** are to be eased with fine abrasive. | E | C | P |
| 1 | 1 | 2 | **TOP FLAT WOOD** surfaces; those that can be sanded with a drum or wide belt sander, requires: | | | |
| 1 | 1 | 2 | 1 Minimum 15 KCPI or 100 grit sanding. | E | C | P |
| 1 | 1 | 2 | 2 120 grit sanding. | E | C | P |
| 1 | 1 | 2 | 3 150 grit sanding. | E | C | P |
| 1 | 1 | 3 | **PROFILED** and **SHAPED WOOD** surfaces require: | | | |
| 1 | 1 | 3 | 1 Minimum 15 KCPI or 100 grit sanding. | E | C | P |
| 1 | 1 | 3 | 2 Minimum 20 KCPI or 120 grit sanding. | E | C | P |
| 1 | 1 | 3 | 3 120 grit sanding. | E | C | P |
| 1 | 1 | 4 | **TURNED WOOD** surfaces require: | | | |
| 1 | 1 | 4 | 1 Minimum 15 KCPI or 100 grit sanding. | E | C | P |
| 1 | 1 | 4 | 2 120 grit sanding. | E | C | P |
| 1 | 1 | 4 | 3 180 grit sanding. | E | C | P |
| 1 | 1 | 5 | **CROSS SANDING**, excluding turned surfaces, is: | | | |
| 1 | 1 | 5 | 1 Not a defect. | E | C | P |
| 1 | 1 | 5 | 2 Not allowed. | E | C | P |
| 1 | 1 | 6 | **TEAR OUTS, KNIFE NICKS**, or **HIT OR MISS** machining are not permitted. | | | |
| 1 | 1 | 7 | **KNIFE MARKS** are not permitted where sanding is required. | | | |
| 1 | 1 | 8 | **GLUE** or **FILLER**, if used, shall be inconspicuous and match adjacent surface for smoothness. | | | |
| 1 | 2 | | **HPDL, PVC,** and **PREFINISHED WOOD** edges shall be machined flush and filed, sanded, or buffed to remove machine marks and sharp edges, and: | | | |
| 1 | 2 | 1 | **OVERLAP** (See Test F illustrations in TESTS) such as, shall not exceed: | | | |
| 1 | 2 | 1 | 1 0.005" (0.13 mm) for a maximum length of 2" (50.8 mm) in any 12" (305 mm) run. | E | C | P |
| 1 | 2 | 1 | 2 0.005" (0.13 mm) for a maximum length of 1" (25.4 mm) in any 24" (610 mm) run. | E | C | P |
| 1 | 2 | 1 | 3 0.003" (0.08 mm) for a maximum length of 1" (25.4 mm) in any 48" (1220 mm) run. | E | C | P |

Continues next column ▼

# SECTION 7
## Stairwork & Rails

GENERAL / **PRODUCT** / INSTALLATION / TEST

**compliance requirements**

Where the **E**, **C**, or **P** icon is not indicated, the rule applies to all Grades equally.

### 7.4.6 Machining Rules

▲ From previous column

| | | | | | | | |
|---|---|---|---|---|---|---|---|
| 1 | | | **EXPOSED SURFACES** (continued): | | | | |
| | 2 | | **HPDL**, **PVC**, and **PREFINISHED WOOD** edges (continued) | | | | |
| | | 2 | **CHIP OUT** (See Test G illustrations in TESTS) such as, 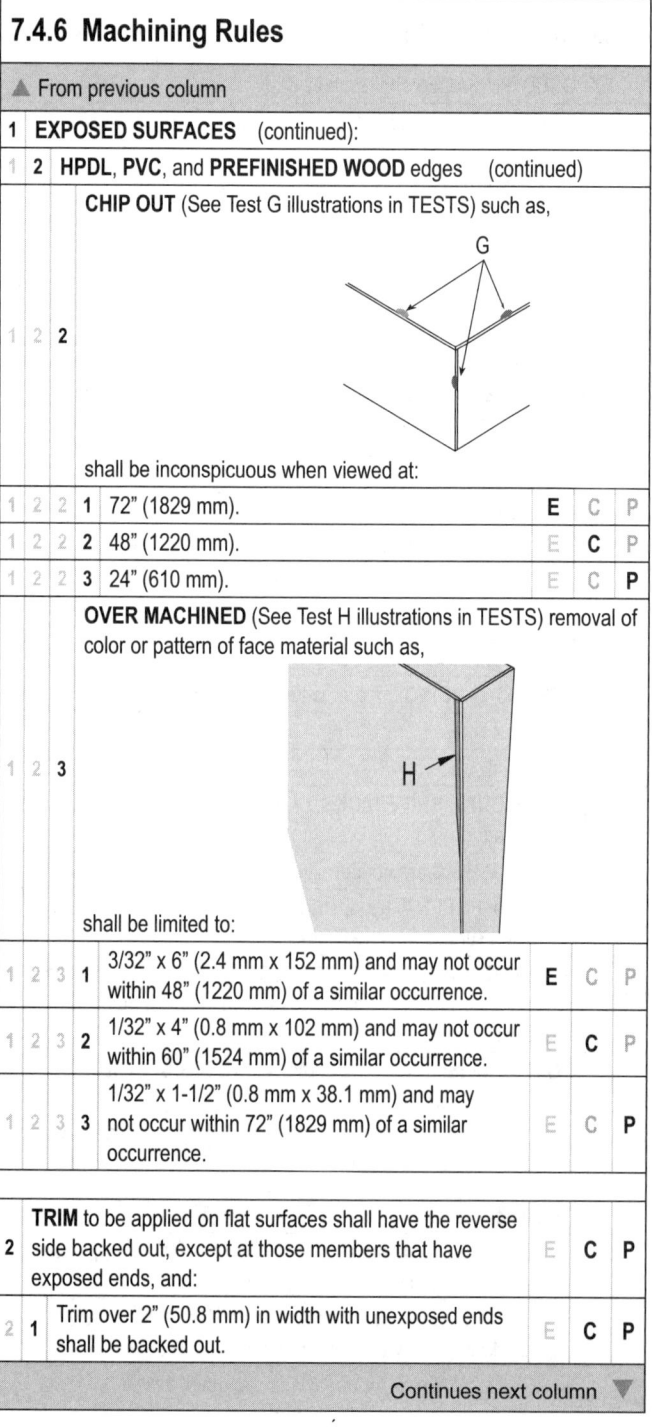 shall be inconspicuous when viewed at: | | | | |
| | 2 | 2 | 1 | 72" (1829 mm). | E | C | P |
| | 2 | 2 | 2 | 48" (1220 mm). | E | C | P |
| | 2 | 2 | 3 | 24" (610 mm). | E | C | P |
| | | 3 | **OVER MACHINED** (See Test H illustrations in TESTS) removal of color or pattern of face material such as, shall be limited to: | | | | |
| | 2 | 3 | 1 | 3/32" x 6" (2.4 mm x 152 mm) and may not occur within 48" (1220 mm) of a similar occurrence. | E | C | P |
| | 2 | 3 | 2 | 1/32" x 4" (0.8 mm x 102 mm) and may not occur within 60" (1524 mm) of a similar occurrence. | E | C | P |
| | 2 | 3 | 3 | 1/32" x 1-1/2" (0.8 mm x 38.1 mm) and may not occur within 72" (1829 mm) of a similar occurrence. | E | C | P |
| 2 | | | **TRIM** to be applied on flat surfaces shall have the reverse side backed out, except at those members that have exposed ends, and: | | | E | C | P |
| 2 | 1 | | Trim over 2" (50.8 mm) in width with unexposed ends shall be backed out. | | | E | C | P |

Continues next column ▼

### 7.4.6 Machining Rules

▲ From previous column

| | | | | | | |
|---|---|---|---|---|---|---|
| 3 | | | **BAND SAWN** and **BLOCK LAMINATED** members shall be divided to minimize the exposure of cross grain in the face of the member, and: | | | |
| 3 | 1 | | Grain angle at the face of curved members shall not exceed 30 degrees, unless a small part size requires otherwise. 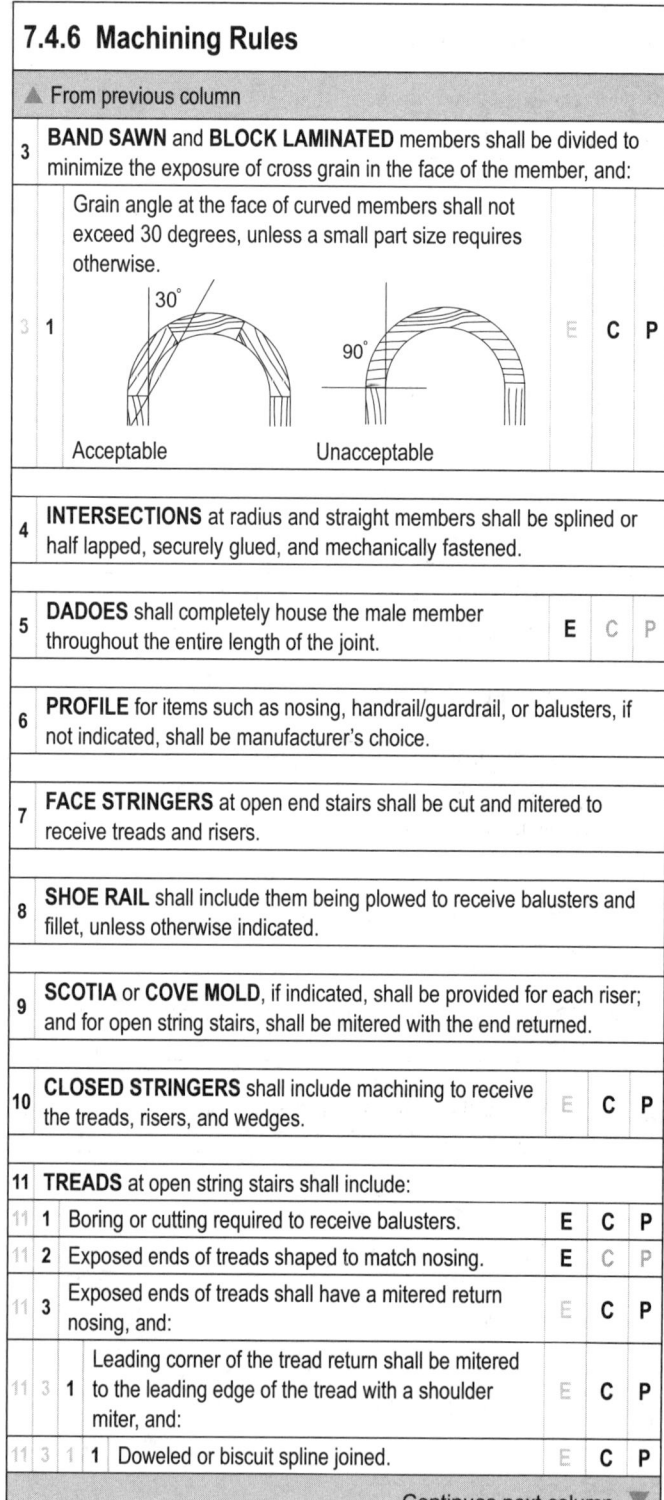 Acceptable — Unacceptable | E | C | P |
| 4 | | | **INTERSECTIONS** at radius and straight members shall be splined or half lapped, securely glued, and mechanically fastened. | | | |
| 5 | | | **DADOES** shall completely house the male member throughout the entire length of the joint. | E | C | P |
| 6 | | | **PROFILE** for items such as nosing, handrail/guardrail, or balusters, if not indicated, shall be manufacturer's choice. | | | |
| 7 | | | **FACE STRINGERS** at open end stairs shall be cut and mitered to receive treads and risers. | | | |
| 8 | | | **SHOE RAIL** shall include them being plowed to receive balusters and fillet, unless otherwise indicated. | | | |
| 9 | | | **SCOTIA** or **COVE MOLD**, if indicated, shall be provided for each riser; and for open string stairs, shall be mitered with the end returned. | | | |
| 10 | | | **CLOSED STRINGERS** shall include machining to receive the treads, risers, and wedges. | E | C | P |
| 11 | | | **TREADS** at open string stairs shall include: | | | |
| 11 | 1 | | Boring or cutting required to receive balusters. | E | C | P |
| 11 | 2 | | Exposed ends of treads shaped to match nosing. | E | C | P |
| 11 | 3 | | Exposed ends of treads shall have a mitered return nosing, and: | E | C | P |
| 11 | 3 | 1 | Leading corner of the tread return shall be mitered to the leading edge of the tread with a shoulder miter, and: | E | C | P |
| 11 | 3 | 1 | 1 | Doweled or biscuit spline joined. | E | C | P |

Continues next column ▼

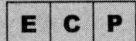 Where the **E**, **C**, or **P** icon is not indicated, the rule applies to all Grades equally

# SECTION 7
## Stairwork & Rails

## compliance requirements

GENERAL / **PRODUCT** / INSTALLATION / TEST

### 7.4.6 Machining Rules

▲ From previous column

| | | | |
|---|---|---|---|
| 12 | | | **RISERS** shall be rabbeted to receive the back edge of the tread, and: |
| 12 | 1 | | **At** open string stairs shall be mitered. |
| 13 | | | **RAILS** to receive balusters with square or rectangular heads shall be plowed on under side and provided with fillet. |
| 14 | | | **NEWEL POSTS**, when built up, shall be of shoulder miter, lock joint, tongues, or splined construction. |

### 7.4.7 Assembly Rules

| | | | | | | | | |
|---|---|---|---|---|---|---|---|---|
| 1 | | | | **THESE STANDARDS** do not establish Grade rules for joint flushness and or gap tolerances for woodwork products installed in a non climate controlled environment: however: | | | | |
| 1 | 1 | | | Prior to installation, the flushness and/or gap tolerances of woodwork products intended for non climate controlled environments shall meet the test requirements herein. | | | | |
| 2 | | | | **JOINTS** at **ASSEMBLED WOODWORK** shall be: | | | | |
| 2 | 1 | | | Neatly and accurately made. | | | | |
| 2 | 2 | | | Securely glued with residue removed from exposed and semi-exposed surfaces, and: | | | | |
| 2 | 2 | 1 | | Reinforced with glue blocks where essential. | | | | |
| 2 | 3 | | | Assembled at stringer aprons, fascias, and flat base with: | | | | |
| 2 | 3 | 1 | | Clamp nail, biscuit spline, spline, butterfly, scarf, or dowel joinery. | | E | **C** | P |
| 2 | 3 | 2 | | Biscuit spline, spline, butterfly, scarf, or dowel joinery. | | E | C | **P** |
| 2 | 4 | | | **HANDRAILS/GUARDRAILS** shall utilize: | | | | |
| 2 | 4 | 1 | | Clamp nails or stair bolts. | | **E** | C | P |
| 2 | 4 | 2 | | Stair bolts. | | | **C** | P |
| 2 | 4 | 3 | | Stair bolts and dowels. | | | | **P** |
| 2 | 4 | 4 | | When mitered, screws if stair bolts are impractical, and | | | | |
| 2 | 4 | 5 | | Have holes plugged, unless covered by fillet, and shall be: | | | | |
| 2 | 4 | 5 | 1 | Compatible for color and grain. | | E | **C** | P |
| 2 | 4 | 5 | 2 | Well matched for color and grain. | | E | C | **P** |
| 2 | 4 | 5 | 3 | Aligned with handrail/guardrail grain. | | E | C | **P** |
| 2 | 5 | | | **MECHANICALLY FASTENED** with nails or screws, where practical, and at solid wood: | | | | |
| 2 | 5 | 1 | | Countersunk. | | | | |
| 2 | 5 | 2 | | In molding quirks or reliefs where possible. | | E | **C** | P |
| 2 | 6 | | | **FREE** of exposed fasteners at exposed surfaces of decorative laminate sheet products. | | | | |
| 2 | 7 | | | Require **FLUSHNESS VARIATIONS** at exposed surfaces (See Test D illustrations in TESTS), when mitered or butted, such as, not to exceed at: | | | | |
| 2 | 7 | 1 | | 0.010" (0.25 mm). | | **E** | C | P |
| 2 | 7 | 2 | | 0.007" (0.18 mm). | | E | **C** | P |
| 2 | 7 | 3 | | 0.005" (0.13 mm). | | E | C | **P** |

Continues next column ▼

# SECTION 7
## Stairwork & Rails

### 7.4.7 Assembly Rules

▲ From previous column

**2 JOINTS at ASSEMBLED WOODWORK** (continued)

| | | | | E | C | P |
|---|---|---|---|---|---|---|
| 2 | 8 | | Allow **GAPS** at exposed surface (see Test A illustrations in TESTS), when mitered or butted, such as, not to exceed: | | | |
| 2 | 8 | 1 | 0.025" (0.64 mm) wide by 20% of the joint length. | E | C | P |
| 2 | 8 | 2 | 0.015" (0.38 mm) wide by 20% of the joint length. | | C | P |
| 2 | 8 | 3 | 0.010" (0.25 mm) wide by 20% of the joint length. | | | P |
| 2 | 9 | | Allow **GAPS** at exposed surface joints of parallel members (See Test B illustrations in TESTS), such as not to exceed: | | | |
| 2 | 9 | 1 | 0.025" x 9" (0.64 mm x 229 mm) shall not occur within 48" (1219 mm) of a similar gap in the same joint. | E | C | P |
| 2 | 9 | 2 | 0.015" x 6" (0.38 mm x 152 mm) shall not occur within 60" (1524 mm) of a similar gap in the same joint. | | C | P |
| 2 | 9 | 3 | 0.010" x 4" (0.25 mm x 102 mm) shall not occur within 72" (1829 mm) of a similar gap in the same joint. | | | P |
| 2 | 10 | | Allow **GAPS** at exposed surface joints (See Test C illustrations in TESTS) when mitered or butted, such as not to exceed at: | | | |
| 2 | 10 | 1 | 0.025" (0.64 mm). | E | C | P |
| 2 | 10 | 2 | 0.015" (0.38 mm). | | C | P |
| 2 | 10 | 3 | 0.010" (0.25 mm). | | | P |

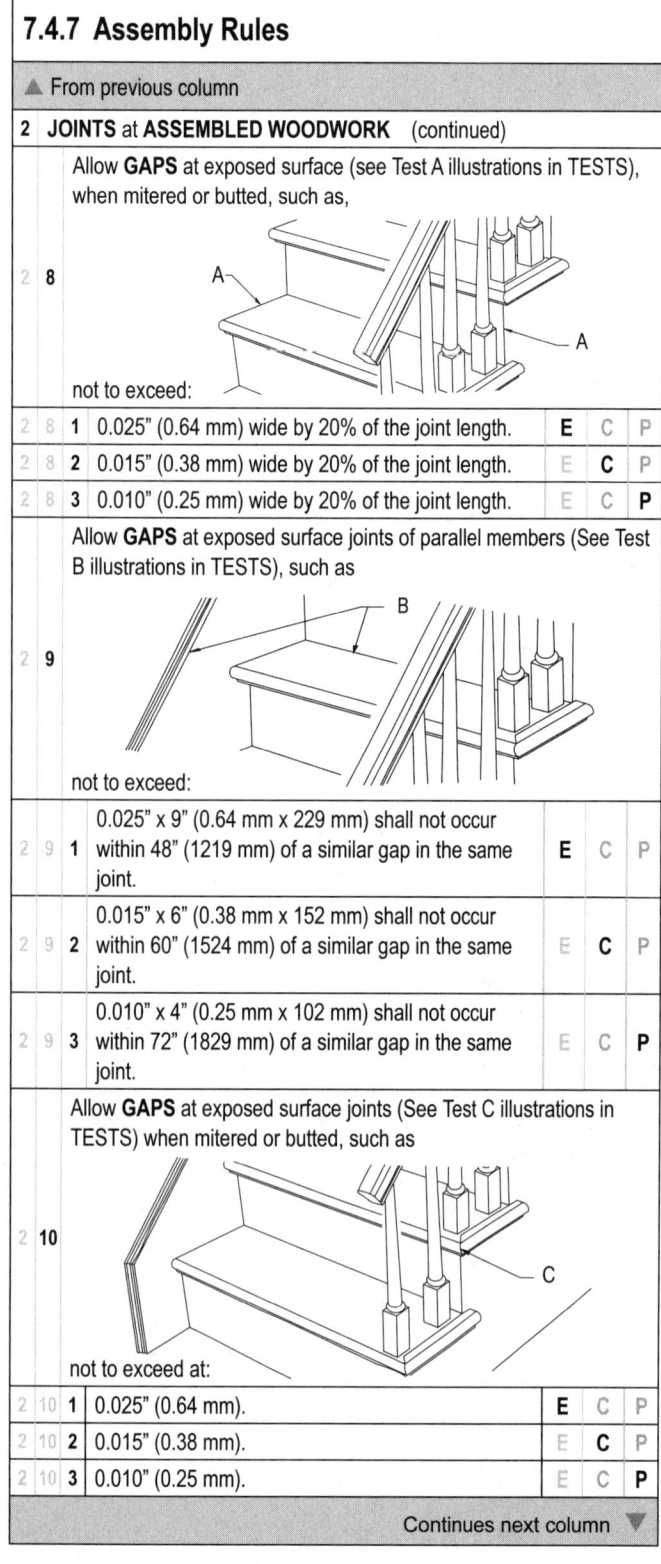

Continues next column ▼

### 7.4.7 Assembly Rules

▲ From previous column

**2 JOINTS at ASSEMBLED WOODWORK** (continued)

| | | | | E | C | P |
|---|---|---|---|---|---|---|
| 2 | 11 | | **FILLER** is permitted: | | | |
| 2 | 11 | 1 | If inconspicuous when viewed at 36" (914 mm). | E | C | P |
| 2 | 11 | 2 | If inconspicuous when viewed at 24" (610 mm). | | C | P |
| 2 | 11 | 3 | Not allowed. | | | P |
| 3 | | | **FLATNESS** or **WARP** of installed and removable sheet products (see Test E illustrations in TESTS) such as shall not to exceed grade tolerance listed for 12" (303 mm) diagonal, width and/or length or as lineal ratio (not geometric ratio) thereof. Example, twice the grade tolerance listed for 24" (610 mm), three times the tolerance for 36" (914 mm): | | | |
| 3 | | 1 | 0.045" (1.1 mm) per 12" (305 mm) or portion thereof. | E | C | P |
| 3 | | 2 | 0.030" (0.8 mm) per 12" (305 mm) or portion thereof. | | C | P |
| 3 | | 3 | 0.020" (0.5 mm) per 12" (305 mm) or portion thereof. | | | P |
| 4 | | | **APPLIED MOLDINGS** shall be spot glued and mechanically fastened. | | | |
| 5 | | | **MITER JOINTS** shall be well fitted and cleaned. | | | |
| 6 | | | **BUILT UP ITEMS** shall be soundly fabricated with half lapped, mitered, shoulder mitered, tonged, or equivalent construction. | | | |
| 7 | | | **SHEET** and **LAMINATED LUMBER PANELS** shall be allowed to move, float, expand or contract in reaction to ambient humidity changes. | | | |
| 8 | | | **STAIRWORK** shall be furnished KD (knocked down), with: | | | |
| 8 | | 1 | **TRIM MEMBERS** cut to required length plus allowance for fitting. | | | |
| 8 | | 2 | **STARTING STEPS** with return riser assembled ready for installation. | | | |
| 8 | | 3 | **SCOTIA** and **SHOE MOLDS** temporarily attached. | | | |
| 8 | | 4 | **BALUSTERS** for open string stairs shall be provided with dowel or tenon to fit into treads. | | | |
| 8 | | 5 | **CROOKS** and **RETURNS** shall be doweled and provided with rail bolts ready for assembly. | | | |
| 7 | | 6 | **GLUE BLOCK**S shall be provided at a minimum of 12" (305 mm) on center for each riser. | | | |

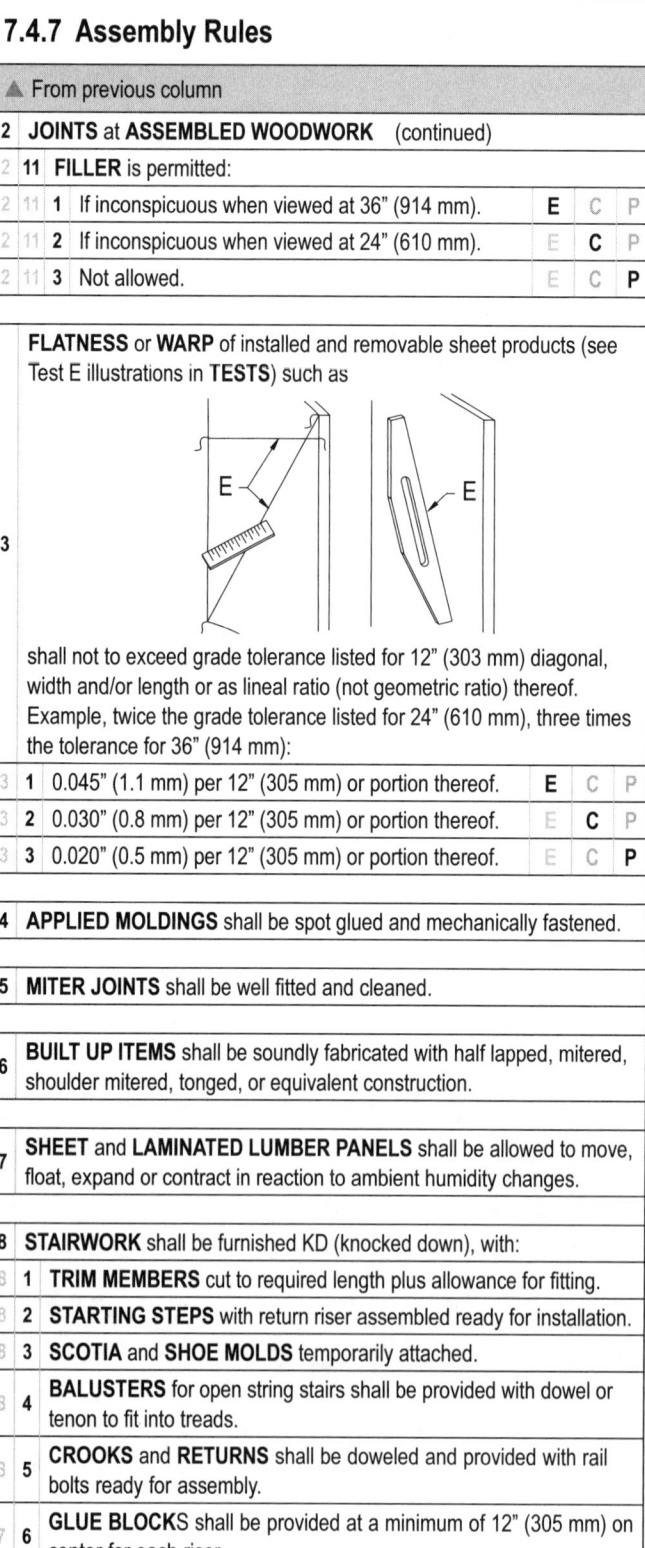

 Where the **E**, **C**, or **P** icon is not indicated, the rule applies to all Grades equally

# SECTION 7
## Stairwork & Rails

## compliance requirements — GENERAL/PRODUCT/INSTALLATION/TEST

### 7.5 PREPARATION and QUALIFICATION REQUIREMENTS (unless otherwise specified)

**1** **CARE, STORAGE,** and **BUILDING CONDITIONS** shall be in compliance with the requirements set forth in Section 2 of these standards.

1.1 Severe damage to the woodwork can result from noncompliance. The manufacturer and/or installer of the woodwork shall not be held responsible for any damage that might develop by not adhering to the requirements.

**2** **CONTRACTOR IS RESPONSIBLE FOR:**

2.1 Furnishing and installing structural members, grounds, in wall blocking, backing, furring, brackets, or other anchorage required for architectural woodwork installation that becomes an integral part of walls, floors, or ceilings to which architectural woodwork shall be installed.

2.1.1 In the absence of contract documents calling for the contractor to supply the necessary in wall blocking/backing in the wall or ceilings, either through inadvertence or otherwise, the architectural woodwork installer shall not proceed with the installation until such time as the in wall blocking/backing is installed by others.

2.1.2 Preparatory work done by others shall be subject to inspection by the architectural woodwork installer, and shall be accepted or rejected for cause prior to installation.

2.1.2.1 **WALL, CEILING,** and/or **OPENING VARIATIONS** in excess of 1/4" (6.4 mm) or **FLOORS** in excess of 1/2" (12.7 mm) in 144" (3658 mm) of being plumb, level, flat, straight, square, or of the correct size are not acceptable for the installation of architectural woodwork, nor is it the responsibility of the installer to scribe or fit to tolerances in excess of such.

2.1.3 Installation site being properly ventilated, protected from direct sunlight, excessive heat and/or moisture, and that the HVAC system is functioning and maintaining the appropriate relative humidity and temperature.

2.1.4 Priming the architectural woodwork in accordance with the contract documents prior to its installation, and:

2.1.4.1 If the architectural woodwork is factory finished, priming by the factory finisher is required.

### 7.5 PREPARATION and QUALIFICATION (continued)

**3** **INSTALLER IS RESPONSIBLE FOR:**

3.1 Having adequate equipment and experienced craftsmen to complete the installation in a first class manner.

3.2 Checking architectural woodwork specified and studying the appropriate portions of the contract documents, including these standards and the reviewed shop drawings to familiarize themselves with the requirements of the Grade specified, understanding that:

3.2.1 Appearance requirements of Grades apply only to surfaces visible after installation.

3.2.2 For transparent finish, special attention needs to be given to the color and the grain of the various woodwork pieces to ensure they are installed in compliance with the Grade specified.

3.3 Verification that installation site is properly ventilated, protected from direct sunlight, excessive heat and/or moisture, and that the HVAC system is functioning and maintaining the appropriate relative humidity and temperature.

3.4 Verification that required priming of woodwork has been completed by others before woodwork is installed.

3.5 Verification that woodwork has been acclimated to the field conditions for a minimum of 72 hours before installation is commenced.

3.6 Woodwork specifically built or assembled in sequence for match of color and grain is installed to maintain that same sequence.

# SECTION 7
## Stairwork & Rails

**GENERAL/PRODUCT/INSTALLATION/TEST** — compliance requirements

Where the **E**, **C**, or **P** icon is not indicated, the rule applies to all Grades equally | E | C | P |

### 7.6 RULES

1. The following rules shall govern unless a project's contract documents require otherwise.

2. These rules are intended to provide a well defined degree of control over a project's quality of installation.

3. **ERRATA**, published on the Associations' websites at www.awinet.org, www.awmac.com, or www.aws-errata.com, **shall take precedence over these rules**, subject to their date of posting and a project's bid date.

### 7.6.4 Basic Rules

| | | | Rule | E | C | P |
|---|---|---|---|---|---|---|
| 1 | | | **AESTHETIC** Grade rules apply only to exposed and semi-exposed surfaces visible after installation. | | | |
| 2 | | | **TRANSPARENT** finished woodwork shall be installed with: | | | |
| 2 | 1 | | **CONSIDERATION** of color and grain. | E | C | P |
| 2 | 1 | | **COMPATIBLE** in color and grain. | E | C | P |
| 2 | 2 | | **WELL MATCHED** for color and grain, and: | E | C | P |
| 2 | 2 | 1 | Sheet products shall be compatible in color with solid stock. | E | C | P |
| 2 | 2 | 2 | Adjacent sheet products shall be well matched for color and grain. | E | C | P |
| 3 | | | **INSTALLER MODIFICATIONS** shall comply to the material, machining, and assembly rules within the **PRODUCT** portion of this section and, if applicable, the finishing rules in Section 5. | | | |
| 4 | | | **REPAIRS** are allowed, provided they are neatly made and inconspicuous when viewed at: | | | |
| 4 | 1 | | 72" (1830 mm). | E | C | P |
| 4 | 2 | | 48" (1219 mm). | E | C | P |
| 4 | 3 | | 24" (610 mm). | E | C | P |
| 5 | | | **WOODWORK** shall be: | | | |
| 5 | 1 | | **SECURELY** fastened and tightly fitted with flush joints, and: | | | |
| 5 | 1 | 1 | Joinery shall be consistent throughout the project. | | | |
| 5 | 2 | | Of maximum available and/or practical length. | E | C | P |
| 5 | 3 | | **TRIMMED EQUALLY** from both sides when fitted for width. | E | C | P |
| 5 | 4 | | **SPLINE** or **DOWELED** when miters are over 4" (100 mm) long. | E | C | P |

*Continues next column*

### 7.6.4 Basic Rules

▲ From previous column

| | | | Rule | E | C | P |
|---|---|---|---|---|---|---|
| 5 | | | **WOODWORK** (continued) | | | |
| 5 | 5 | | **PROFILED** or **SELF MITERED** when trim ends are exposed. | E | C | P |
| 5 | 6 | | **SELF MITERED** when trim ends are exposed. | E | C | P |
| 5 | 7 | | **MITERED** at outside corners. | | | |
| 5 | 8 | | **MITERED** at inside corners. | E | C | P |
| 5 | 9 | | **COPED** at inside corners. | E | C | P |
| 5 | 10 | | **INSTALLED** plumb, level, square, and flat within 1/8" (3.2 mm) in 96" (2438 mm), and when required: | | | |
| 5 | 10 | 1 | **GROUNDS** and **HANGING SYSTEMS** set plumb and true. | E | C | P |
| 5 | 11 | | Installed **FREE** of: | | | |
| 5 | 11 | 1 | Warp, twisting, cupping, and/or bowing that cannot be held true. | | | |
| 5 | 11 | 2 | Open joints, visible machine marks, cross sanding, tears, nicks, chips, and/or scratches. | | | |
| 5 | 11 | 3 | Natural defects exceeding the quantity or size limits defined in Sections 3 & 4. | | | |
| 5 | 12 | | **SMOOTH** and **SANDED** without **CROSS SCRATCHES** in conformance to the **PRODUCT** portion of this section. | | | |
| 5 | 13 | | **SCRIBED** at: | | | |
| 5 | 13 | 1 | Flat surfaces. | E | C | P |
| 5 | 13 | 2 | Shaped surfaces. | E | C | P |
| 6 | | | **THESE STANDARDS** do not establish Grade rules for joint flushness and or gap tolerances for woodwork products installed in a non climate controlled environment. | | | |

*Continues next column* ▼

Where the **E**, **C**, or **P** icon is not indicated, the rule applies to all Grades equally

# SECTION 7
## Stairwork & Rails

## compliance requirements

GENERAL/PRODUCT/**INSTALLATION**/TEST

### 7.6.4 Basic Rules

▲ From previous column

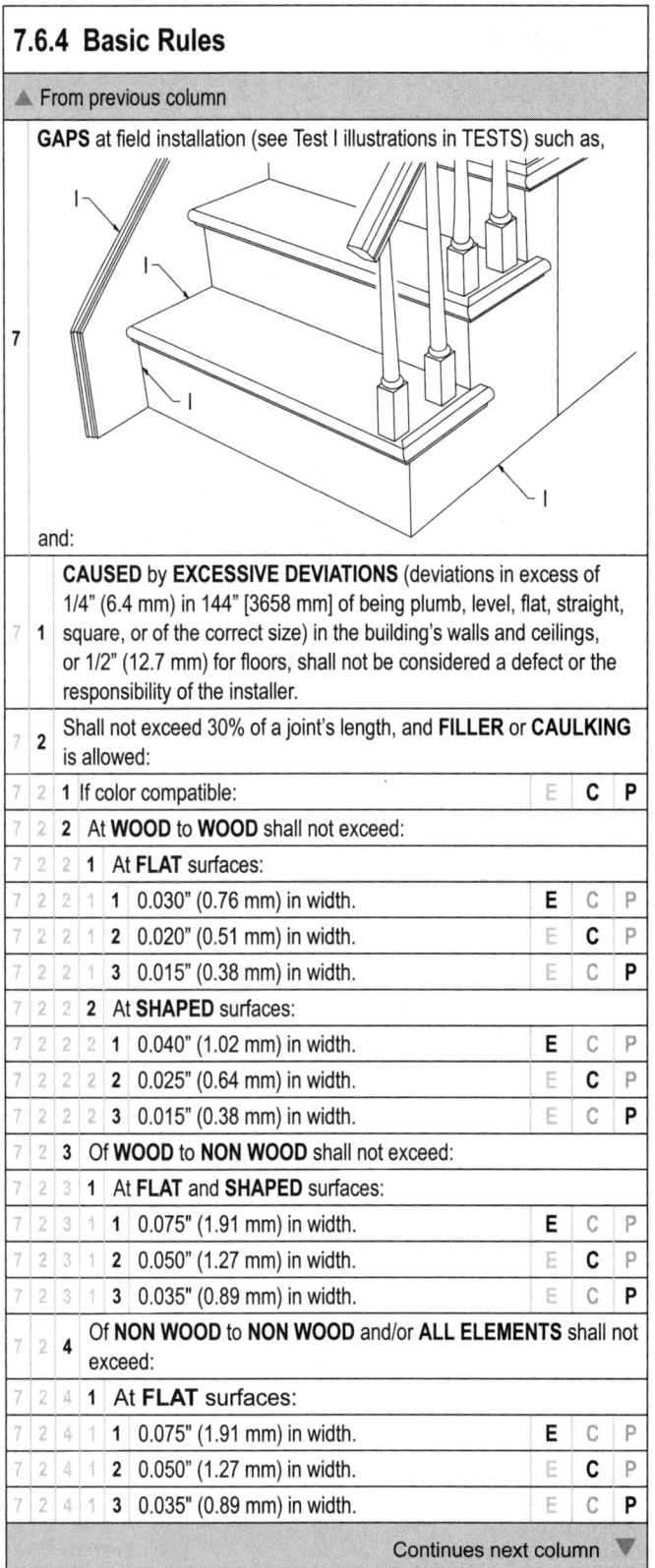

| 7 | | | | GAPS at field installation (see Test I illustrations in TESTS) such as, and: | | | |
|---|---|---|---|---|---|---|---|
| 7 | 1 | | | CAUSED by EXCESSIVE DEVIATIONS (deviations in excess of 1/4" (6.4 mm) in 144" [3658 mm] of being plumb, level, flat, straight, square, or of the correct size) in the building's walls and ceilings, or 1/2" (12.7 mm) for floors, shall not be considered a defect or the responsibility of the installer. | | | |
| 7 | 2 | | | Shall not exceed 30% of a joint's length, and FILLER or CAULKING is allowed: | | | |
| 7 | 2 | 1 | | If color compatible: | E | C | P |
| 7 | 2 | 2 | | At WOOD to WOOD shall not exceed: | | | |
| 7 | 2 | 2 | 1 | At FLAT surfaces: | | | |
| 7 | 2 | 2 | 1 | 1 0.030" (0.76 mm) in width. | E | C | P |
| 7 | 2 | 2 | 1 | 2 0.020" (0.51 mm) in width. | E | C | P |
| 7 | 2 | 2 | 1 | 3 0.015" (0.38 mm) in width. | E | C | P |
| 7 | 2 | 2 | 2 | At SHAPED surfaces: | | | |
| 7 | 2 | 2 | 2 | 1 0.040" (1.02 mm) in width. | E | C | P |
| 7 | 2 | 2 | 2 | 2 0.025" (0.64 mm) in width. | E | C | P |
| 7 | 2 | 2 | 2 | 3 0.015" (0.38 mm) in width. | E | C | P |
| 7 | 2 | 3 | | Of WOOD to NON WOOD shall not exceed: | | | |
| 7 | 2 | 3 | 1 | At FLAT and SHAPED surfaces: | | | |
| 7 | 2 | 3 | 1 | 1 0.075" (1.91 mm) in width. | E | C | P |
| 7 | 2 | 3 | 1 | 2 0.050" (1.27 mm) in width. | E | C | P |
| 7 | 2 | 3 | 1 | 3 0.035" (0.89 mm) in width. | E | C | P |
| 7 | 2 | 4 | | Of NON WOOD to NON WOOD and/or ALL ELEMENTS shall not exceed: | | | |
| 7 | 2 | 4 | 1 | At FLAT surfaces: | | | |
| 7 | 2 | 4 | 1 | 1 0.075" (1.91 mm) in width. | E | C | P |
| 7 | 2 | 4 | 1 | 2 0.050" (1.27 mm) in width. | E | C | P |
| 7 | 2 | 4 | 1 | 3 0.035" (0.89 mm) in width. | E | C | P |

Continues next column ▼

### 7.6.4 Basic Rules

▲ From previous column

| 7 | | | | GAPS (continued) | | | |
|---|---|---|---|---|---|---|---|
| 7 | 2 | | | Shall not exceed (continued) | | | |
| 7 | 2 | 4 | | Of NON WOOD to NON WOOD and/or ALL ELEMENTS (continued): | | | |
| 7 | 2 | 4 | 2 | At SHAPED surfaces: | | | |
| 7 | 2 | 4 | 2 | 1 0.120" (3.05 mm). | E | C | P |
| 7 | 2 | 4 | 2 | 2 0.075" (1.91 mm). | E | C | P |
| 7 | 2 | 4 | 2 | 3 0.050" (1.27 mm). | E | C | P |
| 8 | | | | FLUSHNESS of field joinery (see Test J illustrations in TESTS), such as, and: | | | |
| 8 | 1 | | | At WOOD to WOOD shall not exceed: | | | |
| 8 | 1 | 1 | | At FLAT surfaces: | | | |
| 8 | 1 | 1 | 1 | 0.025" (0.64 mm). | E | C | P |
| 8 | 1 | 1 | 2 | 0.015" (0.38 mm). | E | C | P |
| 8 | 1 | 1 | 3 | 0.010" (0.25 mm). | E | C | P |
| 8 | 1 | 2 | | At SHAPED surfaces: | | | |
| 8 | 1 | 2 | 1 | 0.40" (0.97 mm). | E | C | P |
| 8 | 1 | 2 | 2 | 0.025" (0.65 mm). | E | C | P |
| 8 | 1 | 2 | 3 | 0.020" (0.51 mm). | E | C | P |
| 8 | 2 | | | At WOOD to NON WOOD shall not exceed: | | | |
| 8 | 2 | 1 | | At FLAT and SHAPED surfaces: | | | |
| 8 | 2 | 1 | 1 | 0.075" (1.91 mm). | E | C | P |
| 8 | 2 | 1 | 2 | 0.050" (1.27 mm). | E | C | P |
| 8 | 2 | 1 | 3 | 0.035" (0.89 mm). | E | C | P |

Continues next column ▼

# SECTION 7
## Stairwork & Rails

GENERAL/PRODUCT/**INSTALLATION**/TEST

**compliance requirements**

Where the **E**, **C**, or **P** icon is not indicated, the rule applies to all Grades equally: **E | C | P**

### 7.6.4 Basic Rules

▲ From previous column

| # | | | Rule | E | C | P |
|---|---|---|---|---|---|---|
| 8 | 3 | | At **NON WOOD** to **NON WOOD** and/or **ALL ELEMENTS** shall not exceed: | | | |
| 8 | 3 | 1 | At **FLAT** surfaces: | | | |
| 8 | 3 | 1 | 1  0.075" (1.91 mm). | E | C | P |
| 8 | 3 | 1 | 2  0.050" (1.27 mm). | | C | P |
| 8 | 3 | 1 | 3  0.035" (0.89 mm). | | | P |
| 8 | 3 | 2 | At **SHAPED** surfaces: | | | |
| 8 | 3 | 2 | 1  0.120" (3.05 mm). | E | C | P |
| 8 | 3 | 2 | 2  0.075" (1.91 mm). | | C | P |
| 8 | 3 | 2 | 3  0.050" (1.27 mm). | | | P |
| 9 | | | **FASTENING and FASTENERS** shall: | | | |
| 9 | 1 | | Include the use of construction adhesive, finish nails, trim screws, and/or pins, and: | | | |
| 9 | 2 | | Not permit the use of drywall, bugle head, or case hardened screws. | | | |
| 9 | 3 | | Be countersunk when through an exposed surface, and: | | | |
| 9 | 3 | 1 | Set in quirks and reliefs where possible. | | C | P |
| 9 | 3 | 2 | Inconspicuous, as defined in the Glossary. | | C | P |
| 9 | 4 | | Allow use of construction adhesive for inconspicuous fastening. | | | |
| 9 | 5 | | Not permit exposed fastening through decorative laminate. | | | |
| 9 | 6 | | **REQUIRE** allowable fastener holes, when: | | | |
| 9 | 6 | 1 | Prefinished materials to be filled by the installer with matching filler furnished by the manufacturer. | | | |
| 9 | 6 | 2 | Unfinished materials to be filled by the paint contractor or others. | | | |
| 10 | | | **GLUE** and filler residue is not permitted on exposed faces. | | | |
| 11 | | | **EQUIPMENT CUTOUTS**, including electrical and plumbing, shall be cut out by the installer, provided any needed templates are furnished prior to installation, and: | | | |
| 11 | 1 | | Shall be neatly cut and properly sized to be covered by standard cover plates or rosettes. | | | |
| 11 | 2 | | Cutouts in HPDL shall have radiused inside corners. | | | |

Continues next column ▼

### 7.6.4 Basic Rules

▲ From previous column

| # | | Rule | E | C | P |
|---|---|---|---|---|---|
| 12 | | **HARDWARE** shall be installed: | | | |
| 12 | 1 | Neatly without tear out of surrounding stock. | E | C | P |
| 12 | 2 | Per manufacturer's instructions. | | | |
| 12 | 3 | Using all furnished fasteners and fasteners' provisions and when fastener provisions are countersunk, fasteners shall be countersunk. | | | |
| 12 | 4 | And adjusted for smooth operation. | | | |
| 13 | | **AREAS** of **INSTALLATION** shall be left broom clean, with: | | | |
| 13 | 1 | Debris removed and dumped in containers provided by the contractor. | | | |
| 13 | 2 | Items installed cleaned of pencil or ink marks. | | | |
| 14 | | **FIRST CLASS WORKMANSHIP** is required in compliance with these standards. | | | |

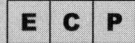

Where the **E**, **C**, or **P** icon is not indicated, the rule applies to all Grades equally

# SECTION 7
## Stairwork & Rails

## compliance requirements

GENERAL/PRODUCT/INSTALLATION/**TEST**

### 7.7 BASIC CONSIDERATIONS

1 The tolerances typically found within the Architectural Woodwork Standards fall into two categories:

1.1 Factory fabricated joinery, assembly and construction found in the **PRODUCT** portion.

1.2 Field installation joinery and assembly found in the **INSTALLATION** portion.

2 Most fabrication and installation assemblies include solid wood to solid wood joints, solid wood to wood veneer joints, solid wood to wood based products (HPDL, LPDL, Solid Phenolic and panel products), solid wood to non wood based products (which can be drywall, glass, metal, stone, acrylics, and other surfaces), and non wood to non wood joints.

3 Tolerances found in the AWS include:

3.1 Flatness of wood based panel products.

3.2 Solid wood to solid wood joints and assemblies.

3.3 Solid wood to wood veneer joints and assemblies.

3.4 Wood veneer to wood veneer joints and assemblies.

3.5 Solid wood to wood based product joints and assemblies.

3.6 Solid surface to solid surface joints and assemblies.

4 Because of the differences of expansion and contraction of non wood products compared to solid wood and wood based products, the AWS does not apply tolerances regarding flatness or joinery to these non wood based products.

5 **FABRICATED** and **INSTALLED** woodwork shall be tested for compliance to these standards as follows:

5.1 **SMOOTHNESS** of exposed surfaces:

5.1.1 **KCPI** (Knife Cuts Per Inch) is determined by holding the surfaced board at an angle to a strong light source and counting the visible ridges per inch, usually perpendicular to the profile.

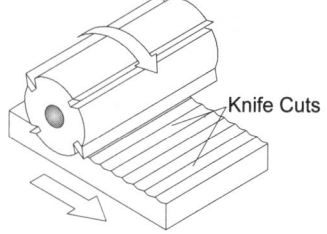

Figure: 07-012

### 7.7 BASIC CONSIDERATIONS (continued)

5.1.2 **SANDING** is checked for compliance by sanding a sample piece of the same species with the required grit of abrasive.

5.1.2.1 Observation with a hand lens of the prepared sample and the material in question will offer a comparison of the scratch marks of the abrasive grit.

5.1.2.2 Reasonable assessment of the performance of the finished product will be weighed against absolute compliance with these standards.

5.1.2.3 A product is sanded sufficiently smooth when knife cuts are removed and any remaining sanding marks are or will be concealed by applied finishing coats.

5.1.2.4 Grain raise at unfinished wood, due to moisture or humidity in excess of the ranges set forth in these standards, shall not be considered a defect and must be sanded prior to finishing.

6 **GAPS, FLUSHNESS, FLATNESS** and **ALIGNMENT** of product and installation:

6.1 Maximum gaps between exposed components shall be tested with a feeler gauge at points designed to join where members contact or touch.

6.2 Joint length shall be measured with a ruler with minimum 1/16" (1 mm) divisions and calculations made accordingly.

6.3 Reasonable assessment of the performance of the finished product will be weighed against absolute compliance with these standards.

# SECTION 7
## Stairwork & Rails

GENERAL/PRODUCT/INSTALLATION/**TEST**

**compliance requirements**

Where the **E**, **C**, or **P** icon is not indicated, the rule applies to all Grades equally | E | C | P |

### 6.7 BASIC CONSIDERATIONS (continued)

6 **GAPS, FLUSHNESS, FLATNESS** and **ALIGNMENT** (continued):

6.4 The following is intended to provide examples of how and where compliance testing is measured:

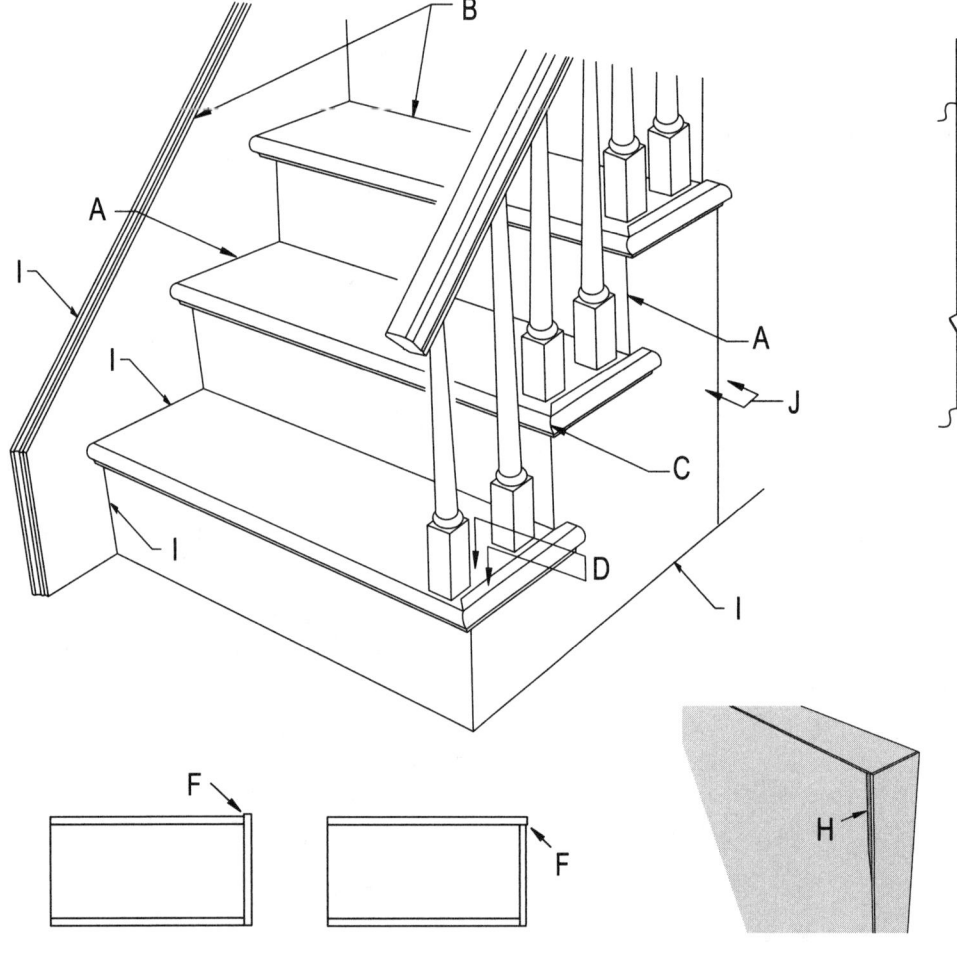
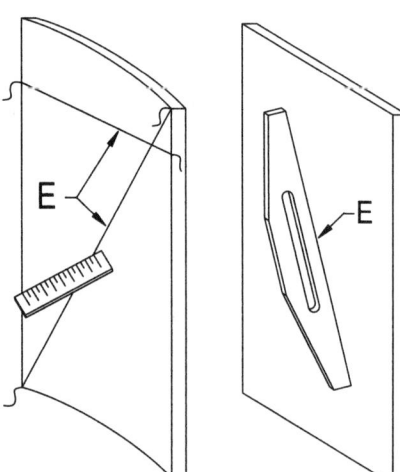

Measured on the concave face

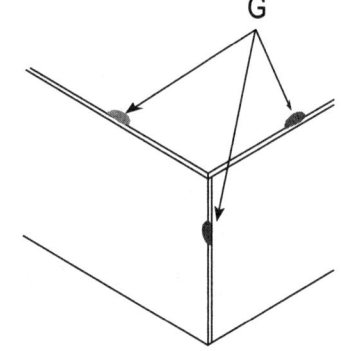

*Figure: 07-013*

A - Fabrication Gaps When Surfaces Are Mitered Or Butted
B - Fabrication Gaps When Parallel Pieces Are Joined
C - Fabrication Gaps When Edges Are Mitered Or Butted
D - Fabrication Flushness Between Two Surfaces
E - Flatness Of Panel Product
F - Overlap
G - Chip Out
H - Over Machined
I - Installation Gaps
J - Installation Flushness

# Architectural Woodwork Standards

# WALL/CEILING SURFACING & PARTITIONS

## SECTION 8

# SECTION 8
## Wall/Ceiling Surfacing and Partitions

## table of contents

### INTRODUCTORY INFORMATION

| | |
|---|---|
| Guide Specifications | 194 |
| Introduction | 195 |
| Wall and Ceiling Surfacing | 195 |
|     Opaque | 195 |
|     Transparent | 195 |
| Contract Documents | 195 |
| Product Advisory | 195 |
| Panel Sequence | 196 |
| Sequencing of Panels Within a Room | 197 |
|     Premanufactured Sequenced Sets | 198 |
|         Full Width Panel Utilization | 198 |
|         Selectively Reduced Panel Utilization | 200 |
|     Made to Order Sequenced Matched Panels | 201 |
|     Made to Order Blueprint Matched Panels and Components | 202 |
| Flitch Selection | 203 |
| Variations in Natural Wood Products | 203 |
| High Pressure Decorative Laminates (HPDL) | 203 |
| Standing and Running Trim | 203 |
| Smoothness of Flat and Molded Surfaces | 204 |
| Installation | 204 |
| Finishing | 204 |
| Fire Retardance and Treatment | 204 |
| Fire Retardant Panel Products | 204 |
| Examples | 205 |
|     Edgebanding | 205 |
|     Field Cut Corner and Transition | 205 |
|     Reveals and Reveal Joint | 205 |
|     Factory Prepared Corner and Transition | 206 |
|     Factory Prepared Transition | 206 |
|     Wall Panels with Millwork | 207 |
|     Stile and Rail Paneling | 208 |
|     Flat Paneling with Reveals within a Niche | 209 |
|     Paneling for Reception Wall with Factory Built Structures | 210 |
|     Specify Requirements For | 211 |
|     Recommendations | 211 |

### COMPLIANCE REQUIREMENTS

**GENERAL**

| | |
|---|---|
| Basic Considerations | 212 |
|     Grades | 212 |
|         Economy | 212 |
|         Custom | 212 |
|         Premium | 212 |
|         Grade Limitations | 212 |
|     Contract Documents | 212 |
|     Acceptable Requirements | 212 |
|     Aesthetic Compliance | 212 |
|     Exposed Surfaces | 213 |
|     Concealed Surfaces | 212 |
|     Solid Surface | 212 |
|     Solid Phenolic | 212 |
|     HPDL Backed Wood Veneers | 212 |
|     Continuous Pressure Laminates | 212 |
|     Furring | 212 |
|     Bleached Veneers | 212 |
|     High Gloss HPDL | 212 |
|     To Prevent Telegraphing | 212 |
|     Industry Practices | 212 |
|         Structural Members | 212 |
|         Wall, Ceiling and Floor | 212 |
|         Priming | 213 |
|         Radius Molding | 213 |
|         Wainscot | 213 |
|         Wall Surfacing | 213 |

**PRODUCT**

| | |
|---|---|
| Scope | 214 |
|     Typical Inclusions | 214 |
|     Typical Exclusions | 214 |
| Default Stipulation | 214 |
|     Wood | 214 |
|     HPDL | 214 |
|     Solid Surface | 214 |
|     Solid Phenolic | 214 |

# SECTION 8
## Wall/Ceiling Surfacing and Partitions

## table of contents

**COMPLIANCE REQUIREMENTS** (continued)

**PRODUCT** (continued)

- Rules ......................................................................... 215
  - Errata .................................................................... 215
  - Basic Rules ........................................................... 215
    - Aesthetic ......................................................... 215
    - Lumber ............................................................ 215
    - Sheet Products ................................................ 215
    - Backing Sheet ................................................. 215
    - Exposed Surfaces ........................................... 215
    - Concealed Surfaces ........................................ 215
    - Wainscot ......................................................... 215
    - Furring ............................................................ 215
    - Defined Grain ................................................. 215
    - Multiple Options ............................................. 215
    - Flame Spread Rating ...................................... 215
    - Specific Profile ............................................... 215
    - If no species is specified for transparent finish .......... 215
    - Where Gluing or Lamination ......................... 215
    - Cut outs .......................................................... 215
    - Cathedral ........................................................ 215
    - Single Source ................................................. 215
    - First Class Workmanship ............................... 215
  - Material Rules ...................................................... 216
    - Species ........................................................... 216
    - Lumber, Veneered Profile or Sheet Products ...... 216
    - Defects ........................................................... 216
    - Figure ............................................................. 216
    - Warp ............................................................... 216
    - Partition Cores ............................................... 216
    - Opaque Finish ................................................ 216
    - Transparent Finish Veneer ............................. 216
    - Exposed Surfaces ........................................... 216
      - Transparent Finish ..................................... 216
    - Concealed Surfaces ........................................ 216
    - Wood Veneer .................................................. 216
      - Cores .......................................................... 217
      - Matching .................................................... 217
      - Opaque ...................................................... 217
      - Transparent ................................................ 217
      - Edge Reveals ............................................. 217
      - Bleed Through ........................................... 217
      - Flame Spread Rated ................................... 217
    - Solid Stile and Rail ........................................ 217
      - Lumber ...................................................... 217
      - Veneer ....................................................... 217
      - Opaque ...................................................... 217
      - Transparent ................................................ 217
      - Panels ........................................................ 217
    - Solid Wood Surfacing .................................... 218
    - Decorative Laminate ...................................... 218
      - Conformance to NEMA LD-3 .................... 218
      - Adjacent Sheets ......................................... 218
      - Flame Spread ............................................. 218
      - Patterned or Wood Grain ........................... 218
      - Cores .......................................................... 218
      - Backing Sheet ............................................ 218
      - Visible Splines and Reveals ...................... 218
      - Edgebanding .............................................. 219
    - Solid Surface ................................................. 219
    - Solid Phenolic ................................................ 219
    - Priming ........................................................... 219
  - Machining Rules ................................................... 219
    - Exposed Surfaces ........................................... 219
      - Sharp Edges ............................................... 219
      - Top Flat Surfaces ...................................... 219
      - Profiled and Shaped Wood ........................ 219
      - HPDL, PVC and Prefinished Wood ............ 219
        - Overlap, Test F ...................................... 219
        - Chip out, Test G .................................... 219
        - Over Machined, Test H ......................... 220
    - Turned Wood .................................................. 220
    - Cross Sanding ................................................ 220
    - Tear out, Knife Nicks .................................... 220
    - Knife Marks ................................................... 220

# SECTION 8
## Wall/Ceiling Surfacing and Partitions

## table of contents

**COMPLIANCE REQUIREMENTS** (continued)

> **PRODUCT** (continued)
>> Rules (continued)
>>> Machining Rules (continued)
>>>> Exposed Surfaces (continued)
>>>>> Glue or Filler .................................................. 220
>>>>> Solid Surface. Solid Phenolic, Epoxy Resin ............. 220
>>> Assembly Rules ............................................................. 220
>>>> These Standards ...................................................... 220
>>>> Joints at Assembled Woodwork ............................... 220
>>>>> Securely Glued ..................................................... 220
>>>>> Reinforced ............................................................ 220
>>>>> Mechanically Fastened ......................................... 220
>>>>> Visible Fasteners .................................................. 220
>>>>> Flushness Variations ............................................ 220
>>>>> Gap Test A ............................................................ 221
>>>>> Gap Test B ............................................................ 221
>>>>> Gap Test C ............................................................ 221
>>>>> Miter Joints ........................................................... 221
>>>>> Built Up Items ....................................................... 221
>>>> Flatness or Warp, Test E .......................................... 221
>>>> Wood Veneer ............................................................ 222
>>>>> Panels ................................................................... 222
>>>>> Veneer Sequence ................................................. 222
>>>>> Butt Joints ............................................................. 222
>>>>> Reveal Joints and Corners ................................... 222
>>>>> Inside Corners ...................................................... 222
>>>>> Mitered ................................................................. 222
>>>>> Field Joinery ......................................................... 222
>>>>> Exposed Corners .................................................. 222
>>>>> Moldings ............................................................... 222
>>>>> Veneer Joints ........................................................ 222
>>>>> Veneer Loss, Side ................................................. 223
>>>>> Veneer Loss, End .................................................. 223
>>>>> End Matched Veneer Misalignment ..................... 223
>>>>> Figure ................................................................... 223
>>>> Solid Stile and Rail Wood ......................................... 223
>>>>> Paneling ................................................................ 223
>>>>>> Field Joints ...................................................... 223
>>>> Decorative Laminate ................................................ 223
>>>>> Alignment Variations ........................................... 223
>>>>> Plumbness ............................................................ 223
>>>>> Gap Test M ........................................................... 223
>>>>> Flushness Test N .................................................. 223
>>>>> Retention Moldings .............................................. 223
>>>>> Vertical Horizontal Joints ..................................... 223
>>>>> Panels ................................................................... 224
>>>>> Butt Joints ............................................................. 224
>>>>> Reveal Joints and Corners ................................... 224
>>>>> Inside Corners ...................................................... 224
>>>>> Mitered Outside Corners ..................................... 224
>>>> Solid Surface ............................................................. 224
>>>>> Butt Joint .............................................................. 224
>>>>> Vertical Joints ....................................................... 224
>>>>> Expansion ............................................................. 224
>>>> Solid Phenolic ........................................................... 224
>>>>> Joint Width ........................................................... 224
>>>>> Joints .................................................................... 224
>>>>> Trims or Gaskets .................................................. 224

**INSTALLATION**
> Care, Storage and Building Conditions ......................... 225
> Contractor is Responsible for ........................................ 225
> Installer is Responsible for ............................................ 225
> Rules ................................................................................ 226
>> Errata ........................................................................... 226
>> Basic Rules .................................................................. 226
>>> Aesthetics ................................................................ 226
>>> Transparent Finished ............................................. 226
>>> Repairs .................................................................... 226
>>> Installer Modifications ........................................... 226
>>> Woodwork ............................................................... 226
>>> These Standards ..................................................... 226

# SECTION 8
## Wall/Ceiling Surfacing and Partitions

## table of contents

- Gaps Test I ......................................................... 227
- Flushness Test J .................................................. 227
- Reveals at Adjoining Panel Gaps Test K ................ 227
- Flushness at Adjoining Panel Flushness Test L ..... 228
- Fastening ............................................................ 228
- Reveal Strips ...................................................... 228
- Expansion Joints ................................................. 228
- Paneling ............................................................. 228
- Joints ................................................................. 228
- Backs ................................................................. 228
- Flatness of Panels Test E .................................... 228
- Glue .................................................................... 229
- Equipment Cutouts .............................................. 229
- Hardware ............................................................ 229
- Areas of Installation ............................................. 229
- First Class Workmanship ..................................... 229
- Specific Rules ......................................................... 229
  - Veneered Panels ................................................ 229
  - Solid Wood Surfacing ......................................... 230
  - Decorative Laminate .......................................... 230
  - Solid Surface ..................................................... 230
  - Solid Phenolic ................................................... 230

**TESTS**
- Basic Considerations ............................................... 231
  - Fabricated and Installed .................................... 231
  - Smoothness ...................................................... 231
    - KCPI ............................................................. 231
    - Sanding ........................................................ 231
  - Gaps, Flushness, Flatness and Alignment ......... 231
    - Illustrations .................................................. 232

# SECTION 8
Wall/Ceiling Surfacing and Partitions

## introductory information

# Guide Specifications

Are available through the Sponsor Associations in interactive digital format including unique and individual quality control options.
The Guide Specifications are located at:

## Architectural Woodwork Institute (AWI)
www.awinet.org

## Architectural Woodwork Manufacturers Association of Canada (AWMAC)
http://awmac.com/aws-guide-specifications

## Woodwork Institute (WI)
www.woodworkinstitute.com/publications/aws_guide_specs.asp

# SECTION 8
## Wall/Ceiling Surfacing and Partitions

## introductory information

### INTRODUCTION:

Section 8 includes information on wood veneer, solid wood, stile and rail wood, decorative laminate, solid surface and solid phenolic products and their related parts.

Quality assurance can be achieved by adherence to the AWS and will provide the owner a quality product at competitive pricing. Use of a qualified Sponsor Member firm to provide your woodwork will help ensure the manufacturer's understanding of the quality level required. Illustrations in this Section are not intended to be all inclusive. Other engineered solutions are acceptable. In the absence of specifications, methods fabrication shall be at the option of the manufacturer. The design professional, by specifying compliance to the AWS increases the probability of receiving the product quality expected.

### WALL and CEILING SURFACING:

Includes wood veneered panels, solid wood, decorative plastic laminate, solid surface, solid phenolic panels and factory built framing for surfacing.

Contract documents, furnished by the design professional, shall clearly indicate or delineate material, fabrication, installation, and applicable building code/regulation requirements.

Shop drawings, engineering, listings and mockups are the means by which the design intent is turned into reality. They shall indicate methods of construction, exact material selections, grain direction(s), methods of attachment and joinery, and exact dimensions. They should also include the manufacturer's technical suggestions. Listings (schedules) are sometimes used to list core, edge and face materials, adhesives etc. when not included on the shop drawings. Mockups may be specified for review as a full scale model showing, materials, joinery and finishes and are often used as the project control sample.

### MATERIAL SELECTIONS:

For **OPAQUE** finishes:
- Medium Density Fiberboard (MDF) is suggested for cost savings and an optimum paintable surface.
- Medium Density Overlay (MDO) which may be machined and detailed with little loss of quality surface characteristics, requires a seal coat prior to application of finish coats with no sheen limitation.
- Medium Density Overlay (MDO) - This provides a paintable surface for panels. The thermosetting resin overlay is designed to take and hold paint. Opaque finish sheens above 40 Satin require special finishing procedures.
- Close Grain Hardwood - Although allowed, extra preparation may be required by the finisher as there may be grain show-through, split veneer joints, and other wood characteristics.
- Manufacturers' option - Face materials are determined by the manufacturer.

For **TRANSPARENT** finishes:
Selection starts by looking at "hand samples," pieces of veneer or lumber representing a particular species, but not necessarily a particular tree or log. Wood is a natural material (unlike a manufactured product), which varies from tree to tree in its color and texture. Rather than simply choosing an appropriate wood for its color, consider the size and availability of the species. A species that grows in smaller diameter, with shorter logs, lends itself to furniture and smaller projects, whereas an abundant species that grows in large diameter lends itself more to larger public spaces. Many projects have run into difficulties because the species availability was not compatible with the project's needs.

### CONTRACT DOCUMENTS SHALL INCLUDE:

Species, Slicing and Matching of individual leaves are reviewed and governed by Section 4, Sheet Products (Note unless otherwise specified; plain sliced and bookmatch are the default standards).

- Species: There are numerous foreign and domestic species available. Involve your manufacturer early in the design and selection process.
- Slicing: Select either rotary, plain sliced, quarter sliced, or (in the case of Oak only) rift sliced.
- Matching of individual leaves: Select either book matched (most appropriate for plain sliced), slip matched (most appropriate for quartered and rift sliced), or random matched (for a rustic look, usually more expensive).
- Matching on each panel face: Select either running match, balance match, or balance and center match. Specify type of end matching for tall elevations.
- Sequence matching between full width pre manufactured panel sets.

### PRODUCT ADVISORY:

Due to adverse reaction of some veneers laminated to fire rated (FR), ultra low emitting formaldehyde (ULEF or NAUF), medium density fiberboard MDF - causing discoloration of the wood veneer even months after installation, major core manufacturers have issued disclaimers in the use of FR cores. They strongly suggest that use of FR ULEF MDF and particleboard cores should be done after testing compatibility of adhesives, wood veneer and cores. Any resulting discoloration with the use of these cores may be exempt in their warranties. Use of FR ULEF cores should only be considered after consultation with the board supplier.

# SECTION 8
## Wall/Ceiling Surfacing and Partitions

# introductory information

**PANEL SEQUENCING:**

- **Running Match** (cannot be end matched) - Each panel face is assembled from as many veneer leaves as necessary. This often results in a non-symmetrical appearance, with some veneer leaves of unequal width. Often the most economical method at the expense of aesthetics.

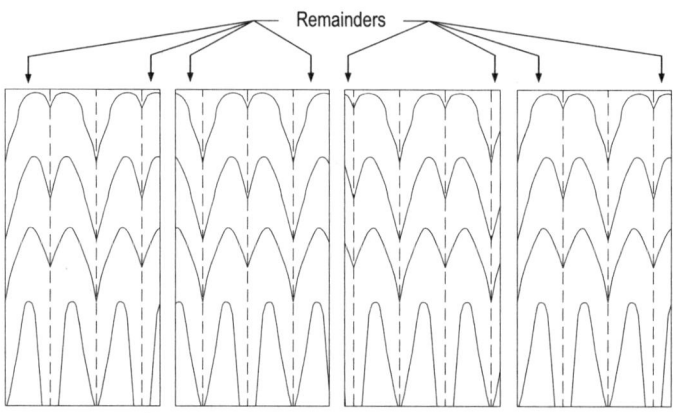

FIGURE: 8-001

- **Balance Match** - Each panel face is assembled from veneer leaves of uniform width before edge trimming. Panels may contain an even (balance and center) or odd (balanced) number of leaves and may change from panel to panel within a sequenced set.

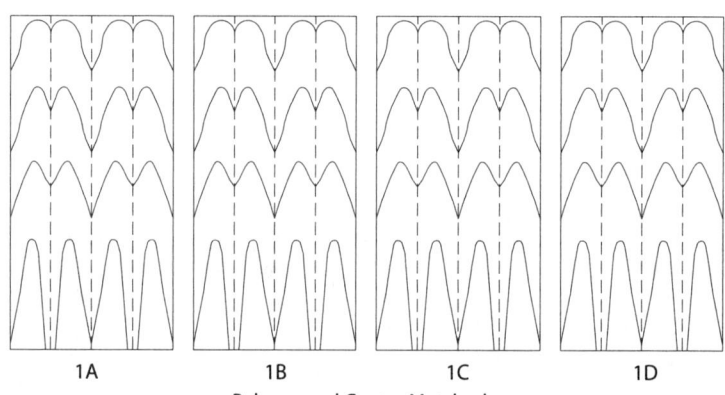

Balance and Center Matched

FIGURE: 8-002

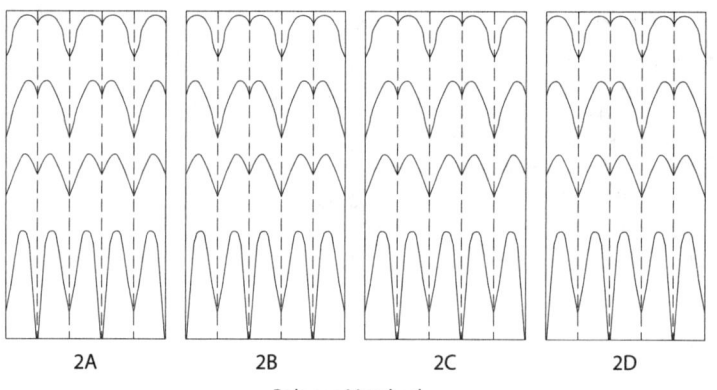

Balance Matched

FIGURE: 8-003

196 Architectural Woodwork Standards ©2014 AWI | AWMAC | WI 2nd Edition, October 1, 2014

# SECTION 8
## Wall/Ceiling Surfacing and Partitions

## introductory information

- Balanced End Match

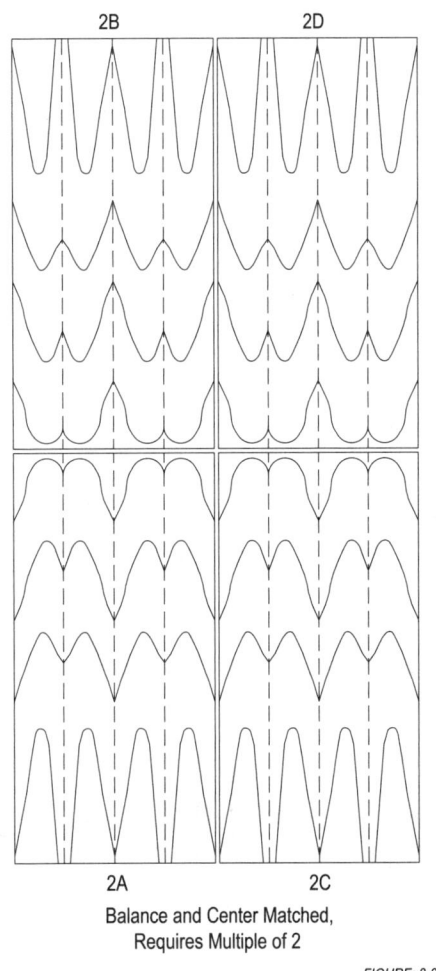

Balance and Center Matched,
Requires Multiple of 2

FIGURE: 8-004

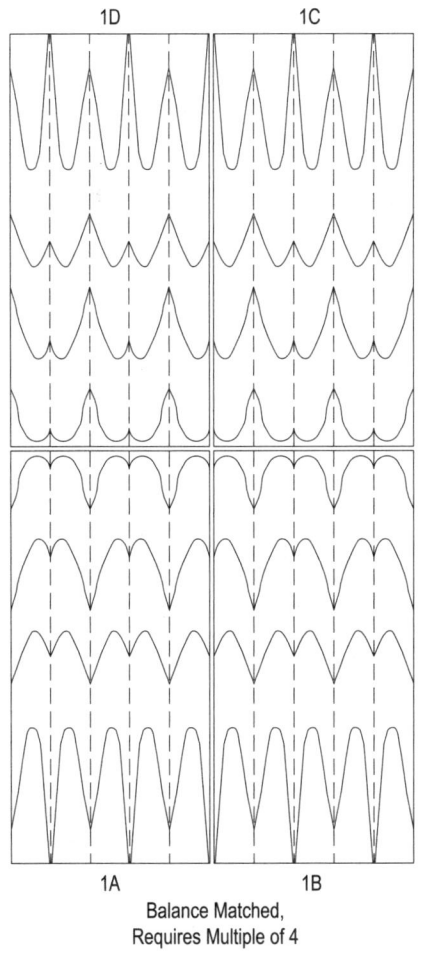

Balance Matched,
Requires Multiple of 4

FIGURE: 8-005

### SEQUENCING of PANELS WITHIN A ROOM:

Selections include: no sequence, pre-manufactured sets - full width, pre-manufactured sets - selectively reduced in width (equally sized), sequenced uniform size set(s), or blueprint sequenced panels and components.

Although many panel distributors maintain a panel inventory of pre-manufactured sets of different species and grades, only a limited quantity of species, cut and grades will be available.

Sequenced custom sized and blueprint sequenced panels offer variables of veneer leaf match and panel width there for panel sequencing shall not be tried with pre-manufactured panel sets.

Sequenced panels and examples of their room layout are as follows:

# SECTION 8
Wall/Ceiling Surfacing and Partitions

## introductory information

**SEQUENCING of PANELS WITHIN A ROOM** (continued):

- **PREMANUFACTURED SEQUENCED SETS**

Full width utilization is composed of a specific quantity of sequenced and numbered panels based on a per room basis for net footage selected from available inventory. They are usually only available in 48" x 96" or 120" (1219 mm x 2438 mm or 3048 mm) sheets in sets varying from 6-12 panels. If more than one set is required, sequencing between sets cannot be expected. Similarly, doors or components cannot be fabricated from the same set.

- **FULL WIDTH PANEL UTILIZATION** with running matched panels.

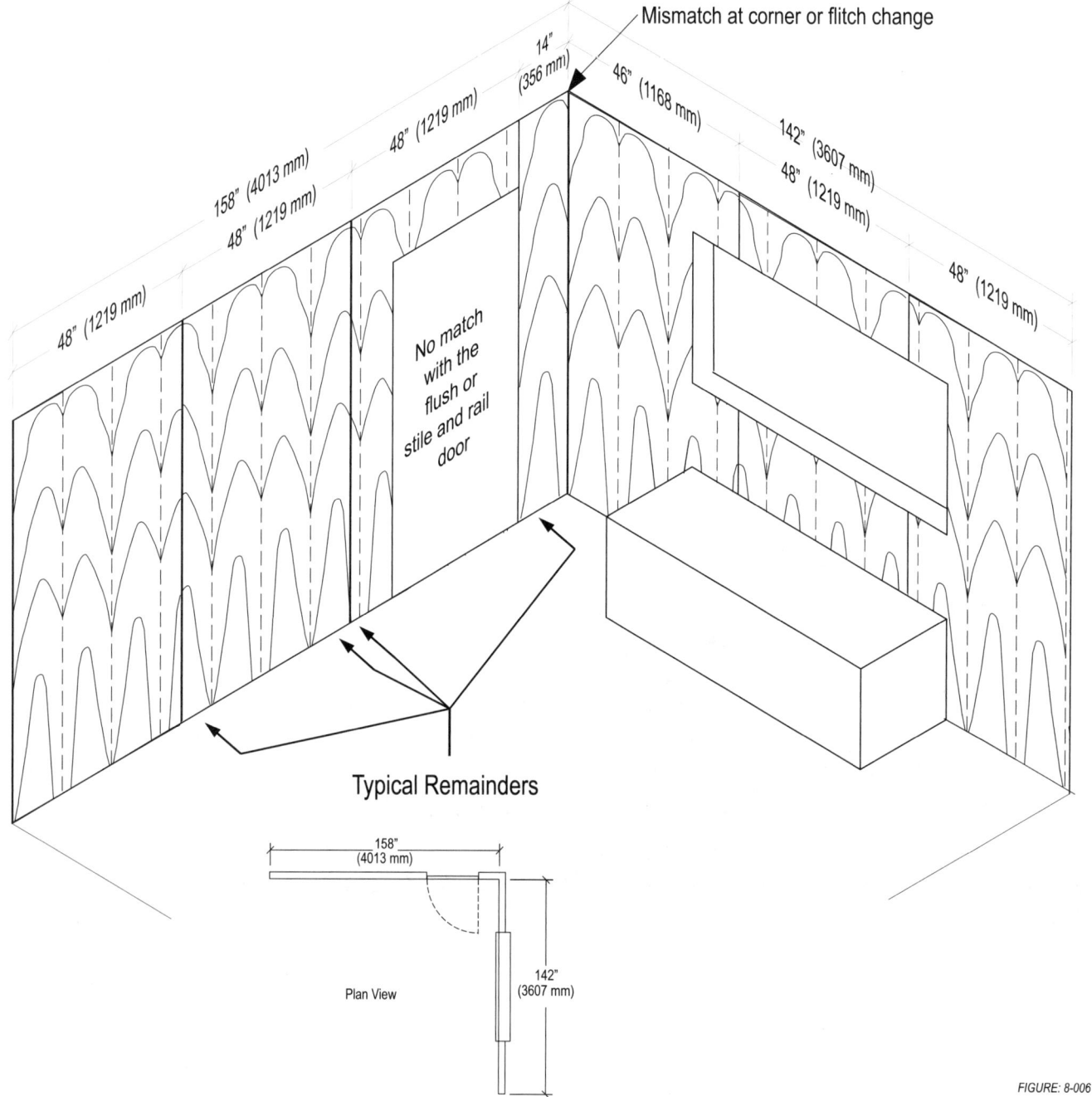

FIGURE: 8-006

198  Architectural Woodwork Standards                    ©2014 AWI | AWMAC | WI  2nd Edition, October 1, 2014

# SECTION 8
## Wall/Ceiling Surfacing and Partitions

# introductory information

## SEQUENCING of PANELS WITHIN A ROOM (continued)

- **PRE-MANUFACTURED SEQUENCED SETS** (continued)
  - **FULL WIDTH PANEL UTILIZATION** with balanced matched panels.

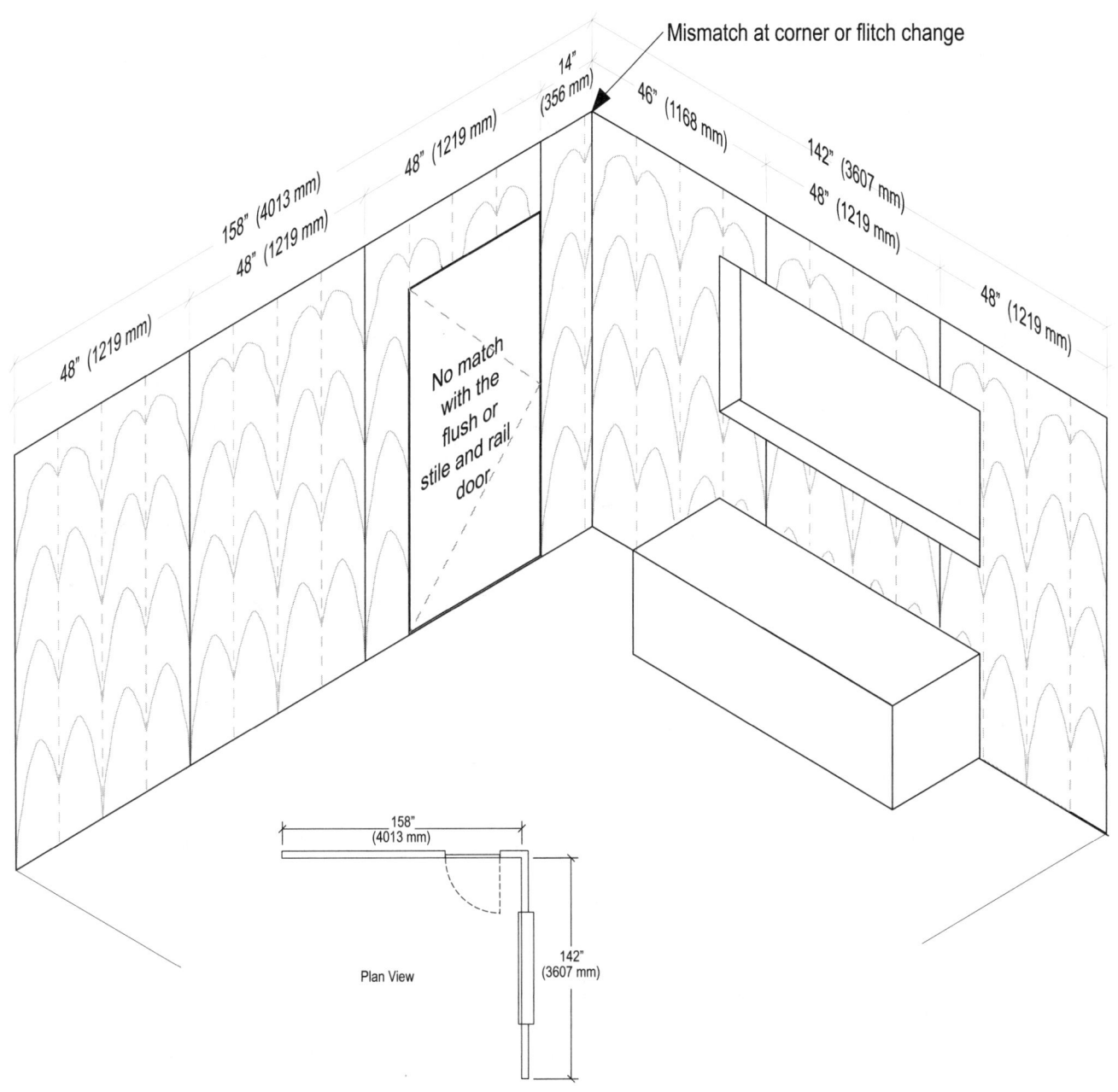

FIGURE: 8-006

# SECTION 8
## Wall/Ceiling Surfacing and Partitions

# introductory information

**SEQUENCING of PANELS WITHIN A ROOM** (continued)

- **PRE-MANUFACTURED SEQUENCED SETS** (continued)
  - **SELECTIVELY REDUCED PANEL UTILIZATION** with balanced matched panels.

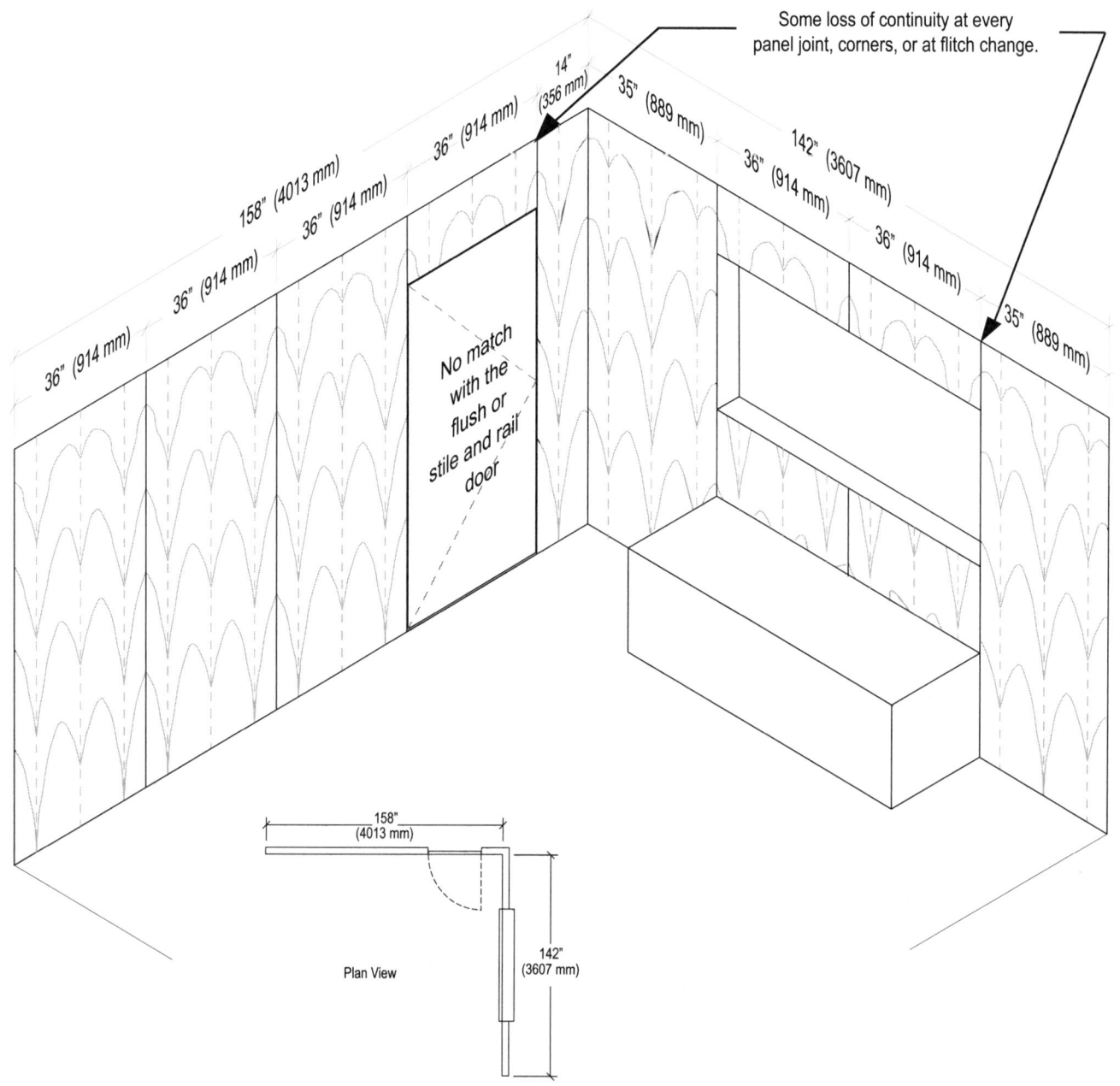

FIGURE: 8-007

# SECTION 8
## Wall/Ceiling Surfacing and Partitions

## introductory information

**SEQUENCING of PANELS WITHIN A ROOM**   (continued)

- **MADE TO ORDER SEQUENCED SETS** (must be specified). Balance or balance and center matched panels are manufactured to exact sizes based on the project's net footage and height requirements.

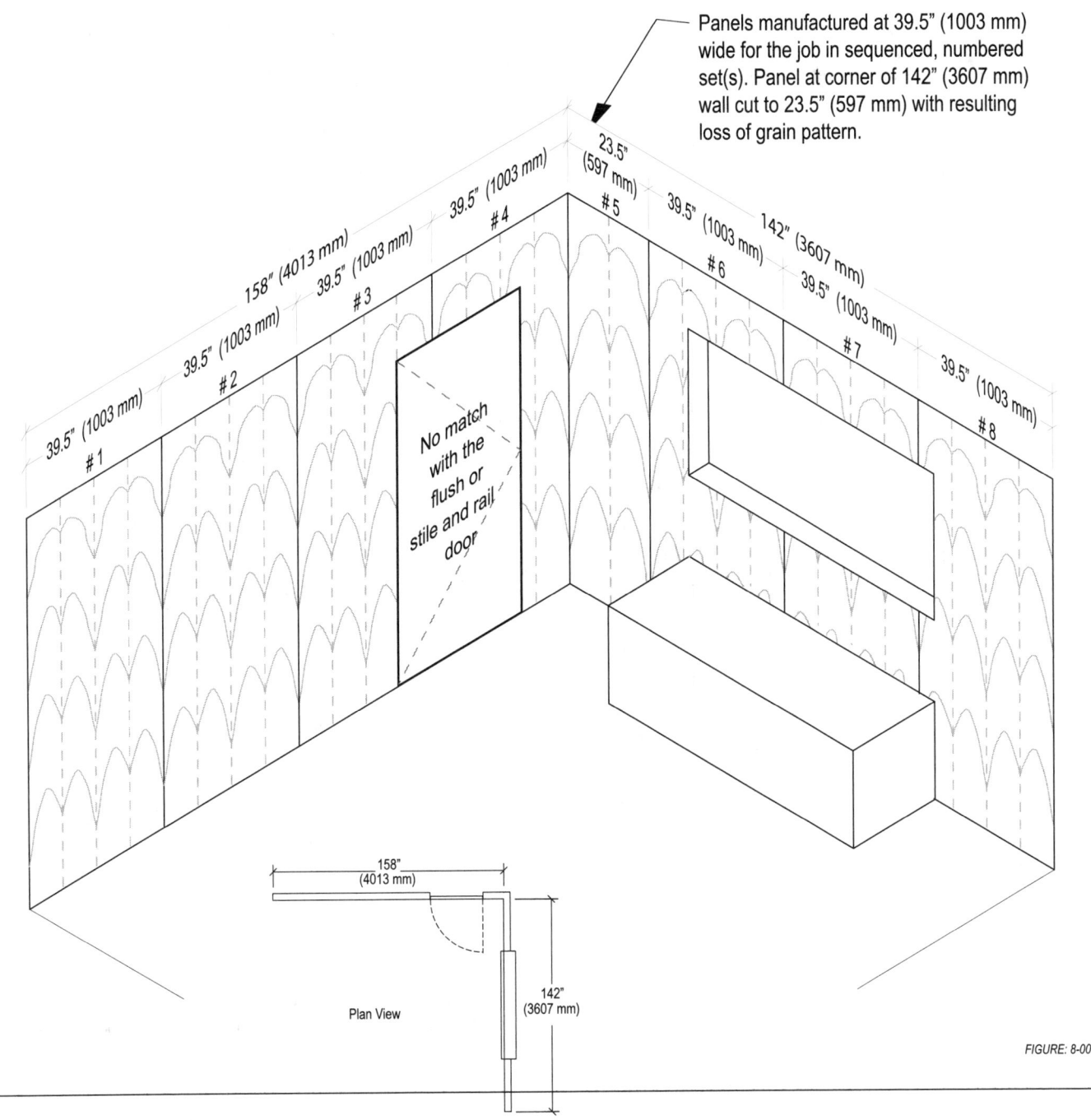

Panels manufactured at 39.5" (1003 mm) wide for the job in sequenced, numbered set(s). Panel at corner of 142" (3607 mm) wall cut to 23.5" (597 mm) with resulting loss of grain pattern.

FIGURE: 8-008

# SECTION 8
## Wall/Ceiling Surfacing and Partitions

# introductory information

### SEQUENCING of PANELS WITHIN A ROOM   (continued)

- **MADE TO ORDER SEQUENCED BLUEPRINT SETS** and **COMPONENTS** (must be specified). Balance and balance and center matched panels are manufactured to the exact sizes the manufacturer determines from the contract drawings, clipping and matching each individual face to the project's specific needs. Each face will be in sequence with adjacent panels, doors, transoms, and cabinet faces as needed for continuity.

  Components such as doors, windows, openings and cabinets plus overall room dimensions are the variables that determine panel width. Either balance and/or balance and center matched panels may be used in conjunction with one another to achieve a blueprint sequence. Therefore, grain continuity is maximized, which enhances the overall aesthetics.

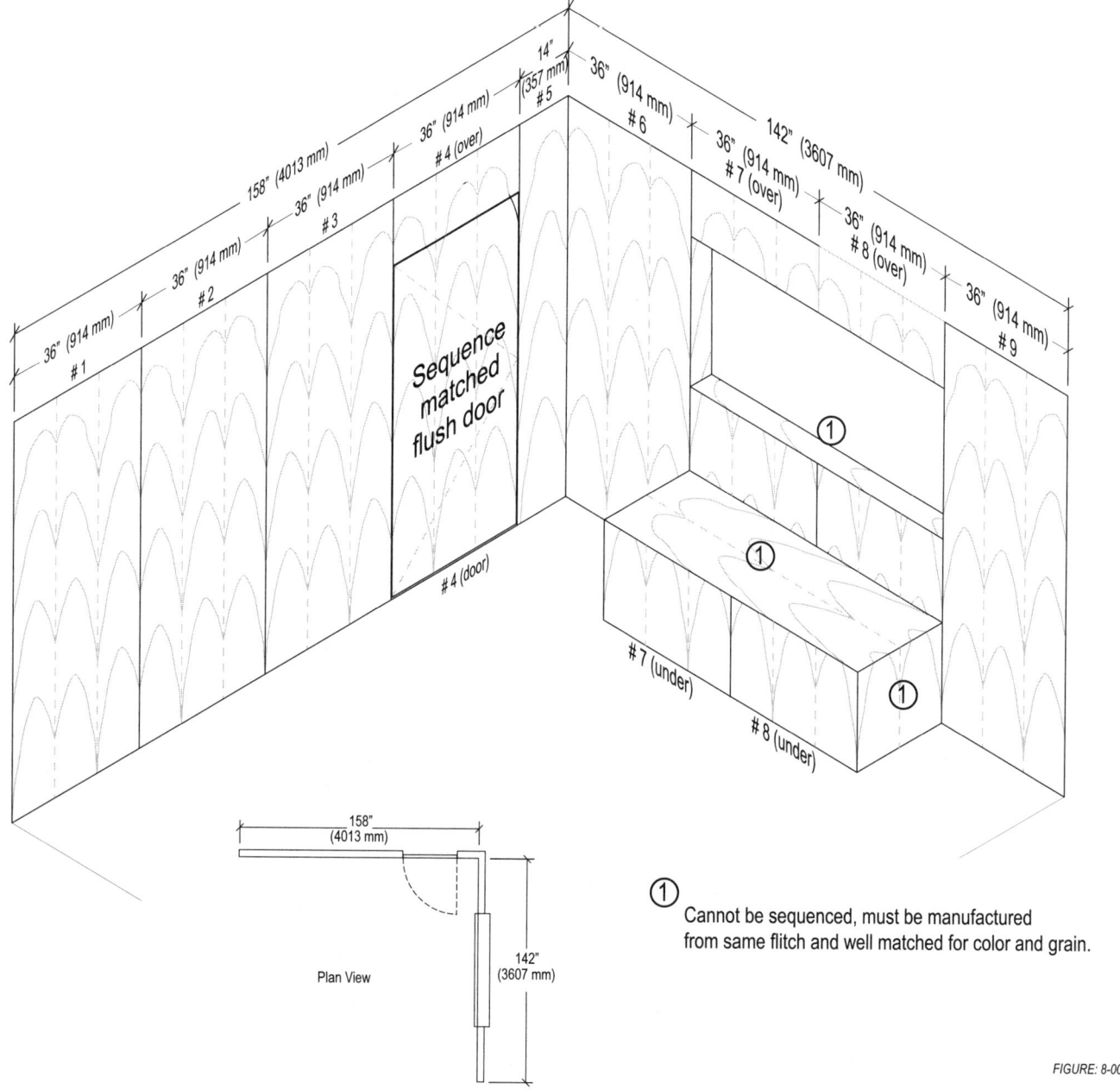

① Cannot be sequenced, must be manufactured from same flitch and well matched for color and grain.

FIGURE: 8-009

# SECTION 8
## Wall/Ceiling Surfacing and Partitions

## introductory information

### FLITCH SELECTION

The design professional may choose to see samples of veneer flitches to evaluate color and grain characteristics for other than pre-manufactured sets. This must be specified. Unless specified, layup is determined by the manufacturer.

When it is determined that the use of pre-manufactured panel sets is not adequate for the scope of the project, then selecting specific veneer flitches is an option to consider.

When sliced from a log, the individual pieces of veneer are referred to as leaves. These leaves are kept in order as they are sliced and then dried. As the leaves come out of the dryer, the log is literally reassembled. This sliced, dried and reassembled log or partial log is called a flitch. The flitch is given a number and the gross square footage of the flitch is tallied.

**To select specific veneer flitches for a project:**
- Determine the net square footage of face veneer required for the project. This should include paneling, casework, built-in furniture, and flush doors items when specifying a blueprint sequenced project.
- Multiply the net square footage times three (this is the average ratio. Some species require a higher multiplier). Example: 5,000 (net square feet) x 3 = 15,000 square feet; this is the gross square footage that should be sampled for this project.

While this may sound like a daunting quantity of veneer to look through, there is an established process that simplifies the task. When a numbered flitch is sampled, typically, three leaves of veneer are removed from the flitch and numbered sequentially. Starting from the top of the flitch, a leaf is removed from one-quarter of the way down, then from one-half, and from three quarters in the flitch. These three sequentially numbered leaves of veneer form a representative sample of that flitch.

- Since it will take at least 6 flitches, with a gross square footage of 2,500 square feet each to meet the project needs, give careful consideration to the following key criteria:

  - **Length** - Is the length adequate for the requirements? The flitch needs to be at least 6" (152 mm) longer than the panel requirements.

  - **Width** - What will the net yield for width be from each flitch?

  - **Gross square footage of each flitch** - total yield must be 15,000 square feet.

  - **Color and grain compatibility** - While exact matching is not possible, from flitch to flitch, this is the opportunity to select the range of color and grain compatibility that will enhance the visual continuity of the entire project.

The reality of this process is that the square footage of individual flitches of veneer will probably range from 1,200 square feet up to 3,000 square feet. This means that one may end up selecting 9 or 10 flitches, instead of just 6. But the goal remains the same as in the example: selecting flitches that will satisfy the aesthetic needs, while fulfilling the face veneer requirements for the project.

It is recommended that specifications be written with the foregoing objective in mind. Then, when the project has been awarded to a qualified manufacturer, talk directly to the manufacturer and be involved in one of the most exciting aspects of bringing the design concepts to reality.

### VARIATIONS in NATURAL WOOD PRODUCTS

Wood is a natural material, with variations in color, texture, and figure. These variations are influenced by the natural growing process and are uncontrollable by the manufacturer. The color of wood within a tree varies between the "sapwood" (the outer layers of the tree which continue to transport sap), which is usually lighter in color than the "heartwood" (the inner layers in which the cells have become filled with natural deposits). Various species produce different grain patterns (figures), which influence the selection process. There will be variations of grain patterns within selected species. The architectural woodwork manufacturer cannot select solid lumber cuttings within a species by grain and color in the same manner in which veneers may be selected. Color, texture, and grain variations will occur in architectural woodworking.

### HIGH PRESSURE DECORATIVE LAMINATES (HPDL)

- High pressure decorative laminate color and texture can be used in the manufacture of architectural panels and doors with the following cautions:

  - High gloss HPDL will highlight minor core and surface imperfections, often unacceptably.

  - HPDL panels and doors are not recommended for exterior use due to the potential differentials in humidity between the faces.

  - Some HPDLs utilize a WHITE BACKGROUND paper to achieve the high fidelity, contrast, and depth of color of their printed pattern, while leaving a white line at exposed edges, which is extremely noticeable with darker colors.

### STANDING AND RUNNING TRIM

Site-applied cornice, chair rail, base, trim, and mouldings are governed by the areas of the Architectural Woodwork Standards covering Standing and Running Trim.

# SECTION 8
Wall/Ceiling Surfacing and Partitions

## introductory information

### SMOOTHNESS of FLAT and MOLDED SURFACES

- **Planers and Molders:** The smoothness of surfaces that have been machine planed or moulded is determined by the closeness of the knife cuts. The closer the cuts to each other (i.e., the more knife cuts per inch [KCPI]), the closer the ridges, and therefore the smoother the resulting appearance.

- **Sanding and Abrasives:** Surfaces can be further smoothed by sanding. Sandpapers come in grits from coarse to fine and are assigned ascending grit numbers. The coarser the grit, the faster the stock removal. The surface will show the striations caused by the grit. Sanding with finer grit papers will produce smoother surfaces.

### INSTALLATION

The methods and skill involved in the installation of paneling and doors in large measure determine the final appearance of the project. The design, detailing, and fabrication should be directed toward achieving installation with a minimum of exposed face fastening. The use of interlocking wood cleats or metal hanging clips combined with accurate furring and shimming will accomplish this. Such hanging of panels has the additional advantage of permitting panel movement that results from humidity changes or building movement. Depending upon local practice, many manufacturers will perform the wall preparation and installation of the paneling and related doors.

### FINISHING

Site conditions and air quality regulations for finishing are rarely conducive to good results. Poor lighting, dust-laden air, and techniques available are limiting factors. Depending upon local practice, many manufacturers will factory finish, yielding better results than can be achieved from field finishing. Unless specified in the Contract Documents, the manufacturer is not responsible for the appearance of field finished panels or doors.

### FIRE RETARDANCE and TREATMENT

The natural fire-retardant qualities and acceptability of treatments vary among the species. Where certain items of architectural woodwork are required to have a flame spread classification to meet applicable building and safety codes, the choice of lumber species must be a consideration. Additional data on various species may be available from U.S. Department of Agriculture Forest Service, Fire Safety of Wood Products Work Unit at (608) 231-9265.

- **Flame Spread Classification:** This is the generally accepted measurement for flame spread rating of materials. It compares the rate of flame spread on a particular species with the rate of flame spread on untreated Oak. Most authorities accept the following classes for flame spread:

  - Class I or A       0-25
  - Class II or B      26-75
  - Class III or C     76-200

- **Fire Retardant Treatments:** Some species may be treated with chemicals to reduce flammability and retard the spread of flame over the surface. This usually involves impregnating the wood, under pressure, with salts suspended in a liquid. The treated wood must be re-dried prior to fabrication. Consult with a manufacturer about the appearance and availability of treated woods prior to specification.

  The sizes and species currently being treated (flame spread less than 25), are very limited, and not available in all markets. Fire-retardant treatment does affect the color and finishing characteristics of the wood.

  Subject to the authority having jurisdiction, untreated wood and wood products may be used. The location and quantity to be determined by the design professional.

- **Intumescent Coatings for Wood:** It is possible to reduce flammability by using intumescent coatings in either opaque or transparent finishes. These are formulated to expand or foam when exposed to high heat, and create an insulating effect that reduces the speed of spread of flame. Improvements are continually being made on these coatings. Consequently, the specifier must ascertain whether they will be permitted under the code governing the project, the relative durability of the finish, and the effect of the coating on the desired color of the finished product.

- **Finishing Of Fire Retardant Treated Lumber:** Fire-retardant treatments may affect the finishes intended to be used on the wood, particularly if transparent finishes are planned. The compatibility of finishes should be tested before they are applied.

### FIRE RETARDANT PANEL PRODUCTS

- **Core** - The flame spread rating of the core material determines the rating of the assembled panel. Fire-retardant veneered panels must have a fire-retardant core. Particleboard core is available with a Class I (Class A) rating. Veneer core and MDF (Medium Density Fiberboard) cores are available with a flame spread rating in some markets.

- **Face** - The International Codes, except where locally amended, provide that facing materials less than 0.036" (0.9mm) or thinner and applied directly to the surface of the walls or ceilings are not required to be tested.

  If a Class I (Class A) panel assembly is specified with a decorative laminate face, the decorative laminate and the laminate balancing sheet must be applied to a Class I (Class A) core material, with the laminate manufacturer's recommended adhesive. It is the responsibility of the specifier to indicate what flame spread rating, if any, is required for the paneling. In the absence of such a specified rating, the manufacturer shall supply un-rated paneling.

# SECTION 8
## Wall/Ceiling Surfacing and Partitions

## introductory information

### EDGEBANDING EXAMPLES

Veneer edgebanded:

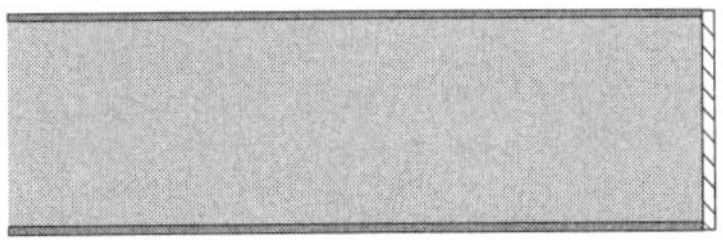

*Figure: 8-010*

Inset Solid Wood edgebanding:

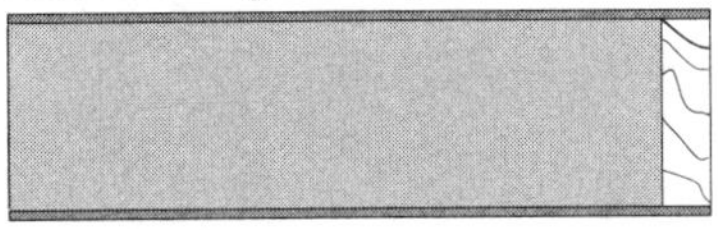

*Figure: 8-011*

Applied Solid Wood with corner joint options:

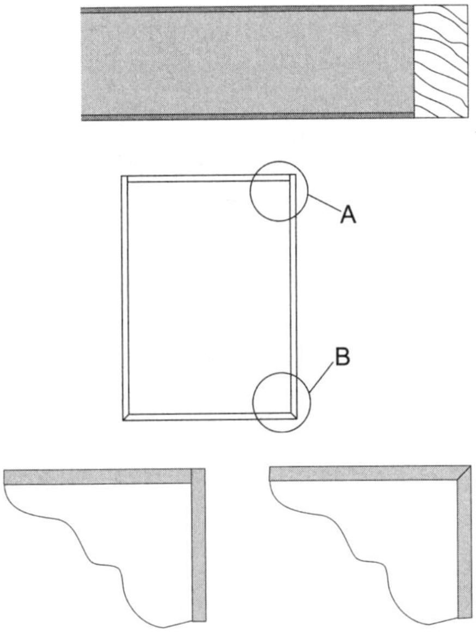

A
B

A - Lapped
B - Mitered

*Figure: 8-012*

For durability, the bottom edge of wall surfacing is edgebanded.

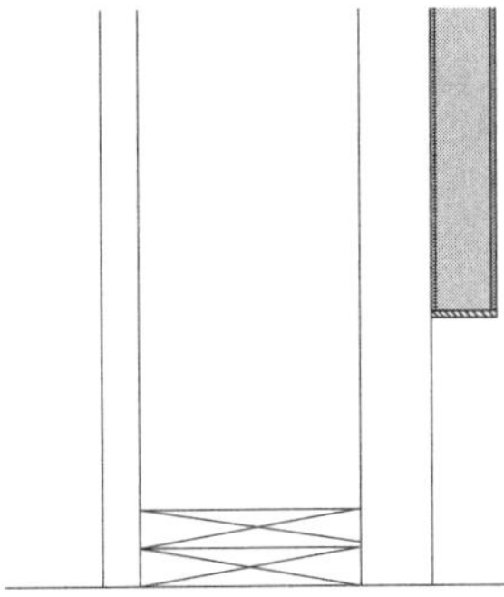

*Figure: 8-013*

### FIELD-CUT CORNER and TRANSITION EXAMPLES

Butt - Outside Corner

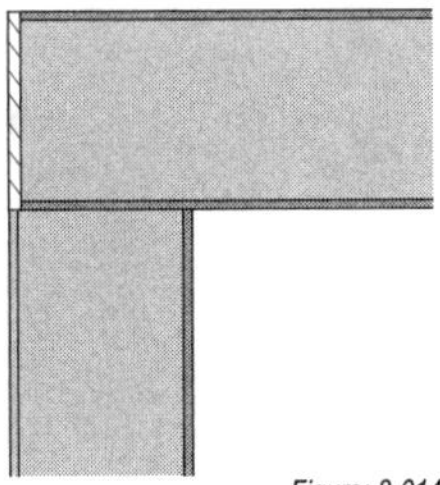

*Figure: 8-014*

Mitered - Outside Corner

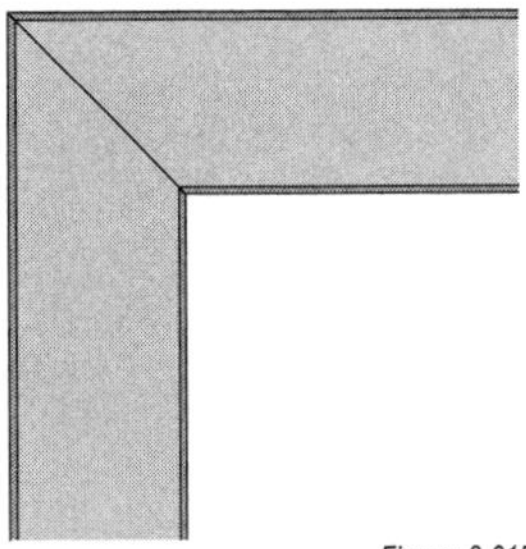

*Figure: 8-015*

Solid Wood - Outside Corner

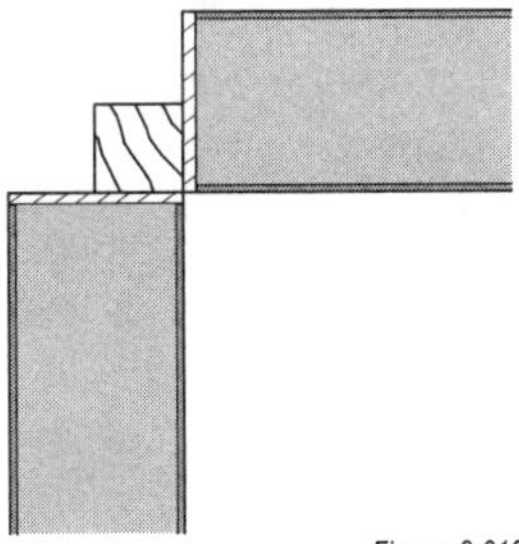

*Figure: 8-016*

Butt - Inside Corner

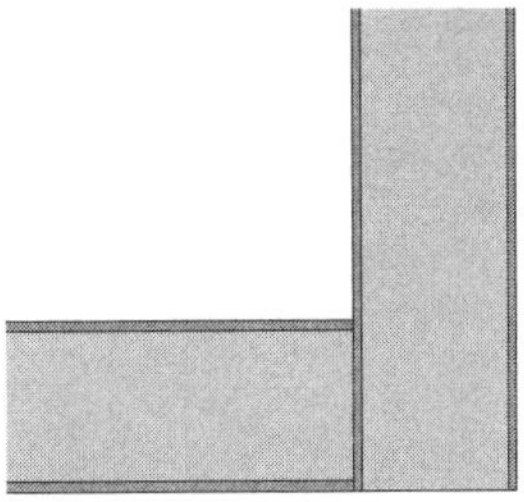

*Figure: 8-017*

Non-reveal - Transition

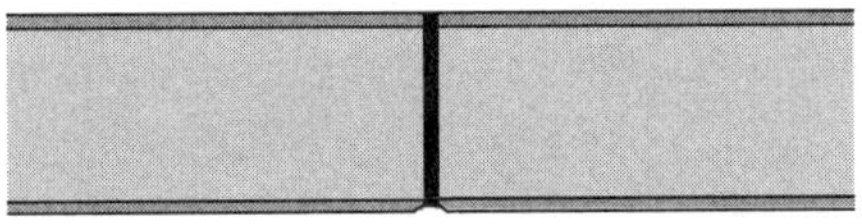

*Figure: 8-018*

### REVEALS and REVEAL JOINT EXAMPLES

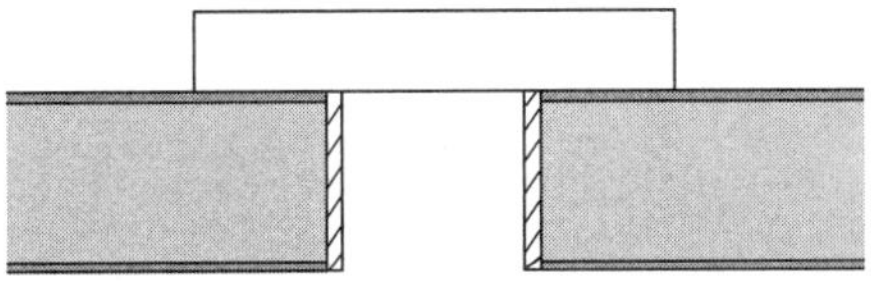

*Figure: 8-019*

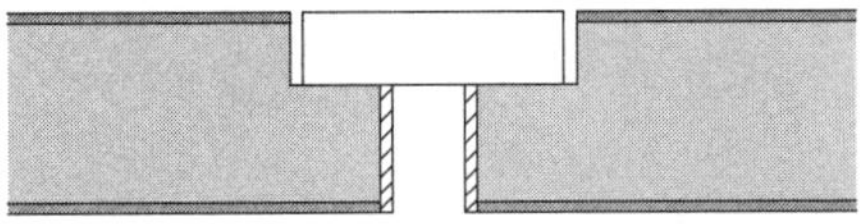

*Figure: 8-020*

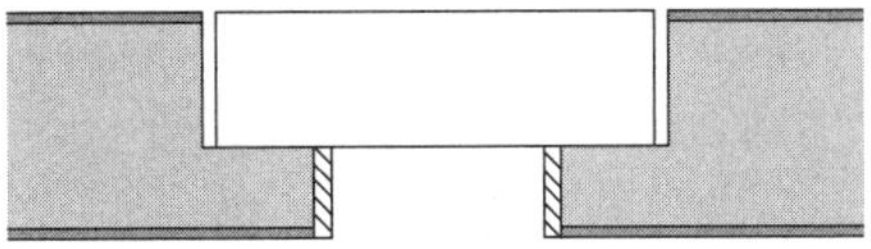

*Figure: 8-021*

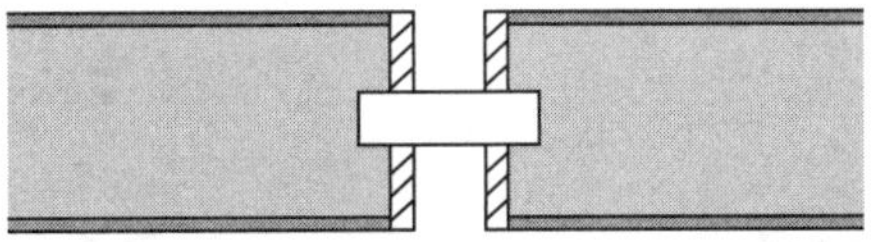

*Figure: 8-022*

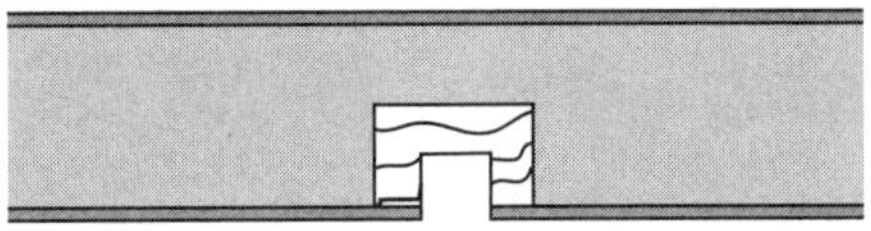

*Figure: 8-023*

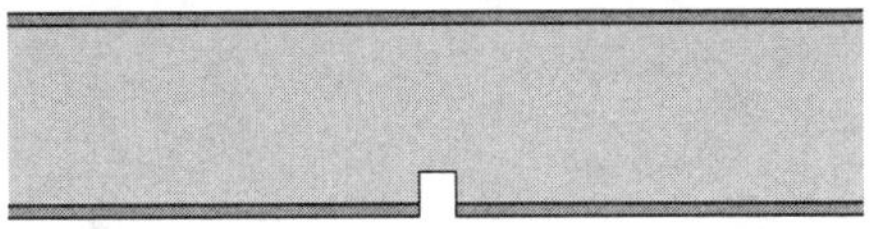

*Figure: 8-024*

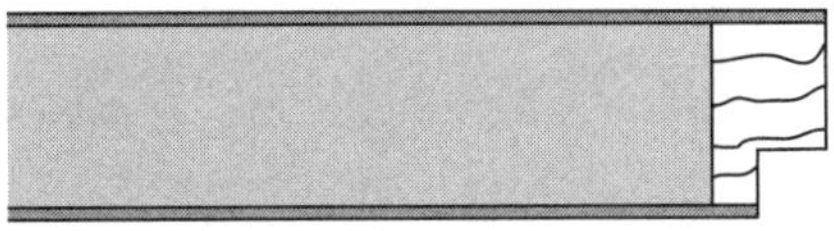

*Figure: 8-025*

To **PREVENT TELEGRAPHING**, inset solid wood edging when used must have similar moisture content as panel core, be glued securely and calibrated with panel core thickness prior to being laminated with a wood veneer on both faces.

# SECTION 8
Wall/Ceiling Surfacing and Partitions

## introductory information

**REVEALS and REVEAL JOINT** (continued)

**FACTORY-PREPARED CORNER and TRANSITION EXAMPLES**

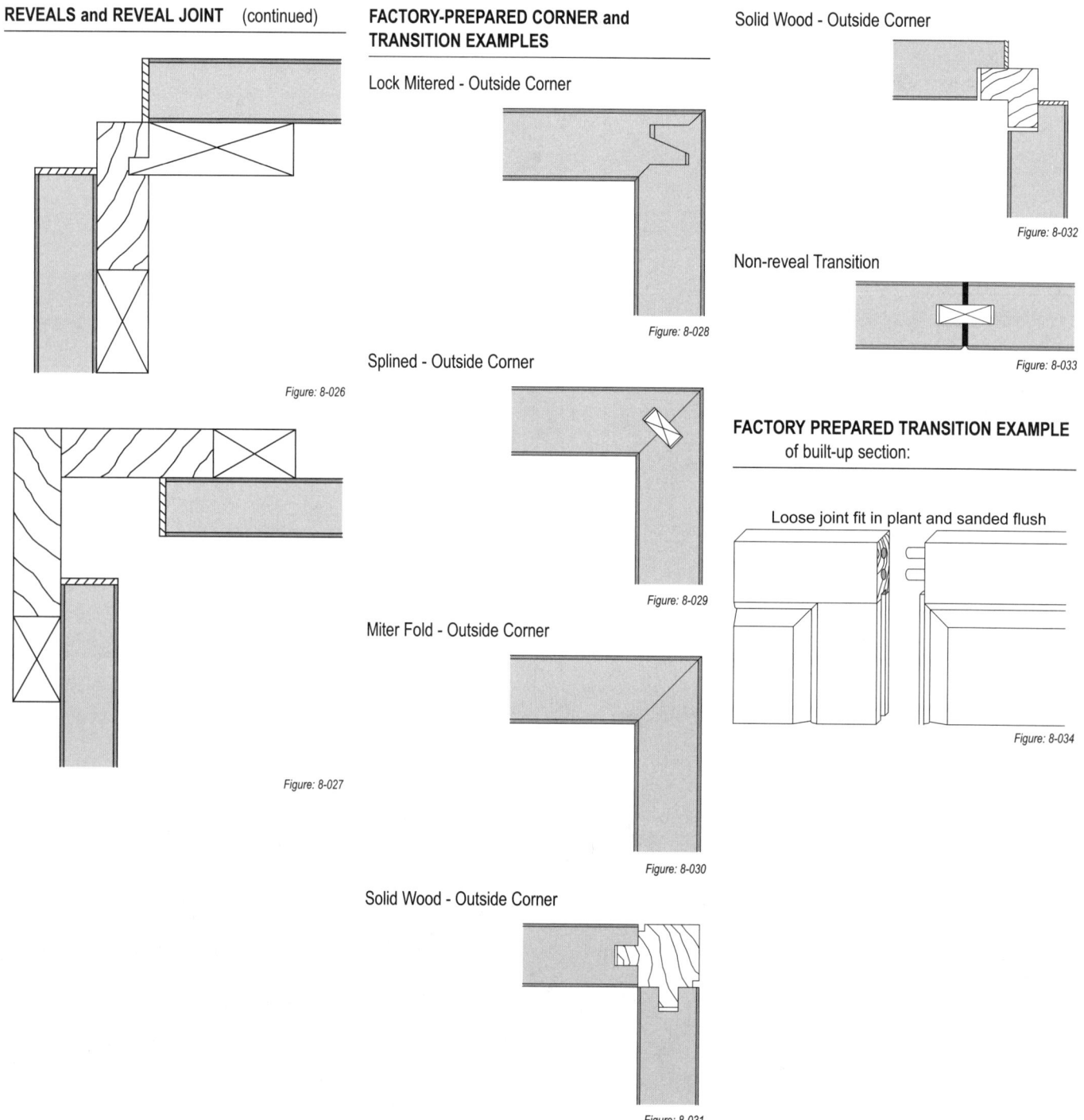

Lock Mitered - Outside Corner
Figure: 8-028

Splined - Outside Corner
Figure: 8-029

Miter Fold - Outside Corner
Figure: 8-030

Solid Wood - Outside Corner
Figure: 8-031

Solid Wood - Outside Corner
Figure: 8-032

Non-reveal Transition
Figure: 8-033

**FACTORY PREPARED TRANSITION EXAMPLE**
of built-up section:

Loose joint fit in plant and sanded flush
Figure: 8-034

Figure: 8-026

Figure: 8-027

# SECTION 8
## Wall/Ceiling Surfacing and Partitions

# introductory information

### STILE and RAIL PANELING

Flat or raised panels with wood veneer faces or of solid lumber, combined with stiles and rails. Design may encompass face application of mouldings. Joints between panels, stiles, rails, and other members to be as designed for functional or decorative purposes.

### EXAMPLES of WALL PANELS WITH MILLWORK

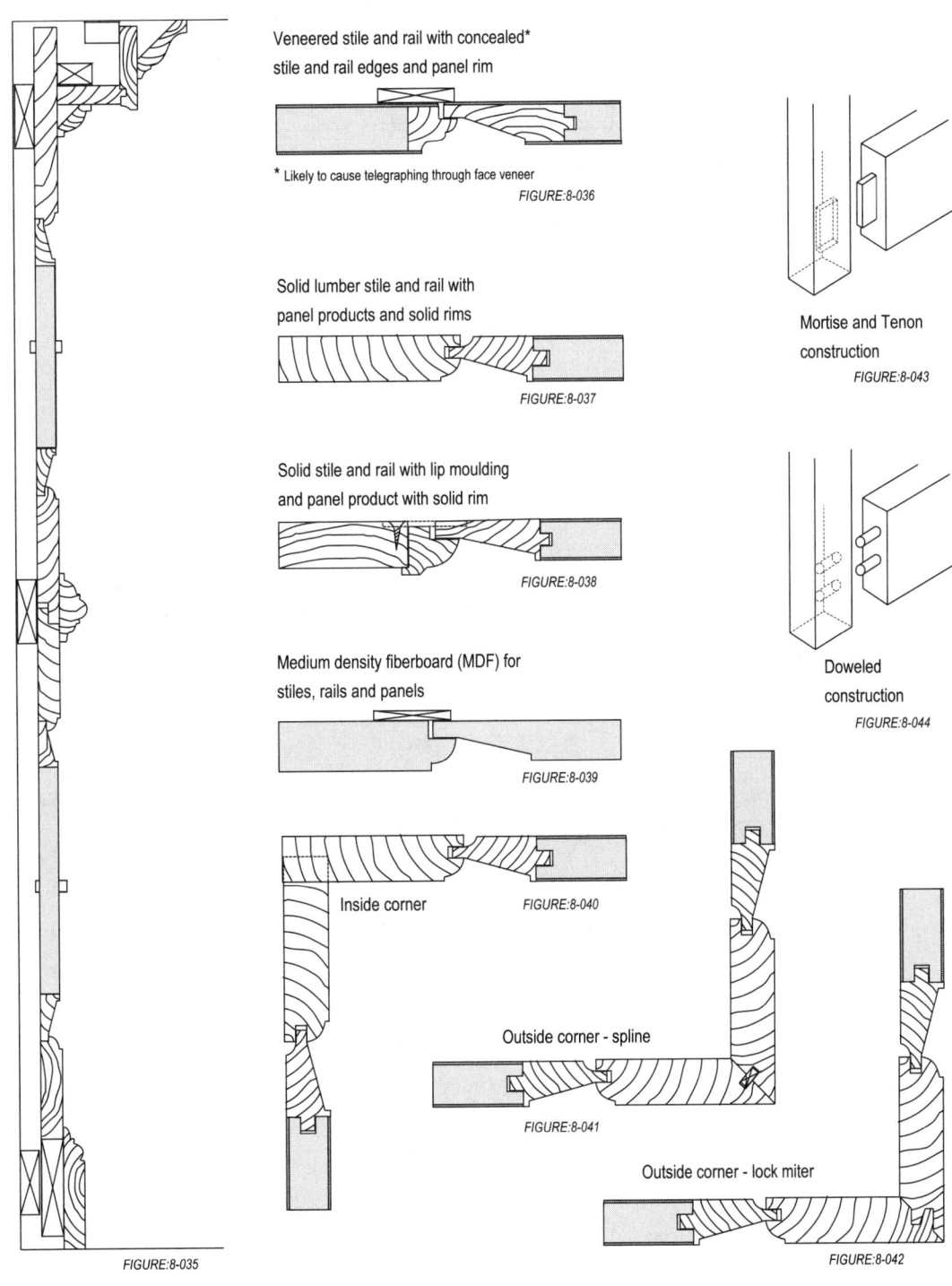

Veneered stile and rail with concealed* stile and rail edges and panel rim
*Likely to cause telegraphing through face veneer*
FIGURE: 8-036

Solid lumber stile and rail with panel products and solid rims
FIGURE: 8-037

Solid stile and rail with lip moulding and panel product with solid rim
FIGURE: 8-038

Medium density fiberboard (MDF) for stiles, rails and panels
FIGURE: 8-039

Inside corner
FIGURE: 8-040

Outside corner - spline
FIGURE: 8-041

Outside corner - lock miter
FIGURE: 8-042

Mortise and Tenon construction
FIGURE: 8-043

Doweled construction
FIGURE: 8-044

FIGURE: 8-035

# SECTION 8
## Wall/Ceiling Surfacing and Partitions

### introductory information

**EXAMPLES of STILE and RAIL PANELING**

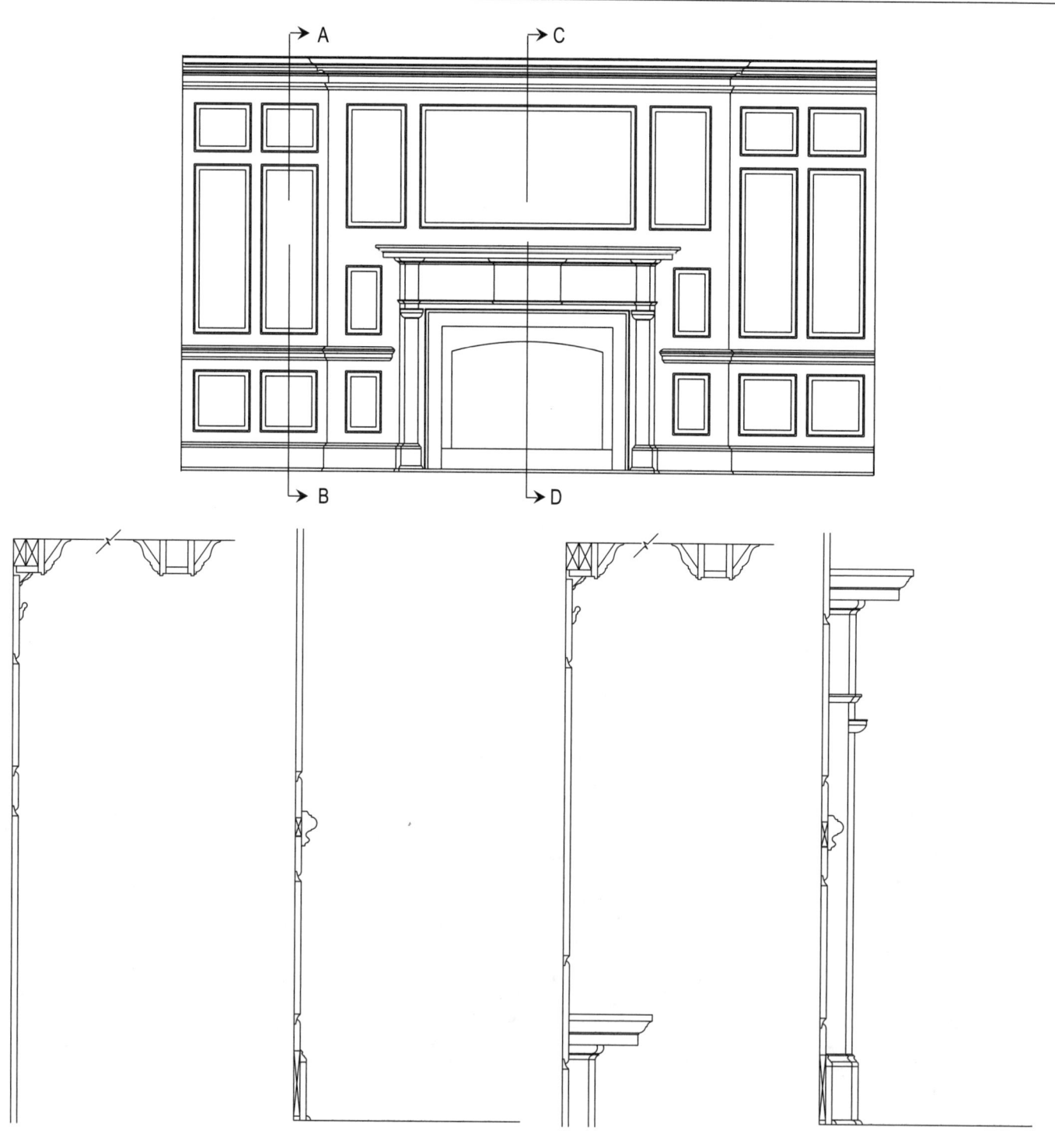

Section A   Section B   Section C   Section D

*Figure: 8-045*

# SECTION 8
## Wall/Ceiling Surfacing and Partitions

## introductory information

**EXAMPLE of FLAT PANELING WITH REVEALS WITHIN A NICHE**

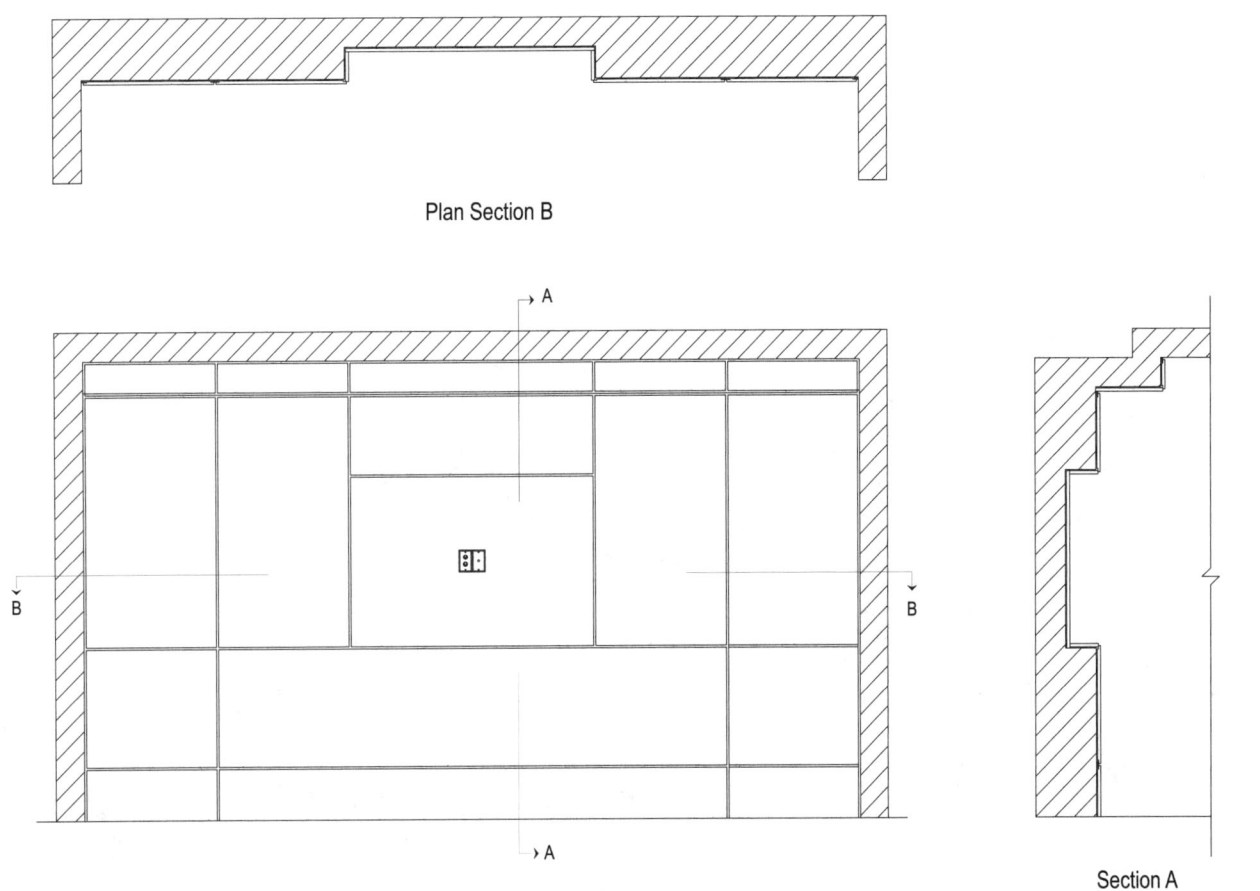

Plan Section B

Section A

*Figure: 8-046*

# SECTION 8
Wall/Ceiling Surfacing and Partitions

## introductory information

**EXAMPLE of PANELING FOR RECEPTION WALLS WITH FACTORY BUILT STRUCTURES**

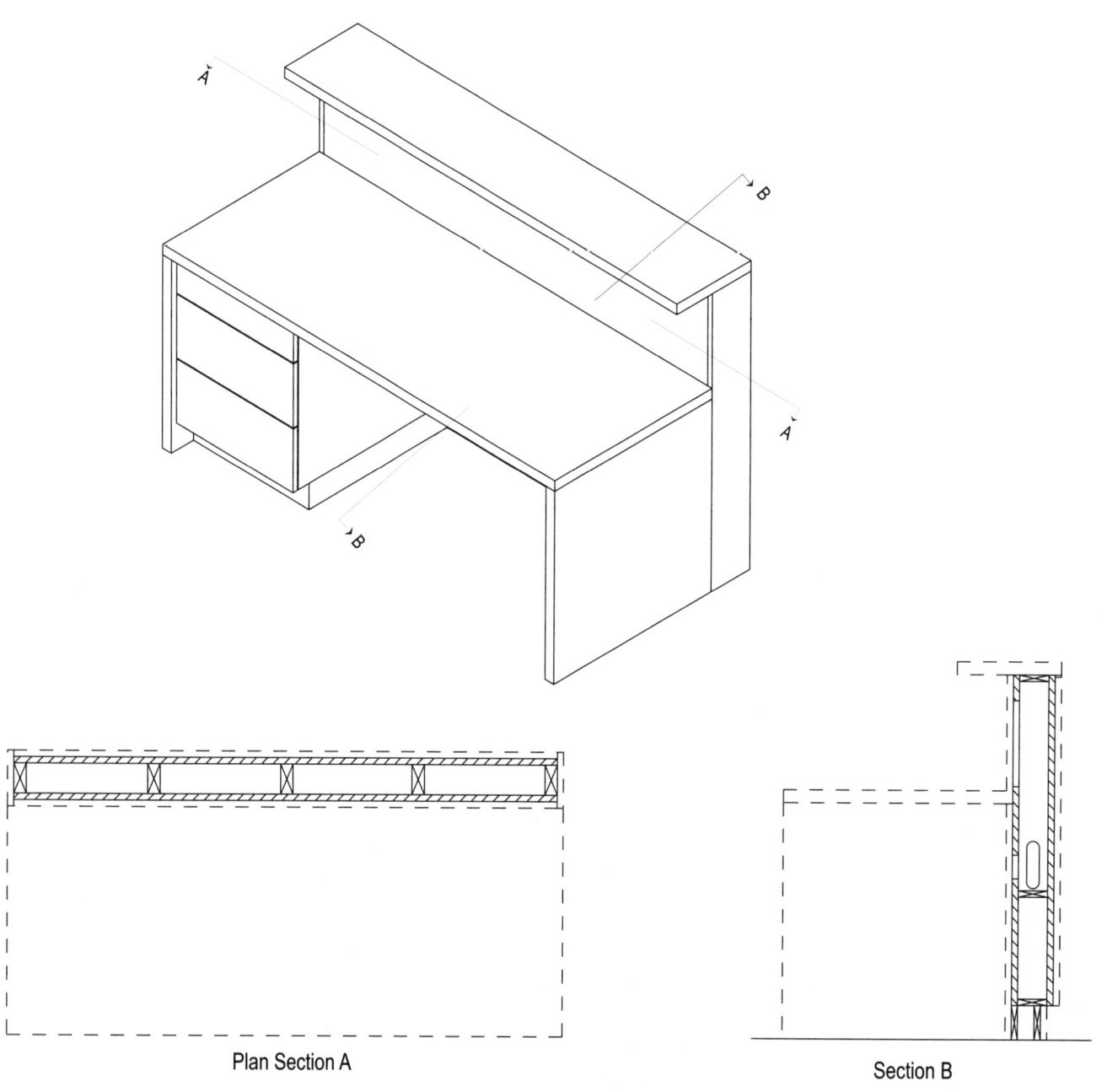

Plan Section A

Section B

Figure: 8-047

# SECTION 8
## Wall/Ceiling Surfacing and Partitions

## introductory information

### SPECIFY REQUIREMENTS FOR

- Flame spread ratings.
- Special code compliance.
- Special molding profile.
- **WOOD VENEER**
  - Species of veneer.
  - Method of slicing (plain, quarter, rotary, or rift).
  - Matching of veneer leaves (book, slip, or random) and veneer leaves within a panel face (running, balance, or center-balanced).
  - Sequence of adjacent panels (non-sequenced, sequenced, or blueprint panels and components) and end-matching.
  - Grain direction, if other than vertical.
  - For selected flitches, the sources, gross footage of flitches, and cost per square foot.
  - Special figure, which is not a function of a species grade, must be specified.
- **SOLID WOOD**
  - Species of wood.
  - Method of cutting (plain, quarter or rift).
  - Grain direction, if other than vertical.
  - Special figure, which is not a function of a species grade, must be specified.
- **LAMINATE, SOLID SURFACE** and **SOLID PHENOLIC**
  - Manufacturer.
  - Pattern or Color.
  - Sheen.
  - Special pattern direction - with lack of specification, pattern direction will be vertical at panels and optional at joints.

### RECOMMENDATIONS

- If **FIELD FINISHED,** include in Division 09 of the specifications:
  - **BEFORE FINISHING**, exposed portions of woodwork shall have handling marks or effects of exposure to moisture, removed with a thorough, final sanding over all surfaces of the exposed portions and shall be cleaned before applying sealer or finish.
  - At **CONCEALED SURFACES** - Architectural woodwork that may be exposed to moisture, such as those adjacent to exterior concrete walls, etc., shall be primed.
- **REVIEW** the GENERAL portion of Sections 3 and 4 for an overview of the characteristics and the minimum acceptable requirements of lumber and/or sheet products that might be used herein.
- **STRUCTURAL MEMBERS**, grounds, in wall blocking, backing, furring, brackets, or other anchorage which becomes an integral part of the building's walls, floors, or ceilings, required for the installation of architectural woodwork are not to be furnished or installed by the architectural woodwork manufacturer or installer.
- **COMPOSITE CORES** (e.g., particleboard, medium-density fiberboard, agrifiber, or combination core products) are recommended in lieu of veneer core, because these cores produce a smoother exposed face, vary less in thickness, and are less likely to warp.
- **SOLID SURFACE**
  - Coordinate material applications within the manufacturer's guidelines.
  - Use of the same batch of materials is important at adjacent sheets to lessen color variations.
  - Thicknesses are nominal and may be a fabrication concern where thickness is critical.
- **SOLID PHENOLIC** performs well in high moisture and heavy use applications**.**

# SECTION 8
## Wall/Ceiling Surfacing and Partitions

GENERAL/PRODUCT/INSTALLATION/TEST

**compliance requirements**

Where the **E**, **C**, or **P** icon is not indicated, the rule applies to all Grades equally | E | C | P |

## Including Wood Veneer, Solid Wood, Stile and Rail Wood, Decorative Laminate, Solid Surface and Solid Phenolic Wall/Ceiling Surfacing and Partition Products

### 8.1 BASIC CONSIDERATIONS

**1 GRADE**

1.1 These standards are characterized in three Grades of quality that might be mixed within a single project. Limitless design possibilities and a wide variety of lumber and veneer species, along with overlays, high-pressure decorative laminates, factory finishes, and profiles are available in all three Grades.

1.2 **ECONOMY GRADE** defines the minimum quality requirements for a project's workmanship, materials, or installation and is typically reserved for woodwork that is not in public view, such as in mechanical rooms and utility areas.

1.3 **CUSTOM GRADE** is typically specified for and adequately covers most high-quality architectural woodwork, providing a well-defined degree of control over a project's quality of materials, workmanship, or installation.

1.4 **PREMIUM GRADE** is typically specified for use in those areas of a project where the highest level of quality, materials, workmanship, and installation is required.

1.5 **GRADE LIMITATIONS**

1.5.1 **SOLID SURFACE** wall surfacing is only defined in Custom and Premium Grade.

1.5.2 **SOLID PHENOLIC CORE** wall surfacing is only defined in Premium Grade.

**2 CONTRACT DOCUMENTS** shall govern if in conflict with these standards.

**3 ACCEPTABLE REQUIREMENTS** of lumber and/or sheet products used within this woodwork product section are established by Sections 3 and 4, unless otherwise modified herein.

**4 AESTHETIC COMPLIANCE REQUIREMENTS** apply only to surfaces visible after fabrication and installation.

**5 EXPOSED SURFACES**

5.1 All visible surfaces of architectural wall surfacing.

### 8.1 BASIC CONSIDERATIONS (continued)

**6 CONCEALED SURFACES**

6.1 All non-visible surfaces attached to and/or covered by another.

6.2 All non-visible blocking or spacers used for attachment.

**7** When **SOLID SURFACE** is referenced in these standards, it refers to filled cast polymeric resin panels per Section 4.

**8** When **SOLID PHENOLIC** (compact laminate) is referenced in these standards, it refers to panels of melamine impregnated decorative sheets over kraft phenolic core sheets per Section 4.

**9** Use of **HPDL-BACKED WOOD VENEERS** is permitted, if so specified or otherwise approved.

**10** Use of **CONTINUOUS PRESSURE LAMINATES** (melamine and polyester-based) as an alternative to HPDL is permitted, provided they conform to the same physical properties and thickness as required for HPDL.

**11 FURRING**, when required, shall be in accordance with the International Building Code (IBC), National Building Code of Canada (NBC)/or regional building code.

**12 BLEACHED VENEERS** may cause finishing problems and are not recommended.

**13 HIGH-GLOSS HPDL** may telegraph minor core and surface imperfections and are not recommended.

**14** To **PREVENT TELEGRAPHING**, inset solid wood edging when used must have similar moisture content as panel core, be glued securely and calibrated with panel core thickness prior to being laminated with a wood veneer on both faces.

**15 INDUSTRY PRACTICES**

15.1 **STRUCTURAL MEMBERS**, grounds, in wall blocking, backing, furring, brackets, or other anchorage that are an integral part of the building's walls, floors, or ceilings, that are required for the installation of architectural woodwork are not furnished or installed by the architectural woodwork manufacturer or installer.

15.2 **WALL, CEILING** and **OPENING** variations in excess of 1/4" (6.4 mm) or **FLOORS** in excess of 1/2" (12.7 mm) in 144" (3658 mm) of being plumb, level, flat, straight, square, or of the correct size are not acceptable for the installation of architectural woodwork, nor is it the responsibility of the installer to scribe or fit to tolerances in excess of such.

## SECTION 8
### Wall/Ceiling Surfacing and Partitions
**GENERAL**/PRODUCT/INSTALLATION/TEST

### 8.1 BASIC CONSIDERATIONS (continued)

**15 INDUSTRY PRACTICES** (continued)

15.3 **PRIMING** of architectural woodwork is not the responsibility of the manufacturer and/or installer, unless the material is being furnished prefinished.

15.4 **RADIUS MOLDINGS** are laminated and formed, preshaped, or machined to the radius and fabricated in the longest practical lengths to minimize field joints.

15.5 **WAINSCOT** is defined as being 48" (1219 mm) or less in height above the finished floor.

15.6 **WALL SURFACING** with a defined grain and/or pattern is installed vertically.

# SECTION 8
## Wall/Ceiling Surfacing and Partitions

GENERAL / **PRODUCT** / INSTALLATION / TEST

Where the **E**, **C**, or **P** icon is not indicated, the rule applies to all Grades equally | **E** | **C** | **P** |

## compliance requirements

### 8.2 SCOPE

1. All decorative, solid or veneered wood, laminated plastic, solid phenolic composite and solid surface for architectural:
   1.1 Wall Surfacing.
   1.2 Ceiling Surfacing.
   1.3 Partitions.

2. **TYPICAL INCLUSIONS:**
   2.1 All decorative, solid or veneered wood, laminated plastic, solid phenolic composite and solid surface wall and ceiling surfacing.
   2.2 All decorative, solid or veneered wood, laminated plastic, solid phenolic composite and solid surface partitions.
   2.3 All doors required to be blueprint matched to wood paneling, not specified otherwise, and:
   2.3.1 If doors are specified to be furnished by others, the paneling supplier shall control matching.
   2.4 If installed, furring, in wall blocking, shims, and methods of attachment from the face of the wall and ceiling out.
   2.5 All exposed decorative solid phenolic composite wall and ceiling surface.
   2.6 Class I Flame Spread Rated HPDL wall and ceiling surfacing assembly.
   2.7 Class I Flame Spread Rated veneered wood wall and ceiling surfacing assembly.

3. **TYPICAL EXCLUSIONS:**
   3.1 Non climate controlled interior or exterior architectural wall and ceiling surfacing.
   3.2 Casework soffits, fascia or filler panels.
   3.3 Room, closet, or access doors, unless sequence matched and blueprint matched with paneling.
   3.4 Any bucks or grounds.
   3.5 Composition or plaster wallboards or coverings.
   3.6 Site built framing or sheathing.
   3.7 Exposed base other than wood, decorative laminate, or solid surface.
   3.8 Fabric wrapped and/or acoustic panels or partitions.

### 8.3 DEFAULT STIPULATION

1. **IF NO FINISH IS SPECIFIED, THE DEFAULT STIPULATION FOR OPAQUE FINISH APPLIES:**
   1.1 **WOOD SURFACING AT OPAQUE FINISH** - unless otherwise specified or detailed, work shall be **CUSTOM GRADE,** panels shall be Medium Density Fiberboard and where details show solid wood components, shall be close grain hardwood.
   1.2 **WOOD SURFACING AT TRANSPARENT FINISH** - unless otherwise specified or detailed, work shall be **CUSTOM GRADE**, panels shall be plain sliced hardwood veneer and where details show solid wood components, shall be plain sawn hardwood.

2. **DECORATIVE LAMINATE SURFACING** - unless otherwise specified or detailed, work shall be **CUSTOM GRADE** with retention moldings at field joints. Colors to be selected from non premium priced standard patterns and texture.

3. **SOLID SURFACE SURFACING** - unless otherwise specified or detailed, work shall be **CUSTOM GRADE**, 1/4" (6.4 mm) minimum thickness, directly applied, with 1/4" x 1" (6.4 mm x 25.4 mm) trim bats at vertical butt joints on continuous horizontal runs. Colors to be selected from non premium priced standard patterns.

4. **SOLID PHENOLIC SURFACING** - unless otherwise specified or detailed, work shall be **PREMIUM GRADE**, 1/8" (3 mm) minimum thickness with 1/8" x 1" (3 mm x 25 mm) battens at vertical joints on continuous horizontal runs. Colors to be selected from the manufacturer's standard patterns and colors.

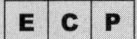 Where the **E**, **C**, or **P** icon is not indicated, the rule applies to all Grades equally

# SECTION 8
## Wall/Ceiling Surfacing and Partitions

## compliance requirements

GENERAL/**PRODUCT**/INSTALLATION/TEST

### 8.4 RULES

1. The following rules shall govern unless a project's contract documents require otherwise.
2. These rules are intended to provide a well defined degree of control over a project's quality of materials and workmanship.
3. **ERRATA**, published on the Sponsor Associations' websites at www.awinet.org, www.awmac.com, or www.aws-errata.com, shall **TAKE PRECEDENCE OVER THESE RULES**, subject to their date of posting and a project's bid date.

### 8.4.4 Basic Rules

1. **AESTHETIC** grade rules apply only to the faces visible after installation.
2. **LUMBER** shall conform to the requirements established in Section 3.
3. **SHEET PRODUCTS** shall conform to the requirements established in Section 4.
4. **BACKING SHEET** shall conform to the requirements established in Section 4.
5. **EXPOSED SURFACES** include:
   1. All visible surfaces of wall and ceiling surfacing.
6. **CONCEALED SURFACES** include:
   1. All non visible surfaces attached to and/or covered by another.
   2. All non visible blocking or spacers used for attachment.
7. **FURRING** shall be used as required, and:
   1. It shall be in accordance with applicable codes and regulations for maximum thickness, fire blocking, and void fills.
8. **DEFINED GRAIN** and/or **PATTERN** of wall surfacing shall be installed with the grain or pattern direction running vertically.
9. **WAINSCOT** shall be 48" (1219 mm) or less in height above the finished floor.
10. **MULTIPLE OPTIONS**, when permitted, shall be the manufacturer's choice.
11. **FLAME SPREAD RATING** requirements shall be specified.

Continues next column ▼

### 8.4.4 Basic Rules

▲ From previous column

12. **SPECIFIC PROFILE**, if required, shall be specified or drawn.
13. For **TRANSPARENT FINISHED WOOD**, if the species is not specified, use of hardwood or softwood (panel product or solid stock) of one species for the entire project is permitted.
14. Where **GLUING** or **LAMINATION** occurs:
    1. Delamination or separation shall not occur beyond that which is allowed in Sections 3 & 4.
    2. Use of **CONTACT ADHESIVE** is not permitted unless otherwise indicated, and:
       1. Complies with the Heat Resistance Test listed in the **APPENDIX**.
       2. Is not allowed at non phenolic backed wood veneer applications.
    3. **HOT MELT APPLIED HPDL** edgebanding shall be primed before application for proper adhesion, unless:
       1. Hot melt adhesive has been especially formulated for the primer less application of **HPDL**.
15. **CUT OUTS** require:
    1. At **SOLID SURFACE** or **HPDL** exposed surfaces have a minimum 1/4" (6.4 mm) radius at inside corners.
16. **CATHEDRAL** type figure shall be achieved by:
    1. A single component in "AA" Face Grade.
    2. The split heart method in Face Grades "A - D", and:
       1. Each half of a split heart shall be subject to the minimum component width requirements for Face Grade "B."
17. **SINGLE SOURCE** is required at blueprint matched doors and panels.
18. **FIRST CLASS WORKMANSHIP** is required in compliance with these standards.

# SECTION 8
## Wall/Ceiling Surfacing and Partitions

GENERAL/**PRODUCT**/INSTALLATION/TEST

**compliance requirements**

Where the **E**, **C**, or **P** icon is not indicated, the rule applies to all Grades equally | E | C | P |

### 8.4.5 Material Rules

| | | | | | |
|---|---|---|---|---|---|
| 1 | | | **LUMBER, VENEERED PROFILE** or **SHEET PRODUCTS** shall be of the species and Grade specified, and: | | |
| 1 | 1 | | Shall not have defects, either natural or manufactured, that exceed those permitted. | | |
| 1 | 2 | | **NATURAL** and **MANUFACTURED DEFECTS** are permitted, if covered by adjoining members or otherwise concealed when installed. | | |
| 1 | 3 | | **FIGURE** is not a function of a species grade and must be specified in the contract document. | | |
| 1 | 4 | | **PERMITS WARP** that can be held flat and straight with methods described in the Installation portion of this Section. | | |
| 5 | | | **PARTITION CORES** of particleboard or medium density fiberboard (MDF) of: | | |
| 5 | 1 | | Up to and including 48" (1219mm) in width or 84" (2137mm) in height shall be a minimum 11/16" (17.5mm) in thickness. | | |
| 5 | 2 | | Over 48" (1219mm) in width or 84" (2137mm) in height shall be a minimum 1" (25.4mm) in thickness. | | |
| 5 | 3 | | Partition doors up to and including 36" (914mm) in width or 72" (1829mm) in height shall be a minimum 11/16" (17.5mm) in thickness. | | |
| 5 | 4 | | Partition doors over 36" (914mm) in width or 72" (1829mm) in height shall be a minimum 1" (25.4mm) in thickness. | | |
| 6 | | | For **OPAQUE FINISH**: | | |
| 6 | 1 | | Medium density fiberboard (MDF) is permitted. | | |
| 6 | 2 | | Veneer is permitted; however: | | |
| 6 | 2 | 1 | **SPECIES** of manufacturer's choice, closed grain hardwood conforming to ANSI/HPHA HP-1 (latest Edition) definitions and characteristics for: | | |
| 6 | 2 | 1 | 1 Grade - **D** | E | C | P |
| 6 | 2 | 1 | 2 Grade - **C** | E | C | P |
| 6 | 2 | 1 | 3 Grade - **B** | E | C | P |
| 7 | | | For **TRANSPARENT FINISH, VENEER**: | | |
| 7 | 1 | | **SPECIES** of manufacturer's choice, hardwood conforming to ANSI/HPHA HP-1 (latest Edition) definitions and characteristics for: | | |
| 7 | 1 | 1 | Grade - **B** | E | C | P |
| 7 | 1 | 2 | Grade - **A** | E | C | P |
| 7 | 1 | 3 | Grade - **AA** | E | C | P |
| 7 | 2 | | **SLICING** of: | | |
| 7 | 2 | 1 | Manufacturer's choice. | E | C | P |
| 7 | 2 | 2 | Plain sliced. | E | C | P |

*Continues next column*

### 8.4.5 Material Rules

*From previous column*

| | | | | | | |
|---|---|---|---|---|---|---|
| 7 | | | For **TRANSPARENT FINISH, VENEER**  (continued) | | | |
| 7 | 3 | | **MATCHING AT ADJACENT LEAVES** shall be: | | | |
| 7 | 3 | 1 | Manufacturer's choice. | E | C | P |
| 7 | 3 | 2 | Book matching. | E | C | P |
| 7 | 4 | | **MATCHING WITHIN PANEL FACE** shall be: | | | |
| 7 | 4 | 1 | Running match. | E | C | P |
| 7 | 4 | 2 | Balance match. | E | C | P |
| 7 | 5 | | At **ADJACENT PANELS** shall be: | | | |
| 7 | 5 | 1 | Sequenced | | | |
| 7 | 5 | 2 | Specified when end matching, made to order sequence sets and blueprint sequencing is required. | E | C | P |
| 8 | | | **EXPOSED SURFACES**: | | | |
| 8 | 1 | | Requires end grain to be kept to a minimum. | E | C | P |
| 8 | 2 | | Requires no end grain showing. | E | C | P |
| 8 | 3 | | Permits medium density fiberboard (MDF) for opaque finish. | | | |
| 8 | 4 | | For **TRANSPARENT FINISH**: | | | |
| 8 | 4 | 1 | Permits hardwood or softwood. | | | |
| 8 | 4 | 2 | Permits only one species for the entire project. | E | C | P |
| 8 | 4 | 3 | Requires adjacent veneer and lumber to be: | | | |
| 8 | 4 | 3 | 1 Manufacturers' choice species. | E | C | P |
| 8 | 4 | 3 | 2 Compatible for color and grain. | E | C | P |
| 8 | 4 | 3 | 3 Well matched for color and grain. | E | C | P |
| 9 | | | **CONCEALED SURFACES**: | | | |
| 9 | 1 | | Permits defects such as voids, wane, or unfilled knots. | | | |
| 9 | 2 | | Requires **STRUCTURAL FRAMING MEMBERS** for items such as reception desk walls, die walls, podiums, benches, partitions etc., to be veneer core plywood, hardwood lumber, particleboard, MDF or SCL. | | | |
| 10 | | | **WOOD VENEER**: | | | |
| 10 | 1 | | Requires **CORES** of particleboard or medium density fiberboard (MDF) to be: | | | |
| 10 | 1 | 1 | A minimum of 1/4" (6.4 mm) in thickness. | E | C | P |
| 10 | 1 | 2 | A minimum of 7/16" (11.1 mm) in thickness. | E | C | P |
| 10 | 1 | 3 | A minimum of 11/16" (17.5 mm) in thickness. | E | C | P |

*Continues next column*

# SECTION 8
## Wall/Ceiling Surfacing and Partitions

**GENERAL / PRODUCT / INSTALLATION / TEST**

Where the **E**, **C**, or **P** icon is not indicated, the rule applies to all Grades equally

## compliance requirements

### 8.4.5 Material Rules

▲ From previous column

**10 WOOD VENEER** (continued)

| | | | | | Description | E | C | P |
|---|---|---|---|---|---|---|---|---|
| 10 | 2 | | | | **MATCHING**, such as book match and end match, slip match and end match, or special sketch faces, to be so specified and detailed. | | | |
| 10 | 3 | | | | For **OPAQUE** finish, face shall: | | | |
| 10 | 3 | 1 | | | **NOT** require the selection of color and/or grain. | | | |
| 10 | 3 | 2 | | | **PERMIT** the use of paint grade hardwood, medium density fiberboard (MDF), or medium density overlay (MDO), and: | | | |
| 10 | 3 | 2 | 1 | | If **MDF** is used, edgebanding is not required. | | | |
| 10 | 3 | 3 | | | Permit manufacturers' choice of veneer slicing. | | | |
| 10 | 3 | 4 | | | **NOT** require matching of veneer leaves. | | | |
| 10 | 3 | 5 | | | **NOT** require matching of adjacent panels. | | | |
| 10 | 3 | 6 | | | Have visible **REVEALS** and **SPLINES** that are: | | | |
| 10 | 3 | 6 | 1 | | Full length. | | | |
| 10 | 3 | 6 | 2 | | Manufacturers' choice of species. | | | |
| 10 | 3 | 7 | | | Have **EDGES**: | | | |
| 10 | 3 | 7 | 1 | | Filled and sanded. | E | C | P |
| 10 | 3 | 7 | 2 | | Edgebanded with close grain material, with: | E | C | P |
| 10 | 3 | 7 | 2 | 1 | **FINGER JOINTS** permitted. | E | C | P |
| 10 | 4 | | | | For **TRANSPARENT** finish, shall: | | | |
| 10 | 4 | 1 | | | Have **FACES** that are: | | | |
| 10 | 4 | 1 | 1 | | Between **ADJACENT PANELS** of: | | | |
| 10 | 4 | 1 | 1 | 1 | Manufacturers' choice. | E | C | P |
| 10 | 4 | 1 | 1 | 2 | Sequenced premanufactured sets. | E | C | P |
| 10 | 4 | 1 | 1 | 3 | Balance matched, sequenced premanufactured sets, except: | E | C | P |
| 10 | 4 | 1 | 1 | 3 | 1 At trimmed ends of sequenced panel sets | | | |
| 10 | 4 | 1 | 1 | 4 | Balance matched when required to be end matched. | E | C | P |
| 10 | 5 | | | | Have visible **EDGES**, **REVEALS**, and/or **SPLINES**, when appropriate, that are: | | | |
| 10 | 5 | 1 | | | Full length. | | | |
| 10 | 5 | 2 | | | **MANUFACTURERS'** choice. | E | C | P |
| 10 | 5 | 3 | | | **MATCH** species of panel face. | E | C | P |
| 10 | 5 | 4 | | | **COMPATIBLE** for color and grain. | E | C | P |
| 10 | 5 | 5 | | | **WELL MATCHED** for color and grain. | E | C | P |
| 10 | 5 | 6 | | | A minimum of 0.020" (0.5 mm) nominal thickness that precludes show through of core. | E | C | P |

Continues next column ▼

### 8.4.5 Material Rules

▲ From previous column

**10 WOOD VENEER** (continued)

| | | | | | Description | E | C | P |
|---|---|---|---|---|---|---|---|---|
| 10 | 5 | 7 | | | **WITHIN A PANEL**, shall have solid wood let into the core before the veneer is applied where the veneer is machined through, however: | E | C | P |
| 10 | 5 | 7 | 1 | | Reveals of 1/8" (3.2 mm) or less in width let into MDF to a maximum depth of one third of the core thickness do not require solid wood if finished same as exposed finish. | | | |
| 10 | 5 | 8 | | | Allows **FINGER JOINTS**: | | | |
| 10 | 5 | 8 | 1 | | At manufacturers' choice. | E | C | P |
| 10 | 5 | 8 | 2 | | One per 96" (2440 mm) of length. | E | C | P |
| 10 | 5 | 8 | 3 | | Not allowed. | E | C | P |
| 10 | 6 | | | | Does not permit **BLEED THROUGH** of adhesive at veneer joints that visually affects an applied finish. | | | |
| 10 | 7 | | | | At **FLAME SPREAD RATED** paneling: | | | |
| 10 | 7 | 1 | | | Shall be of the construction standard of the panel manufacturer and conform to the requirements of applicable labeling agencies. | | | |

**11 SOLID STILE** and **RAIL WOOD SURFACING** permits:

| | | | | | Description | E | C | P |
|---|---|---|---|---|---|---|---|---|
| 11 | 1 | | | | No adhesive bleed through at joints. | | | |
| 11 | 2 | | | | **LUMBER** be plain sawn only. | | | |
| 11 | 3 | | | | **VENEERED** sheet products that comply with those requirements spelled out for Veneered Wall Surfacing within this section. | | | |
| 11 | 4 | | | | At **OPAQUE** finish: | | | |
| 11 | 4 | 1 | | | Medium density fiberboard. | | | |
| 11 | 4 | 2 | | | Paint grade hardwood or softwood at manufacturer's choice. | E | C | P |
| 11 | 4 | 3 | | | Paint grade hardwood. | E | C | P |
| 11 | 4 | 4 | | | Finger joints. | E | C | P |
| 11 | 5 | | | | At **TRANSPARENT** finish, finger joints. | E | C | P |
| 11 | 6 | | | | **PANELS**: | | | |
| 11 | 6 | 1 | | | **SHALL BE** solid stock or veneered construction, at the manufacturer's choice. | | | |
| 11 | 6 | 2 | | | If **FLAT** shall be: | | | |
| 11 | 6 | 1 | 1 | | **SOLID WOOD**: | | | |
| 11 | 6 | 1 | 1 | 1 | Minimum 1/2" (12.7 mm) in thickness and maximum 23-3/4" (603 mm) across the grain in width. | E | C | P |
| 11 | 6 | 1 | 1 | 2 | Minimum 3/4" (19 mm) in thickness and maximum 13-3/4" (350 mm) across the grain in width. | E | C | P |
| 11 | 6 | 1 | 1 | 3 | Not permitted. | E | C | P |

Continues next column ▼

©2014 AWI | AWMAC | WI 2nd Edition, October 1, 2014
As may be updated by errata at awinet.org, awmac.com, or aws-errata.com

Architectural Woodwork Standards

# SECTION 8
## Wall/Ceiling Surfacing and Partitions

GENERAL / **PRODUCT** / INSTALLATION / TEST

**compliance requirements**

Where the **E**, **C**, or **P** icon is not indicated, the rule applies to all Grades equally | **E** | **C** | **P** |

### 8.4.5 Material Rules
▲ From previous column

| | | | | | | E | C | P |
|---|---|---|---|---|---|---|---|---|
| 11 | | | | **SOLID STILE** and **RAIL WOOD SURFACING** (continued) | | | | |
| 11 | 6 | | | **PANELS** (continued) | | | | |
| 11 | 6 | 2 | | If **FLAT** shall be (continued) | | | | |
| 11 | 6 | 2 | 2 | **SHEET PRODUCT:** | | | | |
| 11 | 6 | 2 | 2 | 1 | Minimum 1/4" (6.4 mm) in thickness. | E | C | P |
| 11 | 6 | 2 | 2 | 2 | Minimum 1/2" (12.7 mm) in thickness. | | C | P |
| 11 | 6 | 3 | | If **RAISED** shall be: | | | | |
| 11 | 6 | 3 | 1 | **SOLID WOOD:** | | | | |
| 11 | 6 | 3 | 1 | 1 | Permitted in any dimension. | E | C | P |
| 11 | 6 | 3 | 1 | 2 | Minimum 3/4" (19 mm) in thickness and maximum 13-3/4" (350 mm) across the grain in width. | E | C | |
| 11 | 6 | 3 | 1 | 3 | Not permitted. | | | P |
| 11 | 6 | 3 | 2 | **VENEERED STILES** and **RAILS** or **SHEET PRODUCT:** | | | | |
| 11 | 6 | 3 | 2 | 1 | Minimum 1/2" (12.7 mm) in thickness. | E | C | P |
| 11 | 6 | 3 | 2 | 2 | Minimum 11/16" (17.5 mm) in thickness. | | C | P |
| 11 | 6 | 4 | | **EDGES** of veneered constructed components shall: | | | | |
| 11 | 6 | 4 | 1 | Be veneer edgebanded with compatible species. | | E | C | P |
| 11 | 6 | 4 | 2 | Be veneer edgebanded with same species as face. | | E | C | P |
| 11 | 6 | 4 | 3 | Not require mitering at corners. | | | | |
| 12 | | | | **SOLID WOOD SURFACING** permits: | | | | |
| 12 | 1 | | | No adhesive bleed through. | | | | |
| 12 | 2 | | | At **OPAQUE** finish, use of: | | | | |
| 12 | 2 | 1 | | Medium Density Fiberboard (MDF). | | | | |
| 12 | 2 | 2 | | Paint grade hardwood or softwood at manufacturer's choice. | | E | C | P |
| 12 | 2 | 3 | | Paint grade hardwood. | | | C | P |
| 12 | 2 | 4 | | Finger joints. | | E | C | P |
| 12 | 3 | | | **TRANSPARENT** finish, finger joints. | | E | C | P |
| 13 | | | | **DECORATIVE LAMINATE** requires: | | | | |
| 13 | 1 | | | **CONFORMANCE** to NEMA LD -3 (latest edition). | | | | |
| 13 | 2 | | | Colors selected from non premium priced standard patterns and texture, and: | | | | |
| 13 | 2 | 1 | | No minimum thickness. | | E | C | P |
| 13 | 2 | 2 | | Minimum 0.028" (0.7 mm) in thickness. | | E | C | P |

Continues next column ▼

### 8.4.5 Material Rules
▲ From previous column

| | | | | | E | C | P |
|---|---|---|---|---|---|---|---|
| 13 | | | | **DECORATIVE LAMINATE** (continued) | | | |
| 13 | 3 | | | **ADJACENT SHEETS** be prematched by the manufacturer and/or installer to minimize color variation within the scope of the manufacturer's guarantee, and: | | | |
| 13 | 3 | 1 | | Be fabricated from the longest sheet lengths available. | | | |
| 13 | 4 | | | If **FLAME SPREAD RATED**, be Class I and: | | | |
| 13 | 4 | 1 | | Be applied with a rigid set, Class I flame spread rated adhesive. | | | |
| 13 | 5 | | | **PATTERNED** or **WOOD GRAIN:** | | | |
| 13 | 5 | 1 | | Shall **MATCH VERTICALLY**, provided the total height does not exceed the maximum length of the available sheet. | | | |
| 13 | 5 | 2 | | Is not required to **MATCH HORIZONTALLY**. | | | |
| 13 | 6 | | | **CORES** of particleboard or medium density fiberboard (MDF) shall be: | | | |
| 13 | 6 | 1 | | A minimum of 1/4" (6.4 mm) in thickness. | E | C | P |
| 13 | 6 | 2 | | A minimum of 7/16" (11.1 mm) in thickness. | | C | P |
| 13 | 6 | 3 | | A minimum of 11/16" (17.5 mm) in thickness. | | | P |
| 13 | 7 | | | **BACKING SHEET** shall be: | | | |
| 13 | 7 | 1 | | A minimum of 0.020" (0.5 mm) thickness conforming to NEMA LD-3 (latest edition) and: | | | |
| 13 | 7 | 1 | 1 | Applied to the backside of the core using the same adhesive as the face lamination. | | | |
| 13 | 7 | 2 | | When **FLAME SPREAD RATED**, a minimum of .028" (0.7 mm) HPDL, Class I Flame Spread Rated and: | | | |
| 13 | 7 | 2 | 1 | Applied with a rigid set, Class I Flame Spread Rated adhesive. | | | |
| 13 | 7 | 3 | | Shall be applied in the same machine or grain direction as the face laminate. | | | |
| 13 | 8 | | | **VISIBLE SPLINES** and **REVEALS** that are: | | | |
| 13 | 8 | 1 | | 1/4" (6.4 mm) or less in face dimension by depth require: | | | |
| 13 | 8 | 1 | 1 | MDF core. | | C | P |
| 13 | 8 | 1 | 2 | No treatment of sides or bottom. | E | C | |
| 13 | 8 | 1 | 3 | Edges and bottom painted to match face. | | C | P |
| 13 | 8 | 2 | | Greater than 1/4" (6.4 mm) in face dimension by depth require: | | | |
| 13 | 8 | 2 | 1 | Manufacturers' choice edgebanding or painting of edges and bottom to preclude show through of core. | E | C | P |
| 13 | 8 | 2 | 2 | Manufacturers' choice edgebanding or painting of bottom to preclude show through of core. | | | P |
| 13 | 8 | 2 | 3 | Matching edgeband of partial edges. | | | P |

Continues next column ▼

# SECTION 8
## Wall/Ceiling Surfacing and Partitions

GENERAL / **PRODUCT** / INSTALLATION / TEST

### 8.4.5 Material Rules

▲ From previous column

| | | | | | |
|---|---|---|---|---|---|
| 13 | | DECORATIVE LAMINATE (continued) | | | |
| 13 | 9 | EDGEBANDING of square edged panel parts: | | | |
| 13 | 9 | 1 | Is required at exposed vertical and horizontal edges. | | |
| 13 | 9 | 2 | Shall be color matched to the exposed face. | | |
| 13 | 9 | 3 | Shall be HPDL or PVC, a minimum of 0.018" (0.5 mm) in thickness. | | |
| 13 | 9 | 4 | Shall be applied before or after the face laminate. | | |
| 13 | 9 | 5 | Does NOT require mitering of corners, and: | | |
| 13 | 9 | 5 | 1 | If MITER FOLDED, they shall be machined with the core. | |
| 14 | | SOLID SURFACE: | | | |
| 14 | 1 | DIRECTLY applied to wall or ceiling surfaces shall be a minimum of: | | | |
| 14 | 1 | 1 | 1/4" (6.4 mm) in thickness. | C | P |
| 14 | 1 | 2 | 1/2" (12.7 mm) in thickness. | C | P |
| 14 | 2 | JOINERY shall be: | | | |
| 14 | 2 | 1 | BUTT JOINTED and caulked or covered with a trim batten. | C | P |
| 14 | 2 | 2 | HARD SEAMED, except at building expansion joints. | C | P |
| 14 | 3 | COLOR selection shall be from the manufacturer's full range of colors available for the thickness required. | | | |
| 14 | 4 | FINISH to be manufacturer's standard matte finish unless otherwise specified. | | | |
| 15 | | SOLID PHENOLIC requires: | | | |
| 15 | 1 | THICKNESS to be a minimum of 1/8" (3.2 mm). | | | |
| 15 | 2 | COLOR to be selected from the manufacturer's standard product line. | | | |
| 15 | 3 | FINISH to be selected from the manufacturer's standard product line. | | | |
| 16 | | PRIMING: | | | |
| 16 | 1 | When FACTORY FINISHING is specified, concealed surfaces shall be factory sealed with two coats at 2 mil dry. | E | C | P |

### 8.4.6 Machining Rules

| | | | | | | |
|---|---|---|---|---|---|---|
| 1 | | EXPOSED SURFACES shall comply with SMOOTHNESS REQUIREMENTS (see SMOOTHNESS in TESTS), and: | | | | |
| 1 | 1 | SHARP EDGES be eased. | | | | |
| 1 | 2 | TOP FLAT WOOD surfaces, those that can be sanded with a drum or wide belt sander, be: | | | | |
| 1 | 2 | 1 | Minimum 15 KCPI or 100 grit sanding. | E | C | P |
| 1 | 2 | 2 | 120 grit sanding. | E | C | P |
| 1 | 2 | 3 | 150 grit sanding. | E | C | P |
| 1 | 3 | PROFILED and SHAPED WOOD surfaces be: | | | | |
| 1 | 3 | 1 | Minimum 15 KCPI or 100 grit sanding. | E | C | P |
| 1 | 3 | 2 | Minimum 20 KCPI or 120 grit sanding. | E | C | P |
| 1 | 3 | 3 | 120 grit sanding. | E | C | P |
| 1 | 4 | HPDL, PVC, and PREFINISHED WOOD edges shall be machined flush and filed, sanded, or buffed to remove machine marks and sharp edges, and: | | | | |
| 1 | 4 | 1 | OVERLAP (See Test F illustrations in TESTS) such as, shall not exceed: | | | |
| 1 | 4 | 1 | 1 | 0.005" (0.13 mm) for a maximum length of 2" (50.8 mm) in any 12" (305 mm) run. | E | C | P |
| 1 | 4 | 1 | 2 | 0.005" (0.13 mm) for a maximum length of 1" (25.4 mm) in any 24" (610 mm) run. | E | C | P |
| 1 | 4 | 1 | 3 | 0.003" (0.08 mm) for a maximum length of 1" (25.4 mm) in any 48" (1220 mm) run. | E | C | P |
| 1 | 4 | 2 | CHIP OUT (See Test G illustrations in TESTS) such as, shall be inconspicuous when viewed at: | | | |
| 1 | 4 | 2 | 1 | 72" (1829 mm). | E | C | P |
| 1 | 4 | 2 | 2 | 48" (1220 mm). | E | C | P |
| 1 | 4 | 2 | 3 | 24" (610 mm). | E | C | P |

Continues next column ▼

# SECTION 8
## Wall/Ceiling Surfacing and Partitions

GENERAL/PRODUCT/INSTALLATION/TEST

Where the **E**, **C**, or **P** icon is not indicated, the rule applies to all Grades equally

**compliance requirements**

### 8.4.6 Machining Rules

▲ From previous column

| | | | | | | | |
|---|---|---|---|---|---|---|---|
| 1 | | | **EXPOSED SURFACES** (continued) | | | | |
| 1 | 4 | 3 | **OVER MACHINED** (See Test H illustrations in TESTS) removal of color or pattern of face material such as, 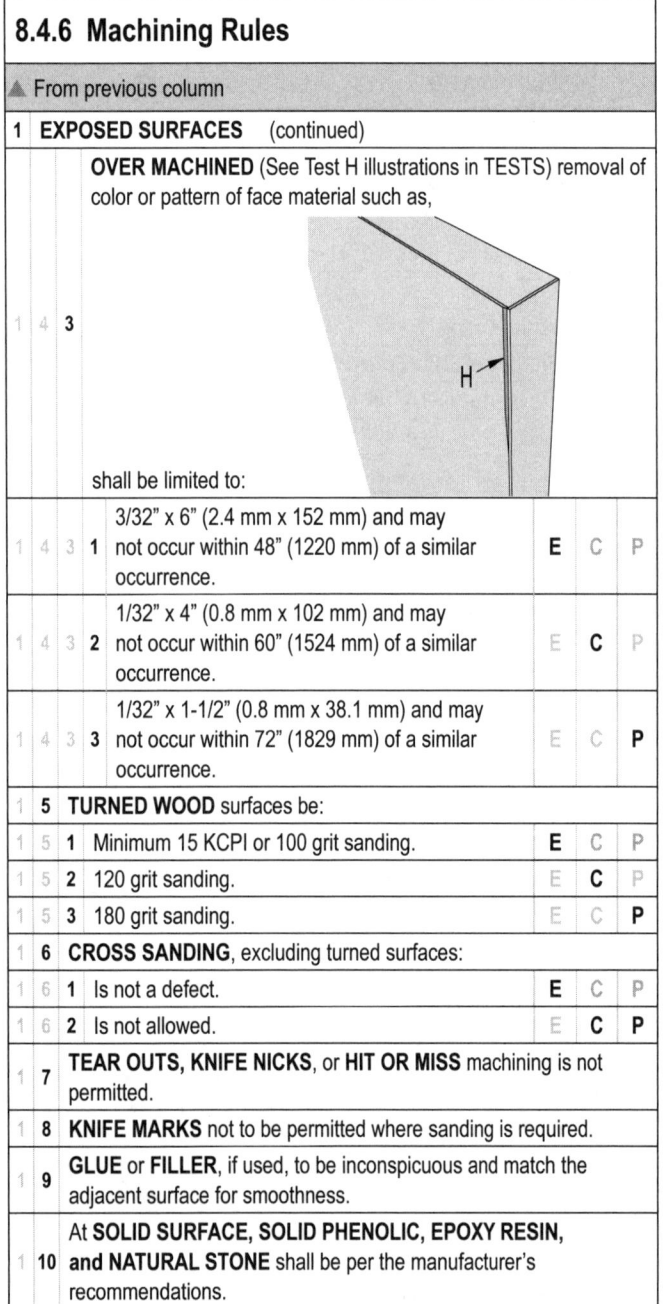 shall be limited to: | | | | |
| 1 | 4 | 3 | 1 | 3/32" x 6" (2.4 mm x 152 mm) and may not occur within 48" (1220 mm) of a similar occurrence. | E | C | P |
| 1 | 4 | 3 | 2 | 1/32" x 4" (0.8 mm x 102 mm) and may not occur within 60" (1524 mm) of a similar occurrence. | E | C | P |
| 1 | 4 | 3 | 3 | 1/32" x 1-1/2" (0.8 mm x 38.1 mm) and may not occur within 72" (1829 mm) of a similar occurrence. | E | C | P |
| 1 | 5 | | **TURNED WOOD** surfaces be: | | | | |
| 1 | 5 | 1 | Minimum 15 KCPI or 100 grit sanding. | | E | C | P |
| 1 | 5 | 2 | 120 grit sanding. | | E | C | P |
| 1 | 5 | 3 | 180 grit sanding. | | E | C | P |
| 1 | 6 | | **CROSS SANDING**, excluding turned surfaces: | | | | |
| 1 | 6 | 1 | Is not a defect. | | E | C | P |
| 1 | 6 | 2 | Is not allowed. | | E | C | P |
| 1 | 7 | | **TEAR OUTS, KNIFE NICKS**, or **HIT OR MISS** machining is not permitted. | | | | |
| 1 | 8 | | **KNIFE MARKS** not to be permitted where sanding is required. | | | | |
| 1 | 9 | | **GLUE** or **FILLER**, if used, to be inconspicuous and match the adjacent surface for smoothness. | | | | |
| 1 | 10 | | At **SOLID SURFACE, SOLID PHENOLIC, EPOXY RESIN, and NATURAL STONE** shall be per the manufacturer's recommendations. | | | | |

### 8.4.7 Assembly Rules

| | | | | | | | |
|---|---|---|---|---|---|---|---|
| 1 | | | **THESE STANDARDS** do not establish grade rules for joint flushness and or gap tolerances for woodwork products installed in a non climate controlled environment: however: | | | | |
| 1 | 1 | | Prior to installation, the flushness and/or gap tolerances of woodwork products intended for non climate controlled environments shall meet the test requirements herein. | | | | |
| 2 | | | **JOINTS** at **ASSEMBLED WOODWORK** shall: | | | | |
| 2 | 1 | | Be neatly and accurately made. | | | | |
| 2 | 2 | | Be **SECURELY GLUED**, with: | | | | |
| 2 | 2 | 1 | Adhesive residue removed from exposed and semi-exposed surfaces. | | | | |
| 2 | 3 | | Be **REINFORCED** with glue blocks where essential. | | | | |
| 2 | 4 | | Utilize biscuit spline, butterfly, scarf, spline, dowel or miter fold joinery. | | E | C | P |
| 2 | 5 | | Be **MECHANICALLY FASTENED** with nails or screws, where practical, with fasteners: | | | | |
| 2 | 5 | 1 | Countersunk. | | | | |
| 2 | 5 | 2 | Located in molding quirks or reliefs where possible. | | E | C | P |
| 2 | 6 | | Not permit **VISIBLE FASTENERS** at exposed surfaces of sheet products. | | | | |
| 2 | 7 | | Require **FLUSHNESS VARIATIONS** at exposed surfaces (See Test D illustrations in TESTS), when mitered or butted, such as, not to exceed at: | | | | |
| 2 | 7 | 1 | Wood to wood: | | | | |
| 2 | 7 | 1 | 1 | 0.010" (0.25 mm). | E | C | P |
| 2 | 7 | 1 | 2 | 0.007" (0.18 mm). | E | C | P |
| 2 | 7 | 1 | 3 | 0.005" (0.13 mm). | E | C | P |
| 2 | 7 | 2 | Non wood to non wood: | | | | |
| 2 | 7 | 2 | 1 | 0.025" (0.64 mm). | E | C | P |
| 2 | 7 | 2 | 2 | 0.015" (0.38 mm). | E | C | P |
| 2 | 7 | 2 | 3 | 0.010" (0.25 mm). | E | C | P |

Continues next column ▼

# SECTION 8
## Wall/Ceiling Surfacing and Partitions

### compliance requirements
GENERAL/**PRODUCT**/INSTALLATION/TEST

### 8.4.7 Assembly Rules

▲ From previous column

| 2 | JOINTS at ASSEMBLED WOODWORK (continued) | | | |
|---|---|---|---|---|
| 2 | 8 | Allow **GAPS** at exposed surface (see Test A illustrations in TESTS), when mitered or butted, such as, 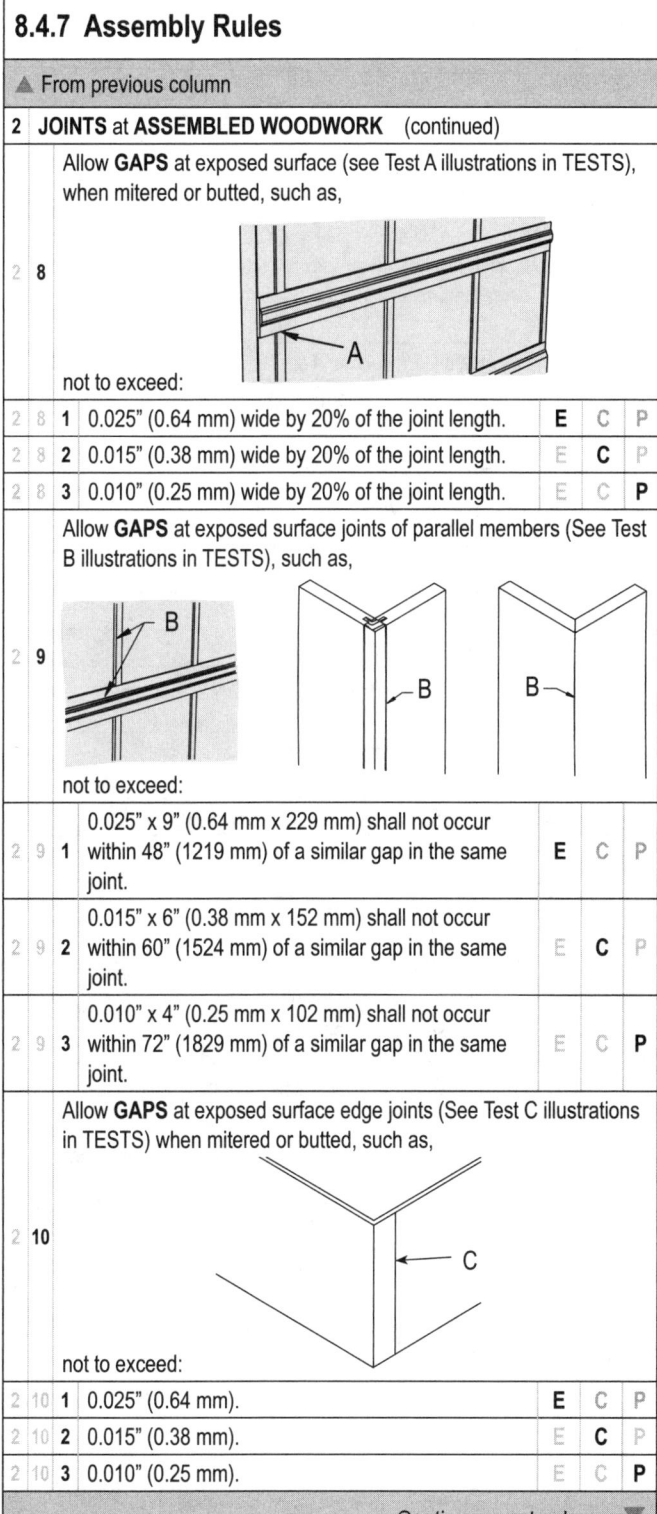 not to exceed: | | | |
| 2 | 8 | 1 | 0.025" (0.64 mm) wide by 20% of the joint length. | E | C | P |
| 2 | 8 | 2 | 0.015" (0.38 mm) wide by 20% of the joint length. | E | **C** | P |
| 2 | 8 | 3 | 0.010" (0.25 mm) wide by 20% of the joint length. | E | C | **P** |
| 2 | 9 | Allow **GAPS** at exposed surface joints of parallel members (See Test B illustrations in TESTS), such as, not to exceed: |
| 2 | 9 | 1 | 0.025" x 9" (0.64 mm x 229 mm) shall not occur within 48" (1219 mm) of a similar gap in the same joint. | **E** | C | P |
| 2 | 9 | 2 | 0.015" x 6" (0.38 mm x 152 mm) shall not occur within 60" (1524 mm) of a similar gap in the same joint. | E | **C** | P |
| 2 | 9 | 3 | 0.010" x 4" (0.25 mm x 102 mm) shall not occur within 72" (1829 mm) of a similar gap in the same joint. | E | C | **P** |
| 2 | 10 | Allow **GAPS** at exposed surface edge joints (See Test C illustrations in TESTS) when mitered or butted, such as, not to exceed: |
| 2 | 10 | 1 | 0.025" (0.64 mm). | **E** | C | P |
| 2 | 10 | 2 | 0.015" (0.38 mm). | E | **C** | P |
| 2 | 10 | 3 | 0.010" (0.25 mm). | E | C | **P** |

Continues next column ▼

### 8.4.7 Assembly Rules

▲ From previous column

| 2 | JOINTS at ASSEMBLED WOODWORK (continued) | | | |
|---|---|---|---|---|
| 2 | 11 | Allows use of **FILLER**, and: | | | |
| 2 | 11 | 1 | If inconspicuous when viewed at 36" (914 mm). | **E** | C | P |
| 2 | 11 | 2 | If inconspicuous when viewed at 24" (610 mm). | E | **C** | P |
| 2 | 11 | 3 | Not be allowed. | E | C | **P** |
| 2 | 12 | Shall be mitered. | | | |
| 2 | 13 | Shall be spot glued and mechanically fastened: | E | **C** | **P** |
| 2 | 13 | 1 | Only to non panel surfaces, panel is required to float. | | | |
| 2 | 13 | 2 | With a maximum of two positioning nails per 12" (300 mm) of length before a joint. | E | **C** | **P** |
| 2 | 13 | 3 | With nails set, and: | E | **C** | **P** |
| 2 | 13 | 3 | 1 | Filled and sanded if prefinished. | | | |
| 2 | 14 | **MITER JOINTS** shall be well fitted and cleaned. | | | |
| 2 | 15 | **BUILT UP ITEMS** shall be soundly fabricated with half lapped, mitered, miter fold, shoulder mitered, tonged, or equivalent construction. | | | |
| 2 | 16 | **SHEET** and **LAMINATED LUMBER PANELS** shall be allowed to move, float, expand or contract in reaction to ambient humidity changes. | | | |
| 3 | Requires **FLATNESS** or **WARP** of installed and removable sheet products (see Test E illustrations in **TESTS**) such as, 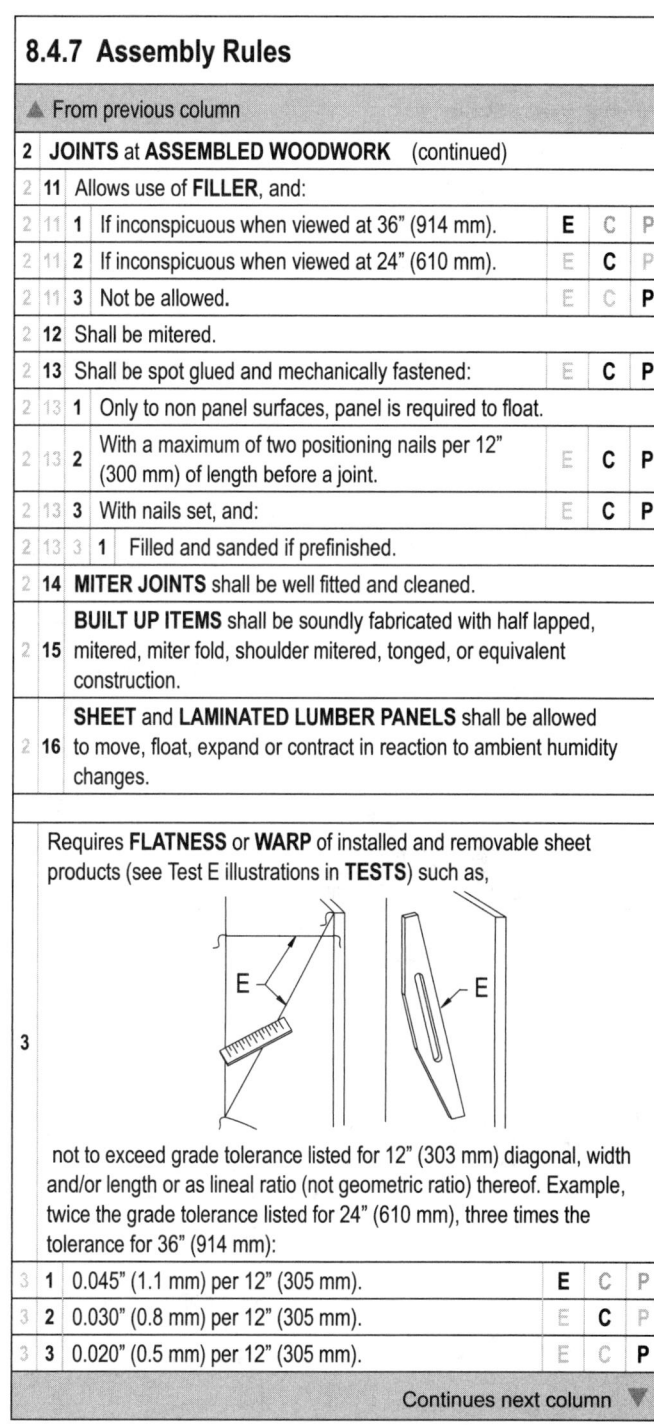 not to exceed grade tolerance listed for 12" (303 mm) diagonal, width and/or length or as lineal ratio (not geometric ratio) thereof. Example, twice the grade tolerance listed for 24" (610 mm), three times the tolerance for 36" (914 mm): |
| 3 | 1 | 0.045" (1.1 mm) per 12" (305 mm). | **E** | C | P |
| 3 | 2 | 0.030" (0.8 mm) per 12" (305 mm). | E | **C** | P |
| 3 | 3 | 0.020" (0.5 mm) per 12" (305 mm). | E | C | **P** |

Continues next column ▼

# SECTION 8
## Wall/Ceiling Surfacing and Partitions

GENERAL/**PRODUCT**/INSTALLATION/TEST

*Where the **E**, **C**, or **P** icon is not indicated, the rule applies to all Grades equally* — **E** | **C** | **P**

**compliance requirements**

### 8.4.7 Assembly Rules

▲ *From previous column*

| # | # | # | # | Rule | E | C | P |
|---|---|---|---|------|---|---|---|
| 4 | | | | **WOOD VENEER:** | | | |
| 4 | 1 | | | **PANELS** are to be cut to size by the: | | | |
| 4 | 1 | 1 | | Installer. | E | C | P |
| 4 | 1 | 2 | | Manufacturer and scribed to fit by installer. | E | C | P |
| 4 | 2 | | | Requires **VENEER SEQUENCE** at: | | | |
| 4 | 2 | 1 | | Premanufactured **BALANCED MATCH** panels with the width of outer leaves after trimming at the edges not to exceed: | | | |
| 4 | 2 | 1 | 1 | Unlimited. | E | C | P |
| 4 | 2 | 1 | 2 | 1-1/2" (38.1 mm) less than the adjoining leaf. | E | C | P |
| 4 | 2 | 1 | 3 | 3/4" (19 mm) less than the adjoining leaf. | E | C | P |
| 4 | 2 | 2 | | Custom made to order **SEQUENCE BALANCE MATCH** panels with the width of outer leaves after trimming at edges not to exceed: | | | |
| 4 | 2 | 2 | 1 | Unlimited. | E | C | P |
| 4 | 2 | 2 | 2 | 1" (25.4 mm) less than the adjoining leaf. | E | C | P |
| 4 | 2 | 2 | 3 | 1/2" (12.7 mm) less than the adjoining leaf. | E | C | P |
| 4 | 2 | 3 | | Panels when divided with **VENEER GRAIN** aligned vertically and/or horizontally within a maximum of: | | | |
| 4 | 2 | 3 | 1 | Unlimited. | E | C | P |
| 4 | 2 | 3 | 2 | 1/4" (6.4 mm) variance. | E | C | P |
| 4 | 2 | 3 | 3 | 1/8" (3.2 mm) variance. | E | C | P |
| 4 | 2 | 4 | | Panels **WITHIN A ROOM** utilizing: | | | |
| 4 | 2 | 4 | 1 | The **FULL WIDTH** of **PREMANUFACTURED SETS**, except the trimmed side of a make up panel, to be: | | | |
| 4 | 2 | 4 | 1 | 1 Running match when panels are not end matched. | E | C | P |
| 4 | 2 | 4 | 1 | 2 Balance match when end matched. | E | C | P |
| 4 | 2 | 4 | 1 | 3 Balance match. | E | C | P |
| 4 | 2 | 4 | 2 | **SELECTIVELY REDUCED WIDTH** of **PREMANUFACTURED SETS**, are **NOT** required to be balance matched; however: | | | |
| 4 | 2 | 4 | 2 | 1 **CUSTOM SEQUENCED** panels are required to be balance matched, including make up panels. | E | C | P |
| 4 | 2 | 4 | 2 | 2 **BLUEPRINT SEQUENCED PANELS** are required to be balance matched with veneer alignment at common size panels, make up panels, and components. | E | C | P |

*Continues next column* ▼

### 8.4.7 Assembly Rules

▲ *From previous column*

| # | # | # | # | Rule | E | C | P |
|---|---|---|---|------|---|---|---|
| 4 | | | | **WOOD VENEER** (continued) | | | |
| 4 | 2 | | | **VENEER SEQUENCE** (continued) | | | |
| 4 | 2 | 4 | | Panels **WITHIN A ROOM** (continued) | | | |
| 4 | 2 | 4 | 3 | When veneer flitch quantity does not allow for sequence matching for the entire room, flitch transition shall be at changes in plane (e.g. corners), and/or wall openings and shall be: | | | |
| 4 | 2 | 4 | 3 | 1 Compatible for color and figure. | E | C | P |
| 4 | 2 | 4 | 3 | 2 Well matched for color and figure. | E | C | P |
| 4 | 3 | | | **BUTT JOINTS** shall: | | | |
| 4 | 3 | 1 | | Not be factory prepared. | E | C | P |
| 4 | 3 | 2 | | Be factory prepared with edges eased. | E | C | P |
| 4 | 3 | 3 | | Be factory prepared and grooved with splines furnished and edges eased. | E | C | P |
| 4 | 4 | | | **REVEAL JOINTS** and **CORNERS** shall: | | | |
| 4 | 4 | 1 | | **NOT** be factory prepared. | E | C | P |
| 4 | 4 | 2 | | Be factory prepared with edges eased and articulation strip(s) furnished. | E | C | P |
| 4 | 4 | 3 | | Be factory prepared and machined for furnished articulation strip(s) with edges eased. | E | C | P |
| 4 | 5 | | | **INSIDE CORNERS** to be shipped oversize for field fitting. | | | |
| 4 | 6 | | | **MITERED** outside corners shall: | | | |
| 4 | 6 | 1 | | **NOT** be factory prepared. | E | C | P |
| 4 | 6 | 2 | | Be factory prepared and shipped loose. | E | C | P |
| 4 | 6 | 3 | | Be factory prepared, and if site conditions permit, glued and braced prior to shipping. | E | C | P |
| 4 | 7 | | | **FIELD JOINERY** shall be factory prepared to the greatest extent possible with feature strips and joint trim furnished oversize, where possible, to allow for jobsite fitting. | E | C | P |
| 4 | 8 | | | **EXPOSED CORNERS** shall be shoulder mitered, lock mitered, spline mitered, mitered with a biscuit spline, or miter folded unless specified and/or detailed otherwise. | | | |
| 4 | 9 | | | **MOLDINGS** within an individual panel face shall be: | | | |
| 4 | 9 | 1 | | Shipped loose. | E | C | P |
| 4 | 9 | 2 | | Factory applied. | E | C | P |
| 4 | 10 | | | **VENEER JOINTS** shall be plumb, within: | | | |
| 4 | 10 | 1 | | 1/4" (6.4 mm). | E | C | P |
| 4 | 10 | 2 | | 3/16" (4.8 mm). | E | C | P |
| 4 | 10 | 3 | | 1/8" (3.2 mm). | E | C | P |

*Continues next column* ▼

# SECTION 8
## Wall/Ceiling Surfacing and Partitions

**GENERAL / PRODUCT / INSTALLATION / TEST**

## compliance requirements

### 8.4.7 Assembly Rules

▲ From previous column

| | | | | E | C | P |
|---|---|---|---|---|---|---|
| 4 | **WOOD VENEER** (continued) | | | | | |
| 4 | 11 | **VENEER LOSS, SIDE** between sequenced adjacent panels shall not exceed: | | | | |
| 4 | 11 | 1 | 1-1/2" (38.1 mm). | E | **C** | P |
| 4 | 11 | 2 | 1" (25.4 mm). | E | C | **P** |
| 4 | 12 | **VENEER LOSS, END** between sequenced adjacent end matched panels shall not exceed: | | | | |
| 4 | 12 | 1 | 2" (50.8 mm). | E | **C** | P |
| 4 | 12 | 2 | 1-1/2" (38.1 mm). | E | C | **P** |
| 4 | 13 | **END MATCHED VENEER MISALIGNMENT** between sequenced adjacent panels shall not exceed: | | | | |
| 4 | 13 | 1 | 3/8" (9.5 mm). | E | **C** | P |
| 4 | 13 | 2 | 3/16" (4.8 mm). | E | C | **P** |
| 4 | 14 | **FIGURE** and/or heart progression shall be uniform and natural between adjacent sequenced panels and not exceed: | | | | |
| 4 | 14 | 1 | 1" (25.4 mm). | E | **C** | P |
| 4 | 14 | 2 | 1/2" (12.7 mm). | E | C | **P** |
| 4 | 14 | 3 | Except at doors and other components that adjoin at blueprint panels shall not exceed: | | | | |
| 4 | 14 | 3 | 1 | 2" (50.8 mm). | E | **C** | P |
| 4 | 14 | 3 | 2 | 1-1/2" (38.1 mm). | E | C | **P** |
| 5 | **SOLID STILE** and **RAIL WOOD** requires: | | | | | |
| 5 | 1 | **PANELING** shall be factory assembled in sections as large as practical for field installation. | E | **C** | **P** |
| 5 | 2 | At **FIELD JOINTS**: | | | | |
| 5 | 2 | 1 | Factory preparation is not required. | **E** | C | P |
| 5 | 2 | 2 | Shall be factory preparation to the greatest extent possible with feature strips and joint trim furnished oversize, where possible, to allow for jobsite fitting. | E | **C** | **P** |

Continues next column ▼

### 8.4.7 Assembly Rules

▲ From previous column

| | | | | E | C | P |
|---|---|---|---|---|---|---|
| 6 | **DECORATIVE LAMINATE** requires: | | | | | |
| 6 | 1 | **ALIGNMENT VARIATIONS** at special patterns not to exceed: | | | | |
| 6 | 1 | 1 | 1/4" (6 mm). | **E** | C | P |
| 6 | 1 | 2 | 1/8" (3 mm). | E | **C** | P |
| 6 | 1 | 3 | 1/16" (1.5 mm). | E | C | **P** |
| 6 | 2 | **PLUMBNESS** at special patterns not to exceed: | | | | |
| 6 | 2 | 1 | 3/8" (9 mm) in 96" (2440 mm). | **E** | C | P |
| 6 | 2 | 2 | 1/4" (6 mm) in 96" (2440 mm). | E | **C** | P |
| 6 | 2 | 3 | 1/8" (3 mm) in 96" (2440 mm). | E | C | **P** |
| 6 | 3 | Allow **GAPS** at butted edges glued to the same piece of core (See Test M illustrations in TESTS) such as, not to exceed: | | | | |
| 6 | 3 | 1 | 3 occurrences of 0.030" x 5" (0.76 mm x 127 mm) in any 65 sq/ft (6 sq/m). | **E** | C | P |
| 6 | 3 | 2 | 2 occurrences of 0.015" x 5" (0.38 mm x 127 mm) in any 65 sq/ft (6 sq/m). | E | **C** | P |
| 6 | 3 | 3 | 1 occurrence of 0.007" x 3" (0.18 mm x 76 mm) in any 65 sq/ft (6 sq/m). | E | C | **P** |
| 6 | 4 | Allow **FLUSHNESS** at butted edges (See Test N illustrations in TESTS) such as, not to exceed: | | | | |
| 6 | 4 | 1 | 0.009" (0.23 mm). | **E** | C | P |
| 6 | 4 | 2 | 0.006" (0.15 mm). | E | **C** | P |
| 6 | 4 | 3 | 0.003" (0.08 mm). | E | C | **P** |
| 6 | 5 | **RETENTION MOLDINGS** are permitted at field joints, and: | | | | |
| 6 | 5 | 1 | Shall be secured to wall studs or in wall blocking. | | | |
| 6 | 6 | **VERTICAL** or **HORIZONTAL JOINTS** shall have a slight "V", and: | | | | |
| 6 | 6 | 1 | Be splined full length or have biscuit splines at a minimum of 12" (305 mm) on center. | | | |

Continues next column ▼

# SECTION 8
## Wall/Ceiling Surfacing and Partitions

GENERAL/**PRODUCT**/INSTALLATION/TEST

## compliance requirements

Where the **E**, **C**, or **P** icon is not indicated, the rule applies to all Grades equally | **E** | **C** | **P** |

### 8.4.7 Assembly Rules

▲ From previous column

| | | | | | | |
|---|---|---|---|---|---|---|
| 6 | | DECORATIVE LAMINATE (continued) | | | | |
| 6 | 7 | | PANELS shall: | | | |
| 6 | 7 | 1 | NOT be factory prepared; panels are to be shipped as full size panels for cutting and fitting in the field. | E | C | P |
| 6 | 7 | 2 | Be factory sized, except where field adjustment is required. | E | C | P |
| 6 | 8 | | BUTT JOINTS shall: | | | |
| 6 | 8 | 1 | NOT be factory prepared. | E | C | P |
| 6 | 8 | 2 | Be factory prepared with edges eased. | E | C | P |
| 6 | 8 | 3 | Be factory prepared and grooved with splines furnished and edges eased. | E | C | P |
| 6 | 9 | | REVEAL JOINTS and CORNERS shall: | | | |
| 6 | 9 | 1 | NOT be factory prepared. | E | C | P |
| 6 | 9 | 2 | Be factory prepared with edges eased and articulation strip(s) furnished. | E | C | P |
| 6 | 9 | 3 | Be factory prepared and machined for furnished articulation strip(s) with edges eased. | E | C | P |
| 6 | 10 | | INSIDE CORNERS to be shipped oversize for field fitting. | | | |
| 6 | 11 | | MITERED OUTSIDE CORNERS shall: | | | |
| 6 | 11 | 1 | NOT be factory prepared. | E | C | P |
| 6 | 11 | 2 | Be factory prepared and shipped loose. | E | C | P |
| 6 | 11 | 3 | Be factory prepared, and if site conditions permit, glued and braced prior to shipping. | E | C | P |

Continues next column ▼

### 8.4.7 Assembly Rules

▲ From previous column

| | | | | | | |
|---|---|---|---|---|---|---|
| 7 | | | SOLID SURFACE (only available in Custom and Premium Grade) requires: | | | |
| 7 | 1 | | BUTT JOINT components to be spaced approximately 1/8 " (3.2 mm) apart to allow satisfactory caulking or seaming: | | | |
| 7 | 1 | 1 | Shall be CAULKED with compatible color matched sealant. | | C | P |
| 7 | 1 | 2 | Shall be SEAMED with compatible hard seam adhesive. | | C | P |
| 7 | 2 | | VERTICAL JOINTS in horizontal panel runs to be: | | | |
| 7 | 2 | 1 | CAULKED or trimmed with an APPLIED 1/4" x 1" (6.4 mm x 25.4 mm) BATTEN using silicone or other manufacturer approved adhesive. | | C | P |
| 7 | 2 | 2 | HARD SEAMED with manufacturer approved hard seam adhesive. | | C | P |
| 7 | 3 | | EXPANSION joints where required by building design or manufacturer recommendation. | | | |
| 8 | | | SOLID PHENOLIC (only available in Premium Grade) requires: | | | |
| 8 | 1 | | JOINT WIDTH shall be at least 1/8 " (3.2 mm) to allow satisfactory caulking penetration. | | | |
| 8 | 2 | | JOINTS shall provide for panel movement in both horizontal and vertical directions, such as by use of: | | | |
| 8 | 2 | 1 | TRIMS or GASKETS made of aluminium, PVC, and neoprene. | | | |
| 8 | 3 | | At rabbeted or tongue and groove joints, panel thickness shall be a minimum of 3/8" (9.5 mm). | | | |

# SECTION 8
## Wall/Ceiling Surfacing and Partitions

**GENERAL/PRODUCT/INSTALLATION/TEST**

### 8.5 PREPARATION AND QUALIFICATION REQUIREMENTS

**1  CARE, STORAGE, and BUILDING CONDITION**S shall be in compliance with the requirements set forth in Section 2 of these standards.

1.1  Severe damage to the woodwork can result from noncompliance. **THE MANUFACTURER AND/OR INSTALLER OF THE WOODWORK SHALL NOT BE HELD RESPONSIBLE FOR DAMAGE THAT MIGHT DEVELOP BY NOT ADHERING TO THE REQUIREMENTS.**

**2  CONTRACTOR IS RESPONSIBLE FOR**

2.1  Furnishing and installing structural members, grounds, in wall blocking, backing, furring, brackets, or other anchorage required for architectural woodwork installation that becomes an integral part of walls, floors, or ceilings to which architectural woodwork shall be installed.

2.1.1  In the absence of contract documents calling for the contractor to supply the necessary in wall blocking/backing in the wall or ceilings, either through inadvertence or otherwise, the architectural woodwork installer shall not proceed with the installation until such time as the in wall blocking/backing is installed by others.

2.1.2  Preparatory work done by others shall be subject to inspection by the architectural woodwork installer and shall be accepted or rejected for cause prior to installation.

2.1.2.1  **WALL, CEILING,** and/or **OPENING VARIATIONS** in excess of 1/4" (6.4 mm) or **FLOORS** in excess of 1/2" (12.7 mm) in 144" (3658 mm) of being plumb, level, flat, straight, square, or of the correct size are not acceptable for the installation of architectural woodwork, nor is it the responsibility of the installer to scribe or fit to tolerances in excess of such.

2.2  Installation site being properly ventilated, protected from direct sunlight, excessive heat and/or moisture, and that the HVAC system is functioning and maintaining the appropriate relative humidity and temperature.

2.3  Priming the architectural woodwork in accordance with the contract documents prior to its installation, and:

2.3.1  Building wall surfaces shall be primed where construction adhesive is used for panelling installation.

2.4  If the architectural woodwork is factory finished, priming by the factory finisher is required.

### 8.5 PREPARATION AND QUALIFICATION REQUIREMENTS (continued)

**3  INSTALLER IS RESPONSIBLE FOR**

3.1  Having adequate equipment and experienced craftsmen to complete the installation in a first class manner.

3.2  Checking architectural woodwork specified and studying the appropriate portions of the contract documents, including these standards and the reviewed shop drawings to familiarize themselves with the requirements of the Grade specified, understanding that:

3.2.1  Appearance requirements of Grades apply only to surfaces visible after installation.

3.2.2  For transparent finish, special attention needs to be given to the color and the grain of the various woodwork pieces to ensure they are installed in compliance with the Grade specified.

3.3  Verification that installation site is properly ventilated, protected from direct sunlight, excessive heat and/or moisture, and that the HVAC system is functioning and maintaining the appropriate relative humidity and temperature.

3.4  Verification that required priming of woodwork has been completed by others before woodwork is installed.

3.5  Verification that woodwork has been acclimated to the field conditions for a minimum of 72 hours before installation is commenced.

3.6  Woodwork specifically built or assembled in sequence for match of color and grain is installed to maintain that same sequence.

# SECTION 8
## Wall/Ceiling Surfacing and Partitions

GENERAL/PRODUCT/**INSTALLATION**/TEST

**compliance requirements**

Where the **E**, **C**, or **P** icon is not indicated, the rule applies to all Grades equally | E | C | P |

### 8.6 RULES

1. The following rules shall govern unless a project's contract documents require otherwise.

2. These rules are intended to provide a well defined degree of control over a project's quality of installation.

3. **ERRATA**, published on the Sponsor Associations' websites at www.awinet.org, www.awmac.com, or www.aws-errata.com, shall **TAKE PRECEDENCE OVER THESE RULES**, subject to their date of posting and a project's bid date.

### 8.6.1 Basic Rules

| | | | Rule | E | C | P |
|---|---|---|---|---|---|---|
| 1 | | | **AESTHETIC** grade rules apply only to exposed and semi-exposed surfaces visible after installation. | | | |
| 2 | | | **TRANSPARENT FINISHED** woodwork shall be installed: | | | |
| 2 | 1 | | With **CONSIDERATION** of color and grain. | E | C | P |
| 2 | 2 | | **COMPATIBLE** in color and grain. | E | C | P |
| 2 | 3 | | **WELL MATCHED** for color and grain, with: | E | C | P |
| 2 | 3 | 1 | **SHEET PRODUCTS** compatible in color with solid stock. | E | C | P |
| 3 | | | **REPAIRS** are allowed, provided they are neatly made and inconspicuous when viewed at: | | | |
| 3 | 1 | | 72" (1830 mm). | E | C | P |
| 3 | 2 | | 48" (1219 mm). | E | C | P |
| 3 | 3 | | 24" (610 mm). | E | C | P |
| 4 | | | **INSTALLER MODIFICATIONS** shall comply to the material, machining, and assembly rules within the **PRODUCT** portion of this section and the applicable finishing rules in Section 5. | | | |
| 5 | | | **WOODWORK** shall be: | | | |
| 5 | 1 | | **SECURELY** fastened and tightly fitted with flush joints. | | | |
| 5 | 1 | 1 | Joinery shall be **CONSISTENT** throughout the project. | | | |
| 5 | 2 | | Of **MAXIMUM** available and/or practical lengths. | E | C | P |
| 5 | 3 | | **TRIMMED EQUALLY** from both sides when fitted for width. | E | C | P |
| 5 | 4 | | **SPLINED** or **DOWELED** when miters are over 4" (100 mm) long. | E | C | P |
| 5 | 5 | | **PROFILED** or **SELF MITERED** when trim ends are exposed. | E | C | P |
| 5 | 6 | | **SELF MITERED** when trim ends are exposed. | E | C | P |

*Continues next column*

### 8.6.1 Basic Rules

▲ From previous column

| | | | Rule | E | C | P |
|---|---|---|---|---|---|---|
| 5 | | | **WOODWORK** (continued) | | | |
| 5 | 7 | | **MITERED** at outside corners. | | | |
| 5 | 8 | | **MITERED** at inside corners. | E | C | P |
| 5 | 9 | | **COPED** at inside corners for shaped surfaces. | E | C | P |
| 5 | 10 | | **INSTALLED** plumb, level, square, and flat within 1/8" (3.2 mm) in 96" (2438 mm), and when required: | | | |
| 5 | 10 | 1 | **GROUNDS** and **HANGING SYSTEMS** set plumb and true. | E | C | P |
| 5 | 11 | | Installed **FREE OF**: | | | |
| 5 | 11 | 1 | Warp, twisting, cupping, and/or bowing that cannot be held true. | | | |
| 5 | 11 | 2 | Open joints, visible machine marks, cross sanding, tear outs, nicks, chips, and/or scratches. | | | |
| 5 | 11 | 3 | Natural defects exceeding the quantity or size limits defined in Sections 3 & 4. | | | |
| 5 | 12 | | **SMOOTH** and **SANDED** without **CROSS SCRATCHES** in conformance to the **PRODUCT** portion of this section. | | | |
| 5 | 13 | | **SCRIBED** at: | | | |
| 5 | 13 | 1 | Flat surfaces. | E | C | P |
| 5 | 13 | 2 | Shaped surfaces. | E | C | P |
| 5 | 14 | | Sealed when in contact with walls and floors and/or wall and floor anchorage. | | | |
| 6 | | | **THESE STANDARDS** do not establish grade rules for joint flushness and or gap tolerances for woodwork products installed in a non climate controlled environment. | | | |
| 7 | | | **GAPS** at field installation (see Test I illustrations in TESTS) such as, and: | | | |
| 7 | 1 | | If caused by excessive deviations in the building's walls and ceilings being in excess of 1/4" (6.4 mm) in 144" (3658 mm) of being plumb, level, flat, straight, square, or of the correct size, or 1/2" (12.7 mm) for floors, shall not be considered a defect or the responsibility of the installer. | | | |
| 7 | 2 | | Not exceed 30% of a joint's **LENGTH** and: | | | |
| 7 | 2 | 1 | Be allowed if filled or caulked, and: | E | C | P |
| 7 | 2 | 1 | If color compatible. | E | C | P |

*Continues next column*

©2014 AWI | AWMAC | WI  2nd Edition, October 1, 2014
As may be updated by errata at awinet.org, awmac.com, or aws-errata.com

| E | C | P | Where the **E**, **C**, or **P** icon is not indicated, the rule applies to all Grades equally |

# compliance requirements

## SECTION 8
### Wall/Ceiling Surfacing and Partitions

GENERAL/PRODUCT/**INSTALLATION**/TEST

### 8.6.1 Basic Rules

▲ From previous column

| | | | | | | |
|---|---|---|---|---|---|---|
| 7 | | | **GAPS** (see Test I illustrations in Tests) (continued) | | | |
| 7 | 3 | | At **WOOD** to **WOOD** shall not exceed: | | | |
| 7 | 3 | 1 | At **FLAT** surfaces: | | | |
| 7 | 3 | 1 | 1 | 0.030" (0.76 mm) in width. | E C | P |
| 7 | 3 | 1 | 2 | 0.020" (0.51mm) in width. | E **C** | P |
| 7 | 3 | 1 | 3 | 0.015" (0.38 mm) in width. | E C | **P** |
| 7 | 3 | 2 | At **SHAPED** surfaces: | | | |
| 7 | 3 | 2 | 1 | 0.040" (1.02mm) in width. | **E** C | P |
| 7 | 3 | 2 | 2 | 0.025" (0.64 mm) in width. | E **C** | P |
| 7 | 3 | 2 | 3 | 0.015" (0.38 mm) in width. | E C | **P** |
| 7 | 4 | | Of **WOOD** to **NON WOOD** shall not exceed: | | | |
| 7 | 4 | 1 | At **FLAT** and **SHAPED** surfaces: | | | |
| 7 | 4 | 1 | 1 | 0.075" (1.91 mm) in width. | **E** C | P |
| 7 | 4 | 1 | 2 | 0.050" (1.27 mm) in width. | E **C** | P |
| 7 | 4 | 1 | 3 | 0.035" (0.89 mm) in width. | E C | **P** |
| 7 | 5 | | Of **NON WOOD** to **NON WOOD** and/or **ALL ELEMENTS** shall not exceed: | | | |
| 7 | 5 | 1 | At **FLAT** surfaces: | | | |
| 7 | 5 | 1 | 1 | 0.075" (1.91 mm) in width. | **E** C | P |
| 7 | 5 | 1 | 2 | 0.050" (1.27 mm) in width. | E **C** | P |
| 7 | 5 | 1 | 3 | 0.035" (0.89 mm) in width. | E C | **P** |
| 7 | 5 | 2 | At **SHAPED** surfaces: | | | |
| 7 | 5 | 2 | 1 | 0.120" (3.05 mm) in width. | **E** C | P |
| 7 | 5 | 2 | 2 | 0.075" (1.91 mm) in width. | E **C** | P |
| 7 | 5 | 2 | 3 | 0.050" (1.27 mm) in width. | E C | **P** |
| 8 | | | **FLUSHNESS** of joinery (see Test J illustrations in TESTS), such as, | | | |

and:

| | | | | | | |
|---|---|---|---|---|---|---|
| 8 | 1 | | Of **WOOD** to **WOOD** shall not exceed: | | | |
| 8 | 1 | 1 | At **FLAT** surfaces: | | | |
| 8 | 1 | 1 | 1 | 0.025" (0.64 mm). | **E** C | P |
| 8 | 1 | 1 | 2 | 0.015" (0.38 mm). | E **C** | P |
| 8 | 1 | 1 | 3 | 0.010" (0.25 mm). | E C | **P** |

Continues next column ▼

### 8.6.1 Basic Rules

▲ From previous column

| | | | | | | |
|---|---|---|---|---|---|---|
| 8 | | | **FLUSHNESS** of joinery (continued) | | | |
| 8 | 1 | 2 | At **SHAPED** surfaces: | | | |
| 8 | 1 | 2 | 1 | 0.040" (0.97 mm). | **E** C | P |
| 8 | 1 | 2 | 2 | 0.025" (0.65 mm). | E **C** | P |
| 8 | 1 | 2 | 3 | 0.020" (0.51 mm). | E C | **P** |
| 8 | 2 | | Of **WOOD** to **NON WOOD** shall not exceed: | | | |
| 8 | 2 | 1 | At **FLAT** and **SHAPED** surfaces: | | | |
| 8 | 2 | 1 | 1 | 0.075" (1.91 mm). | **E** C | P |
| 8 | 2 | 1 | 2 | 0.050" (1.27 mm). | E **C** | P |
| 8 | 2 | 1 | 3 | 0.035" (0.89 mm). | E C | **P** |
| 8 | 3 | | Of **NON WOOD** to **NON WOOD** and/or **ALL ELEMENTS** shall not exceed: | | | |
| 8 | 3 | 1 | At **FLAT** surfaces: | | | |
| 8 | 3 | 1 | 1 | 0.075" (1.91 mm). | **E** C | P |
| 8 | 3 | 1 | 2 | 0.050" (1.27 mm). | E **C** | P |
| 8 | 3 | 1 | 3 | 0.035" (0.89 mm). | E C | **P** |
| 8 | 3 | 2 | At **SHAPED** surfaces: | | | |
| 8 | 3 | 2 | 1 | 0.120" (3.05 mm). | **E** C | P |
| 8 | 3 | 2 | 2 | 0.075" (1.91 mm). | E **C** | P |
| 8 | 3 | 2 | 3 | 0.050" (1.27 mm). | E C | **P** |
| 9 | | | **REVEALS** at **ADJOINING PANELS** (see Test K illustrations in TESTS), such as, shall not exceed a maximum variance of: | | | |
| 9 | 1 | | 0.040" (1.02 mm). | | **E** C | P |
| 9 | 2 | | 0.025" (0.64 mm). | | E **C** | P |
| 9 | 3 | | 0.015" (0.38 mm). | | E C | **P** |

Continues next column ▼

# SECTION 8
## Wall/Ceiling Surfacing and Partitions

GENERAL/PRODUCT/**INSTALLATION**/TEST

**compliance requirements**

Where the **E**, **C**, or **P** icon is not indicated, the rule applies to all Grades equally | E | C | P |

### 8.6.1 Basic Rules

▲ From previous column

| 10 | **FLUSHNESS** at **ADJOINING PANELS** (see Test L illustrations in TESTS) such as, <br><br> shall not exceed a maximum variance of: | | | |
|---|---|---|---|---|
| 10 | 1 | 0.040" (1.02 mm). | E | | |
| 10 | 2 | 0.025" (0.64 mm). | | C | |
| 10 | 3 | 0.015" (0.38 mm). | | | P |
| 11 | **FASTENING** shall: | | | |
| 11 | 1 | Use mechanical fasteners at wall panels installed at 108" (2743 mm) or more above finished floor, and ceiling panels regardless of height. | | | |
| 11 | 2 | Use **CONCEALED** fastening wherever possible. | | | |
| 11 | 2 | 1 | If exposed fastening is required to complete the installation: | | | |
| 11 | 2 | 1 | 1 | Fasteners shall be set in quirks or reliefs (where possible), countersunk, and kept to a minimum. | | | |
| 11 | 2 | 1 | 2 | **PERMIT** use of construction adhesive, finish nails, trim screws, and/or pins. | | | |
| 11 | 2 | 1 | 2 | 1 | Trim screws. | E | | |
| 11 | 2 | 1 | 2 | 2 | Finish nails. | | C | |
| 11 | 2 | 1 | 2 | 3 | Pins and/or construction adhesive. | | | P |
| 11 | 2 | 1 | 3 | **DO NOT PERMIT** the use of drywall, bugle head, or case hardened screws. | | | |
| 11 | 2 | 1 | 4 | Require exposed fasteners to be inconspicuous, as defined in the glossary. | | | |
| 11 | 2 | 1 | 5 | **DO NOT PERMIT** exposed fastening through decorative laminate. | | | |
| 11 | 2 | 2 | Use of metal Z-clips or hanging cleats are acceptable for blind installation. | | | |
| 11 | 3 | A maximum of 3/4" (19 mm) reveal is permitted at the top of panels to allow lift on clearance of the panel. | | | |
| 11 | 4 | **REQUIRE** allowable fastener holes, when: | | | |
| 11 | 4 | 1 | Prefinished materials to be filled by the installer with matching filler furnished by the woodwork supplier. | | | |
| 11 | 4 | 2 | Unfinished or primed materials to be filled and caulked by the paint contractor or others. | | | |

Continues next column ▼

### 8.6.1 Basic Rules

▲ From previous column

| 12 | **REVEAL STRIPS** that are grooved into paneling are to be left floating and allowed to expand and contract in reaction to changing relative humidity. | | | |
|---|---|---|---|---|
| 13 | **EXPANSION JOINTS** shall be provided equivalent to 3/16" (4.8 mm) per 47" (1194 mm) of linear elevation. | | | |
| 13 | 1 | The minimum reveal gap between panels shall be calculated as the length of the panel times: | | | |
| 13 | 1 | 1 | 0.004 for particleboard core. | | | |
| 13 | 1 | 2 | 0.0033 for medium density fiberboard (MDF) core. | | | |
| 14 | **PANELING** shall be: | | | |
| 14 | 1 | Furred and installed in such a way as to avoid deflection when normal pressure is applied. | | | |
| 14 | 2 | Free of warp exceeding: | | | |
| 14 | 2 | 1 | 1/16" (1.6 mm) per linear foot (305 mm). | E | | |
| 14 | 2 | 2 | 3/64" (1.2 mm) per linear foot (305 mm). | | C | |
| 14 | 2 | 3 | 1/32" (0.8 mm) per linear foot (305 mm). | | | P |
| 15 | **JOINTS** shall be: | | | |
| 15 | 1 | Smooth and flush to create a homogenous look. | | | |
| 15 | 2 | Plumb within 1/16" (1.6 mm) in 96" (2438 mm). | | | |
| 16 | **BACKS** of wood wall and ceiling surfacing shall be sealed at 2 mil dry. | | C | P |
| 17 | Requires **FLATNESS** or **WARP** of installed and removable sheet products (see Test E illustrations in **TESTS**) such as, <br><br>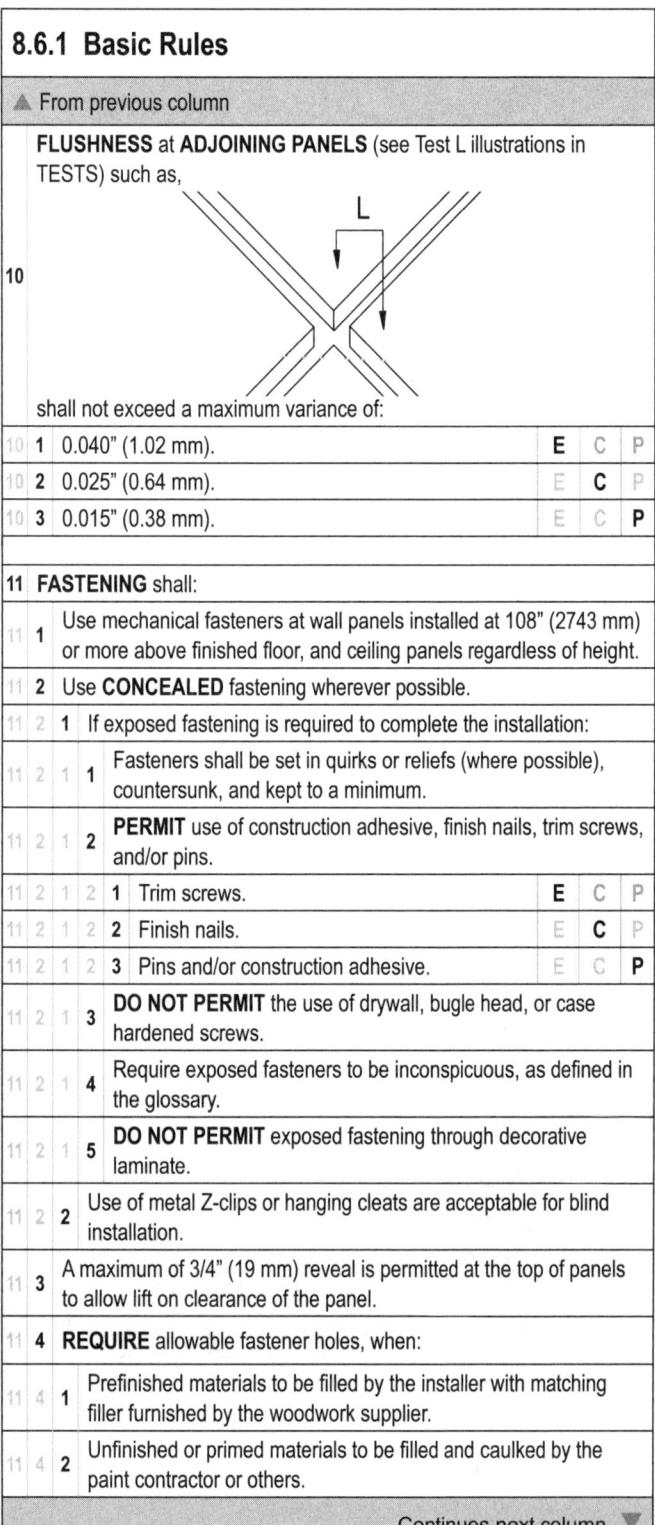<br><br> not to exceed grade tolerance listed for 12" (303 mm) diagonal, width and/or length or as lineal ratio (not geometric ratio) thereof. Example, twice the grade tolerance listed for 24" (610 mm), three times the tolerance for 36" (914 mm): | | | |
| 17 | 1 | 0.050" (1.3 mm) per 12" (305 mm) or portion thereof. | E | | |
| 17 | 2 | 0.036" (0.9 mm) per 12" (305 mm) or portion thereof. | | C | |
| 17 | 3 | 0.027" (0.7 mm) per 12" (305 mm) or portion thereof. | | | P |

Continues next column ▼

| E | C | P | Where the E, C, or P icon is not indicated, the rule applies to all Grades equally |

# compliance requirements

**SECTION 8**
Wall/Ceiling Surfacing and Partitions

GENERAL/PRODUCT/**INSTALLATION**/TEST

## 8.6.1 Basic Rules

▲ From previous column

| | | |
|---|---|---|
| 18 | **GLUE** and filler residue is not permitted on exposed faces. | |
| 19 | **EQUIPMENT CUTOUTS**, including electrical and plumbing, shall be cut out by the installer, provided needed templates are furnished prior to installation, and: | |
| 19 | 1 | Shall be neatly cut and properly sized. |
| 19 | 2 | Cutouts in HPDL shall have radiused inside corners. |
| 20 | **HARDWARE** shall be: | |
| 20 | 1 | Installed neatly without tear out of surrounding stock. |
| 20 | 2 | Installed per the manufacturer's instructions. |
| 20 | 3 | Installed using furnished fasteners and fastener's provisions and when fastener provisions are countersunk, fasteners shall be countersunk. |
| 20 | 4 | Adjusted for smooth operation. |
| 21 | **AREAS** of installation shall be left broom clean. | |
| 21 | 1 | Debris shall be removed and dumped in containers provided by the contractor. |
| 21 | 2 | Items installed shall be cleaned of pencil or ink marks. |
| 22 | **FIRST CLASS WORKMANSHIP** is required in compliance with these standards. | |

## 8.6.2 Product Specific Rules

| | | | | | | |
|---|---|---|---|---|---|---|
| 1 | | | **VENEERED PANELS** | | | |
| 1 | 1 | | For **TRANSPARENT FINISH**, the installer shall pay special attention to the **COLOR** and the **GRAIN** of the various panels and trim pieces to ensure they are installed in compliance with the **GRADE** specified. | | | |
| 1 | 2 | | **PANELS** shall be installed as specified. | | | |
| 1 | 3 | | **GLUING** with construction adhesive is permitted. | | | |
| 1 | 4 | | **CONCEALED FASTENING** shall be used wherever possible, and: | | | |
| 1 | 4 | 1 | A maximum of 3/4" (19 mm) reveal is permitted at the top of panels either under casework or at ceiling to facilitate such. | | | |
| 1 | 5 | | **EDGES** of core that are not self edged shall have one coat sealer applied before installation. | | | |
| 1 | 6 | | Veneer joints shall be plumb, within: | | | |
| 1 | 6 | 1 | 1/4" (6.4 mm). | E | C | P |
| 1 | 6 | 2 | 3/16" (4.8 mm). | E | C | P |
| 1 | 6 | 3 | 1/8" (3.2 mm). | E | C | P |
| 1 | 7 | | **VENEER LOSS** (side) between sequenced adjacent panels shall not exceed: | | | |
| 1 | 7 | 1 | 1-1/2" (38.1 mm). | E | C | P |
| 1 | 7 | 2 | 1" (25.4 mm). | E | C | P |
| 1 | 8 | | **VENEER LOSS** (end) between sequenced adjacent panels at end match shall not exceed: | | | |
| 1 | 8 | 1 | 2" (50.8 mm). | E | C | P |
| 1 | 8 | 2 | 1-1/2" (38.1 mm). | E | C | P |
| 1 | 9 | | End matched veneer alignment between sequenced adjacent panels shall not exceed: | | | |
| 1 | 9 | 1 | 3/8" (9.5 mm). | E | C | P |
| 1 | 9 | 2 | 3/16" (4.8 mm). | E | C | P |
| 1 | 10 | | Figure and/or heart progression shall be uniform and natural between adjacent sequenced panels and not exceed: | | | |
| 1 | 10 | 1 | 1" (25.4 mm). | E | C | P |
| 1 | 10 | 2 | 1/2" (12.7 mm). | E | C | P |
| 1 | 10 | 3 | Except at doors and other components that adjoin at blueprint panels shall not exceed: | | | |
| 1 | 10 | 3 | 1 | 2" (50.8 mm). | E | C | P |
| 1 | 10 | 3 | 2 | 1-1/2" (38.1 mm). | E | C | P |

Continues next column ▼

# SECTION 8
## Wall/Ceiling Surfacing and Partitions

GENERAL/PRODUCT/**INSTALLATION**/TEST

*Where the E, C, or P icon is not indicated, the rule applies to all Grades equally* | E | C | P |

**compliance requirements**

### 8.6.2 Product Specific Rules

▲ From previous column

| | | | | | E | C | P |
|---|---|---|---|---|---|---|---|
| 2 | | | SOLID WOOD SURFACING: | | | | |
| 2 | 1 | | FIELD JOINTS require: | | | | |
| 2 | 1 | 1 | No preparation. | | E | C | P |
| 2 | 1 | 2 | Shall be factory prepared to the greatest extent possible with feature strips and joint trim furnished oversize, where possible. | | E | C | P |
| 3 | | | DECORATIVE LAMINATE: | | | | |
| 3 | 2 | | EXPOSED FASTENING is not permitted, except: | | | | |
| 3 | 2 | 1 | At removable panels. | | | | |
| 3 | 3 | | PANELS shall be installed as specified. | | | | |
| 3 | 4 | | EDGES of core that are not self edged shall have one coat sealer applied before installation. | | | | |
| 3 | 5 | | SCRATCHES and CHIP OUT shall be inconspicuous beyond: | | | | |
| 3 | 5 | 1 | 72" (1830 mm). | | E | C | P |
| 3 | 5 | 2 | 48" (1220 mm). | | | C | P |
| 3 | 5 | 3 | 24" (610 mm). | | | | P |
| 3 | 6 | | PATTERN LINES shall be plumb, within: | | | | |
| 3 | 6 | 1 | 1/4" (6.4 mm). | | E | C | P |
| 3 | 6 | 2 | 3/16" (4.8 mm). | | | C | P |
| 3 | 6 | 3 | 1/8" (3.2 mm). | | | | P |
| 4 | | | SOLID SURFACE (only available in Custom and Premium Grade): | | | | |
| 4 | 1 | | SEALANTS and ADHESIVES shall be compatible with the individual manufacturer's recommendations or specially developed sealants to achieve the best color match. | | | | |
| 4 | 2 | | VERTICAL SURFACING shall be installed over suitable cores based on the manufacturer's recommendations. | | | | |
| 4 | 3 | | EXPANSION joints shall be furnished where required by building design or manufacturer recommendations. | | | | |
| 4 | 4 | | FIELD SEAMS: | | | | |
| 4 | 4 | 1 | Shall be CAULKED with compatible color matched sealant. | | | C | P |
| 4 | 4 | 2 | Shall be SEAMED with compatible hard seam adhesive. | | | | P |
| 4 | 5 | | EXPOSED FASTENING is not permitted, except: | | | | |
| 4 | 5 | 1 | At removable panels. | | | | |
| 4 | 5 | 2 | Where decorative fasteners are specified. | | | | |
| 4 | 6 | | SCRATCHES and CHIP OUTS shall be inconspicuous beyond: | | | | |
| 4 | 6 | 1 | 48" (1220 mm). | | | C | P |
| 4 | 6 | 2 | 24" (610 mm). | | | | P |

*Continues next column* ▼

### 8.6.2 Product Specific Rules

▲ From previous column

| | | | | | E | C | P |
|---|---|---|---|---|---|---|---|
| 5 | | | SOLID PHENOLIC (only available in Premium Grade): | | | | |
| 5 | 1 | | SEALANTS and ADHESIVES shall be compatible with the individual manufacturer's recommendations or specially developed sealants to achieve the best color match. | | | | |
| 5 | 2 | | VERTICAL SURFACING shall be installed over suitable cores based on the manufacturer's recommendations. | | | | |
| 5 | 3 | | EXPANSION CLEARANCE of at least 3/32" (2.4 mm) for every 120" (3048 mm) in length is required. | | | | |
| 5 | 4 | | CAULKED JOINTS shall be approximately 1/8" (3.2 mm) wide to allow satisfactory caulking penetration and expansion. | | | | |
| 5 | 5 | | EXPOSED FASTENING is not permitted, except: | | | | |
| 5 | 5 | 1 | At removable panels. | | | | |
| 5 | 5 | 2 | Where decorative fasteners are specified. | | | | |
| 5 | 6 | | CONCEALED FASTENING shall be used wherever possible, and: | | | | |
| 5 | 6 | 1 | A maximum of 3/4" (19 mm) reveal is permitted at the top of panels either under casework or at ceiling to facilitate such. | | | | |
| 5 | 7 | | SCRATCHES and CHIP OUTS shall be inconspicuous beyond: | | | | |
| 5 | 7 | 1 | 24" (610 mm). | | | | |

# SECTION 8
## Wall/Ceiling Surfacing and Partitions

**GENERAL/PRODUCT/INSTALLATION/TEST**

### 8.7 BASIC CONSIDERATIONS

1. The tolerances typically found within the Architectural Woodwork Standards fall into two categories:

    1.1 Factory fabricated joinery, assembly and construction - found in the **PRODUCT** portion.

    1.2 Field installation joinery and assembly - found in the **INSTALLATION** portion.

2. Most fabrication and installation assemblies include solid wood to solid wood joints, solid wood to wood veneer joints, solid wood to wood based products (decorative laminate Solid Phenolic and panel products), solid wood to non-wood based products (which can be drywall, glass, metal, stone, acrylics, and other surfaces), and non-wood to non-wood joints.

3. Tolerances found in the AWS include:

    3.1 Flatness of wood based panel products.

    3.2 Solid wood to solid wood joints and assemblies.

    3.3 Solid wood to wood veneer joints and assemblies.

    3.4 Wood veneer to wood veneer joints and assemblies.

    3.5 Solid wood to wood based product joints and assemblies.

    3.6 Solid surface to solid surface joints and assemblies.

4. Because of the differences of expansion and contraction of non-wood products compared to solid wood and wood based products, the AWS does not apply tolerances regarding flatness or joinery to these non-wood based products.

5. **FABRICATED** and **INSTALLED** woodwork shall be tested for compliance to these standards as follows.

    5.1 **SMOOTHNESS** of exposed surfaces:

    5.1.1 **KCPI** (Knife Cuts Per Inch) is determined by holding the surfaced board at an angle to a strong light source and counting the visible ridges per inch, usually perpendicular to the profile.

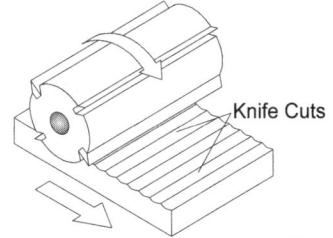

*Figure: 8-048*

### 8.7 BASIC CONSIDERATIONS (continued)

5.1.2 **SANDING** is checked for compliance by sanding a sample piece of the same species with the required grit of abrasive, and:

5.1.2.1 Observation with a hand lens of the prepared sample and the material in question will offer a comparison of the scratch marks of the abrasive grit.

5.1.2.2 Reasonable assessment of the performance of the finished product will be weighed against absolute compliance with the standard.

5.1.2.3 A product is sanded sufficiently smooth when knife cuts are removed and remaining sanding marks are or will be concealed by applied finishing coats.

5.1.2.4 Grain raise at unfinished wood, due to moisture or humidity in excess of the ranges set forth in this standard, shall not be considered a defect and must be sanded prior to finishing.

6. **TESTS FOR SEQUENCED AND BLUEPRINT-MATCHED PANELS, COMPONENTS, AND RELATED DOORS:**

    6.1 These tests do not apply to flush doors specified under Section 9 or specified using other standards, and they are in addition to those requirements covered above.

    6.2 At **END-MATCHED JOINTS:**

    6.2.1 Tested by separating end-matched panels and visually testing grain void for continuity.

    6.3 At **SIDE-MATCHED JOINTS:**

    6.3.1 Tested by separating side-matched panels and visually testing grain void for continuity.

    6.4 **HEART FIGURE PROGRESSION** - The full heart figure of plain-sliced veneer shall develop in uniform and natural progression.

    6.4.1 Split or cut hearts are permitted, provided they are used to maintain sequence or to achieve special effects.

7. **GAPS, FLUSHNESS, FLATNESS** and **ALIGNMENT** of product and installation:

    7.1 Maximum gaps between exposed components shall be tested with a feeler gauge at points designed to join, where members contact or touch.

    7.2 Joint length shall be measured with a ruler with minimum 1/16" (1 mm) divisions and calculations made accordingly.

# SECTION 8
## Wall/Ceiling Surfacing and Partitions

GENERAL/PRODUCT/INSTALLATION/TEST

**compliance requirements**

Where the **E**, **C**, or **P** icon is not indicated, the rule applies to all Grades equally — **E** **C** **P**

### 8.7 BASIC CONSIDERATIONS (continued)

**7 GAPS, FLUSHNESS, FLATNESS and ALIGNMENT** (continued)

7.3 The following is intended to provide examples of how and where compliance testing is measured:

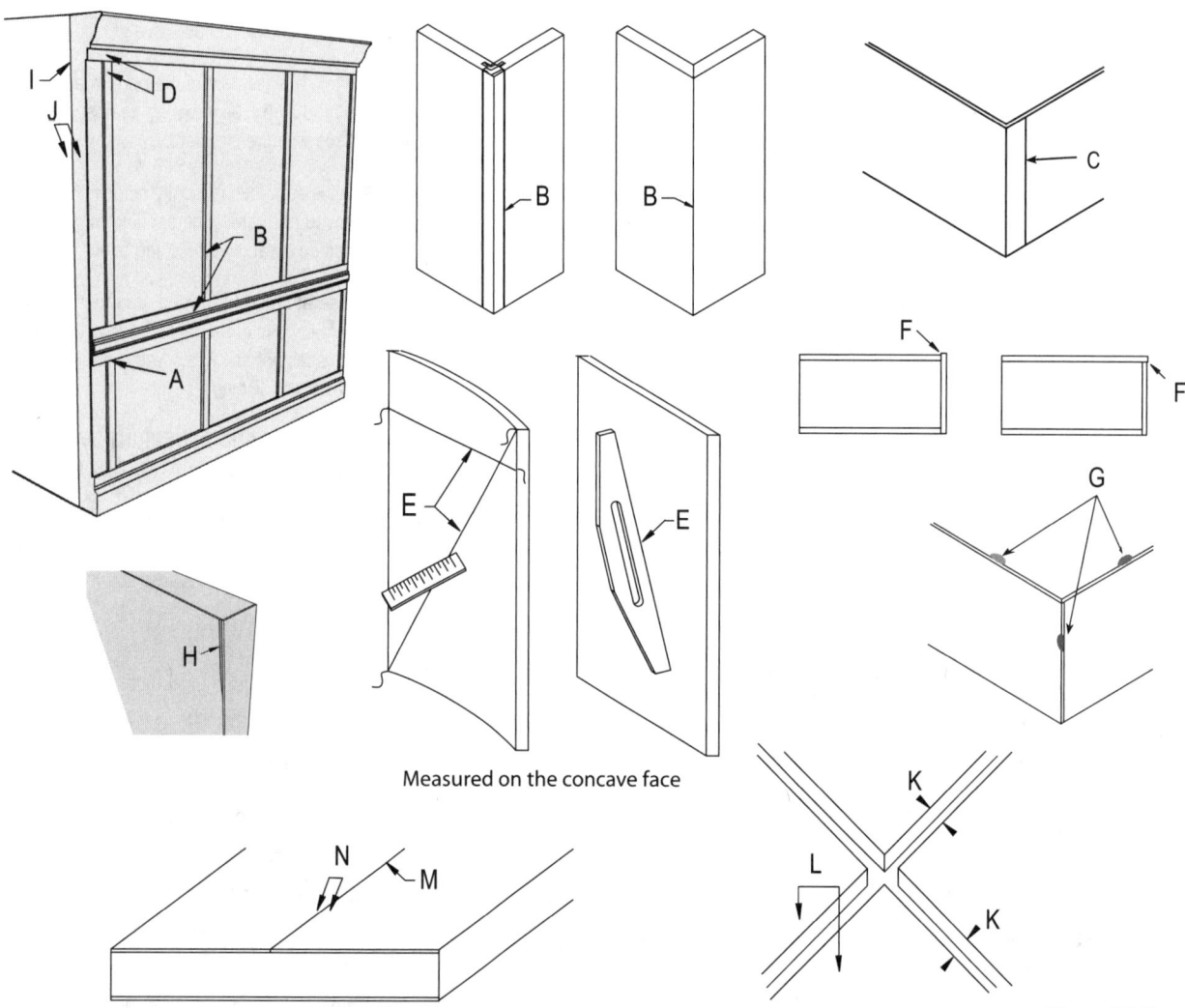

Measured on the concave face

*Figure: 8-049*

- A - Fabrication Gaps When Surfaces Are Mitered Or Butted
- B - Fabrication Gaps When Parallel Pieces Are Joined
- C - Fabrication Gaps When Edges Are Mitered Or Butted
- D - Fabrication Flushness Between Two Surfaces
- E - Flatness Of Panel Product
- F - Overlap (Flushness Of Laminate)
- G - Chip Out
- H - Over Machining
- I - Installation Gaps
- J - Installation Flushness
- K - Installation Reveal At Adjacent Panels
- L - Installation Flushness At Adjacent Panels
- M - Fabrication Gap At Laminate Butt Jointed On The Same Piece Of Core
- N - Fabrication Flushness At Butt Jointed Laminate

# Architectural Woodwork Standards

# DOORS

## SECTION 9

# SECTION 9
## Doors

## table of contents

### INTRODUCTORY INFORMATION

- Guide Specifications .................................................. 238
- Introduction ............................................................. 239
- Exterior Doors .......................................................... 239
- Code and Rule Requirements .................................. 239
- Face Material Selection ............................................ 239
- Veneers for Transparent Finish ................................ 239
- Materials for Opaque Finishes ................................. 239
- High Pressure Decorative Laminates (HPDL) .......... 239
- Door Symbols and Abbreviations ............................. 240
- Basic Core Types ..................................................... 240
- Speciality Cores ....................................................... 241
    - Fire Rated .......................................................... 241
    - Sound Resistant ................................................ 241
    - X-ray .................................................................. 241
    - Bullet Resistant ................................................. 241
    - Electrostatic Shielded ....................................... 241
- Core to Edge Assembly ........................................... 241
- Fire Ratings ............................................................. 241
- Code and Rule Requirements .................................. 241
- Special Function Doors ............................................ 241
- Veneer Faces ........................................................... 241
- Veneer Face Grade Summary ................................. 241
- Doors in Pairs or Sets ............................................. 242
    - Pair Match .......................................................... 242
    - Set Match .......................................................... 242
    - Doors with Transoms ........................................ 242
        - Continuous Match ....................................... 242
        - End Match .................................................. 242
        - No Match .................................................... 242
- Door Edge Construction and Types ......................... 242
- Construction Definitions .......................................... 243
    - Wood Face ........................................................ 243
        - 5 Ply ........................................................... 243
        - 7 Ply ........................................................... 243
    - HPDL Face ........................................................ 243
        - 3 Ply ........................................................... 243
        - 5 Ply ........................................................... 243
- Door Construction Cutaway Examples .................... 243
    - Wood Veneer Face, PC-7/PC-7 ........................ 243
    - HPDL Face, PC-HPDL-3 or PC-HPDL-5 ........... 243
    - Wood Veneer Face, SLC-5 or SLC-7 ............... 243
    - Wood Veneer Face, SCLC-5 or SCLC-7 .......... 243
    - Wood Veneer Face, FD-5 or FD-7 ................... 243
    - HPDL Face, FD-HPDL ...................................... 244
    - Wood Veneer Face, HC-7 ................................ 244
- Construction Details ................................................ 244
    - General Molding Requirements ....................... 244
    - Horizontal or Transom Meeting Edge Options . 244
    - Meeting Edge Options ..................................... 244
    - Glazing Options ................................................ 244
    - Louver Options ................................................. 245
    - Flashing Options .............................................. 245
    - Dutch Door Options ......................................... 245
    - Blocking Options .............................................. 245
- Hand and Bevel of Doors ........................................ 246
- Factory Finishing ..................................................... 246
- Stile and Rail Door Components .............................. 246
    - Stiles ................................................................. 246
    - Rails .................................................................. 246
    - Mullions ............................................................. 246
    - Panels ............................................................... 246
    - Muntins and Bars .............................................. 247
- Stile and Rail Door Design ...................................... 247
- Stile and Rail Door Joinery Examples ..................... 247
- Sticking Profiles ....................................................... 247
- Thickness ................................................................. 247
- Grain Direction and Layout ...................................... 247
- Stile & Rail Door Panel Layout and Grain Patterns . 248
- Stile & Rail Door Construction ................................. 248
- Stile & Rail Panel Construction ............................... 249
- Panel and Glass Retention Illustrations .................. 249
- Design Ideas ............................................................ 249
- Specify Requirements For ....................................... 250
- Recommendations ................................................... 250

# SECTION 9
## Doors

## table of contents

### COMPLIANCE REQUIREMENTS

#### GENERAL
- Basic Considerations ............................................. 251
  - Grades .......................................................... 251
    - Exclusion ................................................... 251
    - Grade Limitations ........................................... 251
  - Contract Documents ............................................. 251
  - Acceptable Requirements ........................................ 251
  - Aesthetic Compliance Requirements .............................. 251
  - Phenolic Backed Wood Veneer .................................... 251
  - Exposed Surfaces ............................................... 251
  - Semi-Exposed Surfaces .......................................... 251
  - NFPA 80 ........................................................ 251
  - Fire Rated Door ................................................ 251
  - Methods of Construction ........................................ 251
  - WDMA Performance Duty .......................................... 252
    - Heavy Duty .................................................. 252
    - Extra Heavy Duty ............................................ 252
    - Standard Duty ............................................... 252
    - Duty Level .................................................. 252
  - Prevent Telegraphing ........................................... 252
  - Industry Practices ............................................. 252
    - Structural Members .......................................... 252
    - Wall, Ceiling and Floor Tolerances .......................... 252
    - Warranty .................................................... 252
    - Handing ..................................................... 253

#### PRODUCT
- Scope .......................................................... 254
- Default Stipulation ............................................ 254
- Rules .......................................................... 254
  - Errata ....................................................... 254
- Basic Rules .................................................... 254
  - WDMA Performance Duty ........................................ 254
    - Flush Solid Core ........................................... 254
    - Flush Hollow Core .......................................... 254
    - Stile and Rail ............................................. 254
    - Responsibility ............................................. 254
  - In Lieu of Testing ........................................... 255
    - Flush Veneered ............................................. 255
    - Stile and Rail ............................................. 255
  - Aesthetic Grade .............................................. 255
  - Lumber ....................................................... 255
  - Sheet Products ............................................... 255
  - Exposed ...................................................... 255
  - Semi-Exposed ................................................. 255
  - Balanced Panel ............................................... 255
  - Cathedral .................................................... 256
  - Fire Rated Doors ............................................. 256
  - Sound Resistant Doors ........................................ 256
  - X-Ray Doors .................................................. 256
  - Bullet Resistant Doors ....................................... 256
  - Electrostatic Shielded Doors ................................. 256
  - Pair and Set Matching ........................................ 256
  - Exposed Faces & Edges ........................................ 256
  - Overall Door Size ............................................ 256
  - Bleed Through ................................................ 256
  - Glass and Glazing ............................................ 256
  - Factory Finished ............................................. 256
  - First Class Workmanship ...................................... 256
- Material Rules ................................................ 257
  - Defects ..................................................... 257
  - Figure ...................................................... 257
  - Hardboard ................................................... 257
    - Exposed ................................................... 257
    - Concealed ................................................. 257

# SECTION 9
## Doors

## table of contents

**COMPLIANCE REQUIREMENTS** (continued)

- **PRODUCT** (continued)
  - Material Rules (continued)
    - Flush Doors ............................................................. 257
      - Veneer Faces ................................................... 257
        - For Opaque ............................................... 257
        - For Transparent ......................................... 257
          - Stand Alone HPVA Door Skin Face Tables .... 257
            - Ash, Beech, Birch, Maple & Poplar ....... 258
            - Mahogany, Anigre, Makore, & Sapele ... 259
            - Oak, Red and White ............................ 260
            - Pecan and Hickory ............................... 261
            - Walnut and Cherry .............................. 262
      - Crossband Veneers ......................................... 263
      - Horizontal Edges ............................................ 263
    - Stile and Rail Doors ............................................ 263
      - For Opaque ..................................................... 263
      - For Transparent .............................................. 263
  - Machine / Assembly Rules ........................................ 264
    - ANSI/HPVA Heavy Duty Performance Duty Level ...... 264
    - Flush and Stile & Rail Table ................................. 264
    - Type I or II Adhesive .......................................... 264
    - Applied Moldings ............................................... 265
    - Glazing Material ................................................ 265
    - Exposed Surface ................................................ 265
      - Glue or Filler .................................................. 265
      - HPDL, PVC and Prefinished Wood ..................... 265
        - Overlap ........................................................ 265
        - Chip Out ...................................................... 265
        - Over Machined ............................................. 266
    - These Standards ................................................ 266
    - Joints at Assembled Woodwork ............................ 266
      - Securely Glued ............................................... 266
      - Reinforced ...................................................... 266
      - Mechanically Fastened .................................... 266
      - Not Permit ..................................................... 266
      - Flushness Variations Test D ............................ 266
      - Gap Test A ..................................................... 266
      - Gap Test B ..................................................... 266
      - Gap Test C ..................................................... 267
    - Flush Doors ....................................................... 267
      - Cores ............................................................. 267
      - Cutouts .......................................................... 267
      - Transom Panels .............................................. 267
      - Dutch Doors ................................................... 267
      - Vertical Edges ................................................ 268
    - Stile and Rail Doors ........................................... 268
      - If Solid Stock ................................................. 268
      - If Veneered .................................................... 268
      - With Panels .................................................... 269
      - Joinery ........................................................... 269

**INSTALLATION**

- Care, Storage and Building Conditions ......................... 270
- Contractor is Responsible for ...................................... 270
- Installer is Responsible for ......................................... 270
- Rules ......................................................................... 270
  - Errata ................................................................... 270
  - Basic Rules ........................................................... 271
    - Aesthetic .......................................................... 271
    - Installers .......................................................... 271
    - Prefit and Premachined ..................................... 271
    - Transparent Finish ............................................ 271
    - Blueprint .......................................................... 271
    - Utility and Structural Strength ........................... 271
    - FireDoor Assemblies ......................................... 271
    - Doors and their Accessories .............................. 271
    - When Installed ................................................. 271
    - Installer Modifications ...................................... 271
    - Door faces ....................................................... 271
    - Fitting .............................................................. 271
    - Clearance ........................................................ 271
    - Hardware ......................................................... 271
    - Leaf Hinges ...................................................... 272
    - Door Cutouts .................................................... 272
    - Temporary Distortions ...................................... 272
    - Repairs ............................................................ 272

# SECTION 9
## Doors

## table of contents

**COMPLIANCE REQUIREMENTS** (continued)

**INSTALLATION** (continued)

    Rules (continued)

        Basic Rules (continued)

            Woodwork .................................................. 272

            Flushness Test D ....................................... 273

            Areas of Installation .................................. 273

            First Class Workmanship ......................... 273

**TESTS**

    Basic Considerations ........................................... 274

    Fabricated and Installed ...................................... 274

    Smoothness ......................................................... 274

        KCPI ............................................................... 274

        Sanding ......................................................... 274

    Gaps, Flushness, Flatness and Alignment ........ 274

        Illustrations .................................................. 275

# SECTION 9
Doors

*introductory information*

# Guide Specifications

Are available through the Sponsor Associations in interactive digital format including unique and individual quality control options. The Guide Specifications are located at:

## Architectural Woodwork Institute (AWI)
www.awinet.org

## Architectural Woodwork Manufacturers Association of Canada (AWMAC)
http://awmac.com/aws-guide-specifications

## Woodwork Institute (WI)
www.woodworkinstitute.com/publications/aws_guide_specs.asp

# SECTION 9
## Doors

## introductory information

### INTRODUCTION

Section 9 includes information on doors using flush and stile & rail construction with wood or HPDL faces and their related parts.

In the past manufacturers have relied on the natural strength of hardwood lumber and veneer to assure long term performance. Many new engineered wood products are now replacing traditional hardwoods; allowing cost reductions, improved production efficiency and allowing the manufacturers the ability to provide better doors.

However, there is a risk some nonconforming products will not perform as well. The materials and construction methods used determine how well a door will resist high use and abuse. With the introduction of engineered wood products this becomes more important. Wood products, whether natural or engineered, have a wide range of strength characteristics and it is important that the door material and construction method meets the performance criteria of the project requirements.

Quality assurance can be achieved by adherence to the AWS and will provide the owner a quality product at competitive pricing. Use of a qualified Sponsor Member firm to provide your woodwork will help ensure the manufacturer's understanding of the quality level required. Illustrations in this Section are not intended to be all inclusive. Other engineered solutions are acceptable. In the absence of specifications; methods of fabrication shall be of the manufacturer's choice. The design professional, by specifying compliance to the AWS increases the probability of receiving the product quality expected.

### EXTERIOR DOORS

Wood doors are not recommended for exterior use. Most flush doors no longer have extended exterior use warranties and some have no warranty at all. Refer to manufacturers' written warranty for specifics.

Wood doors used in an exterior environment should be water repellent treated at the factory after manufacturing. They should be protected according to manufacturers' requirements, which may include flashing of top, bottom and cut outs. Additionally, they should be protected from the sun and other weather elements by overhangs, deep recesses, etc.

While wood stile and rail entry doors have performed well for centuries, the selection of a wood door places a burden on the owner to maintain the door by keeping it painted or sealed, protected from moisture, and properly adjusted in the opening. Medium density overlay faced doors are strongly recommended for severe exposure conditions and all surfaces should be primed with an exterior enamel primer, followed by a minimum of two additional coats of exterior enamel.

### CODE and RULE REQUIREMENTS

The design professional shall be responsible for contract documents which clearly detail products which will comply with local or national applicable codes and rules including, but not limited to: positive pressure requirements and labeling; glass or glazing; prefitting and/or machining for hardware; prehanging and/or machining for weather stripping; priming, sealing and/or transparent finishing; and flashing and/or metal edge guards. The door manufacturer is often a valuable assistant in these matters.

Contract documents shall:

- Specify neutral pressure or positive pressure compliance.

- If positive pressure, specify the category of door: A or B assembly.

- Specify whether the smoke and draft label (S label) is validated or not.

### FACE MATERIAL SELECTION

The panel face veneer standards of the Hardwood Plywood & Veneer Association HP-1, latest edition, is adopted as the minimum standard for face veneers. Specifiers need to determine and specify the following:

### VENEERS FOR TRANSPARENT FINISHES

Species: There are numerous foreign and domestic species available. Involve your manufacturer early in the design and selection process.

Matching: Many different visual effects can be obtained by face veneer matching.

- Appearance and layout of individual pieces of veneer.

- Matching between pieces (leaves) of veneer.

- Orientation of spliced veneer on a door face.

- Appearance of doors in pairs or sets.

- Appearance of doors with transoms.

### MATERIALS FOR OPAQUE FINISHES

**Medium Density Overlay, MDF or Hardboard.** These provide the optimum paintable surface for architectural doors.

**Close Grain Hardwood.** Extra preparation will be required by the finisher as there will be grain show through, open appearing veneer joints, and other wood characteristics when using this product for a painted finish.

**Manufacturers' option.** Face materials are determined by the manufacturer.

### HIGH PRESSURE DECORATIVE LAMINATES (HPDL)

Virtually any high pressure decorative laminate color and texture can be used in the manufacture of architectural doors with the following cautions:

- High gloss and Vertical Grades of decorative laminate will highlight minor core and surface imperfections, often unacceptably.

- Decorative laminate doors are not recommended for use in non climate controlled interior or exterior environment due to the potential differences in lineal expansion between the faces and wood components when exposed to the elements.

# SECTION 9
## Doors

## introductory information

### DOOR SYMBOLS and ABBREVIATIONS

Your door manufacturer is the best source of specific guidance when writing door specifications. The following short list of abbreviations applies to some door companies:

- ME = Matching edges; i.e., vertical edges same as decorative faces.

- CE = Compatible edges; i.e., vertical edges selected for compatibility with decorative faces.

- PC = Particleboard, MDF, or agrifiber core, solid core door with stiles and rails bonded to the core and abrasive planed flat prior to the application of the faces, including:
  - PC-5 = Core with 2 layers on each side.
  - PC-7 = Core with 3 layers on each side.
  - PC-HPDL-3 = Core with laminate to each side.
  - PC-HPDL-5 = Core with crossband and laminate each side.

- SCLC = Structural composite lumber core, solid core door with stiles and rails bonded to the core and abrasive planed flat prior to the application of the faces, including:
  - SCLC-5 = Core with 2 layers on each side.
  - SCLC-7 = Core with 3 layers on each side.
  - SCLC-HPDL-5 = Core with crossband and laminate each side.

- SLC = Staved lumber core, solid core door with stiles and rails bonded to the core and abrasive planed flat prior to the application of the faces.
  - SLC-5 = Core with 2 layers on each side.
  - SLC-7 = Core with 3 layers on each side.
  - SLC-HPDL-5 = Core with crossband and laminate each side.

- FPC = Floating particleboard core, solid core placed within a stile and rail frame, bonded together by the faces, including:
  - FPC-5 = Core with 2 layers on each side.
  - FPC-7 = Core with 3 layers on each side.

- FSLC = Floating staved lumber core, solid core placed within a stile and rail frame, bonded together by the faces, including:
  - FSLC-7 = Core with 3 layers on each side.

- FD = Fire resistant core, fire resistant materials assembled to stiles and rails according to methods prescribed by the testing agency based on rigorous smoke, flame, and pressure tests. Labeled fire doors are specified by their resistance ratings:
  - FD-5 = Core with 2 layers on each side.
  - FD-7 = Core with 3 layers on each side.
  - FD-HPDL-3 = Core with laminate to each side.
  - FD-HPDL-5 = Core with crossband and laminate each side.

- IHC-7 = Institutional hollow core, honey comb, ladder, or grid type cores inside stiles and rails, bonded together by the faces.

- SHC-7 = Standard hollow core, honey comb, ladder, or grid type cores inside stiles and rails, bonded together by the faces.

- SR = Sound retardant doors, specified by their performance characteristics.

- LL = Lead lined doors, designed to resist penetration by radiation of various types, and specified by their performance.

- ES = Electrostatic shielded doors.

- BR = Ballistic resistant doors.

### BASIC CORE TYPES

The design professional or specification writer has the opportunity to select the door core type. In the absence of specification, PC shall be furnished, complying with particleboard standard ANSI A208.1 Particleboard, Grade LD-1 or LD-2.

The five most common core types are PC, SLC, SCLC, HC, and fire resistant door core, conforming to the minimum requirements of WDMA - I.S. 1-A (latest edition).

Specify one, or a combination of, solid core, hollow core, or fire resistant core, and acoustical, ballistic resistant, or lead lining where and when required. The requirements for each core type are illustrated in Section 9. In the absence of clear specifications, the core shall be of the manufacturer's choice. SCLC may be specified in any Grade.

- When solid core is selected, specify one of the following: PC, SLC, or SCLC. When the weight of the door is a design factor, consult the door manufacturer to determine the differences between PC, SLC, and SCLC core types.

- When HC, specify the honey comb, with the minimum cell size required, grid core, or ladder construction.

- When fire resistant core is required beyond the 20 minute label level, consult your door manufacturer for code compliant core types, blocking options, metal edges, cut outs, and astragals.

The use of SCLC for top and/or bottom rails, and blocking is acceptable. SCLC is proving to have excellent performance characteristics as a replacement for stave core, as it often minimizes or eliminates telegraphing of the lumber blocks through the face veneers or overlays. When the edge of an SCL core door will be visible after installation, design professionals may wish to specify a fill and paint treatment, or the application of a veneer edgeband to conceal the coarse texture of the edge of the SCL material. It is the responsibility of the design professional to make a selection in the best interests of the client.

# SECTION 9
## Doors

## introductory information

### SPECIALITY CORES

Such as fire rated, sound resistant, x-ray, bullet resistant, or electrostatic shielded doors shall be properly specified, including the fire rating, sound class, lead thickness, and/or protection rating.

- At **FIRE RATED** doors, the type of construction, core type, thickness, edgebands, moldings, blocking, and use of intumescent coatings shall be the standard of the door manufacturer, conforming to the labeling authority granted to them by their labeling agency.

- At **SOUND RESISTANT** doors, the type of construction, thickness, edgebanding, applied moldings, special stops, stop adjusters, gaskets, and automatic threshold closing devices shall be the standard of the door manufacturer conforming to the STC (Sound Transmission Class) specified when tested as an opening unit (rather than sealed in place).

- At **X-RAY DOORS**, construction, thickness, edgebands, and moldings shall be of the manufacturer's standard.

- At **BULLET RESISTANT** doors, the type of construction, thickness, edgebands, and moldings shall be of the manufacturer's standard.

- At **ELECTROSTATIC SHIELDED** doors, the type of construction, thickness, edgebands, and moldings shall be of the manufacturer's standard.

Cores other than those enumerated herein are manufactured to individual specifications and are not dealt with in these standards for that reason.

### CORE TO EDGE ASSEMBLY

These standards provide for multiple types of assembly between the core and the vertical and horizontal edges in doors:

- Stiles and rails securely bonded to core, prior to application of faces.

- Stiles and rails **NOT** bonded to core prior to application of faces.

- Stiles and rails placed (not bonded) around hollow core inserts.

### FIRE RATINGS

The Model Codes have established a fire door rating and operating classification system for use in protecting door openings in fire rated wall constructions. Fire doors must meet certain requirements and bear certifying labels of an independent testing agency approved by the building official.

### CODE AND RULE REQUIREMENTS

The design professional shall be responsible for contract documents which clearly detail products which will comply with applicable codes and rules including, but not limited to, NFPA 80 requirements; ADA national and federal guidelines; local, state/provincial and federal building codes; positive pressure requirements and labeling; glass or glazing; prefitting and/or machining for hardware; prehanging and/or machining for weatherstripping; priming, sealing and/or transparent finishing; and flashing and/or metal edge guards. The door manufacturer is often a valuable assistant in these matters.

Fire doors shall be installed per NFPA 80.

**Critical note** and **warning:** The status of fire resistant doors and openings continue to change. The design professional shall verify that the total opening complies with both international and local code requirements before finalizing the specification for fire rated doors, hardware, and openings.

### SPECIAL FUNCTION DOORS

Sound retardant (acoustical), lead lined (X-ray), ballistic resistant, and electrostatic shield doors are manufactured by some companies to meet these special needs. Refer to manufacturer's literature for details.

Transom panels and special function doors are available and should be specified carefully, with particular attention to the meeting edge details, operational functions and accessories, and veneer match options. In the absence of clear and complete specifications, fabrication details will be of the manufacturer's choice.

### VENEER FACES

At stand alone doors with face species of Anigre, Ash, Beech, Birch, Cherry, Hickory, African Mahogany, American Mahogany, Makore, Maple, Red Oak, White Oak, Pecan, Poplar, or Walnut shall conform to the HPVA Door Skin Face tables included within the Materials portion of this section. Doors of a species not listed above shall conform to the HPVA Door Skin Faces as agreed on between buyer and seller.

- Doors adjacent to or that become a component of other architectural woodwork shall conform to the applicable requirements of Section 4.

- Stand alone, Center Balanced Matched doors, shall not have the width of outer leaves after trimming exceed 1" (25.4 mm) less than its adjoining leaf for Custom Grade, or 1/2" (12.7 mm) less than its adjoining leaf for Premium Grade.

- Before specifying, check with the door manufacturer for availability.

Special matching shall be so specified, such as: All doors on the same project are to be manufactured using the same or similar flitches.

Sequence matched face veneers required at pairs or sets of doors and adjacent panels.

### VENEER FACE GRADE SUMMARY

Read Section 4 for the complete description of veneer face grades.

When veneers are specified as "natural," they may contain any amount or combination of sapwood and heartwood, with the resultant contrast in color in many species.

The industry recognizes that cost is an important factor, and having lower veneer standards can result in some savings. Specifying Architectural Woodwork Standards Custom Grade meets that need. However, when doors are a part of an overall design scheme and/or are adjacent to other architectural woodwork specified under these standards, the level of quality of those doors must be consistent with other millwork components.

# SECTION 9
## Doors

### introductory information

**DOORS IN PAIRS OR SETS**

- **Pair Match -** Two doors hung adjacent may be (and in some Grades, must be) specified as a Pair Match. Note to specifying authority: Specifying Pair Matched only means the two doors are to be considered Pair Matched as per the AWS Grade specified, it does not mean the veneer is sequenced, nor does it designate the veneer cut or layup. The Grade specified will determine the type of Match required. Sequencing, veneer cut and layup if different from the Grade Rules must be specified. The illustration in Figure 9-001 shows flat or plain cut, book matched, center matched faces.

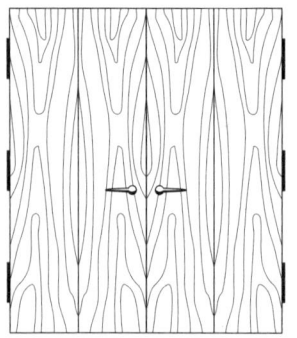

*Figure: 9-001*

- **Set Match -** Three or more doors or two or more Pair Matched doors hung adjacent may be (and in some Grades, must be) specified as a Set Match. Note to specifying authority: Specifying Set Matched only means the three or more doors are to be considered Set Matched as per the AWS Grade specified, it does not mean the veneer is sequenced, nor does it designate the veneer cut or layup. The Grade specified will determine the type of Match required. Sequencing, veneer cut and layup if different from the Grade Rules must be specified. The illustration in Figure 9-002 shows flat or plain cut, book matched, center matched faces.

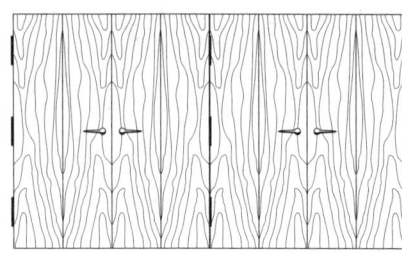

*Figure: 9-002*

- **Doors with Transoms**

The use of the transom increases the apparent height of the door and often enhances the appearance of the opening. The type of match should be specified, and a slight misalignment of veneer grain may occur between the transom and the door. Industry practice allows a variation in grain alignment from side to side of 3/8" (9.5 mm) on a single door, and 1/2" (12.7 mm) on pairs of doors with a single transom. If tighter tolerances are desired, they must be specified.

Grain pattern alignment between the door and transom, even when cut from the same panel, will vary to some extent. This is due to the natural progression of the annual rings which create the figure in the wood. Misalignment will be more apparent in doors veneered with open grain species than with close grain. Misalignment of up to 3/8" (9 mm) is permitted in every Grade.

- **Continuous Match -** Provides optimum veneer utilization as each single piece of veneer extends from the top of the transom to the bottom of the door. Available veneer length in the species may limit this option.

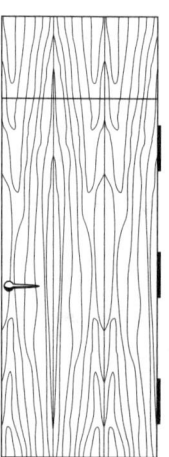

*Figure: 9-003*

- **End Match -** A single piece of veneer extends from the bottom to the top of the door with a mirror image at the transom.

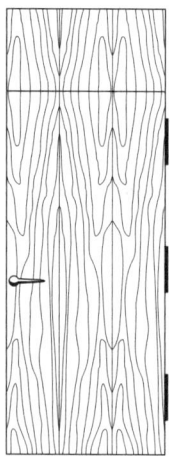

*Figure: 9-004*

- **No Match**

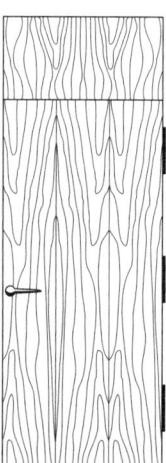

*Figure: 9-005*

**DOOR EDGE CONSTRUCTION AND TYPES**

Edge construction is the manufacturer's choice unless specified otherwise.

- **Type - A -** Solid Wood edgeband, face, and cross band edges show.

*Figure: 9-006*

# SECTION 9
## Doors

## introductory information

- **Type - B** - Wood Veneer edgeband, face, and cross band edges covered.

*Figure: 9-007*

- **Type - C** - HPDL or PVC edgeband, face, and cross band edges covered.

*Figure: 9-008*

- **Type - D** - Solid Wood edgeband, veneer face edge shows.

*Figure: 9-009*

- **Type - E** - Solid Wood edgeband, veneer face edge shows.

*Figure: 9-010*

To **PREVENT TELEGRAPHING**, inset solid wood edging when used must have similar moisture content as panel core, be glued securely and calibrated with panel core thickness prior to being laminated with a wood veneer on both faces.

- **Type - F** - Solid Wood edgeband, face, and cross band edges covered.

*Figure: 9-011*

### CONSTRUCTION DEFINITIONS

- **Wood Face:**
  - **5-Ply** consists of a center core on which is applied to each side a wood veneer or composite cross band with a face veneer applied over the cross band.
  - **7-Ply** consists of a center core on which is applied to each side 3-ply face skins.

- **HPDL-Face:**
  - **3-Ply** consists of a core with a plastic laminate face applied over both sides of the core.
  - **5-Ply** consists of a wood veneer or composite cross band applied over the core before application of the face laminate.

### DOOR CONSTRUCTION CUTAWAY EXAMPLES

Illustrations of grain direction is only applicable to wood veneer.

- **WOOD VENEER FACE** with particleboard, MDF, or agrifiber core (PC-5 / PC-7).

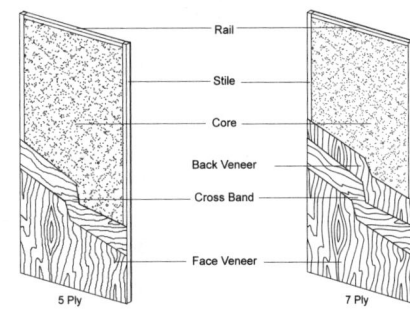

*Figure: 9-012*

- **HPDL FACE** with particleboard, MDF, or agrifiber core (PC-HPDL-3 / PC-HPDL-5).

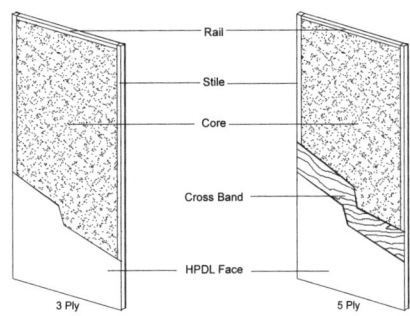

*Figure: 9-013*

- **WOOD VENEER FACE** with staved lumber core (SLC-5 / SLC-7).

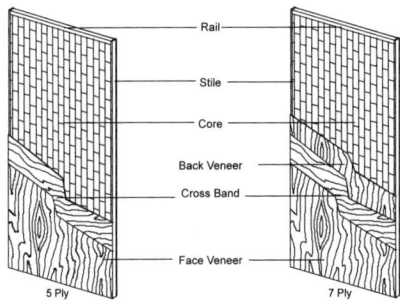

*Figure: 9-014*

- **WOOD VENEER FACE** with structural composite lumber (SCL) core (SCLC-5 / SCLC-7).

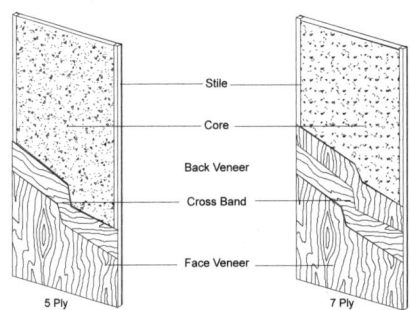

*Figure: 9-015*

- **WOOD VENEER FACE** with fire resistant composite core (FD-5 / FD-7).

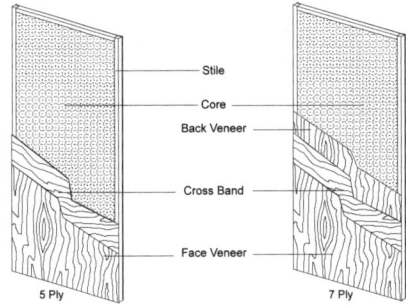

*Figure: 9-016*

# SECTION 9
## Doors

### introductory information

**DOOR CONSTRUCTION CUTAWAY EXAMPLES**
(continued)

- **HPDL** with fire resistant composite core (FD-HPDL).

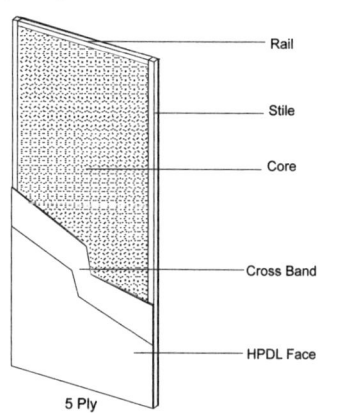

*Figure: 9-017*

- **WOOD VENEER/HPDL FACE** with hollow core (HC-7).

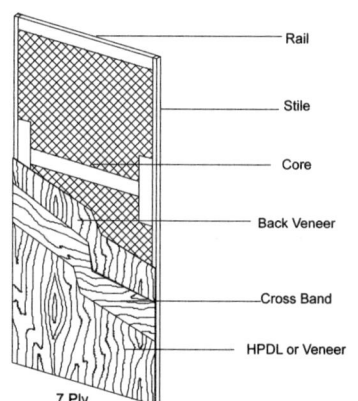

*Figure: 9-018*

### CONSTRUCTION DETAILS

- **General Molding Requirements**

  - Species shall match or be compatible with face veneer or laminate.
  - Specify transparent or opaque finish.
  - Molding shall be free of open defects, shake, splits, or doze.
  - Molding must be smooth and free of visible knife, saw, or sanding marks. Specify from following options:

- **Horizontal or Transom Meeting Edge Options**

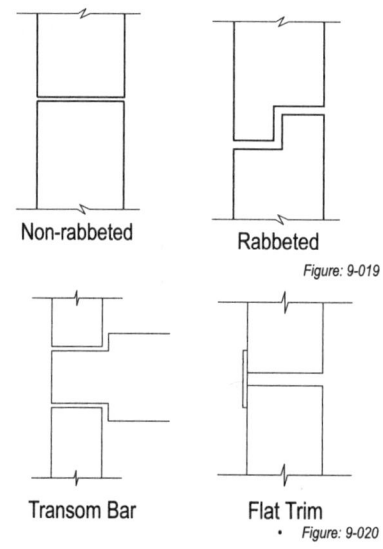

*Figure: 9-019*

*Figure: 9-020*

- **Meeting Edge Options**

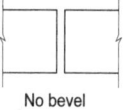
No bevel     Bevel

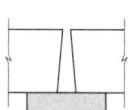
Flat astragal     Tee astragal

*Figure: 9-021*

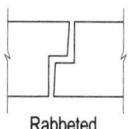
Rabbeted     Parallel bevel Double egress

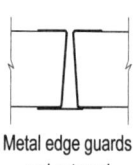
Metal edge guards and astragal     Metal edge guards

*Figure: 9-022*

- **Glazing Options**

*Figure: 9-023*

244 Architectural Woodwork Standards     ©2014 AWI | AWMAC | WI 2nd Edition, October 1, 2014

# SECTION 9
## Doors

## introductory information

### CONSTRUCTION DETAILS (continued)

- **Glazing Options** (continued)

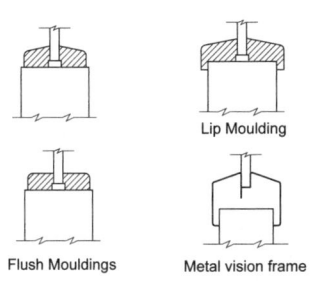

Figure: 9-024

All cutouts for metal or wood vision panels typically should be a minimum of 6" (152 mm) from the edge of the door and/or other cutouts for louvers, locks, closers, or other hardware.

This distance should be maintained or the fire label and warranty may be voided.

- **Louver Options**

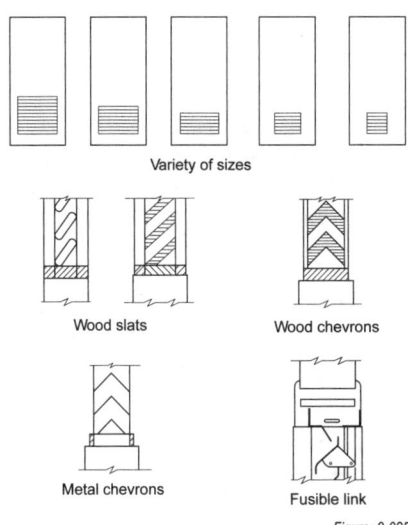

Figure: 9-025

Generally, fusible link louvers installed in 45, 60, and 90 minute fire rated doors must comply with individual fire door authorities. Wood louvers are not allowed by NFPA 80 in fire rated doors. All doors must comply to accessibility requirements.

Fusible link (FL) louvers must be minimum 10" (254 mm) from the bottom of the door to the bottom of the louver cutout, and 6" (152 mm) from the edge of the louver cutout to the edge of the door and/or other cutouts for vision panels, locks, closers, or other hardware. These minimum dimensions should be maintained or the fire rating label and warranty may be voided. Sizes and details other than those illustrated are available.

- **Flashing Options**

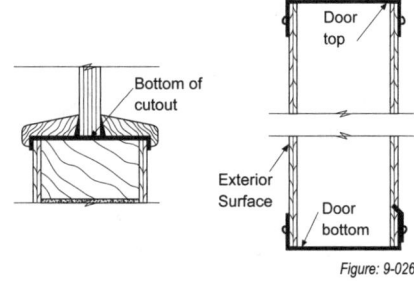

Figure: 9-026

If the manufacturer is to flash the top of the door or the bottom edge of cutouts for exterior doors, it must be specified.

- **Dutch Door Options**

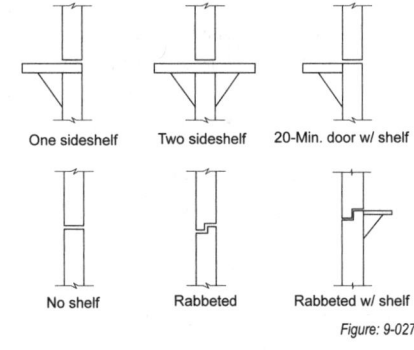

Figure: 9-027

- **Blocking Options**

For undercutting flexibility and specialized hardware applications, a number of internal blocking options are available from most manufacturers. When blocking is required it is typically at particle core and fire resistant core doors. Options such as 5" (127 mm) top rail, 5" (127 mm) bottom rail, 5" x 18" (127 x 457 mm) lock blocks (may be one side only), 2-1/2" (64 mm) cross blocking are available, but there are other options are available. Consult your manufacturer early in the design process to determine requirements.

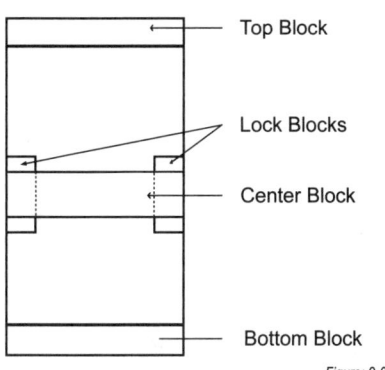

Figure: 9-028

Hardware Blocking, if desired, shall be specified from the following typical options:

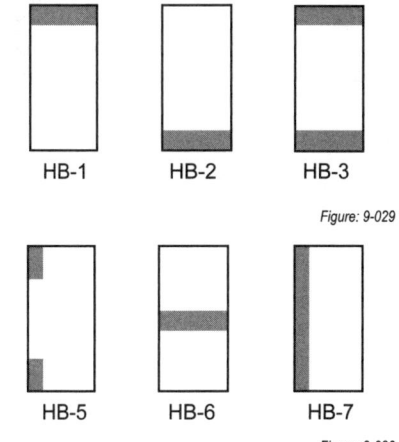

Figure: 9-029

Figure: 9-030

Top Blocking may be full or partial width as required by its application.

# SECTION 9
Doors

## introductory information

### HAND and BEVEL OF DOORS

The "hand" of a door is always determined from the outside. The outside of an exterior door is the street or entrance (key) side. The outside of an interior room or auditorium door is the corridor or hall (key or imaginary key) side. The outside of a closet door is the side opposite the closet; the room, corridor or hall side. The outside of a single communicating door is the side from which the butts are invisible when the door is closed. The outside of twin communicating doors is the space between the two doors.

Standard handed doors push away from the person standing on the outside/key side. Reverse handed doors pull toward the person standing on the outside/key side.

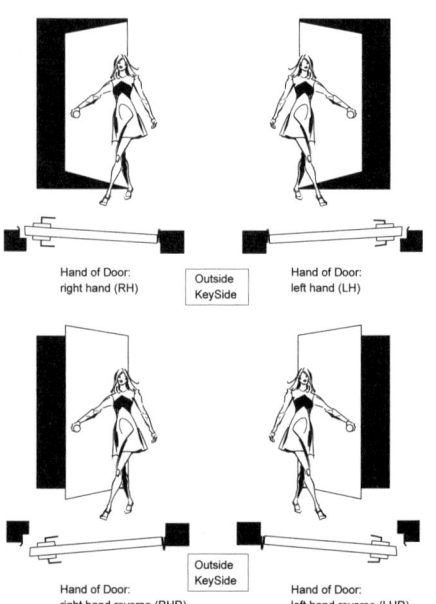

*Figure: 9-031*

### FACTORY FINISHING (when specified)

Firms differ in the variety of factory finishes offered. Some finishes may not be available from all manufacturers. Finishes protect wood from moisture, handling, or harsh chemicals. The sooner moisture is restricted from entering or leaving, the longer wood lasts and the finer it looks. Transparent finishes without stain provide a protective coating for the wood, maintaining its natural look. Transparent finishes with stain provide the architect or designer an opportunity to create a striking visual effect by modifying color, texture, and sheen.

Finishing Options
Section 5 of the AWS defines the finishing systems and performance characteristics.

Carefully studying Section 5 with your manufacturer early in the design phase can result in both high quality and cost savings.

Factory finishing is generally specified when a project requires high quality performance and superior appearance.

Factory finishing offers many benefits, including:

- State of the art equipment in a well lighted, dust free environment (conditions normally not available in the field), which provides uniform color, texture, and sheen.

- Proper sanding prior to the application of stains and finishes. Field conditions often hinder surface preparation resulting in a lack of clarity and uniformity in finish and color.

- Protection from unfavorable relative humidity conditions at the earliest possible time.

- Cost savings (in most cases) over the total cost of field applied finishes by a separate contractor.

- Shorter installation time on the job site, resulting in faster project completion.

### STILE and RAIL DOOR COMPONENTS

- **Stiles** - are the vertical outside members. They may be solid wood or veneered. Stiles usually have solid sticking (solid stuck, solid molded). Sticking is usually of three profiles: "ovolo", "ogee" or "quarter round". Other profiles may be used. The stiles are ploughed or grooved along the edge to receive the panels, rails, and/or glass. If the door is to be assembled by dowelled construction, the stiles are bored to receive the dowels. If the door is to be assembled by lag screw construction, the stiles shall be solid hardwood lumber. The stiles will contain much of the hardware for the door, and must be sized and fabricated to fit the intended hardware, locks, and latches.

- **Rails** - are the cross or horizontal members of the door. They may be solid wood or veneered. Rails are coped on both ends to fit the sticking of the stile. Tenons or dowels are machined into the rails to fit mortises or dowel boring in the stiles.

  - The top and bottom rails are required, with the addition of intermediate cross rails or lock rails as appropriate. The bottom rail is usually the widest of the members, made of edge glued lumber or veneered, depending on the door construction. The top rail is often the same face dimension as the stiles.

  - The lock rail, if there is one, is usually a wide member located at lock height. In the case of narrow stiles or large hardware, this rail serves to house the lock and latch mechanisms.

- **Mullions** - an upright or vertical member between panels. It is similar to a cross rail in the way it is fit and machined.

- **Panels** - are either solid lumber or panel products that fill the frame formed by the stiles, rails, and mullions. When the figure of the wood is visible in the finished product, the grain direction of the panels usually runs vertically.

# SECTION 9
## Doors

## introductory information

### STILE and RAIL DOOR COMPONENTS
(continued)

- **Muntins and Bars** - Stile and rail door with glass panels often utilize muntins and bars, which are smaller in section than mullions. A bar is a rabbeted molding, which extends the total height or width of the glass opening. A muntin is a short bar, either horizontal or vertical, extending from a full bar to a stile, rail, or another bar. Muntins and bars are traditionally coped and mortised joinery.

### STILE and RAIL DOOR DESIGN

Custom stile and rail door design offer many opportunities for creativity and choice. Some of the variables include:

- Panel layout.
- Grain patterns and relationships.
- Stile and rail construction.
- Molding details.
- Panel construction.
- Joinery techniques.

Selection among these variables requires some knowledge of their relative performance characteristics. The following drawings illustrate some of the options. Many manufacturers feel veneered and laminated constructions offer the lowest risk of warp for most species of wood. Consult your manufacturer early in the design process for assistance in making selections.

The strength of a stile and rail door is primarily dependent on the shoulders and joints between the stiles and rails. A wide bottom rail will increase significantly the strength and stability of a door far beyond that of a narrow rail.

Care should be taken to ensure that the design of a door's stiles and rails is large enough to structurally accommodate the intended hardware, provide a strong and stable door, and accommodate the usage and size of the opening.

Because of warpage and twist characteristics of heavy, one piece, solid hardwood members, that method of construction is not recommended for stile and rail door construction.

Door panels of either flush/flat or raised design are typically of the same species as the stiles and rails.

### STILE and RAIL DOOR JOINERY EXAMPLES

- **Haunched Mortise and Tenon**

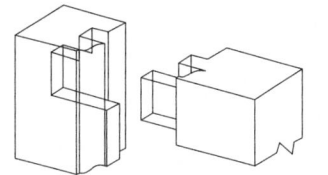

*Figure: 9-033*

- **Slot Mortise and Tenon**

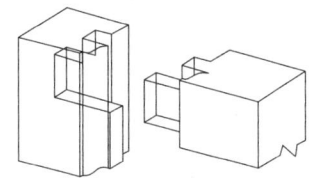

*Figure: 9-034*

- **Loose Tenon**

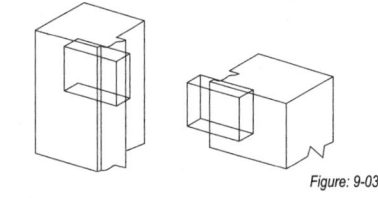

*Figure: 9-035*

- **Dowel**

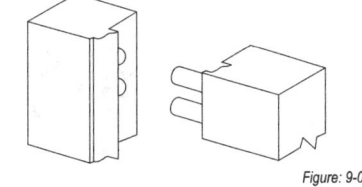

*Figure: 9-036*

### STICKING PROFILES:

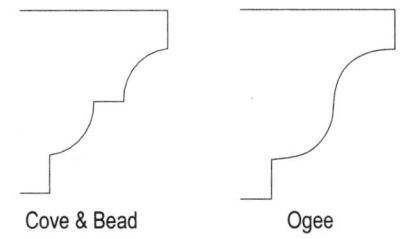

Cove & Bead     Ogee

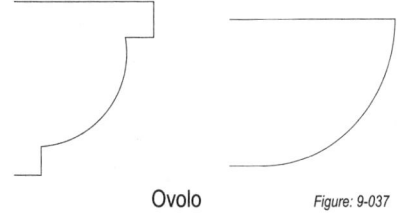

Ovolo     *Figure: 9-037*

### THICKNESS

Stile and rail doors are usually 1-3/4" (44 mm) thick. For doors over 3'-6" (1067 mm) in width or 8'-0" (2440 mm) in height, it is recommended they be 2 1/4" (57 mm) minimum thickness.

### GRAIN DIRECTION and LAYOUT

Traditionally, the grain direction flows with the longest dimension of the stile or rail. Panel grain typically runs vertical: however, it can be altered for design purposes. If raised panels are to be rim raised veneered construction, the grain of the rims will flow around the panel with the long dimension of the rim material.

There are a variety of methods of stile and rail fabrication. It is possible to fabricate stile and rail doors that will perform within the tests established in this Standard using any of the illustrated techniques and others. The illustrations are intended as guidelines for the design professional and should not limit the potential for creative solutions. Glass cannot always be centered on stiles and rails, depending on the thickness. Moldings and stop are usually applied with small brads or finish nails.

# SECTION 9
## Doors

### introductory information

**STILE AND RAIL DOOR PANEL LAYOUT and GRAIN PATTERNS**

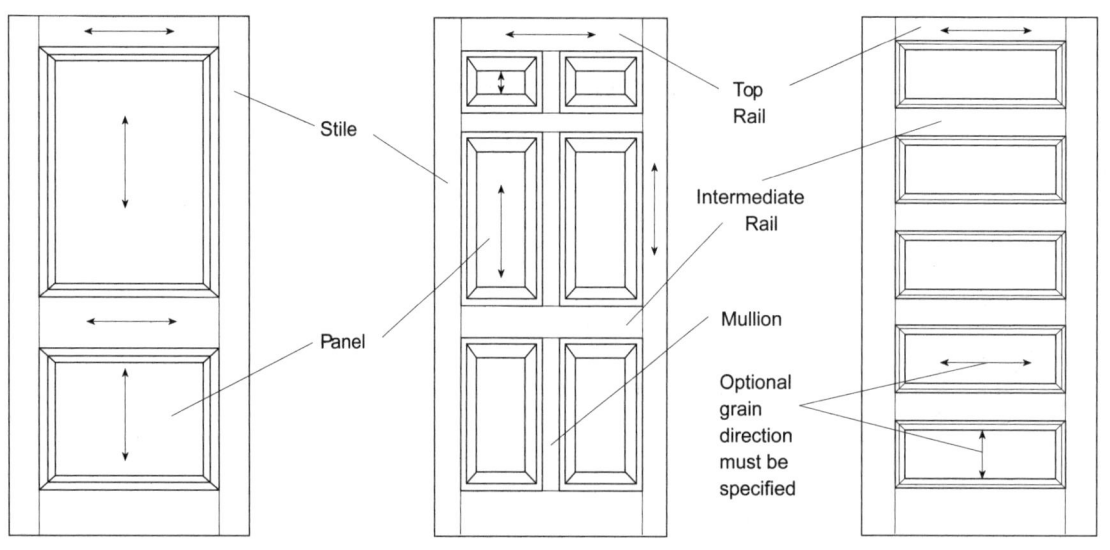

*Figure: 9-038*

**STILE and RAIL DOOR CONSTRUCTION**

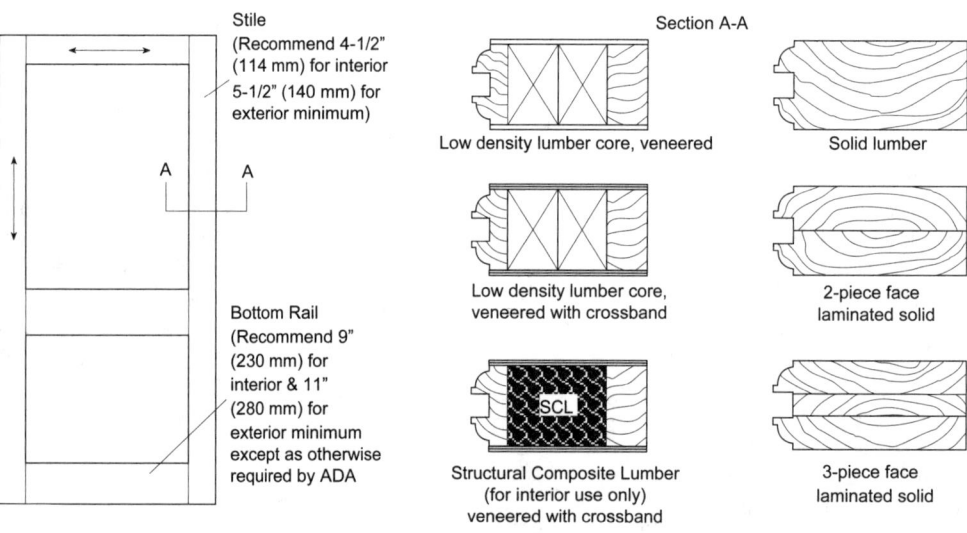

*Figure: 9-039*

# SECTION 9
## Doors

# introductory information

### STILE and RAIL PANEL CONSTRUCTION

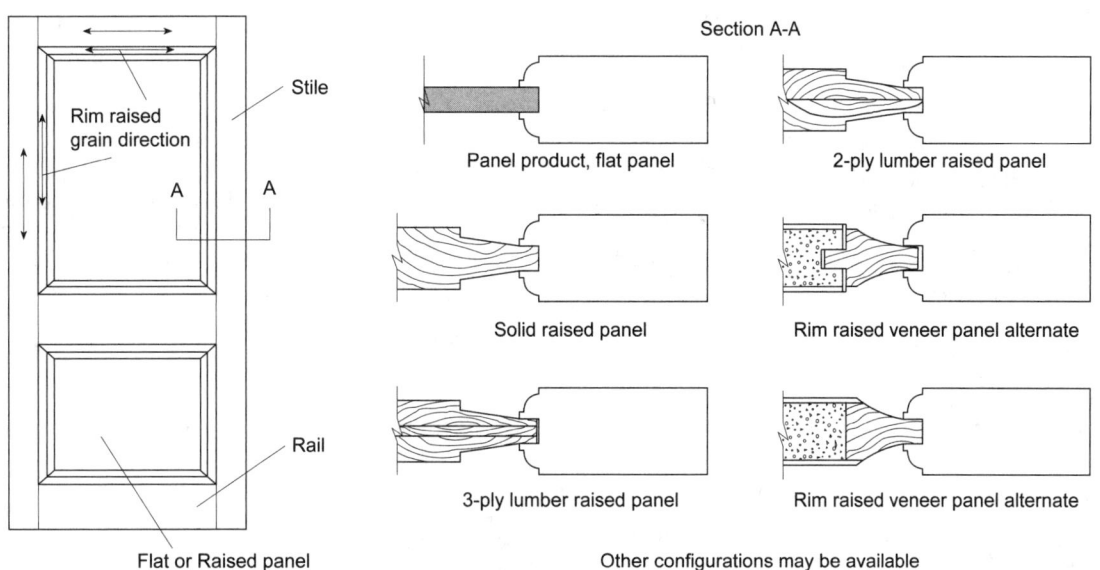

Figure: 9-040

### PANEL and GLASS RETENTION

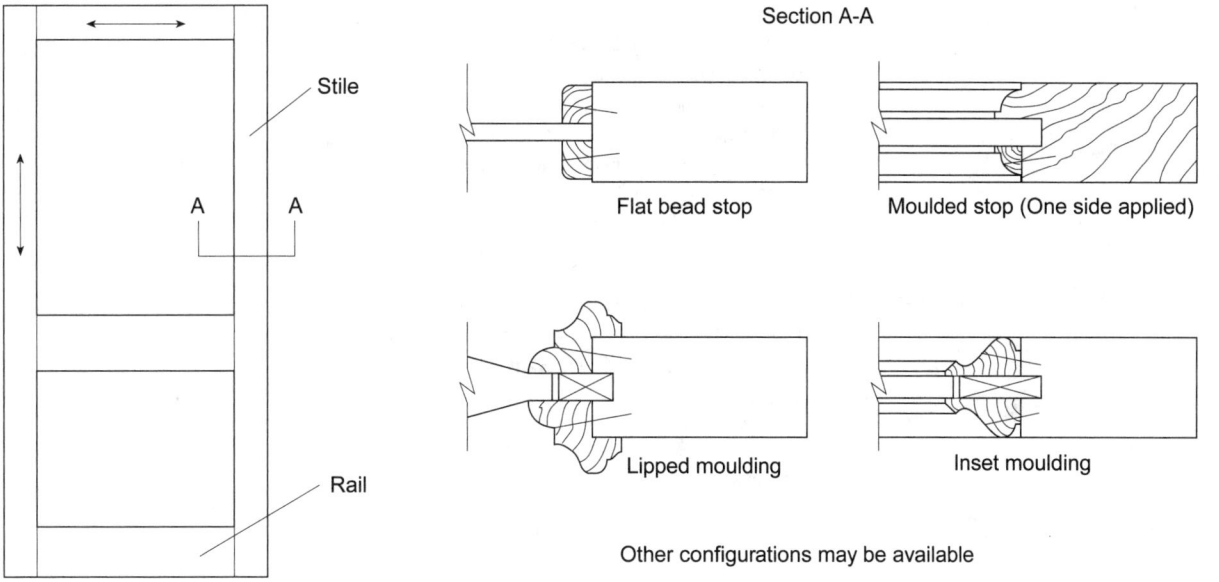

Figure: 9-041

### DESIGN IDEAS

Includes examples of Stile and Rail door configurations. These design ideas are not comprehensive and are for the reader to use as a starting guide.

# SECTION 9
Doors

## introductory information

### SPECIFY REQUIREMENTS FOR

- **FIRE RATINGS.**

- **CODE** or **REGULATION** compliance, and

  - If they require certain design accommodations, and it is the responsibility of the design professional to employ such within their door designs and schedule.

- **HARDWARE** such as kick plates, door closers, hinges, panic hardware, locks, etc.

- Prohibition of **FINGER JOINTS**, which are otherwise allowed at edges.

- At **STILE** and **RAIL DOORS**:

  - Stile or rail widths and/or construction.

  - Ornamental detail or joinery.

  - Panel layout and grain direction.

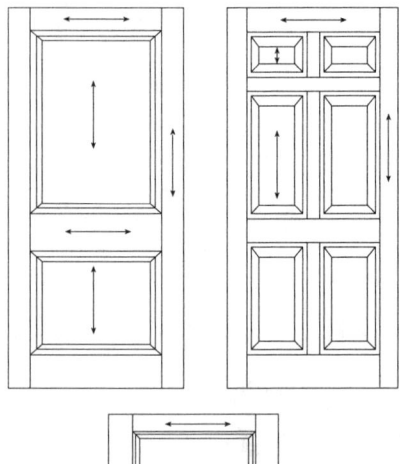

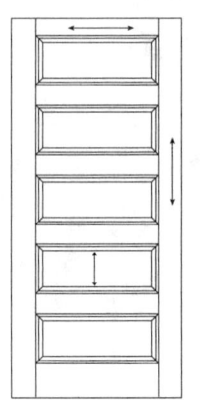

Figure: 9-043

### RECOMMENDATIONS

- If **FIELD FINISHED,** include in Division 09 of the specifications:

  - **BEFORE FINISHING**, exposed portions of woodwork shall have handling marks or effects of exposure to moisture, removed with a thorough, final sanding over all surfaces of the exposed portions and shall be cleaned before applying sealer or finish.

- **THOROUGHLY REVIEW** Sections 3 and 4, especially Basic Considerations, Recommendations, Acknowledgements, and Industry Practices within GENERAL for an overview of the characteristics and minimum acceptable requirements of lumber and/or sheet products that might be used herein.

- **REVIEW** the GENERAL portion of Sections 3 and 4 for an overview of the characteristics and the minimum acceptable requirements of lumber and/or sheet products that might be used herein.

- **STRUCTURAL MEMBERS**, grounds, in wall blocking, backing, furring, brackets, or other anchorage which becomes an integral part of the building's walls, floors, or ceilings, required for the installation of architectural woodwork are not to be furnished or installed by the architectural woodwork manufacturer or installer.

- For an excellent **PAINT GRADE SURFACE** Medium Density Overlay (MDO), Medium Density Fiberboard (MDF) or Hardboard should be specified.

- **WOOD DOORS** should be avoided in exterior applications.

- At **GLASS LIGHTS** - To create the proper seal against weather, wind, and rain, the finish coats on doors should be allowed to flow onto the glass area at least 1/16" (1.6 mm), and:

  - When cleaning, a razor should not be used to scrape the glass because it will destroy the seal; a broad blade putty knife should be used to protect the seal between the paint and the glass. See illustration below showing the finish lapped on the glass.

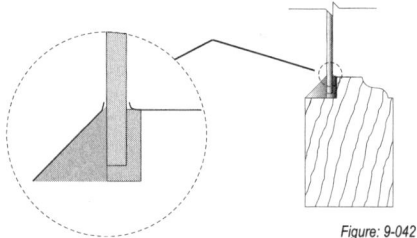

Figure: 9-042

# SECTION 9
## Doors

**GENERAL**/PRODUCT/INSTALLATION/TEST

**compliance requirements**

| C | P | Where the **C**, or **P** icon is not indicated, the rule applies to all Grades equally |

Including: Passage Doors of Flush and Stile & Rail Construction with Wood and HPDL Faces

## 9.1 BASIC CONSIDERATIONS

1 **GRADES**

1.1 These Standards are characterized in three Grades of quality that may be mixed within a single project; however, only Custom and Premium are used in this door Section. Limitless design possibilities and a wide variety of lumber and veneer species, along with overlays, high-pressure decorative laminates, factory finishes, and profiles are available in both Grades.

1.2 **CUSTOM GRADE** is typically specified for and adequately covers most high-quality architectural woodwork, providing a well-defined degree of control over a project's quality of materials, workmanship, or installation.

1.3 **PREMIUM GRADE** is typically specified for use in those areas of a project where the highest level of quality, materials, workmanship, and installation is required.

1.4 **EXCLUSION**, these standards do not cover the re-lamination/re-surfacing of flush doors with decorative laminate or other surfacing.

1.5 **GRADE LIMITATIONS:**

1.5.1 Flush and Stile & Rail doors are offered only in Custom and Premium grades.

2 **CONTRACT DOCUMENTS** shall govern if in conflict with these standards.

3 **ACCEPTABLE REQUIREMENTS** of lumber and/or sheet products used within this woodwork product section are established by Sections 3 and 4, unless otherwise modified herein.

4 **AESTHETIC COMPLIANCE REQUIREMENTS** apply only to surfaces visible after fabrication and installation.

5 Use of **PHENOLIC-BACKED WOOD VENEER** is permitted, if specified or otherwise approved.

6 **EXPOSED SURFACES** include:

6.1 Both visible faces of doors, including applied moldings, lights, and louvers.

6.2 Both vertical edges of doors.

6.3 Top edge, if visible from above.

## 9.1 BASIC CONSIDERATIONS (continued)

7 **SEMI-EXPOSED SURFACES** include:

7.1 Top and bottom edges of doors, unless:

7.1.1 The top edge is visible from above.

8 **NFPA 80** requires design accommodations, and:

8.1 Preparation of **FIRE-RATED DOOR ASSEMBLIES** for locks, latches, hinges, remotely operated or monitored hardware, concealed closers, glass lights, vision panels, louvers, astragals, and laminated overlays shall be performed by the manufacturer or its agent in conformance with the manufacturer's **LICENSING** and **LABEL SERVICE AGREEMENT.**

8.2 Preparation of **SURFACE-APPLIED** hardware, function holes for mortise locks, holes for labeled viewers, allowable undercutting, and application of protection plates may be performed at the jobsite.

8.3 Fire-rated wood doors to be glazed under license.

9 **FIRE-RATED DOORS:**

9.1 Are **AVAILABLE** in 20, 45, 60, and 90 minute labels.

9.2 Shall be of **CONSTRUCTION STANDARD** to the door manufacturer and conform with the requirements of applicable labeling agencies.

9.3 Shall permit **EDGES** on 45, 60, and 90 minute fire-rated doors, regardless of the species of material on the door face and be the standard of the door manufacturer; and the species, width, and fire-retardant treatment shall conform to the requirements of the labeling agency acceptable to the authority with jurisdiction for the label specified.

9.4 **HANGING** shall be compliant with the manufacturer's requirements.

10 Specific **METHODS OF CONSTRUCTION** for flush, excluding hollow core, and stile and rail doors illustrated in this section may not represent all types available. Variations of construction and materials are permitted, as long as the appropriate minimum WDMA duty performance levels are met or exceeded.

# SECTION 9
## Doors
GENERAL/PRODUCT/INSTALLATION/TEST

**compliance requirements**

*Where the C, or P icon is not indicated, the rule applies to all Grades equally* | C | P |

### 9.1 BASIC CONSIDERATIONS (continued)

**11** ANSI/WDMA I.S. 1A (latest edition) **PERFORMANCE DUTY LEVELS.**

**11.1** **HEAVY DUTY** performance level has been adopted for these Standards.

**11.1.1** The heavy duty level typically involves doors for moderate usage and requires intermediate minimum performance standards.

**11.1.2** Typical usage examples:

| | |
|---|---|
| Assisted living room entry | Storage |
| Office - Interior passage stairwell | Apartment/condo entry |
| Mechanical service | X-ray |
| Hallway | Acoustic |
| Medical exam room | Stairwell |

**11.1.3** If a higher or lower Performance Duty Level is desired, it shall be so specified.

**11.2** **EXTRA HEAVY DUTY** level typically involves doors where use is considered heavy and frequent, and requires the highest minimum performance standards.

**11.2.1** Typical usage examples:

| | |
|---|---|
| Classrooms | Detention/correctional |
| Patient rooms | Bullet-resistant |
| Bathrooms - Public | Gym/locker rooms |
| Dorm rooms | Surgical entry |
| Assembly areas | Trauma centers |
| Auditorium entry | Hotel/motel room entry |

**11.3** **STANDARD DUTY** level typically involves doors where frequency of use is low and requires the lowest minimum performance.

Typical usage examples:
| | |
|---|---|
| Closet | Bath - Private |
| Wardrobe | Small, low-usage office |

**11.4** **DUTY LEVEL** performance requirements are spelled out within the Product portion of this Section.

**12** **TYPICAL STILE and RAIL DOOR ILLUSTRATIONS** are provided in **DESIGN IDEAS.**

**13** To **PREVENT TELEGRAPHING**, inset solid wood edging when used must have similar moisture content as panel core, be glued securely and calibrated with panel core thickness prior to being laminated with a wood veneer on both faces.

### 9.1 BASIC CONSIDERATIONS (continued)

**14** **INDUSTRY PRACTICES**

**14.1** **STRUCTURAL MEMBERS**, grounds, in wall blocking, backing, furring, brackets, or other anchorage that becomes an integral part of the building's walls, floors, or ceilings, that are required for the installation of architectural woodwork are not furnished or installed by the architectural woodwork manufacturer or installer.

**14.2** **WALL, CEILING,** and/or opening variations in excess of 1/4" (6.4 mm) or **FLOORS** in excess of 1/2" (12.7 mm) in 144" (3658 mm) of being plumb, level, flat, straight, square, or of the correct size are not acceptable for the installation of architectural woodwork, nor is it the responsibility of the installer to scribe or fit to tolerances in excess of such.

**14.3** **WARRANTY** shall be to the terms, conditions, and duration of the door manufacturer, unless specified otherwise. Check with individual door manufacturers for warranty and fire approval requirements.

**14.3.1** Warranties vary between manufacturers-as to the:

**14.3.1.1** Coverage.

**14.3.1.2** Duration.

**14.3.1.3** Items and conditions that void it.

**14.3.1.4** Extent of replacement and cost coverage.

**14.3.2** Typically, manufacturers do not warranty doors with:

**14.3.2.1** Different Species, face materials, finishes, or laminates on opposite sides.

**14.3.2.2** Different temperature and/or humidity conditions on opposite sides.

**14.3.2.3** **LESS THAN** 5" (127 mm) between cutouts or a cutout and the edge of a door, or:

**14.3.2.4** **LESS THAN** 6" (152.4 mm) at fire-rated doors between cutouts or a cutout and the edge of a door, unless approved by authorities with jurisdiction.

## compliance requirements

**SECTION 9**
Doors

GENERAL/PRODUCT/INSTALLATION/TEST

| C | P | Where the **C**, or **P** icon is not indicated, the rule applies to all Grades equally |

### 9.1 BASIC CONSIDERATIONS (Continued)

**14**    **INDUSTRY PRACTICES** (continued)

**14.4**    **HANDING** of a door is always determined from the outside:

**14.4.1**    The key side is as symbolized below:

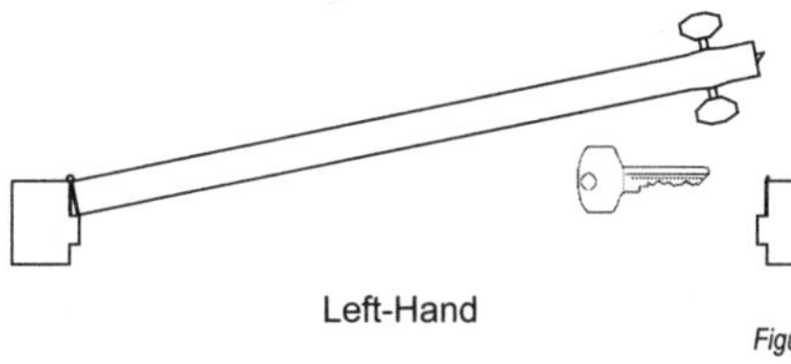

Left-Hand
*Figure: 9-044*

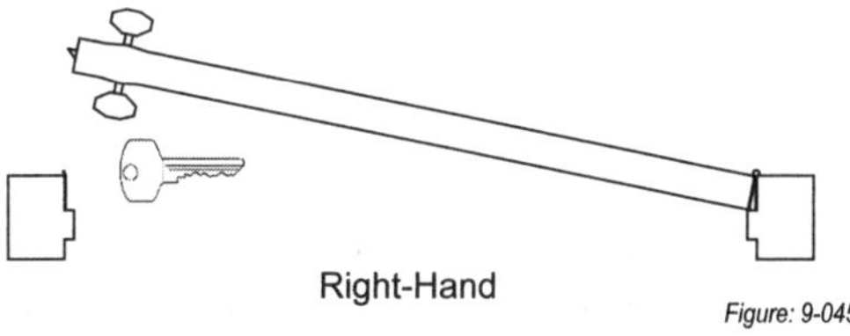

Right-Hand
*Figure: 9-045*

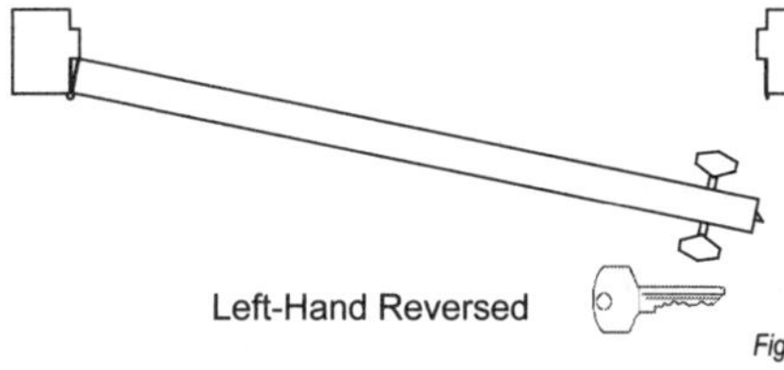

Left-Hand Reversed
*Figure: 9-046*

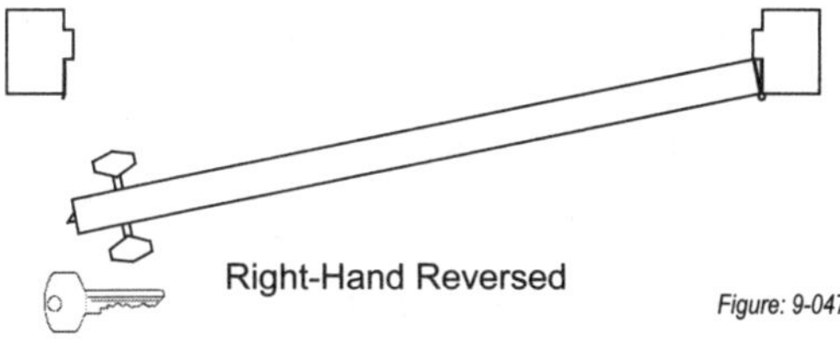

Right-Hand Reversed
*Figure: 9-047*

**Bottom Of Drawings Represent Outside.**

# SECTION 9
## Doors

GENERAL/**PRODUCT**/INSTALLATION/TEST

**compliance requirements**

Where the **C**, or **P** icon is not indicated, the rule applies to all Grades equally | C | P |

### 9.2 SCOPE

1. All flush and stile and rail wood doors with corresponding and adjacent transoms, fixed panels, and/or side lights.

2. **TYPICAL INCLUSIONS:**

2.1 Flush doors, solid, hollow, fire rated, sound resistant, x-ray, or bullet resistant.

2.2 Stile and rail doors of veneered, solid, and/or laminated (solid) construction with or without fire, sound, or bullet resistant ratings.

2.3 Accessories required to comply with the door manufacturer's fire rated door approval, including treated or metal edges at pairs of fire rated doors as required.

2.4 Accessories required to comply with the door manufacturer's sound resistant certification, including gaskets and automatic door bottoms.

2.5 Glass stops.

2.6 Wood louvers.

2.7 **IF SPECIFIED:**

2.7.1 Glass or glazing.

2.7.2 Pre fitting and machining for hardware.

2.7.3 Pre hanging and machining for weather stripping.

2.7.4 Priming, sealing, and/or finishing.

2.7.5 Flashing and/or metal edge guards.

3. **TYPICAL EXCLUSIONS:**

3.1 Cabinet doors included with casework.

3.2 Wood cores for metal or vinyl clad doors.

3.3 Garage, metal, and fiberglass doors.

3.4 Access doors.

3.5 Metal grills or louvers.

3.6 LPDL or vinyl faced doors.

### 9.3 DEFAULT STIPULATION

1. If not otherwise specified or indicated in the contract documents, work shall be **CUSTOM GRADE**, solid core, with paint grade faces and edges.

1.1 Core selection is manufacturer's choice.

1.2 If transparent finish is specified, doors shall be factory clear finished.

### 9.4 RULES

1. The following rules shall govern unless a project's contract documents require otherwise.

2. These rules are intended to provide a well defined degree of control over a project's quality of materials, workmanship, or installation.

3. **ERRATA**, published on the Sponsor Associations' websites at www.awinet.org, www.awmac.com, or www.aws-errata.com, **shall take precedence over these rules**, subject to their date of posting and a project's bid date.

#### 9.4.4 Basic Rules

| | | |
|---|---|---|
| | 1 | These standards are primarily performance based rather than prescriptive based, allowing a wide variance of construction methods and/or component configurations, provided the end product meets or exceeds **WDMA's HEAVY DUTY PERFORMANCE VALUES** contained within these standards, and: |
| 1 | 1 | **FLUSH SOLID CORE**, fire rated, sound resistant, bullet resistant, lead lined, and electrostatic shielded doors - ANSI/WDMA I.S. - 1A, (latest edition), **EXCEPT** as **MODIFIED HEREIN**. |
| 1 | 2 | **FLUSH HOLLOW CORE** doors shall comply with WDMA's Standard Duty performance values. |
| 1 | 3 | For **STILE** and **RAIL** doors with or without fire, sound, or bullet resistant ratings - ANSI/WDMA I.S. - 6A, (latest edition), **EXCEPT AS MODIFIED HEREIN**. |
| 1 | 4 | It is the **RESPONSIBILITY** of the door manufacturer to provide evidence of compliance upon request. |

Continues next column ▼

## SECTION 9 — Doors

### compliance requirements — GENERAL / PRODUCT / INSTALLATION / TEST

#### 9.4.4 Basic Rules

▲ From previous column

| | | | | | |
|---|---|---|---|---|---|
| 2 | | | | | **IN LIEU OF TESTING** for WDMA TM-7 (Slam Cycle) & 8 (Hinge Loading), compliance to the following prescriptive requirements is acceptable: |
| 2 | 1 | | | | Composite cross bands shall have minimum 55 lbs (24.9 kgs) density. |
| 2 | 2 | | | | **FACES** on both sides of the door shall be of the same material and construction detail. |
| 2 | 3 | | | | **FLUSH VENEERED**, solid core door shall include: |
| 2 | 3 | 1 | | | Bonded (stiles and rails securely glued to core) construction. |
| 2 | 3 | 2 | | | Core shall be SCLC, SLC, particleboard, MDF, or agrifiber core conforming to ANSI A208.1 Grade LD-1 or LD-2. |
| 2 | 3 | 3 | | | Stiles and rails with minimum of 1" (25.4 mm) hardwood or material that has been qualified in accordance with WDMA TM 15 (latest edition). |
| 2 | 3 | 4 | | | Blocking for screw attached hardware, and: |
| 2 | 3 | 4 | 1 | | Blocking is not required at SCLC or SLC. |
| 2 | 3 | 5 | | | Calibration (sanding) of core to uniform thickness. |
| 2 | 3 | 6 | | | For **OPAQUE FINISH**: |
| 2 | 3 | 6 | 1 | | Composite face requires minimum 3 ply construction. |
| 2 | 3 | 6 | 2 | | Veneer face requires minimum 5 ply construction. |
| 2 | 3 | 7 | | | For **TRANSPARENT FINISH**: |
| 2 | 3 | 7 | 1 | | Minimum 5 ply construction. |
| 2 | 3 | 7 | 2 | | When veneer is applied to solid wood edge, cross band shall not be set back greater that 1/4" (6.4 mm) from door edge. |
| 2 | 3 | 8 | | | For **HPDL**, minimum 5 ply construction. |
| 2 | 4 | | | | **STILE** and **RAIL** doors with or without fire, sound, or bullet resistant ratings shall: |
| 2 | 4 | 1 | | | Be of solid lumber, SCL, LVL, or staved block core construction, with: |
| 2 | 4 | 1 | 1 | | A minimum of 5/8" (15.9 mm) hardwood edgebands and lock and hinge edges, if not solid lumber. |
| 2 | 4 | 2 | | | Be a minimum of 5" (127 mm) wide stiles, top and intermediate rails. |
| 2 | 4 | 3 | | | Be a minimum of 10" (255 mm) wide bottom rail. |

Continues next column ▼

#### 9.4.4 Basic Rules

▲ From previous column

| | | | | |
|---|---|---|---|---|
| 2 | | | | **IN LIEU OF TESTING** (continued) |
| 2 | 4 | | | **STILE** and **RAIL** doors (continued) |
| 2 | 4 | 4 | | Be of dowel, mortise, and tenon joinery, and: |
| 2 | 4 | 4 | 1 | Dowels shall be a minimum of 1/2" (12.7 mm) in diameter by 5" (127 mm) long, spaced a maximum of 2-1/2" (63.5 mm) on center. |
| 2 | 4 | 4 | 2 | Top and intermediate rails shall have a minimum of two dowels per joint; and the bottom rail, a minimum of three per joint. |
| 2 | 4 | 5 | | Have flat or raised panels a minimum of 5/8" (15.9 mm) in thickness at the tongue of solid lumber or M2 Grade particleboard. |
| 3 | | | | **AESTHETIC GRADE RULES** apply only to the faces visible after installation. |
| 4 | | | | **LUMBER** shall conform to the requirements established in Section 3, and: |
| 4 | 1 | | | **HEARTWOOD** or **SAPWOOD** is permitted in Ash, Birch, Maple, Cherry, Elm, and Red Oak; however: |
| 4 | 1 | 1 | | If only **HEARTWOOD** or **SAPWOOD** is desired, it shall be so specified. |
| 5 | | | | **SHEET PRODUCTS** shall conform to the requirements established in Section 4, and: |
| 5 | 1 | | | Use of **HPDL BACKED WOOD VENEERS** is permitted if specified or otherwise approved. |
| 6 | | | | **EXPOSED SURFACES INCLUDE:** |
| 6 | 1 | | | Both visible faces of doors, including applied moldings, lights, and louvers. |
| 6 | 2 | | | Both vertical edges of doors. |
| 6 | 3 | | | Top edge, if visible from above. |
| 7 | | | | **SEMI-EXPOSED SURFACES INCLUDE:** |
| 7 | 1 | | | Top and bottom edges of doors, unless: |
| 7 | 1 | 1 | | Top edge is visible from above. |
| 8 | | | | For the purpose of this standard, a **BALANCED PANEL** is one that is free from warp that affects serviceability for its intended purpose. |

Continues next column ▼

# SECTION 9
## Doors

GENERAL/PRODUCT/INSTALLATION/TEST — compliance requirements

Where the **C**, or **P** icon is not indicated, the rule applies to all Grades equally

### 9.4.4 Basic Rules

*From previous column*

| | | | |
|---|---|---|---|
| 9 | | | **CATHEDRAL** type figure shall be achieved by: |
| 9 | 1 | | A single component in "AA" Face Grade. |
| 9 | 2 | | The split heart method in Face Grades "A - D", and: |
| 9 | 2 | 1 | Each half of a split heart shall be subject to the minimum component width requirements for Face Grade "B". |
| 10 | | | **FIRE RATED** doors shall be: |
| 10 | 1 | | Of the fire rating specified. |
| 10 | 2 | | Constructed to the manufacturer's standard, conforming with the requirements of their applicable labeling service, with: |
| 10 | 3 | 1 | **EDGES**, regardless of face species, must conform to the manufacturer's approved labeling service. |
| 10 | 4 | | **PREPARED**, in accordance with NFPA 80, for locks, latches, hinges, remotely operated or monitored hardware, concealed closures, glass lights, vision panels, louvers, astragals, and laminated overlays to be performed in conformance with the manufacturer's licensing and label service agreement; however: |
| 10 | 4 | 1 | Preparation for surface applied hardware, function holes for mortise locks, holes for labeled viewers, a maximum of 3/4" (19 mm) wood and composite door undercutting, and protection plates may be performed at the jobsite. |
| 10 | 5 | | Furnished with the **MANUFACTURER'S** basic hanging and finishing instructions. |
| 11 | | | **SOUND RESISTANT** doors shall: |
| 11 | 1 | | Be constructed to the manufacturer's standard, conforming to the requirements for a minimum STC 50 (Sound Transmission Class) or as specified when tested as an opening unit (versus sealed in place), and: |
| 11 | 2 | 1 | Include required special stops, stop adjusters, gaskets, and automatic threshold closing devices of the manufacturer's standard. |
| 12 | | | **X-RAY** doors shall be: |
| 12 | 1 | | Constructed to the manufacturer's standard for the type of construction, thickness, edgebands, and moldings, and: |
| 12 | 1 | 1 | **LEAD** thickness shall be a minimum of 1/16" (1.6 mm) or as specified. |
| 13 | | | **BULLET RESISTANT** doors shall be: |
| 13 | 1 | | Constructed to the manufacturer's standard, conforming to the requirements of UL 752 "Bullet Resisting Equipment" or NIJ (National Institute of Justice) 0108.01 Performance Standards, and: |
| 13 | 1 | 1 | Have a minimum NIJ Level 2 protection rating. |

*Continues next column*

### 9.4.4 Basic Rules

*From previous column*

| | | | |
|---|---|---|---|
| 14 | | | **ELECTROSTATIC SHIELDED** doors shall be: |
| 14 | 1 | | Constructed to the manufacturer's standard for type of construction, thickness, edgebands, and moldings, and: |
| 14 | 2 | 1 | Have the number and location of electrical leads as specified. |
| 15 | | | **PAIR** and **SET MATCHING** is required for flush wood veneer, and shall be: |
| 15 | 1 | | **COMPATIBLE** for **COLOR** and **GRAIN**.    C   P |
| 15 | 2 | | **SEQUENCED** and **WELL MATCHED** for **COLOR** and **GRAIN**.    C   P |
| 16 | | | **PAIR** and **SET MATCHING** cannot be achieved at **STILE** and **RAIL** and is not required. |
| 17 | | | **EXPOSED FACES** and **EDGES** shall be thoroughly sanded using a minimum of 120 grit sandpaper, and: |
| 17 | 1 | | All **EDGES** shall be slightly eased. |
| 18 | | | Overall **DOOR SIZE** for: |
| 10 | 1 | | **NON PREFIT DOORS** (blank) shall be furnished within plus or minus of 1/16" (1.6 mm) for **HEIGHT**, **WIDTH**, and **THICKNESS**. |
| 10 | 2 | | **PREFIT DOORS** shall be furnished, sized in: |
| 10 | 2 | 1 | **WIDTH** within 1/32" (0.8 mm) plus or minus of the specified **FRAME** size, less 1/4" (6.4 mm) in width with a 3 degree bevel on both edges. |
| 10 | 2 | 2 | **HEIGHT**, within 1/16" (1.6 mm), plus or minus the specified size less the undercut. |
| 19 | | | **BLEED THROUGH** of glue at a veneer joint that visually affects an applied finish is not permitted. |
| 20 | | | **GLASS** and **GLAZING** requires: |
| 20 | 1 | | Wood glass stops to be manufacturer prepared and bundled in appropriately labeled sets or prefit and tacked in the appropriate light opening, and: |
| 20 | 1 | 1 | In the absence of specifications or detail, profile shall be manufacturer's choice. |
| 21 | | | **FACTORY FINISHED, DOORS** require both faces and vertical edges to be finished, and: |
| 21 | 1 | | The top/bottom edges and hardware preparation areas shall be sealed. |
| 22 | | | **FIRST CLASS WORKMANSHIP** is required in compliance with these standards. |

# SECTION 9
## Doors

**compliance requirements** — GENERAL/**PRODUCT**/INSTALLATION/TEST

| C | P | Where the **C**, or **P** icon is not indicated, the rule applies to all Grades equally |

### 9.4.5 Material Rules

| # | | | | | Rule | C | P |
|---|---|---|---|---|---|---|---|
| 1 | | | | | Shall be free of **DEFECTS**, both natural and from manufacturing, in excess of those permitted herein. | | |
| 2 | | | | | **FIGURE** (including no figure) is not a function of a species grade, and special requirements must be specified. | | |
| 3 | | | | | **HARDBOARD** faces shall be standard grade, a minimum of 1/8" (3.2 mm) in thickness. | | |
| 4 | | | | | **EXPOSED** surfaces shall be: | | |
| 4 | 1 | | | | Compatible for color and grain. | C | P |
| 4 | 2 | | | | Well matched for color and grain. | C | P |
| 5 | | | | | **CONCEALED** surfaces shall allow non structural defects and voids; blocking may be of a compatible species or material other than that of the exposed or semi-exposed surface. | | |
| 6 | | | | | **FLUSH** door: | | |
| 6 | 1 | | | | **VENEER FACES** shall be of the species and Grade specified and of sufficient thickness so as not to permit show through of cross banding after sanding and/or final finishing. | | |
| 6 | 1 | 1 | | | **OPAQUE** finish shall be: | | |
| 6 | 1 | 1 | 1 | | Sound close grain hardwood veneer, MDO, MDF or hardboard at manufacturer's choice, and: | C | P |
| 6 | 1 | 1 | 1 | 1 | If veneer, it shall be: | | |
| 6 | 1 | 1 | 1 | 1 | HPVA "C" Grade. | C | P |
| 6 | 1 | 1 | 1 | 2 | HPVA "B" Grade. | C | P |
| 6 | 1 | 1 | 2 | | MDO, MDF or hardboard, at manufacturer's choice. | C | P |
| 6 | 1 | 2 | | | **TRANSPARENT** finish requires: | | |
| 6 | 1 | 2 | 1 | | Pairs or sets be compatible for color and grain. | C | P |
| 6 | 1 | 2 | 2 | | Transoms be end matched for color and grain. | C | P |
| 6 | 1 | 2 | 3 | | Pairs or sets be sequenced and well matched for color and grain. | C | P |
| 6 | 1 | 2 | 4 | | Transoms be continuous match for color and grain. | C | P |
| 6 | 1 | 2 | 5 | | **COMPATIBILITY** in color and grain to the other door faces in the same room or area, and: | C | P |
| 6 | 1 | 2 | 5 | 1 | Coordination of compatibility is the responsibility of the door furnisher. | C | P |
| 6 | 1 | 2 | 6 | | Doors that are specified as adjacent to or are specified as a component of other architectural woodwork shall conform to the applicable requirements of Section 4 and 8 for the Grade specified. | | |

*Continues next column*

### 9.4.5 Material Rules

*From previous column*

| # | | | | | Rule | C | P |
|---|---|---|---|---|---|---|---|
| 6 | | | | | **FLUSH** doors (continued) | | |
| 6 | 1 | | | | **VENEER FACES** shall (continued) | | |
| 6 | 1 | 2 | | | **TRANSPARENT** (continued) | | |
| 6 | 1 | 2 | 7 | | Shall be HPVA "A" Grade, with: | C | P |
| 6 | 1 | 2 | 7 | 1 | Running match and end component less than the HPVA requirement. | C | P |
| 6 | 1 | 2 | 8 | | Shall be HPVA "AA" Grade, with: | C | P |
| 6 | 1 | 2 | 8 | 1 | Balanced center matched. | C | P |
| 6 | 1 | 2 | 9 | | Have visible edges and reveals, when appropriate, that are: | | |
| 6 | 1 | 2 | 9 | 1 | Matched to species of face, except: | | |
| 6 | 1 | 2 | 9 | 1 | Maple may be used as an alternate when a Birch face is specified. | | |
| 6 | 1 | 2 | 9 | 2 | Compatible for color and grain. | C | P |
| 6 | 1 | 2 | 9 | 3 | Well matched for color and grain. | C | P |
| 6 | 1 | 2 | 9 | 4 | A minimum of 0.020" (0.5 mm) nominal **THICKNESS** that precludes show through of core. | | |
| 6 | 1 | 2 | 10 | | **STAND ALONE** doors, face species of Anigre, Ash, Beech, Birch, Cherry, Hickory, African Mahogany, American Mahogany, Makore, Maple, Red Oak, White Oak, Pecan, Poplar, or Walnut shall conform to the following **HPVA DOOR SKIN FACE TABLES** for the allowable veneer characteristics for the Grade required, and: | | |
| 6 | 1 | 2 | 10 | 1 | If not of a species listed above shall conform to HPVA Door Skin Face Table as agreed on between the design professional and the manufacturer. | | |
| 6 | 1 | 2 | 10 | 2 | Including those in pairs and sets. | | |
| 6 | 1 | 2 | 10 | 3 | When balance matched, the width of the outer leaves after trimming shall not exceed: | | |
| 6 | 1 | 2 | 10 | 3 | 1" (25.4 mm) less than its adjoining leaf. | C | P |
| 6 | 1 | 2 | 10 | 3 | 1/2" (12.7 mm) less than its adjoining leaf. | C | P |
| 6 | 1 | 2 | 10 | 4 | Table: 9-048 - **ASH, BEECH** (American or European), **BIRCH, MAPLE,** and **POPLAR.** | | |
| 6 | 1 | 2 | 10 | 5 | Table: 9-049 - **MAHOGANY** (African or American), **ANIGRE, MAKORE,** and **SAPELE.** | | |
| 6 | 1 | 2 | 10 | 6 | Table: 9-050 - **RED OAK** and **WHITE OAK.** | | |
| 6 | 1 | 2 | 10 | 7 | Table: 9-051 - **PECAN** and **HICKORY.** | | |
| 6 | 1 | 2 | 10 | 8 | Table: 9-052 - **WALNUT** and **CHERRY.** | | |

*Continues next column*

# SECTION 9
## Doors

GENERAL/**PRODUCT**/INSTALLATION/TEST

**compliance requirements**

Where the **C**, or **P** icon is not indicated, the rule applies to all Grades equally | **C** | **P** |

*Table: 9-048* - **ASH**, **BEECH** [b], **BIRCH**, **MAPLE**, and **POPLAR** (ANSI/HPVA - HP1 - latest edition)

| Cut | Plain Sliced (Flat Cut), Quarter Cut, Rotary Cut ||||||
|---|---|---|---|---|---|---|
| Grade Description | AA ||| A |||
| Color and Matching | Sap (White) | Heart (Red/Brown) | Natural | Sap (White) | Heart (Red/Brown) | Natural |
| Sapwood | Yes | No | Yes | Yes | No | Yes |
| Heartwood | No | Yes | Yes | No | Yes | Yes |
| Color Streaks or Spots | Slight ||| Slight || Yes |
| Color Variation | Slight || Yes | Slight || Yes |
| Sharp Color Contrast at Joints | Yes, if Slip, Plank, or Random Matched ||| Yes, if Slip, Plank, or Random Matched |||
| Type of Matching<br>  Book Matched<br>  Slip Matched<br>  Pleasing Matched | Yes<br>Specify<br>Not applicable ||| Yes<br>Specify<br>Not applicable |||
| Nominal Minimum Width of Face Components [a]<br>  Plain Sliced<br>  Quarter<br>  Rotary | 5" (127 mm)<br>3" (76 mm)<br>5" (127 mm) ||| 4" (102 mm)<br>3" (76 mm)<br>4" (102 mm) |||
| **Natural Characteristics** |||||||
| Small Conspicuous Burls & Pin Knots, Combined Average Number | 1 per 5 sq ft (2 per 1 m²) ||| 1 per 3 sq ft (4 per 1 m²) |||
| Conspicuous Burls, Maximum Size | 1/4" (6.4 mm) ||| 3/8" (9.5 mm) |||
| Conspicuous Pin Knots<br>  Average Number<br>  Maximum Size: Dark Part<br>                  Total | No ||| 1 per 8 sq ft (4 per 3 m²)<br>1/8" (3.2 mm)<br>1/4" (6.4 mm) |||
| Scattered Sound and Repaired Knots | No ||| No |||
| Mineral Streaks | No at Maple, Slight ||| Slight |||
| Bark Pockets | No ||| No |||
| Worm Tracks | Slight ||| Slight |||
| Vine Marks | Slight ||| Slight |||
| Cross Bars | Slight ||| Slight |||
| **Manufacturing Characteristics** |||||||
| Rough Cut/Ruptured Grain | No ||| No |||
| Blended Repaired Tapering Hairline Splits | Two 1/32" x 3" (0.8 mm x 76 mm) on ends only ||| Two 1/16" x 6" (1.6 mm x 152 mm) |||
| Repairs | Very small blending ||| Small blending |||
| **Special Characteristics** |||||||
| Quartered | 1" in 12" (25.4 mm in 305 mm) maximum grain slope; 2-1/2" in 12" (63.5 mm in 305 mm) maximum grain sweep ||||||

Unfilled worm holes, open splits, open joints, open bark pockets, shake, and doze are not allowed in the above grades.
[a] Outside components will be a different size to allow for edge trim loss and certain types of matching.
[b] American or European.

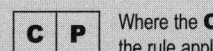

Where the **C**, or **P** icon is not indicated, the rule applies to all Grades equally

# SECTION 9
## Doors

**compliance requirements** — GENERAL/**PRODUCT**/INSTALLATION/TEST

| Table: 9-049 - MAHOGANY (African or American), ANIGRE, MAKORE, and SAPELE (ANSI/HPVA - HP1 - latest edition) | | |
|---|---|---|
| Cut | Plain Sliced (Flat Cut), Quarter Cut, Rotary Cut | |
| Grade Description | AA | A |
| **Color and Matching** | | |
| Sapwood | No | No |
| Heartwood | Yes | Yes |
| Color Streaks or Spots | Slight | Slight |
| Color Variation | Slight | Slight |
| Sharp Color Contrast at Joints | Yes, if Slip, Plank, or Random Matched | Yes, if Slip, Plank, or Random Matched |
| Type of Matching<br>　Book Matched<br>　Slip Matched<br>　Pleasing Matched | Yes<br>Specify<br>Not Applicable | Yes<br>Specify<br>Not Applicable |
| Nominal Minimum Width of Face Components [a]<br>　Plain Sliced<br>　Quarter<br>　Rotary | 5" (127 mm)　3" (76 mm)<br><br>5" (127 mm) | 4" (102 mm)<br>3" (76 mm)<br>4" (102 mm) |
| **Natural Characteristics** | | |
| Small Conspicuous Burls & Pin Knots, Combined Average Number | 1 per 5 sq ft (2 per 1 m²) | 1 per 3 sq ft (4 per 1 m²) |
| Conspicuous Burls, Maximum Size | 1/4" (6.4 mm) | 3/8" (9.5 mm) |
| Conspicuous Pin Knots<br>　Average Number<br>　Maximum Size:　Dark Part<br>　　　　　　　　　Total | No | 1 per 8 sq ft (4 per 3 m²)<br>1/8" (3.2 mm)<br>1/4" (6.4 mm) |
| Scattered Sound and Repaired Knots | No | No |
| Mineral Streaks | No | Slight |
| Bark Pockets | No | No |
| Worm Tracks | No | No |
| Vine Marks | Slight | Slight |
| Cross Bars | Occasional | Occasional |
| **Manufacturing Characteristics** | | |
| Rough Cut/Ruptured Grain | No | No |
| Blended Repaired Tapering Hairline Splits | Two 1/32" x 3" (0.8 mm x 76 mm) on ends only | Two 1/16" x 6" (1.6 mm x 152 mm) |
| Repairs | Very Small Blending | Small Blending |
| **Special Characteristics** | | |
| Quartered | 1" in 12" (25.4 mm in 305 mm) maximum grain slope; 2-1/2" in 12" (63.5 mm in 305 mm) maximum grain sweep | |

Unfilled worm holes, open splits, open joints, open bark pockets, shake, and doze are not allowed in the above grades.
[a] Outside components will be a different size to allow for edge trim loss and certain types of matching.

# SECTION 9
Doors

GENERAL/**PRODUCT**/INSTALLATION/TEST

## compliance requirements

Where the **C**, or **P** icon is not indicated, the rule applies to all Grades equally | **C** | **P** |

*Table: 9-050* - **RED OAK** and **WHITE OAK** (ANSI/HPVA - HP1 - latest edition)

| Cut | Plain Sliced (Flat Cut), Quarter Cut, Rift and Comb Grade, Rotary Cut | | | |
|---|---|---|---|---|
| Grade Description | AA | | A | |
| | Red Oak | White Oak | Red Oak | White Oak |
| **Color and Matching** | | | | |
| Sapwood | No | No | 5%[a] | Yes[a] |
| Heartwood | Yes | Yes | Yes | Yes |
| Color Streaks or Spots | Yes | Yes | Yes | Yes |
| Color Variation | Slight | Slight | Slight | Slight |
| Sharp Color Contrast at Joints | Yes, if Slip, Plank, or Random Matched | | Yes, if Slip, Plank, or Random Matched | |
| Type of Matching<br>  Book Matched<br>  Slip Matched<br>  Pleasing Matched | Yes<br>Specify<br>Not Applicable | | Yes<br>Specify<br>Not Applicable | |
| Nominal Minimum Width of Face Components [a, b, c]<br>  Plain Sliced<br>  Quarter<br>  Rotary | 5" (127 mm)<br>3" (76 mm)<br>5" (127 mm) | | 4" (102 mm)<br>3" (76 mm)<br>4" (102 mm) | |
| **Natural Characteristics** | | | | |
| Small Conspicuous Burls & Pin Knots, Combined Average Number | 1 per 4 sq ft (3 per 1 m²) | | 1 per 2-2/3 sq ft (4 per 1 m²) | |
| Conspicuous Burls - Maximum Size | 1/4" (6.4 mm) | | 3/8" (9.5 mm) | |
| Conspicuous Pin Knots<br>  Average Number<br>  Maximum Size: Dark Part<br>                  Total | No | | 1 per 3 sq ft (4 per 1 m²)<br>1/8" (3.2 mm)<br>1/4" (6.4 mm) | |
| Scattered Sound and Repaired Knots | No | | No | |
| Mineral Streaks | No | | Slight, Blending | |
| Bark Pockets | No | | No | |
| Worm Tracks | No | | No | |
| Vine Marks | No | | Slight | |
| Cross Bars | Slight | | Slight | |
| **Manufacturing Characteristics** | | | | |
| Rough Cut/Ruptured Grain | No | | No | |
| Blended Repaired Tapering Hairline Splits | Two 1/32" x 3" on (0.8 mm x 76 mm) at ends only | | Two 1/16" x 6" (1.6 mm x 152 mm) | |
| Repairs | Very Small Blending | | Small Blending | |
| **Special Characteristics** | | | | |
| Ray Fleck (Flake) | Slight, Blending<br>Quarter Cut Unlimited | | Slight, Blending<br>Quarter Cut Unlimited | |
| Slope and Sweep - Quarter & Rift | 1 inch in 12 inches (25.4 mm in 305mm) max. grain slope, 2-1/2 inch in 12 inches (63.5 mm in 305mm) max. grain sweep | | | |
|   Comb Grain | 1/2 inch in 12 inches (12.7 mm in 305mm) max. grain slope, 1/2 inch in 12 inches (12.7 mm in 305mm) max. grain sweep | | | |

Unfilled worm holes, open splits, open joints, open bark pockets, shake, and doze are not allowed in the above grades.
[a] Sap is allowed in rotary only, unless otherwise specified.
[b] 10% sap is allowed in rift, comb, and plain sliced; 20% sap is allowed in rotary.
[c] Outside components will be a different size to allow for the edge trim loss and certain types of matching.

| CP | Where the **C**, or **P** icon is not indicated, the rule applies to all Grades equally |

# SECTION 9
## Doors

## compliance requirements — GENERAL/PRODUCT/INSTALLATION/TEST

*Table: 9-051* - **PECAN** and **HICKORY** (ANSI/HPVA - HP1 - latest edition)

| Cut | Plain Sliced (Flat Cut), Quarter Cut, Rotary Cut | |
|---|---|---|
| **Grade Description** | AA | A |
| **Color and Matching** | | |
| Sapwood | Yes | Yes |
| Heartwood | Yes | Yes |
| Color Streaks or Spots | Yes | Yes |
| Color Variation | Yes | Yes |
| Sharp Color Contrast at Joints | Yes, if Slip, Plank, or Random Matched | Yes, if Slip, Plank, or Random Matched |
| Type of Matching<br>  Book Matched<br>  Slip Matched<br>  Pleasing Matched | <br>Yes<br>Specify<br>Not Applicable | <br>Yes<br>Specify<br>Not Applicable |
| Nominal Minimum Width of Face Components [a]<br>  Plain Sliced<br>  Quarter<br>  Rotary | <br>5" (127 mm)<br>3" (76 mm)<br>5" (127 mm) | <br>4" (102 mm)<br>3" (76 mm)<br>4" (102 mm) |
| **Natural Characteristics** | | |
| Small Conspicuous Burls & Pin Knots, Combined Average Number | 1 per 1 sq ft (11 per 1 m²) | 2 per 1 sq ft (22 per 1 m²) |
| Conspicuous Burls - Maximum Size | 1/4" | 3/8" |
| Conspicuous Pin Knots [b]<br>  Average Number<br>  Maximum Size: Dark Part<br>                 Total | <br>1 per 2 sq ft (6 per 1 m²)<br>1/8" (3.2 mm)<br>1/4" (6.4 mm) | <br>2 per 1 sq ft (22 per 1 m²)<br>1/8" (3.2 mm)<br>1/4" (6.4 mm)" |
| Scattered Sound and Repaired Knots | No | No |
| Mineral Streaks | Slight | Slight |
| Bark Pockets | No | Small, Occasional |
| Worm Tracks | No | Slight |
| Vine Marks | Slight | Occasional |
| Cross Bars | Slight | Occasional |
| **Manufacturing Characteristics** | | |
| Rough Cut/Ruptured Grain | No | No |
| Blended Repaired<br>  Tapering Hairline Splits | Two 1/32" x 3" (0.8 mm x 76 mm) at ends only | Two 1/16" x 6" (1.6 mm x 152 mm) |
| Repairs | Very Small Blending | Small Blending |
| **Special Characteristics** | | |
| Bird Peck [c] | No | Slight |
| Knife Marks | Knife marks might occur in these dense species. | |
| Quartered | 1" in 12" (25.4 mm in 305 mm) maximum grain slope; 2-1/2" in 12" (63.5 mm in 305 mm) maximum grain sweep | |

Unfilled worm holes, open splits, open joints, open bark pockets, and doze are not allowed in the above grades.
[a] Outside components will be a different size to allow for edge trim loss and certain types of matching.
[b] For Pecan and Hickory, conspicuous pin knots mean sound knots 1/4" (6.4 mm) or less in diameter with dark centers larger than 1/16" (1.6 mm). Blending pin knots are sound knots 1/4" (6.4 mm) or less in diameter with dark centers 1/16" (1.6 mm) or less and are allowed in all grades.
[c] To achieve a more rustic appearance, bird peck shall be specified.

# SECTION 9
## Doors

GENERAL / **PRODUCT** / INSTALLATION / TEST

**compliance requirements**

Where the **C**, or **P** icon is not indicated, the rule applies to all Grades equally

*Table: 9-052* - **WALNUT** and **CHERRY** (ANSI/HPVA - HP1 - latest edition)

| Cut | Plain Sliced (Flat Cut), Quarter Cut, Rotary Cut | |
|---|---|---|
| Grade Description | AA | A |
| **Color and Matching** | | |
| Sapwood [a] | No | No [a] |
| Heartwood | Yes | Yes |
| Color Streaks or Spots | Slight | Slight |
| Color Variation | Slight | Slight |
| Sharp Color Contrast at Joints | Yes if Slip, Plank, or Random Matched | Yes if Slip, Plank, or Random Matched |
| Type of Matching<br>　Book Matched<br>　Slip Matched<br>　Pleasing Matched | <br>Yes<br>Specify<br>n/a | <br>Yes<br>Specify<br>n/a |
| Nominal Minimum Width of Face Components [b]<br>　Plain Sliced<br>　Quarter<br>　Rotary | <br>5" (127 mm)<br>3" (76 mm)<br>5" (127 mm) | <br>4" (102 mm)<br>3" (76 mm)<br>4" (102 mm) |
| **Natural Characteristics (except as listed below, natural characteristics are not restricted)** | | |
| Small Conspicuous Burls & Pin Knots - Combined Average Number | 1 per 4 sq ft<br>(3 per 1 m$^2$) | 1 per 1-1/3 sq ft<br>(8 per 1 m$^2$) |
| Conspicuous Burls - Maximum Size | 1/4" (6.4 mm) | 3/8" (9.5 mm) |
| Conspicuous Pin Knots [c]<br>　Average Number<br>　Maximum Size:　Dark Part<br>　　　　　　　　　Total | <br>1 per 5 sq ft<br>(3 per 1 m$^2$)<br>1/8" (3.2 mm)<br>1/4" (6.4 mm) | <br>1 per 2 sq ft<br>(6 per 1 m$^2$)<br>1/8" (3.2 mm)<br>1/4" (6.4 mm) |
| Scattered Sound and Repaired Knots | No | No |
| Mineral Streaks | Slight | Slight |
| Bark Pockets | No | No |
| Worm Tracks | No | No |
| Vine Marks | Slight | Occasional |
| Cross Bars | Slight | Occasional |
| **Manufacturing Characteristics** | | |
| Rough Cut/Ruptured Grain | No | No |
| Blended Repaired Tapering Hairline Splits | Two 1/32" x 3"<br>(0.8 mm x 76 mm) on panel ends only | Two 1/16" x 6"<br>(1.6 mm x 152 mm) |
| Repairs | Very Small Blending | Small Blending |
| **Special Characteristics (except as listed below, natural characteristics are not restricted)** | | |
| Gum Spots | Occasional Gum Spots permitted in Cherry | Occasional Gum Spots permitted in Cherry |
| Quartered | 1" in 12" (25.4 mm in 305 mm) maximum grain slope; 2-1/2" in 12" (63.4 mm in 305 mm) maximum grain sweep | |

Unfilled worm holes, open splits, open joints, open bark pockets, and doze are not allowed in the above grades.
[a] Sapwood is allowed in Grades A and B; however, the percentage shall be agreed upon between the buyer and the seller.
[b] Outside components will be a different size to allow for edge trim loss and certain types of matching.
[c] For Walnut and Cherry, conspicuous pin knots mean sound knots 1/4" (6.4 mm) or less in diameter with dark centers larger than 1/16" (1.6 mm). Blending pin knots are sound knots 1/4" (6.4 mm) or less in diameter with dark centers 1/16" (1.6 mm) or less and are allowed in all grades.

| C | P | Where the **C**, or **P** icon is not indicated, the rule applies to all Grades equally |

# SECTION 9
## Doors

**compliance requirements** — GENERAL/**PRODUCT**/INSTALLATION/TEST

### 9.4.5 Material Rules

▲ From previous column

| | | | | | |
|---|---|---|---|---|---|
| 6 | | At **FLUSH** doors (continued) | | | |
| 6 | 2 | | **CROSS BAND VENEERS** shall be of wood veneer or composite, and: | | |
| 6 | 2 | 1 | Particleboard cross band veneers are not permitted. | | |
| 6 | 3 | | **HORIZONTAL EDGES** shall run the full width between stiles without a gap. | | |
| 7 | | | **STILE and RAIL** doors: | | |
| 7 | 1 | | For **OPAQUE** finish, face and edges shall be solid stock of close grain hardwood, veneer of sound close grain hardwood or MDO, at the manufacturer's choice. | | |
| 7 | 2 | | For **TRANSPARENT** finish, face and edges shall be: | | |
| 7 | 2 | 1 | Solid stock of species specified. | | |
| 7 | 2 | 2 | Veneer of HPVA "A" Grade. | C | P |
| 7 | 2 | 3 | Veneer of HPVA "AA" Grade. | C | P |

# SECTION 9
## Doors

GENERAL/**PRODUCT**/INSTALLATION/TEST

**compliance requirements**

Where the **C**, or **P** icon is not indicated, the rule applies to all Grades equally [C] [P]

### 9.4.6 Machine/Assembly Rules

**1** — **ANSI/WDMA HEAVY DUTY PERFORMANCE DUTY LEVEL** is required for both Flush and Stile and Rail doors, and:

- **1.1** If a higher Extra Heavy Duty or lower Standard Duty Performance Duty Level is required, it shall be specified.
- **1.2** A minimum 1" (25.4 mm) hardwood or material that has been qualified in accordance with WDMA TM 15 (latest edition) is required at flush doors stiles and rails.

**2** — **FLUSH** - *Table: - 9-053 -* below sets out the Minimum WDMA Performance Duty Values as published by ANSI/WDMA I.S. 1A (latest edition).

*Table: 9-053* - **FLUSH WOOD DOOR MINIMUM PERFORMANCE STANDARDS** - (Reprinted with permission from ANSI/WDMA I.S. 1A latest edition)

| Performance Attribute | Performance Duty Level | | |
|---|---|---|---|
| | **EXTRA HEAVY DUTY** | **HEAVY DUTY** | **STANDARD DUTY** |
| Adhesive Bond Durability, WDMA TM-6 | Type I or Type II | | |
| Cycle Slam, WDMA TM-7 | 1,000,000 cycles | 500,000 cycles | 250,000 cycles |
| Hinge Loading, WDMA TM-8 | 550 lbs (2440 N) | 475 lbs (2110 N) | 400 lbs (1780 N) |
| Door Finish, Various ASTM test methods | TR-6 & OP-6 or equal * *(Catalyzed Polyurethane AWS System -11)* | TR-4 & OP-4 or equal * *(Conversion Varnish AWS System -5)* | TR-2 & OP-2 or equal * *(Catalyzed Lacquer AWS System -2 or 3)* |
| Screwholding, WDMA TM-10 | | | |
|    Door Face (blocked or unblocked) | 550 lbs (2440 N) | 475 lbs (2110 N) | 400 lbs (1780 N) |
|    Vertical Door Edge | 550 lbs (2440 N) | 475 lbs (2110 N) | 400 lbs (1780 N) |
|    Horizontal Door Edge ** | 300 lbs (1330 N) | 240 lbs (1060 N) | 180 lbs (810 N) |
| Telegraph, Section T-1    *See AWS Test N in TEST* | Maximum 0.010" in any 3" span (0.25 mm in any 76 mm span) | | |
| Warp Tolerance, Section T-2    *See AWS Test E in TEST* | Maximum 0.25" per 3'6" x 7'0" (6.4 mm in any 1050 mm x 2100 mm) door section | | |
| Squareness, Section T-3    *See AWS Test M in TEST* | Diagonal variance 1/8" (3.2 mm) | | |

\* Other formulations may exhibit similar performance characteristics, but must meet or exceed the performance levels for the systems specified to be considered equal.
\*\* Horizontal door edge screwholding applies when hardware is to be attached.

**3** — **TYPE I** or **II ADHESIVE** use at the manufacturer's choice.

*Continues next column* ▼

| C | P | Where the **C**, or **P** icon is not indicated, the rule applies to all Grades equally |

# SECTION 9
## Doors

**compliance requirements** — GENERAL/**PRODUCT**/INSTALLATION/TEST

## 9.4.6 Machine/Assembly Rules

▲ *From previous column*

| 4 | | | | **APPLIED MOLDINGS** require: | | |
|---|---|---|---|---|---|---|
| 4 | 1 | | | Solid stock, free of finger joints. | | |
| 4 | 2 | | | Securely and soundly attached, in contact with the adjacent surface. | | |
| 4 | 2 | 1 | | For **OPAQUE** finish: | | |
| 4 | 2 | 1 | 1 | To be **CLOSE GRAIN HARDWOOD** of a species of the manufacturer's choice. | | |
| 4 | 2 | 1 | 2 | Require moldings to be **PRIMED** when the doors are factory primed. | | |
| 4 | 2 | 2 | | For **TRANSPARENT** finish: | | |
| 4 | 2 | 2 | 1 | To be of the **SAME SPECIES** and **LUMBER** or **VENEER GRADE** as the face veneer, except: | | |
| 4 | 2 | 2 | 1 | Maple may be used as an alternate when a Birch face is specified. | | |
| 4 | 2 | 2 | 2 | Require molding to be prefinished if doors are factory finished. | | |
| 4 | 2 | 3 | | At **HPDL** faced doors: | | |
| 4 | 2 | 3 | 1 | To be **CLOSE GRAIN HARDWOOD** of the manufacturer's choice. | | |
| 4 | 2 | 3 | 2 | Require molding to be **STAINED** or **PAINTED** to match the face, if so specified. | | |
| 5 | | | | **GLAZING MATERIAL** required be secured in place with mitered wood glazing beads or clips with glass bedded in sealant that squeezes out on both sides, and/or: | | |
| 5 | 1 | | | Sealant shall be a quality, elastic type compound, which is designed for bedding glazing materials or is recommended for such use by the sealant manufacturer. | | |
| 5 | 2 | | | Use of glazing gaskets, tape or high density foam is acceptable. | | |
| 6 | | | | **EXPOSED SURFACES** shall comply with the following smoothness requirements (see Item 9.87.1 in TESTS): | | |
| 6 | 1 | | | **SHARP EDGES** shall be eased with a fine abrasive. | | |
| 6 | 2 | | | **TOP FLAT WOOD** surfaces; those that can be sanded with a drum or wide belt sander: | | |
| 6 | 2 | 1 | | 120 grit sanding. | C | P |
| 6 | 2 | 2 | | 150 grit sanding. | C | P |
| 6 | 3 | | | **PROFILED** and **SHAPED WOOD** surfaces: | | |
| 6 | 3 | 1 | | 120 grit sanding. | | |
| 6 | 4 | | | **TURNED WOOD** surfaces: | | |
| 6 | 4 | 1 | | 120 grit sanding. | C | P |
| 6 | 4 | 2 | | 180 grit sanding. | C | P |
| 6 | 5 | | | **CROSS SANDING**, excluding turned surfaces, is not allowed. | | |

*Continues next column ▼*

## 9.4.6 Machine/Assembly Rules

▲ *From previous column*

| 6 | | | | **EXPOSED SURFACES**   (continued) | | |
|---|---|---|---|---|---|---|
| 6 | 6 | | | **TEAR OUTS**, **KNIFE NICKS**, or **HIT OR MISS** machining is not permitted. | | |
| 6 | 7 | | | **KNIFE MARKS** are not permitted where sanding is required. | | |
| 6 | 8 | | | **GLUE** or **FILLER**, if used, shall be inconspicuous and match the adjacent surface for smoothness. | | |
| 6 | 9 | | | **HPDL**, **PVC**, and **PREFINISHED WOOD** edges shall be machined flush and filed, sanded, or buffed to remove machine marks and sharp edges, and: | | |
| 6 | 9 | 1 | | **OVERLAP** (See Test F illustrations in TESTS) such as, shall not exceed: | | |
| 6 | 9 | 1 | 1 | 0.005" (0.13 mm) for a maximum length of 1" (25.4 mm) in any 24" (610 mm) run. | C | P |
| 6 | 9 | 1 | 2 | 0.003" (0.08 mm) for a maximum length of 1" (25.4 mm) in any 48" (1220 mm) run. | C | P |
| 6 | 9 | 2 | | **CHIP OUT** (See Test G illustrations in TESTS) such as shall be inconspicuous when viewed at: | | |
| 6 | 9 | 2 | 1 | 48" (1220 mm). | C | P |
| 6 | 9 | 2 | 2 | 24" (610 mm). | C | P |

*Continues next column ▼*

# SECTION 9
## Doors

GENERAL/**PRODUCT**/INSTALLATION/TEST

**compliance requirements**

Where the **C**, or **P** icon is not indicated, the rule applies to all Grades equally

### 9.4.6 Machine/Assembly Rules

▲ From previous column

| | | | | | |
|---|---|---|---|---|---|
| 6 | | **EXPOSED SURFACES** (continued) | | | |
| 6 | 9 | **HPDL**, **PVC**, and **PREFINISHED WOOD** edges (continued) | | | |
| 6 | 9 | 3 | **OVER MACHINED** (See Test H illustrations in TESTS) removal of color or pattern of face material such as, 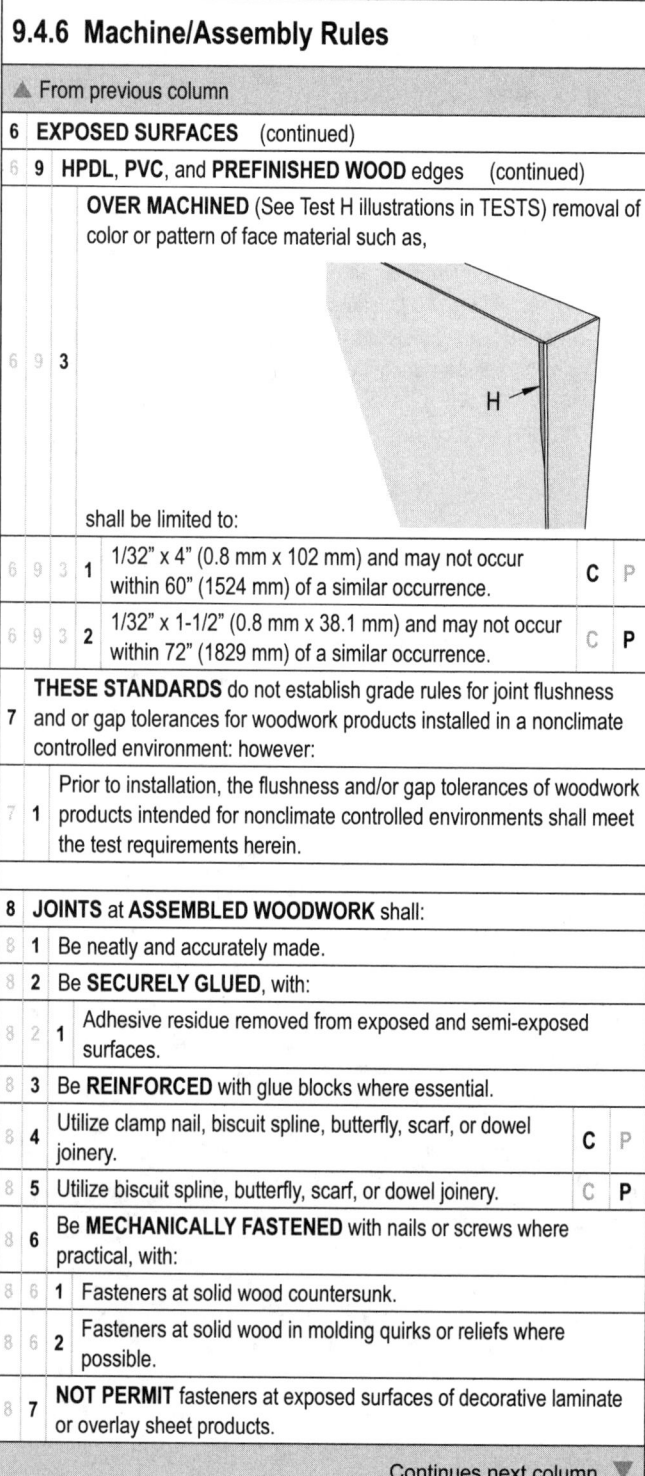 shall be limited to: | | |
| 6 | 9 | 3 | 1 | 1/32" x 4" (0.8 mm x 102 mm) and may not occur within 60" (1524 mm) of a similar occurrence. | C P |
| 6 | 9 | 3 | 2 | 1/32" x 1-1/2" (0.8 mm x 38.1 mm) and may not occur within 72" (1829 mm) of a similar occurrence. | C P |
| 7 | | **THESE STANDARDS** do not establish grade rules for joint flushness and or gap tolerances for woodwork products installed in a nonclimate controlled environment: however, | | | |
| 7 | 1 | Prior to installation, the flushness and/or gap tolerances of woodwork products intended for nonclimate controlled environments shall meet the test requirements herein. | | | |
| 8 | | **JOINTS** at **ASSEMBLED WOODWORK** shall: | | | |
| 8 | 1 | Be neatly and accurately made. | | | |
| 8 | 2 | Be **SECURELY GLUED**, with: | | | |
| 8 | 2 | 1 | Adhesive residue removed from exposed and semi-exposed surfaces. | | |
| 8 | 3 | Be **REINFORCED** with glue blocks where essential. | | | |
| 8 | 4 | Utilize clamp nail, biscuit spline, butterfly, scarf, or dowel joinery. | | | C P |
| 8 | 5 | Utilize biscuit spline, butterfly, scarf, or dowel joinery. | | | C P |
| 8 | 6 | Be **MECHANICALLY FASTENED** with nails or screws where practical, with: | | | |
| 8 | 6 | 1 | Fasteners at solid wood countersunk. | | |
| 8 | 6 | 2 | Fasteners at solid wood in molding quirks or reliefs where possible. | | |
| 8 | 7 | **NOT PERMIT** fasteners at exposed surfaces of decorative laminate or overlay sheet products. | | | |

Continues next column ▼

### 9.4.6 Machine/Assembly Rules

▲ From previous column

| | | | | |
|---|---|---|---|---|
| 8 | | **JOINTS** at **ASSEMBLED WOODWORK** (continued) | | |
| 8 | 8 | Require **FLUSHNESS VARIATIONS** at exposed surfaces (See Test D illustrations in TESTS), when mitered or butted, such as, 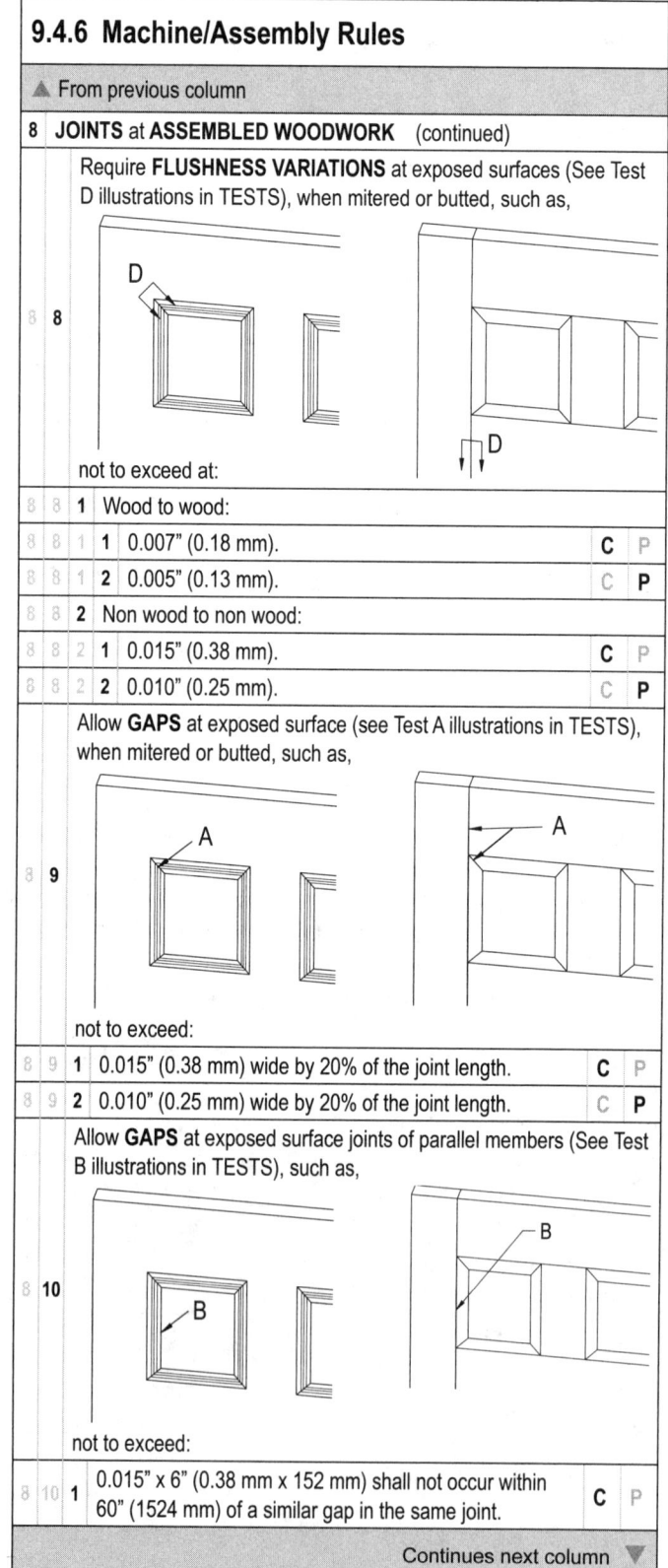 not to exceed at: | | |
| 8 | 8 | 1 | Wood to wood: | |
| 8 | 8 | 1 | 1 | 0.007" (0.18 mm). | C P |
| 8 | 8 | 1 | 2 | 0.005" (0.13 mm). | C P |
| 8 | 8 | 2 | Non wood to non wood: | |
| 8 | 8 | 2 | 1 | 0.015" (0.38 mm). | C P |
| 8 | 8 | 2 | 2 | 0.010" (0.25 mm). | C P |
| 8 | 9 | Allow **GAPS** at exposed surface (see Test A illustrations in TESTS), when mitered or butted, such as, not to exceed: | | |
| 8 | 9 | 1 | 0.015" (0.38 mm) wide by 20% of the joint length. | C P |
| 8 | 9 | 2 | 0.010" (0.25 mm) wide by 20% of the joint length. | C P |
| 8 | 10 | Allow **GAPS** at exposed surface joints of parallel members (See Test B illustrations in TESTS), such as, not to exceed: | | |
| 8 | 10 | 1 | 0.015" x 6" (0.38 mm x 152 mm) shall not occur within 60" (1524 mm) of a similar gap in the same joint. | C P |

Continues next column ▼

# SECTION 9
## Doors

**compliance requirements** — GENERAL/**PRODUCT**/INSTALLATION/TEST

| C | P | Where the **C**, or **P** icon is not indicated, the rule applies to all Grades equally |

## 9.4.6 Machine/Assembly Rules

▲ From previous column

| | | | | | |
|---|---|---|---|---|---|
| 8 | | | **JOINTS** at **ASSEMBLED WOODWORK** (continued) | | |
| 8 | 10 | | Allow **GAPS** at exposed surface joints of parallel (continued) | | |
| 8 | 10 | 2 | 0.010" x 4" (0.25 mm x 102 mm) shall not occur within 72" (1829 mm) of a similar gap in the same joint. | C | P |
| 8 | 11 | | Allow **GAPS** at exposed surface joints (See Test C illustrations in TESTS) when mitered or butted, such as, [illustration] not to exceed: | | |
| 8 | 11 | 1 | 0.015" (0.38 mm). | C | P |
| 8 | 11 | 2 | 0.010" (0.25 mm). | C | P |
| 8 | 12 | | Allows use of filler: | | |
| 8 | 12 | 1 | If inconspicuous when viewed at 24" (610 mm). | C | P |
| 8 | 12 | 2 | Not allowed. | C | P |
| 9 | | | **FLUSH** doors: | | |
| 9 | 1 | | Shall be 3, 5, OR 7 PLY of the manufacturer's choice, unless specified otherwise. | | |
| 9 | 2 | | **CORES**, conforming to the minimum requirements of WDMA - I.S. 1-A (latest edition), at: | | |
| 9 | 2 | 1 | Solid core, shall be particleboard, MDF, agrifiber, staved lumber, SCL, or fire resistant composite. | | |
| 9 | 2 | 2 | Hollow core, shall be honey comb, and the: | | |
| 9 | 2 | 2 | 1 | Stile and/or rail widths remaining after sizing or prefitting to be no less than: | |
| 9 | 2 | 2 | 1 | 1" (25.4 mm) at lock and hinge stiles. | |
| 9 | 2 | 2 | 2 | 6" (152.4 mm) at top, bottom, and intermediate lock rails. | |
| 9 | 3 | | Require **CUTOUTS**: | | |
| 9 | 3 | 1 | At **NON RATED** doors to (unless allowed by individual manufacturer's warranty): | | |
| 9 | 3 | 1 | 1 | Not exceed 40% of the door area, for the combined area of all cutouts for lights or louvers. | |
| 9 | 3 | 1 | 2 | Not exceed one half the door height. | |
| 9 | 3 | 1 | 3 | Be at least 5" (127 mm) from door edges, adjacent cutouts, or hardware mortises. | |

Continues next column ▼

## 9.4.6 Machine/Assembly Rules

▲ From previous column

| | | | | | |
|---|---|---|---|---|---|
| 9 | | | **FLUSH** doors (continued) | | |
| 9 | 3 | | Require **CUTOUTS** (continued) | | |
| 9 | 3 | 2 | At **RATED** doors: | | |
| 9 | 3 | 2 | 1 | Be governed by the individual manufacturer's fire rated approval and/or NFPA 80 for the combined area and location of cutouts for lights or louvers. | |
| 9 | 3 | 3 | At **HPDL** exposed surfaces have a minimum 1/4" (6.4 mm) radius at all inside corners. | | |
| 9 | 4 | | Require **TRANSOM PANEL**: | | |
| 9 | 4 | 1 | **BOTTOM RAILS** to be: | | |
| 9 | 4 | 1 | 1 | **TYPE 2**, which allows side rails to run through. | C | P |
| 9 | 4 | 1 | 2 | Compatible for color to the vertical edgeband of the door. | C | P |
| 9 | 4 | 1 | 3 | **TYPE 1**, full width. | C | P |
| 9 | 4 | 1 | 4 | Well matched for color to the vertical edgeband of the door. | C | P |
| 9 | 4 | 2 | **TOP RAILS** of doors with rabbeted transoms to be: | | |
| 9 | 4 | 2 | 1 | Compatible in color to the vertical edgeband of the door. | C | P |
| 9 | 4 | 2 | 2 | Of the same species as the vertical edgeband of the door. | C | P |
| 9 | 4 | 3 | **FACES**, for transparent finish be: | | |
| 9 | 4 | 3 | 1 | End matched to the door. | C | P |
| 9 | 4 | 3 | 2 | Continuous matched to the door. | C | P |
| 9 | 4 | 4 | **END MATCHED VENEER MISALIGNMENT** between sequenced adjacent panels shall not exceed: | | |
| 4 | 4 | 4 | 1 | 3/8" (9.5 mm). | C | P |
| 4 | 4 | 4 | 2 | 3/16" (4.8 mm). | C | P |
| 9 | 5 | | Requires **DUTCH DOORS** without an applied shelf to have the top edge of the bottom leaf and the bottom edge of the top leaf, if rabbeted: | | |
| 9 | 5 | 1 | For **OPAQUE** finish to be close grain hardwood of a species of the manufacturer's choice. | | |
| 9 | 5 | 2 | For **HPDL**, to be close grain hardwood of a species of the manufacturer's choice, and: | | |
| 9 | 5 | 2 | 1 | Painted or stained to match the face laminate, if edges are so required. | |

Continues next column ▼

# SECTION 9
## Doors

GENERAL/**PRODUCT**/INSTALLATION/TEST

compliance requirements

Where the **C**, or **P** icon is not indicated, the rule applies to all Grades equally | **C** | **P** |

### 9.4.6 Machine/Assembly Rules

▲ From previous column

| | | | | | C | P |
|---|---|---|---|---|---|---|
| 9 | | | | FLUSH doors (continued) | | |
| 9 | 6 | | | Require VERTICAL EDGES: | | |
| 9 | 6 | 1 | | For OPAQUE finished doors: | | |
| 9 | 6 | 1 | 1 | Be primed, if doors are factory primed. | | |
| 9 | 6 | 1 | 2 | Be close grain hardwood lumber, veneer, or MDO over backer of the manufacturer's choice. | | |
| 9 | 6 | 1 | 3 | Permit one finger joint at either veneer edge that is tight, not raised, or not visible from a distance of 48" (1219 mm). | C | P |
| 9 | 6 | 1 | 4 | Finger joints are not permitted. | C | P |
| 9 | 6 | 2 | | For TRANSPARENT finished doors: | | |
| 9 | 6 | 2 | 1 | Permit one finger joint at each edge that is tight, not raised, uniform in color and grain, without discoloration, or not visible from a distance of 48" (1219 mm). | C | P |
| 9 | 6 | 2 | 2 | Finger joint are not permitted. | C | P |
| 9 | 6 | 2 | 3 | Be hardwood lumber or veneer over backer, compatible in color with the face veneer. | C | P |
| 9 | 6 | 2 | 4 | Allow flat grain Douglas Fir at VG Douglas Fir faced doors. | C | P |
| 9 | 6 | 2 | 5 | Be the same species as the face veneer. | C | P |
| 9 | 6 | 2 | 6 | Be prefinished, if the doors are prefinished. | | |
| 9 | 6 | 2 | 7 | If the manufacturer's fire rated door approval prevents the use of matching vertical edges, then the species permitted under their approval shall be allowed. | C | P |
| 9 | 6 | 2 | 8 | Require VG Grain Douglas Fir at VG Douglas Fir faced doors. | C | P |
| 9 | 6 | 3 | | For HPDL FACED doors: | | |
| 9 | 6 | 3 | 1 | Be unfinished close grain hardwood of manufacturer's choice, and: | C | P |
| 9 | 6 | 3 | 1 | At opaque finish, permit finger joints at either edge that are tight, not raised, or not visible from a distance of 48" (1219 mm). | C | P |
| 9 | 6 | 3 | 2 | At transparent finish, permit one finger joint at either edge that is tight, not raised, uniform in color and grain, without discoloration, and not visible from a distance of 24" (610 mm). | C | P |
| 9 | 6 | 3 | 2 | Be HPDL or PVC to match the face laminate or hardwood stained/painted and finished to match the face laminate at the manufacturer's choice. | C | P |

Continues next column ▼

### 9.4.6 Machine/Assembly Rules

▲ From previous column

| | | | | | C | P |
|---|---|---|---|---|---|---|
| 10 | | | | STILE and RAIL doors: | | |
| 10 | 1 | | | Shall be glued up with Type I or II Adhesive at the manufacturer's choice. | | |
| 10 | 2 | | | Special stile or rail requirements to accommodate specified hardware shall prevail. | | |
| 10 | 3 | | | Of softwood shall be solid stock or veneer construction. | | |
| 10 | 4 | | | Of hardwood shall be: | | |
| 10 | 4 | 1 | | Solid stock or veneer construction. | C | P |
| 10 | 4 | 2 | | Veneer construction. | C | P |
| 10 | 5 | | | The construction of the STILES and RAILS: | | |
| 10 | 5 | 1 | | If SOLID STOCK requires: | | |
| 10 | 5 | 1 | 1 | One piece solid stock. | C | P |
| 10 | 5 | 1 | 2 | Two piece balanced lamination for thickness, with opposing grain. | | |
| 10 | 5 | 1 | 3 | Three piece lamination for thickness, balanced outer pieces, with opposing grain, and: | | |
| 10 | 5 | 1 | 1 | Face veneers shall be uniform in thickness. | | |
| 10 | 5 | 1 | 4 | No finger joints. | | |
| 10 | 5 | 1 | 5 | Edge gluing in accordance with Section 3. | | |
| 10 | 5 | 2 | | If VENEERED requires: | | |
| 10 | 5 | 2 | 1 | CORES of either MDF (medium density fiberboard), SCL (structural composite lumber), edge glued wood blocks/strips (staved core), particleboard, agrifiber, laminated veneer lumber core, fire resistant composite core, and specialty door core types, and: | | |
| 10 | 5 | 2 | 1 | If STAVED CORE (edge glued wood block/strips), it shall be of one species in any one door, and the staves (block/strips): | | |
| 10 | 5 | 2 | 1 | 1 | Shall not exceed 2" (50.8 mm) in width. | | |
| 10 | 5 | 2 | 1 | 2 | May be of any length. | | |
| 10 | 5 | 2 | 1 | 3 | Shall have staggered end joints in adjacent rows. | | |
| 10 | 5 | 2 | 1 | 4 | Shall not permit voids between end joints. | | |
| 10 | 5 | 2 | 1 | 5 | Shall not permit open surface defects. | | |
| 10 | 5 | 2 | 1 | 6 | Shall be bonded together under pressure. | | |

Continues next column ▼

# SECTION 9
## Doors

**compliance requirements** — GENERAL/PRODUCT/INSTALLATION/TEST

### 9.4.6 Machine/Assembly Rules

▲ From previous column

| | | | | |  |
|---|---|---|---|---|---|
| 10 | | | | | **STILE** and **RAIL** (continued) |
| 10 | 6 | | | | With **PANELS** require: |
| 10 | 6 | 1 | | | They be finished to a uniform thickness and fit snuggly into the stile and rail retention groves, and that: |
| 10 | 7 | 1 | | | They float in their method of retention, and that: |
| 10 | 7 | 1 | 1 | | Mechanical fastening is not permitted. |
| 10 | 7 | 2 | | | MDF (medium density fiberboard) may be used for opaque finish, and: |
| 10 | 7 | 3 | | | Grain shall run vertically. |
| 10 | 7 | 4 | | | At flat type, they be at least: |
| 10 | 7 | 4 | 1 | | 1/4" (6.4 mm) in thickness at 1-3/8" (35 mm) thick doors. |
| 10 | 7 | 4 | 2 | | 1/2" (12.7 mm) in thickness at 1-3/4" (44 mm) thick doors. |
| 10 | 7 | 4 | 3 | | 5/8" (16 mm) in thickness at 2-1/4" (57 mm) thick doors. |
| 10 | 6 | 5 | | | At **RAISED** type, they shall be: |
| 10 | 6 | 5 | 1 | | At least 3/4" (19 mm) in thickness at 1-3/8" (35 mm) thick doors. |
| 10 | 6 | 5 | 2 | | At least 1-1/8" (28.6 mm) in thickness at 1-3/4" (44 mm) thick doors. |
| 10 | 6 | 5 | 3 | | At least 1-1/2" (38.1 mm) in thickness at 2-1/4" (57 mm) thick doors. |
| 10 | 6 | 5 | 4 | | Constructed of either: |
| 10 | 6 | 5 | 4 | 1 | Solid stock in opening widths not to exceeding 14" (356 mm). |
| 10 | 6 | 5 | 4 | 2 | Rim banded or membrane-pressed panel construction, and: |
| 10 | 6 | 5 | 4 | 1 | Mitered when rim banded. |
| 10 | 7 | | | | Require **JOINERY**: |
| 10 | 7 | 1 | | | To be either mortise and tenon or doweled and glued under pressure so that the stiles, rails, mullions, and muntins are bonded together. |
| 10 | 7 | 2 | | | At faces to finish true, with stile and rail intersections and other copes well fitted. |
| 10 | 7 | 3 | | | Stickings to be clean cut and smooth. |

# SECTION 9
## Doors

GENERAL/PRODUCT/**INSTALLATION**/TEST

**compliance requirements**

### 9.5 Preparation and Qualification Requirements

**1 CARE, STORAGE, and BUILDING CONDITIONS** shall be in compliance with the requirements set forth in Section 2 of these standards, and doors shall be:

1.1 Sealed at earliest possible moment. Edge sealing is particularly important.

1.2 Lift or carry door. Do not drag one door against another.

1.3 Handle doors with clean hands or clean gloves.

1.4 Severe damage to the woodwork can result from noncompliance. The manufacturer and/or installer of the woodwork shall not be held responsible for damage that might develop by not adhering to the requirements.

**2 CONTRACTOR IS RESPONSIBLE FOR**

2.1 Furnishing and installing structural members, grounds, in wall blocking, backing, furring, brackets, or other anchorage required for architectural woodwork installation that becomes an integral part of walls, floors, or ceilings to which architectural woodwork shall be installed.

2.1.1 In the absence of contract documents calling for the contractor to supply the necessary in wall blocking/backing in the wall or ceilings, either through inadvertence or otherwise, the architectural woodwork installer shall not proceed with the installation until such time as the in wall blocking/backing is installed by others.

2.1.2 Preparatory work done by others shall be subject to inspection by the architectural woodwork installer, and may be accepted or rejected for cause prior to installation.

2.1.2.1 **WALL, CEILING,** and/or **OPENING VARIATION**s in excess of 1/4" (6.4 mm) or **FLOORS** in excess of 1/2" (12.7 mm) in 144" (3658 mm) of being plumb, level, flat, straight, square, or of the correct size are not acceptable for the installation of architectural woodwork, nor is it the responsibility of the installer to scribe or fit to tolerances in excess of such.

2.1.3 Installation site being properly ventilated, protected from direct sunlight, excessive heat and/or moisture, and that the HVAC system is functioning and maintaining the appropriate relative humidity and temperature.

2.2 Priming the architectural woodwork in accordance with the contract documents prior to its installation.

### 9.5 Preparation and Qualification Requirements (continued)

**3 INSTALLER IS RESPONSIBLE FOR**

3.1 Having adequate equipment and experienced craftsmen to complete the installation in a first class manner.

3.2 Checking architectural woodwork specified and studying the appropriate portions of the contract documents, including these standards and the reviewed shop drawings to familiarize themselves with the requirements of the Grade specified, understanding that:

3.2.1 Appearance requirements of Grades apply only to surfaces visible after installation.

3.2.2 For transparent finish, special attention needs to be given to the color and the grain of the various woodwork pieces to ensure they are installed in compliance with the Grade specified.

3.3 Verification that installation site is properly ventilated, protected from direct sunlight, excessive heat and/or moisture, and that the HVAC system is functioning and maintaining the appropriate relative humidity and temperature.

3.4 Verification that required priming of woodwork has been completed by others before woodwork is installed.

3.5 Verification that woodwork has been acclimated to the field conditions for a minimum of 72 hours before installation is commenced.

3.6 Woodwork specifically built or assembled in sequence for match of color and grain is installed to maintain that same sequence.

### 9.6 RULES

1 The following rules shall govern unless a project's contract documents require otherwise.

2 These rules are intended to provide a well defined degree of control over a project's quality of materials, workmanship, or installation.

3 **ERRATA**, published on the Sponsor Associations' websites at www.awinet.org, www.awmac.com, or www.aws-errata.com, **shall take precedence over these rules**, subject to their date of posting and a project's bid date.

# SECTION 9
## Doors

**GENERAL / PRODUCT / INSTALLATION / TEST**

**compliance requirements**

> **C** **P** Where the **C**, or **P** icon is not indicated, the rule applies to all Grades equally

### 9.6.4 Basic Rules

| 1 | **AESTHETIC** Grade rules apply only to exposed and semi-exposed surfaces visible after installation. | | |
|---|---|---|---|
| 2 | **INSTALLERS** shall be furnished with an approved: | | |
| 2 | 1 | Hardware schedule and required templates. | |
| 2 | 2 | Set of metal frame shop drawings, including the locations of the hardware preparations. | |
| 3 | **PREFIT** and **PREMACHINED** doors are to be installed in accordance with the manufacturer's data. | | |
| 4 | **TRANSPARENT FINISH** doors insets or with transoms shall be installed: | | |
| 4 | 1 | Compatible in color and grain. | C P |
| 4 | 2 | Well matched for color and grain. | C P |
| 5 | **BLUEPRINT** matched doors and panels shall be single sourced. | | |
| 6 | **UTILITY** or **STRUCTURAL STRENGTH** of doors shall not be impaired in fitting them to the opening, applying hardware, preparing for lights, louvers, plant ons, or other detailing. | | |
| 7 | **FIRE DOOR ASSEMBLIES**, including 20, 30, 45, 60, and 90 minute rated, shall be prepared for locks, latches, hinges, remotely operated or monitored hardware, concealed closers, glass lights, vision panels, louvers, astragals, and laminated overlays in conformance to the manufacturer's Label Service requirements, and: | | |
| 7 | 1 | **LABELS** are prohibited from being removed. | |
| 8 | **DOORS** and their **ACCESSORIES** shall be hung plumb and level within 1/16" (1.6 mm) of the height and width of the door assembly. | | |
| 9 | **WHEN INSTALLED**, doors shall operate smoothly and easily without binding, and: | | |
| 9 | 1 | **PAIRS** of doors, when closed, shall be within 1/16" (1.6 mm) of flush at the meeting edge. | |
| 10 | **INSTALLER MODIFICATIONS** shall comply to the material, machining, and assembly rules within the **PRODUCT** portion of this section and the applicable finishing rules in Section 5. | | |
| 11 | Door **FACES** shall not extend more than: | | |
| 11 | 1 | 1/16" (1.6 mm) beyond the face of the jamb. | |
| 11 | 2 | 1/8" (3.2 mm) behind the face of the jamb. | |

*Continues next column* ▼

### 9.6.4 Basic Rules

▲ *From previous column*

| 12 | **FITTING** for: | | |
|---|---|---|---|
| 12 | 1 | **WIDTH** requires the door to be trimmed equally from both sides; however, on: | |
| 12 | 1 | 1 | **FIRE RATED DOORS**, in order to preserve the label, they shall be trimmed per the manufacturer's requirements. |
| 12 | 2 | **HEIGHT** prohibits trimming top or bottom rails more than 3/4" (19 mm), and: | |
| 12 | 2 | 1 | **FIRE RATED DOORS** shall only be trimmed on the bottom rail only. |
| 12 | 2 | 2 | When cutting to length, extreme care shall be used to prevent chipping of veneer. |
| 13 | **CLEARANCE** between the door and frame members shall be a maximum of 1/8" (3.2 mm) on the hinge and lock sides, the top of the door, and between the meeting edges of doors in pairs, and: | | |
| 13 | 1 | Installer shall not be responsible for clearances in excess of these dimensions if the door manufacturer made an error on prefit widths or locations for mortise hardware. | |
| 13 | 2 | Clearance at the bottom of fire rated doors shall conform to NFPA 80 and at non rated doors shall be a minimum of 1/4" and a maximum of 5/8" measured from the bottom of the door to the highest point of the finish floor that the door swings over. | |
| 14 | **HARDWARE** shall be installed: | | |
| 14 | 1 | In locations and by methods of attachment appropriate for the specific door construction. | |
| 14 | 1 | 1 | Templates for specific hardware preparation and installation are typically available from the manufacturer or the Door Hardware Institute (DHI). |
| 14 | 2 | With appropriate fasteners, and: | |
| 14 | 2 | 1 | Operate as intended. |
| 14 | 2 | 2 | Preferably use threaded to the head wood screws on nonrated doors. |
| 14 | 2 | 3 | Use threaded to the head wood screws on fire rated doors. |
| 14 | 2 | 4 | Require pilot holes to be drilled for screws. |
| 14 | 2 | 5 | Installed using furnished fasteners or fastener provisions and when fastener provisions are countersunk, fasteners shall be countersunk. |

*Continues next column* ▼

# SECTION 9
## Doors

GENERAL / PRODUCT / **INSTALLATION** / TEST — compliance requirements

### 9.6.4 Basic Rules

▲ From previous column

**15** **LEAF HINGES** on:
- **15.1** **SOLID CORE** doors shall require:
  - **15.1.1** A minimum of two hinges for doors up to 60" (1524 mm) in height.
  - **15.1.2** A minimum of three hinges for doors over 60" (1524 mm) in height, and:
    - **15.1.2.1** An additional hinge for each additional 30" (762 mm) or portion thereof in door height.
  - **15.1.3** Space between hinges be equal.
- **15.2** **HOLLOW CORE** doors weighing less than 50 lbs (22.7 kg) and not exceeding 90" (2286 mm) in height shall require only two hinges.

**16** **DOOR CUTOUTS** for lights or louvers, if applicable, shall be protected from water entering the door core by a satisfactory method such as metal flashing at the bottom of the cutout.

**17** **TEMPORARY DISTORTIONS** (warp) will usually disappear when humidity is equalized, and doors seldom need to be replaced.

**18** **REPAIRS** are allowed, provided they are made neatly and are inconspicuous when viewed at:

| | | | C | P |
|---|---|---|---|---|
| 18.1 | 48" (1219 mm). | | C | P |
| 18.2 | 24" (610 mm). | | C | P |

**19** **WOODWORK** such as **APPLIED TRIM** shall be:
- **19.1** **SECURELY** fastened and tightly fitted with flush joints.
  - **19.1.1** Joinery shall be consistent throughout the project.
- **19.2** Of **MAXIMUM** available and/or practical lengths.

| | | | C | P |
|---|---|---|---|---|
| 19.3 | **PROFILED** or **SELF MITERED** when trim ends are exposed. | | C | P |
| 19.4 | **SELF MITERED** when trim ends are exposed. | | C | P |
| 19.5 | **MITERED** at outside corners. | | | |
| 19.6 | **MITERED** at inside corners. | | C | P |
| 19.7 | **COPED** at inside corners. | | C | P |

- **19.8** **INSTALLED** plumb, level, square, and flat within 1/8" (3.2 mm) in 96" (2438 mm).
  - **19.8.1** Grounds and hanging systems set plumb and true.

Continues next column ▼

---

### 9.6.4 Basic Rules

▲ From previous column

**19** **WOODWORK** such as **APPLIED TRIM** (continued)
- **19.9** **INSTALLED FREE OF:**
  - **19.9.1** Warp, twisting, cupping, and/or bowing that cannot be held true.
  - **19.9.2** Open joints, visible machine marks, cross sanding, tear outs, nicks, chips, and/or scratches.
  - **19.9.3** Natural defects exceeding the quantity and/or size limits defined in Sections 3 and 4.
- **19.10** **SMOOTH** and **SANDED** without cross scratches in conformance to the Product portion of this section.

**20** These standards do not establish Grade rules for joint flushness and or gap tolerances for woodwork products installed in a non climate controlled environment.

**21** **GAPS** (see Test I illustrations in TESTS) such as,

and:

| | | | | C | P |
|---|---|---|---|---|---|
| 21.1 | Shall **NOT EXCEED** 30% of a joint's length, and: | | | | |
| 21.1.1 | **FILLER** or **CAULKING** is allowed, if color compatible. | | | | |
| 21.2 | Of **WOOD** to **WOOD** shall not exceed: | | | | |
| 21.2.1 | At **FLAT** surfaces: | | | | |
| 21.2.1.1 | 0.020" (0.51 mm) in width. | | | C | P |
| 21.2.1.2 | 0.015" (0.38 mm) in width. | | | C | P |
| 21.2.2 | At **SHAPED** surfaces: | | | | |
| 21.2.2.1 | 0.025" (0.64 mm) in width. | | | C | P |
| 21.2.2.2 | 0.015" (0.38 mm) in width. | | | C | P |

Continues next column ▼

## 9.6.4 Basic Rules

▲ From previous column

| | | | | | |
|---|---|---|---|---|---|
| 22 | **FLUSHNESS** of joinery (see Test J illustrations in TESTS), such as, and: | | | | |
| 22 | 1 | Of **WOOD** to **WOOD** shall not exceed: | | | |
| 22 | 1 | 1 | At **FLAT** surfaces: | | |
| 22 | 1 | 1 | 1 | 0.015" (0.38 mm) in width. | C P |
| 22 | 1 | 1 | 2 | 0.010" (0.25 mm) in width. | C **P** |
| 22 | 1 | 2 | At **SHAPED** surfaces: | | |
| 22 | 1 | 2 | 1 | 0.025" (0.65 mm) in width. | C P |
| 22 | 1 | 2 | 2 | 0.030" (0.51 mm) in width. | C **P** |
| 23 | **AREAS** of installation shall be left broom clean. | | | | |
| 23 | 1 | Debris shall be removed and dumped in containers provided by the general contractor. | | | |
| 23 | 2 | Items installed shall be cleaned of pencil or ink marks. | | | |
| 24 | **FIRST CLASS WORKMANSHIP** is required in compliance with these standards. | | | | |

# SECTION 9
## Doors

GENERAL/PRODUCT/INSTALLATION/**TEST**

**compliance requirements**

Where the **C**, or **P** icon is not indicated, the rule applies to all Grades equally [C][P]

### 9.7 BASIC CONSIDERATIONS

1. The tolerances typically found within the Architectural Woodwork Standards fall into two categories:

   1.1 Factory fabricated joinery, assembly and construction found in the **PRODUCT** portion.

   1.2 Field installation joinery and assembly found in the **INSTALLATION** portion.

2. Most fabrication and installation assemblies include solid wood to solid wood joints, solid wood to wood veneer joints, solid wood to wood based products (HPDL, LPDL, Solid Phenolic and panel products), solid wood to non wood based products (which can be drywall, glass, metal, stone, acrylics, and other surfaces), and non wood to non wood joints.

3. Tolerances found in the AWS include:

   3.1 Flatness of wood based panel products.

   3.2 Solid wood to solid wood joints and assemblies.

   3.3 Solid wood to wood veneer joints and assemblies.

   3.4 Wood veneer to wood veneer joints and assemblies.

   3.5 Solid wood to wood based product joints and assemblies.

   3.6 Solid surface to solid surface joints and assemblies.

4. Because of the differences of expansion and contraction of non wood products compared to solid wood and wood based products, the AWS does not apply tolerances regarding flatness or joinery to these non wood based products.

5. **FABRICATED** and **INSTALLED** woodwork shall be tested for compliance to these standards as follows:

   5.1 **SMOOTHNESS** of exposed surfaces:

   5.1.1 **KCPI** (Knife Cuts Per Inch) is determined by holding the surfaced board at an angle to a strong light source and counting the visible ridges per inch, usually perpendicular to the profile.

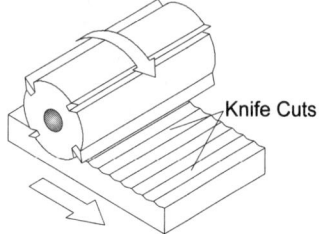

*Figure: 9-054*

### 9.7 BASIC CONSIDERATIONS (continued)

5. **FABRICATED** and **INSTALLED** (continued)

   5.1.2 **SANDING** is checked for compliance by sanding a sample piece of the same species with the required grit of abrasive.

   5.1.2.1 Observation with a hand lens of the prepared sample and the material in question will offer a comparison of the scratch marks of the abrasive grit.

   5.1.2.2 Reasonable assessment of the performance of the finished product will be weighed against absolute compliance with the standard.

   5.1.2.3 A product is sanded sufficiently smooth when knife cuts are removed and remaining sanding marks are or will be concealed by applied finishing coats.

   5.1.2.4 Grain raise at unfinished wood, due to moisture or humidity in excess of the ranges set forth in this standard, shall not be considered a defect and must be sanded prior to finishing.

6. **GAPS, FLUSHNESS, FLATNESS** and **ALIGNMENT** of product and installation:

   6.1 Maximum gaps between exposed components shall be tested with a feeler gauge at points designed to join where members contact or touch.

   6.2 Joint length shall be measured with a ruler with minimum 1/16" (1 mm) divisions and calculations made accordingly.

   6.3 Reasonable assessment of the performance of the finished product will be weighed against absolute compliance with the standards.

# SECTION 9
## Doors

GENERAL/PRODUCT/INSTALLATION/TEST

### compliance requirements

**9.7    BASIC CONSIDERATIONS** (continued)

**6    GAPS, FLUSHNESS, FLATNESS and ALIGNMENT** (continued)

6.4    The following is intended to provide examples of how and where testing is measured:

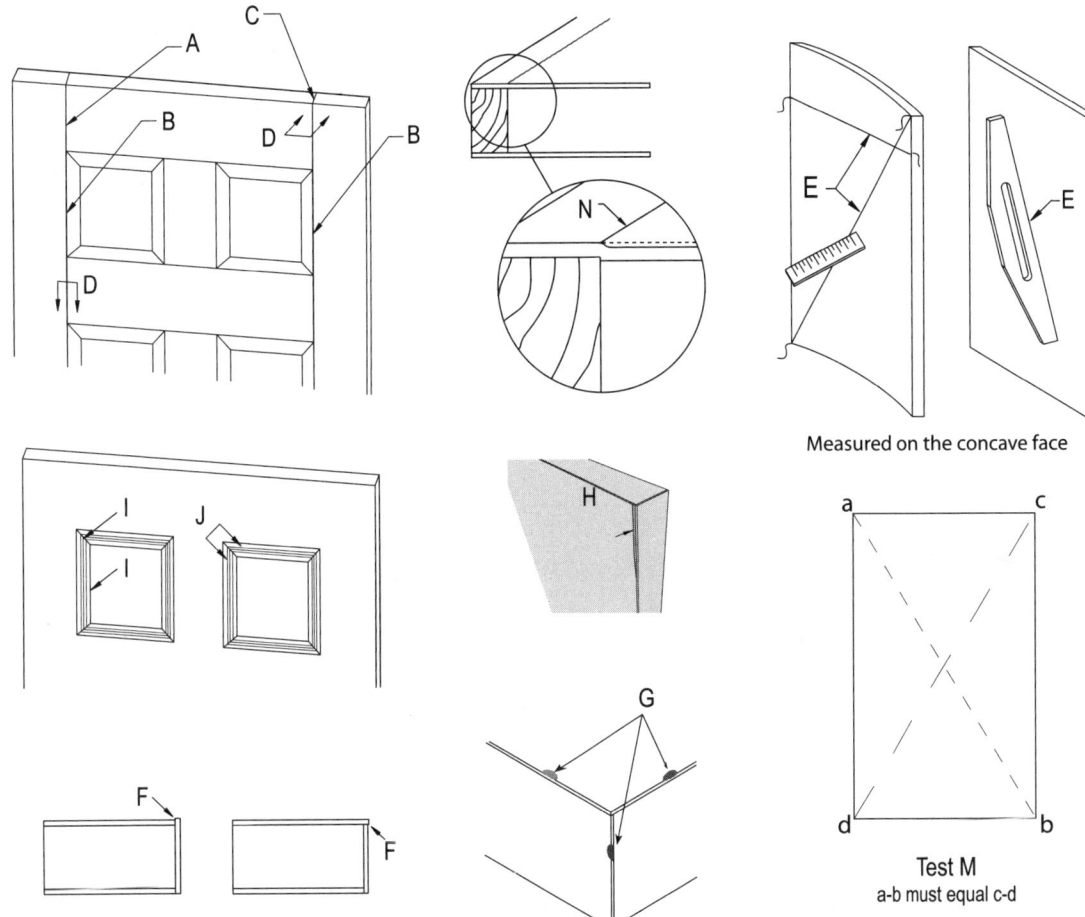

Figure: 9-055

A - Fabrication Gaps When Surfaces Are Mitered Or Butted
B - Fabrication Gaps When Parallel Pieces Are Joined
C - Fabrication Gaps When Edges Are Mitered Or Butted
D - Fabrication Flushness Between Two Surfaces
E - Flatness Of Panel Product
F - Overlap (Flushness Of Laminate)
G - Chip Out
H - Over Machining
I - Installation Gaps
J - Installation Flushness
M - Squareness
N - Show-Through Or Telegraphing

# SECTION 9
Doors

notes

# Architectural Woodwork Standards

# CASEWORK

## 10

SECTION

# SECTION 10
## Casework

### table of contents

**INTRODUCTORY INFORMATION**

- Guide Specifications ................................................. 284
- Introduction ............................................................. 285
- Casework Categories .............................................. 285
  - Wood Casework ................................................. 285
  - Decorative Laminate Casework ......................... 285
  - Solid Phenolic Casework .................................... 285
- Contract Documents ................................................ 285
  - Design Professional's Responsibility ................. 285
  - Complaince to Seismic Requirements ............... 285
  - Chemical and Stain Resistance ......................... 285
  - Abrasion Resistance .......................................... 285
- Unless Specified Otherwise ..................................... 285
  - Corners .............................................................. 285
  - Finished Ends .................................................... 285
  - Base/Toe ............................................................ 285
  - Storage, Janitor Closet and Utility Room Cabinets ..... 285
  - Presentation Panels ........................................... 285
  - Toe Base Height Variance .................................. 285
- Surface Terminologies ............................................. 285
  - Exposed Exterior Surfaces ................................. 285
  - Exposed Interior Surfaces .................................. 286
  - Semi-Exposed Surfaces ..................................... 286
  - Concealed Surfaces ........................................... 286
- Surface Terminology by Illustration ......................... 286
- Surface Finish Requirements .................................. 287
  - Exposed Exterior Surfaces ................................. 287
  - Exposed Interior Surfaces .................................. 287
  - Premium Grade .................................................. 287
  - Semi-Exposed Surfaces ..................................... 287
  - Concealed Surfaces ........................................... 287
- Construction Terminology ........................................ 288
  - Frameless .......................................................... 288
  - Face Frame ........................................................ 288
  - Selection ............................................................ 288

- Cabinet and Door Interface Style Terminology ........ 288
  - Flush Overlay ..................................................... 288
  - Overlay ............................................................... 288
  - Face Frame Construction ................................... 288
  - Flush Inset .......................................................... 288
- Layout Requirements of Grained or Patterned Faces by Grade ........ 289
  - Stile and Rail ...................................................... 289
  - Flush Panel ........................................................ 289
    - Economy Grade ............................................ 289
    - Custom Grade ............................................... 289
    - Premium Grade ............................................. 289
- Door and Applied Drawer Front Profiles ................. 289
  - Edge Profiles ..................................................... 289
  - Retention Profiles ............................................... 289
  - Cabinet Design Series ....................................... 290
  - Casework Integrity ............................................. 290
  - Cabinet Hardware .............................................. 290
  - Drawer Slide Selection Guide ............................ 290
    - Degree of Extension ..................................... 290
    - Static Load Capacity ..................................... 290
    - Dynamic Load Capacity ................................ 290
    - Removal ........................................................ 290
    - Closing .......................................................... 290
    - Metal Sided Drawer Systems ........................ 290
- Hinge Selection Guide ............................................. 291
  - European style hinge ......................................... 291
  - Wraparound hinge .............................................. 291
  - Butt hinge ........................................................... 291
- Adjustable Shelf Loading and Deflection ................ 291
  - Construction Detail Nomenclature ..................... 292
  - Stub Tenon ......................................................... 292
  - Haunch Mortise and Tenon Joint ....................... 292
  - Conventional Mortise and Tenon Joint .............. 292
  - Dowel Joint ......................................................... 292
  - French Dovetail Joint ......................................... 292
  - Conventional Dovetail Joint ............................... 292
  - Drawer Lock Joint .............................................. 292
  - Exposed End Details ......................................... 292

# SECTION 10
## Casework

## table of contents

### INTRODUCTORY INFORMATION (continued)

- Butt Joint .................................................................. 292
- Shoulder Mitered Joint ............................................. 292
- Pocket Screw Joint .................................................. 292
- Through Dado .............................................................. 293
- Blind Dado .................................................................... 293
- Stop Dado ..................................................................... 293
- Dowel Joint .................................................................. 293
- Dowel Screw Joint ....................................................... 293
- Edgebanding ................................................................ 293
- Miter/Miter Fold Joint ................................................. 293
- Spline Joint .................................................................. 293
- Paneled Door Details ................................................. 293
- Specify Requirements For ............................................... 294
  - Construction ............................................................. 294
  - Door and drawer front Interface ............................. 294
  - Door and drawer front edge profile ........................ 294
  - Toe base finish ......................................................... 294
  - Grain direction ......................................................... 294
  - Inside clearance ....................................................... 294
  - Seismic Fabrication and/or installation .................. 294
  - Flame Spread ........................................................... 294
  - Moisture resistance ................................................. 294
  - Insulation from adjacent heating cooling sources .. 294
  - Hardware .................................................................. 294
  - Laboratory features ................................................. 294
- Recommendations ............................................................ 294
  - If Field Finished ....................................................... 294
    - Before Finishing .................................................. 294
    - Concealed Surfaces ............................................ 294
  - Review ...................................................................... 294
  - Structural Members ................................................ 294

### COMPLIANCE REQUIREMENTS

#### GENERAL

- Basic Considerations ...................................................... 295
  - Grades ...................................................................... 295
    - Economy .............................................................. 295
    - Custom ................................................................. 295
    - Premium ............................................................... 295
    - Grade Limitations ................................................ 295
  - Contract Documents ............................................... 295
  - Acceptable Requirements ...................................... 295
  - Aesthetic Requirements ......................................... 295
  - Surface Categories ................................................. 295
    - Cabinet Surface Terminology Illustrations ....... 295
    - Exposed Exterior ................................................. 296
    - Exposed Interior .................................................. 296
    - Semi-exposed ...................................................... 296
    - Concelaed ............................................................ 296
  - Solid Phenolic ......................................................... 296
  - Cabinet Construction ............................................. 296
    - Frameless ............................................................ 296
    - Face Frame ......................................................... 297
  - Cabinet and Door Interface ................................... 297
    - Overlay ................................................................ 297
    - Flush Inset .......................................................... 297
    - Flush Overlay ...................................................... 297
  - Casework Integerity ................................................ 297
  - Hardware .................................................................. 297
  - Cabinet Design Series ............................................. 297
  - Casework Concept Drawings ................................. 297
  - To Prevent Telegraphing ......................................... 297
  - Industry Practices ................................................... 298
    - Structural Members ............................................ 298
    - Wall Ceiling and Floor ........................................ 298
    - Priming ................................................................ 298
    - Surfacing ............................................................. 298

# SECTION 10
## Casework

## table of contents

**COMPLIANCE REQUIREMENTS** (continued)

- **GENERAL** (continued)
  - Basic Considerations (continued)
    - Industry Practices .................................................. 298
      - Casework Dimension Ranges ......................... 298
        - Base ........................................................ 298
        - Wall Hung .............................................. 298
        - Tall Storage ........................................... 298
        - Reception ............................................... 298
        - Tellers Counter ..................................... 298
      - Base Cabinet, Stretcher, Layout and Construction .......... 299
      - Corners ........................................................... 299
      - Finish Ends ..................................................... 299
      - Base/Toe ......................................................... 299
      - Storage, Janitors Closet and Unility Room Cabinets ....... 299
      - Presentation Panels ....................................... 299
      - Toe Base Height Variances ............................ 299
      - Layout ........................................................... 300
        - Stile and Rail ....................................... 300
        - Flush Panel .......................................... 300

**PRODUCT**

- Scope ........................................................................ 301
  - Typical Inclusions ................................................ 301
  - Typical Exclusions .............................................. 301
- Default Stipulation .................................................. 302
  - Exposed Knuckle Hinges ................................... 302
  - Reveal Overlay ................................................... 302
- Rules ......................................................................... 302
  - Errata ................................................................... 302
  - Basic Rules ......................................................... 302
    - Aesthetic ........................................................ 302
    - Woodwork ..................................................... 302
    - Lumber .......................................................... 302
    - Sheet Products ............................................. 302
    - Backing Sheet .............................................. 302
    - All Materials ................................................. 302
  - Surface Categories ........................................... 302
    - Exposed Exterior ......................................... 302
    - Exposed Interior .......................................... 302
    - Semi-Exposed ............................................. 302
  - Concealed .......................................................... 303
  - Hardware ............................................................ 303
    - Conform To .................................................. 303
    - Furnished and Installed ............................. 303
    - Uniform Plated / Power Coated ................ 303
    - Manufacturer's Name ................................ 303
    - First Class Workmanship .......................... 303
    - Locks ............................................................ 303
    - Drawer Slides ............................................. 303
    - Shelf Rests ................................................. 303
    - Pocket Door Hardware ............................. 303
    - Base Adjusters ........................................... 304
    - Multiple Hardware Options ...................... 304
  - Casework ............................................................ 304
  - Panel Components ........................................... 304
  - Frameless Construction .................................. 304
  - Separately Applied Countertops .................. 304
  - Storage ............................................................... 304
  - Cabinets over 72" ............................................. 304
  - Sliding Presentation Boards .......................... 304
  - Hot Melt Applied ............................................... 304
  - Prefinishing ........................................................ 304
  - Cut Outs .............................................................. 304
  - Cathedral ............................................................ 304
  - Cabinet Doors with Glass Lights .................. 304
  - First Class Workmanship ............................... 304
- Material Rules ......................................................... 305
  - Grain or Directional Patterned ..................... 305
  - Light Valance ..................................................... 305
  - Vinyl ..................................................................... 305
  - Glass Shelves .................................................... 305
  - Opaque Finish .................................................... 305
  - Transparent Finish, Veneer ............................ 305
  - Semi-Exposed ................................................... 305
  - Concealed .......................................................... 305

# SECTION 10
## Casework

## table of contents

**COMPLIANCE REQUIREMENTS** (continued)

**PRODUCT** (continued)

Material Rules (continued)

- Wood Casework ................................................... 306
  - Exposed Exterior ............................................. 306
    - Transparent Finish ..................................... 306
    - Opaque Finish ........................................... 306
  - Exposed Interior .............................................. 306
    - Transparent Finish ..................................... 306
    - Opaque Finish ........................................... 306
  - Semi-Exposed ................................................. 306
  - Drawer Box .................................................... 306
    - Surfaces ..................................................... 306
    - Dividers ..................................................... 306
    - Sides, Backs and Subfront ......................... 307
      - Cores ..................................................... 307
      - Minimum Thickness ............................... 307
    - Bottoms .................................................... 307
      - Cores ..................................................... 307
      - Minimum Thickness ............................... 307
- Decorative Laminate Casework ........................... 307
  - Exposed Exterior ............................................. 307
  - Exposed Interior .............................................. 307
  - Semi-Exposed ................................................. 307
  - Drawer Box .................................................... 307
    - Surfaces ..................................................... 307
    - Dividers ..................................................... 308
    - Sides, Backs and Subfront ......................... 308
      - Cores ..................................................... 308
      - Minimum Thickness ............................... 308
    - Bottoms .................................................... 308
      - Cores ..................................................... 308
      - Minimum Thickness ............................... 308
- Solid Phenolic Casework ..................................... 308
  - Exposed Exterior ............................................. 308
  - Exposed Interior .............................................. 308
  - Semi-Exposed ................................................. 308

Machining Rules ......................................................... 309
- Exposed Surfaces and Semi-exposed ................. 309
  - Smoothness .................................................... 309
    - Sharp Edges .............................................. 309
    - Top Flat ..................................................... 309
    - Profiled ..................................................... 309
    - Turned ...................................................... 309
    - Cross Sanding ........................................... 309
    - Tear Outs, Knife Nicks .............................. 309
    - Knife Marks ............................................... 309
    - Glue or Filler ............................................. 309
- HPDL, PVC, and Prefinished Wood ..................... 309
  - Overlap .......................................................... 309
  - Chip Out ........................................................ 309
  - Over Machined .............................................. 309

Assembly Rules .......................................................... 310
- These Standards ................................................ 310
- Joints at Assembled Woodwork ......................... 310
  - Flushness Horizontal ..................................... 310
  - Fixed Horizontal ............................................ 310
  - Gap Test A ..................................................... 310
  - Gap Test B ..................................................... 311
  - Gap Test C ..................................................... 311
  - Joinery ........................................................... 311
  - Bottom Edges ................................................ 311
  - Visible Edges ................................................. 311
    - Adjustable Shelves .................................... 311
    - Bottom Edge ............................................. 311
    - Top Edge ................................................... 311
    - Edgebanding ............................................. 311
    - Dadoes or Lock Joints .............................. 311
    - Tee Banding .............................................. 311
- Drawers ............................................................. 312
  - Sides .............................................................. 312
  - Flush Overlay ................................................. 312

# SECTION 10
Casework

## table of contents

**COMPLIANCE REQUIREMENTS** (continued)

- **PRODUCT** (continued)
  - Assembly Rules (continued)
    - Drawers (continued)
      - Joints ............................................................. 312
      - Slides ............................................................ 312
      - File Drawers ................................................. 312
      - Locks ............................................................ 312
      - Trays, Bins .................................................... 312
      - Fronts and False Fronts ................................ 312
      - Bottoms ........................................................ 313
    - Doors .................................................................. 313
      - Flush Overlay ................................................ 313
      - Back Beveled ............................................... 313
      - Core Thickness ............................................ 313
      - Maximum door size ...................................... 313
      - Door Thickness ............................................ 313
      - Stop Silencers .............................................. 313
      - Core ............................................................. 313
      - Locks ............................................................ 313
      - Glass ............................................................ 313
      - Hinged .......................................................... 313
      - Stile and Rail ................................................ 315
        - Panel ...................................................... 315
        - Sliding .................................................... 315
      - Frameless Glass .......................................... 316
    - Aprons ................................................................ 316
    - Ends and Divisions ............................................. 316
    - Tops and Bottoms .............................................. 316
    - Security and Dust Panels ................................... 317
    - Stretchers .......................................................... 317
    - Backs .................................................................. 317
    - Toe Bases, Kicks, and Sleepers ........................ 317
      - Levelers ........................................................ 317
      - Moveable Toes ............................................. 318

- Shelves ........................................................................ 318
  - Thickness ............................................................ 318
  - Grain and Directional Pattern ............................. 318
  - Dividers ............................................................... 318
  - Uniform Thickness .............................................. 318
  - HardboardCabinets over 72" ............................. 318
  - Glass ................................................................... 318
  - Fixed Shelves ..................................................... 318
  - Adjustable Shelves ............................................. 318
    - Conformance in Thickness ........................... 318
    - Length ............................................................ 321
    - Depth ............................................................. 321
    - Supported ...................................................... 321
    - Metal Shelf Standards ................................... 321
    - Bored Hole Shelf Rest System ..................... 321
- Pullout Shelves ........................................................... 321
  - Bread/Cutting Boards ......................................... 321
  - Writing and Utility Shelves .................................. 321
- Clothes Poles or Rods ............................................... 321
- Wardrobes .................................................................. 321
- Anchor Strips .............................................................. 321
- Moveable Cabinets .................................................... 322
  - Glides .................................................................. 322
  - Casters ................................................................ 322
  - Metal Frame or Diagram Type Double Bottom .. 322
  - Lock Joint Corners ............................................. 322
- Joinery ........................................................................ 322
  - Securely Fastened ............................................. 322
  - Assembled Square and True .............................. 322
  - Securely Glued ................................................... 322
- Scribing ...................................................................... 323
  - None .................................................................... 323
  - Furnished ............................................................ 323
  - Fillers and Molds ................................................ 323
  - Trim Members .................................................... 323
  - Soffit and Facia Panels ...................................... 323
  - Options ............................................................... 323
- Closure ....................................................................... 323

# SECTION 10
## Casework

## table of contents

### COMPLIANCE REQUIREMENTS (continued)

#### PRODUCT (continued)

##### Assembly Rules (continued)

- Clearance and Tolerances .................................................. 323
  - Edge Alignment and Flushness ..................................... 323
  - Maximum Uniform Gap ................................................. 324
    - Reveal Overlay Frameless ....................................... 324
    - Flush Overlay Frameless ......................................... 324
    - Reveal Overlay Face Frame .................................... 324
- Warp and Twist .................................................................... 325
- Wood Casework ................................................................... 325
  - Visible Edges ................................................................. 325
  - Drawers ......................................................................... 325
  - Doors ............................................................................. 325
  - Face Frames ................................................................. 326
  - Tops and Bottoms ......................................................... 326
  - Flush Inset Doors .......................................................... 326
- For Decorative Laminate Casework ................................... 326
  - Exposed Edges ............................................................. 326
  - Drawers ......................................................................... 326
  - Doors ............................................................................. 326
- Solid Phenolic Casework ..................................................... 326
  - Edgebanding ................................................................. 326
  - Drawer .......................................................................... 326
  - Door .............................................................................. 326
  - Aprons ........................................................................... 326
  - Shelves ......................................................................... 326
  - Tops and Fixed Bottoms ............................................... 326
  - Ends and Divisions ....................................................... 326
  - Security and Dust Panels ............................................. 326
  - Stretchers ..................................................................... 326
  - Bread/Cutting Boards ................................................... 326
  - Joinery ........................................................................... 326

### INSTALLATION

- Care, Storage and Building Conditions ............................. 327
- Contractor is Responsible For ............................................ 327
- Installer is Responsible For ................................................ 327
- Rules ..................................................................................... 328
  - Errata ............................................................................. 328
  - Basic Rules ................................................................... 328
    - Aesthetic .................................................................. 328
    - Transparent Finished ............................................. 328
    - Repairs .................................................................... 328
    - Installer Modifications ........................................... 328
    - Casework ................................................................ 328
    - These Standards .................................................... 328
    - Gaps Test I .............................................................. 328
    - Flushness Test J ..................................................... 329
    - Gaps, Edge Alignment and Flushness ................ 329
    - Scribing ................................................................... 329
    - Closure ................................................................... 330
    - Exposed Fasteners ............................................... 330
    - Casework Wall Anchorage ................................... 330
    - Nail Holes ............................................................... 331
    - Glue ......................................................................... 331
    - Caulking .................................................................. 332
    - Require allowable fastener holes ........................ 332
    - Equipment Cutouts ................................................ 332
    - Hardware ................................................................ 332
    - Areas of Installation .............................................. 332

### TESTS

- Basic Considerations .......................................................... 333
  - Fabricated and Installed .............................................. 333
  - Smoothness .................................................................. 333
    - KCPI ........................................................................ 333
    - Sanding ................................................................... 333
  - Gaps, Flushness, Flatness and Alignment .................. 333
    - Illustrations ............................................................. 334

# SECTION 10
Casework

## introductory information

# Guide Specifications

Are available through the Sponsor Associations in interactive digital format including unique and individual quality control options. The Guide Specifications are located at:

## Architectural Woodwork Institute (AWI)
www.awinet.org

## Architectural Woodwork Manufacturers Association of Canada (AWMAC)
http://awmac.com/aws-guide-specifications

## Woodwork Institute (WI)
www.woodworkinstitute.com/publications/aws_guide_specs.asp

# SECTION 10
## Casework

## introductory information

### INTRODUCTION

Section 10 includes information on Wood, Decorative Laminate, and Solid Phenolic Faced Casework and their related parts.

Quality assurance can be achieved by adherence to the AWS and will provide the owner a quality product at competitive pricing. Use of a qualified Sponsor Member firm to provide your woodwork will help ensure the manufacturer's understanding of the quality level required. Illustrations in this Section are not intended to be all inclusive. Other engineered solutions are acceptable. In the absence of specifications; methods of fabrication shall be manufacturer's choice. The design professional, by specifying compliance to the AWS increases the probability of receiving the product quality expected.

### CASEWORK CATEGORIES

This section addresses three distinct categories of casework based on the exterior exposed face:

- **WOOD CASEWORK** with wood faces for transparent or opaque finish.

- **DECORATIVE LAMINATE CASEWORK** with HPDL or LPDL faces.

- **SOLID PHENOLIC CASEWORK** with solid phenolic faces.

### CONTRACT DOCUMENTS

Shall clearly indicate or delineate all material, fabrication, installation, and applicable building code/regulation requirements, and:

- It is the design professional's responsibility to evaluate the fastening methods required and modify as appropriate to ensure adequate in wall blocking and fasteners are used for the project conditions.

- Compliance to **SEISMIC** requirements for casework fabrication and restraint, where required, shall be so specified. Within the United States, the International Building Code (IBC) establishes these minimum requirements; however, some states have expanded on the U.S. requirements. Within Canada, the National Building Code (NBC) establishes these minimum requirements; however, some provinces and cities have expanded on the Canadian requirements.

- Any **CHEMICAL** or **STAIN RESISTANT** surface requirements must be specified. Consider the chemical and staining agents that might be used on or near the surfaces. Chemical resistance and stain resistance are affected by concentration, time, temperature, humidity, housekeeping, and other factors. It is recommended that actual samples are tested in a similar environment with those agents.

- Any **ABRASION RESISTANT** surface requirements must be specified. Consider the abrasive elements that might be used on or near the surfaces. Common guidelines can be found at:

  - ASTM C501 (latest edition).
  - NEMA LD3-3.13 (latest edition).
  - NEMA LD3.7 (latest edition).

### UNLESS SPECIFIED OTHERWISE

- **CORNERS** created by tall, wall, or base casework will create non usable space.

- **FINISHED ENDS** shall be integral, not applied secondarily, except:

  - **APPLIED END PANELS** are allowed at Solid Phenolic casework and at teaching wall assemblies.

- **BASE/TOE** shall be integral (constructed as an integral part of the cabinet body) or separate (constructed as a separate member) at manufacturer's choice.

- **STORAGE, JANITOR CLOSET**, and/or **UTILITY ROOM CABINETS** shall be built in conformance to Economy Grade, regardless of the overall project's Grade requirement, unless specified otherwise.

- Surfaces behind **PRESENTATION PANELS** (such as white board or tack board) are treated as:

  - Semi Exposed at Economy Grade and Custom Grade.
  - Exposed at Premium Grade.

- **TOE BASE HEIGHT VARIANCE** due to floor variations is not considered a defect. Casework is required to be installed level; shimming of the toe base, not to exceed 1/2" (12.7 mm), is acceptable. Floor variations exceeding 1/2" (12.7 mm) shall be corrected before cabinets are installed; however, correction of such is not the responsibility of the cabinet installer.

### SURFACE TERMINOLOGIES

**Cabinet surfaces** are defined in four distinct categories, three for exposed surfaces with very specific minimum surface requirements and one for concealed surfaces subject to manufacturer's choice, as follows:

- **EXPOSED EXTERIOR SURFACES**, defined as all exterior surfaces exposed to view, including:

  - All surfaces visible when doors and drawers are closed, including knee spaces.

  - Underside of cabinet bottoms over 42" (1067 mm) above the finished floor, including cabinet bottoms behind light valances and the bottom edge of light valances.

  - Cabinet tops under 80" (2032 mm) above the finished floor, or if 80" (2032 mm) and over and visible from an upper building level or floor.

  - Front edges of stretchers, ends, divisions, tops, and bottoms.

  - Sloping tops of cabinets that are visible.

# SECTION 10
## Casework

### introductory information

**SURFACE TERMINOLOGIES** (continued)

- **EXPOSED INTERIOR SURFACES**, defined as all interior surfaces exposed to view in open casework or behind transparent doors, include:

  - Shelves, including edgebanding.
  - Divisions and partitions (front edge is an exposed surface).
  - Interior face of ends (sides), backs, and bottoms (including pull outs). Also included are the interior surfaces of cabinet top members 36" (914 mm) or more above the finished floor.
  - Interior face of door and applied drawer fronts.

- **SEMI-EXPOSED SURFACES**, defined as those interior surfaces only exposed to view when doors or drawers are opened, include:

  - Tops and bottoms of shelves, including front edgebanding (front edge is an exposed surface).
  - Divisions and partitions (front edge is an exposed surface).
  - Interior face of ends (sides), backs, and bottoms (including a bank of drawers). Also included are the interior surfaces of cabinet top members 36" (914 mm) or more above the finished floor.
  - Drawer sides, sub fronts, backs, and bottoms.
  - The underside of cabinet bottoms between 24" (610 mm) and 42" (1067 mm) above the finished floor.
  - Security and dust panels or drawer stretchers.

- **CONCEALED SURFACES**, defined as those exterior or interior surfaces that are covered or not normally exposed to view including:

  - Toe space unless otherwise specified.
  - Sleepers, stretchers, and solid sub tops.
  - The underside of cabinet bottoms less than 24" (610 mm) above the finished floor.

- The underside of countertops, knee spaces, and drawer aprons.
- The flat tops of cabinets 80" (2032 mm) or more above the finished floor, except if visible from an upper floor or building level.
- The three non visible edges of adjustable shelves.
- The faces of cabinet ends of adjoining units that butt together.

### SURFACE TERMINOLOGY BY ILLUSTRATION

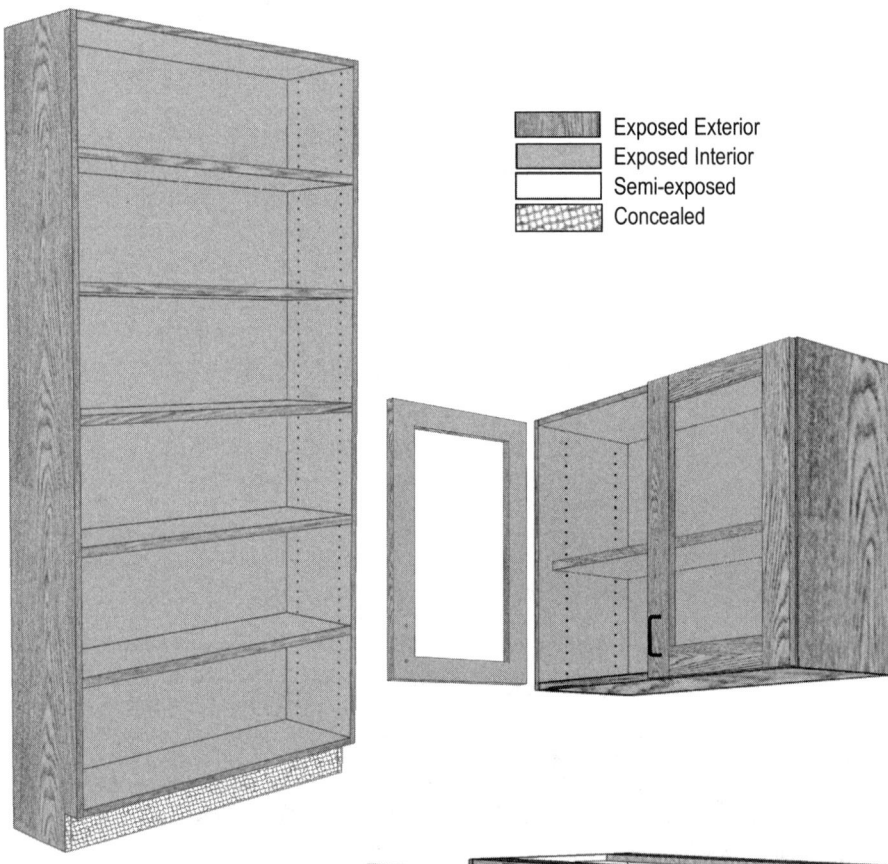
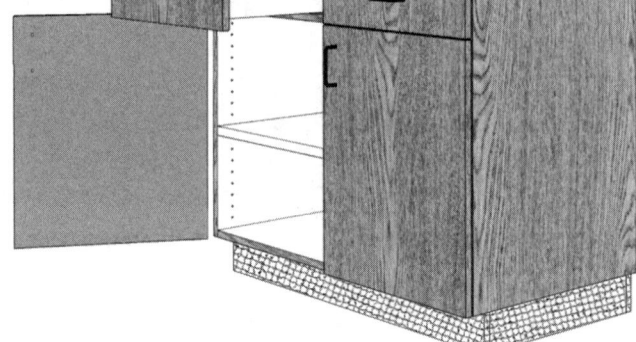

*Figure: 10-001*

# SECTION 10
## Casework

## introductory information

### SURFACE FINISH REQUIREMENTS

- **EXPOSED EXTERIOR SURFACES** for:

  - **WOOD** casework requires:

    - For **TRANSPARENT** finish, wood of specified species, cut, and match.

    - For **OPAQUE** finish at:

      - **ECONOMY GRADE**, Particleboard, MDF, MDO, softwood plywood, hardwood plywood, or solid stock.

      - **CUSTOM GRADE**, MDF, MDO, close grain hardwood plywood, or solid stock.

      - **PREMIUM GRADE**, MDF and MDO.

  - **DECORATIVE LAMINATE** casework requires at:

    - **ECONOMY GRADE**, LPDL of specified color or pattern.

    - **CUSTOM** and **PREMIUM GRADE**, HPDL of specified color or pattern.

  - **SOLID PHENOLIC** casework requires for **PREMIUM GRADE**, solid phenolic of specified color or pattern.

- **EXPOSED INTERIOR SURFACES** for:

  - **ECONOMY GRADE** at:

    - **WOOD** casework requires:

      - For **TRANSPARENT** finish, LPDL or wood of the manufacturer's choice.

      - For **OPAQUE** finish at, Particleboard, MDF, MDO, softwood plywood, hardwood plywood, or solid stock of manufacturer's choice.

    - **DECORATIVE LAMINATE** casework requires, LPDL of the manufacturer's choice.

  - **CUSTOM GRADE** at:

    - **WOOD** casework requires:

      - For **TRANSPARENT** finish, wood of the same species as the exposed exterior surface.

      - For **OPAQUE** finish at, MDF, MDO, close grain hardwood plywood, or solid stock of manufacturer's choice.

    - **DECORATIVE LAMINATE** casework requires HPDL or LPDL compatible to exposed exterior surface in color, grain, or pattern of manufacturer's choice.

  - **PREMIUM GRADE** at:

    - **WOOD** casework requires:

      - For **TRANSPARENT** finish, wood of same the species and cut as the exposed exterior surface.

      - For **OPAQUE** finish, use of MDF and MDO of manufacturer's choice.

    - **DECORATIVE LAMINATE** casework requires, HPDL, the same as the exposed exterior surface.

    - **SOLID PHENOLIC** casework requires, solid phenolic, the same as the exposed exterior surface.

- **SEMI-EXPOSED SURFACES** for:

  - **WOOD** casework require for both **TRANSPARENT** and **OPAQUE** finish at:

    - **ECONOMY GRADE**, wood of the manufacturer's choice of species, MDO, MDF, particleboard, or LPDL of the manufacturer's choice of color.

    - **CUSTOM GRADE**, wood of the manufacturer's choice of species, or LPDL of the manufacturer's choice of color.

    - **PREMIUM GRADE**, wood of a compatible species to the exposed.

  - **DECORATIVE LAMINATE** casework at all grades requires, LPDL of the manufacturer's choice of color.

  - **SOLID PHENOLIC** casework requires, solid phenolic of the mill's choice of color.

- **CONCEALED SURFACES** for all grades at, decorative laminate, wood, and solid phenolic casework require the manufacturer's choice.

# SECTION 10
## Casework

### introductory information

#### CABINET CONSTRUCTION TERMINOLOGY

**FRAMELESS** construction where the front edge of the cabinet body components are edgebanded.

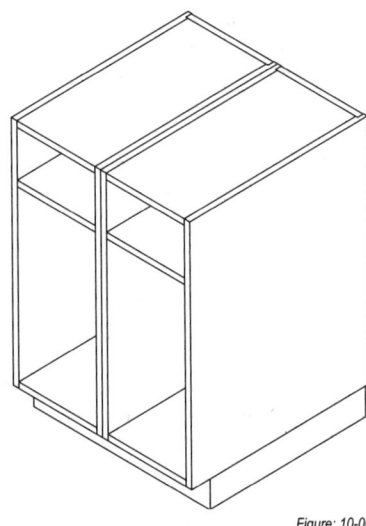

*Figure: 10-003*

**FACE FRAME** construction where the front edge of the cabinet body components are overlaid with a frame.

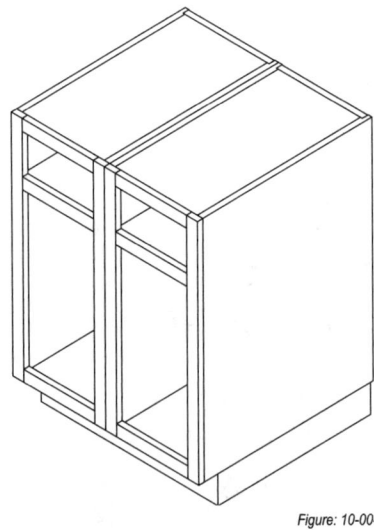

*Figure: 10-004*

**SELECTION** shall be manufacturer's choice, unless specified otherwise.

#### CABINET AND DOOR INTERFACE TERMINOLOGY

**FLUSH OVERLAY** is the default for either **FRAMELESS** or **FACE FRAME** casework:

- **OVERLAY** including flush, reveal, or lipped, as illustrated below:

  - **FRAMELESS Construction:**

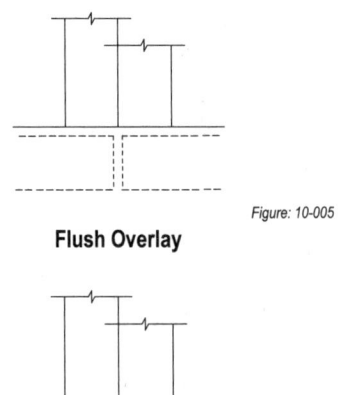

*Figure: 10-005*

**Flush Overlay**

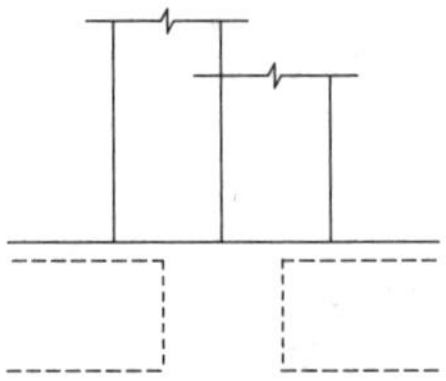

*Figure: 10-006*

**Reveal Overlay**

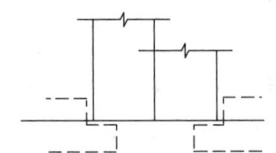

*Figure: 10-007*

**Lipped**

- **FACE FRAME Construction:**

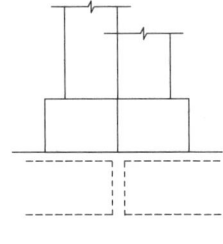

*Figure: 10-008*

**Flush Overlay**

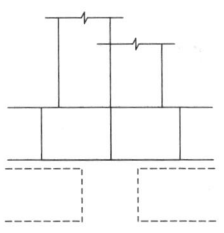

*Figure: 10-009*

**Reveal Overlay**

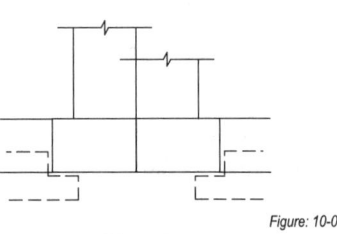

*Figure: 10-010*

**Lipped**

- **FLUSH INSET**, as illustrated below:

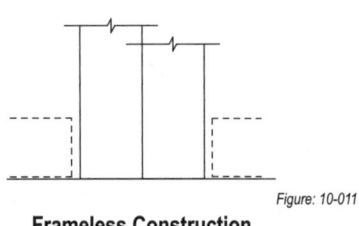

*Figure: 10-011*

**Frameless Construction**

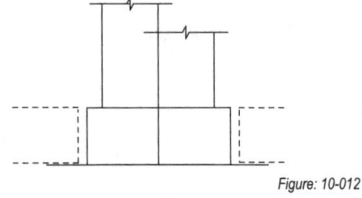

*Figure: 10-012*

**Face Frame Construction**

# SECTION 10
## Casework

## introductory information

### LAYOUT REQUIREMENTS OF GRAINED OR PATTERNED FACES BY GRADE

- **STILE** and **RAIL** doors and drawer fronts for all Grades, drawer fronts shall run either vertically or horizontally at the manufacturer's choice for the entire project. Doors shall be vertical.

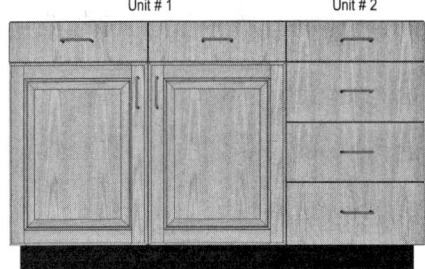

*Figure: 10-013*

*Figure: 10-014*

- **FLUSH PANEL** doors and drawer fronts:

  - **ECONOMY GRADE** - drawer fronts shall run either vertically or horizontally at the manufacturer's choice for the entire project. Doors shall be vertical. Mismatch is allowed:

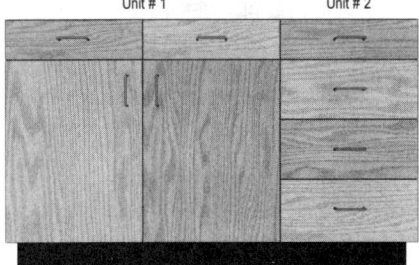

*Figure: 10-015*

- **CUSTOM GRADE** - doors, drawer fronts, and false fronts shall run and match vertically within each cabinet unit:

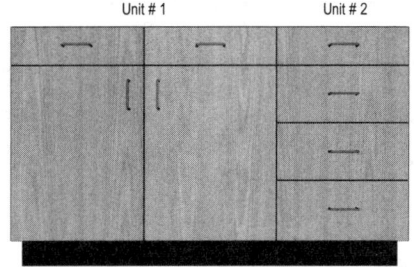

*Figure: 10-016*

- **PREMIUM GRADE** - doors, drawer fronts, and false fronts shall run and match vertically and be sequenced horizontally within each cabinet unit; and at cathedral grain, the crown shall be pointing up and run in the same direction for the entire project. Doors, drawer fronts, and false fronts shall be well matched for color and grain across multiple cabinet faces in one elevation. Requirement for blueprint or sequencing between cabinet units must be so specified.

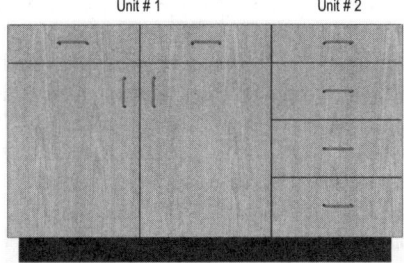

*Figure: 10-017*

### DOOR AND APPLIED DRAWER FRONT PROFILES

For illustration purposes only and are not intended to be duplicated exactly:

- Common **EDGE PROFILES**:

  - Square edge with thin applied edgeband.

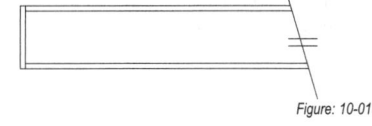

*Figure: 10-018*

- Radius edge with thick applied edgeband.

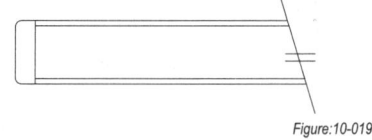

*Figure: 10-019*

- Square edge with thick applied edgeband:

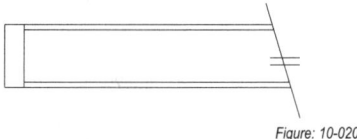

*Figure: 10-020*

- Square edge with inset edgeband.

*Figure: 10-021*

- Lipped edge with inset edgeband:

*Figure: 10-022*

To **PREVENT TELEGRAPHING**, inset solid wood edging when used must have similar moisture content as panel core, be glued securely and calibrated with panel core thickness prior to being laminated with a wood veneer on both faces.

- Common **RETENTION PROFILES**:

  - Fixed panel.

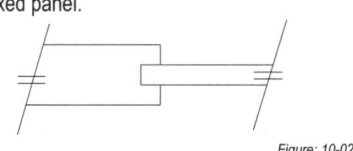

*Figure: 10-023*

- Removable stop.

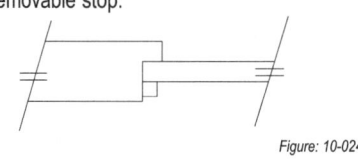

*Figure: 10-024*

- Removable stop at HPDL face.

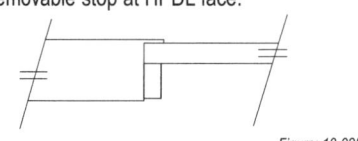

*Figure: 10-025*

# SECTION 10
## Casework

### introductory information

#### DOOR AND APPLIED DRAWER FRONT PROFILES (continued)

- Removable stop, synthetic.

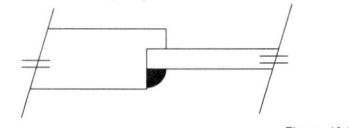

*Figure: 10-026*

- Removable retainer, synthetic.

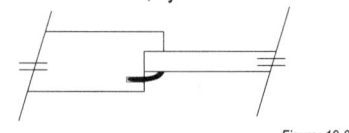

*Figure: 10-027*

- Removable clips.

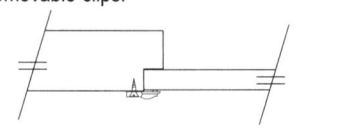

*Figure: 10-028*

#### CABINET DESIGN SERIES (CDS)

Details were developed by the industry and represent a series of numbered cabinet designs that are available for ease of specification and drawing. A numerical/elevation key to the CDS may be found in **DESIGN IDEAS**.

CAD details are available in both Autodesk Revit Families and AutoCAD ".dwg / .dxf" files of the elevations may be found on the Sponsor Associations' websites:

- Architectural Woodwork Institute - www.awinet.org.
- Architectural Woodwork Manufacturers Association of Canada - www.awmac.com.
- Woodwork Institute - www.woodworkinstitute.com.

These cabinets may be specified by number to a specific size requirement on the plan view drawings without having to draw elevations. They are drawn as Frameless Construction, flush overlay Interface', with integral finished ends and scribes at wall to wall installations not exceeding 1-1/2" (38.1 mm) in width.

#### CASEWORK INTEGRITY

These standards have adopted a portion of SEFA's (Scientific Equipment and Fixture Association) methods of testing and acceptable results as the minimum acceptable level of integrity for casework, as found in the **APPENDIX**.

#### CABINET HARDWARE

These standards have adopted ANSI/BHMA Standards (latest edition), Grade 2, as the basic minimum requirement. For more specific details, see the PRODUCT portion of this Section. Choice of product should be made on the basis of utility, aesthetics, security objectives, and the end use desired. As a general guide:

- **GRADE 1** is the highest and is suitable for most institutional applications.
- **GRADE 2** is used in most other applications.

#### DRAWER SLIDE SELECTION GUIDE

The following serves as both a checklist and a starting point for the discussion of a wide variety of drawer slide systems. While by no means exhaustive, the characteristics described below are often considered the most important by the client, the design professional, and the woodwork manufacturer. The selection of the slide characteristics will affect the usefulness of the cabinets. Careful consideration should be given to avoid "over specifying" for the purpose intended:

- **DEGREE OF EXTENSION:**
  - **STANDARD EXTENSION**, all but 4" - 6" (101.6 - 152.4 mm) of drawer body extends out of the cabinet.
  - **FULL EXTENSION**, entire drawer body extends out to the face of cabinet.
  - **FULL EXTENSION with over travel**, entire drawer body extends beyond the face of cabinet.

- **STATIC LOAD CAPACITY:**
  - 50 pounds, residential and light commercial.
  - 75 pounds, commercial.
  - 100 pounds, heavy duty.
  - Over 100 pounds, special conditions, extra heavy duty.

- **DYNAMIC LOAD CAPACITY:**
  - 30 pounds for 35,000 cycles, residential and light commercial.
  - 50 pounds for 50,000 cycles, commercial.
  - 75 pounds for 100,000 cycles, heavy duty.

- **REMOVAL:**
  - **Passive disconnect** - A means of drawer removal that does not require active disconnecting.
  - **Positive disconnect** - A means of removing a drawer that requires active disconnection or removal of hardware.

- **CLOSING:**
  - **Self closing/stay closed**, drawer slides will self close with the related dynamic load when the drawer is 2" (50.8 mm) from the fully closed position and not bounce open when properly adjusted.

- **METAL SIDED DRAWER SYSTEMS** must be specified and should require:
  - **Positive stop**, drawer must stop within itself and not rely on the drawer front to stop it.
  - **Pullout strength**, system must demonstrate sufficient strength of attachment of front to sides, design professional should evaluate and approve individually.

# SECTION 10
## Casework

# introductory information

## HINGE SELECTION GUIDE

Architectural cabinet hinges will usually be furnished from the manufacturer's stock unless otherwise specified. The three most common hinge types are illustrated below.

European hinges with the screws set in synthetic inserts are an established industry standard. These hinges have been found to be cost effective alternatives to the more traditional hinges shown below. Follow hinge manufacturers' recommendations on number and spacing of hinges. There are conditions, however, in which the use of butt or wraparound hinges will continue to be the best solution. Pivot hinges often require a cut in center hinge. Consult manufacturer's recommendations:

- **European style hinge**, typically used in conventional flush without face frame and reveal or flush overlay application offering moderate strength, full concealment, moderate cost, ease of installation and adjustment.

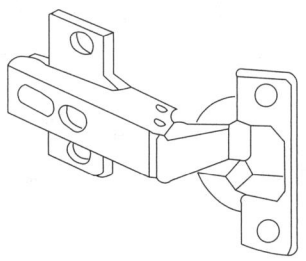

*Figure: 10-029*

- **Wraparound hinge (3 & 5 knuckle)**, typically used in flush and reveal overlay applications offering very high strength, moderate cost, ease of installation and moderate ease of adjustment; however, can require mortising and shows an exposed knuckle and hinge body.

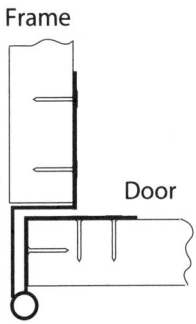

*Figure: 10-030*

- **Butt hinge**, typically used in conventional flush with face frame application, offering high strength, low cost, moderate ease of installation and adjustment; however, can require mortising and shows an exposed knuckle.

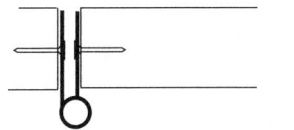

*Figure: 10-031*

## ADJUSTABLE SHELF LOADING and DEFLECTION

Proper specification can balance aesthetic needs with load requirements.

Load is the total applied weight, uniformly dispersed on an individual shelf, not to exceed 200 lbs (90.7 Kg) on any one shelf. These standards have adopted the following load capacities:

- 50 lbs per sq ft (244.1 kg/m2) for school, hospital, and library or book shelving.

- 40 lbs per sq ft (195.3 kg/m2) for all other shelving.

Shelving specification requires consideration of deflection, the measured distance from a straight line that a shelf will deflect under load. L/144 (the length of the shelf divided by 144) is the industry standard for the maximum acceptable deflection of a shelf, which permits 1/4" (6.4 mm) deflection in a 36" (914 mm) shelf.

Creep is the increase in deflection over time, which fluctuates with temperature, humidity, and load stress. Creep is not considered a defect; if it is a concern, it can be reduced by:

- Reduced loading of shelves.

- Use of material with a higher (stiffer) modulus of elasticity (MOE).

- Use of alternate construction (support) techniques.

- Use of a decreased factor of acceptable deflection.

# SECTION 10
## Casework

### introductory information

**CONSTRUCTION DETAIL NOMENCLATURE**

Familiarity with the labeled details on this and following pages will facilitate communication between architects, designers, specifiers, and woodwork manufacturers by establishing common technical language:

- **Stub Tenon** - Joinery method for assembling stile and rail type frames that are additionally supported, such as web or skeleton case frames.

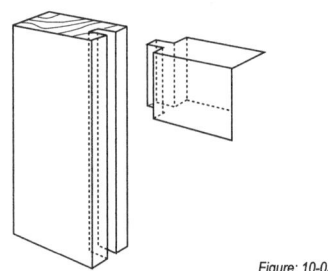

Figure: 10-032

- **Haunch Mortise and Tenon Joint** - Joinery method for assembling paneled doors or stile and rail type paneling.

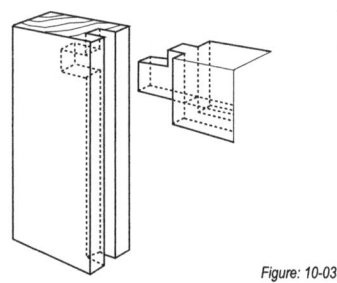

Figure: 10-033

- **Conventional Mortise and Tenon Joint** - Joinery method for assembling square edged surfaces such as case face frames.

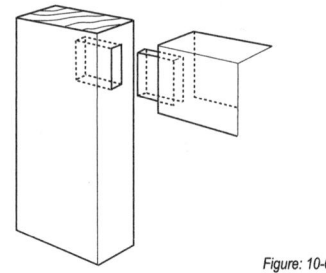

Figure: 10-034

- **Dowel Joint** - Alternative joinery method serving same function as Conventional Mortise and Tenon.

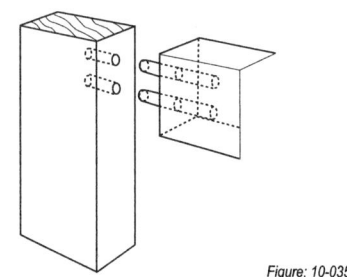

Figure: 10-035

- **French Dovetail Joint** - Method for joining drawer sides to fronts when fronts conceal metal extension slides or overlay the case faces.

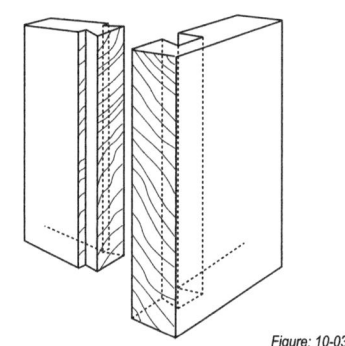

Figure: 10-036

- **Conventional Dovetail Joint** - Traditional method for joining drawer sides to fronts or backs. Usually limited to flush or lipped type drawers.

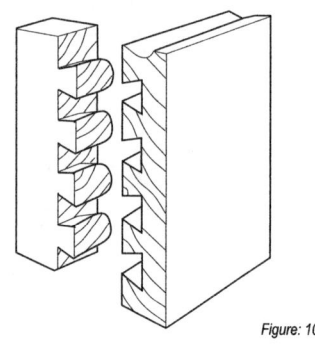

Figure: 10-037

- **Drawer Lock Joint** - Another joinery method for joining drawer sides to fronts. Usually used for flush type installation, but can be adapted to lip or overlay type drawers.

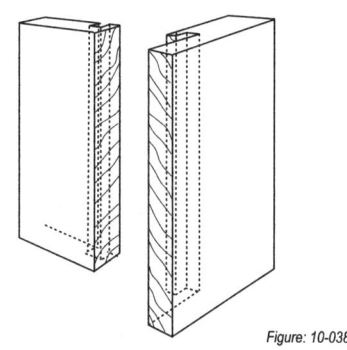

Figure: 10-038

- **Exposed End Details** - Illustrates attachment of finished end of case body to front frame using:

  - **Butt Joint**

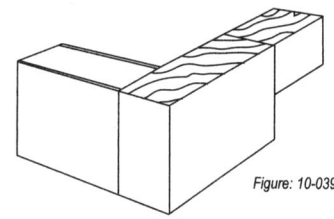

Figure: 10-039

  - **Shoulder mitered joint.**

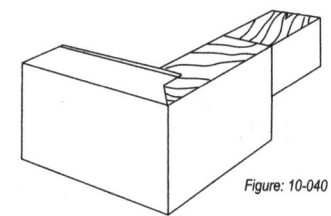

Figure: 10-040

- **Pocket Screw Joint.**

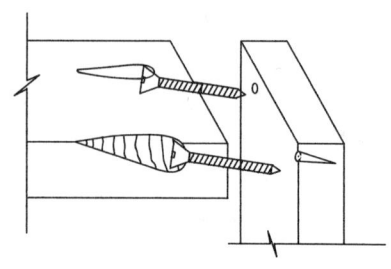

Figure: 10-041

# SECTION 10
## Casework

## introductory information

- **Through Dado** - Conventional joint used for assembly of case body members. Dado not concealed by application of case face frame.

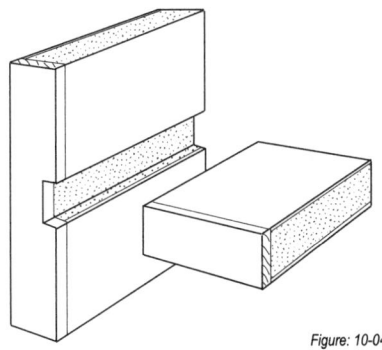

*Figure: 10-042*

- **Blind Dado** - Variation of Through Dado with applied edge "stopping" or concealing dado groove.

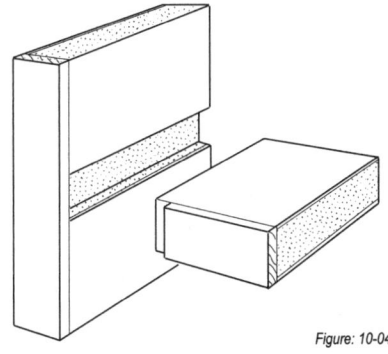

*Figure: 10-043*

- **Stop Dado** - Another method of concealing dado exposure. Applicable when veneer edging or solid lumber is used. Exposed end detail illustrates attachment of finished end of case body to front frame using butt joint.

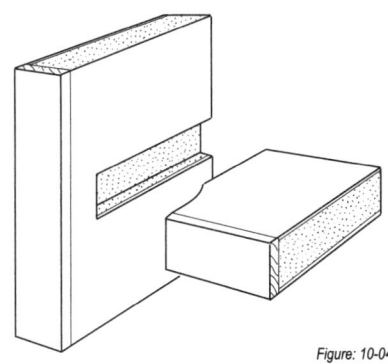

*Figure: 10-044*

- **Dowel Joint** - An established industry standard assembly method, this versatile joinery technique is often based on 1-1/4" (32 mm) spacing of dowels.

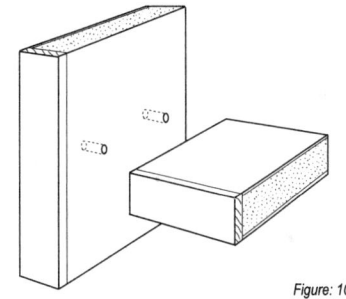

*Figure: 10-045*

- **Dowel Screw Joint** - An alternative to the dowel joint above.

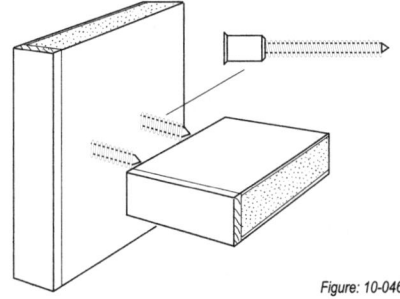

*Figure: 10-046*

- **Edgebanding** - Method of concealing plies or inner cores of plywood or particleboard when edges are exposed. Thickness or configuration will vary with manufacturers' practices.

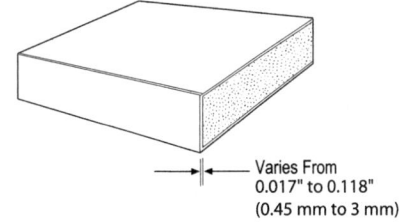

Varies From 0.017" to 0.118" (0.45 mm to 3 mm)

*Figure: 10-047*

- **Miter / Miter Fold Joint.**

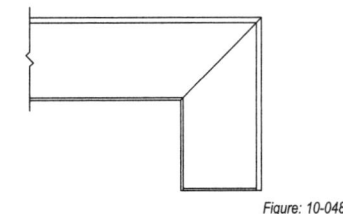

*Figure: 10-048*

- **Spline Joint**: Used to strengthen and align faces when gluing panels in width or length, including items requiring site assembly.

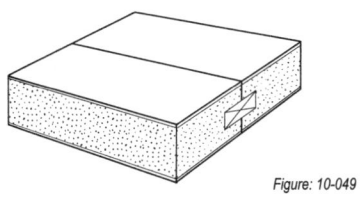

*Figure: 10-049*

- **Paneled Door Details** - Joinery techniques when paneled effect is desired. Profiles are optional as is the use of flat or raised panels. Solid lumber raised panels may be used when width does not exceed Custom Grade standard. Rim raised panels are required for Premium Grade or when widths exceed Custom Grade or when transparent finish is used.

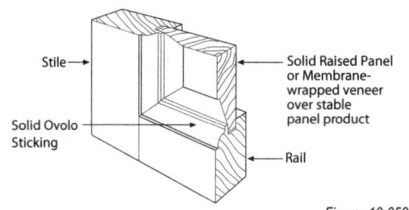

*Figure: 10-050*

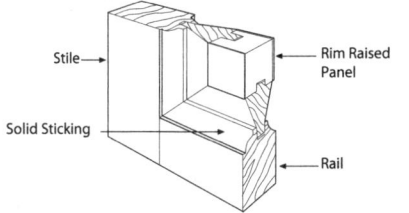

*Figure: 10-051*

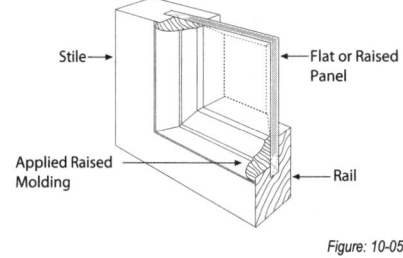

*Figure: 10-052*

# SECTION 10
## Casework

### introductory information

#### SPECIFY REQUIREMENTS FOR

- Construction type.
- Door and drawer front Interface style.
- Door and drawer front edge profile.
- Toe base finish.
- Grain direction, if other than vertical.
- Inside clearance.
- Seismic fabrication and/or installation.
- Flame spread rating.
- Moisture resistance.
- Insulation from adjacent heating cooling sources.
- Hardware.
- Laboratory features, such as:
  - Pipe chase allowance and/or removable backs behind base cabinets.
  - Removable top at countertop splash.
  - Moisture resistant base.
  - Chemical resistant finish or surfaces.
- At wood casework:
  - Species of veneer.
  - Method of slicing (plain, quarter, rift, or rotary).
  - Matching of veneer leaves (book, slip, or random).
  - Matching of veneer leaves within the face of a cabinet unit.
  - Matching between doors, drawers, and adjacent panels (non sequenced, sequenced, or blueprint).
  - End matching.
  - Grain direction, if other than vertical.

#### RECOMMENDATIONS

- If **FIELD FINISHED**, include in Division 09 of the specifications:
  - **BEFORE FINISHING**, exposed portions of woodwork shall have handling marks or effects of exposure to moisture, removed with a thorough, final sanding over all surfaces of the exposed portions and shall be cleaned before applying sealer or finish.
- At **CONCEALED SURFACES** - Architectural woodwork that may be exposed to moisture, such as those adjacent to exterior concrete walls, etc., shall be primed.
- **REVIEW** the **GENERAL** portion of Sections 3 and 4 for an overview of the characteristics and the minimum acceptable requirements of lumber and/or sheet products that might be used herein.
- **STRUCTURAL MEMBERS**, grounds, in wall blocking, backing, furring, brackets, or other anchorage which becomes an integral part of the building's walls, floors, or ceilings, required for the installation of architectural woodwork are not to be furnished or installed by the architectural woodwork manufacturer or installer.

# SECTION 10
## Casework

**GENERAL**/PRODUCT/INSTALLATION/TEST

## compliance requirements

**Including: Wood, Decorative Laminate, and Solid Phenolic Faced Casework**

### 10.1  BASIC CONSIDERATIONS

**1  GRADE**

1.1  These standards are characterized in three Grades of quality that may be mixed within a single project. Limitless design possibilities and a wide variety of lumber and veneer species, along with decorative laminates, factory finishes, and profiles are available in all three Grades.

1.2  **ECONOMY GRADE** defines the minimum quality requirements for a project's workmanship, materials, or installation and is typically reserved for woodwork that is not in public view, such as in mechanical rooms and utility areas.

1.3  **CUSTOM GRADE** is typically specified for and adequately covers most high quality architectural woodwork, providing a well defined degree of control over a project's quality of materials, workmanship, or installation.

1.4  **PREMIUM GRADE** is typically specified for use in those areas of a project where the highest level of quality, materials, workmanship, and installation is required.

1.5  **GRADE LIMITATIONS:**

1.5.1  **SOLID PHENOLIC** faced Casework is only offered in **PREMIUM GRADE**.

2  **CONTRACT DOCUMENTS** shall govern if in conflict with these standards.

3  **ACCEPTABLE REQUIREMENTS** of lumber and/or sheet products used within this woodwork product section are established by Sections 3 and 4, unless otherwise modified herein.

4  **AESTHETIC COMPLIANCE REQUIREMENTS APPLY ONLY TO SURFACES VISIBLE AFTER MANUFACTURE AND INSTALLATION.**

### 10.1  BASIC CONSIDERATIONS  (continued)

5  **SURFACE CATEGORIES:**

5.1  **CABINET SURFACE TERMINOLOGY ILLUSTRATIONS:**

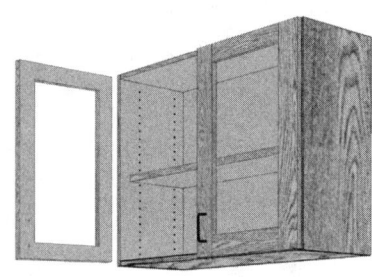

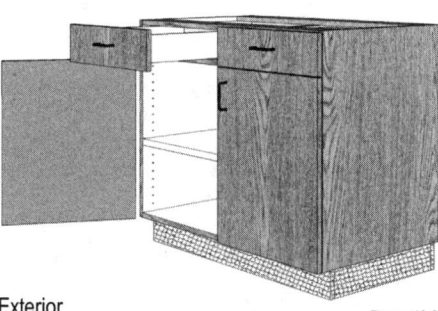

- Exposed Exterior
- Exposed Interior
- Semi-exposed
- Concealed

*Figure: 10-053*

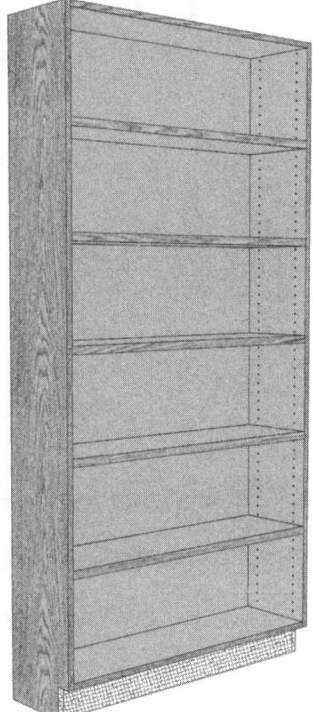

*Figure: 10-054*

# SECTION 10
## Casework

GENERAL/PRODUCT/INSTALLATION/TEST

**compliance requirements**

Where the **E**, **C**, or **P** icon is not indicated, the rule applies to all Grades equally | **E** | **C** | **P** |

### 10.1 BASIC CONSIDERATIONS (continued)

**5 SURFACE CATEGORIES** (continued)

**5.2 EXPOSED EXTERIOR** surfaces, defined as all exterior surfaces exposed to view, include:

5.2.1 All surfaces visible when doors and drawers are closed, including knee spaces.

5.2.2 Underside of cabinet bottoms over 42" (1067 mm) above the finished floor, including cabinet bottoms behind light valances and the bottom edge of light valances.

5.2.3 Cabinet tops under 80" (2032 mm) above the finished floor, or if 80" (2032 mm) and over and visible from an upper building level or floor.

5.2.4 Front edges of stretchers, ends, divisions, tops, and bottoms.

5.2.5 Sloping tops of cabinets that are visible.

**5.3 EXPOSED INTERIOR** surfaces, defined as all interior surfaces exposed to view in open casework or behind transparent doors, include:

5.3.1 Shelves, including edgebanding.

5.3.2 Divisions and partitions (front edge is an exposed surface).

5.3.3 Interior face of ends (sides), backs, and bottoms (including pull outs). Also included are the interior surfaces of cabinet top members 36" (914 mm) or more above the finished floor.

5.3.4 Interior face of door and applied drawer fronts.

**5.4 SEMI-EXPOSED** surfaces, defined as those interior surfaces only exposed to view when doors or drawers are opened, include:

5.4.1 Tops and bottoms of shelves, including front edgebanding (front edge is an exposed surface).

5.4.2 Divisions and partitions (front edge is an exposed surface).

5.4.3 Interior face of ends (sides), backs, and bottoms (including a bank of drawers). Also included are the interior surfaces of cabinet top members 36" (914 mm) or more above the finished floor.

5.4.4 Drawer sides, sub fronts, backs, and bottoms.

5.4.5 The underside of cabinet bottoms between 24" (610 mm) and 42" (1067 mm) above the finished floor.

5.4.6 Security and dust panels or drawer stretchers.

### 10.1 BASIC CONSIDERATIONS (continued)

**5 SURFACE CATEGORIES** (continued)

**5.5 CONCEALED** surfaces, defined as those exterior or interior surfaces that are covered or not normally exposed to view, include:

5.5.1 Toe space unless otherwise specified.

5.5.2 Sleepers, stretchers, and solid sub tops.

5.5.3 The underside of cabinet bottoms less than 24" (610 mm) above the finished floor.

5.5.4 The flat tops of cabinets 80" (2032 mm) or more above the finished floor, except if visible from an upper floor or building level.

5.5.5 The three non visible edges of adjustable shelves.

5.5.6 The underside of countertops, knee spaces, aprons and drawer boxes that are less than 36" (914 mm) above the finished floor.

5.5.7 The faces of cabinet ends of adjoining units that butt together.

**6** When **SOLID PHENOLIC** (compact laminate) is referenced in these standards, it refers to panels of melamine impregnated decorative overlay sheets over a kraft phenolic core sheets per Section 4.

**7 CABINET CONSTRUCTION** terminology is defined as:

**7.1 FRAMELESS** construction where the front edge of the cabinet body components are edgebanded.

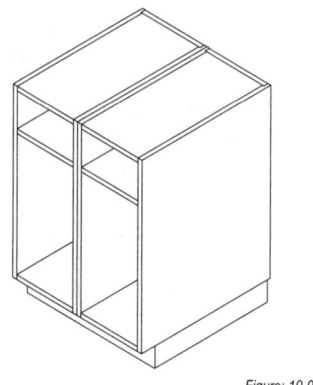

*Figure: 10-055*

## 10.1 BASIC CONSIDERATIONS (continued)

**7.2**    **FACE FRAME** construction where the front edge of the cabinet body components are overlaid with a frame.

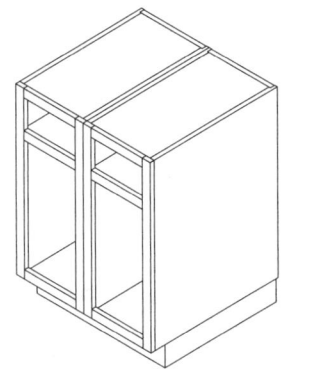

*Figure: 10-056*

**7.3**    **CONSTRUCTION** shall be the manufacturer's choice, unless specified otherwise.

**8**    **CABINET** and **DOOR INTERFACE** terminology is defined as:

**8.1**    **OVERLAY** including flush, reveal, or lipped, as illustrated below:

**8.1.1**    **FRAMELESS CONSTRUCTION:**

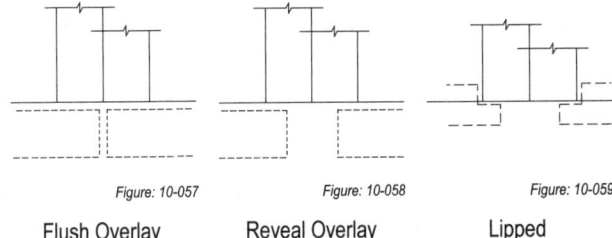

*Figure: 10-057*    *Figure: 10-058*    *Figure: 10-059*

Flush Overlay    Reveal Overlay    Lipped

**8.1.2**    **FACE FRAME CONSTRUCTION:**

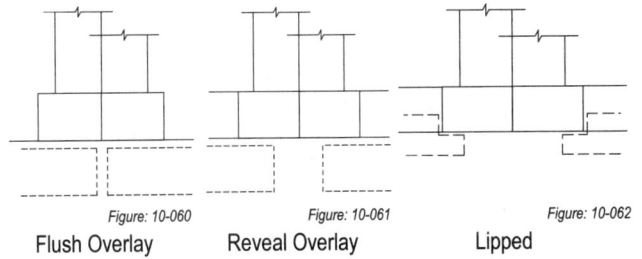

*Figure: 10-060*    *Figure: 10-061*    *Figure: 10-062*

Flush Overlay    Reveal Overlay    Lipped

## 10.1 BASIC CONSIDERATIONS (continued)

**8**    **CABINET** and **DOOR INTERFACE** terminology (continued)

**8.2**    **FLUSH INSET**, as illustrated below:

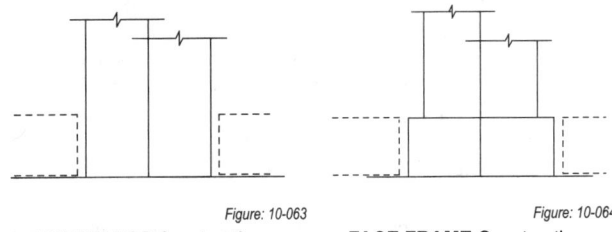

*Figure: 10-063*    *Figure: 10-064*

**FRAMELESS** Construction    **FACE FRAME** Construction

**8.3**    **FLUSH OVERLAY** is the default for either **FRAMELESS** or **FACE FRAME** casework, except:

**8.3.1**    At **EXPOSED KNUCKLE HINGES**, defaulting to **REVEAL OVERLAY** is at the option of the manufacturer, and:

**8.3.1.1**    If reveal overlay, the reveal shall be determined by the hinge overlay.

**9**    **CASEWORK INTEGRITY** - These standards have adopted a portion of SEFA's (Scientific Equipment and Fixture Association) methods of testing and acceptable results as the minimum acceptable level of integrity for casework, as found in the APPENDIX.

**10**    **HARDWARE** - These standards have adopted ANSI/BHMA Standards (latest edition), Grade 2, as the basic minimum requirement for casework hardware.

**11**    **CABINET DESIGN SERIES (CDS):**

**11.1**    The Sponsor Associations have developed a series of numbered cabinet designs that are available for ease of specification and drawing.

**11.1.1**    A numerical/elevation key to the drawings may be found in **DESIGN IDEAS**.

**11.1.2**    Autodesk Revit Families and AutoCad ".DWG/ DXE /.DXF" files of the elevations may be found on each of the Sponsor Associations' **websites at www.awinet.org, www.awmac.com, www.woodworkinstitute.com or at www.aws-errata.com.**

**12**    **CASEWORK CONCEPT DRAWINGS** may be found in **DESIGN IDEAS**.

**13**    To **PREVENT TELEGRAPHING**, inset solid wood edging when used must have similar moisture content as panel core, be glued securely and calibrated with panel core thickness prior to being laminated with a wood veneer on both faces.

# SECTION 10
## Casework

**GENERAL/PRODUCT/INSTALLATION/TEST**

**compliance requirements**

Where the **E**, **C**, or **P** icon is not indicated, the rule applies to all Grades equally | E | C | P |

### 10.1 BASIC CONSIDERATIONS (continued)

**14 INDUSTRY PRACTICES**

**4.1 STRUCTURAL MEMBERS**, grounds, in wall blocking, backing, furring, brackets, or other anchorage that becomes an integral part of the building's walls, floors, or ceilings, that are required for the installation of architectural woodwork are not furnished or installed by the architectural woodwork manufacturer or installer.

**14.2 WALL, CEILING**, and/or opening variations in excess of 1/4" (6.4 mm) or **FLOORS** in excess of 1/2" (12.7 mm) in 144" (3658 mm) of being plumb, level, flat, straight, square, or of the correct size are not acceptable for the installation of architectural woodwork, nor is it the responsibility of the installer to scribe or fit to tolerances in excess of such.

**14.3 PRIMING** of architectural casework is not the responsibility of the manufacturer and/or installer, unless the material is being furnished prefinished.

**14.4 SURFACING** with a defined grain and/or pattern is installed vertically, unless otherwise specified.

**14.5 CASEWORK DIMENSION RANGES** have developed over time with consideration of materials, ergonomics, construction techniques, and general intended usage. It is the responsibility of the design professional to coordinate accessibility requirements, appliance and equipment sizes, and/or storage requirements with the casework manufacturer and adjust the following dimensions accordingly:

**14.5.1 BASE:**

**14.5.1.1 HEIGHT** - from the finished floor to the top of the countertop deck ranges from:

**14.5.1.1.1** 34" (864 mm) to 36" (914 mm) at stand up counters.

**14.5.1.1.2** 31" (787 mm) to 38" (965 mm) at vanities.

**14.5.1.1.3** 28" (711 mm) to 32" (812 mm) at sit down counters, providing a clear knee space height of 24-1/2" (622 mm).

**14.5.1.1.4** 25-1/4" (641 mm) to 28" (711 mm) at keyboard recesses, providing a clear knee space height of 24-1/2" (622 mm).

**14.5.1.2 DEPTH** - from the front of the cabinet door/drawer to the face of the wall ranges from 22" (559 mm) to 30" (762 mm).

### 10.1 BASIC CONSIDERATIONS (continued)

**14 INDUSTRY PRACTICES (continued)**

**14.5 CASEWORK DIMENSION RANGES (continued)**

**14.5.2 WALL HUNG:**

**14.5.2.1 HEIGHT** - including the light apron ranges from 12" (305 mm) to 48" (1219 mm).

**14.5.2.2 DEPTH** - from the front of the cabinet door to the face of the wall ranges from 12-1/2" (318 mm) to 14" (356 mm).

**14.5.3 TALL STORAGE:**

**14.5.3.1 HEIGHT** - from the finished floor to the cabinet top ranges from 72" (1829 mm) to 96" (2438 mm).

**14.5.3.2 DEPTH** - from the front of the cabinet door to the face of the wall ranges from 12-1/2" (318 mm) to 30" (762 mm).

**14.5.4 RECEPTION COUNTER:**

**14.5.4.1 HEIGHT** - from the finished floor to the top of the countertop deck ranges from:

**14.5.4.1.1** 34" (864 mm) to 42" (1067 mm) at the standing side.

**14.5.4.1.2** 28" (711 mm) to 32" (812 mm) at the sit down side, providing a clear knee space height of 24-1/2" (622 mm).

**14.5.4.1.3** 25-1/4" (641 mm) to 28" (711 mm) at the sit down keyboard recesses, providing a clear knee space height of 24-1/2" (622 mm).

**14.5.4.2 DEPTH:**

**14.5.4.2.1** 24" (610 mm) to 30" (762 mm) overall countertop on the sit down side, plus an additional 8" (203 mm) of countertop at the stand up side.

**14.5.5 TELLER COUNTER:**

**14.5.5.1 HEIGHT** - from the finished floor ranges from:

**14.5.5.1.1** 50" (1270 mm) to 54" (1372 mm) on the customer side at the security hood.

**14.5.5.1.2** 40" (1016 mm) to 42" (1067 mm) on the teller's side transaction countertop.

## 10.1 BASIC CONSIDERATIONS (continued)

### 14 INDUSTRY PRACTICES (continued)

**14.5 CASEWORK DIMENSION RANGES** (continued)

**14.5.5 TELLER COUNTER** (continued)

**14.5.5.2 DEPTH:**

14.5.5.2.1    24" (610 mm) to 32" (813 mm) at the countertop on the teller side, plus:

14.5.5.2.1.1    An additional 8" (203 mm) of countertop at the customer side.

**14.6 BASE CABINET, STRETCHER, LAYOUT, and CONSTRUCTION:**

14.6.1    **CASEWORK MANUFACTURER** is responsible for coordinating the following with the countertop manufacturer, and:

14.6.2    **COUNTERTOP MANUFACTURER** is responsible for furnishing wall cleating necessary for proper setting of their countertops where there is no casework for support.

14.6.3    At **FRAMELESS CONSTRUCTION** doors, drawer fronts, and false fronts creating a 1/8" (3.2 mm) to 1/4" (6.4 mm) horizontal reveal with the countertop's bottom edge, shall be consistent across elevations, except:

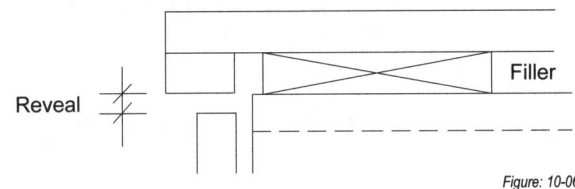

*Figure: 10-065*

14.6.4    At **FACE FRAME CONSTRUCTION**, reveal shall be 1/4" (6.4 mm) to 1" (25.4 mm) and shall be consistent across elevations.

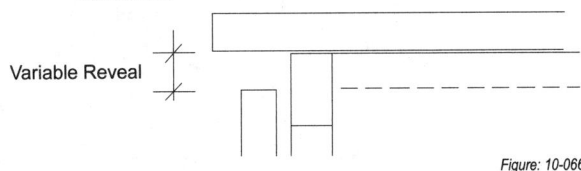

*Figure: 10-066*

14.6.5    At **LABORATORY APPLICATION**, reveal shall be 1/4" (6.4 mm) to 1" (25.4 mm) and shall be consistent across elevations.

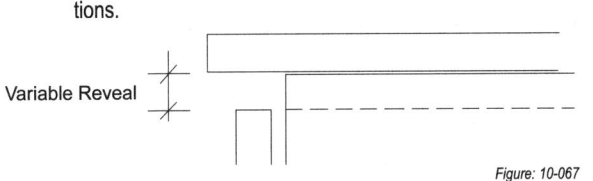

*Figure: 10-067*

## 10.1 BASIC CONSIDERATIONS (continued)

### 14 INDUSTRY PRACTICES (continued)

14.7    **CORNERS** created by adjoining casework will create non usable space.

14.8    **FINISHED ENDS** shall be **INTEGRAL**, not applied secondarily, except:

14.8.1    Applied end panels are allowed at Solid Phenolic casework.

14.9    **BASE/TOE** shall be **INTEGRAL** (constructed as an integral part of the cabinet body) or **SEPARATE** (constructed as a separate member) at the option of the manufacturer.

14.10    **STORAGE, JANITOR CLOSET**, and/or **UTILITY ROOM CABINETS** shall be built in conformance to **ECONOMY GRADE**, regardless of the overall project's Grade requirement, unless specified otherwise, except:

14.10.1    If specified material is **SOLID PHENOLIC, PREMIUM GRADE** shall be provided.

14.11    Surfaces behind **PRESENTATION PANELS** (such as white board or tack board) are treated as:

14.11.1    **SEMI-EXPOSED** at Economy Grade and Custom Grade.

14.11.2    **EXPOSED** at Premium Grade.

14.12    **TOE BASE HEIGHT VARIANCE** due to floor variations is not considered a defect. Casework is required to be installed level; shimming of the toe base, not to exceed 1/2" (12.7 mm), is acceptable. Floor variations exceeding 1/2" (12.7 mm) shall be corrected before cabinets are installed; however, correction of such is not the responsibility of the cabinet installer.

# SECTION 10
## Casework

GENERAL/PRODUCT/INSTALLATION/TEST

Where the **E**, **C**, or **P** icon is not indicated, the rule applies to all Grades equally | E | C | P |

compliance requirements

### 10.1 BASIC CONSIDERATIONS (continued)

**4  INDUSTRY PRACTICES** (continued)

**14.13** **LAYOUT** requirements of grained or patterned faces by Grade:

**14.13.1** **STILE** and **RAIL** doors and drawer fronts for all Grades, drawer fronts shall run either vertically or horizontally at the manufacturer's choice for the entire project. Doors shall be vertical.

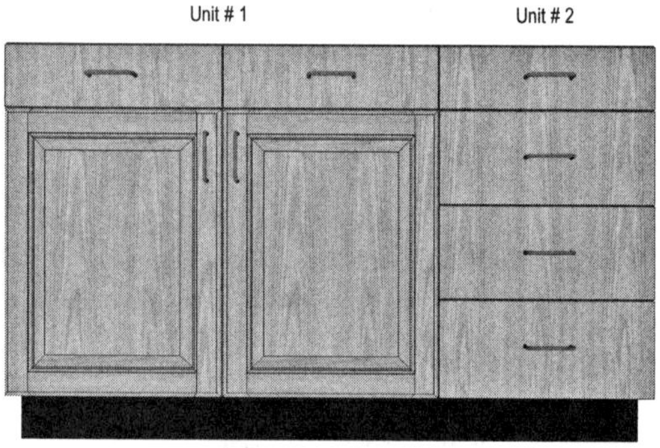

*Figure: 10-068*

*Figure: 10-069*

**14.13.2** **FLUSH PANEL** doors and drawer fronts:

**14.13.2.1** **ECONOMY GRADE** - drawer fronts shall run either vertically or horizontally at the manufacturer's choice for the entire project. Doors shall be vertical. Mismatch is allowed.

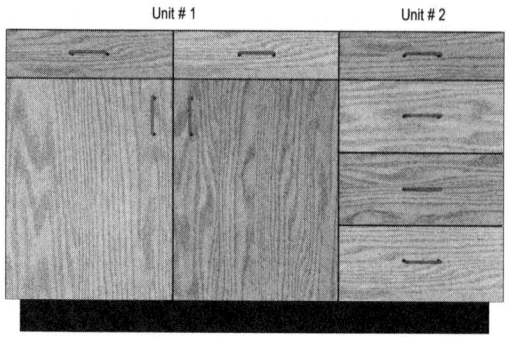

*Figure: 10-070*

### 10.1 BASIC CONSIDERATIONS (continued)

**14  INDUSTRY PRACTICES** (continued)

**14.13** **LAYOUT** requirements of grained or patterned (continued)

**14.13.2** **FLUSH PANEL** doors and drawer fronts (continued)

**14.13.2.2** **CUSTOM GRADE** - doors, drawer fronts, and false fronts shall run and match vertically within each cabinet unit:

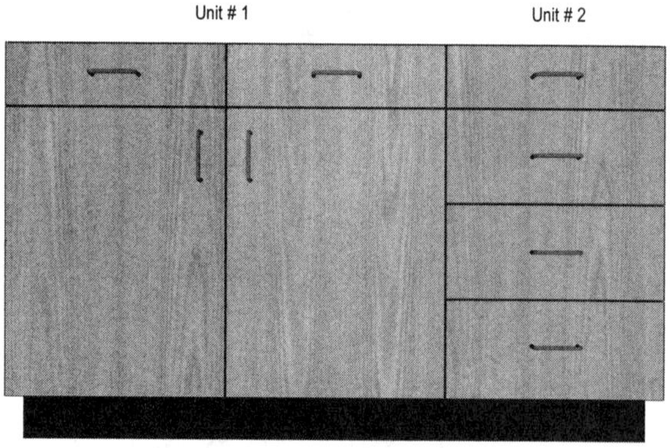

*Figure: 10-071*

**14.13.2.3** **PREMIUM GRADE** - doors, drawer fronts, and false fronts shall run and match vertically and be sequenced horizontally within each cabinet unit; and at cathedral grain, the crown shall be pointing up and run in the same direction for the entire project. Doors, drawer fronts, and false fronts shall be well matched for color and grain across multiple cabinet faces in one elevation. Requirement for blueprint or sequencing between cabinet units must be so specified.

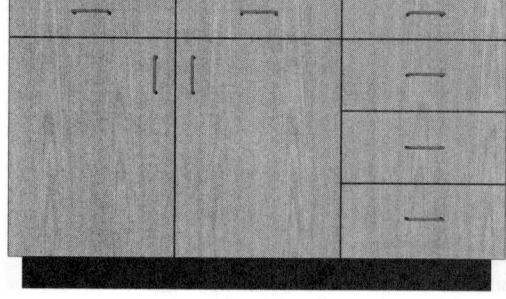

*Figure: 10-072*

300 Architectural Woodwork Standards

# SECTION 10
## Casework

**compliance requirements** — GENERAL/**PRODUCT**/INSTALLATION/TEST

*Where the E, C, or P icon is not indicated, the rule applies to all Grades equally*

### 10.2 SCOPE

1. All wood, high pressure decorative laminate (HPDL), and/or solid phenolic casework, cabinets, and components of face frame or frameless construction, fabricated complete in the manufacturer's facilities to field dimensions, as qualified below.

2. **TYPICAL INCLUSIONS:**

   - 2.1 Altars.
   - 2.2 Bars and back bars.
   - 2.3 Bulletin boards, built up.
   - 2.4 Bookcases, cabinets, carrels, counters, display cases, lecterns, and pulpits.
   - 2.5 Shelving, built up or machined and knocked down.
   - 2.6 Wardrobes.
   - 2.7 Modular cabinets.
   - 2.8 Cabinet doors.
   - 2.9 Clothes poles and supports.
   - 2.10 Shelf standards and rests.
   - 2.11 Track and hardware for sliding doors.
   - 2.12 Casters.
   - 2.13 File drawer rods and followers.
   - 2.14 Hinges.
   - 2.15 Drawer guides and slides.
   - 2.16 Pulls or knobs.
   - 2.17 Glass, mirrors, and glass doors (including hardware) that is integral to millwork.
   - 2.18 Filler panels, scribe strips, trim and moldings necessary for cabinet installation.
   - 2.19 Rough and finish hardware, which is part of the cabinet.
   - 2.20 Metal brackets and fittings, which are an integral part of the cabinet, unless specified elsewhere.
   - 2.21 Cut outs for sinks or similar units.
   - 2.22 Linoleum, vinyl, cork, or resilient covering integral to cabinet.
   - 2.23 Prefinishing, priming, painting, or sealing if so specified.
   - 2.24 Die walls that become integral to millwork.
   - 2.25 Soffit or fascia panels constructed from cabinet material.

3. **TYPICAL EXCLUSIONS:**

   - 3.1 Field installation, unless specified to be included in this scope of work.
   - 3.2 Cutting of holes for field applied vents, weeps, or grills, unless part of the cabinet.
   - 3.3 Fillers, build up, or sub tops for countertops, including tile and natural stone.
   - 3.4 Cutting for field applied hardware, unless part of the cabinet.
   - 3.5 Vinyl, rubber, or carpet base.
   - 3.6 Metal support brackets and fittings that are part of the building structure.
   - 3.7 Security panels, unless so specified.
   - 3.8 Tote trays (except at Cabinet Design Series) and base leveling adjusters, unless so specified.
   - 3.9 Furring, stripping, in wall blocking, grounds, or stub walls.
   - 3.10 Mirrors, glass, or glazing, unless part of the cabinet.
   - 3.11 Plumbing, electrical fixtures, and telephone equipment.
   - 3.12 Metal or ceramic tile for countertops.
   - 3.13 Sink rims.
   - 3.14 Special equipment housed in cabinets.
   - 3.15 Work not directly associated with the casework.
   - 3.16 Sliding presentation boards.
   - 3.17 Metal grills.
   - 3.18 Chalkboards and tack boards that are a part of the cabinet, with the necessary trim and trays.
   - 3.19 Easel trays of plastic or metal.
   - 3.20 Caulking of casework to work of others.

# SECTION 10
## Casework

GENERAL / **PRODUCT** / INSTALLATION / TEST

*compliance requirements*

Where the **E**, **C**, or **P** icon is not indicated, the rule applies to all Grades equally | E | C | P |

## 10.3 DEFAULT STIPULATION

1. If not otherwise specified or indicated, all work shall be Custom Grade, frameless construction with adjustable shelves and Flush Overlay doors of unfinished close grain hardwood intended for an opaque finish, non premium priced standard pattern, color, and finish decorative laminate or solid phenolic, as covered by Sections 3 and 4, except:

   1.1 At **EXPOSED KNUCKLE HINGES**, defaulting to **REVEAL OVERLAY** is manufacturer's choice, and:

   1.1.1 If reveal overlay the reveal shall be determined by the hinge overlay.

## 10.4 RULES

1. The following rules shall govern unless a project's contract documents require otherwise.

2. These rules are intended to provide a well defined degree of control over a project's quality of materials, workmanship, or installation.

3. **ERRATA**, published on the Sponsor Associations' websites at www.awinet.org, www.awmac.com, or www.aws-errata.com, shall **TAKE PRECEDENCE OVER THESE RULES**, subject to their date of posting and a project's bid date.

### 10.4.4 Basic Rules

1. **AESTHETIC** grade rules apply only to exposed and semi-exposed surfaces visible after installation.

2. **WOODWORK** not addressed herein shall be manufactured from solid stock, laminated stock, veneered stock, or a combination thereof.

3. **LUMBER** shall conform to the requirements established in Section 3.

4. **SHEET PRODUCTS** shall conform to the requirements established in Section 4.

5. **BACKING SHEET** shall conform to the requirements established in Section 4.

6. **ALL MATERIALS** shall be securely attached/fastened/bonded.

*Continues next column*

### 10.4.4 Basic Rules

▲ From previous column

7. **SURFACE CATEGORIES** Include:

   7.1 **EXPOSED EXTERIOR** surfaces, defined as all exterior surfaces exposed to view, including:

   7.1.1 All surfaces visible when doors and drawers are closed, including knee spaces.

   7.1.2 Underside of cabinet bottoms over 42" (1067 mm) above the finished floor, including cabinet bottoms behind light valances and the bottom edge of light valances.

   7.1.3 Cabinet tops under 80" (2032 mm) above the finished floor, or if 80" (2032 mm) and over and visible from an upper building level or floor.

   7.1.4 Front edges of stretchers, ends, divisions, tops, and bottoms.

   7.1.5 Sloping tops of cabinets that are visible.

   7.2 **EXPOSED INTERIOR** surfaces, defined as all interior surfaces exposed to view in open casework or behind transparent doors, include:

   7.2.1 Shelves, including edgebanding.

   7.2.2 Divisions and partitions (front edge is an exposed surface).

   7.2.3 Interior face of ends (sides), backs, and bottoms (including pull outs). Also included are the interior surfaces of cabinet top members 36" (914 mm) or more above the finished floor.

   7.2.4 Interior face of door and applied drawer fronts.

   7.3 **SEMI-EXPOSED** surfaces, defined as those interior surfaces only exposed to view when doors or drawers are opened, include:

   7.3.1 Tops and bottoms of shelves, including front edgebanding (front edge is an exposed surface).

   7.3.2 Divisions and partitions (front edge is an exposed surface).

   7.3.3 Interior face of ends (sides), backs, and bottoms (including a bank of drawers). Also included are the interior surfaces of cabinet top members 36" (914 mm) or more above the finished floor.

   7.3.4 Drawer sides, sub fronts, backs, and bottoms.

   7.3.5 The underside of cabinet bottoms between 24" (610 mm) and 42" (1067 mm) above the finished floor.

   7.3.6 Security and dust panels or drawer stretchers.

*Continues next column* ▼

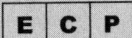

Where the E, C, or P icon is not indicated, the rule applies to all Grades equally

# SECTION 10
## Casework

## compliance requirements

GENERAL / **PRODUCT** / INSTALLATION / TEST

### 10.4.4 Basic Rules

▲ From previous column

| | | | |
|---|---|---|---|
| 7 | | | **SURFACE CATEGORIES** (continued) |
| 7 | 4 | | **CONCEALED** surfaces, defined as those exterior or interior surfaces that are covered or not normally exposed to view, include: |
| 7 | 4 | 1 | Toe space unless otherwise specified. |
| 7 | 4 | 2 | Sleepers, stretchers, and solid sub tops. |
| 7 | 4 | 3 | The underside of cabinet bottoms less than 24" (610 mm) above the finished floor. |
| 7 | 4 | 4 | The flat tops of cabinets 80" (2032 mm) or more above the finished floor, except if visible from an upper floor or building level. |
| 7 | 4 | 5 | The three non visible edges of adjustable shelves. |
| 7 | 4 | 6 | The underside of countertops, knee spaces, aprons and drawer boxes that are less than 36" (914 mm) above the finished floor. |
| 7 | 4 | 7 | The faces of cabinet ends of adjoining units that butt together. |
| 8 | | | **HARDWARE** shall: |
| 8 | 1 | | **CONFORM TO** ANSI/BHMA Standards (latest edition), Grade 2 requirements with the exception of requiring "dynamic" load testing for a minimum of 50,000 cycles, and: |
| 8 | 1 | 1 | **SCHOOLS** and **HOSPITAL** hinges shall be of all metal construction, meeting or exceeding the ANSI/BHMA Grade 1 "performance" and "permanent set" test requirements.. |
| 8 | 1 | 2 | **DRAWER SLIDE TESTING** shall be based on a drawer slide nominal length of 22" or 550 mm mounted on a drawer box 22" (550 mm) in depth with a minimum width of 18" (457 mm) for load ratings up to 125 lbs (56.7 kg) and 24" (610 mm) for load ratings of 125 lbs (56.7 kg) and above, and: |
| 8 | 1 | 2 | 1 | Slides not manufactured in lengths up to 22" (559 mm) shall be tested in their longest production length. |
| 8 | 1 | 3 | **KEYBOARD TRAYS** shall conform to section 4.13 (Test 12, Drawers and Trays) of ANSI/BHMA A156.9 (latest edition). |
| 8 | 1 | 4 | **HINGES** shall have a minimum 120 degree of opening capacity. |
| 8 | 2 | | Be **FURNISHED** and **INSTALLED** per manufacturer's recommendations and as required to provide a complete casework assembly without impairment of the cabinet's structural integrity and/or functionality, and: |
| 8 | 2 | 1 | When fastener provisions are countersunk, fasteners shall be countersunk. |

Continues next column ▼

### 10.4.4 Basic Rules

▲ From previous column

| | | | |
|---|---|---|---|
| 8 | | | **HARDWARE** shall (continued) |
| 8 | 3 | | Be of a **UNIFORM PLATED** BHMA 626 or similar **POWDER COATED** finish on exposed surfaces and: |
| 8 | 3 | 1 | Conform to applicable ANSI/BHMA standards (latest edition). |
| 8 | 3 | 2 | Powder coat finish shall be of a chemical family with sufficient chemical/solvent resistance to not be affected by a rubdown of the solvents or cleaning materials used for final cleanup of the fabricated product, including removal of over spray, glue. |
| 8 | 3 | 3 | Finishes will vary between manufacturers, and it can be expected to see variations from the same manufacturer between different production runs. These variations are not considered a defect, as long as they are compatible with the overall finish of the installed hardware. |
| 8 | 4 | | Have the **MANUFACTURER'S NAME** or unique brand marking stamped on hinges, slides, and locks for identification purposes. |
| 8 | 5 | | Be of **FIRST CLASS WORKMANSHIP**, free of manufacturing imperfections (such as tool or machine marks), and consistent in exposed finish appearance. |
| 8 | 6 | | At **LOCKS**, be furnished when indicated on the contract documents, and: |
| 8 | 6 | 1 | Be keyed differently, only if so specified. |
| 8 | 6 | 2 | Be master keyed, only if so specified. |
| 8 | 7 | | At **DRAWER SLIDES** shall conform to the following minimum load capacity requirements: |
| 8 | 7 | 1 | 50 lbs (22.7 kg) at pencil drawers. |
| 8 | 7 | 2 | 75 lbs (34 kg) at general purpose drawers. |
| 8 | 7 | 3 | 100 lbs (45.4 kg) at file drawers, except: |
| 8 | 7 | 3 | 1 | 150 lbs (68 kg) at lateral file drawers wider than 24" (610 mm) and less than 30" (762 mm). |
| 8 | 7 | 4 | 200 lbs (68 kg) at lateral file drawers wider than 30" (762 mm). |
| 8 | 7 | 5 | Metal Sided Slide Systems must be specified. |
| 8 | 8 | | At **SHELF RESTS** for bored holes, either include a minimum of 0.1969" (5 mm) metal pin or double 0.1969" (5 mm) plastic pins (meeting ANSI/BHMA Grade 1 requirements) and: |
| 8 | 8 | 1 | Meet or exceed these standards' maximum shelf load requirement of 200 lbs (90.7 kg). |
| 8 | 9 | | At **POCKET DOOR HARDWARE,** cabinet doors shall be a maximum of 23-5/8" (600 mm) in width and the maximum door height and weight shall be within the manufacturer's listed capacity. |

Continues next column ▼

# SECTION 10
## Casework

GENERAL / **PRODUCT** / INSTALLATION / TEST

**compliance requirements**

Where the **E**, **C**, or **P** icon is not indicated, the rule applies to all Grades equally | **E** | **C** | **P** |

### 10.4.4 Basic Rules

▲ From previous column

| 8 | | **HARDWARE** shall (continued) | | | |
|---|---|---|---|---|---|
| 8 | 10 | | At **BASE ADJUSTERS** shall be of the adjustable screw type, having a floor bearing surface of at least 1-1/8" (28.6 mm) in diameter at each foot, and: | | |
| 8 | 10 | 1 | Shall provide for leveling the cabinet from inside of the case through holes in the cabinet bottom with cover caps. | | |
| 8 | 11 | | **MULTIPLE HARDWARE OPTIONS**, when specified, shall be the manufacturer's choice. | | |
| 9 | | | **CASEWORK** shall be: | | |
| 9 | 1 | | Assembled complete by the manufacturer, with doors, drawers, and hardware installed. | | |
| 9 | 2 | | Assembled with mechanical fasteners and adhesive. | | |
| 9 | 3 | | Free of adhesive over spray, fabrication marks, and debris. | | |
| 10 | | | **PANEL COMPONENTS** shall be: | | |
| 10 | 1 | | Constructed of particleboard, MDF, or a non telegraphing core. | | |
| 10 | 2 | | Of balanced construction, constructed in such a way as not to warp in its intended use. | | |
| 11 | | | **FRAMELESS CONSTRUCTION** requires self edging of adjoining units be beveled a maximum of 15° for the thickness of the edgebanding, and if adjoined, the total beveled "V" shall not exceed 30°. | | |
| 12 | | | **SEPARATELY APPLIED COUNTERTOPS** are required at base cabinets 48" (1219 mm) or less in height. | | |
| 13 | | | **STORAGE, JANITOR, CLOSET**, and **UTILITY ROOM CABINETS** shall be of hardboard, particleboard, MDF, or decorative laminate, at the manufacturer's choice. | E | C | P |
| 14 | | | **CABINETS OVER** 72" (1829 mm) high (excluding wardrobe cabinets) not abutting a structural wall or another cabinet shall have a fixed shelf approximately mid height, and: | | |
| 14 | 1 | | At seismic compliant construction, have a fixed shelf and anchor strip approximately mid height, and: | | |
| 14 | 1 | 1 | Anchor strip and back shall be securely fastened to the fixed shelf with #10 x 2-1/2" (50.8 mm) screws a maximum of 7" (178 mm) on center. | | |
| 15 | | | **SLIDING PRESENTATION BOARDS** require an integral stop be provided within the top and bottom track to prevent their stopping against the casework. | | |

▼ Continues next column

### 10.4.4 Basic Rules

▲ From previous column

| 16 | | **HOT MELT APPLIED** decorative laminate edgebanding shall be primed before application for proper adhesion, unless the hot melt adhesive used has been specially formulated for the application of decorative laminate without requiring pre-application of a primer. | | | |
|---|---|---|---|---|---|
| 17 | | **PREFINISHING** of wood faced casework requires wall abutting surfaces shall be factory sealed with two coats at 2 mil dry. | E | C | P |
| 18 | | **CUT OUTS** require: | | | |
| 18 | 1 | At **HPDL** exposed surfaces have a minimum 1/4" (6.4 mm) radius at inside corners. | | | |
| 19 | | **CATHEDRAL** type figure shall be achieved by: | | | |
| 19 | 1 | A single component in "AA" Face Grade. | | | |
| 19 | 2 | The split heart method in Face Grades "A - D", and: | | | |
| 19 | 2 | 1 | Each half of a split heart shall be subject to the minimum component width requirements for Face Grade "B". | | |
| 20 | | At cabinet doors with **GLASS LIGHTS**, the exposed groove the glass sits in is considered an Exposed Interior Surface. | | | |
| 21 | | **FIRST CLASS WORKMANSHIP** is required in compliance with these standards. | | | |

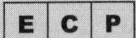

Where the **E**, **C**, or **P** icon is not indicated, the rule applies to all Grades equally

# SECTION 10
## Casework

**compliance requirements**

GENERAL/**PRODUCT**/INSTALLATION/TEST

### 10.4.5 Material Rules

| | | | | | | |
|---|---|---|---|---|---|---|
| 1 | | **GRAIN** or **DIRECTIONAL PATTERNED** sheet products: | | | | |
| 1 | 1 | | Shall run either vertically or horizontally at the manufacturer's choice, and: | E | C | P |
| 1 | 1 | 1 | Drawer fronts shall run either vertically or horizontally for the entire project. | E | C | P |
| 1 | 2 | | Shall run and match vertically within each cabinet unit, including doors, drawers, false fronts, and finished ends. | E | C | |
| 1 | 3 | | Shall run and match vertically and horizontally within each cabinet unit, including doors, drawers, false fronts, and: | E | C | P |
| 1 | 3 | 1 | Cathedral grain shall have the crown pointing up and run the same direction for the entire project. | E | C | P |
| 1 | 3 | 2 | Shall be well matched for color and grain across multiple cabinet faces in each room. | E | C | P |
| 1 | 3 | 3 | Wood veneer blueprint or sequencing requirement for cabinet elevation must be so specified. | | | |
| 1 | 4 | | At **STILE** and **RAIL DOOR** and **DRAWER FRONT** panels shall run either vertically or horizontally at the manufacturer's choice. | | | |
| 2 | | | **LIGHT VALANCE** bottom edge shall be considered an exposed surface. | | | |
| 3 | | | **VINYL** covered material is acceptable for cabinet construction. | E | C | P |
| 4 | | | **GLASS SHELVES** shall be tempered or laminated safety glass, with all four edges polished. | | | |
| 5 | | | For **OPAQUE FINISH**: | | | |
| 5 | 1 | | Medium density fiberboard (MDF) is permitted. | | | |
| 5 | 2 | | Veneer is permitted; however: | | | |
| 5 | 2 | 1 | **SPECIES** of manufacturer's choice, closed grain hardwood conforming to HPVA definitions and characteristics for: | | | |
| 5 | 2 | 1 | 1 Grade **D**. | E | C | P |
| 5 | 2 | 1 | 2 Grade **C**. | E | C | P |
| 5 | 2 | 1 | 3 Grade **B**. | E | C | P |
| 6 | | | For **TRANSPARENT FINISH, VENEER**: | | | |
| 6 | 1 | | **SPECIES** of manufacturer's choice, hardwood conforming to HPVA definitions and characteristics for: | | | |
| 6 | 1 | 1 | Grade **B**. | E | C | P |
| 6 | 1 | 2 | Grade **A**. | E | C | P |
| 6 | 1 | 3 | Grade **AA**. | E | C | P |

Continues next column ▼

### 10.4.5 Material Rules

▲ From previous column

| | | | | | | |
|---|---|---|---|---|---|---|
| 6 | | | For **TRANSPARENT FINISH, VENEER** (continued) | | | |
| 6 | 2 | | **SLICING** of: | | | |
| 6 | 2 | 1 | Manufacturer's choice. | E | C | P |
| 6 | 2 | 2 | Plain sliced. | E | C | P |
| 6 | 3 | | **MATCHING ADJACENT LEAVES** be: | | | |
| 6 | 3 | 1 | Manufacturer's choice. | E | C | P |
| 6 | 3 | 2 | Book matching. | E | C | P |
| 6 | 4 | | **MATCHING WITHIN PANEL FACE** be running match. | | | |
| 6 | 5 | | **MATCHING BETWEEN ADJACENT PANELS** be: | | | |
| 6 | 5 | 1 | Manufacturer's choice. | E | C | P |
| 6 | 5 | 2 | Compatible for color and grain. | E | C | P |
| 6 | 5 | 3 | Well matched for color and grain. | E | C | P |
| 6 | 5 | 4 | **END MATCH, BLUEPRINT** and **SEQUENCING** shall be specified. | | | |
| 7 | | | **SEMI-EXPOSED** surfaces, require: | | | |
| 7 | 1 | | Consistent color or species to be used throughout entire project. | | | |
| 7 | 2 | | Matching to exposed surface is only required if so specified. | | | |
| 7 | 3 | | Vinyl overlay is acceptable at cabinet backs if matched in color to other semi-exposed materials. | | | |
| 7 | 4 | | Hardboard used as vertical or horizontal shelves and/or dividers shall be tempered and smooth on both sides, and: | E | C | P |
| 7 | 4 | 1 | Painted to match other semi-exposed portions is only required if so specified. | E | C | P |
| 7 | 5 | | Vertical or horizontal shelves and/or dividers shall match other semi-exposed surfaces. | E | C | P |
| 8 | | | **CONCEALED** surfaces shall be the manufacturer's choice: | | | |
| 8 | 1 | | If specifications require a moisture resistant base, base components shall be material complying with the base cabinet submersion test, as explained in the **APPENDIX**. | | | **a** |

Continues next column ▼

# SECTION 10
## Casework

GENERAL / **PRODUCT** / INSTALLATION / TEST

Where the **E**, **C**, or **P** icon is not indicated, the rule applies to all Grades equally — | E | C | P |

**compliance requirements**

### 10.4.5 Material Rules

▲ From previous column

| | | | | | | | | |
|---|---|---|---|---|---|---|---|---|
| 9 | | | | At **WOOD CASEWORK**: | | | | |
| 9 | 1 | | | **EXPOSED EXTERIOR** surfaces: | | | | |
| 9 | 1 | 1 | | Requires wood of the specified species, cut, and match. | | | | |
| 9 | 1 | 2 | | **TRANSPARENT FINISH** requires: | | | | |
| 9 | 1 | 2 | 1 | Use of one species for the entire project. | | | | |
| 9 | 1 | 2 | 2 | Solid stock and/or plywood to be **COMPATIBLE** in color and grain. | | E | C | P |
| 9 | 1 | 2 | 3 | Solid stock to be **WELL MATCHED** for color and grain; plywood shall be **COMPATIBLE** in color with solid stock; and adjacent plywood panels shall be **WELL MATCHED** for color and grain. | | E | C | P |
| 9 | 1 | 3 | | **OPAQUE FINISH** permits: | | | | |
| 9 | 1 | 3 | 1 | Use of particleboard, MDF, MDO, softwood plywood, hardwood plywood, and solid stock. | | E | C | P |
| 9 | 1 | 3 | 2 | Use of MDF, MDO, close grain hardwood plywood, and solid stock. | | E | C | P |
| 9 | 1 | 3 | 3 | Use of MDF and MDO. | | E | C | P |
| 9 | 2 | | | **EXPOSED INTERIOR** surfaces, except at doors and drawer fronts, requires: | | | | |
| 9 | 2 | 1 | | **TRANSPARENT FINISH** requires: | | | | |
| 9 | 2 | 1 | 1 | LPDL or wood of the manufacturer's choice. | | E | C | P |
| 9 | 2 | 1 | 2 | Wood, the same species as the exposed exterior surface. | | E | C | P |
| 9 | 2 | 1 | 3 | Wood, the same species and cut as the exposed exterior surface, and be: | | E | C | P |
| 9 | 2 | 1 | 3 | 1 | HPVA Grade **C**. | E | C | P |
| 9 | 2 | 1 | 3 | 2 | HPVA Grade **B**. | E | C | P |
| 9 | 2 | 1 | 3 | 3 | HPVA Grade **A**. | E | C | P |
| 9 | 2 | 2 | | **OPAQUE FINISH** permits: | | | | |
| 9 | 2 | 2 | 1 | Use of particleboard, MDF, MDO, softwood plywood, hardwood plywood, and solid stock. | | E | C | P |
| 9 | 2 | 2 | 2 | Use of MDF, MDO, close grain hardwood plywood, and solid stock. | | E | C | P |
| 9 | 2 | 2 | 3 | Use of MDF and MDO. | | E | C | P |
| 9 | 2 | 3 | | At **INSIDE FACE** of door and drawer fronts permits: | | | | |
| 9 | 2 | 3 | 1 | Manufacturers' choice of species. | | E | C | P |
| 9 | 2 | 3 | 2 | HPVA Grade **B** face of the same species and cut as the exposed exterior surface. | | E | C | P |
| 9 | 2 | 3 | 3 | HPVA Grade **A** face of the same species and cut as the exposed exterior surface. | | E | C | P |

Continues next column ▼

### 10.4.5 Material Rules

▲ From previous column

| | | | | | | | | |
|---|---|---|---|---|---|---|---|---|
| 9 | | | | At **WOOD CASEWORK** (continued) | | | | |
| 9 | 3 | | | **SEMI-EXPOSED** surfaces for both transparent and opaque finishes require: | | | | |
| 9 | 3 | 1 | | Solid wood, veneer of manufacturers' choice of species, MDO, MDF, particleboard, or LPDL of the manufacturer's choice of color. | | E | C | P |
| 9 | 3 | 2 | | Solid wood, veneer of minimum HPVA Grade C of manufacturer's choice of species or LPDL of the manufacturer's choice of color. | | E | C | P |
| 9 | 3 | 3 | | Solid wood, veneer of minimum HPVA Grade C of compatible species to the exposed surface. | | E | C | P |
| 9 | 3 | 4 | | **DRAWER BOX** | | | | |
| 9 | 3 | 4 | 1 | **SURFACES** to be: | | | | |
| 9 | 3 | 4 | 1 | 1 | Consistent color or species to be used throughout entire project. | | | |
| 9 | 3 | 4 | 1 | 1 | Solid hardwood, veneer of manufacturers' choice of species, MDO, MDF, or LPDL of the manufacturer's choice of color. | E | C | P |
| 9 | 3 | 4 | 1 | 2 | Solid hardwood, veneer of minimum HPVA Grade C of manufacturer's species choice or LPDL of the manufacturer's color choice. | E | C | P |
| 9 | 3 | 4 | 1 | 3 | Solid hardwood, veneer of minimum HPVA Grade C of compatible species to the exposed surface, and: | E | C | P |
| 9 | 3 | 4 | 1 | 3 | 1 | For **OPAQUE FINISH** shall be prefinished and of solid wood or veneer of manufacturer's choice of species or MDO. | E | C | P |
| 9 | 3 | 4 | 1 | 3 | 2 | For **TRANSPARENT FINISH** shall be prefinished and of solid wood or veneer of manufacturer's choice of species. | E | C | P |
| 9 | 3 | 4 | 2 | **DIVIDERS**: | | | | |
| 9 | 3 | 4 | 2 | 1 | If hardboard, to be tempered, smooth on both sides, and: | | E | C | P |
| 9 | 3 | 4 | 2 | 1 | Matching other drawer box surfaces is only required if so specified. | | E | C | P |
| 9 | 3 | 4 | 2 | 2 | To match other drawer box surfaces. | | E | C | P |

Continues next column ▼

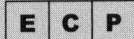

Where the **E**, **C**, or **P** icon is not indicated, the rule applies to all Grades equally

# SECTION 10
## Casework

**compliance requirements** — GENERAL/PRODUCT/INSTALLATION/TEST

### 10.4.5 Material Rules

▲ From previous column

| | | | | | | | | |
|---|---|---|---|---|---|---|---|---|
| 9 | | | | At **WOOD CASEWORK** (continued) | | | | |
| 9 | 3 | | | **SEMI-EXPOSED** (continued) | | | | |
| 9 | 3 | 4 | | **DRAWER BOX** (continued) | | | | |
| 9 | 3 | 4 | 3 | **SIDES, BACK and SUB FRONTS** with: | | | | |
| 9 | 3 | 4 | 3 | 1 | **CORES** of: | | | |
| 9 | 3 | 4 | 3 | 1 | 1 | Solid wood, minimum 7-ply hardwood plywood with no inner core voids of manufacturer's choice of species, MDO, MDF, particleboard. | E | C | P |
| 9 | 3 | 4 | 3 | 1 | 2 | Solid wood, minimum 7-ply hardwood plywood with no inner core voids of manufacturer's choice of species, MDF, particleboard. | E | **C** | P |
| 9 | 3 | 4 | 3 | 1 | 3 | Solid wood or minimum 7-ply hardwood plywood with no inner core voids of manufacturer's choice of species. | E | C | **P** |
| 9 | 3 | 4 | 3 | 2 | **MINIMUM THICKNESS** of: | | | |
| 9 | 3 | 4 | 3 | 2 | 1 | 7/16" (11.1 mm). | **E** | C | P |
| 9 | 3 | 4 | 3 | 2 | 2 | 15/32" (12 mm), except: | E | **C** | P |
| 9 | 3 | 4 | 3 | 2 | 2 | 1 | 5/8" (16 mm) at drawer boxes wider than 30" (762 mm) when constructed of particleboard or MDF core. | E | **C** | **P** |
| 9 | 3 | 4 | 4 | **BOTTOMS** with: | | | | |
| 9 | 3 | 4 | 4 | 1 | **CORES** of: | | | |
| 9 | 3 | 4 | 4 | 1 | 1 | Veneer core plywood, tempered hardboard, or MDF. | **E** | **C** | P |
| 9 | 3 | 4 | 4 | 1 | 2 | Veneer core plywood. | E | C | **P** |
| 9 | 3 | 4 | 4 | 2 | **MINIMUM THICKNESS** of: | | | |
| 9 | 3 | 4 | 4 | 2 | 1 | 13/64" (5.2 mm), except: | | | |
| 9 | 3 | 4 | 4 | 2 | 1 | 1 | 1/4" (6.4 mm) at MDF. | | | |
| 9 | 3 | 4 | 4 | 2 | 2 | 3/8" (9.5 mm) at drawers boxes wider than 30" (762 mm). | E | **C** | **P** |

Continues next column ▼

### 10.4.5 Material Rules

▲ From previous column

| | | | | | | | | |
|---|---|---|---|---|---|---|---|---|
| 10 | | | | At **DECORATIVE LAMINATE CASEWORK**: | | | | |
| 10 | 1 | | | **EXPOSED EXTERIOR** surfaces require: | | | | |
| 10 | 1 | 1 | | LPDL of specified color or pattern. | **E** | C | P |
| 10 | 1 | 2 | | HPDL of specified color or pattern. | E | **C** | **P** |
| 10 | 1 | 3 | | Material, pattern, and color to be as specified, and: | | | |
| 10 | 1 | 3 | 1 | If not specified, to be a non premium priced, standard pattern or color of manufacturer's choice. | | | |
| 10 | 1 | 3 | 2 | Decorative laminate, to be a minimum VGS or VGP HPDL type, and: | | | |
| 10 | 1 | 3 | 2 | 1 | To be of one color or pattern per room, with a maximum of five different colors or patterns per project. | | | |
| 10 | 2 | | | **EXPOSED INTERIOR** surfaces, except at doors and drawer fronts, require: | | | |
| 10 | 2 | 1 | | LPDL of the manufacturer's choice. | **E** | C | P |
| 10 | 2 | 2 | | HPDL or LPDL compatible to exposed exterior surface in color, grain, or pattern. | E | **C** | P |
| 10 | 2 | 3 | | HPDL, the same as the exposed exterior surface. | E | C | **P** |
| 10 | 2 | 4 | | Inside face of solid door and drawer fronts to be: | | | |
| 10 | 2 | 4 | 1 | The same material and thickness as the face. | **E** | **C** | P |
| 10 | 2 | 4 | 2 | The same material, pattern, color, and thickness as the door face. | E | C | **P** |
| 10 | 2 | 5 | | Inside face of framed glass doors to be: | | | |
| 10 | 2 | 5 | 1 | The same material and thickness as the face. | **E** | C | P |
| 10 | 2 | 5 | 2 | The same material, pattern, color, and thickness as the door face. | E | **C** | **P** |
| 10 | 3 | | | **SEMI-EXPOSED** surfaces require: | | | |
| 10 | 3 | 1 | | LPDL or HPDL of the manufacturer's choice of color. | | | |
| 10 | 3 | 2 | | **DRAWER BOX**: | | | |
| 10 | 3 | 2 | 1 | **SURFACES** to be: | | | |
| 10 | 3 | 2 | 1 | 1 | Consistent color to be used throughout entire project. | | | |
| 10 | 3 | 2 | 1 | 2 | MDO, HPDL or LPDL of the manufacturer's color choice. | **E** | C | P |
| 10 | 3 | 2 | 1 | 3 | HPDL or LPDL of the manufacturer's color choice. | E | **C** | P |
| 10 | 3 | 2 | 1 | 4 | HPDL or LPDL matching the color of other semi-exposed surfaces. | E | C | **P** |
| 10 | 3 | 2 | 1 | 5 | Allows vinyl overlay at drawer bottoms if matched in color to other drawer surfaces. | | | |

Continues next column ▼

# SECTION 10
## Casework

**GENERAL / PRODUCT / INSTALLATION / TEST**

*Where the E, C, or P icon is not indicated, the rule applies to all Grades equally* — E | C | P

**compliance requirements**

### 10.4.5 Material Rules
▲ From previous column

| | | | | | | | | E | C | P |
|---|---|---|---|---|---|---|---|---|---|---|
| 10 | | | | | At **DECORATIVE LAMINATE CASEWORK** (continued) | | | | | |
| 10 | 3 | | | | **SEMI-EXPOSED** surfaces (continued) | | | | | |
| 10 | 3 | 2 | | | **DRAWER BOX** (continued) | | | | | |
| 10 | 3 | 2 | 2 | | **DIVIDERS:** | | | | | |
| 10 | 3 | 2 | 2 | 1 | If hardboard, be tempered, smooth on both sides, and: | | | E | C | P |
| 10 | 3 | 2 | 2 | 1 | 1 | Matching other drawer box surfaces is only required if so specified. | | E | C | P |
| 10 | 3 | 2 | 2 | 2 | Match other drawer box surfaces. | | | E | C | P |
| 10 | 3 | 2 | 3 | | **SIDES, BACK and SUB FRONTS** with: | | | | | |
| 10 | 3 | 2 | 3 | 1 | **CORES** of: | | | | | |
| 10 | 3 | 2 | 3 | 1 | 1 | Minimum 7-ply hardwood plywood with no inner core voids of manufacturer's choice of species, MDO, MDF, particleboard. | | E | C | P |
| 10 | 3 | 2 | 3 | 1 | 2 | Minimum 7-ply hardwood plywood with no inner core voids of manufacturer's choice of species, MDF, particleboard. | | E | C | P |
| 10 | 3 | 2 | 3 | 1 | 3 | Minimum 7-ply hardwood plywood with no inner core voids of manufacturer's choice of species. | | E | C | P |
| 10 | 3 | 2 | 3 | | **MINIMUM THICKNESS** of: | | | | | |
| 10 | 3 | 2 | 3 | 1 | 7/16" (11.1 mm). | | | E | C | P |
| 10 | 3 | 2 | 3 | 2 | 15/32" (12 mm), except: | | | E | C | P |
| 10 | 3 | 2 | 3 | 1 | 1 | 5/8" (16 mm) at drawer boxes wider than 30" (762 mm) when constructed of particleboard or MDF core. | | E | C | P |
| 10 | 3 | 2 | 4 | | **BOTTOMS** with: | | | | | |
| 10 | 3 | 2 | 4 | 1 | **CORES** of: | | | | | |
| 10 | 3 | 2 | 4 | 1 | 1 | Veneer core plywood, tempered hardboard, or MDF. | | E | C | P |
| 10 | 3 | 2 | 4 | 1 | 2 | Veneer core plywood. | | E | C | P |
| 10 | 3 | 2 | 4 | 2 | **MINIMUM THICKNESS** of: | | | | | |
| 10 | 3 | 2 | 4 | 2 | 1 | 13/64" (5.2 mm), except: | | | E | C | P |
| 10 | 3 | 2 | 4 | 2 | 1 | 1/4" (6.4 mm) at MDF. | | | E | C | P |
| 10 | 3 | 2 | 4 | 2 | 2 | 3/8" (9.5 mm) at drawers boxes wider than 30" (762 mm) | | E | C | P |

Continues next column ▼

### 10.4.5 Material Rules
▲ From previous column

| | | | | | | E | C | P |
|---|---|---|---|---|---|---|---|---|
| 11 | | | | | At **SOLID PHENOLIC CASEWORK** (Only applicable to Custom and Premium Grade): | | | |
| 11 | 1 | | | | **EXPOSED EXTERIOR** surfaces require: | | | |
| 11 | 1 | 1 | | | Material, pattern, and color to be as specified, and: | | | |
| 11 | 1 | 1 | 1 | | If not specified, to be a non premium priced, standard pattern, minimum 3/8" (9.5 mm) thick at the manufacturer's choice. | | | |
| 11 | 1 | 1 | 2 | | To be of one color per room, with a maximum of five different colors per project. | | | |
| 11 | 2 | | | | **EXPOSED INTERIOR** surfaces shall be the same as the exposed exterior surface. | | | |
| 11 | 3 | | | | **SEMI-EXPOSED** surfaces, including drawer boxes, require manufacturers' choice color, and: | | | |
| 11 | 3 | 1 | | | **DRAWER** sides, back, and sub fronts, a minimum thickness of 1/2" (12.7 mm). | | | |
| 11 | 3 | 2 | | | Drawer bottoms shall be a minimum of 1/4" (6.3 mm). | | | |

# SECTION 10
## Casework

**GENERAL / PRODUCT / INSTALLATION / TEST**

[ECP] Where the **E**, **C**, or **P** icon is not indicated, the rule applies to all Grades equally

## compliance requirements

### 10.4.6 Machining Rules

| | | | | | E | C | P |
|---|---|---|---|---|---|---|---|
| 1 | | | Of **EXPOSED** and **SEMI-EXPOSED** surfaces shall comply with: | | | | |
| 1 | 1 | | **SMOOTHNESS** requirements (see Item 5.1 in Tests) for: | | | | |
| 1 | 1 | 1 | **SHARP EDGES** to be eased with fine abrasive. | | E | C | P |
| 1 | 1 | 2 | **TOP FLAT** wood surfaces; those that can be sanded with a drum or wide belt sander: | | | | |
| 1 | 1 | 2 | 1 | Minimum 15 KCPI or 100 grit sanding. | E | C | P |
| 1 | 1 | 2 | 2 | 120 grit sanding. | E | C | P |
| 1 | 1 | 2 | 3 | 150 grit sanding. | E | C | P |
| 1 | 1 | 3 | **PROFILED** and shaped wood surfaces: | | | | |
| 1 | 1 | 3 | 1 | Minimum 15 KCPI or 100 grit sanding. | E | C | P |
| 1 | 1 | 3 | 2 | Minimum 20 KCPI or 120 grit sanding. | E | C | P |
| 1 | 1 | 3 | 3 | 120 grit sanding. | E | C | P |
| 1 | 1 | 4 | **TURNED** wood surfaces: | | | | |
| 1 | 1 | 4 | 1 | Minimum 15 KCPI or 100 grit sanding. | E | C | P |
| 1 | 1 | 4 | 2 | 120 grit sanding. | E | C | P |
| 1 | 1 | 4 | 3 | 180 grit sanding. | E | C | P |
| 1 | 1 | 5 | **CROSS SANDING**, excluding turned surfaces: | | | | |
| 1 | 1 | 5 | 1 | Is not a defect. | E | C | P |
| 1 | 1 | 5 | 2 | Is not permitted. | E | C | P |
| 1 | 1 | 6 | **TEAR OUTS**, **KNIFE NICKS**, or **HIT OR MISS** machining is not permitted. | | | | |
| 1 | 1 | 7 | **KNIFE MARKS** are not to be permitted where sanding is required. | | | | |
| 1 | 1 | 8 | **GLUE** or **FILLER**, if used, to be inconspicuous and match the adjacent surface for smoothness. | | | | |
| 1 | 2 | | **HPDL**, **PVC**, and **PREFINISHED WOOD** edges shall be machined flush and filed, sanded, or buffed to remove machine marks and sharp edges, and: | | | | |
| 1 | 2 | 1 | **OVERLAP** (See Test F illustrations in TESTS) such as shall not exceed: | | | | |
| 1 | 2 | 1 | 1 | 0.005" (0.13 mm) for a maximum length of 2" (50.8 mm) in any 12" (305 mm) run. | E | C | P |
| 1 | 2 | 1 | 2 | 0.005" (0.13 mm) for a maximum length of 1" (25.4 mm) in any 24" (610 mm) run. | E | C | P |
| 1 | 2 | 1 | 3 | 0.003" (0.08 mm) for a maximum length of 1" (25.4 mm) in any 48" (1220 mm) run. | E | C | P |

Continues next column ▼

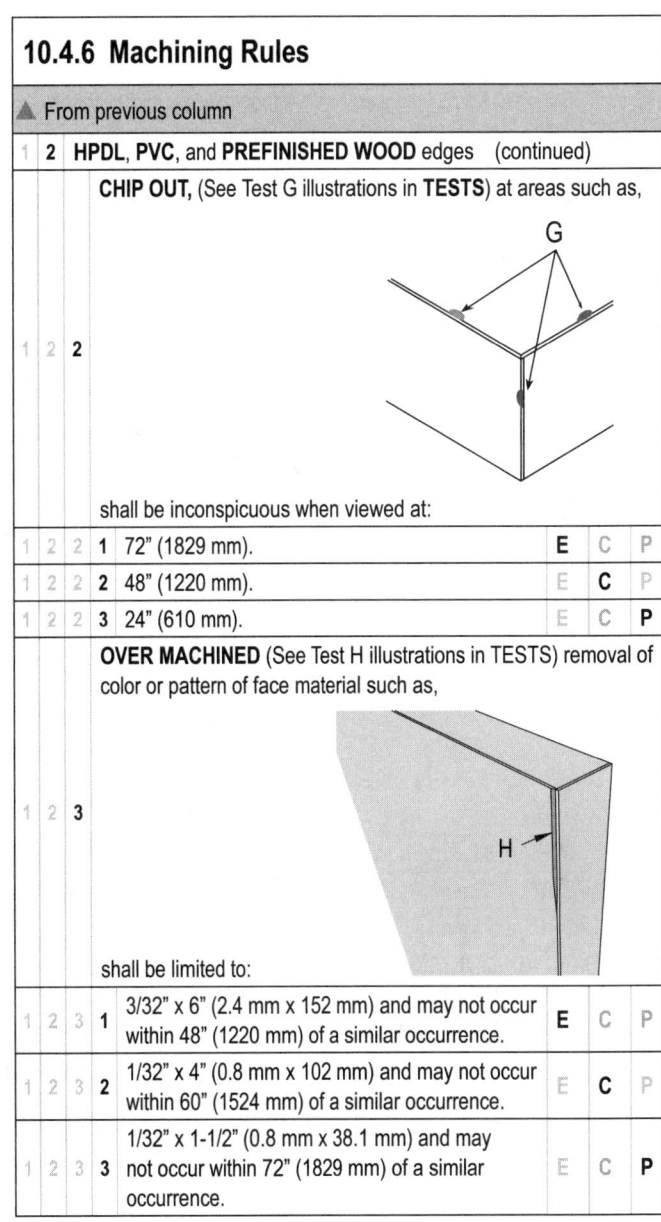

### 10.4.6 Machining Rules

▲ From previous column

| | | | | | E | C | P |
|---|---|---|---|---|---|---|---|
| 1 | 2 | | **HPDL**, **PVC**, and **PREFINISHED WOOD** edges (continued) | | | | |
| 1 | 2 | 2 | **CHIP OUT**, (See Test G illustrations in **TESTS**) at areas such as, shall be inconspicuous when viewed at: | | | | |
| 1 | 2 | 2 | 1 | 72" (1829 mm). | E | C | P |
| 1 | 2 | 2 | 2 | 48" (1220 mm). | E | C | P |
| 1 | 2 | 2 | 3 | 24" (610 mm). | E | C | P |
| 1 | 2 | 3 | **OVER MACHINED** (See Test H illustrations in **TESTS**) removal of color or pattern of face material such as, shall be limited to: | | | | |
| 1 | 2 | 3 | 1 | 3/32" x 6" (2.4 mm x 152 mm) and may not occur within 48" (1220 mm) of a similar occurrence. | E | C | P |
| 1 | 2 | 3 | 2 | 1/32" x 4" (0.8 mm x 102 mm) and may not occur within 60" (1524 mm) of a similar occurrence. | E | C | P |
| 1 | 2 | 3 | 3 | 1/32" x 1-1/2" (0.8 mm x 38.1 mm) and may not occur within 72" (1829 mm) of a similar occurrence. | E | C | P |

# SECTION 10
## Casework

**GENERAL / PRODUCT / INSTALLATION / TEST**

**compliance requirements**

Where the **E**, **C**, or **P** icon is not indicated, the rule applies to all Grades equally

### 10.4.7 Assembly Rules

| 2 | | | | | |
|---|---|---|---|---|---|
| 1 | | | **THESE STANDARDS** do not establish Grade rules for joint flushness and or gap tolerances for woodwork products installed in a non climate controlled environment: however: | | |
| 1 | 1 | | Prior to installation, the flushness and/or gap tolerances of woodwork products intended for non climate controlled environments shall meet the test requirements herein. | | |
| 2 | | | **JOINTS** at assembled woodwork shall: | | |
| 2 | 1 | | Be neatly and accurately made. | | |
| 2 | 2 | | Be securely glued, with: | | |
| 2 | 2 | 1 | Adhesive residue removed from exposed and semi-exposed surfaces. | | |
| 2 | 3 | | Require **FLUSHNESS VARIATIONS** at exposed and semi-exposed surfaces (see Test D illustrations in Tests) when mitered or butted such as, | | |

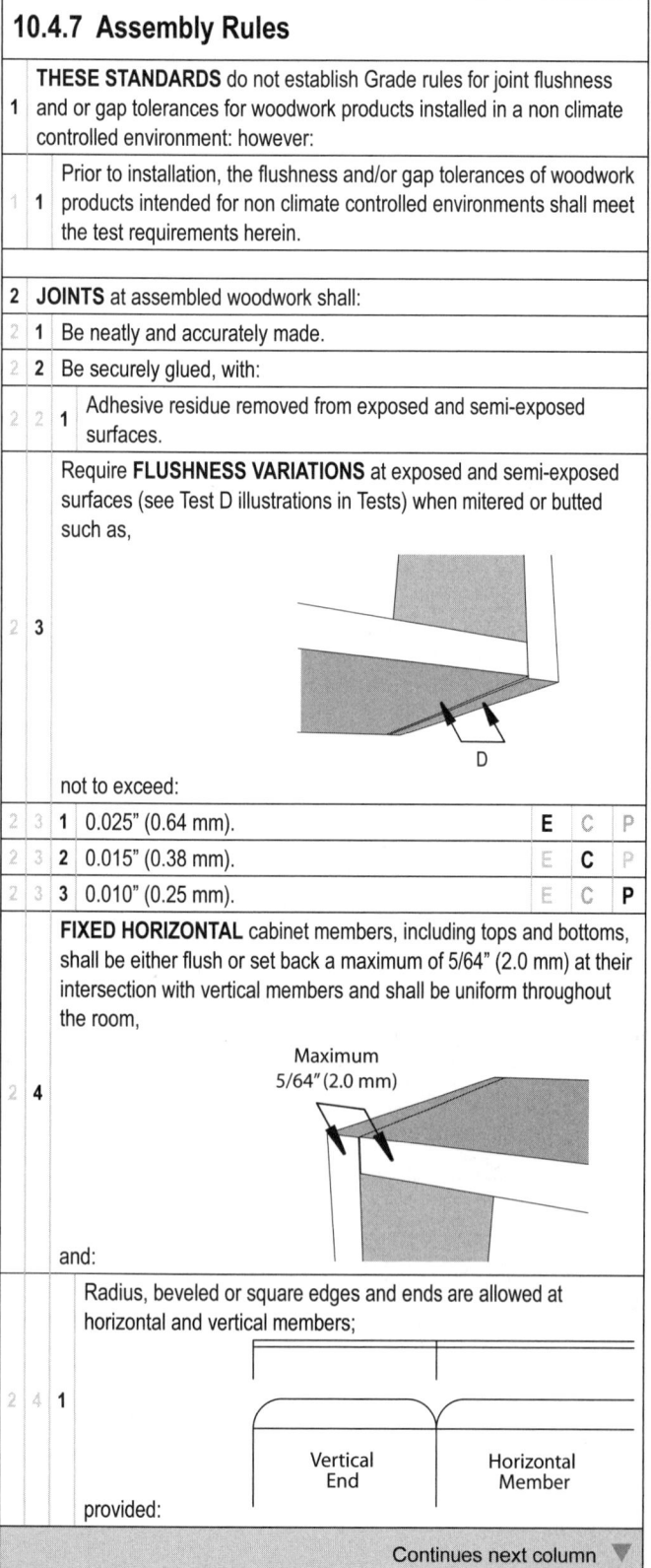

not to exceed:

| 2 | 3 | 1 | 0.025" (0.64 mm). | E | C | P |
| 2 | 3 | 2 | 0.015" (0.38 mm). | E | C | P |
| 2 | 3 | 3 | 0.010" (0.25 mm). | E | C | P |

| 2 | 4 | | **FIXED HORIZONTAL** cabinet members, including tops and bottoms, shall be either flush or set back a maximum of 5/64" (2.0 mm) at their intersection with vertical members and shall be uniform throughout the room, |

Maximum 5/64" (2.0 mm)

and:

| 2 | 4 | 1 | Radius, beveled or square edges and ends are allowed at horizontal and vertical members; provided: |

Continues next column

### 10.4.7 Assembly Rules

▲ From previous column

| 2 | | | | JOINTS (continued) |
| 2 | 4 | | | **FIXED HORIZONTAL** (continued) |
| | | | | Radius or square edges and ends (continued) |
| 2 | 4 | 4 | 1 | The "V" or gap that is formed where a member with a square end meets a member with a radius |

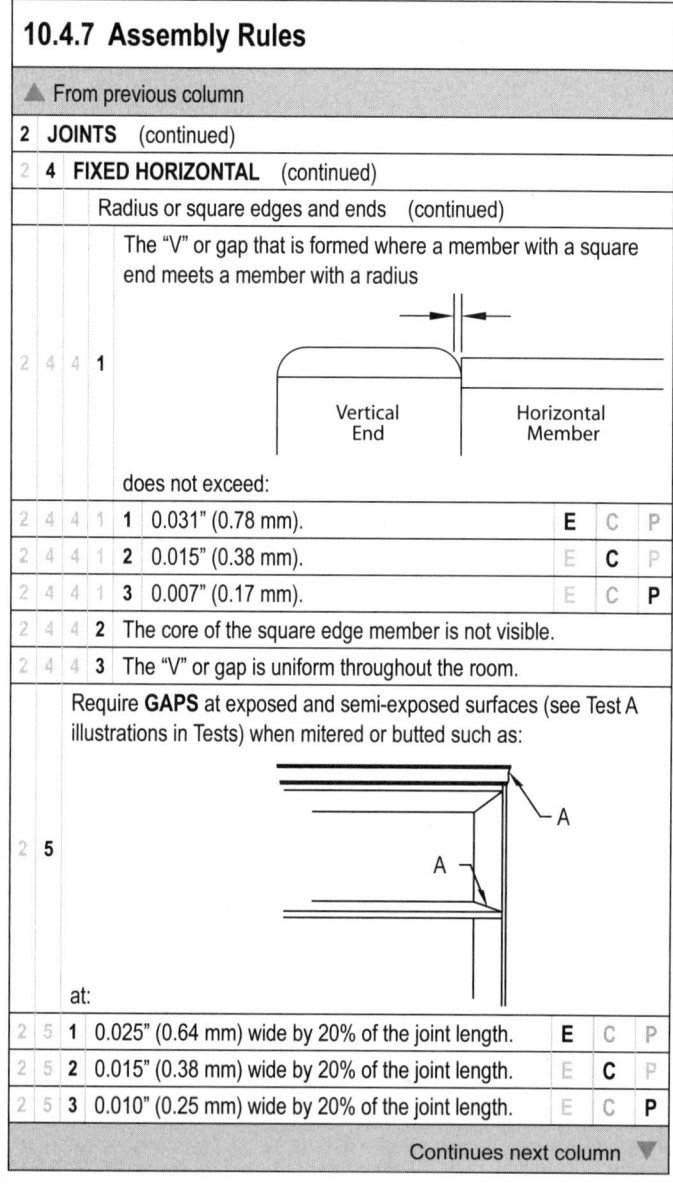

does not exceed:

| 2 | 4 | 4 | 1 | 1 | 0.031" (0.78 mm). | E | C | P |
| 2 | 4 | 4 | 1 | 2 | 0.015" (0.38 mm). | E | C | P |
| 2 | 4 | 4 | 1 | 3 | 0.007" (0.17 mm). | E | C | P |
| 2 | 4 | 4 | 2 | | The core of the square edge member is not visible. | | | |
| 2 | 4 | 4 | 3 | | The "V" or gap is uniform throughout the room. | | | |

| 2 | 5 | | Require **GAPS** at exposed and semi-exposed surfaces (see Test A illustrations in Tests) when mitered or butted such as: |

at:

| 2 | 5 | 1 | 0.025" (0.64 mm) wide by 20% of the joint length. | E | C | P |
| 2 | 5 | 2 | 0.015" (0.38 mm) wide by 20% of the joint length. | E | C | P |
| 2 | 5 | 3 | 0.010" (0.25 mm) wide by 20% of the joint length. | E | C | P |

Continues next column ▼

## SECTION 10
### Casework

**compliance requirements** — GENERAL / PRODUCT / INSTALLATION / TEST

Where the **E**, **C**, or **P** icon is not indicated, the rule applies to all Grades equally

### 10.4.7 Assembly Rules

▲ From previous column

| | | | | | | |
|---|---|---|---|---|---|---|
| 2 | JOINT (continued) | | | | | |
| 2 | 6 | | Require **GAPS** at exposed and semi-exposed surfaces (see Test B illustrations in Tests) at parallel members such as: 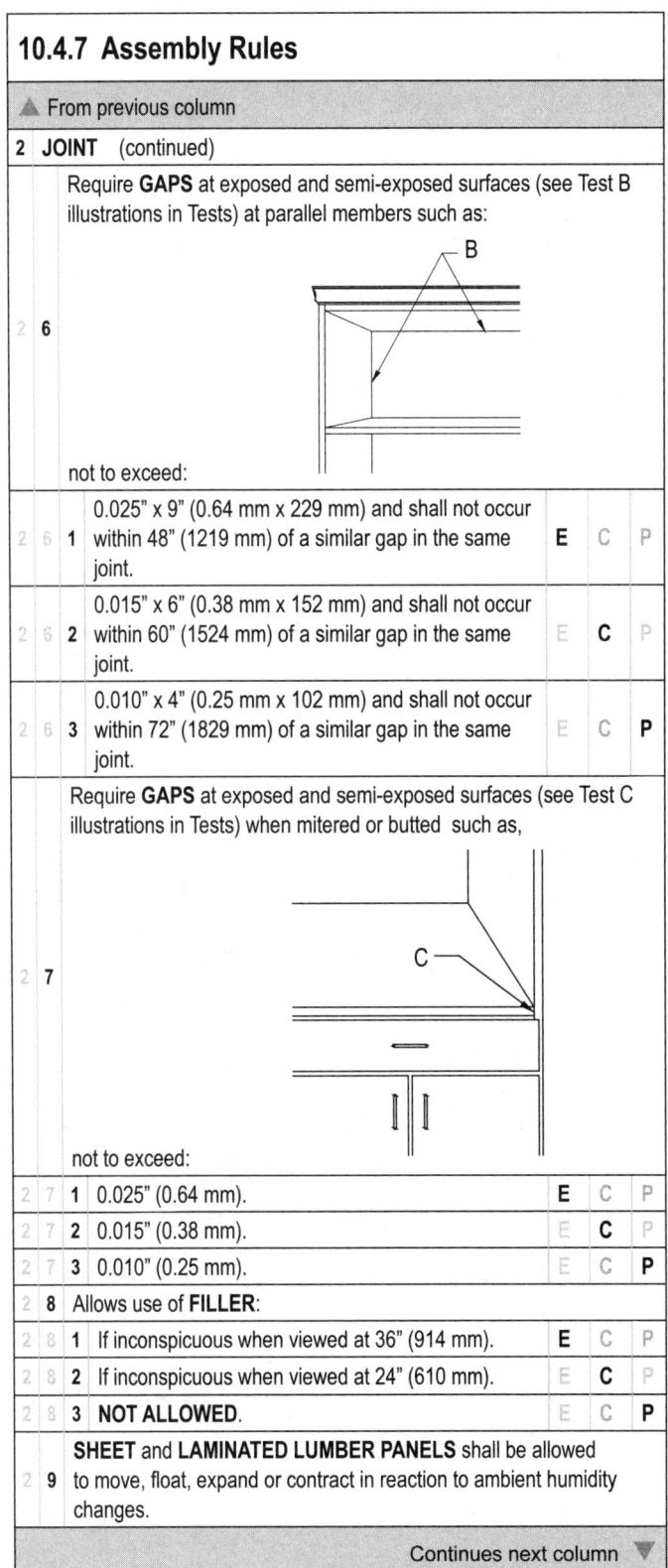 not to exceed: | | | | |
| 2 | 6 | 1 | 0.025" x 9" (0.64 mm x 229 mm) and shall not occur within 48" (1219 mm) of a similar gap in the same joint. | E | C | P |
| 2 | 6 | 2 | 0.015" x 6" (0.38 mm x 152 mm) and shall not occur within 60" (1524 mm) of a similar gap in the same joint. | E | C | |
| 2 | 6 | 3 | 0.010" x 4" (0.25 mm x 102 mm) and shall not occur within 72" (1829 mm) of a similar gap in the same joint. | E | C | P |
| 2 | 7 | | Require **GAPS** at exposed and semi-exposed surfaces (see Test C illustrations in Tests) when mitered or butted such as, not to exceed: | | | | |
| 2 | 7 | 1 | 0.025" (0.64 mm). | E | C | P |
| 2 | 7 | 2 | 0.015" (0.38 mm). | E | C | |
| 2 | 7 | 3 | 0.010" (0.25 mm). | E | C | P |
| 2 | 8 | | Allows use of **FILLER**: | | | |
| 2 | 8 | 1 | If inconspicuous when viewed at 36" (914 mm). | E | C | |
| 2 | 8 | 2 | If inconspicuous when viewed at 24" (610 mm). | E | C | |
| 2 | 8 | 3 | NOT ALLOWED. | E | C | P |
| 2 | 9 | | **SHEET** and **LAMINATED LUMBER PANELS** shall be allowed to move, float, expand or contract in reaction to ambient humidity changes. | | | |

Continues next column ▼

### 10.4.7 Assembly Rules

▲ From previous column

| | | | | | | |
|---|---|---|---|---|---|---|
| 3 | | | Require **FLATNESS** of installed and removable sheet products (see Test E illustrations in Tests) 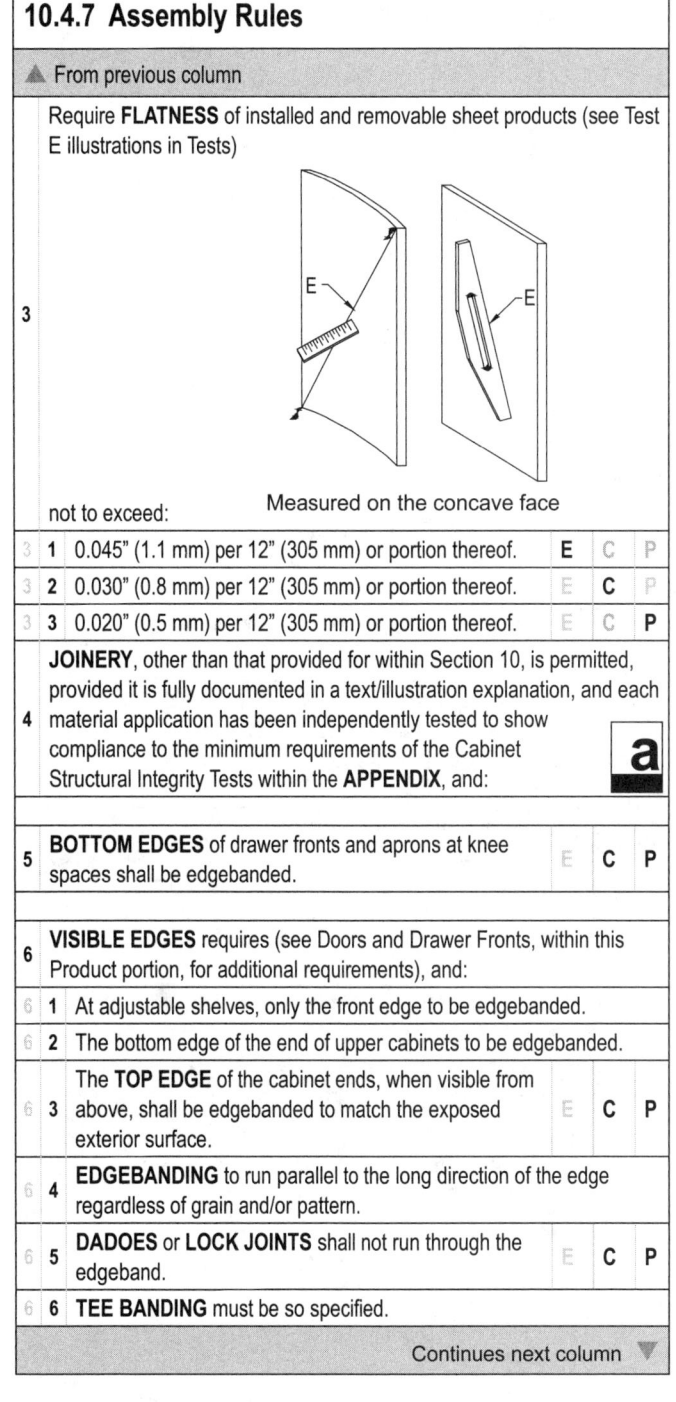 Measured on the concave face not to exceed: | | | |
| 3 | 1 | | 0.045" (1.1 mm) per 12" (305 mm) or portion thereof. | E | C | P |
| 3 | 2 | | 0.030" (0.8 mm) per 12" (305 mm) or portion thereof. | E | C | |
| 3 | 3 | | 0.020" (0.5 mm) per 12" (305 mm) or portion thereof. | E | C | P |
| 4 | | | **JOINERY**, other than that provided for within Section 10, is permitted, provided it is fully documented in a text/illustration explanation, and each material application has been independently tested to show compliance to the minimum requirements of the Cabinet Structural Integrity Tests within the **APPENDIX**, and: | | | a |
| 5 | | | **BOTTOM EDGES** of drawer fronts and aprons at knee spaces shall be edgebanded. | E | C | P |
| 6 | | | **VISIBLE EDGES** requires (see Doors and Drawer Fronts, within this Product portion, for additional requirements), and: | | | |
| 6 | 1 | | At adjustable shelves, only the front edge to be edgebanded. | | | |
| 6 | 2 | | The bottom edge of the end of upper cabinets to be edgebanded. | | | |
| 6 | 3 | | The **TOP EDGE** of the cabinet ends, when visible from above, shall be edgebanded to match the exposed exterior surface. | E | C | P |
| 6 | 4 | | **EDGEBANDING** to run parallel to the long direction of the edge regardless of grain and/or pattern. | | | |
| 6 | 5 | | **DADOES** or **LOCK JOINTS** shall not run through the edgeband. | E | C | P |
| 6 | 6 | | **TEE BANDING** must be so specified. | | | |

Continues next column ▼

Architectural Woodwork Standards

# SECTION 10
## Casework

GENERAL/**PRODUCT**/INSTALLATION/TEST

**compliance requirements**

Where the **E**, **C**, or **P** icon is not indicated, the rule applies to all Grades equally — **E** | **C** | **P**

### 10.4.7 Assembly Rules

▲ From previous column

| 7 | | | DRAWERS (including trays and sliding bins) requires: | | | |
|---|---|---|---|---|---|---|
| 7 | 1 | | Components to be of the same material and color for the entire project, and: | | | |
| 7 | 1 | 1 | Bottoms may be vinyl if matching in color. | | | |
| 7 | 2 | | SIDES to be manufacturer's choice, and shall be: | | | |
| 7 | 2 | 1 | Nailed to sub fronts and backs. | E | C | P |
| 7 | 2 | 2 | Rabbeted to the fronts or sub fronts and backs. | E | C | P |
| 7 | 2 | 3 | Miter folded sides, back, front, and bottom, with: | E | C | P |
| 7 | 2 | 3 | 1 | Core of particleboard or medium density fiberboard. | | | |
| 7 | 2 | 3 | 2 | Side directional grain or pattern running horizontal. | | | |
| 7 | 2 | 4 | Multiple dovetailed, which is limited to solid wood or minimum 7-ply hardwood veneer core plywood with exposed core, without additional mechanical fasteners. | E | C | P |
| 7 | 2 | 5 | Doweled or Dowel screwed. | E | C | P |
| 7 | 2 | 6 | Biscuit splined. | E | C | P |
| 7 | 2 | 7 | Lock jointed and nailed. | E | C | P |
| 7 | 3 | | At FLUSH OVERLAY construction without sub front, sides to be blind dovetail dadoed to the front. | | | |
| 7 | 4 | | Minimum of two mechanical fasteners (dowels, biscuit splines, nails, screws) per joint, and: | | | |
| 7 | 4 | 1 | A maximum of 3" (76 mm) on center for biscuit splines, nails, or screws. | | | |
| 7 | 4 | 2 | A maximum of 1-1/4" (32 mm) on center for joints up to 4" (102 mm) in length and 2-1/2" (64 mm) on center for joints over 4" (102 mm) in length for dowels. | | | |
| 7 | 5 | | JOINTS to be securely glued. | | | |
| 7 | 6 | | To be PROPERLY FITTED to the cabinet without excessive play, and: | | | |
| 7 | 6 | 1 | Fit front to back, less a maximum of 2" (50.8 mm) of interior cabinet depth. | | | |
| 7 | 6 | 2 | Fill opening top to bottom to the greatest extent possible, while remaining fully functional. | | | |

Continues next column ▼

### 10.4.7 Assembly Rules

▲ From previous column

| 7 | | | DRAWERS (continued) |
|---|---|---|---|
| 7 | 7 | | SLIDES to operate smoothly. |
| 7 | 8 | | CLOSING STOPS to be provided at the rear of both drawer sides, unless such is built into the slides to prevent the drawer front from impacting the cabinet body. |
| 7 | 9 | | SPRING LOADED TIP DOWN STOPS to be provided (design permitting) to prevent the drawer from pulling out of the cabinet, unless such is built into the drawer slides. |
| 7 | 10 | | FILE DRAWERS require: |
| 7 | 10 | 1 | Full extension slides. |
| 7 | 10 | 2 | CLEAR INSIDE HEIGHT sufficient for hanging file folder tabs. |
| 7 | 10 | 3 | File direction of manufacturer's choice. |
| 7 | 10 | 4 | System stand or rails shall be at option of the manufacturer, and: |
| 7 | 10 | 4 | 1 | At legal sized drawers they shall accommodate both legal and letter sized files. |
| 7 | 11 | | LOCKS to be furnished only where shown on contract documents, unless specifications denote specific location requirements, and: |
| 7 | 11 | 1 | They shall withstand a minimum of 50 lb (22.7 kg) pull force in the locked position, or: |
| 7 | 11 | 1 | 1 | Strikes are required. |
| 7 | 11 | 2 | Strikes are required at spring loaded latches. |
| 7 | 11 | 3 | Security or dust panels are required at locked banks of drawers when each drawer is keyed differently. |
| 7 | 12 | | TRAYS, BINS and similar items shall be similarly constructed. |
| 7 | 13 | | FRONTS and FALSE FRONTS shall: |
| 7 | 13 | 1 | Match the cabinet doors, except: |
| 7 | 13 | 1 | 1 | Where the drawer and false fronts are too small to allow a match. |
| 7 | 13 | 2 | Be securely attached to drawer sub front with pan/binder head, countersunk flathead, or ovalhead screws with a minimum of two screws at each end a maximum of 1-1/2" (38.1 mm) from the inside corners of the drawer box and a maximum of 12" (305 mm) on center, and: |
| 7 | 13 | 2 | 1 | Fasteners used to attach drawer pulls or knobs through both the sub front and drawer front shall be considered a fastener. |
| 7 | 13 | 3 | At false fronts, be securely attached to the cabinet body. |

Continues next column ▼

# SECTION 10
## Casework

**compliance requirements** — GENERAL / **PRODUCT** / INSTALLATION / TEST

Where the **E**, **C**, or **P** icon is not indicated, the rule applies to all Grades equally.

### 10.4.7 Assembly Rules

*From previous column*

| | | | | Rule | E | C | P |
|---|---|---|---|---|---|---|---|
| 7 | | | | **DRAWERS** (continued) | | | |
| 7 | 14 | | | **BOTTOMS**, excluding integral miter folded, shall: | | | |
| 7 | 14 | 1 | | Be plowed into sides, fronts, or sub fronts, and: | | | |
| 7 | 14 | 1 | 1 | Be securely glued or glue blocked to form a rigid unit. | | | |
| 7 | 14 | 1 | 2 | If 1/2" (12.7 mm) or greater in thickness, they are not required to be plowed into drawer fronts or sub fronts with the use of integral metal drawer side/slide systems. | | | |
| 7 | 14 | 1 | 3 | Plow to be a minimum of 3/8" (9.5 mm) from the bottom of the drawer sides, front, or sub front. | | | |
| 7 | 14 | 2 | | Be securely attached to the drawer box back, either by plow or if run through, by mechanical fastening (maximum of 4" [102 mm] on center). | E | C | P |
| 7 | 14 | 3 | | If surface applied, be mechanically fastened (maximum of 4" [102 mm] on center) to the entire box. | E | C | P |
| 8 | | | | **DOORS** requires: | | | |
| 8 | 1 | | | **FLUSH OVERLAY** is the default for either **FRAMELESS** or **FACE FRAME** casework, except: | | | |
| 8 | 1 | 1 | | At **EXPOSED KNUCKLE HINGES**, defaulting to **REVEAL OVERLAY** is at the option of the manufacturer, and: | | | |
| 8 | 1 | 1 | 1 | If reveal overlay, the reveal shall be determined by the hinge overlay. | | | |
| 8 | 2 | | | At **BACK BEVELED DOORS**, edgebanding: | | | |
| 8 | 2 | 1 | | Is not required. | E | C | P |
| 8 | 2 | 2 | | Is required. | E | C | P |
| 8 | 3 | | | **CORE THICKNESS** to be a minimum of 11/16" (17.5 mm). | | | |
| 8 | 4 | | | **MAXIMUM CABINET DOOR SIZE** shall be 24" (610 mm) in width and 84" (2134 mm) in height, and: | | | |
| 8 | 4 | 1 | | Larger doors are more susceptible to warp, which shall not be the responsibility of the manufacturer/installer. | | | |
| 8 | 5 | | | **DOOR THICKNESS** of 1-3/8" (34.9 mm) or greater be governed by Section 9. | | | |
| 8 | 6 | | | **STOP SILENCERS** to be installed at the top and bottom of hinged cabinet doors (on the closing edge) to properly align the door and silence its closing. | E | C | P |

*Continues next column*

### 10.4.7 Assembly Rules

*From previous column*

| | | | | Rule | E | C | P |
|---|---|---|---|---|---|---|---|
| 8 | | | | **DOORS** requires (continued) | | | |
| 8 | 7 | | | **CORE** to be of an approved particleboard or medium density fiberboard, and: | | | |
| 8 | 7 | 1 | | Veneer, OSB, or lumber cores are not guaranteed against warping, telegraphing, or delamination. | | | |
| 8 | 8 | | | **LOCKS** to be furnished ONLY where shown on cabinet elevations of contract documents, unless specifications denote specific location requirements, and: | | | |
| 8 | 8 | 1 | | Shall withstand a minimum of 50 lb (22.7 kg) pull force in the locked position, or: | | | |
| 8 | 8 | 1 | 1 | Strikes are required. | | | |
| 8 | 8 | 2 | | Strikes are required at spring loaded latches. | | | |
| 8 | 9 | | | **GLASS** shall be clear laminated or tempered. | | | |
| 8 | 9 | 1 | | Stops shall: | | | |
| 8 | 9 | 1 | 1 | Be continuous, removable, on inside only, and: Glass clips are permitted, with a minimum of 6 per door. | | | |
| 8 | 9 | 1 | 2 | For opaque finish, be synthetic or solid stock of the manufacturer's choice. | | | |
| 8 | 9 | 1 | 3 | For transparent finish, be synthetic or solid stock of compatible species to adjacent surface and compatible color to the Exposed Interior surface. | | | |
| 8 | 9 | 1 | 4 | For decorative laminate, be synthetic or solid stock and compatible color to Interior Exposed surface. | | | |
| 8 | 9 | 1 | 5 | Exposed rabbet shall be compatible color painted or finished to the Interior Exposed surface. | | | |
| 8 | 10 | | | When **HINGED**: | | | |
| 8 | 10 | 1 | | Doors shall stop, as applicable, against the cabinet body at the bottom (except at handicapped units), sides, and top stretcher; however: | | | |
| 8 | 10 | 1 | 1 | Flush inset doors, a positive stop or hardware member acting as such is permitted, and: | | | |
| 8 | 10 | 1 | 1 | Stops shall be provided at both sides of the door opening. | E | C | P |
| 8 | 10 | 1 | 2 | Paired doors below a drawer require a rail, stretcher, or partition (full or partial) be provided. | E | C | P |

*Continues next column*

# SECTION 10
## Casework

GENERAL / **PRODUCT** / INSTALLATION / TEST

**compliance requirements**

Where the **E**, **C**, or **P** icon is not indicated, the rule applies to all Grades equally — **E | C | P**

### 10.4.7 Assembly Rules

▲ From previous column

| 8 | | | | | DOORS (continued) | | | |
|---|---|---|---|---|---|---|---|---|
| 8 | 10 | | | | When **HINGED** (continued) | | | |
| 8 | 10 | 2 | | | Hinges shall be installed by the manufacturer, and shall: | | | |
| 8 | 10 | 2 | 1 | | Operate properly without binding. | | | |
| 8 | 10 | 2 | 2 | | Align horizontally, when adjacent and exposed. | | | |
| 8 | 10 | 2 | 3 | | Be self closing or provided with a catch. | E | C | P |
| 8 | 10 | 2 | 4 | | At **Grade I** hinges, doors: | | | |
| 8 | 10 | 2 | 4 | 1 | Under 48" (1219 mm) in height shall have a minimum of two hinges. | | | |
| 8 | 10 | 2 | 4 | 2 | 48" (1219 mm) to 84" (2134 mm) height shall have a minimum of three hinges. | | | |
| 8 | 10 | 2 | 4 | 3 | Over 84" (2134 mm) in height shall have a minimum of four hinges. | | | |
| 8 | 10 | 2 | 5 | | At **Grade II** hinges, doors: | | | |
| 8 | 10 | 2 | 5 | 1 | Under 40" (1016 mm) in height shall have a minimum of two hinges. | | | |
| 8 | 10 | 2 | 5 | 2 | 40" (1016 mm) to 60" (1524 mm) in height shall have a minimum of three hinges. | | | |
| 8 | 10 | 2 | 5 | 3 | 60" (1524 mm) to 80" (2032 mm) in height shall have a minimum of four hinges. | | | |
| 8 | 10 | 2 | 5 | 4 | Over 80" (2031 mm) in height shall have a minimum of five hinges and an additional hinge for every 18" (457 mm) of additional height. | | | |
| 8 | 10 | 2 | 6 | | At **FLUSH OVERLAY** construction, wrap around hinges shall be let into the edge of the door to maintain proper gap tolerance, and: | | | |
| 8 | 10 | 2 | 6 | 1 | Exposed door edges resulting from the notching for hinges are not required to be finished. | E | C | P |
| 8 | 10 | 2 | 6 | 2 | Exposed door edges resulting from the notching for hinges are required to be painted or stained to match. | E | C | P |

Continues next column ▼

### 10.4.7 Assembly Rules

▲ From previous column

| 8 | | | | DOORS requires (continued) | | | |
|---|---|---|---|---|---|---|---|
| 8 | 10 | | | When **HINGED** (continued) | | | |
| 8 | 10 | 2 | | Hinges shall be installed (continued) | | | |
| 8 | 10 | 2 | 7 | **REVEAL OVERLAY** construction, wrap around hinges are not required to be let into the edge of the door, and: | | | |
| 8 | 10 | 2 | 7 | 1 | The reveal shall be determined by the hinge overlay. | | | |
| 8 | 10 | 2 | 8 | **CONCEALED CUP HINGE** assembly installation, when required to be installed with screws, requires dowel/euro screws or screws recommended by the manufacturer. | | | |
| 8 | 10 | 3 | | **LOCKING PAIRS**: | | | |
| 8 | 10 | 3 | 1 | Shall be equipped with an elbow catch/latch and a stop block on the inactive leaf, and: | | | |
| 8 | 10 | 3 | 1 | 1 | Stop block shall be adequate to prevent the latch of the elbow catch/latch from being defeated by applying vertical pressure on the door. | | | |
| 8 | 10 | 3 | 2 | Elbow catch/latch is required on the inactive leaf at the fixed shelf on cabinets with full height doors and a fixed mid height shelf. | | | |
| 8 | 10 | 3 | 3 | Slide bolt or spring actuated chain bolt with shelf depth adjusted accordingly is required on cabinets with full height doors (without fixed shelf). | E | C | P |

Continues next column ▼

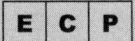

Where the **E**, **C**, or **P** icon is not indicated, the rule applies to all Grades equally

# SECTION 10
## Casework

## compliance requirements

GENERAL/**PRODUCT**/INSTALLATION/TEST

### 10.4.7 Assembly Rules

▲ From previous column

| 8 | | | | | DOORS requires (continued) | | | |
|---|---|---|---|---|---|---|---|---|
| 8 | 11 | | | | When **STILE** and **RAIL CONSTRUCTION** (see the Hinged and Sliding sub headings for additional requirements as applicable): | | | |
| 8 | 11 | 1 | | | **STILES** and **RAILS**: | | | |
| 8 | 11 | 1 | 1 | | Molded profile (sticking) shall be the manufacturer's choice, unless specified otherwise. | | | |
| 8 | 11 | 1 | 2 | | Solid lumber shall be a minimum of 2-1/2" (63.5 mm) in width. | | | |
| 8 | 11 | 1 | 3 | | Shall be a minimum of 3/4" (19 mm) in thickness, and: | | | |
| 8 | 11 | 1 | 3 | 1 | To a tolerance of +/- 1/32" (0.8 mm) of specified thickness. | | | |
| 8 | 11 | 1 | 4 | | Veneered or overlaid construction shall be MDF or particleboard core a minimum of 3-1/2" (88.9 mm) in width, and: | | | |
| 8 | 11 | 1 | 4 | 1 | With approval, framed glass doors may be manufactured from flush panels without stile and rail considerations, provided all other door requirements are met, and: | | | |
| 8 | 11 | 1 | 4 | 1 | All exposed edges shall be edgebanded or finished to match adjacent surfaces. | | | |
| 8 | 11 | 1 | 5 | | Doors over 60" (1524 mm) in height shall have an intermediate rail. | | | |
| 8 | 11 | 1 | 6 | | Stiles shall run the full height of the door, and: | | | |
| 8 | 11 | 1 | 6 | 1 | Rails, including top, cross, and bottom shall run between stiles. | E | C | P |
| 8 | 11 | 1 | 6 | 2 | Mullions shall run between rails. | E | C | P |
| 8 | 11 | 1 | 7 | | Grain or directional pattern shall run vertically on stiles and horizontally on rails. | | | |
| 8 | 11 | 1 | 8 | | Clearance shall be a minimum of 3/8" (9.5 mm) between hardware machining and glass cutout. | | | |
| 8 | 11 | 1 | 9 | | Joinery shall be: | | | |
| 8 | 11 | 1 | 9 | 1 | The manufacturer's choice. | E | C | P |
| 8 | 11 | 1 | 9 | 2 | Mating male/female sticking glued under pressure. | E | C | P |
| 8 | 11 | 1 | 9 | 3 | Mortise and tenon, dowels or loose tenon glued under pressure. | E | C | P |
| 8 | 11 | 2 | | | **PANEL**: | | | |
| 8 | 11 | 2 | 1 | | Direction of grain or pattern shall be the manufacturer's choice. | E | C | P |
| 8 | 11 | 2 | 2 | | Direction of grain or pattern shall run vertically, and: | E | C | P |
| 8 | 11 | 2 | 2 | 1 | Adjacent door panels for transparent finish shall have a pleasing match for color and grain. | E | C | P |
| 8 | 11 | 2 | 3 | | Core shall be covered by veneer, overlay, or rim banding. | | | |

Continues next column ▼

### 10.4.7 Assembly Rules

▲ From previous column

| 8 | | | | | DOORS requires (continued) | | | |
|---|---|---|---|---|---|---|---|---|
| 8 | 11 | | | | When **STILE** and **RAIL CONSTRUCTION** (continued) | | | |
| 8 | 11 | 2 | | | **PANEL** (continued) | | | |
| 8 | 11 | 2 | 4 | | When flat shall be a minimum of 1/4" (6.4 mm) in thickness, and: | | | |
| 8 | 11 | 2 | 4 | 1 | Edge glued solid lumber is permitted if at least 1/2" (12.7 mm) in thickness and width across grain is 13-3/4" (350 mm) or less. | E | C | P |
| 8 | 11 | 2 | 4 | 2 | Solid lumber is not permitted. | E | C | P |
| 8 | 11 | 2 | 5 | | When raised shall be a minimum of 1/2" (12.7 mm) in thickness, and: | | | |
| 8 | 11 | 2 | 5 | 1 | Edge glued solid lumber is permitted for panels less than 13-3/4" (350 mm) in width across grain. | E | C | P |
| 8 | 11 | 2 | 5 | 2 | Solid lumber is not permitted for panels. | E | C | P |
| 8 | 11 | 2 | 5 | 3 | Solid lumber is permitted for rimming panels if mitered and glued under pressure. | | | |
| 8 | 11 | 2 | 6 | | Regardless of retention method, shall have the freedom and room to expand and contract in reaction to ambient humidity changes. | | | |
| 8 | 11 | 2 | 7 | | Applied moldings shall be spot glued and finish nailed. | | | |
| 8 | 12 | | | | When **SLIDING**: | | | |
| 8 | 12 | 1 | | | Thickness to be a minimum of: | | | |
| 8 | 12 | 1 | 1 | | 1/4" (6.4 mm) for doors 24" (610 mm) and under in height. | | | |
| 8 | 12 | 1 | 2 | | 3/4" (19 mm) for doors over 24" (610 mm) in height. | | | |
| 8 | 12 | 2 | | | Vertical edges are considered exposed. | | | |
| 8 | 12 | 3 | | | Top and bottom edges are concealed and not required to be edgebanded or filled. | | | |
| 8 | 12 | 4 | | | Doors more than 1.5 times as tall as they are wide shall be mounted with overhead metal track and roller hanger to prevent tipping and binding. | | | |
| 8 | 12 | 5 | | | At hanging track systems, exposed track is acceptable and door heights of: | | | |
| 8 | 12 | 5 | 1 | | 36" (914 mm) or less shall be equipped with adequate top and/or bottom guides or runs. Sliding doors in excess of 36" (914 mm) in height shall be installed on hardware of a type optional with the manufacturer. | E | C | P |
| 8 | 12 | 5 | 2 | | 34" (864 mm) or less shall be installed on the appropriate fiber or metal track, with top guide. | E | C | P |

Continues next column ▼

# SECTION 10
## Casework

GENERAL/**PRODUCT**/INSTALLATION/TEST

**compliance requirements**

Where the **E**, **C**, or **P** icon is not indicated, the rule applies to all Grades equally | **E** | **C** | **P** |

### 10.4.7 Assembly Rules

▲ From previous column

| | | | | | | | E | C | P |
|---|---|---|---|---|---|---|---|---|---|
| 8 | **DOORS** requires   (continued) | | | | | | | | |
| 8 | 12 | When **SLIDING**   (continued) | | | | | | | |
| 8 | 12 | 5 | At hanging track systems   (continued) | | | | | | |
| 8 | 12 | 5 | 3 | Over 34" (864 mm) shall be installed on either the overhead metal track with nylon roller hangers, or the metal bottom track with sheaves and top guide. | | | E | C | P |
| 8 | 12 | 6 | | At **FACE FRAME CONSTRUCTION**, a continuous vertical filler strip shall be provided in the opening behind the face frame and in front of the rear sliding door. | | | E | C | P |
| 8 | 13 | When **FRAMELESS GLASS**: | | | | | | | |
| 8 | 13 | 1 | Be a minimum of 1/4" (6.4 mm) thick. | | | | | | |
| 8 | 13 | 2 | Be clear tempered glass, with: | | | | | | |
| 8 | 13 | 2 | 1 | Exposed edges ground. | | | E | C | P |
| 8 | 13 | 2 | 2 | Exposed edges flat polished. | | | E | C | P |
| 8 | 13 | 3 | Laminated glass must be specified. | | | | | | |
| 8 | 13 | 4 | Carriers with metal track and top guide, and: | | | | | | |
| 8 | 13 | 4 | 1 | If needed to prevent sagging, bottoms of upper cabinets shall be increased in thickness, provided with a hardwood track member of sufficient thickness, or provided with a strong back support screwed and glued to the underside. | | | | | |
| 9 | **APRONS** require: | | | | | | | | |
| 9 | 1 | Minimum thickness of 3/4" (19 mm), and: | | | | | | | |
| 9 | 1 | 1 | Edgebanding of bottom edge. | | | | E | C | P |
| 10 | **ENDS** and **DIVISIONS** require: | | | | | | | | |
| 10 | 1 | Cabinet ends are required, including: | | | | | | | |
| 10 | 1 | 1 | Against walls. | | | | | | |
| 10 | 2 | Minimum thickness of 3/4" (19 mm), except: | | | | | | | |
| 10 | 2 | 1 | 1/2" (12.7 mm) at face frame construction. | | | | E | C | P |
| 10 | 3 | Exposed ends be of integral construction, rabbeted or plowed to receive backs, and horizontal members (excluding countertops) shall not extend beyond the exposed end. | | | | | | | |
| 10 | 4 | Concealed ends allow tops and bottoms to extend past, if applicable. | | | | | | | |
| 10 | 5 | Top edges of the end of cabinets: | | | | | | | |
| 10 | 5 | 1 | If exposed or visible from above be edgebanded with material of matching color and pattern to exposed exterior surface. | | | | | | |
| 10 | 5 | 2 | If open above; however, not visible, at 80" (2032 mm) or more above the floor be edgebanded with the manufacturer's choice of edge material. | | | | | | |

Continues next column ▼

### 10.4.7 Assembly Rules

▲ From previous column

| | | | | | E | C | P |
|---|---|---|---|---|---|---|---|
| 10 | **ENDS** and **DIVISIONS**   (continued) | | | | | | |
| 10 | 6 | Bottom edges of wall cabinet ends shall be edgebanded with: | | | | | |
| 10 | 6 | 1 | Material compatible to the exposed faces. | | E | C | P |
| 10 | 6 | 2 | The same material as the exposed surfaces. | | E | C | P |
| 10 | 7 | Solid divisions behind vertical face frame members or hanging stiles. | | | E | C | P |
| 10 | 8 | **DRAWER COMPARTMENTS** to be separated from shelf or open compartments by a solid vertical division unless prevented by design or usage. | | | | | |
| 10 | 9 | **PANELED CONSTRUCTION**, stiles and rails be a minimum of 3/4" (19 mm) thickness, with: | | | | | |
| 10 | 9 | 1 | Minimum of 1/4" (6.4 mm) panel thickness. | | | | |
| 10 | 9 | 2 | Hardboard is not permitted for transparent finish. | | | | |
| 10 | 10 | **FREE STANDING** end panels shall be installed with concealed fasteners. | | | E | C | P |
| 11 | **TOPS** and **BOTTOMS** requires: (Note: Base cabinets with separate countertops are not covered within this heading; see "Stretchers"). | | | | | | |
| 11 | 1 | Minimum thickness of 3/4" (19 mm), design permitting. | | | | | |
| 11 | 2 | **BOTTOMS** of wall hung cabinets, and: | | | | | |
| 11 | 2 | 1 | When unsupported, not to exceed 46-1/2" (1181 mm) in width. | | | | |
| 11 | 2 | 2 | Joints are permitted where ends are flush with bottoms in each unit. | | | | |
| 11 | 2 | 4 | Cores be subject to a 40 lb (18.1 kg) load capacity of the manufacturer's choice, with: | | E | C | P |
| 11 | 2 | 4 | 1 | A 50 lb (22.7 kg) load capacity at schools, hospitals, and library bookshelves. | E | C | P |
| 11 | 2 | 5 | Be secured to ends, divisions, and back. | | E | C | P |
| 11 | 2 | 6 | Thickness of at least 1" (25.4 mm) when made of particleboard or MDF core and 42" (1067 mm) or more in length. | | E | C | P |
| 11 | 2 | 7 | If cabinet ends extend below the bottom, the interior exposed surface of the end shall be: | | | | |
| 11 | 2 | 7 | 1 | Material compatible to the exposed surface. | E | C | P |
| 11 | 2 | 7 | 2 | The same material as the exposed surface. | E | C | P |
| 11 | 2 | 8 | If thicker core is desired due to heavy loads, it shall be specified. | | | | |
| 11 | 2 | 9 | At exposed interior shall be uniform in thickness for the entire elevation or connected elevations, except: | | E | C | P |
| 11 | 2 | 9 | 1 | When concealed behind a minimum 1-1/2" (38.1 mm) face frame member. | E | C | P |

Continues next column ▼

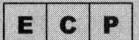

Where the **E**, **C**, or **P** icon is not indicated, the rule applies to all Grades equally

# SECTION 10
## Casework

**compliance requirements**  GENERAL/**PRODUCT**/INSTALLATION/TEST

## 10.4.7 Assembly Rules

▲ From previous column

| | | | | | | |
|---|---|---|---|---|---|---|
| 11 | | **TOPS** and **BOTTOMS** requires (continued) | | | | |
| 11 | 3 | **TOPS** of wall hung and tall cabinets: | | | | |
| 11 | 3 | 1 | Are not considered load bearing. | | | |
| 11 | 3 | 2 | **FRAMELESS CONSTRUCTION**, permit joints where exposed ends are flush with tops, and: | | | |
| 11 | 3 | 2 | 1 | Cabinet end shall be edgebanded to match other exposed surfaces. | | |
| 12 | | **SECURITY** and **DUST PANELS** shall: | | | | |
| 12 | 1 | Be furnished above locked doors and drawers, only if each drawer or door is keyed differently. | | | | |
| 12 | 2 | Be a solid piece of plywood, particleboard, MDF, or solid phenolic, a minimum of 1/2" (12.7 m) in thickness, and: | | | | |
| 12 | 2 | 1 | If front and rear stretchers are used, a 1/4" (6.4 mm) panel may be let into the stretchers. | | | |
| 13 | | **STRETCHERS** shall be: (Note: This is only applicable to base cabinets with separate countertops): | | | | |
| 13 | 1 | Provided at both the front and the back of the cabinet body, except: | | | | |
| 13 | 1 | 1 | At sink compartments, they may run front to back. | | | |
| 13 | 2 | Solid stock or veneer core plywood a minimum of 3/4" (19 mm) in thickness and 2" (50.8 mm) in width. | | | | |
| 13 | 3 | Particleboard or MDF a minimum of 3/4" (19 mm) in thickness and 5" (127 mm) in width and reinforced as necessary to support the countertop. | | | | |
| 13 | 4 | In lieu of stretchers, a panel member a minimum of 3/4" (19 mm) in thickness, the full length and depth of the cabinet opening may be used. | | | | |
| 13 | 5 | At drawer banks, when the total drawer opening height exceeds 30" (762 mm), an intermediate front stretcher is required. | | E | C | P |
| 14 | | **BACKS**: | | | | |
| 14 | 1 | Are required only where the cabinet will be set in an unfinished recess or where the back would be exposed to view, and: | | E | C | P |
| 14 | 1 | 1 | Be hardboard or plywood a minimum of 1/8" (3.2 mm) in thickness. | | E | C | P |

Continues next column ▼

## 10.4.7 Assembly Rules

▲ From previous column

| | | | | | | |
|---|---|---|---|---|---|---|
| 14 | | **BACKS** (continued) | | | | |
| 14 | 2 | Are required and: | | E | C | P |
| 14 | 2 | 1 | Shall be a minimum of 1/4" (6.4 mm) in thickness. | E | C | P |
| 14 | 2 | 2 | Shall be of an approved semi-exposed material. | E | C | P |
| 14 | 2 | 3 | Vinyl is permitted, provided it is of the same color as the other semi-exposed surfaces. | | | |
| 14 | 4 | At exposed exterior shall be a minimum of 1/2" (12.7 mm) in thickness. | | | | |
| 14 | 5 | Where non plowed/dadoed in shall be screwed to the case body, divisions, and/or fixed shelves at a maximum of 4" (101.6 mm) on center. | | | | |
| 14 | 6 | Where plowed/dadoed in, with a minimum shoulder of 1/2" (12.7 mm), shall be securely nailed or stapled to the case body at a maximum of 4" (101.6 mm) on center. | | | | |
| 14 | 7 | Attachment of base, tall, and wall hung cabinet backs by other than the above requirements for non plowed/dadoed or plowed/dadoed in is permitted, provided it has been independently tested to show compliance to the Structural Integrity (Test-Wall Cabinet) as shown in the **APPENDIX**. | | | | **a** |
| 14 | 8 | Are not required to be glued. | | | | |
| 14 | 9 | Shall be rabbeted or dadoed into exposed ends. | | E | C | P |
| 14 | 10 | Shall be removable, if so specified. | | | | |
| 14 | 11 | **VISIBLE JOINTS** are not permitted at exposed interior or semi exposed interior cabinet backs. | | | | |
| 15 | | **TOE BASES, KICKS,** and **SLEEPERS**: | | | | |
| 15 | 1 | Shall be either separate from or integral to the cabinet body at the manufacturer's choice. | | | | |
| 15 | 2 | Shall be a minimum of 4" (101.6 mm) high. | | | | |
| 15 | 3 | Shall be a minimum of 3/4" (19 mm) in thickness. | | | | |
| 15 | 4 | Sleepers shall be provided at separate toe bases a maximum of 48" (1219 mm) on center. | | | | |
| 15 | 5 | Moisture resistant base, if specified, requires base components be material complying with the Base Cabinet Submersion Test, as explained in the **APPENDIX**. | | | | **a** |
| 15 | 6 | **LEVELERS**: | | | | |
| 15 | 6 | 1 | May be used at the manufacturer's choice. | | | |
| 15 | 6 | 2 | At cabinets over 15-1/2" (394 mm) in depth, shall require four levelers per unit up to 37-1/2" (953 mm) in width and six per unit up to 48" (1219 mm) in width. | | | |

Continues next column ▼

# SECTION 10
## Casework

GENERAL / **PRODUCT** / INSTALLATION / TEST

**compliance requirements**

Where the **E**, **C**, or **P** icon is not indicated, the rule applies to all Grades equally | E | C | P |

### 10.4.7 Assembly Rules

▲ From previous column

| 15 | | | **TOE BASES, KICKS**, and **SLEEPERS** (continued) | | | |
|---|---|---|---|---|---|---|
| 15 | 6 | | **LEVELERS** (continued) | | | |
| 15 | 6 | 3 | At cabinets less than 15-1/2" (394 mm) in depth, levelers are only required at the front and shall require two levelers per unit up to 37-1/2" (953 mm) in width and three per unit up to 48" (1219 mm) in width. | | | |
| 15 | 7 | | **MOVEABLE TOES** at ADA base cabinets shall not have a vertical gap exceeding that allowable for the doors above. | | | |
| 16 | | | **SHELVES** require: | | | |
| 16 | 1 | | **THICKNESS** be a minimum of 3/4" (19 mm), and: | | | |
| 16 | 1 | 1 | If thicker shelf is desired due to heavy loads, it shall be specified. | | | |
| 16 | 2 | | **GRAIN** or **DIRECTIONAL PATTERN** of the face to run the length of the shelf. | | | |
| 16 | 3 | | **DIVIDERS**, vertical or horizontal, to match the exposed or the semi-exposed surface, as applicable. | E | C | P |
| 16 | 4 | | **UNIFORM THICKNESS** at each elevation or connected elevations at open casework. | E | C | P |
| 16 | 5 | | **HARDBOARD** used for shelves or vertical/horizontal dividers be tempered and smooth on both sides. | E | C | P |
| 16 | 6 | | **CABINETS OVER 72"** (1829) high, not immediately abutting a structural wall or another cabinet at both ends, shall have a fixed shelf at approximate mid height. | | | |
| 16 | 7 | | **GLASS** shelving shall be supplied as specified, and: | E | C | P |
| 16 | 7 | 1 | Have all four edges polished. | E | C | P |
| 16 | 8 | | At **FIXED SHELVES**: | | | |
| 16 | 8 | 1 | Thickness of 1" (25.4 mm) minimum when made with particleboard or MDF core and are unsupported for 42" (1069 mm) or more. | E | C | P |
| 16 | 8 | 2 | Cores to be subject to a 40 lb per sq ft (195.3 kg/m2) load capacity of the manufacturer's choice, except requires: | E | C | P |
| 16 | 8 | 2 | 1 | 50 lb per sq ft (244.1 kg/m2) load capacity at schools, hospitals, and library bookshelves. | E | C | P |
| 16 | 8 | 3 | Be secured to ends and divisions, and: | | | |
| 16 | 8 | 3 | 1 | When over 48" (1219 mm) in length, be secured to back. | E | C | P |
| 16 | 8 | 3 | 2 | Be secured to back. | E | C | P |
| 16 | 8 | 3 | 3 | When over 48" (1219 mm) have a center support. | E | C | P |

Continues next column ▼

### 10.4.7 Assembly Rules

▲ From previous column

| 16 | | | **SHELVES** require (continued) | | | |
|---|---|---|---|---|---|---|
| 16 | 9 | | At **ADJUSTABLE SHELVES**: | | | |
| 16 | 9 | 1 | **CONFORMANCE IN THICKNESS** to the following maximum adjustable shelf length listings, based on: | | | |
| 16 | 9 | 1 | 1 | Length and grain direction running left to right. | | | |
| 16 | 9 | 1 | 2 | Creep not taken into consideration or considered a defect. | | | |
| 16 | 9 | 1 | 3 | Information and ratings represented in calculations are believed to be reliable; however, due to variations in use not known or out of our control, no warranties or guarantees are made as to the end results. | | | |
| 16 | 9 | 1 | 4 | Laminations of a rigid glue line; contact adhesive is not permitted unless otherwise indicated, and: | | | |
| 16 | 9 | 1 | 4 | 1 | Contact adhesive shall comply with the Heat Resistance Test listed in the **APPENDIX**. **a** |
| 16 | 9 | 1 | 5 | Total applied weight uniformly dispersed on an individual shelf not exceeding 200 lbs (90.7 kg) on any one shelf while being subject to load capacities of: | | | |
| 16 | 9 | 1 | 5 | 1 | **40 lbs** per sq ft (195.3 kg/m2) for commercial shelving. |
| 16 | 9 | 1 | 5 | 2 | **50 lbs** per sq ft (244.1 kg/m2) for schools, hospitals, and library book shelves. |
| 16 | 9 | 1 | 6 | The formula below is used to determine the shelf spans, subject to a maximum 1/4" (6.4 mm) deflection, in the table on the following pages: $$L = \frac{(DEWt^3)/(0.1563s^4)}{W/144}$$ L = lbs/SF of uniformly distributed load<br>D = deflection (inches)<br>E = MOE (psi)<br>t = thickness (inches)<br>W = width (front to back) of shelf (inches)<br>s = span of shelf (inches) | | | |
| 16 | 9 | 1 | 7 | **MOE** (Modulus of Elasticity) figures are referenced in the following table. | | | |

Continues next column ▼

# SECTION 10
## Casework

### compliance requirements
GENERAL/**PRODUCT**/INSTALLATION/TEST

| E | C | P | Where the **E**, **C**, or **P** icon is not indicated, the rule applies to all Grades equally |

## 10.4.7 Assembly Rules

▲ From previous column

| 16 | | | | **SHELVES** require (continued) |
|---|---|---|---|---|
| 16 | 9 | | | At **ADJUSTABLE SHELVES** (continued) |
| 16 | 9 | 1 | | **CONFORMANCE IN THICKNESS** (continued) |

**MAXIMUM ALLOWABLE ADJUSTABLE SHELF LENGTH** based on material compositions.

Capacity Legend: ■ 40 lbs/sf  ▨ 50 lbs/sf

| 16 | 9 | 1 | 8 | |

Chart data (Maximum shelf length in inches by material, thickness, and capacity):

| Material | Thickness | 50 lbs/sf | 40 lbs/sf |
|---|---|---|---|
| 1-M-2 Particleboard with LPDL two sides (MOE: 400,000) | 3/4" | 30 | 32 |
| | 1" | 37 | 39 |
| 1-M-2 Particleboard with hardwood veneer two sides (MOE: 640,000) | 3/4" | 34 | 36 |
| | 1" | 42 | 44 |
| 1-M-2 Particleboard with vertical grade HPDL two sides (MOE: 710,000) | 3/4" | 35 | 37 |
| | 1" | 43 | 45 |
| MDF (Medium Density Fiberboard) with LPDL two sides (MOE: 500,000) | 3/4" | 32 | 34 |
| | 1" | 39 | 42 |
| MDF (Medium Density Fiberboard) with hardwood veneer two sides (MOE: 580,000) | 3/4" | 33 | 35 |
| | 1" | 41 | 43 |
| MDF (Medium Density Fiberboard) with vertical grade HPDL two sides (MOE: 710,000) | 3/4" | 35 | 37 |
| | 1" | 43 | 45 |

Continues next column ▼

©2014 AWI | AWMAC | WI  2nd Edition, October 1, 2014
As may be updated by errata at **awinet.org**, **awmac.com**, or **aws-errata.com**

# SECTION 10
## Casework

### 10.4.7 Assembly Rules

| 16 | | | SHELVES require (continued) |
|---|---|---|---|
| 16 | 9 | | At ADJUSTABLE SHELVES (continued) |
| 16 | 9 | 1 | CONFORMANCE IN THICKNESS (continued) |

MAXIMUM ALLOWABLE ADJUSTABLE SHELF LENGTH based on material compositions (continued)

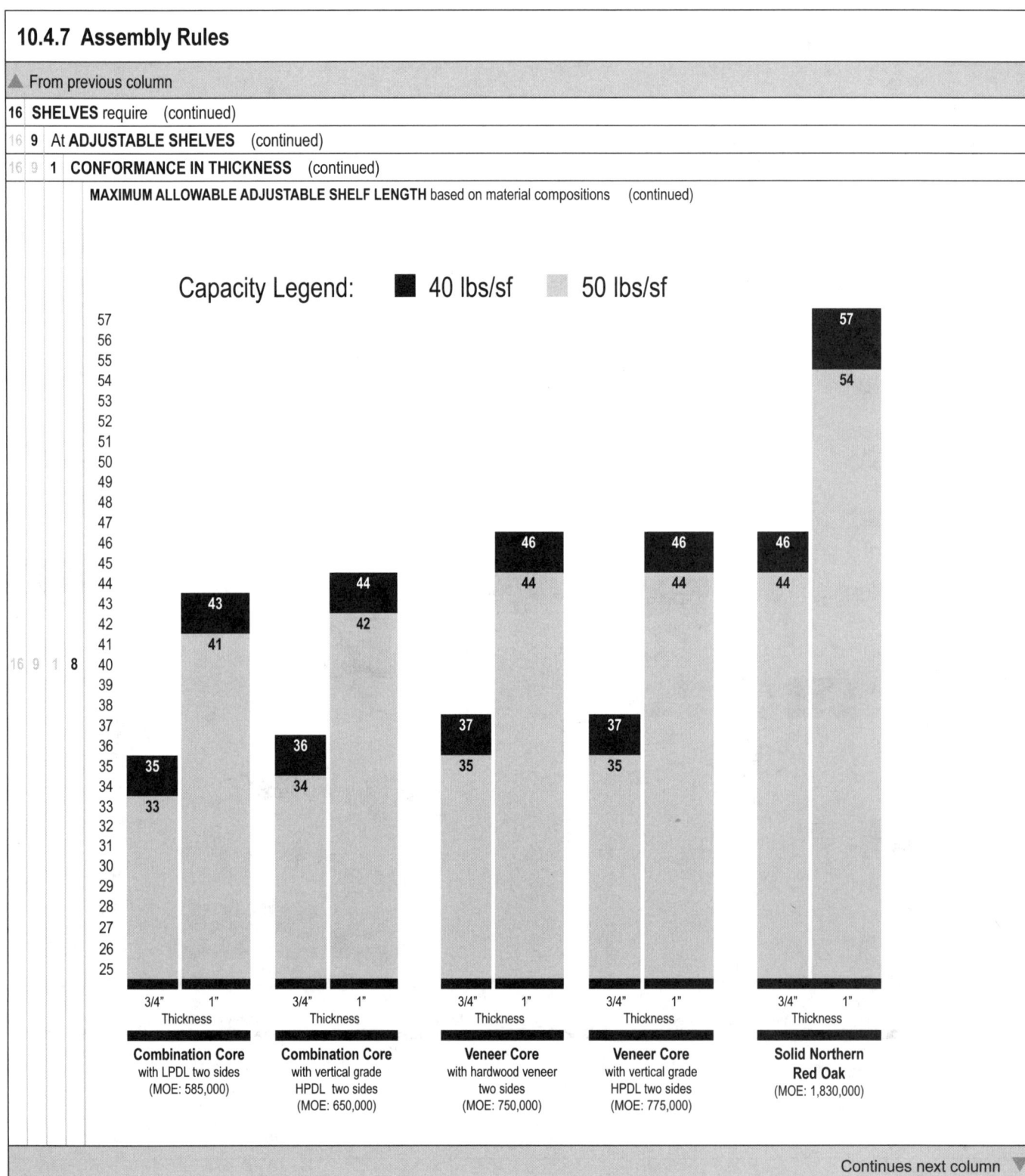

## SECTION 10
### Casework

**compliance requirements** — GENERAL/**PRODUCT**/INSTALLATION/TEST

### 10.4.7 Assembly Rules

▲ From previous column

| | | | | | | | |
|---|---|---|---|---|---|---|---|
| 16 | | **SHELVES** require (continued) | | | | | |
| 16 | 9 | | At **ADJUSTABLE SHELVES** (continued): | | | | |
| 16 | 9 | 2 | Length be a maximum of 1/8" (3.2 mm) less than the inside cabinet width plus any additional offset created by the shelf rests used, | | E | C | P |

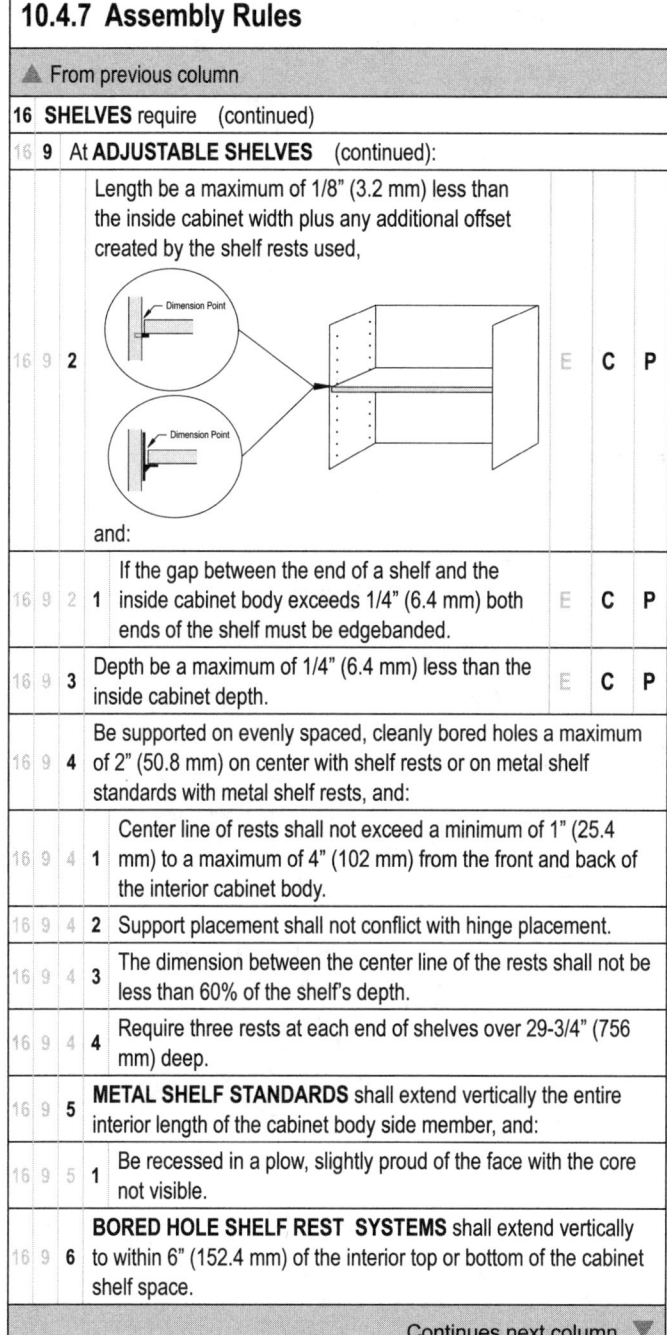

and:

| | | | | | | | |
|---|---|---|---|---|---|---|---|
| 16 | 9 | 2 | 1 | If the gap between the end of a shelf and the inside cabinet body exceeds 1/4" (6.4 mm) both ends of the shelf must be edgebanded. | E | C | P |
| 16 | 9 | 3 | | Depth be a maximum of 1/4" (6.4 mm) less than the inside cabinet depth. | E | C | P |
| 16 | 9 | 4 | | Be supported on evenly spaced, cleanly bored holes a maximum of 2" (50.8 mm) on center with shelf rests or on metal shelf standards with metal shelf rests, and: | | | |
| 16 | 9 | 4 | 1 | Center line of rests shall not exceed a minimum of 1" (25.4 mm) to a maximum of 4" (102 mm) from the front and back of the interior cabinet body. | | | |
| 16 | 9 | 4 | 2 | Support placement shall not conflict with hinge placement. | | | |
| 16 | 9 | 4 | 3 | The dimension between the center line of the rests shall not be less than 60% of the shelf's depth. | | | |
| 16 | 9 | 4 | 4 | Require three rests at each end of shelves over 29-3/4" (756 mm) deep. | | | |
| 16 | 9 | 5 | | **METAL SHELF STANDARDS** shall extend vertically the entire interior length of the cabinet body side member, and: | | | |
| 16 | 9 | 5 | 1 | Be recessed in a plow, slightly proud of the face with the core not visible. | | | |
| 16 | 9 | 6 | | **BORED HOLE SHELF REST SYSTEMS** shall extend vertically to within 6" (152.4 mm) of the interior top or bottom of the cabinet shelf space. | | | |

Continues next column ▼

### 10.4.7 Assembly Rules

▲ From previous column

| | | | | | | | |
|---|---|---|---|---|---|---|---|
| 17 | | | **PULLOUT SHELVES** require: | | | | |
| 17 | 1 | | | **BREAD/CUTTING BOARDS** to be solid stock a minimum of 3/4" (19 mm) in thickness, with: | | | |
| 17 | 1 | 1 | | Tongue and groove edgebands front and back, securely glued with type I adhesive. | | | |
| 17 | 1 | 2 | | Use of exterior plywood is permitted. | E | C | P |
| 17 | 2 | | | **WRITING or UTILITY SHELVES** be a minimum of 3/4" (19 mm) in thickness, and: | | | |
| 17 | 2 | 1 | | Be edgebanded three edges. | | | |
| 17 | 2 | 2 | | Extend a minimum of 15" (381 mm) in cabinets 22" (559 mm) or greater, or 2/3 of the cabinet depth in shallower cabinets. | | | |
| 17 | 2 | 3 | | Be a smooth compatible material to the exposed interior surface. | | | |
| 17 | 2 | 4 | | Operate smoothly in channels or other rigid guides. | | | |
| 18 | | | | **CLOTHES POLES** or **RODS** require: | | | |
| 18 | 1 | | | Wood, a minimum of 1-1/4" (31.8 mm) in diameter, or metal, a minimum of 1-1/16" (27 mm) diameter, at the manufacturers's choice, and supported at: | | | |
| 18 | 1 | 1 | | Each end by rosettes or hook strips with bored holes. | | | |
| 18 | 1 | 2 | | A maximum of 48" (1219 mm) on center. | | | |
| 19 | | | | **WARDROBES:** | | | |
| 19 | 1 | | | 60" (1524 mm) or wider require a horizontal member at the top rail of sliding doors rigidly supported with a vertical 1-3/8" (28.6 mm) round pole or two strips a minimum of 3/4" x 1-1/4" (19 mm x 31.8 mm) forming a "T" member securely positioned behind the door lap. | | | |
| 20 | | | | **ANCHOR STRIPS** (nailers) are required and: | | | |
| 20 | 1 | | | Shall be of solid stock, plywood, particleboard, or medium density fiberboard, a minimum of 1/2" (12.7 mm) in thickness, 2-1/2" (63.5 mm) in width, and: | | | |
| 20 | 1 | 1 | | Be securely glued and mechanically fastened at 4" (101.6 mm) on center. | | | |
| 20 | 2 | | | Where backs, 1/2" (12.7 mm) or thicker are used, anchor strips are not required. | | | |
| 20 | 3 | | | Cabinet heights over 60" (1524 mm) require an intermediate anchor strip. | | | |
| 20 | 4 | | | Shall be provided at the top and bottom of the wall side of the cabinet back, or: | | | |
| 20 | 4 | 1 | | At the inside if semi-exposed material is used, provided they are attached to the cabinet body as well as the back and they are flush with the top, bottom, and ends of the cabinet body. | E | C | P |

Continues next column ▼

# SECTION 10
## Casework

GENERAL / **PRODUCT** / INSTALLATION / TEST

**compliance requirements**

Where the **E**, **C**, or **P** icon is not indicated, the rule applies to all Grades equally — **E | C | P**

### 10.4.7 Assembly Rules

▲ From previous column

**21 MOVEABLE CABINETS require:**

- 21.1 **GLIDES** to be metal and adjustable.
- 21.2 **CASTERS** to have a minimum weight capacity of 90 lbs (40.8 kg) per caster.
- 21.3 **METAL FRAME** or **DIAPHRAGM TYPE DOUBLE BOTTOM** (see **DESIGN IDEAS**, **CDS** drawings) at cabinets over 42" (1067 mm) in height, with doors and without fixed vertical or horizontal stabilizing partitions.
- 21.4 **LOCK JOINT CORNERS** at bottoms or tops be reinforced with a continuous metal angle or wood cleat securely screwed and set with adhesive into the inside of both corner sides.

**22 JOINERY requires:**

- 22.1 Cabinet members to be **SECURELY FASTENED** together, using one or more of the approved methods, at the manufacturer's choice, including:
  - 22.1.1 Dadoes, lock joints, plows, rabbets, dowels, dowel screws, or biscuit splines.
- 22.2 Casework be **ASSEMBLED SQUARE** and **TRUE**, within a tolerance not to exceed 1/32" (0.8 mm) difference in measurement at top versus bottom, and 1/16" (1.6 mm) diagonally.
- 22.3 All joints be **SECURELY GLUED**, with:
  - 22.3.1 Mechanical fasteners for cabinet body, back, and/or drawer construction, a maximum of 4" (101.6 mm) on center with a minimum of two fasteners per joint, except:
    - 22.3.1.1 At face frames, a maximum of 8" (203 mm) on center is permitted.
    - 22.3.1.2 Exposed fasteners are not permitted at exposed exterior surfaces.
    - 22.3.1.3 Exposed fasteners, where permitted, shall be plated, and:
      - 22.3.1.3.1 Bugle drywall screws are not permitted.
      - 22.3.1.3.2 Are permitted for access panels. **E | C | P**
    - 22.3.1.4 Mechanical fasteners are not required at dovetail, miter fold, mortise and tenon, and lock miter joints.
    - 22.3.1.5 At **DOWEL** joints (see end view diagram below):
      - 22.3.1.5.1 Dowel to be a minimum of 5/16" x 1-3/16" (8 mm x 30 mm), and:
        - 22.3.1.5.1.1 Be glued and clamped.
      - 22.3.1.5.2 Minimum of two dowels per joint.
      - 22.3.1.5.3 Spaced with first dowel a maximum of 2" (51 mm) from the front.

Continues next column ▼

---

### 10.4.7 Assembly Rules

▲ From previous column

**22 JOINERY requires** (continued)

- 22.3 All joints be securely glued (continued)
  - 22.3.1 Mechanical fasteners (continued):
    - 22.3.1.5 At **DOWEL** joints (continued):
      - 22.3.1.5.4 [diagram]
        - 3-21/32" (96 mm) Maximum
        - 5/16" (8 mm) X 1-3/16" (30 mm) Minimum Dowels
        - 2" (50.8 mm) Maximum
    - 22.3.1.6 At **DOWEL SCREW** joints (see end view diagram below):
      - 22.3.1.6.1 Dowel screw to be a minimum of 9/32" x 2" (7 mm x 50 mm).
      - 22.3.1.6.2 First dowel screw shall be spaced a maximum of 2" (51 mm) from the front.
      - 22.3.1.6.3 Subsequent dowel screws shall be spaced a maximum of 5" (127 mm) on center.
      - 22.3.1.6.4 Glue is not required.
      - 22.3.1.6.5 [diagram]
        - 5" (128 mm) Maximum
        - 9/32" (7 mm) X 2" (51 mm) Minimum Dowel Screw
        - 2" (50.8 mm) Maximum
    - 22.3.1.7 At **BISCUIT SPLINE** joints:
      - 22.3.1.7.1 Biscuits shall be a minimum #20 or equal, located a maximum of 2" (51 mm) from each edge or end to the center of the plate, and:
        - 22.3.1.7.1.1 Be glued and clamped.
      - 22.3.1.7.2 Subsequent plates shall be spaced a maximum of 6" (152 mm) on center.

Continues next column ▼

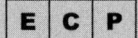

Where the **E**, **C**, or **P** icon is not indicated, the rule applies to all Grades equally

# SECTION 10
## Casework

## compliance requirements

GENERAL/**PRODUCT**/INSTALLATION/TEST

### 10.4.7 Assembly Rules

▲ From previous column

| | | | | | | E | C | P |
|---|---|---|---|---|---|---|---|---|
| 23 | **SCRIBING**: | | | | | | | |
| 23 | 1 | Is **NOT** required. | | | | E | C | P |
| 23 | 2 | Shall be **FURNISHED** by the manufacturer, and: | | | | | C | P |
| 23 | 2 | 1 | Scribe **FILLERS** shall not exceed 1-1/2" (38.1 mm) in width. | | | E | C | P |
| 23 | 2 | 2 | Scribe **MOLDS** shall not exceed 1-1/2" (38.1 mm) in width, and: | | | E | C | |
| 23 | 2 | 2 | 1 | Are not **NOT ALLOWED**. | | E | C | P |
| 23 | 3 | Match exposed surfaces. | | | | | | |
| 23 | 4 | Be furnished in maximum available lengths, joints not allowed in material less than 96" (2438 mm). | | | | | | |
| 23 | 5 | Permits **COLOR COMPATIBLE CAULKING** not to exceed 1/8" (3.2 mm). | | | | E | C | P |
| 23 | 6 | Requires **TRIM MEMBERS** used at the inside corner of the adjoining angled cabinets (which is not a scribe or subject to the 1-1/2" [38.1 mm] maximum scribe allowance) be equal and not exceed 2" (50.8 mm) beyond the cabinet front and/or drawer pull. | | | | | | |
| 23 | 7 | Requires **SOFFIT** or **FASCIA PANELS** to be furnished in maximum available lengths, joints not allowed in material less than 96" (2438 mm) at horizontal grain or directional pattern and 48" (1219 mm) at vertical grain or directional pattern, and: | | | | E | C | P |
| 23 | 7 | 1 | Be a minimum of 3/4" (19 mm) in thickness. | | | | | |
| 23 | 7 | 2 | Grain direction (if any) shall run vertical, or be manufacturer's choice if less than: | | | | | |
| 23 | 7 | 2 | 1 | 12" (305 mm) tall. | | E | C | P |
| 23 | 7 | 2 | 2 | 1-1/2" (38.1 mm) tall. | | E | C | P |
| 23 | 8 | **OPTIONS**: | | | | | | |
| 23 | 8 | 1 | Scribe Filler. | | | | | |
| 23 | 8 | 2 | Scribe Mold. | | | | | |

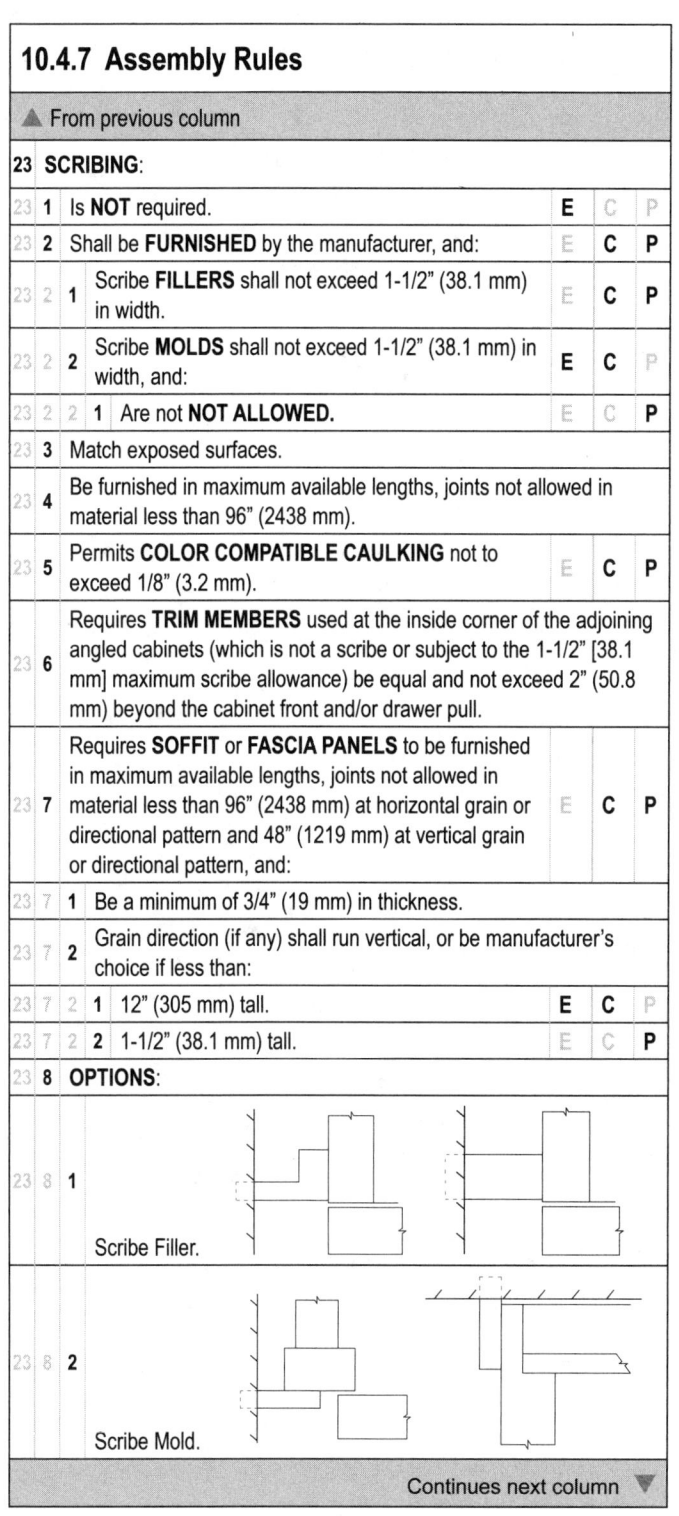

Continues next column ▼

### 10.4.7 Assembly Rules

▲ From previous column

| | | | | E | C | P |
|---|---|---|---|---|---|---|
| 23 | **SCRIBING** (continued) | | | | | |
| 23 | 8 | **OPTIONS** (continued) | | | | |
| 23 | 8 | 3 | Scribe Allowance. | | | |
| 24 | **CLOSURE** provision is required at voids or open spaces between cabinets and walls, such as at the top of tall and upper cabinets and the bottom of upper cabinets caused by scribing or angle turns, and: | | | | | |
| 24 | 1 | At non visible voids, 1-1/2" (38 mm) or less in width, a piece of standard grade laminate may be used as a closure cap. | | | | |
| 24 | 2 | At non visible voids, exceeding 1-1/2" (38 mm) in width, a minimum 3/4" (19 mm) closure filler shall be provided of manufacturer's choice. | | | | |
| 24 | 3 | At visible voids, a minimum 3/4" (19 mm) closure filler shall be provided matching the adjacent surface. | | | | |
| 25 | **CLEARANCES** and **TOLERANCES** requires: | | | | | |
| 25 | 1 | **EDGE ALIGNMENT** and **FLUSHNESS** of doors and drawers (see Test I illustrations in Tests) in both the vertical and horizontal plane, such as, shall not exceed: | | | | |
| 25 | 1 | 1 | 1/16" (1.6 mm). | | E | C | P |
| 25 | 1 | 2 | 1/32" (0.8 mm). | | E | C | P |

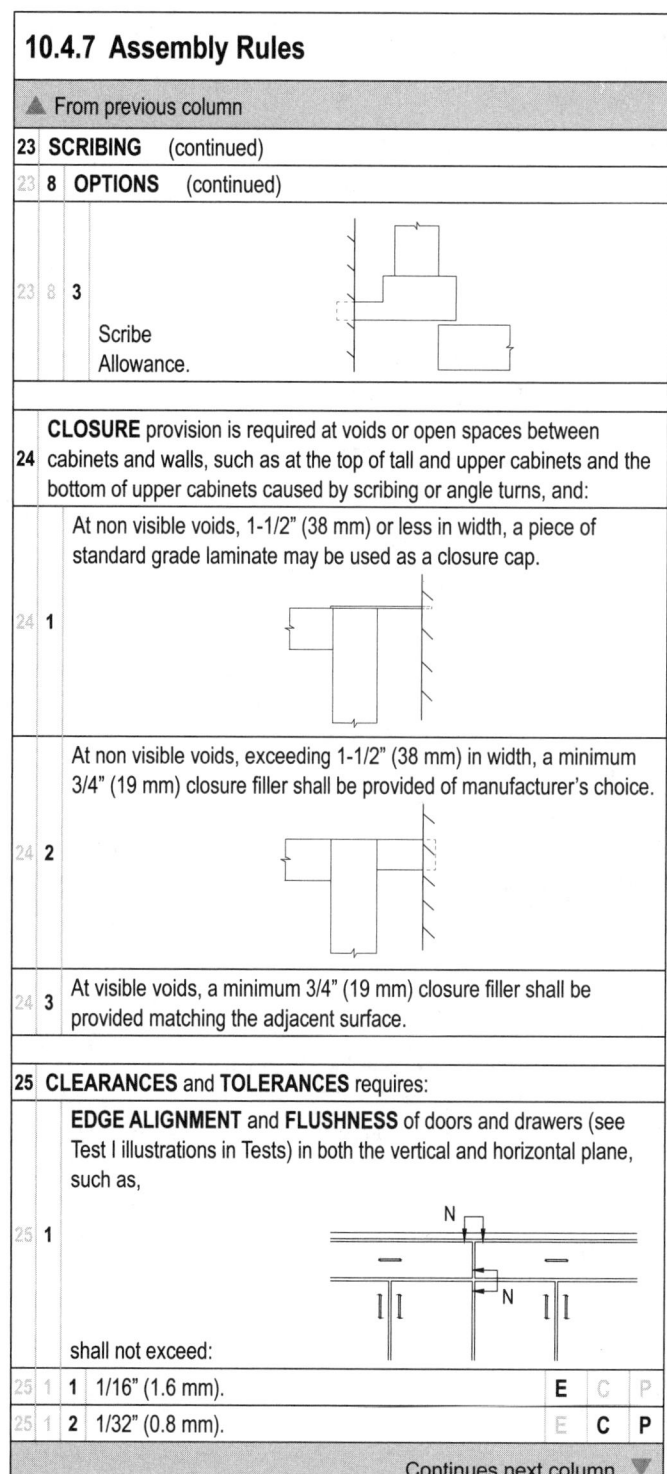

Continues next column ▼

©2014 AWI | AWMAC | WI 2nd Edition, October 1, 2014
As may be updated by errata at awinet.org, awmac.com, or aws-errata.com

Architectural Woodwork Standards **323**

# SECTION 10
## Casework

GENERAL/PRODUCT/INSTALLATION/TEST — compliance requirements

Where the **E**, **C**, or **P** icon is not indicated, the rule applies to all Grades equally | E | C | P

### 10.4.7 Assembly Rules

▲ From previous column

| 25 | | | | CLEARANCES and TOLERANCES (continued) | | | |
|----|---|---|---|---|---|---|---|
| 25 | 2 | | | Doors and drawers shall be on the same plane as one another, and shall not exceed: | | | |
| 25 | 2 | 1 | | 1/8" (3.18 mm). | E | C | P |
| 25 | 2 | 2 | | 1/16" (1.59 mm). | | C | P |
| 25 | 2 | 3 | | 1/32" (0.79 mm). | | | P |
| 25 | 3 | | | The **MAXIMUM UNIFORM GAP** variance (see Test H illustrations in Tests) within a cabinet elevation, between doors hung in pairs, shall be based on the following elevations: | | | |

At **REVEAL OVERLAY FRAMELESS** construction, the maximum uniform reveal (see Test H illustrations in Tests) within a cabinet elevation, between any edge of a door and/or drawer and another door and/or drawer or finished end, and doors hung in pairs,

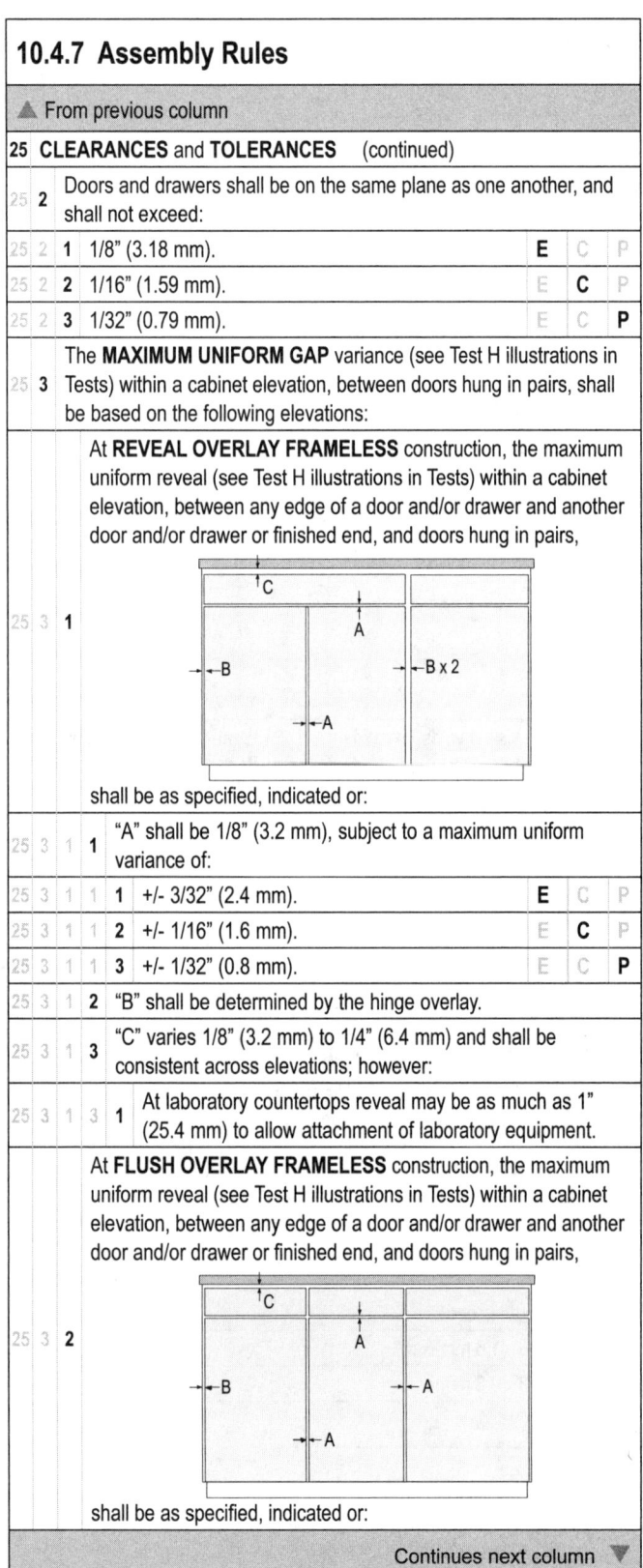

| 25 | 3 | 1 | | shall be as specified, indicated or: | | | |
|----|---|---|---|---|---|---|---|
| 25 | 3 | 1 | 1 | "A" shall be 1/8" (3.2 mm), subject to a maximum uniform variance of: | | | |
| 25 | 3 | 1 | 1 | +/- 3/32" (2.4 mm). | E | | |
| 25 | 3 | 1 | 2 | +/- 1/16" (1.6 mm). | | C | |
| 25 | 3 | 1 | 3 | +/- 1/32" (0.8 mm). | | | P |
| 25 | 3 | 1 | 2 | "B" shall be determined by the hinge overlay. | | | |
| 25 | 3 | 1 | 3 | "C" varies 1/8" (3.2 mm) to 1/4" (6.4 mm) and shall be consistent across elevations; however: | | | |
| 25 | 3 | 1 | 3 | 1 | At laboratory countertops reveal may be as much as 1" (25.4 mm) to allow attachment of laboratory equipment. | | |

At **FLUSH OVERLAY FRAMELESS** construction, the maximum uniform reveal (see Test H illustrations in Tests) within a cabinet elevation, between any edge of a door and/or drawer and another door and/or drawer or finished end, and doors hung in pairs,

| 25 | 3 | 2 | shall be as specified, indicated or: |
|----|---|---|---|

*Continues next column ▼*

### 10.4.7 Assembly Rules

▲ From previous column

| 25 | | | | CLEARANCES and TOLERANCES (continued) | | | |
|----|---|---|---|---|---|---|---|
| 25 | 3 | | | The **MAXIMUM UNIFORM GAP** variance (continued) | | | |
| 25 | 3 | 2 | | At **FLUSH OVERLAY FRAMELESS** construction (continued) | | | |
| 25 | 3 | 2 | 1 | "A" shall not exceed 1/8" (3.2 mm). | | | |
| 25 | 3 | 2 | 2 | "B" shall not exceed 1/16" (1.6 mm). | | | |
| 25 | 3 | 2 | 3 | "A" and "B" are subject to a maximum uniform variance of: | | | |
| 25 | 3 | 2 | 3 | 1 | +/- 3/32" (2.4 mm). | E | | |
| 25 | 3 | 2 | 3 | 2 | +/- 1/16" (1.6 mm). | | C | |
| 25 | 3 | 2 | 3 | 3 | +/- 1/32" (0.8 mm). | | | P |
| 25 | 3 | 2 | 4 | "C" varies from 1/8" (3.2 mm) to 1/4" (6.4 mm) and shall be consistent across elevations, except: | | | |
| 25 | 3 | 2 | 4 | 1 | At laboratory countertops, reveal may be as much as 1" (25.4 mm) to allow attachment of laboratory equipment. | | |

At **REVEAL OVERLAY FACE FRAME** construction, the maximum uniform reveal (see Test H illustrations in Tests) within a cabinet elevation, between any edge of a door and/or drawer and another door and/or drawer or cabinet member, and doors hung in pairs,

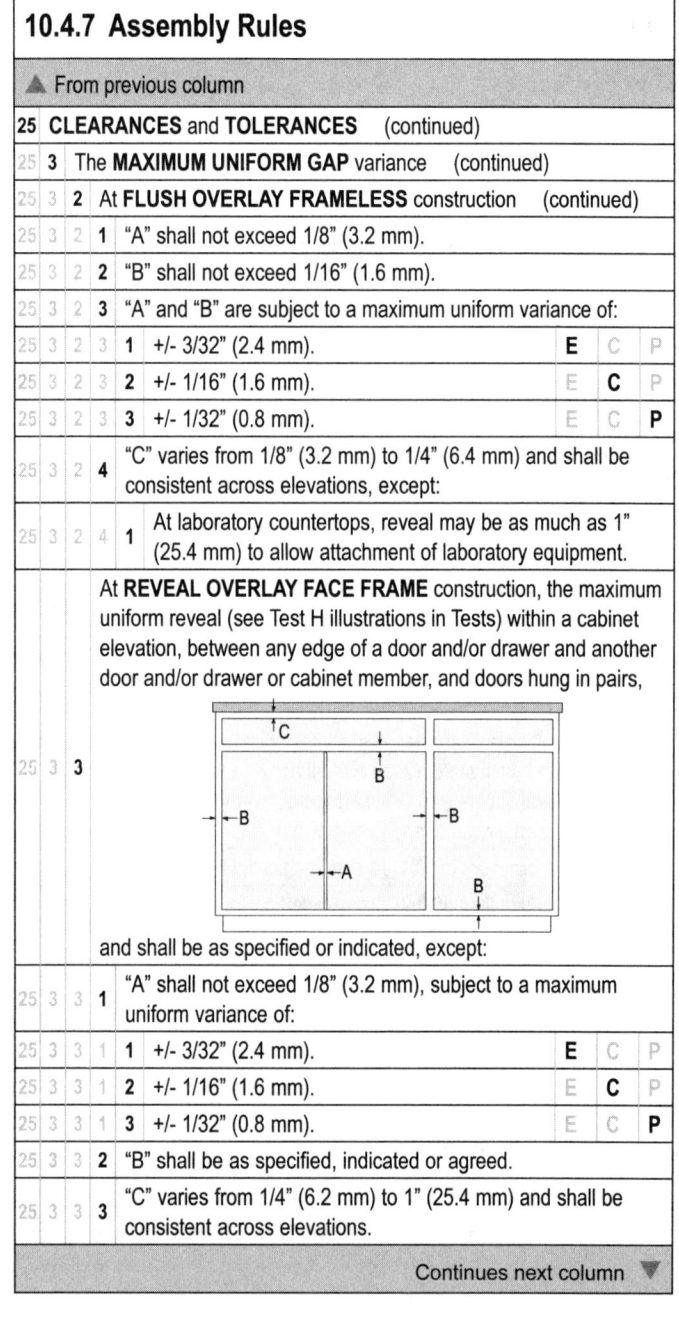

and shall be as specified or indicated, except:

| 25 | 3 | 3 | 1 | "A" shall not exceed 1/8" (3.2 mm), subject to a maximum uniform variance of: | | | |
|----|---|---|---|---|---|---|---|
| 25 | 3 | 3 | 1 | 1 | +/- 3/32" (2.4 mm). | E | | |
| 25 | 3 | 3 | 1 | 2 | +/- 1/16" (1.6 mm). | | C | |
| 25 | 3 | 3 | 1 | 3 | +/- 1/32" (0.8 mm). | | | P |
| 25 | 3 | 3 | 2 | "B" shall be as specified, indicated or agreed. | | | |
| 25 | 3 | 3 | 3 | "C" varies from 1/4" (6.2 mm) to 1" (25.4 mm) and shall be consistent across elevations. | | | |

*Continues next column ▼*

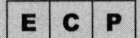

Where the E, C, or P icon is not indicated, the rule applies to all Grades equally

# SECTION 10
## Casework

**compliance requirements** — GENERAL/**PRODUCT**/INSTALLATION/TEST

## 10.4.7 Assembly Rules

▲ From previous column

| | | | | | | | | E | C | P |
|---|---|---|---|---|---|---|---|---|---|---|
| 25 | | **CLEARANCES** and **TOLERANCES** (continued) | | | | | | | | |
| 25 | 3 | The **MAXIMUM UNIFORM GAP** variance (continued) | | | | | | | | |
| 25 | 3 | 4 | At **INSET FACE FRAME** construction, the maximum uniform reveal (see Test H illustrations in Tests) within a cabinet elevation, between any edge of a door and/or drawer and another door and/or drawer or cabinet member, and doors hung in pairs, 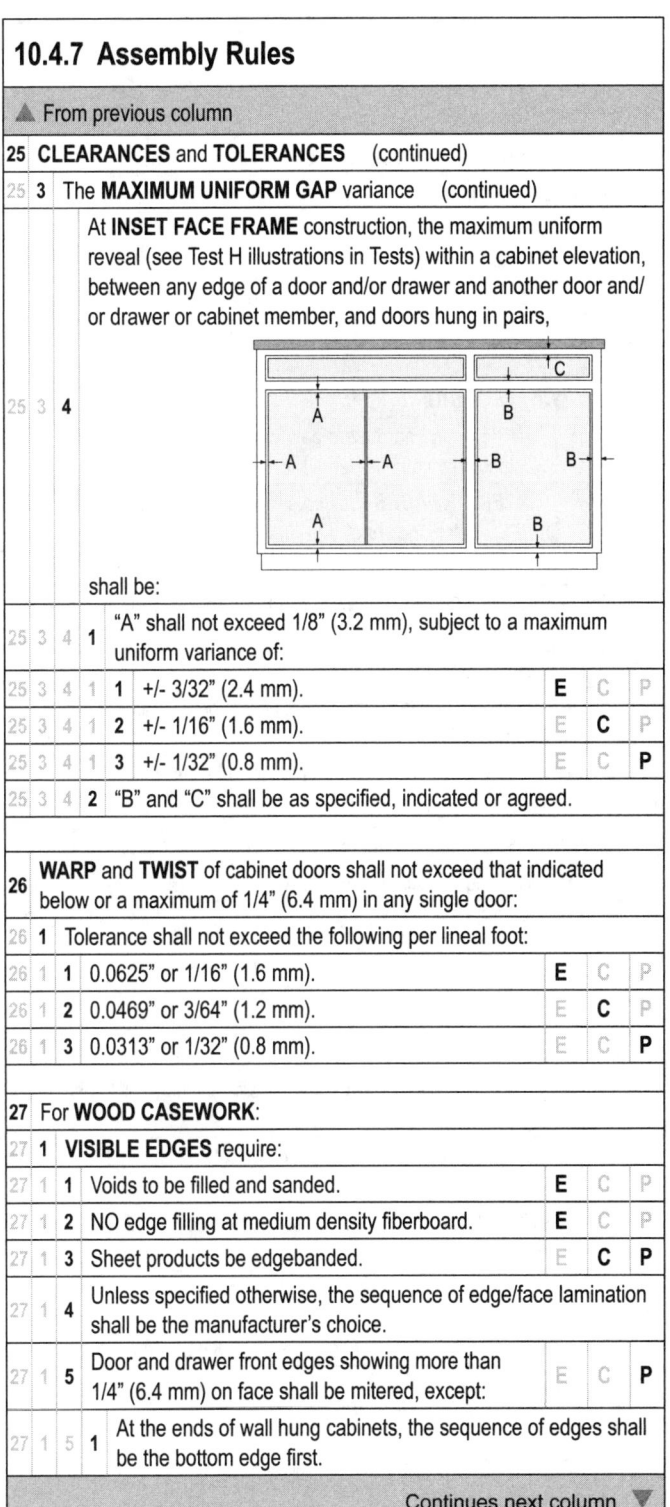 shall be: | | | | | | | | |
| 25 | 3 | 4 | 1 | "A" shall not exceed 1/8" (3.2 mm), subject to a maximum uniform variance of: | | | | | | |
| 25 | 3 | 4 | 1 | 1 | +/- 3/32" (2.4 mm). | | | E | | P |
| 25 | 3 | 4 | 1 | 2 | +/- 1/16" (1.6 mm). | | | E | C | P |
| 25 | 3 | 4 | 1 | 3 | +/- 1/32" (0.8 mm). | | | E | | P |
| 25 | 3 | 4 | 2 | "B" and "C" shall be as specified, indicated or agreed. | | | | | | |
| 26 | | **WARP** and **TWIST** of cabinet doors shall not exceed that indicated below or a maximum of 1/4" (6.4 mm) in any single door: | | | | | | | | |
| 26 | 1 | Tolerance shall not exceed the following per lineal foot: | | | | | | | | |
| 26 | 1 | 1 | 0.0625" or 1/16" (1.6 mm). | | | | | E | | P |
| 26 | 1 | 2 | 0.0469" or 3/64" (1.2 mm). | | | | | E | C | P |
| 26 | 1 | 3 | 0.0313" or 1/32" (0.8 mm). | | | | | E | | P |
| 27 | | For **WOOD CASEWORK**: | | | | | | | | |
| 27 | 1 | **VISIBLE EDGES** require: | | | | | | | | |
| 27 | 1 | 1 | Voids to be filled and sanded. | | | | | E | | P |
| 27 | 1 | 2 | NO edge filling at medium density fiberboard. | | | | | E | | P |
| 27 | 1 | 3 | Sheet products be edgebanded. | | | | | E | C | P |
| 27 | 1 | 4 | Unless specified otherwise, the sequence of edge/face lamination shall be the manufacturer's choice. | | | | | | | |
| 27 | 1 | 5 | Door and drawer front edges showing more than 1/4" (6.4 mm) on face shall be mitered, except: | | | | | E | | P |
| 27 | 1 | 5 | 1 | At the ends of wall hung cabinets, the sequence of edges shall be the bottom edge first. | | | | | | |

Continues next column ▼

## 10.4.7 Assembly Rules

▲ From previous column

| | | | | | | E | C | P |
|---|---|---|---|---|---|---|---|---|
| 27 | | For **WOOD CASEWORK** (continued) | | | | | | |
| 27 | 1 | 6 | Finger joints to be: | | | | | |
| 27 | 1 | 6 | 1 | Unlimited. | | E | C | P |
| 27 | 1 | 6 | 2 | Permitted if adjoining pieces are compatible for color and grain. | | E | C | |
| 27 | 1 | 6 | 3 | Permitted if well matched for color and grain with a maximum of one in 96" (2438 mm) of length. | | E | C | P |
| 27 | 2 | **DRAWERS** require (including trays and sliding bins): | | | | | | |
| 27 | 2 | 1 | Wood shall be finished with a finishing system (see Section 5), at the manufacturer's choice. | | | | | |
| 27 | 2 | 2 | At solid stock, top edges of sides shall be stop shaped. | | | E | C | P |
| 27 | 2 | 3 | Permits horizontal grain at stile and rail door cabinets. | | | | | |
| 27 | 2 | 4 | Permits horizontal grain at solid wood drawer fronts. | | | | | |
| 27 | 2 | 5 | **FRONT** and **FALSE FRONT**: | | | | | |
| 27 | 2 | 5 | 1 | Be **EDGEBANDED** at all four edges, except: | | | | |
| 27 | 2 | 5 | 1 | 1 | When back beveled. | | | |
| 27 | 2 | 5 | 1 | 2 | When of solid wood. | | | |
| 27 | 2 | 5 | 2 | For **OPAQUE** finish, have: | | | | |
| 27 | 2 | 5 | 2 | 1 | Filled and sanded edges at minimum 7-ply hardwood plywood and particleboard. | E | C | P |
| 27 | 2 | 5 | 2 | 2 | No edgebanding at medium density fiberboard. | E | C | P |
| 27 | 2 | 4 | 2 | 3 | Edgebanding at medium density fiberboard shall be at the option of the manufacturer. | E | | P |
| 27 | 2 | 5 | 3 | At **TRANSPARENT** finish, have: | | | | |
| 27 | 2 | 5 | 3 | 1 | Filled and sanded edges at minimum 7-ply hardwood plywood and particleboard. | E | C | P |
| 27 | 2 | 5 | 3 | 2 | Edgebanding matched to exposed surfaces. | | E | C | P |
| 27 | 3 | **DOORS** require: | | | | | | |
| 27 | 3 | 1 | Solid lumber not be permitted, except at stile and rail doors. | | | | | |
| 27 | 3 | 2 | At transparent finish, edgebanding on all four edges matching exposed surfaces. | | | | | |
| 27 | 3 | 3 | Glass stops for transparent finish be of the same species and grade as the exposed surfaces. | | E | C | P |
| 27 | 3 | 4 | When sliding interior faces shall be of balancing species. | | | | | |

Continues next column ▼

# SECTION 10
## Casework

GENERAL / **PRODUCT** / INSTALLATION / TEST — compliance requirements

*Where the E, C, or P icon is not indicated, the rule applies to all Grades equally* | E | C | P |

### 10.4.7 Assembly Rules

▲ From previous column

| # | Rule | E | C | P |
|---|------|---|---|---|
| 27 | For **WOOD CASEWORK** (continued) | | | |
| 27.4 | **FACE FRAMES** require (not applicable to decorative laminate casework): | | | |
| 27.4.1 | Thickness, a minimum of 3/4" (19 mm). | | | |
| 27.4.2 | Solid stock. | | | |
| 27.4.3 | Grain to run vertically on stiles and horizontally on rails. | | | |
| 27.4.4 | Joints to be mortised and tenoned, doweled, metal dowel screwed, pocket screwed or biscuit splined, and: | | | |
| 27.4.4.1 | To be securely glued. | | | |
| 27.4.5 | Frames to be securely glued to cabinet bodies, and: | | | |
| 27.4.5.1 | May be face nailed. | E | C | P |
| 27.4.5.2 | Exposed nailing is not permitted. | E | C | P |
| 27.4.5.3 | Exposed corners shall be shoulder mitered, lock mitered, spline mitered, or mitered with a biscuit spline. | E | C | P |
| 27.5 | **TOPS** and **BOTTOMS**: | | | |
| 27.5.1 | Minimum of 1/2" (12.7 mm). | E | | |
| 27.5.2 | Minimum of 3/4" (19 mm). | | C | P |
| 27.6 | At **FLUSH INSET DOORS**: | | | |
| 27.6.1 | Use of a bottom member of the face frame is the manufacturer's choice. | E | C | |
| 27.6.2 | Use of a bottom member of the face frame is required. | | | P |
| 28 | For **DECORATIVE LAMINATE CASEWORK**: | | | |
| 28.1 | **EXPOSED EDGES** require: | | | |
| 28.1.1 | Unless specified otherwise, the sequence of the edge/face lamination shall be the manufacturer's choice. | | | |
| 28.1.2 | HPDL or PVC a minimum of 0.018" (0.5 mm) and maximum of 0.12" (3 mm) at the manufacturer's choice, well matched to the exposed face. | | | |
| 28.1.3 | PVC and ABS edgebanding thicker than 0.04" (1 mm) be radiused on edges and corners. | | | |
| 28.2 | **DRAWERS** require: | | | |
| 28.2.1 | Front and false front: | | | |
| 28.2.1.1 | To be edgebanded at all four edges, except when back beveled. | | | |

Continues next column ▼

### 10.4.7 Assembly Rules

▲ From previous column

| # | Rule | E | C | P |
|---|------|---|---|---|
| 28 | For **DECORATIVE LAMINATE CASEWORK** (continued) | | | |
| 28.3 | **DOORS** require: | | | |
| 28.3.1 | Edgebanding on all four edges matching exposed surfaces. | E | C | P |
| 28.3.2 | Glass stops to be hardwood solid stock painted to match plastic or a synthetic (vinyl, neoprene, plastic) gasket/retainer; however: | | | |
| 28.3.2.1 | Synthetic stops are acceptable on the inside only. | | | |
| 28.3.3 | When **SLIDING**: | | | |
| 28.3.3.1 | 1/4" (6.4 mm) hardboard painted to match adjacent laminate is permitted. | E | C | P |
| 28.3.3.2 | **INTERIOR FACES** shall be a minimum of 0.020" (0.5 mm) thick HPDL balancing sheet. | | | |
| 29 | For **SOLID PHENOLIC CASEWORK** (Only applicable to Custom and Premium Grade): | | | |
| 29.1 | **EDGEBANDING** is not required. | | | |
| 29.2 | **DRAWER** front and false front thickness to be a minimum of 1/2" (12.7 mm). | | | |
| 29.3 | **DOOR** thickness to be a minimum of 1/2" (12.7 mm), and: | | | |
| 29.3.1 | Glass clips are permitted. | | | |
| 29.4 | **APRONS** require a minimum thickness of 1/2" (12.7 mm). | | | |
| 29.5 | **SHELVES** require a minimum thickness of 3/8" (9.5 mm). | | | |
| 29.6 | **TOPS** and **FIXED BOTTOMS** require a minimum thickness of 1/2" (12.7 mm). | | | |
| 29.7 | **END** and **DIVISIONS** require a minimum of 1/2" (12.7 mm) in thickness, and: | | | |
| 29.7.1 | Applied ends are permitted. | | | |
| 29.8 | **SECURITY** and **DUST PANELS** require a minimum thickness of 1/4" (6.4 mm). | | | |
| 29.9 | **STRETCHERS** require a minimum of 1/2" (12.7 mm) in thickness and 2" (50.8 mm) in width. | | | |
| 29.10 | **BREAD/CUTTING BOARDS** require a minimum of 1/2" (12.7 mm) in thickness. | | | |
| 29.11 | For **JOINERY**, use of a 9/32" x 1-1/4" (7 mm x 32 mm) sheet metal screw is permitted with the first screw 1-15/16" (37 mm) from each edge or end and subsequent screws 5" (128 mm) on center, and: | | | |
| 29.11.1 | Glue is not required. | | | |

 Where the **E**, **C**, or **P** icon is not indicated, the rule applies to all Grades equally

# SECTION 10
## Casework

**compliance requirements** — GENERAL/PRODUCT/**INSTALLATION**/TEST

### 10.5 PREPARATION and QUALIFICATION REQUIREMENTS

**1** **CARE, STORAGE,** and **BUILDING CONDITIONS** shall be in compliance with the requirements set forth in Section 2 of these standards.

1.1 Severe damage to the woodwork can result from noncompliance. The manufacturer and/or installer of the woodwork shall not be held responsible for damage that might develop by not adhering to the requirements.

**2** **CONTRACTOR IS RESPONSIBLE FOR**

2.1 Furnishing and installing structural members, grounds, in wall blocking, backing, furring, brackets, or other anchorage required for architectural woodwork installation that becomes an integral part of walls, floors, or ceilings to which architectural woodwork shall be installed.

2.1.1 In the absence of contract documents calling for the contractor to supply the necessary in wall blocking/backing in the wall or ceilings, either through inadvertence or otherwise, the architectural woodwork installer shall not proceed with the installation until such time as the in wall blocking/backing is installed by others.

2.1.2 Preparatory work done by others shall be subject to inspection by the architectural woodwork installer and may be accepted or rejected for cause prior to installation.

2.1.2.1 **WALL, CEILING,** and/or opening variations in excess of 1/4" (6.4 mm) or **FLOORS** in excess of 1/2" (12.7 mm) in 144" (3658 mm) of being plumb, level, flat, straight, square, or of the correct size are not acceptable for the installation of architectural woodwork, nor is it the responsibility of the installer to scribe or fit to tolerances in excess of such.

2.2 Installation site being properly ventilated, protected from direct sunlight, excessive heat and/or moisture, and that the HVAC system is functioning and maintaining the appropriate relative humidity and temperature.

2.3 Priming architectural woodwork in accordance with the contract documents prior to its installation:

2.3.1 If the architectural woodwork is factory finished, priming by the factory finisher is required.

### 10.5 PREPARATION and QUALIFICATION (continued)

**3** **INSTALLER IS RESPONSIBLE FOR**

3.1 Having adequate equipment and experienced craftsmen to complete the installation.

3.2 Checking architectural woodwork specified and studying the appropriate portions of the contract documents, including these standards and the reviewed shop drawings to familiarize themselves with the requirements of the Grade specified, understanding that:

3.2.1 Appearance requirements of Grades apply only to surfaces visible after installation.

3.2.2 For transparent finish, special attention needs to be given to the color and the grain of the various woodwork pieces to ensure they are installed in compliance with the Grade specified.

3.3 Verification that installation site is properly ventilated, protected from direct sunlight, excessive heat and/or moisture, and that the HVAC system is functioning and maintaining the appropriate relative humidity and temperature.

3.4 Verification that required priming of woodwork has been completed by others before woodwork is installed.

3.5 Verification that woodwork has been acclimated to the field conditions for a minimum of 72 hours before installation is commenced.

3.6 Woodwork specifically built or assembled in sequence for match of color and grain is installed to maintain that same sequence.

# SECTION 10
## Casework

GENERAL/PRODUCT/**INSTALLATION**/TEST

**compliance requirements**

Where the **E**, **C**, or **P** icon is not indicated, the rule applies to all Grades equally | E | C | P |

## 10.6 RULES

1. The following rules shall govern unless a project's contract documents require otherwise.

2. These rules are intended to provide a well defined degree of control over a project's quality of installation.

3. ERRATA, published on the Sponsor Associations' websites at www.awinet.org, www.awmac.com, or www.aws-errata.com, shall TAKE PRECEDENCE OVER THESE RULES, subject to their date of posting and a project's bid date.

### 10.6.1 Basic Rules

| | | | Rule | E | C | P |
|---|---|---|---|---|---|---|
| 1 | | | **AESTHETIC** grade rules apply only to exposed and semi-exposed surfaces visible after installation. | | | |
| 2 | | | For **TRANSPARENT** finish, woodwork shall be installed: | | | |
| 2 | 1 | | With consideration of color and grain. | E | C | P |
| 2 | 2 | | **COMPATIBLE** in color and grain. | E | **C** | P |
| 2 | 3 | | **WELL MATCHED** for color and grain. | E | C | **P** |
| 3 | | | **REPAIRS** are allowed, provided they are neatly made and inconspicuous when viewed at: | | | |
| 3 | 1 | | 72" (1830 mm). | **E** | C | P |
| 3 | 2 | | 48" (1219 mm). | E | **C** | P |
| 3 | 3 | | 24" (610 mm). | E | C | **P** |
| 4 | | | **INSTALLER MODIFICATIONS** shall comply to the material, machining, and assembly rules within the PRODUCT portion of this section and the applicable finishing rules in Section 5. | | | |
| 5 | | | **CASEWORK** or related items: | | | |
| 5 | 1 | | Shall be securely fastened and tightly fitted with flush joint tolerances as set forth in these standards. | | | |
| 5 | 1 | 1 | Joinery shall be consistent throughout the project. | | | |
| 5 | 2 | | Such as scribe molds shall be of maximum available and/or practical lengths and: | | | |
| 5 | 2 | 1 | Mitered at outside corners. | | | |
| 5 | 3 | | Shall be Installed plumb, level, square, flat and in plane within 1/8" (3.2 mm) in 96" (2438 mm), and when required: | | | |
| 5 | 3 | 1 | Grounds and hanging systems set plumb and true. | | | |
| 5 | 4 | | Shall be Installed free of: | | | |
| 5 | 4 | 1 | Warp, twisting, cupping, and/or bowing that cannot be held true. | | | |
| 5 | 4 | 2 | Open joints, visible machine marks, cross sanding, tear outs, nicks, chips, and/or scratches. | | | |

Continues next column ▼

### 10.6.1 Basic Rules

▲ From previous column

| | | | Rule | E | C | P |
|---|---|---|---|---|---|---|
| 5 | | | **CASEWORK** or related items (continued) | | | |
| 5 | 4 | | Shall be Installed free of (continued): | | | |
| 5 | 4 | 3 | Natural defects exceeding the quantity or size limits defined in Sections 3 and 4. | | | |
| 5 | 4 | 4 | Exposed fasteners at exposed exterior surfaces. | | | |
| 5 | 5 | | Shall be smooth and sanded without cross scratches in conformance to the Product portion of this section. | | | |
| 5 | 6 | | Shall be **SCRIBED** at: | | | |
| 5 | 6 | 1 | Flat surfaces. | E | C | P |
| 5 | 6 | 2 | Shaped surfaces. | E | C | P |
| 6 | | | **THESE STANDARDS** do not establish grade rules for joint flushness and or gap tolerances for woodwork products installed in a non climate controlled environment. | | | |
| 7 | | | **GAPS** (see Test I illustrations in TESTS) such as, and: | | | |
| 7 | 1 | | If caused by excessive deviations in the building's walls and ceilings being in excess of 1/4" (6.4 mm) in 144" (3658 mm) of being plumb, level, flat, straight, square, or of the correct size, or 1/2" (12.7 mm) for floors, shall not be considered a defect or the responsibility of the installer. | | | |
| 7 | 2 | | Shall not exceed 30% of a joint's length, with: | | | |
| 7 | 2 | 1 | Be allowed if filled or caulked, and: | E | C | P |
| 7 | 2 | 1 | If color compatible. | E | **C** | **P** |
| 7 | 3 | | Of **WOOD** to **WOOD** shall not exceed: | | | |
| 7 | 3 | 1 | At **FLAT** surfaces: | | | |
| 7 | 3 | 1 | 0.030" (0.76 mm) in width. | **E** | C | P |
| 7 | 3 | 2 | 0.020" (0.51 mm) in width. | E | **C** | P |
| 7 | 3 | 3 | 0.015" (0.38 mm) in width. | E | C | **P** |
| 7 | 3 | 2 | At **SHAPED** surfaces: | | | |
| 7 | 3 | 2 | 1 | 0.040" (1.02 mm) in width. | **E** | C | P |
| 7 | 3 | 2 | 2 | 0.025" (0.64 mm) in width. | E | **C** | P |
| 7 | 3 | 2 | 3 | 0.015" (0.38 mm) in width. | E | C | **P** |

Continues next column ▼

# SECTION 10
## Casework

**compliance requirements** — GENERAL/PRODUCT/**INSTALLATION**/TEST

### 10.6.1 Basic Rules

▲ From previous column

| | | | | | | E | C | P |
|---|---|---|---|---|---|---|---|---|
| 7 | | **GAPS** (continued) | | | | | | |
| 7 | 4 | | Of **WOOD** to **NON WOOD** shall not exceed: | | | | | |
| 7 | 4 | 1 | At **FLAT** and **SHAPED** surfaces: | | | | | |
| 7 | 4 | 1 | 1 | 0.075" (1.91 mm) in width. | | E | C | P |
| 7 | 4 | 1 | 2 | 0.050" (1.27 mm) in width. | | E | **C** | P |
| 7 | 4 | 1 | 3 | 0.035" (0.89 mm) in width. | | E | C | **P** |
| 7 | 5 | | Of **NON WOOD** to **NON WOOD** and/or **ALL ELEMENTS** shall not exceed: | | | | | |
| 7 | 5 | 1 | At **FLAT** surfaces: | | | | | |
| 7 | 5 | 1 | 1 | 0.075" (1.91 mm) in width. | | E | C | P |
| 7 | 5 | 1 | 2 | 0.050" (1.27 mm) in width. | | E | **C** | P |
| 7 | 5 | 1 | 3 | 0.035" (0.89 mm) in width. | | E | C | **P** |
| 7 | 5 | 2 | At **SHAPED** surfaces. | | | | | |
| 7 | 5 | 2 | 1 | 0.120" (3.05 mm) in width. | | E | C | P |
| 7 | 5 | 2 | 2 | 0.075" (1.91 mm) in width. | | E | **C** | P |
| 7 | 5 | 2 | 3 | 0.050" (1.27 mm) in width. | | E | C | **P** |
| 8 | | **FLUSHNESS** of joinery (see Test J illustrations in TESTS), such as, and: | | | | | | |
| 8 | 1 | | Of **WOOD** to **WOOD** shall not exceed: | | | | | |
| 8 | 1 | 1 | At **FLAT** surfaces: | | | | | |
| 8 | 1 | 1 | 1 | 0.025" (0.64 mm). | | E | C | P |
| 8 | 1 | 1 | 2 | 0.015" (0.38 mm). | | E | **C** | P |
| 8 | 1 | 1 | 3 | 0.010" (0.25 mm). | | E | C | **P** |
| 8 | 1 | 2 | At **SHAPED** surfaces: | | | | | |
| 8 | 1 | 2 | 1 | 0.040" (0.97 mm). | | E | C | P |
| 8 | 1 | 2 | 2 | 0.025" (0.65 mm). | | E | **C** | P |
| 8 | 1 | 2 | 3 | 0.020" (0.51 mm). | | E | C | **P** |

Continues next column ▼

### 10.6.1 Basic Rules

▲ From previous column

| | | | | | | E | C | P |
|---|---|---|---|---|---|---|---|---|
| 8 | | **FLUSHNESS** (continued): | | | | | | |
| 8 | 2 | | Of **WOOD** to **NON WOOD** shall not exceed: | | | | | |
| 8 | 2 | 1 | At **FLAT** and **SHAPED** surfaces: | | | | | |
| 8 | 2 | 1 | 1 | 0.075" (1.91 mm). | | E | C | P |
| 8 | 2 | 1 | 2 | 0.050" (1.27 mm). | | E | **C** | P |
| 8 | 2 | 1 | 3 | 0.035" (0.89 mm). | | E | C | **P** |
| 8 | 3 | | Of **NON WOOD** to **NON WOOD** and/or **ALL ELEMENTS** shall not exceed: | | | | | |
| 8 | 3 | 1 | At **FLAT** surfaces: | | | | | |
| 8 | 3 | 1 | 1 | 0.075" (1.91 mm). | | E | C | P |
| 8 | 3 | 1 | 2 | 0.050" (1.27 mm). | | E | **C** | P |
| 8 | 3 | 1 | 3 | 0.035" (0.89 mm). | | E | C | **P** |
| 8 | 3 | 2 | At **SHAPED** surfaces: | | | | | |
| 8 | 3 | 2 | 1 | 0.120" (3.05 mm). | | E | C | P |
| 8 | 3 | 2 | 2 | 0.075" (1.91 mm). | | E | **C** | P |
| 8 | 3 | 2 | 3 | 0.050" (1.27 mm). | | E | C | **P** |
| 9 | | **GAPS, EDGE ALIGNMENT** and **FLUSHNESS** of doors and drawers shall be uniform and within the tolerances set forth in the Product portion of this section, and: | | | | | | |
| 9 | 1 | Door and drawer fronts shall align vertically and horizontally, and: | | | | | | |
| 9 | 1 | 1 | Be flush (on the same plane) to one another. | | | | | |
| 9 | 1 | 2 | Minor adjustments are the responsibility of the installer. | | | | | |
| 10 | | **SCRIBING** shall be provided where cabinets contact finished walls or ceiling as elaborated below and in the Product portion of this section, and: | | | | | | |
| 10 | 1 | Is not required. | | | | E | C | P |
| 10 | 2 | Shall be **FURNISHED** by the manufacturer, and: | | | | E | **C** | **P** |
| 10 | 2 | 1 | Scribe **FILLERS** shall not exceed 1-1/2" (38.1 mm) in width. | | | E | **C** | **P** |
| 10 | 2 | 2 | Scribe **MOLDS** shall not exceed 1-1/2" (38.1 mm) in width, and; | | | E | C | P |
| 10 | 2 | 2 | 1 | End joints may be butt jointed. | | E | C | P |
| 10 | 2 | 2 | 2 | End joints shall be beveled, and: | | E | **C** | P |
| 10 | 2 | 2 | 2 | 1 | Corners shall be mitered or coped. | E | **C** | P |
| 10 | 2 | 2 | 3 | Are not **NOT ALLOWED.** | | E | C | **P** |
| 10 | 3 | Match exposed surfaces. | | | | | | |
| 10 | 4 | Be furnished in maximum available lengths, joints not allowed in material less than 96" (2438 mm). | | | | | | |

Continues next column ▼

# SECTION 10
## Casework

GENERAL / PRODUCT / **INSTALLATION** / TEST

**compliance requirements**

Where the **E**, **C**, or **P** icon is not indicated, the rule applies to all Grades equally | **E** | **C** | **P** |

### 10.6.1 Basic Rules

▲ From previous column

| | | | | E | C | P |
|---|---|---|---|---|---|---|
| 10 | | | **SCRIBING** (continued): | | | |
| 10 | 5 | | Permits **COLOR COMPATIBLE CAULKING** not to exceed 1/8" (3.2 mm). | E | C | P |
| 10 | 6 | | Fillers at inside corners where two elevations of casework meet must be equal in width, and: | | | |
| 10 | 6 | 1 | Not to exceed a maximum of 3" in width unless required for hardware clearance during operation. | | | |
| 10 | 7 | | Requires **SOFFIT** or **FASCIA PANELS** to be furnished in maximum available lengths, joints not allowed in material less than 96" (2438 mm) at horizontal grain or directional pattern and 48" (1219 mm) at vertical grain or directional pattern, and: | E | C | P |
| 10 | 7 | 1 | Be a minimum of 3/4" (19 mm) in thickness. | | | |
| 10 | 7 | 2 | Grain direction (if any) shall run vertical, or be manufacturer's choice if less than: | | | |
| 10 | 7 | 2 | 1 | 12" (305 mm) tall. | E | C | P |
| 10 | 7 | 2 | 2 | 1-1/2" (38.1 mm) tall. | E | C | P |
| 10 | 8 | | **TYPICAL SCRIBING OPTIONS:** | | | |

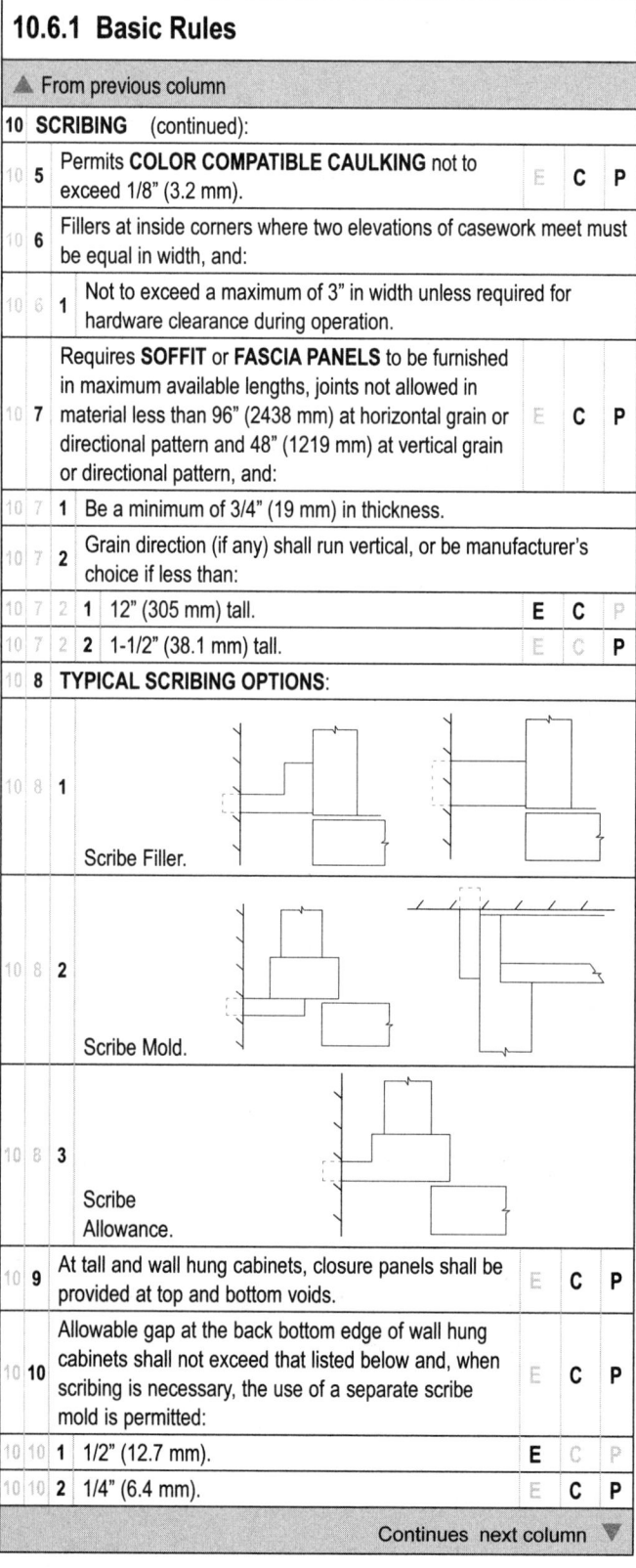

| 10 | 8 | 1 | Scribe Filler. |
| 10 | 8 | 2 | Scribe Mold. |
| 10 | 8 | 3 | Scribe Allowance. |

| | | | | E | C | P |
|---|---|---|---|---|---|---|
| 10 | 9 | | At tall and wall hung cabinets, closure panels shall be provided at top and bottom voids. | E | C | P |
| 10 | 10 | | Allowable gap at the back bottom edge of wall hung cabinets shall not exceed that listed below and, when scribing is necessary, the use of a separate scribe mold is permitted: | E | C | P |
| 10 | 10 | 1 | 1/2" (12.7 mm). | E | C | P |
| 10 | 10 | 2 | 1/4" (6.4 mm). | E | C | P |

Continues next column ▼

### 10.6.1 Basic Rules

▲ From previous column

| | | | | E | C | P |
|---|---|---|---|---|---|---|
| 11 | | | **CLOSURE** provision is required at voids or open spaces between cabinets and walls, such as at the top of tall and upper cabinets and the bottom of upper cabinets caused by scribing or angle turns, and: | | | |
| 11 | 1 | | At non visible voids, 1-1/2" (38 mm) or less in width, a piece of standard grade laminate may be used as a closure cap. | | | |
| 11 | 2 | | At non visible voids, exceeding 1-1/2" (38 mm) in width, a minimum 3/4" (19 mm) closure filler shall be provided of manufacturer's choice. | | | |
| 12 | | | **EXPOSED FASTENERS** are not permitted at exposed exterior surfaces, except: | E | C | P |
| 12 | 1 | | At access panels. | | | |
| 13 | | | **CASEWORK WALL ANCHORAGE**, except for peninsula/island or base casework with mechanical spacing allowances (because of the need to be engineered on an individual basis), requires: | | | |
| 13 | 1 | | **CONTINUOUS IN WALL BLOCKING** or **BACKING** of at least 2" x 6" (51 mm x 152 mm) nominal wood or 6" x 16 ga (152 mm x 1.4 mm) sheet metal, installed by others, shall be appropriately located in all wood or metal stud walls as shown below: | | | |

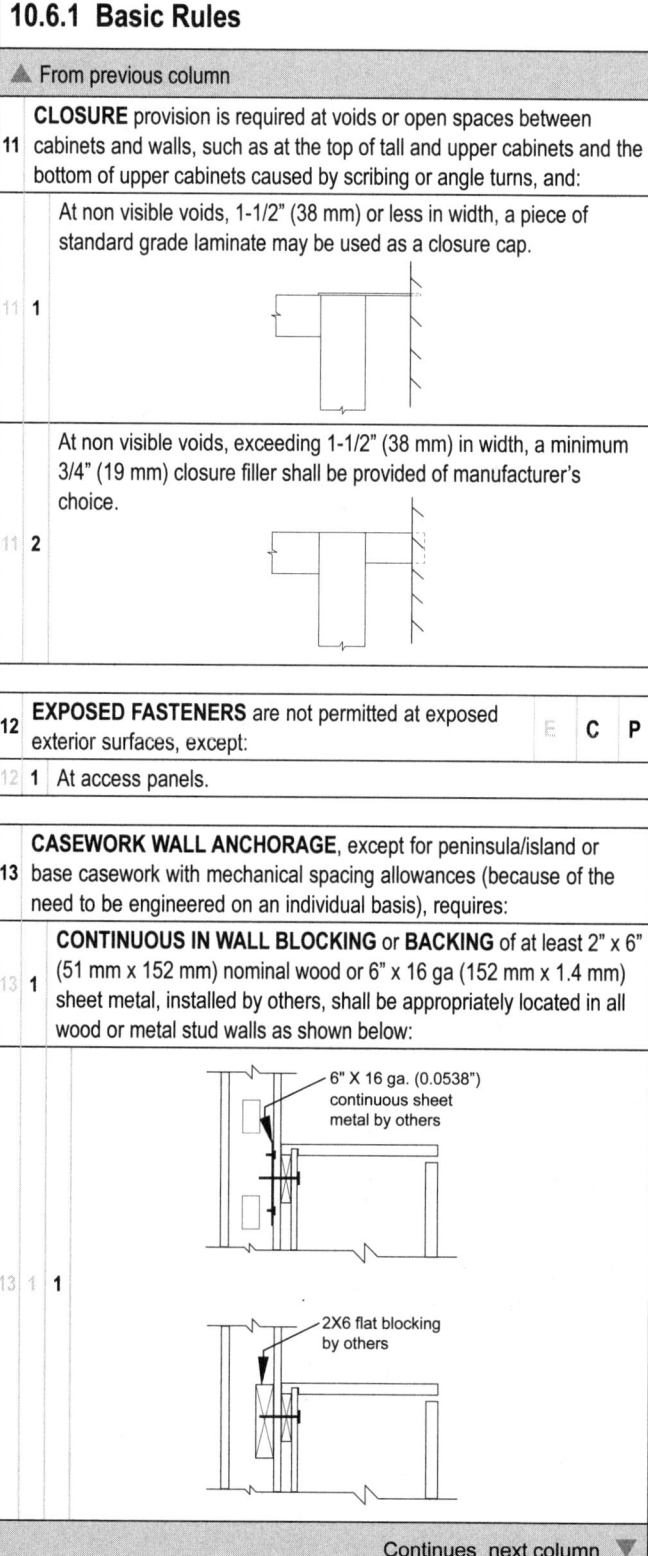

6" X 16 ga. (0.0538") continuous sheet metal by others

2X6 flat blocking by others

| 13 | 1 | 1 | | | | |

Continues next column ▼

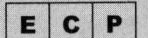

Where the **E**, **C**, or **P** icon is not indicated, the rule applies to all Grades equally

# SECTION 10
## Casework

## compliance requirements

GENERAL/PRODUCT/**INSTALLATION**/TEST

### 10.6.1 Basic Rules

▲ From previous column

| | | | | | |
|---|---|---|---|---|---|
| 13 | | CASEWORK WALL ANCHORAGE (continued): | | | |
| 13 | 2 | **MANUFACTURER** to provide appropriate location layouts on their shop drawings for in wall blocking or backing for all tall, base, and wall hung casework for both top and bottom runs of fasteners, as shown below: | | | |
| 13 | 2 | 1 | 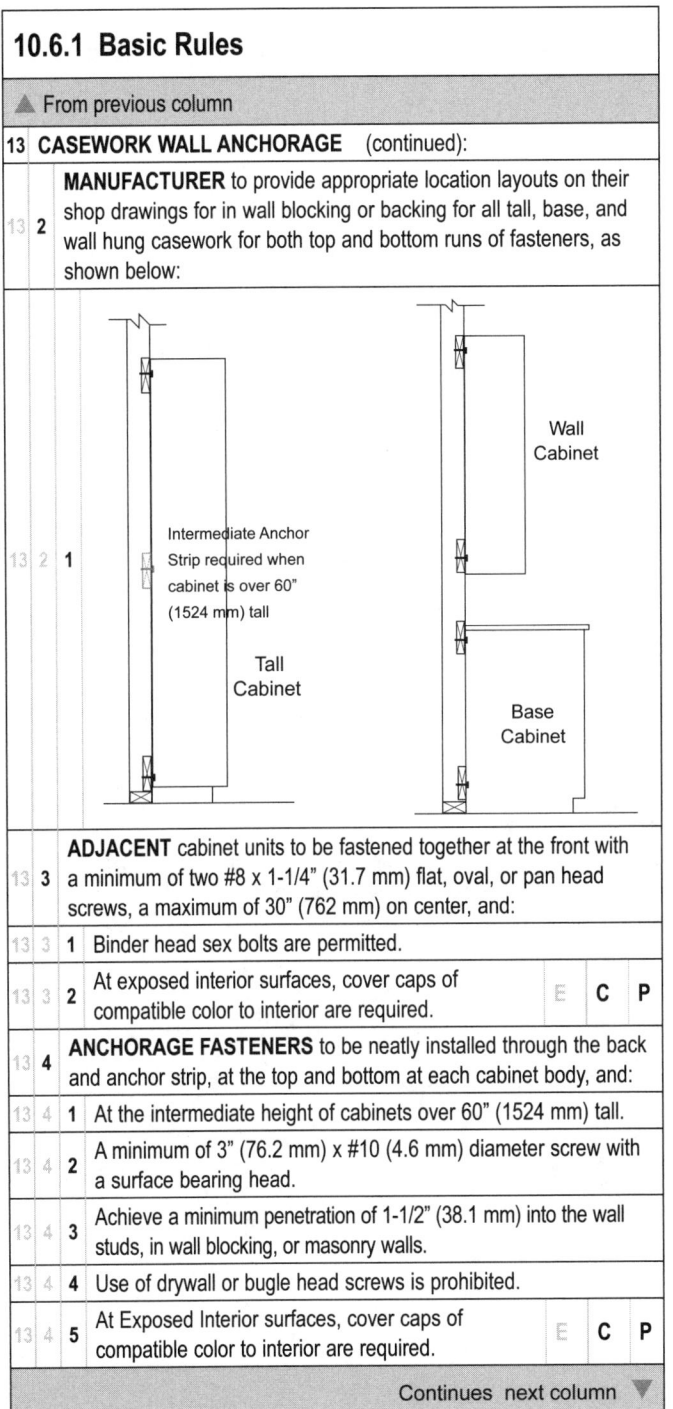 | | |
| 13 | 3 | **ADJACENT** cabinet units to be fastened together at the front with a minimum of two #8 x 1-1/4" (31.7 mm) flat, oval, or pan head screws, a maximum of 30" (762 mm) on center, and: | | | |
| 13 | 3 | 1 | Binder head sex bolts are permitted. | | |
| 13 | 3 | 2 | At exposed interior surfaces, cover caps of compatible color to interior are required. | E | C | P |
| 13 | 4 | **ANCHORAGE FASTENERS** to be neatly installed through the back and anchor strip, at the top and bottom at each cabinet body, and: | | | |
| 13 | 4 | 1 | At the intermediate height of cabinets over 60" (1524 mm) tall. | | |
| 13 | 4 | 2 | A minimum of 3" (76.2 mm) x #10 (4.6 mm) diameter screw with a surface bearing head. | | |
| 13 | 4 | 3 | Achieve a minimum penetration of 1-1/2" (38.1 mm) into the wall studs, in wall blocking, or masonry walls. | | |
| 13 | 4 | 4 | Use of drywall or bugle head screws is prohibited. | | |
| 13 | 4 | 5 | At Exposed Interior surfaces, cover caps of compatible color to interior are required. | E | C | P |

Continues next column ▼

### 10.6.1 Basic Rules

▲ From previous column

| | | | | |
|---|---|---|---|---|
| 13 | | CASEWORK WALL ANCHORAGE (continued): | | |
| 13 | 6 | Each cabinet unit or undivided span shall have a minimum of four anchorage fasteners; two at the top and two at the bottom, subject to: | | |
| 13 | 6 | 1 | Horizontally, within 3" (76.2 mm) of the outside end and equally spaced, at: | |
| 13 | 6 | 1 | 1 | A maximum spacing of 16" (406 mm) on center, except: |
| 13 | 6 | 1 | 1 | 1 | Wall cabinet units over 48" (1,219 mm) in height shall be 12" (305 mm). |
| 13 | 6 | 2 | Vertically, within 3" (76.2 mm) of the outside top or bottom of the cabinet unit and must penetrate the anchor strip. | |
| 13 | 6 | 3 | A locking hanging cleat, or other concealed method of installation may be used, provided it has been independently tested to show compliance to the Wall Cabinet Structural Integrity Test shown in the **APPENDIX**. | **a** |
| 13 | 6 | 3 | 1 | 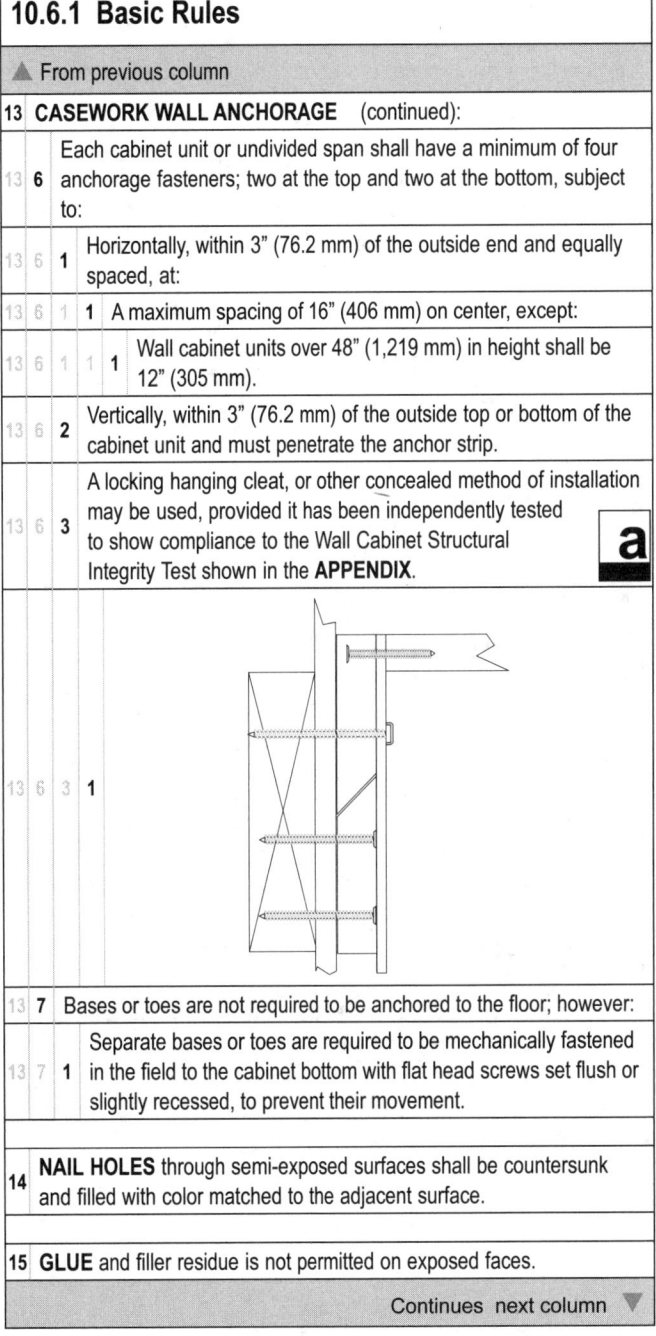 |
| 13 | 7 | Bases or toes are not required to be anchored to the floor; however: | | |
| 13 | 7 | 1 | Separate bases or toes are required to be mechanically fastened in the field to the cabinet bottom with flat head screws set flush or slightly recessed, to prevent their movement. | |
| 14 | | **NAIL HOLES** through semi-exposed surfaces shall be countersunk and filled with color matched to the adjacent surface. | | |
| 15 | | **GLUE** and filler residue is not permitted on exposed faces. | | |

Continues next column ▼

# SECTION 10
## Casework

GENERAL / PRODUCT / **INSTALLATION** / TEST

**compliance requirements**

Where the **E**, **C**, or **P** icon is not indicated, the rule applies to all Grades equally — **E C P**

### 10.6.1 Basic Rules

▲ From previous column

| | | |
|---|---|---|
| 16 | | **CAULKING**, when used to fill gaps and/or voids, shall be color compatible and installed neatly. |
| 17 | | **REQUIRE** allowable fastener holes, when: |
| 17 | 1 | Prefinished materials to be filled by the installer with matching filler furnished by the manufacturer. |
| 17 | 2 | Unfinished materials to be filled by the paint contractor or others. |
| 18 | | **EQUIPMENT CUTOUTS**, including electrical and plumbing, shall be cut out by the installer, provided templates are furnished prior to installation, and: |
| 18 | 1 | Shall be neatly cut and properly sized to be covered by standard cover plates or rosettes. |
| 18 | 2 | Cutouts in HPDL shall have radiused inside corners. |
| 19 | | **HARDWARE** shall be installed: |
| 19 | 1 | Neatly without tear out of surrounding stock. |
| 19 | 2 | Per the manufacturer's instructions. |
| 19 | 3 | Using all furnished fasteners or fastener provisions and when fastener provisions are countersunk, fasteners shall be countersunk. |
| 19 | 4 | Properly, fitted and adjusted to ensure correct and smooth operation. |
| 20 | | **AREAS** of **INSTALLATION** shall be left broom clean of: |
| 20 | 1 | Debris shall be removed and dumped in containers provided by the contractor. |
| 20 | 2 | Items installed shall be cleaned of pencil or ink marks. |
| 21 | | Entire installation shall present **FIRST CLASS WORKMANSHIP** in compliance with these standards. |

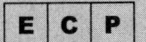 Where the **E**, **C**, or **P** icon is not indicated, the rule applies to all Grades equally

# SECTION 10
## Casework

## compliance requirements
GENERAL/PRODUCT/INSTALLATION/**TEST**

### 10.7 BASIC CONSIDERATIONS

1. The tolerances typically found within the Architectural Woodwork Standards fall into two categories:

   1.1 Factory fabricated joinery, assembly and construction found in the **PRODUCT** portion.

   1.2 Field installation joinery and assembly found in the **INSTALLATION** portion.

2. Most fabrication and installation assemblies include solid wood to solid wood joints, solid wood to wood veneer joints, solid wood to wood based products (HPDL, LPDL, Solid Phenolic and panel products), solid wood to non wood based products (which can be drywall, glass, metal, stone, acrylics, and other surfaces), and non wood to non wood joints.

3. Tolerances found in the AWS include:

   3.1 Flatness of wood based panel products.

   3.2 Solid wood to solid wood joints and assemblies.

   3.3 Solid wood to wood veneer joints and assemblies.

   3.4 Wood veneer to wood veneer joints and assemblies.

   3.5 Solid wood to wood based product joints and assemblies.

   3.6 Solid surface to solid surface joints and assemblies.

4. Because of the differences of expansion and contraction of non wood products compared to solid wood and wood based products, the AWS does not apply tolerances regarding flatness or joinery to these non wood based products.

### 10.7 BASIC CONSIDERATIONS

5. **FABRICATED** and **INSTALLED** woodwork shall be tested for compliance to these standards as follows:

   5.1 **SMOOTHNESS** of exposed surfaces:

   5.1.1 **KCPI** (Knife Cuts Per Inch) is determined by holding the surfaced board at an angle to a strong light source and counting the visible ridges per inch, usually perpendicular to the profile.

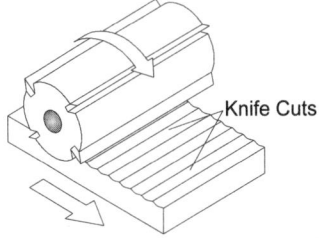

*Figure: 10-073*

   5.1.2 **SANDING** is checked for compliance by sanding a sample piece of the same species with the required grit of abrasive:

   5.1.2.1 Observation with a hand lens of the prepared sample and the material in question will offer a comparison of the scratch marks of the abrasive grit.

   5.1.2.2 Reasonable assessment of the performance of the finished product will be weighed against absolute compliance with the standard.

   5.1.2.3 A product is sanded sufficiently smooth when knife cuts are removed and remaining sanding marks are or will be concealed by applied finishing coats.

   5.1.2.4 Grain raise at unfinished wood, due to moisture or humidity in excess of the ranges set forth in this standard, shall not be considered a defect and must be sanded prior to finishing.

6. **GAPS, FLUSHNESS, FLATNESS** and **ALIGNMENT** of product and installation:

   6.1 Maximum gaps between exposed components shall be tested with a feeler gauge at points designed to join where members contact or touch.

   6.2 Joint length shall be measured with a ruler with minimum 1/16" (1 mm) divisions and calculations made accordingly.

   6.3 Reasonable assessment of the performance of the finished product will be weighed against absolute compliance with the standards.

# SECTION 10
## Casework

GENERAL/PRODUCT/INSTALLATION/**TEST**

**compliance requirements**

Where the **E**, **C**, or **P** icon is not indicated, the rule applies to all Grades equally | **E** | **C** | **P** |

### 10.7 BASIC CONSIDERATIONS

6 **GAPS, FLUSHNESS, FLATNESS** and **ALIGNMENT**
(continued)

6.4 The following is intended to provide examples of how and where testing is measured:

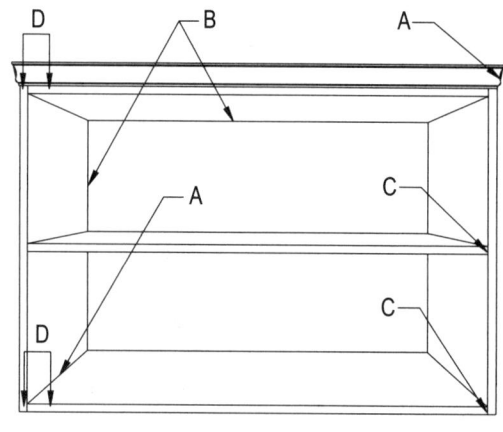

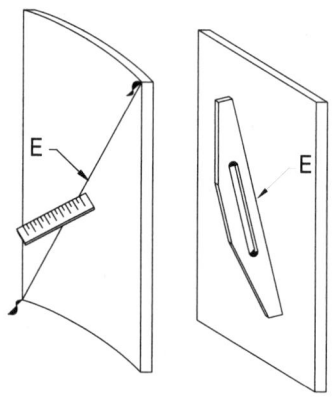

Measured on the concave face

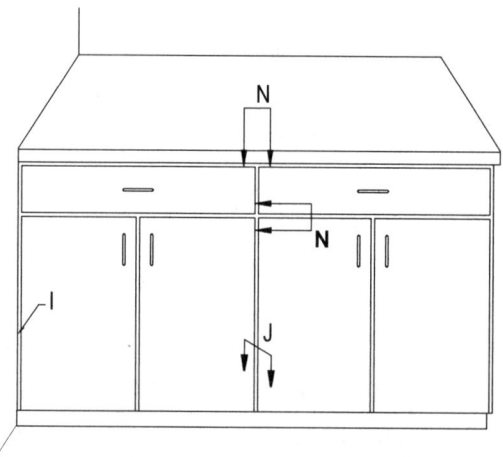

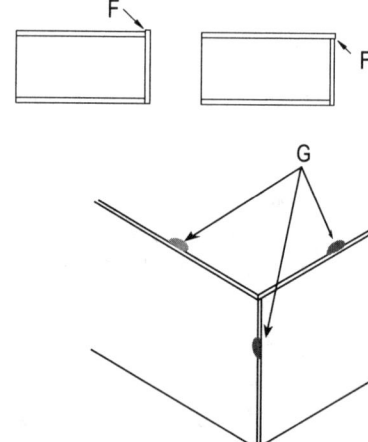

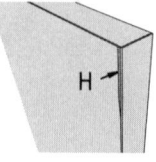

A - Gaps when surfaces are mitered or butted
B - Gaps when parallel pieces are joined
C - Gaps when edges are mitered or butted
D - Flushness between two surfaces
E - Flatness of panel product
F - Overlap (flushness of laminate)
G - Chip Out
H - Over Machining
I - Installation Gaps
J - Installation Flushness
N - Alignment of doors and drawer fronts

Figure: 10-074

# Architectural Woodwork Standards

# COUNTERTOPS

## SECTION 11

# SECTION 11
## Countertops

## table of contents

### INTRODUCTORY INFORMATION

- Guide Specifications .................................................. 341
- Introduction ............................................................. 342
- Typical Countertop Configurations ............................ 342
- Guidelines for Fabrication/Installation of HPDL Tops ... 343
- Typical Problems at HPDL countertops - Causes and Prevention ... 344
- Chemical or Stain Resistance ................................... 345
- Abrasion Resistance ................................................ 345
- HPDL Countertops ................................................... 345
  - Assembly - 1 ..................................................... 345
  - Assembly - 2 ..................................................... 345
  - White Background Paper .................................... 345
  - Flame Spread Rated .......................................... 345
  - Countertop Configuration Options ....................... 345
  - Options at Top of Splash .................................... 346
  - Deck Options at Splash ...................................... 346
  - Front Edge Option ............................................. 346
  - Typical Mechanical Tight Joint Fastener .............. 347
- Solid Surface Countertops ........................................ 347
  - Color and Pattern Match .................................... 347
  - Repairs ............................................................. 347
  - Precautions ....................................................... 347
  - Machinability ..................................................... 347
  - Configuration Options ........................................ 347
  - Top Options at Splash ........................................ 347
  - Deck Options at Splash ...................................... 347
  - Edge Options .................................................... 347
- Solid Phenolic, Epoxy Resin, and Natural/Engineered Stone Countertops ............................................................ 348
  - Configuration Options ........................................ 348
  - Top and Deck Option sat Splash ......................... 348
  - Edge Options .................................................... 348
- Wood Countertops ................................................... 348
  - Configuration Options ........................................ 348
- To Prevent Telegraphing .......................................... 349
- Specify Requirements For ........................................ 349
- Recommendations ................................................... 349
  - If Field Finished ................................................. 349
  - Review .............................................................. 349
  - Structural Members ........................................... 348
  - At HPDL Sink Tops ............................................ 349

# SECTION 11
## Countertops

## table of contents

**COMPLIANCE REQUIREMENTS**

**GENERAL**
- Basic Considerations ..................................................................350
    - Grade ................................................................................350
        - Economy Grade ..........................................................350
        - Custom Grade .............................................................350
        - Premium Grade ............................................................350
        - Grade Limitations .........................................................350
    - Contract Documents ..........................................................350
    - Acceptable Requirements ...................................................350
    - Aesthetic Compliance Requirements ...................................350
    - Exposed Surfaces ..............................................................350
    - Concealed Surfaces ..........................................................350
    - Solid Surface ....................................................................350
    - Solid Phenolic ...................................................................350
    - Epoxy Resin .....................................................................350
    - Natural Stone ...................................................................350
    - Engineered Stone .............................................................350
    - To Prevent Telegraphing ....................................................350
    - Industry Practices .............................................................350
        - Structural Members .....................................................350
        - Wall, Ceilings and Floor Tolerances ..............................351
        - Priming ........................................................................351
        - Build Up ......................................................................351
        - Grain and Pattern ........................................................351
        - Horizontal Reveals ......................................................351

**PRODUCT**
- Scope .................................................................................351
    - Typical Inclusions ..............................................................351
    - Typical Exclusions .............................................................351
- Default Stipulation ................................................................352
    - HPDL Countertop ..............................................................352
    - Wood Countertop ..............................................................352
    - Solid Surface Countertop ...................................................352
    - Solid Phenolic, Epoxy resin, Natural/Engineered Stone Countertop ..........................................................................352

- Rules ....................................................................................352
    - Errata ................................................................................352
    - Basic Rules .......................................................................352
        - Aesthetic ......................................................................352
        - Lumber .........................................................................352
        - Sheet Products .............................................................352
        - Backing Sheet ..............................................................352
        - Exposed Surfaces ........................................................352
        - Concealed Surfaces .....................................................352
        - Balanced Panel ............................................................352
        - Grain or Pattern Surfacing ............................................352
        - Exposed Fastening .......................................................352
        - Fire Retardant or Moisture Resistant ............................352
        - HPDL edgebanding ......................................................353
        - Gluing or Lamination ....................................................353
        - First Class Workmanship .............................................353
    - Material Rules ...................................................................353
        - Factory Finishing ..........................................................353
        - Opaque Finish ..............................................................353
        - Transparent Finish Veneer ...........................................353
            - Species ..................................................................353
            - Slicing .....................................................................353
            - Matching Adjacent Leaves .....................................353
            - Matching within a Panel Face .................................353
            - Matching Between Adjacent Panels .......................353
        - Exposed Surfaces ........................................................353
            - Transparent Finished Wood ...................................353
        - Concealed Surfaces .....................................................353
        - Wood ............................................................................353
            - Core ........................................................................353
                - At Sink Tops .....................................................354
        - HPDL ............................................................................354
            - Core ........................................................................354
                - At Sink Tops .....................................................354
        - Solid Surface ................................................................354
        - Solid Phenolic ..............................................................354
        - Epoxy Resin .................................................................354
        - Natural/Engineered Stone ............................................354

# SECTION 11
## Countertops

## table of contents

**COMPLIANCE REQUIREMENTS**  (continued)

**PRODUCT**  (continued)

Rules  (continued)

- Machining Rules .................................................................. 354
  - Exposed Surfaces ............................................................ 354
    - HPDL, PVC and Prefinished Wood ......................... 354
      - Overlap, Test F ................................................. 354
      - Chip Out, Test G ............................................... 354
      - Over Machined - Test H .................................. 354
    - Cutouts ........................................................................ 355
    - Tear Outs, Knife Nicks, or Hit or Miss ........................... 355
    - Knife Marks ................................................................. 355
    - Sharp Edges ................................................................ 355
    - At Wood ...................................................................... 355
      - Occasional Patches .......................................... 355
      - Finger Joints ..................................................... 355
      - Smoothness Requirements .............................. 355
    - At HPDL ...................................................................... 355
      - Cutouts ............................................................. 355
      - Coves ................................................................ 355
      - Drip Groove ...................................................... 355
      - Miter Fold ......................................................... 355
    - At Solid Surface .......................................................... 355
      - Manufactured Joints ........................................ 355
      - Edge .................................................................. 355
      - Cove .................................................................. 355
    - At Solid Phenolic ........................................................ 356
      - Joints ................................................................. 356
      - Front Edges ...................................................... 356
    - At Epoxy Resin ............................................................ 356
      - Exposed Edges ................................................. 356
      - Lipped Top ....................................................... 356
    - At Natural or Engineered Stone ................................. 356
- Assembly Rules .................................................................. 356
  - These Standards ............................................................ 356
  - Adhesive or Joint Filler .................................................. 356
  - Squareness .................................................................... 356
  - Cutouts ........................................................................... 356
  - Scribing .......................................................................... 356
  - Fillers .............................................................................. 356
  - Edge Application Sequence ......................................... 356
  - Back Splashes ................................................................ 356
  - Removable Ledges and/or Access Panels ................... 356
  - Joints, excluding Soild Phenolic, Epoxy Resin and Natural/Engineered Stone ............................................................. 356
    - Flushness Variations, Test D ................................... 357
    - Gaps, Test A ............................................................. 357
    - Gaps, Test B ............................................................. 357
    - Gaps, Test C ............................................................. 357
    - Flatness, Test E ....................................................... 358
  - Overhang ....................................................................... 358
  - Unsupported Span ........................................................ 358
  - Wall Hung or Cantilever Countertops .......................... 358
  - Exposed Edges .............................................................. 358
  - Metal Trim Rings ........................................................... 358
  - At Wood ......................................................................... 358
    - Joints ......................................................................... 358
    - Wide Width Glue Up ............................................... 358
    - Solid Wood Edges ................................................... 358
    - Built up Members ................................................... 359
  - At HPDL ......................................................................... 359
    - Backing Sheets ........................................................ 359
    - Laminations ............................................................. 359
    - Flame Spread Rated ............................................... 359
    - Joints ......................................................................... 359
    - Bottom of Edge ....................................................... 359
    - Built up Members ................................................... 359
    - Assembly 1 ............................................................... 359
    - Assembly 2 ............................................................... 359
    - Prefinished End Caps ............................................. 359
    - Cantilever ................................................................. 360
    - Removable Components ....................................... 360

# SECTION 11
## Countertops

## table of contents

**COMPLIANCE REQUIREMENTS** (continued)

**PRODUCT** (continued)

Rules (continued)

Assembly Rules (continued)

At Solid Surface ................................................................360
- Flushness Variations, Test D ....................................360
- Gaps, Test A, B and C ..............................................360
- Flatness .....................................................................360
- Joints .........................................................................360
- Exposed Finish .........................................................360
- Seam Joints ..............................................................360
- Expansion Clearances ..............................................360
- Sealants and Adhesives ...........................................360
- Cantilever .................................................................360

At Solid Phenolic ..............................................................361
- Flushness Variations, Test D ....................................361
- Gaps, Test A .............................................................361
- Gaps, Test B .............................................................361
- Gaps, Test C .............................................................361
- Flatness, Test E ........................................................361
- Edge Finish ...............................................................361
- Lipped Tops ..............................................................361
- Back Splashes ..........................................................361
- Cantilever .................................................................361

At Epoxy Resin .................................................................362
- Flushness Variations, Test D ....................................362
- Gaps, Test A, B and C ..............................................362
- Flatness, Test E ........................................................362
- Back Splashes ..........................................................362
- Cantilever .................................................................362

At Natural and Engineered Stone ....................................362
- Flushness Variations, Test D ....................................362
- Gaps, Test A .............................................................362
- Gaps, Test B .............................................................362
- Gaps, Test C .............................................................363
- Thickness .................................................................363
- Flatness, Test E ........................................................363

Back Splashes ..................................................................363
Cantilever .........................................................................363

**INSTALLATION**

Care, Storage and Building Conditions ...........................364
Contractor is Responsible For .........................................364
Installer is Responsible For ..............................................364
Rules ................................................................................364

Basic Rules ......................................................................365
- Aesthetic Grade Rules ..............................................365
- Installed ....................................................................365
- Transparent ..............................................................365
- Repairs .....................................................................365
- Installer Modifications ..............................................365
- Build Up ....................................................................365
- Horizontal Reveal .....................................................365
- Countertops ..............................................................365
  - Securely Fastened ..............................................365
  - Installed ...............................................................365
  - Smooth ................................................................365
  - Scribed ................................................................365
- Glue ..........................................................................365
- Cutouts and Holes ....................................................365
- Mirrors ......................................................................365
- These Standards ......................................................365
- Gaps, Test A, B, and C .............................................366
- Flushness, Test D ....................................................366
- Fastening .................................................................366
- Equipment Cutouts ...................................................367
- Hardware ..................................................................367
- Areas of Installation ..................................................367
- First Class Workmanship .........................................367

At Solid and Veneered Wood ..........................................367
- Edges .......................................................................367
- Waterproof Caulk .....................................................367
- Installer Assembled Joints .......................................367
- Sink Cutouts .............................................................367
- Cutouts .....................................................................367

# SECTION 11
## Countertops

### table of contents

**COMPLIANCE REQUIREMENTS** (continued)

- **INSTALLATION** (continued)
  - Rules (continued)
    - Basic Rules (continued)
      - At HPDL ................................................................... 367
        - Countertops ......................................................... 367
        - Waterproof Caulk ................................................ 367
        - Assembly 1 .......................................................... 367
        - Assembly 2 .......................................................... 368
        - Cutouts ................................................................ 368
      - At Solid Surface ..................................................... 368
        - Sealants and Adhesives ..................................... 368
        - Expansion ............................................................ 368
        - Support ................................................................ 368
        - Joints .................................................................... 368
        - Cutout Corners .................................................... 368
        - Back and End Splashes ..................................... 368
        - Countertop Adhesion .......................................... 368
        - Hard Seams ........................................................ 368
      - At Solid Phenolic .................................................... 369
        - Countertop .......................................................... 369
        - Joints .................................................................... 369
        - Sinks .................................................................... 369
      - At Epoxy Resin, and Natural/Engineered Stone ........ 369
        - Countertop .......................................................... 369
        - Overhang ............................................................ 369
        - Cantilever ............................................................ 369
        - Back and End Splashes ..................................... 369
        - Hard Seams ........................................................ 369
        - Scribing ................................................................ 369
        - Sinks .................................................................... 369

**TESTS**
- Basic Considerations ................................................... 370
  - Fabricated and Installed ........................................... 370
  - Smoothness ............................................................... 370
    - KCPI .................................................................... 370
    - Sanding ............................................................... 370
  - Gaps, Flushness, Flatness and Alignment ............. 370
    - Illustrations ......................................................... 371

## introductory information

# SECTION 11
## Countertops

# Guide Specifications

Are available through the Sponsor Associations in interactive digital format including unique and individual quality control options. The Guide Specifications are located at:

## Architectural Woodwork Institute (AWI)
www.awinet.org

## Architectural Woodwork Manufacturers Association of Canada (AWMAC)
http://awmac.com/aws-guide-specifications

## Woodwork Institute (WI)
www.woodworkinstitute.com/publications/aws_guide_specs.asp

# SECTION 11
## Countertops

### introductory information

**INTRODUCTION**

Section 11 includes information on Countertops and Window Sills manufactured of Wood, High Pressure Decorative Laminate (HPDL), Solid Surface, Engineered Stone, Epoxy Resin, Solid Phenolic and Natural Stone Products and their related parts.

Quality assurance can be achieved by adherence to the AWS and will provide the owner a quality product at competitive pricing. Use of a qualified Sponsor Member firm to provide your woodwork will help ensure the manufacturer's understanding of the quality level required. Illustrations in this Section are not intended to be all inclusive. Other engineered solutions are acceptable. In the absence of specifications; methods of fabrication shall be the manufacturer choice. The design professional, by specifying compliance to the AWS increases the probability of receiving the product quality expected.

**TYPICAL COUNTERTOP CONFIGURATIONS**

- Wood Veneer Tops - This type of top consists of wood veneer laid up over a stable core, veneer edged, solid wood edged or with an applied decorative edge of another material as specified.

- HPDL Tops - This type of top consists of plastic laminate over a stable core, self edged or with an applied decorative edge of another material as specified.

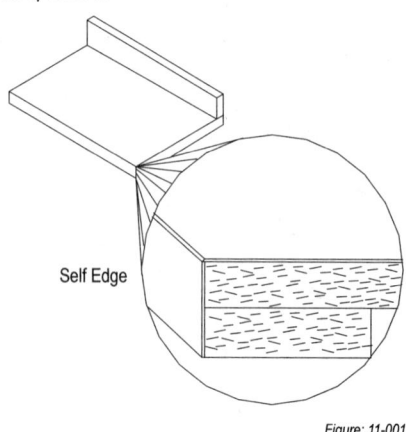

*Figure: 11-001*  — Self Edge

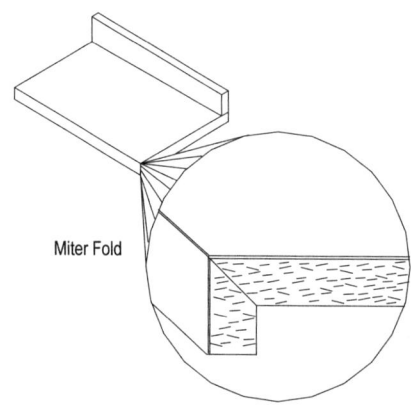

*Figure: 11-002* — Miter Fold

- Post formed high pressure decorative laminated tops - This type of top consists of plastic laminate formed with heat and pressure over a stable core typically with a coved integral backsplash and must be specified.

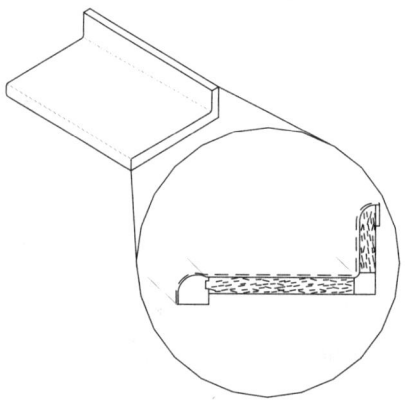

*Figure: 11-003*

- Combination Material Tops - This type of top may consist of a mixture of materials, such as wood, high pressure decorative laminate, inlays, etc.

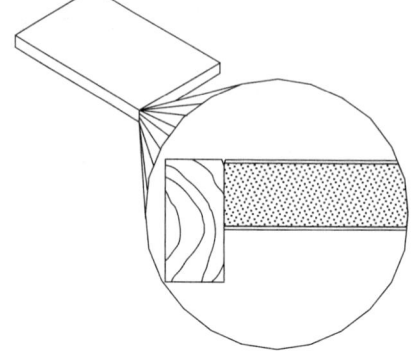

*Figure: 11-004*

- Solid Surfacing Materials - This type of top requires special fabrication techniques, depending upon the composition of the product. Many manufacturers fabricate and install the products. Must be specified by brand name and manufacturer. Typically only available in 1/2" nominal (11-13 mm) thickness.

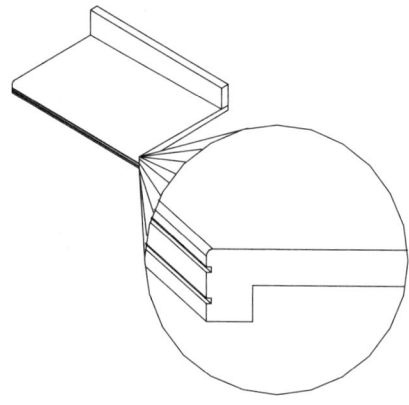

*Figure: 11-005*

Solid Laminated Tops - This type of top consists of narrow strips of wood, face glued together, similar to "butcher block," but custom manufactured to contract documents.

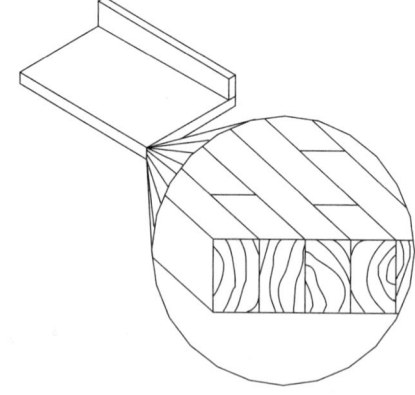

*Figure: 11-006*

# SECTION 11
## Countertops

## introductory information

### TYPICAL COUNTERTOP CONFIGURATIONS
(continued)

- **Solid Wood Tops** - This type of top consists of boards edge glued to a desired width. In this kind of top there is no assurance of matching grain or color at the edges or individual ends of the boards.

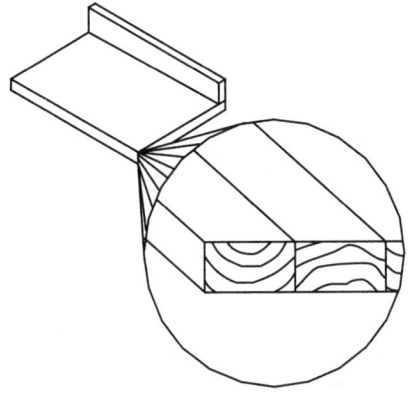

*Figure: 11-007*

- **Epoxy Resin Laboratory Tops and Splashes** - Specially formulated resin tops designed to resist harsh chemicals. Must be specified by brand name and manufacturer.

### GUIDELINES FOR FABRICATION / INSTALLATION OF HPDL COUNTERTOPS

The following was taken in part from the National Electrical Manufacturers Association (NEMA).:

- When making a cutout (as for electrical receptacles, ranges, sinks, grills, windows, chopping blocks, L shaped counter tops, and so forth), inside corners should be smoothly rounded using a minimum corner radius of 1/8" (3 mm). A router is an ideal tool for making cutouts.

- When removing large areas from a sheet of laminate (e.g., a sink cutout), the connecting strips between the remaining areas should be left as wide as possible.

- Factory-trimmed sheet edges and saw-cut edges should be routed and filed. Original edges on factory cut laminates are not finished edges since oversized laminates are supplied to allow for proper fabrication.

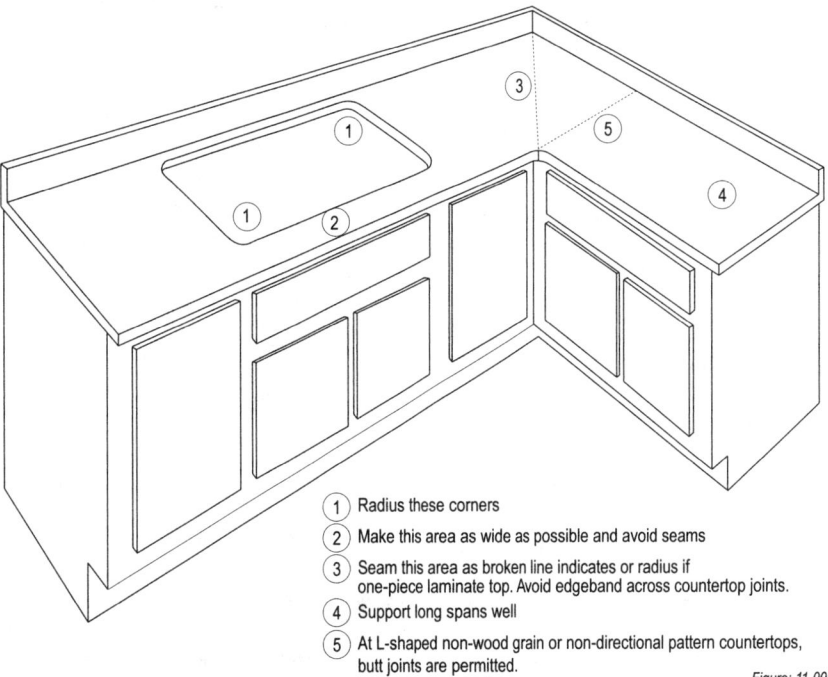

1. Radius these corners
2. Make this area as wide as possible and avoid seams
3. Seam this area as broken line indicates or radius if one-piece laminate top. Avoid edgeband across countertop joints.
4. Support long spans well
5. At L-shaped non-wood grain or non-directional pattern countertops, butt joints are permitted.

*Figure: 11-008*

- All chips, saw marks, and hairline cracks should be removed from cuts by filing, sanding, or routing.

- Backsplash seam areas on countertops which are exposed to spilled water or other fluids should be sealed with caulking to ensure a tight seal.

- When laminate is bonded to a core, precaution should be taken to prevent warping of the assembly. Laminates used on shelves or in long unsupported spans should make use of a backer. A thick backer (approximately the same thickness as the face sheet), can provide more stability than a thin backer. Thicker laminates can offer better dimensional stability and resistance to stress (corner) cracking. Paint, varnish, vinyl film, and fiber backers will not balance HPDL.

- Before using nails or screws, oversized holes should be drilled through the laminate with a sharp drill bit.

# SECTION 11
## Countertops

## introductory information

### TYPICAL PROBLEMS AT HPDL COUNTERTOPS - CAUSES AND PREVENTION

Some of the problems that may arise after laminates have been fabricated and installed are the following:

- **Cracking of the laminate at corners and around cutouts** may be caused by improper climate control, improper bonding and, sometimes, poor planning, or combination of these reasons. Cracking may be caused by shrinkage; proper climate control helps to prevent it. Rough edges, inside corners that have not been rounded, binding and/or forced fits can contribute to cracking. If the seams are properly placed in the layout of the laminate, stresses can be minimized.

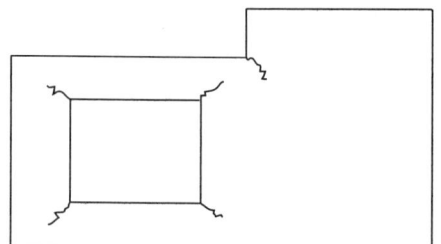

Figure: 11-009

- **Separation of the laminate** from the core may generally be caused by a poor adhesive bond. The bonding procedure should be reviewed with close attention to uniform glue line, uniform pressure and cleanliness of mating surfaces. If the edges fail to bond, extra adhesive may be applied and the product re-clamped.

Some cleaning agents, excess heat, and moisture can contribute to bond failure at joints and edges.

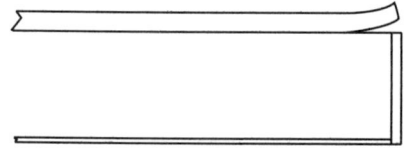

Figure: 11-010

- **Blistering or Bubbling** of the laminate surface away from the core can be caused by excessive heat, starved glue line, improper conditioning, and inadequate pressure or drying. Use of a PVA glue line and pressure over clean, conditioned laminates and core might have prevented the problem.

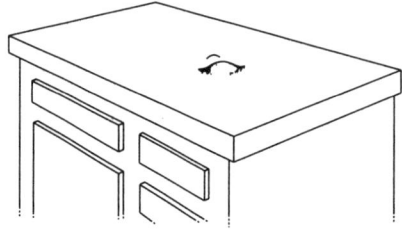

Figure: 11-011

The forming of a blister or bubble over a small area, often accompanied by a darkening of the laminate can be caused by continual exposure to a source of heat. Electrical appliances which produce heat and light bulbs should not be placed in contact with or close proximity to laminate surfaces.

- **Repeated Heating** may cause the laminate and adhesive to react and finally deteriorate after continual exposure to temperatures above 150° F (66° C).

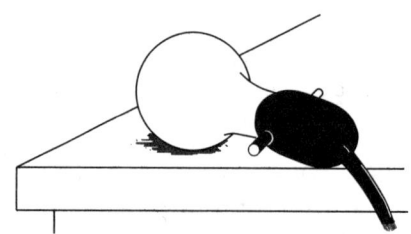

Figure: 11-012

- **Cracking of the laminate in the center of the sheet** may be caused by flexing of the core when it covers a wide span or by spot gluing. Wide spans call for sturdy framework, and special attention should be given to the uniformity of glue lines and gluing pressures. Also, care should be taken to avoid trapping foreign objects between the laminate and the core.

Cantilevered overhangs in excess of 6" (152mm) should be designed with appropriate supports.

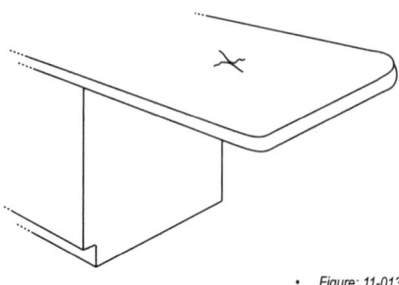

Figure: 11-013

Long, unsupported spans are generally avoided. Most manufacturers limit spans to between 30 - 36" (760 - 915 mm) before the addition of a support of some type. A wide variety of engineering solutions are available.

- **Warping of the assembly** may be generally caused by unbalanced construction or unbalanced glue lines. Proper HPDL backer sheets should be chosen and aligned so that their grain direction is parallel to that of the face laminate. Proper gluing is also important. If the core is secured to a framework, the framework should be designed to hold the assembly to a flat plane. Conditioning is also helpful.

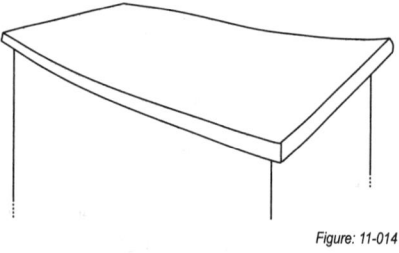

Figure: 11-014

# SECTION 11
## Countertops

## introductory information

### CHEMICAL or STAIN RESISTANCE

Requirements must be specified. Consider the chemical and staining agents that might be used on or near the surfaces. Chemical and stain resistance is affected by concentration, time, temperature, humidity, housekeeping, and other factors; it is recommended that actual samples are tested in a similar environment with those agents. Common guidelines can be found by referring to:

- NEMA LD3 (latest edition) for chemical resistance.
- ASTM D3023 and C1378 (latest editions) for stain resistance.
- SEFA #3 - Recommendations for work surfaces.
- SEFA #8 - PH, PL and W - Recommendations for phenolic, plastic laminate and wood casework.

### ABRASION RESISTANCE

Requirements must be specified. When abrasion resistance requirements are a concern, users should consider the abrasive elements that might be used on or near the countertop surfaces. Common guidelines can be found in:

- ASTM C501 (latest edition)
- NEMA LD3-3.13 (latest edition)
- NEMA LD3.7 (latest edition)

### HIGH PRESSURE DECORATIVE LAMINATE (HPDL) COUNTERTOPS

- **HPDL BACK AND END SPLASH CONSTRUCTION TYPES** - if not otherwise specified, shall be manufacturer's choice:

  - **ASSEMBLY - 1,** Wall Mount, Jobsite Assembled

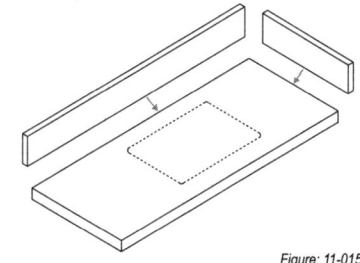

*Figure: 11-015*

- **ASSEMBLY - 2,** Deck Mount, Manufacturer Assembled

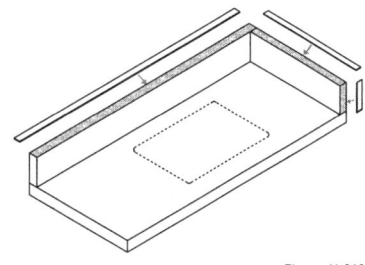

*Figure: 11-016*

- **WHITE BACKGROUND PAPER** is utilized in some HPDLs to achieve the high fidelity, contrast, and depth of color of their printed pattern, leaving a white line at exposed edges that is extremely noticeable with darker colors.

- **FLAME SPREAD RATED** - Class I Flame Spread Architectural HPDL countertops are available. Countertops desired to be certified as a flame spread rated assembly (versus simply having been built with a flame spread rated laminate surface) shall be specified as a "Class I Flame spread Rated HPDL Countertop."

The term "Class I Flame spread Rated HPDL Countertop" shall mean that the entire countertop assembly, including surface HPDL, backer, core, and adhesive, has been tested and certified as to its Class I Flame spread Rating by an authorized organization, such as Underwriters Laboratories, and must be manufactured by an approved company of the certifying agency.

Manufacturers of "Class I Flame Spread Rated Countertop Assemblies" require specific methods of installation and trimming in order to label and certify their product. Design professionals desiring to use a "Class I Flame Spread Countertop Assembly" should coordinate with an approved manufacturer during the design stage.

- **COUNTERTOP CONFIGURATION OPTIONS**

  - Self Edged w/ No Splash

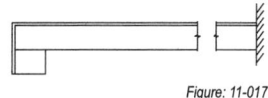

*Figure: 11-017*

  - Self Edged w/ Butt Splash

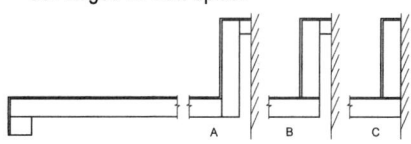

*Figure: 11-018*

  - Self Edged w/ Coved Splash

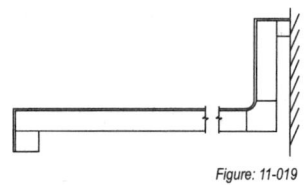

*Figure: 11-019*

  - Post Formed Edge w/ No Splash

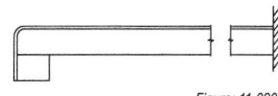

*Figure: 11-020*

  - Post Formed Edge w/ Butt Splash

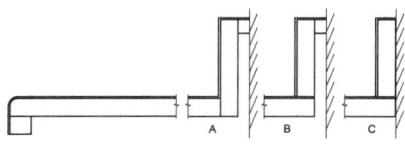

*Figure: 11-021*

  - Post Formed Edge w/ Coved Splash

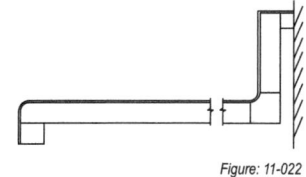

*Figure: 11-022*

  - Fully Formed w/ Coved Splash

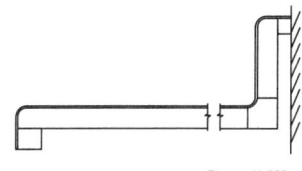

*Figure: 11-023*

# SECTION 11
## Countertops

### introductory information

**HIGH PRESSURE DECORATIVE LAMINATE (HPDL) COUNTERTOPS** (continued)

- **COUNTERTOP CONFIGURATION OPTIONS** (continued)

  - No Drip Edge w/ Coved Splash

    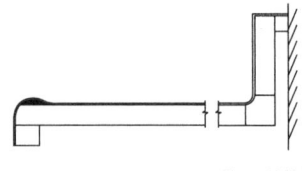
    Figure: 11-024

  - Wood Edge w/ No Splash

    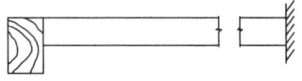
    Figure: 11-025

- **OPTIONS AT TOP OF SPLASH:**

  - Waterfall w/ Scribe

    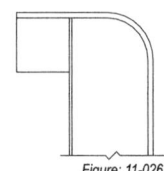
    Figure: 11-026

  - Square w/ Scribe

    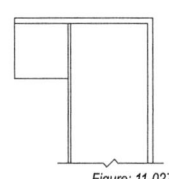
    Figure: 11-027

  - Square

    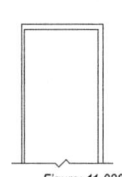
    Figure: 11-028

- **DECK OPTIONS AT SPLASH:**

  - Horizontal Butt

    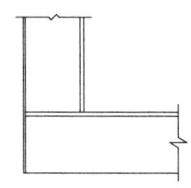
    Figure: 11-029

  - Vertical Butt

    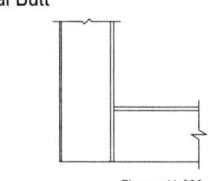
    Figure: 11-030

  - Coved

    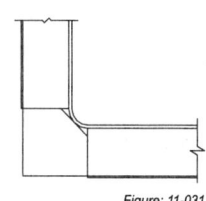
    Figure: 11-031

- **FRONT EDGE OPTIONS:**

  - Self Edgeband w/ Wide Build Up

    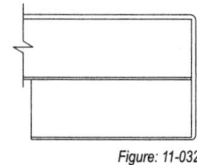
    Figure: 11-032

  - Self Edgeband Narrow Build Up

    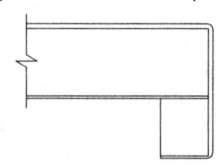
    Figure: 11-033

  - Self Edgeband w/ Drip Groove

    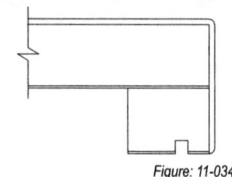
    Figure: 11-034

- Waterfall

  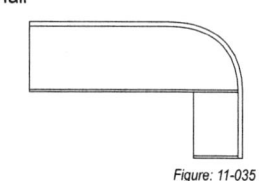
  Figure: 11-035

- No Drip

  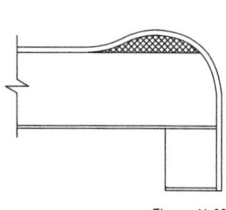
  Figure: 11-036

- Full Round

  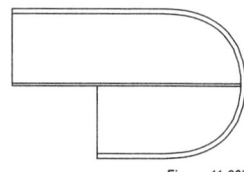
  Figure: 11-037

- Solid Wood Edgeband w/ V Groove

  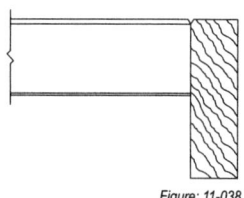
  Figure: 11-038

- Solid Wood Edgeband w/o V Groove

  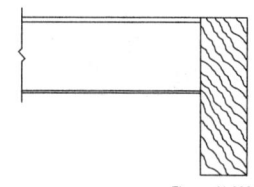
  Figure: 11-039

- Solid Wood Edgeband w/ Overlaid Laminate

  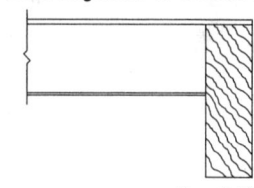
  Figure: 11-040

# SECTION 11
## Countertops

## introductory information

### HIGH PRESSURE DECORATIVE LAMINATE (HPDL) COUNTERTOPS   (continued)

- **FRONT EDGE OPTIONS**   (continued)

  - Miter Fold

    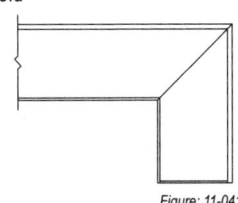
    Figure: 11-041

  - Thick PVC Edgeband

    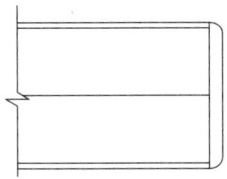
    Figure: 11-042

  - T Mold Edgeband

    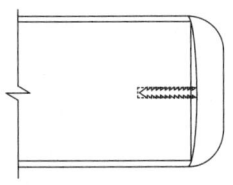
    Figure: 11-043

- **TYPICAL MECHANICAL TIGHT JOINT FASTENER**

  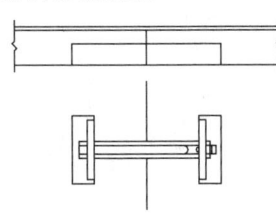
  Figure: 11-044

### SOLID SURFACE COUNTERTOPS

- **COLOR** and **PATTERN MATCH:** Some slight color variation may exist from sheet to sheet, sheet to bowl, or sink products. In sheet stock, use of the same batch material will reduce these variations.

- **REPAIRS:** When allowed, repairability varies from material to material and may be visible.

- **PRECAUTIONS:** Product dimensions are nominal. If tolerances are critical, review them with your manufacturer and/or installer.

- **MACHINABILTY** is an issue with some materials and shall be taken into consideration on selection.

- **CONFIGURATION OPTIONS:**

  - Built Up Edge

    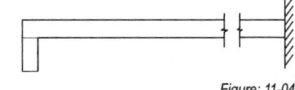
    Figure: 11-045

  - Built Up Edge w/ Butt Splash

    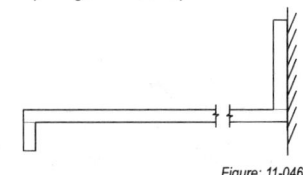
    Figure: 11-046

  - Built Up Edge w/ Coved Splash

    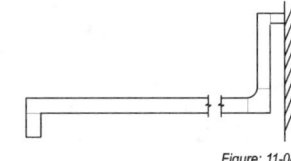
    Figure: 11-047

- **TOP OPTIONS AT SPLASH:**

  - Waterfall

    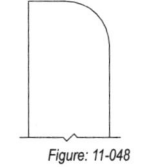
    Figure: 11-048

  - Square

    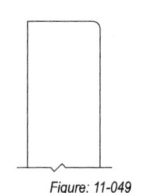
    Figure: 11-049

- **DECK OPTIONS AT SPLASH:**

  - Butt

    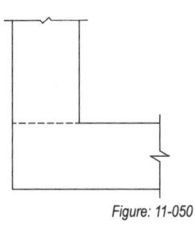
    Figure: 11-050

  - Coved

    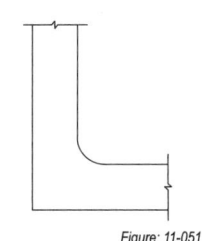
    Figure: 11-051

- **EDGE OPTIONS:**

  - Waterfall

    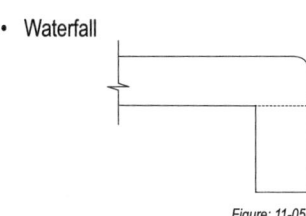
    Figure: 11-052

  - No Drip

    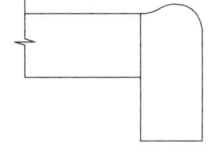
    Figure: 11-053

  - Build Up w/ Drip Groove

    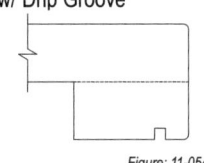
    Figure: 11-054

# SECTION 11
## Countertops

### introductory information

**SOLID PHENOLIC, EPOXY RESIN, AND NATURAL/ENGINEERED STONE COUNTERTOPS**

- **CONFIGURATION OPTIONS:**

  - Butt Splash

  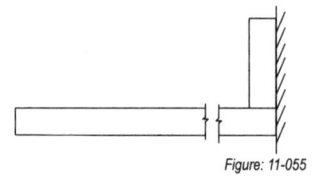
  Figure: 11-055

  - Build Up

  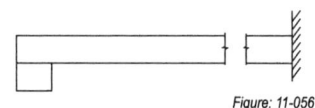
  Figure: 11-056

  - Build Up w/ Butt Splash

  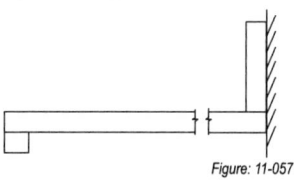
  Figure: 11-057

- **TOP AND DECK OPTIONS AT SPLASH:**

  - Waterfall

  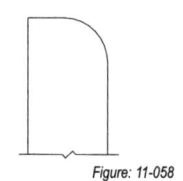
  Figure: 11-058

  - Square

  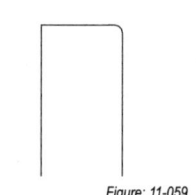
  Figure: 11-059

  - Butt

  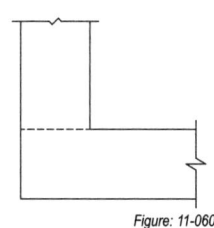
  Figure: 11-060

- Removable Ledge

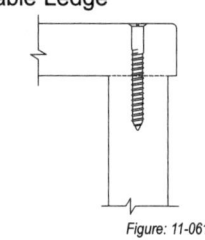
Figure: 11-061

- **EDGE OPTIONS:**

  - Drip Groove

  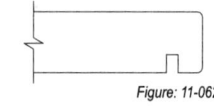
  Figure: 11-062

  - Marine Edge

  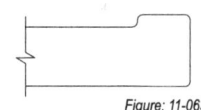
  Figure: 11-063

  - Waterfall

  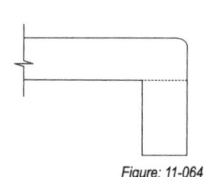
  Figure: 11-064

  - Champher Edge

  Figure: 11-064

  - Bull Nose Edge

  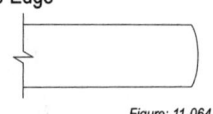
  Figure: 11-064

  - Build Up w/ Drip Groove

  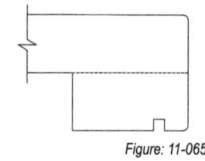
  Figure: 11-065

**WOOD COUNTERTOPS**

- **CONFIGURATION OPTIONS:**

  - Solid Butcher Block

  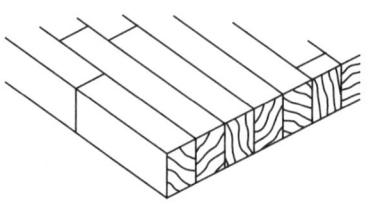
  Figure: 11-066

  - Solid Wide Width

  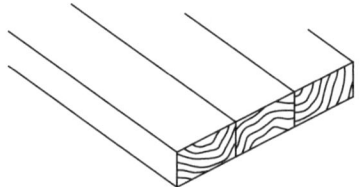
  Figure: 11-067

  - Solid, Splined Wide Width

  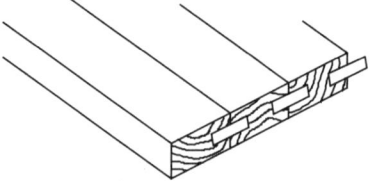
  Figure: 11-068

  - Veneer Edgebanded

  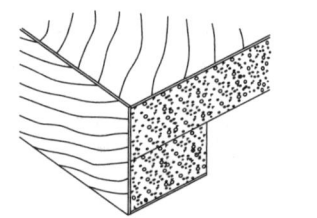
  Figure: 11-069

  - Solid Edgebanded

  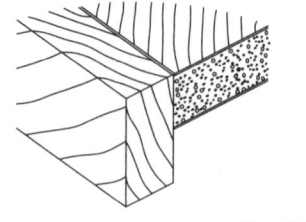
  Figure: 11-070

# SECTION 11
## Countertops

## introductory information

### WOOD COUNTERTOP (continued)

- Solid Edgebanded w/ Overlaid Veneer

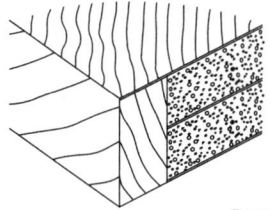

*Figure: 11-071*

To **PREVENT TELEGRAPHING**, inset solid wood edging when used must have similar moisture content as panel core, be glued securely and calibrated with panel core thickness prior to being laminated with a wood veneer on both faces.

### SPECIFY REQUIREMENTS FOR

- Back and end-splash **ASSEMBLY** type.
- Flame Spread requirements.
- Laboratory use, such as:
  - Chemical-resistant work-surface material requirements or finish.
  - Abrasion-resistant work-surface material requirement.
- Removable splash ledger.
- Special splash/deck or top or edge profiles.

### RECOMMENDATIONS

- If FIELD FINISHED, INCLUDE IN THE DIVISION 09 OF THE SPECIFICATIONS:

  - **BEFORE FINISHING**, exposed portions of woodwork shall have handling marks or effects of exposure to moisture removed with a thorough, final sanding over surfaces of the exposed portions and shall be cleaned before applying sealer or finish.

  - **CONCEALED SURFACES** - Architectural woodwork that may be exposed to moisture, such as those adjacent to exterior concrete walls, etc., shall be primed.

  - The underside of wood countertops shall be sealed with at least one coat of primer or sealer.

- **REVIEW** the GENERAL portion of Sections 3 and 4 for an overview of the characteristics and the minimum acceptable requirements of lumber and/or sheet products that might be used herein.

- **STRUCTURAL MEMBERS**, grounds, in wall blocking, backing, furring, brackets, or other anchorage which becomes an integral part of the building's walls, floors, or ceilings, required for the installation of architectural woodwork are not to be furnished or installed by the architectural woodwork manufacturer or installer.

- At **HPDL SINK TOPS**, use of under-mount sinks is not recommended because of the potential for moisture problems, even with proper preparation and installation, and:

  - Use of veneer core plywood with Type II adhesive, industrial-grade particleboard or fiberboard with a 24 hour thickness swell factor of 5.5% or less.

  - Either self-rimming sinks or sinks with surface-mounted metal retention rings are recommended.

# SECTION 11
## Countertops

**GENERAL**/PRODUCT/INSTALLATION/TEST

Where the **E**, **C**, or **P** icon is not indicated, the rule applies to all Grades equally | **E** | **C** | **P** |

## compliance requirements

Including: Tops, Wall Caps, Splashes, and Sills of High-Pressure Decorative Laminate, Wood, Solid Surface, Solid Phenolic, Epoxy Resin, and Natural/Engineered Stone

### 11.1 BASIC CONSIDERATIONS

**1 GRADE**

1.1 These standards are characterized in three Grades of quality that may be mixed within a single project. Limitless design possibilities and a wide variety of lumber and veneer species, along with overlays, high-pressure decorative laminates, factory finishes, and profiles are available in all three Grades.

1.2 **ECONOMY GRADE** defines the minimum quality requirements for a project's workmanship, materials, or installation and is typically reserved for woodwork that is not in public view, such as in mechanical rooms and utility areas.

1.3 **CUSTOM GRADE** is typically specified for and adequately covers most high-quality architectural woodwork, providing a well-defined degree of control over a project's quality of materials, workmanship, or installation.

1.4 **PREMIUM GRADE** is typically specified for use in those areas of a project where the highest level of quality, materials, workmanship, and installation is required.

15 **GRADE LIMITATIONS**

1.5.1 **SOLID SURFACE** countertops are offered only in custom grade and premium grade.

1.5.2 **SOLID PHENOLIC, EPOXY RESIN,** and **NATURAL/ENGINEERED STONE** countertops are offered only in premium grade.

2 **CONTRACT DOCUMENTS** shall govern if in conflict with these standards.

3 **ACCEPTABLE REQUIREMENTS** of lumber and/or sheet products used within this woodwork product section are established by Sections 3 and 4, unless otherwise modified herein.

4 **AESTHETIC COMPLIANCE REQUIREMENTS** apply only to surfaces visible after manufacturer and installation.

5 **EXPOSED SURFACES**

5.1 All visible surfaces of an installed countertop.

5.2 The exposed underside surface over 42" (1067 mm) off the finish floor.

### 11.1 BASIC CONSIDERATIONS (continued)

6 **CONCEALED SURFACES**

6.1 The underside surface 42" (1067 mm) or less off the finished floor.

6.2 All non-visible surfaces attached to and/or covered by another.

6.3 All non-visible blocking, spacers, etc., used for attachment.

7 When **SOLID SURFACE** is referenced in these standards, it refers to filled cast polymeric resin panels per Section 4.

8 When **SOLID PHENOLIC** (compact laminate) is referenced in these standards, it refers to panels of melamine impregnated decorative overlay sheets over kraft phenolic core sheets per Section 4.

9 When **EPOXY RESIN** is referenced in these standards, it refers to homogenous, nonabsorbent, heat cured composite of panels per Section 4.

10 When **NATURAL STONE** is referenced in these standards, it typically refers to granite, marble, slate, soapstone, and limestone. Natural stone countertops are cut directly from the earth and have little processing besides smoothing and shape formation, and will often need to be sealed because natural materials are porous (soapstone is a notable exception to this generalization).

11 When **ENGINEERED STONE** is referenced in these standards, it typically refers to quartz (a man made substance derived from mineral dust) or quartz based and is entirely a man-made surface designed to mimic the beautiful appearance of natural stone. Engineered stone does not have natural defects and is a more uniform design.

12 To **PREVENT TELEGRAPHING**, inset solid wood edging when used must have similar moisture content as panel core, be glued securely and calibrated with panel core thickness prior to being laminated with a wood veneer on both faces.

13 **INDUSTRY PRACTICES**

13.1 **STRUCTURAL MEMBERS**, grounds, in wall blocking, backing, furring, brackets, or other anchorage that becomes an integral part of the building's walls, floors, or ceilings, required for the installation of architectural woodwork is not furnished or installed by the architectural woodwork manufacturer or installer.

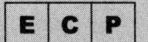

Where the **E**, **C**, or **P** icon is not indicated, the rule applies to all Grades equally

# SECTION 11
## Countertops

**compliance requirements**

**GENERAL**/PRODUCT/INSTALLATION/TEST

## 11.1 BASIC CONSIDERATIONS (continued)

**13 INDUSTRY PRACTICES** (continued)

13.2 **WALL, CEILING**, and/or opening variations in excess of 1/4" (6.4 mm) or FLOORS in excess of 1/2" (12.7 mm) in 144" (3658 mm) of being plumb, level, flat, straight, square, or of the correct size are not acceptable for the installation of architectural woodwork, nor is it the responsibility of the installer to scribe or fit to tolerances in excess of such.

13.3 **PRIMING** of architectural woodwork is not the responsibility of the manufacturer and/or installer, unless the material is being furnished prefinished.

13.4 **BUILD-UP** or spacing materials required for installation of a countertop are the responsibility of the countertop manufacturer.

13.5 Defined **GRAIN** and/or **PATTERN** are installed running with the length of the countertop.

13.6 The **HORIZONTAL REVEAL** between the lower edge of the countertop and the upper edge of the adjacent door or drawer front shall be consistent. Coordination of such is the responsibility of the cabinet manufacturer.

## 11.2 SCOPE

1 All decorative laminate, including Class I Flame Spread-Rated and Chemical-Resistant, Solid Surface, Natural/Engineered Stone, Epoxy Resin, Solid Phenolic, and wood facings, tops, splashes, sills, and ledges.

1.2 **TYPICAL INCLUSIONS**

1.2.1 HPDL, Class I Flame Spread-Rated HPDL, Chemical-Resistant HPDL, Solid Surface, Natural/Engineered Stone, Epoxy Resin, Solid Phenolic, and Wood Countertops with approved backing sheet, as applicable.

1.2.2 Splashes, sills, and ledges.

1.2.3 Solid lumber, metal, or self-edge trim; cutouts for sinks; electrical boxes; and fixtures indicated on drawings.

1.2.4 Installation, if specified.

1.2.5 Solid surface and/or epoxy sinks.

1.2.6 Window sills.

1.2.7 Support members that are surface-mounted.

1.3 **TYPICAL EXCLUSIONS**

1.3.1 Stripping, furring, in wall blocking, or grounds.

1.3.2 Furnishing or installation of sink rims or sinks not listed above.

1.3.3 In-wall support members.

1.3.4 All grounds, backing members, or other items unrelated to the furnishing and installation of countertops and sinks.

1.3.5 Fixtures, plumbing, and data equipment.

1.3.6 Sink outlets and fittings, except at epoxy sinks.

1.3.7 Welded metal support material or structure.

# SECTION 11
## Countertops

GENERAL/**PRODUCT**/INSTALLATION/TEST

**compliance requirements**

Where the **E**, **C**, or **P** icon is not indicated, the rule applies to all Grades equally | **E** | **C** | **P** |

## 11.3 DEFAULT STIPULATION

1      If not otherwise specified or indicated in the contract documents:

1.1      **HPDL COUNTERTOPS** - shall be **CUSTOM GRADE** (unless the related casework is premium grade, then the countertops shall be **PREMIUM GRADE**); of desired HPDL colors selected from the manufacturer's non-premium-priced standard patterns and readily available sheet sizes; with standard self-edge, square butt splash a minimum of 4" (102 mm) above deck of Assembly Type 1 or 2 with square self-edge.

1.2      **WOOD COUNTERTOPS** - shall be **CUSTOM GRADE** (unless the related casework is Premium Grade, then the countertops shall be **PREMIUM GRADE**) hardwood plywood intended for an opaque finish.

1.3      **SOLID SURFACE COUNTERTOPS** - shall be **CUSTOM GRADE** of the manufacturer's choice of brand name and edge treatment. Desired colors to be selected from the manufacturer's standard, non-premium-priced line with standard matte finish; a minimum of 1/2" nominal (11-13 mm) thick; with a minimum of a 3" (76 mm) high splash above the deck surface.

1.4      **SOLID PHENOLIC, EPOXY RESIN, and NATURAL/ENGINEERED STONE COUNTERTOPS** - shall be **PREMIUM GRADE** of manufacturer's choice of brand name and edge treatment; colors to be selected from the manufacturer's standard, non-premium-priced line with standard satin finish, and with compatible sink and accessories.

## 11.4 RULES

1      The following rules shall govern unless a project's contract documents require otherwise.

2      These rules are intended to provide a well-defined degree of control over a project's quality of materials, workmanship, or installation.

3      **ERRATA**, published on the Sponsor Associations' websites at www.awinet.org, www.awmac.com, or www.aws-errata.com, shall **TAKE PRECEDENCE OVER THESE RULES**, subject to their date of posting and a project's bid date.

### 11.4.4 Basic Rules

| | | |
|---|---|---|
| 1 | | **AESTHETIC** grade rules apply only to exposed surfaces visible after installation. |
| 2 | | **LUMBER** shall conform to the requirements established in Section 3. |
| 3 | | **SHEET PRODUCTS** shall conform to the requirements established in Section 4. |
| 4 | | **BACKER MATERIAL** shall conform to the requirements established in Section 4. |
| 5 | | **EXPOSED SURFACES** include: |
| 5 | 1 | All visible surfaces on an exposed countertop. |
| 5 | 2 | The exposed underside surface over 42" (1067 mm) off the finish floor. |
| 6 | | **CONCEALED SURFACES** include: |
| 6 | 1 | The underside surface 42" (1067 mm) or less off the finished floor. |
| 6 | 2 | All non-visible surfaces attached to and/or covered by another. |
| 6 | 3 | All non-visible blocking, spacers, etc., used for attachment. |
| 7 | | A **BALANCED PANEL**, for the purpose of this standard, is one that is free from warp that affects serviceability for its intended purpose. |
| 8 | | **GRAIN** and/or **PATTERN SURFACING** shall be installed with the grain or pattern direction running length-wise. |
| 9 | | **EXPOSED FASTENING** is prohibited, except for access panels. |
| 10 | | Where **FIRE-RETARDANT** or **MOISTURE-RESISTANT** core is required, documentation shall be furnished, if requested. |

Continues next column ▼

# SECTION 11
## Countertops

**compliance requirements** — GENERAL / PRODUCT / INSTALLATION / TEST

*Where the E, C, or P icon is not indicated, the rule applies to all Grades equally*

### 11.4.4 Basic Rules

▲ *From previous column*

| | | | Rule | E | C | P |
|---|---|---|---|---|---|---|
| 11 | | | If **HPDL EDGEBANDING** is not applied with a hot-melt adhesive formulated for its application; the laminate shall be primed before application. | | | |
| 12 | | | Where **GLUING** or **LAMINATION** occurs: | | | |
| 12 | 1 | | **DELAMINATION** or **SEPARATION** shall not occur beyond what is allowed in Sections 3 & 4. | | | |
| 13 | | | **FIRST-CLASS WORKMANSHIP** is required in compliance with these standards. | | | |

### 11.4.5 Material Rules

| | | | | Rule | E | C | P |
|---|---|---|---|---|---|---|---|
| 1 | | | | When **FACTORY FINISHING** is specified, concealed surfaces shall be factory sealed with one coat at 2 mil dry. | E | C | P |
| 2 | | | | For **OPAQUE FINISH**: | | | |
| 2 | 1 | | | Medium-density fiberboard (MDF) is permitted | | | |
| 2 | 2 | | | Veneer is permitted; however: | | | |
| 2 | 2 | 1 | | **SPECIES** of manufacturer's choice, closed grain hardwood conforming to HPVA definitions and characteristics for: | | | |
| 2 | 2 | 1 | 1 | Grade **D** | E | C | P |
| 2 | 2 | 1 | 2 | Grade **C** | | C | |
| 2 | 2 | 1 | 3 | Grade **B** | E | C | P |
| 3 | | | | For **TRANSPARENT FINISH, VENEER**: | | | |
| 3 | 1 | | | **SPECIES** of manufacturer's choice, hardwood conforming to HPVA definitions and characteristics for: | | | |
| 3 | 1 | 1 | | Grade **B** | E | C | P |
| 3 | 1 | 2 | | Grade **A** | | C | |
| 3 | 1 | 3 | | Grade **AA** | | | P |
| 3 | 2 | | | **SLICING** of: | | | |
| 3 | 2 | 1 | | Manufacturer's choice. | | | |
| 3 | 2 | 2 | | Plain-sliced. | | | |
| 3 | 3 | | | **MATCHING ADJACENT LEAVES** be: | | | |
| 3 | 3 | 1 | | Manufacturer's choice. | E | C | |
| 3 | 3 | 2 | | Book matching. | E | C | P |
| 3 | 4 | | | **MATCHING WITHIN PANEL FACE** be: | | | |
| 3 | 4 | 1 | | Running | E | C | |
| 3 | 4 | 2 | | Balance | E | | P |

*Continues next column*

### 11.4.5 Material Rules

▲ *From previous column*

| | | | | Rule | E | C | P |
|---|---|---|---|---|---|---|---|
| 3 | | | | For **TRANSPARENT FINISH, VENEER**: (continued) | | | |
| 3 | 5 | | | **MATCHING BETWEEN ADJACENT PANELS** be: | | | |
| 3 | 5 | 1 | | Manufacturer's choice. | E | C | P |
| 3 | 5 | 2 | | Compatible for color and grain | E | C | P |
| 3 | 5 | 3 | | Well matched for color and grain | E | C | P |
| 3 | 5 | 4 | | **END, SEQUENCE,** and **BLUEPRINT MATCHING** shall be specified | | | |
| 4 | | | | At **EXPOSED SURFACES**: | | | |
| 4 | 1 | | | Shall be free of manufacturing defects. | | | |
| 4 | 1 | | | **TRANSPARENT FINISHED WOOD**: | | | |
| 4 | 1 | 1 | | Permits hardwood or softwood. | | | |
| 4 | 1 | 2 | | Permits only one species for the entire project. | | C | P |
| 4 | 1 | 3 | | Adjacent veneer and lumber shall be: | | | |
| 4 | 1 | 3 | 1 | Manufacturers' choice of species. | E | C | P |
| 4 | 1 | 3 | 2 | Compatible for color and grain. | E | C | P |
| 4 | 1 | 3 | 3 | Well-matched for color and grain. | E | C | P |
| 4 | 1 | 4 | | Have visible edges, reveals, and/or splines that: | | | |
| 4 | 1 | 4 | 1 | Are full length. | | | |
| 4 | 1 | 4 | 2 | Are manufacturers' choice. | E | C | P |
| 4 | 1 | 4 | 3 | Match the species of the panel face. | E | C | P |
| 4 | 1 | 4 | 4 | Are **COMPATIBLE** for color and grain. | E | C | P |
| 4 | 1 | 4 | 5 | Are **WELL-MATCHED** for color and grain. | E | C | P |
| 4 | 1 | 4 | 6 | Are a minimum of 0.020" (0.5 mm) nominal **THICKNESS** that precludes show-through of core. | E | C | P |
| 5 | | | | At **CONCEALED SURFACES** shall allow defects, and: | | | |
| 5 | 1 | | | Blocking, fillers, and shim stock may be of any sound material. | | | |
| 6 | | | | At **WOOD** shall be: | | | |
| 6 | 1 | | | 3/4" (19 mm) minimum thickness hardwood (plywood or solid stock) of one species for the entire project, and: | | | |
| 6 | 1 | 1 | | **CORE** at veneer faced, shall be a minimum of 3/4" (19 mm) particleboard, medium-density fiberboard, veneer core, or otherwise approved engineered core, and: | | | |
| 6 | 1 | 1 | 1 | At **SINK TOPS** and their splashes, use of veneer core plywood with Type II adhesive, industrial-grade particleboard or fiberboard with a 24-hour thickness swell factor of 5.5% or less is required. | | | |

*Continues next column*

# SECTION 11
## Countertops

GENERAL/**PRODUCT**/INSTALLATION/TEST

**compliance requirements**

Where the **E**, **C**, or **P** icon is not indicated, the rule applies to all Grades equally — E | C | P

### 11.4.5 Material Rules

▲ From previous column

| 7 | | | At **HPDL**: |
|---|---|---|---|
| 7 | 1 | | Shall be HPDL, a minimum of .039" (0.99 mm) in thickness, or: |
| 7 | 2 | | Use of continuous-pressure laminates (melamine and polyester-based) as an alternative to HPDL is permitted, provided that they conform to the same physical properties and thickness as required for HPDL. |
| 7 | 3 | | **CORE** shall be a minimum of 3/4" (19 mm) particleboard, medium-density fiberboard, veneer core, or otherwise approved engineered core, and: |
| 7 | 3 | 1 | At **SINK TOPS** and their splashes, use of veneer core plywood with Type II adhesive, industrial-grade particleboard or fiberboard with a 24-hour thickness swell factor of 5.5% or less is required. |
| 7 | 4 | | **FLAME SPREAD RATED** countertops require Class I Flame Spread Rated HPDL and: |
| 7 | 4 | 1 | **CORE**, a minimum of 11/16" (17.5 mm) thick, Class I Flame Spread. |
| 7 | 4 | 2 | **BACKING SHEET**, a minimum of 0.028" (0.7 mm) high-pressure phenolic Class I Flame Spread Rated. |
| 8 | | | At **SOLID SURFACE** shall be: |
| 8 | 1 | | Nominal 1/4" (6-7 mm) minimum thickness for use as wall panels, tub enclosures, or other vertical surfaces. |
| 8 | 2 | | Nominal 1/2" (11-13 mm) minimum thickness for countertops and back splashes. |
| 9 | | | At **SOLID PHENOLIC** shall be: |
| 9 | 1 | | Minimum 3/4" (19 mm) in thickness. |
| 10 | | | At **EPOXY RESIN** shall be: |
| 10 | 1 | | Minimum 1" (25.4 mm) in thickness. |
| 11 | | | At **NATURAL/ENGINEERED STONE** shall be: |
| 11 | 1 | | Minimum 2 cm (13/16" (20 mm)) thick material. |

### 11.4.6 Machining Rules

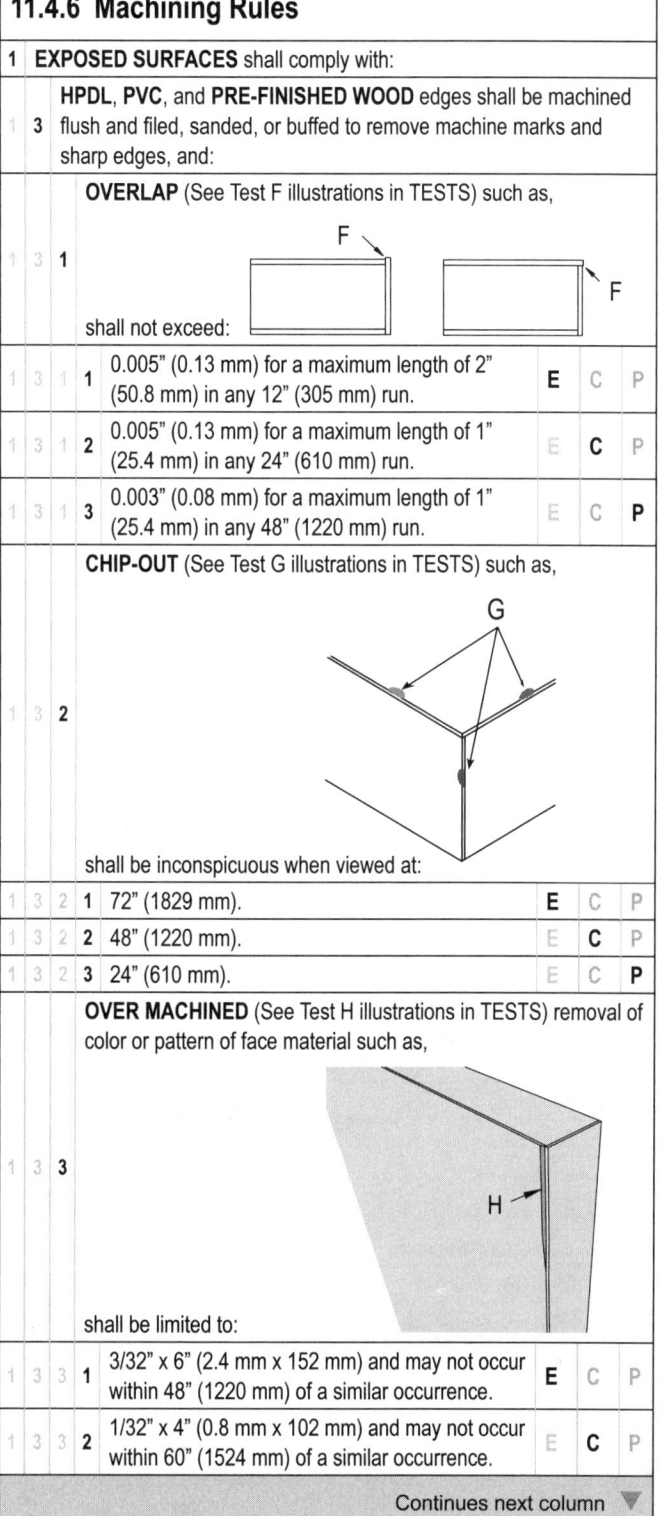

| 1 | | | **EXPOSED SURFACES** shall comply with: |
|---|---|---|---|
| 1 | 3 | | **HPDL**, **PVC**, and **PRE-FINISHED WOOD** edges shall be machined flush and filed, sanded, or buffed to remove machine marks and sharp edges, and: |
| 1 | 3 | 1 | **OVERLAP** (See Test F illustrations in TESTS) such as, shall not exceed: |
| 1 | 3 | 1 | 1 | 0.005" (0.13 mm) for a maximum length of 2" (50.8 mm) in any 12" (305 mm) run. | E | C | P |
| 1 | 3 | 1 | 2 | 0.005" (0.13 mm) for a maximum length of 1" (25.4 mm) in any 24" (610 mm) run. | E | C | P |
| 1 | 3 | 1 | 3 | 0.003" (0.08 mm) for a maximum length of 1" (25.4 mm) in any 48" (1220 mm) run. | E | C | P |
| 1 | 3 | 2 | **CHIP-OUT** (See Test G illustrations in TESTS) such as, shall be inconspicuous when viewed at: |
| 1 | 3 | 2 | 1 | 72" (1829 mm). | E | C | P |
| 1 | 3 | 2 | 2 | 48" (1220 mm). | E | C | P |
| 1 | 3 | 2 | 3 | 24" (610 mm). | E | C | P |
| 1 | 3 | 3 | **OVER MACHINED** (See Test H illustrations in TESTS) removal of color or pattern of face material such as, shall be limited to: |
| 1 | 3 | 3 | 1 | 3/32" x 6" (2.4 mm x 152 mm) and may not occur within 48" (1220 mm) of a similar occurrence. | E | C | P |
| 1 | 3 | 3 | 2 | 1/32" x 4" (0.8 mm x 102 mm) and may not occur within 60" (1524 mm) of a similar occurrence. | E | C | P |

Continues next column ▼

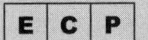

Where the **E**, **C**, or **P** icon is not indicated, the rule applies to all Grades equally

# SECTION 11
## Countertops

**compliance requirements** — GENERAL / **PRODUCT** / INSTALLATION / TEST

## 11.4.6 Machining Rules

▲ From previous column

| | | | | | | | | |
|---|---|---|---|---|---|---|---|---|
| 1 | | **EXPOSED SURFACES**: (continued) | | | | | | |
| 1 | 3 | 3 | 3 | 1/32" x 1-1/2" (0.8 mm x 38.1 mm) and may not occur within 72" (1829 mm) of a similar occurrence. | | E | C | P |
| 2 | | Of **CUTOUTS** within a top, shall be made by either manufacturer or installer, and: | | | | | | |
| 2 | 1 | Sink cutouts shall not fall within 18" (457 mm) of a joint. | | | | | | |
| 3 | | **TEAR-OUTS**, **KNIFE NICKS**, or **HIT-OR-MISS** machining is not permitted. | | | | | | |
| 4 | | **KNIFE MARKS** not to be permitted where sanding is required. | | | | | | |
| 5 | | Requires **SHARP EDGES** be eased. | | | | | | |
| 6 | | At **WOOD**: | | | | | | |
| 6 | 1 | **OCCASIONAL PATCHES** are allowed. | | | | E | C | P |
| 6 | 2 | **FINGER JOINTS** are permitted in solid lumber for opaque or transparent finish. | | | | E | C | P |
| 6 | 3 | **SMOOTHNESS REQUIREMENTS** (see Item 7.1 in TESTS) require: | | | | | | |
| 6 | 3 | 1 | **TOP FLAT WOOD** surfaces; those that can be sanded with a drum or wide belt sander: | | | | | |
| 6 | 3 | 1 | 1 | Minimum of 15 KCPI or 100-grit sanding. | | E | C | P |
| 6 | 3 | 1 | 2 | 120-grit sanding. | | E | C | |
| 6 | 3 | 1 | 3 | 150-grit sanding. | | E | C | P |
| 6 | 3 | 2 | **PROFILED** and **SHAPED WOOD** surfaces: | | | | | |
| 6 | 3 | 2 | 1 | Minimum of 15 KCPI or 100-grit sanding. | | E | C | P |
| 6 | 3 | 2 | 2 | Minimum of 20 KCPI. | | E | C | |
| 6 | 3 | 2 | 3 | 120-grit sanding. | | E | C | P |
| 6 | 3 | 3 | **CROSS-SANDING**: | | | | | |
| 6 | 3 | 3 | 1 | Is not a defect. | | E | C | P |
| 6 | 3 | 3 | 2 | Is not allowed. | | E | C | P |
| 6 | 4 | | **CURVED** front edges shall be solid machined, steam bent, bent solid lumber or laminated plies at the option of the manufacturer, and; | | | | | |
| 6 | 4 | 1 | In full compliance with all other applicable requirements of the AWS including Section 6. | | | | | |

Continues next column ▼

## 11.4.6 Machining Rules

▲ From previous column

| | | | | | |
|---|---|---|---|---|---|
| 7 | | At **HPDL**: | | | |
| 7 | 1 | | **CUTOUTS** shall have a minimum of 1/4" (6.4 mm) radius at inside corners, and: | | |
| 7 | 1 | 1 | Edges subject to excessive moisture shall be sealed with a color-toned (for verification), water-resistant sealer before trim or sink rims are installed. | | |
| 7 | 2 | | **COVES** at splashes of: | | |
| 7 | 2 | 1 | 1/4" (6.4 mm) radius permits a square cove stick the same thickness as the core material with voids filled with glue between the HPDL and the cove stick. | | |
| 7 | 2 | 2 | 3/4" (19 mm) radius requires a molded cove stick glued and mechanically fastened a maximum of 12" (305 mm) on center, with no voids permitted between the HPDL or core and the cove stick. | | |
| 7 | 3 | | **DRIP GROOVE**, when specified, shall be continuous and 1/8" x 1/8" (3.2 mm x 3.2 mm) approximately 3/8" (9.5 mm) from the front edge and sealed with a color-toned (for verification), water-resistant sealer: | | |
| 7 | 3 | 1 | Groove edges shall be smoothly sanded. | | |
| 7 | 4 | | **MITER-FOLD** self edge is acceptable. | | |
| 7 | | At **SOLID SURFACE** (only available in Custom and Premium Grade): | | | |
| 7 | 1 | | Shall conform to the manufacturer's recommendations. | | |
| 7 | 2 | | **MANUFACTURED JOINTS** shall be precision-machined and glued with the manufacturer's hard seaming material or equal: | | |
| 7 | 2 | 1 | Silicone is not permitted at joints, except: | | |
| 7 | 2 | 1 | 1 | Where hot areas meet cold areas. | |
| 7 | 3 | | **EDGE** detail requires a: | | |
| 7 | 3 | 1 | Single drop or build-up with manufacturers' choice of profile, a minimum of 1" (25.4 mm) thick. | C | P |
| 7 | 3 | 2 | Build-up with manufacturers' choice of profile, a minimum of 1-1/2" (38.1 mm) thick. | C | P |
| 7 | 3 | 3 | Miter-fold with manufacturers' choice of profile, a minimum of 1-1/2" (38.1 mm) thick. | | |
| 7 | 4 | | **COVED** splash is only required when so specified, with: | | |
| 7 | 4 | 1 | Ends sent loose without cove. | | |

Continues next column ▼

©2014 AWI | AWMAC | WI 2nd Edition, October 1, 2014
As may be updated by errata at awinet.org, awmac.com, or aws-errata.com

Architectural Woodwork Standards   **355**

# SECTION 11
## Countertops

**GENERAL / PRODUCT / INSTALLATION / TEST**

Where the **E**, **C**, or **P** icon is not indicated, the rule applies to all Grades equally | E | C | P |

**compliance requirements**

### 11.4.6 Machining Rules

▲ From previous column

| | | |
|---|---|---|
| 8 | | At **SOLID PHENOLIC** (only available in Premium Grade): |
| 8 | 1 | **JOINTS** shall be precision-machined with tight joint fasteners and sealed with a biocide silicon prior to tightening (producing an almost invisible joint). |
| 8 | 2 | **FRONT EDGES** shall be a minimum of 3/4" (19 mm) in thickness. |
| 9 | | At **EPOXY RESIN** (only available in Premium Grade): |
| 9 | 1 | **EXPOSED EDGES** shall be smoothly machined and finished to be compatible with the top face. |
| 9 | 2 | **LIPPED TOPS** shall be raised a minimum of 3/16" (4.8 mm) above the work surface, and: |
| 9 | 2 | 1 | Drip groove is not required. |
| 10 | | At **NATURAL** and **ENGINEERED STONE**: (only available in Premium Grade): |
| 10 | 1 | **EXPOSED EDGES** shall be finished the same as the top surface. |

### 11.4.7 Assembly Rules

| | | |
|---|---|---|
| 1 | | **THESE STANDARDS** do not establish grade rules for joint flushness and or gap tolerances for woodwork products installed in a non-climate controlled environment: however: |
| 1 | 1 | Prior to installation, the flushness and/or gap tolerances of woodwork products intended for non-climate controlled environments shall meet the test requirements herein. |
| 2 | | **ADHESIVE** or **JOINT FILLER** material, if used, shall be inconspicuous and match the adjacent surface for smoothness. |
| 3 | | **SQUARENESS** shall be within ±1/64" (0.4 mm) for each 12" (305 mm). |
| 4 | | **CUTOUTS** shall be within ±1/8" for locations and +1/8" to 0" (3.2 to 0 mm) for size. |
| 5 | | For **SCRIBING**, countertop shall be provided with extra length. |
| 6 | | Tops requiring more than one sheet of surface material shall be prematched to minimize color variation within the scope of the manufacturer's guarantee and: | E | C | P |
| 6 | 1 | Shall be fabricated from the longest lengths available. | E | C | P |
| 6 | 2 | Top widths exceeding product availability shall have manufacturer-assembled joints. |
| 7 | | **FILLERS** shall be furnished by the countertop manufacturer. |
| 8 | | **EDGE APPLICATION SEQUENCE** shall be the manufacturer's choice, except at HPDL. |
| 9 | | **BACK SPLASHES** require end splashes at wall ends. |
| 10 | | **REMOVABLE LEDGES** and/or **ACCESS PANELS** shall be attached with flat-head screws, set flush, and: |
| 10 | 1 | If chemical resistance is required, screws shall be stainless steel. |
| 11 | | Of **JOINTS** at assembled work, **EXCLUDING SOLID PHENOLIC, EPOXY RESIN,** and **NATURAL/ENGINEERED STONE**, shall: |
| 11 | 1 | Be neatly and accurately made. |
| 11 | 2 | Be securely glued, with: |
| 11 | 2 | 1 | Adhesive residue removed from exposed surfaces. |
| 11 | 3 | Be reinforced with glue blocks where essential. |
| 11 | 4 | Not permit fasteners at exposed surfaces of decorative laminate. |

▼ Continues next column

## SECTION 11
### Countertops

## 11.4.7 Assembly Rules

▲ From previous column

**11 Of JOINTS at assembled work** (continued)

**11 5** Require **FLUSHNESS VARIATIONS** at exposed surfaces (See Test D illustrations in TESTS), when mitered or butted, such as,

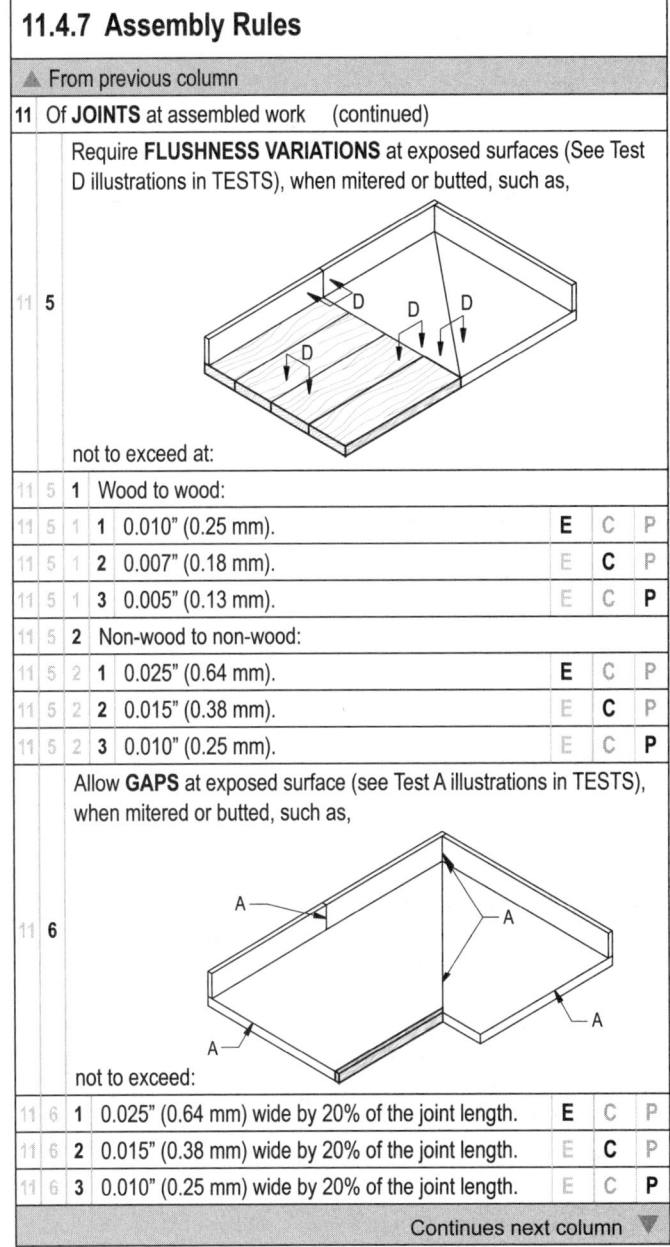

not to exceed at:

| | | | | | | |
|---|---|---|---|---|---|---|
| 11 | 5 | 1 | Wood to wood: | | | |
| 11 | 5 | 1 | 1 | 0.010" (0.25 mm). | E | C | P |
| 11 | 5 | 1 | 2 | 0.007" (0.18 mm). | E | **C** | P |
| 11 | 5 | 1 | 3 | 0.005" (0.13 mm). | E | C | **P** |
| 11 | 5 | 2 | Non-wood to non-wood: | | | |
| 11 | 5 | 2 | 1 | 0.025" (0.64 mm). | **E** | C | P |
| 11 | 5 | 2 | 2 | 0.015" (0.38 mm). | E | **C** | P |
| 11 | 5 | 2 | 3 | 0.010" (0.25 mm). | E | C | **P** |

**11 6** Allow **GAPS** at exposed surface (see Test A illustrations in TESTS), when mitered or butted, such as,

not to exceed:

| 11 | 6 | 1 | 0.025" (0.64 mm) wide by 20% of the joint length. | **E** | C | P |
| 11 | 6 | 2 | 0.015" (0.38 mm) wide by 20% of the joint length. | E | **C** | P |
| 11 | 6 | 3 | 0.010" (0.25 mm) wide by 20% of the joint length. | E | C | **P** |

Continues next column ▼

---

## 11.4.7 Assembly Rules

▲ From previous column

**11 Of JOINTS at assembled work** (continued)

**11 7** Allow **GAPS** at exposed surface joints of parallel members (See Test B illustrations in TESTS), such as,

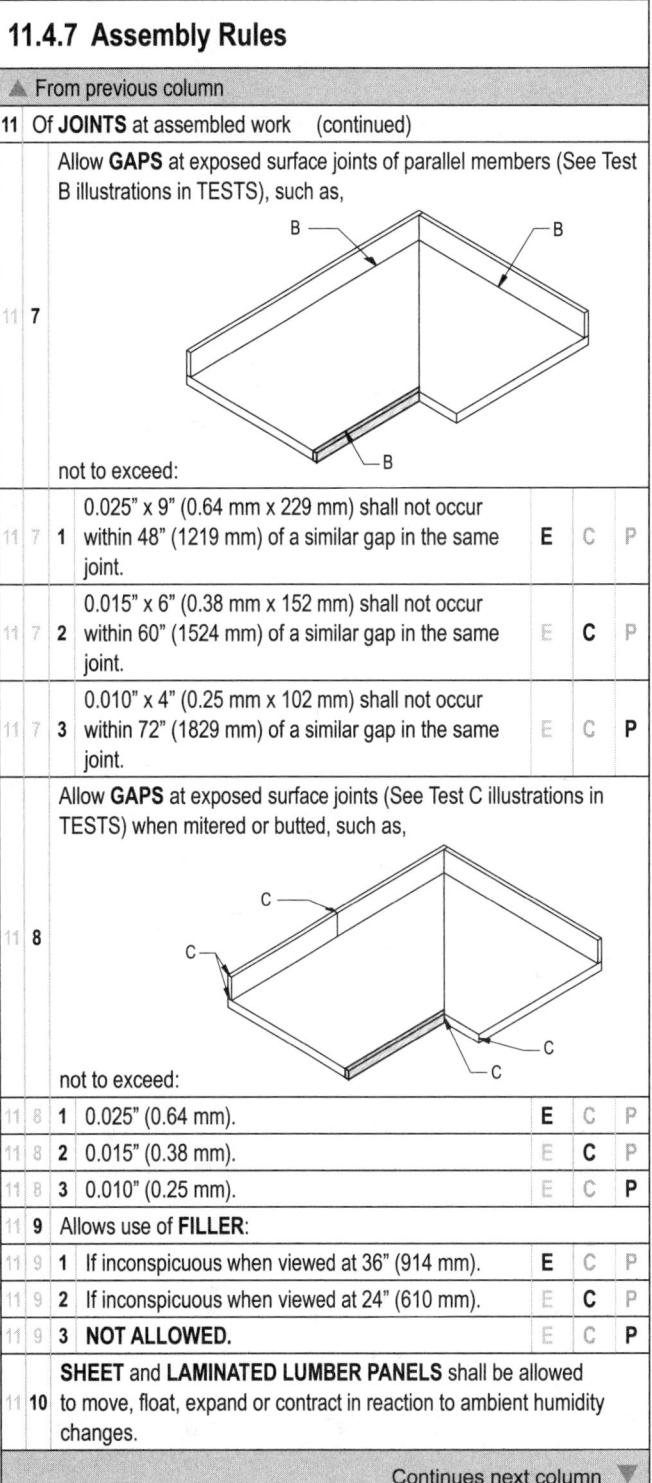

not to exceed:

| 11 | 7 | 1 | 0.025" x 9" (0.64 mm x 229 mm) shall not occur within 48" (1219 mm) of a similar gap in the same joint. | **E** | C | P |
| 11 | 7 | 2 | 0.015" x 6" (0.38 mm x 152 mm) shall not occur within 60" (1524 mm) of a similar gap in the same joint. | E | **C** | P |
| 11 | 7 | 3 | 0.010" x 4" (0.25 mm x 102 mm) shall not occur within 72" (1829 mm) of a similar gap in the same joint. | E | C | **P** |

**11 8** Allow **GAPS** at exposed surface joints (See Test C illustrations in TESTS) when mitered or butted, such as,

not to exceed:

| 11 | 8 | 1 | 0.025" (0.64 mm). | **E** | C | P |
| 11 | 8 | 2 | 0.015" (0.38 mm). | E | **C** | P |
| 11 | 8 | 3 | 0.010" (0.25 mm). | E | C | **P** |

**11 9** Allows use of **FILLER**:

| 11 | 9 | 1 | If inconspicuous when viewed at 36" (914 mm). | **E** | C | P |
| 11 | 9 | 2 | If inconspicuous when viewed at 24" (610 mm). | E | **C** | P |
| 11 | 9 | 3 | **NOT ALLOWED**. | E | C | **P** |

**11 10** **SHEET** and **LAMINATED LUMBER PANELS** shall be allowed to move, float, expand or contract in reaction to ambient humidity changes.

Continues next column ▼

# SECTION 11
## Countertops

GENERAL/PRODUCT/INSTALLATION/TEST

compliance requirements

Where the **E**, **C**, or **P** icon is not indicated, the rule applies to all Grades equally | E | C | P |

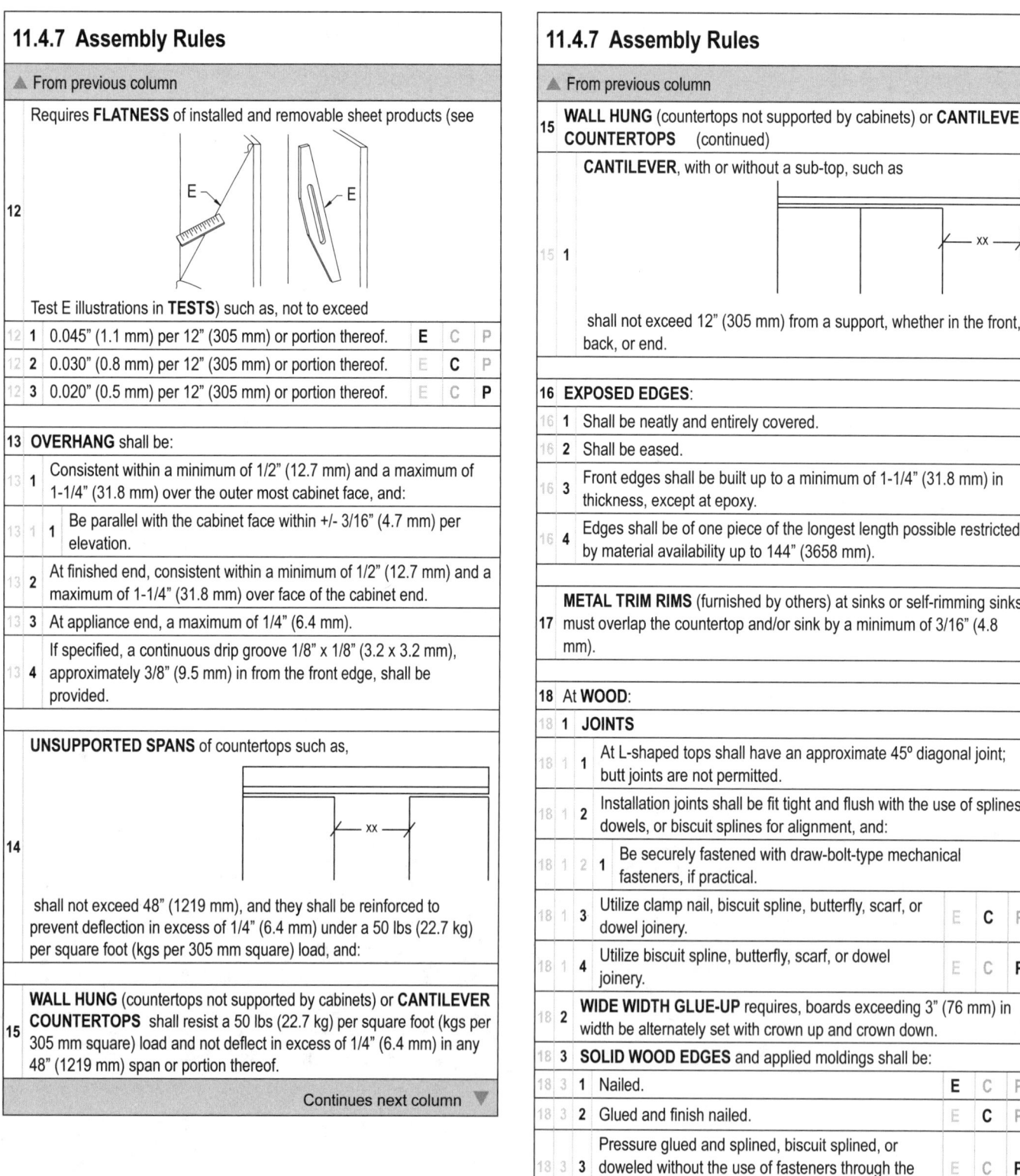

### 11.4.7 Assembly Rules

▲ From previous column

**12** Requires **FLATNESS** of installed and removable sheet products (see Test E illustrations in **TESTS**) such as, not to exceed

| 12 | 1 | 0.045" (1.1 mm) per 12" (305 mm) or portion thereof. | E | C | P |
| 12 | 2 | 0.030" (0.8 mm) per 12" (305 mm) or portion thereof. | | C | P |
| 12 | 3 | 0.020" (0.5 mm) per 12" (305 mm) or portion thereof. | | | P |

**13** **OVERHANG** shall be:

| 13 | 1 | Consistent within a minimum of 1/2" (12.7 mm) and a maximum of 1-1/4" (31.8 mm) over the outer most cabinet face, and: |
| 13 | 1 | 1 | Be parallel with the cabinet face within +/- 3/16" (4.7 mm) per elevation. |
| 13 | 2 | At finished end, consistent within a minimum of 1/2" (12.7 mm) and a maximum of 1-1/4" (31.8 mm) over face of the cabinet end. |
| 13 | 3 | At appliance end, a maximum of 1/4" (6.4 mm). |
| 13 | 4 | If specified, a continuous drip groove 1/8" x 1/8" (3.2 x 3.2 mm), approximately 3/8" (9.5 mm) in from the front edge, shall be provided. |

**14** **UNSUPPORTED SPANS** of countertops such as, shall not exceed 48" (1219 mm), and they shall be reinforced to prevent deflection in excess of 1/4" (6.4 mm) under a 50 lbs (22.7 kg) per square foot (kgs per 305 mm square) load, and:

**15** **WALL HUNG** (countertops not supported by cabinets) or **CANTILEVER COUNTERTOPS** shall resist a 50 lbs (22.7 kg) per square foot (kgs per 305 mm square) load and not deflect in excess of 1/4" (6.4 mm) in any 48" (1219 mm) span or portion thereof.

Continues next column ▼

### 11.4.7 Assembly Rules

▲ From previous column

**15** **WALL HUNG** (countertops not supported by cabinets) or **CANTILEVER COUNTERTOPS** (continued)

| 15 | 1 | **CANTILEVER**, with or without a sub-top, such as shall not exceed 12" (305 mm) from a support, whether in the front, back, or end. |

**16** **EXPOSED EDGES**:

| 16 | 1 | Shall be neatly and entirely covered. |
| 16 | 2 | Shall be eased. |
| 16 | 3 | Front edges shall be built up to a minimum of 1-1/4" (31.8 mm) in thickness, except at epoxy. |
| 16 | 4 | Edges shall be of one piece of the longest length possible restricted by material availability up to 144" (3658 mm). |

**17** **METAL TRIM RIMS** (furnished by others) at sinks or self-rimming sinks must overlap the countertop and/or sink by a minimum of 3/16" (4.8 mm).

**18** At **WOOD**:

| 18 | 1 | **JOINTS** |
| 18 | 1 | 1 | At L-shaped tops shall have an approximate 45° diagonal joint; butt joints are not permitted. |
| 18 | 1 | 2 | Installation joints shall be fit tight and flush with the use of splines, dowels, or biscuit splines for alignment, and: |
| 18 | 1 | 2 | 1 | Be securely fastened with draw-bolt-type mechanical fasteners, if practical. |
| 18 | 1 | 3 | Utilize clamp nail, biscuit spline, butterfly, scarf, or dowel joinery. | E | C | P |
| 18 | 1 | 4 | Utilize biscuit spline, butterfly, scarf, or dowel joinery. | E | C | P |
| 18 | 2 | **WIDE WIDTH GLUE-UP** requires, boards exceeding 3" (76 mm) in width be alternately set with crown up and crown down. |
| 18 | 3 | **SOLID WOOD EDGES** and applied moldings shall be: |
| 18 | 3 | 1 | Nailed. | E | | |
| 18 | 3 | 2 | Glued and finish nailed. | | C | |
| 18 | 3 | 3 | Pressure glued and splined, biscuit splined, or doweled without the use of fasteners through the exposed face. | | | P |

Continues next column ▼

358 Architectural Woodwork Standards

©2014 AWI | AWMAC | WI 2nd Edition, October 1, 2014
As may be updated by errata at awinet.org, awmac.com, or aws-errata.com

# SECTION 11
## Countertops

**compliance requirements** — GENERAL/PRODUCT/INSTALLATION/TEST

Where the **E**, **C**, or **P** icon is not indicated, the rule applies to all Grades equally

### 11.4.7 Assembly Rules

▲ From previous column

**18** At **WOOD** (continued):

| | | | E | C | P |
|---|---|---|---|---|---|
| 18 | 4 | **BUILT-UP MEMBERS** shall be of acceptable core material with backing sheet applied, or: | E | C | P |
| 18 | 4 | 1 — The use of moisture-resistant core or a color-coded, water-resistant sealer may be substituted for backing sheet. | E | C | P |

**19** At **HPDL**:

| 19 | 1 | **BACKING SHEET** shall cover the underside of countertops, the backside of splashes and be the same for the entire project. | | | |
|---|---|---|---|---|---|
| 19 | 2 | **LAMINATIONS** shall be made securely to the core with Type II adhesive applied as recommended by the adhesive manufacturer, and: | | | |
| 19 | 2 | 1 — Contact adhesive shall comply with the Heat Resistance Test listed in the **APPENDIX**. [a] | | | |
| 19 | 2 | 2 — Adhesive for solid color core laminate application shall conform to the manufacturer's recommendation. | | | |
| 19 | 3 | **FLAME SPREAD-RATED** countertops require: | | | |
| 19 | 3 | 1 — Non-formed self-edged. | | | |
| 19 | 3 | 2 — Screwed-on back splash. | | | |
| 19 | 3 | 3 — Minimum custom grade conformance. | | | |
| 19 | 3 | 4 — Adhesive be rigid set with Class I Flame Spread. | | | |
| 19 | 4 | **Self-edge**: | | | |
| 19 | 4 | 1 — Applied after top laminate. | E | C | P |
| 19 | 4 | 2 — Applied before top laminate. | E | C | P |
| 19 | 5 | **JOINTS**: | | | |
| 19 | 5 | 1 — At L-shaped wood grain or directional pattern countertops shall have an approximate 45° diagonal joint, butt joints are not permitted, except: | | | |
| 19 | 5 | 1 — At L-shaped non-wood grain or non-directional pattern countertops, butt joints are permitted. | | | |
| 19 | 5 | 2 — Installation joints shall be fit tight and flush with the use of splines, dowels, or biscuit splines for alignment, and: | | | |
| 19 | 5 | 2 — Be securely fastened with draw-bolt-type mechanical fasteners, if practical. | | | |
| 19 | 6 | **BOTTOM OF EDGING** and its build-up shall be free of dents, torn grain, glue, and sanded smooth with sharp edges removed. | | | |
| 19 | 7 | **BUILT-UP MEMBERS** shall be of acceptable core material with backing sheet applied, or: | E | C | P |
| 19 | 7 | 1 — The use of moisture-resistant core or a color-coded, water-resistant sealer may be substituted for backing sheet. | E | C | P |

Continues next column ▼

### 11.4.7 Assembly Rules

▲ From previous column

**19** At **HPDL** (continued):

At **ASSEMBLY 1** (wall mount) back and end-splash construction,

| 19 | 8 | | | | |
|---|---|---|---|---|---|

and:

| 19 | 8 | 1 — Top edge to be edgebanded. | | | |
|---|---|---|---|---|---|
| 19 | 8 | 2 — Front edge of end splash to be edgebanded. | | | |
| 19 | 8 | 3 — Splash members to be bundled and shipped loose to project. | | | |
| 19 | 8 | 4 — Mechanical fasteners are required between splash members and deck. | E | C | P |

At **ASSEMBLY 2** (deck mount) back and end-splash construction,

| 19 | 9 | | | | |

and:

| 19 | 9 | 1 — Raw core at joint between the countertop deck and end splash or butt joint-applied back splash shall be sealed before assembly. | | | |
|---|---|---|---|---|---|
| 19 | 9 | 2 — End splashes at cove or butt back splashes shall be butt-jointed and securely attached with mechanical fasteners, and: | | | |
| 19 | 9 | 2 — 1 Mechanical fasteners are not required at wall or cabinet abutments that are not as deep as the countertop return. | | | |
| 19 | 9 | 2 — 2 Shall be caulked with clear or compatible color waterproof caulking so as to leave a visual bead not exceeding 1/8" (3.2 mm). | | | |
| 19 | 9 | 3 — Scribe allowance shall be provided, as appropriate, and: | | | |
| 19 | 9 | 3 — 1 Un-backed scribe span shall not exceed 1/2" (12.7 mm) at ends and back walls. | | | |
| 19 | 10 | **FINISHED END CAPS** may be applied after top laminate. | | | |

Continues next column ▼

# SECTION 11
## Countertops

GENERAL/**PRODUCT**/INSTALLATION/TEST

compliance requirements

Where the **E**, **C**, or **P** icon is not indicated, the rule applies to all Grades equally | **E** | **C** | **P** |

### 11.4.7 Assembly Rules
▲ From previous column

**19** At **HPDL** (continued)

**19 | 11** — **CANTILEVER**, with or without a sub-top, such as,

shall not exceed 12" (305 mm) from a support, whether in the front, back, or end.

**19 | 12** — **REMOVABLE COMPONENTS** shall be attached with flat-head screws, set flush, and:

**19 | 12 | 1** — If chemical resistance is required, the screws shall be stainless steel.

**20** At **SOLID SURFACE** (only available in Custom and Premium Grade):

**20 | 1** — **FLUSHNESS VARIATIONS** at exposed surfaces when mitered or butted (see Test D illustrations in TESTS) such as,

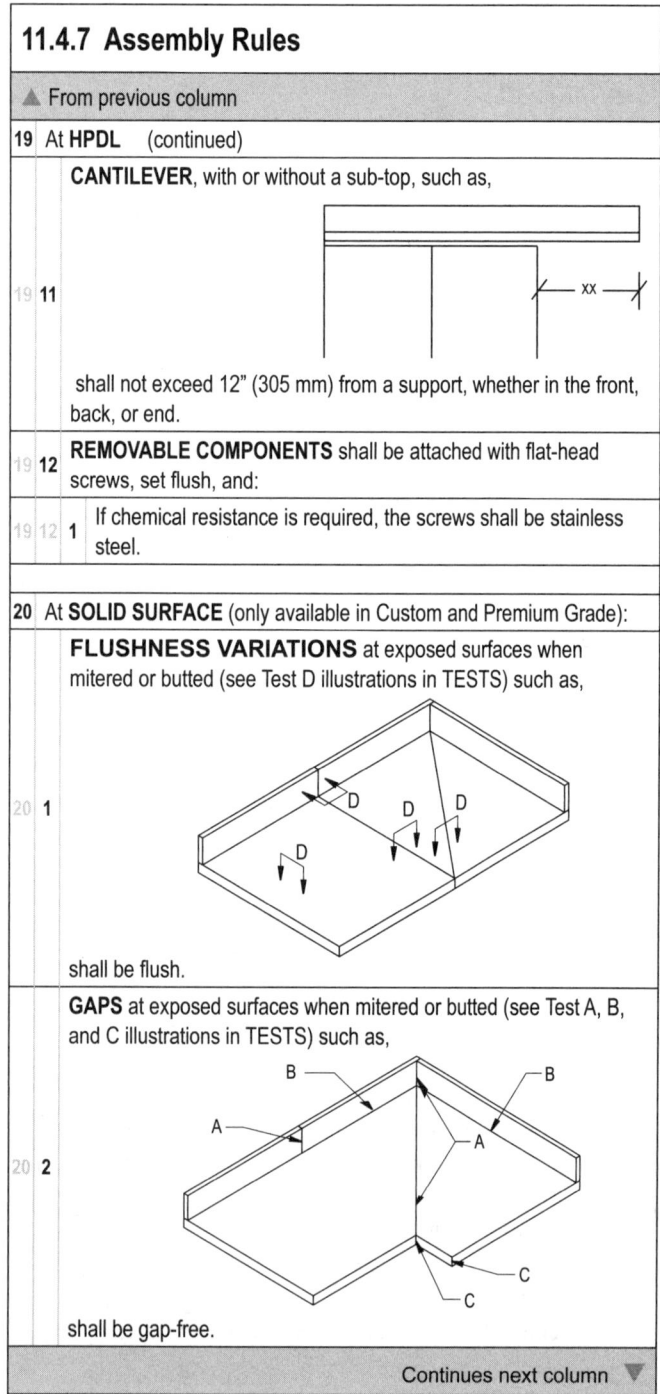

shall be flush.

**20 | 2** — **GAPS** at exposed surfaces when mitered or butted (see Test A, B, and C illustrations in TESTS) such as,

shall be gap-free.

Continues next column ▼

### 11.4.7 Assembly Rules
▲ From previous column

**20** At **SOLID SURFACE** (continued)

**20 | 3** — **FLATNESS** of installed and removable sheet products (See Test E illustrations in TESTS) such as,

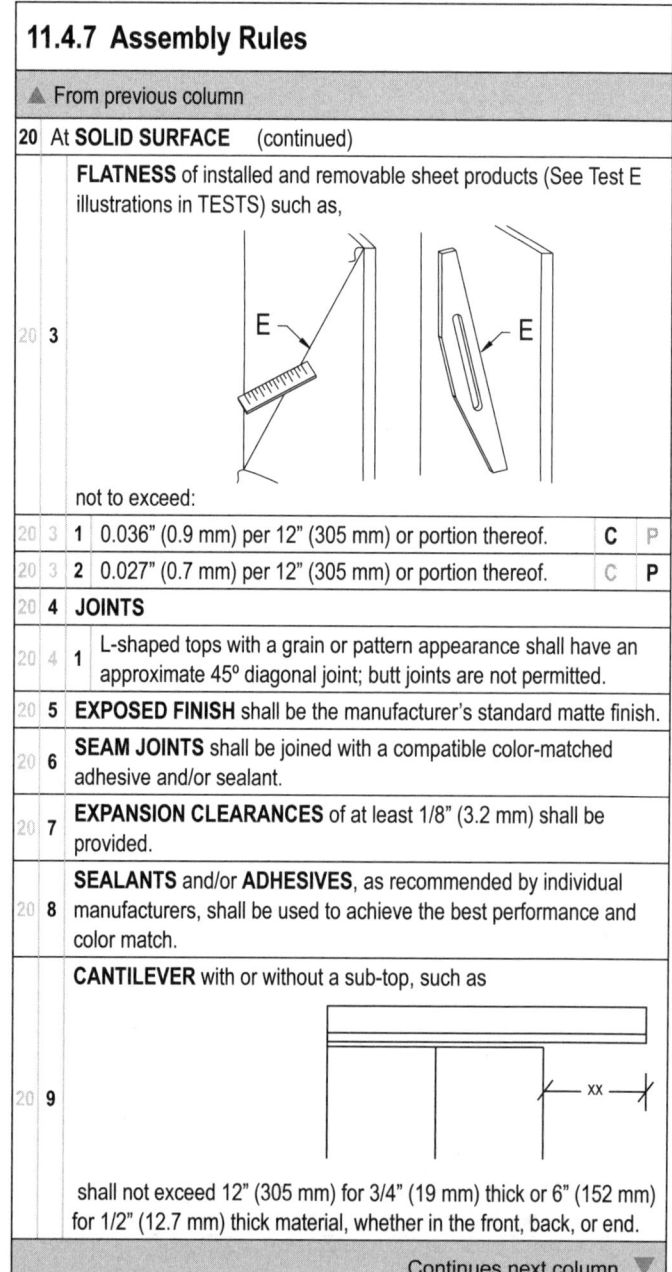

not to exceed:

| | | | | | |
|---|---|---|---|---|---|
| 20 | 3 | 1 | 0.036" (0.9 mm) per 12" (305 mm) or portion thereof. | C | P |
| 20 | 3 | 2 | 0.027" (0.7 mm) per 12" (305 mm) or portion thereof. | C | P |

**20 | 4** — **JOINTS**

**20 | 4 | 1** — L-shaped tops with a grain or pattern appearance shall have an approximate 45° diagonal joint; butt joints are not permitted.

**20 | 5** — **EXPOSED FINISH** shall be the manufacturer's standard matte finish.

**20 | 6** — **SEAM JOINTS** shall be joined with a compatible color-matched adhesive and/or sealant.

**20 | 7** — **EXPANSION CLEARANCES** of at least 1/8" (3.2 mm) shall be provided.

**20 | 8** — **SEALANTS** and/or **ADHESIVES**, as recommended by individual manufacturers, shall be used to achieve the best performance and color match.

**20 | 9** — **CANTILEVER** with or without a sub-top, such as

shall not exceed 12" (305 mm) for 3/4" (19 mm) thick or 6" (152 mm) for 1/2" (12.7 mm) thick material, whether in the front, back, or end.

Continues next column ▼

## SECTION 11
### Countertops

**GENERAL / PRODUCT / INSTALLATION / TEST**

### 11.4.7 Assembly Rules

▲ From previous column

**21** At **SOLID PHENOLIC** (only available in Premium Grade):

| 21 | 1 | **FLUSHNESS VARIATIONS** at exposed surfaces when mitered or butted (see Test D illustrations in TESTS) such as, 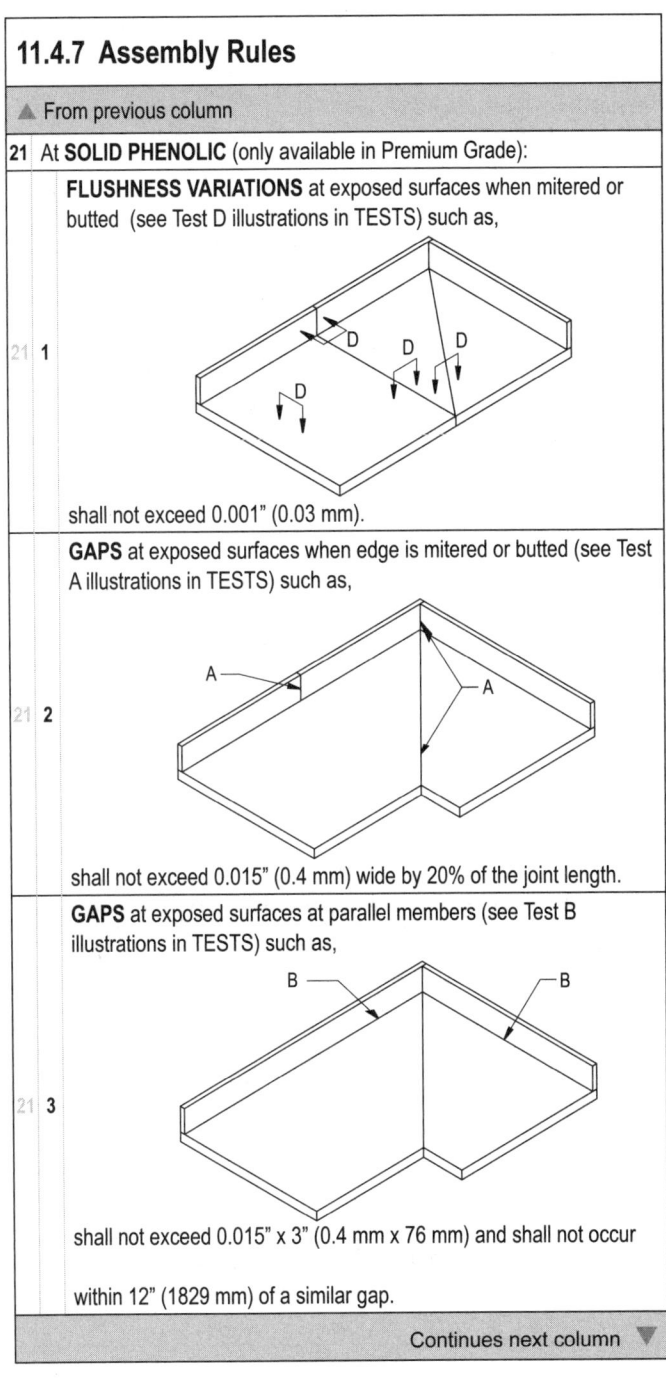 shall not exceed 0.001" (0.03 mm). |

| 21 | 2 | **GAPS** at exposed surfaces when edge is mitered or butted (see Test A illustrations in TESTS) such as, shall not exceed 0.015" (0.4 mm) wide by 20% of the joint length. |

| 21 | 3 | **GAPS** at exposed surfaces at parallel members (see Test B illustrations in TESTS) such as, shall not exceed 0.015" x 3" (0.4 mm x 76 mm) and shall not occur within 12" (1829 mm) of a similar gap. |

*Continues next column* ▼

### 11.4.7 Assembly Rules

▲ From previous column

**21** At **SOLID PHENOLIC** (continued)

| 21 | 4 | **GAPS** at exposed surfaces when mitered or butted (see Test C illustrations in TESTS), such as, 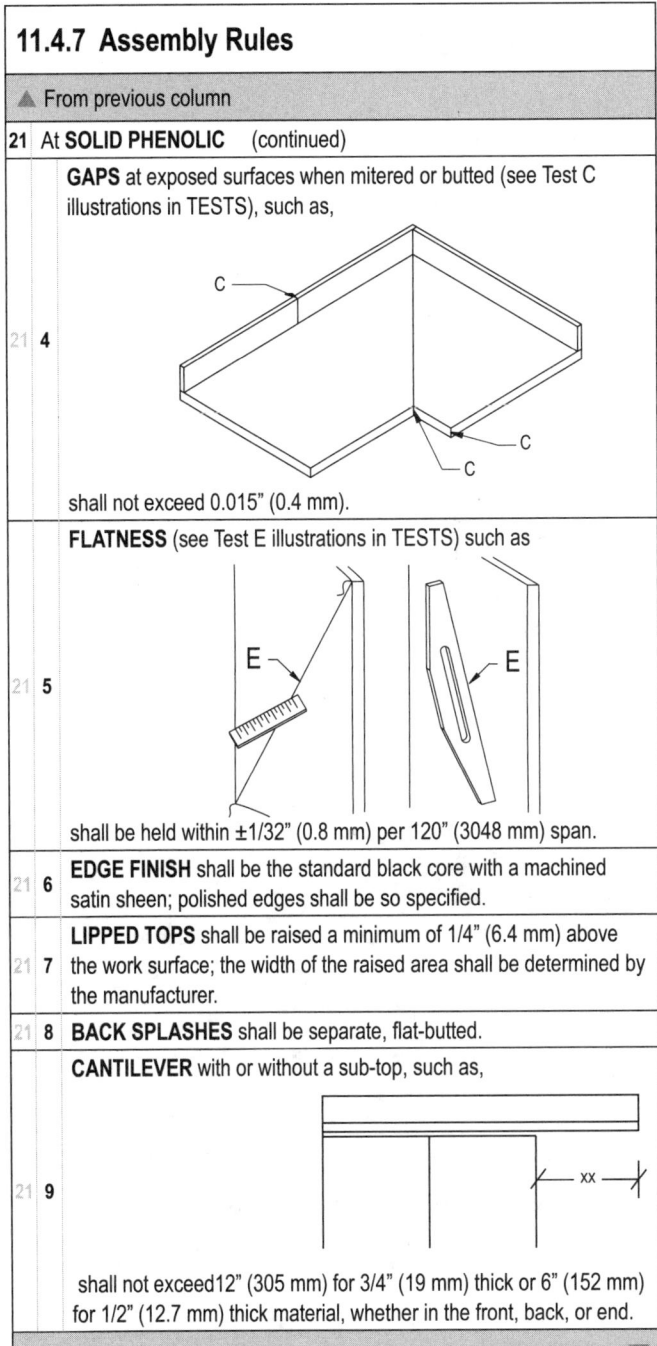 shall not exceed 0.015" (0.4 mm). |

| 21 | 5 | **FLATNESS** (see Test E illustrations in TESTS) such as shall be held within ±1/32" (0.8 mm) per 120" (3048 mm) span. |

| 21 | 6 | **EDGE FINISH** shall be the standard black core with a machined satin sheen; polished edges shall be so specified. |

| 21 | 7 | **LIPPED TOPS** shall be raised a minimum of 1/4" (6.4 mm) above the work surface; the width of the raised area shall be determined by the manufacturer. |

| 21 | 8 | **BACK SPLASHES** shall be separate, flat-butted. |

| 21 | 9 | **CANTILEVER** with or without a sub-top, such as, shall not exceed 12" (305 mm) for 3/4" (19 mm) thick or 6" (152 mm) for 1/2" (12.7 mm) thick material, whether in the front, back, or end. |

*Continues next column* ▼

# SECTION 11
## Countertops

### 11.4.7 Assembly Rules

**From previous column**

**22** At **EPOXY RESIN** (only available in Premium Grade):

- **22.1** **FLUSHNESS VARIATIONS** at exposed surfaces when mitered or butted (see Test D illustrations in TESTS) such as,

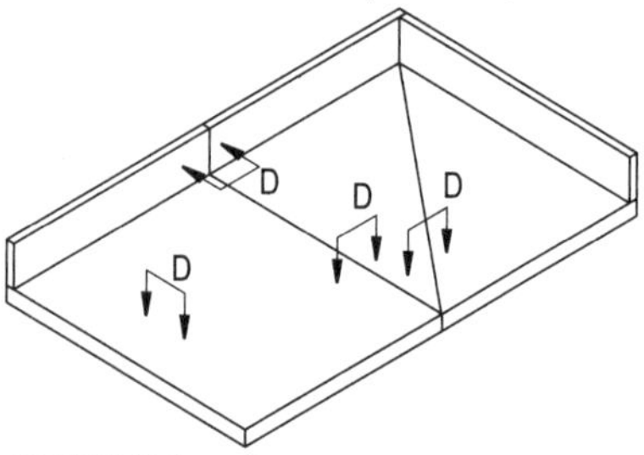

  shall not exceed 0.050" (0.8 mm).

- **22.2** **GAPS** at exposed surfaces when edge is mitered or butted shall be per the manufacturer's recommendation and shall be neatly filled with recommended filler material (see Test A, B, and C illustrations in TESTS) such as,

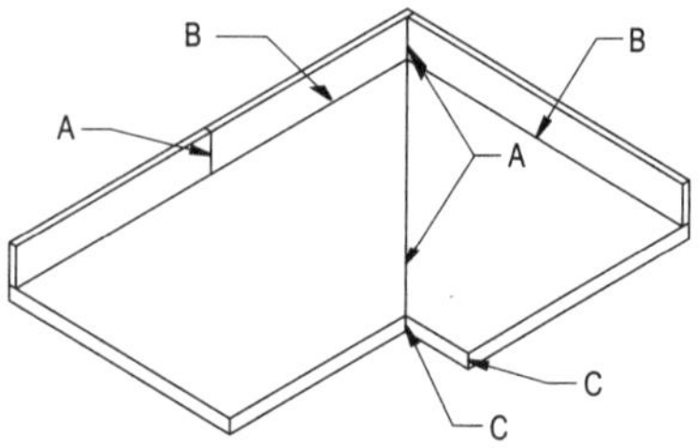

  shall be gap-free.

- **22.3** **FLATNESS** (see Test E illustrations in TESTS) such as,

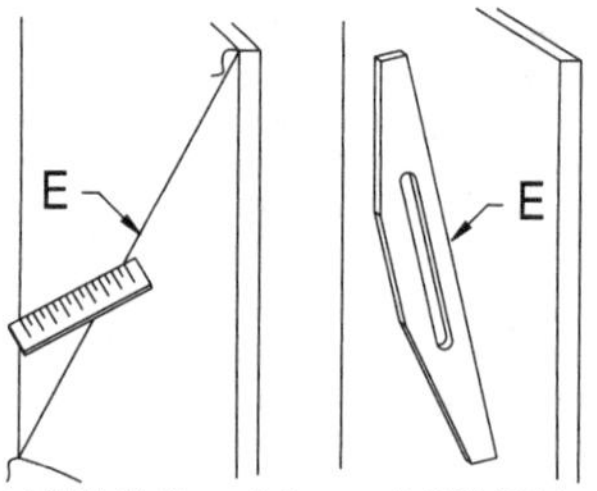

  shall be held within ±1/16" (1.6 mm) for each 36" (914 mm) span.

- **22.4** **BACK SPLASHES** shall be separate, flat-butted.

- **22.5** **CANTILEVER** with or without a sub-top, such as,

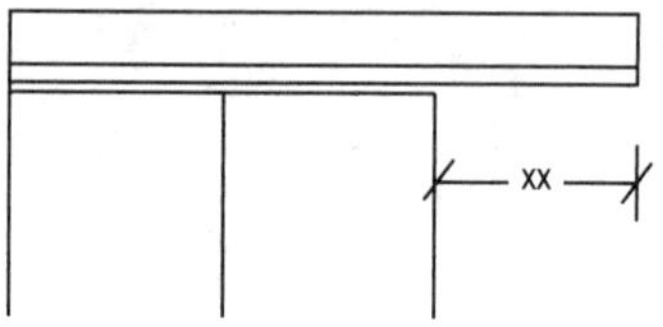

  shall not exceed 12" (305 mm) for 1" (25.4 mm) thick or 6" (152 mm) for 3/4" (19 mm) thick material, whether in the front, back, or end.

*Continues next column*

### 11.4.7 Assembly Rules

**From previous column**

**23** At **NATURAL** and **ENGINEERED STONE** (only available in Premium Grade):

- **23.1** **FLUSHNESS** or **LIPPAGE VARIATIONS** at exposed surfaces when mitered or butted (see Test D illustrations in TESTS) such as,

  shall not exceed 1/32" (0.8 mm) at the center of the joint.

- **23.2** **GAPS** at exposed surfaces when mitered or butted (see Test A illustrations in TESTS) such as,

  shall not exceed 0.015" (0.4 mm) wide by 20% of the joint length.

- **23.3** **GAPS** at exposed surfaces at parallel members (see Test B illustrations in TESTS) such as,

  shall not exceed 0.015" x 3" (0.4 mm x 76 mm) and shall not occur within 12" (1829 mm) of a similar gap.

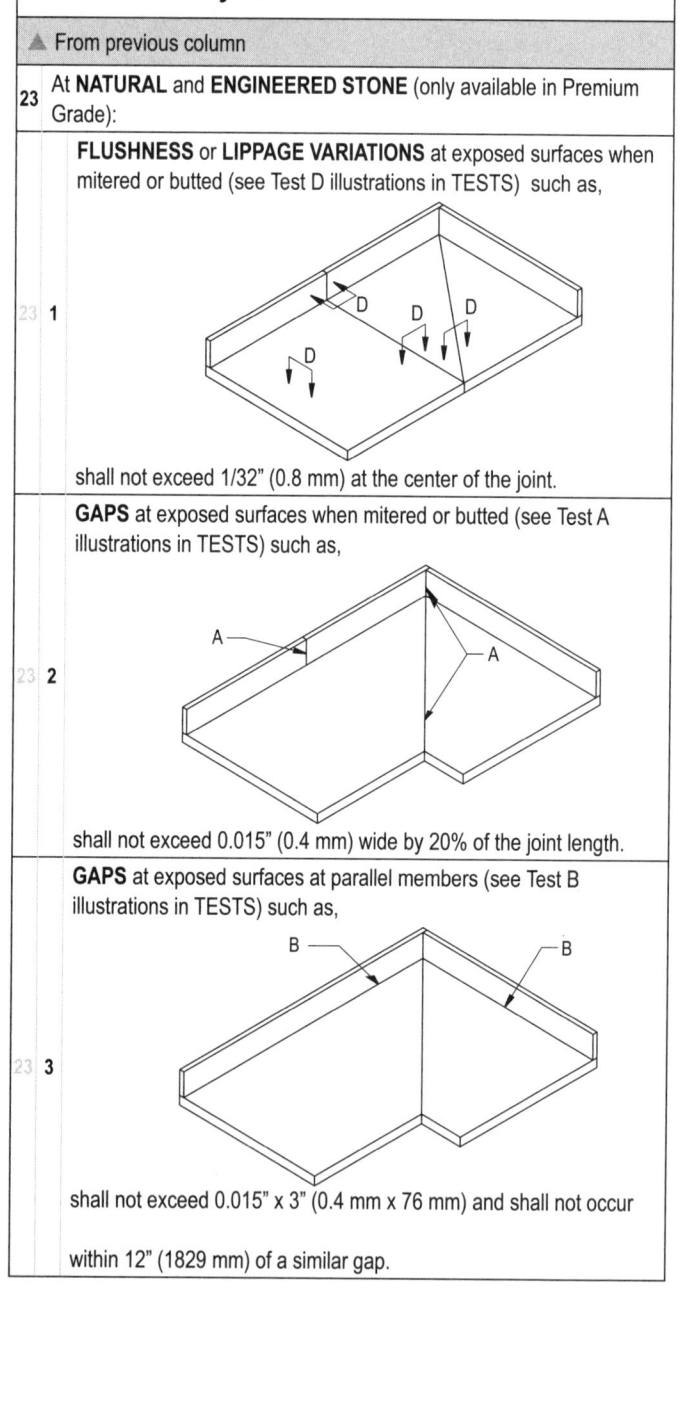

## 11.4.7 Assembly Rules

### 23 At NATURAL and ENGINEERED STONE (continued)

**4. GAPS** at exposed surfaces when mitered or butted (see Test C illustrations in TESTS) such as,

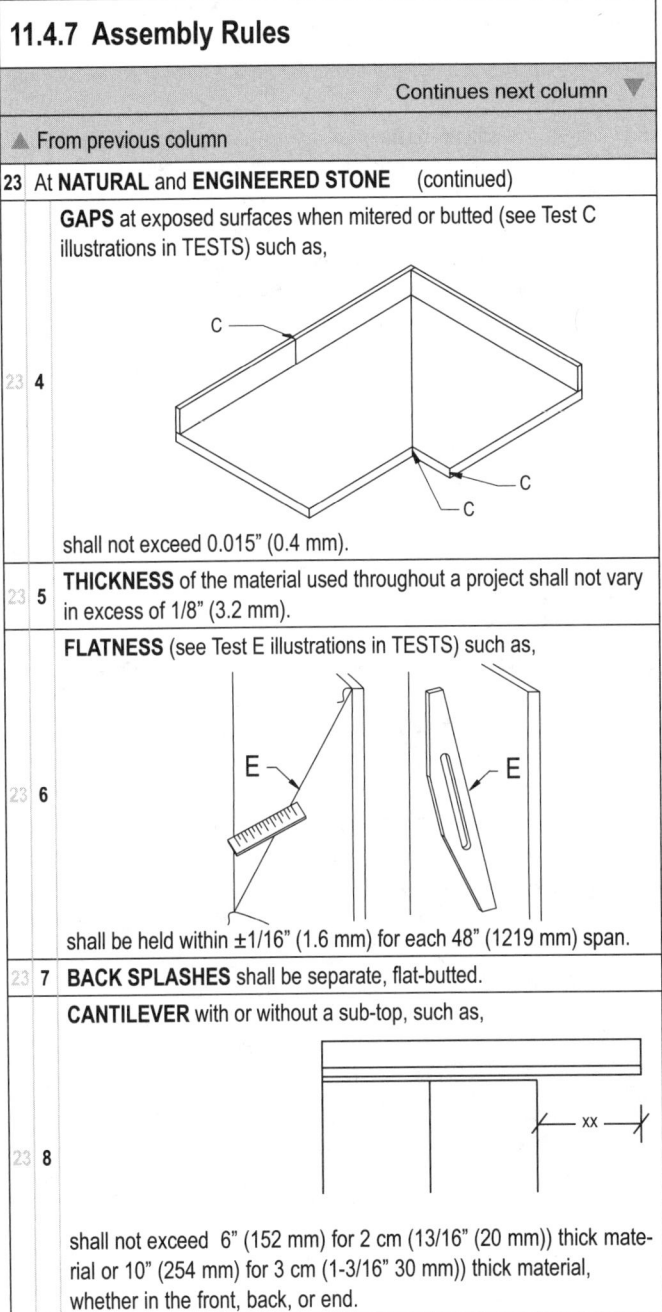

shall not exceed 0.015" (0.4 mm).

**5. THICKNESS** of the material used throughout a project shall not vary in excess of 1/8" (3.2 mm).

**6. FLATNESS** (see Test E illustrations in TESTS) such as,

shall be held within ±1/16" (1.6 mm) for each 48" (1219 mm) span.

**7. BACK SPLASHES** shall be separate, flat-butted.

**8. CANTILEVER** with or without a sub-top, such as,

shall not exceed 6" (152 mm) for 2 cm (13/16" (20 mm)) thick material or 10" (254 mm) for 3 cm (1-3/16" 30 mm)) thick material, whether in the front, back, or end.

# SECTION 11
## Countertops

GENERAL / PRODUCT / **INSTALLATION** / TEST

**compliance requirements**

Where the **E**, **C**, or **P** icon is not indicated, the rule applies to all Grades equally | E | C | P |

### 11.5  Preparation and Qualification requirements

**1.** **CARE, STORAGE, and BUILDING CONDITIONS** shall be in compliance with the requirements set forth in Section 2 of these standards.

1.1  Severe damage to the woodwork can result from noncompliance. **THE MANUFACTURER AND/OR INSTALLER OF THE WOODWORK SHALL NOT BE HELD RESPONSIBLE FOR DAMAGE THAT MIGHT DEVELOP BY NOT ADHERING TO THE REQUIREMENTS.**

**2**  **CONTRACTOR IS RESPONSIBLE FOR**

2.1  Furnishing and installing structural members, grounds, in wall blocking, backing, furring, brackets, or other anchorage required for architectural woodwork installation that becomes an integral part of walls, floors, or ceilings to which architectural woodwork shall be installed.

2.1.1  In the absence of contract documents calling for the contractor to supply the necessary in wall blocking/backing in the wall or ceilings, either through inadvertence or otherwise, the architectural woodwork installer shall not proceed with the installation until such time as the in wall blocking/backing is installed by others.

2.1.2  Preparatory work done by others shall be subject to inspection by the architectural woodwork installer and may be accepted or rejected for cause prior to installation.

2.1.2.1  **WALL, CEILING**, and/or opening variations in excess of 1/4" (6.4 mm) or **FLOORS** in excess of 1/2" (12.7 mm) in 144" (3658 mm) of being plumb, level, flat, straight, square, or of the correct size are not acceptable for the installation of architectural woodwork, nor is it the responsibility of the installer to scribe or fit to tolerances in excess of such.

2.2  Installation site being properly ventilated, protected from direct sunlight, excessive heat and/or moisture, and that the HVAC system is functioning and maintaining the appropriate relative humidity and temperature.

2.3  Priming the architectural woodwork in accordance with the contract documents prior to its installation.

2.3.1  If the architectural woodwork is factory finished, priming by the factory finisher is required.

### 11.5  Preparation and Qualification requirements  (continued)

**3**  **INSTALLER IS RESPONSIBLE FOR**

3.1  Having adequate equipment and experienced craftsmen to complete the installation in a first class manner.

3.2  Checking architectural woodwork specified and studying the appropriate portions of the contract documents, including these standards and the reviewed shop drawings to familiarize themselves with the requirements of the Grade specified, understanding that:

3.2.1  Appearance requirements of Grades apply only to surfaces visible after installation.

3.2.2  For transparent finish, special attention needs to be given to the color and the grain of the various woodwork pieces to ensure they are installed in compliance with the Grade specified.

3.3  Verification that installation site is properly ventilated, protected from direct sunlight, excessive heat and/or moisture, and that the HVAC system is functioning and maintaining the appropriate relative humidity and temperature.

3.4  Verification that required priming of woodwork has been completed by others before woodwork is install.

3.5  Verification that woodwork has been acclimated to the field conditions for a minimum of 72 hours before installation is commenced.

3.6  Woodwork specifically built or assembled in sequence for match of color and grain is installed to maintain that same sequence.

### 11.6  RULES

1  The following rules shall govern unless a project's contract documents require otherwise.

2  These rules are intended to provide a well defined degree of control over a project's quality of installation.

3  **ERRATA**, published on the Sponsor Associations' websites at www.awinet.org, www.awmac.com, or www.aws-errata.com, shall **TAKE PRECEDENCE OVER THESE RULES**, subject to their date of posting and a project's bid date.

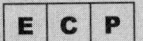 Where the E, C, or P icon is not indicated, the rule applies to all Grades equally

# SECTION 11
## Countertops

**compliance requirements** — GENERAL/PRODUCT/**INSTALLATION**/TEST

## 11.6.4 Basic Rules

| # | | | Rule | E | C | P |
|---|---|---|---|---|---|---|
| 1 | | | **AESTHETIC GRADE RULES** apply only to exposed surfaces visible after installation. | | | |
| 2 | | | **INSTALLED** plumb, level, square, and flat within 1/8" (3.2 mm) in 96" (2438 mm), and when required: | | | |
| 2 | 1 | | **GROUNDS** and hanging systems set plumb and true. | | | |
| 3 | | | **TRANSPARENT** finished woodwork shall be installed: | | | |
| 3 | 1 | | With consideration of color and grain. | E | C | P |
| 3 | 2 | | **COMPATIBLE** in color and grain. | | E | C | P |
| 3 | 3 | | **WELL MATCHED** for color and grain. | | | E | C | P |
| 3 | 3 | 1 | Sheet products shall be compatible in color with solid stock. | E | C | P |
| 3 | 3 | 2 | Adjacent sheet products shall be well matched for color and grain. | | E | C | P |
| 4 | | | **REPAIRS** are allowed, provided they are neatly made and inconspicuous when viewed at: | | | |
| 4 | 1 | | 72" (1829 mm). | E | C | P |
| 4 | 2 | | 48" (1220 mm). | | E | C | P |
| 4 | 3 | | 24" (610 mm). | | | E | C | P |
| 5 | | | **INSTALLER MODIFICATIONS** shall comply to the material, machining, and assembly rules within the PRODUCT portion of this section and the applicable finishing rules in Section 5. | | | |
| 6 | | | **BUILD UP** or spacing materials required for installation of a countertop are the responsibility of the countertop manufacturer. | | | |
| 7 | | | **HORIZONTAL REVEAL** between the lower edge of the countertop and the upper edge of the adjacent door or drawer front at base cabinets with countertops shall be a consistent 1/4" (6.4 mm) +/- 1/8" (3.2 mm), except: | | | |
| 7 | 1 | | At laboratory casework, it shall be 1/4" (6.4 mm) to 1" (25.4 mm) and shall be consistent across elevations, except: | | | |
| 7 | 1 | 1 | At sink locations. | | | |
| 7 | 2 | | Coordination of such is the responsibility of the cabinet manufacturer. | | | |
| 8 | | | **CURVED** front edges shall be solid machined, steam bent, bent solid lumber or laminated plies at the option of the manufacturer, and; | | | |
| 8 | 1 | | In full compliance with all other applicable requirements of the AWS including Section 6. | | | |

*Continues next column*

## 11.6.4 Basic Rules

▲ From previous column

| # | | | Rule | E | C | P |
|---|---|---|---|---|---|---|
| 8 | | | **COUNTERTOPS** shall be: | | | |
| 8 | 1 | | Installed within 1/4" (6.4 mm) plus or minus the industry standard for height specified (see Section 10), except where ADA compliance is required. | | | |
| 8 | 2 | | **SECURELY FASTENED** and tightly fitted with flush joints. | | | |
| 8 | 2 | 1 | The manufacturer's recommended CAULK and SEALANTS shall be used to achieve the best performance and color match. | | | |
| 8 | 2 | 2 | Joinery shall be consistent throughout the project. | | | |
| 8 | 3 | | Of **MAXIMUM** available and/or practical lengths. | E | C | P |
| 8 | 4 | | **INSTALLED** free of: | | | |
| 8 | 4 | 1 | Warp, twisting, cupping, and/or bowing that cannot be held true. | | | |
| 8 | 4 | 2 | Open joints, visible machine marks, cross sanding, tear outs, nicks, chips, and/or scratches. | | | |
| 8 | 4 | 3 | Natural defects exceeding the quantity and/or size limits defined in Sections 3 and 4. | | | |
| 8 | 5 | | **SMOOTH** and sanded without cross scratches in conformance to the product portion of this section. | | | |
| 8 | 6 | | **SCRIBED** at: | | | |
| 8 | 6 | 1 | Flat surfaces. | E | C | P |
| 8 | 6 | 2 | Shaped surfaces. | | E | C | P |
| 9 | | | **GLUE** and filler residue is not permitted on exposed faces. | | | |
| 10 | | | **CUTOUTS** and **HOLES** shall be provided for as indicated on the plans. | | | |
| 11 | | | **MIRRORS**, that are wall mounted, shall not be supported by the countertop or back splash. | | | |
| 12 | | | **THESE STANDARDS** do not establish grade rules for joint flushness and or gap tolerances for woodwork products installed in a non climate controlled environment. | | | |

*Continues next column* ▼

# SECTION 11
## Countertops

**GENERAL/PRODUCT/INSTALLATION/TEST** — compliance requirements

Where the **E**, **C**, or **P** icon is not indicated, the rule applies to all Grades equally

### 11.6.4 Basic Rules

▲ From previous column

**GAPS** (see Test A illustrations in TESTS) such as,

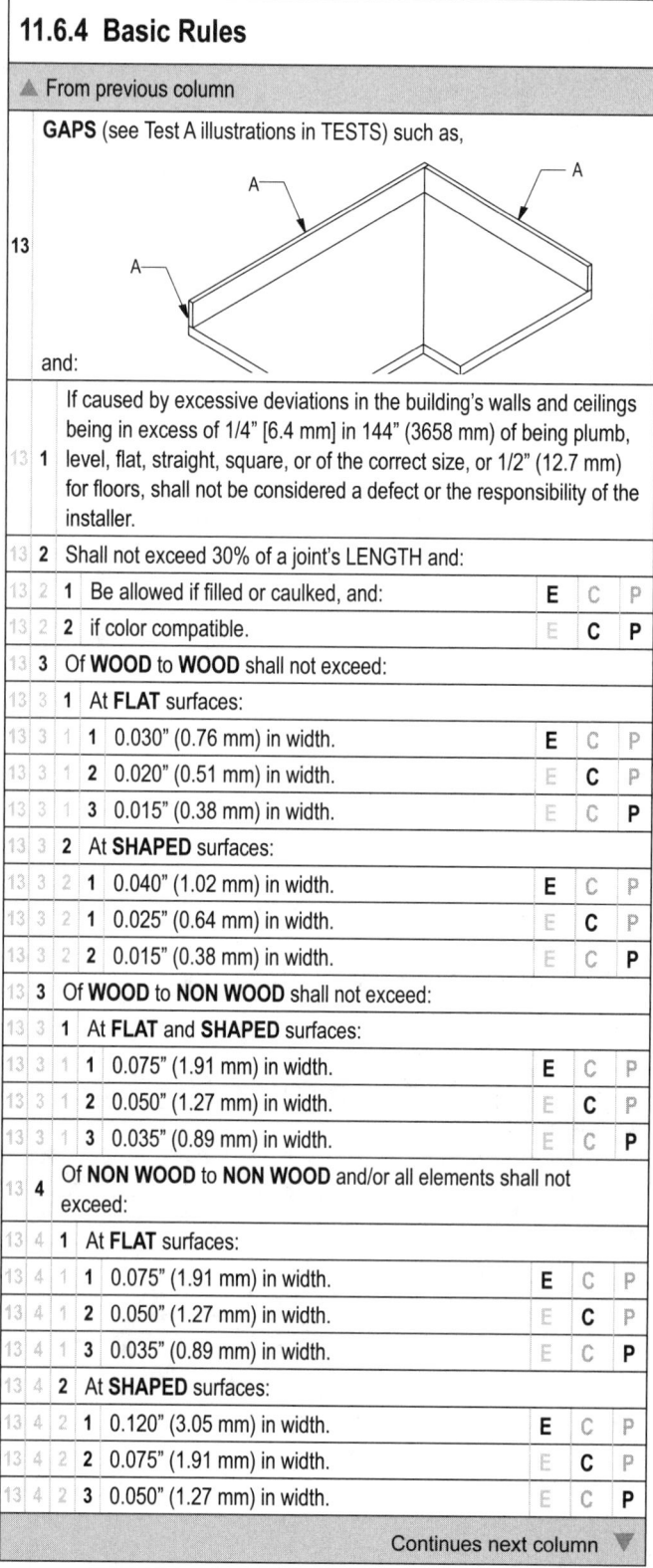

and:

| 13 | | | | | E | C | P |
|---|---|---|---|---|---|---|---|
| | 1 | | | If caused by excessive deviations in the building's walls and ceilings being in excess of 1/4" [6.4 mm] in 144" (3658 mm) of being plumb, level, flat, straight, square, or of the correct size, or 1/2" (12.7 mm) for floors, shall not be considered a defect or the responsibility of the installer. | | | | |
| | 2 | | | Shall not exceed 30% of a joint's LENGTH and: | | | |
| | | 1 | | Be allowed if filled or caulked, and: | E | C | P |
| | | 2 | | if color compatible. | E | C | P |
| | 3 | | | Of **WOOD** to **WOOD** shall not exceed: | | | |
| | | 1 | | At **FLAT** surfaces: | | | |
| | | | 1 | 0.030" (0.76 mm) in width. | E | C | P |
| | | | 2 | 0.020" (0.51 mm) in width. | E | C | P |
| | | | 3 | 0.015" (0.38 mm) in width. | E | C | P |
| | | 2 | | At **SHAPED** surfaces: | | | |
| | | | 1 | 0.040" (1.02 mm) in width. | E | C | P |
| | | | 1 | 0.025" (0.64 mm) in width. | E | C | P |
| | | | 2 | 0.015" (0.38 mm) in width. | E | C | P |
| | 3 | | | Of **WOOD** to **NON WOOD** shall not exceed: | | | |
| | | 1 | | At **FLAT** and **SHAPED** surfaces: | | | |
| | | | 1 | 0.075" (1.91 mm) in width. | E | C | P |
| | | | 2 | 0.050" (1.27 mm) in width. | E | C | P |
| | | | 3 | 0.035" (0.89 mm) in width. | E | C | P |
| | 4 | | | Of **NON WOOD** to **NON WOOD** and/or all elements shall not exceed: | | | |
| | | 1 | | At **FLAT** surfaces: | | | |
| | | | 1 | 0.075" (1.91 mm) in width. | E | C | P |
| | | | 2 | 0.050" (1.27 mm) in width. | E | C | P |
| | | | 3 | 0.035" (0.89 mm) in width. | E | C | P |
| | | 2 | | At **SHAPED** surfaces: | | | |
| | | | 1 | 0.120" (3.05 mm) in width. | E | C | P |
| | | | 2 | 0.075" (1.91 mm) in width. | E | C | P |
| | | | 3 | 0.050" (1.27 mm) in width. | E | C | P |

Continues next column ▼

---

### 11.6.4 Basic Rules

▲ From previous column

**FLUSHNESS** of joinery (see Test D illustrations in TESTS), such as

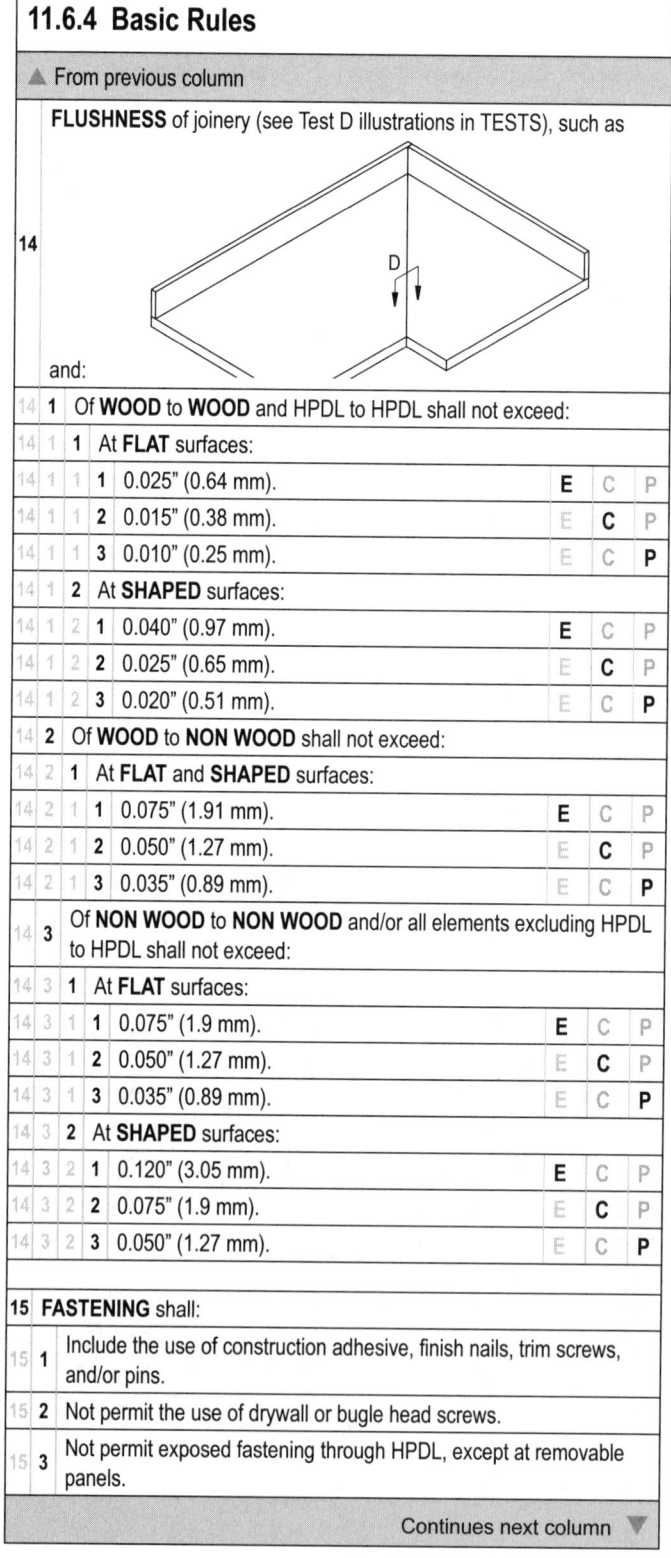

and:

| 14 | | | | | E | C | P |
|---|---|---|---|---|---|---|---|
| | 1 | | | Of **WOOD** to **WOOD** and HPDL to HPDL shall not exceed: | | | |
| | | 1 | | At **FLAT** surfaces: | | | |
| | | | 1 | 0.025" (0.64 mm). | E | C | P |
| | | | 2 | 0.015" (0.38 mm). | E | C | P |
| | | | 3 | 0.010" (0.25 mm). | E | C | P |
| | | 2 | | At **SHAPED** surfaces: | | | |
| | | | 1 | 0.040" (0.97 mm). | E | C | P |
| | | | 2 | 0.025" (0.65 mm). | E | C | P |
| | | | 3 | 0.020" (0.51 mm). | E | C | P |
| | 2 | | | Of **WOOD** to **NON WOOD** shall not exceed: | | | |
| | | 1 | | At **FLAT** and **SHAPED** surfaces: | | | |
| | | | 1 | 0.075" (1.91 mm). | E | C | P |
| | | | 2 | 0.050" (1.27 mm). | E | C | P |
| | | | 3 | 0.035" (0.89 mm). | E | C | P |
| | 3 | | | Of **NON WOOD** to **NON WOOD** and/or all elements excluding HPDL to HPDL shall not exceed: | | | |
| | | 1 | | At **FLAT** surfaces: | | | |
| | | | 1 | 0.075" (1.9 mm). | E | C | P |
| | | | 2 | 0.050" (1.27 mm). | E | C | P |
| | | | 3 | 0.035" (0.89 mm). | E | C | P |
| | | 2 | | At **SHAPED** surfaces: | | | |
| | | | 1 | 0.120" (3.05 mm). | E | C | P |
| | | | 2 | 0.075" (1.9 mm). | E | C | P |
| | | | 3 | 0.050" (1.27 mm). | E | C | P |
| 15 | | | | **FASTENING** shall: | | | |
| | 1 | | | Include the use of construction adhesive, finish nails, trim screws, and/or pins. | | | |
| | 2 | | | Not permit the use of drywall or bugle head screws. | | | |
| | 3 | | | Not permit exposed fastening through HPDL, except at removable panels. | | | |

Continues next column ▼

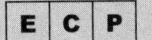

Where the **E**, **C**, or **P** icon is not indicated, the rule applies to all Grades equally

# SECTION 11
## Countertops

## compliance requirements

GENERAL / PRODUCT / **INSTALLATION** / TEST

### 11.6.4 Basic Rules

▲ From previous column

| | | | | |
|---|---|---|---|---|
| 16 | **EQUIPMENT CUTOUTS** shall be neatly cut out by the installer, provided templates are furnished in a timely manner. | | | |
| 16 | 1 | Cutouts in HPDL shall have radiused inside corners. | | |
| 17 | **HARDWARE** shall be: | | | |
| 17 | 1 | Installed neatly without tear out of surrounding stock. | | |
| 17 | 2 | Installed per the manufacturer's instructions. | | |
| 17 | 3 | Installed using all furnished fasteners and fasteners' provisions and when fastener provisions are countersunk, fasteners shall be countersunk. | | |
| 17 | 4 | Adjusted for smooth operation. | | |
| 18 | **AREAS OF INSTALLATION** shall be left broom clean. | | | |
| 18 | 1 | Debris shall be removed and dumped in containers provided by the contractor. | | |
| 18 | 2 | Items installed shall be cleaned of pencil or ink marks. | | |
| 19 | **FIRST CLASS WORKMANSHIP** is required in compliance with these standards. | | | |
| 20 | At **SOLID** or **VENEERED WOOD**: | | | |
| 20 | 1 | **EDGES**, both Front and leading of countertop to withstand a 75 lb (34 kg) pull up pressure. | | |
| 20 | 2 | **WATERPROOF CAULK** shall be used at square butt joints including splashes and return ends, and: | | |
| 20 | 2 | 1 | Shall not exceed 1/16" (6.4 mm). | |
| 20 | 2 | 2 | Shall be furnished by installation contractor, unless otherwise specified. | |
| 20 | 3 | **INSTALLER ASSEMBLED JOINTS** shall be fastened together with a mechanical tightening system either routed into or mounted on the bottom side of the countertop. | | |
| 20 | 4 | **SINK CUTOUTS** shall not fall within 18" (457 mm) of discretionary installer joints. | | |
| 20 | 5 | **CUTOUTS**, subject to excessive moisture, shall have edges sealed with a color toned (for verification), water resistant sealer before trim or sink rims are installed. | | |

Continues next column ▼

### 11.6.4 Basic Rules

▲ From previous column

| | | | | | | |
|---|---|---|---|---|---|---|
| 21 | At **HPDL**: | | | | | |
| 21 | 1 | **COUNTERTOPS** shall be scribed to walls, and: | | | | |
| 21 | 1 | 1 | Securely anchored to base cabinets with proper length screws, and: | | | |
| 21 | 1 | 1 | 1 | Properly aligned with uniform front edge overhang. | | |
| 21 | 1 | 1 | 2 | **INSTALLER ASSEMBLED JOINTS** shall be glued and fastened together with a mechanical tightening system either routed into or surface mounted on the bottom side of the countertop. | | |
| 21 | 1 | 2 | **EDGES**, both Front and leading of countertop to withstand a 75 lb (34 kg) pull up pressure. | | | |
| 21 | 2 | **WATERPROOF CAULK** shall be used at square butt joints including splashes and return ends, and: | | | | |
| 21 | 2 | 1 | Shall not exceed 1/4" (6.4 mm). | E | C | P |
| 21 | 2 | 2 | Shall not exceed 1/8" (3.2 mm). | E | C | P |
| 21 | 2 | 3 | Shall be furnished by installation contractor, unless otherwise specified. | | | |
| 21 | 3 | At **ASSEMBLY 1** (wall mount) back and end splash (wall mount) construction, splash components shall be securely adhered to the wall, butt joined to the countertop, and: | | | | |
| 21 | 3 | 1 | Shall be caulked with clear or compatible color waterproof caulking (furnished by installer), so as to leave a visual bead not exceeding 1/8" (3.2 mm) between the bottom of the splash and the countertop. | | | |
| 21 | 3 | 2 | Variation in building walls in excess of 1/2" (12.7 mm) in 144" (3658 mm) may result in gaps between splash and walls and shall not be considered a defect or the responsibility of the installer. | | | |

Continues next column ▼

# SECTION 11
## Countertops

GENERAL/PRODUCT/**INSTALLATION**/TEST

**compliance requirements**

Where the **E**, **C**, or **P** icon is not indicated, the rule applies to all Grades equally | E | C | P |

### 11.6.4 Basic Rules

▲ From previous column

**21** At **HPDL** (continued)

**21 4** At **ASSEMBLY 2** (deck mount) back and end splash (deck mount) construction, exposed top and ends shall be scribed to the wall configuration.

**21 4 1** Unbacked scribe spans shall not exceed 1/2" (12.7 mm) at ends and back walls, and gaps shall:

| | | | | | | |
|---|---|---|---|---|---|---|
| 21 | 4 | 1 | 1 | Not exceed 1/16" (1.6 mm) and be caulked. | E | C | P |
| 21 | 4 | 1 | 2 | Not exceed 1/32" (0.8 mm) and be caulked. | | E | C | P |

**21 5** **CUTOUTS** shall have a minimum of 1/4" (6.4 mm) radius at inside corners, and:

**21 5 1** Sink cutouts shall not fall within 18" (457 mm) of discretionary installer joints.

**21 5 2** Cutouts, subject to excessive moisture, shall have edges sealed with a color toned (for verification), water resistant sealer before trim or sink rims are installed.

**22** At **SOLID SURFACE** (only available in Custom and Premium Grade):

**22 1** **SEALANTS** and **ADHESIVES** shall be compatible with the individual manufacturer's recommendations or specially developed sealants to achieve the best color match.

**22 2** **EXPANSION** joints shall be furnished where required by building design or manufacturer recommendations.

**22 3** **SUPPORT** shall be adequately furnished to minimize stresses, and:

**22 3 1** Minimum full perimeter and joint support is required on horizontal applications, with:

**22 3 1 1** A maximum on center separation between supports of 30" (750 mm) for acrylic and 24" (610 mm) for non acrylic materials.

**22 3 1 2** A maximum unsupported and unloaded overhang of 12" (305 mm) for 3/4" (19 mm) and 6" (152 mm) for 1/2" (12.7 mm) sheet thickness.

Continues next column ▼

### 11.6.4 Basic Rules

▲ From previous column

**22** At **SOLID SURFACE** (continued)

**22 4** **JOINTS** shall be:

**22 4 1** Square (butt) rather than mitered near corners to minimize material and facilitate installation.

**22 4 2** Be fully supported.

**22 4 3** Edges to be joined shall be straight, smooth, and clean.

**22 4 3 1** All joints shall be made using the manufacturer's recommended adhesive.

**22 4 4** L and U shaped corners shall have smooth, rounded inside corners, and:

**22 4 4 1** Seams shall be offset a minimum of 3 times the inside corner radius.

**22 5** **CUTOUT CORNERS** shall be rounded, 1/4" (6.4 mm) minimum radius, with edges smoothed, and:

**22 5 1** At heat producing areas, corners shall be reinforced per the manufacturer's requirements and protected with approved heat reflective tape.

**22 6** **BACK** and **END SPLASHES** shall be securely adhered to the wall, butt joined to the countertop, and shall be:

**22 6 1** **CAULKED** with clear or compatible color waterproof caulking (furnished by the installer) so as to leave a visual bead not exceeding 1/8" (3.2 mm) between the bottom of the splash and the countertop.

**22 6 2** Variation in building walls in excess of 1/2" (12.7 mm) in 144" (3658 mm) may result in gaps between splash and walls and shall not be considered a defect or the responsibility of the installer.

**22 6 3** **COVED SPLASHES**, If specified, shall be hard seamed and integral to the countertop.

**22 7** **COUNTERTOP ADHESION** shall be made using a clear silicone sealant placed a maximum of 12" (12.7 mm) on center.

**22 8** **HARD SEAMS** shall be water tight and gap free.

Continues next column ▼

| E | C | P | Where the **E, C,** or **P** icon is not indicated, the rule applies to all Grades equally |

# SECTION 11
## Countertops

**compliance requirements** — GENERAL/PRODUCT/**INSTALLATION**/TEST

### 11.6.4 Basic Rules

▲ From previous column

| | | | |
|---|---|---|---|
| 23 | | | At **SOLID PHENOLIC** (only available in Premium Grade): |
| 23 | 1 | | **COUNTERTOP** shall be secured to supports with silicone cement or appropriately sized machine screws applied to each corner and along the perimeter edge at not more than 48" (1219 mm) on center. |
| 23 | 2 | | **JOINTS** shall be precision machined with tight joint fasteners and sealed with a biocide silicon prior to tightening. |
| 23 | 3 | | **SINKS** shall be stainless steel, polypropylene, or epoxy resin; either lipped or under mount, and: |
| 23 | 3 | 1 | **LIPPED** shall be set in a rabbeted cutout in the countertop. |
| 23 | 3 | 2 | **UNDER MOUNT** shall be installed using adjustable metal sink supports for underside installation or fastened directly to the underside of the countertop using machine screws and silicone adhesive. |
| 23 | 3 | 3 | A biocide silicone adhesive shall be used at the juncture of the sink and countertop to produce a leak proof joint. |

Continues next column ▼

### 11.6.4 Basic Rules

▲ From previous column

| | | | | |
|---|---|---|---|---|
| 24 | | | | At **EPOXY RESIN, NATURAL/ENGINEERED STONE** (only available in Premium Grade): |
| 24 | 1 | | | **COUNTERTOP** shall be secured to supports with epoxy cement applied to each corner and along the perimeter edge at not more than 48" (1219 mm) on center, and: |
| 24 | 1 | 1 | | **SUPPORT** must be adequate to prevent deflection in excess of 1/4" (6.4 mm) with a 50 lb (22.7 kg) per square foot load or 250 lb (113 kg) at any given point. |
| 24 | 1 | 2 | | **UNSUPPORTED SPANS** shall not exceed 48" (1219 mm), unless otherwise specified. |
| 24 | 1 | 4 | | **JOINTS** shall be butted and filled with a color matched epoxy cement. |
| 24 | 2 | | | **OVERHANG** shall be provided on the front and ends of 1" (25.4 mm) nominal. |
| 24 | 3 | | | **CANTILEVER**, of unsupported and unloaded overhang shall not exceed 12" (305 mm) for 3/4" (19 mm) and 6" (152 mm) for 1/2" (12.7 mm) sheet thickness. |
| 24 | 4 | | | **BACK** and **END SPLASHES** shall be securely adhered to the wall, butt joined to the countertop, and: |
| 24 | 4 | 1 | | Shall be caulked with clear or compatible color waterproof caulking (furnished by the installer) so as to leave a visual bead not exceeding 1/8" (3.2 mm) between the bottom of the splash and the countertop. |
| 24 | 4 | 2 | | Variation in building walls in excess of 1/2" (12.7 mm) in 144" (3658 mm) may result in gaps between the splash and the walls and shall not be considered a defect or the responsibility of the installer. |
| 24 | 5 | | | **HARD SEAMS** shall be water tight and gap free. |
| 24 | 6 | | | **SCRIBING** is not required. |
| 24 | 7 | | | **SINKS** shall be either lipped or under mounted, and: |
| 24 | 8 | 1 | | **LIPPED** shall be set in a rabbeted cutout in the countertop. |
| 24 | 8 | 2 | | **UNDER MOUNT** shall be installed using adjustable metal sink supports, and: |
| 24 | 8 | 2 | 1 | An epoxy cement is required at the juncture of the sink and countertop to produce a leak proof joint. |
| 24 | 8 | 2 | 2 | The maximum gap between the countertop edge of the sink and underside of the countertop shall not exceed 3/16" (4.8 mm). |

# SECTION 11
## Countertops

GENERAL/PRODUCT/INSTALLATION/TEST — compliance requirements

### 11.7 BASIC CONSIDERATIONS

1 The tolerances typically found within the Architectural Woodwork Standards fall into two categories:

1.1 Factory fabricated joinery, assembly and construction found in the **PRODUCT** portion.

1.2 Field installation joinery and assembly found in the **INSTALLATION** portion.

2 Most fabrication and installation assemblies include solid wood to solid wood joints, solid wood to wood veneer joints, solid wood to wood based products (HPDL, LPDL, Solid Phenolic and panel products), solid wood to non wood based products (which can be drywall, glass, metal, stone, acrylics, and other surfaces), and non wood to non wood joints.

3 Tolerances found in the AWS include:

3.1 Flatness of wood based panel products.

3.2 Solid wood to solid wood joints and assemblies.

3.3 Solid wood to wood veneer joints and assemblies.

3.4 Wood veneer to wood veneer joints and assemblies.

3.5 Solid wood to wood based product joints and assemblies.

3.6 Solid surface to solid surface joints and assemblies.

4 Because of the differences of expansion and contraction of non wood products compared to solid wood and wood based products, the AWS does not apply tolerances regarding flatness or joinery to these non wood based products.

### 11.7 BASIC CONSIDERATIONS

5 **FABRICATED** and **INSTALLED** woodwork shall be tested for compliance to these standards as follows:

5.1 **SMOOTHNESS** of exposed surfaces:

5.1.1 **KCPI** (Knife Cuts Per Inch) is determined by holding the surfaced board at an angle to a strong light source and counting the visible ridges per inch, usually perpendicular to the profile.

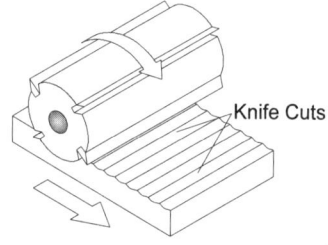

Figure: 11-072

5.1.2 **SANDING** is checked for compliance by sanding a sample piece of the same species with the required grit of abrasive.

5.1.2.1 Observation with a hand lens of the prepared sample and the material in question will offer a comparison of the scratch marks of the abrasive grit.

5.1.2.2 Reasonable assessment of the performance of the finished product will be weighed against absolute compliance with the standard.

5.1.2.3 A product is sanded sufficiently smooth when knife cuts are removed and remaining sanding marks are or will be concealed by applied finishing coats.

5.1.2.4 Grain raise at unfinished wood, due to moisture or humidity in excess of the ranges set forth in this standard, shall not be considered a defect and must be sanded prior to finishing.

6 **GAPS, FLUSHNESS, FLATNESS** and **ALIGNMENT** of product and installation:

6.1 Maximum gaps between exposed components shall be tested with a feeler gauge at points designed to join where members contact or touch.

6.2 Joint length shall be measured with a ruler with minimum 1/16" (1 mm) divisions and calculations made accordingly.

# SECTION 11
## Countertops

GENERAL/PRODUCT/INSTALLATION/**TEST**

**compliance requirements**

Where the **E**, **C**, or **P** icon is not indicated, the rule applies to all Grades equally

## 11.7 BASIC CONSIDERATIONS

**6    GAPS, FLUSHNESS, FLATNESS** and (continued)

6.3    Reasonable assessment of the performance of the finished product will be weighed against absolute compliance with the standards.

6.4    The following is intended to provide examples of how and where compliance testing is measured:

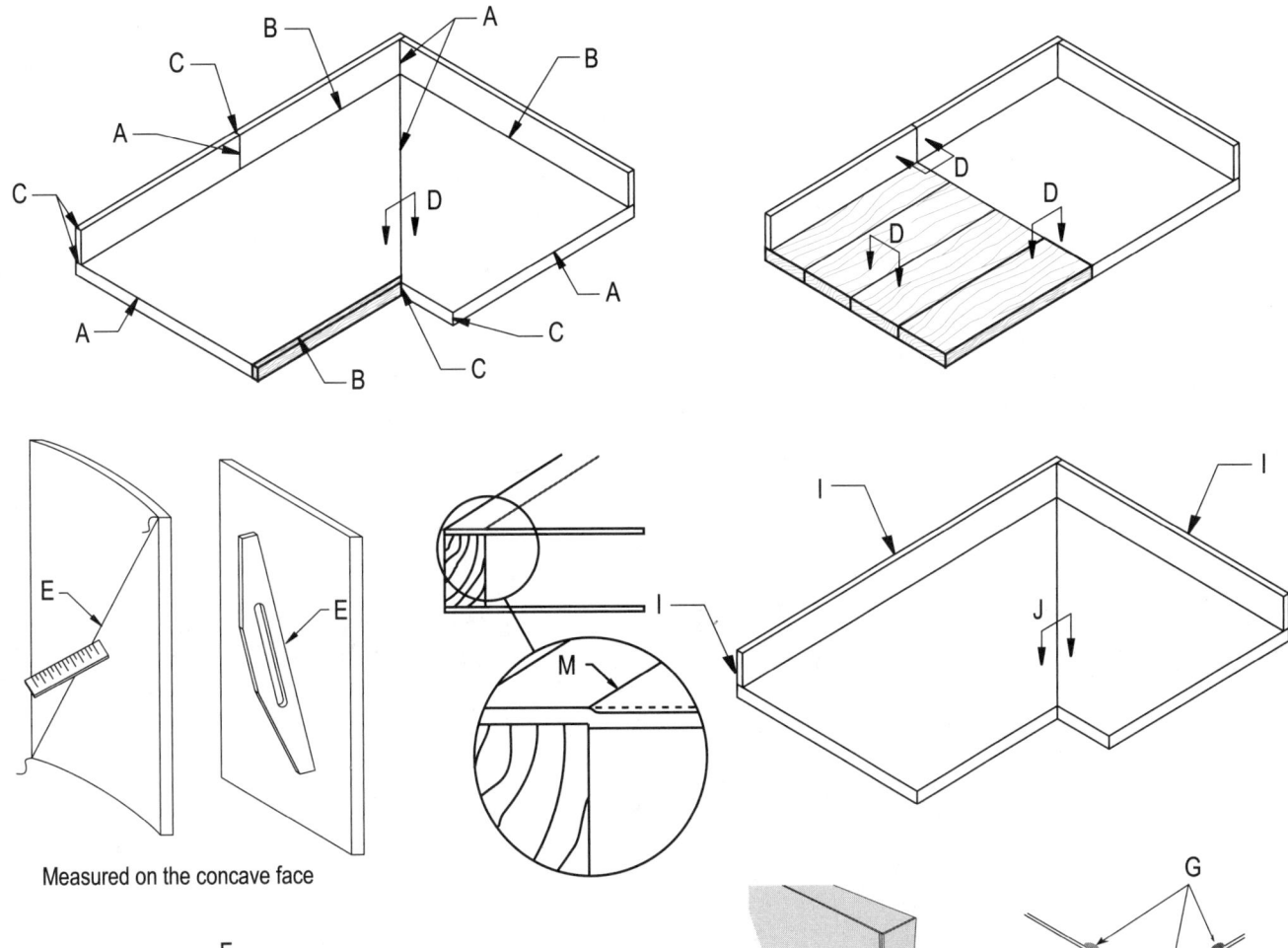

Measured on the concave face

- A - Gaps when surfaces are mitered or butted
- B - Gaps when parallel pieces are joined
- C - Gaps when edges are mitered or butted
- D - Flushness between two surfaces
- E - Flatness of panel product
- F - Overlap (flushness of laminate)
- G - Chip Out
- H - Over Machining
- I - Installation Gaps
- J - Installation Flushness
- M - Show through or telegraphing

*Figure: 11-073*

©2014 AWI | AWMAC | WI  2nd Edition, October 1, 2014
As may be updated by errata at **awinet.org**, **awmac.com**, or **aws-errata.com**

Architectural Woodwork Standards  **371**

# SECTION 11
Countertops

notes

# Architectural Woodwork Standards

# HISTORIC RESTORATION WORK

## SECTION 12

# SECTION 12
## Historic Restoration Work

## table of contents

### INTRODUCTORY INFORMATION

| | |
|---|---|
| Guide Specifications | 376 |
| Introduction | 377 |
| Resources and References | 377 |
| Design Ideas | 377 |
| Specify Requirements For | 378 |
| Recommendations | 378 |
|     If Field Finished | 378 |
|     Review | 378 |
|     Structural Members | 378 |

### COMPLIANCE REQUIREMENTS

#### GENERAL
| | |
|---|---|
| Basic Considerations | 379 |
|     Grades | 379 |
|     Acceptable Requirements | 379 |
|     Contract Documents | 379 |
|     Aesthetic Compliance | 379 |

#### PRODUCT
| | |
|---|---|
| Scope | 380 |
|     Typical Inclusions | 380 |
|     Typical Exclusions | 380 |
| Default Stipulation | 380 |
| Rules | 380 |
|     Errata | 380 |
|     Basic Rules | 380 |
|         Aesthetic | 380 |
|         First Class Workmanship | 380 |
|     Material Rules | 380 |
|         Wood | 380 |
|         Comply with Section 3 - 11 | 380 |
|         Members | 380 |
|         Defects | 380 |
|     Machining Rules | 380 |
|         Comply with Section 6 - 11 | 380 |
|         Machine | 380 |
|         Existing Moldings | 380 |
|     Assembly Rules | 380 |
|         Comply with Section 6 - 11 | 380 |
|         Plywood Backing | 380 |
|     Repair Rules | 381 |
|         Match Existing | 381 |
|         At Transparent Finish | 381 |
|         Carpentry Methods | 381 |
|         Fasteners | 381 |
|         Wood Patches | 381 |

# SECTION 12
## Historic Restoration Work

## introductory information

### COMPLIANCE REQUIREMENTS (continued)

**PRODUCT** (continued)

Rules (continued)

- Stripping Rules .................................................. 381
  - Coating Strippers ........................................... 381
  - Before Stripping ............................................ 381
  - Completely Remove ...................................... 381
  - Stripping Residuals ....................................... 381
  - Sand ............................................................. 381
  - Seal .............................................................. 381
- Finishing Rules ................................................. 381
  - Comply with Section 5 .................................. 381
  - Require ......................................................... 381

**INSTALLATION**

- Care, Storage and Building Conditions ............. 382
- Contractor is Responsible for ........................... 382
- Installer is Responsible for ............................... 382
- Rules ................................................................. 382
  - Errata ............................................................ 382
  - Basic Rules ................................................... 383
    - Aesthetic .................................................. 383
    - Match Existing ......................................... 383
    - Transparent ............................................. 383
    - Repairs .................................................... 383
    - Installer Modifications .............................. 383
    - First Class Workmanship ......................... 383

# SECTION 12
Historic Restoration Work

## introductory information

# Guide Specifications

Are available through the Sponsor Associations in interactive digital format including unique and individual quality control options. The Guide Specifications are located at:

## Architectural Woodwork Institute (AWI)
www.awinet.org

## Architectural Woodwork Manufacturers Association of Canada (AWMAC)
http://awmac.com/aws-guide-specifications

## Woodwork Institute (WI)
www.woodworkinstitute.com/publications/aws_guide_specs.asp

# SECTION 12
## Historic Restoration Work

## introductory information

### INTRODUCTION

The United States Department of the Interior (www.doi.gov/), the National Park Service (www.nps.gov/), and the Historic Sites and Monuments Board of Canada (www.parkscanada.gc.ca/) publish documents related to work under their jurisdiction. The most recent publications from these entities will provide valuable information for the design professional and the woodwork fabrication, finishing, and installation.

The rationale and intent of this section is to assist in compliance with the U.S. Secretary of the Interior's "STANDARDS FOR THE TREATMENT OF HISTORIC PROPERTIES (The Standards) with Guidelines for Preserving, Rehabilitation, Restoring, and Reconstructing Historic Buildings (The Guidelines)" or the STANDARDS AND GUIDELINES FOR THE CONSERVATION OF HISTORIC PLACES IN CANADA which spell out requirements such as:

- The historic character of a property will be retained and preserved. The removal of distinctive materials or alterations of features, spaces, and spatial relationships that characterize a property will be avoided.

- Each property will be recognized as a physical record of its time, place, and use. Changes that create a false sense of historical development, such as adding conjectural features or elements from other historic properties, will not be undertaken.

- Changes to property that have acquired historic significance in their own right will be retained and preserved. Distinctive materials, features, finishes, and construction techniques or examples of craftsmanship that characterize a historic property will be preserved.

- Deteriorated historic features will be repaired rather than replaced. Where the severity of deterioration requires replacement of a distinctive feature, the new feature will match the old in design, color, texture, and, where possible, materials. Replacement of missing features will be substantiated by documentary and physical evidence.

- Chemical or physical treatments, if appropriate, will be undertaken using the gentlest means possible Treatments that cause damage to historic properties will not be used.

- New additions, exterior alterations, or related new construction will not destroy historic materials and spatial relationships that characterize the property. The new work shall be differentiated from the old and will be compatible with the historic materials, features, size, scale, proportion, and massing to protect the historic integrity of the property and its environment.

- New additions and adjacent or related new construction will be undertaken in such a manner that if they are removed in the future, the essential form and integrity of the historic property and its environment will be unimpaired.

- Acceptable requirements of lumber and/or sheet products used within this woodwork product section are established by Sections 3 and 4, unless otherwise modified herein.

- Contract documents, furnished by the design professional, shall clearly indicate or delineate all material, fabrication, installation, and applicable building code/regulation requirements.

### RESOURCES AND REFERENCES

**Museums with period rooms** - There are many historic houses around the country which are open to the public. Eighteenth Century homes such as Gunston Hall in VA, and Drayton Hall, near Charleston, SC, along the Eastern Seaboard and Neoclassical houses as one moves West. There are museums with period rooms as well. The Metropolitan Museum in New York, the Philadelphia Museum of Art, and Colonial Williamsburg are only a few.

**Publications** - Dover Publications, Inc., 31 East Second Street, Mineola, NY 11501.

Dover Publications has an incomparable listing of books which, for the most part, are reprintings of older publications; from Andrea Palladio's Four Books of Architecture to Augustus Charles Pugin's Gothic Ornament as well as handbooks and specialized subjects.

One invaluable Dover handbook is Illustrated Dictionary of Historic Architecture by Cyril M. Harris. It is from Harris that the definitions and many of the illustrations in the Glossary have been used with permission.

Three others which offer good illustrations are:

- Colling, James K. Medieval Decorative Ornament, New York, (Reprint of 1874 edition); Dover Publications, Inc. 1995

- Griesbach, C.B. Historic Ornament: A Pictorial Archive, New York, Dover Publications, Inc., 1975.

- Speltz, Alesander. The Styles of Ornament, (Reprint of German Edition of 1906), New York, Dover Publications, Inc., 1959.

Several books explaining in detail the orders of architecture are:

- Adam, Robert. Classical Architecture: A Comprehensive Handbook to the Tradition of Classical Style, New York: Harry N. Abrams, Inc., Publishers, 1990.

- Chitham, Robert. The Classical Orders of Architecture, New York: Rizzoli International Publications, Inc., 1985 (may be out of print).

- Ware, William R. The American Vignola: A Guide to the Making of Classical Architecture, New York: Dover Publications, Inc., 1994.

A definitive history of architecture is:

- Fletcher, Sir Banister. A History of Architecture on the Comparative Method, 20th edition ed., Dan Cruickshank and Andrew Saint, Oxford: Architectural Press, 1996.

For carving classical architectural elements: Wilbur, Frederick. Carving Architectural Detail in Wood: the Classical Tradition, Lewes, UK: Guild of Master Craftsmen Publications, Ltd. 2000.

### DESIGN IDEAS

Includes Architectural Ornamentation terminology, discussion and illustrations.

# SECTION 12
Historic Restoration Work

## introductory information

### SPECIFY REQUIREMENTS FOR

- Flame spread ratings.
- Special code compliance.

### RECOMMENDATION

- **If FIELD FINISHED, INCLUDE IN THE DIVISION 09 OF THE SPECIFICATIONS:**

  - **BEFORE FINISHING**, all exposed portions of woodwork shall have handling marks or effects of exposure to moisture removed with a thorough, final sanding over all surfaces of the exposed portions using an appropriate grit sandpaper, and shall be cleaned before applying sealer or finish.

  - At **CONCEALED SURFACES** - Architectural woodwork that may be exposed to moisture, such as those adjacent to exterior concrete walls, etc., shall be primed.

- **REVIEW** the GENERAL portion of Sections 3 and 4 for an overview of the characteristics and the minimum acceptable requirements of lumber and/or sheet products that might be used herein.

- **STRUCTURAL MEMBERS**, grounds, in wall blocking, backing, furring, brackets, or other anchorage which becomes an integral part of the building's walls, floors, or ceilings, required for the installation of architectural woodwork are not to be furnished or installed by the architectural woodwork manufacturer or installer.

- **EXPOSED SURFACES** shall include those defined within Sections 6 - 11, as applicable.

- **SEMI-EXPOSED SURFACES** shall include those delineated within Sections 6 - 11, as applicable.

- **CONCEALED SURFACES** shall include those define within Sections 6 - 11, as applicable.

# SECTION 12
## Historic Restoration Work

**compliance requirements** — GENERAL/PRODUCT/INSTALLATION/TEST

### Including: Stripping, Repairs, and Finishing

## 12.1 BASIC CONSIDERATIONS

**1  GRADE**

1.1  Because of the nature of historic woodwork, a specific grade classification is not applicable to this section.

**2  ACCEPTABLE REQUIREMENTS** of lumber and/or sheet products used within this woodwork product section are established by Sections 3 and 4, unless otherwise modified herein.

**3  CONTRACT DOCUMENTS** shall govern if in conflict with these standards.

**4  AESTHETIC COMPLIANCE** requirements apply only to surfaces visible after manufacture and installation.

**5**  Historic woodwork restoration, including stripping, repairs, reconstruction, materials, new fabrication, installation, and finishing, shall be of a **SINGLE SOURCE RESPONSIBILITY**.

**6  INDUSTRY PRACTICES**

6.1  **STRUCTURAL MEMBERS**, grounds, in wall blocking, backing, furring, brackets, or other anchorage that becomes an integral part of the building's walls, floors, or ceilings, that are required for the installation of architectural woodwork are not furnished or installed by the architectural woodwork manufacturer or installer.

6.2  **WALL, CEILING**, and/or opening variations in excess of 1/4" (6.4 mm) or FLOORS in excess of 1/2" (12.7 mm) in 144" (3658 mm) of being plumb, level, flat, straight, square, or of the correct size are not acceptable for the installation of architectural woodwork, nor is it the responsibility of the installer to scribe or fit to tolerances in excess of such.

6.3  **PRIMING** of architectural woodwork is not the responsibility of the manufacturer and/or installer, unless the material is being furnished prefinished.

# SECTION 12
## Historic Restoration Work

GENERAL/**PRODUCT**/INSTALLATION/TEST — compliance requirements

### 12.2 SCOPE

1. All restoration, fabrication, installation, and finishing of all existing and/or new historic architectural woodwork.

2. **TYPICAL INCLUSIONS**

   2.1. Shall include those delineated within Sections 6 - 11, as applicable.

3. **TYPICAL EXCLUSIONS**

   3.1. Shall include those delineated within Sections 6 - 11, as applicable.

### 12.3 DEFAULT STIPULATION

1. If not otherwise specified or indicated in the contract documents, all specified or detailed, all work shall match existing.

   1.1. It is the responsibility of the manufacturer to observe the project before bid and match all materials for species, grain, and overall appearance.

### 12.4 RULES

1. The following rules shall govern unless a project's contract documents require otherwise.

2. These rules are intended to provide a well defined degree of control over a project's quality of materials, workmanship, or installation.

3. **ERRATA**, published on the Sponsor Associations' websites at www.awinet.org, www.awmac.com, or www.aws-errata.com, shall **TAKE PRECEDENCE OVER THESE RULES**, subject to their date of posting and a project's bid date.

### 12.4.4 Basic Rules

1. **AESTHETIC** grade rules apply only to exposed and semi-exposed surfaces visible after installation.

2. **FIRST CLASS WORKMANSHIP** is required in compliance with these standards.

### 12.4.5 Material Rules

1. **WOOD** shall match the species, grain, general pattern, and cut of existing, similar, and/or adjacent woodwork, and shall so be identified by the designer.

2. Shall **COMPLY** with **SECTIONS 3 - 11**, as applicable.

3. **MEMBERS** shall be of the same profile and dimension as existing; however, they may be glued up to achieve this.

4. **DEFECTS**, either natural or manufactured, shall not exceed those permitted by the contract documents.

### 12.4.6 Machining Rules

1. Shall **COMPLY** with **SECTIONS 6 - 11**, as applicable.

2. **MACHINE** new and replacement woodwork to dimensions, profiles, and details to match existing.

3. **EXISTING MOLDINGS**, when hand made and not necessarily uniform in profile, replacement moldings shall be profiled to an agreed representative sample.

### 12.4.7 Assembly Rules

1. Shall **COMPLY** with **SECTIONS** 6 - 11, as applicable.

2. **PLYWOOD BACKING**, if approved, may be used in the fabrication of built up panel assemblies, door and/or window frames, and stacked base trim, provided the exposed profile and configuration matches existing.

# SECTION 12
## Historic Restoration Work

**compliance requirements** — GENERAL/**PRODUCT**/INSTALLATION/TEST

### 12.4.8 Repair Rules

| # | |
|---|---|
| 1 | **MATCH EXISTING** for recommended methods of repair by governing authorities. |
| 2 | At **TRANSPARENT FINISH**, be made with wood of the same species, grade, cut, color tone, and grain pattern. |
| 3 | **CARPENTRY METHODS** shall be the same as exhibited in the existing work. |
| 4 | **FASTENERS** shall be nonferrous, and: |
| 4.1 | Dissimilar metals shall be isolated from one another. |
| 5 | **WOOD PATCHES** of boat and/or diamond shape shall be used so as to minimize those joint surfaces at 90 degrees to the member's grain direction. |

### 12.4.9 Stripping Rules

| # | |
|---|---|
| 1 | **COATING STRIPPERS** shall be environmentally approved, and: |
| 2 | **BEFORE STRIPPING** procedures begin, all surfaces shall be tested (with the process and results recorded) to provide the least intrusive and damaging methods, and: |
| 2.1 | Approval by the design professional or conservator is required for the selected method. |
| 2.2 | Heat based methods of coating removal are permitted, provided the recommendations found in the National Park Service - Preservation Brief 10 Exterior Paint Problems On Historic Woodwork are followed or as allowed by the Historic Sites and Monuments Board of Canada. |
| 3 | **COMPLETELY REMOVE existing finish** using multiple applications of stripper and hand scrapers without gouging, splintering, or otherwise damaging sound wood. |
| 4 | **STRIPPING RESIDUALS** shall be thoroughly removed, including wax. |
| 4.1 | **STRIPPED SURFACES** shall be tested for evidence of acid and alkali, and: |
| 4.1.1 | All stripped surfaces found not to be pH neutral shall be neutralized and retested. |
| 4.1.2 | A written summary report, including before and after pH levels, shall be submitted to the design professional. |

*Continues next column*

### 12.4.9 Stripping Rules

*From previous column*

| # | |
|---|---|
| 5 | **SAND** all surfaces by hand with steel wool and the appropriate grit sandpaper to remove all signs of raised grain. |
| 6 | **SEAL** all exposed surfaces with an approved sanding sealer. |

### 12.4.10 Finishing Rules

| # | |
|---|---|
| 1 | Shall **COMPLY** with **SECTIONS 5** as modified by the plans and specifications. |
| 2 | **REQUIRE** use of applications and techniques best suited to match the existing and/or desired finish. |

# SECTION 12
## Historic Restoration Work

GENERAL / PRODUCT / **INSTALLATION** / TEST — compliance requirements

### 12.5  Preparation and Qualification requirements

**1.** **CARE, STORAGE, and BUILDING CONDITIONS** shall be in compliance with the requirements set forth in Section 2 of these standards.

1.1 Severe damage to the woodwork can result from noncompliance. The manufacturer and/or installer of the woodwork shall not be held responsible for damage that might develop by not adhering to the requirements.

**2** **CONTRACTOR IS RESPONSIBLE FOR**

2.1 Furnishing and installing structural members, grounds, in wall or ceiling blocking, backing, furring, brackets, or other anchorage required for architectural woodwork installation that becomes an integral part of walls, floors, or ceilings to which architectural woodwork shall be installed.

2.1.1 In the absence of contract documents calling for the contractor to supply the necessary blocking/backing in the wall or ceilings, either through inadvertence or otherwise, the architectural woodwork installer shall not proceed with the installation until such time as the in wall or ceiling blocking/backing is installed by others.

2.1.2 Preparatory work done by others shall be subject to inspection by the architectural woodwork installer and may be accepted or rejected for cause prior to installation.

2.1.2.1 **WALL, CEILING**, and/or opening variations in excess of 1/4" (6.4 mm) or **FLOORS** in excess of 1/2" (12.7 mm) in 144" (3658 mm) of being plumb, level, flat, straight, square, or of the correct size are not acceptable for the installation of architectural woodwork, nor is it the responsibility of the installer to scribe or fit to tolerances in excess of such.

2.2 Installation site being properly ventilated, protected from direct sunlight, excessive heat and/or moisture, and that the HVAC system is functioning and maintaining the appropriate relative humidity and temperature.

2.3 Priming the architectural woodwork in accordance with the contract documents prior to its installation.

2.3.1 If the architectural woodwork is factory finished, priming by the factory finisher is required.

### 12.5  Preparation and Qualification requirements (continued)

**3** **INSTALLER IS RESPONSIBLE FOR**

3.1 Having adequate equipment and experienced craftsmen to complete the installation in a first class manner.

3.2 Checking all architectural woodwork specified and studying the appropriate portions of the contract documents, including these standards and the reviewed shop drawings, to familiarize themselves with the requirements of the Grade specified, understanding that:

3.2.1 For transparent finish, special attention needs to be given to the color and grain of the various woodwork pieces to ensure they are installed in compliance to match existing.

3.2.2 Installation site is properly ventilated, protected from direct sunlight, excessive heat and/or moisture, and that the HVAC system is functioning and maintaining the appropriate relative humidity and temperature.

3.3 Verification that installation site is properly ventilated, protected from direct sunlight, excessive heat and/or moisture, and that the HVAC system is functioning and maintaining the appropriate relative humidity and temperature.

3.4 Verification that required priming of woodwork has been completed by others before woodwork is installed.

3.5 Verification that woodwork has been acclimated to the field conditions for a minimum of 72 hours before installation is commenced.

3.6 Woodwork specifically built or assembled in sequence for match of color and grain is installed to maintain that same sequence.

### 12.6  RULES

1 The following rules shall govern unless a project's contract documents require otherwise.

2 These rules are intended to provide a well defined degree of control over a project's quality of materials, workmanship, or installation.

3 **ERRATA**, published on the Sponsor Associations' websites at www.awinet.org, www.awmac.com, or www.aws-errata.com, shall **TAKE PRECEDENCE OVER THESE RULES**, subject to their date of posting and a project's bid date.

# SECTION 12
## Historic Restoration Work

**compliance requirements** — GENERAL/PRODUCT/**INSTALLATION**/TEST

### 12.6.4 Basic Rules

|  | | |  |
|---|---|---|---|
| 1 | | | **AESTHETIC** grade rules apply only to exposed and semi-exposed surfaces visible after installation. |
| 2 | | | **MATCH** of **EXISTING** installation methods is required, in: |
| 2 | 1 | | Compliance with Sections 3 - 11, as applicable. |
| 3 | | | Where new materials are required to be distressed to blend seamlessly with original, mock ups shall be approved by the design professional or conservator before proceeding. |
| 4 | | | **GROUNDS, BUCKS,** or **HANGING SYSTEMS** shall be installed plumb and true. |
| 5 | | | **TRANSPARENT** finished woodwork shall be installed: |
| 5 | 1 | | Well matched for color and grain. |
| 5 | 1 | 1 | Sheet products shall be compatible in color with solid stock. |
| 5 | 1 | 2 | Adjacent sheet products shall be well matched for color and grain. |
| 5 | 2 | | Installer shall pay special attention to the color and the grain of the various trim pieces to ensure they are installed in compliance with Premium Grade. |
| 6 | | | **REPAIRS** are allowed, provided they are neatly made and inconspicuous when viewed at 24" (610 mm). |
| 7 | | | **INSTALLER MODIFICATIONS** shall comply to the material, machining, and assembly rules within the Product portion of this section and the applicable finishing rules in Section 5. |
| 8 | | | **FIRST CLASS WORKMANSHIP** is required in compliance with these standards. |

**Applicable TESTS, may be found in Sections 6 - 11; however, these tests are only applicable to the exposed and semi-exposed portions of installed millwork products.**

# SECTION 12
Historic Restoration Work

notes

# Architectural Woodwork Standards

# APPENDIX

# APPENDIX

## introduction & table of contents

### INTRODUCTION

This **APPENDIX** is provided as additional resources to the manufacturer, design professional, educator, user, or certifying organization and is only part of the standards (compliance requirements) when referenced. For your convenience where referenced it is flagged by the following icon:

### TABLE OF CONTENTS

| | |
|---|---|
| Reference Source Directory | 387 |
| Reference Source Listings | 388 |
| Preservative & Water Repellent Treatments | 390 |
| Fire Retardant Coatings | 390 |
| Fire Codes | 390 |
| ADA Requirements | 390 |
| Rated Fire Door Assemblies | 390 |
| Building Code Requirements | 390 |
| Seismic Fabrication & Installation Requirements | 390 |
| Adhesives Guidelines | 391 |
| Specific Gravity & Weight Of Hardwoods | 392 |
| Joinery Details | 394 |
| Chemical And Stain Resistance (Adapted From SEFA) | 396 |
| Casework Integrity (Adapted From SEFA) | 398 |
| Casework Refinishing/Refacing/Refurbishing Guidelines | 403 |
| Fraction/Decimal/Millimeter Conversion Table | 404 |
| Miscellaneous Conversion Factors | 405 |

# APPENDIX

## reference source directory

**CONTINUING EDUCATION**
- **AIA** - American Institute of Architects
- **AIBD** - American Institute of Building Design
- **BHMA** - Builders Hardware Manufacturers Association
- **CRA** - California Redwood Association
- **IDC** - Interior Design of Canada
- **IIDA** - International Interior Design Association
- **RAIC** - Royal Architectural Institute of Canada

**STANDARDS & REGULATION**
- **ANSI** - American National Standards Institute
- **ARE** - Association for Retail Environments
- **ASID** - American Society of Interior Designers
- **AWI** - Architectural Woodwork Institute
- **AWMAC** - Architectural Woodwork Manufacturers Association of Canada
- **BIFMA** - Business + Institutional Furniture Manufacturers Association
- **CPA** - Composite Panel Association
- **CSC** - Construction Specifications Canada
- **CSI** - Construction Specifications Institute
- **DHI** - The Door and Hardware Institute
- **HPVA** - Hardwood Plywood & Veneer Association
- **ICC** - International Code Council
- **IWPA** - International Wood Products Association
- **NFPA** - National Fire Protection Association
- **NHLA** - National Hardwood Lumber Association
- **NIST** - National Institute of Standards & Technology
- **SEFA** - Scientific Equipment & Furniture Association
- **SFI** - Sustainable Forest Initiative
- **UL** - Underwriters' Laboratories
- **WI** - Woodwork Institute
- **WWPA** - Western Wood Products Association

**MANUFACTURING**
- **AF&PA** - American Forest & Paper Association
- **AHFA** - American Home Furnishings Alliance
- **NAM** - National Association of Manufacturers
- **NEMA** - National Electrical Manufacturers Association
- **WDMA** - Window & Door Manufacturers Association

**TESTING AND GRADING**
- **APA** - The Engineered Wood Association
- **ASTM** - American Society for Testing and Materials
- **ITS** - Intertek Testing Services/Warnock Hersey

**SUSTAINABLE BUILDING**
- **CaGBC** - Canada Green Building Council
- **FSC** - Forest Stewardship Council - U.S.
- **Green Globes**:
    - USA - The Green Building Initiative
    - Canada - ECD Energy and Environment
- **Rainforest Alliance**
- **SAW** - Sustainable Architectural Woodwork
- **SFI** - Sustainable Forestry Initiative Inc.
- **TFF** - Tropical Forest Foundation
- **USGBC** - U.S. Green Building Council

**SPECIALIZED PRODUCT**
- **KCMA** - Kitchen Cabinet Manufacturers Association
- **LMA** - Laminating Materials Association, Inc.
- **MMPA** - Moulding and Millwork Producers Association
- **NHLA** - National Hardwood Lumber Association
- **WDMA** - Window & Door Manufacturers Association
- **WRCLA** - Western Red Cedar Lumber Association

# APPENDIX

## reference source listings

**AF&PA** - American Forest & Paper Association
1111 19th Street NW, Suite 800
Washington, DC 20036
Ph: 800-878-8878 - Fax: 202-463-2700
www.afandpa.org

**AHFA** - American Home Furnishings Alliance
Box HP-7
High Point, NC 27261
Ph: 336-884-5000 - Fax: 336-884-5303
www.ahfa.us

**AIA** - American Institute of Architects
1735 New York Avenue NW
Washington, DC 20006
Ph: 800-242-3837 - Fax: 202-626-7547
www.aia.org

**AIBD** - American Institute of Building Design
529 14th Street, NW, Suite 750
Washington, DC 20045
Ph: 800-366-2423 - Fax: 855-204-0293
www.aibd.org

**ANSI** - American National Standards Institute
25 West 23rd Street, 4th Floor
New York, NY 10036
Ph: 212-642-4900 - Fax: 212-398-0023
www.ansi.org

**APA** - The Engineered Wood Association
7011 South 19th Street
Tacoma, WA 98466
Ph: 253-565-6600 - Fax: 253-565-7265
www.apawood.org

**ARE** - Association for Retail Environments
4651 Sheridan Street, Suite 407
Hollywood, FL 33021-3657
Ph: 954-893-7300 - Fax: 954-893-7500
www.nasfm.org

**ASID** - American Society of Interior Designers
608 Massachusetts Avenue NE
Washington, DC 20002-6006
Ph: 202-546-3480 - Fax: 202-546-3240
www.asid.org

**ASTM** - American Society for Testing and Materials
100 Barr Harbor Drive
West Conshohocken, PA 19428-2959
Ph: 610-832-9585 - Fax: 610-832-9555
www.astm.org

**AWI** - Architectural Woodwork Institute
46179 Westlake Drive, Suite 120
Potomac Falls, VA 20165
Ph: 571-323-3636 - Fax: 571-323-3630
www.awinet.org

**AWMAC** - Architectural Woodwork Manufacturers Association of Canada
Unit 02A 4803 Centre Street NW
Calgary, AB T2E 2Z6
Ph: 403-652-7685
www.awmac.com

**BHMA** - Builders Hardware Manufacturers Association
355 Lexington Avenue, 15th Floor
New York, NY 10017
Ph: 212-297-2122 - Fax: 212-370-9047
www.buildershardware.com

**BIFMA** - Business + Institutional Furniture Manufacturers Association
678 Front Avenue, NW Suite 150
Grand Rapids, MI 49504-5368
Ph: 616-285-3968 - Fax: 616-265-3765
www.bifma.org

**CPA** - Composite Panel Association
19465 Deerfield Avenue, Suite 306
Leesburg, VA 20176
Ph: 703-724-1128 - Fax: 703-724-1588
www.compositepanel.org

**CRA** - California Redwood Association
818 Grayson Road, Suite 201
Pleasant Hill, CA 94523
Ph: 925-935-1499 - Fax: 925-935-1496
www.calredwood.org

**CSC** - Construction Specifications Canada
120 Carlton Street, Suite 312
Toronto, ON, M5A 4K2, Canada
Ph: 416-777-2198 - Fax: 416-777-2197
www.csc-dcc.ca

**CSI** - Construction Specifications Institute
99 Canal Center Plaza, Suite 300
Alexandria, VA 22314
Ph: 800-689-2900 - Fax: 703-684-8436
www.csinet.org

**DHI** - The Door and Hardware Institute
14150 Newbrook Drive, Suite 200
Chantilly, VA 20151-2223
Ph: 703-222-2010 - Fax: 703-222-2410
www.dhi.org

**FSC** - Forest Stewardship Council
**USA:**
212 Third Avenue North, Suite 445
Minneapolis, MN 55401
Ph: 612-353-4511 - Fax: 612-208-1565
www.fscus.org
**Canada:**
70 The Esplanade, Suite 400
Toronto, ON M5E 1R2
Ph: 514-394-1137
www.fsccanada.org

**GREEN GLOBES:**
**USA:**
The Green Building Initiative
2104 SE Morrison,
Portland, Oregon 97214
Ph: 877-424-4241 - Fax: 503-961-8991
www.thegbi.org
**Canada:**
ECD Energy and Environment
165 Kenilworth Avenue
Toronto, ON M4L 3S7
Ph: 416-699-6671
www.greenglobes.com

**HPVA** - Hardwood Plywood & Veneer Association
1825 Michael Faraday Drive
Reston, VA 20190
Ph: 703-435-2900 - Fax: 703-435-2537
www.hpva.org

**ICC** - International Code Council
500 New Jersey Avenue NW, 6th Floor
Washington, DC 20001-2070
Ph: 888-422-7233 - Fax: 202-783-2348
www.iccsafe.org

**IDC** - Interior Design of Canada
C 536-43 Hanna Avenue
Toronto, Ontario, M6K 1X1, Canada
Ph: 416-649-4425 - Fax: 416-921-3660
www.idcanada.org

# APPENDIX

## reference source listings

**IIDA** - International Interior Design Association
13-122 Merchandise Mart
Chicago, IL 60654-1104
Ph: 312-467-1950 - Fax: 312-467-0779
www.iida.org

**ITS** - Intertek Testing Services
Ph: 800-967-5352
www.intertek.com

**IWPA** - International Wood Products Association
4214 King Street West
Alexandria, VA 22302
Ph: 703-820-6696 - Fax: 703-820-8550
www.iwpawood.org

**KCMA** - Kitchen Cabinet Manufacturers Assoc.
1899 Preston White Drive
Reston VA 20191-5435
Ph: 703-264-1690 - Fax: 703-620-6530
www.kcma.org

**LEED®** - Leadership in Energy and Environmental Design
   **USGBC** - U.S. Green Building Council
     2101 L Street, NW, Suite 500
     Washington, DC 20037
     Ph: 800-795-1747 - Fax: 202-828-5110
     www.usgbc.org
   **CaGBC** - Canada Green Building Council
     47 Clarence Street, Suite 202
     Ottawa, ON K1N 9K1
     Ph: 866-941-1184 - Fax: 613-241-4782
     www.cagbc.org

**LMA** - Laminating Materials Association
116 Lawrence Street
Lillsdale, NJ 07642-2730
Ph: 201-664-2700 - Fax: 201-666-5665
www.lma.org

**MMPA** - Moulding and Millwork Producers Association
507 First Street
Woodland, CA 95695
Ph: 530-661-9591 - Fax: 530-661-9586
www.wmmpa.com

**NAM** - National Association of Manufacturers
733 10th Street, NW, Suite 700
Washington, DC 20001
Ph: 800-814-8468 - Fax: 202-637-3182
www.nam.org

**NEMA** - National Electrical Manufacturers Association
1300 North 17th Street, Suite 1752
Rosslyn, Virginia 22209
Ph: 703-841-3200 - Fax: 703-841-5900
www.nema.org

**NFPA** - National Fire Protection Association
1 Batterymarch Park
Quincy, MA 02169-7471
Ph: 617-770-3000 - Fax: 617-770-0700
www.nfpa.org

**NHLA** - National Hardwood Lumber Association
6830 Raleigh-Lagrange Road
Memphis, TN 38184-0518
Ph: 901-377-1818 - Fax:901-382-6419
www.nhla.com

**NIST** - National Institute of Standards & Technology
100 Bureau Drive, Stop 3460
Gaithersburg, MD 20899-3460
Ph: 301-975-6478 - Fax: 301-926-1630
www.nist.gov

**RAIC** - Royal Architectural Institute of Canada
330-55 Murray Street
Ottawa, Ontario, K1N 5M3, Canada
Ph: 631-241-3600 - Fax: 613-241-5750
www.raic.org

**SEFA** - Scientific Equipment & Furniture Association
65 Hilton Avenue
Garden City, NJ 11530
Ph: 877-294-5424 - Fax: 516-294-4765
www.sefalabs.com

**SFI** - Sustainable Forest Initiative, Inc.
  **USA:**
    900 17th street, NW, Suite 700
    Washington, DC 20006
    Ph: 202-596-3450 - Fax: 202-596-3451
    www.sfiprogram.org
  **Canada:**
    1309 Carling Ave., PO Box 35043
    Westgate
    Ottawa, ON K1Z 1A2
    Ph: 613-722-8734 - Fax: 613-792-1470
    www.certificationcanada.org/

**RAINFOREST ALLIANCE**
233 Broadway, 28th Floor
New York, NY 10279
Ph: 212-677-1900 - Fax: 212-677-2187
www.rainforest-alliance.org

**SAW** - Sustainable Architectural Woodwork
PO Box 980248
West Sacramento, CA 95798-0248
Ph: 916-372-8242 - Fax: 916-372-9950
www.sawcertified.org

**TFF** - Tropical Forest Foundation
2121 Eisenhower Avenue, Suite 200
Alexandria, VA 22314
Ph: 703-518-8834 - Fax: 703-518-8974
www.tropicalforestfoundation.org

**UL** - Underwriters' Laboratories
333 Pfingsten Road
Northbrook, IL 60062-2096
Ph: 847-272-8800 - Fax: 847-272-8129
www.ul.com

**WDMA** - Window & Door Manufacturers Association
2025 M Street, NW, Suite 800
Washington DC, 20036-3309
Ph: 800-223-2301 - Fax: 847-299-1286
www.wdma.com

**WI** - Woodwork Institute
P.O. Box 980247
West Sacramento, CA 95798
Ph: 916-372-9943 - Fax: 916-372-9950
www.woodworkinstitute.com

**WRCLA** - Western Red Cedar Lumber Association
1501-700 West Pender Place 1, Business Building
Vancouver, BC, Canada V6C 1G8
Ph: 866-778-9096
www.realcedar.org.

**WWPA** - Western Wood Products Association
Yeon Building, 522 SW Fifth Avenue
Portland, OR 97204-2122
Ph: 503-224-3930 - Fax: 503-224-3934
www2.wwpa.org

# APPENDIX

## miscellaneous

### PRESERVATIVE & WATER REPELLENT TREATMENTS

Within the U.S., preservative and water repellent treatments are governed under I.S. - 4, latest edition, as published by the Window and Door Manufacturers Association (WDMA), www.wdma.com, subject to any applicable EPA or local Air Quality Management District's restrictions on what may be used for the project location. Within Canada, they are governed by the National Building Code of Canada, Section 3.8, Appendix A. Contact the National Research Council Canada at www.nrc.ca.

### FIRE RETARDANT COATINGS

Fire retardant coatings are typically subject to listing by an accredited testing laboratory and require a registration number for approval recognized by fire inspectors.

### FIRE CODES

Within the U.S., fire codes are primarily governed by the International Code Council, Inc. (ICC), www.iccsafe.org, and the National Fire Protection Association (NFPA), www.nfpa.org. Within Canada, they are governed by the National Building Code of Canada, Section 3.8, Appendix A. Contact the National Research Council Canada at www.nrc.ca.

### ADA REQUIREMENTS

Within the U.S., ADA requirements are governed by the Federal Americans with Disabilities Act (ADA) subject to any applicable state or local requirements that might be more stringent for the project location. For further information regarding national regulations: a) in the U.S., contact the Access Board at www.access-board.gov, and b) in Canada, see the National Building Code of Canada, Section 3.8, Appendix A. Contact the National Research Council Canada at www.nrc.ca.

### RATED FIRE DOOR ASSEMBLIES

Within the U.S., rated fire door assemblies are governed in accordance with the National Fire Protection Association's Publication NFPA 80, "Standard for Fire Doors and Fire Windows," subject to any applicable state or local requirements that might be more stringent for the project location. Within Canada, governance is by the National Building Code of Canada, Section 3.8, Appendix A, which can be reviewed at www.nrc.ca.

### BUILDING CODE REQUIREMENTS

Within the U.S., building code requirements are governed by the International Building Code (IBC), subject to any applicable state or local requirements that might be more stringent for the project location. Within Canada, they are governed by the National Building Code of Canada, Section 3.8, Appendix A. Contact the National Research Council Canada at www.nrc.ca.

### SEISMIC FABRICATION & INSTALLATION REQUIREMENTS

Within the U.S., seismic fabrication and installation requirements are governed by the International Building Code (IBC), subject to any applicable state or local requirements that might be more stringent for the project location. Within Canada, they are governed by the National Building Code of Canada, Section 3.8, Appendix A. Contact the National Research Council Canada at www.nrc.ca.

# APPENDIX

## adhesive guidelines

### PERFORMANCE RATINGS:

**Type I** Fully Waterproof (Exterior) Two Cycle Boil/Shear Test

**Type II** Water Resistant (Interior) Three Cycle Soak Test

### GENERAL INFORMATION:

| GENERIC NAME | BONDING | RATING | CHARACTERISTICS |
|---|---|---|---|
| **ALIPHATIC** (Carpenter's Glue) | Wood to wood | Type II | Non toxic; non flammable; non staining; water resistant. |
| **CASEIN** | Wood to wood | Type II | Water resistant. |
| **CONTACT ADHESIVE** | HPDL and wood veneer to wood | Type II | Water resistant. |
| **EPOXY** | Wide range; wood; wood to metals | Type I | Two part system; fully waterproof. |
| **HOT MELT** Polyurethane Reactive (PUR) | Wide variety of materials | * | Liquefies when heated; bonds in a liquid state; solidifies as it cools. |
| **PVA** (Polyvinyl Acetate) | Wood to wood Wood to HPDL | * | General purpose. |
| **PVA** (Polyvinyl Acetate - Catalyzed) | Wood to wood | Type I | Fully waterproof. |
| **PVC** (Polyvinyl Chloride) | Wide variety of materials | * | Crystal clear; fast drying. |
| **RESORCINOL RESIN** | Wood to wood and laminates | Type I | Fully waterproof; purple glue line; two part system; limited pot life (3 hours). |
| **UREA RESIN** | Wood to wood | Type II | Mixes with water; must be clamped; 3 to 7 hours of drying time at 70° F (21.1° C). |
| **PANEL/CONSTRUCTION ADHESIVE** | Wide variety of materials | Type II | Plastic epoxy base; liquid state; dries fast; difficult to remove; can be used to set adjustment screws in European type hinges. |

* Check manufacturer's rating.

### HEAT RESISTANCE TEST:

A sample of the laminated plastic approximately 12" x 12" (305 x 305 mm), glued to the substrate for a minimum of 21 days shall be used for this test. A hot air gun rayed at 14 amperes, 120 volts, with a nozzle temperature of 500° F or 274° C shall be directed at the test panel. A thermometer set at the panel surface shall register 356° F or 180° C for an exposure time of 5 minutes. The formation of a blister or void between the overlay and the substrate shall constitute a failure of the adhesive. A metal straightedge shall be used to determine if a blister has occurred. This determination shall be made within 30 seconds of heat removal.

# APPENDIX

## specific gravity and weight of hardwoods

| SPECIES | SPECIFIC GRAVITY [1] | WEIGHT [2] |
|---|---|---|
| ALDER, RED<br>Alnus rubra | .37 | 28 |
| ASH, WHITE<br>Average of 4 species | .54 | 41 |
| ASPEN<br>Populus tremuloides | .35 | 27 |
| AVODIRE<br>Turraeanthus africanus | n/a | 36 |
| BASSWOOD<br>Tilia americana | .32 | 26 |
| BEECH<br>Fagus grandifolia | .56 | 45 |
| BIRCH, SWEET<br>Betula lenta | .60 | 46 |
| BIRCH, YELLOW<br>Betula alleghaniensis | .55 | 43 |
| BUBINGA<br>Guibourtia demeusil | n/a | 55 |
| BUTTERNUT<br>Juglans cinerea | .36 | 27 |
| CATALPA, NORTHERN<br>Catalpa speciosa | .38 | 29 |
| CATIVO<br>Prioria copaifera | .40 | 29 |
| CHERRY, BLACK<br>Prunus serotina | .47 | 35 |
| CHESTNUT<br>Castanea dentata | .40 | 30 |
| COTTONWOOD, EASTERN<br>Populus deltoides | .37 | 28 |
| CUCUMBER TREE, YELLOW<br>Magnolia acuminata | .44 | 34 |
| CYPRESS (BALD CYPRESS)<br>Taxodium distichum | .42 | 32 |

| SPECIES | SPECIFIC GRAVITY [1] | WEIGHT [2] |
|---|---|---|
| DOGWOOD, FLOWERING<br>Cornus florida | .64 | 51 |
| EBONY (NIGERIAN)<br>Diospyros crassiflora | n/a | 63 |
| ELM, AMERICAN<br>Ulmus Americana | .46 | 36 |
| SWEETGUM (RED AND SAP)<br>Liquidambar styraciflua | .44 | 34 |
| TUPELO, WATER<br>Nyssa aquatica | .46 | 35 |
| HACKBERRY<br>Celtis occidentalis | .49 | 37 |
| HICKORIES, TRUE<br>Average of 4 species | .65 | 51 |
| HOLLY<br>Ilex opaca | .50 | 40 |
| LIMBA<br>Terminalia superba | .45 | 34 |
| LOCUST, BLACK<br>Robinia pseudoacacia | .66 | 48 |
| MAHOGANY, AFRICAN<br>Khaya ivorensis | .43 | 31 |
| MAHOGANY, CUBAN<br>Swietenia mahogany | .57 | 41 |
| MAHOGANY, CENTRAL AMERICAN<br>Swietenia species | .45 | 32 |
| MAKORE<br>Tieghemella heckelii | | 40 |
| MAPLE, RED<br>Acer rubrum | .49 | 38 |
| MAPLE, SILVER<br>Acer saccharinum | .44 | 33 |
| MAPLE, SUGAR<br>Acer saccharum | .57 | 44 |

# APPENDIX

## specific gravity and weight of hardwoods

| SPECIES | SPECIFIC GRAVITY [1] | WEIGHT [2] |
|---|---|---|
| **MYRTLE** Umbellularia Californica | .51 | 39 |
| **NARRA** Pterocarpus indicus | .52 | 42 |
| **OAK, COMMERCIAL RED** Average of 9 species | .56 | 44 |
| **OAK, COMMERCIAL WHITE** Average of 6 species | .59 | 47 |
| **ORIENTAL WOOD** Endiandro palmerstoni | n/a | 44 |
| **OSAGE ORANGE** Maclura pomifera | .76 | n/a |
| **PADUAK (AFRICAN)** Pterocarpus soyauxii | n/a | 43 |
| **PADUAK (ANDAMAN)** Pterocarpus dalbergioides | .62 | 45 |
| **PADUAK (BURMA)** Pterocarpus macrocarpus | .75 | 54 |
| **PALDAO** Dracontomelum dao | .59 | 44 |
| **PECAN** Carya illinoensis | .60 | 47 |
| **PEARWOOD (EUROPEAN)** Purus communis | n/a | 43 |
| **PHILIPPINE HARDWOODS** | | |
|    **RED LAUAN** Shorea negrosensis | .40 | 36 |
|    **WHITE LAUAN** Pentacme contorta | n/a | 36 |
|    **TANGUILE** Shorea polysperma | .53 | 39 |
| **POPLAR, YELLOW (TULIPTREE)** Liriodendron tulipifera | .38 | 28 |
| **PRIMAVERA** Cybistax donnell-smithii | .40 | 30 |

| SPECIES | SPECIFIC GRAVITY [1] | WEIGHT [2] |
|---|---|---|
| **ROSEWOOD (BRAZIL)** Dalbergia nigra | n/a | 50 |
| **SAPELE** Entandrophragma cylindricum | .54 | 40 |
| **SATINWOOD (EAST INDIAN)** Chloroxylon swientenio | .83 | 67 |
| **SONORA (MANGGASINORO)** Shorea philippinensis | .42 | 31 |
| **SYCAMORE** Platanus accidentalis | .46 | 35 |
| **TEAK** Tectona grandis | .60 | 43 |
| **TIGERWOOD** Lavoa klaineana | .45 | 34 |
| **WALNUT, AMERICAN (BLACK)** Juglans nigra | .51 | 39 |
| **WILLOW, BLACK** Salix nigra | .34 | 26 |
| **ZEBRAWOOD** Microberlinia brazzavillensis | .62 | 48 |

The data for native species as furnished on this chart are from the U.S. Forest Products Laboratory's Technical Bulletin 158.
[1] Based on green volume and oven dry weight.
[2] Based on pounds per cubic foot at 12% moisture content.

# APPENDIX

## joinery details

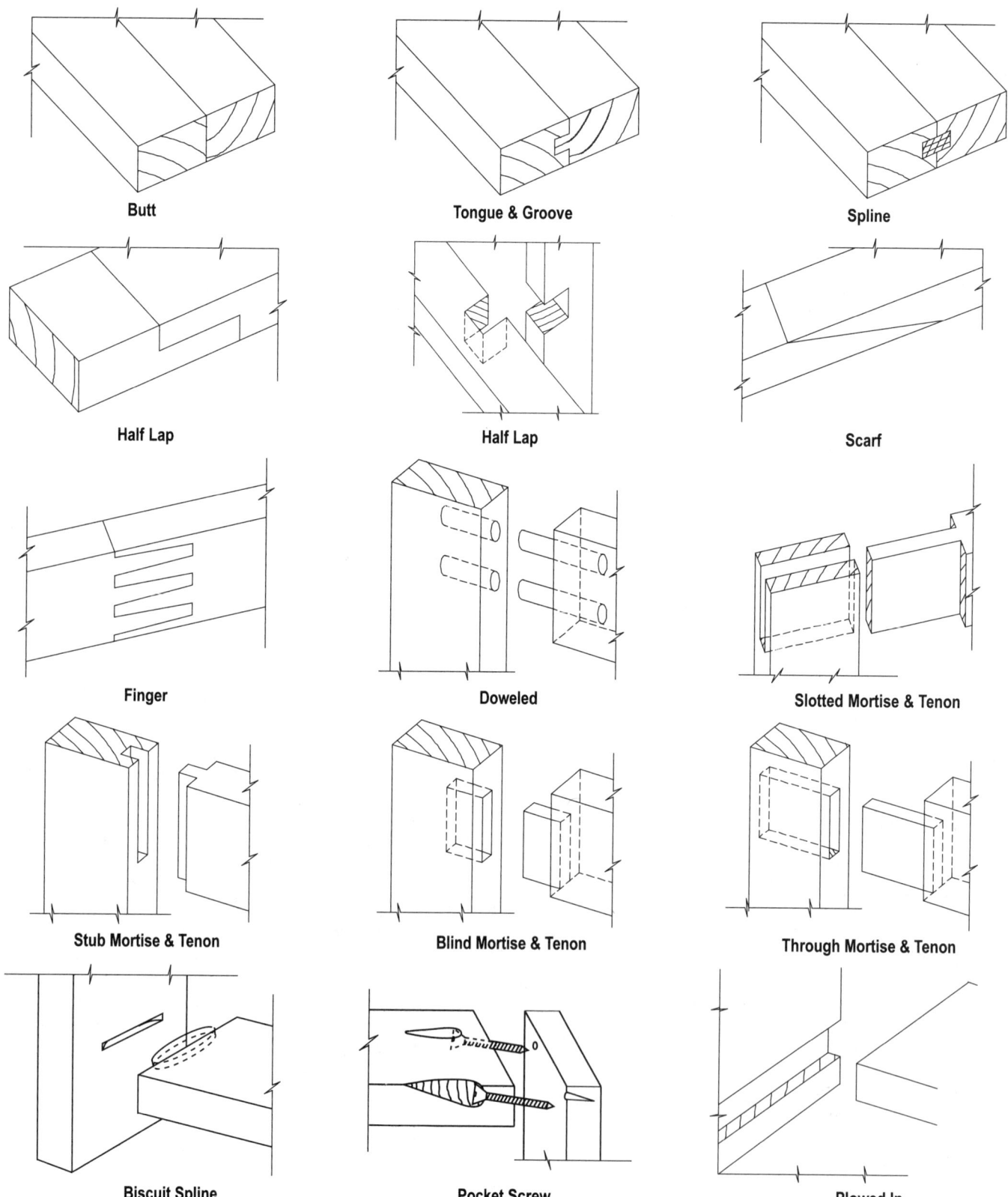

# APPENDIX

## joinery details

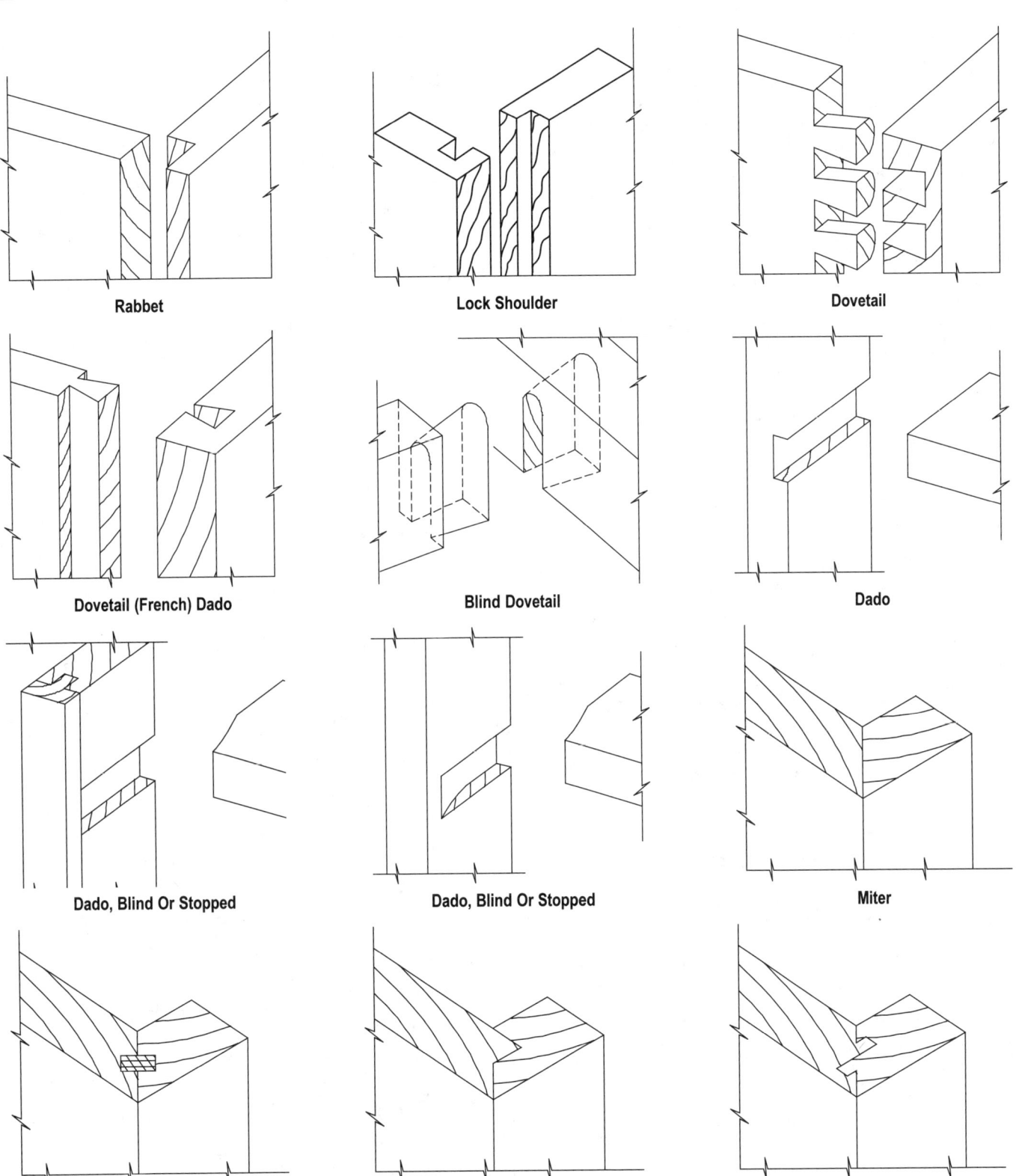

# APPENDIX

## chemical and stain resistance

If chemical and/or stain resistance is a concern, users should consider the chemical and staining agents that might be used on or near casework or countertop surfaces. Common guidelines can be found in NEMA LD3 (latest edition) for chemical resistance and ASTM D3023 and C1378 (latest editions) for stain resistance. Because chemical and stain resistance is affected by concentration, time, temperature, humidity, housekeeping, and other factors, it is recommended that actual samples are tested in a similar environment with those agents that are of concern.

In lieu of actual sample testing to evaluate the resistance a finish has to chemical spills, the SEFA 8-1999 (Scientific Equipment and Fixture Association) standard list of 49 chemicals/concentrations, their required methods of testing, and their minimum acceptable results have been adapted for use in these standards as the means of establishing a minimum acceptable chemical resistance for exposed and semi-exposed surfaces where required by contract documents.

**REQUIREMENT:** Exposed horizontal surfaces, such as countertops, are required to pass a 24 hour exposure test, whereas exposed vertical surfaces and semi-exposed surfaces are required to pass a 1 hour exposure test.

**TEST PROCEDURE:** Obtain one sample panel measuring 14" x 24" (356 mm x 610 mm) and test for chemical resistance as described herein:

Place the panel on a flat surface, clean with soap and water, and blot dry. Condition the panel for 48 hours at 73° ±3° F (20° ±2° C) and 50% ±5% relative humidity. Test the panel for chemical resistance using the following 49 different chemical reagents by one of the following methods:

- **METHOD A** - Test volatile chemicals by placing a cotton ball saturated with reagent in the mouth of a 1 oz. (29.574 cc) bottle and inverting the bottle on the surface of the panel.

- **METHOD B** - Test non volatile chemicals by placing five drops of the reagent on the surface of the panel and covering with a 24 mm watch glass, convex side down.

For both of the above methods, leave the reagents on the panel for a period of:

- One (1) hour for exposed vertical surfaces and semi-exposed surfaces.

- Twenty four (24) hours for exposed horizontal surfaces such as countertops.

Wash off the panel with water, clean with detergent and naphtha, and rinse with deionized water. Dry with a towel and evaluate after 24 hours at 73° ±3° F (20° ±2° C) and 50% ±5% relative humidity using the following rating system:

**RESULT CLASSIFICATIONS:**

- **LEVEL 0** - No detectable change.
- **LEVEL 1** - Slight change in color or gloss.
- **LEVEL 2** - Slight surface etching or severe staining.
- **LEVEL 3** - Pitting, cratering, swelling, or erosion of coating; obvious and significant deterioration.

**ACCEPTANCE LEVEL:** Results will vary from product to product, and suitability for a given application is dependent upon the chemicals used in a given laboratory setting. Without contract documents requiring otherwise, an acceptable level of chemical and stain resistance for products requiring such in accordance with these standards and a project's contract documents shall be finishes with test results SHOWING NO MORE THAN four of the Level 3 Result Classifications.

| | CHEMICAL REAGENT | TEST METHOD |
|---|---|---|
| 1 | Acetate, Amyl | A |
| 2 | Acetate, Ethyl | A |
| 3 | Acetic Acid, 98% | B |
| 4 | Acetone | A |
| 5 | Acid Dichromate, 5% | B |
| 6 | Alcohol, Butyl | A |
| 7 | Alcohol, Ethyl | A |
| 8 | Alcohol, Methyl | A |
| 9 | Ammonium Hydroxide, 28% | B |
| 10 | Benzene | A |
| 11 | Carbon Tetrachloride | A |
| 12 | Chloroform | A |
| 13 | Chromic Acid, 60% | B |
| 14 | Cresol | A |
| 15 | Dichlor Acetic Acid | A |
| 16 | Dimethylformanide | A |
| 17 | Dioxane | A |
| 18 | Ethyl Ether | A |
| 19 | Formaldehyde, 37% | A |
| 20 | Formic Acid, 90% | B |
| 21 | Furfural | A |
| 22 | Gasoline | A |
| 22 | Hydrochloric Acid, 37% | B |
| 24 | Hydrofluoric Acid, 48% | B |
| 25 | Hydrogen Peroxide, 3% | B |
| 26 | Iodine, Tincture of | B |
| 27 | Methyl Ethyl Ketone | A |
| 28 | Methylene Chloride | A |
| 29 | Mono Chlorobenzene | A |
| 30 | Naphthalene | A |

# chemical and stain resistance

| 31 | Nitric Acid, 20% | B |
|---|---|---|
| 32 | Nitric Acid, 30% | B |
| 33 | Nitric Acid, 70% | B |
| 34 | Phenol, 90% | A |
| 35 | Phosphoric Acid, 85% | B |
| 36 | Silver Nitrate, Saturated | B |
| 37 | Sodium Hydroxide, 10% | B |
| 38 | Sodium Hydroxide, 20% | B |
| 39 | Sodium Hydroxide, 40% | B |
| 40 | Sodium Hydroxide, Flake | B |
| 41 | Sodium Sulfide, Saturated | B |
| 42 | Sulfuric Acid, 33% | B |
| 43 | Sulfuric Acid, 77% | B |
| 44 | Sulfuric Acid, 96% | B |
| 45 | Sulfuric Acid, 77% and Nitric Acid, 70% - equal parts | B |
| 46 | Toluene | A |
| 47 | Trichloroethylene | A |
| 48 | Xylene | A |
| 49 | Zinc Chloride, Saturated | B |

# APPENDIX

## casework integrity

To evaluate the overall integrity of casework, portions of SEFA 8-1999 (Scientific Equipment and Fixture Association) methods of testing and acceptable results have been adapted for use in these standards as the minimum acceptable level of integrity for casework conforming to all grades.

### TEST LISTING

- Structural Integrity - Base Cabinet
- Concentrated Load - Base Cabinet
- Torsion - Base Cabinet
- Base Submersion
- Structural Integrity - Wall Cabinet
- Door and Door Hinge Durability
- Door Impact
- Drawer Bottom Impact
- Drawer Support
- Drawer and Door Pull
- Drawer Rolling Load
- Shelf Load
- Structural Integrity - Table

**SHELF TEST UNIT** - Shelves, both fixed and/or adjustable, regardless of material or application, shall be tested using the following procedure. This is inclusive of shelves in wall cabinets, base cabinets, full height cabinets, wall mounted shelves, and free standing shelves.

**TABLE TEST UNIT** - Shall be 48" (1219 mm) long, 24" (610 mm) deep, and 36" (914 mm) high. A top of 1" (25.4 mm) thick medium density fiberboard shall be positioned on the table so that it will overhang the frame perimeter by 1" (25.4 mm), and its weight shall be included in the test as live load. Tables are represented by a large range of styles and designs, including free standing tables, desks, aprons mounted between two fixed areas (such as a wall or casework), mobile tables (free standing tables on wheels or casters), and mobile under counter units.

**BASE CABINET TEST UNIT** - Shall be 48" (1219 mm) wide, 36" (914 mm) high, and 22" (559 mm) deep with one full width drawer (approximately one fourth the height of the cabinet's face opening) and two doors. Cabinet shall be designed to provide unobstructed entry into the cabinet interior with the doors open and shall contain one adjustable shelf. For LABORATORY USE, the cabinet back shall be removable and tested with the cabinet back removed.

The cabinet shall be free standing, squared, and set level. A piece of 1" (25.4 mm) thick medium density fiberboard shall be positioned on the cabinet without glue or fasteners of any kind, of such dimensions that it will overhang the cabinet perimeter by 1" (25.4 mm), and its weight shall be included in the test as live load. Doors and the drawer should be free moving, and the door shall latch properly.

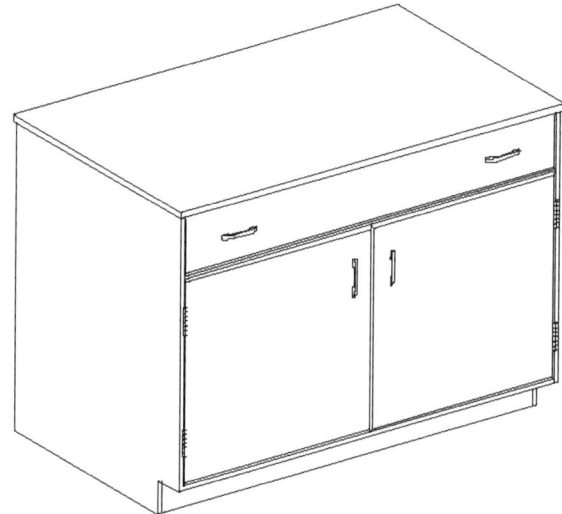

**WALL CABINET TEST UNIT** - Shall be 48" (1219 mm) wide, 36" (914 mm) high, and 12" (305 mm) deep with two swinging doors and one shelf, and shall be designed in such a way that when the doors are open, access to the cabinet is unobstructed.

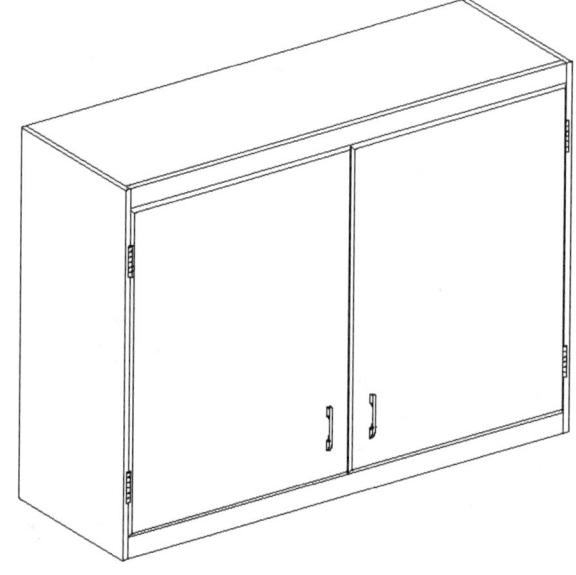

# APPENDIX

## casework integrity

### STRUCTURAL INTEGRITY TEST - BASE CABINET

- **CHALLENGES** the load bearing capability of a cabinet's construction.

- **PROCEDURE** - Load the cabinet top by using 2000 lbs (907 kg) of solid steel bars stacked eight high and evenly spaced for a time period of 10 minutes, then unload the cabinet.

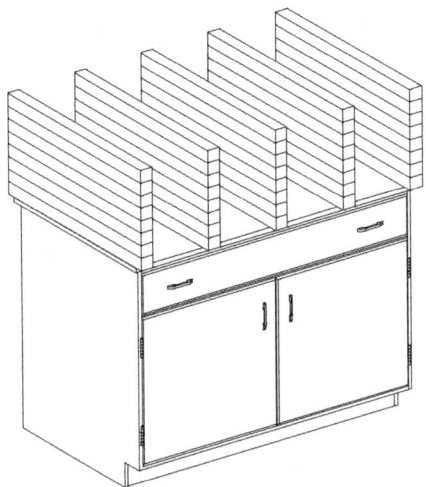

- **ACCEPTANCE LEVEL** - Cabinet shall have no signs of permanent failure. If used, inspect the levelers; any deformation shall not interfere with the function of the leveling system.

### CONCENTRATED LOAD TEST - BASE CABINET

- **CHALLENGES** the functional characteristics of the cabinet when subjected to a concentrated load on the center of the cabinet top.

- **PROCEDURE** - Using solid weights or 10 lb (4.53kg) sand bags, apply a total of 200 lbs (90.7 kg) to the top of the cabinet along the cabinet centerline. Operate the doors and the drawer.

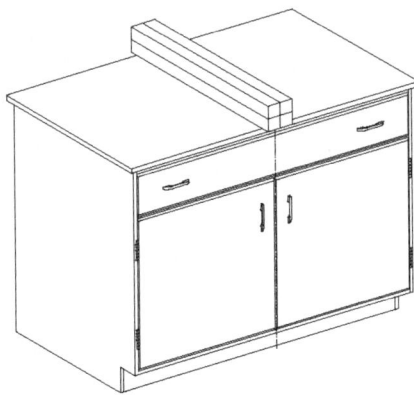

- **ACCEPTANCE LEVEL** - Door and drawer operation shall be normal under condition of test load and there shall be no signs of permanent distortion to the front rail, cabinet joinery, doors, or the drawer after load is removed.

### TORSION TEST - BASE CABINET

- **CHALLENGES** the structural integrity of the cabinet construction when subjected to a torsional load.

- **PROCEDURE** - The cabinet shall be tested in its normal upright position, raised not less than 4" (101.6 mm) off the floor, and supported on both rear corners and one front corner. The area of support under the cabinet shall be located not more than 6" (152.4 mm) in from each supported corner. Secure the cabinet diagonally from the unsupported corner with seven solid steel bars (350 lbs [159 kg]) on the top of the cabinet to prevent overturning. Apply four solid steel bars (200 lbs [90.7 kg]) to the unsupported corner for a period of 15 minutes. Remove the weight, and place the cabinet on the floor in its normal upright position. Observe the cabinet joinery. Level the cabinet and measure the face and back of the cabinet across the diagonal corners.

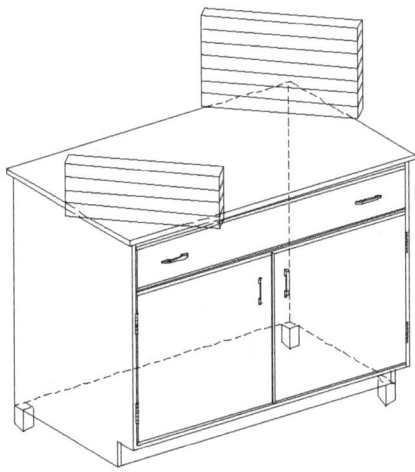

- **ACCEPTANCE LEVEL** - When returned to the normal position, the operation of the cabinet shall be normal without any signs of permanent damage. The difference between the two measurements taken from measuring the diagonal corners shall be no more than 1/8" (3.2mm).

# APPENDIX

## casework integrity

**SUBMERSION TEST - BASE CABINET** (Only applicable to casework specified for moisture resistant or laboratory use)

- **CHALLENGES** the cabinet's resistance to standing water and is only applicable to cabinets whose bases are within 2" (50.8 mm) of the finished floor.

- **PROCEDURE** - The material thickness along the perimeter of the cabinet shall be measured on 6" (152.4 mm) increments. Record the thickness of the material to be submerged in water. Calculate the arithmetic mean of the data taken. Place the entire test cabinet in its upright position so that the cabinet is submerged in a pan filled with 2" (50.8 mm) of water. After 4 hours, remove the unit from the water and immediately measure the thickness of the material at the same points measured initially. Calculate the new arithmetic mean. After the unit has been allowed to dry, inspect for other damage.

- **ACCEPTANCE LEVEL** - The cabinet will show no signs of permanent deformation or deterioration. Any increase in thickness of the base material shall not exceed 4% of the initial mean measurements.

**STRUCTURAL INTEGRITY TEST - WALL CABINET**

- **CHALLENGES** the strength of the back of the wall cabinet as well as the joinery of the cabinet and the function of the doors when the wall mounted unit is subjected to load.

- **PROCEDURE** - Using sand or shot bags weighing 10 lbs (4.5 kg) each, load the cabinet bottom, shelf, and top uniformly to a maximum of 200 lbs (90.7 kg) each, with the maximum load not exceeding 600 lbs (272 kg).

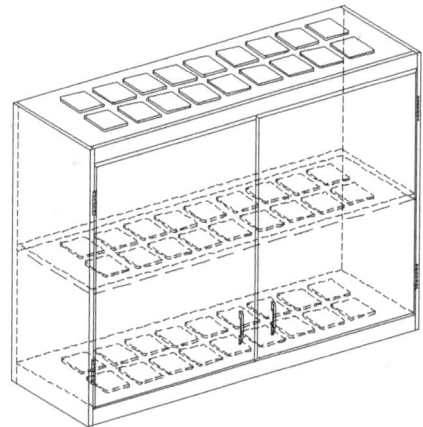

- **ACCEPTANCE LEVEL** - With weights in place, operate the doors through full travel to verify the normal operation of the doors. Remove the weights and operate the doors to verify normal operation. Verify that there is no significant permanent deflection of the cabinet top, cabinet back, cabinet bottom, or shelf. After the weights are removed, the cabinet shall show no permanent damage to the cabinet, cabinet bottom, or shelf.

**DOOR and DOOR HINGE DURABILITY TEST**

- **CHALLENGES** the durability of the door and its hardware (hinge leaf, screws, etc.) to an applied load of 200 lbs (90.7 kg).

- **PROCEDURE** - Remove the shelf for this test. With the unit and top set, add sufficient weight to the top in order to prevent overturning. With the cabinet door open 90 degrees, hang a sling made up of two 100 lb (45.4 kg) weights (shot bags or solid weights) over the top of the door at a point 12" (305 mm) out from the hinge center line. Slowly move the door through the full cycle of the hinge, up to a 160 degree arc. Remove the weight, swing the door through its full intended range of motion, and close the door.

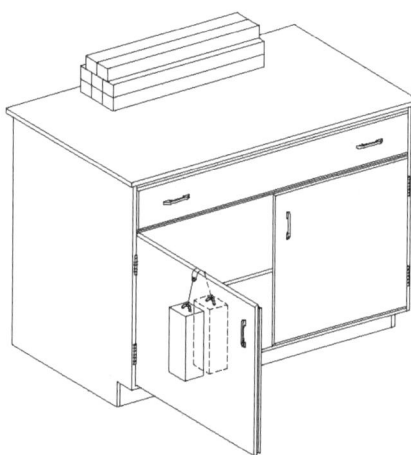

- **ACCEPTANCE LEVEL** - The open door shall withstand a load of 200 lbs (90.7 kg) when applied at a point 12" (305 mm) from the hinge centerline without significant permanent distortion that will cause binding of the door or hinges or that will adversely affect the operation of the catch.

# APPENDIX

## casework integrity

### DOOR IMPACT TEST

- **CHALLENGES** the resistance of a 240 inch pound impact to the door face and is applicable only to cabinet doors that extend below the work surface, excluding glass doors.

- **PROCEDURE** - With the unit and top set, add sufficient weight to the top in order to prevent overturning. A 20 lb (9 kg) sand bag shall be suspended and dropped to provide an impact of 240 inch pounds at the center of the closed door.

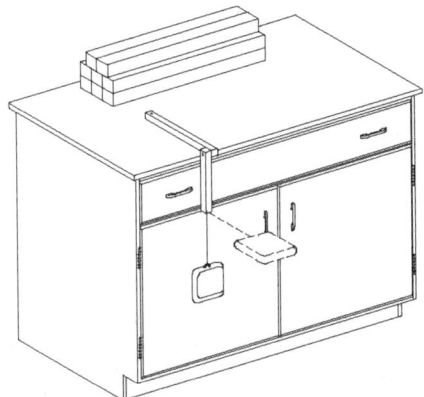

- **ACCEPTANCE LEVEL** - After the test, the door and catch shall operate normally and show no signs of permanent damage.

### DRAWER BOTTOM IMPACT TEST

- **CHALLENGES** the resistance to impact of the drawer bottom and slide mechanism.

- **PROCEDURE** - Open the drawer to 13" (330 mm) of travel. Drop a 10 lb (4.5 kg) sand or shot bag from a height of 24" (610 mm) into the bottom of the drawer at the center of the width of the drawer and 6" (152 mm) back from the inside face of the drawer. Remove the sand or shot bag.

- **ACCEPTANCE LEVEL** - Operate the drawer through the full cycle. The drawer shall operate normally. Any deformation will not cause binding or interfere with the operation of the drawer.

### DRAWER SUPPORT TEST

- **CHALLENGES** the ability to support a point load given to the front of the drawer and will challenge the attachment of the drawer head to the drawer.

- **PROCEDURE** - With the unit and top set, add sufficient weight to the top in order to prevent overturning. Open the drawer to 13" (330 mm) of travel and hang 150 lbs (68 kg) from the drawer head at the centerline of the drawer for 5 minutes. Remove the weight and operate the drawer through the full cycle.

- **ACCEPTANCE LEVEL** - There shall be no interference with the normal operation of the drawer.

### DRAWER AND DOOR PULL TEST

- **CHALLENGES** the strength of the pull hardware.

- **PROCEDURE** - Pulls are to be installed in accordance with the manufacturer's practice, using the specified attaching hardware and method. Block the door and the drawer closed. Using a cable pulley and weight assembly, apply a force of 50 lbs (22.7 kg) perpendicular to each pull. Revise the setup to hang weight from each pull.

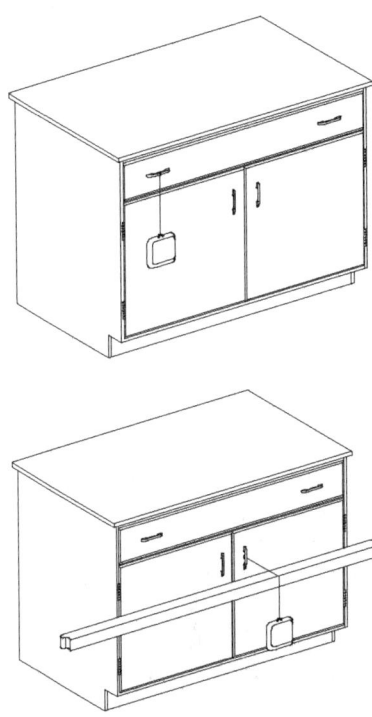

- **ACCEPTANCE LEVEL** - The pulls shall resist force and support weight without breakage. After completion of the test and removal of the weight, there shall be no significant permanent distortion. Some pull designs will require variations to set up apparatus. These pulls shall be tested in conformance to the applied pull forces.

# APPENDIX

## casework integrity

### DRAWER ROLLING LOAD TEST

- **CHALLENGES** the strength of the drawer head, bottom, and back as a result of opening and closing the drawer with a rolling load.

- **PROCEDURE** - Position the drawer on a table at a 45 degree angle. Place a 2" (50.8 mm) diameter by 12" (305 mm) long steel rod (approximately 10 lbs [4.5 kg]) 13" (330 mm) from the target impact area (so that the rod will roll freely to impact the back) of the drawer. Subject the back to three impacts, and reverse the drawer to subject the front to three additional impacts.

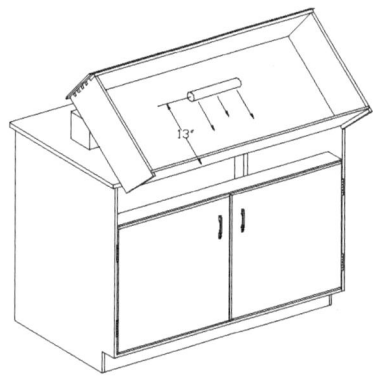

- **ACCEPTANCE LEVEL** - The drawer shall show no signs (other than minor scratches and dents) of permanent damage. All joinery shall be intact, and the drawer, when replaced in the unit, shall operate normally. Minor scratches and dents are acceptable.

### SHELF LOAD TEST

- **CHALLENGES** the ability of a shelf and its mounting hardware to support normal loads.

- **PROCEDURE** - The shelf shall be mounted as designed. Measure the distance from the underside of the shelf to a reference point perpendicular to the center of the shelf. Using shot or sand bags weighing 10 lbs (4.5 kg) each, uniformly load the shelf to a maximum of 200 lbs (90.7 kg). Measure the deflection on the shelf by measuring the distance to the reference point and calculating the difference between the two measurements.

- **ACCEPTANCE LEVEL** - The maximum deflection shall be 1/180 of the span, not to exceed 1/4" (6.4 mm).

### TABLE STRUCTURAL INTEGRITY TEST

- **CHALLENGES** the table components to a normal load.

- **PROCEDURE** - Load the table top with an evenly distributed load of no less than 300 lbs (136 kg) for mobile, 600 lbs (272 kg) for free standing, and 2000 lbs (907 kg) for fixed. Include the weight of the working surface as a live load by using solid steel bars, each weighing 50 lbs (22.7 kg).

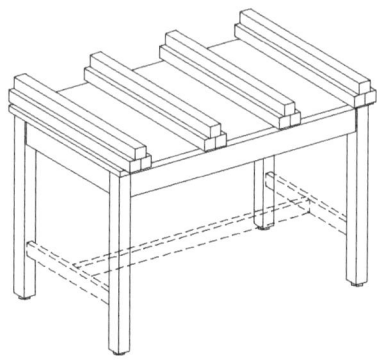

- **ACCEPTANCE LEVEL** - No structural breakage shall occur, and the apron rails shall not deflect more than 1/8" (3.2 mm). In the case of a table with a drawer, the deflection of the rail shall not interfere with the function of the drawer.

# APPENDIX

## casework refinishing/refacing/refurbishing - guidelines

**THIS TYPE OF WORK** is typically required to be done in the field and without specific contract document requirements to the contrary:

- Will not update any seismic fabrication and/or installation deficiencies.

- Lead and/or toxic material abatement shall not be the responsibility of the woodwork manufacturer/installer.

**SPECIFICATIONS** shall clearly indicate whether refinishing, refacing, refurbishing, or a combination thereof is required.

**ARCHITECTURAL PLANS** shall clearly indicate all casework to be refinished, refaced, and/or refurbished. The casework elevations shall also indicate any unusual or special requirements (such as structural repair or component replacement).

It is the design professional's responsibility to specify any and all modifications required for code compliance.

Including the means, methods, and materials required to retrofit casework for UBC Title 24 or other national compliance code(s).

The requirement for reinstallation of existing casework (if needed to be removed), in a manner other than the original, shall be so specified.

If new or additional wall blocking is required, it shall be so specified and be the responsibility of the contractor.

All refinishing, refacing, and/or refurbishing of casework governed by these standards shall generally be in accordance with these standards as applicable, with the following exception:

- Repair or modification of existing casework shall be in compliance with accepted methods of joinery as contained in these standards.

The method of repair used shall be optional with the manufacturer/installer.

**REFINISHING** can be as simple as the application of a new finish over the existing cabinet surfaces or as extensive as the removal of the existing finish, repair or patch of all physical defects, and the application of a new finish; however: does not include the replacement of hardware, unless so specified.

**REFACING** is usually more involved and very field labor intensive, and existing surfaces, including doors, drawer fronts, cabinet face, and finished ends:

- If HPDL, shall be removed with any damaged core areas repaired and core surface suitably prepared for proper adhesion of the new surface material.

- If paint, shall be stripped to the original surface with any damaged areas repaired and resurfaced with the specified material.

Does not include the replacement of hardware, unless so specified.

**REFURBISHING** includes either the refinishing or refacing of the exterior cabinet body, replacement of the cabinet doors and drawer fronts, and replacement of all exposed cabinet hardware, including hinges, pulls, catches, and locks; however:

- It does not include the repair or replacement of interior components such as shelves, drawer boxes, or drawer slides unless so specified.

New components, such as doors, drawer fronts, drawer boxes, and shelves, shall be compliant to these standards.

Gaps and tolerances shall match that of the existing casework within an elevation and within a room.

Hardware replacement for refurbished casework, or when specified to be included with refinishing or refacing, shall include door hinges, door and drawer pulls, and locks (keying requirement to be as specified).

Drawer slide replacement is not included unless specifically required in the contract documents.

Match of existing hardware is contingent on the availability of such from a manufacturer's current stock.

The method of repair or patching of tear outs used for proper hardware replacement shall be optional with the manufacturer/installer.

All work shall meet the requirements of first class workmanship.

# APPENDIX

## fraction/decimal/millimeter conversions

| FRACTION | DECIMAL | MILLIMETER | FRACTION | DECIMAL | MILLIMETER |
|---|---|---|---|---|---|
| 1/64 | 0.01563 | 0.3969 | 33/64 | 0.51563 | 13.0969 |
| 1/32 | 0.03125 | 0.7938 | 17/32 | 0.53125 | 13.4938 |
| 3/64 | 0.04688 | 1.1906 | 35/64 | 0.54688 | 13.8906 |
| 1/16 | 0.06250 | 1.5875 | 9/16 | 0.56250 | 14.2875 |
| 5/64 | 0.07813 | 1.9844 | 37/64 | 0.57813 | 14.6844 |
| 3/32 | 0.09375 | 2.3813 | 19/32 | 0.59375 | 15.0813 |
| 7/64 | 0.10937 | 2.7781 | 39/64 | 0.60938 | 15.4781 |
| 1/8 | 0.12500 | 3.1750 | 5/8 | 0.62500 | 15.8750 |
| 9/64 | 0.14063 | 3.5719 | 41/64 | 0.64063 | 16.2719 |
| 5/32 | 0.15625 | 3.9688 | 21/32 | 0.65625 | 16.6688 |
| 11/64 | 0.17188 | 4.3656 | 43/64 | 0.67188 | 17.0656 |
| 3/16 | 0.18750 | 4.7625 | 11/16 | 0.68750 | 17.4625 |
| 13/64 | 0.20312 | 5.1594 | 45/64 | 0.70313 | 17.8594 |
| 7/32 | 0.21875 | 5.5563 | 23/32 | 0.71875 | 18.2563 |
| 15/64 | 0.23438 | 5.9531 | 47/64 | 0.73438 | 18.6531 |
| 1/4 | 0.25000 | 6.3500 | 3/4 | 0.75000 | 19.0500 |
| 17/64 | 0.26563 | 6.7469 | 49/64 | 0.76563 | 19.4469 |
| 9/32 | 0.28125 | 7.1438 | 25/32 | 0.78125 | 19.8438 |
| 19/64 | 0.29688 | 7.5406 | 51/64 | 0.79688 | 20.2406 |
| 5/16 | 0.31250 | 7.9375 | 13/16 | 0.81250 | 20.6375 |
| 21/64 | 0.32813 | 8.3344 | 53/64 | 0.82813 | 21.0344 |
| 11/32 | 0.34375 | 8.7313 | 27/32 | 0.84375 | 21.4313 |
| 23/64 | 0.35938 | 9.1281 | 55/64 | 0.85938 | 21.8281 |
| 3/8 | 0.37500 | 9.5250 | 7/8 | 0.87500 | 22.2250 |
| 25/64 | 0.39063 | 9.9219 | 57/64 | 0.89063 | 22.6219 |
| 13/32 | 0.40625 | 10.3188 | 29/32 | 0.90625 | 23.0188 |
| 27/64 | 0.42188 | 10.7156 | 59/64 | 0.92188 | 23.4156 |
| 7/16 | 0.43750 | 11.1125 | 15/16 | 0.93750 | 23.8125 |
| 29/64 | 0.45313 | 11.5094 | 61/64 | 0.95313 | 24.2094 |
| 15/32 | 0.46875 | 11.9063 | 31/32 | 0.96875 | 24.6063 |
| 31/64 | 0.48438 | 12.3031 | 63/64 | 0.98438 | 25.0031 |
| 1/2 | 0.50000 | 12.7000 | 1 | 1.00000 | 25.4000 |

# APPENDIX

## miscellaneous conversions

| WHEN KNOWN | MULTIPLY BY | TO FIND |
|---|---|---|
| Inches | 2.54 | Centimeters |
| Inches | 25.4 | Millimeters |
| Square Inches | 6.452 | Square Centimeters |
| Feet | 30.48 | Centimeters |
| Square Feet | .0929 | Square Meters |
| Yards | .9144 | Meters |
| Square Yards | .8361 | Square Meters |
| Miles | 1.6 | Kilometers |
| Square Miles | 2.59 | Square Kilometers |
| Acres | .4047 | Hectares |
| Ounces | 28.349527 | Grams |
| Pounds | .4536 | Kilograms |
| Pressure | .0703 | Bar |
| Radius | 2 | Diameter |
| Diameter | .5 | Radius |
| Diameter | 3.1416 | Circumference |
| Diameter | .8862 | Side of an Equal Square |
| Circumference | .31831 | Diameter |
| Circumference | .15915 | Radius |
| Circumference | .2821 | Side of an Equal Square |
| Square of Diameter | .7854 | Area of Circle |
| Square of Diameter | 3.1416 | Square of Sphere of Globe |
| Square of Circumference | .07958 | Area of Circle |
| Square of Radius | 3.1416 | Area of Circle |
| TO FIND | DIVIDE BY | WHEN KNOWN |

| WHEN KNOWN | MULTIPLY BY | TO FIND |
|---|---|---|
| Fahrenheit | 0.556 after subtracting 32 | Celsius |
| Celsius | 1.8 and add 32 | Fahrenheit |

# APPENDIX

notes

# Architectural Woodwork Standards

# DESIGN IDEAS

# DESIGN IDEAS

## introduction & table of contents

### TABLE OF CONTENTS

- Base and Base Cap Patterns ............................................. 409
- Picture Mold Patterns ....................................................... 412
- Casing Patterns ................................................................ 413
- Panel Mold Patterns ......................................................... 416
- Crown Mold Patterns ........................................................ 417
- Bed Mold Patterns ............................................................ 419
- Handrail Patterns .............................................................. 420
- Chair Rail Patterns ............................................................ 421
- Architectural Ornamentation ............................................. 423
  - Terminology ................................................................. 423
  - Historic Woodwork Glossary ....................................... 424
  - Classic Orders ............................................................. 428
- Stile & Rail Door Design Examples ................................... 436
- Casework Design Examples .............................................. 440
  - Schools and Libraries .................................................. 440
  - Banks and Courts ........................................................ 444
  - Judge's Bench ............................................................. 447
  - Corporate Woodwork .................................................. 448
  - Furniture and Fixtures ................................................. 453
  - Reception .................................................................... 461
  - Church Fittings ............................................................ 466
  - Basic Cabinetry ........................................................... 467
- Cabinet Design Series (CDS) ............................................ 469
  - CDS Overview ............................................................. 469
  - General Notes ............................................................. 469
  - Special Base Casework Heights .................................. 469
  - 100 Series - Base Cabinets w/o Drawers ..................... 470
  - 200 Series - Base Cabinets w/ Drawers ....................... 473
  - 300 Series - Wall Hung Cabinets .................................. 475
  - 400 Series - Tall Storage Cabinets ............................... 477
  - 500 Series - Wardrobe Cabinets .................................. 481
  - 600 Series - Library Cabinets ....................................... 483
  - 700 Series - Moveable Cabinets ................................... 485

### INTRODUCTION

This section of the Architectural Woodwork Standards contains valuable content that will assist the design professional in the use and specification of fine woodworking. Much more than ideas, it contains comprehensive sets of drawings for mouldings, stile and rail doors, custom casework and ornamental woodwork as well as the complete Casework Design Series. All casework drawings shown are diagrammatic only. This information will assist even the most seasoned specifier in the application of an extensive array of wood products. Moulding profiles and door designs are numbered for call outs in architectural drawings. The Cabinet Design Series has been used for years as a system to identify cabinet types and configurations. The ornamental woodwork portion of this section gives a history and a primer, tracking the classic architectural elements used throughout the ages and extensively today.

These standards are meant to be a tool to enhance and empower the creative use of architectural woodwork and this section uniquely provides applicable drawings and terminology to support and contribute to the design process.

For your convenience where referenced it is flagged by the following **DESIGN IDEAS** icon: **di**

# DESIGN IDEAS

## standing & running trim design examples

**BASE AND BASE CAP PATTERNS**

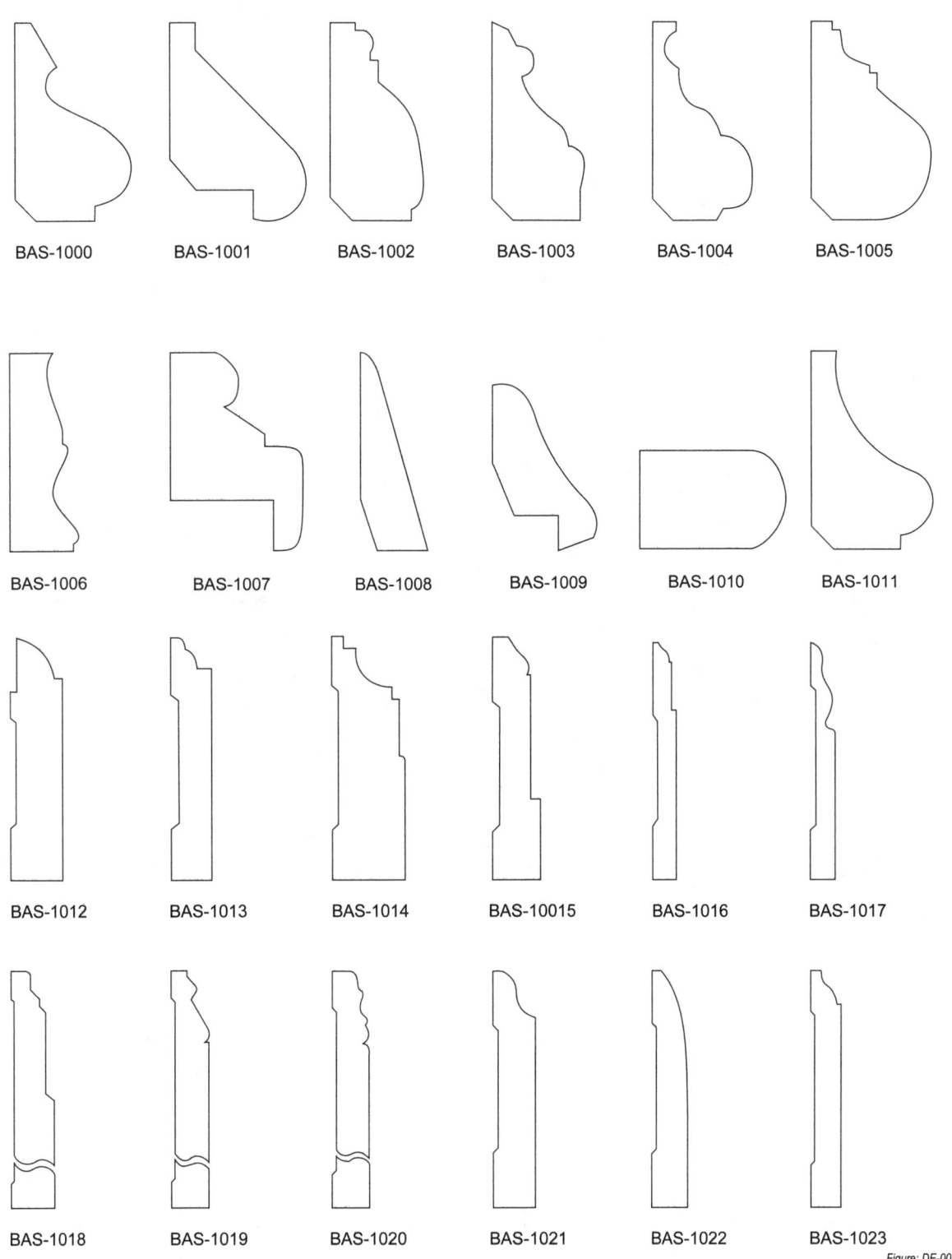

Figure: DE-001

# DESIGN IDEAS

## standing & running trim design examples

**BASE AND BASE CAP PATTERNS**

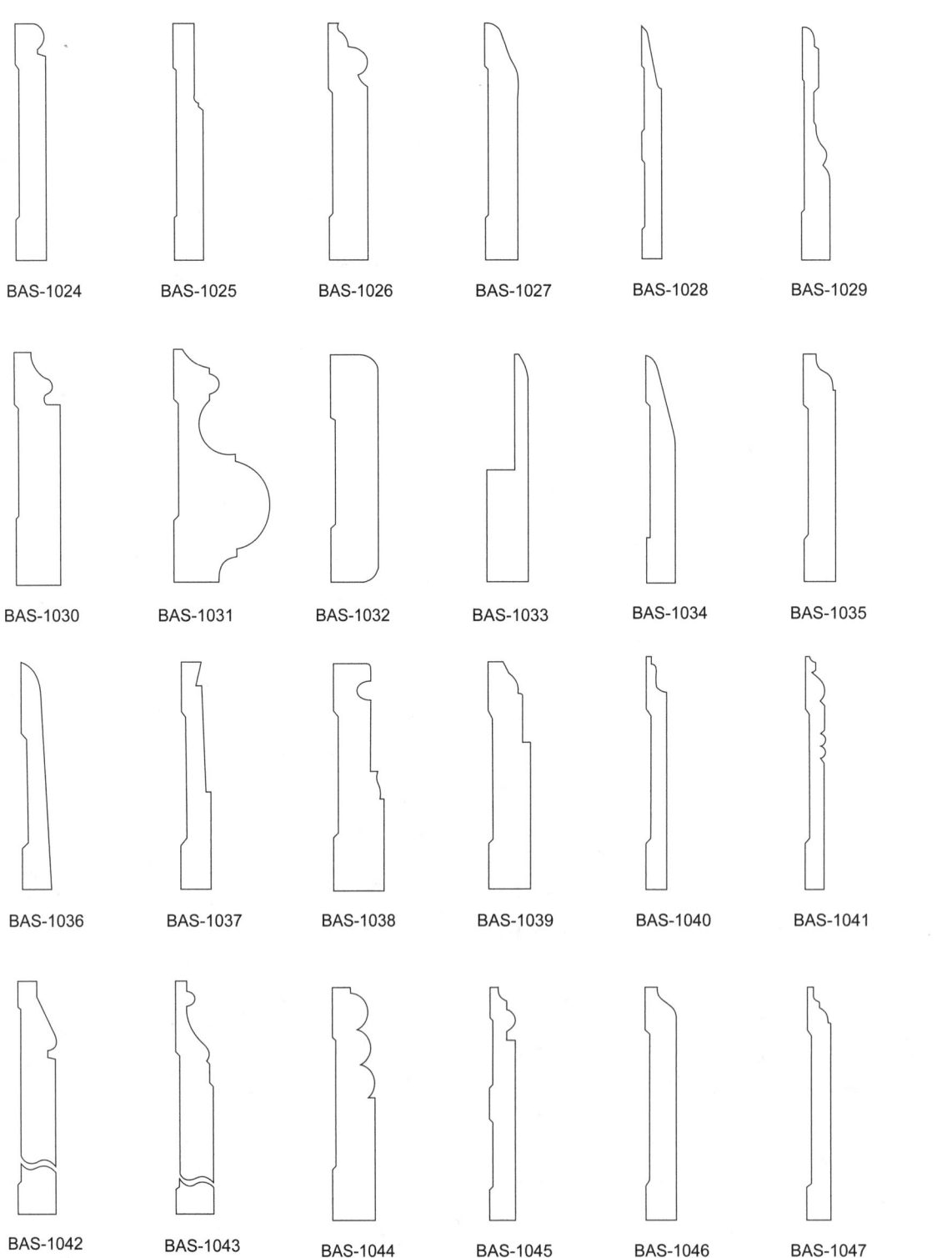

Figure: DE-002

# DESIGN IDEAS

## standing & running trim design examples

**BASE AND BASE CAP PATTERNS**

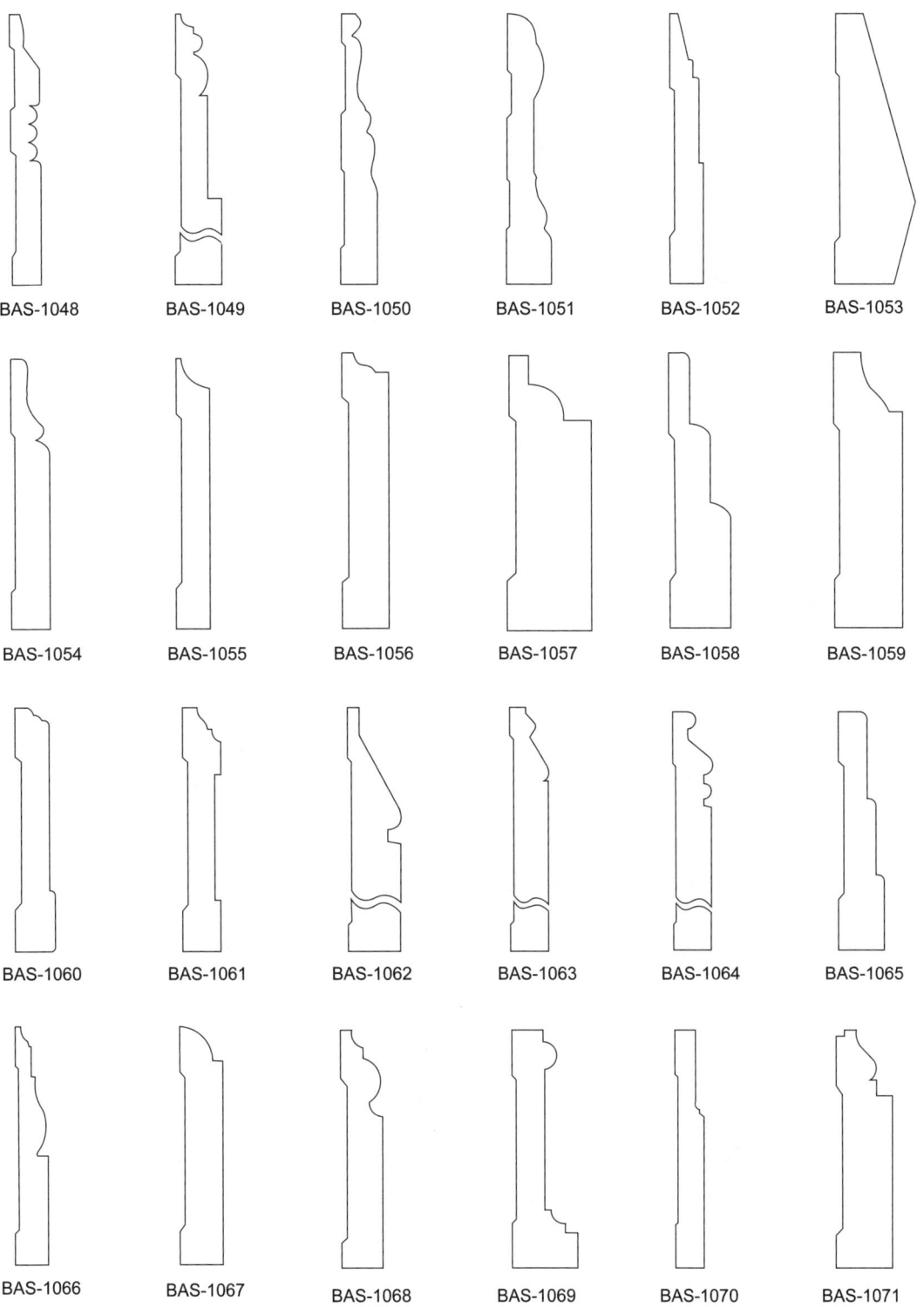

Figure: DE-003

# DESIGN IDEAS

## standing & running trim design examples

**BASE AND BASE CAP PATTERNS**

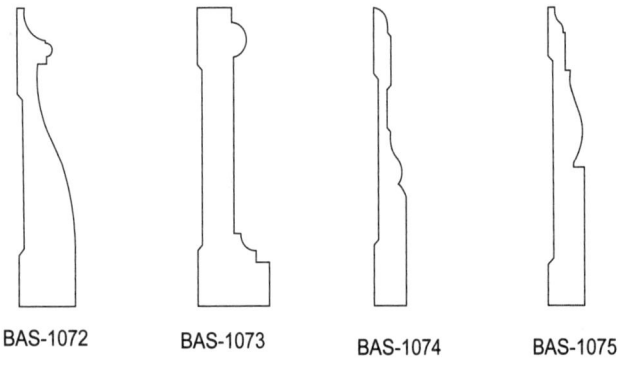

BAS-1072    BAS-1073    BAS-1074    BAS-1075

*Figure: DE-004*

**PICTURE MOLD PATTERNS**

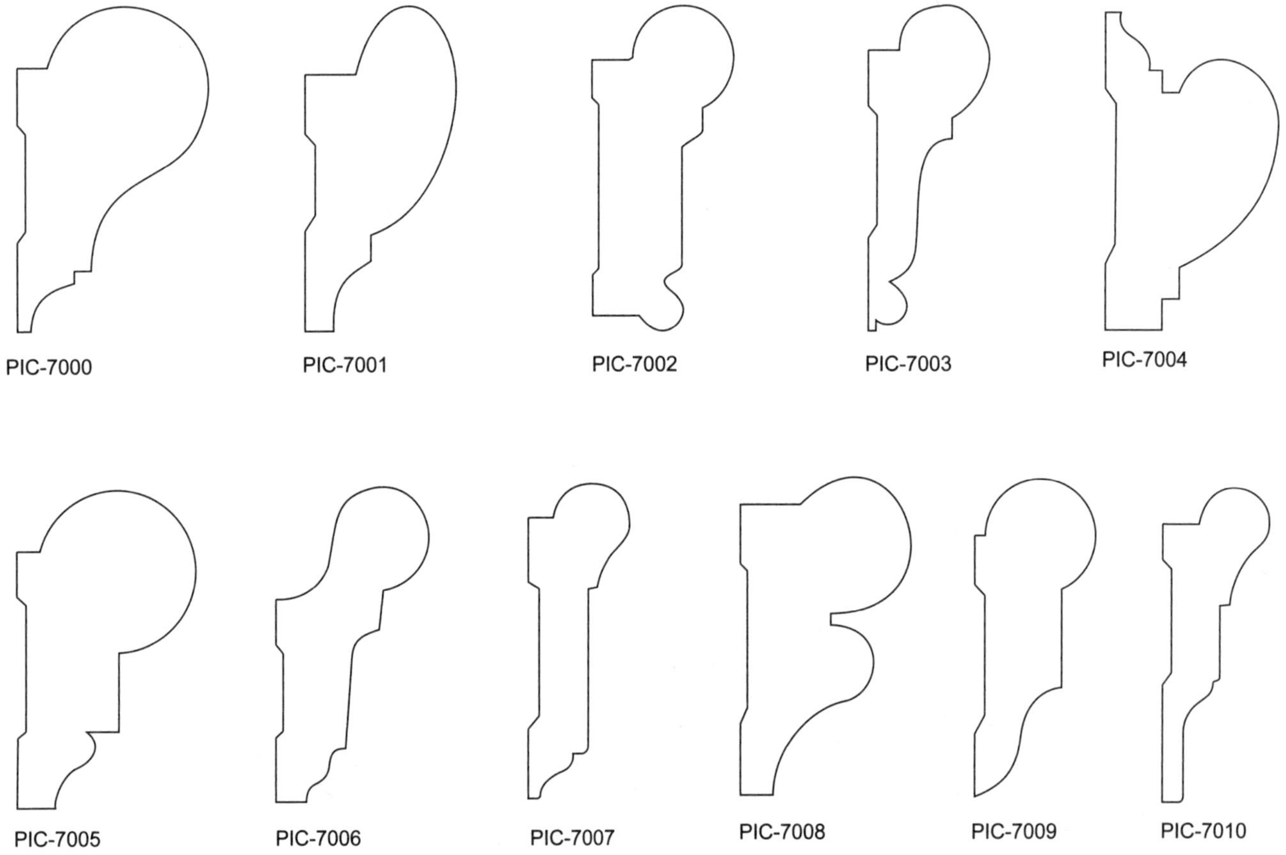

PIC-7000    PIC-7001    PIC-7002    PIC-7003    PIC-7004

PIC-7005    PIC-7006    PIC-7007    PIC-7008    PIC-7009    PIC-7010

*Figure: DE-005*

# DESIGN IDEAS

## standing & running trim design examples

**CASING PATTERNS**

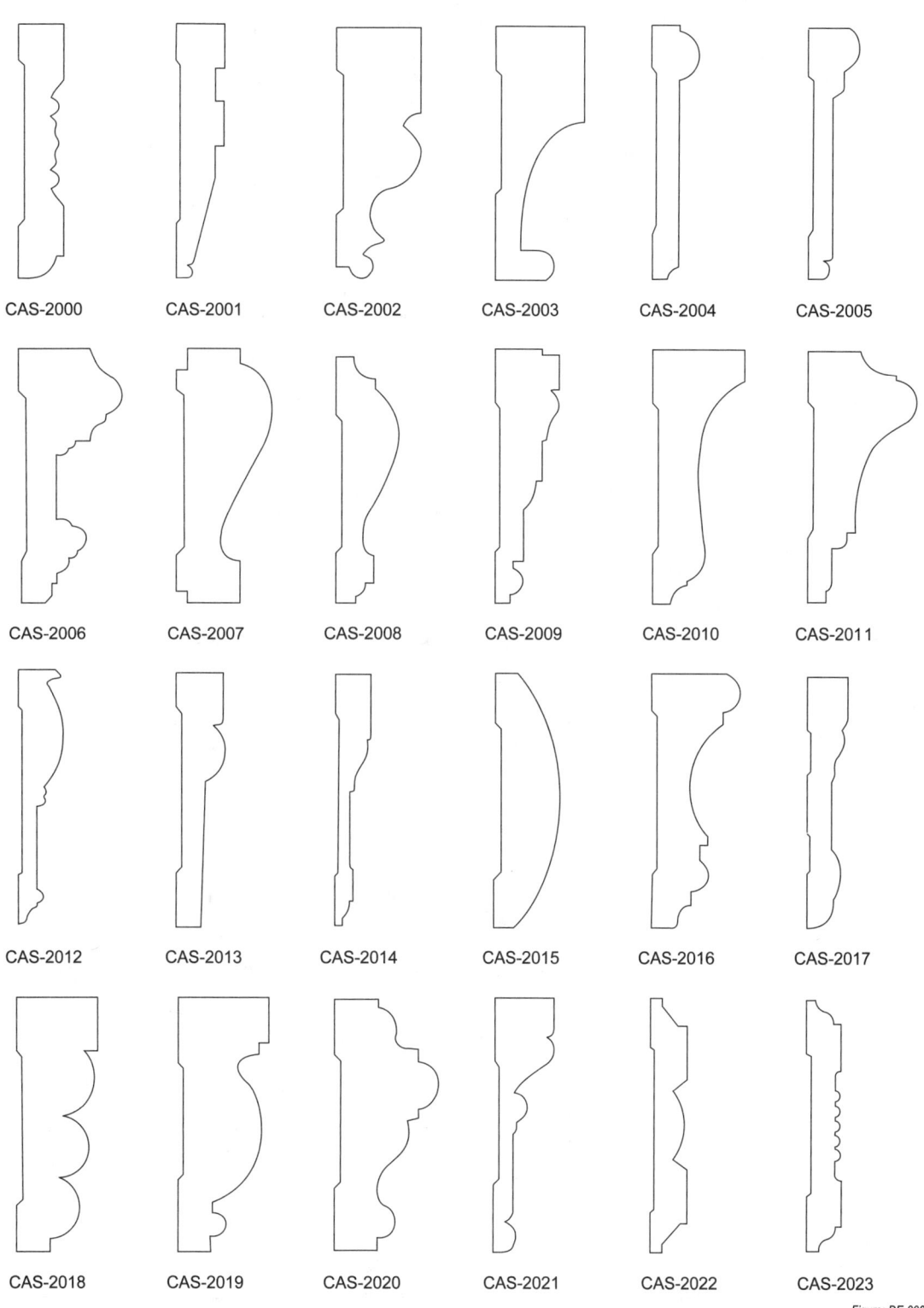

Figure: DE-006

# DESIGN IDEAS

## standing & running trim design examples

**CASING PATTERNS**

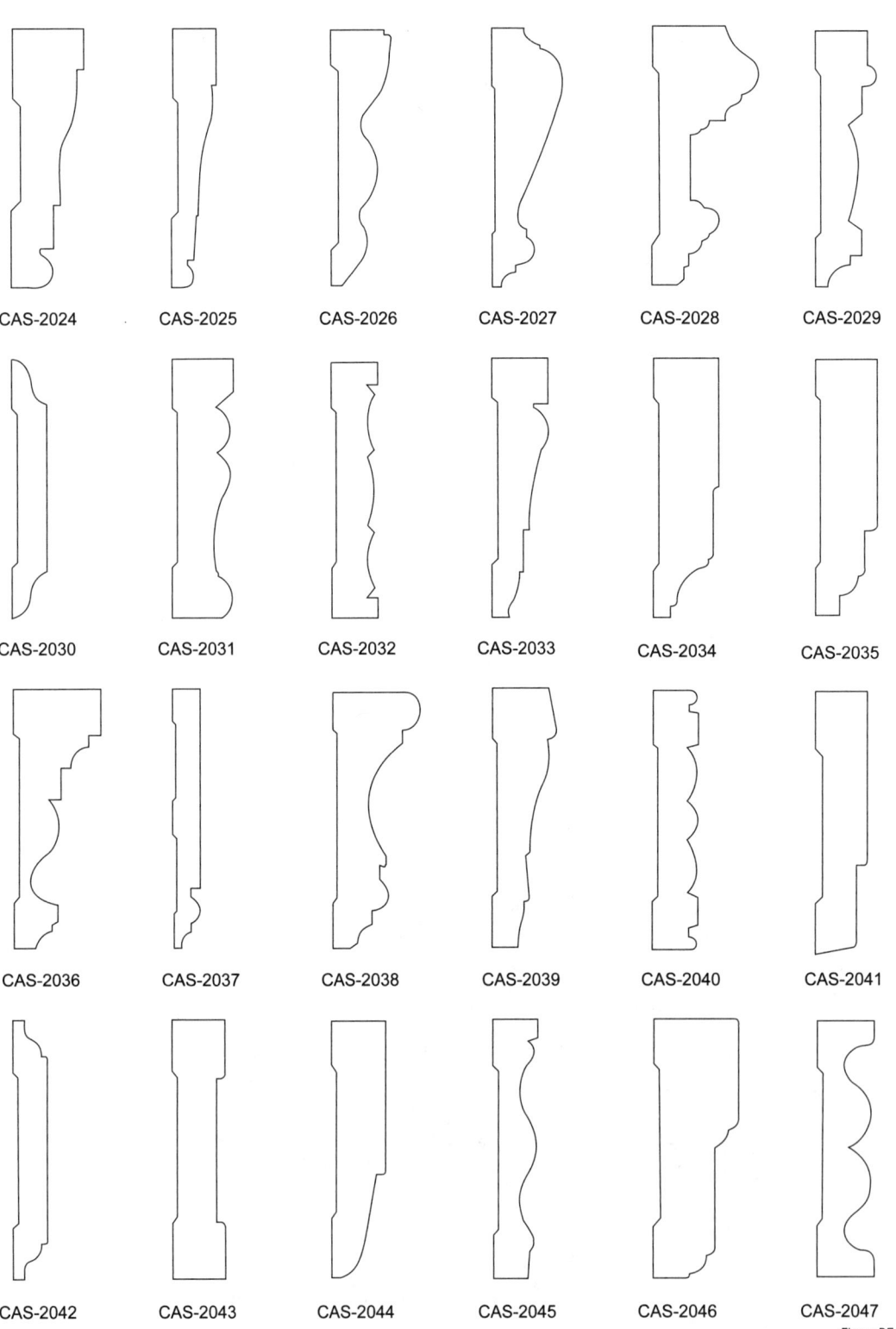

Figure: DE-007

# DESIGN IDEAS

## standing & running trim design examples

**CASING PATTERNS**

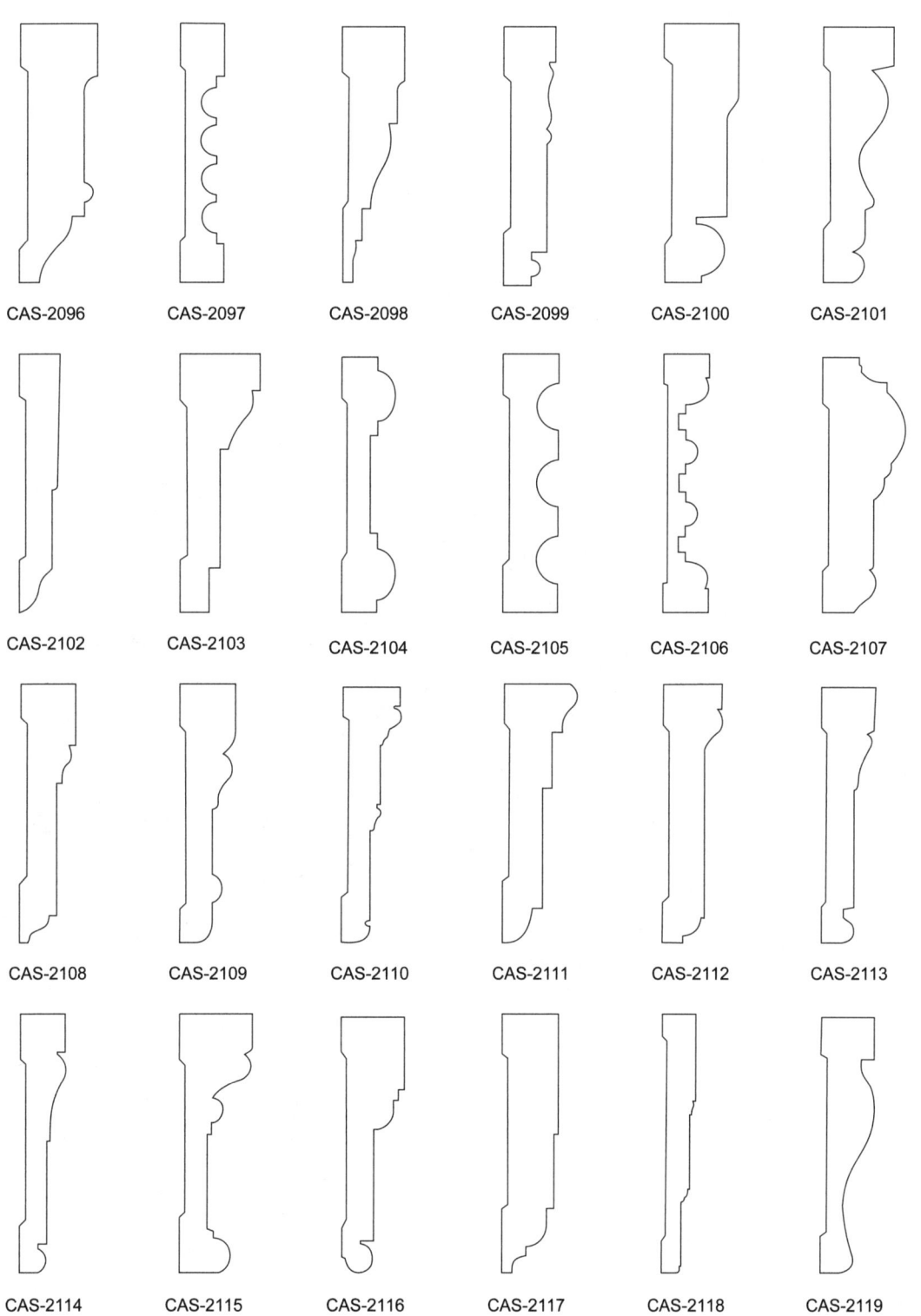

Figure: DE-008

# DESIGN IDEAS

## standing & running trim design examples

**CASING and PANEL MOLDING PATTERNS**

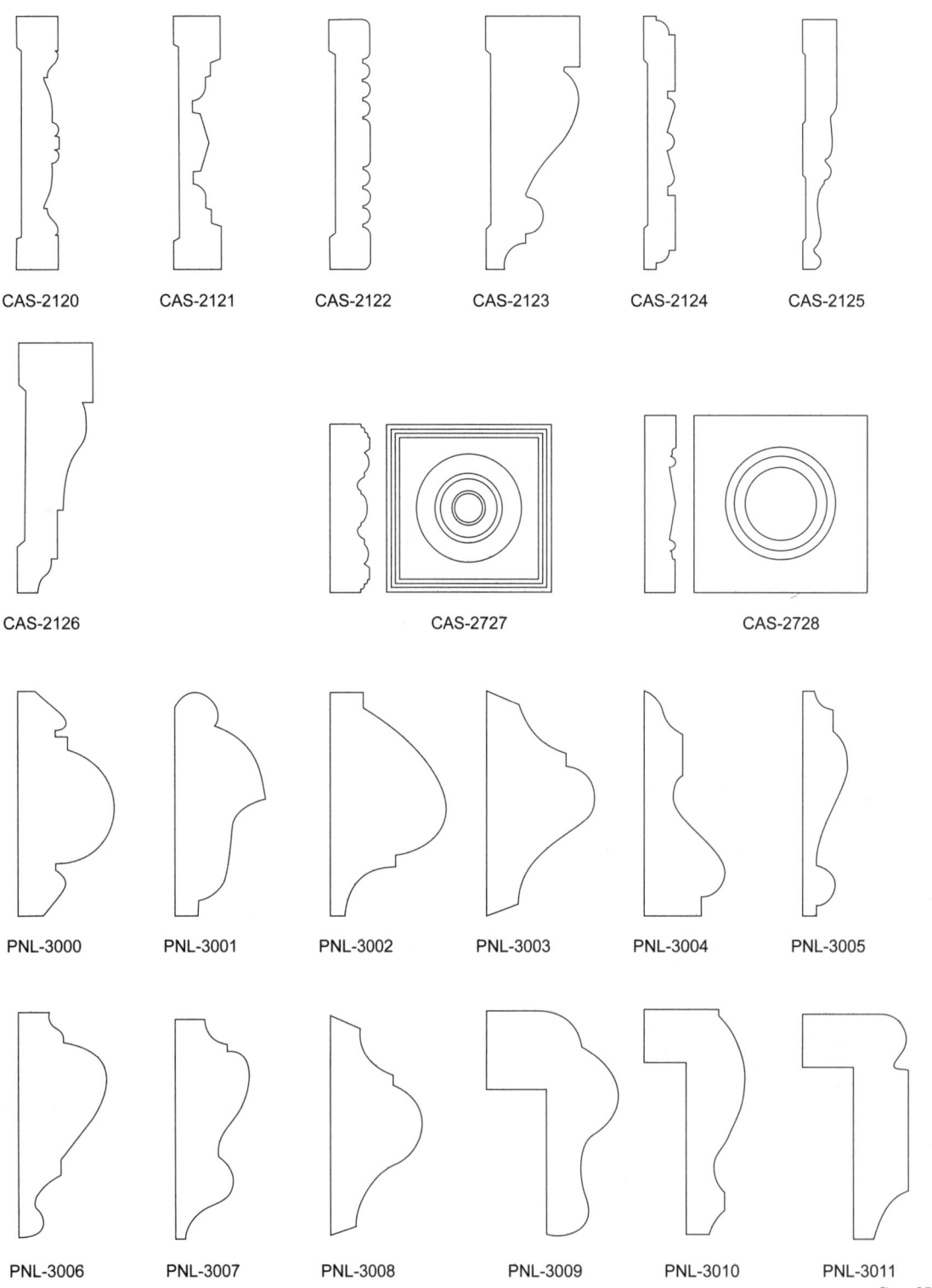

Figure: DE-009

# DESIGN IDEAS

## standing & running trim design examples

**CROWN MOLD PATTERNS**

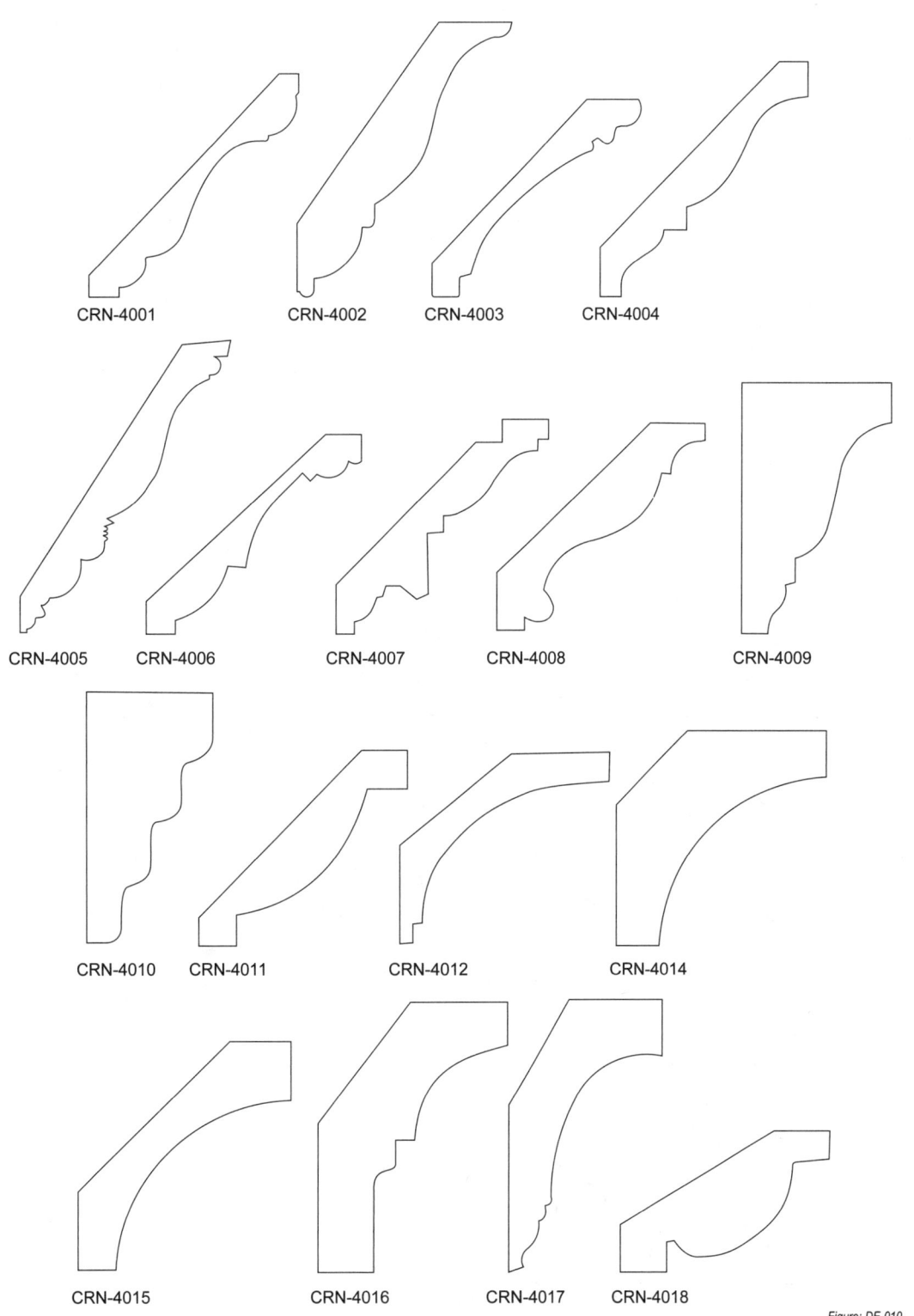

Figure: DE-010

# DESIGN IDEAS

## standing & running trim design examples

**CROWN MOLD PATTERNS**

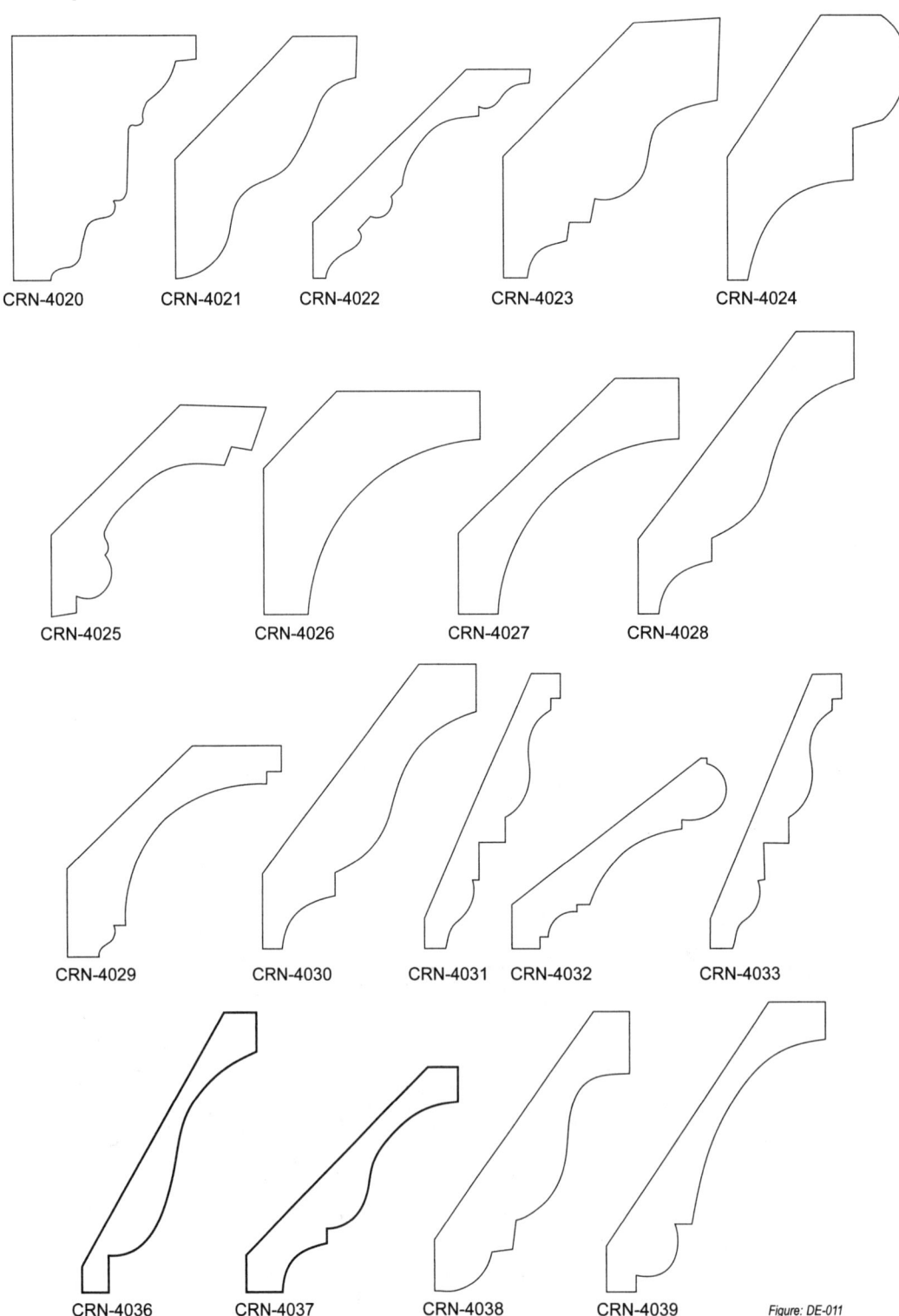

Figure: DE-011

# DESIGN IDEAS

## standing & running trim design examples

**BED MOLD PATTERNS**

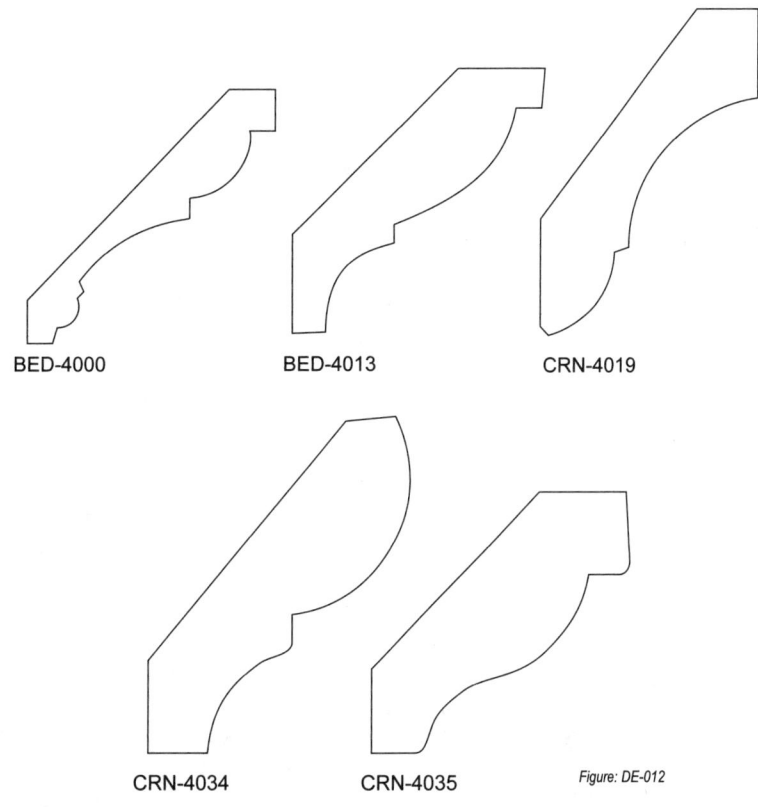

Figure: DE-012

# DESIGN IDEAS

## standing & running trim design examples

**HANDRAIL PATTERNS**

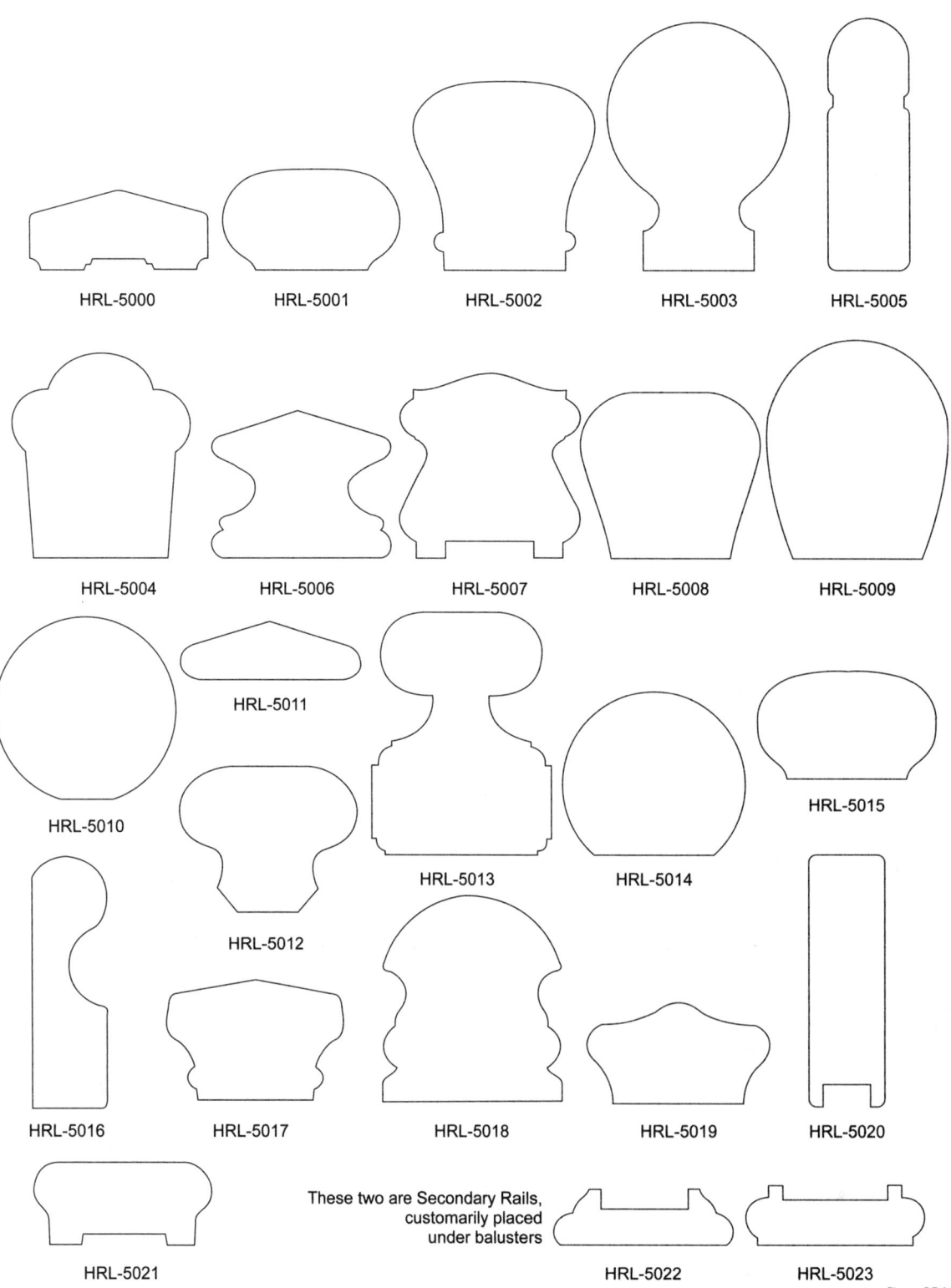

Figure: DE-013

# DESIGN IDEAS

## standing & running trim design examples

**CHAIR RAIL PATTERNS**

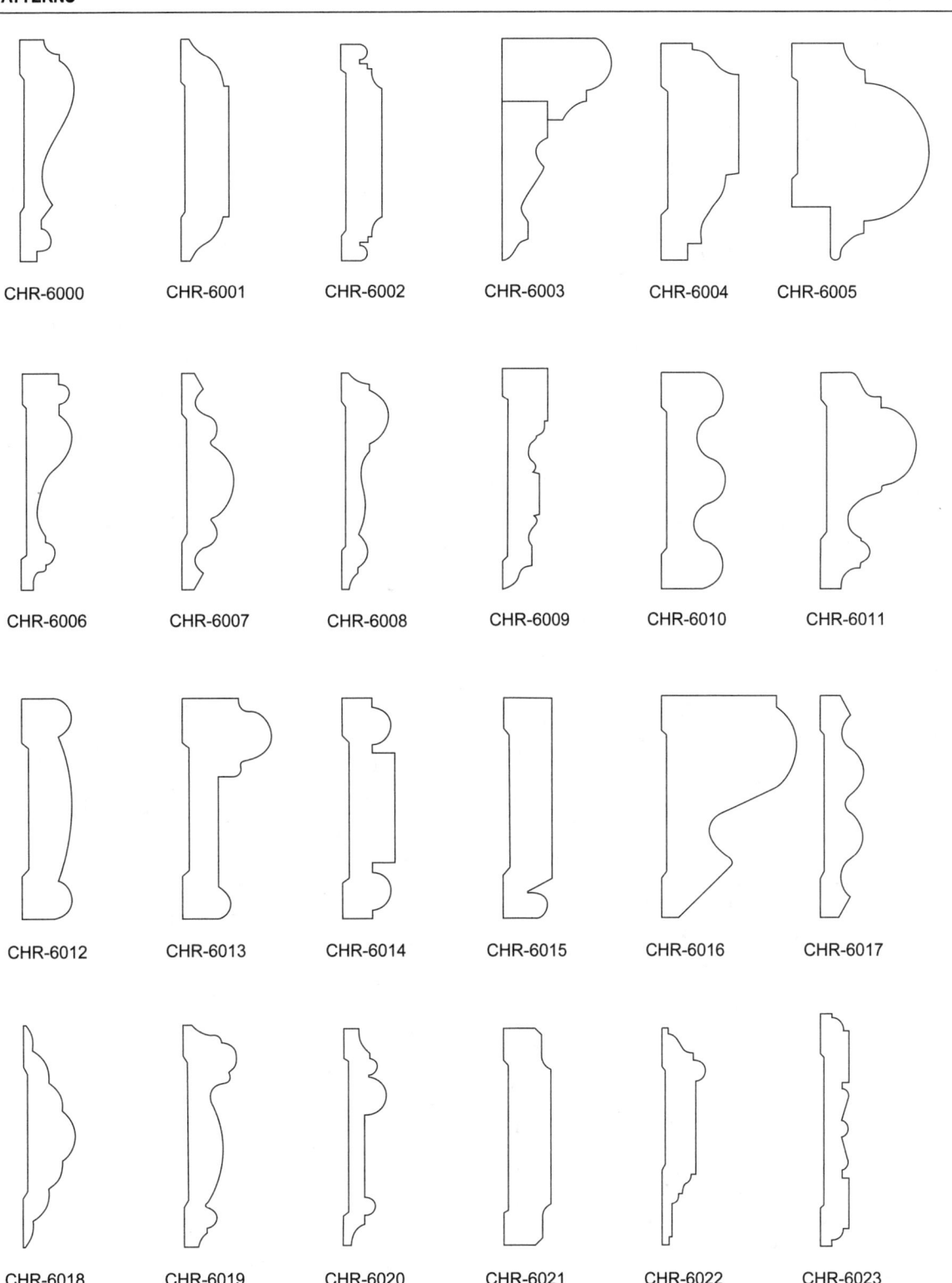

Figure: DE-014

# DESIGN IDEAS

## standing & running trim design examples

**CHAIR RAIL PATTERNS**

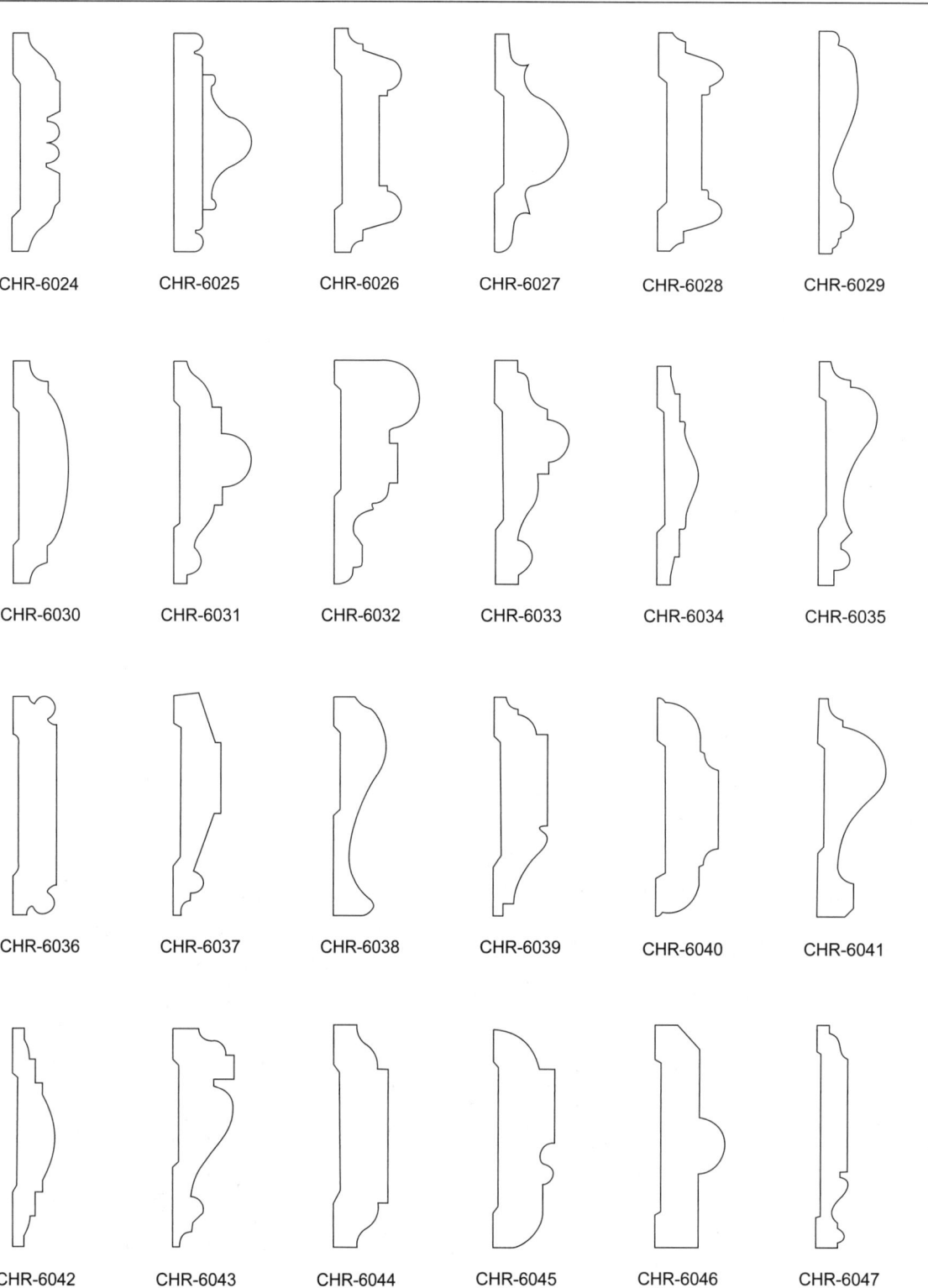

Figure: DE-015

# architectural ornamentation

## ARCHITECTURAL ORNAMENTATION

Discussing ornamental style is a difficult endeavor because it is historically complex and subject to interpretation. North America is made up of ethnic groups from around the world and each has brought its own cultural history to the mix. The notes here do not intend to exclude any style of ornamentation, but concentrate on the predominant influence of Western Art and Architecture. Risking over simplification, style tends to vacillate over time between two extremes:

- Formal, restrained classicism, and

- Emotional and vivacious Romanticism.

Much of Western Architecture derives from the art and architecture of ancient Greece and Rome. Classicism is based on symmetry and proportion providing mathematical relationships among all elements of the building. One characteristic is the use of columns for support, though engaged columns and pilasters were used, sometimes in conjunction with arches. The orders of architecture, have been codified and reinterpreted ever since Vitruvious wrote a treatise on architecture in 30 BCE. In reality there was wide variation and great adaptability over a thousand years of evolution in many disparate geographical areas. The Parthenon in Athens, the Maison Carrée in Nîmes, France, or the Pantheon in Rome are familiar examples. In succeeding revivals an abundance of government and academic buildings reflect these archetypes - the United States Capitol building, many state and county courthouses, and Jefferson's University of Virginia.

Romanticism, on the other hand, is subjective, derived from the randomness of nature, spiritual, and introduces asymmetry, exuberance, and complex lines. Many designs are eclectic, fantastic and mix a number of exotic motifs. Though there are many of the same mathematical concerns in Romanesque and Gothic buildings as there are in Classical buildings, the ornamentation conveys a different feeling. The achievement of Gothic architecture was the introduction of the pointed arch which solved some structural limitations of Romanesque vaulting. While Classicism appears to be simple in concept, romanticism seems to relish complexity.

A Gothic cathedral when viewed from any angle except frontally does not seem to have much order, with flying buttresses and pinnacles and windows complicating one's perception of the form of the building.

Reacting to Gothic embellishments, Renaissance architects rediscovered classicism, but in time the Classical tenets were corrupted (Mannerism) and the Baroque, which emphasized undulating surfaces, complicated interior spaces and dramatic decoration, permeated Europe. As a reaction to the flamboyance of the Baroque, interest in Classicism reemerged in the 18th Century. But in this era the Rococo style and the "Chinese" style, (Chinoiserie), especially in furniture, were also in vogue. The 19th Century saw continued C Lunch: Tuesday – Saturday 11:00-2:30
Bar Menu: Tuesday – Saturday 2:30-5:00
Dinner: Monday – Sunday 5:00-10:30
lassicism, but also an eclectic mix of revivals - Romanesque, Gothic and Eastern styles.

## TERMINOLOGY

A rudimentary explanation of some carving terms will assist the design professional in communicating with the custom carver:

There are four methods of depicting a design in wood.

- Incised: Incised designs are simply made by shallow grooves in the surface of the material.

- Relief: Most architectural carving is carved in relief. The degree to which the design is lifted off the surface is described as low or high relief.

- Pierced: Some voids in the design are literally cut through the material and are termed pierced carvings.

- Sculpture: Carving in the round or sculptural works are also incorporated into architectural surroundings.

Moldings have multiple uses but one important one is to visually set apart various elements. For instance, they are transitions between the parts of the entablature. They accentuate the trim (architrave) around doors and windows, and around an arch (archivolt). The various terms depend primarily on the profiles, but there are a few terms which indicate use, location or size.

The curving profiles are often separated or off set by a relatively small flat called a fillet.

The small half round is an astragal, often decorated with beads or bead and billet. A larger half round, usually associated with the base of a column or base of a structure is called a torus (plural tori) molding, sometimes decorated with ribbon bundled Bay Laurel, Oak leaves, or reeds.

The ovolo is a quarter ellipse (Greek) or quarter round (Roman) profile, most often carved with egg and dart design, but many other possibilities make it a very popular molding.

The cyma recta is a double curved molding with the concave curve on the outside of the molding, pointing toward the viewer as if reaching, outward. The cyma reversa is the opposite, the convexity nearer the viewer and seems to support or bolster the element to which it is attached. Both profiles are often carved with foliage, generically termed acanthus leaf. Both of these profiles as well as the ovolo often have the curved portion separated from the fillet by deep valleys or quirks.

Medieval moldings were often made of a number of closely placed profiles, often with deep hollows and repeated rounds.

Romanesque architecture continued many of the same principles of classical architecture, though much of the decoration; such as column capitals became more idiosyncratic and depicted the profusion of natural foliage. The innovation of the pointed arch (loosely called the Gothic arch), ubiquitous in Gothic architecture, allowed buildings to soar to great heights and to redistribute weight. This allowed larger windows and the lacy stone work termed tracery. The designs of this tracery are geometrically derived from, for the most part, overlapping and intersecting circles. The circular voids are called foils and the pointed intersections cusps; thus a three lobbed design is a trefoil, while one of four is a quatrefoil, one of five is a cinquefoil. Tracery was found incorporated into the woodwork of choir stalls, paneling and memorial structures.

# DESIGN IDEAS

## architectural ornamentation

### TERMINOLOGY (continued)

Much decoration was derived from nature in depictions of vines and animals. Of course, religious figures and symbols were also a primary motif. Foliage climbing the edges of pinnacles and spires consists of the leaves, called crockets, and the terminating leaves, a finial or (especially on pew ends) poppyhead. Moldings were made of multiple profiles and combined with running vines and crestings, or stylized leaves. Square flowers and ballflowers were often spaced along moldings. At intersections of the ribbed vaults were bosses, which depict foliage (like a rosette), figures, or heraldic devises. A selected partially illustrated glossary related to ornament and architecture follows.

### HISTORIC WOODWORK GLOSSARY

**abacus** - The uppermost member of the capital of a column; often a plain square slab, but sometimes moulded or carved. The plate or bearing surface at the top of a column upon which the architrave rests.

**acanthus** - An indigenous plant of the Mediterranean area depicted on the Corinthian capital and used as a decorative motif on many objects throughout history. Today nearly a generic term for any multi leafleted foliage.

**angle bead** - A vertical molding that protects or decorates the projecting angle of a wall or partition.

**arch** - A curved construction which spans an opening; usually consists of wedge shaped blocks called voussoirs and a keystone, or a curved or pointed structural member which is supported at the sides or ends (often contrasted to trabeated construction of post and lintel).

**architrave** -
- In the classical orders, the lowest members of the entablature; the beam that spans from column to column, resting directly on their capitals.
- The ornamental moldings around the faces of the jambs and lintel of a doorway or other opening.

**archivolt** - The face molding of an arch (the architrave of an arch).

**astragal** - A bead, usually half round, with a fillet on one or both sides. It may be plain, but the term is more correctly used to describe the classical molding decorated with a string of beads or bead and reel shapes. A small molding of half round section, often carved with beads; often referred to as a bead by furniture makers.

**baguette** - A simple, narrow, convex molding.

**bead** -
- A bead molding.
- A narrow wood strip, moulded on one edge, against which a door or window sash closes; a stop bead.
- A pearl shaped carved decoration on moldings or other ornaments, usually in a series, or in conjunction with other shapes; a beading.

**bead and reel** - A semi-round convex molding carved with a pattern of disks alternating with round or elongated beads.

Figure: DE-016

**belt and base courses** - Horizontal flat members, either decorative or protective, on the exterior of a building. Typically, a belt course is approximately mid range in height and a base course is at the bottom of the siding.

**bolection molding** - A molding which covers the joint between panel and stile and projects above the surface of stile; a molding applied to a flat ground.

**boss** -
- A projecting, usually richly carved ornament, decorative rosette, portrait, heraldic devise or similar motif, placed at the intersection of ribs, groins, beams, etc., or at the termination of a molding.
- In masonry, a roughly shaped stone set to project for carving in place.

**bracket** - A general term for an element projecting from a wall or other surface to support another element such as a beam or cornice.

**brattishing** - An ornamental crest along the top of a cornice or screen, often carved with leaves and flowers.

**bead and reel** - A molding with a profile of half a circle or more, in which beads form alternate design forms seen edge on.

**billet** - A molding made of several bands of raised cylinders or rectangular segments.

**bolection molding** - A molding which projects beyond the face of a panel or frame usually found in paneling, doors and fireplaces, especially when the meeting surfaces are at different levels.

**cable molding** - Carved spirally to resemble a rope or cable.

**capital** - The topmost member, usually decorated, of a column or pilaster, etc., it provides a larger bearing surface for the architrave; different in appearance according to the order of the building.

**cavetto** - A cove; a molding profile whose arc is a segment of a circle, (unlike scotia whose profile has two centers).

**cinquefoil** - A five lobed pattern divided by cusps; in Gothic tracery a geometric design with five round open areas.

**column** -
- In structures, a relatively long, slender structural compression member such as a post, pillar, or strut; usually vertical, supporting a load which acts in (or near) the direction of its longitudinal axis.
- In classical architecture, a cylindrical support of the entablature, consisting of a base (except Greek Doric), shaft, and capital.

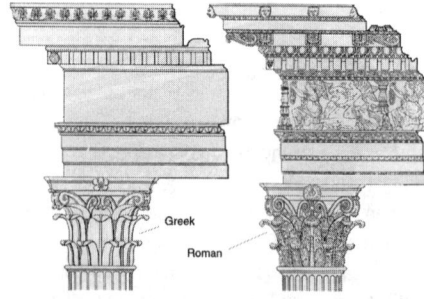

*The Classical Orders of Architecture*, Second Edition, Robert Chitham, © 1985, 2005, Architectural Press. Reproduced by permission of Taylor & Francis Books UK.
Figure: DE-017

**console** - A scrolled bracket used to support an architectural element such as a cornice, entablature over a door, mantel shelf or in furniture, a table top.

# DESIGN IDEAS

## architectural ornamentation

**corbel** - A projection from a wall which supports a beam, arch or vault ribbing.

**Corinthian order** - One of the Greek orders characterized by slender proportions; the column shaft is fluted, with a capital depicting acanthus leaves and scrolled sprouts (caulicoli) and with an entablature with dentil course and medallions under the soffit. Roman adaptations often highly decorated.

**Cornice** -
- A moulded projection which crowns or finishes the parts to which it is affixed.
- The third or uppermost division of an entablature, resting on the frieze consisting of corona and cymatium.
- An ornamental molding, usually of wood or plaster, running round the walls of a room just below the ceiling; a crown molding; the molding forming the top member of a door or a window frame.

**corona** - The overhanging vertical member of a cornice.

**crockets** - Regularly spaced leaves projecting along the gable of a Gothic arch, spire, or pinnacle. Sometimes as terminations of the interior cusps of an arch or trefoil, quarterfoil, etc.

**cusp** - In Gothic tracery, the intersection or termination of arcs which define foliations or spaces.

**cyma molding** - Has an S shaped profile.

**cyma recta** - A molding with an S curve section; orientation is with concave curve foremost toward viewer. Example is cymatium of cornice; opposite of cyma reversa.

**cyma reversa** - A molding with a S curve section; orientation is with convex curve foremost toward viewer. Example is panel (bolection) molding.

**cymatium** - The top molding of the cornice; usually a cym profile, but can be an ovolo or (rarely) a cavetto.

**dart** - A conventionalized arrowhead shape, often alternating with egg or other forms in moldings.

**dentil** - One of a band or small, square, tooth like blocks forming part of the characteristic ornamentation of the Ionic, Corinthian, and Composite orders.

**dentil molding** - Composed of a series of small rectangular blocks.

**doric order** - One of the Greek orders; the sturdiest order with stout proportions; the column has no base, is fluted and has a relatively simple flaring capital; the frieze of the entablature is divided into triglyphs and metopes. Example is the Parthenon.

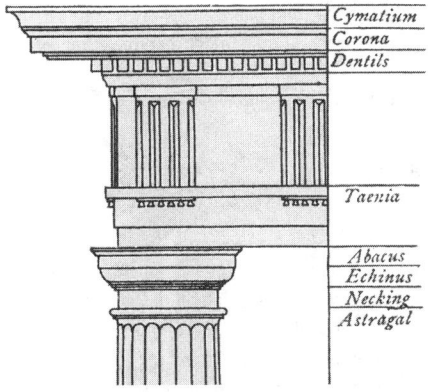

*The Classical Orders of Architecture*, Second Edition, Robert Chitham, © 1985, 2005, Architectural Press. Reproduced by permission of Taylor & Francis Books UK.
Figure: DE-018

**dovetail molding** - Carved with interlocked triangles.

**echinus** - The bulging or flaring of a capital; of elliptical section as in the Doric order, often an ovolo molding.

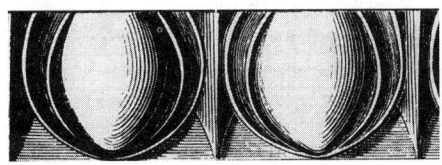

*The Classical Orders of Architecture*, Second Edition, Robert Chitham, © 1985, 2005, Architectural Press. Reproduced by permission of Taylor & Francis Books UK.
Figure: DE-019

**egg and anchor molding** - Composed of alternating oval and anchor like shapes.

**egg and dart molding** - Composed of alternating egg and arrowhead shapes.

**egg and tongue molding** - Composed of alternating egg and pointed elements

**entablature** - In classical architecture, the elaborated beam member carried by the columns, horizontally divided into architrave (below), frieze, and cornice (above).

**entasis** - The intentional slight convex curving of the vertical profile of a tapered column used to overcome the optical illusion of concavity that characterized straight sided columns.

**fillet** - A molding consisting of a narrow flat band, often square in section; the term is loosely applied to rectangular molding used to visually separate molding profiles.

**finial** - An ornament which terminates the point of a spire, pinnacle, etc., often turned or carved (downward pointing decorations are called drops).

**foil** - In tracery, any of several lobes, circular or nearly so, tangent to the inner side of a larger arc, as of an arch, and meeting each other in points, called cusps, projecting inward from the arch, or circle. Five foils make a cinquefoil.

**frieze** -
- The middle horizontal member of a classical entablature, above the architrave and below the cornice.
- A similar decorative band near the top of an interior wall below the cornice.
- A broad horizontal band near the top of the wall or element (such as a mantelpiece).

**fret** - An essentially two dimensional geometric design consisting of shallow bands; example is Greek key.

**fretwork** - A repeated, symmetrical, interlaced design of small bars.

**gadroon** - Elongated bulbous shapes in series, as on decorative urns and turnings; a molding of repeated tear drop shaped elements, often on a thumbnail profile.

# DESIGN IDEAS

# architectural ornamentation

## HISTORIC WOODWORK GLOSSARY
(continued)

**gothic arch** - A loose term denoting a pointed arch consisting of two (or more centers) as opposed to Roman or Romanesque arch which is semicircular.

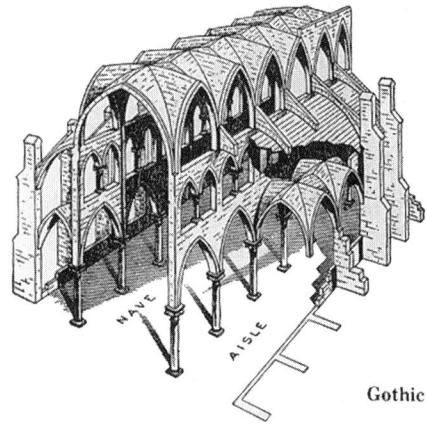

Figure: DE-020

**groin** - The ridge, edge, or curved line formed by the intersection of the surfaces of two intersecting vaults.

**guilloche** - Shallow design of overlapping circles, sometimes in filled with rosettes.

**inlay** - A surface decoration composed of small pieces of contrasting woods or other materials set flush with a wood surface.

**intarsia:** A surface decoration of wood consisting of solid wood inlays or projections in various colors (see marquetry).

**Ionic order** - The classical order originated by the Ionian Greeks, characterized by its capital with large volutes, a fasciated entablature, continuous frieze, usually dentils in the cornice, and by its elegant detailing.

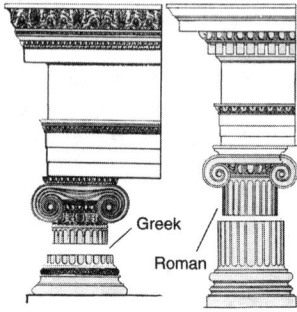

*The Classical Orders of Architecture*, Second Edition, Robert Chitham, © 1985, 2005, Architectural Press. Reproduced by permission of Taylor & Francis Books UK.

Figure: DE-021

**leaf and dart molding** - Composed of alternating leaf like and arrowhead shapes.

**lininfold** - A carved wood surface that may give a three dimensional affect similar to folded fabric.

**marquetry** - An inlaid mosaic pattern or picture made of various multicolored veneers, sometimes interspersed with other materials, such as mother of pearl.

**metopes** - The panel between the triglyphs in the Doric frieze, often carved.

**modillions** - A horizontal bracket or console, usually in the form of a scroll with acanthus, supporting the corona under a cornice.

**mutule** - A sloping flat block on the soffit of the Doric cornice

**order** -
- An arrangement of columns with an entablature.
- In classical architecture, a particular style of column with its entablature, having standardized details. The Greek orders were the Doric, Ionic, and Corinthian; the Romans added the Tuscan and Composite orders.

**ovolo** - A convex molding, less than a semicircle in profile; usually a quarter of a circle or approximately a quarter ellipse in profile, often decorated with egg and dart design.

**pediment** -
- In classical architecture, the triangular gable end of the roof above the horizontal cornice, often filled with sculpture.
- In later work, a surface used ornamentally over doors or windows; usually triangular but may be curved.

*The Classical Orders of Architecture*, Second Edition, Robert Chitham, © 1985, 2005, Architectural Press. Reproduced by permission of Taylor & Francis Books UK.

Figure: DE-022

**pearl molding** - Carved to imitate a string of pearls.

**pellet molding** - Carved in a series of discs, with the flat surfaces facing the viewer.

**pilaster** - An engaged pier or pillar, often with capital and base.

**poppyhead** - A carved foliage ornament generally used for the finials of pew ends and similar pieces of church furniture.

**plinth** -
- A square or rectangular base for column, pilaster, or door framing.
- A solid monumental base, often ornamented with moldings, etc.

**quatrefoil** - A four lobed pattern divided by cusps.

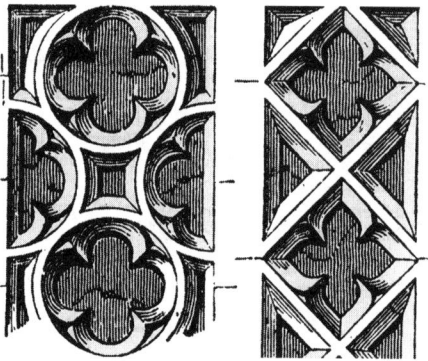

Figure: DE-023

**quirk** - An indentation separating one element from another, as between moldings; a valley between fillet and profile of a molding; between abacus and echinus of Doric capital.

**reed, reeding** - A molding made of closely spaced, parallel, half round convex profiles.

**reglet** - Defines a flat, narrow molding, used chiefly to separate the parts or members of compartments or panels from one another.

**rope molding** - Carved to imitate the twisted strands of cordage.

**roundel** - One of the series of elements in a bead molding.

# DESIGN IDEAS

## architectural ornamentation

**Romanesque** - The style emerging in Western Europe in the early 11th century, characterized by massive articulated wall structures, round arches, and powerful vaults, and lasting until the advent of Gothic architecture in the middle of the 12th century.

*Figure: DE-024*

**rosette -**
- A round pattern with a carved or painted conventionalized floral and/or foliage design where petals/leaves radiate from center.
- A circular or oval decorative wood plaque used in joinery, such as one applied to a wall to receive the end of a stair rail.

**scotia** - A deep concave molding defined by two varying arcs, especially one at the base of a column in Classical architecture.

**shaft** - The portion of a column or pilaster between the base and the capital.

**soffit** - The exposed undersurface of an overhead component of a building, such as an arch, balcony, beam, cornice, lintel, etc.

**stylobate** - The floor of classical temple; top step of crepidoma.

**torus, tori** - A bold projecting molding, convex in shape, generally forming the lowest member of a base over the plinth.

**trabeated -**
- Descriptive of construction using beams or lintels, following the principle of post and lintel construction, as distinguished from construction using arches and vaults.
- Furnished with an entablature.

**tracery** - The pierced designs of window mullions in the Medieval period consisting of geometrically derived curving shapes; the same designs on furniture panels, walls and the decorative arts.

**trefoil** - A three lobed pattern divided by cusps.

**treenail** - A hardwood pin, peg, or spike used to fasten beams and planking, usually made of dry compressed lumber so that it will expand when moistened; sometimes pronounced and spelled "trunnel."

**triglyph** - The characteristic ornament of the Doric frieze, consisting of slightly raised blocks of three vertical bands separated by V shaped grooves. The triglyphs alternate with plain or sculptured panels called metopes.

**Tuscan order** - A simplified version of the Roman Doric order, having a plain frieze and no mutules in the cornice.

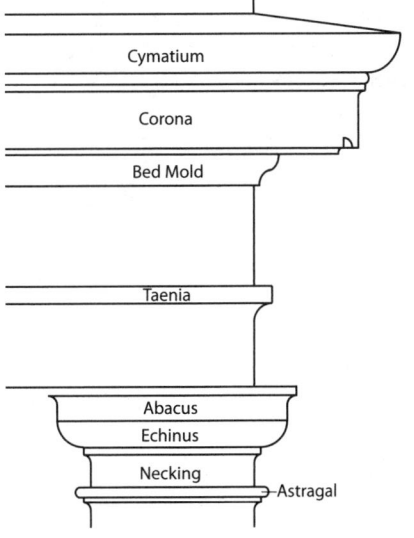

*The Classical Orders of Architecture*, Second Edition, Robert Chitham, © 1985, 2005, Architectural Press. Reproduced by permission of Taylor & Francis Books UK.

*Figure: DE-025*

**verge board** - An exposed member attached along the rake of a gable end roof open cornice; also implies the larger rake member of an exterior cornice; sometimes referred to as a "barge board".

**Volutes -**
- A spiral scroll, as on Ionic, Corinthian, or Composite capitals, etc.
- A stair crook having an easement with a spiral section of stair rail.

**voussoir** - A wedge shaped masonry unit in an arch or vault whose converging sides are cut as radii of one of the centers of the arch or vault.

Tracery with Trefoils

*Figure: DE-026*

# DESIGN IDEAS

## architectural ornamentation

**CLASSICAL ORDERS**

The orders of architecture refer to the configurations and relationship of parts of Greek and Roman buildings. (See illustrations on the following pages.) Over the centuries, the relationship of parts of the classical building have been systematized, but one should keep in mind that Greek and Roman architecture had many variations and evolved through time. Generally, the orders refer to the proportions of the building; some being squarish or heavy, while others are taller and therefore lighter. The trabeated or post and lintel system of building consists of columns and a superstructure supporting the roof. This entablature is made up of the architrave, the frieze and the cornice. The architrave is the beam, which spans from column to column. The frieze is derived from the band covering the joist ends, while the cornice creates the eaves. The columns have base moldings (except the Doric order) a shaft, plain or fluted, and a capital, which supports the architrave. Because the capitals are very different in appearance for each order it is an easy way to distinguish among them. Because the roof line ran the length of the building the triangular area above the entablature is called the pediment.

**Three Greek orders:**

- The Doric column has no base but rests directly on the stylobate or floor, of the building, is fluted and has a simple turned bowl-like capital. The bulging shape is the echinus. The frieze of the Doric is divided into triglyphs and metopes; the latter often decorated with sculptural figures (as on the Parthenon). This order appears sturdy and well planted, having a horizontal appearance.

- The Ionic order has a column which has several rounds of base moldings, usually consisting of two tori or half-round moldings, divided by a scotia or concave recess, a shaft which is fluted and a capital with distinctive scrolls or volutes. The frieze is relatively plain, or contains sculptural figures in an uninterrupted procession. Above the frieze is the characteristic dentil molding.

- The Corinthian order proportionally is similar to the Ionic though some examples have very slender proportions. The column is similar, but the capital has acanthus leaves, and volutes spring like sprouts from the foliage. The entablature is similar to the Ionic, but the use of medallions or brackets in the eaves (separating rosettes in the soffit) sets this order apart.

**Two Roman orders:**

- The Tuscan column is derived from native antecedents and is a relatively plain style with unfluted columns, simply echinus capital and entablature like the Ionic without the dentil course.

- The Composite column has a capital, which is an amalgamation of the Ionic volutes, and the Corinthian acanthus leaves. The entablature is similar to the Corinthian. The Romans introduced several building innovations, but the use of the arch (the arcuated system), and therefore vaults and domes, changed architecture immeasurably.

The columns of the classical orders of Greek and Roman architecture are often adapted for modern construction. These orders are Tuscan, Doric, Ionic, Corinthian, and Composite. The following composite figures names the basic features of a classical order and gives some of the proportions of the column in relation to the shaft diameter as a basic unit of measurement. Pilasters are rectangular in plan, without taper from top to bottom. If used structurally they are usually referred to as piers, but are treated architecturally as columns. The typical pilaster extends a third or less of its width from the wall surface behind it.

# DESIGN IDEAS

## architectural ornamentation

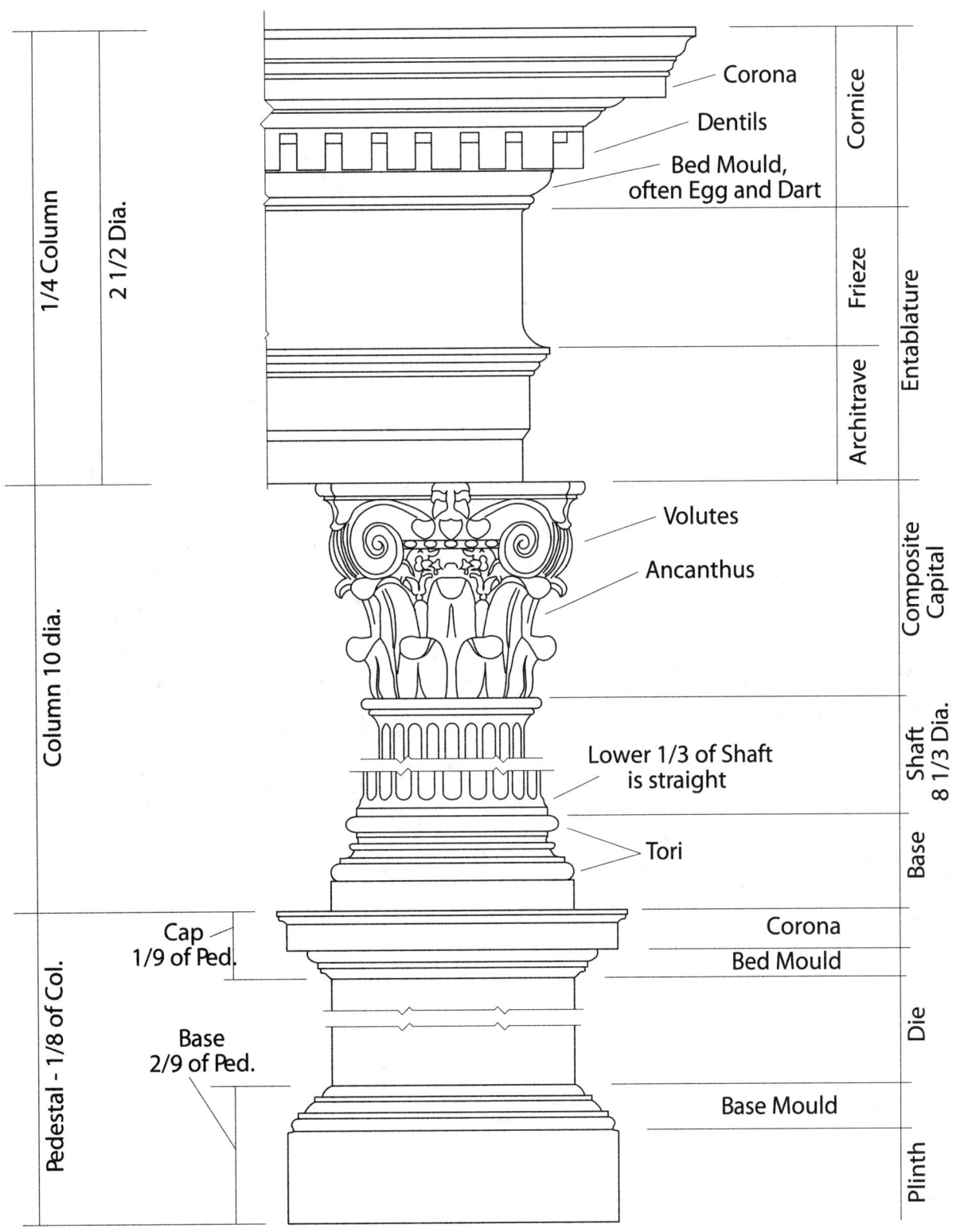

Figure: DE-027

# DESIGN IDEAS

## architectural ornamentation

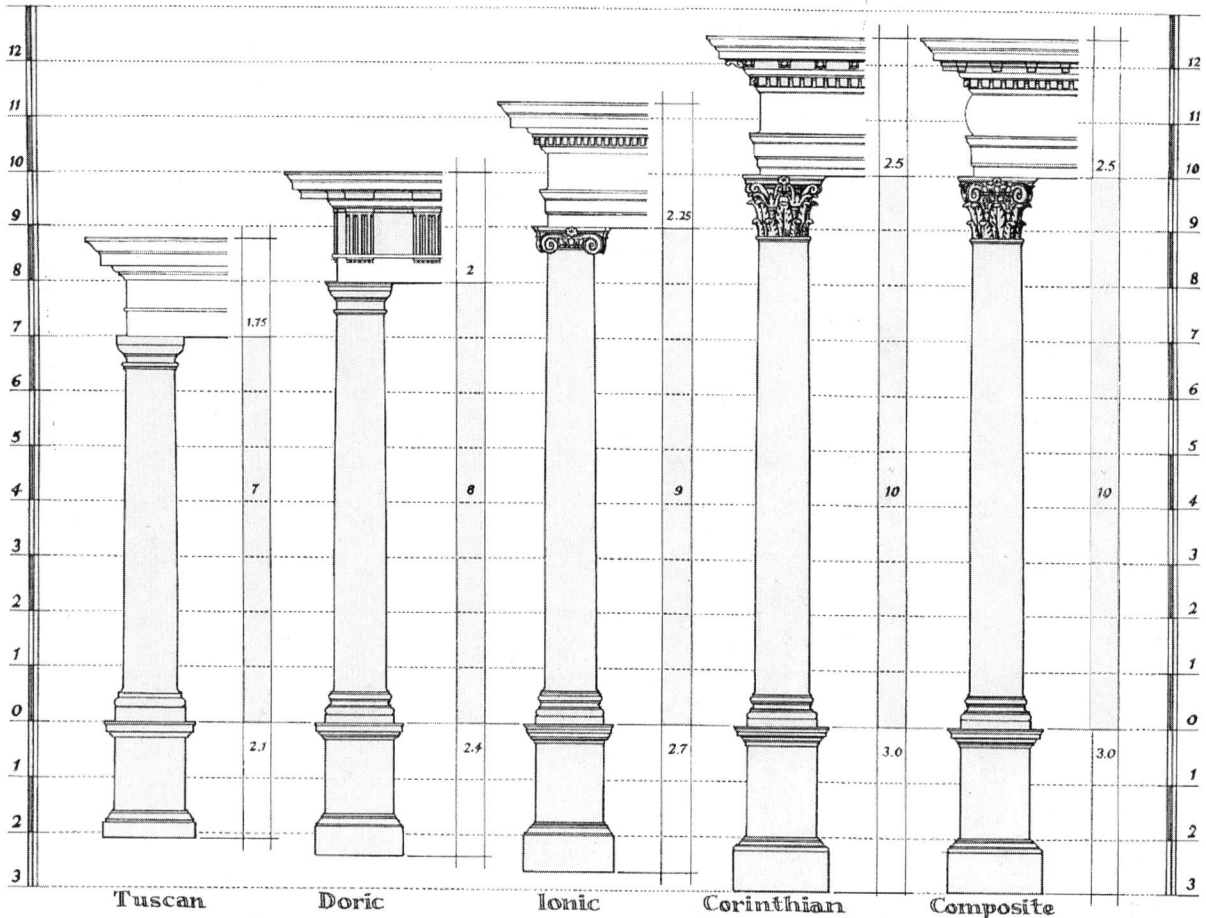

The Five Orders - *The Classical Orders of Architecture*, Second Edition, Robert Chitham, © 1985, 2005, Architectural Press. Reproduced by permission of Taylor & Francis Books UK

Figure: DE-028

# DESIGN IDEAS

## architectural ornamentation

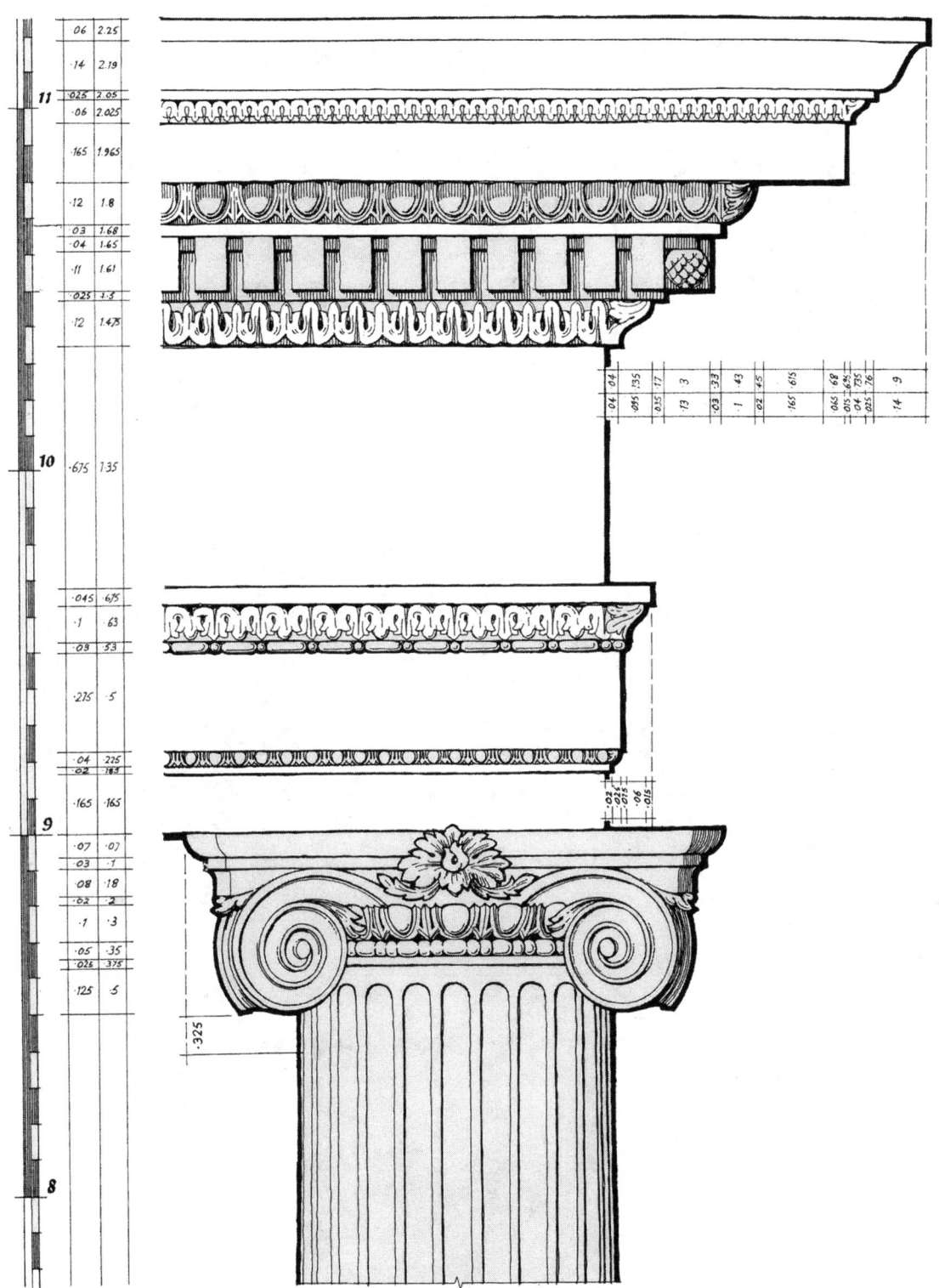

The Ionic Capital and Entablature - *The Classical Orders of Architecture*, Second Edition, Robert Chitham, © 1985, 2005, Architectural Press. Reproduced by permission of Taylor & Francis Books UK.

Figure: DE-029

# DESIGN IDEAS

## architectural ornamentation

Elevation
.475 to centre of eye
.675 over volute
.525 over abacus

Half Plan

End Elevation

Ionic Capital detail - *The Classical Orders of Architecture*, Second Edition, Robert Chitham, © 1985, 2005, Architectural Press. Reproduced by permission of Taylor & Francis Books UK.

Figure: DE-030

# DESIGN IDEAS

## architectural ornamentation

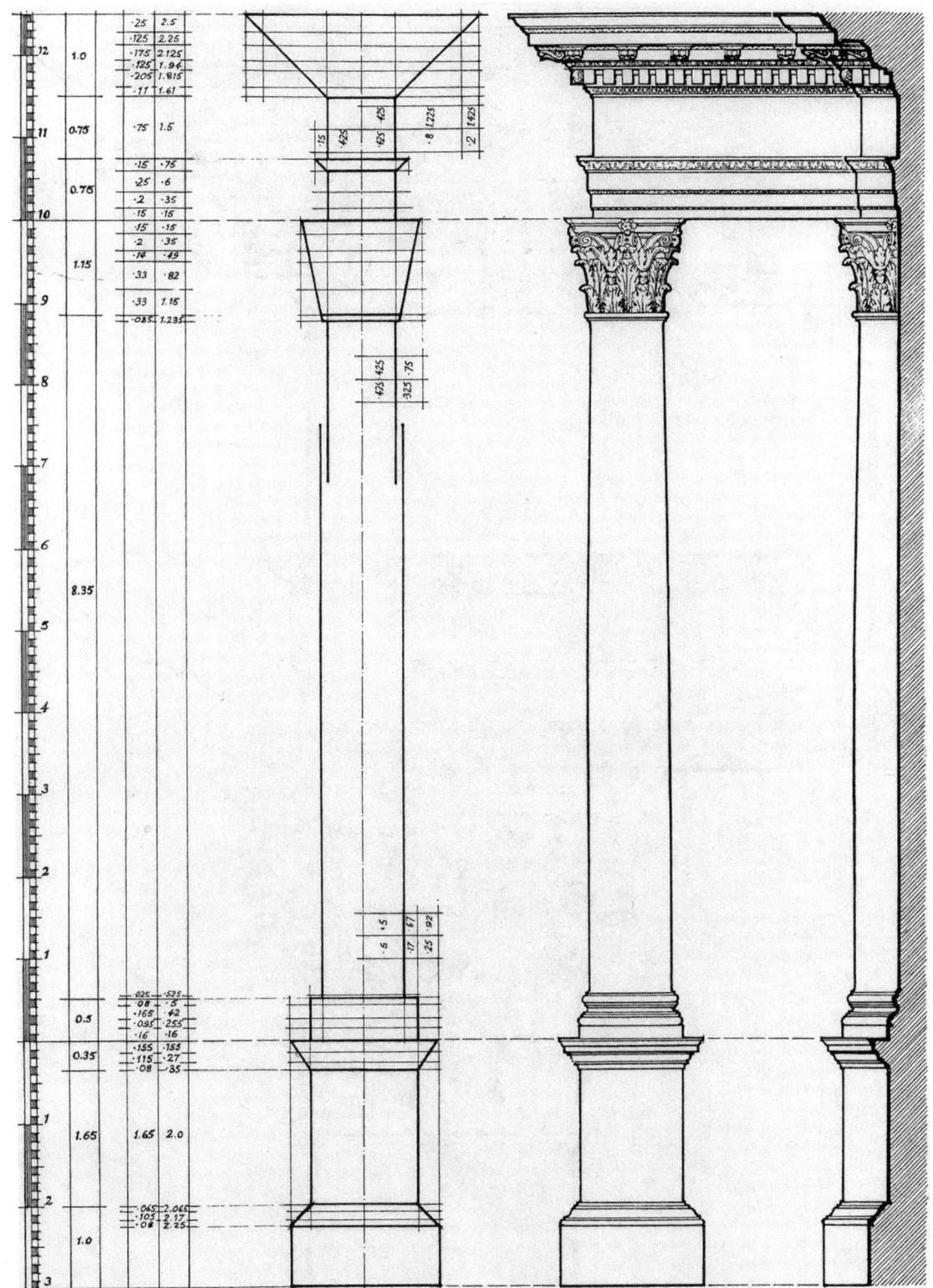

Corinthian Order proportions - *The Classical Orders of Architecture*, Second Edition, Robert Chitham, © 1985, 2005, Architectural Press. Reproduced by permission of Taylor & Francis Books UK.

Figure: DE-031

# DESIGN IDEAS

## architectural ornamentation

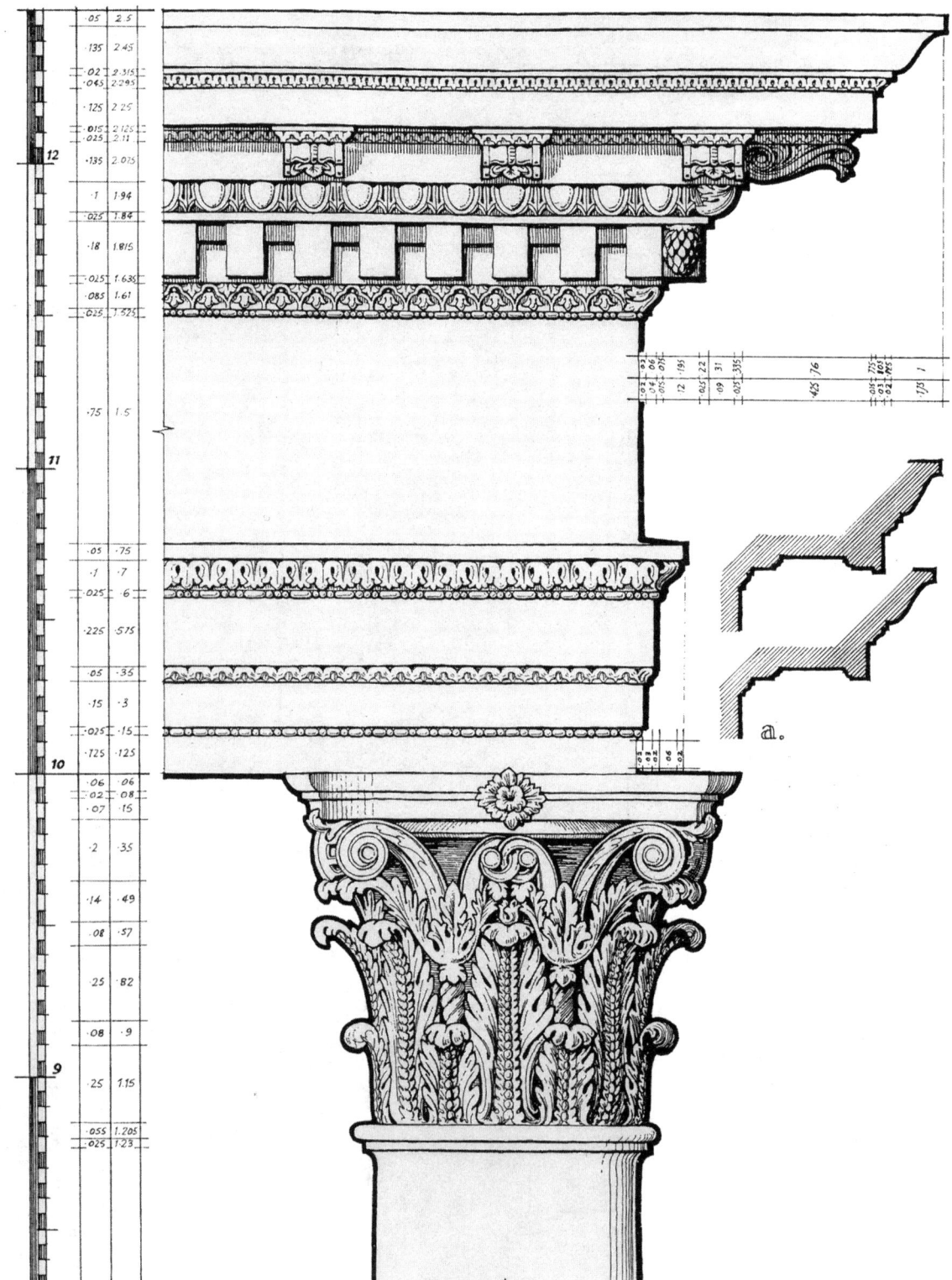

Ionic Capital detail - *The Classical Orders of Architecture*, Second Edition, Robert Chitham, © 1985, 2005, Architectural Press. Reproduced by permission of Taylor & Francis Books UK.

Figure: DE-032

# DESIGN IDEAS

## architectural ornamentation

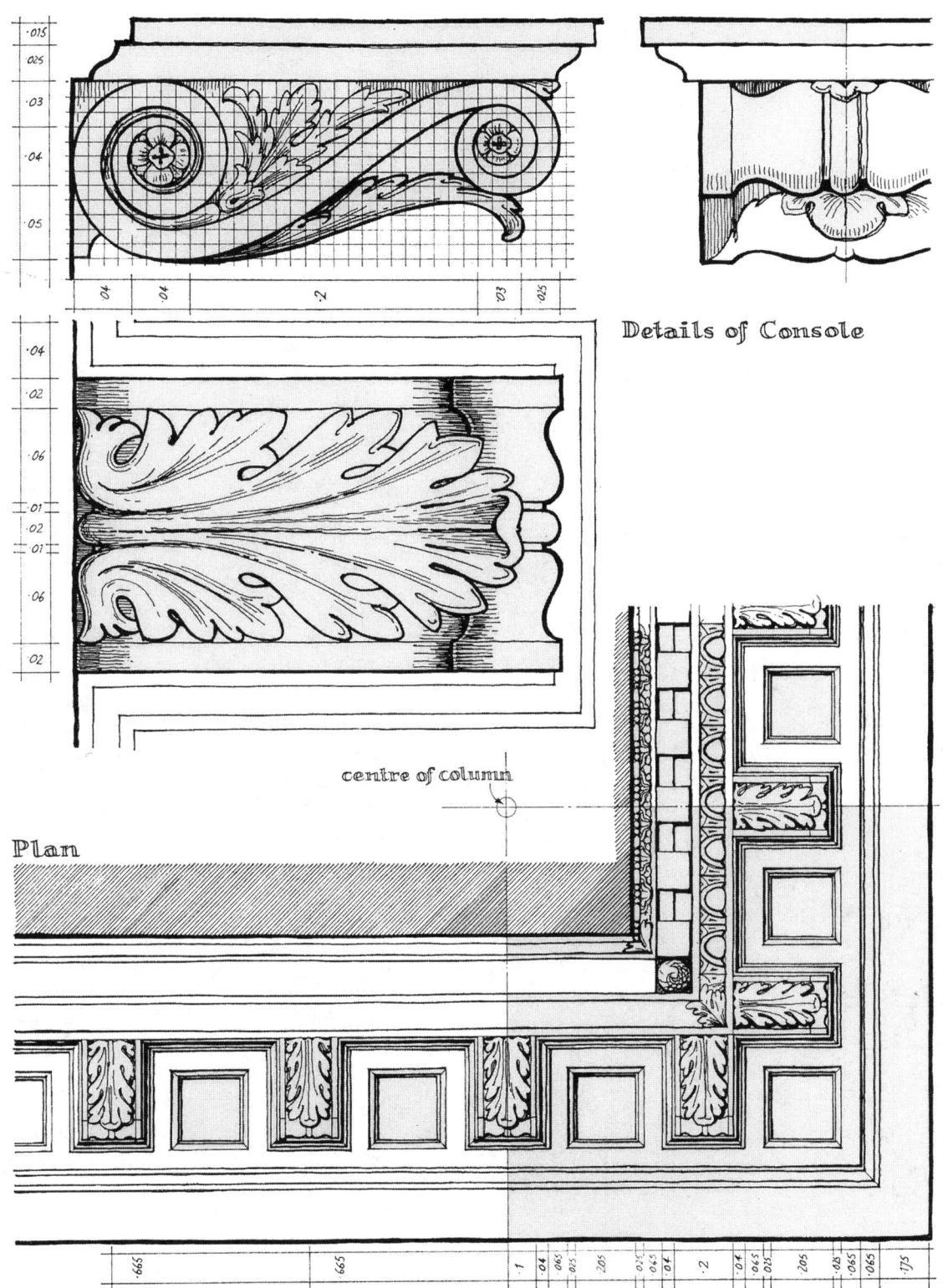

Details of Console

Plan

centre of column

Corinthian Entablature detail - *The Classical Orders of Architecture*, Second Edition, Robert Chitham, © 1985, 2005, Architectural Press. Reproduced by permission of Taylor & Francis Books UK.

Figure: DE-033

# DESIGN IDEAS

## stile & rail doors design examples

Figure: DE-034

# DESIGN IDEAS

## stile & rail doors design examples

Figure:DE-035

# DESIGN IDEAS

## stile & rail doors design examples

*Figure: DE-036*

# DESIGN IDEAS

## stile & rail doors design examples

Figure: DE-037

# DESIGN IDEAS

## casework design examples

**Schools and Libraries**

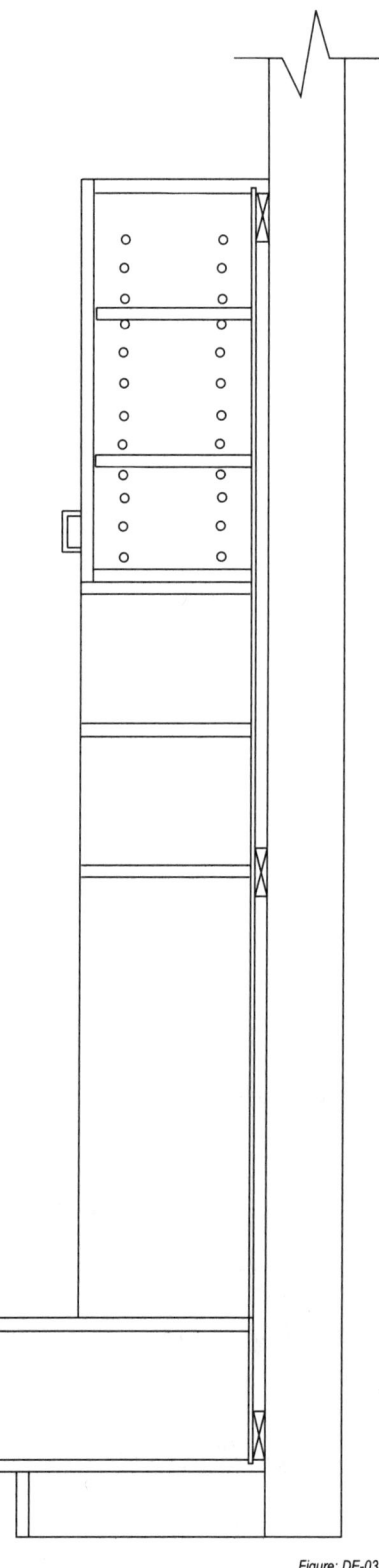

Figure: DE-038

# DESIGN IDEAS

## casework design examples

### Schools and Libraries

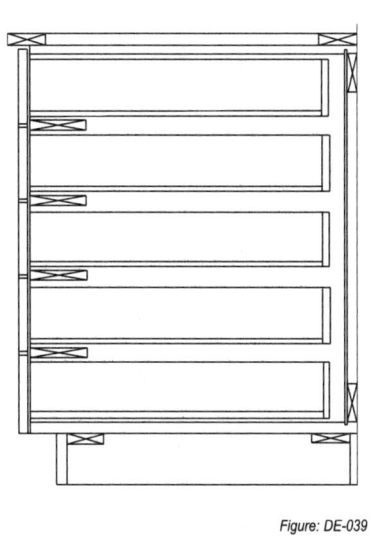

Figure: DE-039

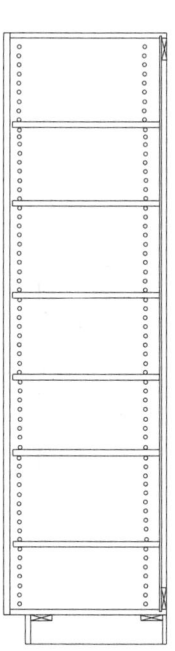

Figure: DE-041

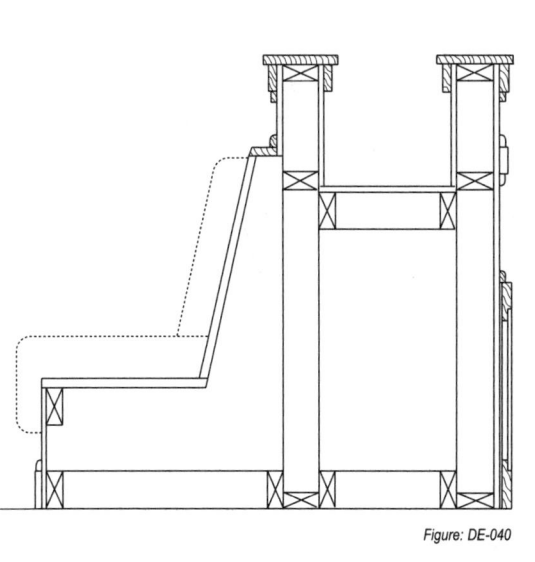

Figure: DE-040

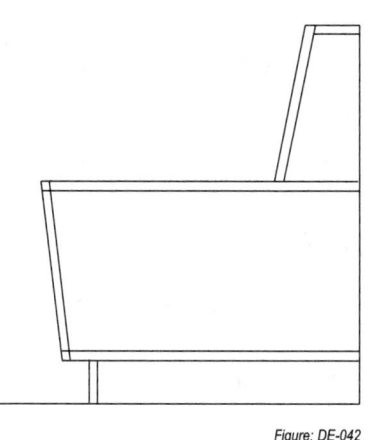

Figure: DE-042

# DESIGN IDEAS

## casework design examples

**Schools and Libraries**

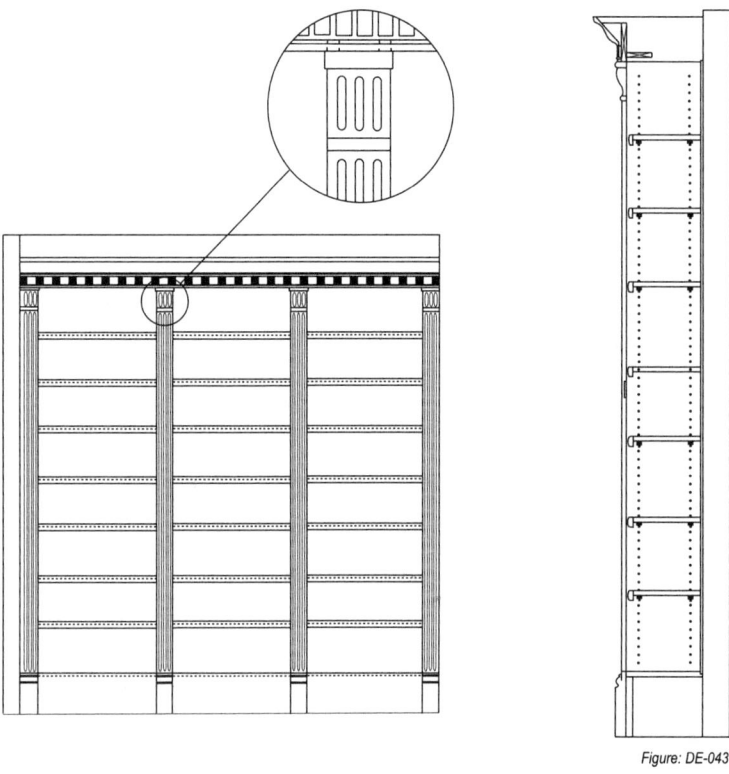

Figure: DE-043

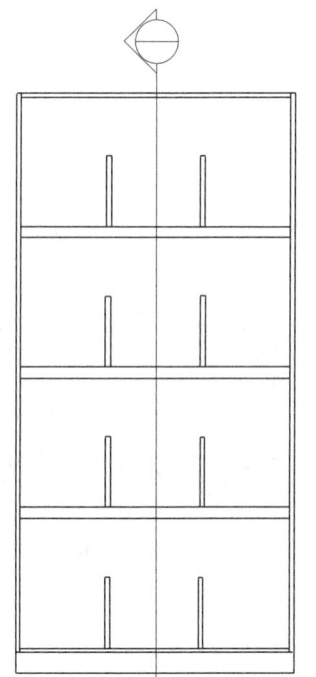 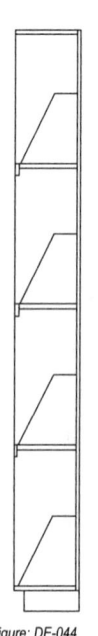

Figure: DE-044

# DESIGN IDEAS

## casework design examples

### Schools and Libraries

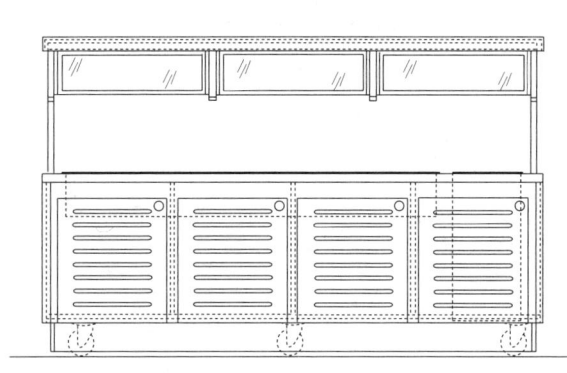

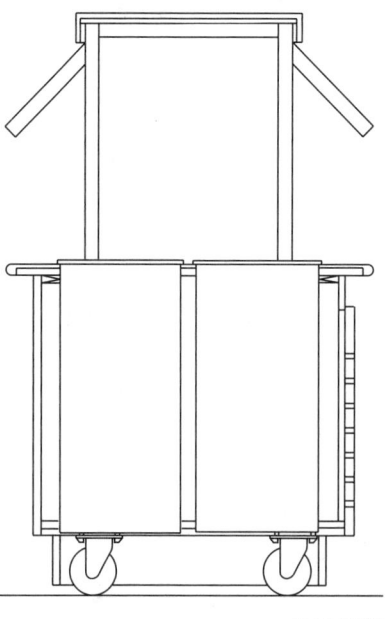

Figure: DE-045

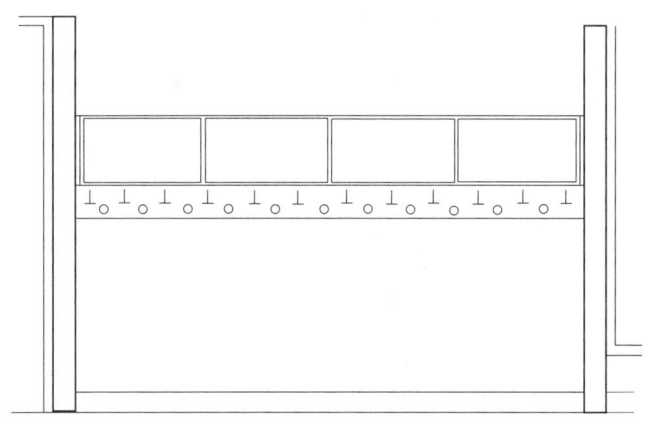

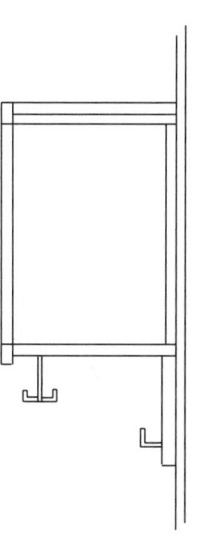

Figure: DE-046

# DESIGN IDEAS

## casework design examples

### Banks and Courts

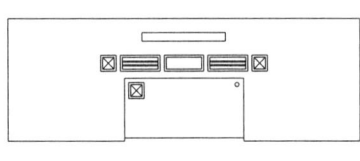

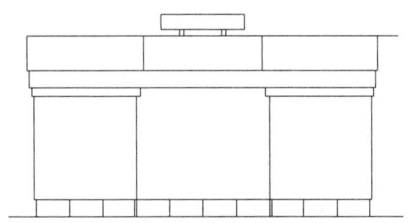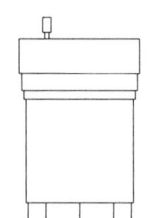

*Figure: DE-047*

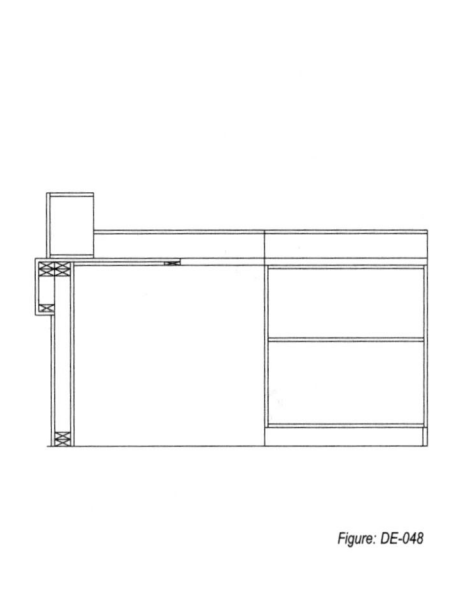

*Figure: DE-048*

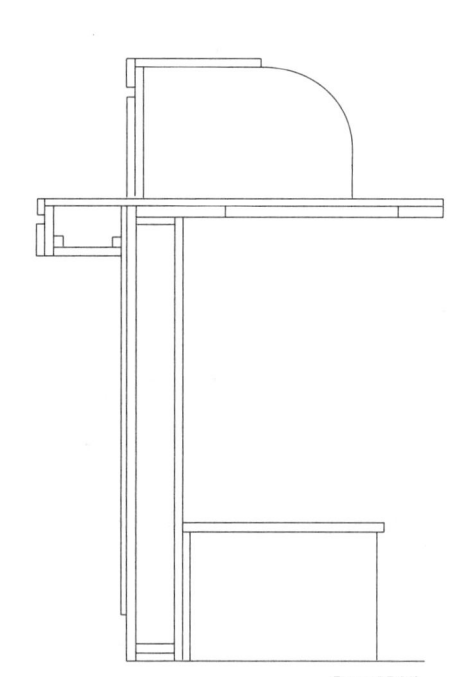

*Figure: DE-049*

# DESIGN IDEAS

## casework design examples

### Banks and Courts

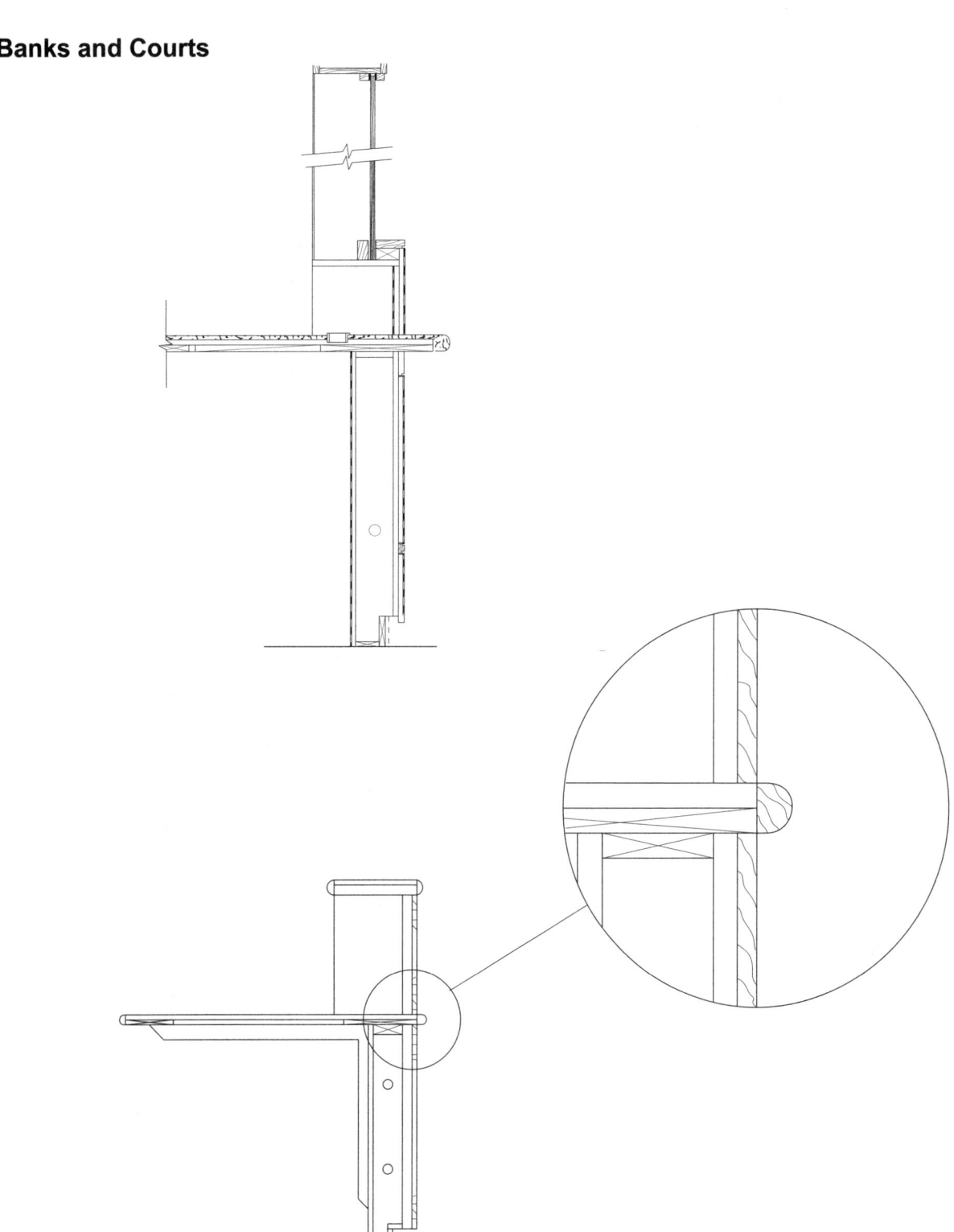

Figure: DE-050

# DESIGN IDEAS

## casework design examples

**Banks and Courts**

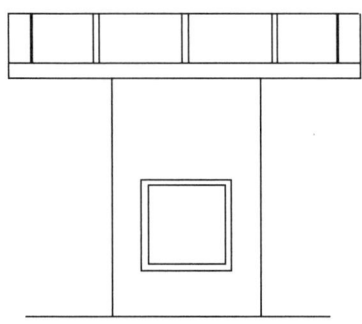

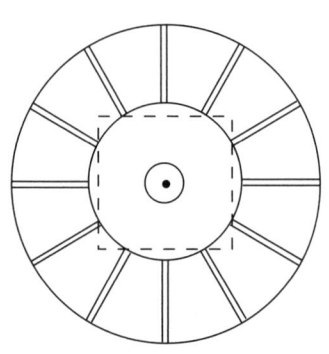

*Figure: DE-051*

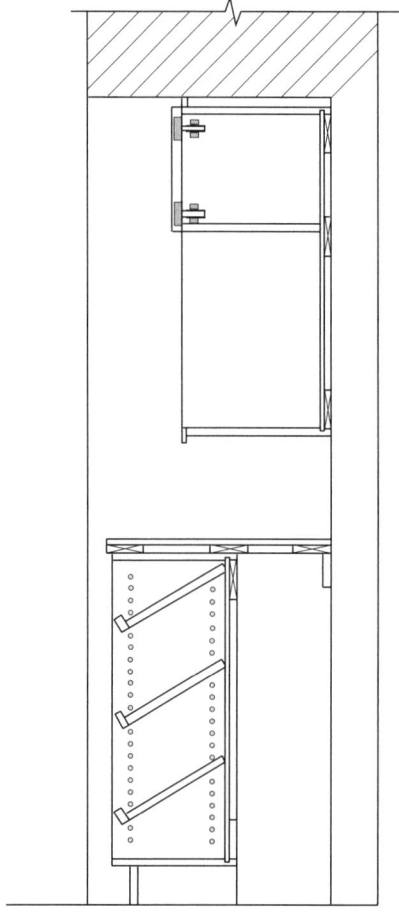

*Figure: DE-052*

# DESIGN IDEAS

## casework design examples

### Judge's Bench

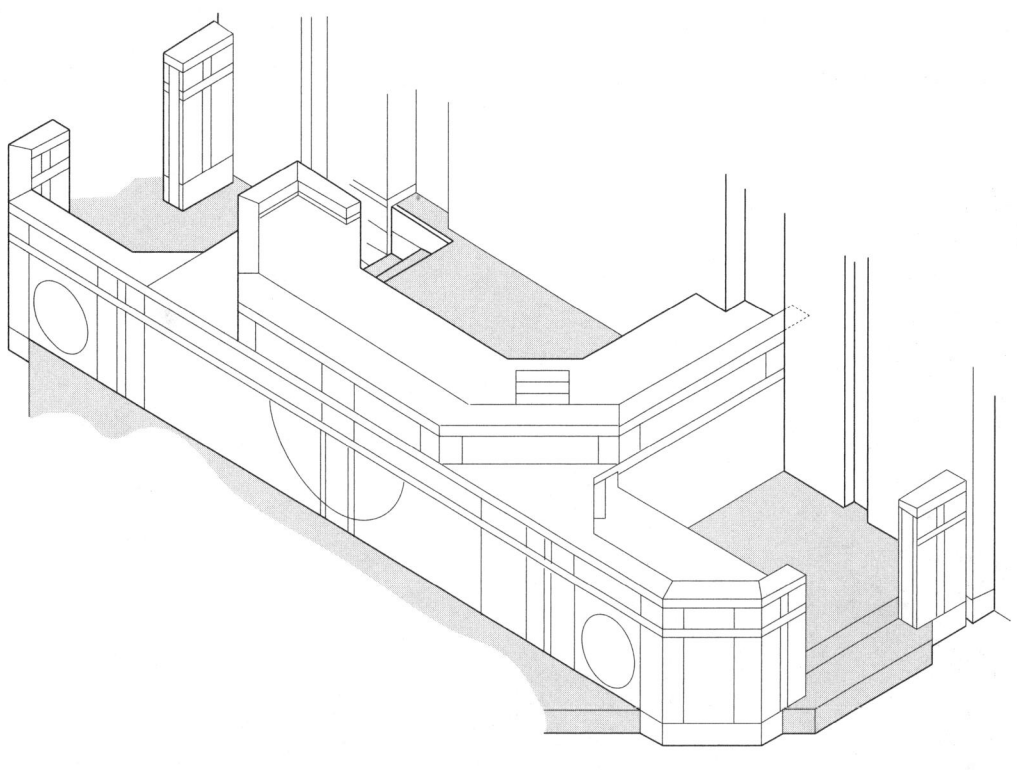

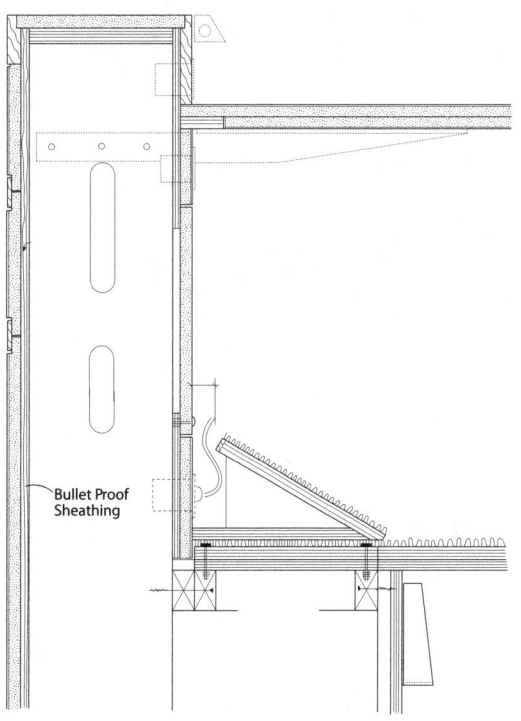

Bullet Proof Sheathing

Figure: DE-053

# DESIGN IDEAS

## casework design examples

**Corporate Woodwork**

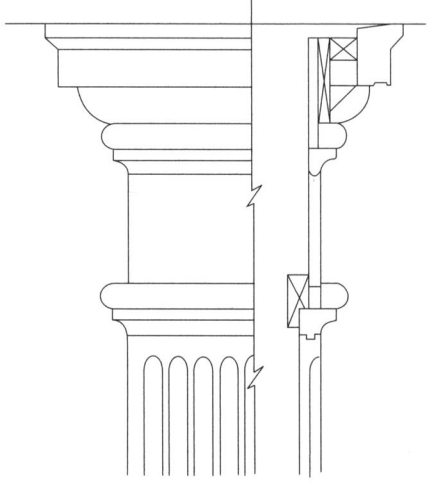

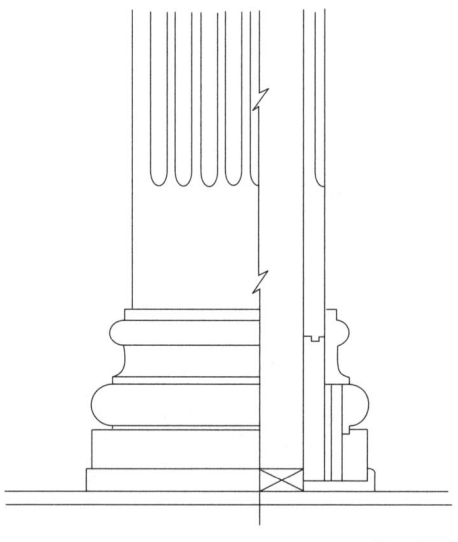

*Figure: DE-054*

# DESIGN IDEAS

## casework design examples

**Corporate Woodwork**

Figure: DE-055

Figure: DE-056

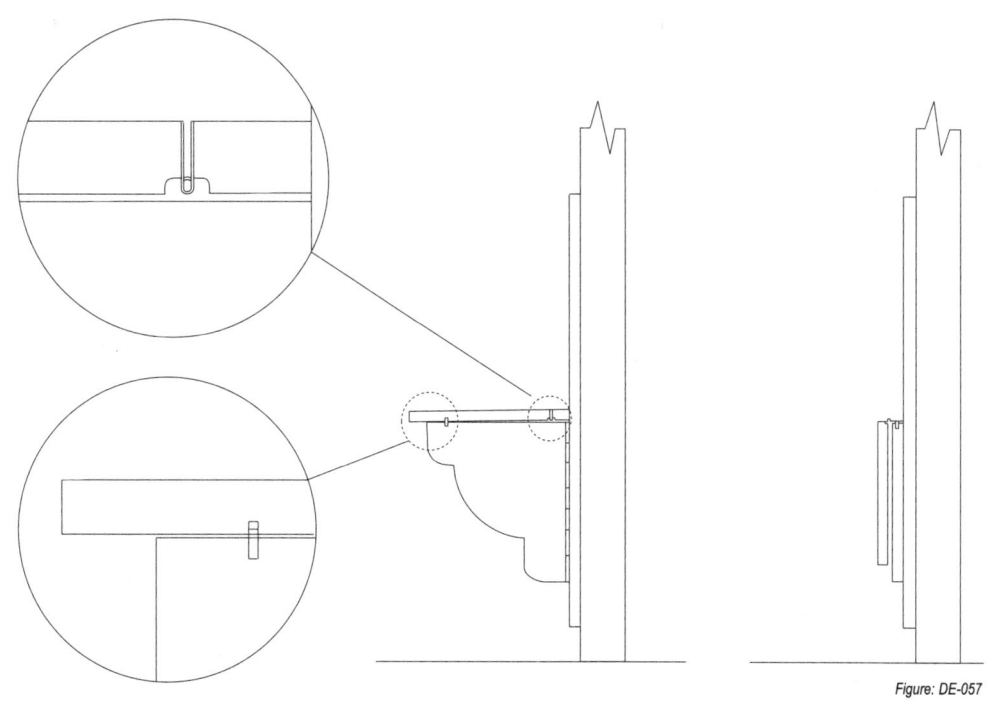

Figure: DE-057

# DESIGN IDEAS

## casework design examples

### Corporate Woodwork

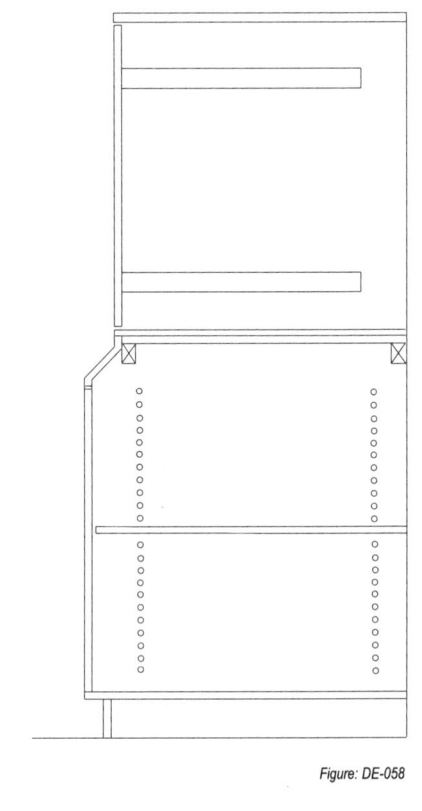

Figure: DE-058

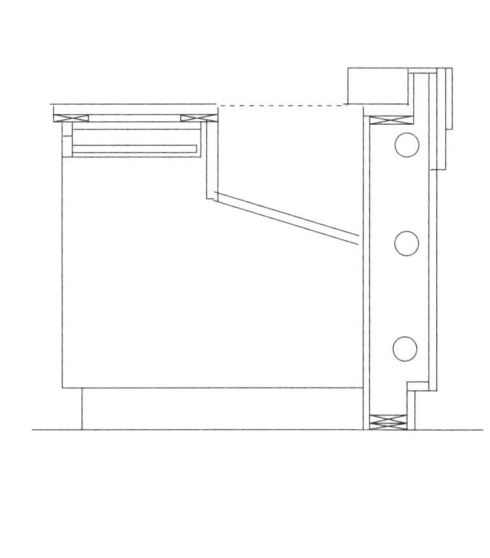

Figure: DE-059

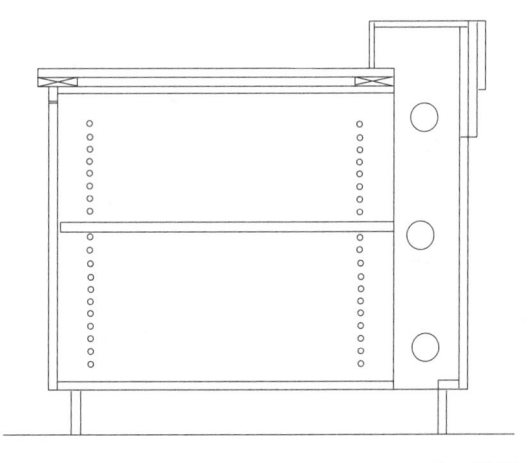

Figure: DE-060

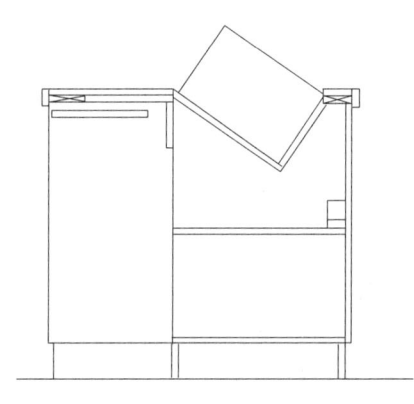

Figure: DE-061

# DESIGN IDEAS

## casework design examples

### Corporate Woodwork

Figure: DE-062

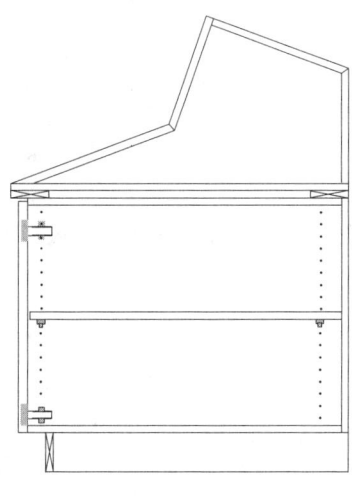

Figure: DE-063

# DESIGN IDEAS

## casework design examples

### Corporate Woodwork

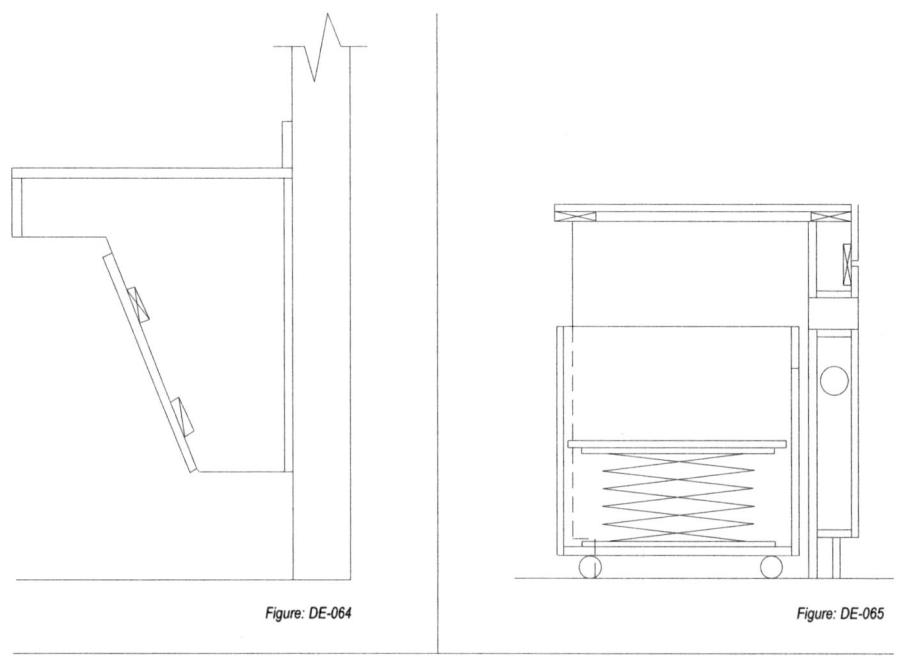

Figure: DE-064

Figure: DE-065

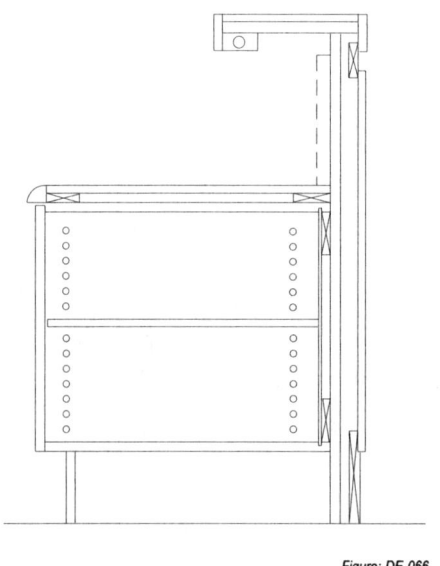

Figure: DE-066

# DESIGN IDEAS

## casework design examples

**Furniture and Fixtures**

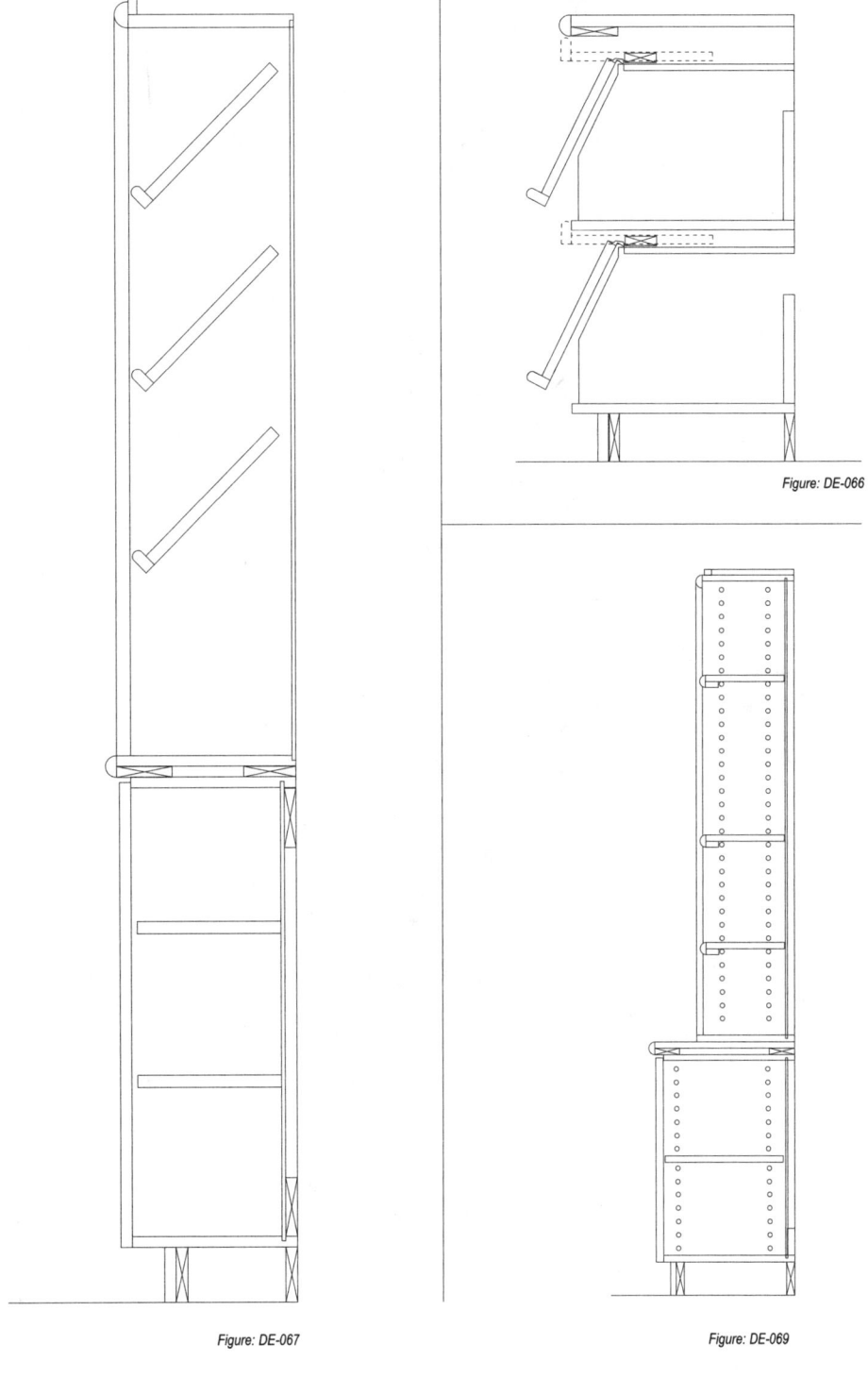

Figure: DE-066

Figure: DE-067

Figure: DE-069

# DESIGN IDEAS

## casework design examples

**Furniture and Fixtures**

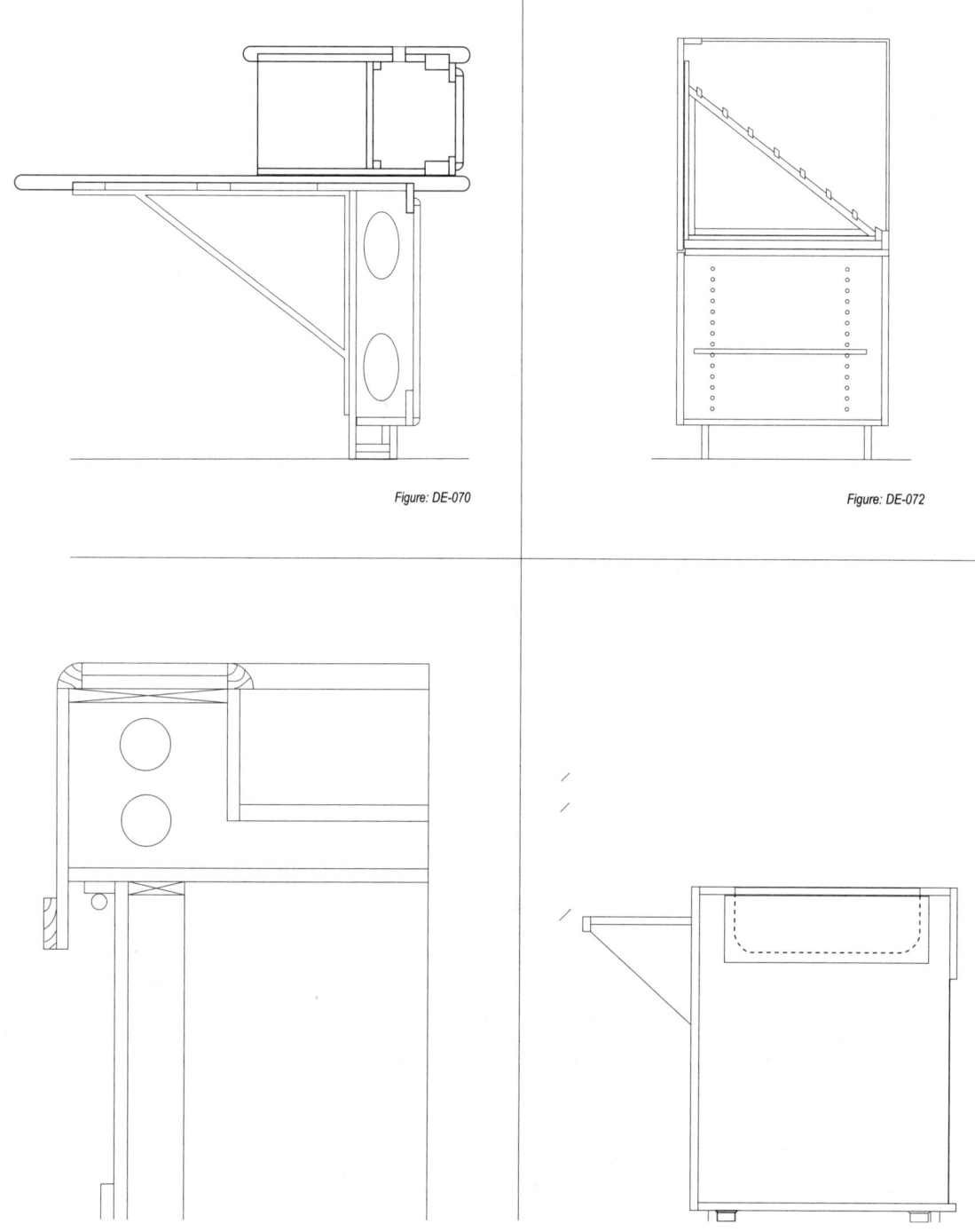

Figure: DE-070

Figure: DE-072

Figure: DE-071

Figure: DE-073

# DESIGN IDEAS

## casework design examples

**Furniture and Fixtures**

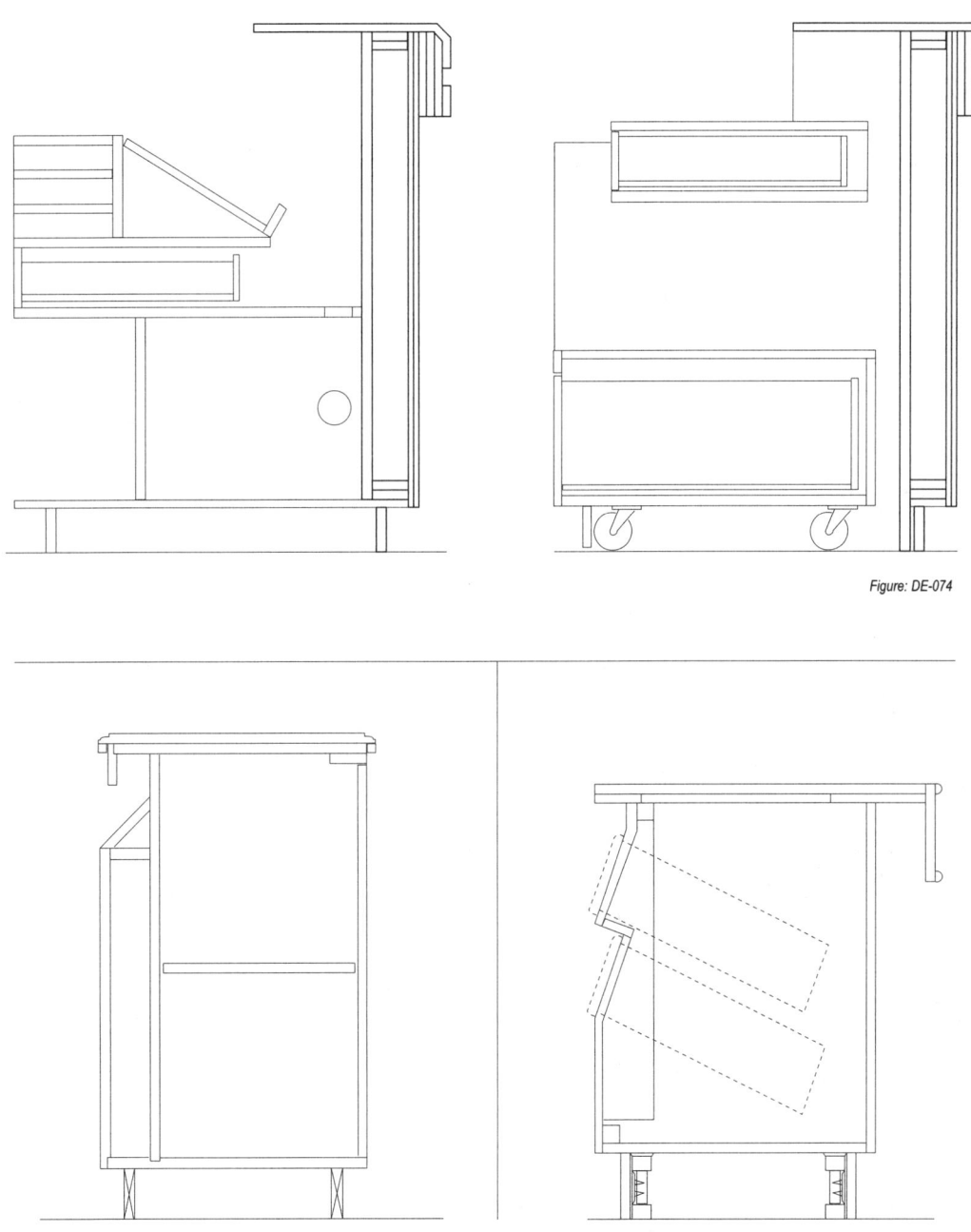

Figure: DE-074

Figure: DE-075

Figure: DE-076

# DESIGN IDEAS

## casework design examples

**Furniture and Fixtures**

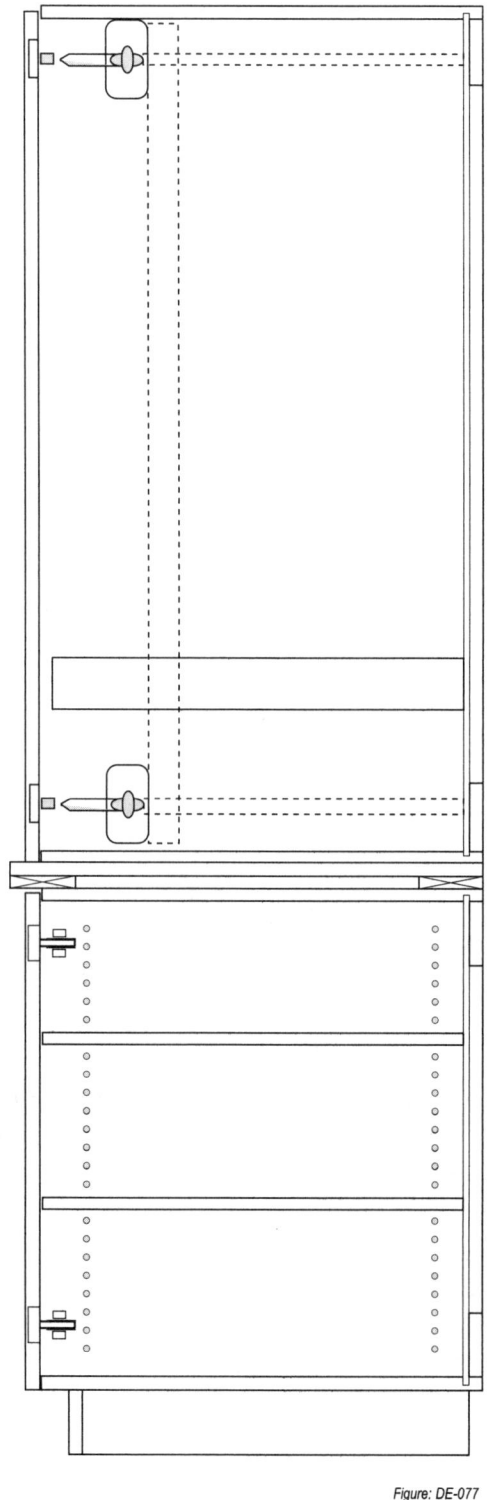

Figure: DE-077

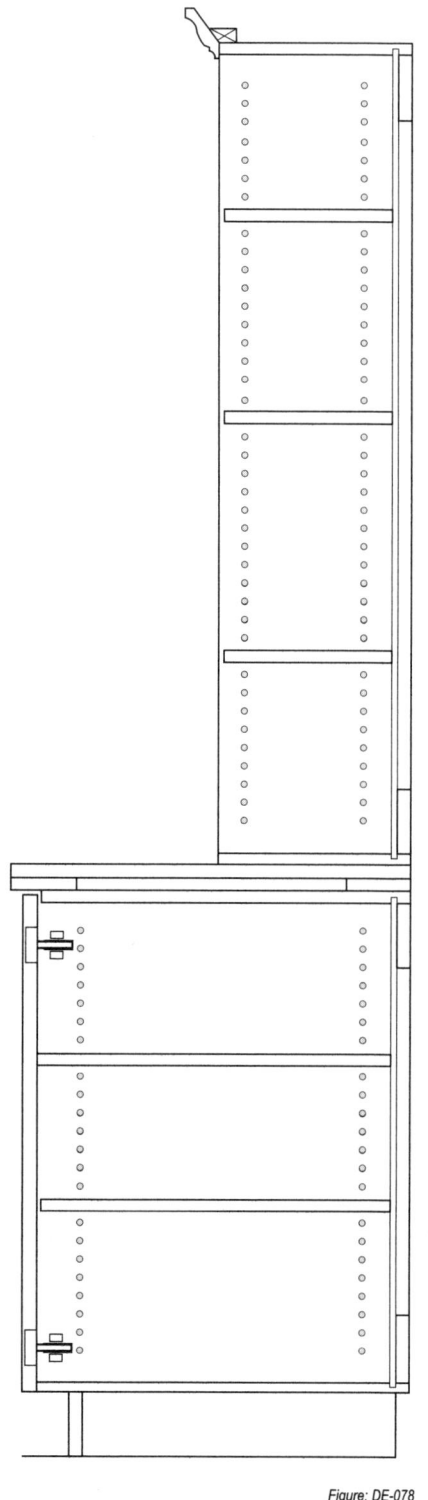

Figure: DE-078

# DESIGN IDEAS

## casework design examples

### Furniture and Fixtures

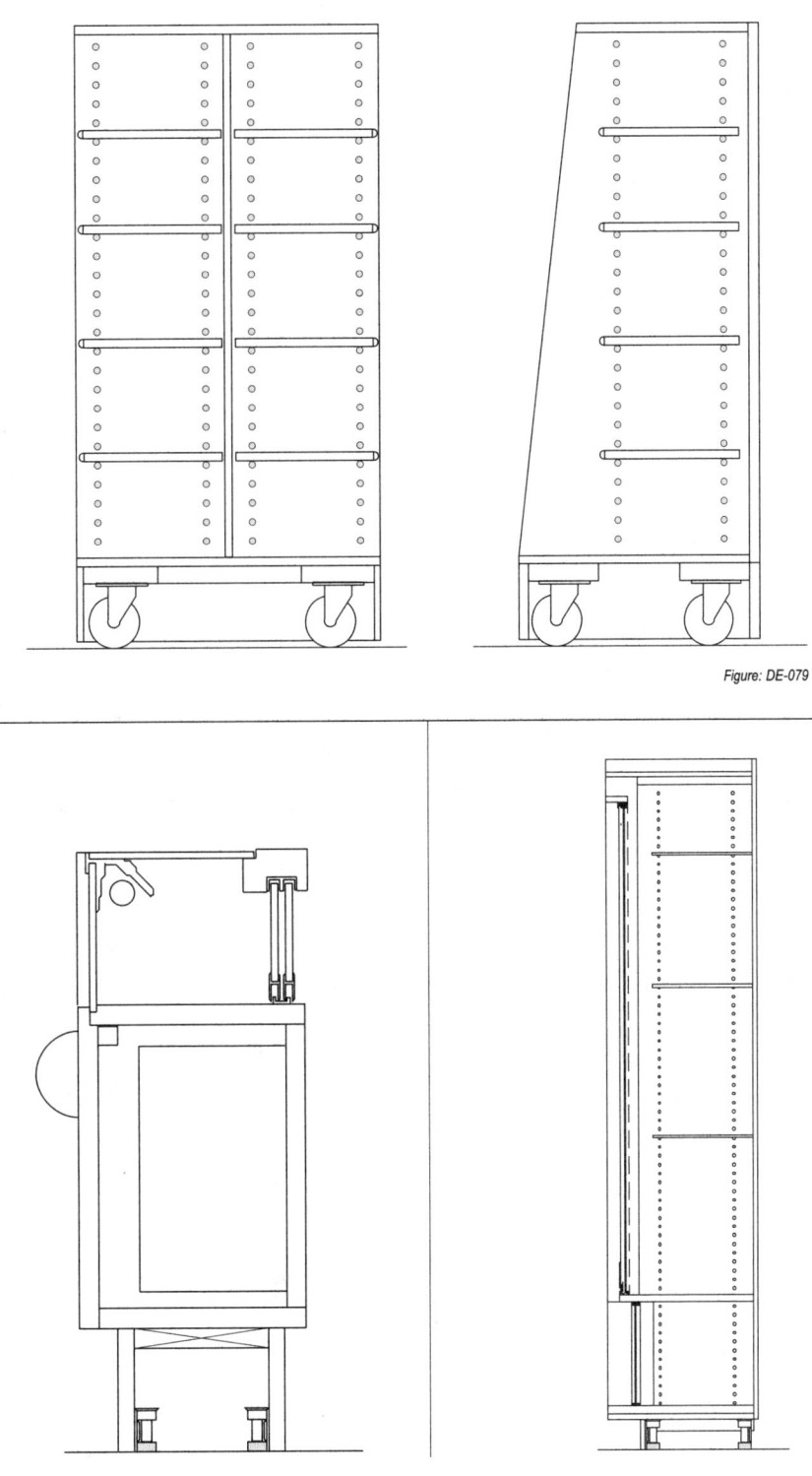

Figure: DE-079

Figure: DE-080

Figure: DE-081

# DESIGN IDEAS

## casework design examples

**Furniture and Fixtures**

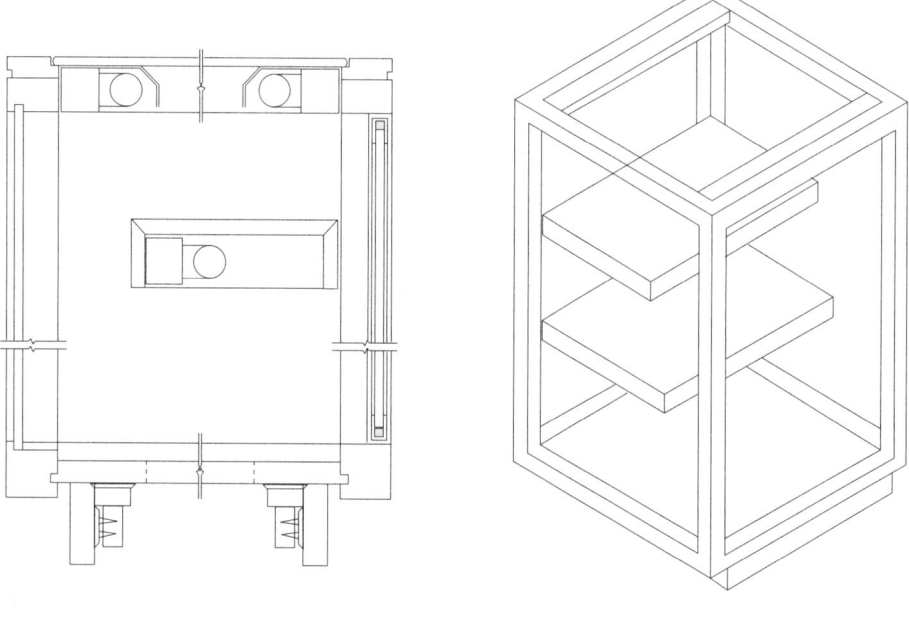

Figure: DE-082

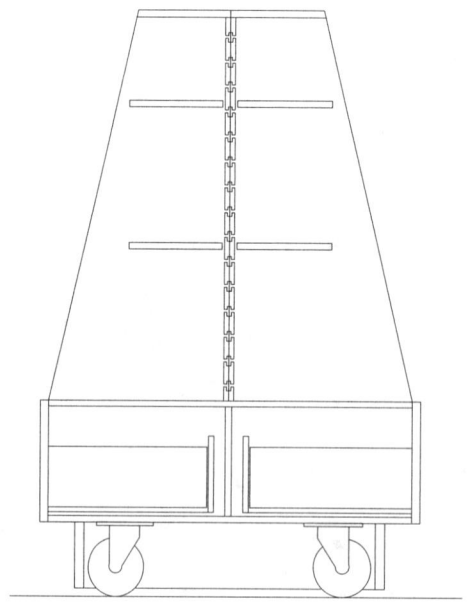

Figure: DE-083

# DESIGN IDEAS

## casework design examples

**Furniture and Fixtures**

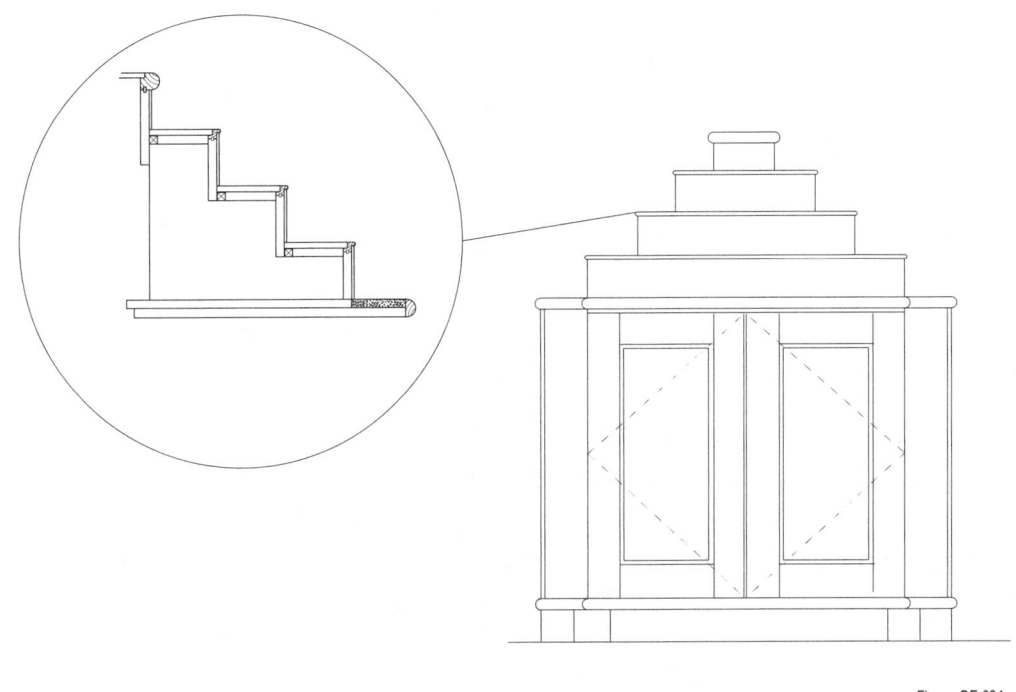

*Figure: DE-084*

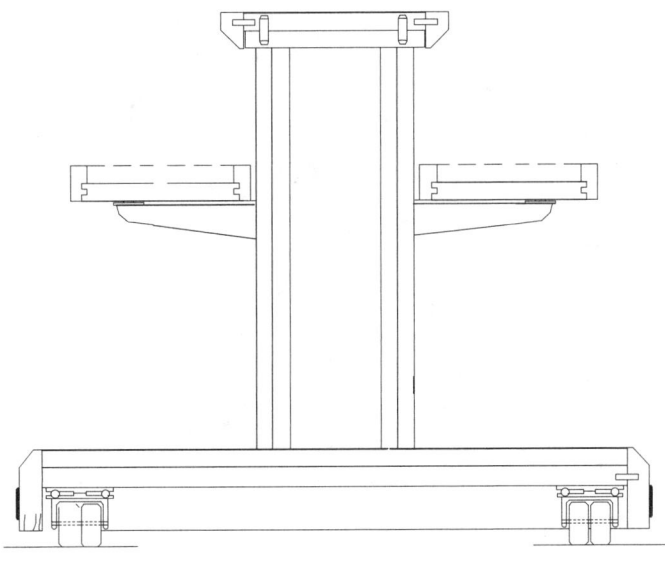

*Figure: DE-085*

# DESIGN IDEAS

## casework design examples

**Furniture and Fixtures**

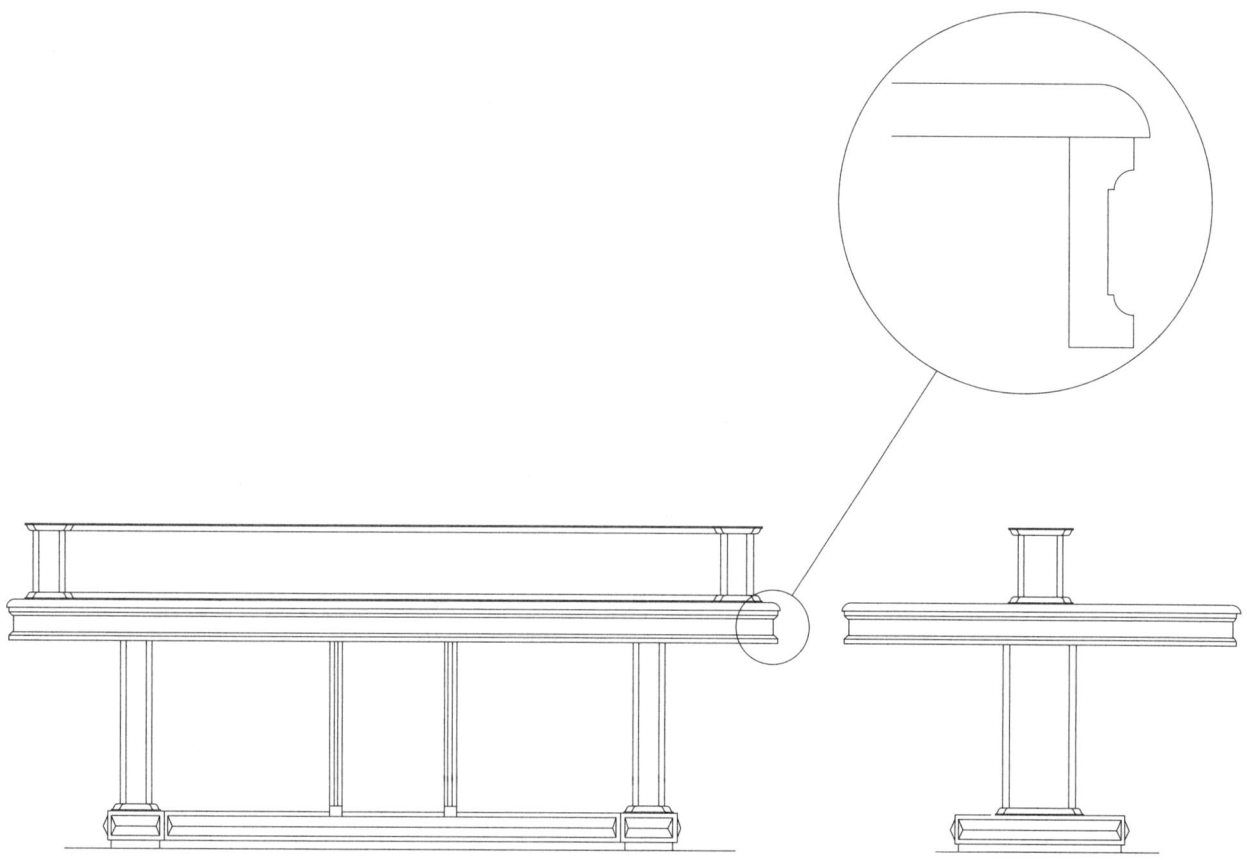

Figure: DE-086

# DESIGN IDEAS

## casework design examples

**Reception**

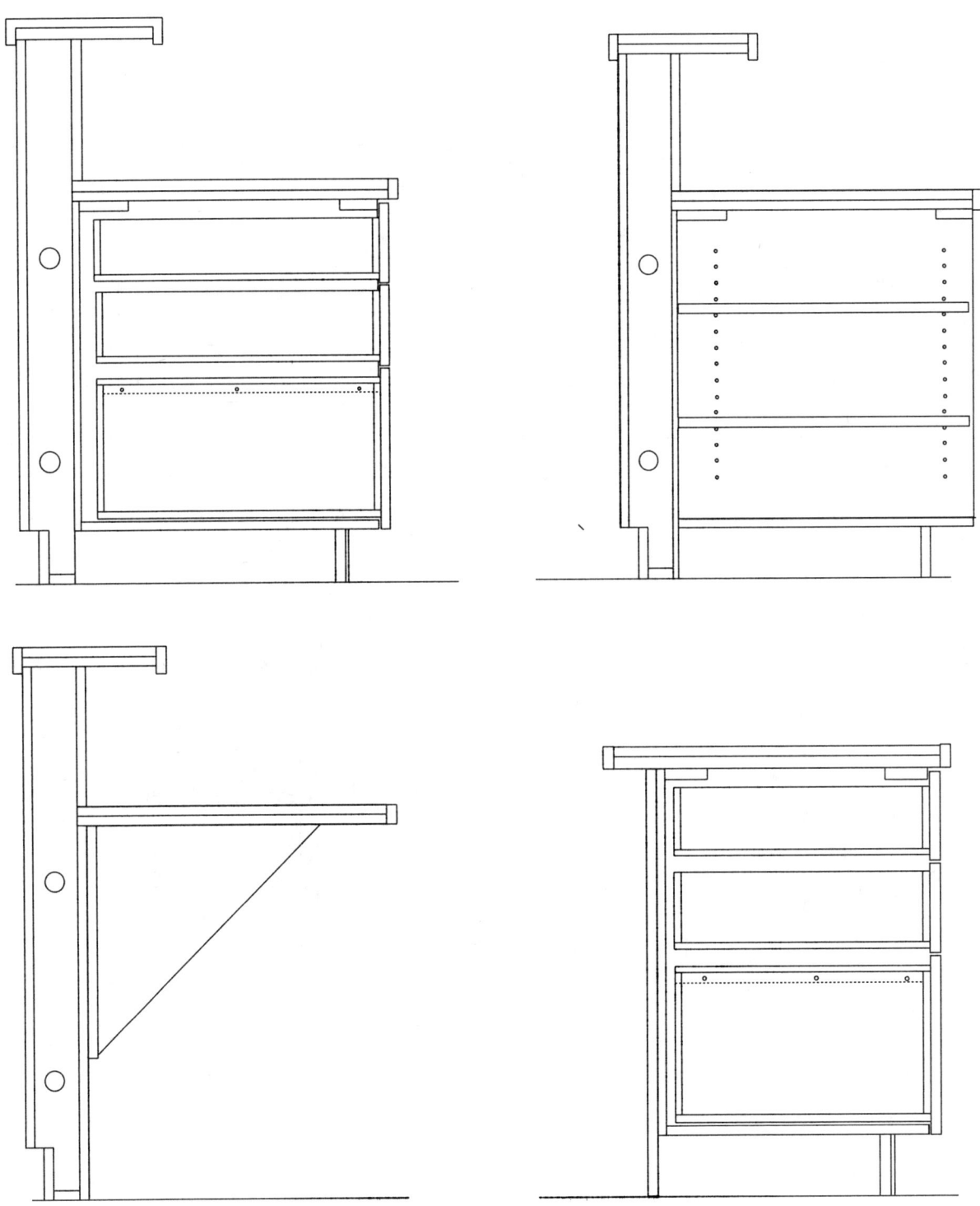

Figure: DE-087

# DESIGN IDEAS

## casework design examples

**Reception**

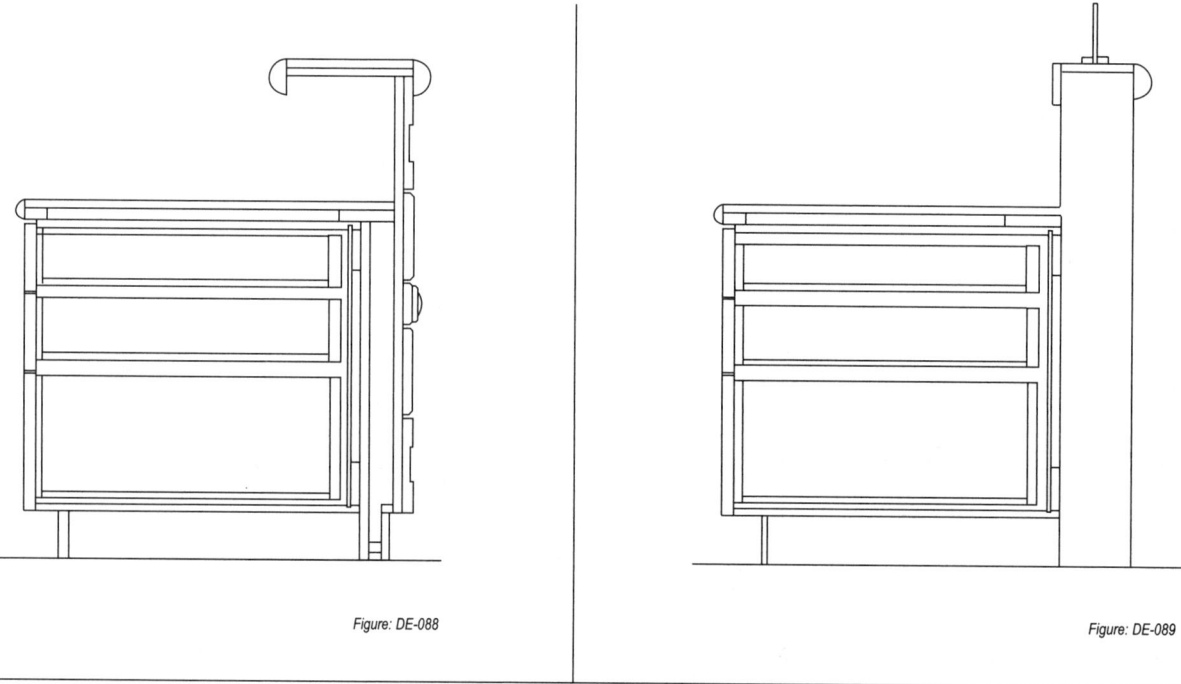

Figure: DE-088

Figure: DE-089

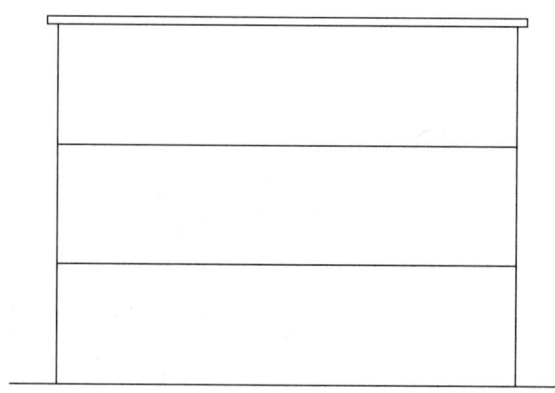

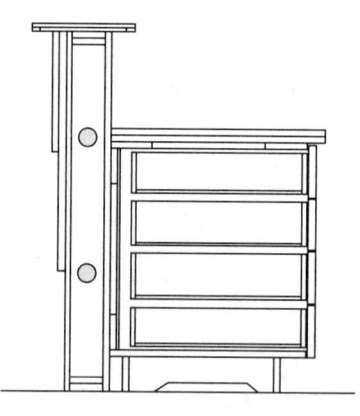

Figure: DE-090

# DESIGN IDEAS

## casework design examples

**Reception**

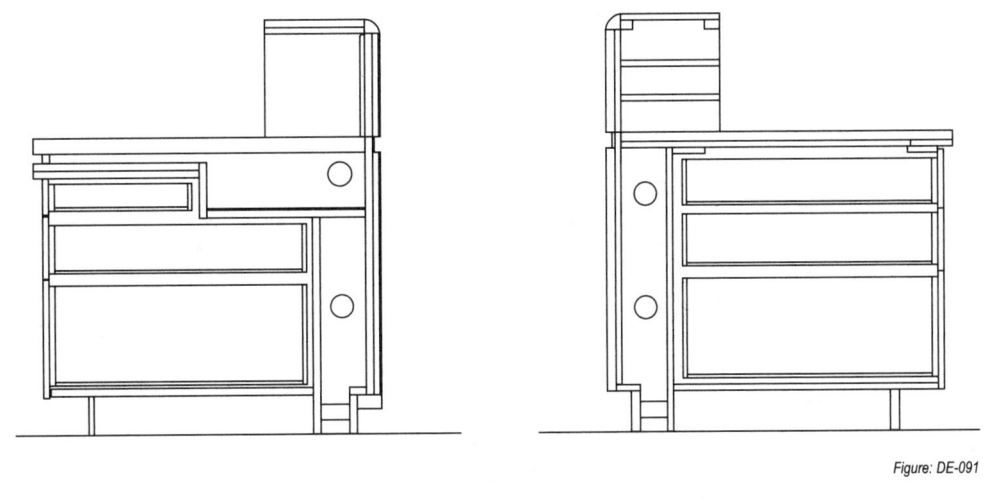

Figure: DE-091

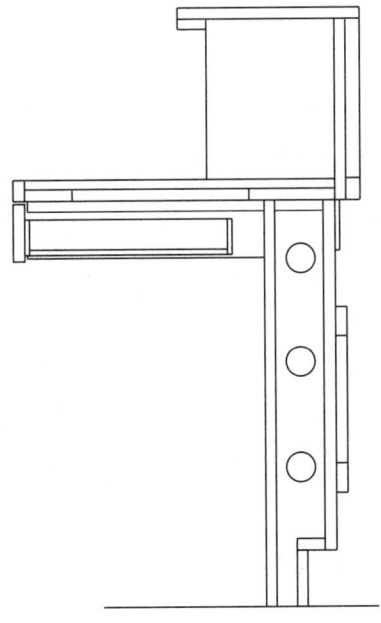
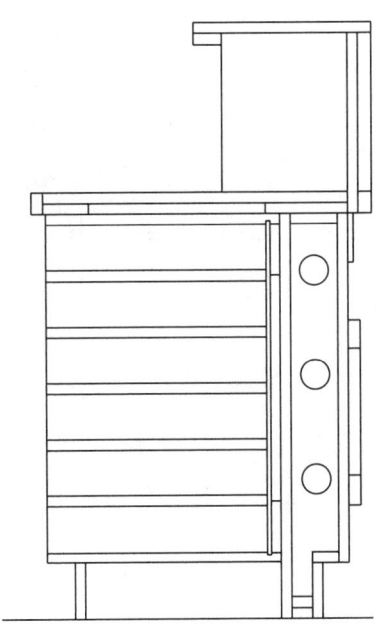

Figure: DE-092

# DESIGN IDEAS

## casework design examples

**Reception**

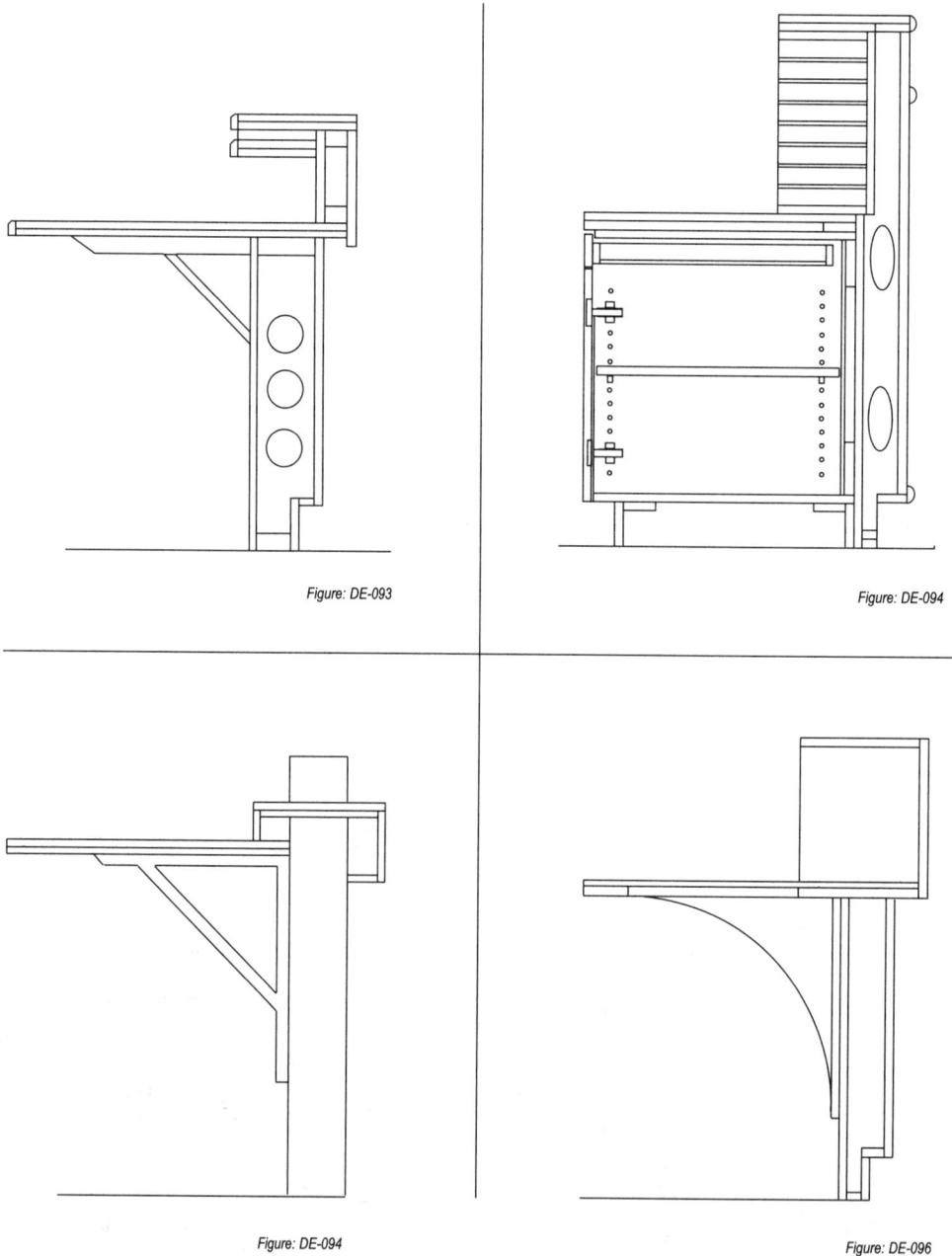

Figure: DE-093

Figure: DE-094

Figure: DE-094

Figure: DE-096

# DESIGN IDEAS

## casework design examples

### Reception

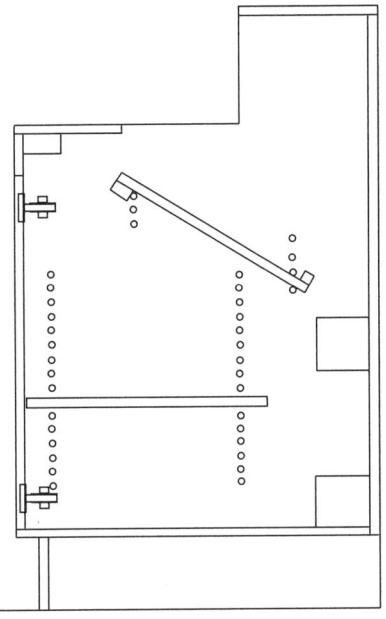
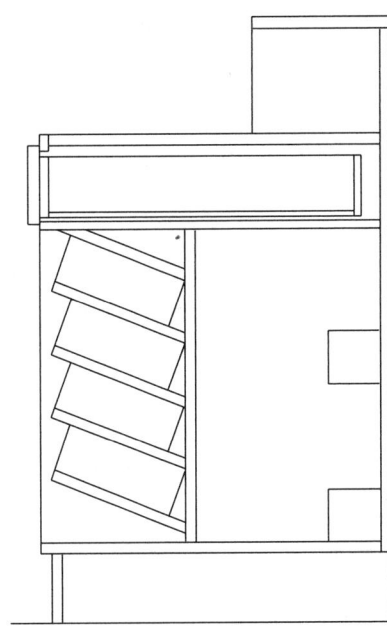

*Figure: DE-097*

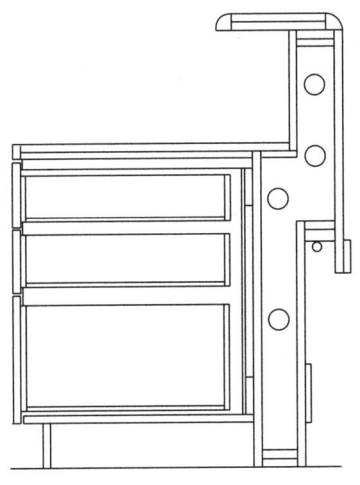
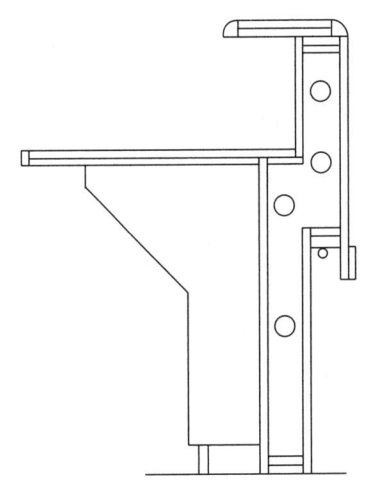

*Figure: DE-098*

# DESIGN IDEAS

## casework design examples

**Church Fittings**

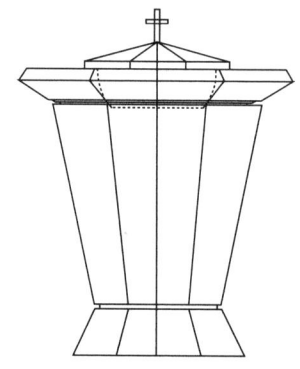
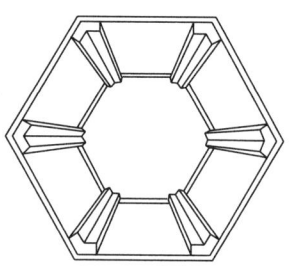

*Figure: DE-099*

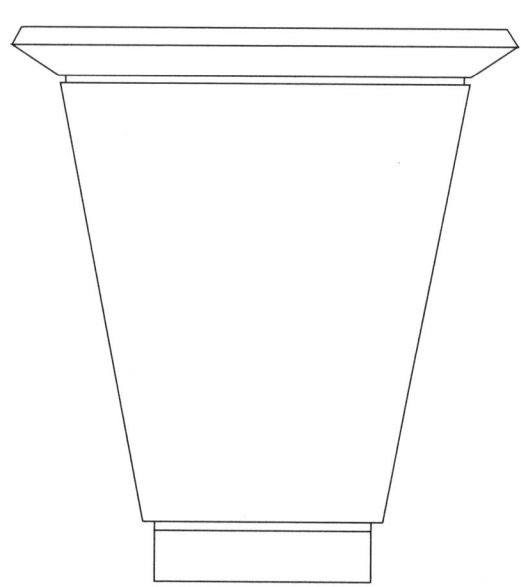
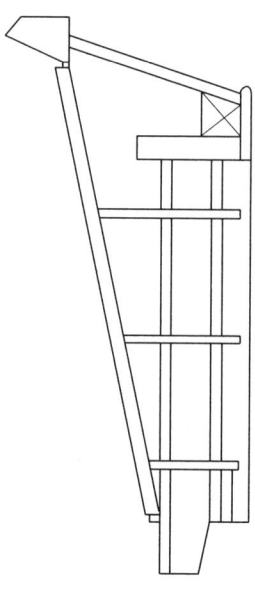

*Figure: DE-100*

# DESIGN IDEAS

## casework design examples

### Basic Cabinetry

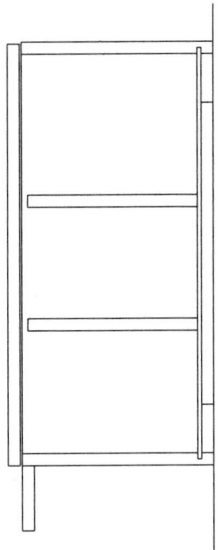

*Figure: DE-101*

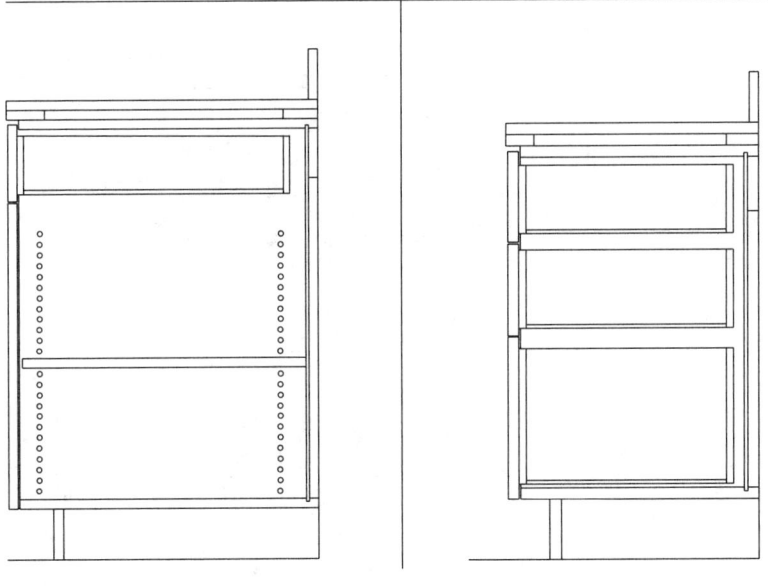

*Figure: DE-102*  *Figure: DE-103*

# DESIGN IDEAS

## casework design examples

**Basic Cabinetry**

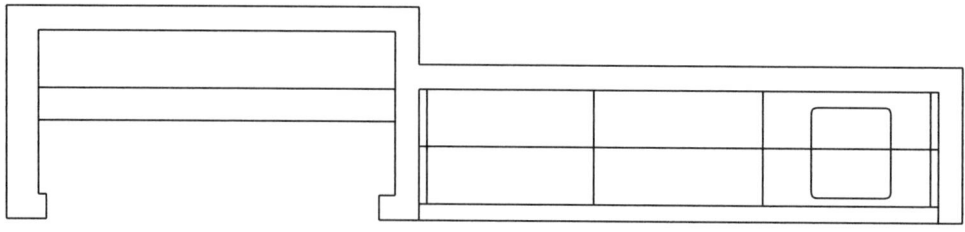

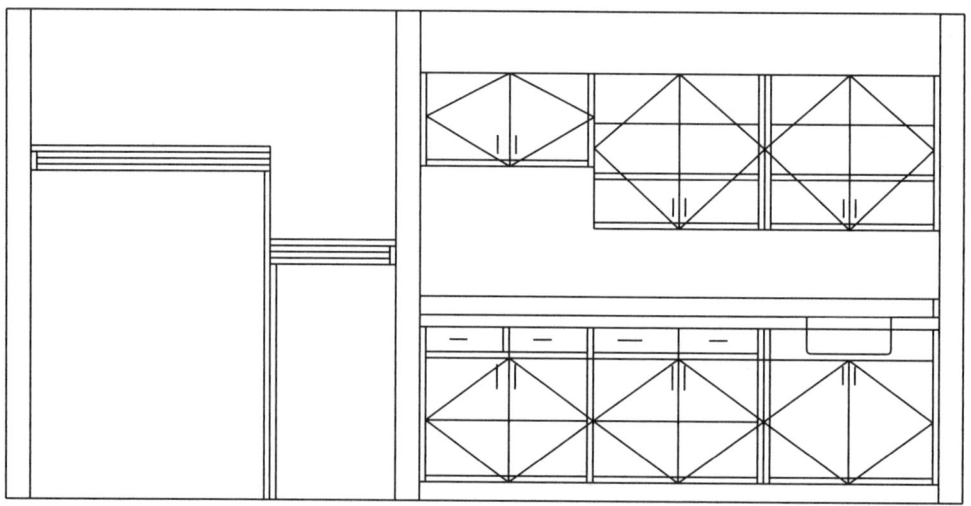

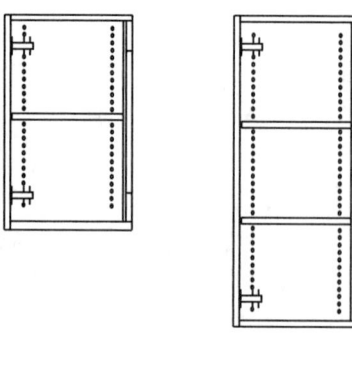
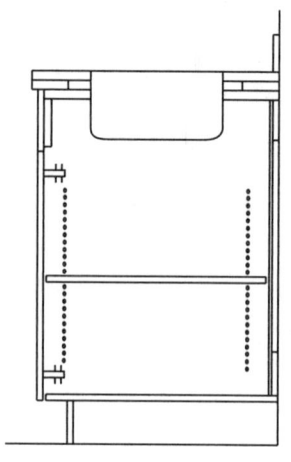
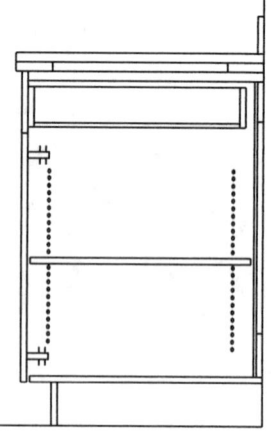

Figure: DE-104

# DESIGN IDEAS

## cabinet design series (CDS)

**CDS** illustrations are provided to assist design professionals and casework users in selecting typical designs. These illustrations are not intended to limit or restrict creativity, or to be all inclusive.

When utilizing the CDS numbering system, it is not necessary to show casework elevations in your contract documents. However, it is necessary to show a plan view with each CDS number indicated along with the width, height, and depth in inches or millimeters (example: 102-36"x 30"x 18" [102-914 mm x 762 mm x 457 mm]). Cabinet dimensions indicate the nominal outside dimension (floor to top of countertop for height and face of finished wall to face of cabinet door for depth). Manufacturers are permitted a tolerance of plus/minus 1/2" (12.7 mm) in width only.

When designs other than those provided for in the CDS system are desired, they may be indicated by selecting the CDS number most closely representing the desired design, followed by the letter "M" and a description or illustration of the design modification (example: 102M - 2 shelves - 36"x 30"x 18" [102M - 2 shelves - 914 mm x 762 mm x 457 mm] or 102M - no shelves -36"x 30"x 18" [102M - no shelves -914 mm x 762 mm x 457 mm]). It is suggested that a standard number/dimension convention similar to that shown below, is used.

If the CDS numbering system is used in conjunction with cabinet elevations on contract documents, the cabinet elevations shall govern on any conflict between the requirements of the elevation and the CDS number.

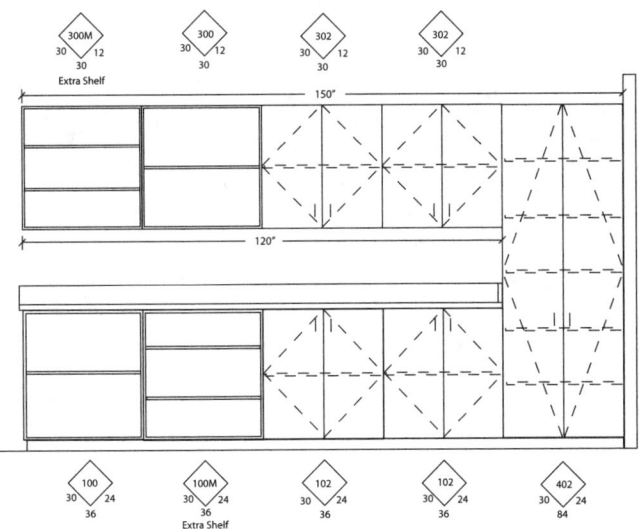

**CDS** cabinets are intended for TYPE A construction with integral finished ends and scribes at wall to wall installations not exceeding 1-1/2" (38.1 mm) in width. Hardware and accessories shall be as provided for in these standards.

**CDS** are subdivided as follows:

- Base Cabinets w/o Drawers        100 Series
- Base Cabinets w/ Drawers         200 Series
- Wall Hung Cabinets               300 Series
- Tall Storage Cabinets            400 Series
- Tall Wardrobe Cabinets           500 Series
- Library Cabinets                 600 Series
- Moveable Cabinets                700 Series

**GENERAL NOTES:**

- 100 or 200 Series cabinets may be converted into moveable cabinets by prefixing a "7" to the number. (Example: 7-102-36"x 30"x 18" [7-102-914 mm x 762 mm x 457 mm]).

- Moveable cabinets shall be equipped with adequate approved casters for the intended load capacity.

- CDS #'s 728, 729, 735, 736, 737, 738, and 739 require metal angle reinforced corners.

- Carts and rolling tall storage cabinets with doors, lacking any horizontal and/or vertical stabilizing dividers, require a diaphragm bottom; specifically CDS #'s 702, 712, 716, 722, 743, 744, 746, 747, 750, and 751.

- Wardrobe cabinets (500 Series) with doors require a framed mirror on one door, and cabinets # 533 and 534 require a paper roller/cutter and slide out tilting paper shelves.

- Cart storage cabinets are required to have hardwood side guides, specifically CDS #'s 160, 161, and 162.

- Ceramics drying cabinets are required to have galvanized metal frame shelves with wire mesh, specifically CDS #'s 198 199, and 459.

- File drawers require full extension slides and a file hanging system, specifically CDS #'s 223, 224, 230, 231, 240, 242, 253, 255, 531, 532, and 533.

- Wardrobe cabinets are required to have a shelf, pole, and framed mirror when closed with hinged doors, specifically CDS #'s 501, 511, 512, 522, 530, 531, 532, and 552.

**SPECIAL BASE CASEWORK HEIGHTS**, the following are recommended for various school grades, subject to ADA requirements:

- Kindergarten - Grade 1     24" (610 mm)
- Grades 2 - 3               27" (686 mm)
- Grades 4 - 6               30" (762 mm)
- Grades 7 - 9               33" (838 mm)
- Grades 10 and above        36" (914 mm)

# DESIGN IDEAS

## cabinet design series (CDS)

**100 SERIES - BASE CABINETS w/o DRAWERS**

| 100 | 101 | 102 | 106 |
| 107 | 110 | 111 | 112 |
| 116 | 117 | 120 | 121 |
| 122 | 130 | 131 | 132 |
| 136 | 140 Removable Back | 141 Removable Back | 142 Removable Back |

**DESIGN IDEAS**

# cabinet design series (CDS)

**100 SERIES - BASE CABINETS w/o DRAWERS**
(continued)

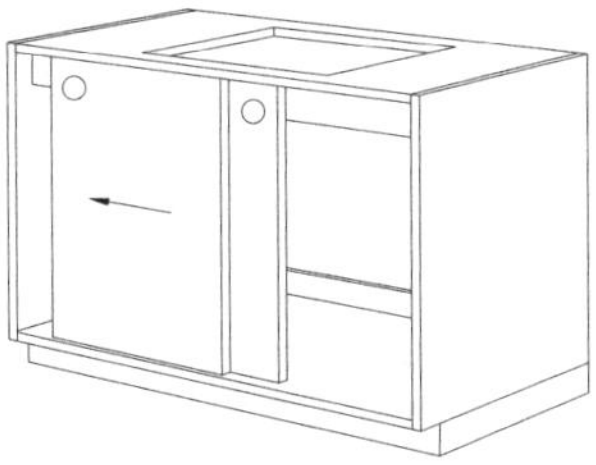

**146**
Removable Back

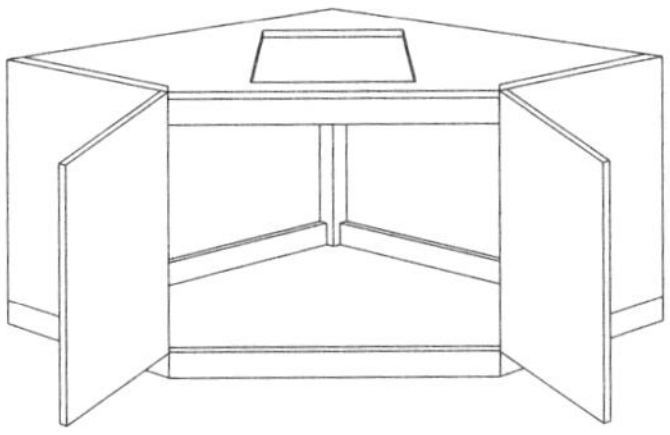

**148**
Removable Back

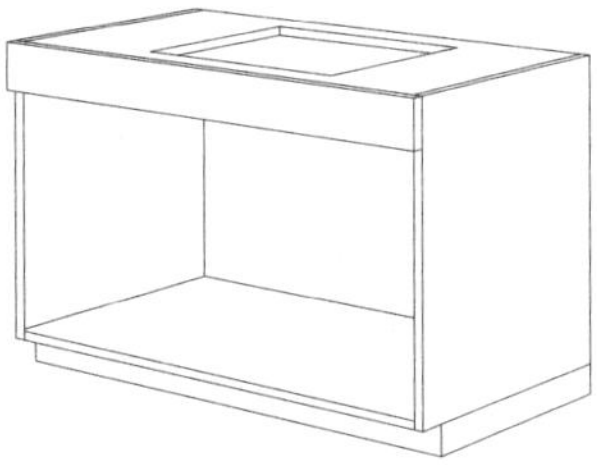

**150**

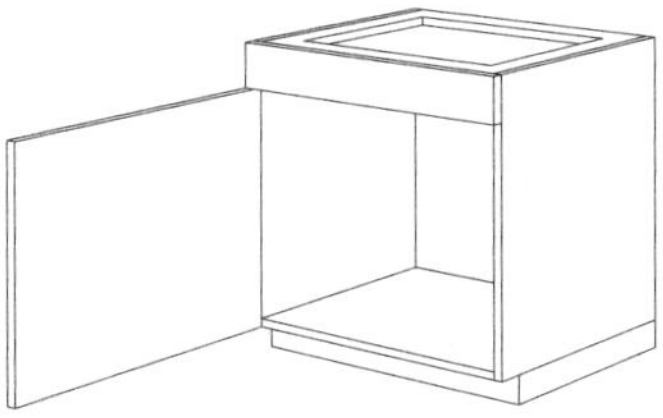

**151**

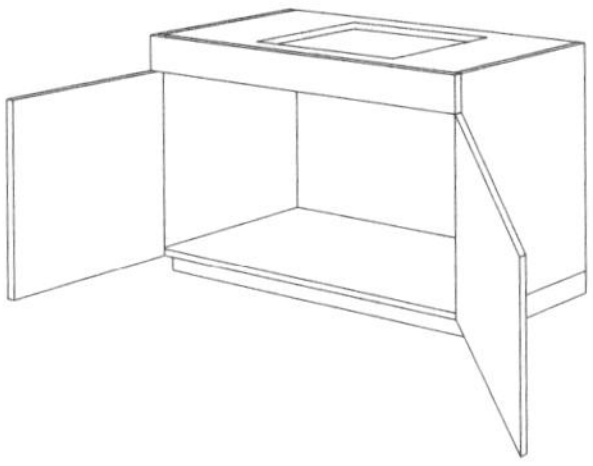

**152**

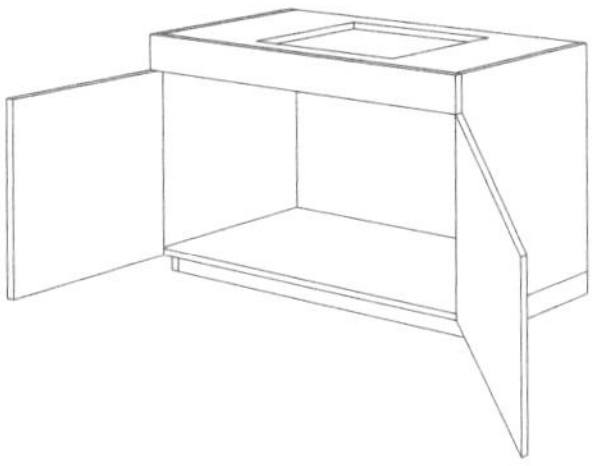

**153**
Removable Base/Toe

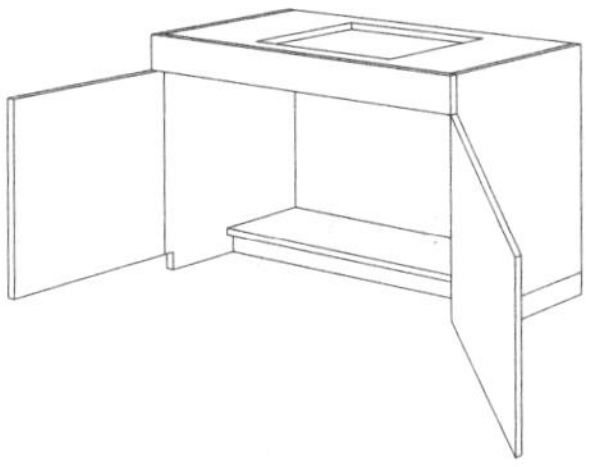

**154**

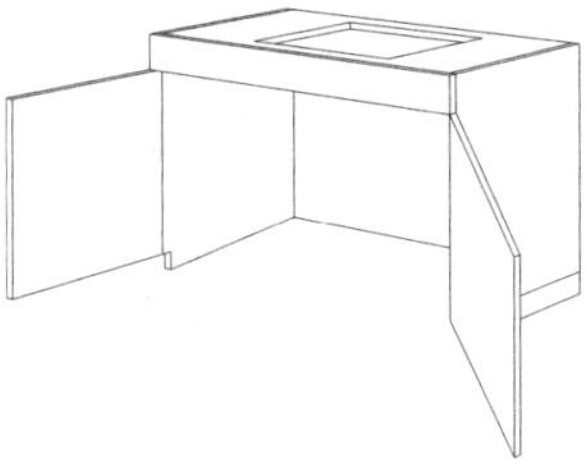

**155**

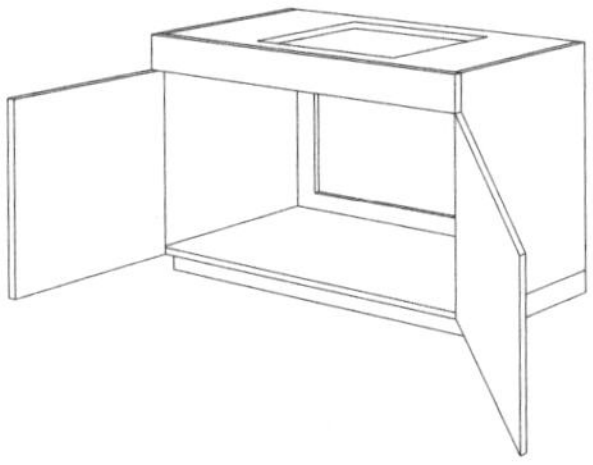

**156**
Removable Back

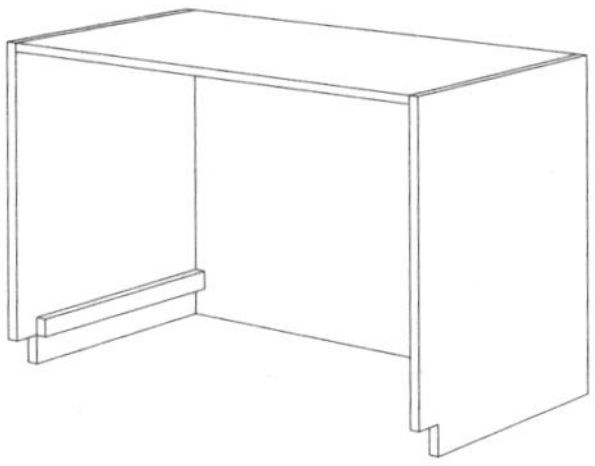

**160**
Cart Storage

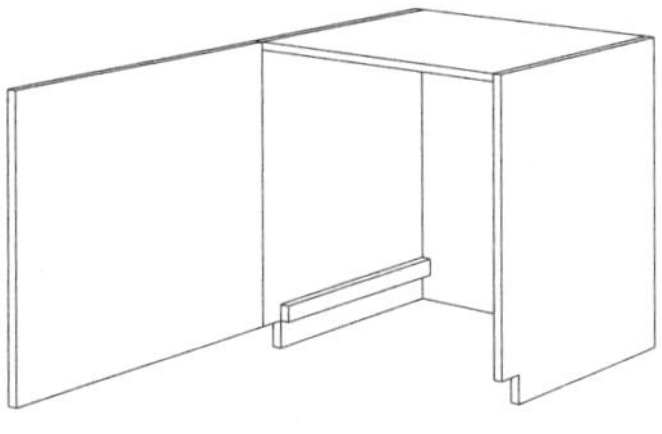

**161**
Cart Storage

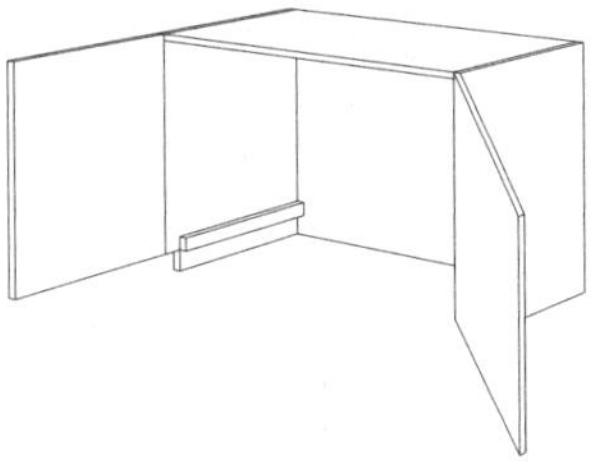

**162**
Cart Storage

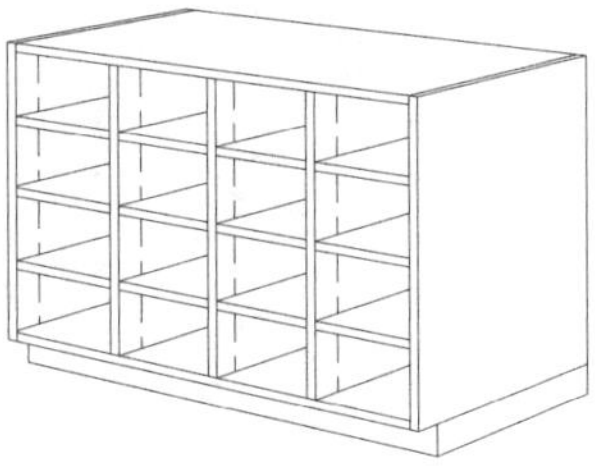

**170**

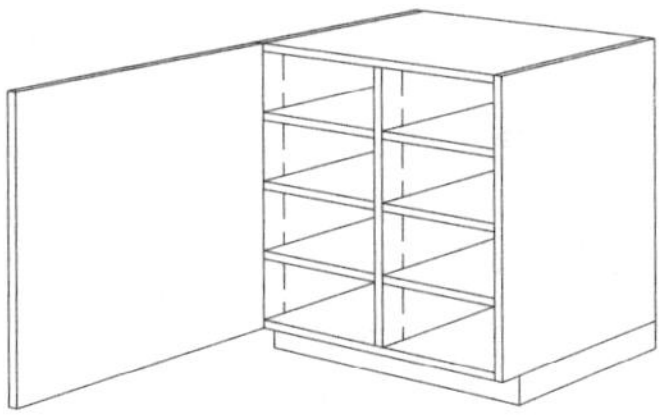

**171**

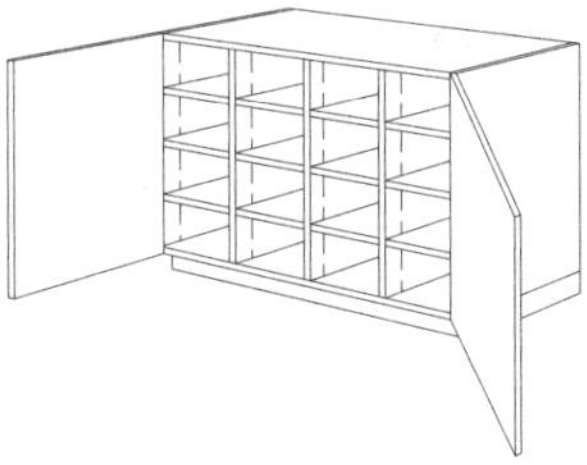

**172**

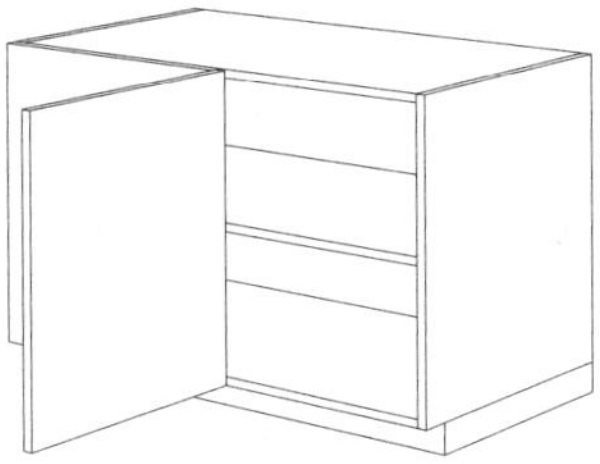

**176**

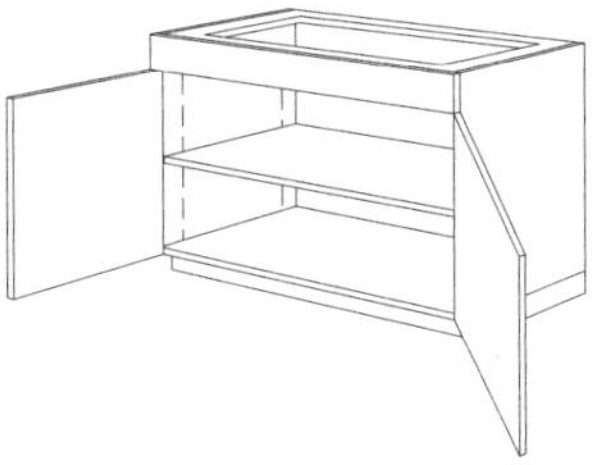

**177**

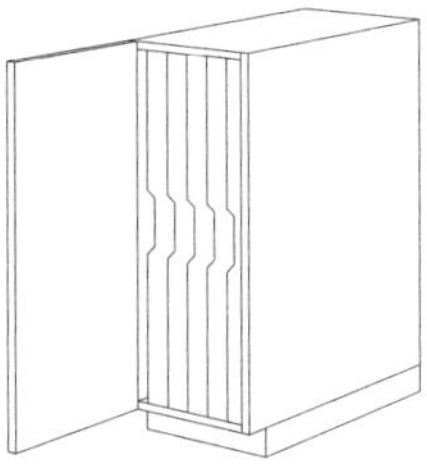

**178**

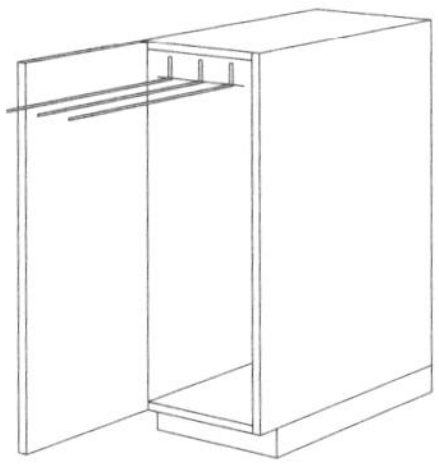

**179**
Retractable Towel Rack

Architectural Woodwork Standards

# DESIGN IDEAS

## cabinet design series (CDS)

**100 SERIES - BASE CABINETS w/o DRAWERS**
(continued)

| 180 | 182 | 186 | 187 Sliding Tray & Lift Shelf |

| 188 | 189 Drawing Board Rack | 190 | 191 |

| 192 | 193 | 194 | 195 |

| 196 | 197 | 198 | 199 |

# DESIGN IDEAS

## cabinet design series (CDS)

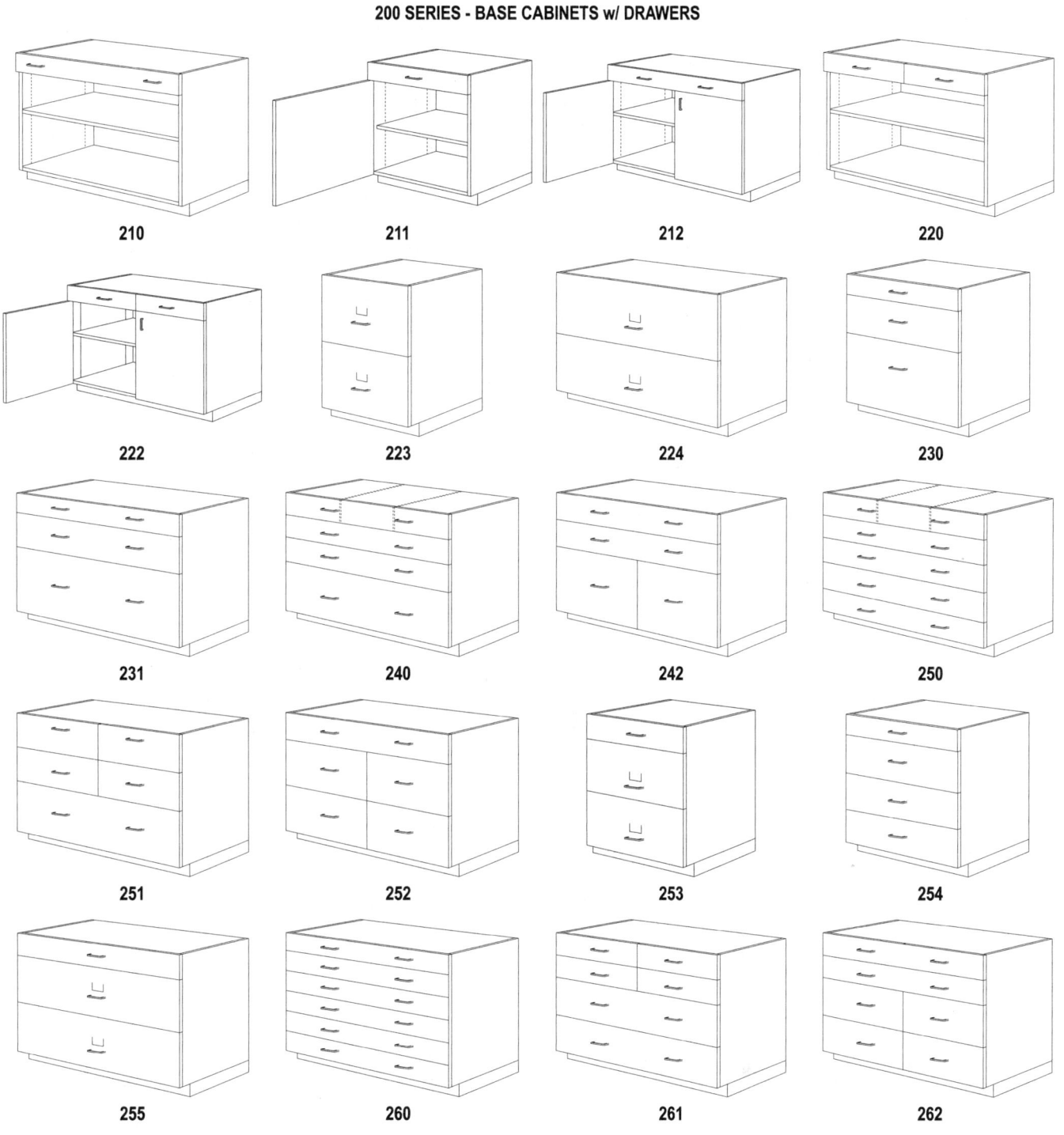

**200 SERIES - BASE CABINETS w/ DRAWERS**

# DESIGN IDEAS

## cabinet design series (CDS)

**200 SERIES - BASE CABINETS w/ DRAWERS**
(continued)

270

271

272

290

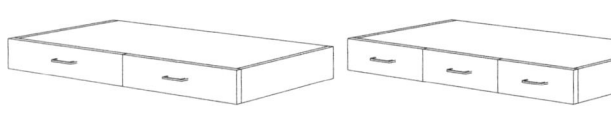

291            292

# DESIGN IDEAS

## cabinet design series (CDS)

**300 SERIES - WALL HUNG CABINETS**

| 300 | 301 | 302 | 306 |

| 307 | 308 Angle Corner | 309 Blind Corner | 310 |

| 311 | 312 | 316 | 317 |

| 318 | 320 | 321 | 322 |

| 323 | 324 | 325 | 326 |

# DESIGN IDEAS

## cabinet design series (CDS)

**300 SERIES - WALL HUNG CABINETS**
(continued)

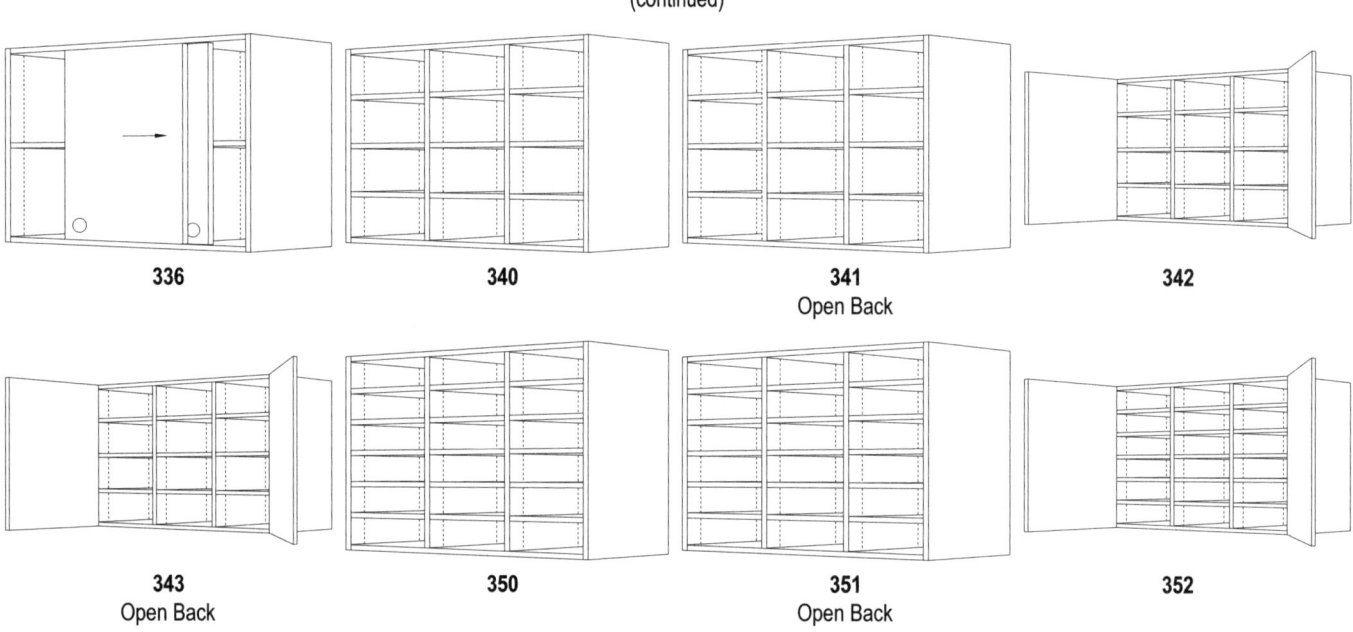

# DESIGN IDEAS

## cabinet design series (CDS)

**400 SERIES - TALL STORAGE CABINETS**

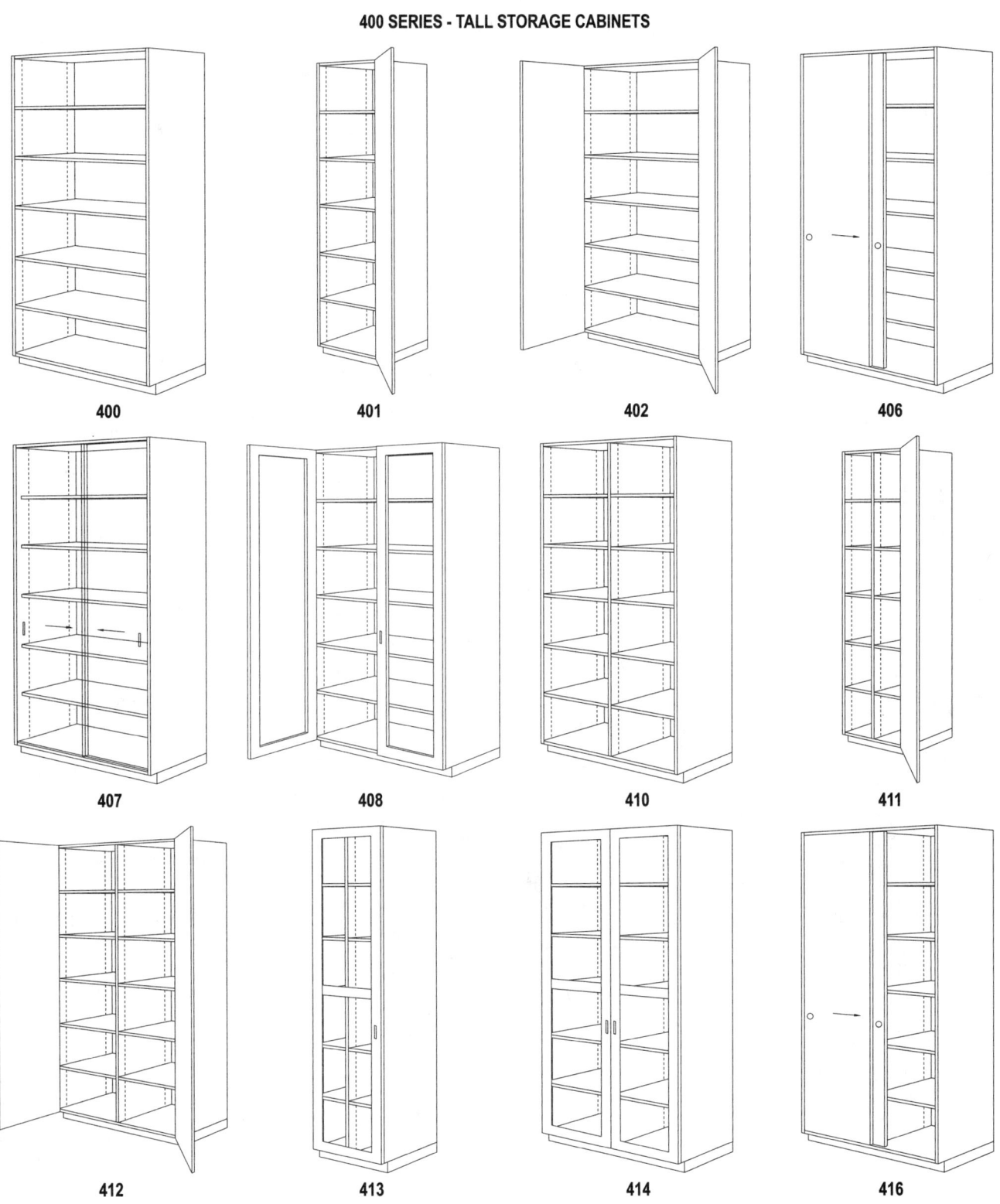

# DESIGN IDEAS

## cabinet design series (CDS)

**400 SERIES - TALL STORAGE CABINETS**
*(continued)*

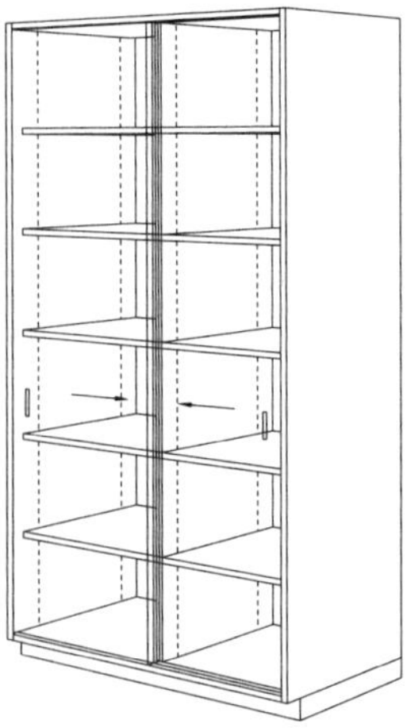

417

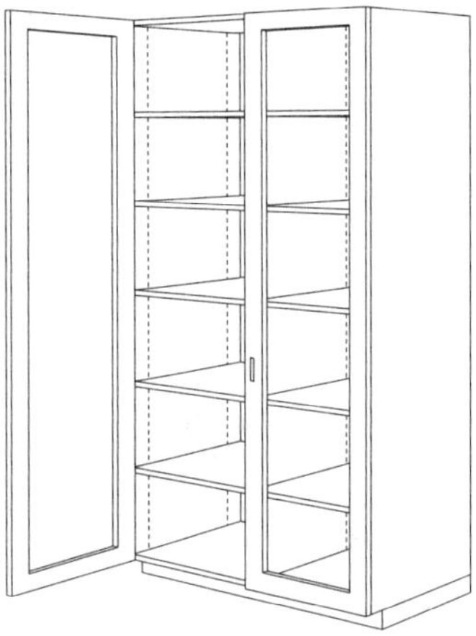

418

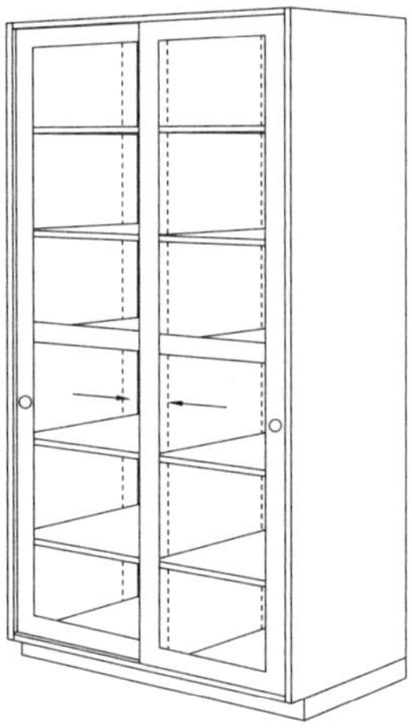

419

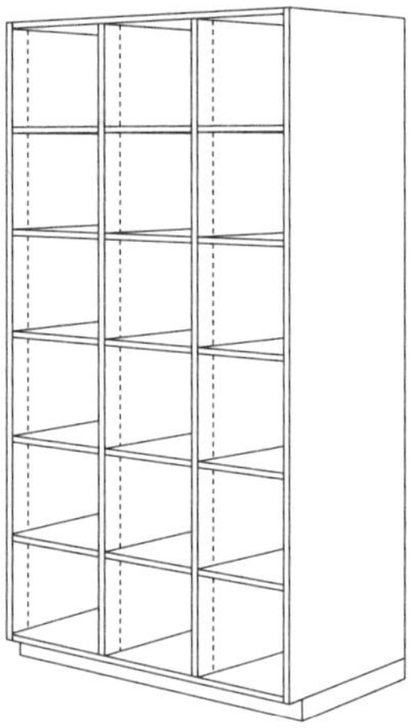

420

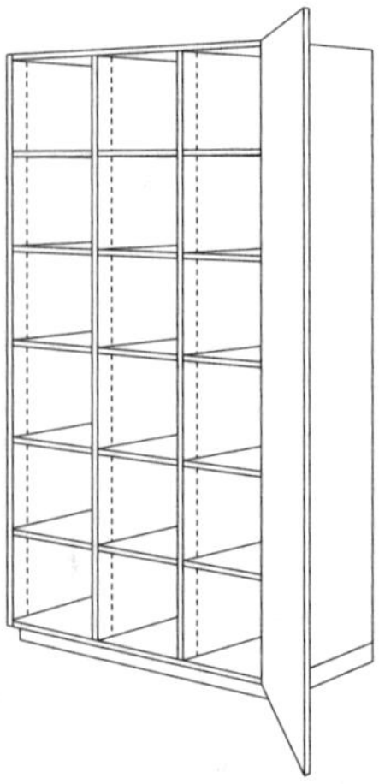

421

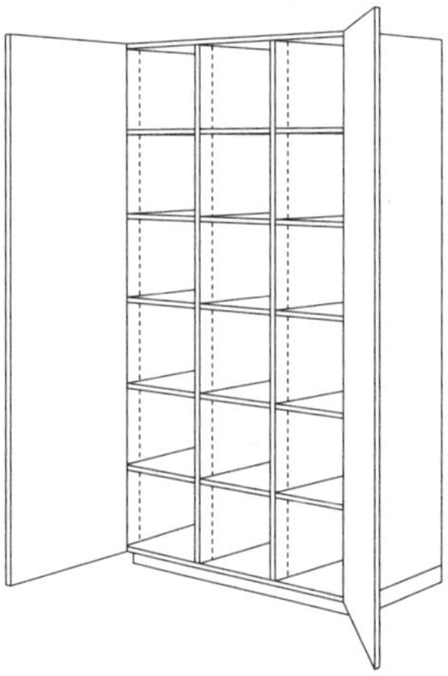

422

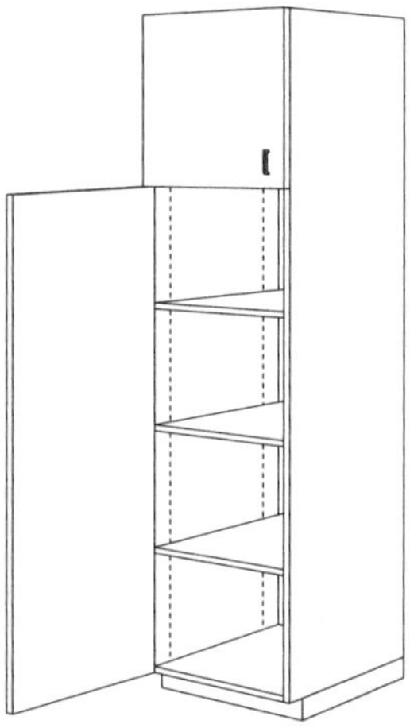

423

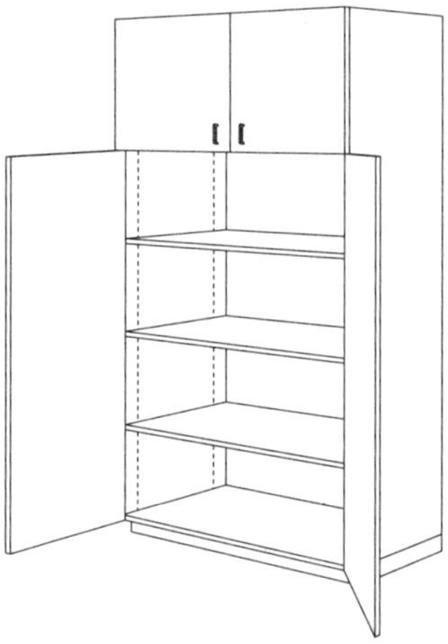

424

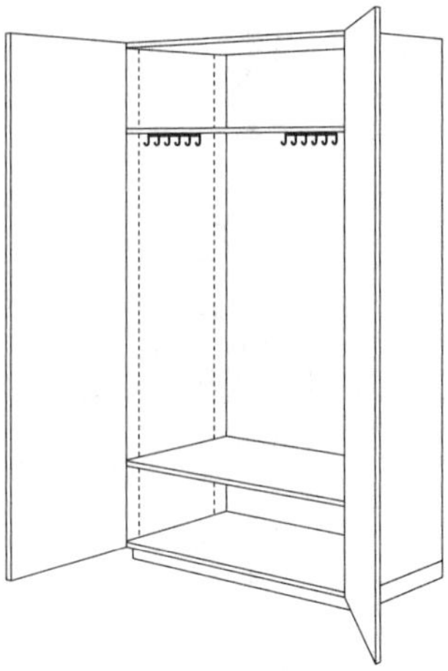

425
Dust Panel, Integral or Separate

426

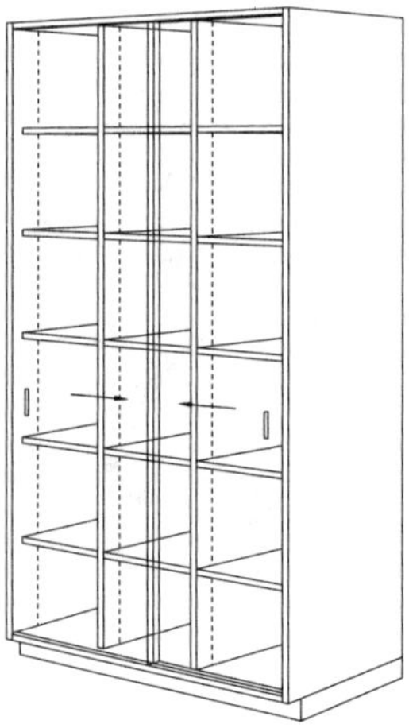

427

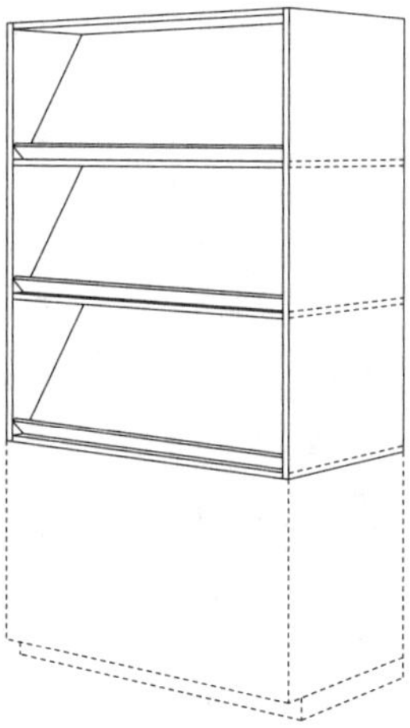

429
Hutch w/ Fixed Shelves

# DESIGN IDEAS

## cabinet design series (CDS)

**400 SERIES - TALL STORAGE CABINETS**
(continued)

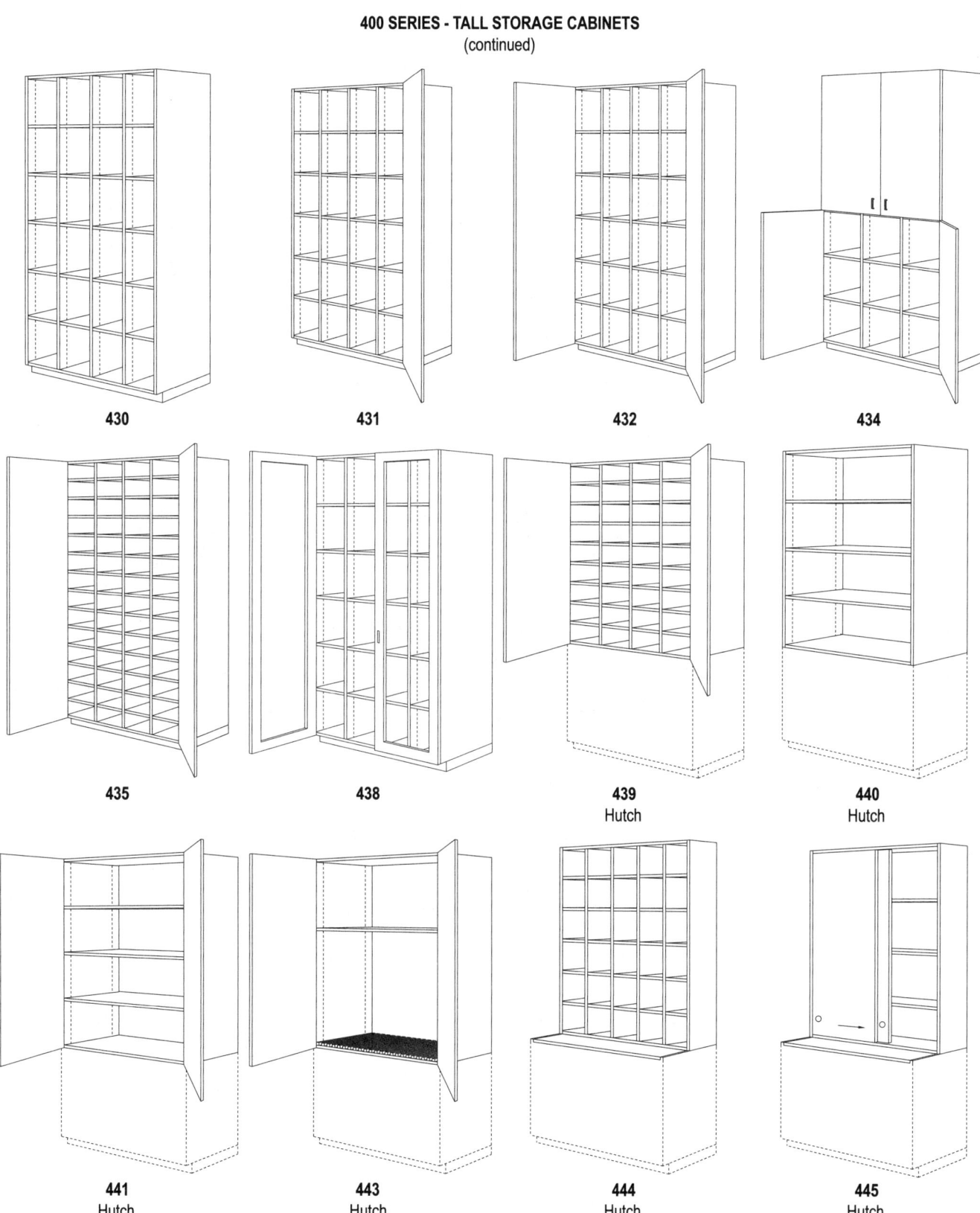

**DESIGN IDEAS**

## cabinet design series (CDS)

**400 SERIES - TALL STORAGE CABINETS**
(continued)

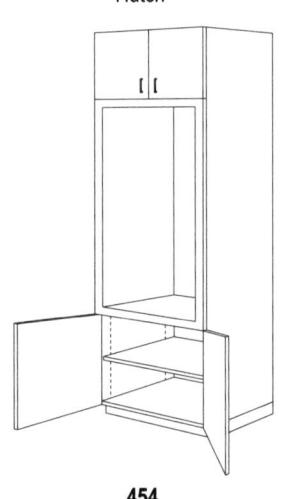
**446**
Hutch

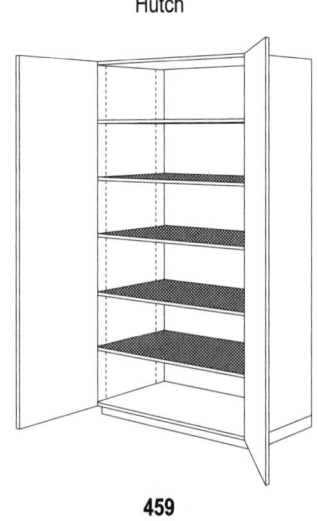
**447**
Hutch

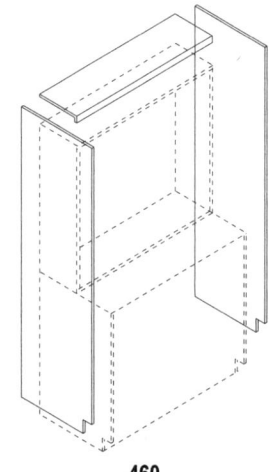
**448**
Hutch

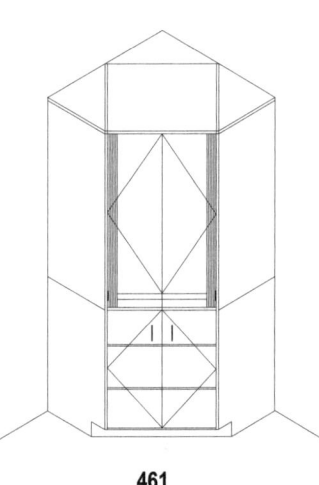
**449**
Hutch

**454**

**459**

**460**

**461**

## DESIGN IDEAS

## cabinet design series (CDS)

**500 SERIES - WARDROBE CABINETS**

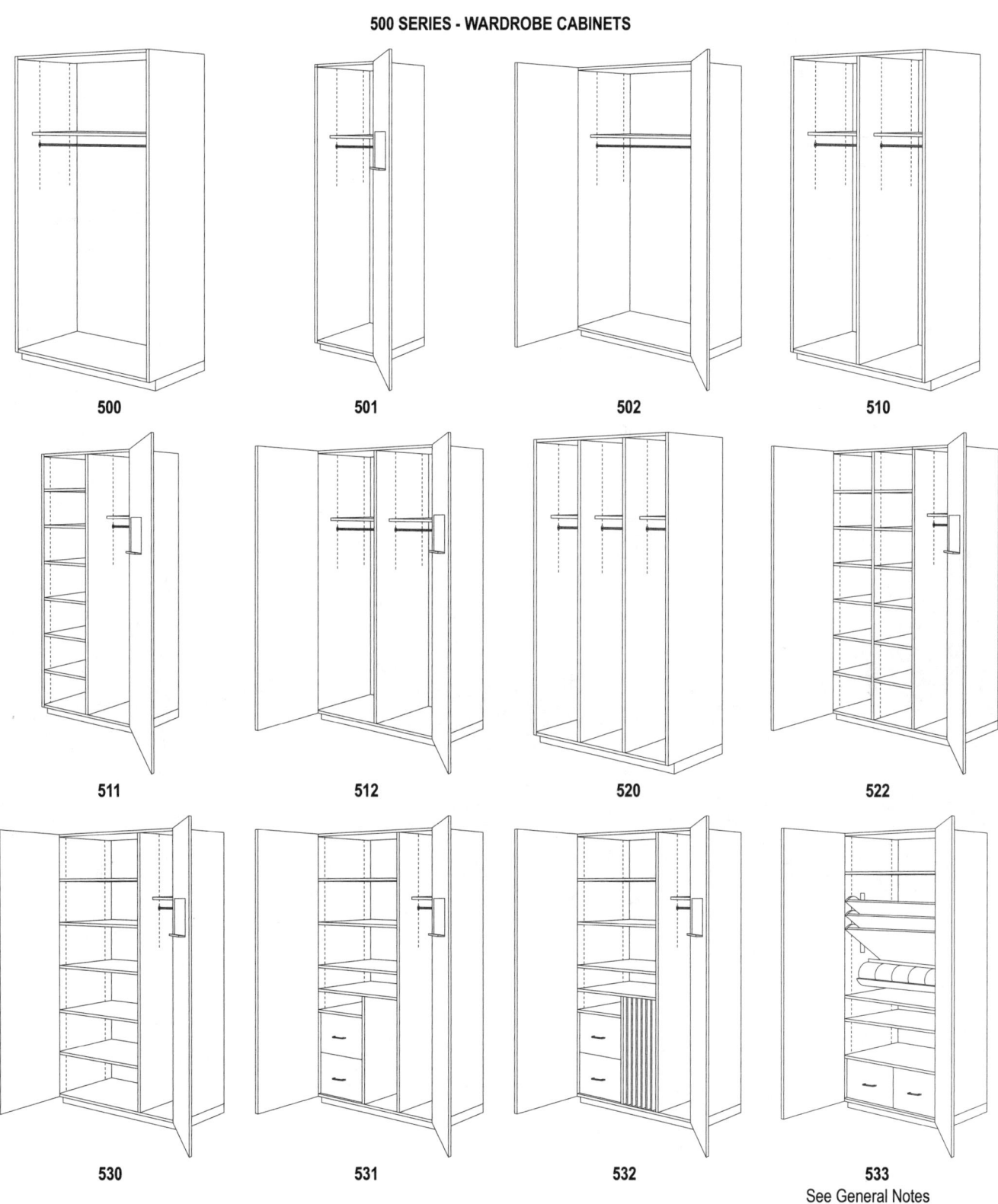

# DESIGN IDEAS

## cabinet design series (CDS)

**500 SERIES - WARDROBE CABINETS**
(continued)

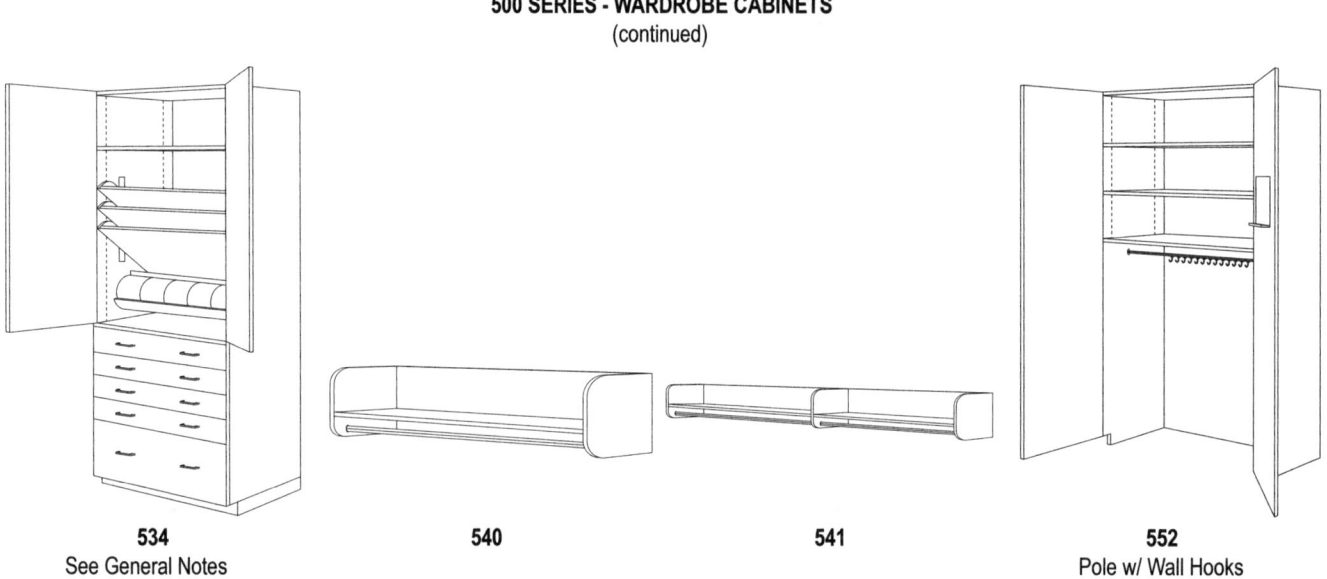

**534**
See General Notes

**540**

**541**

**552**
Pole w/ Wall Hooks

# DESIGN IDEAS

## cabinet design series (CDS)

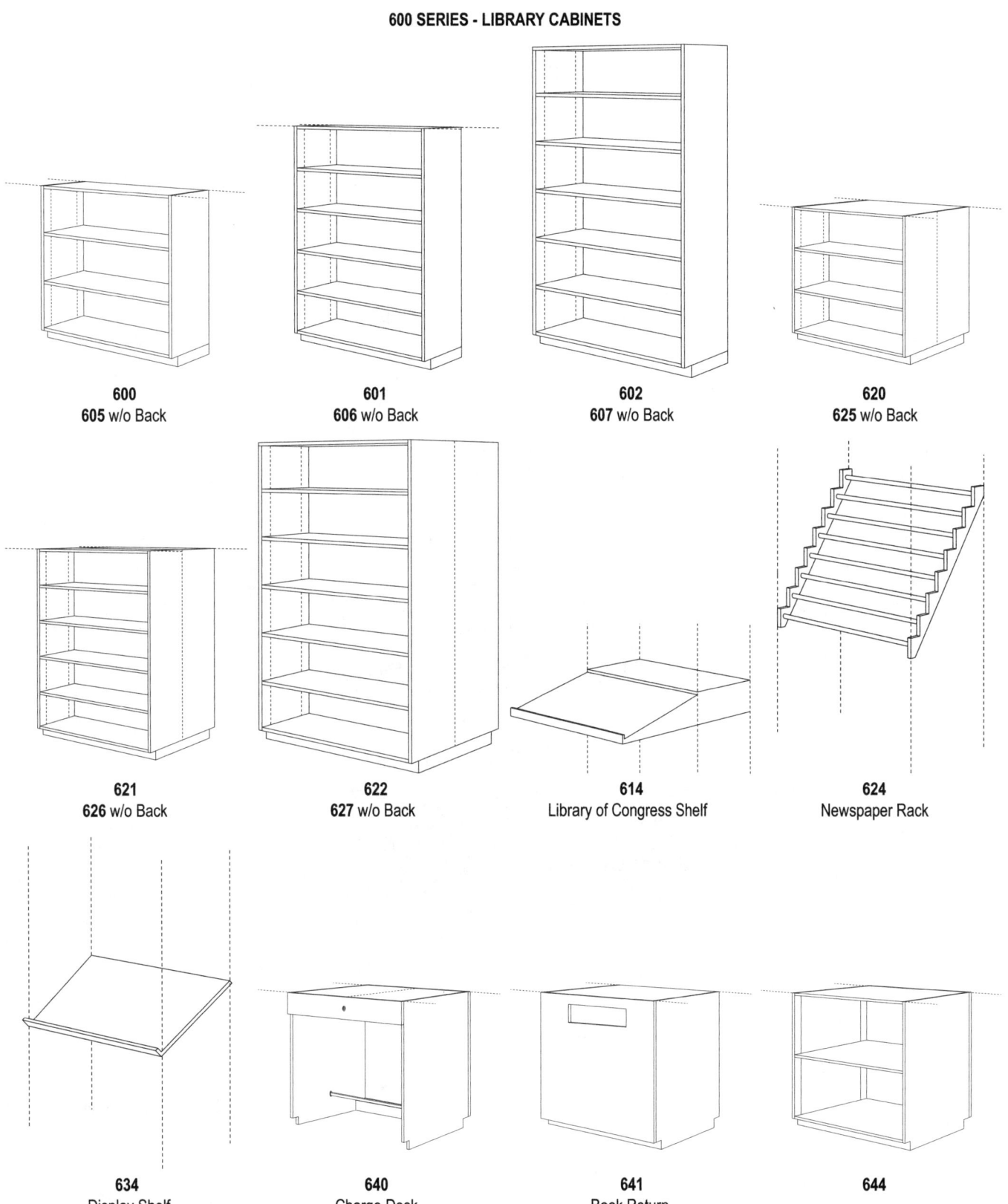

**600 SERIES - LIBRARY CABINETS**

**600** / **605** w/o Back
**601** / **606** w/o Back
**602** / **607** w/o Back
**620** / **625** w/o Back
**621** / **626** w/o Back
**622** / **627** w/o Back
**614** Library of Congress Shelf
**624** Newspaper Rack
**634** Display Shelf
**640** Charge Desk
**641** Book Return
**644**

# DESIGN IDEAS

## cabinet design series (CDS)

**600 SERIES - LIBRARY CABINETS**
(continued)

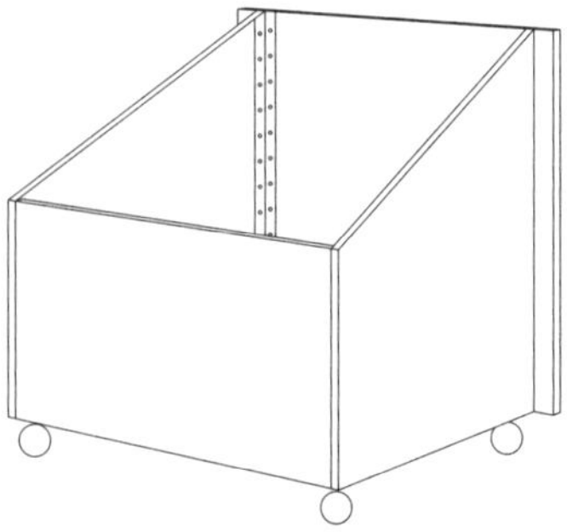

**651**
Book Cart

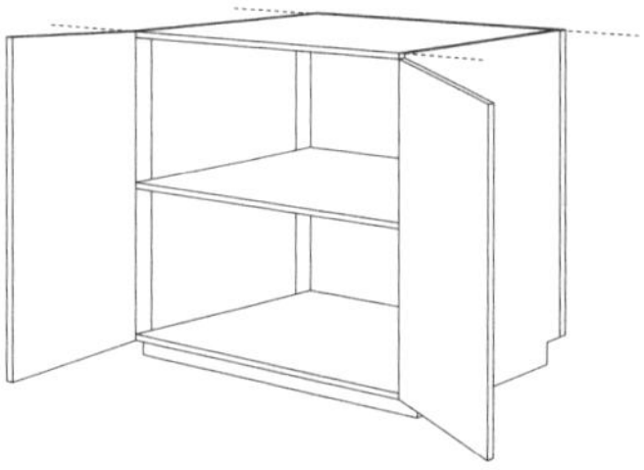

**654**

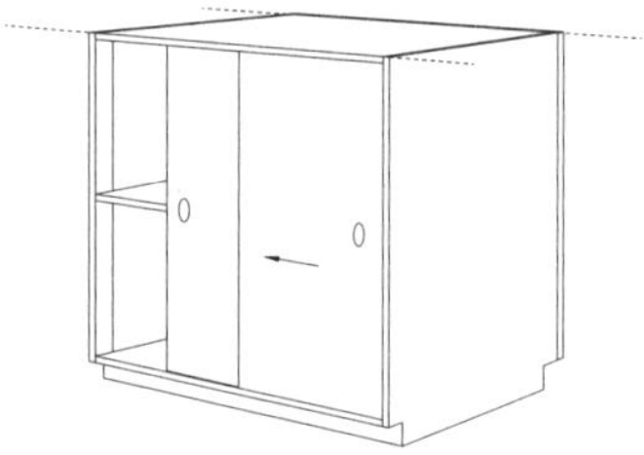

**664**

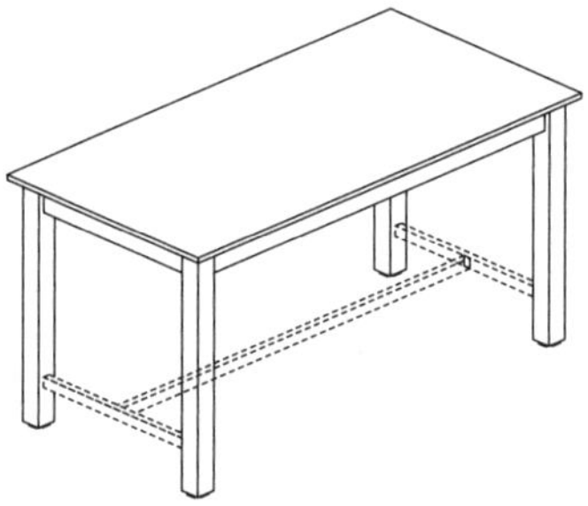

**671a**
**671b** w/ Lateral Bracing

**672**

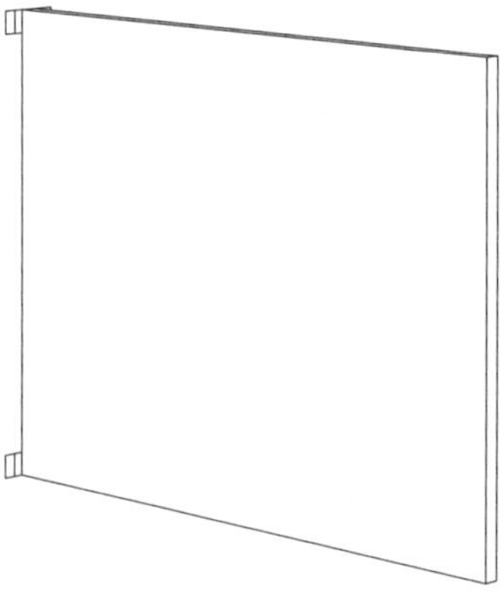

**673**
Gate

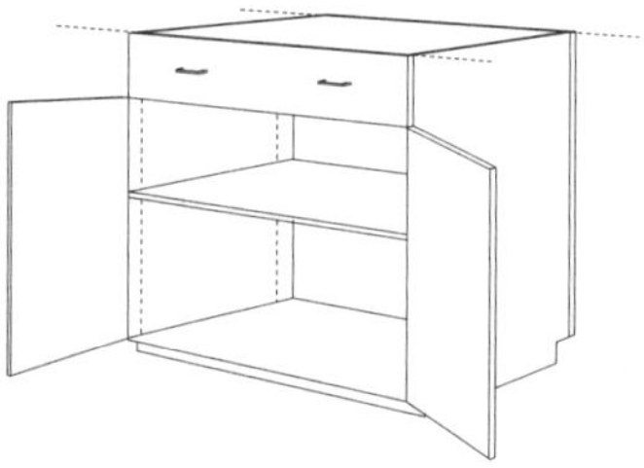

**674**

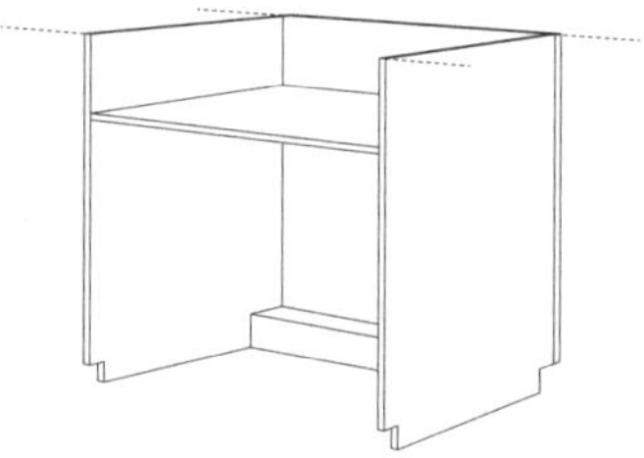

**681**

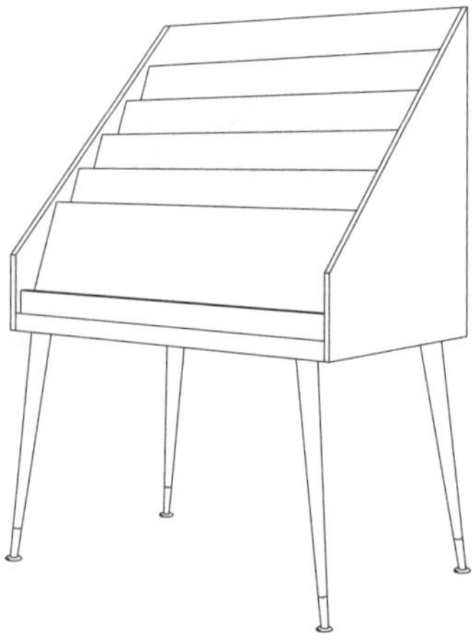

**682 / 692**
Magazine Rack

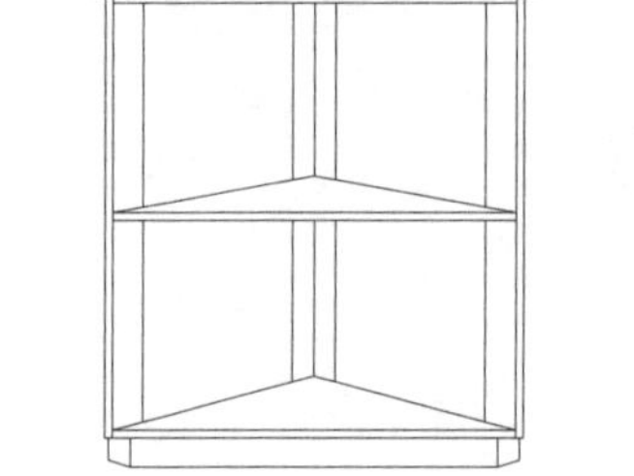

**683**

**684**

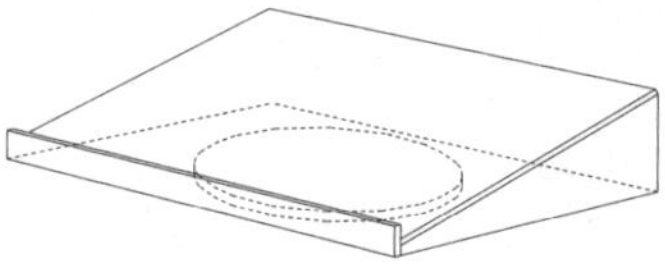

**693**
Dictionary Stand

# DESIGN IDEAS

## cabinet design series (CDS)

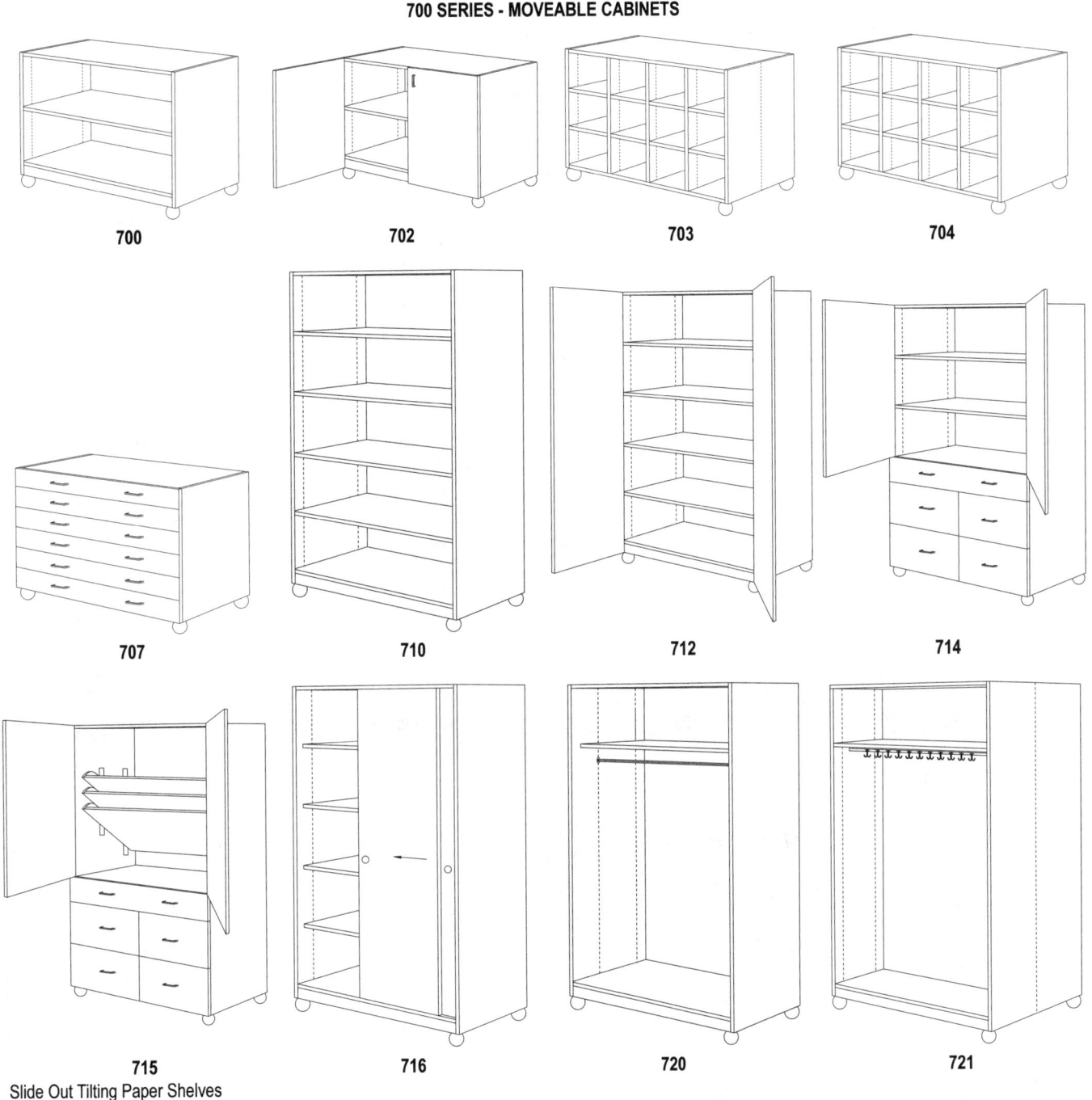

700 SERIES - MOVEABLE CABINETS

715 Slide Out Tilting Paper Shelves

# DESIGN IDEAS

## cabinet design series (CDS)

**700 SERIES - MOVEABLE CABINETS**
(continued)

722

724

725

726

728
Toy Cart

729
Toy Cart

730

731

732

734

735
Clay Cart, Tin NIC

736
Metal Lined Clay Cart

# DESIGN IDEAS

## cabinet design series (CDS)

**700 SERIES - MOVEABLE CABINETS**
(continued)

**737** Block Cart

**738** Block Cart

**739** Ball & Bat Cart

**742** Lab Demonstration Cart

**743** Two Sided Easel

**744** Single Sided Easel

**746** Cooking Demonstration Cart

**747** Nature Demonstration Cart

**750**

**751**

**752**

**753**

# DESIGN IDEAS

## cabinet design series (CDS)

**700 SERIES - MOVEABLE CABINETS**
(continued)

**754**

**755**

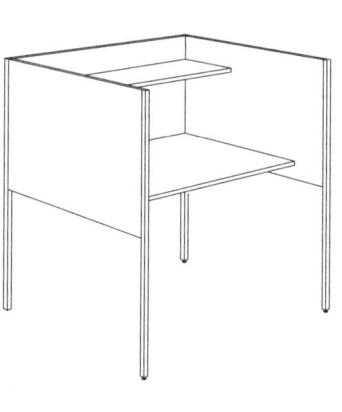

**760**
Study Carrel

Typical Diaphragm Bottom Detail

# Architectural Woodwork Standards

# GLOSSARY

# GLOSSARY

## INTRODUCTION

The Glossary portion of the *Architectural Woodwork Standards* provides definitions of words and is intended to clarify terms and usage with regard to specific application within the standards. The Design Ideas portion includes an additional Historic Woodwork Glossary, listing terms and definitions relating to ornamental woodwork and architectural moldings.

**1 MIL:** A mil is 1/1000" or 0.001" (0.00254 mm).

**ABRASION RESISTANCE:** Resistance to friction wear.

**ABS:** Abbreviation for "Acrylonitrile butadiene styrene," a synthetic decorative coating or edgebanding.

**ACRYLIC LACQUER:** In finishing, a high quality clear system for finishing furniture.

**ADHESION:** The degree of attachment between a finish step and the underlying material.

**ADHESIVE:** A substance capable of bonding materials together by surface attachment. It is a general term and includes all cements and glues.

**ADHESIVE, COLD PRESS AND HOT PRESS:** "Cold press" means no heat is applied to the press and will include the use of pinch rollers. "Hot press" means heat is applied at the time the press is in operation.

**ADHESIVE, TYPE I FULLY WATERPROOF:** Forms a bond that will retain practically all of its strength when occasionally subjected to a thorough wetting and drying; bond shall be of such quality that specimens will withstand shear and the two cycle boil test specified in ANSI/HPVA HP (latest edition).

**ADHESIVE, TYPE II WATER RESISTANT:** Forms a bond that will retain practically all of its strength when occasionally subjected to a thorough wetting and drying; bond shall be of such quality that specimens will withstand the three cycle cold soak test specified in ANSI/HPVA HP (latest edition).

**ADJACENT:** When one surface is directly next to or touching another surface with no other surfaces in between the two.

**ADJACENT PANEL:** When one panel surface is within 6" (152 mm) of another panel surface on the same plane within a room.

**ADJUSTABLE SHELVES:** Generally accomplished through the use of multiple holes with either plastic or metal pins to hold the shelves. Some metal or plastic shelf standards are still in use. The adjustment method is the manufacturer's option unless otherwise specified.

**AGROFIBER:** Refers to core products made from the residual material from a grain crop similar in composition to particleboard.

**AIR DRIED:** Seasoned by controlled exposure to the atmosphere, in the open or under cover, without artificial heat.

**ALL HEART:** Of heartwood throughout; free of sapwood.

**ANCHOR STRIPS:** Used to mount woodwork; other names include nailers, mounting cleats, hanging strips, and wall cleats.

**ANCHORAGE FASTENER:** Installation screws used to attach casework to walls. Screw requirements are as described in section 10.

**ANILINE DYE:** A synthetic dye often used to impart enhanced clarity of color to wood.

**APRON:** For purposes of these standards, means a horizontal trim member below the countertop typically at knee spaces or open sink areas.

**ARCHITECTURAL WOODWORK:** Custom woodworking, so varied in design and complexity that it becomes difficult to define; specified for special applications and functions by design professionals and created by manufacturers. It includes all exterior and interior woodwork exposed to view in a finished building (except specialty items of flooring, shingles, exposed roof decking, ceiling, siding, structural wood trusses and rafters, and overhead type doors), including all exposed wood, plywood, high and low pressure decorative laminates, and doors. Items made of other materials are included only if called for in the specifications. Finishing may be included if specified. Site installation may also be included if specified.

**ARRIS:** In architecture, a sharp edge formed by the meeting of two flat or curved surfaces.

**ARTICULATED JOINT:** In architectural paneling, joint details that allow for field variations.

**ASSEMBLY-1:** A wall mounted method of decorative laminate back and end splash countertop construction.

**ASSEMBLY-2:** A deck mounted method of back and end splash countertop construction.

**B-STAGE CURING:** Is a process that utilizes heat or UV light to remove the majority of solvent from a substance, thereby allowing application to be "staged." In between application, coating and curing can be held for a period of time, without sacrificing performance.

**BACK:** The side reverse to the face of a panel, or the poorer side of a panel in any Grade of plywood calling for a face and a back.

**BACK PRIMING:** A finish coating typically applied to concealed surfaces of architectural woodwork to minimize moisture penetration.

**BACK VENEER:** The veneer placed on the semi-exposed or concealed face of a veneered panel construction to balance the construction. Also, the side reverse to the face of a panel, or the poorer side of panel in any Grade calling for a face and a back.

# GLOSSARY

**BACKED OUT:** Wide, shallow area machined on the back surface of wide solid moldings and some frames. Allows the item to span irregular surfaces.

**BACKER MATERIAL:** A sheet product with performance properties determined by its material composition. Because material composition types vary then backer sheet types accordingly vary in performance properties. Which backer sheet material is used should be based on overall product demands. When used as a balancing sheet a backer must have performance properties equal to an opposing surface with a similar adhesive and application process as the face sheet. (See BALANCING SHEET) Otherwise a backer sheet need not have performance properties equal to an opposing surface.

**BALANCED CONSTRUCTION:** To achieve balanced construction, panels should be absolutely symmetrical from the center line; i.e., use materials on either side that contract or expand, or are moisture permeable, at the same rate. Balanced finishing coats on the back of veneered panels are also highly recommended. Balancing sheet requirements for decorative laminate fabrication vary with the product. Doors and panels should have a balancing sheet on the back side and be applied in the same machine direction. Countertops or cabinet members, on the other hand, merely require some form of balancing material.

**BALANCED MATCH:** A common term in book matching that uses two or more leaves of uniform width on the face of a panel, wherein the two outermost leaves in a panel or face are of the same width.

**BALANCING SHEET:** A sheet product with performance properties equal to an opposing surface. A balancing sheet is laminated to the secondary surface of a core with the same adhesive and application process as the primary surface material (i.e., face material) to maintain the panel's flatness. Typically a balance sheet is used to balance a panel that will not be captured or restrained (e.g., doors).

**BALANCING SPECIES:** A species of similar density to achieve balance by equalizing the rate of moisture absorption or emission.

**BALUSTER:** One of the repetitive vertical members below a handrail or guardrail to provide support and a functional barrier.

**BALUSTRADE:** The assembly of newels, balusters, and rails that make up the safety barrier along balconies and open sides of stairways and ramps.

**BANDED:** Usually refers to the application of a similar material to the edge of a built up member to cover or hide the otherwise exposed core, such as on plywood.

**BARBER POLE:** An effect in book matching of veneers resulting from tight and loose sides of veneers causing different light reflections when finished.

**BARK POCKET:** Bark around which normal wood has grown.

**BEDDING IN PUTTY:** Glazing whereby a thin layer of putty or bedding compound is placed in the glass rabbet, and the glass is inserted and pressed onto this bed.

**BEVEL:** A machine angle other than a right angle; e.g., a 3 degree bevel, which is equivalent to a 1/8" (3.2 mm) drop in a 2" (50.8 mm) span. Also, in flooring or wall paneling, a V shaped groove between strips, planks, or panels.

**BEVELED EDGE:** An edge of the door that forms an angle of less than 90 degrees with the wide face of the door, such as a 3 degree beveled edge.

**BIRD'S EYE:** Decorative figure due to small conical depressions in the outer annual rings, which appear to follow the same contour in subsequent growth rings, probably for many years. Rotary slicing cuts the depressions crosswise, exposing a series of circlets called bird's eyes.

**BISCUIT SPLINE:** A concealed oblong shaped spline used to join adjacent members.

**BLEACHING:** The chemical process used to remove color or whiten solid wood or wood veneered panels. This process may be used to lighten an extremely dark wood or to whiten a lighter colored wood. Most woods do not turn completely white when bleached.

**BLEEDING:** When the color of one coating material migrates up through the finishing layer to the succeeding coat, imparting some of its characteristics.

**BLENDING:** Color change that is detectable at a distance of 6' to 8' (1829 mm to 2438 mm) but that does not detract from the overall appearance of the panel.

**BLIND CORNER:** The space created by abutting cabinets at an approximate 90 degree angle.

**BLISTERING:** The formation of bubbles on the surface of a coating, caused by trapping air or vapors beneath the surface; an area where veneer does not adhere; a figure resembling an uneven collection of rounded or blister like bulges caused by the uneven contour of annual growth rings.

**BLOCKING:** Commonly understood as the wooden support material placed within or upon gypsum board and plaster walls to support casework.

**BLUEPRINT SEQUENCED PANELS AND COMPONENTS:** Each panel for walls and components (e.g., desk, doors) is custom manufactured to the specific size required. All panels are balance matched and sequenced to the adjacent panels.

**BLUSHING:** The whitish, cloud like haze that occurs in fast drying finishes, especially lacquer, when they are sprayed in very humid conditions. Blushing is most often due to moisture (water vapor) trapped in the film or to resin precipitating out of solution.

**BOARD:** A piece of lumber before gluing for width or thickness.

# GLOSSARY

**BOARD FOOT:** A unit of measurement of lumber represented by a board 12" (305 mm) long, 12" (305 mm) wide, and 1" (25.4 mm) thick. Abbreviated BF, Bf, bf. When stock is less than 1" (25.4 mm) thick, it is usually calculated as if it were a full 1" (25.4 mm) thick.

**BOOK MATCH:** Matching between adjacent veneer leaves on one panel face. Every other piece of veneer is turned over so that the adjacent leaves are "opened" as two pages in a book. The fibers of the wood, slanting in opposite directions in the adjacent leaves, create a characteristic light and dark effect when the surface is seen from an angle.

**BOW:** A deviation, flatwise, from a straight line drawn from end to end of a piece. It is measured at the point of greatest distance from the straight line.

**BOX STRINGER:** See closed stringer.

**BRASHNESS:** Condition of wood characterized by low resistance to shock and by abrupt failure across the grain without splintering.

**BUCKS:** In wall blocking used for the installation of door/window jambs and other woodwork in conjunction with metal framing and/or block walls.

**BUGLE HEAD SCREW:** Is similar to countersunk; however, there is a smooth progression from the shaft to the angle of the head, similar to the bell of a bugle. This term is generally used in referencing drywall screws.

**BULLNOSE:** A convex, rounded shape such as the front edge of a stair step.

**BURL:** A figure created by abnormal growth or response to injury that forms an interwoven, contorted, or gnarly mass of dense woody tissue on the trunk or branch of the tree. Burls are usually small and characterized by eye like markings surrounded by swirls and clusters of distorted tissues. The measurement of the burl is the average of the maximum and minimum dimensions of the burl.

**BURL, BLENDING:** A swirl, twist, or distortion in the grain of the wood which usually occurs near a knot or crotch but does not contain a knot and does not contain abrupt color variation. A blending burl is detectable at 1.8 m to 2.4 m (6 feet to 8 feet) as a swirl or roundel.

**BURL, CONSPICUOUS:** A swirl, twist, or distortion in the grain of the wood which usually occurs near a knot or crotch. A conspicuous burl is associated with abrupt color variation and/or a cluster of small dark piths caused by a cluster of adventitious buds.

**BUTCHER BLOCK:** Generally refers to face laminate hardwoods (usually Maple) forming a work surface in which the edge grain is exposed to wear.

**BUTT JOINT:** A joint formed by square edged surfaces (ends, edges, faces) coming together; end butt joint, edge butt joint.

**CABINET FACE:** The outermost surface of a cabinet unit that allows access to the interior of the cabinet unit, including door faces, drawer faces or false front faces. Does not include ends, sides, top, bottom or back. If the cabinet is an open cabinet the cabinet face is the outermost front exposed edges of the cabinet box.

**CABINET LINER:** As used within these standards, shall describe 0.020" (0.5 mm) high pressure decorative laminate (HPDL).

**CABINET UNIT:** A single manufactured case typically consisting of two ends, a top, a bottom, and may include back, stretchers, anchor strips, shelves, doors, drawer fronts, drawers, dividers, and hardware.

**CANTILEVER:** A projecting structure that is attached or supported at only one end, such as an extended countertop.

**CANT STRIP:** A triangular shaped or beveled strip of material used to ease the transition from a horizontal plane to a vertical plane.

**CAPTURED:** A component whose perimeter is mechanically fastened or joined to other components so that it's not allowed to warp independent of those attached components.

**CASEWORK:** Base and wall cabinets, display fixtures, and storage shelves. The generic term for both "boxes" and special desks, reception counters, nurses stations, and the like. Generally includes the countertops and work surfaces.

**CATALYZED:** In finishing, an ingredient added to a basic product to provide additional performance characteristics.

**CATHEDRAL GRAIN:** A grain appearance characterized by a series of stacked and inverted "V" or cathedral type of springwood (early wood)/summerwood (late wood) patterns common in plain sliced (flat cut) veneer.

**CAULK:** Either the action of making a watertight or airtight seal between two adjacent surfaces by filling the area between the surfaces with a sealant, or the sealant itself.

**CENTER MATCHED:** A form of veneer matching that uses two or more even numbered leaves of equal width, matched with a joint occurring in the center of the panel. A small amount of the figure is lost.

**CHAIN OF CUSTODY:** A method of tracking the handling of a wood product from forest to delivery of a finished product. Each step of transportation and manufacturing is documented for verification of the handling process.

**CHAMFER:** To cut away the edge where two surfaces meet in an exterior angle, leaving a bevel at the junction.

**CHARACTER MARK:** As an element of nature, a distinctive feature in a hardwood surface produced by minerals and other elements that are absorbed as a tree grows.

**CHARACTERISTICS:** The natural irregularities found in wood, whether solid or veneered. Their acceptance is a function of each particular Grade.

**CHATTER:** Lines appearing across the panel or board at right angles to the grain, giving the appearance of one or more corrugations resulting from bad setting of sanding equipment or planing knives.

# GLOSSARY

**CHECKING:** Cracks that appear in a finishing film due to lack of cohesion, often caused by too heavy of a coat being applied or a poor grade of finish being used. Also called cold checking.

**CHECKS:** Small slits running parallel to the grain of wood, caused chiefly by strains produced in seasoning and drying.

**CHIP MARKS:** Shallow depressions or indentations on or in the surface of dressed lumber caused by shavings or chips getting embedded in the surface during dressing.

**CLIMATE:** Conditions found inside or outside a building that include temperature, humidity and barometric pressure.

**CLIMATE CONTROLLED:** Referring to the inside areas of a building where heat or air conditioning systems are installed and actively used for environmental controls.

**CLOSED GRAIN AND OPEN GRAIN:** The size and distribution of the cellular structure of the wood influences the appearance and uniformity. Open grain hardwoods, such as Elm, Oak, Ash, and Chestnut, are "ring porous" species. These species have distinct figure and grain patterns. Close grain hardwoods, such as Cherry, Maple, Birch, and Yellow Poplar, are "diffuse porous" species. Most North American diffuse porous woods have small, dense pores resulting in less distinct figure and grain. Some tropical diffuse porous species (e.g., Mahogany) have rather large pores.

**CLOSED STRINGER:** In stairwork, a stringer that boxes in the treads and risers.

**COFFER:** A sunken, decorative panel in a ceiling.

**COMB GRAIN:** A quality of rift cut veneer with exceptionally straight grain and closely spaced growth increments resembling the appearance of long strands of combed hair.

**COMBINATION CORE:** Panels are a hybridization of veneer and composition cores offering the advantages of both. Typically these cores have internal layers which are constructed of three or five plies of veneer or a center layer of wafer board (randomly oriented wafers) or other wood fiber which are sandwiched between thin laminations of a composite product like MDF, particleboard, hardboard, etc. Typically these products result in stronger, lighter weight, dimensionally stable panels with increased screw holding ability and superior surface flatness.

**COMPATIBLE FOR COLOR AND GRAIN:** For purposes of these standards, means members shall be selected so that:
- Lighter than average color members will not be adjacent to darker than average color members, and there will be no sharp contrast in color between the adjacent members, and
- The grain of adjacent members shall not vary widely or be dissimilar in grain, character, and figure.

**COMPATIBLE SPECIES:** For purposes of these standards, means different species which are able to exist in a harmonious combination of color and grain.

**CONCEALED SURFACE:** Surface not normally visible after installation.

**CONSPICUOUS:** Detectable; readily visible with the naked eye when observed in normal light at a distance stated within these standards.

**CONTACT ADHESIVE:** Normally used for bonding high pressure decorative laminates to a core.

**CONTRACTOR:** A general contractor, normally holding the legal agreement for construction of an owner's building project.

**CONVERSION VARNISH:** In finishing, a class of coatings that are tough and exhibit excellent resistance to household chemicals.

**COPE/COPED:** To cut the end of one member to match the profile of another molded member.

**CHORD SEGMENTATION:** The process of cutting short lengths of straight molding and joining them around a curve core which is not permitted under these standards.

**CORE:** The material (typically, veneer, lumber, particleboard, medium density fiberboard, or a combination of these) on which an exposed surface material (typically, veneer or decorative laminate) is applied.

**CORE, HOLLOW:** A core assembly of strips or other units of wood, wood derivative, or insulation board with intervening hollow cells or spaces that support the outer faces.

**CORE, MINERAL:** A fire resistant core material generally used in doors requiring fire rating of 3/4 hours or more.

**CORE, SOLID:** The innermost layer or section in flush door construction. Typical constructions are as follows:
- **PARTICLEBOARD** - A solid core of wood or other lignocellulose particles bonded together with a suitable binder, cured under heat, and pressed into a rigid panel in a flat platen press.
- **STAVE** - A solid core of wood blocks or strips.
- **WOOD BLOCK, LINED** - A solid core of two parts; a central wood block core bonded to two core liners of wood or other lignocellulose materials.

**CRATERING:** The formation of small depressions in a finish, sometimes called fish eye. Often caused by the contamination of the finish material or the core with silicone, oil, or other substances.

**CREEP:** The deflection over time of loaded or unloaded adjustable shelves, which fluctuates with temperature, humidity and load stress.

**CROOK:** A deviation, edgewise, from a straight line drawn from end to end of a piece. It is measured at the point of greatest distance from the straight line.

# GLOSSARY

**CROSSBANDING:** A ply placed between the core and face veneer in 5 ply construction, or a ply placed between the back and face of a 3 ply skin in 7 ply construction. When the crossbanding has directional grain, it is placed at right angles to the grain of the face veneer. When used with laminate face doors, crossbanding may consist of more than one ply.

**CROSS BAR:** Irregularity of grain resembling a dip in the grain running at right angles, or nearly so, to the length of the veneer.

**CROSS GRAIN:** Applied to wood in which the grain is not running lengthwise of the material in one direction. The irregularity is due to interlocked fiber, uneven annual rings, or to the intersection of branch and stem.

**CROTCH:** Comes from the portion of a tree just below the point where it forks into two limbs. The grain is crushed and twisted, creating a variety of plume and flame figures, often resembling a well formed feather. The outside of the block produces a swirl figure that changes to full crotch figure as the cutting approaches the center of the block.

**CUP:** A deviation in the face of a piece from a straight line drawn from edge to edge of that piece. It is measured at the point of greatest distance from the straight line.

**CURB STRINGER:** See closed stringer.

**CURING:** The complete drying of a finish to the ultimate development of its properties.

**CURLY:** Figure that occurs when the fibers are distorted, producing a wavy or curly effect in the lumber or veneer. Primarily found in Maple or Birch.

**CUSTOM GRADE:** The middle or normal Grade in both material and workmanship, and intended for high quality, conventional work.

**CUT HEART:** See split heart.

**DADO, BLIND, OR STOPPED JOINT:** A dado that is not visible when the joint is completed.

**DADO JOINT:** A rectangular groove across the grain of a wood member into which the end of the joining member is inserted; also a housed joint. Variations include "mortise and tenon" and "stopped or blind dado" joints.

**DECAY:** Disintegration of wood due to the action of wood destroying fungi; "doze", "rot", and "unsound wood" mean the same as "decay."

**DECORATIVE COMPOSITE PANELS:** For the purposes of these standards, a thermally fused panel flat pressed from a thermoset polyester or melamine resin impregnated paper (minimum 30%); see low pressure decorative laminates.

**DEFECT:** Fault that detracts from the quality, appearance, or utility of the piece. Handling marks and/or grain raising due to moisture shall not be considered a defect.

**DEFECT, OPEN:** Open joints, knotholes, cracks, loose knots, wormholes, gaps, voids, or other openings interrupting the smooth continuity of the wood surface.

**DEFLECTION:** When weight is applied to a flat panel supported at two opposing ends in a horizontal position, such as a shelf, and the weight causes the shelf surface to become concave. Deflection is affected by the weight applied as well as the shelf core and finish materials.

**DELAMINATION:** Separation of plies or layers of wood or other materials through failure of the adhesive joint.

**DESIGN PROFESSIONAL:** An architect, interior designer, specification writer, or other individual qualified by virtue of education and/or training to provide services for the design of buildings, interiors, and furnishings.

**DIE WALL:** A millwork assembly, typically vertical, that includes sub framing and a finish face on one or more sides. Die walls are commonly used at reception desks, nurse stations and low walls dividing areas within a larger room. They are typically self supported or attached to floors or walls. A die wall typically allows other millwork items to be attached, such as countertops, transaction countertops and casework.

**DIMENSION LUMBER:** Material that is precut in width and thickness to a standard size.

**DIRECTIONAL PATTERN OR VENEER GRAIN MATCH:** (see Veneer Grain or directional pattern Match).

**DISCOLORATIONS:** Stains in wood substances. Common veneer stains are sap stains, blue stains, stains produced by chemical action caused by the iron in the cutting knife coming in contact with the tannic acid of the wood, and those resulting from exposure of natural wood extractives to oxygen and light, to chemical action of vat treatments or the adhesive components, and/or to the surface finish.

**DISTRESSING:** In finishing, either a mechanical or chemical special effect.

**DISTRIBUTOR:** A person or organization that provides products on a wholesale basis to a manufacturer of woodwork.

**DIVISION:** A cabinet component that is not one of the two sides, top or bottom. A division divides a cabinet into sections. Divisions may be horizontal or vertical.

**DOOR FURNISHER:** As used in PRODUCT of section 09, is defined as the party responsible for the taking off, ordering and supplying of the doors to a project.

**DOVETAIL JOINT:** A joint formed by inserting a projecting wedge shaped member (dovetail tenon) into a correspondingly shaped cut out member (dovetail mortise); variations include the "dovetail dado" and the "blind dovetail dado."

**DOWEL:** Cylindrical peg used to strengthen a wood joint.

**DOWELED JOINT:** A joint using "dowels" (doweled construction); also "doweled edge joint."

# GLOSSARY

**DOUG FIR:** Referring to Douglas Fir. Douglas fir is a common name for softwood evergreen coniferous trees of the genus Pseudotsuga in the family Pinaceae. Also known as Douglas Tree, False Hemlock and Oregon Pine. The heartwood of Doug Fir is moderately resistant to decay and is often used in exterior applications that require a smooth finish. The grain is typically straight and used as small parts for millwork where straightness is a consideration.

**DOZE:** A form of incipient decay characterized by a dull and lifeless appearance of the wood, accompanied by a loss of strength and softening of the wood substance.

**DRAWINGS:** Part of a project's design documents which, in combination with written specifications, define the scope, quality assurance, requirements, submittals, dimensions, product handling, and product specifications to the manufacturer. See Shop Drawings.

**EASED EDGES:** For the vast majority of work, a sharp arris or edge is not permitted. Such edges are traditionally "eased" by lightly striking the edge with a fine abrasive. Less often, or as a design element, such edges are machined to a small radius.

**EASEMENTS:** Short curved segments of handrail that provide for changes in pitch, elevation, or direction.

**ECONOMY GRADE:** The lowest Grade in both material and workmanship, and intended for work where price outweighs quality considerations.

**EDGEBANDING:** The process of attaching a finished material to the edge of panels. Typically machine applied with hot melt glue, however hand attachment is allowed. Edgeband application is subject to tolerances found in these Standards.

**EDGE GRAIN (EG) OR VERTICAL GRAIN (VG):** A piece or pieces sawn at approximately right angles to the annual growth rings so that the rings form an angle of 45 degrees or more with the surface of the piece.

**EDGE JOINT:** When the edges of boards are glued together to increase the width.

**EFFECT:** The final result achieved in a finished wood surface, after the application of a clearly specified series of finishing procedures (steps) have been completed. Successfully achieving a specified "effect" requires the active participation of the design professional and the woodwork finisher.

**ELEVATION:** As used within these standards, a view of the front, back or end of an assembly or grouping of architectural woodwork components.

**END BUTT JOINT:** When:
- One end is glued to an edge or face of another board to form an angle (e.g., stiles and rails of a face frame)
- The end of one board is fastened to the end of another to increase its length (e.g., running trim).

**END GRAIN:** The grain seen in a cut made at a right angle to the direction of the fibers in a board.

**END MATCH:** Butting adjacent veneer leaves on one panel end to end in sequence. Veneer leaves are book matched end to end. Generally used for very long panels or for projects in which only short length veneers are available.

**EQUILIBRIUM MOISTURE CONTENT:** The moisture content at which wood neither gains nor loses moisture when surrounded by air at a given relative humidity and temperature.

**ESCUTCHEON:** A protective fitting around a keyhole; also a shield like ornament.

**EXPOSED EXTERIOR SURFACES:** For purposes of these standards, specifically casework, means all exterior surfaces exposed to view.

**EXPOSED FASTENERS:** Any mechanical fastening device, filled or unfilled, that can be seen on exposed or semi-exposed surfaces of woodwork.

**EXPOSED INTERIOR SURFACES:** For purposes of these standards, specifically casework, means all interior surfaces exposed to view in open casework or behind transparent doors.

**EXPOSED SURFACES:** Surfaces normally visible after installation.

**EXTERIOR (Building):** That portion of the structure that is outside of the weather proofing of the building, including the weather proofing (non climate controlled).

**FACE:** The better side of any panel in which the outer plies are of different veneer grades; also either side of a panel in which there is no difference in veneer grade of the outer plies.

**FACE FRAME CONSTRUCTION:** A type of construction, where the front edge of the cabinet body components is overlaid with a frame.

**FACE VENEER:** The outermost exposed wood veneer surface of a veneered door, panel, or other component exposed to view when the project is completed.

**FASTENER, MECHANICAL:** The generic term for securing devices that are used in the fabrication and/or installation of architectural woodwork, such as dowels, dowel screws, splines, nails, screws, bolts, shot pins, etc.

**FEW:** A small number without regard to their arrangement in the panel.

**FIBER:** One of the long, thick walled cells that give strength and support to hardwoods.

**FIBERBOARD CORE:** Manufactured from wood reduced to fine fibers mixed with binders and formed by the use of heat and pressure into panels.

**FIDDLEBACK:** A fine, strong, even ripple figure as frequently seen on the backs of violins. The figure is found principally in Mahogany and Maple, but occurs sometimes in other species.

**FIELD:** With reference to work location, meaning in the field or jobsite versus in the manufacturing plant or shop.

**FIGURE:** The natural pattern produced in the wood surface by annual growth rings, rays, knots, and natural deviations from the normal grain, such as interlocked and wavy grain, and irregular coloration.

# GLOSSARY

**FILLER:** In finishing, ground inert solids specifically designed to fill pores or small cavities in wood as one step in the overall finishing process. In casework, paneling, ornamental work, stairwork, frames, and some other architectural woodwork applications, an additional piece of trim material between woodwork members or between woodwork and some other material used to create a fill or transition between the members.

**FINGER JOINT:** When the ends of two pieces of lumber are cut to an identically matching set. Used most commonly to increase the length of the board. A series of interlocking fingers are precision cut on the ends of two pieces of wood that mesh together and are held rigidly in place with adhesive.

**FIRE RETARDANT TREATMENT:** Only a few species are treated with chemicals to reduce flammability and retard the spread of flame over the surface. This usually involves impregnation of the wood, under pressure, with salts and other chemicals. White Oak is untreatable.

**FIRE RATED DOOR:** A door that has been constructed in such a manner that when installed in an assembly and tested will pass ASTM E-152 "Fire Test of Door Assemblies," and can be rated as resisting fire for 20 minutes (1/3 hour), 30 minutes (1/2 hour), 45 minutes (3/4 hour) (C), 1 hour (B), or 1-1/2 hours (B). The door must be tested and carry an identifying label from a qualified testing and inspection agency.

**FIRST CLASS WORKMANSHIP:** For architectural woodwork, the finest or highest class of workmanship for the Grade specified, and shall be free of manufacturing and natural defects covered under grading rules in these standards.

**FLAKE:** See "Fleck, Ray".

**FLAKEBOARD:** See "particleboard."

**FLAME SPREAD:** Fire retardant particleboard is available with an Underwriters' Laboratory (UL) stamp for Class 1 Flame Spread 20 (Smoke Developed 25). Fire Rated doors are available with particleboard and mineral cores for ratings up to 1-1/2 hours. It is the responsibility of the specifier to indicate which fire retardant classification is required for a particular product. In the absence of such a specified rating, the manufacturer may supply unrated product.

**FLAME SPREAD CLASSIFICATION:** The generally accepted measurement for flame spread rating of materials. It compares the rate of flame spread on a particular species with the rate of flame spread on untreated Red Oak.

**FLAT GRAIN (FG) OR SLASH GRAIN (SG):** A piece or pieces sawn approximately parallel to the annual growth rings so that all or some of the rings form an angle of less than 45 degrees with the surface of the piece.

**FLAT SLICING:** See "Plain Slicing".

**FLATNESS:** A panel face having an even or smooth surface in one plane without depressions or projections.

**FLECK, RAY:** Portion of a ray as it appears on the quartered or rift cut surface. Fleck is often a dominant appearance feature in Oak.

**FLITCH:** A hewn or sawn log made ready for veneer production or the actual veneer slices of one half log, kept in order, and used for the production of plywood panels.

**FLUSH INSET:** Cabinet construction in which the door and drawer faces are set within and flush with the body members or face frames of the cabinet with spaces between face surfaces sufficient for operating clearance.

**FLUSH OVERLAY:** Cabinet construction in which door and drawer faces cover the body members of the cabinet with spaces between face surfaces sufficient for operating clearance.

**FLUTE:** One of a series of parallel, lengthwise channels or grooves in a column, cornice molding, band, or furniture leg.

**FRAMELESS CONSTRUCTION:** A type of construction, where no frame is attached to the front edge of the cabinet body components which are typically edgebanded.

**FRENCH CLEAT:** A method of concealed panel or trim hanging where one component is screwed to the wall and the other component is screwed to the back of a millwork product. Each cleat has an opposing 45 degree edge, causing the two pieces to interlock. French cleats may be used for cabinet hanging provided it has been independently tested to show compliance to the Wall Cabinet Structural Integrity Test shown in Appendix.

**FURRING:** Material added to a building surface to create a true plane in order to install woodwork plumb and level.

**GABLE:** Aside from the traditional usage referring to the end of a building, in casework the end or side of a cabinet.

**GAP:** An unfilled opening in a continuous surface or between adjoining surfaces.

**GENERAL CONTRACTOR:** See contractor.

**GLAZING:** In finishing, an added step for achieving color or to heighten grain appearance.

**GLOSS:** See sheen.

**GLUE BLOCK:** A wood block, usually triangular in cross section, securely glued to an angular joint between two members for a greater glue bond area.

**GLUE SPOTS:** The discoloration or barrier to finish penetration caused by the bleed through or unremoved glue on an exposed or semi-exposed wood surface.

**GLUED, SECURELY:** The bonding of two members with an adhesive forming a tight joint with no visible delamination at the lines of application.

**GRADE:** Unless otherwise noted, this term means Grade rules for Economy, Custom, and/or Premium Grade.

# GLOSSARY

**GRADING RULES:** Most hardwoods are graded utilizing the rules established by the National Hardwood Lumber Association. Softwoods, on the other hand, are graded by several grading associations. The three primary softwood grading associations are Western Wood Products Association, Southern Pine Inspection Bureau, and Redwood Inspection Service.

- Although lumber must be purchased by the manufacturer according to these grading rules, these rules should not be used to specify lumber for architectural woodwork. Specify the Grade of Work for the fabricated products under these standards.

- Softwood plywood is graded by the American Plywood Association (APA, The Engineered Wood Association). Grade markings are stamped on the back or edge of each sheet.

- Hardwood plywood is made under the standards of the Hardwood Plywood and Veneer Association (HPVA). These Grades are rarely marked on the panels.

**GRAIN:** The fibers in wood and their direction, size, arrangement, appearance, or quality. When severed, the annual growth rings become quite pronounced and the effect is referred to as "grain":

- **FLAT GRAIN (FG) or SLASH GRAIN (SG)** - lumber or veneer is a piece sawn or sliced approximately parallel to the annual growth rings so that some or all of the rings form an angle of less than 45 degrees with the surface of the piece.

- **MIXED GRAIN (MG)** - is any combination of vertical or flat grain in the same member. Vertical grain lumber or veneer is a piece sawn or sliced at approximately right angles to the annual growth rings so that the rings form an angle of 45 degrees or more with the surface of the piece.

- **QUARTERED GRAIN** - is a method of sawing or slicing to bring out certain figures produced by the medullary or pith rays, which are especially conspicuous in Oak. The log is flitched in several different ways to allow the cutting of the veneer in a radial direction. Rift or comb grain is lumber or veneer that is obtained by cutting at an angle of about 15 degrees off of the quartered position. Twenty-five percent (25%) of the exposed surface area of each piece of veneer may contain medullary ray flake.

- **OPEN GRAIN AND CLOSED GRAIN** - The size and distribution of the cellular structure of the wood influences the appearance and uniformity. Open grain hardwoods, such as Elm, Oak, Ash, and Chestnut are "ring porous" species. These species have distinct figure and grain patterns. Close grain hardwoods, such as Cherry, Maple, Birch, and Yellow Poplar, are "diffuse porous" species. Most North American diffuse porous woods have small, dense pores resulting in less distinct figure and grain. Some tropical diffuse porous species (e.g., Mahogany) have rather large pores.

- **GRAIN RAISE** - When moisture in a finish swells and lifts wood fibers away from the surface of the wood being finished. The wood surface should be further sanded to eliminate grain raise.

- **RAISED GRAIN** - Roughened condition of the surface of dressed lumber on which hard summerwood is raised above the softer springwood, but is not torn loose from it.

**GRAIN CHARACTER:** A varying pattern produced by cutting through growth rings, exposing various layers. It is most pronounced in veneer cut tangentially or rotary.

**GRAIN FIGURE:** The pattern produced in a wood surface by annual growth rings, rays, knots, or deviations from natural grain, such as interlocked and wavy grain and irregular coloration.

**GRAIN RAISE:** See Grain.

**GRAIN SLOPE:** Expression of the angle of the grain to the long edges of the veneer component.

**GRAIN SWEEP:** Expression of the angle of the grain to the long edges of the veneer component over the area extending one-eighth of the length of the piece from the ends.

**GROOVE:** Rectangular slot of three surfaces cut parallel with the grain of the wood.

**GROUND:** A narrow strip of wood that serves as a guide for plaster as well as a base to which trim members are secured. Grounds are applied to rough interior openings especially doors and windows; along interior walls at the finish floor line; and wherever wainscot may be installed. The thickness of a ground is that of the combined lath and plaster, while the width varies from 1" (25.4 mm) to 3" (76.2 mm), which is often called plaster grounds (around interior or exterior openings) and base grounds (when used around base of rooms).

**GROWTH RINGS:** The layer of wood added by a tree in a single growing season, the markings of which contribute to the figure in finished woods. Annual growth rings include both summer and winter growth.

**GUM POCKETS:** Well defined openings between rings of annual growth, containing gum or evidence of prior gum accumulations.

**GUM SPOTS AND STREAKS:** Gum or resinous material or color spots and streaks often dark brown, black or golden, caused by prior resin accumulations sometimes found on veneer or lumber surfaces.

**HAIRLINE:** A thin, perceptible line showing at the joint of two pieces of wood.

**HALF LAP JOINT:** A joint formed by extending (lapping) the joining part of one member over the joining part of another.

**HALF ROUND:** A method of cutting veneers on an off center lathe that results in modified characteristics of both rotary and plain sliced veneers; often used in Red and White Oak.

# GLOSSARY

**HALF ROUND SLICING:** A method of veneer cutting similar to rotary cutting, except that the piece being cut is secured to a "stay log," a device that permits the cutting of the log on a wider sweep than when mounted with its center secured in the lathe to produce rotary sliced veneer. A type of half round cutting is used to achieve plain sliced or flat cut veneer.

**HANDLING MARKS:** Scratches, dents, blemishes, mars, or scuffs left or created by physical handling or packaging.

**HANDRAIL:** See "Molding".

**HAND RUBBED FINISH:** In finishing, a manual step performed to smooth, flatten, or dull the topcoat.

**HARDBOARD:** A generic term for a panel manufactured primarily from inter felted lignocellulose fibers consolidated under heat and pressure in a hot press and conforming to the requirements of ANSI/AHA A 135.4 (latest edition).

**HARDBOARD, TEMPERED:** Hardboard that has been coated or impregnated with an oil and then baked to give it more impact resistance, hardness, rigidity, tensile strength, and more resistance to scratches and moisture. Tempered hardboard is typically smooth on both sides and may have a dark smooth finish.

**HARDNESS** (in finishing): The property of a coating that causes it to resist denting or penetration by a hard object.

**HARDWOOD:** General term used to designate lumber or veneer produced from temperate zone deciduous or tropical broad leaved trees in contrast to softwood, which is produced from trees that are usually needle bearing or coniferous. The term does not imply hardness in its physical sense.

**HEARTWOOD:** The non active or dormant center of a tree, generally distinguishable from the outer portion (sapwood) by its darker color, sometime referred to as heart.

**HEAT RESISTANCE TEST:** See "Appendix."

**HIGH DENSITY OVERLAY:** The standard grades of high density overlay shall be as listed in PS 1, latest edition. The surface of the finished product shall be hard, smooth, or uniformly textured, although some evidence of underlying grain may appear. The surface shall be of such a character that further finishing by paint or protective coating is not necessary.

**HIGH PRESSURE CABINET LINER:** Conforms to NEMA LD-3 (latest edition), has a color or pattern sheet to enhance its appearance, and is intended for use in cabinet interiors.

**HIGH PRESSURE DECORATIVE LAMINATE (HPDL):** Laminated thermosetting decorative sheets intended for decorative purposes. The sheets consist essentially of layers of a fibrous sheet material, such as paper, impregnated with a thermosetting condensation resin and consolidation under heat and pressure. The top layers have a decorative color or a printed design. The resulting product has an attractive exposed surface that is durable and resistant to damage from abrasion and mild alkalies, acids, and solvents, meeting the requirements of the National Electrical Manufacturers Association (NEMA) LD-3 (latest edition).

**HOLE:** Applies to holes from any cause.

**HOLES, WORM:** Holes resulting from infestation by worms greater than 1/16" (1.6 mm) in diameter.

**HONEYCOMB DOOR CORE:** A method of using lightweight paper, wood or other material based products to form a door core. The honeycomb provides some structural integrity and is a base for attachment of back bands or cross bands.

**HONEYCOMB IN RED OAK:** A structural defect found in Red Oak caused by bacterial heartwood infection resulting in abnormal odors in kiln dried lumber and an appearance of voids within the lumber.

**HOUSED CABINET BACK:** When a cabinet back is set in a three sided groove such as a plow or groove.

**HPDL:** See "high pressure decorative laminate."

**HPDL COMPACT:** See "Solid Phenolic".

**HUMIDITY:** The common term for relative humidity; the amount of moisture in an atmosphere in relation to temperature.

**INCONSPICUOUS:** Not readily visible without careful inspection (as a measurement of natural or machining characteristics).

**INDENTATIONS:** Areas in the face that have been compressed as the result of residue on the platens of the hot press or handling damage through the factory.

**INNER PLIES:** Plies other than face or back plies in a panel construction. Crossbands and centers are classed as inner plies (see core).

**INSTALLER:** A person or organization that regularly engages in the practice of installing architectural woodwork.

**INTERIOR** (Building): That portion of a building that is inside the building weather proofing, not including the weather proofing (can be climate controlled).

**INTUMESCENT COATINGS:** Can be applied to the surface of flammable products to reduce flammability.

**JOINT:** The line of juncture between the edges or ends of two adjacent pieces of lumber or sheets of veneer, such as butt, dado (blind, stopped), dovetail, blind dovetail, finger, half lap, lock, miter (shoulder, lock, spline), mortise and tenon (blind slotted, stub, or through), rabbet, scarf, spline, and tongue and groove joint.

**JOINT, OPEN:** Joint in which two adjacent pieces of lumber or veneer do not fit tightly together.

**JOINTS TIGHT, FACTORY:** Any joints or a combination of joints and/or mechanical fasteners, that are used to join two members in the shop. Distance between members shall not exceed those set forth in these standards.

**JOINTS TIGHT, FIELD:** Any joints or a combination of joints and/or mechanical fasteners that are used to join two members in the field. Distance between members shall not exceed those set forth in these standards.

# GLOSSARY

**KCPI:** Stands for "knife cuts per inch"; generally used when describing the result of molded profiles or S4S materials.

**KERF:** The groove or notch made as a saw passes through wood; also the wood removed by the saw in parting the material.

**KILN DRIED:** Lumber dried in a closed chamber in which the removal of moisture is controlled by artificial heat and usually by controlled relative humidity.

**KNIFE MARKS:** The imprints or markings of the machine knives on the surface of dressed lumber.

**KNOCKED DOWN (KD):** Unassembled, as contrasted to assembled.

**KNOT:** Cross section of tree branch or limb with grain usually running at right angles to that of the piece of wood in which it occurs

- **CONSPICUOUS PIN** - Sound knots 6.4 mm (1/4 inch) or less in diameter containing dark centers.
- **HOLES** - Openings produced when knots drop from the wood in which they were embedded.
- **OPEN** - Opening produced when a portion of the wood substance of a knot has dropped out or where cross checks have occurred to produce an opening.
- **SOUND TIGHT** - Knots that are solid across their face and fixed by growth to retain their place.
- **SPIKE** - Knots cut from 0° to 45° to the long axis of limbs.

**LACQUER:** A coating composed of synthetic film forming materials such as nitrocellulose, ethylcellulose, natural and synthetic resins, which are dissolved in organic solvents and are dried by solvent evaporation.

**LEAF:** The individual pieces of wood veneer that make up a flitch.

**LEED®:** An environmental building rating system created by United States Green Building Council (USGBC) to encourage and certify the environmental and energy saving attributes of a building and its operations.

**LIFTING:** In finishing, the softening of a dried film by the solvents of a succeeding coat, which causes raising and wrinkling of the first coat.

**LIGHTS (LITES):** In door construction, openings to receive glazing.

**LIPPAGE:** Variation in the height of adjoining stone or epoxy resin counter top joints. The differences in elevation between edges of adjacent tile modules.

**LISTING:** A tabular method of describing materials or methods that do not require drawings.

**LOCK BLOCK:** A concealed block the same thickness as the door stile or core that is adjacent to the stile at a location corresponding to the lock location and into which a lock is fitted.

**LOCK JOINT:** Interlocking machine joint between two members.

**LOOSE SIDE** (of leaf): In knife cut veneer, that side of the leaf that was in contact with the knife as the veneer was being cut, and containing cutting checks (lathe checks) because of the bending of the wood at the knife edge.

**LOUVER:** A slat or slats installed in a panel or door at an angle to the panel allowing various degrees of light, air or sound passage. May be constructed as adjustable.

**LOW PRESSURE DECORATIVE LAMINATE:** A general term referring to a variety of melamine or polyester enhanced surface papers and foils laminated to a core, typically referred to as melamine or polyester overlays.

**LPDL:** See "low pressure decorative laminate."

**LUMBER:** Pieces of wood no further manufactured than by sawing, planing, crosscutting to length, and perhaps edge machining.

**LUSTER:** See "Sheen".

**MADE TO ORDER SEQUENCED PANELS:** All panels are manufactured to width and/or height according to each elevation. All panels are balanced matched and sequenced to the adjacent panels.

**MAHOGANY:** The term "Mahogany" should not be specified without further definition. It must be understood that there are different species of Mahogany that should be specified.

African, Central and South American, or Tropical American, including American Mahogany, are genuine and true Mahoganies. American Mahogany varies in color from light pink to light red; reddish brown to golden brown or yellowish tan. Some Mahogany turns darker and some lighter in color after machining.

The figure or grain in American Mahogany runs from plain sliced, plain stripe to broken stripe, mottled, fiddleback, swirl, and crotches. As uniform color is not a natural characteristic of this species, if a uniform color is desired it is recommended that the finishing specification include a statement that toner or tint must be applied so that color variation shall be kept to a minimum.

Lauan White and Red, Tanguile, and other species are native to the Philippine Islands and are sometimes referred to as Philippine Mahogany. Those species are not a true Mahogany.

When only the word "Mahogany" is specified, it usually (but not always) means a true Mahogany as selected by the manufacturer unless a specific species is called for in the specifications. When Philippine Mahogany is specified, it nearly always means Lauan, Tanguile, and other natural Philippine species of wood.

**MANUFACTURER:** A person or organization that regularly engages in the practice of manufacturing, prefinishing, and/or installing architectural woodwork.

**MATCHING EDGEBAND:** See "self edge."

**MECHANICAL FASTENER:** The generic term for securing devices that are used in the fabrication and/or installation of architectural woodwork such as dowels, dowel screws, splines, biscuit splines nails, screws, bolts, pins, etc.

**MEDIUM DENSITY FIBERBOARD (MDF):** See particleboard for a basic description. As used in these standards, whether as MDF alone or as core material, the MDF shall meet the requirements of ANSI A-208.2 (latest edition).

# GLOSSARY

**MEDIUM DENSITY OVERLAY (MDO):** A panel product particularly well suited for opaque (paint) finishes; most versions are highly weather resistant.

**MEDIUM DENSITY PARTICLEBOARD:** Generally refers to particleboard manufactured to an approximate density of 45 lbs per cubic foot (20.41 kg per cubic cm); the type of particleboard used for architectural woodworking cores.

**MEDULLARY RAY:** Extends radially from the center of a log toward the outer circumference. These rays serve primarily to store food and transport it horizontally. These rays vary in height from a few cells in some species to an excess of 4" (102 mm) in Oaks. In Oak, it produces the flake effect common to quarter sawn lumber.

**MELAMINE:** Resin impregnated paper used in decorative composite panel products (see thermally fused decorative laminate panel).

**MEMBER:** An individual piece of solid stock or plywood that forms an item of woodwork.

**METAMERISM:** An apparent change in color when exposed to differing wavelengths of light; the human perception of color (see Barber Pole and Book Match).

**MILL RUN:** Molding run to pattern only, not assembled, machined for assembly, or cut to length. The terms "material only" and "loose and long" mean the same as "mill run."

**MILLWORK:** See "architectural woodwork."

**MINERAL STREAK:** An olive to greenish black or brown discoloration of undetermined cause in hardwoods.

**MIRROR POLISH FINISH:** In finishing, several steps of wet sanding, mechanical buffing, and polishing.

**MISMATCH:** An uneven fit in worked lumber when adjoining pieces do not meet tightly at all points of contact or when the surfaces of adjoining pieces are not in the same plane.

**MITERFOLD:** Made from a single panel in one machining process; includes placement of tape, machining, application of adhesive, folding, glue, clamp, and clean.

**MITER JOINT:** The joining of two members at an angle that bisects the angle of junction.

**MITER, LOCK JOINT:** A miter joint employing a tongue and groove to further strengthen it.

**MITER, SHOULDER JOINT:** Any type of miter joint that presents a shoulder, such as a lock miter or a splined miter.

**MOCK UP:** A sample made by the manufacturer to demonstrate materials, assembly, finish and/or tolerances proposed for a project. A mock up does not eliminate the requirements found in section 1 for shop drawings. Mock ups, if approved, may be allowed to become part of the finished project.

**MODULAR CASEWORK:** Casework produced from a manufacturer's standard details adapted to use for a particular project.

**MODULUS OF ELASTICITY (MOE):** As referenced in this standard, the theoretically recoverable longitudinal deflection value of a material from an applied load.

**MODULUS OF RUPTURE (MOR):** The maximum load carrying capacity of a member under bending load.

**MOISTURE CONTENT:** The weight of the water in the wood expressed in percentage of the weight of the oven dry wood.

**MOLDED EDGE:** Edge of piece machined to any profile other than a square or eased edge.

**MOLDING (MOULDING):** A decorative strip, usually having a curved or projecting surface. Some common moldings used are listed below. (Additional ornamental and architectural moldings are listed in the Design Ideas Section under Historic Woodwork Glossary):

- **ASTRAGAL -** A molding attached to one door of a pair of doors covering the gap between the doors.
- **BACK BAND -** Used in conjunction with casing or baseboard to create a wide variety of trim options for windows and doors. Generally backband moldings create thicker or wider moldings than single piece components.
- **BASE BLOCK -** The square block terminating a molded baseboard at a doorway; a plinth block.
- **BASE CAP -** A molding applied to the top edge of a base molding to add aesthetic affect.
- **BASE or BASEBOARD -** Moldings used to trim the intersection of a wall or cabinet and the floor.
- **BASE SHOE -** A small molding combined with a base molding to complete the trimming of the wall and floor intersection.
- **BEAD MOLDING -** A narrow half round molding that is continuous or divided into bead like forms.
- **CASING -** Generally, a molding placed around a door frame or window frame.
- **BED MOLDING -** A molding or group of moldings used immediately beneath a projection.
- **CHAIR RAIL -** Applied along a wall for protection or as a design element between wall treatments, such as paneling, wallpaper, or paint. Traditionally placed at the horizontal location on the wall at a height that would be rubbed by a chair back, to protect the wall.
- **CORNICE -** A wood or composite wood molding detail along the top edge of a piece of a millwork assembly or a building. May be built up of several moldings or components to create one large profile.
- **COVE -** Similar to crown moldings, often smaller in size and less decorative.
- **CROWN -** Used to accent ceiling intersections and traditional pediments and casework tops.
- **FILLET -** A thin molding used to separate or decorate larger moldings and also refers to the infill strip that fits between the balusters on a stair case.

# GLOSSARY

- **HANDRAIL** - A molding used along a hallway or corridor designed to be grasped by the hand to provide stability or support.
- **LATTICE** - A thin, flat molding, rectangular in cross-section, used to build decorative screening or conceal joinery.
- **OGEE** - A molding with reverse curved face that is concave above and convex below.
- **QUARTER ROUND** - A molding with a convex, quarter cylindrical shape.
- **PANEL MOLDING** - A decorative molding used to trim out raised or recessed wall panels.
- **SHOE** - A small molding with a concave channel and a square back.
- **TRANSITION MOLDING** - A molding that conceals the joint between uneven surfaces.

**MORTISE AND TENON, BLIND JOINT:** A mortise and tenon joint in which the tenon does not extend through the mortise and does not remain visible once the joint is completed; also "blind tenoned."

**MORTISE AND TENON, SLOTTED JOINT:** A mortise and tenon right angle joint in which the tenon is visible on two edges once the joint is completed.

**MORTISE AND TENON, STUB JOINT:** A short tenon inserted in a plow or groove.

**MORTISE AND TENON, THROUGH JOINT:** A mortise and tenon joint in which the inserted tenon extends completely through the mortise and the end of the tenon remains visible once the joint is completed.

**MOTTLE:** Broken wavy patches across the face of the wood that give the impression of an uneven, although smooth, surface caused by a twisted interwoven grain with irregular cross figure, which is the mottle. The effect is due to reflected light on the uneven arrangement of the fibers. Other terms used to describe variations include bee's wing, fiddle, peacock, plum, ram, block, or stop mottle.

**NAILED:** Members secured together with nails, including power driven nails or staples. On exposed surfaces, staples and tee nails shall run parallel to the grain.

**NATURAL:** When referring to color and matching, veneers containing any amount of sapwood and/or heartwood.

**NEWEL POST:** In stairwork, an upright post that supports or receives the handrail at critical points of the stair, such as starting, landing, or top; the central vertical support of a spiral staircase.

**NGR STAINS:** Refers to non grain raising stains.

**NOMINAL:** The average sizes (width and thickness) of lumber just out of the sawmill before being processed into usable board stock. Always larger than "finished" dimensions. Also, a term that designates a stated dimension as being approximate and subject to allowances for variation.

**NON CLIMATE CONTROLLED:** Referring to the inside or outside areas of a building where heat or air condition systems are not used for environmental controls.

**NON HOUSED CABINET BACK:** When a cabinet back is set in a rabbet or is plant on back style.

**NON WOOD:** As used in INSTALLATION sections of this Standard refers to components made of material other than wood and that are subject to this Standard's tolerance threshold values.

**NON WOOD BASED PRODUCTS:** Any material that is not made of wood, veneer or paper based materials. Common non wood based products include: solid surface, stone, metals, fabrics, drywall, and masonry.

**NON WOOD TO NON WOOD:** A two or more component joint or assembly containing products that are not made of wood or wood based products.

**NOSING:** A rounded convex edge, as on a stair step.

**OCCASIONAL:** A small number of characteristics that are arranged somewhat diversely within the panel face.

**OPAQUE FINISH:** A paint or pigmented stain finish that hides the natural characteristics and color of the grain of the wood surface and is not transparent.

**OPEN GRAIN AND CLOSED GRAIN:** See Grain.

**ORANGE PEEL:** The description of a coating that does not flow out smoothly, exhibiting the texture of an orange.

**ORIENTED STRAND BOARD (OSB):** is an engineered wood product formed by layering strands (flakes) of wood in specific orientations. In appearance it may have a rough and variegated surface with the individual strips lying unevenly across each other.

**OVER FILING:** In manufacturing, rough edges are required to be filed or sanded smooth. Over filing exposes the core of the decorative laminate or otherwise causes defects in the finished product.

**OVERLAP:** A condition where the veneers comprising plywood are so misplaced that one piece overlaps the other and does not make a smooth joint.

**OVERLAY:** To superimpose or laminate a wood veneer of various species or a decorative item, such as melamine, polyester, or high pressure decorative laminate to one or both sides of a given core, such as plywood, particleboard, or medium density fiberboard.

**OVERSPRAY:** The dry, pebble like surface caused when the sprayed finish begins to dry in the air before it hits the surface.

# GLOSSARY

**OXIDATION:** The effect on the appearance of exposed wood faces caused by exposure to atmosphere. This is analogous to browning reactions in freshly cut fruit; for instance, apples. Hardwoods can develop deep yellow to reddish brown discolorations on the surface of the wood when exposed to air immediately after sawing or peeling. These discolorations are especially noticeable on Cherry, Birch, Red Alder, Sycamore, Oak, Maple, and Sweet Gum. Some species, such as Alder, Oak, Birch, and Maple, develop these discolorations during air seasoning. A related gray stain on several varieties of Southern Oaks also appears to be oxidative in nature. Proper selection, sanding, and finishing can minimize the effects of oxidation. Care should be taken when using filler, as it might not change the same as the wood.

**PAIR MATCH:** Relating to passage doors, means doors are adjacent to each other or are next to each other with only a door frame member separating the two doors.

**PANEL:** Panels are consistent in thickness, with edges that are at right angles to the face and are either homogeneous or made up of three or more layers.

**PANEL MATCH:** Establishes the leaf layout in each individual panel.

**PARTICLEBOARD:** A generic term for a panel manufactured from lignocellulosic materials (usually wood), primarily in the form of discrete pieces of particles, as distinguished from fibers, combined with a synthetic resin or other suitable binder, and bonded together under heat and pressure in a hot press by a process in which the entire interparticle bond is created by the added binder, and to which other materials may have been added during manufacturing to improve certain properties. Particles are further defined by the method of pressing. When pressure is applied in the direction perpendicular to the faces as in a conventional multi platen hot press, they are defined as flat platen pressed; and when the applied pressure is parallel to the faces, they are defined as extruded.

**PARTICLEBOARD, FIRE RETARDANT TREATED:** Particleboard treated to obtain Class I or Class II flame spread.

**PARTITION:** A panel that is securely attached to floor, ceiling, walls or a supported frame used to divide room spaces.

**PATCH:** A repair made by inserting and securely gluing a sound piece of wood of the same species in place of a defect that has been removed. The edges shall be cut clean and sharp and fit tight with no voids. "Boat" patches are oval shaped with sides tapering in each direction to a point or to a small rounded end; "router" patches have parallel sides and rounded ends; "sled" patches are rectangular with feathered ends.

**PECKY:** Pockets of disintegrated wood caused by localized decay or wood areas with abrupt color change related to localized injury such as bird peck. Peck is sometimes considered a decorative effect, such as bird peck in Pecan and Hickory or pecky in Cypress.

**PEDIMENT:** A triangular ornament above a cornice.

**PENETRATING OIL:** In finishing, an oil based material designed to penetrate the wood.

**PERFORMANCE BASED:** With reference to these standards, and in contrast to prescriptive based, refers to the lack of dictated or specifically required technical processes in lieu of a concept that allows innovation as long as the required outcomes are achieved.

**PHENOL FORMALDEHYDE RESIN:** Typically used for exterior type construction. Plywood and doors bonded with this adhesive have a high resistance to moisture. The most common types require high temperatures during pressing to aid in the curing process.

**PHOTODEGRADATION:** The effect on the appearance of exposed wood faces caused by exposure to both sun and artificial light sources. Obviously, if an entire face is exposed to a light source, it will photodegrade somewhat uniformly and hardly be noticeable; whereas partially exposed surfaces or surfaces with shadow lines may show nonuniform photodegradation. Some woods, such as American Cherry and Walnut, are more susceptible than others to photodegradation.

**PILASTER:** A fluted or carved, flat, decorative column vertically attached to a building or furniture.

**PIN HOLES:** All circular or nearly circular holes in the exposed surface.

**PITCH:** An accumulation of resin that occurs in separations in the wood or in the wood cells themselves.

**PITCH POCKET:** A well defined opening between the annual growth rings that contains pitch.

**PITCH STREAK:** A well defined accumulation of pitch in the wood cells in a more or less regular streak.

**PITH:** A small, soft core occurring in the center of the log.

**PLAIN SAWN:** A hardwood figure developed by sawing a log lengthwise at a tangent to the annual growth rings. It appears as U shaped or straight markings in the board's face.

**PLAIN SLICING:** Most commonly used for hardwood plywood. The log is cut in half, and one half is placed onto a carriage and moved up and down past a fixed knife to produce the veneers. Veneer is sliced parallel to the pith of the log and approximately tangent to the growth rings to achieve flat cut veneer. Each piece is generally placed in a stack and kept in order. One half log, sliced this way, is called a "flitch."

**PLANK:** A board, usually between 1-1/2" to 3-1/2" (38.1 to 88.9 mm) thick and 6" (152 mm) or more wide, laid with its wide dimension horizontal and used as a bearing surface.

**PLANT ON BACK:** When a cabinet back is applied and fastened to the back edges of a cabinet box. The back is not set in grooves, plows or rabbets.

**PLASTIC LAMINATE FINISH:** See "high pressure decorative laminate."

# GLOSSARY

**PLEASING MATCHED:** A face containing components that provide a pleasing overall appearance. The grain of the various components need not be matched at the joints, but will not be widely dissimilar in character and/or figure. Sharp color contrasts at the joints of the components are not permitted. Members are selected so that lighter than average color members are not placed adjacent to darker than average members.

**PLOW:** A rectangular groove or slot of three surfaces cut parallel to the grain of a wood member, in contrast to a dado, which is cut across the grain.

**PLY:** A single sheet of veneer or several strips laid with adjoining edges that may or may not be glued, which forms one veneer laminate in a glued panel (see layer). In some constructions, a ply is used to refer to other wood components such as particleboard or MDF.

**PLYWOOD:** A panel composed of a crossbanded assembly of layers or plies of veneer, or veneers in combination with a lumber core or particleboard core, that are joined with an adhesive. Except for special constructions, the grain of alternate plies is always approximately at right angles, and the thickness and species on either side of the core are identical for balanced effect. An odd number of plies is always used.

**POCKET SCREW:** Pocket screw joints are created by aligning two pieces perpendicular, drilling angled pocket and pilot holes and then driving cabinet assembly screws to connect the pieces. These screws are used in concealed surface locations only.

**POLYESTER:** In finishing, a very high solids content plastic coating, leaving a deep, wet look.

**POLYURETHANE:** A very hard and wear resistant finish, which is very difficult to repair. Most commonly used as a two component system, comprising multifunctional isocyanate or moisture cured urethane, with a higher solids content than lacquers. Single component (excluding moisture cured) products are usually composed of precatalyzed urethane.

**PREFINISHED:** Product that is delivered with finish as opposed to field finishing.

**PREMANUFACTURED SETS:** Each panel, usually 4' x 8' (1219 mm x 2438 mm) or 4' x 10' (1219 mm x 3048 mm), is part of a sequenced set of balanced matched, premanufactured panels to be installed full width with the sequencing maintained. The panel's balanced match becomes unequal at the start, end, and any other opening or change in plane when trimmed.

**PREMIUM GRADE:** The highest Grade available in both material and workmanship intended for the finest work. This is naturally the most expensive Grade.

**PRESCRIPTIVE BASED:** With reference to these standards, and in contrast to performance based, refers to the manner in which regulations are expressed that dictate the technical processes by which the required outcomes are to be achieved.

**PRESERVATIVE:** (n.) A treating solution that prevents decay in wood; (adj.) having the ability to preserve wood by inhibiting the growth of decay fungi.

**PRESSED:** As in panel layup, hot, cold, vacuum or mechanical requires pressure until glue sets and becomes rigid.

**PROFILE:** A trim that has a shaped detail along one or more edges. Eased edges are included in profiles. Ends or faces may also have profiles.

**PUR:** Is a general adhesive with polyurethane as its primary component used in the woodwork industry. It is also referred to as PU and polyurethane reactive.

**PUTTIED:** See "fill."

**PVA:** Is a wood adhesive with polyvinyl acetate as its primary component and is commonly referred to as wood glue, white glue, carpenter's glue, or PVA glue.

**PVC:** Abbreviation for "polyvinyl chloride," a synthetic decorative coating or edgebanding.

**PVC EDGING:** A polyvinyl chloride edging, usually in seamless rolls, typically applied by edgebanding machines using hot melt adhesives. Available in a variety of solid colors, patterns, and wood grain designs, in both textured and smooth finish.

**QUARTER SAWN (QUARTERED LUMBER):** Refers to solid lumber cutting. Available in limited amounts in certain species. Yields straight grain, narrow boards with "flake" or figure in some species (particularly in Red and White Oak).

**QUARTER SLICING:** Produces a striped grain pattern, straight in some woods, varied in others. Veneer produced by cutting in a radial direction to the pith to the extent that fleck or ray flake is produced, and the amount may be unlimited. In some woods, principally Oak, fleck results from cutting through the radial medullary rays.

**QUARTERS:** The commercial thicknesses usually associated with the purchase or specification of hardwoods, such as "five quarter" (5/4 of 1"), meaning 1-1/4" (31.8 mm) in thickness.

**QUIRK:** For purposes of these standards, means a sharp incision or kerf in moldings or trim that can hide the use of mechanical fastener.

**RABBET:** Rectangular cut on the edge of a member; a "rabbet" has two surfaces, and a "plow" has three.

**RABBET JOINT:** A groove cut across the grain of the face of a member at an edge or end to receive the edge or end thickness of another member.

**RAIL:** The cross or horizontal pieces of a stile and rail assembly or the cross pieces of the core assembly of a wood flush door or panel.

**RAILING:** In stairwork, the member that follows the pitch of the stair for grasping by the hand.

**RAISED GRAIN:** See "Grain".

**RAISED PANEL:** Traditional door or wall panel with a bevel edge captured in a stile and rail frame.

**RANDOM MATCH:** Matching between adjacent veneer leaves on one panel face. Random selection in the arrangement of veneer leaves from one or more flitches producing a deliberate mismatch between the pieces of veneer.

**RAY:** One of the radial structures in a tree that stores nourishment and transports it horizontally through the trunk. In quarter sawn Oak, the rays form a figure called fleck.

# GLOSSARY

**RECONSTITUTED VENEER:** Logs that are first sliced into veneer leaves, the leaves may be dyed, then glued under pressure in a mold to produce a large laminated block. The laminated block is then sliced across the glue line to create a faux grain with a designed appearance that is highly repeatable.

**RED/BROWN:** When referring to color and matching, veneers containing all heartwood, ranging in color from light to dark.

**RED BIRCH:** The heartwood of the Yellow Birch tree.

**RELIEF:** Defined as the difference in elevation between the high and the low parts of an area or where a form is raised (or alternatively lowered) from a flattened background without being disconnected from it.

**REPAIRS:** A patch, shim, or filler material inserted and/or glued into veneer or a panel to achieve a sound surface.

**REPAIRS, BLENDING:** Wood or filler insertions similar in color to adjacent wood so as to blend well.

**RESORCINOL FORMALDEHYDE RESIN:** For woodworking, formulated into water resistant glues.

**RESTRAINED:** See "Captured".

**RETENTION MOLDING:** A molding used to capture or hold in place another material such as a panel, glass, metal or other millwork product.

**RETURN:** Continuation in a different direction of a molding or projection, usually right angles.

**REVEAL, CABINET:** The space between door edges and inset frames. The amount of viewable case edge when a door is in the closed position in flush overlay or reveal overlay cabinet construction.

**REVEAL, PANEL:** A detail used in wall and ceiling surfacing panel design that allows for expansion and contraction between adjacent panels. The reveal is a space between adjacent panels or other architectural features that allows for panel expansion and contraction.

**REVEAL OVERLAY:** Cabinet construction in which the door and drawer faces partially cover the body members or face frames of the cabinet with spaces between face surfaces creating decorative reveals.

**RIFT CUT:** A straight grain appearance achieved through the process of cutting at a slight angle, approximately 15 degrees, to the radial on the half round stay log or through the use of veneer cut in any fashion that produces a straight grain with minimal ray fleck.

**RING, ANNUAL GROWTH:** The growth layer put on in a growth year.

**RISER:** The board at the back of a tread that "rises" to the bottom of the next tread above. In an "open riser" stair, this element is left out, and the gap between the treads is open. Open riser stairs are prohibited by code in many circumstances.

**ROOM MATCH:** Refers to the matching of panel faces within a room.

**ROTARY SLICING:** Most common method for preparing veneers for softwood plywood. The log is placed in a lathe and rotated against a stationary knife. This produces a more or less continuous sheet of veneer, similar to pulling a long sheet off a roll of paper towels.

**ROUGH CUT:** Irregular shaped areas of generally uneven corrugation on the surface of veneer, differing from the surrounding smooth veneer and occurring as the veneer is cut by the lathe or slicer.

**RUNNING MATCH:** Each panel face is assembled from as many veneer leaves as necessary. Any portion left over from one panel may be used to start the next.

**RUNNING TRIM:** Generally combined in the term "standing and running trim" and refers to random, longer length trims delivered to the jobsite (e.g., baseboard, chair rail, crown molding). Running trim is generally installed horizontally. Standing trim installed vertically.

**RUNS:** The result of spraying a heavier coat on a vertical, or nearly vertical, surface than the viscosity of the finish will allow to hold without movement; when in close multiples are also called "sags."

**RUPTURED GRAIN:** A break or breaks in the grain or between springwood and summerwood caused or aggravated by excessive pressure on the wood by seasoning, manufacturing, or natural processes. Ruptured grain appears as a single or series of distinct separations in the wood such as when springwood is crushed leaving the summerwood to separate in one or more growth increments.

**S4S:** Means "Surfaced Four Sides," and generally refers to the process of reducing nominal sized rough lumber to finished widths and thicknesses.

**SAGS:** In finishing, partial slipping of finish film creating a "curtain" effect.

**SAND THROUGH:** A defect on the exposed visible surface, such as depressions, bumps, marks, or core usually caused by thin veneers or over sanding.

**SANDED, CROSS:** Sanded across, rather than parallel to, the grain of a wood surface.

**SANDED, MACHINE:** Sanded by a drum or equivalent sander to remove knife or machine marks.

**SANDED, SMOOTHLY:** Sanded sufficiently smooth so that all machining, machine sanding marks, cross sanding, and other sanding imperfections will be concealed by the painter's applied finish work. The proper sanding grit varies with the species of material; however, it generally runs in the 120 to 150 grit range and grade of workmanship specified.

# GLOSSARY

**SAPWOOD:** The living wood of lighter color occurring in the outer portion of a tree, sometimes referred to as sap.

**SASH:** A single assembly of stiles and rails into a frame for holding glass, with or without dividing bars, to fill a given opening. It may be either open or glazed.

**SCARF JOINT:** When the ends of two boards are cut on an angle and glued together to increase the length of the board.

**SCL:** See "Structural Composite Lumber".

**SCRIBE:** To mark and cut an item of woodwork so that it will abut an uneven wall, floor, or other adjoining surface.

**SEALING:** The process of applying a moisture resistant finish to the edges of sink cut outs. The process of applying a finish to concealed areas of factory finished millwork. Sealing is a part of proper factory finished panel balancing.

**SEALERS:** Compounds that provide a sandable coating and a smooth surface for final topcoat application, provide system toughness and moisture resistance, and contribute to build and clarity.

**SEASONING:** The process of allowing new cut wood to release moisture and achieve optimal moisture content without the aid of mechanical drying processes such as kiln drying.

**SECURELY ATTACHED:** The attachment of one member to another by means of approved joinery, adhesive, mechanical fasteners, or by a combination of these means. Members shall not be considered securely attached if they disassemble during standard usage and stress.

**SECURELY FASTENED OR BONDED:** See "securely attached."

**SELECT:** A lumber grading term. Also, in architectural specifications, the term "select" is frequently used to describe, clarify, or qualify specific characteristics of the hardwood lumber being specified; for example, Select White Maple or Select White Birch, by using "select" as a descriptor, Natural, Brown, and Red Maple/Birch are excluded.

**SELF EDGE:** Application of an edge that matches the face.

**SEMI-EXPOSED SURFACES:** Surfaces that are only visible under closer examination.

**SET MATCH -** Relating to passage doors, means three or more doors that are adjacent to each other or are next to each other with only a door frame member separating any of the doors.

**SHADING:** In finishing, transparent color used for highlighting and uniform color.

**SHAKE:** A separation or rupture along the grain of wood in which the greater part occurs between the rings of annual growth (see ruptured grain).

**SHARP CONTRAST:** For the purpose of this standard, this term applies to woodwork such as veneer of lighter than average color joined with the veneer of darker than average color. Two adjacent pieces of woodwork should not be widely dissimilar in grain, figure, and natural character markings.

**SHEEN:** Finish shine or brightness; luster, patina, and radiance. The sheen or gloss level of a cured finish is traditionally measured with a 60 degree gloss meter. The words used to describe various sheens are not standardized between companies.

**SHELF CLEAT:** A piece of wood or other solid material attached directly to in wall blocking just below the bottom edge of a shelf.

**SHELF DEFLECTION:** Shelf deflection is the deviation from true flat of a shelf when placed under load.

**SHELF LOAD:** The amount of weight a shelf is designed to carry based on shelf core material, Modulus of Elasticity and surface materials.

**SHELLAC:** A coating made from purified lac, a secretion from an insect (laccifera lacca) that is dissolved in alcohol and often bleached white.

**SHOP DRAWINGS:** Shop drawings are detailed engineering drawings produced by the manufacturer for the fabrication of the architectural woodwork products, and are often submitted to the design professional for review and comment. See Drawings.

**SHOW THROUGH:** Irregular surfaces visible on the face of a veneered panel (such as depressions, bumps, mechanical marks, or core or frame outlines).

**SKIN:** The hardwood plywood (usually 3 ply), hardboard, or composition panel, whether flat or configured, that is used for facings for flush doors, bending laminations, finished end panels, and the like.

**SKIRT BOARD:** A trim member similar to base, run on the rake along the wall adjoining a stairway. The skirt board covers the joint between the treads and risers and the wall. Also, the similar member below the treads at the open side of a stairway. A wall routed to receive the treads and risers may replace a skirt board.

**SLEEPER:** A support member, usually vertical in placement, between the front and rear members of a non integral toe base or kick assembly.

**SLICED (SLICE):** See "Veneer, Sliced".

**SLIGHT:** Visible on observation, but does not interfere with the overall aesthetic appearance with consideration of the applicable grade of the panel.

**SLIP MATCHED:** Each leaf from a flitch is laid out in sequence from their place in the bundle, all faces in one direction. The result is that all the faces are either loose or tight, therefore reflect light the same minimizing the barber pole or metamerism effect.

**SMOOTH, TIGHT CUT:** Veneer cut to minimize lathe checks.

**SMOOTHNESS:** The degree to which a surface has had machining and handling effects removed. Typically accomplished by sanding with progressively finer sanding grits until the required surface texture is achieved.

**SOFT CONVERSION:** An inch measurement is mathematically converted to its exact, or nearly exact metric equivalent. Inches are multiplied by 25.4 to determine millimeters. Example: 48" x 25.4 = 1219.2 mm, commonly rounded to 1219 mm.

# GLOSSARY

**SOFTWOOD:** General term used to describe lumber or veneer produced from needle and/or cone bearing trees (see hardwood).

**SOLID PHENOLIC:** A composite of solid phenolic resins molded with a homogenous core of organic fiber reinforced phenolic and one or more integrally cured surfaces of compatible thermoset nonabsorbent resins.

**SOLID STOCK:** Solid, sound lumber (as opposed to plywood), that may be more than one piece of the same species, securely glued for width or thickness.

**SOLID SURFACE:** Filled cast polymeric resin panel. The fillers enhance both its performance properties and aesthetics. With a homogeneous composition throughout its thickness, solid surface requires no finish coat and is capable of being fabricated with inconspicuous seams and repaired to its original finish.

**SOUND:** In reference to lumber or veneer, the absence of decay, pith, shake, doze and wane.

**SP:** See "Solid Phenolic".

**SPANDREL:** The triangular element in a staircase between the stringer and the baseboard.

**SPECIES:** A distinct kind of wood.

**SPECIFIC GRAVITY:** The ratio of the weight of a certain volume of a substance to the weight of an equal volume of water, the temperature of which is 39.2 degrees Fahrenheit (4 degrees Celsius).

**SPECIFICATION:** Directions provided by the design professional and found within a given project's contract documents, or addendum. Specifications may be modified by agreements such as change orders or field directives from the Design Professional.

**SPECIFIED:** See "Specification".

**SPECIFY:** See "Specification".

**SPLINE:** A thin narrow strip forming a key between two members, usually of plywood, inserted into matching grooves that have been machined in abutting edges of panels or lumber to ensure a flush alignment and a secure joint.

**SPLINE JOINT:** A joint formed by the use of a "spline." Splines customarily run the entire length of the joint.

**SPLIT:** Separations of wood fiber running parallel to the grain.

**SPLIT HEART:** A method of achieving an inverted "V" or cathedral type of springwood (earlywood)/summerwood (latewood), plain sliced (flat cut) figure by joining two face components of similar color and grain.

**STAIN:** A variation (normally blue or brown) from the natural color of the wood. It should not be confused with natural red heart. In finishing, produces the desired undertone color with proper distribution, depth, and clarity of grain. Selection of the type of stain used is governed by the desired artistic result. In natural wood, a variation in the color tending toward blue or brown, but not to be confused with naturally occurring heartwood.

**STAINING:** An optional operation in wood finishing to achieve the desired undertone color and complement the wood with proper distribution of color, depth of color, and clarity of grain.

**STAIRWORK:** Wood material to form a stair or to clad stair parts constructed of materials other than wood, and that are custom manufactured to a design for a particular project.

**STANDING TRIM:** Generally combined in the term "standing and running trim" and refers to vertically installed moldings of fixed length delivered to the jobsite (e.g., door jambs and casings, premachined window stools).

**STAPLED:** Members secured together with nails, including power driven nails or staples. On exposed surfaces, staples shall run parallel to the grain.

**STAVED CORE:** Typically refers to a core used in flush doors made up of end and edge glued wood blocks.

**STICKING:** A term used to describe shaped or molded solid wood members.

**STILE AND RAIL CONSTRUCTION:** A technique often used in the making of doors, wainscoting, and other decorative features for cabinets and furniture. The basic concept is to capture a panel within a frame, and in its most basic form it consists of five members: the panel and the four members that make up the frame. The vertical members of the frame are called stiles, while the horizontal members are known as rails.

**STILES AND VERTICAL EDGES:** The upright or vertical pieces of stile and rail assemblies; the vertical members of the core assembly of a wood flush door.

**STOPS:** Generally a molding used to "stop" a door or window in its frame.

**STREAKS, MINERAL:** Sharply contrasting elongated discolorations of the wood substance.

**STRETCHER:** An upper support member of base cabinet fabrication, used in lieu of a solid cabinet top, to space the end panels.

**STRINGER:** A diagonal element supporting the treads and risers in a flight of stairs.

**STRINGER TURNOUT:** In stairwork, that portion of a stringer that curves or angles away from the basic run, typically used at the beginning tread.

**STRIPE:** Stripe figure is a ribbon grain:
- **BROKEN STRIPE** - A modification of ribbon stripe. The figure markings taper in and out, due to twisted or interlocked grain, so that the ribbon stripe is not continuous as it runs more or less the full length of the flitch.
- **PLAIN STRIPE** - Alternating darker and lighter stripes running continuously along the length of a piece, due to cutting wood with definite growth rings on the quarter.
- **RAINDROP** - When the waves of the fibers occur singly or in groups with considerable intervals between, the figure looks like streaks made by raindrops striking a window pane at a slant.
- **RIBBON STRIPE** - In some wood with interwoven grain, such as Mahogany, wide unbroken stripes can be produced by cutting on the quarter.

# GLOSSARY

- **ROE** - Also called "roey." Short, broken ribbon or stripe figure in quarter sliced or sawn wood, due to the spiral formation of the fibers, or interlocked grain, in the growth rings. The irregular growth produces alternate bands of varying shades of color and degrees of luster.

**STRIPPING:** For purposes of these standards, means the process of removing an old or existing finish from a surface.

**STRUCTURAL COMPOSITE LUMBER (SCL):** A man made composite that utilizes stranded wood fibers from a variety of tree species, providing an alternative to dimension lumber. The material is engineered for strength and stability. While not really "lumber", it is marketed as a lumber substitute to be used in place of stave lumber core materials.

**SUB FRONT:** A front drawer box member over which another front is placed.

**SUBTOP:** A separate support member for countertops.

**SURFACE BEARING HEAD:** A screw with a homogeneous head that has a flat bottom surface at least two times the diameter of the screw shaft and when tightened applies distributed pressure on the surfaces being screwed. Screws and washers are not considered surface bearing heads for the purpose of this Standard.

**SURFACE CHECK:** The separation of a wood, normally occurring across the rings of annual growth; usually as a result of seasoning, and occurring only on one surface of the piece.

**SWIRL:** Figure obtained from that part of a tree where the crotch figure fades into the figure of the normal stem.

**TAMBOUR:** A rolling top or front in casework enclosing a storage space. It consists of narrow strips of wood fastened to canvas or a similar material.

**TELEGRAPH OR TELEGRAPHING:** In veneer or laminated work, the variations in surface refraction as a result of the stile, rail, core, core laps, glue, voids, or extraneous matter show through to the face of a panel or a door. The selection of high gloss laminates and finishes should be avoided because they tend to accentuate natural telegraphing.

**TENON:** The projecting tongue like part of a wood member to be inserted into a slot (mortise) of another member to form a mortise and tenon joint.

**TEXTURE:** A term used to describe relative size and distribution of the wood elements. Coarse texture in veneer is associated with fast growth and harder, more difficult wood to cut. Soft or fine texture in veneer is associated with slower growth and with less summerwood, resulting in wood fibers that are easier to cut.

**THERMALLY FUSED DECORATIVE LAMINATE PANEL:** A polyester or melamine resin impregnated paper, thermally fused under pressure to a composite core.

**THICK PHENOLIC:** See solid phenolic.

**TIGHT:** Set together so that there is no opening between members.

**TIGHT SIDE** (of leaf): In knife cut veneer, that side of the leaf that was farthest from the knife as the veneer was being cut and containing no cutting checks (lathe checks).

**TONGUE:** Projection on the edge or end of a wood member that is inserted into the groove or plow of a similar size to form a joint.

**TONGUE AND GROOVE JOINT:** A joint formed by the insertion of the "tongue" of one wood member into the "groove" of the other.

**TOPCOAT:** The final protective film of a finish system. There are various topcoats with different properties.

**TOP FLAT SURFACE:** The flat surface that can be sanded with a drum sander.

**TORN GRAIN:** A roughened area caused by machine work in processing.

**TRANSPARENT FINISH:** A stain or a clear finish that allows the natural characteristics and color of the grain of the wood surface to show through the finish.

**TREAD:** The horizontal surface of a staircase step.

**TREAD RETURN:** A narrow piece of tread stock applied to the open end of a tread so that the end grain is not exposed. The leading corner of the return is mitered to the leading edge of the tread with a shoulder miter.

**TWIST:** A distortion caused by the turning or winding of the edges of the surface, so that the four corners of any face are no longer in the same plane.

**UREA FORMALDEHYDE RESIN:** Commonly used for Type I assemblies; relatively water resistant. Often requires curing by heat, but will cure at room temperature over time.

**V GROOVED:** Narrow and shallow V or U shaped channels machined on a surface to achieve a decorative effect. V grooving is most commonly encountered in mismatched or random matched wall panels as the grooves fall on the edge joints of the pieces of veneer, making the face appear as planking.

**VARNISH:** An oil based finish used to coat a surface with a hard, glossy film.

**VENEER:** A thin layer of wood, rotary cut or sliced from a log or flitch. Thickness may vary from 1/100" (0.3 mm) to 1/4" (6.4 mm).

**VENEER CORE:** Plywood constructed using a core of an odd number of veneer plies, with face and back veneers of overlays adhered thereto.

**VENEER GRAIN OR DIRECTIONAL PATTERN MATCH:** Produced by cutting one or more components from the same panel and assembled maintaining grain or pattern alignment.

**VENEER, RIFT CUT:** Veneer in which the rift or comb grain effect is obtained by cutting at an angle of about 15 degrees off of the quartered position. Twenty-five percent (25%) of the exposed surface area of each piece of veneer may contain medullary ray flake.

# GLOSSARY

**VENEER, ROTARY CUT:** Veneer in which the entire log is centered in a lathe and is turned against a broad cutting knife that is set into the log at a slight angle.

**VENEER, SLICED:** Veneer in which a log or sawn flitch is held securely in a slicing machine and is thrust downward into a large knife that shears off the veneer.

**VERTICAL GRAIN:** Produced by cutting perpendicular to a log's growth rings, where the member's face is no more than 45 degrees to the rings. This produces a pleasing straight grain line. Vertical grain is defined as having no less than an average of five growth rings per inch on its exposed face.

**VINE MARK:** Bands of irregular grain running across or diagonally to the grain which are caused by the growth of climbing vines around the tree.

**VINYL:** Heavy film, minimum of 4 mils in thickness, opaque or reverse printed.

**VINYL LACQUERS:** In finishing, catalyzed lacquers with a plastic rather than a nitrocellulose base.

**VISCOSITY:** The property of resistance to flow in a fluid or semi fluid.

**VOLUTE:** The spiral decorative element terminating the lower end of a stair rail.

**WAFERBOARD:** See "particleboard."

**WAINSCOT:** A lower interior wall surface that contrasts with the wall surface above it.

**WANE:** Defect in lumber defined as bark or lack of wood from any cause on the edge or corner, except eased edges.

**WARP:** Any deviation from a true or plane surface, including bow, crook, cup, twist, or any combination thereof. Warp restrictions are based on the average form of warp as it occurs normally, and any variation from this average form, such as short kinks, shall be appraised according to its equivalent effect. Pieces containing two or more forms of warp shall be appraised according to the combined effect in determining the amount permissible.

- **BOW -** A deviation flatwise from a straight line drawn from end to end of a piece. It is measured at the point of greatest distance from the straight line.
- **CROOK -** A deviation edgewise from a straight line drawn from end to end of a piece. It is measured at the point of greatest distance from the straight line.
- **CUP -** A deviation in the face of a piece from a straight line drawn from edge to edge of a piece. It is measured at the point of greatest distance from the straight line.
- **TWIST -** A deviation flatwise, or a combination of flatwise and edgewise, in the form of a curl or spiral, and the amount is the distance an edge of a piece at one end is raised above a flat surface against which both edges at the opposite end are resting snugly. In passage doors, any distortion in the door itself and not its relationship to the frame or jamb in which it is to be hung, measured by placing a straight edge or a taut string on the concave face.

**WASH COATS:** Thin solutions applied as a barrier coat to wood. Used prior to wiping stains for color uniformity.

**WATER REPELLENT:** A wood treating solution that deposits waterproof or water resistant solids on the walls of wood fibers and ray cells, thereby retarding their absorption of water; having the quality of retarding the absorption of water by wood fibers and ray cells.

**WAVY:** Curly grain with large undulations; sometimes referred to as "finger roll" when the waves are about the width of a finger.

**WELL HOLE:** In stairwork, the open space in which the stair is set.

**WELL MATCHED FOR COLOR AND GRAIN:** For the purpose of these standards, means that the members that make up the components of an assembly and components of an adjacent assembly are:
- Similar and nearly uniform in color, and
- Have similar grain, figure, and character. Adjacent members must be of the same grain type whether flat grain (plain sliced), vertical grain (quarter cut), rift grain, or mixed grain.

**WHITE:** When referring to color and matching, veneers containing all sapwood ranging in color from pink to yellow.

**WHITE BIRCH:** Term used to specify the sapwood of the Yellow Birch tree.

**WINDOWS:** In architectural woodwork, all frames and sashes for double hung, casement, awning, sidelights, clerestory, and fixed windows. Stock and name brand units are not included.

**WIPING STAINS:** Refers to pigmented oils or solvents applied to wood.

**WOOD BASED PRODUCTS:** Products made of wood, veneer or paper based materials such as plastic laminate and engineered panels.

**WOOD FILLER:** An aggregate of resin and strands, shreds, or flour of wood, which is used to fill openings in wood and provide a smooth, durable surface.

**WOOD FLUSH DOOR:** An assembly consisting of a core, stiles and rails, and/or edgebands, with two or three plies of overlay on each side of the core assembly. All parts are composed of wood, wood derivatives, or high pressure decorative laminates.

**WOOD TO NON WOOD:** A two or more component joint or assembly containing wood or wood based products being installed next to non wood based components.

**WOOD TO WOOD:** A two or more component joint or assembly containing wood or wood based products.

**WOODWORK:** See "Architectural Woodwork".

# GLOSSARY

**WOODWORKER:** See "Manufacturer".

**WORKMANSHIP:** See f"First Class Workmanship".

**WORMHOLES:** Holes resulting from infestation of worms.

**WORM TRACK:** Marks caused by various types of wood attacking larvae. Often appear as sound discolorations running with or across the grain in straight to wavy streaks. Sometimes referred to as "pith flecks" in certain species of Maple, Birch and other hardwoods because of a resemblance to the color of pith.

# GLOSSARY

notes